Lecture Notes in Computer Science   13121

Services Science

Subline of Lectures Notes in Computer Science

More information about this subseries at http://www.springer.com/series/7408

Hakim Hacid · Odej Kao ·
Massimo Mecella · Naouel Moha ·
Hye-young Paik (Eds.)

Service-Oriented Computing

19th International Conference, ICSOC 2021
Virtual Event, November 22–25, 2021
Proceedings

 Springer

Editors
Hakim Hacid (iD)
Zayed University
Dubai, United Arab Emirates

Odej Kao
Technical University of Berlin
Berlin, Germany

Massimo Mecella (iD)
Informatica Automatica Gestio
Sapienza University of Rome
Rome, Italy

Naouel Moha
Departement d'Informatique
University of Quebec
Montreal, QC, Canada

Hye-young Paik (iD)
UNSW Sydney
Sydney, NSW, Australia

ISSN 0302-9743   ISSN 1611-3349 (electronic)
Lecture Notes in Computer Science
ISBN 978-3-030-91430-1   ISBN 978-3-030-91431-8 (eBook)
https://doi.org/10.1007/978-3-030-91431-8

LNCS Sublibrary: SL2 – Programming and Software Engineering

This Springer imprint is published by the registered company Springer Nature Switzerland AG
The registered company address is: Gewerbestrasse 11, 6330 Cham, Switzerland

Preface

Welcome to the proceedings of the 19th International Conference on Service-Oriented Computing (ICSOC 2021). Following ICSOC 2020, which was held virtually due to COVID-19, ICSOC 2021 has also become a virtual event, held in November 22–25, 2021. The conference series aims to bring together academics, industry researchers, developers and practitioners to report and share ground-breaking work in the area of Service Oriented Computing (SOC). The objective of ICSOC 2021 was to foster cross-community scientific excellence by gathering experts from various existing and emerging disciplines with the following four focus areas: *(i)* trends in service-oriented technology, *(ii)* distributed ledger and blockchain technologies, *(iii)* industry 4.0 technologies and *(iv)* smart services and smart data, including many emerging AI applications in SOC. This edition of ICSOC built upon a history of successful series of previous editions in Toulouse (France), Hangzhou (China), Malaga (Spain), Banff (Canada), Goa (India), Paris (France), Berlin (Germany), Shanghai (China), Paphos (Cyprus), San Francisco (USA), Stockholm (Sweden), Sydney (Australia), Vienna (Austria), Chicago (USA), Amsterdam (the Netherlands), New York (USA), and Trento (Italy).

ICSOC 2021 introduced a new two-rounds submission and reviewing process for both research and industry papers. In the research track, 61 papers were initially submitted in the first round, of which 14 were suggested for "minor revision and resubmission", while 31 were judged as "fair paper, considerably improve and resubmit", and 16 were rejected. In the second submission round, we received 128 research papers and 40 resubmissions from the previous round. All the submissions went through a rigorous review process that involved on average three reviewers and a discussion moderated by one senior PC member. For papers resubmitted from the early round, the letter detailing the authors' responses to the reviewers, and the quality of the revision results were assessed. The final outcomes were as it follows: 14 "minor revision and resubmission" papers were finally accepted; out of the 26 "fair paper, considerably improve and resubmit", 12 papers were accepted and 2 were judged worthy of acceptance as short papers; 11 papers out of the newly submitted in the second round were accepted and other 24 were judged worthy of acceptance as short papers. The acceptance rate is 16.2% for full papers.

For the industry track, 5 papers originally were submitted in the early round, and 14 in the second round (one of them a resubmission of the previous round). In the end, 2 papers were accepted as full papers and 2 as short papers.

This book also includes 3 papers accepted for the vision track, which underwent a simplified review process aimed at judging futuristic ideas that can drive and guide ongoing research efforts.

The conference program also included three keynotes from distinguished speakers:

- *AI Augmented Service Enablement: Challenges and Directions*, given by Boualem Benatallah (University of New South Wales, Australia);

- *Intelligent Knowledge Discovery for Reliable Cloud Operations*, given by Michael R. Lyu (Chinese University of Hong Kong, China);
- *Cloud-Edge Coopetition: A Win-Win Partnership*, given by Zakaria Maamar (Zaayed University, UAE)

Finally, a PhD symposium, a demo session and different workshops completed the program. The workshops were:

- 2nd International Workshop on Artificial Intelligence for IT Operations (AIOPS 2021)
- 3rd International Workshop on Smart daTa integRation And Processing on Service- based environments (STRAPS 2021)
- 2nd International Workshop on AI-enabled Process Automation (AI-PA 2021)

The ICSOC 2021 Organizing Committee is also grateful to the workshop organizers for their great efforts to help promote SOC research to broader domains.

Special thanks are due to the members of the Senior Program Committee, the International Program Committee, and the external reviewers for a rigorous and robust reviewing process.

We are also grateful to Zayed University for their technical and organizational support, ensuring a successful virtual conference. We would also like to acknowledge all the members of the Organizing Committee and who contributed to make ICSOC 2021 a successful event.

We also acknowledge the prompt and professional support from Springer, who publishes these proceedings as part of the Lecture Notes in Computer Science series.

Most importantly, we would like to thank all authors and participants of ICSOC 2021 for their insightful work and discussions.

We expect that the ideas that have emerged in ICSOC 2021 will result in the development of further innovations for the benefit of scientific, industrial and social communities.

November 2021

Massimo Mecella
Naouel Moha
Hye-young Paik
Hakim Hacid
Odej Kao

Organization

General Co-chairs

Hakim Hacid   Zayed University, UAE
Odej Kao   TU Berlin, Germany

Program Co-chairs

Massimo Mecella   Sapienza Università di Roma, Italy
Naouel Moha   École de Technologie Supérieure, Canada
Hye-young (Helen) Paik   University of New South Wales, Australia

Industrial Track Co-chairs

Jorge Cardoso   Huawei and University of Coimbra, Portugal
Anup K. Kalia   IBM T. J. Watson Research Center, USA

Workshop Co-chairs

Monther Aldwairi   Zayed University, UAE
Reda Bouadjenek   Deakin University, Australia
Marinella Petrocchi   Institute of Informatics and Telematics, CNR, Italy

Special Sessions and Tutorials Co-chairs

Amin Beheshti   Macquarie University, Australia
Zhihui Lv   Fudan University, China
Lauritz Thamsen   TU Berlin, Germany

Demonstrations Co-chairs

Hai Dong   RMIT, Australia
Yucong (Henry) Duan   Hainan University, China
Imran Junejo   Zayed University, UAE

PhD Symposium Co-chairs

Noura Faci   Claude Bernard Lyon 1 University, France
Honghao Gao   University of Shanghai, China
Fatma Outay   Zayed University, UAE

Sponsorship Co-chair

Haseena Al Katheeri   Zayed University, UAE

Finance Chair

Hakim Hacid   Zaycd University, UAE

Local Arrangement Co-chairs

Ons AL-Shamaileh   Zayed University, UAE
Eleana Kafeza   Zayed University, UAE
Andrew Leonce   Zayed University, UAE

Publication Chair

Francis Palma   Linnaeus University, Sweden

Publicity, Website, and Social Media Co-Chairs

Manel Abdellatif   École Polytechnique de Montréal, Canada
Andrew Leonce   Zayed University, UAE
Xiao Xue   Tianjin University, China
Sami Yangui   IRIT, Toulouse, France

ICSOC Steering Committee Representative

Michael Papazoglou   University of Tilburg, The Netherlands

Program Committee

Senior Program Committee Members

Carlos Carnal   University of Malaga, Spain
Fabio Casati   Servicenow, USA
Flavio De Paoli   Università di Milano Bicocca, Italy
Schahram Dustdar   Vienna University of Technology, Austria
Aditya Ghose   University of Wollongong, Australia
Mohad-Said Hacid   Université Lyon 1, France
Zakaria Maamar   Zayed University, UAE
Cesare Pautasso   University of Lugano, Switzerland
Barbara Pernici   Politecnico di Milano, Italy
Gustavo Rossi   Universidad Nacional La Plata, Argentina
Antonio Ruiz-Cortés   University of Seville, Spain
Mohamed Adel Serhani   United Arab Emirates University, UAE
Michael Q. Sheng   Macquarie University, Australia
Stefan Tai   TU Berlin, Germany

Farouk Toumani Limos	Blaise Pascal University, France
Mathias Weske	University of Potsdam, Germany
Jian Yang	Macquarie University, Australia
Liang Zhang	Fudan University, China

Program Committee Members

Marco Aiello	University of Stuttgart, Germany
Alessandro Aldini	University of Urbino "Carlo Bo", Italy
Mohammad Allahbakhsh	The University of New South Wales, Australia
Filipe Araujo	University of Coimbra, Portugal
Alvaro Arenas	IE Business School, Spain
Marcos Baez	University of Trento, Italy
Luciano Baresi	Politecnico di Milano, Italy
Thais Batista	Federal University of Rio Grande do Norte, Brazil
Raghav Batta	Vmware, USA
Amin Beheshti	Macquarie University, Australia
Ladjel Bellatreche	LIAS and ENSMA, France
Moez Ben	Université de Tunis-ElManar, Tunisia
Boualem Benatallah	UNSW, Australia
Salima Benbernou	Université de Paris, France
Djamal Benslimane	Lyon 1 University, France
Walter Binder	University of Lugano, Switzerland
Juan Boubeta-Puig	University of Cádiz, Spain
Omar Boucelma	LSIS, Aix-Marseille University, France
Athman Bouguettaya	The University of Sydney, Australia
Lars Braubach	City University of Applied Sciences Bremen, Germany
Antonio Brogi	Università di Pisa, Italy
Antonio Bucchiarone	FBK-IRST, Italy
Muhammed Bulut	IBM, USA
Christoph Bussler	Google, USA
François Charoy	Université de Lorraine, LORIA and Inria, France
Sanjay Chaudhary	Ahmedabad University, India
Liang Chen	Sun Yat-Sen University, China
Lawrence Chung	The University of Texas at Dallas, USA
Rolland Colette	Université Paris 1 Panthéon-Sorbonne, France
Gianpiero Costantino	IIT-CNR, Italy
Carlos E. Cuesta	Rey Juan Carlos University, Spain
Hoa Khanh Dam	University of Wollongong, Australia
Martina De Sanctis	Gran Sasso Science Institute, Italy
Bruno Defude	Télécom SudParis, France
Shuiguang Deng	Zhejiang University, China
Hai Dong	RMIT University, Australia
Monica Dragoicea	Politehnica University of Bucharest, Romania
Khalil Drira	LAAS-CNRS, France
Yucong Duan	Hainan University, China

Brahim Medjahed   University of Michigan, USA
Sumaira Sultan Minhas   Fatima Jinnah Women University, Pakistan
Raffaela Mirandola   Politecnico di Milano, Italy
Sajib Mistry   Curtin University, Australia
Lars Moench   University of Hagen, Germany
Prateeti Mohapatra   IBM, India
Michael Mrissa   InnoRenew CoE, University of Primorska, Slovenia
Juan M. Murillo Rodríguez   University of Extremadura, Spain
Nanjangud Narendra   Ericsson Research, India
Surya Nepal   CSIRO, Australia
Anne Ngu   Texas State University, USA
Talal H. Noor   Taibah University, Saudi Arabia
Alex Norta   Tallinn University of Technology, Estonia
Paolo Notaro   Huawei Technologies Inc., Germany
Guadalupe Ortiz   UCASE Software Engineering Group, Spain
Olivier Perrin   Loria, France
Ernesto Pimente   University of Malaga, Spain
Pierluigi Plebani   Politecnico di Milano, Italy
Pascal Poizat   Université Paris Nanterre and LIP6, France
Omer Rana   Cardiff University, UK
Manfred Reichert   University of Ulm, Germany
Stefanie Rinderle-Ma   Technical University of Munich, Germany
Stefan Schulte   TU Hamburg, Germany
Lionel Seinturier   University of Lille, France
Mohamed Sellami   Telecom SudParis, France, France
Jun Shen   University of Wollongong, Australia
Sergey Smirnov   SAP Research, Germany
George Spanoudakis   City, University of London, UK
Le Sun Nanjing   University of Information Science and Technology,
                                  China
Marco Vieira   University of Coimbra, Portugal
Monica Vitali   Politecnico di Milano, Italy
Guiling Wang   North China University of Technology, China
Jianmin Wang   Tsinghua University, China
Jianwu Wang   University of Maryland, USA
Xianzhi Wang   University of Technology, Sydney, Australia
Yan Wang   Macquarie University, Australia
Zhongjie Wang   Harbin Institute of Technology, China
Jun Wei   Institute of Software, Chinese Academy of Sciences,
                                  China
Matthias Weidlich   Humboldt-Universität zu Berlin, Germany
Lijie Wen   Tsinghua University, China
Jin Xiao   IBM, USA
Hanchuan Xu   Harbin Institute of Technology, China
Sami Yangui   CNRS-LAAS, France
Lina Yao   University of New South Wales, Australia

Sira Yongchareon	Auckland University of Technology, New Zealand
Muhammad Younas	Oxford Brookes University, UK
Jian Yu	Auckland University of Technology, New Zealand
Qi Yu	Rochester Institute of Technology, USA
Gianluigi Zavattaro	University of Bologna, Italy
Uwe Zdun	University of Vienna, Austria
Mingwei Zhang	Northeastern University, China
Pengcheng Zhang	Hohai University, China
Weiliang Zhao	Macquarie University, Australia
Zhangbing Zhou	China University of Geosciences Beijing, China
Christian Zirpins	Karlsruhe University of Applied Sciences, Germany

External Reviewers

Prabath Abeysekara
Amani Abusafia
Simone Agostinelli
Ahmed Alharbi
Balsam Alkouz
Ebaa Alnazer
Matteo Basso
Mohamed Bouguessa
Abdel Kader Chabi Sika Boni
Juan Chafla
Jaime Correia
Mohamed Hedi Fourati
Ikram Garfatta
Kawsar Haghshenas
Amolkirat Singh Mangat
Jose Antonio Peregrina Perez

Jorge Ramírez
Mohammadreza Rasolroveicy
Andrea Rosà
Subhash Sagar
Francesco Sapio
Beate Scheibel
Babar Shahzaad
Yingnan Shi
Nour El Houda Sioud
Nafiseh Soveizi
Nan Wang
Shoujin Wang
Karolin Winter
Arash Yadegari
Munazza Zaib
Stefano Pio Zingaro

Contents

Architectures, Microservices and APIs

Applications and Miscellanea

Internet-of-Things, Crowdsourced, Social, and Conversational Services

Service Composition and Recommendation

Cloud/edge Computing

Vision Papers

Short Papers

Cloud/Edge/Fog Computing and Internet-of-Things

Microservices and APIs

Industry Papers

Processes

Assessing the Impact of Context Data on Process Outcomes During Runtime

Matthias Ehrendorfer[1], Juergen Mangler[2], and Stefanie Rinderle-Ma[2]($\boxtimes$)

[1] Faculty of Computer Science, University of Vienna, Vienna, Austria
matthias.ehrendorfer@univie.ac.at
[2] Department of Informatics, Technical University of Munich, Garching, Germany
{juergen.mangler,stefanie.rinderle-ma}@tum.de

Abstract. The outcome of a process e.g., the quality of a produced part, constitutes a key performance indicator for process analysis and monitoring. Process outcomes are not only affected by process data, but also by data that is not associated with the process logic through decisions or task input. The rising temperature in a machine, for example, might cause deterioration of part quality. Assessing the impact of context data on the process outcome at runtime is particularly useful to reduce the reaction time to possible errors or deviations. However, as process models contain loops and decisions, grouping and making context data streams interpretable is not always straight-forward, especially under the condition that describing dependencies between context data and process data should be simple and flexible. The contribution of this paper is a classification of context data types, how they are connected to a process model, and how process models can be segmented into stages to group semantically related tasks. The impact of context data on the process outcome is then determined during runtime, i.e., as a process instance is progressing through these segments at runtime, impact calculations using context data can be gradually refined. The approach is prototypically implemented and applied to an artificial logistics and a real-world manufacturing data set.

Keywords: Manufacturing intelligence · Runtime process analysis · Process outcomes · Process context data · Impact factors

1 Introduction

Business processes are specified in the form of process models containing necessary tasks to reach a goal as well as the sequence of their execution. The process logic typically depends on data elements (e.g., the amount of a loan

This work has been partly funded by the Austrian Research Promotion Agency (FFG) via the "Austrian Competence Center for Digital Production" (CDP) under the contract number 881843. This work has been supported by the Pilot Factory Industry 4.0, Seestadtstrasse 27, Vienna, Austria.

© Springer Nature Switzerland AG 2021
H. Hacid et al. (Eds.): ICSOC 2021, LNCS 13121, pp. 3–18, 2021.
https://doi.org/10.1007/978-3-030-91431-8_1

or the decision of process actors) that are available in the process. While tasks implementing a database access typically only receive data that can be utilised in the process logic as a whole, tasks such as starting a machine and waiting for the machine to finish typically receive raw machine telemetry data that is discarded as it is not important for the process logic. Explicitly dealing with such telemetry data in the business logic is often not desirable (even to implement standardised data collection), as it complicates the process models and makes them much harder to maintain and improve. Another category of context data, is data that is never part of the process execution, but instead exists entirely outside of the scope of any process model. For example a hardware temperature sensor might continuously collect data while a machine is running, but the resulting data stream is never connected to a particular process instance.

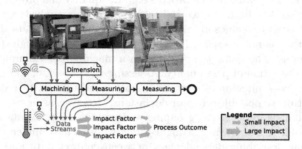

Fig. 1. Sample process with data streams collected during process run

Figure 1 shows a sample process from the manufacturing domain, which waits for (a) the machining of a part, (b) measurement results of a laser based optical micrometer, and finally (c) the tactile measurement results. While (a) from the perspective of the process is just about waiting until the task is finished, it yields gigabytes of data from the machining process itself and additional power and temperature measurement sensors. (b) on the other hand collects measurement information, that could be used for early termination of the process, but additionally gathers information about the temperature of the produced part. A part being too hot or too cold can have a serious impact on measurements, although this is not considered in the process. With (c) finished, a machined part as well as a detailed report about its quality is available. This is referred to as **process outcome**. Individual **data streams** (e.g., machining, power, temperature) are not part of the **data flow**, but nonetheless are important when reasoning why a certain outcome has been reached. Hence, **data streams** can be considered as **impact factors** for quantifying the process outcome.

Online (runtime) analysis of impact factors has the potential to predict outcomes, thus holding the possibility for optimising production processes regarding time and quality. Furthermore, analysing processes during their execution instead of ex-post enables to utilise information from unfinished process instances running in parallel. Another important aspect when dealing with impact factors is relevance. Not all impact factors might contribute equally to the quantification of the output. In previous work [2], first ex post analysis means for impact factors of process outcomes based on annotating the process model is provided. However, methods for determining the importance of individual impact factors at runtime are missing. We tackle this research gap based on the following research questions:

- How can relevant impact factors be found in an online setting where process instances are only partly executed? How can we deal with decisions and loops?
- How does the completion of a trace including its outcome contribute to the confirmation or contradiction of the determined impact factors?
- How does the order in which traces are completed influence the certainty of the determined impact factors? How can this be used to reorder the traces to achieve a higher certainty in a faster way?

To tackle the above research questions, we introduce stages as a means to group tasks and their impact factors. Based on comparing information between stages of different instances we present static stage clustering and dynamic stage analysis approaches to predict the process outcome.

In order to evaluate the concepts presented in this paper, two data sets are analysed: (1) a synthetic simple logistic data set that comprehensibly demonstrates the main concepts, and (2) a real-world manufacturing data set with a multitude of sensors and high velocity machining data, that shows how complex multi-faceted data streams can be handled.

The remainder of the paper is structured as follows: Sect. 2 introduces fundamentals, Sect. 3 presents the approach, and Sect. 4 delves Into how the clustering of impact factors can be realised, and how forecasts can be achieved. The approach is evaluated in Sect. 5 and the results are discussed in Sect. 6. Finally, related work is shown in Sect. 7 and the paper is concluded in Sect. 8.

2 Context Data Fundamentals

In general, impact factors are determined based on data that is available in the process. This data can stem from different data sources and ranges from data determining the control flow of the process to independent sensors measuring data streams that can influence the process. To handle these different types, **context data probes** are introduced to abstract from the underlying type of data when determining impact factors.

2.1 Context Data Probe Types

To track data in a process, different types of data probes can be distinguished (cf. Fig. 2):

(1) **Intrinsic Context Data Probes** (cmp. ⓐ in Fig. 2) describe data collected inside the process where an intrinsic motivation to obtain this data

exists stemming from the execution semantic of the process (i.e., a data element that is used to make a decision in the process or gives the termination condition for a loop). In literature this is often referred to as "process data" or "data elements".

(2) **Extrinsic Context Data Probes** (cmp. **b** in Fig. 2) describe data provided by tasks enacted in the process, but not manifesting in data elements of the process. Examples include tasks that interact with a machine or worklist where data is returned to the process.

(3) **Discrete Context Data Probes** are directly connected to the continuous stream of data from external sources not used in tasks of the process. Examples include data from temperature sensors or twitter feeds which might influence the execution of the process. Two different types exist:

- **Instance Based Discrete Context Data Probes** (cmp. **c** in Fig. 2) track the continuous data stream during the whole execution time of the instance. This allows for the collection of data streams from continuous data streams not connected to any of the tasks in particular but possibly being able to influence the process instance during its runtime.
- **Task Based Discrete Context Data Probes** (cmp. **d** in Fig. 2) only track the continuous data stream during the execution of a specific task. This enables collecting parts of data streams from autonomous sources that only have an influence when certain operations are performed.

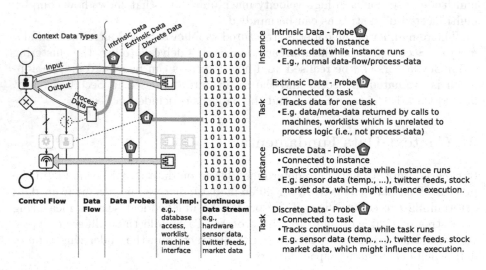

Fig. 2. Types of data in the process context

2.2   Impact Factors and Impact Profiles

This section explains impact factors and profiles as introduced in [2] and depicted in Fig. 3. Data probes produce homogeneous data streams, which are then aggregated. This can happen either with simple (avg, median) or complex domain specific aggregation functions depending on the use case, similarly to calculating key performance indicators, cf. [7]. An impact factor itself can be an aggregation, e.g., inside a machine the temperature might be taken at various locations to account for local heat build-up. The impact factor combines the data from all temperature sensors. Finally, different impact factors are weighted and combined to form profiles. Profiles can either exist for individual tasks or at the instance level.

How to derive the weights between impact factors is one of the contributions of this paper, and will be explained in detail in the next chapters. It is assumed that there is a notion of good or bad outcome: i.e., in a manufacturing process, after quality control it is known if a part is good or bad. We can thus summarise that the following domain specific input to derive impact profiles is necessary:

- A superset/list of data streams which might potentially influence outcome.
- A function how to aggregate each homogeneous data stream.
- A function how to aggregate one or more data impact values (even if the values e.g., derive from different sensor types).
- A set of impact factors that contribute to an impact profile.
- A binary notion of process outcome: good/bad.

The weights for the impact profile function are then calculated in a way so that good parts yield a result that tends towards 1 and bad parts 0.

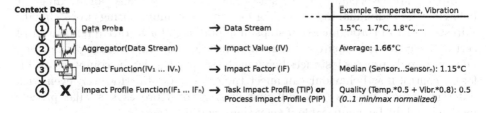

Fig. 3. Impact profiles and related concepts

3 Runtime Context Data Analysis

The fundamentals of context data as used in this paper are explained in Figs. 2 and 3: (a) which data types can occur in the process context and (b) how to handle data streams that are collected during process execution. Figure 4 shows a concrete example of a process in the manufacturing domain where external data is collected in some tasks. Individual data streams can then be aggregated and combined as outlined in Fig. 3 and performed in the example in Fig. 4 where different ways of building impact factors from data streams are shown. The impact factors are then used in further steps of the approach.

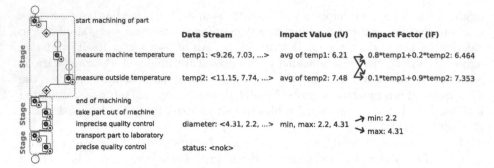

Fig. 4. Running example process

3.1   Comparing Process Instances - Stages

During runtime, a multitude of process instances might be active and in different states of their execution. An execution state is defined by the set of tasks that are currently executed. As the definition of impact factors depends on the tasks, the different execution states result in a varying number of impact factors for the currently active process instances. This can aggravate the comparison of the impact factors over a set of process instances. Hence, we suggest the usage of *stages* that reflect certain execution states in a process and enable to cluster the running instances along these states. Figure 4 depicts the running example process with three stages reflected by boxes.

Stages are especially important when process models allow different behaviour for individual instances. For example, a manufacturing process might skip steps or run through certain steps in a loop, e.g., for iterative refinement of certain aspects that require constant adaptation of manufacturing parameters. Obviously, only process instances being in the same stage can be compared as different control flow behaviour can affect the collected data. However, even with different process models (e.g., different versions of a process), similar process instances might be comparable if they share certain stages.

Stages are user defined at the process model level, and consist of one or several tasks, based on semantic affiliation of included data (e.g., same source, collected in same step)[1]. If, for example, one overall machining operation consists of multiple tasks which represent different machining programs applied on a single piece of raw material, and supervised by a set temperature and vibration sensors, they can be grouped in a stage by the process designer. At the process instance level, a stage is complete, when all tasks contained in the stage have been completed. This constitutes a trigger point for (a) forecasting the next stage, and (b) refining the forecasting data set for the finished stage (see Sect. 4.2).

Predicting how an upcoming stage might contribute to the outcome depends on one or several stages that have been already finished. When analysing the data modified in finished stages, two types of data can be identified.

---

[1] In future work, we aim at the automatic definition of stages based on process abstractions [9] or inspired by automatic approaches such as [6].

Static Stage Clustering: If data points in a set of stages are similar, they can be grouped. Future stages of instances being in the same groups might also contribute to outcome similarly. Therefore instances with such static stages are clustered (see Sect. 4.1 on how a data stream is analysed to cluster instances).

Dynamic Stage Analysis: If a process instance has new data points compared to instances that are in an earlier stage, the difference constitutes a potential progression an early-stage instance might take. An outcome prediction based on this potential progression is possible when comparing instances which are in different stages (see Sect. 4.2).

4 Realisation

Two techniques are employed to realise the introduced concepts, i.e., clustering and refinement of the importance of impact factors when a process instance progresses from one stage to the next one.

4.1 Clustering

Data streams need to be grouped to find out which ones are important for the outcome of a process instance. Without results from earlier process executions it is necessary to identify the streams being similar for "normal" process executions and others deviating from the norm. During clustering, points being close to each other based on a distance metric are grouped. This grouping is utilised by assuming that data streams that can easily be clustered are more important for the outcome. Therefore, the following steps are performed:

```
process_instance = ((DS,A)+,IFU)*) # each process instance contains all
     impact factor (IF) definitions consisting of data streams (DS),
     aggregations (A), and impact functions (IFU)
possible_DS_combinations = all possible combinations of data streams

for DS_set in possible_DS_combinations
   all_IF_lists =[]
   for process_instance in all_process_instances
      IF_list =[]
      for ((DS,A)+,IFU) in process_instance
         if((DS,A)+ contains_all_DS_of DS_set)
            IV_list =[]
            for (DS,A) in (DS,A)+
               IV = aggregate(DS,A)
               IV_list . push(IV)
            IF = create_impact_factor(IV_list ,IFU)
            IF_list . push(IF)
      all_IF_lists . push(IF_list)
   params = determine_clustering_params(all_IF_lists) # kNN plot
   cluster_assignment = build_clusters(all_IF_lists ,params) # assign
        cluster to each process_instance using DBSCAN
   for cluster in cluster_assignment
      cluster_quality(all_IF_lists , cluster) # silhouette value
add list of assigned clusters & their quality  to each process_instance
```

Algorithm 1.1: Static stage clustering

Looking at the running example (Fig. 4), two temperature based impact factors and two impact factors based on the diamater are available. Therefore, a process instance is assigned to two clusters (one for the temperature data streams and one for the diameter data stream). The concrete clustering technique is not important for the general idea. However, as different techniques require different information to perform them, two techniques are considered for this paper:

- The k-means algorithm, following the argumentation in [3], is a well explored approach. On the flip side, it requires the number of clusters (and their initial centre points) as input. Using this clustering technique for finding similar data streams is therefore difficult as it is not known beforehand how many clusters should be found as stream data can show a multitude of different behaviours. Even with methods existing for determining the number of clusters, this technique is not suitable for the intended purpose.
- The DBSCAN algorithm [8] finds clusters based on the distance between data points. These distances are used to determine which points form a cluster and which are too far apart. Therefore, it is not necessary to provide the number of clusters as input. However, the *epsilon* value needs to be provided which defines the neighbourhood of points used for finding points being in the same cluster. This value can be found using a k Nearest Neighbours (kNN) graph if no value from expert knowledge is available.

Based on these considerations we opt for the DBSCAN algorithm. Concerning a quality measure for the whole clustering as well as for individual clusters, the silhouette value is used. The silhouette value can be calculated for each data point and is between -1 and 1. Low values are obtained if points from other clusters are closer than the ones of the same cluster and high values are gained if the point is close to points from its own cluster. Therefore, the silhouette value of a cluster or of all points gives an idea of how close data points are to other points in the same cluster (i.e., how well clustering works).

4.2 Stage Progression

All steps described before are performed in one go where some data streams are already available while other information is not. The final step of the approach presented in this paper is to have individual instances progress in their execution. Two cases exist: for a stage where some instances already have impact factors/data clusters, a forecast for the outcome of the stage can be derived. For stages, where this is not the case, forecast is not possible. The information about available clusters is used (as described in Algorithm 1.2) to determine the overall score of a process instance (representing the impact profile) taking into account the importance of different impact factors and their values for the specific instance.

```
process_instance = ((DS,A)+,IFU)*, cluster_assignment) #
    process_instances additionally contain their cluster assignment
possible_DS_combinations = all possible combinations of data streams

for DS_set in possible_DS_combinations
  for cluster in clusters
    stat_value = get_static_value(cluster)
    if(cluster in cluster_assignment)
      dyn_value = get_dynamic_value(cluster)
      update_overall_score(stat_value,dyn_value)
```

Algorithm 1.2: Dynamic stage analysis

As also described in Sect. 4, the static value of stages is obtained by using the silhouette value of the corresponding cluster based on the group of unfinished process instances. The dynamic value, is based on already finished process instances. Therefore, the share of positive outcomes of the corresponding clusters represents the dynamic value and is combined with the static value to determine the value added to the overall score for determining the outcome of the examined process instance.

5 Evaluation

5.1 Settings

One evaluation scenario is a manufacturing process where a part is produced by a machine tool and afterwards measured twice. Data about the manufacturing process is therefore collected (1) during the manufacturing of a part, (2) during the fast, but imprecise measurement directly after the manufacturing of a part, and (3) during the slow, but precise measurement of the part performed independent of the manufacturing of a part. Parts being taken out of the machine can have a metal chip from the machining on it requiring special handling. After the production step, process instances of the manufacturing process are in a stage where all data (i.e., machining and the fast, but imprecise measurement data) is already collected, but the outcome (i.e., chip occurrence or quality control test result) is still unknown. The data streams used for the evaluation are the workload of the drive (aaLoad) and the axis speed (aaVactB) for the X, Y, and Z axis together with the actual speed of the spindle (actSpeed) and the workload of the spindle (driveLoad) from the machining of the part and the measurement values from the fast, but imprecise measurement which measures the silhouette of the part. For all of these values the minimum, maximum, average, and weighted average (which tries to tackle irregular machine tool measurements) are used to get characteristic values of the timeseries for clustering. Furthermore, the weighted average of an important segment of the fast, but imprecise measurement is used for determining the outcome of a quality control test.

Another data set used for the evaluation is adapted from a realistic container transportation case described in [1]. The process includes the loading of a vehicle which afterwards moves towards its destination. During this journey, the temperature is constantly measured. When the temperature is beyond a certain point for a certain period of time, the vehicle has to return to its origin. Otherwise it continues towards the destination where the container is unloaded. As this process only contains one data stream that is measured (i.e., the temperature) it was decided to additionally use the temperature of each third of the measurement interval as an individual data probe (resulting in 4 data probes) to showcase the approach. Again, minimum, maximum, and average are chosen for obtaining values for clustering the time series. The outcome of the process is defined by normal cases and exceptional cases (i.e., cases where the vehicle has to return to its origin). The process instances are in a stage where the temperature is already measured. However, it is not known if the vehicle has to return to its origin (negative case) or if it is able to stay on the route to its final destination (positive case).

5.2   Evaluation Process

As described in Sects. 3 and 4, the first step of assessing the impact factors of data streams on process outcomes during runtime is to obtain the static characteristics by clustering traces based on the available data. This is done individually for each data stream meaning process instances are clustered multiple times (i.e., once per data stream). The DBSCAN clustering algorithm is used because the number of clusters is not previously known. The *epsilon* value (needed for performing DBSCAN) is determined using kNN plots and finding the elbow in the graph.

Clustering provides a silhouette score describing how close data points in one cluster are together compared to other clusters. The silhouette value can be given for the overall clustering result of a data stream as well as for individual clusters. As explained in Sects. 3 and 4, clusters sticking closer together are assumed to also be more important impact factors for the outcome of a process.

The first example from the manufacturing scenario is shown in Fig. 5. Here, the outcome is represented by the occurrence of a chip on the part. Figure 5a shows the development of the importance of data streams for the outcome after the specified number of process instances have been continued (therefore considering the static characteristics as well as the change of the dynamic characteristics of different data streams). Obviously, the imprecise measurement is the most important impact factor for this outcome. The development of the overall score of process instances based on static and dynamic characteristics is shown in Fig. 5b. The scores of process instances with positive (i.e., no chip on the part) and negative (i.e., chip on the part) outcomes differ from a certain point on. This is depicted by green (positive outcome) and red (negative outcome) boxplots for different numbers of finished process instances. Lower scores signal a negative outcome while higher scores signal a positive outcome.

However, it is also important to get to a point where cases can be distinguished as fast as possible (i.e., by having to finish as few process instances as possible). The approach presented in this paper selects the next process instance up for continuing execution based on the clusters to which the data streams are assigned by choosing the one having the overall highest impact. In contrast to this strategy, continuing the execution of process instances randomly (Fig. 5c) or always choosing the one with the lowest overall impact (Fig. 5d) leads to different behaviour. It can be seen that process instances with positive outcomes can be distinguished from ones with negative ones at an earlier point in time (approximately after 15 process instances have been finished) when choosing

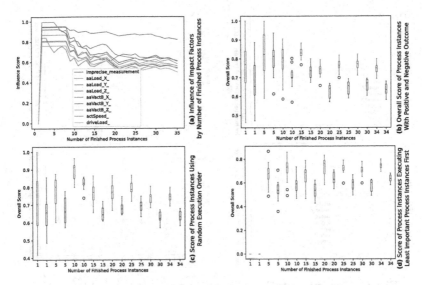

Fig. 5. Chip occurrence in parts of batch 15

process instances with high impact for execution as shown in Fig. 5b in contrast to different ordering techniques as shown in Figs. 5c and 5d. Additionally, the order of process instances can be chosen before any process instances are starting to continue or it can be adapted each time another process instance finishes and therefore more information is available. However, this difference is not discussed due to shortage of space. If not specifically described otherwise all following figures show the approach when the most impactful process instance is chosen and continued after the previous process instance has finished.

Using the same data set as above, but another outcome (i.e., the passing of a specific quality control test) leads to the results shown in Fig. 6. For batch 15 positive and negative outcomes are not clearly distinguishable (see Fig. 6b) and no data stream clearly important for the outcome can be found (see Fig. 6a). However, for batch 14, the overall score of individual process instances can be used to distinguish between cases with different outcomes (see Fig. 6d). Furthermore, it can be seen in Fig. 6c that even if no single important data stream can be identified, there is a group of data streams (actSpeed, aaLoad_Z, and aaVactB_X) being more important than the other ones.

Using the logistics data set for the evaluation leads to the results shown in Fig. 7. Figure 7a shows the development of the impact factors of the data streams that are chosen for the logistics data set as given in the scenario description. Furthermore, Fig. 7b shows that the overall score of process instances with a positive outcome (i.e., normal cases) achieve higher values than ones with a negative outcome (i.e., exceptions) after the initial information gained from clustering is refined by executing additional traces (i.e., about half the process instances have been executed). However, as with the last example, no single data stream can be highlighted as most important.

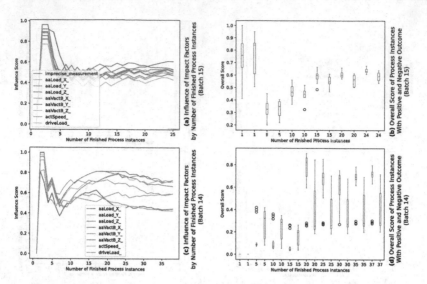

Fig. 6. Quality control test result in parts of batch 14 and 15

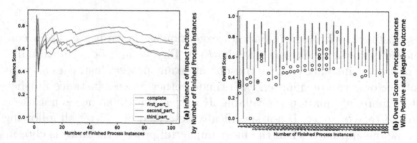

Fig. 7. Completion of route for logistics use case

Overall, the evaluation shows, that it is possible to identify the importance of different impact factors for outcomes of a process at runtime. Using the identified influence of the impact factors on the outcomes allows to calculate an overall score. The approach is evaluated using different domains and shows its applicability by making it possible to distinguish between process instances with a positive outcome and ones with a negative outcome after the initial importance of impact factors has been refined by finishing some initially unfinished process instances. The evaluation also shows that the order in which traces are finished has an effect on how early different outcomes can be identified.

Code and data used for the evaluation along with instructions how to use it is available on gitlab[2]. The manufacturing data is based on the process logs available at cpee.org[34]. The logistics data is based on the case described in [1].

6 Discussion

The evaluation shows that impact factors along with their influence on the outcome can be found. However, supposing that the order in which process instances are continued can be freely defined, the question emerges how the determination of impact factors can be sped up. A possibility is to reorder process instances such that always the one for which the data streams are assigned to the most promising clusters is continued next. As shown in the evaluation this allows to faster distinguish between process instances having a positive/negative outcome. The order can be set either before executing any process instances or it can dynamically change each time new information is available (i.e., when a process instance is continued). This also has implications for real-world applications. In the manufacturing domain it might be necessary to know the order in which parts should be measured beforehand. For static processes this cannot be adapted. However, more dynamic processes which allow to adapt processes based on new insights may support changing the order during the process. An example for a static scenario where the order in which process instances are executed has to be known beforehand would be a robot taking parts from a conveyor belt in the order in which they have been placed. In contrast to this, a robot which picks parts from a tray based on the information available in the process only needs the information which part to pick right before picking.

Concerning the data set of the manufacturing process, two batches are used for the evaluation. One is used to evaluate the described approach for finding impact factors and their importance for two different outcomes (i.e., occurrence of a chip and passing of a quality control test). The other one is used to perform the evaluation for passing a quality control test with different data and the results are compared to each other for validation. The logistics data set is used to show that the approach is applicable to multiple areas where data inside a process is measured over a time period. Another area matching this description is the medical domain where process instances correspond to the treatment of one person and different data such as the temperature or the blood pressure of the patient is measured multiple times. Other domains where the impact of different data streams on the outcome should be determined could also be suitable.

As discussed, the presented approach has certain limitations regarding the scenario. To use the knowledge gained from process instances being slightly ahead of others it has to be possible to intervene in the latter ones. This allows to use information gained from further advanced process instances to adapt process

---

[2] https://gitlab.com/me33551/runtime_impact_factor_assessment [Online; accessed 12-Aug-2021].

[3] https://cpee.org/~demo/DaSH/batch14.zip [Online; accessed 12-Aug-2021].

[4] https://cpee.org/~demo/DaSH/batch15.zip [Online; accessed 12-Aug-2021].

instances which are similar to improve the outcome or at least be prepared for formerly unexpected events. However, this does not necessarily mean that process instances influence each other, it is just about identifying similar instances to improve prediction of the outcome. Regarding the complexity of the proposed algorithms, Algorithm 1.1 analyses each instance for every combination of data streams which may lead to long execution times for big data sets with many data streams. Algorithm 1.2 is also depending on the number of possible data stream combinations (but only once because instances progress individually).

Future work will deal with how stages are best defined and if there is a way to identify them automatically instead of manually. Furthermore, the composition of impact factors based on data probes needs to be developed towards the direction of finding meaningful combinations instead of needing domain knowledge.

7   Related Work

Recently, process mining and predictive process monitoring approaches have started to consider and analyze process perspectives beyond control flow, including process data [5]. Also external data such as time series data is exploited for detecting concept drifts during runtime [10]. In contrast to these approaches, this paper tries to determine how much impact data streams collected during the process have on the outcome. The survey presented in [11] compares different outcome-oriented predictive process monitoring techniques. However, existing approaches do not consider the impact of continuous data streams from external data sources on the outcome of the process. Anomaly detection for manufacturing systems based on sensor data is, for example, tackled by [4]. However, the process aspect and particularly the impact of the sensor streams on the process outcome are not considered. [7] defines an ontology for process performance indicators (PPIs), together with templates and patterns. The PPIs can be defined to aggregate observations in the process. This constitutes valuable input for aggregating impact factors after being transferred to work on external data streams. [6] presents an approach to find stages in a process by automatically maximising the measure of modularity which describes a high density of connections within a stage and a low number of edges between stages. However, [6] only considers the control flow of processes. Therefore, external data which is important for the definition of stages, is not taken into account. The definition of stages is also connected to process abstractions. A survey on process abstractions is provided in [9], also discussing why, when, and how abstraction is applied. For this paper, abstraction supports the focus on the data perspective. The abstraction is done by identifying tasks containing data streams applying to the same abstract steps of the process and group them together in one stage.

8   Conclusion

Knowing the outcomes of process instances while they are still executed bears advantages for process operators. This paper presents an approach to assess the impact of data streams on process outcomes during runtime. Clustering individual data streams allows to determine the initial importance of different impact factors i.e., their share in influencing the outcomes. This is initially only based on the available data from unfinished process instances. Afterwards, process instances being continued are used to refine the initial assessment. Furthermore, it is shown that when the reordering of traces is possible, it is beneficial to finish process instances where the data streams belong to clusters that are promising candidates for important impact factors.

To answer the research questions three concepts are presented in this paper. Firstly, in order to reduce the complexity of a high number of process instances being executed until a certain task, stages are used to support the comparison between different instances that are comparable regarding the collected data. Secondly, static characteristics of impact factors for the process outcome are used to describe their maximum impact on the outcome. Thirdly, dynamic characteristics are used to deduce the actual impact of different factors on the outcome. In contrast to static characteristics which are determined only with unfinished process instances and stay the same, dynamic characteristics are adapted based on the actual outcomes of process instances finished over time.

The approach presented in this paper is evaluated using two batches of a real-world data set from the manufacturing domain including multiple data streams as well as one data set from the logistics domain to show the applicability of the approach for other domains where continuous data streams are included.

References

1. Dunkl, R., Rinderle-Ma, S., Grossmann, W., Fröschl, K.A.: A method for analyzing time series data in process mining: application and extension of decision point analysis. In: Advanced Information Systems Engineering, pp. 68–84 (2014)
2. Ehrendorfer, M., Mangler, J., Rinderle-Ma, S.: Sensor data stream selection and aggregation for the ex post discovery of impact factors on process outcomes. In: CAiSE Forum, pp. 29–37 (2021)
3. Faber, V.: Clustering and the continuous K-means algorithm. Los Alamos Science **22** (1994)
4. Kammerer, K., Hoppenstedt, B., Pryss, R., Stökler, S., Allgaier, J., Reichert, M.: Anomaly detections for manufacturing systems based on sensor data-insights into two challenging real-world production settings. Sensors **19**(24), 5370 (2019)
5. Mannhardt, F.: Multi-perspective Process Mining. Ph.D. thesis, Technische Universiteit Eindhoven, Eindhoven, February 2018
6. Nguyen, H., Dumas, M., ter Hofstede, A.H.M., La Rosa, M., Maggi, F.M.: Mining business process stages from event logs. In: Advanced Information Systems Engineering, pp. 577–594 (2017)
7. del Río-Ortega, A., Resinas Arias de Reyna, M., Durán Toro, A., Ruiz-Cortés, A.: Defining process performance indicators by using templates and patterns. In: Business Process Management, pp. 223–228 (2012)
8. Schubert, E., Sander, J., Ester, M., Kriegel, H.P., Xu, X.: DBSCAN revisited, revisited. ACM Trans. Database Syst. **42**(3), 1–21 (2017)

 9. Smirnov, S., Reijers, H.A., Weske, M., Nugteren, T.: Business process model abstraction: a definition, catalog, and survey. Distributed Parallel Databases **30**(1), 63–99 (2012)
10. Stertz, F., Rinderle-Ma, S., Mangler, J.: Analyzing process concept drifts based on sensor event streams during runtime. In: Business Process Management, pp. 202–219 (2020)
11. Teinemaa, I., Dumas, M., Rosa, M.L., Maggi, F.M.: Outcome-oriented predictive process monitoring: review and benchmark. ACM Trans. Knowl. Discov. Data **13**(2) (2019)

DeepProcess: Supporting Business Process Execution Using a MANN-Based Recommender System

Asjad Khan[1], Hung Le[2(✉)], Kien Do[2], Truyen Tran[2], Aditya Ghose[1],
Hoa Dam[1], and Renuka Sindhgatta[3]

[1] University of Wollongong, Wollongong, Australia
maak458@uowmail.edu.au, {aditya,hoa}@uow.edu.au
[2] Deakin University, Geelong, Australia
{lethai,dkdo,truyen.tran}@deakin.edu.au
[3] IBM India Research Laboratory, Bangalore, India
renuka.sr@in.ibm.com

Abstract. Process-aware Recommender systems can provide critical decision support functionality to aid business process execution by recommending what actions to take next. Based on recent advances in the field of deep learning, we present a novel memory-augmented neural network (MANN) based approach for constructing a process-aware recommender system. We propose a novel network architecture, namely Write-Protected Dual Controller Memory-Augmented Neural Network(DCw-MANN), for building prescriptive models. To evaluate the feasibility and usefulness of our approach, we consider three real-world datasets and show that our approach leads to better performance on several baselines for the task of suffix recommendation and next task prediction.

1 Introduction

Business process management assists organizations in planning and executing activities that collectively deliver business value, usually in the form of a product or a service. Flexible execution of business process instances entails multiple critical decisions, involving various actors and objects, which can have a major impact process performance and achieving desired process outcomes [32]. These decisions therefore require careful attention, as sub-optimal decisions during process execution, can lead to cost overruns, missed deadlines and the risk of failure [11]. While the problem of predicting the behaviour of a given process instance has been studied extensively, using these predictions to support operational decision-making of the kinds outlined above remains a challenge [6,22]. *Process-Aware Recommender Systems* have been proposed to assist knowledge workers in operational decision-making, for instance, by recommending actions leading to process end, managing resource allocation policies and so on [1,28]. In this work, we present a novel *Process-Aware Recommender System* for supporting organizations and process owners in operational decision-making (related to control-flow).

© Springer Nature Switzerland AG 2021
H. Hacid et al. (Eds.): ICSOC 2021, LNCS 13121, pp. 19–33, 2021.
https://doi.org/10.1007/978-3-030-91431-8_2

Recent advances in neural network architectures and learning algorithms have led to the popularization of *Deep Learning* methods which are particularly good at automated feature discovery and learning robust representations from large quantities of raw data, thus significantly reducing the need to hand-craft features which is typically required when using traditional machine learning techniques [20]. Deep Learning based techniques such as Long Short-Term Memory (LSTM) and Gated Recurrent Units (GRUs) have generated considerable interest recently for tackling various Process Analytics tasks (e.g. predictive monitoring). However, LSTMs and GRU methods lack the capacity to solve complex, structured tasks that, for example, require reasoning and planning [10,13]. To tackle such complex tasks, two promising approaches based on neural networks have been proposed: Memory Networks and Neural Turing Machines, both being instantiations of *Memory-Augmented Neural Networks* (MANN) [12]. In this paper, we investigate the applicability of MANNs for building a *Process-Aware Recommender System* that can provide process execution decision support of the kind discussed above.

Contributions: We propose a novel neural network architecture, namely *Write-Protected Dual Controller Memory-Augmented Neural Network(DCw-MANN)*, for building a Process-Aware Recommender System, where we introduce several modifications to the existing Differential Neural Computer(DNC) architecture: (i) *separating the encoding phase and decoding phase, resulting in dual controllers, one for each phase*; (ii) *implementing a write-protected policy for memory during the decoding phase*. We evaluate the effectiveness of our approach on three world datasets for the task of *generating suffix recommendations* that lead to optimal outcomes.

The paper is organized as follows: In Sect. 2, we provide the necessary background on Process Analytics and Deep Learning techniques upon which our proposed method is built. In Sect. 3, we explain the technical workings of our Process-Aware Recommender System, designed to tackle a number of prescriptive process analytics tasks. Implementation details and experimental results are reported in Sect. 4. Finally, Sect. 5 discusses related work, followed by Sect. 6 which concludes the paper and outlines future work.

2 Preliminaries

We first briefly present the existing work upon which our method is built, including event log presentation, recurrent neural networks, and Long Short-Term Memory (LSTM).

2.1 Process Analytics

Process analytics involves a sophisticated layer of data analytics built over the traditional notion of process mining [33]. Compared to Process mining, Process analytics addresses the more general problem of leveraging data generated by, or associated with, process execution to obtain actionable insights about business processes. Process analytics leverages a range of data, including, but not limited to process logs, event logs [26], provisioning logs, decision logs and process context [29] and answers queries that have a number of real world applications particularly related to prescriptive analytics such as resource optimisation and instance prioritisation. In this paper we focus on event logs and assume that when a business process instance is executed, its execution trace is recorded as an event log. An event log is a sequence of events, naturally ordered by the associating timestamps.

In predictive analytics, we study techniques that allow us to predict how the future of a given process instance will unfold and the likely occurrence of future process events [10]. It can be considered as computing (a) a set of functions and (b) a set of computer programs that carry out computation, over a (partially executed) process instance. An example of case (a) is computing remaining time of a process instance, which is the *sequence-to-vector* setting. An example of case (b) is a continuation of a partially executed process, which is the *sequence-to-sequence* setting.

Prescriptive business process monitoring techniques and Process Aware Recommender systems are for providing decision-support to process users. Applications of such system include, offering recommendations about: *(i)* next activities to execute, *(ii)* resource allocation support, *(iii)* Cost and time optimization and *(iv)* risk-mitigation by raising alarms or recommending actions to prevent undesired outcomes [8,35].

2.2   Sequence Modeling with Deep Learning

Recurrent Neural Nets(RNNs), especially the Long Short-Term Memory (LSTM) have brought about breakthroughs in solving complex sequence modelling tasks in various domains such as video understanding, speech recognition and natural language processing [20,27]. Similarly, it has been shown that LSTM can consistently outperform classical techniques for a number of process analytics tasks such as predicting the next activity, time to the next activity etc. [24,31].

Recurrent neural network (RNN) is a model of dynamic processes, and to some degree, a model of computer programs. At each time step t, a RNN reads an *input vector* $\boldsymbol{x}_t$ into a *hidden state vector* $\boldsymbol{h}_t$ and predicts an *output vector* $\boldsymbol{y}_t$. The state dynamic can be abstracted as a recurrent relation: $\boldsymbol{h}_t = \text{RNN}(\boldsymbol{h}_{t-1}, \boldsymbol{x}_t)$. The vanilla RNN is parameterized as follows:

$$\boldsymbol{h}_t = \sigma\left(W_h \boldsymbol{h}_{t-1} + V\boldsymbol{x}_t + \boldsymbol{b}_h\right)$$
$$\boldsymbol{y}_t = W_y \boldsymbol{h}_t + \boldsymbol{b}_y$$

where $(W_h, W_y, V, \boldsymbol{b}_h, \boldsymbol{b}_y)$ are learnable parameters, and σ is a point-wise non-linear function.

Although theoretically powerful, vanilla RNNs cannot learn from long-sequences due to a problem known as vanishing or exploding gradients. A powerful solution is Long Short-Term Memory (LSTM) [16]. LSTM introduces one more vector called "memory" $\boldsymbol{c}_t$, which, together with the state $\boldsymbol{h}_t$, specify the dynamic as: $(\boldsymbol{h}_t, \boldsymbol{c}_t) = \text{LSTM}\,(\boldsymbol{h}_{t-1}, \boldsymbol{c}_{t-1}, \boldsymbol{x}_t)$. In most implementations, this is decomposed further as:

$$\boldsymbol{c}_t = \boldsymbol{f}_t * \boldsymbol{c}_{t-1} + i_t * \tilde{\boldsymbol{c}}_t$$
$$\boldsymbol{h}_t = \boldsymbol{o}_t * \tanh(\boldsymbol{c}_t)$$

where $\tilde{\boldsymbol{c}}_t$ is a candidate memory computed from the input, $\boldsymbol{f}_t, i_t, \boldsymbol{o}_t \in (0, 1)$ are gates, and $*$ denotes point-wise multiplication. $\boldsymbol{f}_t$ determines how much the previous memory is maintained; i_t controls how much new information is stored into memory, and $\boldsymbol{o}_t$ controls how much memory is read out. The candidate memory and the gates are typically parameterized as:

$$\tilde{\boldsymbol{c}}_t = \tanh\,(W_c \boldsymbol{h}_{t-1} + V_c \boldsymbol{x}_t + \boldsymbol{b}_c)$$

$$\begin{bmatrix} \boldsymbol{f}_t \\ i_t \\ \boldsymbol{o}_t \end{bmatrix} = \text{sigm}\left(\begin{bmatrix} W_f \\ W_i \\ W_o \end{bmatrix} \boldsymbol{h}_{t-1} + \begin{bmatrix} V_f \\ V_i \\ V_o \end{bmatrix} \boldsymbol{x}_t + \begin{bmatrix} \boldsymbol{b}_f \\ \boldsymbol{b}_i \\ \boldsymbol{b}_o \end{bmatrix} \right)$$

where $(W_{c,f,i,o}, V_{c,f,i,o}, \boldsymbol{b}_{c,f,i,o})$ are learnable parameters.

3   Approach

While LSTMs can theoretically deal with long event sequences, the long-term dependencies between distant events in a process get diffused into the memory vector. LSTM partly solves the gradient issue associated with the vanilla RNN but it may not be very effective on complex process executions that contain multiple computational steps and long-range dependencies. Keeping this in mind, we explore the application of an expressive sequential process model, that would allow storing and retrieval of intermediate process states in a long-term memory. This is akin to the capability of a trainable Turing machine. Closest to a Turing machine is an instantiation of MANN, known as Differential Neural Computer (DCN) [13]. MANNs can be considered as a recurrent net augmented with an external memory module [13,30]. Because of this memory module MANNs have certain advantages over traditional LSTMs when tackling highly complex sequence modeling problems such as question answering [30] and algorithmic tasks [13]. The memory $\boldsymbol{c}_t$ compresses the entire history into a single vector, and thus the process structure is somewhat lost. For example, if two distant events are highly dependent, there are no easy ways to enforce this relationship through the forgetting gates. Another critical issue is that if a process involves multiple intermediate results for latter use, there are no mechanism to store these results into the flat memory vector $\boldsymbol{c}_t$. These drawbacks demand an external memory to store temporary computational results, akin to the role of RAM in modern computers. The key idea behind these architectures is that all memory operations, including addressing, reading and writing are differentiable. This enables end-to-end gradient-based training. MANNs have found many applications, e.g., question answering [18,30] and simple algorithmic tasks [12]. Overall, Encoder-decoder architectures like *memory-augmented neural nets* are geared to solve sequence to-sequence problems and are naturally a good fit for tackling the problem of *optimal path recommendation.*

We adapted the most advanced variant of MANNs to date, the Differential Neural Computer (DNC) [13]. In most popular implementations, DNC can be considered as a LSTM augmented with an external memory module M. The LSTM plays the role of a controller, which is akin to a CPU, where the memory c_t is akin to registers in the CPU. At each time step, the controller (i) reads an input, (ii) updates its own internal memory and states, (iii) writes the new information data into the external memory, and (iv) finally reads the updated memory to produce an output. In a typically implementation, the external memory is a matrix of N slots, each slot is a vector. To interface with the external memory, the controller computes keys k_t for locating slots for reading and writing. The memory slot is found using cosine similarity between the key and the slot content. This mechanism of locating memory slot is known as *content-based addressing.* In addition, DNC also supports *dynamic memory allocation* and *temporal memory linkage* mechanisms for computing one final write-weight and several read-weights. The read-weights are then used to produce a read content from the memory. Multiple reads are then combined with the controller state to produce an output vector o_t. For readability, we omit the mathematical details here. Readers are referred to the original paper [13].

We now describe how the DNC can be adapted for prescriptive process analytic tasks, starting from event coding into the model and decoding from it, to specific modifications of the DNC to make it suitable for solving a variety of prescriptive tasks in business processes.

3.1   Events/Resources Coding and Decoding

Discrete events/resources in event log can be coded into MANN in several ways. If the number of unique events/resources is large, embedding into a low-dimensional space is typically employed, that is $a \rightarrow x_a$. Otherwise, a simple one-hot coding will suffice, that is, $a \rightarrow [0, 0, ...1, ...0]$. Continuous resources such as time can be normalized as input variables. Alternatively, these continuous variables can be discretized into symbols that represent intervals. This could enable true *end-to-end* learning. However, we can also employ a certain degree of feature engineering to enhance the input signals as in [31], which has been shown to be highly effective.

For discrete symbol prediction at time t, we can use a softmax:

$$P_t \left(a \mid \text{history} \right) = \frac{\exp \left(w_a \cdot o_t \right)}{\sum_{a'} \exp \left(w_{a'} \cdot o_t \right)} \tag{1}$$

where o_t is the output vector generated by the controller, and w_a is a trainable parameter vector. The discrete output is simply: $a^* = \arg \max_a P_t \left(a \mid \text{history} \right)$. Continuous prediction is through a function $y_t = f \left(o_t \right)$, which can be itself a feedforward neural net.

Application of these decoding settings in Eq. (1) allows us to solve a variety of predictive and prescriptive tasks like next-activity recommendation, suffix recommendation and so on. Likewise time-to-event estimation is simply continuous prediction.

3.2 Sequence Prediction with Dual-Controllers and Write-Protected Policy

We assume that at the decision point, we are given a partially executed process instance, and we want to prescribe actions for the continuation of a process instance based and optimize for KPIs based on remaining time, or the set of resources needed for completing the instance. Under the MANN formulation, many of those prescriptive tasks can be cast into *sequence prediction*, that is, we generate a sequence of discrete symbols. For example, process continuation is a natural case, where each symbol is an event.

In case of resources prediction, even though there may or may not natural ordering among resources, we can still produce a sequence. Due to the availability of the external memory which stores all the previous knowledge, the strict ordering in the output sequence is not of a major issue, because at any point in the prediction time, the controller can just make use of the external memory (which can be order-free since it is read-only), and relies less on its own internal memory (which is order-dependent). Note that this property is not possible in LSTM, which is sequential by design.

In the DNC setting, this task can be decomposed into dual phases: the *encoding phase*, in which the prefix is read into the memory, and the *decoding phase*, in which the suffix is sequentially generated. Second, in standard DNC operations, the memory is constantly modified at each time step. In the dual-phase setting, there is no need to update the memory since there are no real inputs. Thus we suggest a simple modification, that is, the memory is read-only during the decoding phase. And finally, since the two phases serve different purposes, it might be useful to separate the *encoding controller* from the *decoding controller*. That is, the encoding controller is specialized in keeping the best description of the process thus far, and the decoding controller is optimized to producing the best suffix, given the information pre-computed by the encoding controller. We call this DNC variant *DCw-MANN*, which stands for Write–Protected Dual Controller Memory–Augmented Neural Network. The proposed system learns a highly compact low-dimensional process representation and captures all variations implicit in the given process execution log to enable *near real-time decision support* for tackling multiple prescriptive monitoring tasks.

Model Operations Over Time: The operations of the modified DNC is illustrated in Fig. 1. There are two controllers, the encoder $LSTM_{enc}$ for the encoding phase and the decoder $LSTM_{dec}$ for the decoding phase. Both share the same external memory M. Each controller maintains their own internal memory c and state h. In the encoding phase, the prefix is fed into the encoder one event at a time. The external memory is updated a long the way. In decoding phase, the state of the encoder and the memory are passed into the decoder. The long-range dependencies between the input prefix and the output suffix are maintained through the memory look-up operations.

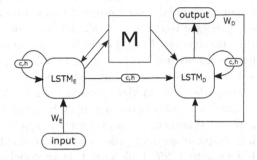

Fig. 1. Write-protected dual controller memory augmented neural network

During the sequence decoding phase, the next symbol at time t is predicted using the information from the memory and previously generated symbols:

$$P_t\left(a \mid a_{l_{pre}+1}, ..., a_{t-1}, \text{history}\right)$$

as in Eq. (1), where the output o_t is generated by the decoder LSTM_{dec}.

3.3   Generating Suffix Recommendations for Decision-Support

Next, our we goal is to learn the task of generating optimal suffix recommendations from partially executed process instances. Process-Aware Recommender Systems, support process users in operational decision-making by continuously monitoring process executions and providing automated recommendations which maximize the likelihood of achieving desired process outcomes. Machine learning based approaches are commonly used to construct data-driven recommender systems where the system attempts to predict the user's interests and recommends items based on those interests. Many of the standard industry recommender systems build a machine learning model by leveraging the user's past behaviour (which is routinely logged) as well as similar actions taken by other users. This model is then used to predict items (or ratings for items) that the users may have an interest in. In Process Analytics, the operative notion of *recommendation*, can be realised by using a machine learning based system, capable of learning from successful (or well-performing) process instances. Weber et al. [28] have explained outcome oriented recommendations based on predictions, as follows: "Recommendations can be considered as predictions about a case, conditioned on the next step that has not been performed yet. In order to recommend to a user what should be the next step in a process, the recommendation service needs to know what the user's target (goal) is, e.g. should the user perform its tasks as soon as possible, or should s/he optimize its outcome in terms of business value".

We have designed our Process-Aware Recommender System to consider the process outcomes by *i)* implementing task conditioning at an architectural level (i.e. using task specific encoders/decoders) *ii)* leveraging past execution data labelled with outcomes (based on performance indicators or non-functional attributes defined for the task). Such labelled data, contains rich knowledge capturing cumulative best practices from the perspective of multiple process users. Our system underpins operational decision support in a manner where good performing instances are leveraged to train a model that can correlate actions with the likelihood of their effectiveness. Here, labels help in differentiating between process instances that performed well based on a pre-defined performance criterion (e.g. through-put time) versus those that performed poorly.

The training examples allow our model to learn the relevant representations from raw data. We trained our proposed machinery in a manner similar to the task of training unsupervised language models, where sequence prediction models are trained with a simple objective: predict the next word, given all of the previous words within some text [25]. Following this approach allows us to learn the prescriptive tasks without the need for explicit supervision. Furthermore, this approach allows us to build a general-purpose model that assumes no domain-specific knowledge of the process, other than the symbolic representation of events (or resources). We finally note that, once the model is trained, it doesn't simply match or repeat the same sequence(recommendations) from training logs rather testing it on an unseen test set(as done in our experiments) shows that our model has learned the task of *recommending an optimal suffix* given a partially executed instance. Good performance on test set also shows that capability of our model to generalise such that it can perform well on a wide variety of future unseen process instances(that were missing from the training data).

4   Evaluation

In the following sections, we explain the experimental setup, we then describe the datasets and pre-processing strategy used for evaluating our proposed approach (Sect. 4.2 and 4.3). We motivate the choice of metrics and describe the baseline methods. We finally present an explanation of model implementation (Sect. 4.4) along with experimental results.

4.1   Datasets

We consider three datasets to evaluate our suffix recommendation engine, whose description is as follows:

– **Moodle Dataset:** This dataset has been created from Moodle's(e-learning platform) issue tracking system. The issue tracking system collects bug reports and allows developers to track the bug resolution process as an issue goes through various development stages. The log contains 10,219 complete processes in total with the number of events in each process ranging from 4 to 23. The preprocessing procedure results in about 32K training prefix/suffix sequences and 8K prefix/suffix sequences. The number of event codes in Moodle dataset is 23.

- **Financial Log:** This log is based on BPI2012 challenge dataset but was pre-processed(see description below) based on a time-based performance metric. After pre-processing we are only left with good performing instances which can be fed to the dataset. The Raw dataset containes about 13,087 cases. The training and testing numbers are approximately 4.2K and 1K, respectively. This dataset has 32 unique type of event codes.
- **IT Incident Management Dataset:** This is an anonymized data set extracted from incident management system supporting an enterprise resource planning (ERP) application. It contains 16,000 tickets(process instances) of IT incident management processes. The log contains the life cycle of a ticket. The ticket is opened by a customer. It is acknowledged typically by a team lead, then it gets assigned to a person working on it and after some analysis and other changes, it gets closed. The group that solved the ticket might not correctly resolve the issue. The log contains the name of the last group that solved the ticket. After splitting, the Incident Mgmt. dataset has about 26K training and 6.5K prefix/suffix sequences. This dataset has 32 unique type of event codes.

4.2 Pre-processing

We take each of these datasets and we split the logs into desirable and undesirable instances (by using the performance of each instance against the stated KPIs) and following the language modeling approach, only train our models using desirable instances. In the Moodle dataset we filter the dataset, by applying a couple of pre-conditions such that each instance should have at least four distinct states[1] and no more than 25 state changes. An undesirable instance examples are chosen with the assumption that bad process instances would shift states back and forth a lot (e.g., issue being reopened multiple times is an Undesirable instance). Hence if more than 25 state changes occur for a given issueID then it would be labelled as an Undesirable instance. Similarly for BPI2012 financial log data we filter cases based on running time. Cases that started in 2012 were filtered out(about 49% because they are not likely to finish. Next, we perform performance filtering using total time duration for each case. Cases with a maximum duration of 1 day 19 h are considered desirable instances while rest of them are labelled as Undesirable performing instances. Each process is a sequence of events and each event is represented by a discrete symbol, which is coded using the one-hot coding scheme introduced in Sect. 3.1. We randomly divide all processes into 80% for training and 20% for testing. Then, we continue splitting each process in the training and test sets into prefix sequence and suffix sequence such that the minimum prefix length is 4.

4.3 Experimental Setup and Modeling

For all experiments, deep learning models are implemented in Tensorflow 1.3.0. Optimizer is Adam [17] with learning rate of 0.001 and other default parameters.

---

[1] https://docs.moodle.org/dev/Process.

Table 2 describes the hyper-parameter settings, as selected through trial and error. To the best of our knowledge, there is no existing ML based technique for suffix recommendation that considers the problem of outcome based optimal path generation. Therefore, for comparison, we implement custom process-agnostic baselines. For the datasets (Moodle, Financial Log and Incident Mgmt.), the baselines are k-NN, and GRU. The k-NN presents a simple but powerful baseline for the case of vector inputs. Thus it is of interest to see if it works well for sequence inputs as in the case of process analytics. The LSTM, on the hand, has been the state-of-the-art for this domain, as shown in recent work [9,31]. The GRU is a recent alternative to LSTM, which has been shown to be equally effective in NLP tasks [4]. The k-NN works by retrieving k most similar prefixes in the training data. Then suffix and other desirable outcomes are computed from the same outcomes of those retrieved cases. The recommendation is either the average of the retrieved outcomes (if continuous), or the most common outcome (if discrete).

Model Evaluation: Numerical evaluations with comparisons to baselines play a central role when judging research for most recommender systems, therefore we rely on baseline comparisons/benchmarks to evaluate the quality of recommendations produced by our machinery. Our recommender system provides operational decision support for process users and on a higher level, performs utility optimization. Gunawardana et al. [15] provide a survey of evaluation metrics for recommender systems. They observe that the task of optimizing utilities is by far the least explored recommendation task. Hence research/industry standard evaluation metrics do not exist for such task. Prescriptive machine learning models for such tasks are predominantly benchmarked by matching samples against a reference solution (e.g. previously well-performing instances representing ground truth). In our case, we have picked Levenshtein distance metric because it aptly summarizes accuracy/precision in terms of the closeness of recommended sequences to the reference(desired) sequences in high-dimensional vector space. It represents a degree of conformity of evaluated predictions to the true value and is sensitive to differences in error rates, making it effective for judging the effectiveness of our process-aware recommendation machinery. However, these distances have a quadratic time complexity of the sequence length, which can be expensive for long sequences. Hence we build a Trie over the training prefixes for fast retrieval. In our experiments, we choose k to be 1 and 5. We append to the end of each complete process a special token <END> signaling its termination. We train the GRU in the same manner as training a language model [23], which is identical to next activity prediction. After training, a test prefix will be fed to the GRU as prior context and the model will continue recommending the next event step-by-step until the <END> symbol is outputted. In our experiment, we use a hidden vector of size 100 for both GRU and MANN methods.

4.4   Results and Discussion

For evaluation, we use the edit distance (Levenshtein distance) as it is a good indication of sequence similarity where deletion, insertion or substitution are available as in the case of business processes. To account for variable sequence lengths, we normalize this distance over the length of the longer sequence (between 2 sequences). Then, the final metric is calculated as the normalized edit similarity that equals $1-$ normalized edit distance. Consequently, the predicted sequence is good if its normalized edit similarity to the target sequence is high.

We observe in Table 1 that our MANN based mode outperforms the state of the art LSTM model across all three datasets. The k-NN works surprisingly well. However, it faces some difficulties in this problem of sequence-to-sequence prediction. First, the prefixes can be slightly different but the suffices can differ drastically, e.g., due to a single decisive event. Second, the k-NN does not capture the continuation of a process, and thus suffices from similar instances do not guarantee to be the right continuation. And third, for $k > 1$, there is no easy way to combine multiple suffix sequences, which shows in the worse result than the case $k = 1$.

Table 1. Suffix recommendation task: the average normalized edit similarity between the target suffixes and the suffixes recommended by different models (higher is better).

Method	Moodle	fin_log	Inc_Mgmt
5-NN	0.817	0.588	0.418
1-NN	0.840	0.631	0.432
GRU	0.875	0.559	0.454
LSTM	0.887	0.683	0.497
MANN	**0.888**	**0.691**	**0.502**

Table 2. MANN hyper-parameters. (*) no duplicate.

Hyper-parameters	Moodle	Financial log	Incident Mgmt.
# memory slots	64	64	64
Memory slot size	100	64	100
Controller hidden dim	100	100	100

Since the authors in [31] shared, only public the code for the two-layer LSTMs (one is shared-weight), we can only calculate the parameter size for this configuration, which is about 208K trainable parameters. It should be noted that the best model configurations consisting of 3 or 4 layers may have even more than that number of parameters. Our MANN, by contrast, is much simpler with two one-layer controllers and an external memory hence has fewer parameters (less than 125K). This suggests the ability of the external memory to compress and capture essential information in order to perform better.

Taken together, the results achieved using MANNs demonstrate that our proposed machinery is well-suited for solving both predictive and prescriptive monitoring tasks, with far fewer parameters. We also note that MANNs are relatively new, and we expect that even better performance could be achieved with greater effort in devising encodings for process analytics problems. As well, we have been able to position a range of process analytics problems to leverage future developments/improvements in MANNs. Our approach based on employing labelled datasets should hopefully lead the community to ask a broader range of prescriptive process analytics questions that could be solved using similar machinery as discussed in this paper.

5   Related Work

Predictive business process monitoring is a family of techniques concerned with predicting the future state, outcomes and behaviour of ongoing cases of a business process [32]. Relevant to our work, the task of *next activity prediction* and *Process Path Prediction* has been tackled by approaches like state-transition models, hidden Markov models(HMM) and Probabilistic Finite Automatons(PFA) models [2,3,19]. Tax et al. [31] point out that such approaches are *'tailor-made for specific prediction tasks and not readily generalizable'*. Recently, Deep Learning methods such as LSTMs have shown an advantage over such classical methods for making accurate predictions and solving various predictive monitoring tasks [31]. Several survey papers have reviewed the literature on predictive process monitoring. e.g. Marquez-Chamorro et al. [22] and Di Francescomarino et al. [7] classify the literature based on input data, classification algorithm and prediction target. Similarly, Teinemaa et al. [32] and Verenich et al. [34] also survey the literature by covering various datasets, propose task definitions and provide benchmark comparison of recently proposed algorithms. The output of Predictive business process monitoring techniques, is just *predictions*. Predictions can be used as *early warnings* for taking risk informed decisions but do not explicitly support answering of question like *What action should we take next to achieve a particular goal?* and *Why should we do it?* [21]. Compared to descriptive and predictive business analytics, prescriptive process analytics remains less mature [8]. Marquez et al. [22] point out that *'little attention has been given to providing recommendations'*. Instead of providing specific action recommendations, literature on business process monitoring focuses on forecasting future process events(and outcomes) while leaving the action implementation part to the subjective judgment of process users and business decision makers [6]. Overall, prescriptive business process monitoring techniques [5,14,28] have largely focused on recommending preventive actions in order to support *risk-informed decision making*.

Eili et al. [8] provide a systematic review of Recommender Systems in Process Mining and classify recommendation approaches as *'pattern optimization'*, *'risk minimization'*, or *'metric-based'*. They highlight the fact that compared to descriptive and predictive business analytics, prescriptive process analytics remains less mature [8]. Existing prescriptive business process monitoring techniques [5,14,28] are used to recommend *preventive actions* in order to support *risk-informed decision making*. To the best of our knowledge, the problem of recommending best path (representing sequence of activities leading to the process end), based on pre-defined KPIs hasn't been addressed. Closely related to our work, Weinzier et al. [35] consider problem of recommending *next best actions* that lead to optimal outcomes. Their work however differs from ours, as their technique relies on explicitly adding control-flow knowledge to their proposed technique via formal process model and uses process simulations to verify and filter the predictions of the trained predictive model. Similarly, Groger et al. [14] introduce the concept of recommendation-based business process optimization for data-driven process optimization. Their data-mining driven solution supports adaptive processes and recommends actions for next process step to take for a given process instance in order to avoid performance deviation. Lastly, Schobel et al. [28] propose a technique for early identification of diverging processes that can support operational decision-making processes by for example taking remedial actions as business processes unfold. Overall, prescriptive business process monitoring techniques [5,14,28] are used to recommend preventive actions in order to support *risk-informed decision making*. However, compared to above mentioned work which focuses on *early warning recommendations* (e.g. predicted metric deviation), our work focuses on *best action recommendations* that maximize the likelihood of achieving desirable outcomes.

6 Conclusion

In this paper, we explored the application of recent advances in deep learning for building a *Process-Aware Recommender System*. We investigated a specific type of neural network known as the *memory–augmented neural network (MANN)* for its applications in prescriptive process monitoring tasks. We adapted a recently developed MANN architecture, namely the Differential Neural Computer [13] and proposed several modifications to the default architecture. We performed evaluations using three labelled datasets to show that our proposed approach performs well on the task of suffix recommendation while taking cognisance of the relevant KPIs. Our future work will involve investigating the behaviour of MANNs on highly complex processes that involve multiple intermediate steps and results, and devising ways to visualise how distant events are remembered and linked together.

References

1. Beheshti, A., Yakhchi, S., Mousaeirad, S., Ghafari, S.M., Goluguri, S.R., Edrisi, M.A.: Towards cognitive recommender systems. Algorithms **13**(8), 176 (2020)
2. Breuker, D., Matzner, M., Delfmann, P., Becker, J.: Comprehensible predictive models for business processes. MIS Q. **40**(4), 1009–1034 (2016)
3. Ceci, M., Lanotte, P.F., Fumarola, F., Cavallo, D.P., Malerba, D.: Completion time and next activity prediction of processes using sequential pattern mining. In: Džeroski, S., Panov, P., Kocev, D., Todorovski, L. (eds.) DS 2014. LNCS (LNAI), vol. 8777, pp. 49–61. Springer, Cham (2014). https://doi.org/10.1007/978-3-319-11812-3_5

4. Cho, K.: Learning phrase representations using RNN encoder-decoder for statistical machine translation. In: Proceedings of the 2014 Conference on Empirical Methods in Natural Language Processing (EMNLP), Doha, Qatar, pp. 1724–1734. Association for Computational Linguistics, October 2014
5. Conforti, R., de Leoni, M., La Rosa, M., van der Aalst, W.M.P.: Supporting risk-informed decisions during business process execution. In: Salinesi, C., Norrie, M.C., Pastor, Ó. (eds.) CAiSE 2013. LNCS, vol. 7908, pp. 116–132. Springer, Heidelberg (2013). https://doi.org/10.1007/978-3-642-38709-8_8
6. Dees, M., de Leoni, M., van der Aalst, W.M.P., Reijers, H.A.: What if process predictions are not followed by good recommendations? (technical report). arXiv preprint arXiv:1905.10173 (2019)
7. Di Francescomarino, C., Ghidini, C., Maggi, F.M., Milani, F.: Predictive process monitoring methods: which one suits me best? In: Weske, M., Montali, M., Weber, I., vom Brocke, J. (eds.) BPM 2018. LNCS, vol. 11080, pp. 462–479. Springer, Cham (2018). https://doi.org/10.1007/978-3-319-98648-7_27
8. Eili, M.Y., Rezaeenour, J., Sani, M.F.: A systematic literature review on process-aware recommender systems. arXiv preprint arXiv:2103.16654 (2021)
9. Evermann, J., Rehse, J.-R., Fettke, P.: A deep learning approach for predicting process behaviour at runtime. In: Dumas, M., Fantinato, M. (eds.) BPM 2016. LNBIP, vol. 281, pp. 327–338. Springer, Cham (2017). https://doi.org/10.1007/978-3-319-58457-7_24
10. Evermann, J., Rehse, J.-R., Fettke, P.: Predicting process behaviour using deep learning. Decis. Support Syst. **100**, 129–140 (2017)
11. Ghattas, J., Soffer, P., Peleg, M.: Improving business process decision making based on past experience. Decis. Support Syst. **59**, 93–107 (2014)
12. Graves, A., Wayne, G., Danihelka, I.: Neural turing machines. arXiv preprint arXiv:1410.5401 (2014)
13. Graves, A., et al.: Hybrid computing using a neural network with dynamic external memory. Nature **538**(7626), 471–476 (2016)
14. Gröger, C., Schwarz, H., Mitschang, B.: Prescriptive analytics for recommendation-based business process optimization. In: Abramowicz, W., Kokkinaki, A. (eds.) BIS 2014. LNBIP, vol. 176, pp. 25–37. Springer, Cham (2014). https://doi.org/10.1007/978-3-319-06695-0_3
15. Gunawardana, A., Shani, G.: A survey of accuracy evaluation metrics of recommendation tasks. J. Mach. Learn. Res. **10**(12) (2009)
16. Hochreiter, S., Schmidhuber, J.: Long short-term memory. Neural Comput. **9**(8), 1735–1780 (1997)
17. Kingma, D.P., Ba, J.: Adam: a method for stochastic optimization. arXiv preprint arXiv:1412.6980 (2014)
18. Kumar, A., et al.: Ask me anything: dynamic memory networks for natural language processing. In: International Conference on Machine Learning, pp. 1378–1387. PMLR (2016)
19. Lakshmanan, G.T., Shamsi, D., Doganata, Y.N., Unuvar, M., Khalaf, R.: A Markov prediction model for data-driven semi-structured business processes. Knowl. Inf. Syst. **42**(1), 97–126 (2013). https://doi.org/10.1007/s10115-013-0697-8
20. LeCun, Y., Bengio, Y., Hinton, G.: Deep learning. Nature **521**(7553), 436–444 (2015)
21. Lepenioti, K., Bousdekis, A., Apostolou, D., Mentzas, G.: Prescriptive analytics: literature review and research challenges. Int. J. Inf. Manage. **50**, 57–70 (2020)
22. Márquez-Chamorro, A.E., Resinas, M., Ruiz-Cortés, A.: Predictive monitoring of business processes: a survey. IEEE Trans. Serv. Comput. **11**(6), 962–977 (2017)

23. Mikolov, T., et al.: Statistical language models based on neural networks. Presentation at Google, Mountain View, 2 April 2012
24. Navarin, N., Vincenzi, B., Polato, M., Sperduti, A.: LSTM networks for data-aware remaining time prediction of business process instances. In: 2017 IEEE Symposium Series on Computational Intelligence (SSCI), pp. 1–7. IEEE (2017)
25. Radford, A., Jeffrey, W., Child, R., Luan, D., Amodei, D., Sutskever, I., et al.: Language models are unsupervised multitask learners. OpenAI Blog 1(8), 9 (2019)
26. Santiputri, M., Ghose, A., Dam, H.K., Automating the acquisition of process semantics: Mining task post-conditions. Data Knowl. Eng. **109**, 112–125 (2017)
27. Schmidhuber, J.: Deep learning in neural networks: an overview. Neural Netw. **61**, 85–117 (2015)
28. Schonenberg, H., Weber, B., van Dongen, B., van der Aalst, W.: Supporting flexible processes through recommendations based on history. In: Dumas, M., Reichert, M., Shan, M.-C. (eds.) BPM 2008. LNCS, vol. 5240, pp. 51–66. Springer, Heidelberg (2008). https://doi.org/10.1007/978-3-540-85758-7_7
29. Sindhgatta, R., Ghose, A., Dam, H.K.: Context-aware analysis of past process executions to aid resource allocation decisions. In: Nurcan, S., Soffer, P., Bajec, M., Eder, J. (eds.) CAiSE 2016. LNCS, vol. 9694, pp. 575–589. Springer, Cham (2016). https://doi.org/10.1007/978-3-319-39696-5_35
30. Sukhbaatar, S., Szlam, A., Weston, J., Fergus, R.: End-to-end memory networks. arXiv preprint arXiv:1503.08895 (2015)
31. Tax, N., Verenich, I., La Rosa, M., Dumas, M.: Predictive business process monitoring with LSTM neural networks. In: Dubois, E., Pohl, K. (eds.) CAiSE 2017. LNCS, vol. 10253, pp. 477–492. Springer, Cham (2017). https://doi.org/10.1007/978-3-319-59536-8_30
32. Teinemaa, I., Dumas, M., Rosa, M.L., Maggi, F.M.: Outcome-oriented predictive process monitoring: Review and benchmark. ACM Trans. Knowl. Discovery Data (TKDD) **13**(2), 1–57 (2019)
33. van der Aalst, W., et al.: Process mining manifesto. In: Daniel, F., Barkaoui, K., Dustdar, S. (eds.) BPM 2011. LNBIP, vol. 99, pp. 169–194. Springer, Heidelberg (2012). https://doi.org/10.1007/978-3-642-28108-2_19
34. Verenich, I., Dumas, M., Rosa, M.L., Maggi, F.M., Teinemaa, I.:. Survey and cross-benchmark comparison of remaining time prediction methods in business process monitoring. ACM Trans. Intell. Syst. Technol. (TIST) **10**(4), 1–34 (2019)
35. Weinzierl, S., Dunzer, S., Zilker, S., Matzner, M.: Prescriptive business process monitoring for recommending next best actions. In: Fahland, D., Ghidini, C., Becker, J., Dumas, M. (eds.) BPM 2020. LNBIP, vol. 392, pp. 193–209. Springer, Cham (2020). https://doi.org/10.1007/978-3-030-58638-6_12

Interval-Based Remaining Time Prediction for Business Processes

Chi Wang(ID) and Jian Cao(✉)(ID)

Shanghai Jiao Tong University, Shanghai, China
cao-jian@cs.sjtu.edu.cn

Abstract. Uncertainty is an unavoidable factor in predictive business process monitoring, especially in terms of remaining time prediction. However, existing methods only give a precise time as the result, which fails to consider and reveal the uncertainty of ongoing processes. As a novel attempt to add quantified uncertainty into process monitoring, this paper proposes a model that provides comprehensive predictive information. Specifically, an interval-based time predictor is constructed to make both an optimistic and a pessimistic forecast of the remaining time for business processes. In addition, a clustering-based method is used to extract trace patterns as prior knowledge to optimize interval prediction. We investigate LSTM networks as an approach to construct qualifying time intervals as well as different trace embedding and clustering methods. Our model achieves acceptable results on real-life event logs according to the measurement of coverage-width criterion.

Keywords: Business process monitoring · Interval-based remaining time prediction · Trace clustering and prefix classification

1 Introduction

Predictive business process monitoring is a group of analytical techniques conducted during the early execution of an ongoing business process, aiming to forecast the future states or properties of a process and assess its performance or reduce possible violations [22]. As an important sub-field of process mining, predictive business process monitoring derives useful insights from historical data and makes real-time predictions in order to ameliorate business processes [17].

Recent research has introduced machine learning and deep learning techniques to the field of process monitoring. While machine learning algorithms like decision trees are often combined with filter which extracts features from business processes, deep learning methods tend to possess end-to-end structures [2]. As business processes take place event after event, recurrent neural networks, particularly the ones with a long short-term memory (LSTM) architecture, have been applied to solve process monitoring problems due to their remarkable performance in sequence modeling tasks [21].

Various methods have been proposed to predict the properties of business processes, for instance, compliance violations [4], and next activity [21]. Of these

© Springer Nature Switzerland AG 2021
H. Hacid et al. (Eds.): ICSOC 2021, LNCS 13121, pp. 34–48, 2021.
https://doi.org/10.1007/978-3-030-91431-8_3

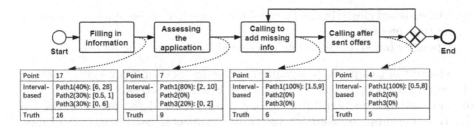

Point	17		Point	7		Point	3		Point	4
Interval-based	Path1(40%): [6, 28] Path2(30%): [0.5, 1] Path3(30%): [0, 6]		Interval-based	Path1(80%): [2, 10] Path2(0%) Path3(20%): [0, 2]		Interval-based	Path1(100%): [1.5,9] Path2(0%) Path3(0%)		Interval-based	Path1(100%): [0.5,8] Path2(0%) Path3(0%)
Truth	16		Truth	9		Truth	6		Truth	5

Fig. 1. The comparison between point prediction and interval-based prediction. The example originates from the dataset BPIC2012. The predictions are presented as day.

different kinds of prediction objectives, remaining time prediction offers an important indicator of a process that enables process administrators to lower the risk of a deadline violation and notifies customers of possible delays in advance.

Although a number of remaining time prediction models are proposed, they all try to present a single point estimation of remaining time and neglect the uncertainty of business process executions. There are many factors that lead to uncertainty in the executions of a business process, which results in uncertainty in relation to the remaining time. A business process often includes multiple alternative execution paths whose execution time may be very different. It is impossible to precisely know which path a process instance will follow at the early phase. Moreover, the execution time of the same paths can still vary widely due to workload and resource differences. Therefore, the remaining time for a business process is uncertain in nature. Fortunately, this kind of uncertainty decreases as the execution draws closer to termination and more information is provided.

Consequently, an 'interval' prediction, in contrast to a 'point' prediction, makes better sense. A time interval consists of a lower bound and an upper bound, representing how much time the process will take to finish at the earliest and the latest. As shown in Fig. 1, the point prediction gives either a shorter or a longer remaining time. An optimistic prediction may lead to deadline violations as well as the impatience of the applicants of the process. A pessimistic prediction may lead to redundant resource allocation. On the contrary, an interval-based prediction gives all the path probabilities and the corresponding time intervals. The midpoint of the interval is basically as accurate as the point prediction. This offers comprehensive information to interested stakeholders and enables them to better allocate resources and manage time.

Therefore, the main purpose of this paper is to propose a model that can predict the remaining time with an uncertainty degree. Instead of merely giving a point value, our model offers a more informative prediction result, i.e., a remaining time interval. The main contributions of this paper are as follows:

– An interval-based remaining time prediction model is proposed, which brings uncertainty into process monitoring tasks.

- A trace-based clustering and prefix-based classifier are combined with remaining time prediction.
- A penalty-based loss function is designed to optimize the model.

The rest of this paper is organized as follows. Section 2 presents a summary of the related work on time prediction of business processes and interval prediction methods. Section 3 gives formal descriptions of the problem. Section 4 describes our proposed methods and the experimental assessments of our model are presented in Sect. 5. Section 6 concludes our work.

2   Related Work

2.1   Remaining Time Prediction

Many approaches have been proposed for remaining time prediction for business processes. State transition systems [1] and stochastic Petri nets [19] are two major tools for process-aware information systems. Non-process-aware approaches rely on machine learning algorithms [25] like regression trees [6]. Generally, traces are pre-processed before prediction models are applied on them. The typical pre-processing step is clustering [7], through which similar traces are grouped according to their control flow similarity so that a specified model can be trained on the traces belonging to each group. However, most clustering-based methods create trace clusters based on full traces and they are unable to classify small fractions of traces of a business process into a correct category [26].

The performance of traditional machine learning methods heavily depends on the features and the encoding of a trace is often conducted by manually selecting features like special trace patterns. On the contrary, neural networks encode raw data into feature representations of a higher level [2]. Complex network structures like recurrent neural networks [9] have been explored given that events in business processes are similar to words in natural language processing. RNNs with an LSTM structure have been applied by Niek Tax [21] to predict the next activity and the cycle time of activities. Existing predictive methods either give a deadline violation warning or a specific predicted remaining time. Unfortunately, the uncertainty of predicted information is not considered.

2.2   Interval Prediction Model

Uncertainty plays a problematic but important role in many scientific and engineering problems. How to represent or quantify the randomness and uncertainty in prediction modeling problems has become a critical task in recent times. Neural networks are an effective way to quantify uncertainty by constructing prediction intervals (PIs). PIs have been used in numerous applications such as economics, medical statistics and renewable energy consumption [11].

Traditional prediction interval constructions such as the delta method [10] often rely on assumptions of normally distributed and homogeneous uncertainty.

Direct prediction interval construction methods provide a way to build PI regardless of distribution [3]. The lower and upper bound estimation (LUBE) method [13] directly predicts the bounds of the interval through the neural network. A neural network controls the quality of the interval by controlling coverage percentage and width. Heuristic optimization methods like annealing are used but they become incompetent as the networks become complex. Some researchers use a penalty-based loss function for PI to apply a gradient-based optimization strategy [20].

3 Problem Formulation

3.1 Event Logs and Traces

Business process monitoring relies on event logs that record the events during the execution of processes [23]. An event log consists of sequences of events called traces. A complete trace corresponds to a case of a process. Every event possesses a set of different attributes, among which three attributes must appear, namely *activity name*, *timestamp* and *case id*. An *activity name* refers to the activity the event executes. A corresponding *timestamp* specifies when the event occurs. The *case id* indicates to which case the event belongs. With other event-wise or case-wise attributes, an event is defined in Definition 1. Events with the same case ID form a chronological sequence called a trace as shown in Definition 2.

Definition 1. *An event is defined as $e = (a, c, t, (d_1, v_1), ..., (d_m, v_m))$, where a is the activity name, c is case ID and t is the timestamp. (d_i, v_i) represents an attribute and its corresponding value. m is the total number of attributes.*

Definition 2. *A trace is defined as $\sigma = [e_1, ..., e_n], e_i.c = e_j.c, \forall i, j \in [1, ..., n]$, where e_i, e_j are the i-th and j-th events in the trace and $e_i.c$ represents the case ID of e_i.*

Predictive business process monitoring makes predictions for ongoing traces in which only a few events, the prefix of a trace (Definition 3), has taken place. A prefix log (Definition 4) can be made from the original event log L. A predictive model can learn the relation between the attributes of the prefixes and the future states of the process.

Definition 3. *A prefix is defined as $prefix(\sigma, l) = [e_1, ..., e_l], l \leq |\sigma|$, where l is the length of the prefix and $|\sigma|$ is the length of the complete trace.*

Definition 4. *A prefix log is defined as $L^* = prefix(\sigma, k) : \sigma \in L, 1 \leq k \leq |\sigma|$, where L is the complete event log.*

3.2 Predictive Business Process Monitoring

A predictive process monitoring system [16] consists of two components, i.e., a trace processor and a predictor. We extend this structure by adding more components so that it can fit our requirements. As shown in Fig. 2, historical

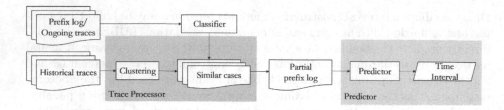

Fig. 2. An overview of the framework.

traces are clustered based on their similarity. We predict the cluster to which an ongoing trace belongs using a classifier, which is trained on the historical traces. A remaining time interval predictor is trained on each cluster.

When a prefix is given, the classifier outputs the probabilities of the prefix falling into different clusters. It is possible that some of the probabilities are similar [24], because, according to the information obtained so far, there is no strong evidence to decide its suffix. As a result, multiple predictors for the possible clusters give the upper and lower bounds of the remaining time.

3.3   Performance Evaluation of Interval Predictions

While point predictions can be assessed by metrics such as mean absolute error, prediction intervals need other indicators to measure quality. An interval must contain the true point value with a not-too-large width. Prediction Interval Coverage Probability ($PICP$) [12] statistically calculates the calibration of PIs.

$$PICP = \frac{1}{n} \sum_{i=1}^{n} c_i, c_i = \begin{cases} 1, t_i \in [y_{li}, y_{ui}] \\ 0, t_i \notin [y_{li}, y_{ui}] \end{cases} \tag{1}$$

t_i is the ground truth of the remaining time point value. y_{li} and y_{ui} are the lower and upper bound. Prediction interval normalized average width ($PINAW$) [14] restricts the width:

$$PINAW = \frac{1}{Rn} \sum_{i=1}^{n} (y_{ui} - y_{li}) \tag{2}$$

where R is the value range of our target. $PINAW$ can be combined with $PICP$ to construct the coverage width-based criterion (CWC) [14].

$$CWC = PINAW(1 + \gamma(PICP)e^{\eta(\mu - PICP)}) \tag{3}$$

where,

$$\gamma(PICP) = \begin{cases} 1, PICP < \mu \\ 0, PICP \geq \mu \end{cases} \tag{4}$$

η is a weight hyper-parameter and μ is the hyper-parameter that represents the target confidence level. In addition, to compare interval prediction with time point values, the midpoint of an interval is chosen to represent the point value prediction and we use mean absolute error to measure the accuracy.

$$MAE = \frac{1}{n} \sum_{i=1}^{n} |\frac{y_{ui} + y_{li}}{2} - t_i| \tag{5}$$

4 Proposed Model

4.1 Trace Clustering and Prefix Classifier

Clustering approaches often use manually selected features like frequencies and specific patterns. Also, the clusters are based on prefixes, leading to blindness to the suffixes. In the sense that different traces take different paths and imply different time-related properties, we directly divide the complete traces into different categories based on their similarity to the event sequences.

As the execution of business processes is analogous to the word flow in natural language processing, sentence embedding skills can be applied to trace embedding. Trace2Vec [5] is a successful adoption of Doc2Vec [15], which uses adjacent words and paragraph IDs (events and case ID in our case) to generate an embedding. The embedding vectors can be used by clustering algorithms like k-means with the measurement of cosine similarity. To incorporate our objective, the completion time of traces are concatenated to the vectors.

The clustering model is based on the complete historical traces, so it cannot be applied to the classification of prefixes. An LSTM network is constructed to classify ongoing traces into different clusters. Apart from the event sequence, other attributes are used to help the multi-class prediction problem. The classifier gives the probabilities of the clusters after a softmax calculation.

4.2 An Interval Prediction Model

The structure of the time prediction model includes an LSTM network with several shared and independent layers referring to the methods in [21]. The model directly gives the upper and lower bounds. The shared layers integrate the information obtained from the embedded features, which helps multi-objective learning. Batch normalization is used after each LSTM layer.

PICP makes gradient descent impossible, so a loss function based on an out-of-bound penalty is designed. The loss function penalizes the model when the upper bound is less than or the lower bound is greater than the true value. It also penalizes intervals that exceed width expectations.

$$lower\_loss = \frac{1}{n} \sum_{i=1}^{n} ReLU(y_{li} - t_i) \tag{6}$$

$$upper\_loss = \frac{1}{n} \sum_{i=1}^{n} ReLU(t_i - y_{ui}) \tag{7}$$

$$width\_loss = \frac{1}{n} \sum_{i=1}^{n} ReLU(|y_{ui} - y_{li}| - w_{exp}) \tag{8}$$

$$MAE = \frac{1}{n} \sum_{i=1}^{n} |\frac{y_{ui} + y_{li}}{2} - t_i| \tag{9}$$

where l_i is the ground truth and y_{li} and y_{ui} are the predicted lower and upper bounds. $ReLU$ is an activation function which only outputs positive input, i.e.

$$ReLU(x) = \begin{cases} x, x > 0 \\ 0, x \le 0 \end{cases} \tag{10}$$

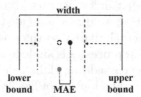

Fig. 3. How the loss function works.

The final loss function (Eq. 11) is a weighted combination. To emphasize the importance of coverage probability, β_2 and β_3 are relatively greater. Figure 3 shows how the loss function controls the bounds [12] by reducing the width and the difference between the midpoint and the ground truth while keeping the truth within the interval.

$$loss = \beta_1 * MAE + \beta_2 * upper\_loss + \beta_3 * lower\_loss + \beta_4 * width\_loss \tag{11}$$

where β_1, β_2, β_3 and β_4 are the hyper-parameters that control the predictions.

5   Experiments

5.1   Datasets

The Business Process Intelligence Challenge 2012 BPIC2012[1] is an event log from the Dutch Financial Institute characterizing the application process for personal loans. The event log incorporates three intertwined sub-processes, namely **A**pplication state changes, **O**ffer state changes and **W**orkflow events. In addition to the activity name and the timestamp, a case-wise attribute indicating the requested amount of money and the resources of events are used as features.

---

[1] https://doi.org/10.4121/uuid:3926db30-f712-4394-aebc-75976070e91f.

Helpdesk. The dataset[2] records the process of a ticketing management of an Italian software company. Each case starts with a ticket insertion and ends with a resolved issue or a closed ticket. Only activity name and timestamp are available.

The Business Process Intelligence Challenge 2015. BPIC2015[3] contains five datasets provided by Dutch municipalities concerning the building permission applications. Case-wise attributes include the type of the case, the responsible actor and the cost of the application. The resources of the events are given.

Credit Requirement. The dataset[4] records credit requirement processes in a bank. The automatic or manual resources are given along with the timestamps. In this dataset, all the event sequences are identical. As a result, clustering is based merely on completion time.

Table 1. Basic information of datasets

Name	Total cases	Trace length	Completion time	Remaining time	Activity types
BPIC2012a	13087	4.64 ± 1.88	8.08 ± 11.86	7.94 ± 11.73	10
BPIC2012o	5015	6.23 ± 3.17	17.17 ± 11.41	12.64 ± 12.02	7
BPIC2012w	9658	7.50 ± 7.28	11.39 ± 12.71	10.83 ± 11.95	6
Helpdesk	3804	3.60 ± 1.19	8.80 ± 11.00	5.51 ± 9.45	9
BPIC2015_1	1199	43.55 ± 16.98	95.72 ± 121.35	53.18 ± 94.96	398
BPIC2015_2	830	53.44 ± 19.75	160.49 ± 168.43	104.21 ± 133.29	410
BPIC2015_3	1409	42.36 ± 16.14	62.23 ± 97.61	26.89 ± 70.07	383
BPIC2015_4	1052	44.95 ± 14.89	116.91 ± 108.16	88.42 ± 88.71	356
BPIC2015_5	1156	51.11 ± 16.03	98.34 ± 108.19	59.76 ± 88.41	389
Credit	10035	8.00 ± 0.00	0.95 ± 0.85	0.44 ± 0.72	8

Basic information on the datasets is given in Table 1. Several intuitive time-related features are added into the input including the duration between two events, the elapsed time from the beginning, the time from midnight and weekdays [8, 21]. One-hot vectors are used to represent categorical attributes such as resources and numerical attributes are normalized by min-max normalization.

As prefixes which are too long slow down the training efficiency [25], we limit the maximum lengths of the prefixes to be tested to 20, i.e.,

$$L^* = prefix(\sigma, k) : \sigma \in L, 1 \leq k \leq min(|\sigma| - 1, 20) \tag{12}$$

where, L is the complete event log. If a trace contains less than 20 events, all other events except the one including the last event are used because the last event represents the completeness of the case. In all the experiments, the first 80% of traces are used to generate a prefix log as the training set (20% of which are used as the validation set), and the rest are used as the test set.

---

[2] https://doi.org/10.17632/39bp3vv62t.1.

[3] https://doi.org/10.4121/uuid:31a308ef-c844-48da-948c-305d167a0ec1.

[4] https://doi.org/10.4121/uuid:453e8ad1-4df0-4511-a916-93f46a37a1b5.

5.2   Comparative Approaches and Settings

We compare our model with the time point prediction methods based on regression tree and XGBoost. The features are encoded by last state and aggregation encoding [25]. All the time-related features and the case-wise attributes are included in the encoding. The 'event' and 'resource' attributes are encoded as one-hot vector for last state encoding and are encoded by the counts of their appearances for aggregation encoding. LSTM networks with the same number of layers are also used for comparison. We apply linear regression to obtain a prediction interval. The time since the last event and the time since the beginning are used to train a multivariate linear regression model.

Table 2. Experiment settings

	Name	Value
Model settings	lstm units	[128, 128] or [128, 128, 64]
	lstm dropout rate	0.3
Training configurations	Optimization	Nadam
	Batch size	32
	Initial learning rate	0.002

Machine learning methods are implemented by sklearn and LSTM-based models are implemented on Keras. Other experiment settings are shown in Table 2. The lists of units mean that there are corresponding numbers of units on the same level of LSTM or dense layers. For instance, if a network has one shared layer and one independent layer, the shared layer has 128 units and each independent layer has 128 units. The width expectation w_{exp} is set to 0.5, 0.5, 10, 0 for the datasets in the order above. The experiments are conducted on i7-10510U CPU.

5.3   Results and Analysis

We first make sure that our proposed model and our optimization strategy can effectively influence the time intervals. According to Fig. 4, while the MAE is similar, doubling the weights of the out-of-bounds penalty leads to a significantly higher $PICP$. Though the intervals become relatively wider, the predictions are more reliable. Moreover, generally, combining shared layers with independent layers is helpful to obtain intervals of a higher overall quality. Only the best configurations are discussed in the following discussions.

As shown in Table 3, the accuracy of interval prediction is generally better than traditional machine learning methods and is comparable to LSTM-based point prediction. The prediction with an optimistic and pessimistic estimate can allow stakeholders to observe the process more thoroughly and reduce the impacts of wrong predictions. The results in Fig. 5 show that as the prefixes

Table 3. Results without clustering

Dataset	Predictor type	configuration	PICP(%)	Width(days)	MAE(days)	CWC
BPIC2012a	XGBoost	agg	–	–	8.55	–
	Point LSTM	3	–	–	**6.23**	–
	Linear	–	80.00	33.08	8.99	0.36
	Interval	2 + 1 1:10:10:1	**87.10**	**25.81**	10.21	**0.28**
BPIC2012o	Tree	agg	–	–	7.89	–
	Point LSTM	3	–	–	**6.15**	–
	Linear	–	**80.00**	29.48	8.31	**0.33**
	Interval	2 + 1 1:10:10:1	76.48	**21.64**	8.13	0.49
BPIC2012w	Tree	ls	–	–	7.20	–
	Point LSTM	2	–	–	**6.26**	–
	Linear	–	80.00	30.96	7.79	0.34
	Interval	2 + 1 1:10:10:1	**88.82**	**23.70**	6.70	**0.26**
Helpdesk	XGBoost	agg	–	–	7.80	–
	Point LSTM	2	–	–	**6.63**	–
	Linear	–	80.00	26.57	7.99	0.48
	Interval	0+2 1:10:10:1	**83.29**	**21.17**	9.02	**0.38**
BPIC2015_1	XGBoost	ls	–	–	58.15	–
	Point LSTM	3	–	–	52.43	–
	Linear	–	**80.00**	301.38	54.10	0.20
	Interval	1 + 1 1:10:10:1	78.49	**115.00**	**48.46**	0.15
BPIC2015_2	Tree	agg	–	–	**93.62**	–
	Point LSTM	3	–	–	96.99	–
	Linear	–	80.00	369.59	105.10	0.27
	Interval	3 + 0 1:10:10:1	**83.21**	**226.51**	94.17	**0.20**
BPIC2015_3	XGBoost	agg	–	–	23.18	–
	Point LSTM	3	–	–	**20.80**	–
	linear	–	80.00	211.04	32.23	0.14
	Interval	3 + 0 1:10:10:1	**88.16**	**69.14**	26.01	**0.04**
BPIC2015_4	Tree	agg	–	–	47.55	–
	Point LSTM	3	–	–	58.60	–
	Linear	–	80.00	276.29	**46.54**	0.30
	Interval	2 + 1 1:10:10:1	**91.55**	**191.97**	48.45	**0.13**
BPIC2015_5	Tree	ls	–	–	69.91	–
	Point LSTM	3	–	–	**63.36**	–
	Linear	–	**80.00**	252.56	69.88	**0.19**
	Interval	1 + 1 1:10:10:1	71.64	**122.65**	64.88	0.19
Credit	XGBoost	ls	–	–	**0.08**	–
	Point LSTM	2	–	–	0.28	–
	Linear	–	80.00	1.69	0.41	0.34
	Interval	1 + 2 1:10:10:1	**89.42**	**0.86**	0.31	**0.17**

'tree', 'XGBoost', and 'linear' refer to regression tree, xgboost, and linear regression respectively. 'agg' and 'ls' refer to the aggregation and the last state encoding. 'Point LSTM' refers to the LSTM point-prediction model with its number of layers. Only the best results of the similar approaches are presented.

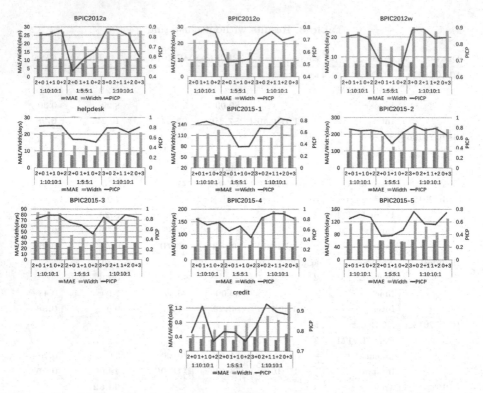

Fig. 4. The results without clustering with different settings. The settings of layers are given in the form of $n + m$ where n and m are the numbers of the shared layers and the independent layers. The ratio are in the order of MAE:upper bound:lower bound:width.

grow longer and the uncertainty in traces decreases, the accuracy of interval prediction becomes closer to that of the point prediction. The valley of MAE (a descent followed by an increase) is due to the finish of some short traces [25].

By fixing the target confidence level at 80%, we can compare the CWC between our proposed model and linear regression. In general, our model offers time intervals with higher quality according to CWC. As the width of prediction intervals are less than twice the deviation in Table 1, the predictions are convincing. As shown in Fig. 5, the widths become smaller when the prefixes become longer except when a part of the ongoing traces ends. $PICP$s are generally higher than the target confidence level. At the beginning of the traces, the predictions easily cover the ground truth by giving a wide interval. As the prefixes grow longer, the model narrows down the intervals, leading to some out-of-bound predictions. $PICP$ increases as the uncertainty gradually decreases. In addition, our model performs the best when the traces are more balanced in length and traces patterns according to the experiment results on BPIC2012w.

We also test the clustering-based interval prediction. The number of clusters for k-means clustering is set to 5. The LSTM-based classifier consists of two LSTM layers with 128 units. Three approaches are used to select the predictors:

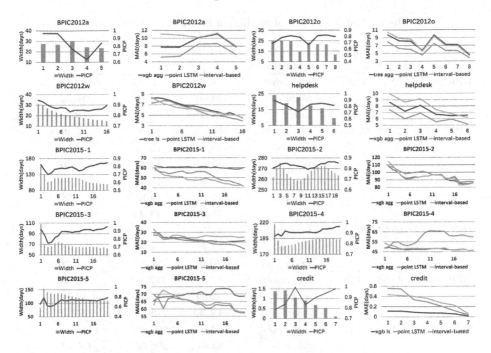

Fig. 5. The trend of criteria along the execution of traces.

max_prob: The predictor from the cluster with the maximum probability given by the classifier is selected.

all_prob: The predictors are all used and the final evaluation is based on the expectation of all the criteria and the absolute error.

prior: The designated cluster labels are used to evaluate the predictor with prior path knowledge to see if the clustering methods can help the prediction.

Unfortunately, as useful interpretative features are difficult to obtain for the classification task in the early stage [27], prefix classification based on trace clustering is not effective enough to boost interval-based remaining time prediction. This is reasonable, since at the early stage, it is not possible to know which pattern a case should follow with insufficient information [18].

If the pattern is known, the interval-based model is confident enough to compress the interval and provides a more accurate prediction, compared to Table 3. The disadvantage is a relatively lower coverage probability. This indicates that the low accuracy of classification greatly restrains the overall performance of our approach. However, the main purpose of trace clustering is that the prediction can incorporate more information of uncertainty, which helps process workers and users to undertake sufficient preparation by considering the probabilities of different path choices and the corresponding time interval predictions.

Finally, we briefly discuss the time performance. The time of one training epoch for LSTM networks is highly related to the dimension of the input and the settings of layers (rangeing from 4 s/epoch for 'helpdesk 2+0' to 80 s/epoch

Table 4. Quality of interval prediction based on trace clustering

Dataset	Acc.	Top2 Acc.	Evaluation method	PICP(%)	Width (days)	MAE (days)
BPIC2012a	54.21	59.20	max_prob	51.45	**6.76**	6.89
			all_prob	43.66	11.52	10.52
			prior	**61.18**	6.93	**4.48**
BPIC2012o	24.82	95.92	max_prob	64.30	14.74	6.49
			all_prob	59.82	15.05	8.57
			prior	**71.43**	**14.67**	**5.97**
BPIC2012w	12.66	23.26	max_prob	**71.95**	18.73	7.78
			all_prob	70.62	19.12	8.04
			prior	58.36	**11.41**	**6.60**
Helpdesk	69.77	76.04	max_prob	61.59	**7.26**	6.97
			all_prob	51.46	9.54	9.38
			prior	**70.90**	7.79	**4.26**
BPIC2015_1	49.08	73.18	max_prob	72.54	**113.50**	60.38
			all_prob	72.09	116.77	59.71
			prior	**77.33**	118.29	**55.26**
BPIC2015_2	34.50	54.22	max_prob	63.37	206.22	114.60
			all_prob	61.97	206.32	116.94
			prior	**65.66**	**203.99**	**109.50**
BPIC2015_3	71.42	90.06	max_prob	79.20	**60.97**	28.17
			all_prob	78.21	62.05	28.59
			prior	**82.61**	62.63	**26.26**
BPIC2015_4	34.96	54.45	max_prob	69.79	161.55	65.53
			all_prob	63.25	**151.20**	67.72
			prior	**79.12**	185.87	**62.65**
BPIC2015_5	41.49	72.75	max_prob	57.33	**93.09**	62.64
			all_prob	55.96	132.62	79.99
			prior	**59.80**	113.97	**59.90**
Credit	76.03	97.13	max_prob	84.23	0.18	0.07
			all_prob	83.04	0.18	0.09
			prior	**94.89**	**0.18**	**0.03**

for 'BPIC2012w 0+3'). The epochs until convergence are relative to the input features (e.g., 26 epochs for BPIC2012w and 148 for helpdesk on average). The clustering is relatively less time-consuming (less than 20 s).

6   Conclusion

Our work is novel for incorporating and quantifying uncertainty in the remaining time prediction for business processes. We mainly consider trace patterns and time interval as two entry points of uncertainty in business process. Through trace clustering and interval estimation, our LSTM-based model is able to provide remaining time prediction with possible path branches. As the first attempt at clustering-based interval prediction in this field, there are still some limitations in our work. The structures of the prediction model and the embedding approach of the traces can be improved. The classification of prefixes is not satisfactory enough despite the fact that trace pattern is theoretically powerful prior knowledge for predictive monitoring. How to use the trace patterns to the greatest extent is worthy of further study.

Acknowledgement. This work is partially supported by National Key Research and Development Plan(No. 2019YFB1704405) and China National Science Foundation (Granted Number 62072301).

References

1. Van der Aalst, W.M., Rubin, V., Verbeek, H., van Dongen, B.F., Kindler, E., Günther, C.W.: Process mining: a two-step approach to balance between underfitting and overfitting. Software Syst. Modeling **9**(1), 87–111 (2010)
2. Bengio, Y., Courville, A., Vincent, P.: Representation learning: a review and new perspectives. IEEE Trans. Pattern Anal. Mach. Intell. **35**(8), 1798–1828 (2013)
3. Chu, Y., Li, M., Pedro, H.T., Coimbra, C.F.: Real-time prediction intervals for intra-hour DNI forecasts. Renew. Energy **83**, 234–244 (2015)
4. Conforti, R., de Leoni, M., La Rosa, M., van der Aalst, W.M., ter Hofstede, A.H.: A recommendation system for predicting risks across multiple business process instances. Decis. Support Syst. **69**, 1–19 (2015)
5. De Koninck, P., vanden Broucke, S., De Weerdt, J.: act2vec, trace2vec, log2vec, and model2vec: representation learning for business processes. In: Weske, M., Montali, M., Weber, I., vom Brocke, J. (eds.) BPM 2018. LNCS, vol. 11080, pp. 305–321. Springer, Cham (2018). https://doi.org/10.1007/978-3-319-98648-7_18
6. De Leoni, M., van der Aalst, W.M.P., Dees, M.: A general framework for correlating business process characteristics. In: Sadiq, S., Soffer, P., Völzer, H. (eds.) BPM 2014. LNCS, vol. 8659, pp. 250–266. Springer, Cham (2014). https://doi.org/10.1007/978-3-319-10172-9_16
7. Di Francescomarino, C., Dumas, M., Maggi, F.M., Teinemaa, I.: Clustering-based predictive process monitoring. IEEE Trans. Serv. Comput. **12**(6), 896–909 (2016)
8. Di Francescomarino, C., Ghidini, C., Maggi, F.M., Petrucci, G., Yeshchenko, A.: An eye into the future: leveraging a-priori knowledge in predictive business process monitoring. In: Carmona, J., Engels, G., Kumar, A. (eds.) BPM 2017. LNCS, vol. 10445, pp. 252–268. Springer, Cham (2017). https://doi.org/10.1007/978-3-319-65000-5_15
9. Evermann, J., Rehse, J.-R., Fettke, P.: A deep learning approach for predicting process behaviour at runtime. In: Dumas, M., Fantinato, M. (eds.) BPM 2016. LNBIP, vol. 281, pp. 327–338. Springer, Cham (2017). https://doi.org/10.1007/978-3-319-58457-7_24
10. Hwang, J.G., Ding, A.A.: Prediction intervals for artificial neural networks. J. Am. Stat. Assoc. **92**(438), 748–757 (1997)
11. Kabir, H.D., Khosravi, A., Hosen, M.A., Nahavandi, S.: Neural network-based uncertainty quantification: a survey of methodologies and applications. IEEE Access **6**, 36218–36234 (2018)

12. Khosravi, A., Nahavandi, S., Creighton, D.: A prediction interval-based approach to determine optimal structures of neural network metamodels. Expert Syst. Appl. **37**(3), 2377–2387 (2010)
13. Khosravi, A., Nahavandi, S., Creighton, D., Atiya, A.F.: Lower upper bound estimation method for construction of neural network-based prediction intervals. IEEE Trans. Neural Networks **22**(3), 337–346 (2010)
14. Khosravi, A., Nahavandi, S., Creighton, D., Atiya, A.F.: Comprehensive review of neural network-based prediction intervals and new advances. IEEE Trans. Neural Networks **22**(9), 1341–1356 (2011)
15. Le, Q., Mikolov, T.: Distributed representations of sentences and documents. In: International Conference on Machine Learning, pp. 1188–1196. PMLR (2014)
16. Maggi, F.M., Di Francescomarino, C., Dumas, M., Ghidini, C., et al.: Predictive monitoring of business processes. In: Jarke, M. (ed.) CAiSE 2014. LNCS, vol. 8484, pp. 457–472. Springer, Cham (2014). https://doi.org/10.1007/978-3-319-07881-6_31
17. Márquez-Chamorro, A.E., Resinas, M., Ruiz-Cortés, A.: Predictive monitoring of business processes: a survey. IEEE Trans. Serv. Comput. **11**(6), 962–977 (2017)
18. Mori, U., Mendiburu, A., Dasgupta, S., Lozano, J.A.: Early classification of time series by simultaneously optimizing the accuracy and earliness. IEEE Trans. Neural Netw. Learn. Syst. **29**(10), 4569–4578 (2018). https://doi.org/10.1109/TNNLS.2017.2764939
19. Rogge-Solti, A., Weske, M.: Prediction of remaining service execution time using stochastic petri nets with arbitrary firing delays. In: Basu, S., Pautasso, C., Zhang, L., Fu, X. (eds.) ICSOC 2013. LNCS, vol. 8274, pp. 389–403. Springer, Heidelberg (2013). https://doi.org/10.1007/978-3-642-45005-1_27
20. Saeed, A., et al.: Hybrid bidirectional LSTM model for short-term wind speed interval prediction. IEEE Access **8**, 182283–182294 (2020)
21. Tax, N., Verenich, I., La Rosa, M., Dumas, M.: Predictive business process monitoring with LSTM neural networks. In: Dubois, E., Pohl, K. (eds.) CAiSE 2017. LNCS, vol. 10253, pp. 477–492. Springer, Cham (2017). https://doi.org/10.1007/978-3-319-59536-8_30
22. Teinemaa, I., Dumas, M., Maggi, F.M., Di Francescomarino, C.: Predictive business process monitoring with structured and unstructured data. In: La Rosa, M., Loos, P., Pastor, O. (eds.) BPM 2016. LNCS, vol. 9850, pp. 401–417. Springer, Cham (2016). https://doi.org/10.1007/978-3-319-45348-4_23
23. Van Der Aalst, W.: Process mining. Commun. ACM **55**(8), 76–83 (2012)
24. Verenich, I., Dumas, M., La Rosa, M., Maggi, F.M., Di Francescomarino, C.: Complex symbolic sequence clustering and multiple classifiers for predictive process monitoring. In: Reichert, M., Reijers, H.A. (eds.) BPM 2015. LNBIP, vol. 256, pp. 218–229. Springer, Cham (2016). https://doi.org/10.1007/978-3-319-42887-1_18
25. Verenich, I., Dumas, M., Rosa, M.L., Maggi, F.M., Teinemaa, I.: Survey and cross-benchmark comparison of remaining time prediction methods in business process monitoring. ACM Trans. Intell. Syst. Technol. (TIST) **10**(4), 1–34 (2019)
26. Xing, Z., Pei, J., Dong, G., Yu, P.S.: Mining sequence classifiers for early prediction. In: Proceedings of the 2008 SIAM International Conference on Data Mining, pp. 644–655. SIAM (2008)
27. Xing, Z., Pei, J., Yu, P.S., Wang, K.: Extracting interpretable features for early classification on time series. In: Proceedings of the 2011 SIAM International Conference on Data Mining, pp. 247–258. SIAM (2011)

Evaluating Stability of Post-hoc Explanations for Business Process Predictions

Mythreyi Velmurugan[1](✉)[iD], Chun Ouyang[1][iD], Catarina Moreira[1][iD], and Renuka Sindhgatta[2][iD]

[1] Queensland University of Technology, Brisbane, Australia
{m.velmurugan,c.ouyang,catarina.pintomoreira}@qut.edu.au
[2] IBM Research, Bangalore, India
renuka.sr@ibm.com

Abstract. Predictive process analytics uses advanced machine learning techniques to accurately predict future states of running business processes. Given the complexity of these predictive models, explainable AI techniques are also required to enable informed decision-making. However, few studies evaluate the quality of explanations provided by existing methods to explain business process predictions. In this paper, we attempt to evaluate the consistency of explanations produced for process predictions by two popular explainable methods. We propose that methods and metrics to assess feature selection algorithms can be used to evaluate explanation stability. We use these metrics to assess explanations produced by LIME and SHAP. Our findings indicate that explanation stability may depend on dataset characteristics, feature construction methods and predictive model characteristics. In addition, we also find that, though stable explanations are needed for informed decision-making, unexpected behaviour in explanation stability can act as a diagnostic tool to determine model quality.

Keywords: Predictive process analytics · Explainable AI · Evaluation metrics · Explanation stability

1 Introduction

Predictive process analytics (PPA) attempts to predict some future state of a business process [6]. It uses event logs, which capture process execution data, to train predictive models. As these models require advanced machine learning algorithms to create accurate predictions, their internal workings are complex, and thus opaque to a human audience. The research field of explainable AI (XAI) provides methods to interpret these opaque, *"black box"* predictive models [3]. Recent studies in PPA have applied existing XAI methods to explain process predictions [2,13] or evaluate process predictive models [11]. However, few works have attempted to evaluate the quality of explanations generated by these methods for process predictions.

© Springer Nature Switzerland AG 2021
H. Hacid et al. (Eds.): ICSOC 2021, LNCS 13121, pp. 49–64, 2021.
https://doi.org/10.1007/978-3-030-91431-8_4

This has motivated us to conduct functionally-grounded evaluation, in which some inherent property of the explanation is evaluated, without input from a human user. Though such evaluations do not reveal the usefulness of the explanation to humans, they are often an essential step in determining the fitness of an explainable method to a dataset and context [1]. A key evaluation measure is *explanation stability*, which is used to assess the consistency of explanations generated for an opaque predictive model [15]. Few methods to measure stability have been proposed in XAI literature, most of which are specific to a single explainable method (such as in [15]), and do not enable comparison between explainable methods. In addition, to the best of our knowledge, no studies have attempted to evaluate explanation stability for process predictions.

In this paper, we aim to use methods and metrics from the field of feature selection to evaluate explanation stability for business process predictions. The evaluation focuses on the stability of *local, post-hoc* explanations, which are provided to individual predictions by an explainable method *after* a predictive model is trained. We apply the proposed metrics to LIME [10] and SHAP [5] in the context of process predictions using real-life event logs.

Furthermore, since event log data is both temporal and case-based, extensive feature construction methods are required to make this data machine readable [14]. Therefore, of particular interest in PPA are not only the dataset and predictive model, but also feature construction techniques used. We aim to understand how the characteristics of this pipeline affect explanation stability. Hence, we design experiments by varying the event log datasets, feature construction methods and classification algorithms used to train a business process predictive model along the pipeline.

Thus, our contributions are two-fold. Firstly, we propose and demonstrate that metrics to evaluate the stability of feature selection algorithms can be used to evaluate the stability of explanations for tabular data such as event logs. Secondly, we apply these metrics to explanations of process predictions to determine the PPA-specific characteristics that affect explanation stability, and in doing so, derive insights into the use of explainable methods for PPA.

2   Background and Related Work

2.1   Process Execution Event Logs

Process execution event logs (or simply *event logs*) are a form of sequential data in tabular format. During business process execution, information is recorded in information systems in the form of event logs. Event log data include the activities that were undertaken (*event*), and the actors, systems and data involved in each event. Events are linked to a particular execution of the process (*process instance* or *case*) through some specific case identifier such as patient ID or order ID. Events form the rows of an event log, in order of occurrence, and attributes associated with an event (*event attributes*), such as case identifier, actors participating in the event, event name or timestamp, form the columns. These attributes may be *static* and unchanging over the course of the case, such as the case identifier, or *dynamic*, such as the timestamps of events. A *trace* is a sequence of events for the same case, and *prefixes* are the features constructed for each trace using both events and event attributes.

2.2 Explainable AI

The field of explainable AI (XAI) has arisen as a means to provide transparency into otherwise opaque predictive models. Although more complex and sophisticated predictive models may be more accurate, this internal complexity also reduces the ability of human agents to understand their decision-making processes, thus requiring interpretation [3]. In this work, we are interested in local, post-hoc explanations – i.e. explanations provided to individual predictions or small data neighbourhoods (*local explanations*) by explainable methods after the predictive model is trained (*post-hoc*) [3]. A variety of explainable methods exist within this category, among which LIME and SHAP well-known and popular. Both provide feature attribution explanations, wherein they determine the contribution of each feature to the final outcome, though they use different mechanisms to determine feature importance. LIME creates a surrogate model to mimic the black box model's behaviour within a particular data neighbourhood, and uses this surrogate model to determine local feature importance [10]. SHAP's approach is based on game theory and attempts to identify the marginal contribution of each feature to the final output of the predictive model for a single instance [5].

2.3 Explainable Predictive Process Analytics

PPA attempts to predict a future state of process instances using prefixes. Common prediction targets in PPA include case outcome prediction, remaining time prediction, next activity prediction and risk prediction, among others [6]. Given the complexity of machine learning models needed for process predictions, as well as the extensive processing required to extract algorithm-readable features from event log data, process predictive models are highly opaque to human agents [13]. Most attempts at explaining or refining process prediction black boxes in literature have generally attempted to use existing post-hoc methods, including LIME [11,13], SHAP [2,11] and Partial Dependence Plots, a method to generate global explanations capturing the overall model behaviour [7].

2.4 Evaluating Explanation Stability

Explanation stability measures the consistency of explanations generated for identical or similar instances in the data [15]. Since explainable methods attempt to provide insight into otherwise "black box" models, the provided explanations must be reliable. But, when the explainable method is subject to randomness, there may be variations in the explanation, calling its reliability into question [4]. Though stability metrics have been proposed for post-hoc explainable methods, these are often specific to a particular explainable method (for example, the metrics proposed in [15] for LIME).

We propose that measures and metrics to assess the stability of feature selection algorithms can be adapted for explainable methods. Feature selection algorithms are used to reduce the dimensions of high-dimensional datasets by determining feature relevance [9]. The outputs of these algorithms – feature subsets, feature rankings or quantification of feature relevance [8] – are similar to feature attribution explanations. Thus, we suggest that approaches and metrics to evaluate feature selection algorithms can be applied in XAI, particularly when evaluating feature attribution explanations.

3   Methods and Metrics

3.1   Evaluation Method

We propose an approach to evaluate the stability of explanations generated by post-hoc explainable methods for business process predictions. Figure 1 depicts an overview of this approach, as well as the standard workflow for building process predictive models using machine learning algorithms [14].

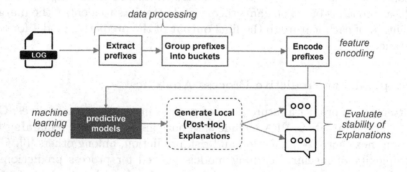

Fig. 1. Approach for evaluating explanation stability for process predictions

Firstly, prefixes are extracted for each trace in the event log, then grouped into *buckets* based on their similarities, such as length or last completed event. The prefixes in each bucket are then encoded into algorithm-readable feature vectors of equal length, and one model is trained per bucket. Once the predictive model/s have been created, local explanations are generated using post-hoc explainable methods for a sample of data. The sample of data for evaluating stability are randomly chosen, primarily from the testing set, but also from the training set when the testing set is small. Around 50 samples are chosen at each prefix length used, though fewer were chosen for the smaller datasets.

During evaluation, we measure the stability of the subset of most important features (*stability by subset*) and the stability of weights applied to each feature (*stability by weight*). Ten explanations are generated for each instance in the sample of data used for evaluation (i.e. $M = 10$ for each instance, see Eqs. 1 and 2 in Sect. 3.2). This follows the general approach in [15], where the stability of variables used by LIME's surrogate models, and the coefficients applied to them, were measured across 10 surrogate models.

We do not specify a certain number of features to measure stability by subset. Rather, we use the features with feature weights that fall into the top quartile of the feature weight distribution. For example, if the feature weights in an explanation range from 0 to 1, only features with feature weights greater than 0.75 are used to evaluate *stability by subset* (see Eq. 1). *Stability by weight* is evaluated using the weights for all features (see Eq. 2).

3.2 Evaluation Metrics

We propose two explanation stability evaluation metrics. Both are applied to test explanation stability for a single instance, but can be averaged out to understand stability at the dataset level.

Stability by Subset. This metric was proposed in [9] to determine the stability of feature selection algorithms, based on the presence or absence of each feature across a number of feature subsets. We calculate the stability of feature subsets ($\phi(\mathcal{Z})$) for a single process instance in an *event log* as follows:

$$\phi(\mathcal{Z}) = 1 - \frac{\frac{1}{d}\sum_{i=1}^{d} s_{f_i}^2}{\frac{\bar{k}}{d}(1 - \frac{k}{d})} \tag{1}$$

where:

- d = number of features encoded from event attributes in the log
- M = number of explanations generated for the process instance
- $\mathcal{Z}$ = binary matrix of size M x d. Each row of the binary matrix represents a feature subset from a single explanation, where a 1 at the ith position means feature f_i is among the most relevant and a 0 means it is not.
- k = number of most relevant features, where relevance or level of importance is determined by an explanation generated for the process instance, for a single explanation
- $\bar{k}$ = average of k across all M explanations for the process instance
- $s_{f_i}^2$ = sample variance of the presence of feature f_i across all M explanations for the process instance (i.e. the the variance of column i in $\mathcal{Z}$)

This measure is bounded between 0 and 1, where 0 indicates no similarity in the feature subsets, and 1 indicates that all subsets are identical.

Stability by Weight. Pearson's correlation coefficient is generally used to measure stability of feature weights in feature selection algorithms [8], but this measures the similarity of trendlines and does not calculate the degree by which a feature's weight may vary. As such, we specify the measure *stability by weight*

– adapted from the statistical measure of relative variance – and calculate the
stability of feature weights ($\phi(\mathcal{W})$) for a single process instance in an *event log*
as follows:

$$\phi(\mathcal{W}) = 1 - \frac{1}{d} \sum_{i=1}^{d} \frac{\sigma_{w_i}^2}{|\mu_{w_i}|} \qquad (2)$$

where:

- d = number of features encoded from event attributes in the log
- M = number of explanations generated for the process instance
- $\mathcal{W}$ = matrix of size M x d. Each row of the matrix records the weight of each
  feature as quantified by a single explanation
- μ_{w_i} = mean of the weights of feature f_i across all M explanations for the
  process instance (i.e. the mean of column i in $\mathcal{W}$)
- $\sigma_{w_i}^2$ = variance of the weights of feature f_i across all M explanations for the
  process instance (i.e. the variance of column i in $\mathcal{W}$)

This measure also has an upper bound of 1 (indicating perfect stability), but no
lower bound. The suitability of these metrics will be assessed through comparison
to previous results in literature and known behaviours of the explainable methods
used.

4 Experimental Design

4.1 Predictive Models

The chosen prediction target for the experiments was the process outcome. This
is a common prediction problem in PPA and a typical example of a classification problem. Two algorithms were used to create the predictive models. One
is XGBoost which generally produces the most accurate models for outcome-
oriented prediction [14]. Given that an aim of this work was to understand the
effects of predictive model on explanation stability, a second prediction algorithm
of different characteristics was also chosen. Logistic regression (Logit) is simpler
in comparison to the significantly more complex models created by XGBoost,
but generally produces less accurate models for outcome prediction.

Three combinations of bucketing and encoding were used to construct features when creating the classifiers:

- Aggregate encoding for dynamic attributes with prefix-length bucketing
- Index-based encoding for dynamic attributes with prefix-length bucketing
- Aggregate encoding for dynamic attributes compiled in a single bucket

In the single bucketing method, all data is compiled as one and a single
classifier is trained on this bucket. When prefix-length bucketing is used, data is
grouped based on the number of activities that have already been completed in
a process instance (the prefix length), and one model is trained for each bucket.

Three different types of encoding are used. Static encoding, where numeric
attributes are used as-is and categorical attributes are one-hot encoded, was

applied to static attributes in all combinations of bucketing and encoding. Aggregate and index-based encoding were applied for dynamic attributes. Aggregate encoding summarises each case, with a single feature indicating frequency of occurrence for each categorical attribute and four features (mean, maximum, minimum and standard deviation) for each numeric attribute. If index-based encoding is used, numeric attributes are encoded as-is and categorical attributes are one-hot encoded at each index (prefix in the process trace). As such, out of the three methods used, combining prefix-length bucketing with index-based encoding best preserves the temporal information in event logs, while using single buckets with aggregate encoding preserves the least.

Two explainable methods are evaluated in this work. SHAP and LIME, two popular post-hoc interpretation methods, were chosen given their relative popularity in explaining process predictions [2,11,13].

We will assess the suitability of the described metrics based on past stability evaluation results in literature. Instability is a known issue of LIME. To generate instances to train the surrogate model, LIME randomly samples the neighbourhood of the input instance to derive a set of perturbed inputs [10]. This random sampling results in a different set of perturbed instances for every explanation, and so the surrogate model and the resulting explanation lack stability, a problem compounded as the length of the input increases [12]. On the other hand, SHAP optimises the interpretation mechanism for certain categories of predictive models, such that they examine the model directly [5]. We will use two such optimisations (TreeSHAP and LinearSHAP). The lack of randomisation in the interpretation mechanism should result in little to no instability in the explanation. Therefore, the metrics can be judged to be appropriate if the following are observed:

1. LIME's explanations will become more unstable as the length of the input increases; and
2. SHAP's explanations show little to no instability.

4.2   Datasets

We use three open-source, real-life event logs. Each event log is from a different domain and has different characteristics (see Table 1 for summary of the three event logs used).

The Production dataset[1] is derived from a manufacturing process. This event log has the fewest cases and the shortest traces out of the three event logs. When using this dataset, we attempt to predict whether at least one work order in the case will be rejected (which occurs in around 55% of cases). This dataset also has a substantial number of attributes, more dynamic that static.

The Sepsis Cases dataset[2] records patients' journeys in a hospital. Using this dataset, we attempt to predict whether a patient returns to the ER within 14 days of discharge, which only 16% do. As such, this dataset was balanced through down-sampling before model training. This dataset also contains a relatively

---

[1] https://doi.org/10.4121/uuid:68726926-5ac5-4fab-b873-ee76ea412399.
[2] https://doi.org/10.4121/uuid:915d2bfb-7e84-49ad-a286-dc35f063a460.

Table 1. A summary of statistics of three event log datasets

Event log		Production	Sepsis cases	BPIC2012
Description		A manufacturing process	Hospital event log showing sepsis cases	Loan application process
No. of cases (before prefix extraction)		220	782	4,685
Proportion of positive cases		55.0%	16.0%	53.4%
Maximum prefix length		23	29	40
Prefix lengths used		1–20	1–20	1–20
Feature vector length	Single bucket & aggregate encoding	166	272	133
	Prefix-length buckets & aggregate encoding	Min: 144 Max: 164	Min: 175 Max: 212	Min: 43 Max: 133
	Prefix-length buckets & index-based encoding	Min: 110 Max: 964	Min: 146 Max: 495	Min: 11 Max: 1257

large number of static attributes, but fewer dynamic attributes, so it produces comparatively longer feature vectors when using aggregate encoding, but shorter feature vectors at higher prefix lengths when using index-based encoding.

The BPIC2012 event log[3] follows a loan process. When using this event log, we attempt to predict whether the loan application is accepted (roughly 53% are rejected). This event log only has one static attribute and several dynamic attributes for each event. As such, it will have comparatively short feature vectors when using aggregate encoding, but comparatively long feature vectors at higher prefix lengths when using index-based encoding.

As a summary, each combination of the above bucketing methods, encoding methods, predictive models and explainable methods are evaluated for each dataset. Only a maximum of 20 prefixes are used to train and explain a predictive model. Each event log was split into training and testing sets (80-20 ratio) prior to feature construction. The split was temporal, such that the cases that finished the earliest were used for model training and the remaining 20% was used as the testing set.

All relevant code associated with the experiments, including the feature construction methods, hyperparamter optimisation, model training and explanation generation and evaluation, are available at https://git.io/Jc9Az.

5   Results and Analysis

5.1   Results and Observations

For SHAP, all experiments return 1.0000 for each stability metric. It is by far the more stable explainable method, both by subset and by weight, producing *perfectly* stable explanations regardless of the dataset, feature construction methods or classification algorithm used. On the other hand, LIME's stability was more variable, and often poor (see Tables 2 and 3).

---

[3] https://doi.org/10.4121/uuid:3926db30-f712-4394-aebc-75976070e91f.

Table 2. Stability by Subset results for LIME (averaged over the dataset)

Classifier	Data encoding	Production	Sepsis cases	BPIC2012
XGBoost	Single bucket & aggregate encoding	0.3959	0.2166	0.8135
	Prefix-length buckets & aggregate encoding	0.6660	0.4067	0.3790
	Prefix-length buckets & index-based encoding	0.5010	0.3520	0.1987
Logit	Single bucket & aggregate encoding	0.8417	0.7260	0.8734
	Prefix-length buckets & aggregate encoding	0.9789	0.7906	0.8155
	Prefix-length buckets & index-based encoding	0.8124	0.7977	0.6598

Table 3. Stability by Weight Results for LIME (averaged over the dataset)

Classifier	Data encoding	Production	Sepsis cases	BPIC2012
XGBoost	Single bucket & aggregate encoding	0.5507	−0.2961	0.5415
	Prefix-length buckets & aggregate encoding	0.5682	0.4694	0.4722
	Prefix-Length buckets & index-based encoding	0.2668	0.1595	−0.1645
Logit	Single bucket & aggregate encoding	−0.0825	0.6926	0.9687
	Prefix-length buckets & aggregate encoding	0.9751	0.7915	0.9450
	Prefix-length buckets & index-based encoding	0.9415	0.8177	−0.1644

The combination of prefix-length bucketing and index-based encoding generally seems to produce the most unstable explanations when using LIME to explain predictions from the BPIC2012 and Production datasets. Using single buckets with aggregate encoding produced the least stable explanations for the Sepsis Cases dataset. The most stable combination varied between the three datasets. The most stable explanations were produced for the Production data set when using prefix-length bucketing with aggregate encoding, but when using single buckets and aggregate encoding for the BPIC2012 dataset.

5.2 Analysis and Findings

Finding 1: Causes of Instability. The returned results are as expected. SHAP is perfectly stable, while LIME shows instability. We further unfold the results for LIME by visualising the stability of explanations for each instance. Instability is closely linked to prefix length and can be seen to increase as the size of the input feature vector increases. This is apparent, both when comparing results across different bucketing and encoding methods for the same dataset and when comparing results between datasets.

For example, we unfold and examine explanation stability for the BPIC 2012 dataset in Fig. 2 and Fig. 3. When using single buckets with aggregate encoding, where the input size remains consistent, stability is also consistent (Fig. 2(a) and (d)). However, in Fig. 2(c) and (f), the results for prefix-length bucketing with index-based encoding indicate a general downward trend in stability as the prefix length increases. When considering the feature vector lengths, rather than the prefix length (Fig. 3(b) and (d)), it becomes clear that this downward trend is

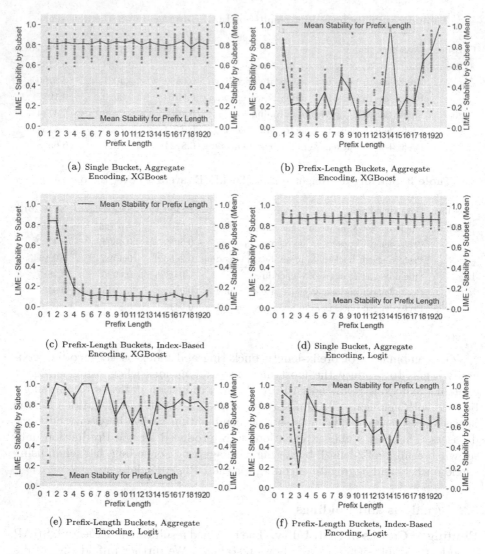

Fig. 2. The stability by subset at each prefix length for LIME using BPIC2012. Stability seems related to prefix length when using prefix-length bucketing.

related to the length of the input. As such, the metrics used can be judged to be suitable.

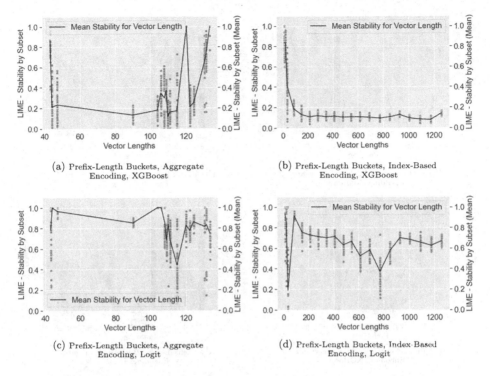

(a) Prefix-Length Buckets, Aggregate
Encoding, XGBoost

(b) Prefix-Length Buckets, Index-Based
Encoding, XGBoost

(c) Prefix-Length Buckets, Aggregate
Encoding, Logit

(d) Prefix-Length Buckets, Index-Based
Encoding, Logit

Fig. 3. The stability by subset at different feature vector lengths for LIME using BPIC2012. Stability generally decreases as the number of features increase.

This relationship between input length and LIME stability is also true to some degree when using prefix-length bucketing with aggregate encoding (Fig. 3(a) and (c)). However, there are spikes in stability at certain prefix lengths when using this bucketing-encoding combination. This notably occurs at bucket 14 when using XGBoost (Fig. 2(b)) and at buckets 2, 5, 6, and 8 when using Logit (Fig. 2(e)), where stability does not follow the described trend. This is likely because a number of "empty" explanations with no feature attribution – where the feature weights of all features were 0 – were produced by LIME where these spikes occurred (see Fig. 4(a) and (b)).

Finding 2: Non-attributive Explanations. Non-attributive explanations, as described above, were seen in explanations for all datasets. They were primarily produced by LIME, and were extremely rare in SHAP, and occurred only when prefix-length bucketing and aggregate encoding were both used. When all explanations produced for an instance were empty, explanation stability was considered to be perfect. As such, in buckets where a large proportion of consistently empty explanations were produced, there was a noticeable spike in stability.

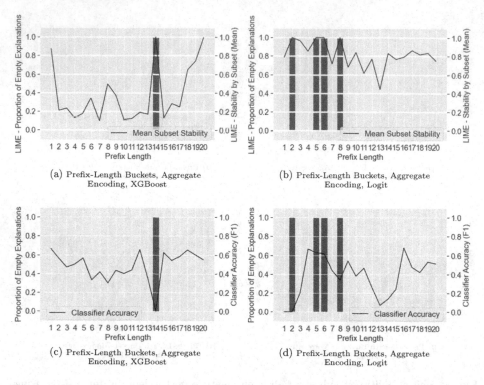

Fig. 4. The number of non-attributive, "empty" explanations generated for BPIC2012 (a and b) and its relationship to accuracy (c and d).

A closer investigation of this phenomena suggests that non-attributive explanations occur when model accuracy is poor. Many buckets with a high proportion of empty explanations also had a predictive model with a poor F1-score. For example, when using the BPIC2012 dataset, the XGBoost model at bucket 14 and the Logit model at bucket 2 both had F1-scores of 0, and all explanations produced for these buckets were non-attributive (see Fig. 4(c) and (d)). This also occurred when accuracy is reasonably high, but the model predicted only a single class for all or a majority of instances. This was the case for the Logit models at buckets 2 and 5 for the BPIC2012 dataset.

Therefore, non-attributive explanations for these classifiers is likely due to model underfitting. A simpler, underfit predictive model can be more easily mimicked by LIME's surrogate models than a more complex, well-fit model. Moreover, in classifiers where only a single class is predicted regardless of the input, any surrogate models produced will also disregard features. As such, when multiple explanations are created, the resulting surrogate models are identical or similar enough to ensure explanation stability.

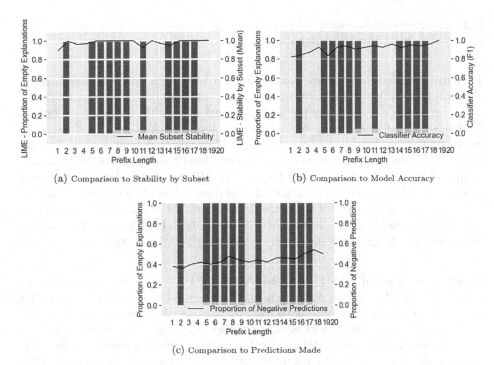

(a) Comparison to Stability by Subset   (b) Comparison to Model Accuracy

(c) Comparison to Predictions Made

Fig. 5. A large proportion of non-attributive explanations when for the Production dataset when using Logit with using prefix-length bucketing and aggregate encoding (a), which is not related to model accuracy (b) or prediction accuracy (c).

Finding 3: Effect of Data on Non-attributive Explanations. A notable exception to this trend of non-attributive explanations, both when explaining XGBoost models and when explaining Logit models, is the Production dataset. When explaining XGBoost models, there were no non-attributive explanations generated, though some classifiers have poor quality or predict only a single class. However, when explaining Logit, explanations provided for around 60% of cases are non-attributive (Fig. 5(a)), though the accuracy of the predictive models are high (Fig. 5(b)), and no classifier predicts primarily a single class (Fig. 5(c)). This indicates that other underlying causes for non-attributive explanations also exist, though they are not immediately apparent. This also occurred in other datasets to a lesser degree. For example, the Logit model for bucket 6 of the BPIC2012 dataset had an F1-Score of 0.62 and a 0.4:0.6 ratio for the predicted class, but all explanations generated for this model were non-attributive.

It is likely that this anomalous behaviour is related to some characteristic of the Production dataset. Out of the three event logs used, Production has fewest events and cases, the shortest traces and a significant number of trace variants in comparison to the number of cases. Some form of one of these may also be present in the data used in other buckets where these exceptions occurred.

Further investigations using other datasets in needed to fully understand the causes of non-attributive explanations.

Finding 4: Effect of Feature Construction Methods on Non-attributive Explanations. We deem it to be significant that empty explanations have so far occurred only when using prefix-length bucketing with aggregate encoding. Prefix-length bucketing aims to preserve the temporal nature of business processes by sorting data based on the number of events that have occurred in the process. However, aggregate encoding is more "lossy" and preserves little of the temporal information in the event log. Firstly, although prefix-length bucketing groups cases based on events completed, this does not imply homogeneity in the traces within each bucket. If there are several variants of traces in each bucket, It is possible that this and the sparsity of data in each bucket, caused by lack of cases and use of aggregate encoding, creates poorly-fitting models.

Finding 5: Use of LIME and SHAP in PPA. It is also interesting to note that SHAP rarely provided non-attributive explanations, even when the predictive model did not appear to use any of the features in the input – that is, where the predictive model always returned the same prediction regardless of input. Given that non-attributive explanations generally appeared to indicate some problem in the underlying predictive model, this is significant. SHAP's stability and consistency may make it more suited to enable end user decision-making in PPA. However, LIME may be of more use to software engineers and data scientists in attempting to inspect and diagnose problems in the underlying process predictive models.

6 Limitations and Future Work

Past evaluations of bucketing and encoding methods and supervised machine learning models for PPA have considered their effects only on prediction accuracy [14]. However, the findings in this work emphasise the importance of the quality of explanations generated by explainable methods for machine learned process predictions. Our study also suggests that predictive model design in PPA must consider not only prediction accuracy but also compatibility with explainable methods. To this end, more extensive benchmarks are required to understand the effects of various configurations and methods used to design predictive models, as well as dataset characteristics, on explanation quality in addition to prediction accuracy.

We can be assured of the applicability of the described approach and the metrics in Sect. 3 for feature attribution explanations as they measure the stability of the output, i.e. the explanation. While the interpretation mechanism may vary across explainable methods, a feature attribution explanation will always produce a list or ranking of features, and weights associated with features. Thus, we measure the stability of these two outputs.

Future work should also consider the stability of other classes of explainable methods. The two methods evaluated in this work are both feature attribution methods, though they use different underlying mechanisms and approaches to generating explanations. Explainable methods of other classes, such as rule-based explanations, also connect features to the output. Thus, we suggest that stability by subset can also be assessed in explainable methods of classes other than feature attribution. However, this does not necessarily cover all possible aspects of the explanation in these classes. For example, the stability of the full predicates, not just features used, in rule-based explanations. As such, other classes of explainable methods, using different approaches and mechanisms of interpretation should also be considered in future works, as should a wider range of predictive models (e.g., those based on deep neural networks).

7 Conclusion

Post-hoc explainable methods are gaining popularity as a means of improving the transparency of process predictive models. However, the fitness of these methods for predictive process analytics is as yet unclear. In this work, we evaluated one aspect of explanation quality: explanation stability. We draw on research fields outside of both PPA and XAI to derive the relevant methods and metrics required for evaluation. Our result suggests that explanation stability is dependent on the characteristics of both the datasets and predictive models. We also find that, though stability may be important in supporting end-user decision-making, unexpected behaviour in explanation stability can also be useful as a diagnostic tool in determining model quality. Hence, we suggest that the choice of feature construction methods and predictive models should consider both prediction accuracy and explainable method compatibility, and as such, more extensive evaluations are required to identify suitable configurations for both.

Acknowledgements. Computational resources and services used in this work were provided by HPC and Research Support Group, Queensland University of Technology (QUT), Brisbane, Australia. The first author's research is sponsored by the Australian Government Research Training Program (RTP) Scholarship. The research is also partly supported by Centre for Data Science's First Byte Funding Program 2021 at QUT.

References

1. Doshi-Velez, F., Kim, B.: Towards a rigorous science of interpretable machine learning (2017). arXiv: 1702.08608v2
2. Galanti, R., Coma-Puig, B., de Leoni, M., Carmona, J., Navarin, N.: Explainable predictive process monitoring. In: 2020 2nd International Conference on Process Mining (ICPM). IEEE, October 2020
3. Guidotti, R., Monreale, A., Ruggieri, S., Turini, F., Giannotti, F., Pedreschi, D.: A survey of methods for explaining black box models. ACM Comput. Surv. **51**(93), 1–42 (2018)

4. Guidotti, R., Ruggieri, S.: On the stability of interpretable models. In: 2019 International Joint Conference on Neural Networks (IJCNN), Budapest, Hungary, 14–19 July 2019 (2019)
5. Lundberg, S.M., Lee, S.I.: A unified approach to interpreting model predictions. In: Proceedings of the 2017 Neural Information Processing Systems Conference, Long Beach, USA, 4–9 December 2017 (2017)
6. Marquez-Chamorro, A.E., Resinas, M., Ruiz-Cortes, A.: Predictive monitoring of business processes: a survey. IEEE Trans. Serv. Comput. **11**(6), 962–977 (2017)
7. Mehdiyev, N., Fettke, P.: Prescriptive process analytics with deep learning and explainable artificial intelligence. In: ECIS 2020 Proceedings, Marrakech, Morocco, 15–17 June 2020 (2020)
8. Mohana Chelvan, P., Perumal, K.: A survey of feature selection stability measures. Int. J. Comput. Inf. Technol. **5**(1) (2016). Article No. 15
9. Nogueira, S., Sechidis, K., Brown, G.: On the stability of feature selection algorithms. J. Mach. Learn. Res. **18**(174), 6345–6398 (2018)
10. Ribeiro, M.T., Singh, S., Guestrin, C.: "Why should I trust you?": explaining the predictions of any classifier. In: Proceedings of the 22nd ACM SIGKDD International Conference on Knowledge Discovery and Data Mining, San Francisco, California, 13–17 August 2016 (2016)
11. Rizzi, W., Di Francescomarino, C., Maggi, F.M.: Explainability in predictive process monitoring: when understanding helps improving. In: Fahland, D., Ghidini, C., Becker, J., Dumas, M. (eds.) BPM 2020. LNBIP, vol. 392, pp. 141–158. Springer, Cham (2020). https://doi.org/10.1007/978-3-030-58638-6_9
12. Shankaranarayana, S.M., Runje, D.: ALIME: autoencoder based approach for local interpretability. In: Yin, H., Camacho, D., Tino, P., Tallón-Ballesteros, A.J., Menezes, R., Allmendinger, R. (eds.) IDEAL 2019. LNCS, vol. 11871, pp. 454–463. Springer, Cham (2019). https://doi.org/10.1007/978-3-030-33607-3_49
13. Sindhgatta, R., Ouyang, C., Moreira, C.: Exploring interpretability for predictive process analytics. In: Kafeza, E., Benatallah, B., Martinelli, F., Hacid, H., Bouguettaya, A., Motahari, H. (eds.) ICSOC 2020. LNCS, vol. 12571, pp. 439–447. Springer, Cham (2020). https://doi.org/10.1007/978-3-030-65310-1_31
14. Teinemaa, I., Dumas, M., La Rosa, M., Maggi, F.M.: Outcome-oriented predictive process monitoring: review and benchmark. ACM Trans. Knowl. Discov. Data **13**(17), 1–57 (2019)
15. Visani, G., Bagli, E., Chesani, F., Poluzzi, A., Capuzzo, D.: Statistical stability indices for LIME: obtaining reliable explanations for machine learning models. J. Oper. Res. Soc., 1–11 (2021)

Interactive Segmentation of User Interface Logs

Simone Agostinelli$^{(\boxtimes)}$, Francesco Leotta, and Andrea Marrella$^{(\boxtimes)}$

Sapienza Università di Roma, Rome, Italy
{agostinelli,leotta,marrella}@diag.uniroma1.it

Abstract. Robotic Process Automation (RPA) is an emerging technology that relies on software (SW) robots to automate intensive and repetitive tasks (i.e., *routines*) performed by human users on the application's User Interface (UI) of their computer systems. RPA tools are able to capture in dedicated *UI logs* the execution of many routines of interest. A UI log consists of user actions that are mixed in some order that reflects the particular order of their execution by the user, thus potentially belonging to different routines. In the RPA literature, the challenge to understand which user actions contribute to which routines and cluster them into well-bounded *routine traces* is known as *segmentation*. In this paper, we present a novel approach to the discovery of routine traces from unsegmented UI logs, which relies on: *(i)* a frequent-pattern identification technique to automatically derive the routine behaviors (a.k.a. *routine segments*) as recorded into a UI log, *(ii)* a human-in-the-loop interaction to filter out those segments not allowed (i.e., wrongly discovered from the UI log) by any real-world routine under analysis, and *(iii)* a trace alignment technique to cluster all those user actions belonging to a specific segment into routine traces. We evaluate our approach showing its effectiveness in terms of supported segmentation variants.

1 Introduction

Robotic Process Automation (RPA) [1] is an emerging technology in the field of Business Process Management (BPM) that relies on software (SW) robots to automate intensive and repetitive tasks (in the following, called *routines*) performed by human users on the application's User Interface (UI) of their computer systems. Similarly to traditional BPM Systems (BPMSs), RPA tools are able to act as effective *service orchestrators*, but without the need of performing the manual configuration steps required by whatever BPMS to run a process, e.g., the definition of specific business rules, the association of resources to the process activities, etc. Since many routine tasks can be implemented through scripting or intelligent recording techniques, RPA projects typically involve comparably little cost than traditional BPM projects [1]. Overall, the target of existing RPA tools is to boost the productivity of organizations by reducing manual labor while improving the operational quality and reducing user input errors.

To take full advantage of this technology, organizations leverage the support of skilled human experts that: *(i)* preliminarily observe how routines are executed

© Springer Nature Switzerland AG 2021
H. Hacid et al. (Eds.): ICSOC 2021, LNCS 13121, pp. 65–80, 2021.
https://doi.org/10.1007/978-3-030-91431-8_5

on the UI of the involved SW applications (by means of walkthroughs, etc.), *(ii)* convert such observations in explicit flowchart diagrams, which are specified to depict all the potential behaviors (i.e., *segments*) of the routines of interest, and *(iii)* finally implement the SW robots that automate the routines enactment on a target computer system. However, the current practice is time-consuming and error-prone, as it strongly relies on the ability of human experts to correctly interpret the routines to automate [14]. Consequently, if SW robots are not designed for the appropriate scope of their work, then their implementation cost will increase while no clear business improvement effect will be achieved [13].

To tackle this challenge, in their Robotic Process Mining framework [16], Leno et al. propose to exploit the User Interface (UI) logs recorded by RPA tools to automatically discover the candidate routines that can be later automated with SW robots. UI logs are sequential data of user actions performed on the UI of a computer system during many routines' executions. Typical user actions are: opening a file, selecting/copying a field in a form or a cell in a spreadsheet, read and write from/to databases, open emails and attachments, etc.

To date, when considering state-of-the-art RPA technology, it is evident that the RPA tools available in the market are not able to learn how to automate routines by only interpreting the user actions stored into UI logs [3]. The main trouble is that in a UI log there is not an exact 1:1 mapping among a recorded user action and the specific routine segment it belongs to. In fact, the UI log usually records information about several routines whose actions are mixed in some order that reflects the particular order of their execution by the user. The issue to automatically understand which user actions contribute to a particular routine segment inside a UI log and cluster them into well-bounded *routine traces* (i.e., complete execution instances of a routine) is known as *segmentation* [3,16].

The majority of state-of-the-art segmentation approaches are able to properly extract routine segments (i.e., repeated routine behaviors) from unsegmented UI logs when the routine executions are not interleaved from each others. Only few works are able to partially untangle unsegmented UI logs consisting of many interleaved routines executions, but with the assumption that any routine provides its own, separate universe of user actions. This is a relevant limitation, since it is quite common that real-world routines may share the same user actions (e.g., copy and paste data across cells of a spreadsheet) to achieve their objectives.

In this paper, we propose a novel approach to the segmentation of UI logs that aims to mitigate the aforementioned issue showing its effectiveness in terms of supported segmentation variants. The approach relies on three key ingredients:

1. a *frequent-pattern identification technique* to automatically discover the observed segments of the routines as recorded into the UI log. In this phase, the risk exists that some wrong segments are discovered, i.e., not allowed from the real-world routines that are known to be valid at the outset.
2. a *human-in-the-loop interaction* that enables human experts to visualize the *declarative constraints* inferred by the discovered routine segments. Such constraints describe the temporally extended relations between user actions that must be satisfied throughout a routine segment (e.g., an action a_1 must be

eventually followed by an action a_2). In a nutshell, they collectively determine the observed behaviors of the routine segments from the UI log. This knowledge allows human experts to identify and remove those constraints that should not be compliant with any real-world routine behavior, thus filtering out the not valid (i.e., wrongly discovered) routine segments;

3. a *trace alignment technique* to cluster all the user actions associated to a valid routine segment into well-bounded routine traces.

We show the feasibility of our approach by employing a dataset of 144 synthetic UI logs covering different segmentation cases to measure to what extent the approach is able to (re)discover the valid routine segments from such UI logs.

The rest of the paper is organized as follows. Section 2 introduces a running example that will be used to explain our approach, and discusses the relevant background on the segmentation of UI logs with all its potential variants. In Sect. 3, we present the details of our approach to the automated segmentation of UI logs. Section 4 evaluates the feasibility of the proposed approach against synthetic UI logs. Finally, Sect. 5 discusses the novelty of our approach against literature works, while Sect. 6 draws conclusions, traces future works and outlines a critical discussion about the general applicability of the approach.

2 Background

2.1 Running Example

In this section, we describe a RPA use case inspired by a real-life scenario at Department of Computer, Control and Management Engineering (DIAG) of Sapienza Università di Roma. The scenario concerns the filling of the travel authorization request form made by personnel of DIAG for travel requiring prior approval. The request applicant must fill a well-structured Excel spreadsheet (cf. Fig. 1(a)) providing some personal information, such as her/his bio-data and the email address, together with further information related to the travel, including the destination, the starting/ending date/time, the means of transport to be used, the travel purpose, and the envisioned amount of travel expenses, associated with the possibility to request an anticipation of the expenses already incurred (e.g., to request in advance a visa). When ready, the spreadsheet is sent via email to an employee of the Administration Office of DIAG, which is in charge of approving and elaborating the request. Concretely, for each row in the spreadsheet, the employee manually copies every cell in that row and pastes that into the corresponding text field in a dedicated Google form (cf. Fig. 1(b)), accessible just by the Administration staff. Once the data transfer for a given travel authorization request has been completed, the employee presses the "Submit" button to submit the data into an internal database.

In addition, if the request applicant declares that s/he would like to use her/his personal car as one of the means of transport for the travel, then s/he has to fill a dedicated web form required for activating a special insurance for the part of the travel that will be performed with the car. This further request will

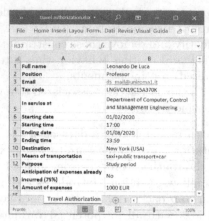

(a) Excel spreadsheet   (b) Google form

Fig. 1. UIs involved in the use case

be delivered to the Administration staff via email, and the employee in charge of processing it can either approve or reject such request. At the end, the applicant will be automatically notified via email of the approval/rejection of the request.

The above procedure, which involves two main routines (in the following, we will denote them as R1 and R2), is performed manually by an employee of the Administration Office of DIAG, and it should be repeated for any new travel request. Routines such as these ones are good candidates to be encoded with executable scripts and enacted by means of a SW robot within a commercial RPA tool. However, unless there is complete a-priori knowledge of the specific routines that are enacted on the UI and of their concrete composition, their automated identification from an UI log is challenging, since the associated user actions may be scattered across the log, interleaved with other actions that are not part of the routine under analysis, and potentially shared by many routines.

Based on the above description, it becomes clear that a proper execution of R1 requires a path on the UI made by the following user actions:[1]

- loginMail, to access the client email;
- accessMail, to access the specific email with the travel request;
- downloadAttachment, to download the Excel file including the travel request;
- openWorkbook, to open the Excel spreadsheet;
- openGoogleForm, to access the Google Form to be filled;
- getCell, to select the cell in the i-th row of the Excel spreadsheet;
- copy, to copy the content of the selected cell;
- clickTextField, to select the specific text field of the Google form where the content of the cell should be pasted;

---

[1] Note that the user actions recorded in a UI log can have a finer granularity than the high-level ones used here just with the purpose of describing the routine's behavior.

– paste, to paste the content of the cell into a text field of the Google form;
– formSubmit, to finally submit the Google form to the internal database.

Note that the user actions openWorkbook and openGoogleForm can be performed in any order. Moreover, the sequence of actions ⟨getCell, copy, clickTextField, paste⟩ will be repeated for any travel information to be moved from the Excel spreadsheet to the Google form. On the other hand, the path of user actions in the UI to properly enact R2 is as follows:

– loginMail, to access the client email;
– accessMail, to access the specific email with the request for travel insurance;
– clickLink, to click the link included in the email that opens the Google form with the request to activate the travel insurance on a web browser;
– approveRequest, to approve the request on the Google form;
– rejectRequest, to reject the request on the Google form;

Note that the execution of approveRequest and rejectRequest is exclusive.

In the rest of the paper, we concisely represent the universe of user actions of interest for R1 and R2 as follows: $Z = \{A, B, C, D, E, F, G, H, I, L, M, N, O\}$, such that: $A = $ loginMail, $B = $ accessMail, $C = $ downloadAttachment, $D = $ openWorkbook, $E = $ openGoogleForm, $F = $ getCell, $G = $ copy, $H = $ clickTextField, $I = $ paste, $L = $ formSubmit, $M = $ clickLink, $N = $ approveRequest, $O = $ rejectRequest.

2.2   Segmentation of UI Logs

In this section, we provide the relevant background on UI logs and we explain in detail the issue of segmentation of UI logs with all its potential variants.

A UI log typically consists of a long sequence of user actions recorded during one user interaction session.[2] Such actions include all the steps required to accomplish one or more relevant routines using the UI of one or many sw application/s. For instance, in Fig. 2, we show a snapshot of a UI log captured using a dedicated action logger[3] during the execution of R1 and R2. The employed action logger enables to record the *events* happened on the UI, enriched with several data fields describing their "anatomy". For a given event, such fields are useful to keep track the name and the timestamp of the user action performed on the UI, the involved sw application, the resource that performed the action, etc.

As shown in Fig. 2, a UI log is not specifically recorded to capture pre-identified routines. A UI log may contain multiple and interleaved executions of one/many routine/s (cf. in Fig. 2 the blue/red boxes that group the user actions belonging to R1 and R2, respectively), as well as redundant behavior and noise. We consider as *redundant* any user action that is unnecessary repeated during the execution of a routine, e.g., a text value that is first pasted in a wrong field and then is moved in the right place through a corrective action on the UI. On the other hand, we

---

[2] We interpret a user session as a group of interactions that a single user takes within a given time frame on the UI of a specific computer system.

[3] https://github.com/bpm-diag/smartRPA.

	A	B	C	D	E	F	G	H	I	J
1	timestamp	user	category	application	event_type	event_src_path	clipboard_content	workbook	worksheet	cell_content
2	2020-04-06 13:47	Simone	Mail	Outlook	loginMail					
3	2020-04-06 13:47	Simone	Mail	Outlook	accessMail					
4	2020-04-06 13:47	Simone	Mail	Outlook	downloadAttachment					
5	2020-04-06 13:47	Simone	MicrosoftOffice	Microsoft Excel	openWorkbook	C:\Users\Simone\Desktop\richiesta missione xc		richiesta missione.xlsx	Foglio1	
6	2020-04-06 13:47	Simone	MicrosoftOffice	Microsoft Excel	openWindow	C:\Users\Simone\Desktop		richiesta missione.xlsx	Foglio1	
7	2020-04-06 13:47	Simone	MicrosoftOffice	Microsoft Excel	afterCalculate					
8	2020-04-06 13:47	Simone	MicrosoftOffice	Microsoft Excel	resizeWindow	C:\Users\Simone\Desktop		richiesta missione.xlsx	Foglio1	
9	2020-04-06 13:47	Simone	Browser	Chrome	openGoogleForm					
10	2020-04-06 13:47	Simone	MicrosoftOffice	Microsoft Excel	getCell			richiesta missione.xlsx	Foglio1	Simone Agostinelli
11	2020-04-06 13:47	Simone	Clipboard	Clipboard	copy		Simone Agostinelli			
12	2020-04-06 13:47	Simone	Browser	Chrome	clickTextField					
13	2020-04-06 13:48	Simone	Mail	Outlook	clickLink					
14	2020-04-06 13:48	Simone	Browser	Chrome	paste		Simone Agostinelli			
15	2020-04-06 13:48	Simone	Browser	Chrome	changeField					
16	2020-04-06 13:48	Simone	Browser	Chrome	approveRequest					
17	2020-04-06 13:48	Simone	MicrosoftOffice	Microsoft Excel	getCell			richiesta missione.xlsx	Foglio1	Dottorando
18	2020-04-06 13:48	Simone	Clipboard	Clipboard	copy		Dottorando			
19	2020-04-06 13:48	Simone	MicrosoftOffice	Microsoft Excel	resizeWindow	C:\Users\Simone\Desktop		richiesta missione.xlsx	Foglio1	
20	2020-04-06 13:48	Simone	Browser	Chrome	clickTextField					
21	2020-04-06 13:48	Simone	Browser	Chrome	paste		Dottorando			

Fig. 2. Snapshot of a UI log captured during the executions of R1 and R2

consider as *noise* all those actions that do not contribute to the achievement of any routine target, e.g., a window that is resized. In Fig. 2, the sequences of user actions that are not surrounded by a blue/red box can be safely labeled as noise.

In this context, *segmentation* techniques aim first to extract from a UI log all those user actions that are compliant with a specific *routine segment*, i.e., with a repetitive routine behavior as observed in the UI log. Then, the target is to cluster such user actions into well-bounded *routine traces*, which are complete and independent execution instances of the routine within the UI log. Such traces are finally stored in a dedicated *routine-based logs*, which capture all the user actions happened during many different executions of the routine and compliant with a specific routine segment, thus achieving the segmentation task. It is worth noticing that a routine-based log obtained in this way can eventually be employed by the commercial RPA tools to synthesize executable scripts in form of SW robots that will emulate the routine behavior.

For example, an allowed routine segment of R1 is $\langle A, B, C, D, E, F, G, H, I, L \rangle$. From the description of the use case, allowed routine segments are also those ones where: *(i)* A is skipped (if the user is already logged in the client email); *(ii)* the pair of actions $\langle D, E \rangle$ is performed in reverse order; *(iii)* the sequence of actions $\langle F, G, H, I \rangle$ is executed several time before submitting the Google form. On the other hand, two allowed routine segments can be observed from R2: $\langle A, B, M, N \rangle$ and $\langle A, B, M, O \rangle$, again with the possibility to skip A, i.e., the access to the client email. Note that A and B can be employed by both R1 and R2 to achieve their targets. By analyzing the log, it can be noted that: A is *potentially involved* in the enactment of any execution of R1 and R2, while B is *required by all* executions of R1 and R2, but it is not clear the association between the single executions of B and the routine segments they belong to. Any observed execution of user actions in the UI log that matches with one of the above routine segments can be considered as a valid routine trace.

According to [5], we can distinguish between three major forms of UI logs, which can be categorized as follows:

- **Case 1**. A UI log captures many not interleaved (*case 1.1*) or interleaved (*case 1.2*) executions of the same routine.
- **Case 2**. A UI log captures many executions of different routines, but with the assumption that different routines do not have any user action in common. Four variants of this case can be identified: clear separation in the UI log between the routines' executions (*case 2.1*); many executions of the same routine can be recorded in an interleaved fashion, but the executions of different routines are separated from each others (*case 2.2*); the executions of different routines can be recorded in an interleaved fashion, but the executions of a specific routine can not be enacted in an interleaved way (*case 2.3*); the executions of any routine can be always interleaved from each others (*case 2.4*).
- **Case 3**. Similarly to Case 2, it provides four variants (cases *3.1*, *3.2*, *3.3*, and *3.4*)), with the only difference that a same kind of user action can be employed by many different routines to achieve their objectives, e.g., the UI log associated with the running example in Sect. 2.1 belongs to Case 3.

While the literature does not provide works able to properly segment UI logs including user actions "shared" by many routine executions, in this paper we propose an approach that is able to relax this assumption and to achieve the following segmentation cases: *1.1*, *2.1*, *2.3*, *3.1* and *3.3*.

3   Approach

Our approach to the segmentation of UI logs can be considered a semi supervised one, as it integrates the usage of automated techniques with the intervention of human experts in some specific points of the approach. To be more precise, as shown in Fig. 3, starting from an unsegmented UI log previously recorded by a RPA tool, the first step is to inject into the UI log the *end-delimiters* of the routines under examination. An end-delimiter is a dummy action added to the UI log immediately after the user action that is known to complete a routine execution. If we consider our running example in Sect. 2.1, an end-delimiter is always required after the final action of R1, i.e., formSubmit, and after one of the final actions or R2, i.e., approveRequest or rejectRequest. In this paper, we assume that the knowledge of the final action(s) of a routine is given at the outset. Such information can be obtained, for example, by interviewing the users that are in charge to execute the routines of interest.

The second step of the approach consists of automatically extracting the observed routines' behaviors (i.e., the routine segments) directly from the UI log with the end-delimiters. To this aim, we employ a *frequent-pattern identification technique* [9], which has been properly customized for this purpose.

Since from the previous step there is the possibility that some (not allowed) segments are identified as if they would be valid, the third step of the approach involves a *human-in-the-loop interaction* to filter out these segments. Specifically, we automatically infer the declarative constraints (i.e., the temporally extended

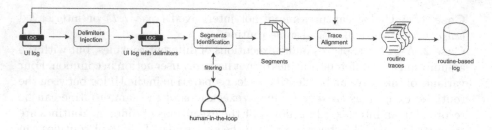

Fig. 3. Overview of our general approach to the segmentation of UI logs

relations between user actions) that must be satisfied throughout a routine segment. In this way, we enable human experts to identify and remove those constraints that should not be compliant with any real-world routine behavior, thus removing the wrongly discovered routine segments from the UI log.

Finally, starting from any of the remaining (valid) routine segments, we employ a customized version of a *trace alignment* technique in Process Mining [2] to automatically detect and extract the *routine traces* by the original UI log. Such traces will be stored in a dedicated *routine-based log*. Therefore, the final outcome of our segmentation approach will be a collection of as many routine-based logs as are the number of valid routine segments. By identifying the routine traces, we are also able to filter out those actions in the UI log that are not part of the routine under observation and hence are redundant or represent noise.

In the following sections, we discuss in detail all the steps of our approach, instantiating them over the running example of Sect. 2.1.

3.1   Segments Discovery Through Frequent-Pattern Identification

Pattern identification is a common task in data sequences analysis. As an example, in the field of smart spaces, patterns are identified in sensor logs representing human routines [17]. These patterns are then used to learn models of human behavior that can be used at runtime for activity recognition or anomaly detection. In such a scenario, authors in [9] proposed an approach based on minimum description length (MDL) principle. In this paper, we have customized the technique presented in [9] for automatically identifying the routine segments from UI logs with the end-delimiters properly converted into ad-hoc datasets.

The algorithm takes as input a dataset of a sequence of sensor events witnessing human interactions with the environment. At each step, the algorithm looks for patterns that best compress the dataset. A pattern consists of a specific sequence of sensor events and all of its occurrences in the dataset. In our RPA application scenario, the sensor events represent the user actions involved in each routine(s) execution(s), and the frequent patterns are the discovered routine segments.

Starting from a single pattern for each different sensor event, the algorithm at each step tries to extend patterns aiming at the best compression possible. Every instance of the pattern, in particular, is replaced by a symbol associated to the pattern. The compression of a dataset D given a pattern P is given

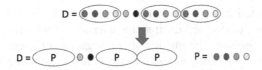

Fig. 4. A dataset compression step in segments discovery

by the formula $\frac{DL(D)}{DL(D|P)+DL(P)}$, where $DL(D)$ represent the description length, measured for example in bits of the dataset with the current patterns, $DL(D|P)$ represents the description length of D if all of the occurrences of P are replaced with a symbol, and $DL(P)$ represents the description length of the pattern, which must be taken into account in compression evaluation. The algorithm stops as soon as no further compression is possible, returning all the patterns found (i.e., all the discovered routine segments). Figure 4 shows a compression step where a pattern P of repeating events (for simplicity colors have been used instead of labels) is identified and the dataset is compressed accordingly. Noteworthy, for certain parts of the dataset, no pattern is found whose definition improve compression (with the exception of the initial patterns of length one).

We show now how an execution instance of the above algorithm can be applied to the following UI log (that already includes the end-delimiters) generated from the running example of Sect. 2.1: $U = \{A, B, C_{11}, D_{11}, E_{11}, F_{11}, G_{11}, H_{11}, I_{11}, L_{11}, X, B, M_{21}, N_{21}, Z, B, C_{12}, D_{12}, E_{12}, F_{12}, G_{12}, H_{12}, I_{12}, L_{12}, X, B, M_{22}, O_{22}, Z, \ldots, A, B, C_{1(i-1)}, Y_1, D_{1(i-1)}, E_{1(i-1)}, F_{1(i-1)}, G_{1(i-1)}, G_{1(i-1)}, G_{1(i-1)}, H_{1(i-1)}, I_{1(i-1)}, L_{1(i-1)}, X, B, M_{2(i-1)}, N_{2(i-1)}, Z, \ldots, B, Y_{n-1}, C_{1i}, D_{1i}, E_{1i}, Y_n, F_{1i}, G_{1i}, H_{1i}, I_{1i}, I_{1i}, I_{1i}, L_{1i}, X, B, M_{2i}, O_{2i}, Z\}$. For the sake of understandability, we use a numerical subscript ji associated to any user action to indicate that it belongs to the $i-th$ execution of the $j-th$ routine under study. This information is not recorded into the UI log, and discovering it (i.e., the identification of the subscripts) is one of the "implicit" effects of segmentation when routine traces are built. Note that A and B are not decorated with subscripts since they can potentially belong to executions of R1 or R2. The log contains elements of noise, i.e., user actions $Y_{k \in \{1,n\}}$ that are not allowed by R1 and R2, and redundant actions like G and I that are unnecessary repeated multiple times. X and Z are the end-delimiters for the executions of R1 and R2.

The delimiters injection stage is crucial to drive the discovery of the largest possible set of valid routine segments, otherwise the technique would detect only a small subset of them. For example, let us suppose that the UI log includes only user actions related to two routines A and B without the presence of any end-delimiter. In this case, the UI log will likely include different sequences of consecutive routine segments of the kind A*, B* or AB*. In this condition, any compression algorithm will likely merge multiple routine segments into cumulative symbols (e.g., AAA, BB, ABAB) rather than highlighting single routine executions. This issue becomes less relevant when between the execution of two separate routines there are no repetitive actions. However, while the latter assumption is reasonable in case of recording of human habits, it is far from being realistic in case of UI logs recording low-level user actions performed during the interaction with a computer system.

Based on the foregoing, the output of the segments discovery stage is represented by a set of identified frequent segments (some of them may not be compliant with the real-world routine behaviors, see the next section), as follows:

– $\{\langle F, G \rangle, \langle C, D, E \rangle, \langle H, I, L \rangle, \langle C, D, E, F, G, H, I, L \rangle, \langle \boldsymbol{B}, C, D, E, F, G, H, I, L \rangle, \langle \boldsymbol{A}, \boldsymbol{B}, C, D, E, F, G, H, I, L \rangle\}$
– $\{\langle \boldsymbol{A}, \boldsymbol{B} \rangle, \langle \boldsymbol{B}, M \rangle, \langle \boldsymbol{B}, M, O \rangle, \langle \boldsymbol{B}, M, N \rangle\}$

3.2 Human-in-the-Loop Interaction

Once the routine segments have been discovered, the possibility exists that many of them represent not allowed routine behaviors. This happens because a UI log combines the execution of several routines that are usually interleaved from each others. In addition, in case of routines that make use of the same kinds of user actions to achieve their goals, it may happen that new patterns of repeated user actions, which represent potential not allowed routine segments, are rather detected as valid ones within the UI log.

On the basis of the experiments performed in Sect. 4, it becomes clear that the employed frequent-pattern identification algorithm is able to (re)discover the allowed routine segments that are known to be recorded in the input UI logs. However, since there is the possibility that some (not allowed) segments are identified as if they would be valid, a *human-in-the-loop interaction* is required to filter out all those routine segments representing behaviors that should not be allowed by any real-world routine of interest. Specifically, starting from the discovered routine segments, we invoke for any of these segments the Declare Miner algorithm implemented in [6] to infer the declarative constraints (i.e., the temporally extended relations between user actions) that must be satisfied throughout the segments. The constraints are represented using Declare, a well-known declarative process modeling language introduced in [10]. Declare constraints can be divided into four main groups: existence, relation, mutual and negative constraints. We notice that the use of declarative notations has been already demonstrated as an effective tool to visually support expert users in the analysis of event logs [21].

At this point, one or more human expert(s) may be involved to evaluate the constraints derived for any routine segment and remove those ones that are considered not compliant with any real-world routine behavior. Detecting and removing these constraints means to filter out all the not allowed (i.e., wrongly discovered) routine segments.

For example, if we consider the discovered segment $\langle C, D, E \rangle$, the following (simple) Declare constraints (among the others) hold: *Init(C)* and *End(E)*, meaning that routines' executions starting with C or ending with E have been discovered into the UI log. An expert user that is aware of the behavior of the real-world routines under analysis can immediately understand that the above Declare constraints should not hold in reality, since R1 and R2 can start only with **A** or **B** and end with L, O or N. For this reason, the above Declare constraints can be considered both as wrongly representative of the routines under analysis. As a consequence, all the discovered segments for which one of the above Declare constraints hold can be immediately discarded. For the sake of space, we do not show here all the Declare constraints that hold for any of the discovered segments. However, we point out that the iterative analysis of the Declare constraints associated to the discovered segments will support the human experts to easily detect and filter out those segments that must not be later emulated by SW robots. The list of allowed segments for our running example is the following:

- $\{\langle \boldsymbol{B}, C, D, E, F, G, H, I, L\rangle, \langle \boldsymbol{A}, \boldsymbol{B}, C, D, E, F, G, H, I, L\rangle\}$
- $\{\langle \boldsymbol{B}, M, O\rangle, \langle \boldsymbol{B}, M, N\rangle\}$

3.3 Trace Alignment

Trace alignment [2] is a conformance checking technique within Process Mining that replays the content of any trace in a log against a process model, one event at a time. For each trace in the log, the technique identifies the closest corresponding trace that can be parsed by the model, i.e., an *alignment*.

We perform trace alignment by constructing an alignment of a UI log U (note that we can consider the entire content of the UI log as a single trace) and a process model W (representing a valid routine segment) as a Petri Net, which allows us to exactly pinpoint where deviations occur. Specifically, we relate "moves" in the log to "moves" in the model in order to establish an alignment between U and W. However, it may be that some of the moves in the log cannot be mimicked by the model and vice versa. In particular, we are interested in synchronous moves between U and W. If they exist, the user actions involved in such synchronous moves are extracted and stored into a routine-based log.

We have implemented a customized version of the above trace alignment algorithm as a supervised segmentation technique [4] that is able to segment a UI log and achieve all variants of cases 1, 2 and (partially) 3 except when there are interleaved executions of shared user actions by many routines. In that case, the risk exists that a shared user action is associated to a wrong routine execution (i.e., case 3.3 and 3.4 are not covered). Thus, while in [4], to make the algorithm works, it is required to know a-priori the structure (i.e., the flowchart) of the routines to identify in the UI log (cf. [20]), the novelty of the proposed approach is to semi-automatically discover such structures in the form of routine segments, and then used them as input for the supervised segmentation technique in [4].

In the case of our running example, starting from the outcome of the previous step (i.e., the valid routine segments), the output of the trace alignment will be a set of four routine-based logs generated as follows:

- $U_{W1} = \{\langle \boldsymbol{A_{11}}, \boldsymbol{B_{11}}, C_{11}, D_{11}, E_{11}, F_{11}, G_{11}, H_{11}, I_{11}, L_{11} \rangle, \ldots, \langle \boldsymbol{A_{1(i-1)}}, \boldsymbol{B_{1(i-1)}}, C_{1(i-1)}, D_{1(i-1)}, E_{1(i-1)}, F_{1(i-1)}, G_{1(i-1)}, H_{1(i-1)}, I_{1(i-1)}, L_{1(i-1)}, \rangle\}$
- $U_{W2} = \{\langle \boldsymbol{B_{12}}, C_{12}, D_{12}, E_{12}, F_{12}, G_{12}, H_{12}, I_{12}, L_{12}, \rangle, \ldots, \langle \boldsymbol{B_{1i}}, C_{1i}, D_{1i}, E_{1i}, F_{1i}, G_{1i}, H_{1i}, I_{1i}, L_{1i} \rangle\}$
- $U_{W3} = \{\langle \boldsymbol{B_{21}}, M_{21}, N_{21}\rangle, \ldots, \langle \boldsymbol{B_{2(i-1)}}, M_{2(i-1)}, N_{2(i-1)}\rangle\}$
- $U_{W4} = \{\langle \boldsymbol{B_{22}}, M_{22}, O_{22}\rangle, \ldots, \langle \boldsymbol{B_{2i}}, M_{2i}, O_{2i}\rangle\}$

Table 1. Experiments' results. For each segmentation case the number of actions is 28, 21 and 20 (resp.). Only logs with 20 different allowed segments are shown here, and the number of valid routine behaviors is the 70% of the 1000 s that were introduced in the UI logs, while the other 30% may be affected by noise.

Case 1	# discovered segments (valid/wrong)		
Noise	0%	10%	20%
No repetitive actions	20/2	20/88	20/118
Repetitive actions	20/11	16/161	16/179
Case 2	# discovered segments (valid/wrong)		
Noise	0%	10%	20%
No repetitive actions	20/2	20/59	20/69
Repetitive actions	20/10	20/132	20/136
Case 3	# discovered segments (valid/wrong)		
Noise	0%	10%	20%
No repetitive actions	20/6	20/53	20/67
Repetitive actions	20/13	20/146	20/170

4 Evaluation

To investigate the feasibility of our approach to the automated segmentation of UI logs, we assessed to what extent it is able to (re)discover routine segments that are known to be recorded into the input UI logs. Specifically, we have synthetically generated 144 different UI logs, in a way that each UI log consisted of 1000 routine executions and was characterized by a unique configuration by varying the following inputs:

- *valid_routine_segments*: number of different routines segments (5/10/15/20), in terms of allowed behaviors, included in the UI log.
- *alphabet_size*: size of the alphabet of user actions for each segmentation case: Case 1 (13/18/23/28); Case 2 (15/16/18/21); Case 3 (13/15/17/20).
- *valid_traces*: percentage of allowed behaviors recorded into the UI log (50%/ 70%/100%). The remaining portion of the UI log (50%/30%) may be dirty, i.e., it contains routine executions potentially affected by noise.
- *percentage of noise* in the remaining (dirty) portion of the UI log (10%/20%).

The synthetic UI logs generated for the test and the complete list of results can be analyzed at: http://tinyurl.com/icsoc2021. The implementation of our approach is available: https://github.com/bpm-diag/INTSEG. For the sake of space, we present in Table 1 only a view of the results in one of the most complex cases to tackle. The results indicate that the approach scales very well in case of an increasing number of different routine segments to be discovered and with an alphabet of user actions of growing size. The computation time is not shown, since it ranges from milliseconds for UI logs with 5 different routine segments up to few seconds for UI logs with 20 segments. This result was expected, since more segments in a UI log means more executions to analyze and interpret.

By analyzing the results, we can infer that the approach is able to discover the same allowed routine segments that were synthetically introduced in the routine executions recorded in the UI logs, achieving the following segmentation cases: *1.1, 2.1, 2.3, 3.1* and *3.3*. On the other hand, our approach seems to lack in the computation of valid routine segments in presence of repetitive user actions (i.e., user actions that are repeated in a loop), when there are several routine segments generated by different executions of the same routine. This is due to the fact that similar sequences of user actions tend to be compressed together, and since they are generated from the same routine, the risk exists that different sequences are wrongly recognized as the same and bounded together, thus leading to a number of routine segments lower than ones that were synthetically introduced.

5   Related Work

Segmentation is currently considered as one of the "hot" key research effort to investigate [3,16] in the RPA field. Concerning RPA-related techniques, Bosco et al. [8] provide a method that exploits rule mining and data transformation techniques, able to discover routines that are fully deterministic and thus amenable for automation directly from UI logs. This approach is effective in case of UI logs that keep track of well-bounded routine executions (cases 1.1 and 2.1), and becomes inadequate when the UI log records information about several routines whose actions are potentially interleaved. In this direction, Leno et al. [15] propose a technique to identify execution traces of a specific routine relying on the automated synthesis of a control-flow graph, describing the observed directly-follow relations between the user actions. This technique is able to achieve cases 1.1, 1.2 and 2.1, and (only) partially the cases 2.2, 2.3 and 2.4, losing in accuracy in presence of recurrent noise and interleaved routine executions. The main limitation of the above techniques is tackled in [4], which presents a supervised segmentation technique that is able to achieve all variants of cases 1, 2 and (partially) 3 except when there are interleaved executions of shared user actions by many routines. In this paper, we exploit the technique presented in [4] to the discovery of routine traces given a set of input routine segments.

Even if more focused on traditional business processes in BPM rather than on RPA routines, Fazzinga et al. [11] employ predefined behavioral models to establish which process activities belong to which process model. The technique works well when there are no interleaved user actions belonging to one or more routines, since it is not able to discriminate which event instance (but just the event type) belongs to which process model. This makes [11] effective to tackle cases 1.1, 2.1 and 3.1. Closely related to [11], there is the work of Liu [18]. The author proposes a probabilistic approach to learn workflow models from interleaved event logs, dealing with noises in the log data. Since each workflow is assigned with a disjoint set of operations, the work [18] is able to achieve both cases 1.1 and 2.1, but partially cases 2.2, 2.3 and 2.4 (the approach can lose accuracy in assigning operations to workflows).

There exist other approaches whose the target is not to exactly resolve the segmentation issue. Many research works exist that analyze UI logs at different levels of abstraction and that can be potentially useful to realize segmentation techniques. With the term "*abstraction*" we mean that groups of user actions to be interpreted as executions of high-level activities. Baier et al. [7] propose a method to find a global one-to-one mapping between the user actions that appear in the UI log and the high-level activities of a given model. Similarly, Ferreira et al. [12], starting from a state-machine model describing the routine of interest in terms of high-level activities, employ heuristic techniques to find a mapping from a "micro-sequence" of user actions to the "macro-sequence" of activities in the state-machine model. Finally, Mannhardt et al. [19] present a technique that map low-level event types to multiple high-level activities (while the event instances, i.e., with a specific timestamp in the log, can be coupled with a single high-level activity). However, segmentation techniques in RPA must enable to associate low-level event instances (i.e., user actions) to multiple routines, making abstractions techniques ineffective to tackle all those cases where is the presence of interleaving user actions of many routines. As a consequence, all abstraction techniques are effective to achieve cases 1.1 and 2.1 only.

6   Discussion and Concluding Remarks

In this paper we have presented an approach that tackles the segmentation challenge relying on three main steps: *(i)* a frequent-pattern identification technique to automatically derive the observed routine behaviors from a UI log, *(ii)* a human-in-the-loop interaction to filter out those behaviors not allowed by any real-world routine execution, and *(iii)* a trace alignment technique in Process Mining to cluster all user actions belonging to a specific routine behavior into well-bounded routine traces. Our approach is based on a semi-supervised assumption, since we know a-priori the end-delimiters to be associated to any user action that ends a routine execution. On the other hand, the approach is not aware of the concrete behavior of the routines of interest, which will be discovered by the approach itself. For this reason, we consider this contribution as an important step towards the development of a more complete and unsupervised technique to the segmentation of UI logs.

The presented approach is able to extract routine traces from unsegmented UI logs that record in an interleaved fashion many different routines but not the routine executions, thus losing in accuracy when there is the presence of interleaving executions of the same routine. In addition, it is also able to properly deal with shared user actions required by all routine executions in the UI log, thus achieving the cases *1.1*, *2.1*, *2.3*, *3.1*, and *3.3*.

As a future work, we are going to perform a robust evaluation: *(i)* on real-world case studies with heterogeneous UI logs, and *(ii)* on the impact of the human-in-the-loop interaction to filter out wrongly discovered routine segments. In addition, we aim at relaxing the semi-supervised assumption by employing *machine learning* and *DNN* techniques to automatically identify the end-delimiters.

Acknowledgments. This work has been supported by the "Dipartimento di Eccellenza" grant, the H2020 project DataCloud and the Sapienza grant BPbots.

References

1. van der Aalst, W.M.P., Bichler, M., Heinzl, A.: Robotic process automation. Bus. Inf. Syst. Eng. **60**(4), 269–272 (2018). https://doi.org/10.1007/s12599-018-0542-4
2. Adriansyah, A., Sidorova, N., van Dongen, B.F.: Cost-based fitness in conformance checking. In: ACSD 2011, pp. 57–66. IEEE (2011)
3. Agostinelli, S., Marrella, A., Mecella, M.: Research challenges for intelligent robotic process automation. In: Di Francescomarino, C., Dijkman, R., Zdun, U. (eds.) BPM 2019. LNBIP, vol. 362, pp. 12–18. Springer, Cham (2019). https://doi.org/10.1007/978-3-030-37453-2_2
4. Agostinelli, S., Marrella, A., Mecella, M.: Automated Segmentation of User Interface Logs. In: RPA. Management, Technology, Applications. De Gruyter (2021)
5. Agostinelli, S., Marrella, A., Mecella, M.: Exploring the challenge of automated segmentation in robotic process automation. In: Cherfi, S., Perini, A., Nurcan, S. (eds.) RCIS 2021. LNBIP, vol. 415, pp. 38–54. Springer, Cham (2021). https://doi.org/10.1007/978-3-030-75018-3_3
6. Alman, A., Di Ciccio, C., Haas, D., Maggi, F.M., Nolte, A.: Rule mining with RuM. In: ICPM 2020. IEEE (2020)
7. Baier, T., Rogge-Solti, A., Mendling, J., Weske, M.: Matching of events and activities: an approach based on behavioral constraint satisfaction. In: SAC (2015)
8. Bosco, A., Augusto, A., Dumas, M., La Rosa, M., Fortino, G.: Discovering automatable routines from user interaction logs. In: Hildebrandt, T., van Dongen, B.F., Röglinger, M., Mendling, J. (eds.) BPM 2019. LNBIP, vol. 360, pp. 144–162. Springer, Cham (2019). https://doi.org/10.1007/978-3-030-26643-1_9
9. Cook, D.J., Krishnan, N.C., Rashidi, P.: Activity discovery and activity recognition: a new partnership. IEEE Trans. Cybern. **43**(3), 820–828 (2013)
10. van Der Aalst, W.M., Pesic, M., Schonenberg, H.: Declarative workflows: balancing between flexibility and support. Comp. Sci. Res. Dev. **23**, 99–113 (2009)
11. Fazzinga, B., Flesca, S., Furfaro, F., Masciari, E., Pontieri, L.: Efficiently interpreting traces of low level events in business process logs. Inf. Syst. **73**, 1–24 (2018)
12. Ferreira, D.R., Szimanski, F., Ralha, C.G.: Improving process models by mining mappings of low-level events to high-level activities. Inf. Syst. **43**, 379–407 (2014). https://doi.org/10.1007/s10844-014-0327-2
13. Gao, J., van Zelst, S.J., Lu, X., van der Aalst, W.M.P.: Automated robotic process automation: a self-learning approach. In: Panetto, H., Debruyne, C., Hepp, M., Lewis, D., Ardagna, C.A., Meersman, R. (eds.) OTM 2019. LNCS, vol. 11877, pp. 95–112. Springer, Cham (2019). https://doi.org/10.1007/978-3-030-33246-4_6
14. Jimenez-Ramirez, A., Reijers, H.A., Barba, I., Del Valle, C.: A method to improve the early stages of the robotic process automation lifecycle. In: Giorgini, P., Weber, B. (eds.) CAiSE 2019. LNCS, vol. 11483, pp. 446–461. Springer, Cham (2019). https://doi.org/10.1007/978-3-030-21290-2_28
15. Leno, V., Augusto, A., Dumas, M., La Rosa, M., Maggi, F.M., Polyvyanyy, A.: Identifying candidate routines for robotic process automation from unsegmented UI logs. In: 2nd International Conference on Process Mining, pp. 153–160 (2020)
16. Leno, V., Polyvyanyy, A., Dumas, M., La Rosa, M., Maggi, F.M.: Robotic process mining: vision and challenges. Bus. Inf. Sys. Eng. **63**(3), 301–314 (2020)

17. Leotta, F., Mecella, M., Sora, D., Catarci, T.: Surveying human habit modeling and mining techniques in smart spaces. Future Internet **11**(1), 23 (2019)
18. Liu, X.: Unraveling and learning workflow models from interleaved event logs. In: 2014 IEEE International Conference on Web Services, pp. 193–200 (2014)
19. Mannhardt, F., de Leoni, M., Reijers, H.A., van der Aalst, W.M., Toussaint, P.J.: Guided process discovery - a pattern-based approach. Inf. Syst. **76**, 1–18 (2018)
20. Marrella, A.: What automated planning can do for business process management. In: Teniente, E., Weidlich, M. (eds.) BPM 2017. LNBIP, vol. 308, pp. 7–19. Springer, Cham (2018). https://doi.org/10.1007/978-3-319-74030-0_1
21. Rovani, M., Maggi, F.M., de Leoni, M., van der Aalst, W.M.: Declarative process mining in healthcare. Expert Syst. Appl. **42**(23), 9236–9251 (2015)

Trustworthy Cross-Organizational Collaborations with Hybrid On/Off-Chain Declarative Choreographies

Tiphaine Henry[1,3](✉), Amina Brahem[2,4], Nassim Laga[1], Julien Hatin[1], Walid Gaaloul[3], and Boualem Benatallah[5]

[1] Orange Labs, Paris, France
tiphaine.henry@orange.fr
[2] OASIS, University Tunis El Manar, Tunis, Tunisia
[3] Telecom SudParis, UMR 5157 Samovar, Institut Polytechnique de Paris, Palaiseau, France
[4] LIFAT, University of Tours, Tours, France
[5] University of New South Wales, Sydney, Australia

Abstract. Business Process Management communities increasingly adopt the blockchain technology to support trustworthy decentralized execution of processes. In this context, the interest in business process choreographies rises as they offer a distributed way to compose and control cross-organizational processes. In choreographies, the process view is distributed between participants to limit privacy leakages. Hence, the process observability (i.e., who knows what) is challenging. On one side, partners have no insight into each other's orchestration and communicate peer-to-peer via the public view. On the other side, they have to maintain their internal orchestrations' states consistent with the choreography's global state. The need to ensure a privacy-preserving method to enforce a blockchain-based execution thus rises. In the present work, we propose a unified solution for the hybrid on/off-chain generation and execution of business process choreographies. The public view, shared understanding of the cross-organizational process, is triggered by the on-chain smart contract. Participants generate their private views off-chain using this on-chain public view. They execute afterward the private views in their off-chain process execution engine. Our prototypical implementation demonstrates the feasibility of the approach.

Keywords: Decentralized choreographies · Business Process Management · Dynamic condition response graphs · Blockchain

1 Introduction

A cross-organizational process can be defined as a process scattered across different organizations. It comprises private processes carried out by individual partners, where internal data such as model and execution logs should not be visible to the other partners. It also includes a public process, where several

© Springer Nature Switzerland AG 2021
H. Hacid et al. (Eds.): ICSOC 2021, LNCS 13121, pp. 81–96, 2021.
https://doi.org/10.1007/978-3-030-91431-8_6

partners collaborate in a coordinated way. All partners should trust the execution state of the public process. A trade-off between ensuring the privacy of partners' private processes and the exposure of the public process thus arises. In cross-organizational processes, model flexibility is also at stake, as processes are dynamic: partners should be able to change their internal processes without impacting the public process [15]. Thus, the following question arises: *(RQ) how to carry out a separation of concerns that preserves the privacy of the private processes, trust of the public process, and flexibility of the whole?*

In the literature, business process choreographies answer the need for such separation of concerns by clearly specifying coordination tasks [1,6]. In addition, the public process is shared between participants to limit privacy leakages. Meanwhile, private views hold the set of (1) internal tasks of a particular partner not disclosed to the other partners, and (2) communication tasks in which this partner is involved, i.e., the projection of the public view over this partner [1]. However, the trustworthy execution of the public view remains challenging as it is often managed centrally [6].

Blockchain has been leveraged in the literature as a trustworthy coordination mechanism for collaborative business processes [5,6]. In [5], a smart contract manages the public workflow of an orchestration. However, in this approach, the execution of private tasks off-chain is only mentioned and the inner mechanism has not been detailed further. Additionally, in [6], the smart contract is used to manage the public view of a choreography, and so doing enforcing the order of messages. Nonetheless, in this work, a private/public separation is suggested but only the public view mechanism is implemented. Additionally, there is no on/off-chain enforcement of projections during deployment of the process instance. Thus, to the best of our knowledge, none of the retrieved works addresses the trustworthy deployment of choreographies. This deployment remains challenging as private information should not be shared between partners at design nor runtime. Moreover, none of the retrieved works proposes a detailed mechanism for the execution of projections using a hybrid on/off-chain mechanism.

In this paper, we contribute to the literature through a unified solution for the design and execution of business process choreographies in a hybrid on/off-chain fashion. The first contribution of this paper is a mechanism for the deployment of the global process which offers trustworthiness while preserving the separation of concerns. At deployment time, participants build incrementally the global process from a public view stored in a smart contract. Each participant will compute off-chain its role projection comprising public events where she is involved, and private events are kept off-chain for privacy concerns. This way, private control-flows remain in the participants' process engines, while blockchain systems ensure a tamper-proof public view. The blockchain has no access to the private events; it is the aggregation of all role projections that will render the global process. The second contribution is a hybrid on/off-chain mechanism for the execution of cross-organizational choreographies. The roles execute their internal tasks off-chain in their local process execution engine. Meanwhile, a smart contract manages public interactions. When the smart contract receives an interaction request initiated from one of the roles (sender or receiver(s)), it executes the task and communicates its state back. The roles update their private states accordingly. Hence, we achieve a trustworthy separation of concerns preserving partners' private processes' privacy. Most existing works use an imperative paradigm such as BPMN. However, we chose to model choreographies with a declarative language that abstracts the control-flow through a set of rules or constraints [3,10], namely Dynamic-Condition-Response (DCR) graphs [11,25]. We believe that the declarative paradigm corresponds to the dynamic nature of choreography interactions, as business modelers cannot predefine all the execution paths of a model in constant evolution. Only essential constraints are specified in the model. We demonstrate our approach's feasibility through an implemented prototype and its effectiveness via a set of experiments.

The remainder of this paper is organized as follows. Section 2 introduces key concepts around blockchain and DCR graphs. Section 3 presents our motivating example. Section 4 details our approach. Section 5 presents an implemented prototype as a validation of our approach. Section 6 reviews the main known related work. Finally, Sect. 7 concludes the paper.

2   Background

A blockchain [26] is a distributed ledger holding a linked list of transactions organized in blocks. Each block contains (1) the reference to the previous block, (2) a tamper-evident digest of the transaction history to attest the integrity and blocks ordering, and (3) the list of the transactions to commit. Independent peers maintain the network. Peers use dedicated consensus algorithms such as proof-of-work or proof-of-stake to append transactions to the chain [13]. Some blockchains host smart contracts, deterministic scripts enforcing the terms of an agreement [14]. Business process approaches use blockchain to monitor in a decentralized fashion an agreed-upon scheme [17].

DCR is a declarative business process modeling language whose formalism is described in [11]. We refer to the following definition (cf [11]):

Definition 1. A DCR graph G is a tuple $(E, M, L, f, \longrightarrow \bullet, \bullet \longrightarrow, \longrightarrow \diamond, \longrightarrow +, \longrightarrow \%)$, where:

- E is a set of events
- $M = (\text{In,Pe,Ex}) \subseteq E \times E \times E$ is a marking
- L is a set of labels
- $f : E \longrightarrow L$ is a labelling function
- $l \subseteq E \times E$ for $l \in \{\longrightarrow \bullet, \bullet \longrightarrow, \longrightarrow \diamond, \longrightarrow +, \longrightarrow \%\}$ are relations between events.

With DCR, processes are modelled as a set of *events* E linked together with *relations*.[1] Markings M capture the graph's state at runtime by referring to the triplet (currently included *events* In, currently pending *responses* Pe, previously

---

[1] A DCR event is equivalent to a BPMN activity.

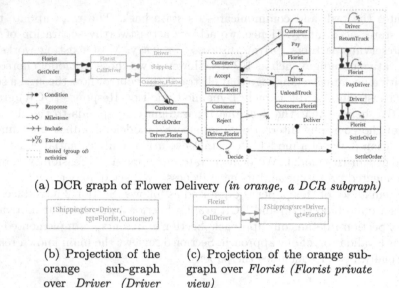

(a) DCR graph of Flower Delivery *(in orange, a DCR subgraph)*

(b) Projection of the orange sub-graph over *Driver (Driver private view)*

(c) Projection of the orange sub-graph over *Florist (Florist private view)*

Fig. 1. DCR graph, and projections of a DCR graph chunk (in orange). (Color figure online)

executed *events Ex*). Relations model in a loosely fashion the constraints linking two *events*. The end-user can enact any enabled activity at any time and more than one time during a process instance execution. DCR graphs hold five types of relations. Two relations, *condition* and *milestone*, model pre-execution constraints. They restrain the enactment of an *event*. The *condition* relation implies that a task must be launched for another to start, while *milestone* requires full task completion. Three relations translate the effects of an *event* execution to the remaining activity markings. *Exclude* and *include* respectively lock or unlock the receiver task. *Response* sets the receiver task to pending upon completion of the source task. A *DCR choreography* [11,23] models and executes DCR graphs in a distributed way. It comprises choreography *events* that ease coordination between independent entities and internal events. We reconcile the definition of a DCR choreography proposed in [11] and formalize it as follows:

Definition 2. A DCR choreography is a triple (G, I, R) where G is a DCR graph, I is a set of interactions and R is a set of roles. An interaction i is a triple (e, r, r') in which the event e is initiated by the role r and received by the roles $r' \subset R \setminus \{r\}$. For an event $e \in E$, e.type is the type of the event, e.type $\in \{\epsilon, \gamma\}$, where (i) ϵ denotes the set of internal events in G, i.e., events having one initiator $r \in R$ and (ii) γ are the set of interactions in G ($\gamma = I$).

In Fig. 1a, *Shipping* is a choreography event sent by Driver and received by Florist and Customer. *GetOrder* is an internal event of the role Florist.

3   Motivating Example

Figure 1a represents a DCR choreography of a delivery process involving three participants: Customer, Florist, and Driver. Table 1 illustrates several executions of the graph instance. Each column corresponds to an event marking of the graph in the form (included, pending, executed). Each line stands for an event query triggered. For example, initially, no event is executed nor pending. The event *GetOrder* is included in the execution set. Thus the initial marking of GetOrder is $(1, 0, 0)$. Each participant has control over the set of internal and choreography events where she is involved. We define this set of events as her private view. For example, the sub-graph in orange in Fig. 1a depicts the global view of a process involving three partners: Florist, Driver, and Customer. Figure 1b and Fig. 1c depict respectively the private views over Driver and Florist.

Requirements arise when dealing with the execution of such choreography. The activities for which some of the participants are not interested in (e.g., *ReturnTruck*) or confidential (e.g., *GetOrder*) must be kept private. The public view must express by design the information and requirements needed to execute the workflow. Moreover, public activities must be tamper-proof, and the execution flow fulfilled to keep on with the agreed-upon flow. The system must offer integrity by design. If a claim occurs, the system becomes the single source of truth. Former works on private and public views have been proposed before blockchain emergence [15, 18]. A separation of concerns is reached by separating public and private views. However, trust in the execution of the public view is still needed. Blockchain brings two interesting properties with regards to our research: decentralization and tamper-proof logs. Thus, the public view of a business process could be completely decentralized by design while ensuring trust through the tamper-proof logs property. Nonetheless, two questions arise in this setting to preserve the separation of concerns between participants. The first question concerns the deployment of the global process in each local BPMS. The deployment shall not be managed by a centralized entity that would then upload the public view on-chain. Otherwise, the trust issue would rise again. Additionally, the question of how to ensure that projections are completed off-chain while avoiding any leakage of information remains. The second question concerns the execution of the global graph. The smart contracts acts as an entry-point to ensure correctness of execution of the public view. The mechanism managing the two-sided public/private execution of tasks needs to be defined to ensure that each participant can manage its projection in a trustworthy fashion.

4   The Approach

4.1   Design Time: Generating Public and Private Views

This section presents the hybrid on/off-chain protocol developed to generate the partners view-based projections (cf Fig. 2). A smart contract comprising (1) DCR execution constraints rules, and (2) a list of workflows initially empty, is used to manage workflow instances. The workflow responsible generates the new

Table 1. Evolution of the markings of the DCR graph in Fig. 1a

	Markings (included, pending, executed)							
	GetOrder	CallDriver	Shipping	CheckOrder	Accept	Reject	Deliver	SettleOrder
(init)	(1, 0, 0)	(0, 0, 0)	(0, 0, 0)	(0, 0, 0)	(0, 0, 0)	(0, 0, 0)	(0, 0, 0)	(0, 0, 0)
GetOrder	(1, 0, 1)	(1, 1, 0)	(0, 0, 0)	(0, 0, 0)	(0, 0, 0)	(0, 0, 0)	(0, 0, 0)	(0, 0, 0)
CallDriver	(1, 0, 1)	(1, 0, 1)	(1, 1, 0)	(0, 0, 0)	(0, 0, 0)	(0, 0, 0)	(0, 0, 0)	(0, 0, 0)

workflow and updates the on-chain smart contract with the new public view. For each instance, the workflow comprises: the relation matrices and markings of the public view (cf. Sect. 2), the role addresses linked to each activity, and the IPFS hash of the textual input. The hash serves as a unique identifier for the workflow. Then, each participant computes its private view by combining the public view with its internal events. The output is a bitvectorized DCR graph. These private views constitute the entry point for the hybrid runtime execution. Finally, once the generation of role projections fulfilled, the smart contract unlocks the process instances for execution.

Used Formalism. Let (G, I, R) be a DCR choreography (cf. **Definition** 2), we define this DCR choreography through its public view G_γ and private views G_r, $\forall\, r \in R$, which are derived from G. We formalize G_γ and G_r, $\forall\, r \in R$ as follows:

Definition 3. Public View G_γ is a tuple $(E_\gamma, M_\gamma, L_\gamma, f_\gamma, \longrightarrow \bullet_\gamma, \bullet \longrightarrow_\gamma, \longrightarrow \diamond_\gamma, \longrightarrow +_\gamma, \longrightarrow \%_\gamma)$, where:

1. $E_\gamma = \{e \in I\}$
2. $M_\gamma = (In_\gamma, Pe_\gamma, Ex_\gamma)$ where $In_\gamma = In \cap E_\gamma$, $Pe_\gamma = Pe \cap E_\gamma$, and $Ex_\gamma = Ex \cap E_\gamma$
3. $f_\gamma(e) = f(e)$
4. $L_\gamma = img(f_\gamma)$
5. $\longrightarrow \bullet_\gamma =\longrightarrow \bullet \cap ((\longrightarrow \bullet\ E_\gamma) \times E_\gamma)$
6. $\bullet \longrightarrow_\gamma = \bullet \longrightarrow \cap ((\bullet \longrightarrow E_\gamma) \times E_\gamma)$
7. $\longrightarrow \diamond_\gamma =\longrightarrow \diamond \cap ((\longrightarrow \diamond\ E_\gamma) \times E_\gamma)$
8. $\longrightarrow +_\gamma =\longrightarrow + \cap ((\longrightarrow + E_\gamma) \times E_\gamma)$
9. $\longrightarrow \%_\gamma =\longrightarrow \% \cap ((\longrightarrow \% E_\gamma) \times E_\gamma)$
   Hence, $l_\gamma \in \{\longrightarrow \bullet_\gamma, \bullet \longrightarrow_\gamma, \longrightarrow \diamond_\gamma, \longrightarrow +_\gamma, \longrightarrow \%_\gamma\}$

Definition 4. Private Views For a role $r \in R$, G_r = a tuple $(E_r, M_r, L_r, f_r, \longrightarrow \bullet_r, \bullet \longrightarrow_r, \longrightarrow \diamond_r, \longrightarrow +_r, \longrightarrow \%_r)$, where:

1. $E_r = \{e \in E \mid Initiator(e) = r \cup Receiver(e) = r\}$
2. $M_r = (In_r, Pe_r, Ex_r)$ where $In_r = In \cap E_r$, $Pe_r = Pe \cap E_r$, and $Ex_r = Ex \cap E_r$
3. $f_r(e) = f(e)$
4. $L_r = img(f_r)$

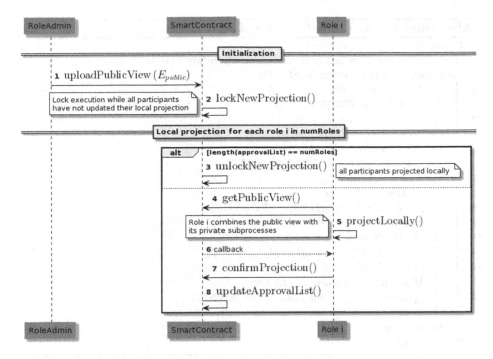

Fig. 2. Sequence diagram of the hybrid on/off-chain design protocol

5. $\longrightarrow \bullet_r = \longrightarrow \bullet \cap ((\longrightarrow \bullet\ E_r) \times E_r)$
6. $\bullet \longrightarrow_r = \bullet \longrightarrow \cap ((\bullet \longrightarrow E_r) \times E_r)$
7. $\longrightarrow \diamond_r = \longrightarrow \diamond \cap ((\longrightarrow \diamond\ E_r) \times E_r)$
8. $\longrightarrow +_r = \longrightarrow + \cap ((\longrightarrow + E_r) \times E_r)$
9. $\longrightarrow \%_r = \longrightarrow \% \cap ((\longrightarrow \% E_r) \times E_r)$
   Hence, $l_r \in \{\longrightarrow \bullet_r, \bullet \longrightarrow_r, \longrightarrow \diamond_r, \longrightarrow +_r, \longrightarrow \%_r\}$

Translating DCR Graphs into Bitvectors. The public and private views
are initially described as a textual input following the semantics prescribed in
[16]. The reader can find input examples in the source code repository of our
prototype.[2] We translate each view into a bitvector representation for execution
in the off-chain and on-chain process execution engines [5,7]. We describe in the
following paragraph the approach computing such representation.

The bitvector representation comprises (1) the five relation matrices of the
DCR graph and (2) the three markings of the graph. The five relation matrices are computed out of an input view. For each relation $[event_i \longrightarrow event_j]$,
the item a_{ij} in the relation matrix is set to one. Besides, we generate the three
initial bit-vector markings of the graph (Algorithm 1, l.3–5). The *executed* and
pending initial markings are set to zero as no event has been executed yet.

---

[2] https://anonymous.4open.science/r/hybridChoreo-1CF8/.

Algorithm 1. Marking Vectorization of a private view

Data: $G_r = (E, l)$
Result: the list of included, executed, and pending marking vectors
1 **Function** initializeMarkings(E, l):
2   var $len \leftarrow length(E)$;
 // INITIALIZE VECTORS
3   var $In \leftarrow Vector(size : len)$;
4   var $Pen \leftarrow Vector(size : len)$;
5   var $Ex \leftarrow Vector(size : len)$;
 // DETECT INITIALLY INCLUDED EVENTS
6   var $i=0$;
7   **forall the** $e \in E.\epsilon$ **do**
8   var $hasPreceedingEvent \leftarrow FALSE$;
9   **forall the** $rel \in l$ **do**
10   **if** $rel.target == e$ **then**
11     $hasPreceedingEvent \leftarrow TRUE$;
12     $break$;
13   **if** $not\ hasPreceedingEvent$ **then**
14    $In[i] \leftarrow 1$; // NO PRECEEDING EVENTS
15   $i=i+1$;
16 **return** $[In, Pen, Ex]$
17 **End Function**

The *included* state of the event is set to one if it has no pre-execution *condition* (Algorithm 1, l.6–15). We now illustrate the Florist projection bitvectorisation. First, we generate the five relation matrices. In the Florist private projection, a *condition* relation links *CallDriver* and *Shipping*. Thus, *Condition* $[id_{CallDriver}, id_{Shipping}] = 1$. The same protocol follows for each relation of the graph. We then compute the three markings of the projection. The *pending* and *executed* bit-vectors are filled with eleven zeros (one for each event of $E_{Florist}$). The Florist included bit-vector is filled similarly, except for *GetOrder* which is set to one (no pre-condition).

Hybrid On/Off-Chain Generation of Views. The generation of views comprises two steps: the on-chain public view first and private views.

The public view managed on-chain, G_γ, is the DCR graph consisting of the set of choreography events, i.e., events having one or many receivers and their relations, that model participants interactions. A representative of all participants first generates the approved bitvector representation of the public view (Fig. 2, step1). The public view consists of choreography events and their relations. Each role has a public blockchain address, and choreography events are mapped to a sender role. Moreover, the representative saves the textual public view input to IPFS to keep track of it, and saves the hash into the smart contract. The smart contract locks the process instance while waiting for each participant projection (Fig. 2, step2). A variable named *cnt*, initially set to zero, keeps track of the number of projections realized. The process instance is unlocked for execution when cnt equals the number of participants. The public events of Fig. 1a are {*Shipping, CheckOrder, Accept, Reject, Pay, UnloadTruck, PayDriver*}. The smart contract stores these events and relations where at least two public events are involved. Internal events such as {*ReturnTruck*} for Driver, or {*GetOrder, CallDriver, SettleOrder*} for Florist are kept off-chain.

Once the public view populates the smart contract, each participant fetches it (Fig. 2, step4). The private projection is generated by extracting all the events of G_γ where the participant is an initiator or a receiver in a choreography event. We conjointly extract relations connecting these events. Afterward, the participant combines off-chain the public view with its internal events (Fig. 2, step4). The obtained projection over the role r is G_r. A dedicated smart contract function named, *confirmProjection()*, enables participants to update cnt after the local projection. The function uses two mapping variables. The first mapping, *approval*, records whether a participant has generated its local projection. The second mapping, *didFetch*, records whether the participant did fetch the public view (necessary condition to realize the projection). The following constraints restrain cnt update: (i) the sender's address must belong to the list of addresses white-listed in the smart contract, (ii) participants can only update the variable once, and (iii) must have fetched the public projection first. In the motivating example, Florist asks the public projection to the smart contract. The smart contract verifies that its address belongs to the white-list, forwards the public view to Florist, and updates cnt to 1. Florist projects the view over her role. She obtains a set of receive events: {*Shipping, CheckOrder, Accept, Reject, Pay, UnloadTruck*}, and one send event {*PayDriver*}. She then adds its internal activities {*GetOrder, CallDriver, SettleOrder*} to the projection. Lastly, Florist triggers *confirmProjection()*.

4.2 Hybrid Off/On-Chain Runtime Execution

Our approach proposes a hybrid execution at runtime: the private DCR execution engine of the involved participants manages the private projections. Meanwhile, a smart contract called S triggers the execution logic of the public tasks on blockchain. An event execution query comprises the name of the event and its class: *internal*, or *choreography*. The execution logic depends on the event class. The private and public projections communicate via choreography events. Participant executes private events off-chain (cf. Fig. 3a). For an internal event, the private process engine looks at its private markings (see Fig. 3a). If the event is enabled,[3] we apply post-execution constraints to the bound events (i.e., events are set to pending, included, or excluded), and update the marking accordingly. For example, the execution request of *GetOrder* (Fig. 1a) will succeed: it does not have any pre-execution constraint. Thus, the executed marking of the event *GetOrder* will be set to one. The post-execution constraints (*condition* and *response*) will unlock *CallDriver* and set its pending marking to one.

---

[3] An event is *enabled* if the following preconditions are fulfilled: the event is included, and the *condition* and *milestone* relations are executed.

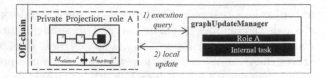

(a) Execution of an internal event

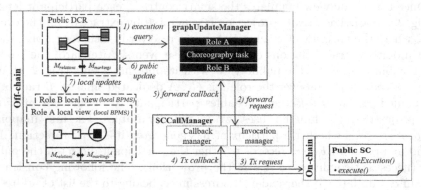

(b) Execution of a choreography event

Fig. 3. The execution scheme logic of DCR choreography events

The smart contract S handles the execution of the choreography send and receive events (cf. Fig. 3b). S holds the bitvector representation of the public view and two functions: *enableExecution()* checks the enabling preconditions, and *execute()* computes the enabled event and updates the marking vectors. The execution of a choreography event follows the subsequent steps (see Fig. 3b). First, the backend receives an execution query (step 1) and forwards it to the smart contract API (step 2). The latter sends a transaction (Tx) to S to call the function *enableExecution()* (step 3). The Tx includes the event's name to execute, the event initiator, the receiver (if it is a choreography event), and the event state (enabled, included, executed). If the activation conditions are verified, the function *execute()* updates the event state (the three bit-vectors) and the public projection state (the five relation matrices). The Tx callback containing the updated states is sent back to the smart contract API (step 4), which forwards it to the local backend (step 5). The backend updates the public projection (step 6). Changes are propagated to the concerned private projections (step 7). Choreography events are by nature of interest to process participants. S makes their execution management trustworthy as its behavior is deterministic, and the choreography states stored into the smart contract are tamper-proof.

5 Evaluation

Our proof of concept is a hybrid on/off-chain business process engine managing declarative choreographies (code repo: cf footnote 2). We use a Ganache testnet to deploy the public smart contract S which manages each process. S comprises (1) execution constraints rules, and (2) a list of workflows initially empty. The initial cost of deployment of S is 0.06413472 ETH (i.e., 137.6$). For each workflow, RoleAdmin (1) generates the public view bitvector representation (Sect. 4.1), (2) saves the textual public view input to IPFS, and (3) registers the new workflow on-chain by calling the function uploadPublicView. The workflow is identified by the IPFS unique hash. Participants interact with the smart contract via API calls to generate their private views. Afterwards, the process instance is released for execution. The local process execution engine executes internal events off-chain and forwards choreography events to the blockchain.

We instantiate three cross-organizational processes in the platform to assess the execution cost in terms of gas fees and time. We test two workflows from the literature: the invoice and oncology workflows [25], and the motivating example. We run the experiments on a personal computer with an Intel i5 core CPU, 4 GB of RAM. At the time of writing, 1ETH = 2,145.73$. We evaluate the public-to-private projection costs of the system for the deployment of the three processes mentioned above (cf. Table 2a). For each workflow, the public view registration cost is worth 0.068352 ETH (146.7$) for the delivery workflow, 0.040947 ETH (87.9$) for the invoice workflow, and 0.065019 ETH (139.5$) for the oncology workflow. Afterwards, each role fetches the public view, and confirms its projection. The delivery and invoice workflows share the same costs for fetching the public view and confirming the projection. Such cost, corresponding to updating *approval* and *didFetch*, is proportional to the number of roles registered. The total cost for instantiating a choreography corresponds to public view upload, and the number of roles $\#R$ times the private projection cost. It is worth 0.078534 ETH (168.5$), 0.051129 ETH (109.7$), and 0.079795 ETH (171.2$) for the delivery, invoice, and oncology workflows respectively. The public-to-private total projection cost depends on the number of roles and events.

We also evaluate the performance of the system at runtime: Table 2a presents the results obtained after the enactment of one trace. The reported execution time factors the transaction confirmation time. The average transaction fees requested for a task execution are smaller than the process instantiation ones. Moreover, the average execution time for a private task is one order of magnitude smaller than the one needed for a public task. Indeed, we compute private activities off-chain. Thus the execution time of a private event corresponds comprises checking the event nature (private or public), and updating private markings. On the opposite, the execution of public activities comprises an interaction with the blockchain network. Against this backdrop, the local execution of private tasks reduces the overall execution time.

Finally, we compare the transaction costs of our approach to the BPMN-based experiments presented in [8]. We translate into DCR choreographies the two open-sourced BPMN choreographies presented in [5], namely *supply chain* and *incident management*. We deploy and execute the choreography in our prototype, and compare the results. Table 3 shows the instantiation and task execution average gas fees; task execution fees correspond to the average cost of

Table 2. Hybrid on/off-chain Projection and execution costs Hybrid on/off-chain Projection and execution costs

(a) Public-to-private projection costs, *W. =Workflow*

Step	Role	Function	Delivery W.	Invoice W.	Oncology W.
A	RoleAdmin	*uploadPublicView()*	0.068352 ETH	0.040947 ETH	0.065019 ETH
B1	Role r in *R*	*fetchPublicView()*	0.002006 ETH	0.002006 ETH	0.002139 ETH
B2	Role r in *R*	*confirmProjection()*	0.001388 ETH	0.001388 ETH	0.001555 ETH
Total Cost = A + #*R*.(B1+B2)			0.078534 ETH	0.051129 ETH	0.079795 ETH

(b) Task execution costs *(Pub/Pri= public/private tasks)*.

Workflow					Tx. Fees	Exec Time	
Name	*#Parties*	*#Pub*	*#Pri*	*#Constraints*	*Task Exec*	*Pub*	*Pri*
Delivery	3	9	1	28	0.0093 ETH	15s	1s
Invoice	3	8	2	15	0.0069 ETH	10s	1s
Oncology	4	10	3	21	0.0117 ETH	19s	2s
				Mean	0.0093 ETH	14.6s	1.3s

Table 3. Gas fees comparison of BPMN [8] and DCR choreographies (our approach) run on the Ethereum blockchain

Workflow	#Tasks	#Gateways	Gas fees	[8] (BPMN)	Our approach
Supply chain [5]	10	2	Instantiation	1,100,590	1,074,178
			Task exec.	566,861	478,527
Incident Mgt. [5]	9	6	Instantiation	1 119,803	930,399
			Task exec.	324,420	456,887

execution of a task. A gain of 26,412 gas for the supply chain workflow, and 189,404 gas for the incident management workflow can be noticed with the DCR approach. Thus, the DCR-based smart-contract requires less fees for instantiation than the BPMN one in these workflows. Regarding task execution costs, the modeling choice does not seem to impact gas fees: a gain can be noticed with DCR in the supply chain workflow, but not in the incident management one. The number of gateways (2 in the supply chain, and six in the incident management workflow) may explain such disparity. Indeed, each exclusive gateway is translated into an include and a response relation for each decision path in the DCR model. Such translation may explain the gas difference.

6   Related Work

Regarding traditional view-based approaches, authors in [15,18] use process views to build an abstracted version of each partners' private processes in order to hide its internal structure. In [18], authors define a SOG (Symbolic Observation Graph) for each choreography participants. A SOG is an abstraction of the reachability state graph of a formally modeled process (e.g., an LTS). The nodes in the SOG are meta-states, i.e., a set of states connected by unobserved (internal) activities, and the edges are labelled with observed (interaction) activities. The SOG of the choreography process is the product of the SOGs of the participants. In [15], roles inter-connect via a set of virtual activities. These virtual activities abstract choreography interactions, and are enacted by a trusted third-party. In these works, partners' privacy is reached by separating public and private views. However, trust issues remain as shared execution logic and data are managed in a centralized fashion, often by a third-party [6].

Blockchains have been leveraged as trusted mechanisms to ensure the public view correctness in recent work. In the following, we classify related works managing collaborative processes on-chain according to (1) the choice of paradigm which impacts the system flexibility and scalability, (2) the public/private views separation which impacts confidentiality, and (3) the deployment which impacts participants trust. The **paradigm** criterion refers to the process modeling choice used to represent collaborative processes on blockchain. In [4–6,19,21,24], the imperative modeling approach is chosen: BPMN business models describe the control flow in a sequential manner. Other works such as [2,7,9,12,20] use the *declarative modeling* approach where only execution constraints are specified. [9,12] propose LTL for smart contract parametrized pre and post-execution conditions, however without including implementations. Authors in [20] use the artifact-centric language, in [2] XML, and in [7] DCR. The **view-based** criterion refers to the separate display of the global process: in a view-based setting, participants only have access to their tasks. [2,4,5,7,9,12,20,21,24] do not consider the public/private view separation. For example, in [5,7,19], authors handle orchestration schemes only. [6] considers a choreography but authors do not expand on the participants' private workflows execution and deployment. Though the generation of the public and private views in [6] is suggested, projections are not enforced in a trustworthy fashion in this work. The **deployment** criterion refers to the deployment model chosen for collaborative processes. *Regarding fully on-chain schemes*, a translator maps directly BPMN [5,6,19], DCR [7], or XML [2] models into Solidity. Additionally, a custom interface binds local execution engines with blockchain in [6]. In [24], authors run choreographies with Bitcoin instead of smart contracts. [9,12] advise the direct end-to-end deployment of public processes. [20] stores the hash of an artifact-based multi-party process in a smart contract but no details are given on off-chain tasks. *Regarding hybrid on/off-chain schemes*, [21] proposed a set of on/off-chain connectors, but processes are intra-organizational and the system allows only monetary operations. In [4], a gateway enables interactions of an off-chain intra-organizational BPMN process with heterogeneous blockchains.

Most blockchain-based collaborative processes cited in the literature do not consider declarative choreographies. When they do, they do not distinguish the partners' internal processes and the public view of the choreography when deployed to the chain. Consequently, the contribution of this paper is to answer cross-organizational needs for process flexibility and trustworthy separation of concerns. To do so, we build a collaborative BPMS that offers modeling flexibility, as well as a trustworthy and privacy-preserving separation of concerns. We chose a declarative language that offers collaboration flexibility, necessary due to the dynamic nature of collaborations. We add to this design choice the public/private view separation and a hybrid deployment to enforce in a trustworthy fashion the separation of concerns.

7   Discussion and Conclusion

This paper leverages the management of business process choreographies using blockchain to address the need for a trustworthy separation of concerns. Additionally, we model choreographies with a declarative language called DCR. This language offers loosely-constrained models to meet the flexibility requirements of cross-organizational processes. To enhance privacy at design time, the public view of the choreography is stored in a smart contract, and participants generate their private view off-chain. On the execution side, internal events are executed locally for privacy concerns, while choreography events are executed on-chain for accountability concerns.

This approach represents a first effort to separate the public and private views of a declarative choreography and proceed with its hybrid off/on-chain management. Results confirm the advantages of separating public from private events to ensure privacy while leveraging blockchain as a decentralized execution infrastructure. Moreover, the local execution of private events leads to time and economic gains. Our approach works if there is no public event. Then, no public projection is generated. Multi-instance choreographies are also possible: for each new instance, a workflow instance is added to the smart contract. Besides, experiments on graphs of alternative complexity (be it the number of participants or activities) should confirm preliminary results. A limitation to our approach concerns the public/private exchange of information. In our setting, the information published in the smart contract is public. Consortium or private blockchains, coupled to off-chain oracles to exchange sensitive information with the smart contract, could answer privacy concerns. Furthermore, we rely on the truthfulness of participants to execute their private projections and do not ensure the correct enforcement of private processes. This concern, inherent to choreographies, is part of ongoing research efforts.

As future work, we plan to use side channels [22] to manage on-chain process instances to save transaction costs and reduce task execution latency. Only two blockchain transactions would be of need: one to instantiate the process execution channel, and one to settle it. Additionally, a need rises regarding the ability of participants to change the global workflow at runtime. An avenue for future work is to propose such functionality to the proposed system, building on the declarative paradigm to define flexibly authorizations and obligations.

References

1. van der Aalst, W.M.P., Weske, M.: The P2P approach to interorganizational work-flows. In: Dittrich, K.R., Geppert, A., Norrie, M.C. (eds.) CAiSE 2001. LNCS, vol. 2068, pp. 140–156. Springer, Heidelberg (2001). https://doi.org/10.1007/3-540-45341-5_10
2. Brahem, A., et al.: Blockchain's fame reaches the execution of personalized touristic itineraries. In: WETICE, pp. 186–191. IEEE (2019)
3. Fahland, D., Mendling, J., Reijers, H.A., Weber, B., Weidlich, M., Zugal, S.: Declarative versus imperative process modeling languages: the issue of maintainability. In: Rinderle-Ma, S., Sadiq, S., Leymann, F. (eds.) BPM 2009. LNBIP, vol. 43, pp. 477–488. Springer, Heidelberg (2010). https://doi.org/10.1007/978-3-642-12186-9_45
4. Falazi, G., et al.: Process-based composition of permissioned and permissionless blockchain smart contracts. In: EDOC (2019)
5. Weber, I., Xu, X., Riveret, R., Governatori, G., Ponomarev, A., Mendling, J.: Untrusted business process monitoring and execution using blockchain. In: La Rosa, M., Loos, P., Pastor, O. (eds.) BPM 2016. LNCS, vol. 9850, pp. 329–347. Springer, Cham (2016). https://doi.org/10.1007/978-3-319-45348-4_19
6. Ladleif, J., Weske, M., Weber, I.: Modeling and enforcing blockchain-based choreographies. In: Hildebrandt, T., van Dongen, B.F., Röglinger, M., Mendling, J. (eds.) BPM 2019. LNCS, vol. 11675, pp. 69–85. Springer, Cham (2019). https://doi.org/10.1007/978-3-030-26619-6_7
7. Madsen et al., M.F.: Collaboration among adversaries: distributed workflow execution on a blockchain. In: FAB, p. 8 (2018)
8. López-Pintado O., et al.: CATERPILLAR: a business process execution engine on the ethereum blockchain. Softw.; Pract. Exp. **49**(7), 1162–1193 (2019)
9. Hull, R., Datra, V.S., Chen, Y.-M., Deutsch, A., Heath III, F.F.T., Vianu, V.: Towards a shared ledger business collaboration language based on data-aware processes. In: Sheng, Q.Z., Stroulia, E., Tata, S., Bhiri, S. (eds.) ICSOC 2016. LNCS, vol. 9936, pp. 18–36. Springer, Cham (2016). https://doi.org/10.1007/978-3-319-46295-0_2
10. Goedertier, S., et al.: Declarative business process modelling: principles and modelling languages. Enterp. Inf. Syst. **9**(2), 161–185 (2015)
11. Hildebrandt, T.T., Slaats, T., López, H.A., Debois, S., Carbone, M.: Declarative choreographies and liveness. In: Pérez, J.A., Yoshida, N. (eds.) FORTE 2019. LNCS, vol. 11535, pp. 129–147. Springer, Cham (2019). https://doi.org/10.1007/978-3-030-21759-4_8
12. de Sousa et al, V.A.: B-MERODE: a model-driven engineering and artifact-centric approach to generate smart contracts. In: CAiSE (2020)
13. Bach, L., Mihaljevic, B., Zagar, M.: Comparative analysis of blockchain consensus algorithms. In: MIPRO, pp. 1545–1550. IEEE (2018)
14. Buterin, V., et al.: A next-generation smart contract and decentralized application platform. White paper, vol. 3, no. 37 (2014)
15. Chebbi, I., Dustdar, S., Tata, S.: The view-based approach to dynamic interorganizational workflow cooperation. Data Knowl. Eng. **56**(2), 139–173 (2006)
16. Debois, S., Hildebrandt, T.: The DCR Workbench: Declarative Choreographies for Collaborative Processes, pp. 99–124. River Publishers (2017)
17. Henry, T., Laga, N., Hatin, J., Gaaloul, W., Boughzala, I.: Cross-collaboration processes based on blockchain and IoT: a survey. In: HICSS (2021)

18. Klai, K., Tata, S., Desel, J.: Symbolic abstraction and deadlock-freeness verification of inter-enterprise processes. In: Dayal, U., Eder, J., Koehler, J., Reijers, H.A. (eds.) BPM 2009. LNCS, vol. 5701, pp. 294–309. Springer, Heidelberg (2009). https://doi.org/10.1007/978-3-642-03848-8_20
19. López-Pintado, O., Dumas, M., García-Bañuelos, L., Weber, I.: Dynamic role binding in blockchain-based collaborative business processes. In: Giorgini, P., Weber, B. (eds.) CAiSE 2019. LNCS, vol. 11483, pp. 399–414. Springer, Cham (2019). https://doi.org/10.1007/978-3-030 21290-2_25
20. Meroni, G., Plebani, P., Vona, F., et al.: Trusted artifact-driven process monitoring of multi-party business processes with blockchain. In: Di Ciccio, C. (ed.) BPM 2019. LNBIP, vol. 361, pp. 55–70. Springer, Cham (2019). https://doi.org/10.1007/978-3-030-30429-4_5
21. Palacin, L.: Accelerate blockchain technology adoption with Bonita BPM and Chain Core, pp. 04–08 (2018)
22. Papadis, N., Tassiulas, L.: Blockchain-based payment channel networks: challenges and recent advances. IEEE Access **8**, 227596–227609 (2020)
23. Peltz, C.: Web services orchestration and choreography. Computer **36**, 46–52 (2003)
24. Prybila, C., Schulte, S., Hochreiner, C., Weber, I.: Runtime verification for business processes utilizing the bitcoin blockchain. FGCS **107**, 816–831 (2020)
25. Slaats, T., Hildebrandt, T.T., Carbone, M., Völzer, H.: Flexible process notations for cross-organizational case management systems. ITU Copenhagen (2015)
26. Underwood, S.: Blockchain beyond bitcoin. ACM **59**(11), 15–17 (2016)

Blockchains and Smart Contracts

Blockchain-Based Result Verification
for Computation Offloading

Benjamin Körbel[1,2], Marten Sigwart[1,2], Philip Frauenthaler[1,2],
Michael Sober[1,2], and Stefan Schulte[1,2(✉)] (iD)

[1] Christian Doppler Laboratory for Blockchain Technologies for the Internet
of Things, TU Hamburg, Hamburg, Germany
{michael.sober,stefan.schulte}@tuhh.de
[2] Christian Doppler Laboratory for Blockchain Technologies for the Internet
of Things, TU Wien, Vienna, Austria
https://www.cdl-bot.at

Abstract. Offloading of computation, e.g., to the cloud, is today a
major task in distributed systems. Usually, consumers which apply offloading have to trust that a particular functionality offered by a service
provider is delivering correct results. While redundancy (i.e., offloading
a task to more than one service provider) or (partial) reprocessing help
to identify correct results, they also lead to significantly higher cost.

Hence, within this paper, we present an approach to verify the results
of offchain computations via the blockchain. For this, we apply zero-
knowledge proofs to provide evidence that results are correct. Using our
approach, it is possible to establish trust between a service consumer
and arbitrary service providers. We evaluate our approach using a very
well-known example task, i.e., the Traveling Salesman Problem.

Keywords: Offloading · Verification · Blockchain

1 Introduction

Offloading of computational tasks has gained a lot of research attention in recent
years [18]. The basic idea of offloading is that a client device outsources resource-
intensive computational tasks to providers, often in exchange for a fee [13].
Hence, when offloading tasks, two parties are involved. Task issuers (i.e., *service consumers*) potentially have limited computational capabilities and therefore are interested in outsourcing particular tasks. Conversely, task processors
(i.e., *service providers*) may have idle computational resources and offer their
CPU-cycles and further computational resources to process these tasks. Typical
examples are the offloading of data processing tasks from lightweight Internet of
Things (IoT) or mobile devices in order to decrease processing time or to save
energy [24]. For instance, machine learning, (combinatorial) optimization tasks,
or the application of heuristics (e.g., genetic algorithms) to solve a complex problem require often resources not available to a potential service consumer. Apart
from overcoming limited computational resources, scalability and fault tolerance
are also major reasons why offloading is applied [10].

© Springer Nature Switzerland AG 2021
H. Hacid et al. (Eds.): ICSOC 2021, LNCS 13121, pp. 99–115, 2021.
https://doi.org/10.1007/978-3-030-91431-8_7

Offloading can be done to resources following the Infrastructure-as-a-Service (IaaS), Platform-as-a-Service (PaaS), or Software-as-a-Service (SaaS) models, depending on the needs of the service consumer. Traditionally, computation offloading leverages the cloud, e.g., [16], but more recently, offloading to resources at the edge of the network has also been widely discussed, e.g., [12].

Regardless of the technological setting, offloading requires a client to trust the service provider to deliver correct results. This is a major market entry barrier, since service consumers naturally trust well-known service providers more than new market participants.

In order to avoid reliance on a particular provider, the usage of blockchain technologies for task offloading has previously been discussed [23]. In such approaches (e.g., Golem or iExec—see Sect. 2), the blockchain is a service broker, which brings together consumers and providers, and often delivers further functionalities, e.g., automated settlement after the offloading task has been carried out. Also, the offloading results are delivered through the blockchain.

However, to the best of our knowledge, none of the existing approaches performs a check of the correctness of the delivered results. Ideally, before service consumers pay the service providers for their work, they have an assurance that the returned results can be fully trusted. Previous studies are aware of this issue and discuss solutions based on, e.g., redundant computing, reprocessing fractions of a task locally, or reputation-based systems in order to ensure correct results [3,6,20]. While these approaches may reduce the risk of receiving wrong results, they cannot proof that a result is correct [23]. In other, non-blockchain solutions, the user needs to trust a third party which provides functionalities ensuring trust in the offloading results, e.g., [17].

Furthermore, it should be noted that many offloading tasks do not deliver a deterministic result. For instance, if offloading machine learning tasks or heuristics to solve NP-complete problems, the computation results can differ. This further complicates checking the correctness of a result, since redundant computing or partial reprocessing may lead to different results.

Within the work at hand, we address this issue by conceptualizing, implementing, and evaluating a blockchain-based offloading approach that can prove the proper execution of a particular computation task. By using a blockchain, we dissolve the dependency on a trusted third party. Using a public blockchain also helps to achieve transparency, since information about the off-chaining procedure is publicly available. To prove the correctness of computational results, we apply zero-knowledge proofs (ZKPs). We evaluate our approach using the well-known Traveling Salesman Problem (TSP), showing in which use case areas the proposed solution is beneficial if compared to other alternative approaches, and assessing the cost and time overhead of our approach.

In brief, we provide the following contributions in this paper:

- We assess approaches to ensure trust in results provided by service providers.
- We discuss the utilization of ZKPs and blockchain technologies in order to verify the results for offloaded tasks.

- We design and implement a blockchain-based solution for computation off-loading with result verification.
- We apply the TSP as a running example and in order to evaluate the overhead resulting from the presented approach.

The remainder of this paper is organized as follows: In Sect. 2, we discuss the related work. In Sect. 3, we assess different approaches to verify the results of offloaded computation tasks. Based on this, we present our design and implementation in Sect. 4. Section 5 shows the results of the evaluation of the presented work, and Sect. 6 concludes this paper.

2 Related Work

To the best of our knowledge, the field of blockchain-based, verifiable task off-loading is still a novel research area, and not too many approaches have been presented so far.

Golem [20], iExec [6], and SONM [21] are three commercial solutions, aiming at decentralizing offloading to the cloud [23]. Their respective primary goal is to provide solutions to decrease market entry barriers, by allowing arbitrary providers to offer computational resources on a blockchain, and arbitrary consumers to use these resources. Notably, the intended providers of cloud resources are not large-scale data centers, but could be anyone with idle computational resources. Golem, iExec and SONM aim at providing marketplace and broker functionalities, and apply a pay-per-use model, i.e., the consumer has to pay for using computational infrastructure or for processing a particular task. Notably, in contrast to the work at hand, which focuses on a SaaS model, these solutions aim at providing computing power in general, i.e., on the IaaS level.

With regard to result verification, Golem supports redundant computation, but also allows to recompute fractions of an offloaded task locally (i.e., at the service consumer's side), and to subsequently compare the results. Also, Golem implements a reputation mechanism, which is based on consumer (e.g., late payments) and provider behavior (e.g., not delivering results in time), respectively [20]. iExec applies a similar approach, where the service consumer can define the needed reliability of the results. If this value is high, a higher degree of redundancy is applied when computing the offloading tasks, and more reliable providers, i.e., with a high reputation, are selected. Notably, iExec also allows to support Software Guard Extension (SGX), which is a kind of enclave-based off-chain computations (see Sect. 3) [6]. So far, SONM does not implement a verification mechanism, but names reputation management as a major enabler to provide reliable computation results [21].

None of the so-far discussed approaches provides a proof that the results of a computation are correct. Instead, redundant computations, recomputing fractions of tasks locally, and reputation-based methods only *decrease* the risk that the results are not correct. Especially redundant computations also increase the cost by quite some degree, since all involved service providers charge a fee for the computations. Reputation systems can be helpful, but provide market entry barriers since new service providers need to build a reputation. Also, it remains unclear how these solutions handle results which are not deterministic, e.g., for machine learning or heuristic tasks.

FlopCoin [3] is a blockchain-based offloading framework with a decentralized incentive and reputation scheme. Among other metrics, the reputation of participants is used as input for the offloading decision, i.e., to which provider of computational resources a particular task is offloaded. EdgeChain [14] uses a blockchain and smart contracts to link computational resources at the edge and IoT devices which need to offload tasks. The blockchain is used to monitor the offloading procedure and to conduct payments. A mechanism to detect malicious nodes based on past behavior is also introduced. Qiu et al. [15] discuss a similar approach, but apply deep reinforcement learning to find an assignment of tasks and available edge resources. Very recently, another approach for offloading to the fog has been presented by Wu et al. [25]. The focus of this work is also on the actual decision making, i.e., where to place which offloaded task. In contrast, we aim primarily on proving that computed results are valid.

To the best of our knowledge, none of the discussed research papers directly address offloading result verification. Hence, the work at hand complements existing work, and could be used within existing solutions in order to proof that an offloaded computation provides valid results.

3   Result Verification for Offloaded Tasks

As discussed above, it is the goal of the work at hand to provide mechanisms that can verify results of offloaded computational tasks. In general, we focus on the SaaS model, but in fact, result verification could also be done for user-deployed services using the IaaS or PaaS model.

To achieve result verification, different schemes could be applied: *Verifiable off-chain computation* entails the provisioning of cryptographic proofs that witness correct processing. After a computation is performed, a cryptographic proof is generated and published together with the result on a blockchain by the processor (here: the service provider). Subsequently, the validity of the computation can be verified on-chain using a smart contract [4].

Verifiable off-chain computation can be realized using ZKPs [7]. The basic idea behind ZKPs is to convince someone that a statement is true without revealing any underlying information needed to proof that the statement is true. This allows to hide the input data for a proof and therefore supports data privacy. Importantly, in the scenario at hand, this facilitates the verification that the results delivered by a service provider are correct, without the need that the provider reveals its applied service or algorithm. Hence, the computation performed by the service provider remains a blackbox from the perspective of result verification. This is even the case for non-deterministic computations, e.g., if a heuristic is applied. As long as it is possible to define rules which describe if an offloading result is valid, ZKPs can be applied successfully.

ZKPs can be realized in the form of Zero-Knowledge Non-Interactive Succinct Arguments of Knowledge (zk-SNARKs), Zero-Knowledge Scalable Transparent Arguments of Knowledge (zk-STARKs), and Bulletproofs [9].

zk-SNARKs are non-interactive and provide relatively cheap verification by their succinctness. Before generating a proof and performing the verification step, a one-time setup must be carried out by a trusted party. Unlike zk-SNARKs, zk-STARKs and Bulletproofs do not require a trusted one-time setup. In zk-SNARKs and Bulletproofs, computations are abstracted with arithmetic circuits, while zk-STARKs leverage higher degree polynomials. Both zk-STARKs and Bulletproofs feature growing proof-size and on-chain verification, while zk-SNARKs are independent of the task complexity and provide compact proves [4]. Due to the succinctness of zk-SNARKs, very short proofs (i.e., in the range of bytes) can be provided, which is very beneficial when blockchain technology is involved. Therefore, we decided to apply zk-SNARKs for result verification.

We have also investigated other result verification schemes: For instance, *Secure Multiparty Computation* (SMPC) protocols enable the construction of privacy-preserving off-chain computation schemes, but are accompanied by high overhead [4]. *Enclave-based off-chain computation* relies on Trusted Execution Environments (TEEs) which enable code execution while preserving confidentiality and integrity. The enclave-based scheme allows universal computations but has potential security issues [8,19]. *Incentive-driven off-chain computing* rewards nodes which are doing verification work to check if a computation is correct. One implementation of this scheme is TrueBit [22]. A challenge when using the described scheme is to keep nodes motivated for performing verifications continuously. Also, the throughput of completed computation tasks and the general service can be hindered by malicious verifiers by marking each computation result as faulty [4].

The selection of zk-SNARKs allows us to make use of the ZoKrates toolbox [5], which supports the entire process of specifying, integrating and deploying ZKPs on Ethereum-based blockchains. The toolbox consists of a Domain-specific Language (DSL), a compiler and generators for proofs as well as smart contracts for verification. In brief, ZoKrates can be used to execute a computational task off-chain. Afterwards, the result of the computation (here: of an offloading task) and the corresponding proof are written back to a blockchain. The proof that attests correct (or incorrect) computation can then be verified on-chain. Therefore, the computational effort on a blockchain is reduced, while privacy can be preserved due to the usage of ZKPs.

4   Design and Implementation

4.1   Overview

After having selected zk-SNARKs as the underlying approach to provide result verification for computation offloading, we are now able to design a solution.

As discussed before, we make use of a blockchain-based approach to offload tasks to service providers. While this has been proposed before (see Sect. 2), there

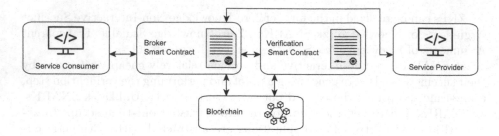

Fig. 1. Blockchain-based computation offloading with result verification

is lack of solutions which allow to verify the results delivered by the service providers. Due to space constraints, we focus on this particular functionality in the work at hand. However, we have in fact designed and implemented a framework which covers the necessary functionality stack, i.e., acts as a blockchain-based broker for service consumers (offloaders) and service providers, and implements an incentive structure, so that fees can be charged and are automatically paid if a result has been verified. Notably, while the implemented solution can be used by traditional cloud providers to offer their resources and services, it could also be used in fog and edge settings, or by private persons who want to offer spare computational resources.

In the case of non-deterministic results, e.g., since a heuristic is applied by a service provider (see Sect. 1), our framework allows to obtain results from different providers and to compare the result quality. The integration of methods to assess the result quality is part of our future work (see Sect. 6).

Figure 1 shows the components of the software solution. As it can be seen, the system consists of the service consumer (i.e., the client software for the task offloader), the service provider (i.e., the according client software), the broker smart contract and the result verification smart contract. In the following subsections, we discuss the core components with a focus on the verification functionalities.

4.2   Blockchain-based Brokering and Result Verification

The blockchain serves two major purposes in our scenario: First, it acts as a broker during the offloading process, i.e., facilitates the cooperation between a service consumer and a service provider. This includes provisioning of results to the service consumer and payment to the service provider. Second, the blockchain delivers the result verification (see Sect. 4.4). Following the approach presented in this work, no preexisting relationship and no position of trust between a service consumer and potential service providers need to exist.

Brokering functionalities and result verification are implemented using smart contracts. Within the work at hand, we use Ethereum for this, since it provides a broad acceptance in the research community as well as industry. It should be noted that the presented approach is per se protocol-agnostic, and could also be implemented using a permissioned blockchain like Hyperledger Fabric. However, we opted to use a public blockchain in the work at hand.

4.3   Broker Smart Contract

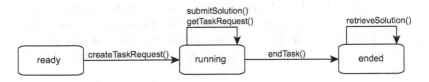

Fig. 2. Simplified state diagram of the broker smart contract

Figure 2 provides an overview of the states the broker smart contract passes through. As it can be seen in the state diagram, the contract may be in the states *ready*, *running*, and *ended*. For the transition between the states, particular functions must be called. Before any interaction is possible, i.e., any function is callable, the smart contract needs to be deployed on the blockchain. After the deployment, it is in state *ready*. At this point, a service consumer can create a new request for offloading, i.e., a new offloading task, using *createTaskRequest()*.

The necessary inputs for *createTaskRequest()* are a stake, which is used as a deposit for the later payment to the service provider, information about the offloaded task, and a boolean value if the result should be verified or not. Once this has been done, the state changes to *running*.

At this point of time, a potential service provider can retrieve all the necessary information to process the task by calling *getTaskRequest()*. Notably, the selection of the service provider could follow different patterns, e.g., based on reputation and/or load balancing as proposed in the related work (see Sect. 2), by applying a reverse auction so that potential service providers compete for the requests, or other allocation techniques.

Since this is not in the focus of the work at hand, we implement a simplified approach, i.e., once a service provider has computed a result, it can be published using *submitSolution()*. When calling this function, the service provider needs to deliver the actual solution to the request. At this point, network participants including the service consumer can see the submitted solution due to the public nature of the blockchain. To circumvent that a service consumer reads the result and does not pay the provider, the stake deposited by the consumer is used.

Any network participant (here: the service consumer or the service providers) may close the task by using *endTask()*, which also means that the state changes to *ended* and that the payment to the service provider is triggered. Notably, this is only possible once a minimum duration has passed, which is also defined by the service consumer. When the task is ended, the service consumer can collect the solution by calling the function *retrieveSolution()*. As written before, the consumer could also read the result simply from the blockchain. We explicitly

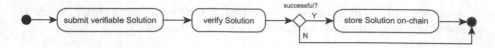

Fig. 3. High level process of the result verification

foresee *retrieveSolution()* as the possibility to implement a more sophisticated function here, e.g., to encrypt and decrypt the result in order to not release the solution publicly on the blockchain, or to provide the solution via a blockchain-external data storage like the InterPlanetary File System (IFPS) [11], in order to save gas cost.

4.4 Result Verification

Figure 3 gives a high level overview of result verification within our approach. As it can be seen, solutions of verifiable tasks are written to the blockchain only if the result verification is successful. Otherwise, the submission is discarded. The activity *verify Solution* is part of the result verification while all other activities in Fig. 3 belong to the broker smart contract discussed in Sect. 4.3. The verification is performed within a separate smart contract generated by ZoKrates. For this, the broker smart contract has to trigger the verification function *verifyTx()* in the verification smart contract. An example implementation of *verifyTx()* is discussed in Sect. 4.6.

The procedure of the result verification is illustrated in Fig. 4. First, a service provider decides to contribute to a particular offloading task, which is the start event for the result verification. For this, the provider retrieves all relevant input data. Based on that, the service provider computes the task locally (and therefore off-chain) with a service running on the provider's computational resources. After a solution has been found, a witness has to be computed. This means that a program specified in DSL code is run with the service provider's result as input; this DSL program is providing important input for the ZoKrates toolbox as discussed in more detail in Sect. 4.6. If the verification succeeds, the DSL program returns a witness that proves proper computation. Otherwise, it can be assumed that an error occurred during the computation phase or a wrong result has been entered. In this case, the computation is repeated. If the computation fails again, the procedure ends unsuccessfully (not shown in Fig. 4).

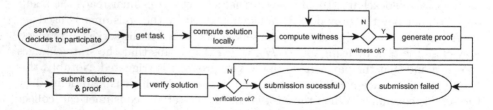

Fig. 4. Result verification procedure

Based on the witness, a proof can be generated, which is needed for the on-chain verification in the next step. Both actions, compute witness and generate proof are performed locally on the service provider's hardware. Afterwards, the solution and the proof can be submitted to the broker smart contract. When a solution is submitted, the broker smart contract calls the verification function *verifyTx()* of the verification smart contract. If the verification function returns true, we can assume that the computation has been executed honestly. As a result, the solution is stored on-chain. Otherwise, if false is returned, the submission of the service provider is discarded entirely. In both cases, the procedure subsequently ends.

4.5   Implementing Result Verification for Specific Use Cases

Result verification is naturally tied to specific computation problems. This means that a certain part of the result verification, more specifically the DSL program implemented using the ZoKrates toolbox, is not generic and must be adapted whenever a different computation problem has to be served.

Accordingly, the DSL code contains appropriate checks to prove that a computation is done correctly. The possibility of creating or adopting these programs enables flexibility and adds universal applicability to the result verification. In other words, new use cases can be added and thus potential demands of service consumers for new computation problems can be met. The mandatory steps to add a new use case are depicted in Fig. 5.

To verify results of a specific computation problem, several one-time preparation steps have to be conducted. As indicated, a program in form of DSL code has to be written. Within the DSL program, some logic, e.g., conditions, has to be specified, which makes the solution for a specific problem true. The DSL program takes a number of inputs (depending on the use case) and verifies if all specified conditions are met. Consider the offloading task of calculating the sum of two integers. In this case, the equation $a + b = c$ must hold and has to be encoded in the DSL. In general, an arbitrary task can be verified, as long as it is possible to define a rule that the result has to follow. As described in Sect. 3, for this, the service provider does not have to disclose any information about the applied algorithm or method.

Then, keys and the verification smart contract have to be generated. For the keys, this means that a trusted setup is necessary. In the work at hand, we assume that the trusted setup is performed by the developers of the smart contracts presented in Sect. 4.2. Afterwards, the on-chain verification for the specific computation problem is ready for deployment. Alternatively, a multiparty computation protocol could be applied, e.g., [2], that prevents fake proofs as long as one participant is honest.

When the result verification scheme is integrated into the broker smart contract, the inputs of the function *submitSolution()*, as well as the storage format for solutions of the new problem, should be kept in mind. Under certain circumstances, it can be useful to draw up a detached broker smart contract for each use case. In this case, the basic functions of the broker smart contract,

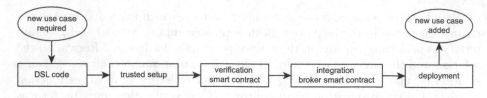

Fig. 5. Process for adding result verification for additional use cases

e.g., *getTaskRequest()* can be copied, but use case-specific data, e.g., necessary fields for the problem instance and solutions, must be considered and adapted as well. Furthermore, the function *submitSolution()* that also calls *verifyTx()* of the verification smart contract has to be tailored. A separation per use case would lead to more compact code artifacts and better maintenance. However, to simplify the description of our solution approach, we only discuss the usage of one broker smart contract in this paper.

When a new use case is added, the main effort consists of rewriting the DSL program and integrating the verification smart contract into the broker smart contract. The aforementioned trusted setup and creation of the verification smart contract is mainly handled by the ZoKrates toolbox. The deployment of new smart contracts is tool-supported as well. This means that merely predefined commands have to be executed.

4.6 Example Implementation

To demonstrate how our blockchain-based offloading approach with result verification can be adopted to specific use cases, we describe the process of implementing an exemplary use case based on the TSP.

The TSP is selected since it is very well-known among computer scientists, and easy to understand, but actually hard to compute. In brief, the TSP describes the problem to find the shortest path to travel a predefined number of cities and to return back to the origin city, but visiting any other city only once. As input, a list of cities and the distances between each pair of cities are given [1]. Once a solution to the TSP has been found, its validity can be verified in little time, e.g., by traversing the path of a solution. Interestingly, it is also easy to assess the quality of the solution, i.e., by comparing the computed path length.

The TSP is an NP-hard problem, which also opens interesting future research direction (see Sect. 6). Notably, the TSP is merely used as an exemplary use case in the work at hand. The presented approach explicitly allows to verify other tasks as well. The according implementation including the broker smart contract can be found at Github[1].

There are some restrictions which have to be taken into account because of the applied ZoKrates toolbox. First, the toolbox only supports numbers, i.e.,

---

[1] https://github.com/ben2048/blockchainBasedComputationOffloading.

Alg. 1. Main function of the DSL program

```
1   def main(
2   private field[10] path, private field mapnumber, field sum,
3   private field[10] cities, field[2] hashOfCities, field[2] hashOfPath
4   ) -> (field):
5
6   1 == basicInputCheck(path, cities, mapnumber)
7   1 == checkCities(path, cities, mapnumber)
8   sum == calculateSum(path, mapnumber)
9
10  field[2] hashedPath = hash(concat(path))
11  hashOfPath[0] == hashedPath[0]
12  hashOfPath[1] == hashedPath[1]
13
14  field[2] hashedCities = hash(concat(cities))
15  hashOfCities[0] == hashedCities[0]
16  hashOfCities[1] == hashedCities[1]
17
18  return 1
```

cities in the TSP have to be represented by numbers, not by their names. Second, ZoKrates does not support any dynamic fields. Accordingly, the size of an array needs to be defined at compile time. Both constraints complicate the implementation a little bit, but do not lead to any significant restrictions. We discuss the impact of the fixed array sizes also in the evaluation in Sect. 5.

As described in Sect. 4.5, the result verification is based on a DSL, which proves program inputs against defined checks. With regard to the TSP, the result verification has to verify whether a solution has been computed properly. In other words, service providers need to prove that they have found a valid solution for an TSP instance. To accomplish that, the produced path has to be Hamiltonian (i.e., each city appears exactly once in the path) and the path length must correspond to the sum of the connections between the cities on the basis of the path and the given distances [1]. As input, the map of cities for the TSP has to be defined, including the cities (represented by numbers) and the distances between the cities, i.e., a complete graph made up from vertices (cities) and edges (distances) between the vertices. This data structure can be stored as an array within the DSL program.

In the following paragraphs, we discuss the example given in Algorithm 1. To verify that a service provider has computed a correct result, the following information needs to be provided (lines 2–3): (i) The computed **path**, consisting of a sequence of numbers representing cities, (ii) an ID **mapnumber** for the map which has been used for solving the TSP instance (this allows to use different maps with the TSP), (iii) the computed length of the path **sum**, (iv) the **cities** for which the minimal distance has been computed, and (v) the hashed path **hashOfPath** and the hashed cities **hashOfCities**. As it can be seen, the example allows a maximum of ten cities on a path, but other lengths are also possible.

The path and the map are needed to calculate the distance and to compare it with the stated length (i.e., the result) from the service provider. Path and cities are used to determine if all cities are covered exactly once in a path. The hashed

Alg. 2. verifyTx()

```
1   function verifyTx(
2   uint[2] memory a, uint[2][2] memory b,
3   uint[2] memory c, uint[6] memory input
4   ) public returns (bool r) {
5       Proof memory proof;
6       proof.a = Pairing.G1Point(a[0], a[1]);
7       proof.b = Pairing.G2Point([b[0][0], b[0][1]], [b[1][0], b[1][1]]);
8       proof.c = Pairing.G1Point(c[0], c[1]);
9       uint[] memory inputValues = new uint[](input.length);
10      for(uint i = 0; i < input.length; i++){
11          inputValues[i] = input[i];
12      }
13      if (verify(inputValues, proof) == 0) {
14          return true;
15      } else {
16          return false;
17      }
18  }
```

path is necessary to prevent malicious behavior originating from the service provider when submitting a solution. Without the hash, it would be possible to decouple the proof from the path. In other words, if the service provider submits a valid proof but an invalid path, it possibly cannot be detected on-chain, i.e., the result verification would succeed even though an incorrect path would be stored on the blockchain. To recognize and prevent such scenarios, we compare the hash and the path within the DSL program and in the broker smart contract.

As it can be seen, the main function first performs an input check (line 6). This is done in order to sort out solutions with invalid indices or map numbers. Next, it is checked if the stated path contains each city exactly once (line 7), i.e., if the path is Hamiltonian. Afterwards, it is checked if the stated path length (field **sum** in line 8) is equal to the sum resulting from the distances of the stated path based on the distances between cities, i.e., the map. Then, it is necessary to embed the hash of the path in the verification procedure (lines 10–12). Therefore, the hash of the path is needed as input. Consequently, we have to compute the hash of the stated path and compare it with the input, to prevent the aforementioned malicious action. For this, we utilize the implementation of SHA256 provided by ZoKrates.

As discussed before, the DSL program shown in Algorithm 1 runs off-chain, while the verification function *verifyTx()* is carried out on-chain. Notably, the number of inputs of *verifyTx()* is a cost factor. With regard to our use case and the specification of the input parameters in the DSL program, the number of cities scales with the instance size. This becomes a crucial cost factor, since the gas cost rise linearly with the number of public inputs provided. Hence, we make use of the hashed cities instead of the number of cities. This allows to make the cities a private input, but also makes it necessary to check the hash of the cities (lines 14–16), analogue to lines 10–12.

Based on the DSL program, ZoKrates is able to define *verifyTx()* as depicted in Algorithm 2. The input array consists of the path length, hash values for the path and the cities plus the expected return value of the DSL program (lines 2–3). Afterwards, a new proof is instantiated (line 5). Then, *verifyTx()* requires three elliptic curve points in form of the arrays a, b, c (lines 6–8). These elliptic curve points actually make the zk-SNARKs proof and are delivered via the DSL program by the ZoKrates toolbox. Hence, the developer who integrates *verifyTx()* does not have to take care of the actual proofs, which is a major reason for using the ZoKrates toolbox.

The array input depicts the public inputs and the expected return value of the DSL code, and is used to fill the inputValues (lines 9–12). Afterwards, the actual verification is carried out (line 13). In the case of a successful verification, the boolean true is returned (line 14), else, the boolean false is returned (line 16). Thus, a service consumer can be sure that a result is valid (or not), and the broker smart contract could carry out the payment. Notably, since only the proof is published on the blockchain, no conclusions regarding the computation and concrete results are possible. This ensures the privacy property regarding the proof. However, as written above, the solution is still available on the chain. To avoid this, a solution could be encrypted (see Sect. 4.3).

5   Evaluation

5.1   Evaluation Setup

In order to evaluate the presented approach, we measure the overhead (regarding time and cost) occurring because of result verification.

As mentioned in Sect. 4, the computation offloading consists of an on-chain and an off-chain part. To evaluate the on-chain activities, the smart contracts have been deployed in a local Ethereum blockchain (using Truffle), while for the off-chain activities, ZoKrates has been installed locally in a Docker container.

5.2   Overhead Analysis

The result verification is part of the solution submission process as presented in Sects. 4.3 and 4.4. Hence, in order to evaluate the overhead with regard to gas cost and time, we implemented a second *submitSolution()* function in the broker smart contract. However, this version of the function does *not* verify the submitted solution. This allows us to compare the gas and time consumption of a benchmark with the according values of our zk-SNARKs-based verification approach. As a second benchmark, we conduct an on-chain result verification, i.e., a solution for a TSP instance is verified by a separate smart contract deployed on the blockchain. We apply two maps with size 30 and 70, respectively, in order to see how the map size (i.e., number of cities) influences the results. To get a complete picture of the cost overhead, TSP instance sizes between 3 and 30 (*map 30*) respectively 3 and 60 (*map 70*) are used.

The results regarding the cost for map 70 are shown in Fig. 6. Not surprisingly, the gas consumption with verification is higher than without verification. If

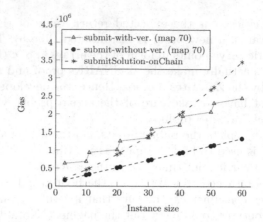

Fig. 6. Gas consumption

no verification is done, there is no difference between the two maps. Hence, there is only one plot for the offloading without verification. Actually, this benchmark also indicates how big the cost become if redundant computation is used (see Sect. 2). In that case, based on the level of redundancy, each submitted solution leads to the same cost. In addition, some overhead for the comparison (e.g., majority voting) of the results needs to be taken into account. This shows that redundant computing is not really an option with regard to the gas consumption for the solution submission.

While not shown in the figure in order not to overload the plot, the submission of solutions based on the smaller map (with 30 cities) is marginally cheaper than solutions based on the larger map (with 70 cities).

It can also be seen that verifying TSP solutions on-chain (*submitSolution-onChain*) is cheaper than the approach presented in this work for small instances, but more expensive for large ones. Up to an instance size of 29, the on-chain verification is cheaper than applying zk-SNARKs. For instances of size 30, the zk-SNARKs-based version should be preferred, whereby on-chain verification is at a lower price for an instance size of 31. Finally, the cost of on-chain verification exceeds the cost of the zk-SNARKs-based variant at instance size 40. Overall, we can clearly see which version is cheaper for instances of size up to 29 and from 40 ascending. Around the instance size 30, three intersections with regard to the on-chain and zk-SNARKs-based variant are visible. To determine the exact break-even point(s) between 29 and 40, we have performed further (not-depicted) measurements showing that the on-chain variant is more cost-efficient for instances of size 31–34. From instance size 35, the zk-SNARKs-based variant should be preferred.

These results show that it is necessary to discuss the line course in more detail: It becomes clear that the gas demand of all three variants shown in Fig. 6 increases with the instance size. It is also noticeable that the cost levels of *submit-without-ver. (map 70)* and *submitSolution-onChain* rise continuously,

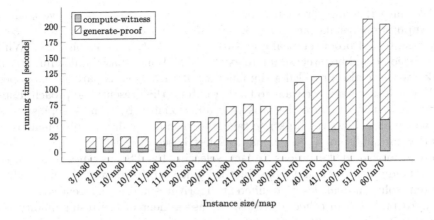

Fig. 7. Time overhead

while the levels of *submit-with-ver. (map 70)* increase step-wise. This is caused by the partitioned verification, due to the lack of dynamic fields and the subsequent fixed array sizes within the DSL of ZoKrates. For solutions of size 3 to 60, separate DSL programs with a varying number of inputs (starting with an instance size of 10, and increased by steps of 10) are provided. For example, if a DSL solution for 11 cities is computed, the resulting path has to be padded, according to the expected number of inputs of the DSL program. Due to the fact that such a padding is not necessary when no verification is performed or the verification is done on-chain, the gas consumption merely rises continuously for these options, but for the zk-SNARKs-based approach, "jumps" in the plot can be seen. A solution to circumvent this would be to have different smart contracts for different TSP instance sizes.

Second, we observe the time overhead. Figure 7 depicts the time needed to execute the *compute-witness* and *generate-proof* step for TSP instances of sizes 3 to 60. The values on the x-axis can be interpreted as follows: 3/m30 means that the instance is of size three and belongs to map 30. As can be seen, the overall run-time increases with the size of instances. The step *generate-proof* takes on average 3.2 (standard dev.: 0.28) times longer than the *compute-witness* step. Considering the increasing runtime of the proof generation and the computation of the witness, it becomes clear that the presented result verification approach should primarily be used in scenarios which are not very time-critical.

6   Conclusion

In order to provide solutions for fully decentralized task offloading, a number of blockchain-based solutions have already been proposed. However, to the best of our knowledge, none of these solutions is able to verify that an offloaded task is computed correctly. Instead, redundant computing or trust models are applied, which however cannot guarantee that a computation is valid.

We have therefore presented an approach which supports the verification of computation results, applying zk-SNARKs. Especially, this allows to compute results and proofs off-chain, and to only verify the proofs on-chain. While our solution could be integrated into existing blockchain-based offloading frameworks, we have also provided a simplified broker solution as part of this paper.

In our future work, we want to further extend the presented approach. Especially, we want to replace the brokering functionality by a more sophisticated one which also allows the broker to take into account quality requirements (e.g., a particular quality of a result), and to select based on this the best result from a number of provided solutions. In fact, selecting the TSP as our evaluation use case already lays the foundations for this, since service providers could deliver different solution qualities with different algorithms and at different cost to this NP-hard problem. In other scenarios, the assessment of the result quality is a more complex task and therefore an interesting direction of future work.

While currently our reference implementation applies a simple pricing scheme, i.e., the service provider is paid with the consumer's stake, more complex pricing might be useful. For instance, a dynamic pricing scheme based on the complexity of an offloaded computational task and the number of available service providers might be helpful. Last but not least, as has been shown in the evaluation, an on-chain verification is sometimes cheaper to conduct than the proposed off-chain result verification. Therefore, we will further investigate in which cases which of these two approaches should be preferred.

Acknowledgments. The financial support by the Austrian Federal Ministry for Digital and Economic Affairs, the National Foundation for Research, Technology and Development and the Christian Doppler Research Association is gratefully acknowledged.

References

1. Applegate, D.L., Bixby, R.E., Chátal, V., Cook, W.J.: The Traveling Salesman Problem - A Computational Study. Princeton University Press, Princeton (2007)
2. Ben-Sasson, E., Chiesa, A., Tromer, E., Virza, M.: Succinct non-interactive zero knowledge for a von Neumann architecture. In: 23rd USENIX Security Symposium, pp. 781–796. USENIX Association (2014)
3. Chatzopoulos, D., Ahmadi, M., Kosta, S., Hui, P.: FlopCoin: a cryptocurrency for computation offloading. IEEE Trans. Mobile Comput. **17**(5), 1062–1075 (2018)
4. Eberhardt, J., Heiss, J.: Off-chaining models and approaches to off-chain computations. In: 2nd Workshop on Scalable and Resilient Infrastructures for Distributed Ledgers, pp. 7–12. ACM (2018)
5. Eberhardt, J., Tai, S.: ZoKrates - scalable privacy-preserving off-chain computations. In: 1st IEEE International Conference on Blockchain, pp. 1084–1091. IEEE (2018)
6. Fedak, G., Bendella, W., Alves, E.: Blockchain-Based Decentralized Cloud Computing. https://iex.ec/wp-content/uploads/pdf/iExec-WPv3.0-English.pdf (2017)
7. Goldreich, O., Micali, S., Wigderson, A.: How to play any mental game or a completeness theorem for protocols with honest majority. In: 19th Annual ACM Symposium on Theory of Computing, pp. 218–229. ACM (1987)

8. Greenberg, A.: Hackers can mess with voltages to steal intel chips' secrets. https://www.wired.com/story/plundervolt-intel-chips-sgx-hack
9. Kosba, A., Papadopoulos, D., Papamanthou, C., Song, D.: MIRAGE: succinct arguments for randomized algorithms with applications to universal zk-SNARKs. In: 29th USENIX Security Symposium, pp. 2129–2146. USENIX Association (2020)
10. Kosta, S., Aucinas, A., Hui, P., Mortier, R., Zhang, X.: ThinkAir: dynamic resource allocation and parallel execution in the cloud for mobile code offloading. In: 31st IEEE International Conference on Computer Communications, pp. 945–953. IEEE (2012)
11. Krejci, S., Sigwart, M., Schulte, S.: Blockchain- and IPFS-based data distribution for the internet of things. In: Brogi, A., Zimmermann, W., Kritikos, K. (eds.) ESOCC 2020. LNCS, vol. 12054, pp. 177–191. Springer, Cham (2020). https://doi.org/10.1007/978-3-030-44769-4_14
12. Mach, P., Becvar, Z.: Mobile edge computing: a survey on architecture and computation offloading. IEEE Commun. Surv. Tutorials 19(3), 1628–1656 (2017)
13. Marston, S., Li, Z., Bandyopadhyay, S., Zhang, J., Ghalsasi, A.: Cloud computing - the business perspective. Decis. Support Syst. 51, 176–189 (2011)
14. Pan, J., Wang, J., Hester, A., AlQerm, I., Liu, Y., Zhao, Y.: EdgeChain: an edge-IoT framework and prototype based on blockchain and smart contracts. IEEE Internet of Things J. 6(3), 4719–4732 (2019)
15. Qiu, X., Liu, L., Chen, W., Hong, Z., Zheng, Z.: Online deep reinforcement learning for computation offloading in blockchain-empowered mobile edge computing. IEEE Trans. Veh. Technol. 68(8), 8050–8062 (2019)
16. ur Rehman Khan, A., Othman, M., Madani, S.A., Khan, S.U.: A survey of mobile cloud computing application models. IEEE Commun. Surv. Tutorials 16(1), 393–413 (2014)
17. Santos, N., Gummadi, K.P., Rodrigues, R.: Towards trusted cloud computing. In: 2009 Conference on Hot Topics in Computing. USENIX Association, Article No. 3 (2009)
18. Satyanarayanan, M.: A brief history of cloud offload: a personal journey from odyssey through cyber foraging to cloudlets. GetMobile Mob. Comput. Commun. 18(4), 19–23 (2014)
19. Schwarz, M., Weiser, S., Gruss, D., Maurice, C., Mangard, S.: Malware guard extension: using SGX to conceal cache attacks. In: Polychronakis, M., Meier, M. (eds.) DIMVA 2017. LNCS, vol. 10327, pp. 3–24. Springer, Cham (2017). https://doi.org/10.1007/978-3-319-60876-1_1
20. Skrzypczak, A.: Golem Architecture. https://blog.golemproject.net/golem-architecture/ (2017). Accessed 20 May 2021
21. Sonm Pte. Ltd.: SONM - Supercomputer Organized by Network Mining. https://whitepaper.io/document/326/sonm-whitepaper
22. Teutsch, J., Reitwießner, C.: A scalable verification solution for blockchains. CoRR abs/1908.04756 (2019). http://arxiv.org/abs/1908.04756
23. Uriarte, R.B., De Nicola, R.: Blockchain-based decentralized cloud/fog solutions: challenges, opportunities, and standards. IEEE Commun. Stand. Mag. 2(3), 22–28 (2018)
24. Wu, H., Sun, Y., Wolter, K.: Energy-efficient decision making for mobile cloud offloading. IEEE Trans. Cloud Comput. 8(2), 570–584 (2020)
25. Wu, H., Wolter, K., Jiao, P., Deng, Y., Zhao, Y., Xu, M.: EEDTO: an energy-efficient dynamic task offloading algorithm for blockchain-enabled IoT-edge-cloud orchestrated computing. IEEE Internet Things J. 8(4), 2163–2176 (2021)

Model Checking of Solidity Smart Contracts Adopted for Business Processes

Ikram Garfatta[1,2]([✉]), Kaïs Klai[2], Mohamed Graïet[3], and Walid Gaaloul[4]

[1] University of Tunis El Manar, National Engineering School of Tunis,
OASIS, Tunis, Tunisia
[2] University Sorbonne Paris North, LIPN UMR CNRS 7030, Villetaneuse, France
ikram.garfatta@lipn.univ-paris13.fr
[3] University of Monastir, Higher Institute for Computer Science and Mathematics,
Monastir, Tunisia
[4] Institut Mines-Télécom, Télécom SudParis, SAMOVAR UMR 5157, Évry, France

Abstract. Several features of the Blockchain technology are well aligned with critical issues in the Business Process Management (BPM) field, and yet adopting Blockchain for BPM should not be taken lightly. In fact, the security of smart contracts, which are one of the main elements of the Blockchain that make the integration with BPM possible, has proved to be vulnerable. It is therefore crucial for the protection of the designed business processes to prove the correctness of the smart contracts to be deployed on a blockchain. In this paper we propose a formal approach based on the transformation of Solidity smart contracts, with consideration of the BPM context in which they are used, into a Hierarchical Coloured Petri net. We express a set of smart contract vulnerabilities as temporal logic formulae and use the *Helena* model checker to, not only detect such vulnerabilities while discerning their exploitability, but also check other temporal-based contract-specific properties.

Keywords: Blockchain · Business process management · Model checking · Solidity · Smart contracts · Hierarchical coloured petri nets · Temporal properties

1 Introduction

Initially featured as the technology behind Bitcoin, Blockchain has soon after escaped the box of cryptocurrencies to find its way into a multitude of application domains, including that of Business Process Management (BPM). In fact, its inherent characteristics, namely its decentralized nature, ability to provide trust among trustless parties, immutability and financial transparency seem to deliver the right tools to contrive adequate solutions for existing problems in BPM, especially for collaborations [20]. One of the promising integration possibilities of these two fields is the design of Blockchain-based business processes (BPs). The general preference has been to use an existing modeling language for BPs and adopt Blockchain for different aspects of their management. For instance, Lorikeet [28] is

© Springer Nature Switzerland AG 2021
H. Hacid et al. (Eds.): ICSOC 2021, LNCS 13121, pp. 116–132, 2021.
https://doi.org/10.1007/978-3-030-91431-8_8

a tool that leverages Blockchain as a message exchange mechanism for BP choreographies. Caterpillar [16], on the other hand, is used to implement the BP model and deploy it on the chain. This has been possible thanks to the concept of *smart contracts* which allow the execution of sequences of interdependent transactions while complying to the rules implemented within. In general, a BP can be analogously viewed as a sequence of tasks linked by causal relationships with the aim of achieving a business goal. Therefore, smart contracts seem to be ideal candidates for the implementation and automation of BPs.

Despite the advance in the adoption of Blockchain for the BPM context, its state is still nascent, and using smart contracts to carry on BPs cannot be considered safe. Many attacks with significant consequences on several blockchains, exploiting hidden vulnerabilities in smart contracts and exposing the defectiveness of the targeted applications bear witness to such a risk. In 2010, 92 billion BTC were generated out of thin air by exploiting an integer vulnerability on the Bitcoin blockchain [1]. The DAO attack on Ethereum exploited a reentrancy vulnerability and resulted in 3.6M of stolen Ether [25]. A vulnerable blockchain-based application does not have to be the target of an attack to malfunction. For instance, the Parity multisig wallet was subject to an accident caused by a self-destruction vulnerability in 2017 and resulting in freezing 500K of Ether [26].

Informal as well as formal methods have been proposed to ensure the correctness of smart contracts. While informal techniques can test a smart contract under certain scenarios, they cannot be relied on to verify specific properties defining its correctness. We note that we are interested in Ethereum smart contracts as it is currently the second largest cryptocurrency platform after Bitcoin besides being the inaugurator of smart contracts, and more particularly those written in Solidity [2] as it is the most popular language used by Ethereum.

In this paper, we propose a model-checking-based approach for the verification of Solidity smart contracts with a particular focus on those used in the BPM context. Thanks to their ability to combine the analysis power of Petri nets with the expressive power of programming languages, Coloured Petri Nets (CPNs) [11] are suitable candidates for the modeling and verification of large and complex systems, and therefore they are employed in our approach to model the smart contracts execution with respect to a behavior specification defining the workflow within which they are used. The result of this modelling step is a hierarchical CPN (HCPN), on which we define a set of temporal properties to express vulnerabilities as well as contract-specific properties relevant to both data- and control-flows of the modelled smart contracts. We implement a prototype that automates the generation of the HCPN model in the specification language of *Helena* [9], the model checker we use for the verification of the defined properties.

The remainder of this paper will be organized as follows: Sect. 2 provides an overview of related studies on formal verification of Solidity smart contracts. Prerequisites on CPN and a brief overview on the representation of BP models are given in Sect. 3, followed by a use case in Sect. 4. An overview of our proposed approach is given in Sects. 5 followed by its detailed steps in Sect. 6. The formal specification of some vulnerabilities and the application on the use case are presented in Sect. 7. Finally, Sect. 8 concludes the paper.

2 Related Work

Existing studies on formal verification of smart contracts follow mainly two streams [10]: The first is based on theorem proving [3,5]. Approaches based on this technique cannot be fully automated as the user usually has to intervene to assist the prover. The second includes studies based on model checking, which is where our work can be situated. Most of the studies under this second category use symbolic model checking coupled with complementary techniques such as symbolic execution [13] and abstraction [4]. The first attempt was Oyente [17], a tool that targets four vulnerabilities and operates at the EVM bytecode level of the contract. It generates symbolic execution traces and analyzes them to detect the satisfaction of certain conditions on the paths which indicates the presence of corresponding vulnerabilities. Numerous studies followed in the footsteps of this work, some of which exploited some of its components in their implementations like GASPER [6] which reuses Oyente's generated control flow graph, while others extended it with the aim of supporting the detection of other vulnerabilities, like Osiris [27]. Also based on symbolic model checking, Zeus [12] operates on the source code of the contract. VeriSolid [18] is an FSM-based approach that aims at producing a correct-by-design contract rather than detecting bugs. The authors propose a transformation of a contract modeled as an FSM into a Solidity code and provide the ability to specify intended behavior in the form of liveness, deadlock freedom and safety properties expressed using templates for CTL properties and checked by a backend symbolic model checker. The proposed approaches usually use under-approximation which means that critical violations can be overlooked. This explains the presence of false negatives and/or positives in their reported results. We note that most of the existing studies target specific vulnerabilities in contracts, and few are those that allow expressing customizable control flow-related properties while none target data-related properties.

More recently, other attempts using CPN have been proposed. The work in [15] shows an example of verification of behavioural properties applied manually on a CPN model for a crowdfunding smart contract. It does not, however, propose a complete approach with generic transformation rules that can be automated and applied to any contract. Another CPN-based proposition was presented in [8]. This approach, despite being based on CPN, cannot be used for the verification of data-flow related properties as the generated model focuses on the representation of the workflow extracted from the contract's CFG.

Our proposed approach aims at overcoming the stated shortcomings by providing the means to elaborate behavioural and contract-specific properties (in the form of temporal properties) that can depend on the data-flow in the contract and hence is not bound to a restricted set of reported vulnerabilities. Besides, our approach relies on explicit model checking and that our transformation algorithm operates on the source code as opposed to the bytecode. Hence, we avoid the consequences of under-approximation and contextual information loss.

3   Preliminaries

3.1   On Coloured Petri Nets

A Petri net [22] is a formal model with mathematics-based execution semantics. It is a directed bipartite graph with two types of nodes: places (drawn as circles) and transitions (drawn as rectangles). Despite its efficiency in modelling and analysing systems, a basic Petri net falls short when the system is too complex, especially when representation of data is required. To overcome such limitations, extensions to basic Petri nets were proposed, equipping the tokens with colours or types and hence allowing them to hold values. A large Petri net model can therefore be represented in a much more compact and manageable manner using a *Coloured Petri net* [11]. The formal definition of a CPN is given in Definition 1 and the main concepts needed to define its dynamics are given in Definition 2.

Definition 1 (Coloured Petri net). *A Coloured Petri Net is a nine-tuple* $CPN = (P, T, A, \Sigma, V, C, G, E, I)$, *where:*

1. *P is a finite set of* places.
2. *T is a finite set of* transitions *such that $P \cap T = \emptyset$.*
3. *$A \subseteq (P \times T) \cup (T \times P)$ is a set of directed arcs.*
4. *Σ is a finite set of non-empty colour sets.*
5. *V is a finite set of typed variables such that $Type[v] \in \Sigma, \forall v \in V$.*
6. *$C : P \to \Sigma$ is a colour set function that assigns a colour set to each place.*
7. *$G : T \to EXPR_V$, where $EXPR_V$ is the set of expressions with variables in V, is a guard function that assigns a guard to each transition t.*
8. *$E : A \to EXPR_V$ is an arc expression function that assigns an arc expression to each arc a such that $Type[E(a)] = C(p)_{MS}$.*
9. *$I : P \to EXPR_\emptyset$ is an initialisation function that assigns an initialisation expression to each place p such that $Type[I(p)] = C(p)_{MS}$.*

Definition 2 (CPN concepts). *For CPN $(P, T, A, \Sigma, V, C, G, E, I)$, we note:*

1. *A marking is a function M that maps each place into a multiset of tokens.*
2. *The initial marking M_0 is defined by $M_0(p) = I(p)\langle\rangle$ for all $p \in P$.*
3. *The variables of a transition t are denoted by $Var(t) \subseteq V$.*
4. *A binding of a transition t is a function b that maps each variable $v \in Var(t)$ into a value $b(v) \in Type[v]$. It is written as $\langle var_1 = val_1, ..., var_n = val_n \rangle$. The set of all bindings for a transition t is denoted $B(t)$.*
5. *A binding element is a pair (t, b) such that $t \in T$ and $b \in B(t)$. The set of all binding elements $BE(t)$ for a transition t is defined by $BE(t) = \{(t, b) | b \in B(t)\}$. The set of all binding elements in a CPN model is denoted BE.*

A transition is said to be *enabled* if a binding of the variables appearing in the surrounding arc inscriptions exists such that the inscription on each input arc evaluates to a multiset of token colours present on the corresponding input place. *Firing* a transition consists in removing (resp. adding), from each input (resp. to each output) place, the multiset of tokens corresponding to the input (resp. output) arc inscription. For more details on CPN we refer readers to [11].

3.2   On Business Process Modeling Representations

When it comes to business process modeling languages, controversy arises as to whether imperative or declarative modeling approaches are better. An empirical investigation [24] states that while imperative languages (e.g., Business Process Model and Notation BPMN [23]) can be considered superior in terms of comprehensibility by end-users, this fact's accuracy can be influenced by the experimental subjects' familiarity with imperative modeling languages. On the other hand, declarative modeling approaches (e.g. Dynamic Condition Response DCR Graphs [21]) are considered less rigid than their counterpart and therefore more suitable for rapidly evolving business processes. In fact, imperative models represent *how* a process is executed by explicitly defining its control flow while declarative models focus on *why* a process is executed in such a way by implicitly defining its control flow as a set of rules. Consequently, making changes to an imperative model is more time-consuming and complex than altering a declarative one, since the former would entail explicitly adding/deleting execution alternatives, which can call into question the correctness of the model, while the latter could be achieved by adding/deleting constraints from the model to discard/add execution alternatives. In our work, we do not support any claims for the supposed superiority of any paradigm over the other.

Definition 3. *A DCR graph is a tuple* $G = (E, M, Act, \rightarrow\bullet, \bullet\rightarrow, \rightarrow+, \rightarrow\%,$ $\rightarrow\diamond, l)$ *where* $\mathcal{M}(G) =_{def} \mathcal{P}(E) \times \mathcal{P}(E) \times \mathcal{P}(E)$ *is the set of all markings:*

1. E *is the set of events, ranged over by* e.
2. $M \in \mathcal{M}(G)$ *is the marking of the graph.*
3. Act *is the set of actions.*
4. $\rightarrow\bullet, \bullet\rightarrow \subseteq E \times E$ *are the condition and response relations, respectively.*
5. $\rightarrow+, \rightarrow\% \subseteq E \times E$ *are the dynamic include and exclude relations, respectively, satisfying that* $\forall e \in E \,.\, e \rightarrow+ \cap\, e \rightarrow\% = \emptyset$.
6. $\rightarrow\diamond \subset E \times E$ *is the milestone relation.*
7. $l : E \rightarrow Act$ *is a labelling function mapping every event to an action.*

A marking $M = (Ex, Re, In) \in \mathcal{M}(G)$ *is a triplet of event sets where* Ex *represents the set of events that have previously been executed,* Re *the set of events that are pending responses required to be executed or excluded, and* In *the set of events that are currently included. The idea conveyed by the dynamic inclusion/exclusion relations is that only the currently included events are considered in evaluating the constraints. In other words, if* e *is a condition for* e' *(*$e \rightarrow\bullet e'$*), but is excluded from the graph then it no longer restricts the execution of* e'*. Moreover, if* e' *is the response for* e *(*$e\bullet\rightarrow e'$*) but is excluded from the graph, then it is no longer required to happen for the flow to be acceptable. The inclusion relation* $e \rightarrow+ e'$ *(resp. exclusion relation* $e \rightarrow\% e'$*) means that, whenever* e *is executed,* e' *becomes included in (resp. excluded from) the graph. The milestone relation is similar to the condition relation in that it is a blocking one. The difference is that it is based on the events in the pending response set. In other words, if* e' *is a milestone of* e *(*$e' \rightarrow\diamond e$*), then* e *cannot be executed as long as* e' *is in* Re*. For more details on DCR Graphs we refer the readers to [21].*

4   Use Case: Blind Auction

Our use case is adapted from [2]. Participants in a blind auction have a bidding window during which they can place their bids. A participant can place more than one bid and the placed bid is blinded. The bidder has to make a deposit along the bid with a value that is supposedly greater than the real bid. Once the bidding window is closed, the revealing window is opened. Participants proceed to reveal their bids by sending the actual values of the bids along with the used keys. The system verifies whether the sent values correspond with the placed blinded bids and potentially updates the highest bid and bidder's values. If the revealed value of a bid does not correspond with its blinded value, or is greater than the deposit, the said bid is considered invalid. Once the revealing window is closed, participants can proceed to withdraw their deposits. A deposit made along a non-winning, invalid or unrevealed bid is wholly restored. In case of a winning bid, the difference between the deposit and the real bid is restored. The auction is terminated when all participants withdraw their deposits. We propose a design for such a blind auction system using a BPMN choreography diagram as well as a DCR graph (Fig. 1). Listing 1.1 is an excerpt of the corresponding Solidity contract. The full Solidity example can be found in our repository[1].

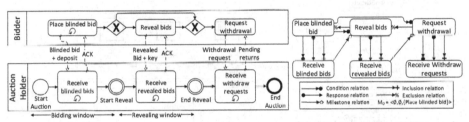

(a) Blind Auction: BPMN choreography   (b) Blind Auction: DCR graph

Fig. 1. Blind auction workflow representations

```
contract BlindAuction {
    struct Bid {bytes32 blindedBid; uint deposit;}
    uint public biddingEnd, revealEnd, highestBid;
    mapping(address => Bid[]) public bids;
    address public highestBidder;
    mapping(address => uint) pendingReturns;
    modifier onlyBefore(uint _time) {require(now<_time);_;}
    modifier onlyAfter(uint _time) {require(now>_time);_;}
    constructor(uint _biddingTime, uint _revealTime) public {...}
    function bid(bytes32 _blindedBid) public payable onlyBefore(
        biddingEnd) {...}
    function reveal(uint[] values, bytes32[] secrets) public
        onlyAfter(biddingEnd) onlyBefore(revealEnd) {...}
    function withdraw() public onlyAfter (revealEnd) {
        uint8 amount = pendingReturns[msg.sender];
        if (amount > 0) {
```

---

[1] https://depot.lipn.univ-paris13.fr/garfatta/sol2cpn.

```
if (msg.sender != highestBidder)
    msg.sender.call.value(amount)("");
else
    msg.sender.call.value(amount-highestBid) ("");
pendingReturns [msg.sender] = 0;}}}
```

Listing 1.1. Excerpt of the Blind Auction smart contract in Solidity

5   Overview of our Formal Verification Approach

Our proposed approach for the verification of smart contracts is based on model checking of CPN models and comprises mainly two phases:

1. A pre-verification phase: consists in transforming the smart contracts' Solidity code into CPN submodels corresponding to their functions.
2. A verification phase: consists in constructing a CPN model w.r.t an LTL property that can express: *(i)* a vulnerability in the code or *(ii)* a contract-specific property, linking it to a CPN model representing the behavior to be considered, and feeding it the model checker to verify the targeted property.

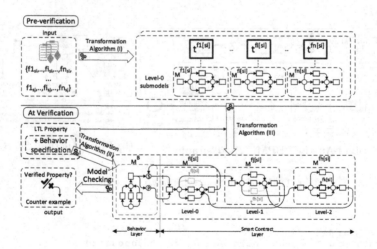

Fig. 2. Overview of the approach

More precisely, we opt for a hierarchical CPN to represent the considered smart contracts' execution and interaction w.r.t the provided behavior specification.

As shown in Fig. 2, we represent each function of a smart contract by an *aggregated transition* that encapsulates a submodel corresponding to the internal workflow of the former. In fact, our aim at this pre-verification phase is to get building blocks for the hierarchical model that will be fed to the model checker. Then, given a behavior specification and an LTL property to be verified, the final CPN model is built by *(1)* linking the aggregated transition representing the targeted function to the behavioral model and *(2)* building a hierarchy by explicitly representing function calls in the submodel in question (if the checked property requires it). In fact, function calls are initially abstracted and therefore represented by aggregated transitions in the model (e.g., $t^{fj[si]}$ in Fig. 2) under the assumption that they do not present behavioral problems (deadlock-free and strong-livelock-free) which can be separately verified for each function. Depending on the property to be verified, an aggregated transition may need to be *unfolded* if any of its corresponding function's instructions or variables are involved in the property, hence the multi-level hierarchy in the model (e.g., in Fig. 2, $t^{fj[si]}$ in $M^{fi[si]}$ is hidden and replaced by its submodel $M^{fj[si]}$). It is kept *folded* otherwise (e.g., $t^{fk[si]}$ in $M^{fh[si]}$). This abstraction leads to a reduction in the size of the state space the model checker needs to explore.

6   Generation of the Hierarchical CPN Model

In order to implement our approach, we propose a transformation algorithm for the generation of the final HCPN model from the provided input artifacts.

6.1   Our HCPN Model: Defining Its Elements

Transitions T. We distinguish two types of transitions in our model:

1. aggregated (T^A): used at the level-0 model for the representation of functions, as well as at higher levels for the modular representation of function calls and can be substituted by a submodel.
2. regular (T^R): simple unsubstitutable CPN transition.

For a transition $t \in T$ we note:

- $t.st$, the Solidity code associated to transition t
- $t.metaColour$, the metaColour associated to the control flow places of t (if $t \in T^A$)
- $t.data$, the set of data places associated to transition t (if $t \in T^A$)
- $t.submodel$, the CPN submodel associated to transition t (if $t \in T^A$), with $t.submodel.inTransitions$ (resp. $t.submodel.outTransitions$) designating its input (resp. output) transitions
- $t.guard$, the guard of the transition t
- $\bullet t[cf], t \bullet [cf] \in P_{CF} \cup P_S$, the input and output control flow places of t
- $\bullet t[input] \in P_P$, the input parameters place of t
- $\bullet t[data], t \bullet [data] \subseteq P_{data}$, the input and output data places of t
- $t \bullet [output] \in P_R$, the output return place of t

Places P. For level-1 submodels, we define 4 types of places:

- *Control flow places* P_{CF} are places created to implement the order of execution of the workflow. We also use them to carry data related to the state of the smart contract which can be defined by its balance and the values of its state variables. Such places have a *metaColour* defined at each aggregated transition t^a of level-0 as the concatenation of the *state* (i.e., the colour of $\bullet t[cf] \in P_S$) and the *input parameters* (i.e., the colour of $\bullet t[input] \in P_P$): *[uint: contractBalance, $typc_{v_1}$: stateVariable₁, ..., $type_{v_n}$: stateVariable$_n$, $type_{p_1}$: inputParameter₁, ... , $type_{p_n}$: inputParameter$_n$].*
- *Data places* P_{data} (for internal local variables) where each place is of a colour corresponding to the represented variable's type.
- *Parameter places* P_P that convey potential inputs of function calls. Each function call has an associated parameter place whose colour is as follows *[$type_{p_1}$: inputParameter₁, ..., $type_{p_n}$: inputParameter$_n$].*
- *Return places* P_R that communicate potential functions' returned data and whose colours correspond to the return type of the called functions.

Two input places are created at the behavioral layer:

- a *state place* $p_s \in P_S$ representing the state of the contract. Its colour is as follows: *[uint: contractBalance, $type_{v_1}$: stateVariable₁, ..., $type_{v_n}$: stateVariable$_n$]*
- a *parameters place* $p_p \in P_P$ representing the input parameters of the function in question.

Expressions E. Expression are constructs made up of literals, variables, function calls and operators, according to the syntax of Solidity, that evaluate to single values:

- expressions with variables E_V: they make use of at least one local variable. In such an expression e_v, the set of variables used is accessible via $e_v.vars$.
- expressions with function calls E_F: they make use of at least one function call. In such an expression e_v, the set of function calls used is accessible via $e_v.fctCalls$
- explicit expressions E_E: they do not make use of variables nor function calls.

Statements S. A statement $st \in \mathbb{S}$ can be either a compound statement $\{st[1]; st[2]; ...; st[N]\}$ (where $\forall i \in [1..N]$, $st[i] \in S$), or a simple statement (st_{LHS}, st_{RHS}) (where $st_{LHS} \in E$ and $st_{RHS} \in E$), or a control statement. A simple statement can be:

- a function call statement, where:
  - $st_{LHS} = \emptyset$
  - $st_{RHS}.vars$ is the set of variables used in the arguments of the call (if $st_{RHS} \in E_V$)
- an assignment statement, where:
  - $st_{LHS} \in E_V$ and $st_{LHS}.vars$ contains the assigned variable
  - $st_{RHS}.vars$ is the set of variables used in the assignment (if $st_{RHS} \in E_V$)
  - $st_{RHS}.fctCalls$ is the set of function calls used in the assignment (if $st_{RHS} \in E_F$)

- a variable declaration statement, where:
  - $st_{LHS} \in E_V$ and $st_{LHS}.vars$ contains the declared variable
  - $st_{LHS}.type$ designates the type of the declared variable
  - $st_{RHS}.vars$ designates the set of variables used in the variable initialization expression (if the variable is initialized and $st_{RHS} \in E_V$)
  - $st_{RHS}.fctCalls$ is the set of function calls used in the variable initialization (if the variable is initialized $st_{RHS} \in E_F$)
- a sending statement, where:
  - st_{LHS} designates the destination account
  - $st_{RHS}.vars$ designates the set of variables in the expression of the value to be sent (if $st_{RHS} \in E_V$)
  - $st_{RHS}.fctCalls$ is the set of function calls in the value to be sent (if $st_{RHS} \in E_F$)
- a returning statement, where:
  - $st_{LHS} = \emptyset$
  - $st_{RHS}.vars$ is the set of variables in the returned value (if $st_{RHS} \in E_V$)
  - $st_{RHS}.fctCalls$ is the set of function calls in the returned value (if $st_{RHS} \in E_F$)

A control statement can be:

- a requirement statement of the form $require(c)$
- a selection statement of the form $if(c)$ then st_T [else st_F]
- a looping statement which can be:
  - a for loop; $for(init; c; inc)$ st_T
  - a while loop: $while(c)$ st_T
- where:
  - c is a boolean expression
  - $c.vars$ designates the set of variables used in the condition (if $c \in E_V$)
  - $c.fctCalls$ is the set of function calls used in the condition (if $c \in E_F$)
  - st_T, st_F, $init$ and inc are statements

6.2   Solidity-to-CPN: Building Blocks for the Smart Contract Layer

The first step is to build the level-0 submodels for the aggregated transitions of the contract's functions. To do so, we propose the algorithm GENERATELEVEL0.

We define a CPN pattern for each Solidity statement type. Considering that a function is a set of statements, CPN snippets are generated according to the defined patterns and linked according to the function's internal workflow. CREATESUBMODEL implements such correspondences. For lack of space, we only include the transformation algorithm for a function call statement and the graphical pattern (Fig. 3) and description of a compound statement. The rest of the algorithms and descriptions are available online (See footnote 1).

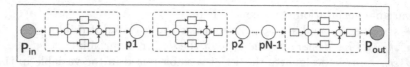

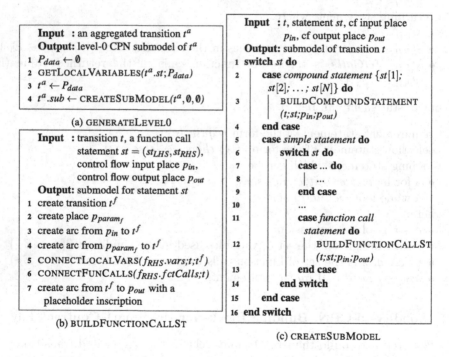

Fig. 3. Compound statement pattern

Compound statement $\{st[1]; st[2]; \ldots; st[N]\}$. The algorithm is re-executed on each component statement $st[i]$, after creating $N-1$ control flow places (of the *metaColour* colour) to interconnect the resulting CPN snippets while merging the entering point of the snippet of $st[1]$ with the entering point of the snippet of st and the exiting point of $st[N]$ to that of the snippet of st.

Input : an aggregated transition t^a
Output: level-0 CPN submodel of t^a
1   $P_{data} \leftarrow \emptyset$
2   GETLOCALVARIABLES($t^a.st; P_{data}$)
3   $t^a \leftarrow P_{data}$
4   $t^a.sub \leftarrow$ CREATESUBMODEL($t^a, \emptyset, \emptyset$)

(a) GENERATELEVEL0

Input : transition t, a function call
       statement $st = (st_{LHS}, st_{RHS})$,
       control flow input place p_{in},
       control flow output place p_{out}
Output: submodel for statement st
1   create transition t^f
2   create place p_{param_f}
3   create arc from p_{in} to t^f
4   create arc from p_{param_f} to t^f
5   CONNECTLOCALVARS($f_{RHS}.vars; t; t^f$)
6   CONNECTFUNCALLS($f_{RHS}.fctCalls; t$)
7   create arc from t^f to p_{out} with a
       placeholder inscription

(b) BUILDFUNCTIONCALLST

Input : t, statement st, cf input place
       p_{in}, cf output place p_{out}
Output: submodel of transition t
1   **switch** st **do**
2   **case** *compound statement* $\{st[1];$
       $st[2]; \ldots; st[N]\}$ **do**
3   BUILDCOMPOUNDSTATEMENT
       $(t; st; p_{in}; p_{out})$
4   **end case**
5   **case** *simple statement* **do**
6   **switch** st **do**
7   **case** ... **do**
8   ...
9   **end case**
10   ...
11   **case** *function call*
        statement **do**
12   BUILDFUNCTIONCALLST
         $(t; st; p_{in}; p_{out})$
13   **end case**
14   **end switch**
15   **end case**
16 **end switch**

(c) CREATESUBMODEL

The hierarchy of the CPN model depends on the LTL property to be verified. Such a hierarchy is achieved by *unfolding* targeted aggregated transitions as well as potential aggregated transitions within their submodels[2].

---

[2] We note that if a place does not exist ($p = \emptyset$) any arc creation involving it does not take effect.

Input : aggregated transition t^a, p_{in}, p_{out}	7 **end for**
Output: submodel replacement of t^a	8 **for** $t' \in t^a.sub.outTransition$ **do**
1 **for** $t' \in t^a.sub.inTransition$ **do**	9 $\quad$ replicate (arc from t^a to p_{out}) to
2 $\quad$ replicate (arc from p_{in} to t^a) to t'	$\quad$ t' with the placeholder inscrip-
3 $\quad$ replicate (arc from $\bullet t[input]$ to t^a) to t'	$\quad$ tion replaced by values from
4 $\quad$ **for** $p \in \bullet t^a[data] \cup \bullet t^a[output]$ **do**	$\quad$ $\bullet t'[cf]$
5 $\quad$ $\quad$ | replicate (arc from p to t^a) to t'	10 **end for**
6 $\quad$ **end for**	11 hide transition t^a and all arcs linked to it

(d) UNFOLDTRANSITION

6.3   Behavior-to-CPN: Generation of the Behavioral Layer

We consider two types of behavior specifications for smart contracts:
(1) completely-free if no information is provided on the execution context of a
contract and *(2) constrained* if the context in which a smart contract is used is
provided (e.g., as a DCR Graph or a BPMN model). A CPN behavioral model
is added as an additional layer and linked to the hierarchical model built using
the previously generated CPN submodels.

Modeling a Completely-Free Behavior. In case no behavior is provided with
the smart contracts to be verified, we define a behavioral model to represent their
execution in a completely-free way. In such a model (see Fig. 4a) a place S is used
to represent the global state of the blockchain environment shared by all of the
smart contracts' functions. For each function f_i a place P_i is used to represent
its input parameters. The marking of a place P_i corresponds to all the possible
calling arguments for f_i.

Modeling a Constrained Behavior. The user may want to define the behavior of smart contracts. This can be captured either imperatively or declaratively.
Existing BPMN-to-CPN transformations [19] could be leveraged for an imperative representation. For an example of a declarative one, we propose in the
following a formal translation of DCR to CPN.

Definition 4 (CPN4DCR). *Given a DCR graph $G = (E, M, Act, \rightarrow\bullet, \bullet\rightarrow, \pm, l)$, a corresponding CPN model $CPN = (P, T, A, \Sigma, V, C, G, E, I)$ is defined s.t.:*

- $P = \{S\}$
- $T = \{t_i, \forall i \in [1, n]\}$, *with* $n = |E|$ *the number of events in* G
- $A = \{(t_i, S), \forall i \in T\} \cup \{(S, t_i), \forall i \in T\}$
- $\Sigma = \{C_E, (C_E \times C_E \times C_E)\}$, *where* C_E *is a colour defined as an integer type* $(C_E = range\ INT)$ *where each event* $e_i \in E$ *is represented in* C_E *by its index.*
- $V = \{Ex, Re, In, Ex', Re', In'\}$, *with* $Type[v] = C_E, \forall v \in V$
- $C = \{S \rightarrow (C_E \times C_E \times C_E)\}$
- $G = \{t_i \rightarrow guard_i, \forall i \in [1, n]\}$, *with* $n = |E|$

- $E = \{a \rightarrow < Ex, Re, In >, \forall a \in A \cap (P \cup T)\} \cup \{a \rightarrow < Ex', Re', In' >, \forall a \in A \cap (T \cup P)\}$ with (1) $Ex' = Ex \cup e_i$, (2) $Re' = (Re \backslash e_i) \cup e \bullet \rightarrow$ and (3) $In' = (In \cup e_i \rightarrow +) \backslash e \rightarrow \%$
- $I = \{S \rightarrow < S_1, S_2, S_3 >\}$ with $< S_1, S_2, S_3 >$ the initial marking M of G

For all $t_i \in T$ representing an event e_i in the DCR graph, we further precise that:

- $guard_i$ is the conjunction of the conditions defining the enabling of the corresponding event (1) $e_i : i \in In$, (2) $(\rightarrow \bullet i \cap In) \in Ex$ and (3) $(\rightarrow \diamond i \cap In) \in E \backslash Re$
- the expression $< Ex', Re', In' >$ on its output arc is defined such that: (1) $Ex' = Ex \cup i$, (2) $Re' = (Re \backslash i) \cup i \bullet \rightarrow$ and (3) $In' = (In \cup i \rightarrow +) \backslash i \rightarrow \%$

Theorem 1. *Let G be a DCR graph and C the corresponding CPN model generated by following definition 4, then G and C are semantically equivalent.*

We include a proof of this theorem in our repository (See footnote 1).

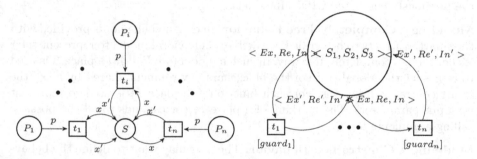

(a) CPN model for a completely-free behavior

(b) CPN model for a DCR Graph

Fig. 4. Behavior representations

7   Model Checking: On the Blind Auction Use Case

Given the HCPN model generated by the application of our transformation algorithm on the input smart contracts along with the LTL property to check and the behavior specification, we use *Helena* [9] to verify the validity of the considered LTL property on our model. Such a property can express either a predefined vulnerability, or a contract-specific property. In fact, many vulnerabilities have been identified in the literature [7], and the user may want to check the presence of certain bugs in a smart contract. To prove the ability of our approach to detect vulnerabilities, we propose LTL formulae to express common vulnerabilities. We then apply our approach on our use case and showcase its capability to detect vulnerabilities as well as check contract-specific properties.

7.1 Expressing Vulnerabilities in LTL

We consider here one of the most common vulnerabilities in Solidity smart contracts. More vulnerabilities are explained and expressed in LTL in our repository (See footnote 1). In the following, $t_{s_i}^f$ denotes the CPN aggregated transition for function f in smart contract s_i.

Integer Overflow/Underflow: Due to Solidity's lack of safeguards on mathematical operators, errors such as overflows and underflows may occur as a result of violation of value limitations of integer data types. For instance, the *uint8 amount* variable in the *BlindAuction* contract can be the source of such a vulnerability when the *pendingReturns* of a bidder exceeds 255. Due to Solidity's wrapping in two's complement integer representation, *amount* will contain a wrong value, causing an incorrect execution.

In our CPN model, we define correspondences between the types used in the Solidity language and those offered by *helena* so that they cover the same ranges. The model checker is therefore able to detect when the smart contract contains an out-of-range expression. It does not, however, pinpoint the source of the anomaly, so the user does not have much information to go on to track it and try to correct it. To overcome this deficiency, we propose to model integer overflows/underflows as a safety LTL property that can be verified on a specific variable x to check:

$$IUO_x = \Box \neg xIsOutOfRange$$

where $xIsOutOfRange$ is a proposition defining the conditions for overflow and underflow for x w.r.t the range of its type which we delimit by defining lower and higher thresholds:

$$xIsOutOfRange = (x < minThreshold) \lor (x > maxThreshold)$$

7.2 Application on the Use Case

The application of our approach on the use case (Sect. 4) yields a HCPN model whose level-0 submodels are created by the execution of CREATESUBMODEL. For lack of space, we choose to include the submodel for *withdraw* in Fig. 5.

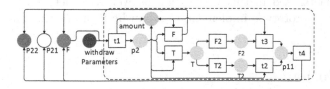

Fig. 5. SubModel of transition *withdraw*

Verifying properties of the contract would come down to verifying properties on the corresponding CPN model. For model checking, we chose *Helena* [9] which offers explicit model checking support for on-the-fly verification of state and LTL properties over CPN models. We have generated the CPN models of our use case in *Helena*'s specification language using our prototype for the transformation algorithm, while considering a free behaviour as well as the BPMN and DCR specifications as presented in Sect. 4. We have then written the corresponding properties in *Helena*'s language for the vulnerabilities in Sect. 7.1 and were able to detect them. We have also established other contract-specific properties that we were able to verify on our example. Figure 6 shows the corresponding property written in *Helena* for the *IUO* LTL property applied on the variable *amount* in *BlindAuction* and Fig. 7 is a snippet of the result of the model checker showing the detection of the vulnerability with a counter example.

```
440 proposition outOfRange : exists (t in S|(t->1).amoUnt > maxThreshold
                                or (t->1).amoUnt < mihThreshold);

1 ltl property IUO:
2     [] not outOfRange;
```

Fig. 6. The integer overflow/underflow LTL property in *Helena*

```
Search report
--------------------------------------------------
 Action performed
    property checking
 Host machine
    Ikramz (pid = 60511)
 Property checked
    IUO
 Termination state
    PROPERTY_VIOLATED
Statistics report
--------------------------------------------------
 Model statistics

    24 places
    28 transitions
    72 arcs
Trace report
--------------------------------------------------
 The following run invalidates the property.
 {
    S = <( {0, 0, 0, ||, false, 0} )>
```

Fig. 7. Model checking result

The artifacts used in this verification as well as a detailed report on the results and the prototype implementation can be found at this repository (See footnote 1).

8   Conclusion

The combination of the Blockchain technology and the BPMN domain has been an evident step, especially considering the assets that the former brings to the latter. It is still crucial, however, to guarantee the correctness of the smart contracts involved in this association to ensure its safety. Existing verification approaches are generally designed to target specific vulnerabilities which have been reported to be the root of some attacks or malfunctions. Checking the absence of vulnerabilities in a smart contract, however necessary, does not guarantee its correctness as a faulty behaviour may stem from a flaw specific to that contract. With our approach we aim to bring a solution to this problem by providing a way to formally verify contracts by both checking for vulnerabilities in the code and offering the possibility to express additional contract-specific properties to check. In this paper, we focus on extending our approach to take into account the context in which the smart contracts to be verified are executed as a behavior specification, while also considering the case where no such specification is provided. To further improve the *Helena*'s performance, we intend to work on *Helena*'s model checker by embedding it with an extension to an existing technique previously developed to deal with the state space explosion problem in regular PNs [14] and applying it on CPNs.

References

1. Overflow incident. en.bitcoin.it/wiki/Value/overflow/incident
2. Solidity documentation. docs.soliditylang.org/en/latest/
3. Amani, S., Bégel, M., Bortin, M., Staples, M.: Towards verifying ethereum smart contract bytecode in isabelle/hol. In: Proceedings of the 7th ACM SIGPLAN International Conference on Certified Programs and Proofs, pp. 66–77. NY, USA (2018)
4. Anand, S., Pasareanu, C.S., Visser, W.: Symbolic execution with abstraction. Int. J. Softw. Tools Technol. Transf. **11**(1), 53–67 (2009)
5. Bhargavan, K., et al.: Formal verification of smart contracts: short paper. In: Proceedings of the 2016 ACM Workshop on Programming Languages and Analysis for Security, PLAS@CCS 2016, Austria (2016)
6. Chen, T., Li, X., Luo, X., Zhang, X.: Under-optimized smart contracts devour your money. In: IEEE 24th International Conference on Software Analysis, Evolution and Reengineering, SANER 2017, Austria, pp. 442–446 (2017)
7. Dingman, W., et al.: Defects and vulnerabilities in smart contracts, a classification using the NIST bugs framework. IJNDC **7**(3), 121–132 (2019)
8. Duo, W., Huang, X., Ma, X.: Formal analysis of smart contract based on colored petri nets. IEEE Intell. Syst. **35**(3), 19–30 (2020)
9. Evangelista, S.: High level petri nets analysis with helena. In: Applications and Theory of Petri Nets 2005, pp. 455–464. Berlin, Heidelberg (2005)
10. Garfatta, I., Klai, K., Gaaloul, W., Graiet, M.: A survey on formal verification for solidity smart contracts. In: ACSW '21: 2021 Australasian Computer Science Week Multiconference, New Zealand, 2021, pp. 1–10. ACM (2021)
11. Jensen, K., Kristensen, L.M.: Coloured petri nets: modelling and validation of concurrent systems, 1st (edn.) Springer Publishing Company, Incorporated (2009)
12. Kalra, S., Goel, S., Dhawan, M., Sharma, S.: ZEUS: analyzing safety of smart contracts. In: 25th Annual Network and Distributed System Security Symposium, NDSS 2018, San Diego, California, USA, 2018 (2018)
13. Khurshid, S., Pasareanu, C.S., Visser, W.: Generalized symbolic execution for model checking and testing. In: Tools and Algorithms for the Construction and Analysis of Systems, 9th International Conference, TACAS 2003, Poland, Proceedings (2003)

14. Klai, K., Poitrenaud, D.: MC-SOG: an LTL model checker based on symbolic observation graphs. In: Applications and Theory of Petri Nets, 29th International Conference, PETRI NETS 2008, Xi'an, China, 2008. Proceedings, pp. 288–306 (2008)
15. Liu, Z., Liu, J.: Formal verification of blockchain smart contract based on colored petri net models. In: 43rd IEEE Annual Computer Software and Applications Conference, COMPSAC 2019, USA, vol. 2, pp. 555–560. IEEE (2019)
16. López-Pintado, O., García-Bañuelos, L., Dumas, M., Weber, I., Ponomarev, A.: Caterpillar: A business process execution engine on the ethereum blockchain. Softw. Pract. Exp. **49**(7), 1162–1193 (2019)
17. Luu, L., Chu, D., Olickel, H., Saxena, P., Hobor, A.: Making smart contracts smarter. In: Proceedings of the 2016 ACM SIGSAC Conference on Computer and Communications Security, Austria, 2016, pp. 254–269 (2016)
18. Mavridou, A., Laszka, A., Stachtiari, E., Dubey, A.: Verisolid: correct-by-design smart contracts for ethereum. In: Financial Cryptography and Data Security - 23rd International Conference, FC 2019, St. Kitts and Nevis, 2019, pp. 446–465 (2019)
19. Meghzili, S., Chaoui, A., Strecker, M., Kerkouche, E.: An approach for the transformation and verification of BPMN models to colored petri nets models. Int. J. Softw. Innov. **8**(1), 17–49 (2020)
20. Mendling, J., et al.: Blockchains for business process management - challenges and opportunities. ACM Trans. Manag. Inf. Syst. **9**(1), 1–16 (2018)
21. Mukkamala, R.R.: A formal model for declarative workflows dynamic condition response graphs. (2012)
22. Murata, T.: Petri nets: properties, analysis and applications. Proc. IEEE **77**(4), 541–580 (1989)
23. OMG: Business process model and notation (bpmn) 2.0. (2011). www.omg.org/spec/BPMN/2.0/
24. Pichler, P., Weber, B., Zugal, S., Pinggera, J., Mendling, J., Reijers, H.A.: Imperative versus declarative process modeling languages: an empirical investigation. In: Business Process Management Workshops - BPM 2011 International Workshopsvol, pp. 383–394. Clermont-Ferrand, France, 2011 (2011)
25. Siegel, D., et al.: The dao attack: understanding what happened (2020). www.coindesk.com/understanding-dao-hack-journalists
26. Team, S.: Parity multi-sig wallets funds frozen (explained) (2021). www.spring works.in/blog/parity-multi-sig-wallets-funds-frozen-explained/
27. Torres, C.F., Schütte, J., State, R.: Osiris: hunting for integer bugs in ethereum smart contracts. In: Proceedings of the 34th Annual Computer Security Applications Conference, pp. 664–676. ACSAC 2018, PR, USA (2018)
28. Tran, A.B., Lu, Q., Weber, I.: Lorikeet: A model-driven engineering tool for blockchain-based business process execution and asset management. In: Proceedings of the Dissertation Award, Demonstration, and Industrial Track at BPM 2018, vol. 2196, pp. 56–60. Sydney, Australia (2018)

Trustworthy Pre-processing of Sensor Data in Data On-Chaining Workflows for Blockchain-Based IoT Applications

Jonathan Heiss[✉], Anselm Busse, and Stefan Tai

Information Systems Engineering (ISE), Berlin, TU, Germany
{jh,ab,st}@ise.tu-berlin.de

Abstract. Prior to provisioning sensor data to smart contracts, a pre-processing of the data on intermediate off-chain nodes is often necessary. When doing so, originally constructed cryptographic signatures cannot be verified on-chain anymore. This exposes an opportunity for undetected manipulation and presents a problem for applications in the Internet of Things where trustworthy sensor data is required on-chain.

In this paper, we propose trustworthy pre-processing as enabler for end-to-end sensor data integrity in data on-chaining workflows. We define requirements for trustworthy pre-processing, present a model and common workflow for data on-chaining, select off-chain computation utilizing Zero-knowledge Proofs (ZKPs) and Trusted Execution Environments (TEEs) as promising solution approaches, and discuss both our proof-of-concept implementations and initial experimental, comparative evaluation results. The importance of trustworthy pre-processing and principle solution approaches are presented, addressing the major problem of end-to-end sensor data integrity in blockchain-based IoT applications.

Keywords: Pre-processing · Sensor data · IoT · Blockchain · Trustworthy · On-chaining · Off-chaining · TEE · zkSNARKs · Zokrates · SGX

1 Introduction

Blockchain technology is increasingly used in the Internet of Things (IoT) to store and process critical sensor data originating from and shared between multiple, often mutually distrusting parties [7,12,15,16,20,23,24]. In local energy grids with blockchain-based energy trading, for example, energy consumers and producers depend on smart meter-generated measurement data [7,19]. In supply chains, product-related manufacturing and shipping events are written to a blockchain to provide a single source of truth for all involved, independent parties [23,24]. In healthcare, blockchain use cases exist for doctors, hospitals, and emergency services to have access to patients' health data collected by wearables [12].

However, the variety and scale of connected IoT devices and the generated data pose new challenges regarding data processing and data on-chaining. Raw

© Springer Nature Switzerland AG 2021
H. Hacid et al. (Eds.): ICSOC 2021, LNCS 13121, pp. 133–149, 2021.
https://doi.org/10.1007/978-3-030-91431-8_9

sensor measurements cannot directly be used on the blockchain because of volume limitations [18] or because sensitive information may be exposed and become accessible to unintended readers [7]. Blockchains inherently have privacy and scalability limitations [6,17] that must be taken into account.

Consequently, the on-chain processing of sensor data is preceded by preprocessing steps to reduce data volume and ensure that confidential information is veiled. Such pre processing typically is executed on intermediate, off-chain nodes as part of multi-staged data provisioning workflows [7,12,15,16,20,24]: data originates on constrained sensor nodes, then moves to more powerful *gateway* nodes for pre-processing, and is finally provisioned to smart contracts as aggregated information. For example, in the healthcare use case described in [12], data is pre-processed by personal computers or smartphones; in energy grids [7] by workstations located within participating households; in supply chains [24] by board computers and mobile devices.

While pre-processing has become an integral element in such *data on-chaining workflows* and is necessary to mitigate scalability and privacy issues, off-chain pre-processing also represents a security risk. Sensor devices typically sign their measurements to provide data integrity. However, sensor data integrity is not end-to-end: once data is pre-processed on middleboxes, signatures constructed on the input do not apply to the output anymore. Contrary to smart contract application logic, application stakeholders cannot validate off-chain processing as part of the blockchain's consensus protocol. Consequently, naive pre-processing can be exploited for malicious data manipulation without being noticed. This attack vector threatens data integrity in data on-chaining workflows and quickly questions the entire blockchain-based IoT system design and data quality.

To address this problem, solutions are needed to ensure *trustworthy preprocessing*, i.e., to make computational correctness verifiable on the blockchain. Off-chain computations have been proposed [6] to outsource blockchain transaction processing to off-chain nodes without compromising trust guarantees. Zero-Knowledge (ZK) computations and Trusted Execution Environments (TEE) are two important approaches here that are also increasingly being used in early-adoption projects and practice [1,7,9,10]. However, using ZK computations and TEEs for trustworthy pre-processing has not been examined so far.

In the face of the rising interest in blockchain-based sensor data management and the need for end-to-end sensor data integrity, in this paper, we analyze the underlying problem of trustworthy pre-processing in data on-chaining workflows, propose a model for integrity-preserving data on-chaining, and examine its practical applicability based on ZK computations and TEEs. Thereby, we make two individual contributions:

1. First, we propose a model for end-to-end sensor data integrity through trustworthy pre-processing. We characterize sensor data pre-processing in on-chaining workflows for blockchain-based IoT applications based on relevant literature. From our findings, we refine our problem statement and introduce trustworthy pre-processing as a workflow element that enables application

stakeholders through participation in the blockchain network to verify data integrity from source to sink.

2. Second, we examine the applicability of zkSNARKs-based and Trusted Execution Environments (TEE)-based off-chain computations for our proposed model. Based on a typical application workflow, we first conceptualize how trustworthy pre-processing can be instantiated with ZoKrates [8], a toolkit for zkSNARKs-based off-chain computation, and with Intel SGX [5], Intel's realization of TEEs. Then, we implement the proposed model with both technologies as a proof of concept and present preliminary experiments in a testbed. While our results attest to the applicability of trustworthy pre-preprocessing with both approaches, they also confirm that, in comparison, zkSNARKs provide stronger integrity guarantees (weaker trust assumptions), whereas TEEs enable more efficient off-chain pre-processing.

2 Pre-processing

To lay the foundation for trustworthy pre-processing, in this section, we first describe the general characteristics of pre-processing in blockchain-based IoT applications that we observed in pertinent research papers. Next, we refine our problem statement and define computational integrity, based on [2]. Finally, we present a model for trustworthy pre-processing on gateway nodes for use in data on-chaining workflows that start with sensor devices and result in smart contracts.

2.1 Characterization

Pre-processing in blockchain-based applications shares common objectives, input types, and functionality.

Objectives. In data on-chaining workflows, off-chain pre-processing helps to mitigate blockchain-inherent scalability and privacy limitations. Thereby, it pursues the following objectives:

- *Offloading Computation*: Outsource on-chain data processing to an off-chain node that is not bound to costly consensus-based transaction processing [7].
- *Reducing Storage*: Reduce the volume of sensor data to minimize the storage footprint on the blockchain [12,18].
- *Enabling Confidentiality*: Hide sensitive information contained in raw measurements or meta-data from stakeholders that do have read permissions [7, 20,24].

Inputs. Pre-processing can be executed on different types of data. We distinguish between the following:

- *Measurements* include all data that is generated by sensor devices. This includes *time series* data collected over a longer period of time [21], for example, temperature or location data, and *event* data that represents externally triggered occurrences [24], for example, the scanning or opening of a container in a logistics context.
- *Meta-data* originates from the sensor device and contains descriptive information about the measurements, such as sensor identities, target storage addresses, or timestamps.
- *Auxiliary data* is added at the gateway node. Examples are filter rules, access control lists, or storage addresses.

Measurements and meta-data are critical for pre-processing and are referred to in the following as sensory data. In contrast, auxiliary data is never processed alone but optionally used to enrich pre-processing.

Types. Without claiming completeness, we identify three general types of data pre-processing which can be observed in relevant applications [12,19,20,24] and which represent typical functionality for operating on sequential data[1].

- *Mapping*: Data is transformed into a target format, e.g., enumeration, encryption, decryption, hashing [20,24].
- *Reducing*: Data of one or multiple sensor devices is consolidated, e.g., the arithmetic average or a total amount is calculated [19].
- *Filtering*: Data is filtered according to predefined rules, e.g., only values below a predefined threshold are returned [12].

2.2   Problem Refinement

Data provisioning is often controlled by one of the stakeholders, e.g., shippers in supply chains [15,24] or producers in energy markets [7]. Stakeholders may have a personal, often economically motivated interest in manipulating the data, e.g., in cooling chains to prevent contractual penalties if perishable fright is perished or to improve accounting positions. Given such motifs, we assume data providing stakeholders as potential attackers.

In data on-chaining workflows, data can take three states: it is *in transit* when it is transmitted from one to another component, it is *at rest* when it is persisted on disk, and it is *in use* when it is processed in memory. During the states in transit and at rest, data integrity and authenticity can be verified using cryptographic signatures. However, when data is processed, it is transformed and signatures constructed on the input do not apply for the output anymore. Furthermore, off-chain pre-processing cannot be validated by stakeholders through the consensus mechanism. An attacker could selfishly execute different functions on the data to manipulate the output and obtain a personal benefit without being noticed. Therefore, we assume manipulation of computation as the potential attack.

---

[1] https://web.mit.edu/6.005/www/fa15/classes/25-map-filter-reduce/.

2.3   Computational Integrity

As a first step towards trustworthy pre-processing, we characterize computational integrity. We adopt the model proposed in [2].

A pre-processing program P is executed on input data D and some auxiliary data A and returns output O such that $P(D, A) \to O$.

A malicious executer may benefit from creating a manipulated program P' such that $P'(D, A) \to O' \mid O' \neq O$. For example, in the supply chain use case, a shipper executes a threshold check P on temperature measurements D using the threshold A. If the shipper knows that the outcome O triggers a contractual penalty, but O' does not, it may change P to P' to obtain O' instead of O. It then reports O' to the blockchain and is exempt from the penalty. Additionally, the executer may leave the program P unchanged but manipulate the input data D such that $P(D', A) \to O' \mid D \neq D' \wedge O' \neq O$ or the auxiliary data A such that $P(D, A') \to O' \mid A \neq A' \wedge O' \neq O$

To prevent both, program and input manipulation, stakeholders should be able to verify computational integrity which is only guaranteed if output O is executed on the right program P and on the right input data (D, A) such that $P(D, A) \to O \mid (P \neq P') \wedge (D \neq D') \wedge (A \neq A')$. Therefore, we assume that program P also generates an *evidence* E that asserts computational integrity such that $P(D, A) \to (O, E)$. To enable third-party stakeholders to verify computational integrity, additionally, an asymmetric key pair is required: the evidence signed with the *proving key* can be verified by any third party with the corresponding *verification key*. The evidence and the evidence key pair represent the major artefacts for trustworthy pre-processing.

2.4   End-to-End Data Integrity

Given that integrity of data can be verified while it is in use, we can define a data on-chaining workflow where integrity is verifiable from its source on the sensor node to its sink on the smart contract as depicted in Fig. 1. Note that instead of a simple signature, verifiable evidence is provided to the blockchain that allows data integrity verification with moderate computational overhead in the blockchain network.

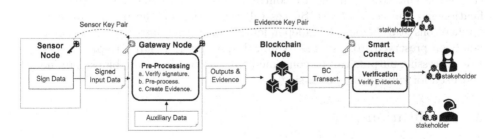

Fig. 1. End-to-End Data Integrity through Trustworthy Pre-Processing

One Time Setup. During an initial one time setup, central system artifacts are generated and deployed on the system components. Given that these artifacts are critical to verify computational integrity, we assume a trusted setup where each stakeholder can verify the integrity of the artifacts. It consists of three steps:

As a first step (*1. Integrity Assertion*), an environment is established that enables the gateway node to generate verifiable evidence of computational integrity as accompanying artefacts of the pre-processing outputs. This includes the integrity of sensory and auxiliary inputs. Examples for such environments are mathematical constraint systems [8] or trusted execution environments [5] as will be described in the subsequent section.

Next (*2. Key Generation*), two key pairs are required: an *evidence key pair* consisting of a proving and verification key for signing and verifying the evidence and a *sensor key pair*, represented as a cryptographic public and private key that is used to sign and verify the sensor data on the sensor node and the gateway node respectively.

As the last setup step (*3. Deployment*), all artefacts are deployed: The gateway node is equipped with the sensor node's public key, the integrity-preserving pre-processing program, the proving key, and optionally auxiliary data. The smart contract receives the verification key that enables evidence verification.

Recurring Operations. Sensory data arrives recurringly at the gateway node in regular intervals, e.g., batches of *time series* data, or in irregular intervals, e.g., externally triggered *events*. Then (*4. Pre-Processing*), the pre-processing program takes the signed sensory data, the sensor's public key, and optionally auxiliary data as inputs and executes the following steps:

(a) The sensory inputs' signature is verified with the sensor device's public key.
(b) Pre-processing functions are executed on the verified inputs. Examples are provided in Sect. 2.1.
(c) An evidence is created and signed with the gateways' proving key. The evidence enables the smart contract to verify computational integrity.

Outputs and signed evidence are transmitted to the smart contract through the blockchain node. The smart contract verifies the evidence using the verification key (*5. Verification*). Successful verification on the blockchain enables applications stakeholders to independently verify that integrity of sensor data has been preserved from source to sink despite intermediate pre-preprocessing. Pre-processing outputs can be consumed through participating blockchain nodes and used for subsequent processing.

3 Application

For trustworthy pre-processing to become easily applicable in practice, technologies are required that enable on-chain verifiability of computational integrity and that can implement the pre-processing characteristics as described in Sect. 2.1.

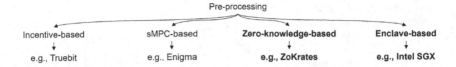

Fig. 2. Off-chain Computation Technologies according to [6]

3.1 Technologies for Trustworthy Pre-processing

Off-chain computation has been proposed to mitigate privacy and scalability limitations of blockchains by outsourcing computation to off-chain nodes without compromising core blockchain properties [6,17]. Thereby, it represents a matching concept for trustworthy pre-processing.

However, the different approaches to off-chain computation presented in [6] and depicted in Fig. 2 are not equally suitable. Both incentive-based and sMPC-based approaches require multiple nodes that execute non-trivial protocols. However, in data on-chaining applications in the IoT [7,12,15,20,24], pre-processing is typically executed on a single node with limited networking and storage capacity. If such a constraint is given, the distributed computation model and interactive nature of incentive- and sMPC-based approaches may be inconsistent with use case specific requirements which restricts general applicability. In contrast, zero-knowledge and enclave-based approaches can be executed non-interactively on a single node and, hence, promise broader applicability for trustworthy pre-processing.

3.2 ZkSNARKs-Based Pre-processing with ZoKrates

Zero-knowledge proofs enable a prover to convince a verifier that it has correctly executed a computation without revealing inputs to the verifier.

zkSNARKs can be summarized as one type of a zero-knowledge protocol that distinguishes through *succinctness*, i.e., resulting artefacts are small in size and can be verified fast, *non-interactivity*, i.e., only one message is required to convince the verifier, and *argument of knowledge*, i.e., the prover is able to prove that she has access to the correct data.

ZoKrates [8] provides a toolbox and a higher-level language to implement a zkSNARKs-proving system where an off-chain prover can convince an on-chain verifier that the computation has been executed correctly.

To describe the ZoKrates-based pre-processing (compare Fig. 3), we leverage the model presented in Sect. 2.1 and build upon the ZoKrates workflow described in [8].

One Time Setup

1. *Integrity Assertion*: To guarantee integrity of auxiliary data and the sensor public key, both are typed as public arguments in the ZoKrates program and,

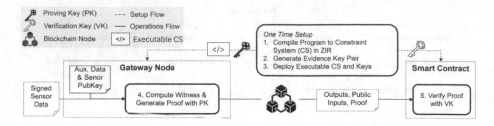

Fig. 3. Trustworthy Pre-Processing with ZoKrates

hence, are required on-chain for evidence verification. Since the verification would fail on different public inputs, their integrity can be determined on-chain.

Once specified, the high-level ZoKrates code is compiled into an executable constraint system (ECS) in the ZoKrates Intermediate Representation (ZIR) format that can be considered as an extension to a Rank-1-Constraint System and enables assertion of computational integrity: if a variable assignment is found that satisfies the defined constraints computational integrity can be proven.

2. *Evidence Key Generation*: An evidence key pair is generated from a Common Reference String (CRS) [8] which enables proof creation and verification. Since the CRS allows construction of fake proofs it must be securely disposed after key generation. The evidence key pair is cryptographically bound to the previously generated ECS.

3. *Deployment*: The ECS, the evidence proving key, auxiliary data, and the sensor public key are deployed to the gateway node which takes the role of the off-chain prover. Verification key and the verification contract are deployed to the blockchain.

Recurring Operations

5. *Execution*: The ZIR program is executed on predefined inputs, through the ZoKrates interpreter. The output is called witness, an artefact representing variable assignments that satisfy the specified constraints for a specific execution. In a separate step, the cryptographic proof is generated based on the execution-specific witness and the program-specific proving key. Finally, outputs and evidence are forwarded to the smart contract through a blockchain node.

6. *Verification*: The verification contract takes the cryptographic proof, the verification key, and public program arguments as input parameters. The verification is only successful if the proof is executed with the right program and on the right (public) inputs.

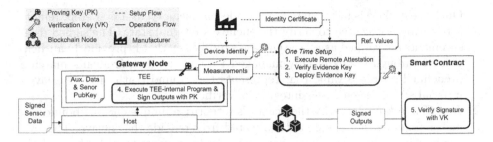

Fig. 4. Trustworthy Pre-Processing with Intel SGX

3.3   Enclave-Based Pre-processing with Intel SGX

Enclave-based computation enables an enclave-external party to verify that an output has been computed by a specific program inside a specific enclave that protects internal integrity. Thereby, it relies on two concepts: Trusted Execution Environments and Remote Attestation.

Trusted Execution Environments (TEE) are hardware-secured parts of a system architecture that protect data and code from external manipulation and disclosure. Programs executed inside such TEEs are running in an isolated and/or encrypted memory region that cannot even be accessed in the highest privilege level of the system. Thus, it protects the content of the TEE from the system owner and guarantees the integrity of computation executed inside the TEE. Intel SGX is Intel's concrete implementation of TEEs. We use the terms TEE and enclave interchangeably.

Remote Attestation enables the external verification of the integrity of the TEE's internal state and the authenticity of messages received from inside. Thus, ensuring that a malicious attacker cannot falsely pose as an trusted enclave. TEE-enabled devices have a device identity key that is embedded into the device hardware during manufacturing and can be verified by external parties through a Public Key Infrastructure (PKI). Using this key, the device creates for each instantiated TEE an identity certificate which can externally be verified through the PKI. This enables evidence key generation. When remote attestation is requested, the enclave returns signed measurements which represent a complete snapshot of the TEEs internal state. With SGX as TEE, remote attestation and the PKI are managed by Intel.

In the following, we describe pre-processing with Intel SGX as depicted in Fig. 4. To achieve comparability with Zokrates-based pre-processing we use the same workflow model as described in Sect. 2.4.

One Time Setup

1. *Integrity Assertion*: To guarantee integrity of auxiliary data and the sensor public key, both must be protected through the TEEs security guarantees. Therefore, they are specified inside the enclave during implementation.

Once the enclave is instantiated and loaded in memory, as a first step, remote attestation is executed to verify the enclave's internal state. The signed measurements are verified using the enclave's public key that is previously authenticated through the externally managed PKI. If the measurements match a predefined reference value that represents the ground truth of the enclave's internal state, the enclave's integrity is verified.

2. *Key Generation*: To verify the enclave's integrity a unique enclave-bound key pair is required that can be authenticated from outside the enclave. This evidence key pair is used to sign program results computed inside the enclave. Given that the enclave's integrity guarantees hold, this signature enables verification of computational integrity on the blockchain. The evidence key is generated inside the enclave and can be authenticated through an externally managed PKI.

3. *Deployment*: The enclave's evidence public key becomes part of the verification contract which implements the signature verification on-chain and is deployed to the blockchain. At this point, the enclave is already instantiated on the gateway node.

Recurring Operations

5. *Execution*: Sensor data is provided through the host program which represents the only interface to the enclave. Auxiliary data and the sensor public key are already part of the enclave and, hence, protected. The program is executed as defined in Sect. 2.4. The computational outputs are signed with the evidence proving key.

6. *Verification*: The verification contract validates the signature with the evidence verification key. A successful validation proves the outputs' authenticity, i.e., they have been signed with the right proving key that is unique to the enclave, and integrity, i.e., the received outputs are computed by the right pre-processing program inside the enclave.

4   Evaluation

Given the two conceptual workflow descriptions, in this section, we evaluate the technical feasibility for each technology.

4.1   Implementation

Our proof-of-concept (PoC) implementations follow the descriptions provided in Sect. 3.2 and 3.3 respectively. Thereby, we focus on the recurring operations steps, *execution* and *verification* which we consider as most relevant to demonstrate feasibility. Aspects of the setup phase are discussed in Sect. 5.

The PoC program should respect the pre-processing characteristics presented in Sect. 2.1. Our program mimics a threshold violation check on sensory data where the threshold represents auxiliary data. The sensory data is *filtered* for violations, then *reduced* by counting the violations, and *mapped* by scaling the filtered values down. The smart contract is only provided with the violation count. Thereby, the program fulfills all three objectives: computation is outsourced to an off-chain node, the data footprint is reduced in size, and the potentially sensitive sensor measurements are not published on-chain.

ZoKrates: For our ZoKrates-based implementation, we simulate the sensor node with a Python script that hashes the data with SHA256 and signs it with EDDSA-based sensor key pair, which ZoKrates support. Plain sensory data is a private input, while the data's hash, signature, and the sensor public key are public inputs to the ZoKrates program. To verify integrity of sensory inputs, the signature's hash input is reconstructed from the plain sensor data and compared to the hash inputs. Only if both signature verification and hash comparison are successful integrity is guaranteed. Hashing and signature verification are implemented using the ZoKrates Standard Library. Pre-processing is executed by two commands provided by the ZoKrates CLI: *compute-witness* that requires the compiled program and *generate-proof* that takes proving key and witness as inputs. The outputs are written to disk.

Intel SGX: For the SGX evaluation, we have implemented two enclaves. The first one simulates a sensor node and signs the sensory input data with an internally generated sensor key pair using the SGX-provided operations *sgx_create _keypair* and *sgx_ecdsa_sign*. The second enclave represents the gateway node that stores auxiliary data and the sensor public key internally. It verifies the sensor data with the sensor public key using the SGX operation *sgx_ecdsa_verify*. Evidence key pair generation and signature construction on computational outputs are realized with the same SGX commands as the sensor enclave. The processing result and the corresponding signature are written to disk.

Ethereum: As blockchain technology, we chose Ethereum [26], which is widely used and finds application both as a public blockchain but also as consortium blockchain based on Proof-of-Authority consensus and non-public deployment. For each, respectively, a verification contract is implemented in Solidity that runs on a locally deployed Ethereum blockchain and is accessed through a Ganache blockchain client. To validate Intel SGX evidence, we build upon an existing ECDSA implementation for the Ethereum blockchain[2]. ZoKrates proofs rely on EdDSA (twisted Edwards curve) and are verified through a dedicated verification contract that is generated by ZoKrates CLI support[3].

4.2 Experiments

Given our proof-of-concept implementations, we can now conduct initial experiments to obtain the first practical insights into trustworthy pre-processing with zkSNARKs and TEEs. At this point, it should be noted that experimental results strongly depend on our non-optimized PoC implementations and, hence, cannot simply be generalized.

---

[2] https://github.com/tdrerup/elliptic-curve-solidity.
[3] https://github.com/Zokrates/ZoKrates.

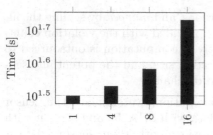 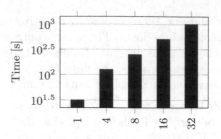

(a) Various Batch Sizes, Count of 1   (b) Various Batch Counts, Size of 1

Fig. 5. Pre-processing with ZoKrates

Exerimental Setup. For our experimental setup, we deploy our implementations on an Intel NUC-Kit NUC7PJYH with an SGX enabled Pentium Silver J5005 CPU, 8 GB of Memory, and an Ubuntu 18.04.5 LTS operating system. To construct workloads, we use smart meter measurements collected in a testbed of an energy grid research project[4] and prepare the measurements such that (1) each measurement consists of four integer values, (2) measurements are collected into batches of different sizes line-wise in plain text, and (3) each batch is signed to represent the sensor's signature.

As mentioned in Sect. 2.1, pre-processing is typically exposed to two types of workloads: event and batch processing. To simulate that in our experimental setup, we turn on two knobs: for events of different sizes, we change the input data size per execution (batch size), for batch processing, we vary the number of subsequent executions (batch count). Latter is executed on size-one-batches which contain a single measurement.

The computational outputs of size-one-batch experiments are used for on-chain verification, which is measured in *Gas*, an Ethereum-specific metric for capturing computational complexity of on-chain transaction processing.

Results. The results summarized for ZoKrates in Fig. 5 and for Intel SGX in Fig. 6 show the overall execution time for off-chain pre-processing in seconds and microseconds, respectively. As expected, the execution time of zkSNARKs-based pre-processing is orders of magnitude higher than that of enclave-based pre-processing. With larger batch sizes, the execution time increases almost gradually. This holds true for each technology individually as shown in Fig. 5a) and Fig. 6a). Similar behaviour can be observed for increasing the batch count as shown in Fig. 5b) and Fig. 6b). However, we can observe that for both ZoKrates and SGX the increase is much steeper for a growing batch count than for a growing batch size (note the different logarithmic y-scales). For this specific implementation example, this would mean that it is preferable to increase the number of processed data through larger batch sizes rather than counts when possible in the actual application scenario.

---

[4] https://blogpv.net/.

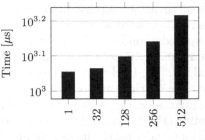
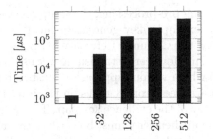

(a) Various Batch Sizes, Count of 1   (b) Various Batch Counts, Size of 1

Fig. 6. Pre-processing with Intel SGX

In ZoKrates-based pre-processing, the accompanying construction of crypto-graphic proofs represents a memory-intensive computation that correlates with the input size. The experiment for the next larger batch size of 32 measurements in ZoKrates ran out of memory during the *proof-generation* on the test system. Given that sensory data can quickly grow very large, the memory capacity of constrained IoT or edge devices may present a limiting factor, but may not be an issue for larger middleboxes.

In contrast, Intel SGX reduces pre-processing overhead. Even though, our implementation was also memory limited regarding a batch size larger than 1024 measurements, this is just a limitation of the current SGX design that might change in the future and can be mitigated, e.g., by splitting up the processes into multiple enclaves on the same machine. Better efficiency and smaller memory consumption distinguishes Intel SGX as a suitable technology for lower IoT layers where computational resources are typically scarce. However, contrary to ZoKrates, SGX-based pre-processing requires an increased trust in the correctness of the hardware implementation and the attestation process that requires trusting Intel regarding a correct attestation.

In our proof-of-concept implementation, on-chain verification costs are cheaper for ZoKrates-generated proofs (567 614 Gas) than for Intel SGX-generated signatures (1 211 443 Gas). However, since on-chain verification costs strongly depend on the implementation of respective signature algorithm our results cannot be generalized, e.g., for other blockchain technologies.

5 Discussion

While in the previous section, initial insights about the performance behavior of each technology were provided, in this section, we discuss security and trust aspects and potential extensions for trustworthy pre-processing.

Integrity and Trust Assumptions: As described in Sect. 2.2, pre-processing is assumed to be executed by non-trusted stakeholders who have an incentive for data manipulation. While off-chain technologies eliminate unnoticed attacks during pre-processing, the setup phase still reveals an attack surface. In Zokrates, for example, key generation must be executed in a trusted setup to guarantee that the Common Reference String is safely disposed to prevent fake proof generation. However, establishing a trusted setup for zkSNARKs is a known problem to which various approaches exist as referenced in [8]. In Intel SGX, the integrity guarantee strongly relies on the internal state of the enclave and on the authenticity of the evidence key pair. To preserve this guarantee, remote attestation and key authenticity must be verified through a trusted third party or by all involved stakeholders individually. Also, auxiliary data and the sensor's public key must be verified before being added to the enclave. Beyond the setup, zkSNARKs-based pre-processing does not rely on further trust assumptions, whereas enclave-based pre-processing heavily relies on a trustworthy manufacturer that ensures that private keys are kept secret and certificates obtained from the PKI are authentic to the device's identities. This distinguishes ZoKrates as particularly suitable for processing critical data with substantial security demands.

Further Attacks: Beyond our attack model described in Sect. 2.2, attacks on data freshness and availability must be considered. While an attacker that controls communication channels, e.g., between gateway and blockchain node, cannot compromise data integrity without being noticed (*Man-in-the-Middle Attack*) due to signature and evidence verification, it can, however, intercept and replay messages in a different order to impact the overall application logic (*Replay Attack*). To prevent this, secure timestamps or challenge-response patterns can be applied. Furthermore, to prevent a malicious executor from compromising availability by withholding messages (*Denial of Service Attack*), gateway nodes can redundantly be deployed to eliminate centralization, similar to this proposal [25].

Multi-stage Pre-processing: In multi-stage data on-chaining workflows, multiple pre-processing tasks may be executed subsequently by different non-trusted stakeholders. To verify integrity on-chain, an evidence chain must be established that allows any subsequent computation to validate the provided evidence of the previous computation. This way, end-to-end integrity could be guaranteed along arbitrarily long on-chaining workflows.

Confidential Pre-processing: While this work focuses on integrity preservation, in some use cases it might be required to keep inputs to pre-processing hidden from the executor. This can, for example, be achieved through Intel SGX, where encrypted inputs can be decrypted inside the enclave, processed, and encrypted again before being returned. Thereby, inputs and outputs would not be accessible by the executor. However, side-channel attacks must be respected that are known to extract confidential information from enclaves [4].

6   Related Work

In this paper, we extend trustworthy data on-chaining as presented in [14] by considering *data in use* as an additional attack vector. Furthermore, we leverage approaches to off-chain computation presented in [6] to realize trustworthy pre-processing. From the proposed off-chain computation technologies in [6], zkSNARKs and Trusted Execution Environments are increasingly adopted in scientific literature on blockchain-based IoT applications.

Recently, many proposals leverage zkSNARKs for off-chain computations through Zokrates; however, only a few intersect blockchain-based sensor data management. While in [7] ZoKrates is applied for off-chain processing of sensor data, i.e., smart meter measurements in local energy grids, other works mainly use Zokrates for privacy-preserving authentication, e.g. in the context of smart vehicle authentication at charging stations [11], consumer authentication for car sharing [13], or in health care for patient authentication [22].

TEEs are leveraged in various papers to implement trustworthy oracles that bridge data provisioning from off-chain data sources to smart contracts. For example, in TownCrier [27], a TEE-based oracle system is proposed to authenticate data provided by HTTPS-enabled off-chain data sources, or in [25], a distributed TEE-enabled oracle system is proposed that improves availability. Beyond scientific usage, e.g., ChainLink[5] works on a solution to implement these concepts for practical usage [3].

While the main focus of these proposals lies in data provisioning, other works instead use TEEs for sensor data management. In [9], for example, a system is proposed that employs TEEs for intermediate processing of sensory data before it is forwarded to the blockchain and the cloud. The authors of [1] use TEEs for trustworthy access management of sensor data in hybrid storage systems where off-chain storage holds encrypted sensor data and the blockchain stores its hashes and access logs. While these proposals do not apply pre-processing as defined in this paper, they underline the need for a systematization of trustworthy pre-processing that we aim to provide with our contributions.

7 Conclusion

End-to-end sensor data integrity is critical to many blockchain-based IoT applications. Data on-chaining workflows accordingly require pre-processing on off-chain nodes to be trustworthy. In this paper, we explored the use of zkSNARKs- and TEE-based computations for trustworthy pre-processing, first, as individual candidate technologies that require non-trivial set-ups for integration in data on-chaining workflows, and second, through a preliminary, comparative experimental evaluation based on two proof-of-concept implementations. We conclude that each presents an important approach that (a) can conceptually be well-integrated in respective workflows and (b) satisfies the requirements and primary objective of end-to-end data integrity. Our proof-of-concept implementations use current, state-of-the-art software, and, since both zero-knowledge proofs and TEEs are very active areas of research, our implementations and the experimental findings must be seen as preliminary. We expect rapid advances regarding the used software stacks and current constraints regarding memory limitations, and, consequently, performance numbers to change. Still, a principal performance gap

---

[5] https://chain.link/.

and performance advantage of TEEs over zkSNARKs is expected to remain. However, as discussed in this paper, the choice of an approach and technology will depend also on other, non-performance criteria like the integrity and trust assumptions or existing attack vectors for the specific IoT application under consideration. Future work will address extensions of the proposed model regarding its computational scalability through parallel execution and its applicability for stream processing.

References

1. Ayoade, G., Karande, V., Khan, L., Hamlen, K.: Decentralized IOT data management using blockchain and trusted execution environment. In: 2018 IEEE International Conference on Information Reuse and Integration (IRI), pp. 15–22 (2018)
2. Ben-Sasson, E., et al.: Computational integrity with a public random string from Quasi-Linear PCPs. In: Coron, J.-S., Nielsen, J.B. (eds.) EUROCRYPT 2017. LNCS, vol. 10212, pp. 551–579. Springer, Cham (2017). https://doi.org/10.1007/978-3-319-56617-7_19
3. Breidenbach, L., et al.: Chainlink 2.0: next steps in the evolution of decentralized oracle networks (2021)
4. Bulck, J.V., et al: Foreshadow: extracting the keys to the intel SGX kingdom with transient out-of-order execution. In: 27th USENIX Security Symposium (USENIX Security 18), pp. 991–1008. USENIX Association, Baltimore, MD (2018)
5. Costan, V., Devadas, S.: Intel SGX explained. IACR Cryptol. ePrint Arch. **86** (2016). eprint.iacr.org/2016/086
6. Eberhardt, J., Heiss, J.: Off-chaining models and approaches to off-chain computations. In: Proceedings of the 2nd Workshop on Scalable and Resilient Infrastructures for Distributed Ledgers. SERIAL'18, ACM (2018)
7. Eberhardt, J., Peise, M., Kim, D.H., Tai, S.: Privacy-preserving netting in local energy grids. In: 2020 IEEE International Conference on Blockchain and Cryptocurrency (ICBC), pp. 1–9 (2020)
8. Eberhardt, J., Tai, S.: Zokrates - scalable privacy-preserving off-chain computations. In: IEEE International Conference on Blockchain (2018)
9. Enkhtaivan, B., Inoue, A.: Mediating data trustworthiness by using trusted hardware between iot devices and blockchain. In: 2020 IEEE International Conference on Smart Internet of Things (SmartIoT), pp. 314–318 (2020)
10. Gabay, D., Akkaya, K., Cebe, M.: A privacy framework for charging connected electric vehicles using blockchain and zero knowledge proofs. In: 2019 IEEE 44th LCN Symposium on Emerging Topics in Networking (LCN Symposium), pp. 66–73 (2019)
11. Gabay, D., Akkaya, K., Cebe, M.: Privacy-preserving authentication scheme for connected electric vehicles using blockchain and zero knowledge proofs. IEEE Trans. Vehic. Technol. **69**(6), 5760–5772 (2020)
12. Griggs, K.N., Ossipova, O., Kohlios, C.P., Baccarini, A.N., Howson, E.A., Hayajneh, T.: Healthcare blockchain system using smart contracts for secure automated remote patient monitoring. J. Med. Syst. **42**, 1–7 (2018)
13. Gudymenko, I., et al.: Privacy-preserving blockchain-based systems for car sharing leveraging zero-knowledge protocols. In: 2020 IEEE International Conference on Decentralized Applications and Infrastructures (DAPPS), pp. 114–119 (2020)

14. Heiss, J., Eberhardt, J., Tai, S.: From oracles to trustworthy data on-chaining systems. In: IEEE International Conference on Blockchain (2019)
15. Helo, P., Shamsuzzoha, A.: Real-time supply chain-a blockchain architecture for project deliveries. Robot. Comput. Integr. Manuf. **63**, 101909 (2020)
16. Huang, S., Wang, G., Yan, Y., Fang, X.: Blockchain-based data management for digital twin of product. J. Manuf. Syst. **54**, 361–371 (2020)
17. Eberhardt, S.T.: On or Off the blockchain? insights on off-chaining computation and data. In: ESOCC 2017: 6th European Conference on Service-Oriented and Cloud Computing (2017)
18. Kurt Peker, Y., Rodriguez, X., Ericsson, J., Lee, S.J., Perez, A.J.: A cost analysis of internet of things sensor data storage on blockchain via smart contracts. Electronics **9**(2) (2020)
19. Peise, M., et al.: Blockchain-based local energy grids: advanced use cases and architectural considerations. In: IEEE 18th ICSA-C, pp. 130–137 (2021)
20. Putz, B., Dietz, M., Empl, P., Pernul, G.: Ethertwin: Blockchain-based secure digital twin information management. Inf. Proc. Manage. **58**(1) (2021)
21. Shafagh, H., Burkhalter, L., Hithnawi, A., Duquennoy, S.: Towards blockchain-based auditable storage and sharing of iot data. In: Proceedings of the 2017 on Cloud Computing Security Workshop. p. 45–50 (2017)
22. Sharma, B., Halder, R., Singh, J.: Blockchain-based interoperable healthcare using zero-knowledge proofs and proxy re-encryption. In: 2020 International Conference on Communication System NetworkS (COMSNETS), pp. 1–6 (2020)
23. Sigwart, M., Borkowski, M., Peise, M., Schulte, S., Tai, S.: Blockchain-based data provenance for the internet of things. In: Proceedings of the 9th International Conference on the Internet of Things (2019)
24. Sund, T., Lööf, C., Nadjm-Tehrani, S., Asplund, M.: Blockchain-based event processing in supply chains-a case study at ikea. Robotics and Computer-Integrated Manufacturing **65**, 101971 (2020)
25. Woo, S., Song, J., Park, S.: A distributed oracle using intel SGX for blockchain-based IOT applications. Sensors **20**(9) (2020)
26. Wood, G.: Ethereum: a secure decentralised generalised transaction ledger. Ethereum Project Yellow Paper (2014)
27. Zhang, F., Cecchetti, E., Croman, K., Juels, A., Shi, E.: Town crier: an authenticated data feed for smart contracts. In: Proceedings of the 2016 ACM SIGSAC Conference on Computer and Communications Security (2016)

Architectures, Microservices and APIs

Formalising Solutions to REST API Practices as Design (Anti)Patterns

Van Tuan Tran[1(✉)], Manel Abdellatif[2], and Yann-Gaël Guéhéneuc[1]

[1] Concordia University, Montreal, QC, Canada
`vantuan.tran@mail.concordia.ca`, `yann-gael.gueheneuc@concordia.ca`
[2] Polytechnique Montréal, Montreal, QC, Canada
`manel.abdellatif@polymtl.ca`

Abstract. REST APIs are nowadays the de-facto standard for Web applications. However, as more systems and services adopt the REST architectural style, many problems arise regularly. To avoid these repetitive problems, developers should follow good practices and avoid bad practices. Thus, research on good and bad practices and how to design a simple but effective REST API are essential. Yet, to the best of our knowledge, there are only a few concrete solutions to recurring REST API practices, like "API Versioning". There are works on defining or detecting some practices, but not on solutions to the practices. We present the most up-to-date list of REST API practices and formalize them in the form of REST API (anti)patterns. We validate our design (anti)patterns with a survey and interviews of 55 developers.

1 Introduction

In the last decade, the information presented on the Internet moved from simple static Web pages to sophisticated interactive Web applications that can be customized by and react to user actions. Users expect to find in their Web browsers the same applications that they run on their local computers, making these Web applications more complicated than ever.

More and more Web applications use the REpresentational State Transfer (REST) architectural style, which separates the concerns of the server (store, process, and serve resources) with the client application (present information). Simple Object Access Protocol (SOAP) used to be the main protocol to expose services to clients. However, starting from the 2000s, many organizations migrated their services from SOAP to REST to widen developers' accessibility to their data. For example, in 2006, Google deprecated SOAP for its Search API and moved to REST[1]. The number of REST API published increased every year, from 445 APIs in 2007 to over 24k APIs in 2021[2].

The word "practice", as defined by Oxford Dictionary, is a way of doing something. In REST API, a good practice is a good way to implement the REST

---

[1] https://groups.google.com/g/google.public.web-apis/c/YOHPWSqcFBA.
[2] https://www.programmableweb.com/apis/directory.

© Springer Nature Switzerland AG 2021
H. Hacid et al. (Eds.): ICSOC 2021, LNCS 13121, pp. 153–170, 2021.
https://doi.org/10.1007/978-3-030-91431-8_10

API for simplicity, mutual understanding, and reusable code. On the other hand, while resolving a problem, a bad practice is not "good" in other aspects.

As with any other architectural style, REST APIs can be more or less "well" used and, therefore, the subjects of good and bad practices. To evaluate how good a REST system is, Richardson proposed a maturity model for REST APIs[3]. Other researchers also proposed good practices to make REST APIs more understandable and reusable [10,14]. The academic and gray literature report 19 problems related to REST APIs and their uses. For example, Rodríguez et al. [15] found out that only a few Web services reach maturity Level 3, which is defined as "Hypermedia as the engine of state".

The literature has so far not systematically described these problems and practices in the form of design (anti)patterns, which are, in general, a problem, a recurring design with bad consequences, and an alternative solution with more positive results [1].

Therefore, we follow the "**Design Science Research Methodology**"[13] to propose three contributions: **(1)** we review the academic and gray literature related to REST APIs and identify 19 common good and bad practices, **(2)** we propose practical solutions to these problems and formalize them in the form of REST API design anti-patterns, and **(3)** we validate our solutions via surveys and interviews of 55 participants.

The rest of the paper is as follows. Section 2 summarises the related work. Section 3 describes the approaches. Section 4 discusses each practices with concrete implementations of the solutions. Section 5 explains how we evaluated our solutions with developers. Section 6 discusses threats to validity as well as our observations. Section 7 conclude the paper with future work.

2   Related Work

Masse, in the book "REST API Design Rulebook" [10], defined 84 rules to design a consistent REST API, some of which became *de facto* standard, e.g., "Amorphous URIs" or "CRUD function name should not be used in URIs" (aka "CRUDy URIs").

Rodriguez et al. [16] proposed the "Content negotiation" good practice: servers should serve different formats of the same resources on request. Fredrich [2] defined three bad practices, including "Context-less resource name", "Non-hierarchical nodes", "Singularized and Pluralized Nodes". He also gave two good practices, which are "List pagination" and "API Versioning".

Evdemon gave examples of bad URIs and proposed the "CRUDy URIs" bad practice, where CRUD verbs are included in the URI[4]. Palma et al. [12] defined the "Non-pertinent documentation" bad practice, where the documentation is not matching the actual REST APIs. Tilkov defined seven REST API bad practices[5], including "Breaking self-descriptiveness", "Forgetting Hypermedia" (bad

---

[3] http://martinfowler.com/articles/richardsonMaturityModel.html.

[4] https://bit.ly/3i5CIsc.

[5] https://www.infoq.com/articles/rest-anti-patterns/.

practice of "Entity Linking"), "Ignoring MIME type" (bad practice of "Content negotiation"), "Ignoring status code", and "Misusing cookies".

For the bad practice "Tunnel everything through GET" and "Tunnel everything through POST", we combine them with other misuses of HTTP Verbs into "Use the wrong HTTP Verbs" for simplicity. "Breaking self-descriptiveness" means developers ignore standardized headers, formats, protocols, and use nonstandard ones. "Ignoring status code" happens when a server does not use status codes or use the wrong ones; "Misusing cookies" when a server store the session's state or cookies, breaking the statelessness of REST APIs.

In addition to these practices, we propose two new good practices: "Server Timeout" and "POST-PUT-PATCH Return", which we discuss in Sect. 4.

Researchers proposed solutions for some bad practices. Frameworks also provide some support to avoid some bad practices. We examine here ASP.NET Core[6] and Java Spring[7] because of their popularity and community support.

For "Content negotiation", Lemlouma et al. [7] designed "Negotiation and adaptation core (NAC)" that works as a proxy between the media servers and the consuming clients. Based on the client profile, the NAC converts the response to an appropriate format. This is a general architecture and its authors do not discuss any implementation.

For "Endpoint Redirection (URL Redirection)", we could not find any academic solution. The gray literature only explains the concept of URL redirection and how to set it up in some servers. Popular servers, like Microsoft IIS or Apache Tomcat, implement URL redirection with some configuration[8].

For "Entity Linking", we could not find any academic work, blog, or technical tutorials with concrete implementations. However, Liskin et al. [8] described a wrapper module to convert a normal response to a response that conforms to "Entity Linking", which allows improving old REST systems not supporting Entity Linking and reaching Level 3 in Richardson's Maturity Model.

For "Server Timeout", Eastbury et al. proposed a design[9], which we extend to maximize its benefit for REST API developers in Sect. 4.5.

"Response caching" is a common good practice. Both of the examined Web frameworks offer multiple built-in caching techniques.

For "List Pagination", both Google and Microsoft[10] suggested that REST APIs returning lists should use pagination. Masse [10] also stated that collections should be returned in chunks. Murphy et al. [11] showed that pagination was proposed in 24 over 32 REST API company guidelines. Both of the examined Web frameworks support this good practice.

In general, previous work mostly identified and defined good and bad REST API practices. A few authors proposed solutions to the bad practices, often with limitations. For each practice, we discuss and compare its solutions with our own. We also provide concrete implementations in two popular frame-

---

[6] https://dotnet.microsoft.com/apps/aspnet.

[7] https://spring.io/projects.

[8] https://bit.ly/34AUbRu and https://bit.ly/3i6X8Ry.

[9] https://bit.ly/2R9clXf.

[10] https://bit.ly/2RY62pW and https://git.io/JGRwC.

works (ASP.NET and Java Spring). We also provide sample implementations for "Response Caching" and "List Pagination", supported by the frameworks.

3   Categories of Good and Bad Practices of REST APIs

To categorize the REST API practices, we extensively reviewed both academic papers and gray literature (i.e., blog posts, technical tutorials, StackOverflow, etc.) and studied the existing open-source REST API systems. In total, we reviewed seven papers and four gray documents (see https://git.io/JwWeh).

We identified 19 REST API practices and divided them into two categories: technical and non-technical. The technical category includes practices that can be solved or made conformed by an architectural solution or some Web framework's features. The non-technical category includes practices that require developers' efforts to conform, which are usually domain- or business-specific.

For example, the URI structures should represent the relationships between the nodes to avoid the "Non-hierarchical Nodes" bad practice. Yet, companies disagree on using URI to show this relationship and even discourage nesting structures. Another example, for the "Using the wrong HTTP Verbs" bad practice, IBM only mentions GET and POST while Google use GET, POST, PUT, DELETE and invents some new verbs like LIST and MOVE [11].

For each practice in the technical category, we propose an architectural solution or good practice in Sect. 4, which should be simple but guarantee the conformance to the good practice with minimal effort. Practices in the non-technical category require developers' inputs and are not directly solvable.

Table 1 summarises the practices. The practices with (+) have built-in or partial solutions in the examined frameworks, which we discuss and compare to our solutions in Sect. 4. The good practices are green; the bad ones red.

Table 1. Categorizing REST API practices

Technical	Non-technical
Content negotiation (+)	Entity Endpoint
Endpoint redirection	Contextless Resource name
Entity Linking	Non-hierarchical Nodes
Response caching (+)	Amorphous URIs
API Versioning	CRUDy URIs
Server Timeout	Singularized Pluralized Nodes
POST-PUT-PATCH Return (+)	Non-pertinent Documentation
List Pagination (+)	Breaking Self-descriptiveness
	Ignoring status code
	Using the wrong HTTP Verbs
	Misusing Cookies

Besides existing solutions, we examined 23 software design patterns for object-oriented programming [3] to design concrete implementations for each of the eight good practices in the technical category. For some practice, we adapted these concrete implementations to fit with the REST API frameworks. If no design pattern could solve a problem, we extended our search to the gray literature.

The Web frameworks already have built-in features for "Response Caching" and "List Pagination". Therefore, we only present these solutions and provide sample usages for the sake of completeness. For "Content negotiation", we compare our solutions with the built-in features. Developers can use the solutions that fit with their projects based on their advantages and disadvantages.

4   REST API Anti-patterns

We now present each practice using the following structure: **(1)** Practice name, **(2)** Problem statement, **(3)** Expected result/output, **(4)** Solution, and **(5)** Sample implementation/source code. For the sake of space, we put out implementations in a GitHub repository: https://github.com/huntertran/restapi-practices-impl.

We exclude the "Response Caching" and "List Pagination" good practices out of this research because they are already well supported by Web frameworks.

4.1   Content Negotiation

Problem: The client can only process and manipulate the resources in some formats. For example, JSON is faster to parse and smaller to transport over the Internet while XML supports namespaces, comments, and metadata. A client may favor one over another.

Expected Result: We expect: **(1)** Resources of a same type should be served in various formats (JSON and XML, image file formats, Base64 encoded, etc.); **(2)** The server should set a default format if the client does not specify a requested format; **(3)** The implementation of each data format should be easily modifiable and expandable for new data formats.

Solution: Based on the request header, the server prepares the data in the requested format, then returns the data in the response body. We could use the Factory design pattern [3]. For each format, there could be a corresponding concrete Factory. In the `ObjectFactory` class[11], developers could set the default format by using the `default:` clause of the `switch` statement. (See https://git.io/JwW08).

Both Java Spring and ASP.NET core support content negotiation with the default set to JSON format. Below is the feature comparison table.

---

[11] https://git.io/JwWC6.

	Java Spring	ASP.NET core	Our
Common media types	Yes	Yes	Yes
Customizable serializer	No	Yes	Yes
Require data annotation on model	Yes	No	No
Built-in support ignorable	Yes	Yes	N/A

ASP.NET Core has the most flexible support for Content Negotiation. In Java Spring, developers cannot override the serializer, but can combine multiple approaches to achieve the desired effect. The XML format in Java requires data annotation to be added to the model classes, which sometimes require changes to the design of the data model.

4.2   Endpoint Redirection

Problem: Resources can be moved to new locations when the data structure changes or developers refactor the URI structure. However, a client could request resources using the old URIs; the server should answer these requests with HTTP Code 3xx and the new locations.

Expected Result: Most of the REST APIs frameworks use the Model-View-Controller pattern (MVC). The solution should be built on or integrated with the MVC pattern. It should satisfy the following: **(1)** There should be a class that handles redirection logic, separated from other classes; **(2)** The redirection logic should have the same interface as the old controller class; **(3)** The new controller class should extend or include the redirection logic, but still conform to the *Single Responsibility Principle* [9].

Solution: There are two possible solutions for this practice. Each solution will have advantages and disadvantages.

Solution 1: Extend a `Redirector` Class: In this solution, the old controller and the redirector implement the same interface. The new controller extends the redirector class. The methods in the new controller and the redirector are exposed as API endpoints to the clients. (See https://git.io/JwWMn).

Solution 2: Nested Class Inside the New Controller: The redirection logic is separated into a stand-alone class, implementing the interface of the old controller class. The difference with the previous solution is that the redirection logic class is a nested class inside the new controller. Thus, the redirector can access methods and variables in the controller. (See https://git.io/JwWDo).

The new controller implements the interface of the old controller and contains a private instance of the redirector class. The interface implementation makes sure all the old methods are properly handled. The private instance works as a proxy to the actual logic of the redirector class.

Comparison Between Both Solutions

	Extend	Nested
Pros	Redirection logic separated in classes	Allows the outer class (the main class) be inherited from another class
	Easier implementation. Can be implemented in multiple languages	The Redirector has access to methods/variables in the controller
Cons	The Redirector cannot access resources in the controller	Redirection logic coded inside the controller
	The controller cannot inherit other classes (w/o multiple inheritance)	Not all languages support nested classes

4.3   Entity Linking

Problem: Developers must find programmatically links to resources related to a current, requested resource. For example, when designing a service for a content management system (CMS), after sending a GET request to retrieve a post, if conforming to the Entity Linking good practice, the server should return the post details, including links to comments and likes. The response below helps developers to post new comments or get the likes on the post.

```
1   {"post": {"title": "Lorem ipsum","content": "Lorem ipsum",
2         "links":[{"rel":"comment","method":"post","uri":"/post/123/comment"},
3               {"rel":"like","method": "get","uri":"/post/123/like"}]}}
```

With the "Forgetting Hypermedia" bad practice, the links in the response are not available. Therefore, developers do not know if they can post a new comment or get the likes on a post. They must make requests to the server to find out, possibly by trial-and-error. If they cannot, for some reason, the server refuses their requests with HTTP Code 4xx.

Expected Result: (1) The current controller should have access to other controllers to check the availability of related resources; **(2)** The current controller should have access to class and method information (names, annotations, public and private variables, etc.) because Web frameworks use naming conventions/annotation to construct URIs.

Solution: The method that handles the current request has a list of related classes containing the related resources. To loop through the list, all these classes should implement a same interface. To access the methods provided by this interface in different classes, we could use the Visitor design pattern [9] with language reflection features to access data annotations.

All the controllers intended to be used for populating links for related resources must implement a LinkedResource interface. This interface has a method accept() that accept a Visitor instance of type ResourceVisitor. For each logic to select the resource to be included, a separate, concrete Visitor is created. These visitors could share some common logic in an abstract class `CommonResourceVisitor`, also a good place for the reflection logic.

A sample implementation with reflection is available for ASP.NET Core and Java Spring. (See https://git.io/JwWjZ and https://git.io/JwleR).

4.4 API Versioning

Problem: REST API system evolves. In traditional software systems, developers can release new versions while old ones continue working. With Web applications, a new version may break the client applications. The client-application developers may not be aware of breaking changes and may not have enough time to adapt to the changes before changes break their application.

In addition to communicating and advertising new versions of some REST APIs, REST API developers must support the old APIs in parallel with the new ones for a time. This parallelisation allows the coexistence of multiple versions of the API. To separate the old APIs from the new ones, developers can choose one of two approaches: **(1)** Include the version of the API in the URI: Version the API globally for all resources or separately for each type of the resources; **(2)** Include the version in the header(s), in the `accept` header or a custom header chosen by the REST API developers.

Expected Result: (1) The URIs of a version should not change over time. The client application always receive the expected results when requesting a resource during the lifetime of that version; **(2)** Client applications can access multiple versions of the APIs simultaneously. The Web application supports multiple versions at a same time; **(3)** The Web application can use a single database. If breaking changes occur in the database, a mechanism should translate the old and new data for any object.

Solution: Section 2 show existing solutions, which we compare to ours below.

We propose using the Proxy design pattern to redirect/convert requests to old versions of the API. For each version of the API, there should be a corresponding interface. The interface does not serve a purpose in the current version but is the contract with the next version. A class contains a private instance of each old API classes that support this next version. The versions of the API may also have common logic that did not change over time and can be factored into an abstract class; then, the API controllers inherit from it. (See https://git.io/JwQKX).

One advantage of this solution is that a new version of an API only implements the interfaces of old versions if they must be supported. For example, if there is a Version 3, which should support both Versions 1 and 2, then a controller for Version 3 implements the interfaces of Versions 1 and 2 only, which does not require a "chain of adapters" and allows developers to support versions not ordered in time, e.g., Version 4 could support Version 1 and 3, when compared to the solution proposed in [4]. In addition, this solution is implemented in the server itself, differently from the solution proposed in [6].

4.5   Server Timeout

Problem: When there is a long-running operation on a REST API server, the client must wait to receive a response. In traditional software systems, the communication between the running operation and the consumer of its results is permanent. However, in a Web application, clients and servers communicate over the Internet, which introduces some potential problems: if the client and the server are disconnected, the operation continues to run on the server, but the result is no longer needed/accessible. Similarly, if the client cancels or abandons its request, wasting the server's resources.

Expected Result: The long-running operation should have a mechanism to cancel itself when needed, releasing resources held by its process.

Solution: Two solutions could solve the problems. The combined implementation of both solutions produces the best results but with increased complexity.

Solution 1: Timeout: The developers define a timeout for the operation. When the time is up, the server cancels the process. However, in some cases, when there are unpredictable factors, this solution is not practical. For example, if the operation depends on data retrieved through the Internet, then its speed is not stable and it is challenging to find an appropriate timeout value.

Since Java 1.5, developers can use `ExecutorService` to start a new single thread in Java. Then, they can submit a long running operation wrapped in a `Callable` object. Similarly, in ASP.NET Core, developers can use `TimeOutAfter` or `CancellationTokenSource.CancelAfter`[12] in .NET 5.0 or later.

Solution 2: Asynchronous Request-Reply Pattern (HTTP Polling): This solution requires some extra work from both server and client developers. First, server developers must implement an operation status checker and a cache system to store the operation result on the server. Then, client developers must implement a polling mechanism that periodically polls the operation status and, finally, gets the response from the `Resource Endpoint`. (See https://git.io/Jw7fS).

Comparisons Between the Two Solutions

	Timeout	Async request-reply
Pros	No requirement on client side	Client and server can re-establish connection after disconnection
	Easier to implement	Serves the same results instantly
	Single system involved	
Cons	Risk of incorrect predefined timeout value	Requires changes in both client and server
		Requires a mechanism to store results
	If the client disconnects early, the server still wastes resources until timeout	

---

[12] https://git.io/JwQPs and https://bit.ly/3vDwdB1.

Combination of Both Solutions

Developers can combine both solutions to maximize their benefits, especially when following the Asynchronous Request-Reply pattern, because they only need a little extra work to combine both solutions. There are three stages: (1) initialisation, (2) polling, and (3) termination. During initialisation, the client sends a request to the server that starts the long-running operation. The server registers the operation status. During polling, the client periodically polls for the result. With each polling request, the server resets the timeout. In case of a disconnection between the client and server, the server timeouts and aborts the process and releases any resources. (See https://git.io/Jw7La).

4.6   POST-PUT-PATCH Return

Problem: When a client application sends a request to modify a database (create, update, or delete), the server usually only returns a simple result indicating success/failure, like HTTP Code 200. The client does not know immediately the added/modified object and whether it was correctly committed to the database until the client makes a new request for that particular object.

When there is a mismatched datatype between the model classes and the data posted by the client, the server may still work by simply ignoring any mismatched data, writing everything else to the database. The server would still signal that the writing process was successful. The client could wrongly believe that the operation was entirely successful although its data and the data written to the database are different.

However, sending the created/modified object in the response body could cost transmission time and network bandwidth, i.e., some clients may not need to know/confirm that the committed data in the database is correct.

Expected Result: The name "POST-PUT-PATCH return" of this practice is based on the HTTP verbs POST, PUT, and PATCH. We expect: **(1)** A mechanism for the client to control the response, if it only needs a HTTP Code 200; **(2)** Separation of database and business logic; **(3)** Minimal requests to the database.

Solution: To separate the database manipulation logic from the business logic, we use the Repository pattern. To make sure a database transaction was successfully executed before returning its result to the client, we could use the Unit of Work pattern[13]. In general, there should be a repository that handles CRUD operations for each resource or groups of related resources. This class is injected into controllers using Dependency Injection. In addition, each repository implements the Unit of Work pattern. (See https://git.io/Jw7q3).

Java Spring has a Repository pattern built-in with basic CRUD operations, see details in https://bit.ly/3c6GFcs. ASP.NET Core does not have this pattern built-in. Still, there is an instruction on how to implement them, see details in https://bit.ly/3uCO9du. Both frameworks support Dependency Injection and

---

[13] https://bit.ly/3uCO9du.

Unit of Work. Sample implementations exist for Java Spring at https://git.io/Jw7md and ASP.NET Core at https://git.io/Jw73w.

5   Evaluations

Although good/bad practices come from a consensus in the academic/professional communities, our solutions must be validated by experienced developers, who only can confirm that our solutions (**1**) solve bad practices, (**2**) conform to good practices, and (**3**) are acceptable in industrial environments.

Consequently, we designed a validation survey and administered it to 55 professional REST API developers. We now describe our methodology and the obtained results, which show that our solutions indeed remove bad practices and are acceptable by professional developers.

5.1   Overview

We obtained an ethics certificate from the Office of Research of our university; university and number hidden for double-blind review. We follow the "Questionnaire Survey" empirical standard by ACM[14]. We divided the survey into sections. Each section contained one practice, problem identification, a short explanation for the good practice, and the concrete implementation in ASP.NET core and Java Spring. To increase the response rates, we split the survey into two Parts A and B.

5.2   Survey Design

In each section, we asked two questions: (**1**) Did you face this/these problem(s) in some of your projects? (**2**) Is it a good design?. Each question has an "Other" option with a text-box if the participant has comments.

Using these two questions, we can know: (**1**) The prevalence of the problem in industrial environments; (**2**) How well received are the solutions to the bad practices; (**3**) Do alternative implementations exist?

At the end of the survey, we asked for age group, education, current profession, and employment status.

5.3   Participants Selection

We selected participants who are: (**1**) Adult; (**2**) Professional developers; (**3**) Use OOP languages. We recruited participants through a convenient sampling of software developers and engineers through e-mail lists, social media (LinkedIn, GitHub), etc.

5.4   Participants' Demographics

Figures 1, 2, 3, 4 and 5 summarise participants' demographic information.

---

[14] https://acmsigsoft.github.io/EmpiricalStandards/docs/.

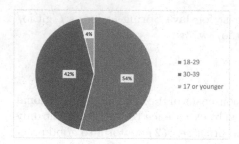

Fig. 1. Participants' age groups

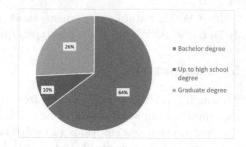

Fig. 2. Participants' education

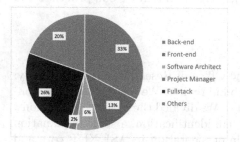

Fig. 3. Participants' profession

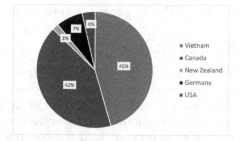

Fig. 4. Participants' country of origin

5.5   Qualitative Analyses

We sent our survey to 55 professional developers. Out of 55, 51 developers completed at least one of the surveys. We received 68 complete surveys (Parts A and B). The number of completed surveys is greater than the number of participants because some participants completed both Parts A and B. We received 17 incomplete responses. Because of the randomized orders of the question, we could still extract valuable data from these responses. Thus, the average completion rate of both surveys is 76%.

We extracted and analyzed the completed parts of the incomplete survey, whose questions were all answered by the participants. Table 2 shows the percentage of positive responses.

Some participants do not use the frameworks considered in this study but different ones, like `nodejs` with JavaScript or `Flask` with Python. Some good practices proposed in this study did not apply to these frameworks. Therefore, participants answered the survey questions using the "Other" option.

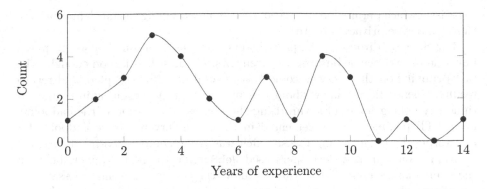

Fig. 5. Participant's years of experience

Table 2. The positive results statistics of the survey

	Face this problem	Std. dev.	Good solution	Std. dev.
Content negotiation	52.4%	2.289	76.2%	1.952
Endpoint redirection	45%	2.225	75%	1.936
Entity linking	47.4%	2.177	57.9%	2.152
API versioning	72.2%	1.901	72.2%	1.901
Server timeout	77.8%	1.763	66.7%	1.999
POST-PUT-PATCH return	58.8%	2.029	82.4%	1.570

5.6 Quantitative Analyses

Landis et al. [5] proposed a scale for the strength of agreement, with 61%–80% labeled as "Substantial". We decided to use the threshold, average value of 70%, to determine which good practices are acceptable or require further analysis.

For the **Content Negotiation, Endpoint Redirection, API Versioning,** and **POST-PUT-PATCH Return** good practices, more than 70% developers agreed that the proposed solutions are good. Further interviews with some of the developers also confirm that the solution for **Content Negotiation** is used in industrial environments even if not publicly published as a good practice.

Two good practices have positive answers below 70%. We interviewed five participants who answered "No" or "Other" for these practices to understand the reasons behind their choices. In addition, we also asked their opinions on other practices to which they give positive responses.

For **Entity Linking**, there is an alternative approach that avoids the actual problem of entity linking. In the first login, the server sends a set of allowed permission to the client, including the API endpoints related to these permissions. Therefore, the client can use this set of permissions and endpoints to know if it can request specific resources or not. This approach frees the server from calculating the related resources (hence linked entities) and endpoints of these resources. In addition, it is easier to implement. Companies that allow third-parties developers to register which permission they need, thus avoid providing too much information that could raise privacy concerns.

For **Server Timeout**, the participants used the solution that we proposed but, due to the specific business requirements, it was still not good enough. The tasks running on their servers could take several hours to complete and return results. Clients did not know about this processing time, resulting in them continuously polling for results, throttling the servers. Furthermore, the endpoints for HTTP polling were implemented in the same servers as the endpoint for registering the long-running tasks, which was not recommended in the original solution. Consequently, developers used `WebSocket` to create tunnels between the clients and servers. These tunnels allow the servers to "send" messages to the clients when the task are completed. Yet, this solution cannot be used when uploading large files. Usually, a dedicated server will be used for this specific case, with HTTP polling or job queue.

6   Discussions

6.1   Threats to Validity

While most developers agreed/somewhat agreed on our solutions, there are some threats to validity that we would like to discuss.

Internal Validity: Our solutions assume that the developers are using object-oriented programming languages, like C# or Java. There are other languages for back-end programming trending in recent years. For example, JavaScript with `nodejs`, Go with `Gin`, etc. In addition, there are other Web frameworks from the community for C# like OpenRasta and NancyFx, although they are not as popular as ASP.NET. For Java, besides Spring, there are multiple Web frameworks, like Struts and Grails. These frameworks could have different approaches to good and bad practices. We could minimize this threat by expanding the survey and ask other framework experts.

We looked for existing solutions in both academic and gray literature, conforming to good practices in reviewing previous work. However, we may have missed some solutions due to inconsistencies in vocabulary, titles and contents, etc. We minimized this threat by using multiple related keywords to search the academic and gray literature.

External Validity: We proposed six solutions to practically implement REST API good practices. To evaluate these solutions, we surveyed back-end developers. Due to the number of proposed solutions, the survey was quite long. The participants could become tired by the end of the survey and answer the questions with lower attention than those near the start. These responses could bias our analysis. To minimize this threat, we divided the survey in two parts and tried to be as concise as possible. We also put the questions of the "Response Caching" and "List Pagination" good practices at the end of the survey, because they are supported or partially supported by the web frameworks.

Developers depend on their experiences and domain knowledge to concretely implement good practices and avoid bad practices. Therefore, their levels of expertise may affect the survey result. More experienced developers could see potential problems in our solutions or evaluate these solutions more thoroughly. Less experienced developers may favor our solutions or not have experienced the practice problems. We tried to minimize this threat by asking and controlling for age groups, education level, and current profession.

In general, we could minimize threats to internal validity in future work by examining more Web frameworks and programming languages. For external threats, we could conduct more one-on-one interviews with developers to find out their experience and ask for their feedback and concrete solutions.

6.2   Developers' Feedback on Solutions

As presented in Sect. 5, for "Content Negotiation", "Endpoint Redirection", "API Versioning", and "POST-PUT-PATCH return", we received more than 70% positive responses. However, some developers commented our solutions and proposed other solutions. We summarise and analyse each participants' comment in the following.

Endpoint Redirection Good Practice
Comment 1: *It is better to use a proxy or a service broker*

Using a proxy server or service could solve the problem but the proxy/service would have to implement the exact resource mapping mechanism proposed by the good practice solution. In addition, it would have to implement mechanisms to "catch" the request that needs redirecting, making it more complex than ours.

API Versioning Good Practice
Comment 1: *At least with the version in URI, I don't have to modify my code as long as that version is available. For the suggested design, I'll have to modify my code and still have to rely on the availability of the old version.*

The suggested solution does not force developers to choose a specific versioning type, see Sect. 4.4. It provides a solution that helps developers to reuse business logic. Besides, developers should apply good practices when designing their applications, not when refactoring or introducing a new feature.

Server Timeout
Comment 1: *Use http2, Web socket for request from frontend, use grpc or a pub/sub if request from back-end*

An interview with the participant helped us understand this comment: the participant's company uses the proposed good practice. Yet, the specific business of the company makes the system perform poorly. Indeed, a single task could run for hours. To address this issue, developers use multiple approaches, including: **http2:** The major next revision of the HTTP network protocol that supports a single connection from the browser to the back-end; **WebSocket:** A communication protocol supporting two-way communication over a single TCP connection; **gRPC:** Google Remote Procedure Calls, an open-source remote procedure call framework that uses `http2`; **publisher/subscriber pattern:** A messaging pattern allowing a publisher to emit multiple events to multiple subscribers interested in these events.

The participant's company has the advantage of controlling both back-end and front-end applications. Therefore, they can use new technologies that are still in beta development or require major changes/complex implementations.

POST-PUT-PATCH Return Good Practice

Comment 1: *If DB doesn't return data for create and update operation, we need to make an additional get operation to DB.*

The focus of the good practice is on the back-end. We explained in Sect. 4.6 that there should be a mechanism to control the response if it only needs a HTTP Code 200. Both considered Web frameworks optimise database requests using "Lazy Loading". Application only query databases when data is needed.

Comment 2: *Depends on the type of requirement. Clean Architecture and applying CQRS is better with a solution that is complex and needs scaling.*

Clean Architecture is an architectural style that splits the concerns of the application into a central domain logic and multiple cross-cutting concerns, like caching, authentication, authorization, rendering, etc. The concerns work with each other via interfaces. This architectural style is not related to the issues tackled by the good practice. *CQRS* stands for *Command Query Responsibility Segregation*, which is a pattern stating that developers should use a different model to update information than the model to read information. Again, this pattern is not directly related to the issue and the good practice.

6.3   Developers and Bad Practices

All the bad practices in the non-technical category require constant review by experienced developers. For example, the "CRUDy URIs" bad practice is not solvable with an architectural design but by continuously watching the API endpoints in development. Therefore, there is a need to develop tools to support developers during development. Such tools are out of the scope of this study.

7   Conclusion

In this paper, we presented an up-to-date list of good and bad practices to design REST API systems, divided into 8 technical and 11 non-technical practices. For each technical practice, we proposed and discussed practical solutions and concrete implementations. For three of the four most common practices, **Content Negotiation**, **API Versioning**, and **Endpoint Redirection**, we compared/supplemented the existing solutions with new solutions and implementations that increase their benefits. To determine how acceptable our solutions were and how well they could be applied in industrial environments, we surveyed and interviewed 55 developers. Results of our survey and one-on-one interviews showed that most of the developers agreed with our solutions. Developers also confirmed that their companies use some good practices and other approaches that fit their specific business. Hence, we contributed by:

1. Reviewing REST API practices usage in the academic and gray literature.
2. Providing solutions and concrete implementations to these practices.
3. Validating our solutions with professional developers.

We conclude that our solutions are relevant to developers and researchers as a basis for implementation and future, quantitative studies (e.g., detection).

In future work, we could extend our approach to provide concrete implementation for Service Oriented Architecture (SOA). Our approach could be generalized by applying it to other good/bad practices. For the practices to which we cannot apply our approach, we could do further research to categorise them based on other criteria, like the numbers of parties involved or the server architectural style. We could also expand the survey and have more one-on-one interviews to qualify more precisely our solutions.

References

1. Brown, W.H., Malveau, R.C., McCormick, H.W.S., Mowbray, T.J.: AntiPatterns: Refactoring Software, Architectures, and Projects in Crisis. Wiley, New York (1998)
2. Fredrich, T.: Restful service best practices. Recommendations for Creating Web Services, pp. 1–34 (2012)
3. Gamma, E., Helm, R., Johnson, R., Vlissides, J.: Design patterns: abstraction and reuse of object-oriented design. In: Nierstrasz, O.M. (ed.) ECOOP 1993. LNCS, vol. 707, pp. 406–431. Springer, Heidelberg (1993). https://doi.org/10.1007/3-540-47910-4_21
4. Kaminski, P., Litoiu, M., Müller, H.: A design technique for evolving web services. In: Proceedings of the 2006 CASCON, p. 23-es (2006)
5. Landis, J.R., Koch, G.G.: The measurement of observer agreement for categorical data. Biometrics **33**, 159–174 (1977)
6. Leitner, P., Michlmayr, A., Rosenberg, F., Dustdar, S.: End-to-end versioning support for web services. In: 2008 IEEE SCC, vol. 1, pp. 59–66 (2008)
7. Lemlouma, T., Layaïda, N.: NAC: a basic core for the adaptation and negotiation of multimedia services. Opera Project, Inria (2001)
8. Liskin, O., Singer, L., Schneider, K.: Teaching old services new tricks: adding HATEOAS support as an afterthought. In: Proceedings of the 2nd WS-REST 2011, pp. 3–10 (2011)
9. Martin, R.C.: Agile Software Development: Principles, Patterns, and Practices. Prentice Hall, Hoboken (2002)
10. Masse, M.: REST API Design Rulebook: Designing Consistent RESTful Web Service Interfaces. O'Reilly Media, Inc., Sebastopol (2011)
11. Murphy, L., Alliyu, T., Macvean, A., Kery, M.B., Myers, B.A.: Preliminary analysis of REST API style guidelines. Ann Arbor **1001**, 48109 (2017)
12. Palma, F., Gonzalez-Huerta, J., Founi, M., Moha, N., Tremblay, G., Guéhéneuc, Y.G.: Semantic analysis of restful APIs for the detection of linguistic patterns and antipatterns. IJCIS **26**(02), 1742001 (2017)
13. Peffers, K., Tuunanen, T., Rothenberger, M.A., Chatterjee, S.: A design science research methodology for information systems research. J. Manag. Inf. Syst. **24**(3), 45–77 (2007)

14. Petrillo, F., Merle, P., Moha, N., Guéhéneuc, Y.-G.: Are REST APIs for cloud computing well-designed? An exploratory study. In: Sheng, Q.Z., Stroulia, E., Tata, S., Bhiri, S. (eds.) ICSOC 2016. LNCS, vol. 9936, pp. 157–170. Springer, Cham (2016). https://doi.org/10.1007/978-3-319-46295-0_10
15. Rodríguez, C., et al.: REST APIs: a large-scale analysis of compliance with principles and best practices. In: Bozzon, A., Cudre-Maroux, P., Pautasso, C. (eds.) ICWE 2016. LNCS, vol. 9671, pp. 21–39. Springer, Cham (2016). https://doi.org/10.1007/978-3-319-38791-8_2
16. Rodriguez, J.M., Crasso, M., Zunino, A., Campo, M.: Automatically detecting opportunities for web service descriptions improvement. In: Cellary, W., Estevez, E. (eds.) I3E 2010. IAICT, vol. 341, pp. 139–150. Springer, Heidelberg (2010). https://doi.org/10.1007/978-3-642-16283-1_18

Are Developers Equally Concerned About Making Their APIs RESTful and the Linguistic Quality? A Study on Google APIs

Francis Palma[(⊠)] [iD], Osama Zarraa, and Ahmad Sadia

SIG, Department of Computer Science and Media Technology,
Linnaeus University, Växjö, Sweden
francis.palma@lnu.se, {oz222am,as224zk}@student.lnu.se
https://lnu.se/en/research/searchresearch/smart-industry-group/

Abstract. REST (REpresentational State Transfer) is an architectural style for distributed, hypermedia systems that allows communication between clients and servers using the HTTP methods and URIs (Uniform Resource Identifiers). In the literature, researchers and practitioners defined best design practices, i.e., REST patterns, violation of which are known as REST antipatterns. Also, clients need to understand the use and purpose of APIs while consuming them. A set of best practices is defined in the literature for APIs to have a better linguistic design, i.e., linguistic patterns, violation of which are known as linguistic antipatterns. For API developers, it is challenging to ensure that their APIs are RESTful and manifest linguistic design quality. This paper investigates whether developers are equally concerned about making their APIs RESTful while also focus on designing APIs with better linguistic quality that may facilitate their comprehension and consumption. Thus, we examine the relation between RESTful and linguistic design quality in RESTful APIs. We analyzed eight Google APIs and performed the detection of 21 patterns and antipatterns on those APIs. Using the quantitative data, we performed a series of statistical tests. Results suggest a negligible relationship between RESTful and linguistic design quality. Thus, developers are unaware of whether they conjointly lack RESTful and linguistic design quality.

Keywords: Patterns · Antipatterns · RESTful APIs · Uniform resource identifiers · Detection · RESTful design · Linguistic quality

1 Introduction

Service-Oriented Architecture (SOA) has become the dominant architectural choice within the industry for its ways of developing, deploying, and consuming service-based systems [10]. One can use two major Web services standards to build service-based systems: Simple Object Access Protocol (SOAP) and REpresentational State Transfer (REST). In recent years, REST has become a standard architectural style adopted by many software organizations [11]. The REST

© Springer Nature Switzerland AG 2021
H. Hacid et al. (Eds.): ICSOC 2021, LNCS 13121, pp. 171–187, 2021.
https://doi.org/10.1007/978-3-030-91431-8_11

architectural style is based on the client-server pattern, and relies on HTTP methods and resource URIs (Uniform Resource Identifiers) for communications between the clients and servers [7].

A well-designed RESTful API can attract client developers to use the service and put the service provider ahead of the competition. A RESTful API needs to be truly RESTful, i.e., must adhere to six REST principles defined by Roy T. Fielding [11]. These principles are explained as best design practices, i.e., REST patterns, when violated, known as REST antipatterns. Another important aspect that attracts and benefits client developers is the linguistic design quality of the RESTful APIs. A resource URI that can be easily understood and reused helps the client developers while designing and developing their services-based systems using the RESTful APIs [20]. A set of best practices for APIs to have a better linguistic design is known as linguistic patterns, violation of which can be referred to as linguistic antipatterns.

Due to many constraints, it might be challenging for API developers to ensure that their APIs are RESTful and manifest high linguistic design quality. However, there has been no evidence of whether poorly designed RESTful APIs also have poor linguistic quality; and vice versa for well-designed APIs. Hence, this paper aims to investigate the relation between RESTful design and linguistic quality in RESTful APIs. We analyzed Google RESTful APIs to see whether APIs that (1) have many REST antipatterns also manifest linguistic antipatterns; (2) have many REST antipatterns also manifest linguistic patterns; (3) have many REST patterns also manifest linguistic patterns; and (4) have many REST patterns also manifest linguistic antipatterns. More specifically, we aim to answer research question **RQ$_1$ What is the relationship between the RESTful design and linguistic quality in RESTful APIs?** RQ$_1$ aims to investigate whether RESTful APIs that suffer from antipatterns (or patterns) with respect to RESTful design are also prone to linguistic antipatterns (or patterns). To answer RQ$_1$, we further answer the following research questions:

RQ$_{1.1}$: What is the relationship between REST antipatterns and linguistic antipatterns in RESTful APIs?

RQ$_{1.2}$: What is the relationship between REST antipatterns and linguistic patterns in RESTful APIs?

RQ$_{1.3}$: What is the relationship between REST patterns and linguistic patterns in RESTful APIs?

RQ$_{1.4}$: What is the relationship between REST patterns and linguistic antipatterns in RESTful APIs?

To find the relationship between REST design quality and linguistic quality in the RESTful APIs, we analyzed eight Google RESTful APIs. We performed the detection of 21 patterns and antipatterns on those eight Google APIs. The results suggest that the relationship between the RESTful design and linguistic design quality is negligible, i.e., developers are aware of whether they conjointly lack RESTful design and linguistic quality.

Thus, the main contributions of this study include (1) empirical evidence that RESTful APIs concurrently lack RESTful design and linguistic design quality,

Table 1. REST patterns and antipatterns.

REST patterns and antipatterns
Breaking Self-descriptiveness (BSD) antipattern occurs when REST developers ignore the standardized headers, formats, or protocols [22]
Forgetting Hypermedia (FH) antipattern occurs due to the lack of proper entity linking and hinders the state transition for REST applications [6,14,22]
Ignoring Caching (IC) antipattern occurs when due to implementation complexity, client and server developers ignore caching capability [6,14,22]
Ignoring MIME Types (IMT) antipattern occurs when server fails to represent resources in various formats, limiting resources reusability and accessibility [6,22]
Ignoring Status Code (ISC) antipattern occurs when API developers avoid using the defined set of application-level status code [6,22]
Misusing Cookies (MC) antipattern occurs when a Set-cookie or a Cookie header contains keys or tokens that supposed to be sent by other standardized means [14,22]
Content Negotiation (CN) pattern allows a service to support multiple resource representations based on the metadata provided by the consumer [6,9,14]
Entity Linking (EL) pattern enables communication by providing hyperlinks to the service consumers in response messages [6,9]
Response Caching (RC) pattern caches all response messages in the local client machine to avoid sending duplicate requests or responses [6,9]

and, as a whole, RESTful APIs that are not (truly) RESTful exhibit poor linguistic design quality, and vice-versa; (2) the extension of SOFA framework [20] by integrating eight Google APIs to the framework and the detection of 21 patterns and antipatterns on those Google APIs.

In the rest of the paper: Sect. 2 provides the background of this work. We provide the study design in Sect. 3 and shows the results in Sect. 4. Section 5 discusses our results in detail while Sect. 6 presents the studies relevant to this study. Finally, Sect. 7 concludes our work and outlines future work.

2   Background

This section briefly introduces REST patterns and antipatterns (Sect. 2) and the SODA approach and SOFA framework (Sect. 2) that we rely on for the detection of REST patterns and antipatterns in this study.

REST Patterns and Antipatterns: This study considers 21 REST and linguistic patterns and antipatterns from the literature. Design patterns and antipatterns in RESTful APIs are considered as best and poor design practices, respectively. For example, Masse [15] in his book discussed numerous rules, i.e., patterns, to design APIs. Practitioners also emphasized many best practices and things to avoid when it comes to designing RESTful APIs [1,6,14,22]. Table 1 introduces nine REST patterns and antipatterns, and Table 2 lists twelve linguistic patterns and antipatterns.

Table 2. Linguistic patterns and antipatterns.

Linguistic patterns and antipatterns
Contextualized vs. Contextless Resource Names: Applying *Contextualized Resource Names* pattern ensures that all nodes in a URI belong to a semantically related context. The corresponding antipattern *Contextless Resource Names* leads to decreased understandability of the API [14, 19]
Hierarchical vs. Non-hierarchical Nodes: The *Hierarchical Nodes* pattern ensures each node in a URI is related, hierarchically, to its adjacent nodes. If not applied, the corresponding antipattern *Non-hierarchical Nodes* occurs that hinders the understandability and usability of an API [14, 19]
Tidy vs. Amorphous URI: A URI is tidy when it has an appropriate lower-case resource naming without any extensions, underscores, or trailing slashes. A URI that does not adhere to this pattern is an *Amorphous URI*. This antipattern may mislead users and decrease readability [1, 19]
Verbless vs. CRUDy URI: A verbless URI does not contain any HTTP method (i.e., Get, Post, Put, or Delete) and their synonyms, rather the action is defined using the HTTP methods. On the other hand, a CRUDy URI uses terms, such as create, read, update, or delete, and their synonyms as part of the URI design, which may confuse API clients and cause an overload on the HTTP methods [1, 6, 14, 19]
Singularised vs. Pluralised Nodes: The singular and plural nouns should be used consistently. The last node of a PUT/DELETE request URI should be singular. The last node should be plural in POST requests. If this pattern is not applied correctly, the *Pluralised Nodes* antipattern occurs, causing unexpected server responses [1, 14, 19]
Versioned vs. Non-versioned URI: As API changes, API versioning is recommended to manage the complexity of these changes. A *Non-versioned URI* antipattern may lead to users' confusion regarding the API version in use and, in worst scenarios, may break existing consumers [1, 6, 14]

SODA Approach and SOFA Framework: The SODA (Service Oriented Detection of Antipatterns) is a rule-based approach proposed in [16, 20] and works in three steps for the detection of antipatterns in service-based systems: (1) specification of rule cards, (2) generation of detection algorithms, and (3) applying detection algorithms on service-based systems. The SOFA (Service Oriented Framework for Antipatterns) implements these steps. Currently, SOFA can detect antipatterns in three service-oriented technologies including SCA (Service Component Architecture) systems, SOAP (Simple Object Access Protocol) Web services, and RESTful Web services. Since the source code for the web services is proprietary, the detection of patterns and antipatterns are at the interface and/or specification level. SOFA performs the detection of both REST patterns and antipatterns [20] and linguistic patterns and antipatterns [16]. In this study, we performed the detection of 21 patterns and antipatterns on eight Google APIs using the SOFA framework.

3   Study Design

This section presents the study design, the RESTful APIs we analyzed, and the dependent and independent variables in this study.

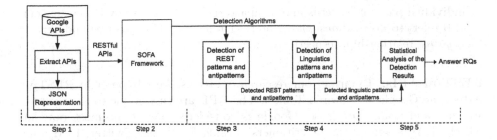

Fig. 1. Study design.

Data Collection and Processing: Figure 1 shows the steps this study adopts to answer our research questions. The remainder of this section briefly describes the steps.

- Step 1: **Extract Google APIs:** In this step, the Google APIs are extracted from https://developers.google.com and stored in a JSON file. Additionally, the required parameters and data-form of each URI are filled into the JSON file. This process is done manually due to the differences among the APIs and URIs in their presentation formats and structures.
- Step 2: **Extend the SOFA framework:** This step involves extending the SOFA framework by adding the collected Google APIs data to detect patterns and antipatterns of both linguistic and RESTful design practices in those APIs. The detection algorithms that we apply are defined in SOFA in the previous studies [19,20]. Thus, in this form, SOFA can be extended for new antipatterns and APIs.
- Step 3: **Detect REST Patterns and Antipatterns:** In this step, the SOFA framework automatically performs the detection of nine REST patterns and antipatterns and export the detection results to CSVs. We further process these CSVs to aggregate the numbers for each REST pattern and antipattern for each Google API.
- Step 4: **Detect Linguistic Patterns and Antipatterns:** Similar to step 3, in this step, the SOFA framework automatically performs the detection of twelve linguistic patterns and antipatterns and exports the detection results to CSVs. Then, we further process the CSVs to aggregate the numbers for each linguistic pattern and antipattern for each Google API.
- Step 5: **Analyze the Data:** Finally, in this last step, the data obtained from steps 3 and 4 are analyzed. The statistical analysis is performed by conducting two types of tests: (1) the Chi-square test of independence and (2) the Phi-coefficient test. The Chi-square test of independence determines if there is a significant relationship between two nominal (categorical) variables [17,21]. We perform a Chi-square test on two groups of patterns and antipatterns at the significance level $p < 0.05$. The Phi-coefficient test, on the other hand, is used to determine the relationship strength between two binary (dichotomous) variables [4,21]. Therefore, it is used when assessing

individual pairs of patterns and antipatterns in this study. A Phi-coefficient of 0 refers to *no relationship*; +1 and −1 refer to *perfect positive* and *perfect negative* relationship, respectively [4,24].

RESTful APIs: To answer our research questions, we rely on eight RESTful APIs from Google as shown in Table 3. The APIs are chosen due to their extensive use and availability. Also, Google is considered one of the most popular RESTful APIs among the practitioners[1] beside Facebook, Twitter, IBM, and Amazon.

Table 3. Google APIs and the number of resource URIs tested.

RESTful APIs	Online documentations	Versions	Resource URIs tested
Google photos API	developers.google.com/photos	v1	17
Google drive API	developers.google.com/drive	v3	42
YouTube API	developers.google.com/youtube	v3	52
Google classroom API	developers.google.com/classroom	v1	56
Gmail API	developers.google.com/gmail/api	v1	74
Google calendar API	developers.google.com/calendar	v3	32
Google sheets API	developers.google.com/sheets/api	v4	17
Google blogger API	developers.google.com/blogger	v3	27

Variable Selection: For each of our research questions, we have a set of independent and dependent variables, as shown in Table 4.

Table 4. Independent variables and dependent variables.

RQs	Independent variables	Dependent variables	Measures
RQ$_1$	REST antipatterns & patterns	Linguistic antipatterns & patterns	*Number of detected instances*
RQ$_{1.1}$	REST antipatterns	Linguistic antipatterns	
RQ$_{1.2}$	REST antipatterns	Linguistic patterns	
RQ$_{1.3}$	REST patterns	Linguistic patterns	
RQ$_{1.4}$	REST patterns	Linguistic antipatterns	

4   Case Study Results

This section shows the results obtained after performing the detection of 21 REST and linguistic patterns and antipatterns on eight Google APIs and the statistical tests performed on the detection results.

---

[1] https://www.creativebloq.com/web-design/apis-developers-need-know-121518469.

4.1 Relationship Between Design and Linguistic Quality

Table 5 shows the contingency table of the REST patterns/antipatterns and the linguistic patterns/antipatterns on eight Google APIs. The first column lists nine REST antipatterns/patterns. The following columns show the number of instances detected as linguistic antipatterns and patterns. For example, in Table 5, 227 URIs that were detected as *Breaking self-descriptiveness* REST antipattern are also detected as *Amorphous URI* linguistic antipattern. We answer RQ$_1$ based on this contingency table using the Chi-squared test. To answer RQ$_1$, we test the null hypothesis H$_{01}$: There is no statistically significant relationship between the RESTful design and linguistic quality in RESTful APIs.

Table 5. Contingency table of REST and linguistic patterns and antipatterns.

		Linguistic antipatterns						Linguistic patterns					
		AMO	CRD	NV	CRN	NHN	SPN	TDY	VBL	VS	CRN	HN	SP
REST antipattern	BSD	227	4	0	41	0	64	88	311	315	274	275	42
	FH	129	1	0	29	0	53	49	177	178	149	154	35
	IMT	0	0	0	0	0	0	0	0	0	0	0	0
	IC	0	0	0	0	0	0	0	0	0	0	0	0
	MC	0	0	0	0	0	0	0	0	0	0	0	0
	ISC	19	0	0	2	0	1	4	23	23	21	23	0
REST pattern	EL	37	3	0	3	0	12	16	50	53	50	47	7
	CN	228	4	0	41	0	65	89	313	317	276	277	42
	RC	0	0	0	0	0	0	0	0	0	0	0	0

* AMO: Amorphous URIs, TDY: Tidy URIs, CRD: CRUDy URIs, VBL: Verbless URI, NV: Non-versioned URI, VS: Versioned URIs, CRN: Contextless Resource Names, CRN: Contextualized Resource Names, NHN: Non-Hierarchical Nodes, HN: Hierarchical Nodes, SPN: Pluralised Nodes, SP: Singularised Nodes.

Table 6. χ^2 test of independence among REST and Linguistic Patterns/Antipatterns.

Test type	p-value
χ^2(**ContingencyTable**(`REST-Patterns-Antipatterns`, `Linguistic-Patterns-Antipatterns`))	*<2.2e−16*

Table 6 shows the result of the Chi-squared test of independence between REST patterns/antipatterns and linguistic patterns/antipatterns. In order to examine whether there is a relationship between REST and linguistic quality, Chi-squared tests are performed on all four groups of REST and linguistic patterns and antipatterns. Our tests yielded a statistically significant relationship overall with the significance level *p-value* < 0.05. Therefore, the H$_{01}$ is rejected, and we can conclude that there is a likely strong relationship between RESTful design and linguistic quality in RESTful APIs. Overall, it is possible that when APIs have more REST antipatterns, they also have higher linguistic antipatterns. This also applies the REST patterns and linguistic patterns.

Summary on RQ$_1$: Chi-squared test performed in a group finds a statistical significant relationship between RESTful design and linguistic quality in Google APIs.

4.2   Relation Between REST and Linguistic Antipatterns

Table 7 shows the results of the Phi-coefficient test for each pair of REST antipattern and linguistic antipattern. To answer $RQ_{1.1}$, we test $H_{01.1}$: There is no statistically significant relationship between REST antipatterns and linguistic antipatterns in RESTful APIs.

When studying the relationship between REST and linguistic antipatterns, the Phi-coefficient test is used. All the tests, except one, ranged from -0.19 to $+0.19$; this means there might be a relationship at a negligible level according to [24]. Thus, the results lead to failure in rejecting $H_{01.1}$ due to insufficient statistical evidence. Therefore, it is concluded that there is no statistically significant relation between REST antipatterns and linguistic antipatterns.

Table 7. Relation between REST and linguistic antipatterns.

Pairs of REST antipatterns and linguistic antipatterns	*Phi* coefficient
Breaking Self-descriptiveness vs. Amorphous URI	0.03887
Breaking Self-descriptiveness vs. CRUDy URI	0.009
Breaking Self-descriptiveness vs. Non-version URI	–
Breaking Self-descriptiveness vs. Contextless Resource Names	0.03071
Breaking Self-descriptiveness vs. Non-hierarchical Nodes	–
Breaking Self-descriptiveness vs. Pluralised Nodes	−0.05821
Forgetting Hypermedia vs. Amorphous URI	0.01379
Forgetting Hypermedia vs. CRUDy URI	−0.07097
Forgetting Hypermedia vs. Non-versioned URI	–
Forgetting Hypermedia vs. Contextless Resource Names	0.11325
Forgetting Hypermedia vs. Non-hierarchical Nodes	–
Forgetting Hypermedia vs. Pluralised Nodes	0.25984
Ignoring MIME Types vs. Amorphous URI	–
Ignoring MIME Types vs. CRUDy URI	–
Ignoring MIME Types vs. Non-version URI	–
Ignoring MIME Types vs. Contextless Resource Names	–
Ignoring MIME Types vs. Non-hierarchical Nodes	–
Ignoring MIME Types vs. Pluralised Nodes	–

(*continued*)

Table 7. (*continued*)

Pairs of REST antipatterns and linguistic antipatterns	*Phi* coefficient
Ignoring Caching vs. Amorphous URI	–
Ignoring Caching vs. CRUDy URI	–
Ignoring Caching vs. Non-version URI	–
Ignoring Caching vs. Contextless Resource Names	–
Ignoring Caching vs. Non-hierarchical Nodes	–
Ignoring Caching vs. Pluralised Nodes	–
Misusing Cookies vs. Amorphous URI	–
Misusing Cookies vs. CRUDy URI	–
Misusing Cookies vs. Non-version URI	–
Misusing Cookies vs. Contextless Resource Names	–
Misusing Cookies vs. Non-hierarchical Nodes	–
Misusing Cookies vs. Pluralised Nodes	–
Ignoring Status Code vs. Amorphous URI	0.0665
Ignoring Status Code vs. CRUDy URI	−0.03161
Ignoring Status Code vs. Non-version URI	–
Ignoring Status Code vs. Contextless Resource Names	−0.03532
Ignoring Status Code vs. Non-hierarchical Nodes	–
Ignoring Status Code vs. Pluralised Nodes	−0.11193

* The "–" symbol means Phi Coefficient is not applicable.

Summary on $RQ_{1.1}$: Phi-coefficient test on each pair of REST and linguistic antipattern finds a negligible relationship between REST and linguistic antipatterns.

4.3 Relation Between REST Antipatterns and Linguistic Patterns

Table 8 shows the results of the Phi-coefficient test for each pair of REST antipattern and linguistic pattern. To answer $RQ_{1.2}$, we test null hypothesis $H_{01.2}$: There is no statistically significant relationship between REST antipatterns and linguistic patterns in RESTful APIs.

Similar to $H_{01.1}$, we use the Phi-coefficient test to examine $H_{01.2}$. Our obtained results exhibit a no or negligible relationship as they ranged from −0.19 to +0.19. One value showed a weak positive relationship with a Phi-coefficient value of 0.21, i.e., between *Forgetting Hypermedia* and *Singularised Nodes*. That is, at times, if an API has *Forgetting Hypermedia* REST antipattern, it may manifest *Singularised Nodes* linguistic pattern. However, the overall test results have failed to reject $H_{01.2}$ due to insufficient statistical evidence.

Table 8. Relation between REST antipatterns and linguistic patterns.

Pairs of REST antipatterns and linguistic patterns	*Phi* coefficient
Breaking Self-descriptiveness vs. Tidy URI	−0.03887
Breaking Self-descriptiveness vs. Verbless URI	0.009
Breaking Self-descriptiveness vs. Versioned URI	–
Breaking Self-descriptiveness vs. Contextualized Resource Names	−0.03071
Breaking Self-descriptiveness vs. Hierarchical Nodes	−0.03027
Breaking Self-descriptiveness vs. Singularised Nodes	0.03113
Forgetting Hypermedia vs. Tidy URI	−0.01379
Forgetting Hypermedia vs. Verbless URI	0.07097
Forgetting Hypermedia vs. Versioned URI	–
Forgetting Hypermedia vs. Contextualized Resource Names	−0.11325
Forgetting Hypermedia vs. Hierarchical Nodes	−0.02947
Forgetting Hypermedia vs. Singularised Nodes	0.21408
Ignoring MIME Types vs. Tidy URI	–
Ignoring MIME Types vs. Verbless URI	–
Ignoring MIME Types vs. Versioned URI	–
Ignoring MIME Types vs. Contextualized Resource Names	–
Ignoring MIME Types vs. Hierarchical Nodes	–
Ignoring MIME Types vs. Singularised Nodes	–
Ignoring Caching vs. Tidy URI	–
Ignoring Caching vs. Verbless URI	–
Ignoring Caching vs. Versioned URI	–
Ignoring Caching vs. Contextualized Resource Names	–
Ignoring Caching vs. Hierarchical Nodes	–
Ignoring Caching vs. Singularised Nodes	–
Misusing Cookies vs. Tidy URI	–
Misusing Cookies vs. Verbless URI	–
Misusing Cookies vs. Versioned URI	–
Misusing Cookies vs. Contextualized Resource Names	–
Misusing Cookies vs. Hierarchical Nodes	–
Misusing Cookies vs. Singularised Nodes	–
Ignoring Status Code vs. Tidy URI	−0.0665
Ignoring Status Code vs. Verbless URI	0.03161
Ignoring Status Code vs. Versioned URI	–
Ignoring Status Code vs. Contextualized Resource Names	0.03532
Ignoring Status Code vs. Hierarchical Nodes	0.10628
Ignoring Status Code vs. Singularised Nodes	−0.1093

Summary on RQ$_{1.2}$: With Phi-coefficient test performed for each pair of REST antipattern and linguistic pattern, there is negligible relation between REST antipatterns and linguistic patterns.

4.4   Relation Between REST and Linguistic Patterns

Table 9 shows the results of the Phi-coefficient test for each pair of REST pattern and linguistic pattern. To answer $RQ_{1.3}$, we test null hypothesis $H_{01.3}$: There is no statistically significant relationship between REST patterns and linguistic patterns in RESTful APIs.

Like the two previous analyses, testing the relationship between REST patterns and linguistic patterns yielded statistically insignificant results using phi-coefficient test ranging from -0.19 to $+0.19$. Thus, a negligible relationship is found between the REST pattern and linguistic pattern. The test results failed to reject $H_{01.3}$ due to insufficient statistical evidence.

Summary on $RQ_{1.3}$: Phi-coefficient test on each pair of REST pattern and linguistic pattern finds a negligible relationship between REST and linguistics patterns.

Table 9. Relation between REST pattern and linguistic pattern.

Pairs of REST patterns and linguistic patterns	*Phi* coefficient
Entity Linking vs. Tidy URI	0.02106
Entity Linking vs. Verbless URI	-0.17656
Entity Linking vs. Versioned URI	–
Entity Linking vs. Contextualized Resource Names	0.09711
Entity Linking vs. Hierarchical Nodes	0.01750
Entity Linking vs. Singularised Nodes	-0.00055
Content Negotiations vs. Tidy URI	–
Content Negotiation vs. Verbless URI	–
Content Negotiation vs. Versioned URI	–
Content Negotiation vs. Contextualized Resource Names	–
Content Negotiation vs. Hierarchical Nodes	–
Content Negotiation vs. Singularised Nodes	–
Response Caching vs. Tidy URI	–
Response Caching vs. Verbless URI	–
Response Caching vs. Versioned URI	–
Response Caching vs. Contextualized Resource Names	–
Response Caching vs. Hierarchical Nodes	–
Response Caching vs. Singularised Nodes	–

Table 10. Relation between REST pattern and linguistic pattern.

Pairs of REST patterns and linguistic antipatterns	Phi coefficient
Entity Linking vs. Amorphous URI	−0.02106
Entity Linking vs. CRUDy URI	0.17656
Entity Linking vs. Non-versioned URI	–
Entity Linking vs. Contextless Resource Names	−0.09711
Entity Linking vs. Non-Hierarchical Nodes	–
Entity Linking vs. Pluralised Nodes	0.02371
Content Negotiations vs. Amorphous URI	–
Content Negotiation vs. CRUDy URI	–
Content Negotiation vs. Non-versioned URI	–
Content Negotiation vs. Contextless Resource Names	–
Content Negotiation vs. Non-Hierarchical Nodes	–
Content Negotiation vs. Pluralised Nodes	–
Response Caching vs. Amorphous URI	–
Response Caching vs. CRUDy URI	–
Response Caching vs. Non-versioned URI	–
Response Caching vs. Contextless Resource Names	–
Response Caching vs. Non-Hierarchical Nodes	–
Response Caching vs. Pluralised Nodes	–

4.5   Relation Between REST Patterns and Linguistic Antipatterns

Table 10 shows the results of the Phi-coefficient test for each pair of REST pattern and linguistic antipattern. To answer $RQ_{1.4}$, we test hypothesis $H_{01.4}$: There is no statistically significant relationship between REST patterns and linguistic antipatterns in RESTful APIs.

When comparing REST patterns and linguistics antipatterns using the Phi-coefficient test, our obtained results exhibit a negligible relation between REST pattern and linguistic pattern with values ranging between −0.19 and +0.19. The results lead to failure in rejecting $H_{01.4}$ for insufficient statistical evidence. Hence, there is no relationship between REST patterns and linguistic antipatterns.

Summary on $RQ_{1.4}$: With Phi-coefficient test performed for each pair of REST pattern and linguistic antipattern, there is no or negligible relation between REST patterns and linguistic antipatterns.

5   Discussions

The detection results for linguistic patterns and antipatterns show that very few URIs are CRUDy and all Google APIs are versioned. Moreover, only a portion of the tested URIs, i.e., 41, have *Contextless Resource Names* antipattern, and no URIs are found to be involved in *Non-Hierarchical Nodes* antipattern. However, there is a considerably higher number of *Amorphous URI* antipattern detected. *Pluralized Nodes* antipattern is also common to some extent, i.e., up to 65 URIs were detected, while *Singularized Nodes* pattern had only 42 instances (13%) detected out of 317 URIs tested. Thus, Google APIs are mostly well-designed in terms of linguistic quality.

The analysis of the RESTful design quality shows that almost all URIs contain *Breaking Self-descriptiveness* antipattern. This is mostly because Google uses some of its non-standard request and response headers. Moreover, the *Forgetting Hypermedia* and *Ignoring Status Code* antipatterns are present in the majority of the URIs. Although, the greater number of the Google APIs follow the *Content Negotiation* REST patterns since Google servers can provide resources in various formats to the clients. These show that when it comes to RESTful design, Google APIs do not display similar RESTful design quality as in linguistic design.

When we examine the relation between REST antipatterns and linguistic antipatterns, we found that the *Forgetting Hypermedia* REST antipattern weak-positively correlates with the *Pluralized Nodes* linguistic antipattern with a Phi-coefficient value of 0.25984 (see Table 7). Also, the *Forgetting Hypermedia* antipattern is positively (but negligible) correlated with the *Contextless Resource Names* linguistic antipattern with a phi-coefficient value of 0.11325.

When we examine the relation between REST antipatterns and linguistic patterns, we again found that the *Forgetting Hypermedia* REST antipattern is weak-positively correlated with the *Singularised Nodes* linguistic pattern with a Phi-coefficient value of 0.21408 (see Table 8). However, the *Forgetting Hypermedia* antipattern is negatively (but negligible) correlated with the *Contextualized Resource Names* linguistic pattern with a Phi-coefficient value of −0.11325. Thus, when a resource URI has *Forgetting Hypermedia*, more often than not, that same URI does not have *Contextualized Resource Names* linguistic pattern. More specifically, when API developers design their resources, they not only miss to include the hyperlinks, but they also design the URIs using (semantically) less correlated nodes.

When we correlate REST patterns with linguistic patterns, we found that *Entity Linking* REST pattern is negatively (but negligible) correlated with the *Verbless URI* linguistic pattern with a Phi-coefficient value of −0.17656. Thus, when API developers provide hyperlinks for their resources, they often do not follow a good URI design practice— *Verbless URI*. As such, we also found a positive but negligible correlation between *Entity Linking* REST pattern and *CRUDy URI* linguistic antipattern when we examine the correlation between REST patterns and linguistic antipatterns (Phi-coefficient value 0.17656, see Table 10). These could be due to various development constraints like a shorter release span or sprint for a large API.

Practical Implications: Client developers who rely on the RESTful APIs to develop their applications face challenges when APIs are not truly RESTful and have poor linguistic design [12,19]. An empirical evidence similar to this study informs client developers that, in practice, APIs that claim to be RESTful are not always RESTful and may lack basic REST principles defined by Fielding [11]. API providers might not always be concerned about the linguistic design quality of their APIs, which, in practice, hinder the comprehension and usability of the APIs. What is more troubling, without proper understanding, client developers may misinterpret and misrepresent a resource URI in an API, as discussed previously by Aghajani et al. [3]. In addition, when the APIs are not truly RESTful, it is possible that client developers build and deliver a not-quite-right product to their clients, albeit unknowingly. Our study provides examples that such proneness persists, i.e., RESTful APIs at the same time are not truly RESTful and have poor design quality and APIs that suffer from poor RESTful design quality also tend to have poor linguistic quality. Although, the latter relation is found to be *negligible* in the context of Google. Nevertheless, client developers should be careful about impulsively relying on the RESTful APIs available in practice.

Threats to Validity: We discuss the threats to validity according to the guidelines by [23]. When it comes to *external validity*, the findings might not be generalized to other RESTful APIs. Also, selecting APIs that only belong to Google may introduce a selection bias, adding another threat to the study. However, we tried to minimize the threats by analyzing eight different Google APIs. To minimize the threats to *construct validity*, all the detection rules were defined and identified according to existing literature and previous research on the REST and linguistic patterns and antipatterns in RESTful APIs [19,20]. The *internal validity* threat presents in this study is the accuracy of SOFA to detect the violations of RESTful API design pattern principles and poor linguistics design. However, SOFA has an average precision of 89% for the detection of REST (anti)patterns and more than 80% in detecting linguistic (anti)patterns [20]. Moreover, the findings on the relation between REST patterns and linguistic patterns might be affected by the fact that fewer REST patterns (i.e., only three) are analyzed than the number of linguistic patterns (i.e., six). A natural extension would be considering more REST patterns to minimize the threats to internal validity. The threats to *reliability validity* concern the possibility of replicating our study. We provided all the detection results required to replicate the study including the raw data to compute the statistics online.[2] *Conclusion validity* threats refer to the relation between the treatment and the outcome. We used the phi-coefficient test at the significance level $p < 0.05$. The phi-coefficient measures and test the strength of association between two categorical variables where each variable has only two groups.

---

[2] https://ufile.io/fpqm4lba.

6   Related Work

Several studies dealt with the analysis of RESTful APIs aimed at detecting patterns and antipatterns towards assessing their design quality. Studies in [18,20] concerned the RESTful design quality while other studies, e.g., [3,5,13,19] analyzed RESTful APIs assessing their structural and linguistic quality and employed syntactic and semantic analysis of the resource URIs. The authors in [18] proposed the first approach for automatic detection of antipatterns in RESTful APIs. They studied 13 patterns and antipatterns related to RESTful design and performed the detection on twelve APIs including DropBox, Facebook, Twitter, and YouTube. The approach performed with an average precision of 89.42%.

Haupt et al. [13] introduced a framework for the structural analysis of RESTful APIs based on their descriptions. The authors validated their framework with 286 APIs available as Swagger documents and performed metrics-based (e.g., share of read-only resources, distribution of API size, etc.) analysis to check the conformance with the REST architectural style. Alshraiedeh and Katuk [5] automatically parsed the URIs and detect antipatterns in RESTful Web services. The detection concerned antipatterns like Amorphous URI and Ambiguous Name with an average accuracy of 82% of precision and 88% recall.

The SARA approach [19] performs the detection of linguistic patterns and antipatterns in RESTful APIs. The authors studied twelve linguistic patterns and antipatterns and performed their detection on 18 RESTful APIs with an average precision of 81%. Brabra et al. [8] provided specification of 21 REST and 24 OCCI (Open Cloud Computing Interface) antipatterns, and performed their detection on five APIs providing cloud services. Abdellatif et al. [2] provided a catalog of poor practices by android REST mobile clients and performed their detection on 1,595 android apps downloaded from the Google Play store. Thus, a magnitude of studies performed the detection of poor linguistic design and consuming practices for REST APIs but did not study the possible relation between linguistic and RESTful design quality.

Aghajani et al. [3] showed that linguistic antipatterns affect the quality of APIs (e.g., introduce bugs) in object-oriented systems. Also, it was found that client developers ask more questions on Stack Overflow when an API has linguistic antipatterns. The authors studied 1.6k releases of 75 Maven libraries used by more than 14k client projects. They concluded that linguistic antipatterns in the APIs could create issues for the client developers who might misinterpret the API and introduce bugs when using it. However, we are not aware of such phenomenon in the domain of service-oriented systems, in particular, RESTful APIs. Thus, we conducted a study investigating whether RESTful APIs suffer from RESTful design quality also lack linguistic quality or vice-versa.

7   Conclusion and Future Work

A well-designed, easy to understand RESTful API attracts more clients. Therefore, RESTful design and linguistic quality are two essential factors an API provider should consider. This empirical study was performed to determine whether API developers are equally concerned about making their APIs 'RESTful' and the linguistic quality of their APIs. More specifically, we examined whether there is a relation between RESTful design and linguistic quality in RESTful APIs. We analyzed eight Google APIs and performed the detection of 21 patterns and antipatterns on those APIs. Using the quantitative data, we performed a series of statistical tests.

A chi-squared test showed there is a statistically significant relationship between RESTful design and linguistic quality in Google RESTful APIs (RQ_1). A phi-coefficient test performed for each pair of REST antipattern and linguistic antipattern showed that there is negligible relation between REST and linguistic antipatterns ($RQ_{1.1}$); a phi-coefficient test performed for each pair of REST antipattern and linguistic pattern also showed a negligible relation between REST antipatterns and linguistic patterns ($RQ_{1.2}$); a phi-coefficient test performed for each pair of REST pattern and linguistic pattern showed that there is also a negligible relation between REST and linguistic patterns ($RQ_{1.3}$); and, finally, a phi-coefficient test performed for each pair of REST pattern and linguistic antipattern showed there is also a negligible relation between REST patterns and linguistic antipatterns ($RQ_{1.4}$). Thus, developers are unaware of whether they conjointly lack RESTful design and linguistic quality. In other words, these could be due to various development constraints like a shorter release span or sprint for a large API.

Further work could involve extending this study on other RESTful APIs to increase the datasets and test our hypotheses, which may provide more statistical significance and reliability when performing the phi-coefficient test on each pair of pattern and antipattern. This may give better insights into why software organizations should emphasize more on RESTful design and linguistic quality. Moreover, other available REST and linguistic patterns and antipatterns need to be considered part of the future study.

References

1. REST Resource Naming Guide (2020). https://restfulapi.net/resource-naming/. Accessed 20 July 2021
2. Abdellatif, M., Tighilt, R., Belkhir, A., Moha, N., Guéhéneuc, Y.-G., Beaudry, É.: A multi-dimensional study on the state of the practice of REST APIs usage in Android apps. Autom. Softw. Eng. **27**(3), 187–228 (2020). https://doi.org/10.1007/s10515-020-00272-9
3. Aghajani, E., Nagy, C., Bavota, G., Lanza, M.: A large-scale empirical study on linguistic antipatterns affecting APIs. In: 2018 IEEE International Conference on Software Maintenance and Evolution (ICSME), pp. 25–35. IEEE (2018)
4. Allen, M.: The SAGE Encyclopedia of Communication Research Methods. SAGE Publications (2017). https://books.google.se/books?id=4GFCDgAAQBAJ
5. Alshraiedeh, F.S., Katuk, N.: A URI parsing technique and algorithm for antipattern detection in RESTful Web services. Int. J. Web Inf. Syst. **17**, 1–17 (2020)

6. Au-Yeung, J., Donovan, R.: Best Practices for REST API Design (2020). https://stackoverflow.blog/2020/03/02/best-practices-for-rest-api-design/. Accessed 20 July 2021

7. Bass, L., Clements, P., Kazman, R.: Software Architecture in Practice, 3rd edn. Addison-Wesley Professional, Boston (2012)

8. Brabra, H., et al.: On semantic detection of cloud API (anti)patterns. Inf. Softw. Technol. **107**, 65–82 (2019). https://doi.org/10.1016/j.infsof.2018.10.012

9. Erl, T.: SOA Design Patterns, 1st edn. Prentice Hall, Hoboken (2009)

10. Erl, T., Merson, P., Stoffers, R.: Service-oriented Architecture: Analysis and Design for Services and Microservices. Prentice Hall Service Technology, Prentice Hall, Service Tech Press (2016). https://books.google.se/books?id=yNmlnQAACAAJ

11. Fielding, R.T., Taylor, R.N.: Architectural styles and the design of network-based software architectures. Ph.D. thesis. University of California, Irvine (2000)

12. Giessler, P., Gebhart, M., Sarancin, D., Steinegger, R., Abeck, S.: Best practices for the design of RESTful web services. In: International Conferences of Software Advances (ICSEA), pp. 392–397 (2015)

13. Haupt, F., Leymann, F., Scherer, A., Vukojevic-Haupt, K.: A framework for the structural analysis of REST APIs. In: 2017 IEEE International Conference on Software Architecture (ICSA), pp. 55–58. IEEE (2017)

14. Kapadnis, J.: REST: good practices for API design - design your REST API so that it will get used (2018). https://medium.com/hashmapinc/rest-good-practices-for-api-design-881439796dc9. Accessed 20 July 2021

15. Masse, M.: REST API Design Rulebook: Designing Consistent RESTful Web Service Interfaces. O'Reilly Media Inc., Newton (2011)

16. Moha, N., et al.: Specification and detection of SOA antipatterns. In: Liu, C., Ludwig, H., Toumani, F., Yu, Q. (eds.) ICSOC 2012. LNCS, vol. 7636, pp. 1–16. Springer, Heidelberg (2012). https://doi.org/10.1007/978-3-642-34321-6_1

17. Moore, D., Notz, W., Fligner, M.: The Basic Practice of Statistics. W.H. Freeman and Company (2013). https://books.google.se/books?id=aw61ygAACAAJ

18. Palma, F., Dubois, J., Moha, N., Guéhéneuc, Y.-G.: Detection of REST patterns and antipatterns: a heuristics-based approach. In: Franch, X., Ghose, A.K., Lewis, G.A., Bhiri, S. (eds.) ICSOC 2014. LNCS, vol. 8831, pp. 230–244. Springer, Heidelberg (2014). https://doi.org/10.1007/978-3-662-45391-9_16

19. Palma, F., Gonzalez-Huerta, J., Founi, M., Moha, N., Tremblay, G., Guéhéneuc, Y.G.: Semantic analysis of RESTful APIs for the detection of linguistic patterns and antipatterns. Int. J. Coop. Inf. Syst. **26**(02), 1742001 (2017)

20. Palma, F., Moha, N., Guéhéneuc, Y.G.: UniDoSA: the unified specification and detection of service antipatterns. IEEE Trans. Softw. Eng. **45**(10), 1024–1053 (2018)

21. Sheskin, D.J.: Handbook of Parametric and Non-parametric Statistical Procedures, 4th edn. Chapman & Hall/CRC, Boca Raton (2007)

22. Tilkov, S.: REST anti-patterns (2008). https://www.infoq.com/articles/rest-anti-patterns. Accessed 20 July 2021

23. Yin, R.: Case Study Research and Applications: Design and Methods. SAGE Publications (2017). https://books.google.se/books?id=fHE3DwAAQBAJ

24. Yule, G.: On the methods of measuring association between two attributes. J. R. Stat. Soc. **75**(6), 579 (1912)

Evaluating and Improving Microservice Architecture Conformance to Architectural Design Decisions

Evangelos Ntentos[1]([✉]), Uwe Zdun[1], Konstantinos Plakidas[1], and Sebastian Geiger[2]

[1] Faculty of Computer Science, Research Group Software Architecture,
University of Vienna, Vienna, Austria
{evangelos.ntentos,uwe.zdun,konstantinos.plakidas}@univie.ac.at
[2] Siemens Corporate Technology, Vienna, Austria
sebastian.geiger@siemens.com

Abstract. Microservices are a commonly used architectural style targeting independent development, deployment, and release of services, as well as supporting polyglot capabilities and rapid release strategies. This depends on the presence of certain software architecture qualities. A number of architecture patterns and best practices that support the required qualities have been proposed in the literature, but usually in isolation of one another. Additionally, in real-world systems, assessing conformance to these patterns and practices and detecting possible violations is a significant challenge. For small-scale systems of a few services, a manual assessment and violation detection by an expert is probably both accurate and sufficient. However, for industrial-scale systems of several hundred or more services, manual assessment and violation detection is laborious and likely leads to inaccurate results. Furthermore, manual assessment is impractical for rapidly evolving and frequently released system architectures. In this work we examine a subset of microservice-relevant patterns, and propose a method for the semi-automatic detection and resolution of conformance violations. Our aim is to assist the software architect by providing a set of possible fix options and generating models of "fixed" architectures.

1 Introduction

Microservices are one of many service-based architecture decomposition approaches (see e.g. [1–4]). The chief features of microservices are that they communicate via message-based remote APIs in a loosely coupled fashion, and that they can be highly polyglot; ideally, microservices should not share their data with other services. This allows the rapid evolution of individual microservices independently of one another, and their independent deployment in lightweight containers or other virtualized environments. These features make microservices ideal for DevOps practices (see e.g. [5,6]).

While a large body of literature has examined architectural patterns and recommended "best practices" in a microservice context [3,7,8], translating these theoretical insights into usable tools to assist the architectural evolution of actual microservice-based systems has lagged behind. While the theoretical tenets proposed in the literature are easy to grasp and maintain in small-scale systems, ensuring conformance in large,

H. Hacid et al. (Eds.): ICSOC 2021, LNCS 13121, pp. 188–203, 2021.
https://doi.org/10.1007/978-3-030-91431-8_12

complex, as well as rapidly and independently evolving systems quickly becomes a laborious affair requiring considerable manual work and resulting in extensive overhead effort. Furthermore, patterns have mutual dependencies, meaning that improvement in one area can result in deterioration in another. Real-world architectures are also impacted by a number of non-microservice-specific requirements, which also can lead to unintended violations of microservice best practices.

This work provides a set of actionable solutions to violations on different aspects of microservice architectures, as part of a larger study on the topic. Three architectural design decisions (ADDs) were selected as representing very different aspects of architecting microservices, so as to demonstrate the wide applicability of our approach. Other ADDs have already been covered in our prior work. More specifically, for covering the best practices of client-system communication we chose the External API decision; for the guaranteed delivery of messages, a critical aspect of many business-critical microservice systems, we used the Inter-Service Message Persistence decision to examine the relevant recommended practices; finally, to cover the logging and monitoring practices that ensure observability of the microservices and their complex interactions, we used the End-to-End Tracing decision. In this context, we aim to study the following research questions:

- **RQ1.** What are the possible architecture violations related to the above-mentioned ADDs and how can they be automatically detected?
- **RQ2.** What are the possible fixes for the violations found in RQ1 and how can architects be assisted in choosing the appropriate solutions and applying them?

We propose a novel architecture refactoring approach that uses empirically validated metrics proposed in our prior work [9] to evaluate the degree of architecture conformance for each of the given ADDs. For every ADD design option, we define every possible violation and propose a corresponding, automated violation detection algorithm, as well as a set of possible fixes. For each microservice-based system, the sets of ADD options, violations, and fixes leads to a search tree of possible architecture designs that partly or entirely enforce conformance to best practices, which we can continually assess using our metrics.

To evaluate our approach we utilized a set of 24 models of microservice-based systems from third-party practitioners (see Table 1). For each of these, we implemented the automated violation detection and refactoring (fix) algorithms to detect the possible violations and to generate all the possible fixes for addressing each violation, resulting in a set of models. Using our metrics, we evaluated the improvements compared with the original version, as well as any outstanding issues. This process was iteratively repeated until all violations were resolved. Each of the violations found in the 24 models can be fully resolved leading to optimal metric values within *at most* 3 refactoring steps, usually with many suggested optimal models provided as options for architects to choose from.

This paper is structured as follows: In Sect. 2 we analyze the ADDs examined in this work, the associated patterns and practices, and the corresponding metrics. Section 3 discusses and compares our approach to existing studies in the literature. Our research methods and the tools we have applied in our study are described in Sect. 4, followed by a detailed explanation of our approach in Sect. 5. The evaluation process is given at Sect. 6, the results are discussed in Sect. 7, and the threats to validity in Sect. 8. Finally, in Sect. 9 we draw conclusions and discuss future work.

2 Background: Decisions and Metrics

In this section, we briefly introduce the three ADDs and the corresponding patterns and practices as decision options, based on our prior work. The decisions have been modeled based on an empirical study of existing best practices and patterns by practitioners [10], while the metrics used to assess the pattern conformance of each given system derive from [9].

External API Decision. A fundamental decision in microservice-based systems is how external clients are connected to the system services. This can affect aspects related to loose coupling, releasability, independent development and deployment, and continuous delivery. The simplest method, but with the highest negative impact, occurs when the *clients can call into system services directly*, resulting in high coupling that impedes releasing, developing, and deploying the clients and system services independently of each other. Another option, that solves possible problems caused by client-service direct connections, is the *API Gateway* [3], which provides a common entry point for the system (Facade component) and all client requests are routed via this component. It is a specialized variant of a *Reverse Proxy*, which covers only the routing aspects of an *API Gateway* but not further API abstractions such as authentication, rate limiting, etc. (see [7]). The *Backends for Frontends* pattern [3] is another variant of *API Gateway* that specializes in handling different types of clients (e.g., mobile and desktop clients). Alternatively, the *API Composition* pattern [3] describes a service that shields other services from the clients by actively gathering and composing their data. In our previous work [9], we have empirically defined two metrics that can be used to assess conformance to each of the decision options:

- *Client-side Communication via Facade utilization metric* measures how many unique client links are using the External API used by one of the Facade components (i.e. offered through patterns such as *API Gateway*, *Reverse Proxy*, *Backends for Frontends*) compared to the total number of unique client links.
- *API Composition utilization metric* measures the proportion of clients connected services which are possibly composing an *External API* using *API Composition*.

Inter-service Message Persistence Decision. The persistence or missing persistence of the inter-service messages is another decision with considerable impact on the qualities of the system. Many real-world systems use *no inter-service message persistence*, while options that support message persistence are the *Messaging* pattern [11], in which persistent message queuing is used to store a producer's messages until the consumer receives them, or alternatively *Stream Processing* [8] components (e.g. Apache Kafka). Another option is *Interaction through a Shared Database*, since it supports some level of message persistence, but not the automated support of *Messaging*. A technique that is more microservice-relevant and able to support a lower level of persistence to *Messaging* or a *Shared Database* is the combination of the *Outbox* and the *Transaction Log Tailing* patterns [3]. A persistence more tailored to event-driven or eventually consistent microservice architectures can be achieved following the *Event Sourcing* pattern [3].

For this decision, too, we have empirically defined three metrics that can be used to assess conformance to each of the decision options:

- *Service Messaging Persistence utilization metric* measures the proportion of all service interconnections that are made persistent through a supporting technology (i.e. *Messaging* or *Stream Processing*).
- *Shared Database utilization metric* measures the proportion of all interconnections via a *Shared Database*.
- *Outbox/Event Sourcing utilization metric* measures the proportion of all interconnections with *Outbox/Event Sourcing*.

End-to-End Tracing Decision. End-to-end tracing is an important aspect in microservice architectures since they are usually highly distributed and polyglot systems with complex interactions. One option, like in the other decisions, is to offer *no tracing support*. Alternatively, traces can be recorded on either the services themselves or facade components (or both) via *Distributed Tracing* [3]. A less comprehensive level of tracing can be achieved when service communication is routed through a central component, which stores some, but not all inter-service communication (e.g., *Publish/Subscribe*, *Message Broker* [11], *API Gateway* or *Event Logging* [3,8]); the exception is *Event Sourcing*, which temporarily stores *all* service events.

For this decision, too, we have empirically defined three metrics that can be used to assess conformance to each of the decision options:

- *Services and Facades Support Distributed Tracing metric* measures the proportion of all services and facades that support distributed tracing.
- *Service Interaction via Central Component utilization w/o Event Sourcing metric* measures the proportion of all service interactions through a central component other than *Event Sourcing*.
- *Service Interaction via Central Component with Event Sourcing metric* measures the proportion of all service interactions through a central component via *Event Sourcing*.

3   Related Work

The fundamentals of the term "microservices" were first discussed by Fowler and Lewis [12], and fundamental tenets by Zimmermann [5]. Richardson [3] has published a collection of microservice patterns and practices, while a mapping study by Pahl and Jamshidi [1] has summarized much of the previous literature on patterns. Skowronski [8] has examined event-driven microservice architectures specifically, and microservice API patterns were studied by Zimmermann et al. [7].

A number of studies have focus on techniques for detecting design or architecture "bad smells" (violations). Taibi and Lenarduzzi [13] defined a list of microservice-specific smells, while Neri et al. [14] have presented an extensive examination of architectural smells for independent deployability, horizontal scalability, fault isolation, and decentralisation of microservices, as well as suggesting refactorings to resolve them. Most similar studies are more generic, but still useful. Le et al. [15] proposed a classification of architectural smells and their impact on different quality attributes. Catalogs of smells have been published by Garcia et al. [16,17] and Azadi et al. [18]. Detection strategies for smell categories related to our study are discussed by Brogi et al. [19], Le et al. [20], Marinescu [21], and especially Neri et al. [14], along with suggested refactorings for resolving them. Although these works study various aspects of architecture violations detection, and some investigate aspects related to the microservice domain, none covers detecting and addressing violations specifically associated with the ADDs covered in this work (external API, persistent messaging, and end-to-end tracing) in a microservice context, which our work investigates in detail.

As a result, we expect that our work produces more accurate detection of decision-specific violations and more targeted suggestions for fixes. On the other hand, our approach requires a model in which the component and connector roles in a microservice architecture have been modeled (as for instance done with stereotypes in the model introduced in Fig. 2). That is, our work requires additional insight into a system's architecture, and some effort in encoding the corresponding models; however, this knowledge is at a relatively high level of abstraction and the resulting models are not impacted by changes in service implementation. We are currently working on a semi-automatic approach for architecture reconstruction and modelling that relies on reusable code abstractions and is thus suitable for complex systems with short delivery cycles.

4   Research and Modeling Methods

In this section, we summarize the main research methods applied in our study. These have been more extensively described in our previous work [22]. For reproducibility, all the code of the algorithms' implementation and the models produced in this study will be made available online, as an open-access dataset in a long-term archive.[1]

4.1   Research Method

Figure 1 shows the structure of the research process of this study. In Sect. 2 we have already explained in detail the architectural decisions and the model-based metrics on which this study is based. In Sect. 5 we present precise definitions and algorithms a) for the detection of possible violations per decision option, and b) for the possible fixes (architecture refactorings) for each violation.

We have tested our approach by applying the algorithms to the 24 models in our data set. First all violations present in each model were detected, and then all possible fixes for each violation were applied in an iterative-exhaustive manner, i.e., on the resulting, refactored models for each violation fix, we again performed *all* violation detection algorithms and applied *all* possible refactorings, until either no more violations were detected, or we arrived at a refactored model identical to a previous version. In the latter case, which we did not encounter here, this would have meant that a violation could not be entirely resolved, as its fix introduced other violations. For each of the final models (the 'leaves' of the iteration tree), we assessed pattern conformance through our metrics on microservice coupling, to judge the improvement compared to the original model.

---

[1] https://doi.org/10.5281/zenodo.5549978.

Table 1. Selected models: size, details, and sources

Model ID	Model size	Description/source
BM1	10 components 14 connectors	Banking-related application based on CQRS and event sourcing (from https://github.com/cer/event-sourcing-examples)
BM2	8 components 9 connectors	Variant of BM1 which uses direct RESTful completely synchronous service invocations instead of event-based communication
BM3	8 components 9 connectors	Variant of BM1 which uses direct RESTful completely asynchronous service invocations instead of event-based communication
CO1	8 components 9 connectors	The common component model E-shop application implemented as microservices directly accessed by a Web frontend (from https://github.com/cocome-community-case-study/cocome-cloud-jee-microservices-rest)
CO2	11 components 17 connectors	Variant of CO1 using a SAGA orchestrator on the order service with a message broker. Added support for Open Tracing. Added an API gateway
CO3	9 components 13 connectors	Variant of CO1 where the reports service does not use inter-service communication, but a shared database for accessing product and store data. Added support for Open Tracing
CI1	11 components 12 connectors	Cinema booking application using RESTful HTTP invocations, databases per service, and an API gateway (from https://codeburst.io/build-a-nodejs-cinema-api-gateway-and-deploying-it-to-docker-part-4-703c2b0dd269)
CI2	11 components 12 connectors	Variant of CI1 routing all interservice communication via the API gateway
CI3	10 components 11 connectors	Variant of CI1 using direct client to service invocations instead of the API gateway
CI4	11 components 12 connectors	Variant of CI1 with a subsystem exposing services directly to the client and another subsystem routing all traffic via the API gateway
EC1	10 components 14 connectors	E-commerce application with a Web UI directly accessing microservices and an API gateway for service-based API (from https://microservices.io/patterns/microservices.html)
EC2	11 components 14 connectors	Variant of EC1 using event-based communication and event sourcing internally
EC3	8 components 11 connectors	Variant of EC1 with a shared database used to handle all but one service interactions
ES1	20 components 36 connectors	E-shop application using pub/sub communication for event-based interaction, a middleware-triggered identity service, databases per service (4 SQL DBs, 1 Mongo DB, and 1 Redis DB), and backends for frontends for two Web app types and one mobile app type (from https://github.com/dotnet-architecture/eShopOnContainers)
ES2	14 components 35 connectors	Variant of ES1 using RESTful communication via the API gateway instead of event-based communication and one shared SQL DB for all 6 of the services using DBs. However, no service interaction via the shared database occurs
ES3	16 components 35 connectors	Variant of ES1 using RESTful communication via the API gateway instead of event-based communication and one shared database for all 4 of the services using SQL DB in ES1. However, no service interaction via the shared database occurs
FM1	15 components 24 connectors	Simple food ordering application based on entity services directly linked to a Web UI (from https://github.com/jferrater/Tap-And-Eat-MicroServices)
FM2	14 components 21 connectors	Variant of FM1 which uses the store service as an API composition and asynchronous interservice communication. Added Jaeger-based tracing per service
HM1	13 components 25 connectors	Hipster shop application using GRPC interservice connection and OpenCensus monitoring & tracing for all but one services as well as on the gateway. (from https://github.com/GoogleCloudPlatform/microservices-demo)
HM2	14 components 26 connectors	Variant of HM1 that uses publish/subscribe interaction with event sourcing, except for one service, and realizes the tracing on all services
RM	11 components 18 connectors	Restaurant order management application based on SAGA messaging and domain event interactions. Rudimentary tracing support (from https://github.com/microservices-patterns/ftgo-application)
RS	18 components 29 connectors	Robot shop application with various kinds of service interconnections, data stores, and Instana tracing on most services (from https://github.com/instana/robot-shop)
TH1	14 components 16 connectors	Taxi hailing application with multiple frontends and databases per services from (https://www.nginx.com/blog/introduction-to-microservices/)
TH2	15 components 18 connectors	Variant of TH1 that uses publish/subscribe interaction with event sourcing for all but one service interactions

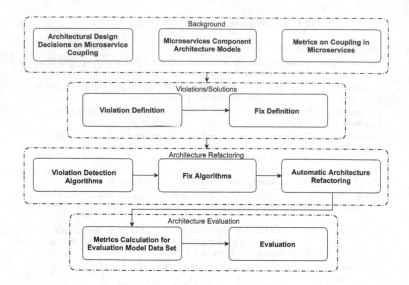

Fig. 1. Overview diagram of the research method followed in this study

5   Architecture Refactoring Approach

From an abstract point of view, a microservice-based system is composed of components and connectors, with distinct sets of component types and connector types. This applies also to indirect or implicit relationships between components, such as indirect dependencies, which can be described as a special set of connectors. For example, in Fig. 2, two components are indirectly linked via the API gateway.

We base our definitions of the violations and fixes on the notion of an architecture model consisting of a directed components and connectors graph. This can be expressed formally as: A microservice architecture model M is a tuple (CP, CN, CPT, CNT, ST) where:

- CP is a finite set of **component nodes**. The operation $components(M)$ returns all components in M.
- $CN \subseteq CP \times CP$ is an ordered finite set of **connectors**. $connectors(M)$ returns all connectors in M.
- CPT is a set of **component types**. The operation $services(M)$ returns all components of type $service$ in M. The operation $service\_connectors(M)$ returns all connectors of components of type $service$ in M.
- CNT is a set of **connector types**.
- ST is a finite set of **stereotype nodes**. The operation $cp\_stereotypes(CP)$ returns all stereotypes of component CP. The operation $cn\_stereotypes(CN)$ returns all stereotypes of connector CN. Stereotypes can be applied to components to denote their type, such as *Service*, *API Gateway*, etc. Stereotypes can be applied to connectors to denote their type, such as *Read_Data*, *RESTful HTTP*, or *Asynchronous*. Some are specialized with tagged values (details omitted here for space reasons).

- $cp\_annotations : CP \rightarrow \{String\}$ is a function that maps an component to its set of annotations. Annotations are used in our approach (in some of the fixes) to document aspects that need further consideration or maybe manual refactoring.
- $cn\_annotations : CN \rightarrow \{String\}$ is a function that maps a connector to its set of annotations.

Please note that we define many additional model traversal operations not detailed here for space reasons.

5.1 Violations and Detection Algorithms

Table 2. Identified violations and violation detection algorithms

Violation	Violation detection algorithm summary
D1: External API	
D1.V1: Services are directly connected to clients	All services in the model are traversed, and it is checked whether services are directly connected to clients or web UIs. If this is the case, a violation is raised. Each service-client connector that is found is returned by the detector operation
D2: Persistent Messaging for Inter-Service Communication	
D2.V1: Services communicate without using an intermediary component that is able to persist the communication (e.g., Message Brokers or a persistent Publish/Subscribe or Stream Processing or Event Sourcing or Outbox/Transaction Log Tailing or Database) and no persistent messaging occurs between them	All service connectors in the model are traversed. If no intermediary component is found, the violation is raised and the list of all relevant connectors is returned by the detector operation
D3: End-to-End Tracing	
D3.V1: Distributed Tracing is not supported on services and/or facades or services communicate without using a central intermediary component (e.g., Message Brokers or persistent Publish/Subscribe or Stream Processing or Event Sourcing or Outbox/Transaction Log Tailing or API Gateway)	All services, facades and the corresponding connectors in the model are traversed, and it is checked whether services and/or facades support tracing or whether an intermediary component is presented. If no intermediary component or tracing support on services/facades is found, the violation is raised and the list of all relevant connectors is returned by the detector operation

Table 2 summarizes the possible violations we have identified for each of the decisions. The table also describes in detail how the algorithms that we use for detecting the violations in the models work. As a detailed example, Algorithm 1 detects the *Services communicate without using an intermediary component* violation of Decision D2. It returns a list of connected service pairs s_i and s_j, that are *not* connected via an intermediary component.

Algorithm 1: Services Communicate w/o Intermediary Component Violation

```
input : Model M
output: Set<Tuple> Component intermediary
begin
    violations ← ∅
    for s_i ∈ services (M):
    for s_j ∈ services (M):
        if (s_i, s_j) ∈ direct_service_connectors (M):
            violations ← violations ∪ (s_i, s_j)
    return violations
end
```

5.2 Fix Options and Algorithms

Table 3 details all the fixes for each identified violation, along with a summary of the fix algorithm. Please note that many algorithms can only be applied fully automatically with their default values. Many of them require human review and decision by the architect. For example, the architects can be presented with a choice of an intermediary component to use to replace services links.

Table 3. Identified fixes and fix algorithms

Violation	Fix	Fix and fix algorithm summary
D1: External API		
D1.V1	D1.V1.F1: Do not fix the violation	The architect should have the option to *not* fix the violation, e.g. because it is not critical
	D1.V1.F2: Introduce a new API Gateway and connect client to services via it	Disconnect client(s) from the services and introduce a new API Gateway. Connect the client(s) to the API Gateway and the API to each former client-connected service
	D1.V1.F3: Introduce API Composition service or service with reverse proxy capabilities and connect client(s) to the services via this component	Disconnect client(s) from the services and introduce a new API composition service. Connect the client(s) to the API composition service and the latter to each former client-connected service
D2: Persistent Messaging for Inter-Service Communication		
D2.V1	D2.V1.F1: Do not fix the violation	The architect should have the option to *not* fix the violation, e.g. because it is not critical
	D2.V1.F2: Remove the non-persistent connectors between services and replace them with persistent messaging-based connectors	Replace non-persistent interconnections with interactions via an intermediary component (e.g., API Gateway, Pub/Sub, Message Broker). The architect has to select if an existing intermediary component can be used for the fix, or a new one has to be created. Replace non-persistent interconnections with persistent interconnections via this component
	D2.V1.F3: Remove the non-persistent connectors between services and replace them by writing to and reading from a common database	The architect has to select if an existing database can be used for the fix, or a new one has to be created For each connector, introduce communication by writing to and reading from this database. Delete the non-persistent interconnections
D3: End-to-End Tracing		
D3.V1	D3.V1.F1: Do not fix the violation	The architect should have the option to *not* fix the violation, e.g. because it is not critical
	D3.V1.F2: Remove the connectors that don't support end-to-end tracing between services and replace them with interactions via an intermediary component (e.g., API Gateway, Pub/Sub, Message Broker)	The architect has to select if an existing intermediary component can be used for the fix, or a new one has to be created. Replace interconnections that don't support end-to-end tracing with interconnections via this component
	D3.V1.F3: Connect services and facades that don't support end-to-end tracing with a tracing component (e.g., Zipkin)	The architect has to select if an existing tracing component can be used for the fix, or a new one has to be created. Introduce interconnections from service and facades to tracing component

The Algorithms 2 and 3 respectively present the fixes F2 and F3, for Decision D2 and its Violation V1. For explanations of each fix, please study Table 3.

Algorithm 2: Remove the non-persistent connectors between services and replace them with persistent messaging-based connectors

```
input: Model M, Set<Tuple> violation , Component intermediary_component
output: -
begin
   for (s_i, s_j) ∈ violation:
      add_connector(s_i, intermediary_component,
         get_applicable_stereotypes(M, (s_i, s_j)))
      add_connector(intermediary, s_m,
         get_applicable_stereotypes(M, (s_i, s_j)))
    delete_direct_connector(M, (s_i, s_j))
end
```

Algorithm 3: Remove the non-persistent connectors between services and replace them by writing to and reading from a common database

```
input: Model M, Set<Tuple> violation , Component database
output: -
begin
   for (s_i, s_j) ∈ violation:
      add_connector(s_i, database,
         get_applicable_stereotypes(M, (s_i, s_j)))
      add_connector(s_j, database,
         get_applicable_stereotypes(M, (s_i, s_j)))
    delete_direct_connector(M, (s_i, s_j))
end
```

5.3   Example Application

In Fig. 2 the model C14 from Table 1 is shown as an illustrative example to demonstrate all three violations and possible fixes. In this model the *Cinema Catalog* service is connected directly with *Movie* and *Booking* services, causing D2.V1 and D3.V1, while *Client* is connected directly with *Cinema Catalog* service, causing D1.V1. In contrast, *Booking Payment* and *Notification* services are connected to each other and with the *Client* through the *API Gateway*, resulting in no violation. If we run our fix algorithms, some of the resulting refactoring suggestions are:

– *Applying Fix D1.V1.F2:* The architect can choose the existing *API Gateway* and connect *Client* to *Cinema Catalog* and *Movie* services through it. The current connectors are removed by this fix.
– *Applying Fix D1.V1.F3:* The architect can introduce an *API composition* service or service with reverse proxy capabilities and connect *Client* to *Cinema Catalog* and *Movie* services through it. The current connectors are removed by this fix.
– *Applying Fix D2.V1.F2:* All services with non-persistent connectors are disconnected and connected to a *Message-based persistent mechanism* (all interactions will be happening via this component). For example, this fix can introduce a new *Pub-/Sub intermediary component* (alternatively *Message Broker* or *API Gateway*), to which all involved services will be connected with *publish* and *subscribe* operations supporting persistent communications.
– *Applying Fix D2.V1.F3:* All services with non-persistent connectors are disconnected from each other as well as from their existing databases and connected to a new *shared database* with *read* and *write* operations.

– *Applying Fix D3.V1.F2:* *Cinema Catalog*, *Movie* and *Booking* services that don't support end-to-end tracing will be disconnected from each other and connected to a new (or existing) *intermediary component* (e.g., *Pub/Sub*, *Message Broker* or *API Gateway*).
– *Applying Fix D3.V1.F3:* A new *tracing component* (e.g., *Zipkin*) is introduced and connected to all services and the *API Gateway*.

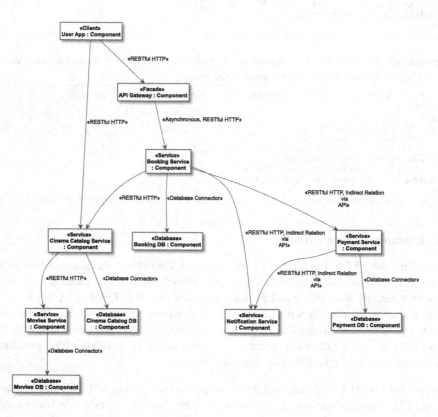

Fig. 2. Example of an architecture component model (CI4 in Table 1): this architecture violates all three ADDs

6   Iterative Application and Evaluation

To evaluate our work, we have fully implemented our algorithms for detecting violations and performing fixes, as well as generating the set of metrics described in Sect. 2 to measure the improvements and the presence of remaining violations, in our model set. In case multiple violations are present in a model, then the algorithms can be employed iteratively, until all violations have been fully resolved.

As an example, let us illustrate this exhaustive iterative refactoring for the previously mentioned CI4 Model (see Fig. 2). CI4 violates all the three decisions as indicated

by the corresponding decision-related measures in Table 4. The incremental refactoring process is illustrated in Fig. 3. At the first iteration, there are three branches, indicating the respective violations. The first refactoring step produces 6 possible model
variants, one for each fix option from Table 3. All resulting models have resolved the
respective violation, but have the other two unresolved, requiring another refactoring
step that produces 18 new model variants. In turn, 7 of the resulting models still violate D1.V1 and D2.V1, requiring a third step to be resolved. At the end of the third
step, we have 29 suggested model variants (M1_1, M2_1, M2_3, M1_2_1–M1_2_2, M2_1_1–
M2_2_2, M2_4_1–M2_4_2, M3_1, M3_2_1–M3_2_2, M4_1, M4_2_1–M4_2_2, M4_3_1–M4_3_2,
M5_1–M5_2, M4_4_1–M4_4_2, M6_1_1–M6_2_2, M6_2_1–M6_2_2, M6_3_1–M6_3_2, M6_4_1–
M6_4_2) which all fully resolve the violations (i.e., scoring 1.00 in our assessment scale).
The architect can choose the refactoring sequence, and from among those final optimal
model variants, but can also choose to not apply certain fixes, e.g. due to other con-
straints that are outside of the scope of our study.

For evaluation purposes, we have performed this procedure for *all* 24 system models
in Table 1. The resulting number of intermediary models and violation instances per
step, and the number of final suggested models with an optimal assessment of 1.00,
are given in Table 4, along with the initial violations and architecture assessment values
for each model. Please note that the metrics reported here are the ones associated with
each of the decisions in Sect. 2. Please also note that for each violation to be fixed, it

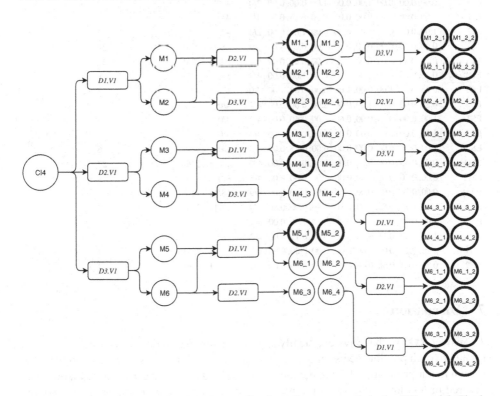

Fig. 3. Example of an exhaustive iterative application of our approach in the CI4 model. Final
(i.e., fully resolved) resulting models are thickly outlined.

is enough that at least one of the corresponding metrics is optimal (1.00). Obviously, the number of steps required to reach optimal models depends on a) the number of the violations present in the initial model and b) on the possible appearance of new violations during the refactoring process, which did not occur in the present case. As can be seen in Table 4, *all* models are *fully resolved*—i.e., all assessment metrics are 1.00—after *at most* three steps.

Table 4. This table shows a) the architecture assessment (per decision/violation pair) of the original models used in our study, b) the number of models generated at each step of an iterative application of our algorithms, and c) the number of violation instances (generated models × violations per model) still remaining, or introduced, after each iteration, plus d) the resulting number of suggested (optimal) models at the end (cf. Fig. 3 for a detailed example).

Model ID	Initial model assessments			Models generated/remaining violation instances per refactoring step			Resulting suggested (optimal) Models
	D1.VI	*D2.VI*	*D3.VI*	*Step 1*	*Step 2*	*Step 3*	
BM1	1.00, 0.00	0.00, 0.00, 1.00	0.00, 0.00, 1.00	–	–	–	–
BM2	1.00, 0.00	0.00, 0.00, 0.00	0.00, 1.00, 0.00	2/0	–	–	2
BM3	1.00, 0.00	0.00, 0.00, 0.00	0.00, 1.00, 0.00	2/0	–	–	2
CO1	0.00, 0.00	0.00, 0.00, 0.00	0.00, 0.00, 0.00	6/9	18/11	22/0	29
CO2	1.00, 0.00	1.00, 0.00, 0.00	1.00, 1.00, 0.00	–	–	–	–
CO3	0.00, 0.00	0.00, 1.00, 0.00	1.00, 0.00, 0.00	2/0	–	–	2
CI1	1.00, 0.00	0.00, 0.00, 0.00	0.00, 0.14, 0.00	4/2	4/0	–	6
CI2	1.00, 0.00	0.00, 0.00, 0.00	0.00, 1.00, 0.00	2/0	–	–	2
CI3	0.00, 0.30	0.00, 0.00, 0.00	0.00, 0.00, 0.00	6/9	18/11	22/0	29
CI4	0.50, 0.10	0.00, 0.00, 0.00	0.00, 0.60, 0.00	6/9	18/11	22/0	29
EC1	0.25, 0.00	0.00, 0.00, 0.00	0.00, 1.00, 0.00	4/4	8/0	–	8
EC2	0.25, 0.00	1.00, 0.00, 1.00	0.00, 0.00, 1.00	2/0	–	–	2
EC3	0.25, 0.00	0.00, 1.00, 0.00	0.00, 0.00, 0.00	4/2	4/0	–	4
ES1	1.00, 0.00	0.60, 0.00, 0.60	0.00, 0.60, 0.00	4/2	4/0	–	6
ES2	1.00, 0.00	0.00, 0.00, 0.00	0.00, 0.45, 0.00	4/2	4/0	–	6
ES3	1.00, 0.00	0.00, 0.00, 0.00	0.00, 0.45, 0.00	4/2	4/0	–	6
FM1	0.00, 0.25	0.00, 0.00, 0.00	0.00, 0.00, 0.00	6/9	18/11	22/0	29
FM2	0.00, 0.50	0.00, 0.00, 0.00	1.00, 0.00, 0.00	4/4	8/0	–	8
HM1	0.00, 0.70	0.00, 0.00, 0.00	0.90, 0.00, 0.00	6/9	18/11	22/0	29
HM2	0.00, 0.70	0.80, 0.00, 0.80	0.90, 0.00, 0.80	6/9	18/11	22/0	29
RM	1.00, 0.00	1.00, 0.00, 0.00	0.14, 1.00, 0.00	–	–	–	–
RS	1.00, 0.00	0.11, 0.00, 0.00	0.62, 0.11, 0.00	4/2	4/0	–	6
TH1	0.25, 0.12	0.00, 0.00, 0.00	0.00, 0.00, 0.00	6/9	18/11	22/0	29
TH2	0.25, 0.04	0.66, 0.00, 0.66	0.00, 0.00, 0.66	6/9	18/11	22/0	29

7   Discussion

To answer **RQ1** we have systematically specified a number of decision-based violations related to each possible decision option, summarized in Table 2. As we have empirically shown in our prior work [9] that the metrics described in Sect. 2 can reliably distinguish favored or less favored design options, the role of the violation detectors is to find the precise locations in the models where the violations occur. For each system model in our evaluation dataset it was possible to suggest fixes that bring the architecture to optimal values, meaning that the algorithms have found the right place(s) to apply the fixes.

Regarding **RQ2** we defined a number of algorithms addressing every possible violation, with multiple fix options (cf. Table 3). If all options are tried out, this results in a search tree of possible architecture models, which can in turn be assessed, using our metrics, to measure improvements to the initial architecture and detect any remaining violations. We have shown (cf. Table 4) that an iterative approach results, within a few steps, in a sufficient variety of possible architecture models that remove all detected violations and ensure pattern conformance of the system architecture. The multiple optimal model variants that result from our approach give architects substantial levels of freedom in their design decisions. As detection is fully automated and human expertise is limited to the fix process, the approach is well suited to be run in a continuous delivery environment, which was one of our research goals.

8   Threats to Validity

The basis material of our study derives from third-party sources: the solutions we propose are gathered from the best practices recommended in the published literature, and our evaluation dataset is a fairly representative set of systems (cf. Table 1), derived from nine different sources and published with the express purpose of demonstrating microservice architecture features. One possible threat to the internal validity of our algorithms is that they depend on the particular modelling approach we have adopted. However, our approach is by design abstract and generic, based on typical component-and-connector models used widely in the literature. The author team, with considerable experience in modeling methods, performed the system modeling as well as, repeatedly and independently cross-checked all models. As the main modelling criterion was the ability to adequately represent the context of our systems, we cannot exclude that other teams might arrive at different interpretations, but we are confident that any resulting models would be broadly similar and compatible with our results. Furthermore, the algorithms we specified could easily be adapted to a different model, as they operate on the level of basic architectural constructs.

Nevertheless, some limitations remain. In order to remove the obstacles provided by the polyglot nature of microservice-based systems, we have chosen to apply our metrics and tools at a relatively high level of abstraction. We also limited our evaluation in the present paper to the patterns, metrics, and concerns applying to the given three ADDs, which in a real-world architecture would be insufficient. This point is addressed in previously published and ongoing parts of our work, which extend the coverage to additional ADDs, and aim to extend and test our approach in a larger set of patterns, design requirements, and more granular parameters. The same concern applies as to the lack of evaluation of the applicability of our approach on larger and more complex systems that are commonly found in industry, but which were not accessible to us for study. The lack of full automation is also a major obstacle to practical application, as the process still requires considerable input by the architect. At the same time, our approach can not match the ability of an experienced architect, familiar with the system, to devise a much more optimal solution. This is a limitation of all generic architecture assistance approaches, and one we intend to improve on. We want to emphasize that the present approach is a starting point from which the question of evaluating and improving microservice architectures can be examined, facilitating and building up to more complex and nuanced methods as more systems and decisions are modelled and tested. The generated models are also not optimal, as they are not evaluated, for example, on the coding/refactoring effort required to implement them. Nevertheless, the existence of a semi-automatic approach that detects and analyzes violations in an architecture remains of great value, since practitioners often ignore best practices, systems are often developed without a conscious effort to follow best practices, or are allowed to drift from the original architecture specifications over time.

9   Conclusion and Future Work

In this paper we present a set of violations for three microservice-related ADDs. Building on previous work, we have defined automatic detectors, which return the location where the violations occur, a set of possible fixes for each violation, and automatic algorithms for refactoring the system in order to fix the violations. We have evaluated our approach on a set of 24 models of various degrees of pattern violations and architecture complexity, and have shown that our approach is capable of resolving these violations in at most 3 refactoring steps. Both metric calculation and violation detection are fully automated, but the choice of fixes and refactoring sequence remains with the human architect. Thus the approach is still flexible enough to let the architect make meaningful architectural design choices.

In our future work, we aim to broaden the set of ADDs and violations included in our approach, enrich it with runtime metrics and other architecture aspects such as deployment environments, and extend our model dataset to include larger and more complex systems. In addition, we hope to experimentally validate our approach by employing it in real-world delivery pipelines as part of a feedback loop.

Acknowledgments. This work was supported by: FFG (Austrian Research Promotion Agency) project DECO, no. 864707; FWF (Austrian Science Fund) project API-ACE: I 4268; FWF (Austrian Science Fund) project IAC²: I 4731-N. Our work has received funding from the European Union's Horizon 2020 research and innovation programme under grant agreement No 952647 (AssureMOSS project).

References

1. Pahl, C., Jamshidi, P.: Microservices: a systematic mapping study. In: 6th International Conference on Cloud Computing and Services Science, pp. 137–146 (2016)
2. Pautasso, C., Wilde, E.: Why is the web loosely coupled?: a multi-faceted metric for service design. In: 18th International Conference on World Wide Web, pp. 911–920. ACM (2009)
3. Richardson, C.: A pattern language for microservices (2017). http://microservices.io/patterns/index.html
4. Zimmermann, O., Gschwind, T., Küster, J., Leymann, F., Schuster, N.: Reusable architectural decision models for enterprise application development. In: Overhage, S., Szyperski, C.A., Reussner, R., Stafford, J.A. (eds.) QoSA 2007. LNCS, vol. 4880, pp. 15–32. Springer, Heidelberg (2007). https://doi.org/10.1007/978-3-540-77619-2_2

5. Zimmermann, O.: Microservices tenets. Comput. Sci. - Res. Dev. **32**(3), 301–310 (2016). https://doi.org/10.1007/s00450-016-0337-0

6. Pautasso, C., Zimmermann, O., Amundsen, M., Lewis, J., Josuttis, N.: Microservices in practice, part 1: reality check and service design. IEEE Softw. **34**(1), 91–98 (2017)

7. Zimmermann, O., Stocker, M., Zdun, U., Luebke, D., Pautasso, C.: Microservice API patterns (2019). https://microservice-api-patterns.org

8. Skowronski, J.: Best practices for event-driven microservice architecture (2019). https://hackernoon.com/best-practices-for-event-driven-microservice-architecture-e034p21lk

9. Ntentos, E., Zdun, U., Plakidas, K., Meixner, S., Geiger, S.: Metrics for assessing architecture conformance to microservice architecture patterns and practices. In: Kafeza, E., Benatallah, B., Martinelli, F., Hacid, H., Bouguettaya, A., Motahari, H. (eds.) ICSOC 2020. LNCS, vol. 12571, pp. 580–596. Springer, Cham (2020). https://doi.org/10.1007/978-3-030-65310-1_42

10. Bures, T., Duchien, L., Inverardi, P. (eds.): ECSA 2019. LNCS, vol. 11681. Springer, Cham (2019). https://doi.org/10.1007/978-3-030-29983-5

11. Hohpe, G., Woolf, B.: Enterprise Integration Patterns. Addison-Wesley, Boston (2003)

12. Lewis, J., Fowler, M.: Microservices: a definition of this new architectural term, March 2004. http://martinfowler.com/articles/microservices.html

13. Taibi, D., Lenarduzzi, V.: On the definition of microservice bad smells. IEEE Softw. **35**(3), 56–62 (2018)

14. Neri, D., Soldani, J., Zimmermann, O., Brogi, A.: Design principles, architectural smells and refactorings for microservices: a multivocal review. SICS Software-Intensive Cyber-Physical Systems **35**(1), 3–15 (2019). https://doi.org/10.1007/s00450-019-00407-8

15. Le, D.M., Carrillo, C., Capilla, R., Medvidovic, N.: Relating architectural decay and sustainability of software systems. In: 2016 13th Working IEEE/IFIP Conference on Software Architecture (WICSA), pp. 178–181 (2016)

16. Garcia, J., Popescu, D., Edwards, G., Medvidovic, N.: Identifying architectural bad smells. In: 2009 13th European Conference on Software Maintenance and Reengineering, pp. 255–258 (2009)

17. Garcia, J., Popescu, D., Edwards, G., Medvidovic, N.: Toward a catalogue of architectural bad smells. In: Mirandola, R., Gorton, I., Hofmeister, C. (eds.) QoSA 2009. LNCS, vol. 5581, pp. 146–162. Springer, Heidelberg (2009). https://doi.org/10.1007/978-3-642-02351-4_10

18. Azadi, U., Fontana, F., Taibi, D.: Architectural smells detected by tools: a catalogue proposal. In: 2019 IEEE/ACM International Conference on Technical Debt (TechDebt), pp. 88–97 (2019)

19. Brogi, A., Neri, D., Soldani, J., et al.: Freshening the air in microservices: resolving architectural smells via refactoring. In: Yangui, S. (ed.) ICSOC 2019. LNCS, vol. 12019, pp. 17–29. Springer, Cham (2020). https://doi.org/10.1007/978-3-030-45989-5_2

20. Le, D.M., Link, D., Shahbazian, A., Medvidovic, N.: An empirical study of architectural decay in open-source software. In: 2018 IEEE International Conference on Software Architecture (ICSA), pp. 176–17609 (2018)

21. Marinescu, R.: Detection strategies: metrics-based rules for detecting design flaws. In: 20th IEEE International Conference on Software Maintenance, 2004. Proceedings, pp. 350–359 (2004)

22. Ntentos, E., Zdun, U., Plakidas, K., Geiger, S.: Semi-automatic feedback for improving architecture conformance to microservice patterns and practices. In: 18th IEEE International Conference on Software Architecture(ICSA 2021), March 2021. http://eprints.cs.univie.ac.at/6763/

ThunQ: A Distributed and Deep Authorization Middleware for Early and Lazy Policy Enforcement in Microservice Applications

Martijn Sauwens[✉], Emad Heydari Beni, Kristof Jannes, Bert Lagaisse, and Wouter Joosen

imec-DistriNet, KU Leuven, Leuven, Belgium
{martijn.sauwens,emad.heydaribeni,kristof.jannes,bert.lagaisse, wouter.joosen}@kuleuven.be

Abstract. Online software services are often designed as multi-tenant, API-based, microservice architectures. However, sharing service instances and storing sensitive data in a shared data store causes significant security risks. Application-level access control plays a key role in mitigating this risk by preventing unauthorized access to the application and data. Moreover, a microservice architecture introduces new challenges for access control on online services, as both the application logic and data are highly distributed. First, unauthorized requests should be denied as soon as possible, preferably at the facade API. Second, sensitive data should stay in the context of its microservice during policy evaluation. Third, the set of policies enforced on a single application request should be consistent for the entire distributed control flow.

To solve these challenges, we present ThunQ, a distributed authorization middleware that enforces authorization policies both early at the facade API, as well as lazily by postponing authorization decisions to the appropriate data context. To achieve this, ThunQ leverages two techniques called partial evaluation and query rewriting, which support policy enforcement both at the facade API, as well as deep in the data tier.

We implemented and open-sourced ThunQ as a set of reusable components for the Spring Cloud and Data ecosystem. Experimental results in an application case study show that ThunQ can efficiently enforce authorization policies in microservice applications, with acceptable increases in latency as the number of tenants and access rules grow.

1 Introduction

Contemporary online services often provide a customer-facing API and adopt an internal architecture based on application-level multi-tenancy and microservices. Application-level multi-tenancy [10], as illustrated in Fig. 1, benefits from

© Springer Nature Switzerland AG 2021
H. Hacid et al. (Eds.): ICSOC 2021, LNCS 13121, pp. 204–220, 2021.
https://doi.org/10.1007/978-3-030-91431-8_13

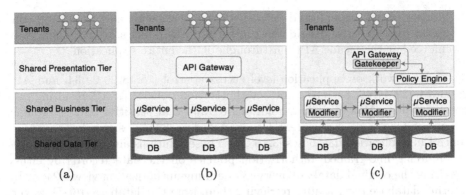

Fig. 1. Overview of application-level multi-tenancy (a) for both microservice applications (b) and applications with ThunQ (c). ThunQ's components are shown in green. (Color figure online)

economies of scale by sharing resources between the tenants, such as the application and database. However, storing sensitive tenant data poses significant security risks. Application-level access control [34] is a key security technique that mitigates these risks by enforcing authorization policies at the application-level to block unauthorized access to resources. Moreover, multi-tenant applications require that both the application provider and tenants can specify these policies. In particular, the provider specifies the basic authorization policies for the platform, while the tenants can provide additional policies that further restrict access by their end-users to comply with internal authorization policies. For example a tenant policy may state that: *"An insurance company employee can only view insurance documents of customers that are assigned to the employee."*

Supporting tenant specific policies requires an appropriate level of modularity, separation of concerns and adaptation of the related software artefacts [8]. While single-tenant applications can embed the authorization logic directly in the database query to enforce fine-grained access control, it is no longer feasible for multi-tenant applications with custom authorization policies per tenant. Custom policies require a more flexible approach where policies can be updated at run-time, as new tenants are continuously added to the application.

A frequently used architectural pattern to realize multi-tenant applications are *microservices* [23]. Microservice applications often adopt the *API gateway* [32] and the *database-per-service* [32] pattern as shown in Fig. 1b. The distribution of application logic and data in multi-tenant microservice applications introduces the following new challenges for access control in such applications:

1. Unauthorized requests should be denied *as soon as possible* (ASAP), such that unauthorized resource usage and control flows in the distributed microservice application are minimized.
2. Sensitive data should stay in the context of its microservice during policy evaluation, i.e. data from the data tier should not flow to the API gateway when evaluating authorization policies.

3. The set of policies enforced on a single application request should be consistent for the entire distributed control flow, as policies are no longer only enforced at the facade API but throughout the entire application.

Existing work on application-level access control [15,18,20,29,34] and API gateways [29,44,46] aims to enforce authorization policies ASAP, resulting in a permit or deny. However, these solutions require that sensitive data is brought outside of its microservice context. Other related work focuses on enforcing access control in application databases [3,16,24]. These solutions aim to restrict access by enforcing fine-grained authorization policies on the data records by either rewriting the original database query [3], defining authorization views [24] or by filtering database records after retrieving them from the database [16]. However, securing database access is only a part of the challenges to enforce a consistent set of authorization policies over a large number of microservices.

To address the challenges and shortcomings above, we present *ThunQ*, a distributed authorization middleware for multi-tenant microservice applications designed to efficiently and consistently enforce a set of authorization policies on distributed application services and data. ThunQ enforces authorization policies early in the distributed control flow, as well as deep down in the *data tier*. ThunQ achieves this by adding the *gatekeeper*, *policy engine* and *query modifier* components to the generic microservice architecture as shown in Fig. 1c. The gatekeeper and policy engine use partial policy evaluation [26] to create *thunks* that are piggybacked on the application request. The thunks are then used by the query modifier to enforce authorization policies deep in the data tier.

We implemented and open-sourced ThunQ [45] as a set of reusable components for the Spring Cloud and Data ecosystem. Our evaluation shows that ThunQ performs notably better than state-of-practice postfiltering approaches. Moreover, ThunQ's overhead is largely independent of the number of application tenants and the complexity of the tenant specific policies.

The remainder of this text is structured as follows. Section 2 presents the motivational use case and provides the reader with background on access control and ThunQ's supporting technologies. Section 3 presents the architecture and the security model of the ThunQ middleware. Section 4 discusses the evaluation and results. Section 5 discusses related work and Sect. 6 concludes this work.

2   Motivational Use Case and Background

This section presents the motivation and background for ThunQ. We start with presenting *e-insurance*, an anonymized industrial case study of a multi-tenant insurance brokering platform with a microservice architecture and API-based online service offering. Next, we discuss background on access control models and ThunQ's enabling technologies.

The E-Insurance Case Study. In the financial industry, insurance companies or insurers do not always sell their insurance products directly to end customers.

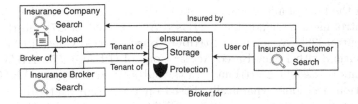

Fig. 2. Participants of the e-insurance application.

Instead, they employ intermediaries, called insurance brokers, to bring their products to the customer. Brokers negotiate insurance contracts with the customers and take care of the paperwork related to the contract. Furthermore, customers should have access to information regarding their insurance products, such as the current balance of their life insurance account. As shown in Fig. 2, e-insurance integrates insurers, brokers, and customers into a single platform that shares their insurance documents. E-insurance is responsible for storing the insurance contracts and their related documents, as well as offering advanced search operations on stored documents. However, as the contents of the insurance documents are sensitive, the results of the search operations should only include the information which the user is authorized to view.

Access Control Analysis. Ensuring the confidentiality of the insurance documents is the primary security goal of e-insurance. To achieve confidentiality, e-insurance must restrict access to only those users who are authorized to access a given document. Whether or not a user is authorized to access a document is determined by *authorization policies*. E-insurance defines two sets of policies: platform policies which are specified by e-insurance itself, and tenant policies, which are specified by the tenants to further restrict access by their end-users. Next, we provide a sample of possible policies.

P1. (platform) Brokers can only view documents assigned to them.
P2. (platform) Customers can only view documents that belong to them.
P3. (broker) Only senior employees can view documents worth over $100k.
P4. (insurer) Employees can only view the documents assigned to them.
P5. (insurer) Employees can only view documents during working hours.

Challenges. Given the discussion above, we can identify the following challenges for e-insurance. First, the application must guarantee the confidentiality of insurance documents by enforcing both platform and tenant policies. Second, e-insurance must offer the performance necessary to support numerous tenants and documents. Searching documents should be fast even as the number of tenants and documents increases. Finally, the set of policies applied to a single application request should be consistent for the entire distributed control flow.

Background. Access control models are models that determine which subjects, such as users and processes, are authorized to access a given object, such as files and other resources. The choice of access control model has a significant impact on the kind of authorization policies that can be expressed. Examples of access control models include Lattice Based Access Control [27] and Role Based Access Control [28]. We focus on Attribute-Based Access Control (ABAC) [12] in combination with Policy-Based Access Control (PBAC) [25]. ABAC models access rights by assigning attributes to the subjects and objects. ABAC makes authorization decisions dynamically, based on the assigned attributes and the environment, such as location and time. PBAC, on the other hand, makes decisions based on authorization policies. These policies are evaluated by a policy engine that uses an access control model, such as the attributes and context assigned by the ABAC model, to reach an authorization decision.

The separation of concerns between authorization policies and the mechanism to enforce them is a key principle in secure software engineering [8]. PBAC [25] decouples policy from mechanism by using policy engines to evaluate policies written in authorization policy languages. The *Open Policy Agent* (OPA) [41] is a policy engine that supports the *Rego* [40] policy language for writing policies. Rego policies use the attributes provided by the authorization request, as well as the access control model stored by OPA. OPA supports both full and *partial evaluation* [26] of authorization policies. Partial evaluation reduces a given policy by substituting the known variables in the policy and evaluating the involved expressions. The result of a partial evaluation is a reduced version of the original policy that only contains unknown variables. We further refer to the reduced version of the policy as the *residual policy*.

The OASIS eXtensible Access Control Markup Language (XACML) [18] is an industry standard for access control. XACML provides a specification for the XACML policy language and a reference architecture for authorization systems. XACML combines PBAC and ABAC, using XML documents to specify authorization policies. The XACML reference architecture contains the following components: (i) a Policy Enforcement Point (PEP), which intercepts incoming application requests, (ii) a Policy Administration Point (PAP), that manages the system's policies, (iii) a Policy Information Point (PIP), that stores the access control attributes, and (iv) a Policy Decision Point (PDP), which takes authorization decisions based on the context provided by the PAP and PIP.

3   ThunQ Middleware

This section presents ThunQ, a distributed authorization middleware for multi-tenant microservice applications. ThunQ is designed to efficiently enforce a consistent set of authorization policies on distributed application services and data. ThunQ combines *partial policy evaluation* [26] and *query rewriting* [2,3] to enforce authorization policies both *early* and *lazily*. Early enforcement denies unauthorized requests as soon as possible, while lazy enforcement pushes access decisions further down the distributed control flow. Next, we define ThunQ's security model, followed by a description of the architecture and its key elements.

Security Model. Figure 1b depicts the system model for applications supported by ThunQ. ThunQ assumes that all application requests pass through an API gateway [32], which is a *facade* for the services in the *business tier*. Microservices in the business tier execute the actual business logic of the application and can call other microservices. Additionally, the services in the business tier rely on the databases in the *data tier* for persistence. ThunQ supports dedicated databases per service, as well as a single database that is shared between microservices. Given this system model, ThunQ makes the following trust assumptions.

A1. All services shown in Fig. 1b are trusted and operate correctly.
A2. Policies defined by the platform's security administrators are correct, meaning that they enforce the intended security policies.
A3. Tenant policies do not impact existing security properties of the system, i.e. policies are defined by the provider's security consultant after a requirements analysis of the tenant.
A4. Security administrators are trusted, i.e. there is no insider threat caused by the security staff.

The primary security goal of ThunQ is to restrict access to the distributed application logic and data by enforcing platform and tenant policies. First, ThunQ should deny unauthorized requests as soon as possible. Second, ThunQ should enable the confidentiality of application data by enforcing the authorization policies on individual data records deep in the data tier. ThunQ only achieves these goals when the following assumptions about the attacker hold.

A5. An attacker can only interact with the system through the APIs provided by the platform.
A6. An attacker cannot impersonate any other user.
A7. The attacker has no access to side-channels in the communication between the system and the attacker.

ThunQ's Overall Architecture. The authorization architecture of ThunQ is shown in Fig. 3. ThunQ adds the following components to realize its security goals. First, ThunQ adds the *gatekeeper* to the API gateway. The gatekeeper performs authorization checks and piggybacks the *thunks* on the application request. Second, ThunQ transparently adds a *query modifier* to the microservices. The modifier intercepts database queries from the application and rewrites them to enforce authorization policies. Next, we discuss the application request flow with distributed policy evaluation, followed by ThunQ's core architectural elements.

Distributed Policy Evaluation. Policy evaluation in ThunQ is distributed, early and lazy. Evaluation is distributed, as ThunQ evaluates policies at different points in the microservice application, early, as unauthorized requests are denied ASAP by partial evaluation, and lazy, as ThunQ postpones access decisions by piggybacking the residual policies to the appropriate data context. More specifically, policy evaluation in ThunQ starts at the API gateway where incoming application requests are intercepted by the gatekeeper (1). The gatekeeper then inspects the request and extracts any information regarding the subject. Next, the gatekeeper selects the policies applicable to the request and calls the *policy*

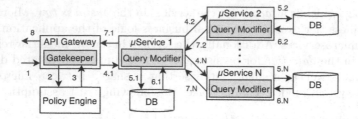

Fig. 3. Authorization architecture. ThunQ's components are shown in green.

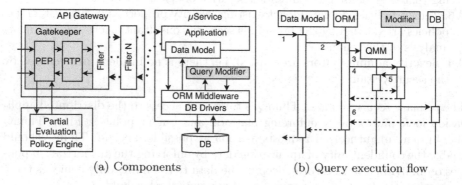

(a) Components   (b) Query execution flow

Fig. 4. Detailed view of ThunQ's interactions with the application components.

engine with the subject information and the selected policies as arguments (2). The policy engine then partially evaluates the policies and returns the *residual policies* to the gatekeeper (3). The gatekeeper transforms the residual policies into a thunk and attaches the thunk to the application request. Alternatively, the policy engine returns a deny, in which case the gateway blocks the request.

Next, the API gateway forwards the request to the relevant microservice (4.1). The microservice then handles the request either by querying the database (5.1–6.1) or by calling other microservices and piggybacking the thunk (4.x–7.x). Each query made by the application gets intercepted by the query modifier, where the query gets rewritten to enforce the authorization policies before being passed to the database (5.1). The result of the rewritten query is then sent back to the application (6.1). After the data is retrieved, the application can perform other operations, eventually finishing the request and replying to the caller (7.1). Eventually, the API gateway receives the response and forwards it to the client (8). Note that the same rewriting procedure (5.x–6.x) is applied when the service calls other microservices to handle the request.

We next discuss the core architectural elements of the ThunQ middleware. The ThunQ middleware consists of two main components the gatekeeper and the query modifier. These components and a policy engine are added transparently to the microservice application as shown in Fig. 4.

Gatekeeper. The gatekeeper enforces the authorization policies on the requests both early and lazily. As depicted in Fig. 4a, the gatekeeper is attached to the API

```
1   allow {                              allow {
2     user.tenant=="insurer"               doc.tenant_id==67
3     doc.tenant_id==user.tenant_id        doc.employee_id==42
4     user.role=="account_manager"     }
5     doc.employee_id==user.id
6   }
```

Fig. 5. Example policy (left) and the residual policy after partial evaluation (right).

gateway as a filter component that intercepts all incoming application requests. The gatekeeper can be further broken down into the *Policy Enforcement Point* or PEP, and the *Request Transformation Point* or RTP. The PEP is a modified version of a XACML PEP [18] and is responsible for sending requests for partial policy evaluation to the policy engine. The policy engine responds with either a set of residual policies or a deny. In the case of a deny, the PEP blocks the application request, denying the request early. Alternatively, the policy engine responds with a residual policy, in which case the PEP sends the residual policies to the RTP, which transforms the residual policies into Boolean expressions and adds the expressions to the thunk. The RTP is a new component in the XACML dataflow that is responsible for augmenting application requests, in particular by attaching a thunk for lazy enforcement.

Figure 5 shows an example of partial policy evaluation at the gateway. The policy consists of rules which are defined by the provider at lines 2 and 3, as well as by the tenant at lines 4 and 5. Note that all subject attributes are available at the gateway such that lines 2 and 4 can be evaluated and, if necessary, denied early. This while lines 3 and 5 must be evaluated lazily in the data tier, as the attributes of *doc* are not accessible from the current evaluation context.

We realized ThunQ's gatekeeper as a *gateway filter* instance for *Spring Cloud Gateway* [44]. The gateway filter is implemented as a *stateless* instance to minimize ThunQ's memory footprint. However, the concept of the gatekeeper is more general and is not limited to this specific software implementation. The policy engine is provided by *Open Policy Agent* (OPA) [41], as it supports partial policy evaluation. OPA can be deployed as either a standalone service or a sidecar of the API gateway, depending on its memory consumption. For e-insurance we deployed OPA as a stateless sidecar, as memory use was limited to 10 MiB.

Thunks. A thunk is the key data structure that enables lazy and consistent policy evaluation in a distributed control flow. Thunks are created by the RTP which transforms the residual policies forwarded by the PEP into Boolean expressions. These expressions are added to a thunk by the RTP and piggybacked on the request. By piggybacking the thunks, the residual policies are able to travel together with distributed control flow, where they can be used by other ThunQ components to enforce fine-grained authorization policies deep in the data tier. As shown in Fig. 6, a thunk is a collection of *URL path selectors* mapped to a Boolean expression. The selectors are used by the query modifier to determine which residual policies are relevant for the intercepted database query. To ensure loose coupling, thunks are forwarded in their entirety between microservices.

```
{
    "/accountStates/*":"doc.tenant_id=67 && doc.employee_id=42",
    "/hospitalBills/*": <BoolExpr#2>,
    "/*": <BoolExpr#3>
}
```

Fig. 6. Example of a thunk encoding the partial policy of Fig. 5 and others.

```
SELECT *                    SELECT *
FROM account_states         FROM account_states
                            WHERE tenant_id=67 AND employee_id=42
                              AND <BoolExpr#3>
```

Fig. 7. Example of query rewriting by the query modifier. The original query on the left is rewritten using the thunk in Fig. 6 with *accountStates/all* as request path.

Note that each application request is processed with a consistent set of policies, as the same thunk is re-used for the entire the distributed control flow.

Query Modifier. The query modifier rewrites database queries such that the queries enforce authorization policies on individual data records. Note that the query modifier only augments search queries since these operate on large result sets. As shown in Fig. 4a, the query modifier is attached to the application as a plugin for the *Object Relational Mapper(ORM) middleware*. ORMs often provide hooks that enable third-party extensions to modify database queries through the *query meta-model* (QMM).

To rewrite queries, the query modifier must first determine the relevant residual policies to enforce. These policies are encoded as Boolean expressions in the thunks that are piggybacked on the application requests. The relevant Boolean expressions are selected by matching the URL path selectors of the thunk against the application request path. The matching expressions are then joined using a conjunction to create a Boolean expression that encodes all the matched residual policies at once. This expression is then woven into the meta-model of the database query by adding the expression to the *predicate* of the query's model. The modified query then gets further processed by the ORM middleware before it is sent to the database. The result of the query then is sent back to the ORM without passing through the modifier. An example of the effect of query rewriting on a SQL query is illustrated in Fig. 7.

Figure 4b shows the flow of a database query in detail. First, the application invokes a search method on the data model (1). Next, the data model contacts the ORM middleware (2) which creates a query meta-model that corresponds to the method call (3). This meta-model is an internal representation of the query that the ORM will map later to a database specific query. Next, the ORM passes the meta-model to the query modifier (4), which rewrites the query as described earlier using the meta-model (5). After calling the modifier, the ORM instantiates the actual database query using the modified meta-model (6) and returns the result back to the data model. ThunQ's query modifier was realized as a component for the *Spring Data* [43] ORM middleware. The query modifier utilizes the Querydsl [35] query meta-model to rewrite database queries. Furthermore, the query modifier is implemented as a stateless component to minimize ThunQ's memory footprint.

4   Evaluation

This section discusses the evaluation of the ThunQ middleware with a key focus on the performance overhead of the middleware solution. We compare ThunQ against two alternative approaches for fine-grained authorization in the data tier, namely *postfiltering* [16] and *hand-crafted queries*. Postfiltering enforces authorization policies on data queries by checking each record in the result set against a policy engine. Hand-crafted queries, on the other hand, encode the authorization policies directly in the application queries. Although the last approach is impractical for multi-tenant applications, it represents the best-case scenario for query-based approaches to enforce fine-grained authorization, as it doesn't have the overhead of ThunQ's middleware components. The evaluation aims to answer the following questions related to multi-tenancy and performance.

Q1. What is the impact of the properties of the enforced policies on the latency? As tenants specify policies that further restrict access by their end-users, it decreases the number of records included in the results. Also, adding policies can increase the number of attributes required for evaluation.

Q2. What is the impact on end-to-end latency when the number of tenants grows? As microservice applications are very sensitive to increases in latency, the overhead of ThunQ should not put limitations on the number of tenants.

Evaluation Setup. All experiments were performed on a proof-of-concept application (PoC) that is based on the e-insurance case study discussed in Sect. 2. The PoC was deployed in an AKS Kubernetes cluster in the Microsoft Azure public cloud. The Kubernetes control plane was hosted on a single Standard_B2s VM with 2 CPUs and 4GiB of memory, while the PoC runs inside a node pool consisting of 3 Standard_D4as_v4 VMs with 4 CPUs and 16GiB of memory. To simulate application users, we used the Locust [6] load generation tool.

The PoC consists of the following services: an *API gateway*, an *account-state service*, a *datastore*, and an *IAM* system. The API gateway is an instance of Spring Cloud Gateway [44] with an additional *gatekeeper* filter as discussed in Sect. 3. The account-state service handles statements of account balances generated by life insurances. The service is realized a Spring Boot [42] application augmented with the *query modifier* from Sect. 3. Furthermore, the datastore is an instance of Azure SQL and the IAM system is provided by Keycloak [39].

Q1. We first investigate the impact of two policy properties called *policy selectivity* and *attribute count*. Policy selectivity is the ratio between the number of data records still included after applying the policy to the result set and the size of the original result set. Policies with low values for selectivity are called *narrow*, as only a small portion of the original result set is included. Policies with high selectivity values are called *broad* as more records remain included.

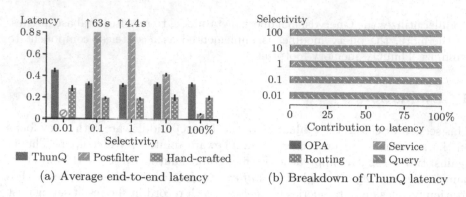

(a) Average end-to-end latency   (b) Breakdown of ThunQ latency

Fig. 8. Latency in function of policy selectivity.

The attribute count of a policy, on the other hand, defines how many attributes are required by a policy for lazy evaluation.

We configured the experiments as follows. Clients send requests through the API gateway to fetch data from the account-state service, which has a database with 1 million records. Application requests are paginated and retrieve only the first 50 accessible records that satisfy the authorization policies. The policies in both scenarios were synthetically generated to show the impact of the different policy properties. The policies for the experiments with varying policy selectivity only have a single attribute, while the experiments with varying attribute count have policies with a selectivity of 10%.

Impact of Policy Selectivity. Figure 8a shows the impact of policy selectivity on the end-to-end latency. For ThunQ and hand-crafted queries, latencies are largely unaffected by policy selectivity, with only a minor increase for very narrow policies. In addition, the breakdown of the ThunQ's request latency shown in Fig. 8b, indicates that ThunQ's latency is dominated by the database query. The results for postfiltering show low latencies for policies with selectivity between 10 and 100%. This is a consequence of paged requests, as filling a page requires that only a limited number of records have to be checked against the policy engine. In contrast, narrow policies have high latencies. The decrease in selectivity means that more database records need to be checked by the policy engine before a single page can be filled, in turn increasing the overhead of the postfilter and the overall latency. A final observation concerns the results for policies with a selectivity of 100%. In this case, postfiltering outperforms both ThunQ and hand-crafted queries. This is caused by the way Spring Data handles request paging for ThunQ and hand-crafted queries.

Impact of Attribute Count. Figure 9 shows the relation between the number of attributes used in the lazy evaluation of a policy and the end-to-end request latency for policies with a 10% selectivity. All three fine-grained authorization methods show a linear increase in latency for higher attribute counts. Although postfiltering initially performs worse than the other techniques, its slope is less steep compared to ThunQ or hand-crafted queries. Consequently it matches or outperforms the other solutions for higher attribute counts. The steeper slope

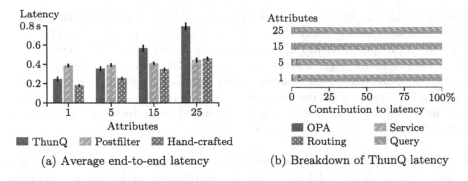

(a) Average end-to-end latency

(b) Breakdown of ThunQ latency

Fig. 9. Latency in function of policy attribute count.

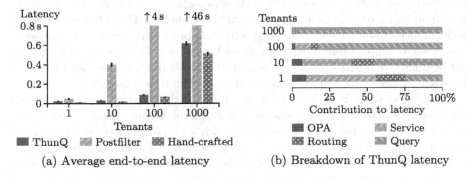

(a) Average end-to-end latency

(b) Breakdown of ThunQ latency

Fig. 10. Latency in function of the number of tenants.

for both ThunQ and hand-crafted queries can be explained by a combination of the extra work required to check extra attributes in the query and request pagination in Spring Data, which generates extra count queries.

Q2. Next, we investigate the impact of the number of tenants on the end-to-end latency. We increased the number of tenants by adding brokers that are each assigned 1000 documents. We also enforced the policy that *"A broker can only view the documents that are assigned to the broker"*. Adding new brokers impacts two dimensions of the system. First, The size of the database increases, as each broker is assigned a fixed number of records. Second, the authorization policy becomes narrower, as the ratio between the records that the broker is authorized to view and the total number of records decreases. As before, application requests are paged with 50 records per page.

Figure 10a shows the impact of the number of brokers in the system on the end-to-end latency. ThunQ closely follows the performance of hand-crafted queries, with the latency of both techniques increasing for a larger number of tenants. As shown earlier in Q1, policy selectivity only has a limited impact on the latency of either fine-grained authorization systems. This implies that the increase in latency can mostly be attributed to the increase in database size. The latency of the postfilter increases sharply once the system exceeds 10 tenants. This increase is mostly likely caused by the increase in policy selectivity. The behavior of the postfilter in Fig. 8a confirms this observation. The performance breakdown of ThunQ's end-to-end latency in Fig. 10b shows that the end-to-end latency is dominated by the database operations of the account-state service. This implies that relative overhead of ThunQ decreases as the number of tenants increases, which makes ThunQ better suited to protect applications with larger databases.

Discussion. Our results indicate that the impact of policy selectivity, attribute count, and the number of tenants on the performance of ThunQ is similar to the impact of these parameters on the performance of hand-crafted queries. However, postfiltering outperforms both approaches in scenarios where policies are broad and have a high attribute count. Nonetheless, ThunQ exhibits better performance characteristics for multi-tenant applications, such as e-insurance, that have to support numerous tenants with narrow policies, while still offering the flexibility required by policy customization. We did not consider the use of database indexes which might greatly enhance ThunQ's performance.

As discussed in Sect. 3, thunks are forwarded in their entirety between microservices to ensure loose coupling. Although this approach can cause thunks to contain policies that are not required by downstream services, we can assume that this overhead is relatively small for two reasons. First, thunks are composed of residual policies, which often reduces the size of the thunks. Second, generalizing our evaluation results, we can assume that the cost of query execution will be the dominant source of overhead in most target systems.

5   Related Work

This section first presents work related to access control for databases, followed by a discussion of security techniques for microservice applications.

Access Control for Databases. Enforcing access control at the level of database records is a non trivial problem. Next, we provide an overview of some techniques proposed by literature for fine-grained access control in database systems.

FGAC [24] enforces authorization policies on individual database records by defining a set of *authorization views* that restrict access to the database. Authorization views scale well to large result sets, but they break separation of concerns between security administration and application development, as authorization views are defined in the database's native query language. Moreover, FGAC scales poorly in terms of administrative overhead. FGAC represents each subject by a separate database user, which not only causes significant administrative overhead but is also problematic for multi-tenant applications, which often integrate with the IAM systems of their tenants.

Bouncer [16] aims to scale fine-grained access control with respect to large groups of users. It does so by inserting an enforcement point between the database and the application The enforcement point first performs an authorization check when a query arrives at the database. The result set of this query is then passed back to Bouncer, which uses a postfilter to exclude any unauthorized records. However, postfiltering does not scale well for large result sets [3].

Sequoia [3] combines the strengths of FGAC and Bouncer by rewriting database queries based on XACML policies. This approach results in low latency enforcement of expressive policies, even in systems with a large number of users. However, Sequoia does not provide an end-to-end solution for access control in applications with distributed application logic and data, such as multi-tenant microservice applications. Moreover, Sequoia instances receive policy updates individually, such that there are no guarantees that multiple Sequoia instances enforce a consistent set of policies on a single distributed control flow.

Securing Microservices. Securing microservice applications [11,19] is challenging, and it requires a holistic approach at different layers of the software stack for in-depth defense. Next, we discuss some security techniques which are put forward by literature to secure microservice applications.

Access control ensures that only authorized entities can interact with the protected system. Most solutions for application-level access control [9,15,20,29] either enforce policies within a single application domain [9,29] or in a setting with multiple parties [15,20]. To ensure interoperability, most solutions use standardized technologies, such as OAuth [15,29], UMA [20] and XACML [15]. The aforementioned systems enforce access control on the level of application requests, while ThunQ also enforces fine-grained policies at the data-record level.

Access control can also be enforced at the network level [21,31,37], either by leveraging Software Defined Networks (SDNs) [31], application containers [37], or a combination of both SDNs and the Host Identity Protocol (HIP) [21].

Managing authorization policies in microservice is challenging due to the multitude of services and the complexity of their interactions. One solution is to mine policies from historical application data [36] and install them at the application services. *AutoArmor* [14] offers a more holistic approach, as it extracts policies from the microservice code and keeps the policies up-to-date.

Application-level access control, such as ABAC, can leak sensitive information about its users. TSAP [38] is a system that is designed to protect the users' attributes by assigning attribute sensitivity and resource server trust levels.

Monitoring and Anomaly Detection aims to completely mediate and monitor application requests [31]. Recent work leverages anomaly detection to detect suspicious behavior through microservice RPC calls [7] or circumvent attacks against auto-scaling infrastructure by identifying cyclic patterns in application load [22].

Deception techniques aim to confuse attackers by setting up decoys and traps in the microservice application. Sandnet [17] leverages SDNs and CRIU (Checkpoint/Restore In Userspace) to create a sandboxed environment for suspicious application containers that are possibly compromised by an attacker.

Moving Target Defense (MTD) targets to reduce an attack's economy of scale by introducing variation in the microservice application. The challenge of MTD is selecting the appropriate variation technique to increase the resiliency of the application in a trade-off between security and performance. Recent work proposes to use vulnerability rating systems such as ORRM (OWASP Risk Rating Methodology) and CVSS (Common Vulnerability Scoring System) to select the appropriate variations [33]. Alternatively, MTD can use custom metrics such as *betweenness centrality* [13] to choose the most suitable variation technique.

A *Trusted Execution Environment* (TEE), such as Intel Secure Guard Extensions (SGX), is another technique to protect microservice applications. Squad [30] leverages TEEs for the secure delivery of application secrets and critical system configuration parameters. *Vert.x Vault* [4] extends the Eclipse *Vert.x* framework for microservices with secure application components that protect specific parts of the application using TEEs.

Integrity Protection aims to protect the integrity of artifacts and configuration of microservice applications from insider threats. Protecting the integrity of these systems often requires a combination of security techniques, such as *remote attestation, access control,* and *audit* [1]. Integrity protection can be used to ensure part of ThunQ's trust requirements presented in Sect. 3.

The discussion above highlights some of the techniques available for securing microservices. Even though ThunQ is able to efficiently enforce access control, it should be used in tandem with other security techniques.

6   Conclusion and Future Work

This work presented ThunQ, a distributed authorization middleware for multi-tenant microservice applications. ThunQ ensures data confidentiality by denying unauthorized requests as soon as possible and enforcing authorization policies *lazily.* ThunQ uses *partial policy evaluation* to make authorization decisions early at the *API gateway* and piggybacks the resulting *residual policies* as a *thunk* on the application request. This scheme moves the policies close to the data that is required to evaluate them, keeping the sensitive records within their local microservice context.

Our evaluation shows that ThunQ's performance is suitable to support large-scale multi-tenant microservice applications. ThunQ has limited overhead and performs better than postfiltering at large scales. Moreover, ThunQ's performance is comparable to the baseline hand-crafted implementation.

As a part of future work, we want to support authorization policies that use data from multiple data-sources for policy evaluation, for example by means of the *Command Query Responsibility Segregation* [23] pattern for microservices. Another effort can be focused on supporting obligations and HBAC policies [5].

Acknowledgement. We would like to thank the R&D team from Xenit Solutions NV and Paul C. Warren for their insightful discussions and contribution to the prototype.

References

1. Ahmadvand, M., Pretschner, A., Ball, K., Eyring, D.: Integrity protection against insiders in microservice-based infrastructures: from threats to a security framework.

In: Mazzara, M., Ober, I., Salaün, G. (eds.) STAF 2018. LNCS, vol. 11176, pp. 573–588. Springer, Cham (2018). https://doi.org/10.1007/978-3-030-04771-9_43

2. Bertino, E., Sandhu, R.: Database security-concepts, approaches, and challenges. IEEE TDSC **2**(1), 2–19 (2005)

3. Bogaerts, J., Lagaisse, B., Joosen, W.: Sequoia: a middleware supporting policy-based access control for search and aggregation in data-driven applications. IEEE TDSC **18**(1) (2021)

4. Brenner, S., Hundt, T., Mazzeo, G., Kapitza, R.: Secure cloud micro services using intel SGX. In: Chen, L.Y., Reiser, H.P. (eds.) DAIS 2017. LNCS, vol. 10320, pp. 177–191. Springer, Cham (2017). https://doi.org/10.1007/978-3-319-59665-5_13

5. Brewer, D., Nash, M.: The Chinese wall security policy. In: Proceedings of IEEE S&P 1989 (1989)

6. Bystr, C., Heyman, J., Hamrén, J., Heyman, H., Holmberg, L.: Locust. https://locust.io/

7. Chen, J., Huang, H., Chen, H.: Informer: irregular traffic detection for containerized microservices RPC in the real world. In: Proceedings of SEC 2019. ACM (2019)

8. De Win, B., Piessens, F., Joosen, W., Verhanneman, T.: On the importance of the separation-of-concerns principle in secure software engineering. In: ACSAC - WAEPSSD (2003)

9. Faravelon, A., Chollet, S., Verdier, C., Front, A.: Configuring private data management as access restrictions: from design to enforcement. In: Liu, C., Ludwig, H., Toumani, F., Yu, Q. (eds.) ICSOC 2012. LNCS, vol. 7636, pp. 344–358. Springer, Heidelberg (2012). https://doi.org/10.1007/978-3-642-34321-6_23

10. Guo, C.J., Sun, W., Huang, Y., Wang, Z.H., Gao, B.: A framework for native multi-tenancy application development and management. In: CEC-EEE (2007)

11. Hannousse, A., Yahiouche, S.: Securing microservices and microservice architectures: a systematic mapping study. Comput. Sci. Rev. **41**, 100415 (2021)

12. Hu, V., et al.: Guide to attribute based access control (ABAC) definition and consideration. Technical report, NIST (2014)

13. Jin, H., Li, Z., Zou, D., Yuan, B.: Dseom: a framework for dynamic security evaluation and optimization of MTD in container-based cloud. IEEE TDSC **18**(3) (2021)

14. Li, X., Chen, Y., Lin, Z., Wang, X., Chen, J.H.: Automatic policy generation for inter-service access control of microservices. In: USENIX Security 21. USENIX Association (2021)

15. Nehme, A., Jesus, V., Mahbub, K., Abdallah, A.: Fine-grained access control for microservices. In: Zincir-Heywood, N., Bonfante, G., Debbabi, M., Garcia-Alfaro, J. (eds.) FPS 2018. LNCS, vol. 11358, pp. 285–300. Springer, Cham (2019). https://doi.org/10.1007/978-3-030-18419-3_19

16. Opyrchal, L., Cooper, J., Poyar, R., Lenahan, B., Daniel, Z.: Bouncer: policy-based fine grained access control in large databases. IJSIA **5**(2), 1–16 (2011)

17. Osman, A., Bruckner, P., Salah, H., Fitzek, F.H.P., Strufe, T., Fischer, M.: Sandnet: towards high quality of deception in container-based microservice architectures. In: IEEE ICC (2019)

18. Parducci, B., Lockhart, H.: Extensible access control markup language (XACML) version 3.0. Standard, OASIS (2013)

19. Pereira-Vale, A., Fernandez, E.B., Monge, R., Astudillo, H., Márquez, G.: Security in microservice-based systems: a multivocal literature review. Comput. Secur. **103**, 102200 (2021)

20. Preuveneers, D., Joosen, W.: Towards multi-party policy-based access control in federations of cloud and edge microservices. In: IEEE Euro S&PW (2019)

21. Ranjbar, A., Komu, M., Salmela, P., Aura, T.: Synaptic: secure and persistent connectivity for containers. In: IEEE/ACM CCGRID (2017)
22. Ravichandiran, R., Bannazadeh, H., Leon-Garcia, A.: Anomaly detection using resource behaviour analysis for autoscaling systems. In: NetSoft and Workshops (2018)
23. Richardson, C.: Microservices Patterns. Manning Publications Co. (2018)
24. Rizvi, S., Mendelzon, A., Sudarshan, S., Roy, P.: Extending query rewriting techniques for fine-grained access control. In: Proceedings of SIGMOD 2004. ACM (2004)
25. Samarati, P., de Vimercati, S.C.: Access control: policies, models, and mechanisms. In: Focardi, R., Gorrieri, R. (eds.) FOSAD 2000. LNCS, vol. 2171, pp. 137–196. Springer, Heidelberg (2001). https://doi.org/10.1007/3-540-45608-2_3
26. Sandall, T.: Partial evaluation. https://blog.openpolicyagent.org/partial-evaluation-162750eaf422
27. Sandhu, R.S.: Lattice-based access control models. Computer **26**(11), 9–19 (1993)
28. Sandhu, R.S., Coyne, E.J., Feinstein, H.L., Youman, C.E.: Role-based access control models. Computer **29**(2), 38–47 (1996)
29. ShuLin, Y., JiePing, H.: Research on unified authentication and authorization in microservice architecture. In: IEEE ICCT (2020)
30. da Silva, M.S.L., de Oliveira Silva, F.F., Brito, A.: Squad: a secure, simple storage service for SGX-based microservices. In: LADC (2019)
31. Sun, Y., Nanda, S., Jaeger, T.: Security-as-a-service for microservices-based cloud applications. In: IEEE CloudCom (2015)
32. Taibi, T., Lenarduzzi, V., Pahl, C.: Architectural patterns for microservices: a systematic mapping study. In: Proceedings of CLOSER. SciTePress (2018)
33. Torkura, K.A., Sukmana, M.I., Kayem, A.V., Cheng, F., Meinel, C.: A cyber risk based moving target defense mechanism for microservice architectures. In: IEEE BDCloud (2018)
34. Verhanneman, T., Piessens, F., De Win, B., Joosen, W.: Uniform application-level access control enforcement of organizationwide policies. In: ACSAC 2005 (2005)
35. Westkämper, T., Dijkstra, R., Tims, J., Bain, R.: Querydsl. http://www.querydsl.com/
36. Xu, Z., Stoller, S.D.: Mining attribute-based access control policies. IEEE TDSC **12**(5), 533–545 (2015)
37. Zaheer, Z., Chang, H., Mukherjee, S., Van der Merwe, J.: Eztrust: network-independent zero-trust perimeterization for microservices. In: Proceedings of SOSR 2019. ACM (2019)
38. Zhang, G., Liu, J., Liu, J., et al.: Protecting sensitive attributes in attribute based access control. In: Ghose, A. (ed.) ICSOC 2012. LNCS, vol. 7759, pp. 294–305. Springer, Heidelberg (2013). https://doi.org/10.1007/978-3-642-37804-1_30
39. Keycloak. https://www.keycloak.org/
40. Rego. https://www.openpolicyagent.org/docs/latest/policy-language/
41. Open policy agent. https://www.openpolicyagent.org/
42. Spring boot. https://spring.io/projects/spring-boot
43. Spring data. https://spring.io/projects/spring-data
44. Spring cloud gateway. https://spring.io/projects/spring-cloud-gateway
45. Thunq. https://distrinet.cs.kuleuven.be/software/thunq
46. Zuul. https://github.com/Netflix/zuul

Boreas – A Service Scheduler for Optimal Kubernetes Deployment

Torgeir Lebesbye[1], Jacopo Mauro[2], Gianluca Turin[1](✉), and Ingrid Chieh Yu[1]

[1] University of Oslo, Oslo, Norway
{torgeirl,gianlutu,ingridcy}@ifi.uio.no
[2] University of Southern Denmark, Odense, Denmark
mauro@imada.sdu.dk

Abstract. The advent of cloud computing radically changed the way organisations operate their applications and allows them to achieve high availability of services at affordable cost. Most cloud-computing platforms fostered Kubernetes for their container orchestration and service management. The scheduler is a key component of Kubernetes, as it is responsible for finding the placement of new service containers when they are deployed. The default scheduler is very fast, although often suboptimal. This can lead to inefficient placement of services, or more severely, inability to deploy.

We present a custom Kubernetes scheduler, dubbed *Boreas*, which is designed to evaluate bursts of deployment requests concurrently. Boreas finds the optimal placements for service containers with their deployment constraints by utilising a configuration optimiser. Results show that Boreas is able to find placements where the default Kubernetes scheduler fails, wasting less computing resources, or proving that no feasible deployment solution is possible.

Keywords: Services on the Cloud · Cloud service management · Kubernetes · Scheduling

1 Introduction

Kubernetes [5] has become the new standard for container orchestration and service management. Originally proposed by Google, Kubernetes is an open source project that provides a layer between the cluster operator and the applications running on the cluster. Its applications are implemented as collections of services, each developed, deployed and scaled individually.

The main components of a Kubernetes systems are the Pods, every one of them representing an instance of a scalable (micro)service. A pod generally hosts one or few containers which are the minimal units containing the service source code to execute with all the code dependencies. This division proved to be extremely useful to avoid software dependencies because when two services have conflicting modules they can be arranged in different containers within the same

© Springer Nature Switzerland AG 2021
H. Hacid et al. (Eds.): ICSOC 2021, LNCS 13121, pp. 221–237, 2021.
https://doi.org/10.1007/978-3-030-91431-8_14

pod. On the other hand, this flexibility is limited by the pod's need of being small so it can be quickly scaled to meet possibly increasing service demand.

Another central component in Kubernetes is the scheduler [14], i.e., the component responsible for finding the placement of new service pods when they need to be deployed. Kubernetes comes with a default scheduler that is very fast, scales to hundreds of nodes, but it is heuristic based. This means that dependency constraints (e.g., pod affinities) are not necessarily optimal, thus leading to possible waste of resources, and more severely, the scheduler may be incomplete, i.e., unable to deploy pods even when a possible schedule is available.

In general, the problem of finding the optimal pod deployment in Kubernetes is an extension of the bin-packing problem and therefore a NP-complete problem [17]. Kubernetes developers prioritized speed over scheduler completeness and optimality in the design of the default scheduler to allow Kubernetes to scale up to thousands of pods and nodes. However, Kubernetes is also used for systems that are not very dynamic and with a limited size. In such deployment scenarios, when speed is not the main priority, one would prefer a scheduler that can lead to more accurate and less resource consuming deployments.

In this paper, we introduce a custom Kubernetes scheduler, dubbed *Boreas*, that ensures optimal pod placements with deployment constraints. Boreas reduces the overall computing resource usage and increases the utilization of cloud computing infrastructure managed by Kubernetes at the cost of slower pod deployment. The core of Boreas is the optimization configuration tool Zephyrus2 [1] that relies on the Aeolus formal model [9] for provably optimal service deployment [6]. Boreas integrates Zephyrus with the architecture of Kubernetes through a proper adapter. When new pod deployment requests arrive, Boreas parses the deployment constraints of the new requests and, based on the available computational resources left, encodes the deployment problem for Zephyrus that is invoked to retrieve the optimal pods deployment solution, if any. In this paper, we describe the design principles and the architecture of Boreas. Moreover, we show empirically that in the presence of standard Kubernetes deployment constraints, Boreas is able to find a placement for the pods in cases where the default scheduler fails, demonstrating that Boreas can be a better alternative than the default scheduler for medium size cost-aware applications.

The rest of the paper is organized as follows. In Sect. 2 we give an introduction of Kubernetes, the pod deployment strategy and the optimization tool Zephyrus2. In Sect. 3 we introduce Boreas, its architecture, how it handles deployment constraints and its batch scheduling. In Sect. 4 we test Boreas and compare it with the default scheduler on some medium size deployment jobs. Section 5 gives related work and we conclude the paper in Sect. 6.

2   Preliminaries

In this section we briefly introduce the two main tools used in our approach: Kubernetes and Zephyrus.

Kubernetes. Kubernetes [5] is the most widely used container orchestration engine for the deployment and maintenance of container based applications.

Containers encapsulate the execution environments of a program, abstracting from the details of physical and virtual machines, and the deployment infrastructure. Compared to virtual machines, they provide the same advantages of virtualization but are more lightweight, offering a better scalability and maintainability. Containers are also *portable* across clouds [10], they require much less storage, and have faster booting time than virtual machines. For all these reasons, containers have recently been widely adopted giving rise to the need of platforms such as Kubernetes to orchestrate them. In the following, we restrict our attention to the main components of Kubernetes related to resource management, with a special focus on the scheduler.

Pods are the basic scheduling unit in Kubernetes. They are high-level abstractions for groups of containerized components which are usually run using a Docker engine [26]. A pod consists of one or more containers that are guaranteed to be co-located on the host machine and can share resources. A pod is deployed according to its resource requirements and has its own specified resource limits. For two or more pods to be deployed in the same node, the sum of the minimum amounts of resources required for the pods needs to be available in the node.

Services represent components that act as basic internal load balancers and ambassadors for pods. A service can be thought as a collection of pods that perform the same function and are viewed as a single entity. Kubernetes can deploy a service, keep track of pods of the service and route all needed communications to them. Services and pods in a Kubernetes cluster are organized within namespaces, allowing multiple applications to share the cluster resources.

Nodes are computing resource on which Kubernetes runs. One node functions as the master node,[1] and acts as a gateway and controller for the cluster by exposing an API for developers and external traffic. The master node carries out the scheduling and orchestrates the communication between other components. The other nodes, called workers, host pods. The worker nodes have explicit resource capabilities given as a set of labels that can specify its version, status, and particular features (e.g., presence of a GPU).

Autoscalers are responsible for ensuring that the number of pods deployed in the cluster matches the number of pods in its configuration. There is one autoscaler for each service, managing a group of identical, replicated pods which are created from pod templates and can be horizontally scaled by deploying or removing pods.

Scheduler is in charge of assigning pods to specific nodes in the cluster. The scheduler matches the operating requirements of a pod's workload to the resources that are available in the current infrastructure environment, and places pods on appropriate nodes. The scheduler is responsible for monitoring the available capacity on each node to make sure that workloads are not scheduled in excess of the available resources. The scheduler needs to know the total capacity of each node and the resources already allocated to the nodes.

---

[1] There can be more master nodes, but one will always be the main master node hosting the cloud controller.

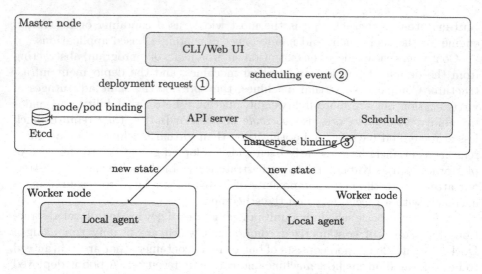

Fig. 1. Pod scheduling orchestration in Kubernetes.

While deploying a pod, it is possible to set deployment constraints that condition how it should be placed in the cluster. For example, it is possible to define pod *affinity* to place the affine pods on the same nodes. Similarly, by defining a pod *anti-affinity* it is possible to avoid deploying the pods on the same node. If the pods have an anti-affinity for themselves, every pod of a service will be deployed on a different node. Pods can also have affinities towards node types.

When a pod deployment is created, a chain of events is generated as illustrated in Fig. 1. When the deployment request is sent to the Kubernetes API server ①, the API server creates and exposes a scheduling event ②. Schedulers listen for such events and when an event targets them they process the request. The scheduler first identifies a node that is suitable for deploying the pod of the scheduling event and then sends a suggestion back to the API server in the form of a namespace binding between the pod and node ③. The API server, at this point, adds the binding to its own distributed storage (i.e., an Etcd server), allowing the local Kubernetes agent running on the selected node to instructs its container runtime to fetch and run the pod's container(s).

A pivotal point in this event chain is when scheduling events are processed by schedulers. The default Kubernetes scheduler iterates unassigned pods one at a time when assigning them to a node. It does so at an incredible speed (i.e., scheduling throughput of more than 50 pods/sec), but its implementation is heuristic-based, and it does not guarantee that pods are placed where they fit best if looking at all deployments as a whole.

The default scheduler identifies the most suitable node in the cluster in two steps [19]:

1. Filter: remove any node that lack any resources required by the pod, doesn't match explicit label or node name requirements, or that report memory or disk pressure.

2. Rank: the remaining nodes are then ranked using a set of priority functions. The ranking is calculated by weighting properties such as highest fraction of free resources (least requested), resource balance, service spread, pre-installed service requirements and affinity requirements.

One consequence of the default weighting of these priority functions is that the ranking will lean towards spread pods as much as possible.

Zephyrus2. Zephyrus2 [1] is a configuration optimizer originally designed to find the optimal placement of applications on virtual machines. Zephyrus2 requires a declarative description as input to specify the software components, the available virtual machines, and the deployment constraints.

The software components are specified in Aeolus [9], i.e., a component model for the definition and reasoning of cloud deployment plans. In Aeolus, software components are modeled as black-boxes that expose require- and provide-ports to capture required and provided functionalities respectively. Every software component consumes a given amount of resources. The virtual machines are modeled instead as locations. Each location has a name, a list of resources that it can provide, and an associated cost. The user can specify (deployment) constraints in an ad-hoc declarative language to define the desired final configuration. The constraints are powerful enough to express, e.g., the presence of a given number of components, their co-installation requirements, and their conflicts.

By exploiting modern SMT and CP technologies, Zephyrus2 finds a configuration distributing components on a set of locations such that: (i) the constraints reflecting the user requirements are satisfied, (ii) every functionality required by a deployed component is provided, (iii) in each location, the available resources are sufficient to cover the resource needs of all components deployed on it, and (iv) the values of some user-defined objective functions are minimized. The default objective-function is to obtain the final configuration with lower cost, choosing the one with the minimal amount of components in case of ties.

Zephyrus2 can be deployed as a Docker container, and it can be invoked by HTTP requests.

3   Boreas - An Optimal Kubernetes Scheduler

In this section we present the salient features of Boreas, how it can be deployed and how the deployment optimization problems are encoded and solved.

Boreas is a custom scheduler for Kubernetes that can replace the default scheduler or run alongside it. The modular system architecture of Kubernetes makes this framework highly configurable and extensible allowing to modify, extend or replace the default scheduler [20].

A graphical representation of the deployment of the Boreas scheduler in a Kubernetes master node is shown in Fig. 2. The Boreas scheduler and Zephyrus2 run in separate Docker containers and are arranged together in a service pod. They run on the master node alongside other Kubernetes system services. The

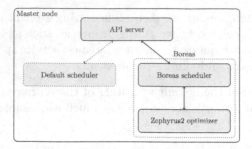

Fig. 2. Boreas from the master node perspective

Boreas scheduler communicates with the API server using the Kubernetes client API, and to Zephyrus2 using regular HTTP requests.

Boreas' workflow starts with collecting the pod deployment requests in batches. The batch size is limited to a maximum amount of events (99 by default). When this limit is reached or if a configurable number of seconds passes (e.g., 30 s by default), the accumulated requests are processed. The Boreas scheduler encodes the deployment of all the pod requests into an optimization problem for Zephyrus2 taking into account the request, the deployment constraints, and the current configuration of the cluster. Zephyrus2 is then invoked, and after processing the problem, it returns the optimal placement for each pod, if any. The Boreas scheduler parses the response and applies it by sending pod deployment instructions to the API server, like the default scheduler.

While Kubernetes is implemented in the Go programming language, any custom component can be implemented in another programming language due to its modular system architecture. Since we were interested in a proof-of-concept implementation, Boreas is implemented in Python. This choice does not call for efficiency, but since the heaviest task is the optimization of the configuration performed by Zephyrus2, the performance of the wrapping layer does not affect the overall scheduling performance. Boreas is constituted by about 400 lines of code and is freely available from the project's Github repository [3].

3.1 Deploying Boreas in Kubernetes

Boreas is deployed as a Kubernetes pod on the master node. The source code includes a deployment script that provides the configurations and privilege required to function as a custom scheduler. The script can be run by using `kubectl`, i.e., the command-line tool to control Kubernetes. Running the deployment script will download the containers and deploy the Boreas pod to the master node, as shown below.

```
$ kubectl create -f deployments/scheduler.yaml
serviceaccount/boreas-scheduler created
clusterrolebinding.rbac.authorization.k8s.io/boreas-
    ↪ scheduler-as-kube-scheduler created
deployment.apps/boreas-scheduler created
```

The Boreas pod will then be listed alongside the default services in the kube-system namespace, i.e., the default namespace used to run the pods implementing the core functionalities of Kubernetes.

```
$ kubectl get pods --namespace=kube-system
NAME                      READY   STATUS    RESTARTS    AGE
boreas-scheduler-<hash>   2/2     Running   0           60s
kube-scheduler-master     1/1     Running   0           1d12h
...
```

3.2 Integration with Zephyrus2

Since the Zephyrus2 container is running in the same pod as the Boreas scheduler, their containers can communicate using HTTP. The Boreas scheduler can therefore retrieve deployment configurations from Zephyrus2 simply by sending an HTTP post request to its container.

The Zephyrus2 tool was originally designed to minimize the cost of application deployment to virtual machines (VMs) [1]. While conceptually there is not a big difference between that problem and the placement of service pods on nodes in a Kubernetes cluster, in practice, extensive adjustments and conversions of the data and constraints had to be made before Zephyrus2 was able to process the placement of Kubernetes pods.

As a first operation, Boreas retrieves the status of every node in the cluster and encodes them into a location, as defined in the Aeolus model [9]. A node with its resources is simply seen as a location in which software components can be deployed. The CPU and the memory available on the node are seen as resources provided by the location. Since Zephyrus2 does not support fractional CPU specification while Kubernetes also allows millicores for pod consumption specification[2], the CPU values had to be rescaled of a factor of 1000. As an example, Listing 1.1 shows the JSON representation gathered for Zephyrus2 of a computation node. Lines 3–6 specifies that there is currently a node ("num": 1) that has a spare capacity of 3972 MB of RAM and 900 millicores.

---

[2] E.g. One CPU equals 1000m where m stands for millicore and a Pod generally occupies few hundreds millicores.

Listing 1.1. Snippet of node encoding for Zephyrus2.

```
1   "locations": {
2     "k8s_worker_1": {
3       "num": 1,
4         "resources": {
5           "RAM": 3972,
6           "cpu": 900 }}}
```

In a Kubernetes cluster, services can be horizontally scaled by defining a number of running copies of pods within the so-called *replica set*. The API server creates individual scheduling events for each pod, including all the pods in a replica set. Passing every single request to Zephyrus2 as a separate request would greatly reduce its performance due to the increased number of components and constraints that would need to be considered. For this reason, Boreas compresses all requests for pods of a replica set into an equivalent unique request while processing events from the API server. The pod requests are then encoded in Zephyrus2 with the notion of a software component and a deployment constraint.

A pod is seen as a black box that requires a given amount of resources. As an example, Listing 1.2 shows the JSON representation of a `frontend` pod that requires 67 MB of RAM and 100 millicores.

Listing 1.2. Snippet of pod encoding for Zephyrus2.

```
12  "components": {
13    "frontend": {
14      "resources": {
15        "RAM": 67,
16        "cpu": 100 }}}
```

The deployment constraint is instead a conjunction of inequality that requires the installation of certain components in a given amount of resources and the metric to minimize. For example the deployment constraints requiring the installation of two frontend pods as encoded in Listing 1.2 is the following.

`"specification": "frontend > 1; cost; (sum ?y in components: ?y)"`

Here the first constraint `frontend > 1` imposes Zephyrus2 to search for configurations in which there are at least 2 `frontend` components. What follows after the semicolon is the definitions of the minimization metric used by Zephyrus2. In this case, Zephyrus2 proceeds to minimize the `cost` of the new deployment. Since no nodes have been defined by specifying a cost, by default, the nodes' costs are treated equally, and therefore this metric simply requires Zephyrus2 to minimize the number of nodes used for the deployment. The last part of the specification string (`sum ?y in components: ?y`) requires Zephyrus2 to break the possible ties between configurations using the same amount of nodes by further minimizing the total number of new pods deployed. In this specific case, since there are no pod dependencies and the frontend was required in an amount strictly greater than 1, Zephyrus will produce a configuration using the least amount of nodes and deploying only two frontends.

The last ingredients taken into consideration by Boreas are affinities and anti-affinities constraints that allow to deploy pods on the same node or only in separate nodes. These constraints were a recent addition to the 1.6 version of Kubernetes [24], but are vital to guarantee the efficiency and reliability of the deployed application and thus frequently used in modern complex applications.

Listing 1.3. Example of affinity and anti-affinity relationships in Kubernetes.

```
1   affinity:
2     podAffinity:
3       requiredDuringSchedulingIgnoredDuringExecution:
4       - labelSelector:
5           matchExpressions:
6           - key: app
7             operator: In
8             values:
9             - frontend
10          topologyKey: "kubernetes.io/hostname"
11    podAntiAffinity:
12      requiredDuringSchedulingIgnoredDuringExecution:
13      - labelSelector:
14          matchExpressions:
15          - key: app
16            operator: In
17            values:
18            - backend
19          topologyKey: "kubernetes.io/hostname"
```

Kubernetes allows to define two types of intra pod affinities, a "hard" one that specifies rules that must be met for a pod to be scheduled and "soft" that specifies preferences that the scheduler will try to enforce but will not guarantee. Boreas, for the time being, considers the "hard" request since these are those that can not be violated and restrict the possible admissible configurations.

In Kubernetes, intra pod affinities and anti-affinities are expressed implicitly using labels assigned to pods, e.g., a pod can be affine to pods having a certain label. Labels allow a certain degree of flexibility but since they are not considered by the Aeolus formal model, Boreas has to compile all the affinity and anti-affinity relationships between pod labels into affinity and anti-affinity between pods. For this reason, Boreas gathers all the labels of batched pods, deployed, pods, and worker nodes and used them to create a reverse look-up function to represent a biunivocal relation between labels and components and nodes names, thus allowing to convert the constraints from labels to components and nodes. The affinity and anti-affinity constraints can thus be precisely defined in the declarative language supported by Zephyrus2.

As an example, Listing 1.3 presents a snippet for the definition of one affinity and one anti-affinity constraint for a `backend` pod deployable in Kubernetes. This snippet assumes that the `backend` has associated a label `app` with value `backend` while the `frontend` pod has associated the label `app` with value `frontend`. The `requiredDuringSchedulingIgnoredDuringExecution` in Lines 3 and 12 specify to Kubernetes that the two constraints are "hard" and must be satisfied during the scheduling. The pod affinity in Lines 4–9 states that the `backend` pod can be scheduled onto a node only if that node has at least one running pod with a label with the key `app` and value `frontend`. Similarly, the pod anti-affinity in Lines 13–18 state that a `backend` pod can not be installed on a node having a pod with a label with key `app` and value `backend`.[3] Finally, the `topologyKey` is used to define the domain of the application of the policy to a topology domain like node, rack, cloud provider zone, or cloud provider region. In this context we can abstract from these details, assuming that the policies apply to all the nodes.

As specified with constraint in Listing 1.3, Boreas detects that there is an affinity between the `backend` and the `frontend`, and an anti-affinity between two `backend` pods. The affinity is encoded as (`forall ?x in locations: (?x.backend` ↪ `> 0 impl ?x.frontend > 0)`) that will require Zephyrus2 to consider configuration in which for all the possible locations x (i.e., for all the Kubernetes nodes), if the number of `backend` pods deployed on x (represented in Zephyrus2 as `?x.backend`) is greater than 0, then also on the same node the number of `frontend` must be greater than 0. This universal quantification of an implication thus excludes the possibility to have a node in which a `backend` is installed but no `frontend` is available. Similarly, Boreas will encode the self anti-affinity constraint as (`forall ?x in locations: (?x.backend <= 1)`). These constraints are added to the specification in conjunction with the constraints specifying the minimal amount of pods required (e.g., in conjunction with the constraint `frontend > 1`).

4   Evaluation

In this section we describe the experiments performed to compare Boreas w.r.t. the default scheduler proving that Boreas can deploy applications that the default scheduler can not.

Due to the lack of established benchmarks for deployment tasks, we set up two kinds of synthetic tests: i) a minimal test to prove that the heuristics of the default scheduler can prevent the full deployment of a simple application, and ii) a more elaborate affinity test using affinity and anti-affinity constraints in which the default scheduler behaves in a nondeterministic way, often preventing the deployment of the application.

---

[3] The Boreas scheduler supports hard pod affinities specified with the `In` operator. The full support of the other operators, e.g., `NotIn`, `Exists` and `DoesNotExist`) is trivial due to the fact that labels are finite at a given point in time and left as a future work.

The scheduling tests are regular Kubernetes deployment scripts, and were initiated with a single Kubernetes command line instruction (i.e., `kubectl create`). A test run is considered successful if the scheduler is able to find placements on worker nodes for all pods requests. Note that the schedulers may fail quite differently. The default scheduler processes as many service pods as possible, leaving some of them in a "Pending" state, meaning that it did not find space to deploy them. Boreas's holistic approach leads instead to the deployment of all the pods or, if all the requests can not be satisfied, leave all pods in a pending state.

Due to the nondeterministic nature of the Kubernetes default scheduler, the evaluation tests were repeated 100 times and run on a small cluster of twelve Ubuntu 20.04 LTS servers running upstream Kubernetes 1.19. Each worker node contributed with 1 CPU and 4 GB of computing resources to the cluster and was built automatically using the open-source *infrastructure as code software tool* Terraform [31]. The Kubernetes software and its dependencies were installed and configured automatically using Ansible playbooks [2]. For solving the optimization problem, Zephyrus2 was configured to rely to OR-Tools [28], i.e., a state-of-the-art constraint solver. To reproduce the deployment, the scripts are available in the project's Github repository [3].

Minimal Test. To verify the difference between Boreas and the default scheduler, the two schedulers were tasked with the deployment of a new system requiring the deployment of two backend pods and three frontend pods on two empty nodes, as visually depicted in Fig. 3. This deployment was set up to require all available CPU resources on two worker nodes.

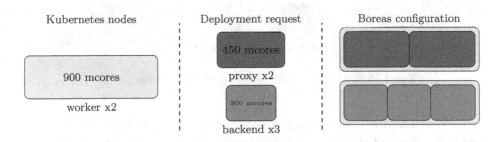

Fig. 3. Minimal test requirements and Boreas configuration

In the Boreas case, the scheduling requests are batched and, as expected, the optimal allocation was always found. On the other hand, the default scheduler had a hard time finding a placement for all five service pods. Its one-at-a-time approach forces it to select a placement for the first service pods without being able to plan for the resources needed for the other service pods. The default scheduler's algorithm for ranking available worker nodes makes it prone to place the first service pods where they will block later service pods in a resource-scarce scenario. Among all the 100 repetitions, none of the deployments were successful when using the default scheduler.

Affinity Test. In the second and more elaborate test we tested the deployment of an application constituted by a reverse proxy server such as Nginx [27] for incoming HTTP requests, frontend and backend components of a web application, and a message broker such as Redis [29] to queue long-running tasks from the backend to separate threads. The application is an instance of the typical web frontend with backend services and cache and is derived from the production ready Online Boutique[4] which can scale up to handle millions of users given the proper amount of resources.

With our deployment constraints, an optimal deployment for this system requires four worker nodes and, differently from the previous test, only 83% of the total amount of the CPU resources are needed. As illustrated in Fig. 4, for redundancy and load balancing purposes 3 backends, 3 frontends, and 3 message brokers are required. Moreover, the system also requires 2 proxy services for communication with the outside world. The backend and frontend have anti-affinity to themselves, thus requiring at most one copy of each in a node. Moreover, the frontend has an affinity to the backend requiring for performance reasons to be deployed in the same node.

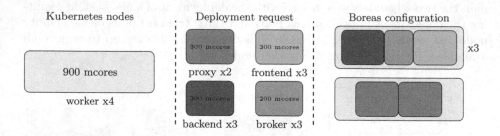

Fig. 4. Affinity test requirements and Boreas configuration

By repeating 100 times the deployment of this system starting from 4 empty nodes, we have noticed that the default scheduler has a success rate of 34%. As with the basic test, its failures result from the earlier placements of service pods blocking the placement of the ones that are scheduled later.[5] When the default scheduler fails, it will not be able to deploy one or two of the pods in the test, usually either a `proxy` or `backend` pod, due to the lack of a suitable node. Boreas, on the other hand, succeeded each test run, giving rise to the

---

[4] https://github.com/GoogleCloudPlatform/microservices-demo

[5] Please note that even though the request are given at once with the command `kubectl create`, the default scheduler sequentializes the requests.

configuration depicted in Fig. 4.[6] The evaluation shows that there are resource-scarce scenarios or complex deployment constraints scenarios where the Boreas scheduler finds placement for services that the default scheduler is unable to find.

In the first set of minimal test, Boreas takes an average of 1.82 s to compute the deployment and 2.15 in the affinity test. Moreover, when the number of replicas in the affinity example is scaled to require a cluster of 8 or 12 nodes, (thus optimizing the placement of a total 22 or 33 pods respectively), Boreas takes 2.92 and 4.22 s in average to compute the optimal placement. For this reason, we conjecture that the majority of the time taken by Boreas for these simple optimization problems is spent on the exchange of messages and in the initialization of Zephyrus2. Trying to reduce the running time by integrating more tightly Zephyrus or an ad-hoc reasoner directly in the Boreas scheduler is beyond the scope of this work and left as future work.

We would like to note that the deployment optimization in Boreas, being an NP-hard problem, does not provide any time guarantee for the returning of the result. The resource consumption of the Boreas scheduler requires less than 50 MB and 400 millicores for scheduling up to 50 pods in 10 nodes. This amount of resources is negligible considering that the current recommended settings for a master node of Kubernetes with 11–100 nodes are 4 vCPUs and 15 GB of memory and slightly above the footprint of the default scheduler that consumes 27 MB and 5 millicore for handling a queue of 50 scheduling events. While the Boreas Scheduler has a low resource consumption, the NP-hardness of the optimization problem solved by Zephyrus2 can also have an impact on the footprint of the Zephyrus2 optimizer container that can vary depending on the nature of the optimization problem and the backend solver used to solve it. Based on Zephyrus2's benchmarks [1] we conjecture that Boreas can be used to deploy up to hundreds of pods in clusters with up to a dozen nodes in less than a minute.[7]

5   Related Work

Kubernetes is a complex ecosystem that rely of a set of plugins and extensions that improve and extend its functionalities. Aside for the scheduler, there are plenty of other approaches that substitute and complement the default implementation. For example, plugins like Istio [18] and Linkerd [22] complement the native handling service-to-service communication with a service mesh.

---

[6] Note that Boreas can compute configurations that are not robust like the one presented in Figure 4 that has two proxies deployed on the same node. It is the user responsibility to define all the constraints to make the final configuration robust stating, e.g., all the anti-affinity constraints.

[7] Additional example of bigger system requiring more computation time from Zephyrus2 (i.e., less than a minute for clusters up to 10 nodes) can be found in the project's Github repository [3].

If we restrict to consider Kubernetes schedulers, different scheduler have been designed to exploit deployment heuristics to try to optimize some resources. As an example, RLSK [15] is a deep Reinforcement Learning Scheduler for Kubernetes that uses reinforcement learning for the refinement of deployment heuristic. To improve resource distribution, Zhang [34] proposed to combine an ant colony and particle swarm optimization algorithms. Li et al. [25] introduced a dynamic Input/Output sensing scheduler for Kubernetes. The scheduler considers the disks pressure in the scheduling process and tries to balance the node disk I/O usage across the cluster dynamically. Similarly, Gaia [30] is a scheduler specifically designed to improve GPUs load distribution, treating GPU resources in the same way Kubernetes treats CPUs. Townend et al. [32] and Wang et al. [33] studied schedulers to reduce energy consumption and heat waste. Poseidon-Firmament [21] is instead a scheduler designed to be faster than the default Kubernetes scheduler on bigger clusters. Differently than Boreas, all these approaches, are neither complete nor optimal, polynomial in the size of the cluster and the number of pods to deploy and thus privileging speed over optimality.

Not focusing on Kubernetes, the closest works to ours is Aeolus Blender [6, 7] that combines the first version of Zephyrus [8] with the Metis planner [23] and the Mandriva Armonic collection into a tool chain that automates ad-hoc deployment tasks. Differently that in our approach, the application domain of Aeolus blender was narrower and they did not combine the configuration optimizer with an established and constraint-rich orchestration tool. Similarly, the Jolie redeployment optimiser [11] used Zephyrus with a reconfiguration coordinator to redeploy micro-services when they are reconfigured. In this case, the service orchestration would be handled by the Jolie redeployment optimiser itself. SmartDepl [13] presents instead an extension to the Abstract Behavioural Specification language (ABS) [16] allowing users to specify costs and other deployment requirements using ABS classes and outputs a deployment configuration by using Zephyrus2. The final configuration can be simulated or formally checked by using the formal methods tools available for ABS.

Also relevant, is the work of Medea [12] that introduces a two-scheduler design for clusters where long-running service containers are deployed together with short-running batch containers. Medea, differently than us, was implemented as an extension to the Apache Hadoop cluster scheduler and finds placement for the long-running containers, leaving the short-running containers for the default scheduler in order to keep scheduling latency low.

6   Conclusion

In this work, we presented an alternative scheduler that optimizes the resource usage and costs of a Kubernetes cluster, i.e., the most used container orchestrator. The new scheduler, Boreas, relies on a configuration optimizer and on a formal model for the cloud deployment. We have shown that Boreas is able to deploy applications that the default scheduler failed to deploy.

Boreas can be used for Kubernetes clusters having only one scheduler per cluster or one scheduler per zone in the case the cluster is divided into zones. Our approach assumes that the components of the application have been profiled to establish their RAM and vCPU consumption, around 50 MB of RAM in the Kubernetes master node, and the selection of a suitable time window for the grouping of the deployment requests and their concurrent deployment. Solving a NP-hard problem, Boreas can not guarantee answers in a short amount of times and therefore, it is mainly targeting clusters encompassing a limited amount of computing nodes (e.g., dozen nodes) and applications that do not require high variability (i.e., less than a hundred new deployment requests per minute).

Boreas is only a proof-of-concept implementation that does not support all the deployment constraints recently introduced in Kubernetes. We plan to extend it further to capture all the possible varieties of deployment constraints (e.g., affinity constraints with different matching criteria for pod labels) and also improve the resolution of the optimization problem. Further evaluations and tests are required to study the impact of possible backup plans for situations in which the solver can not prove the optimality of the solution in time (e.g., use the best solution so far retrieved or the solution produced by the default scheduler). In particular, we are interested in leveraging Boreas to solve the local deployment problems created when topology spread constraints are used. These constraints, introduced in the 1.19 recent version of Kubernetes, are used to control how pods are spread across the cluster regions, zones, or nodes and can split the global problem of scheduling pods into smaller sub-problems that can be solved independently.

Aside from improving Boreas, we are also interested in providing comprehensible explanations for the DevOps operators managing a Kubernetes cluster when a system is not deployable. This can be achieved by exploiting the conflicting constraints found by Boreas when solving the deployment problem. Moreover, inspired by [4,13], we are also interested in introducing more complex deployment constraint directly in Kubernetes to describe dependencies between the pods that allow the cluster operators to avoid "domino" effects due to unstructured scaling actions that may cause cascading slowdowns or outages [35].

References

1. Ábrahám, E., Corzilius, F., Johnsen, E.B., Kremer, G., Mauro, J.: Zephyrus2: on the fly deployment optimization using SMT and CP technologies. In: Fränzle, M., Kapur, D., Zhan, N. (eds.) SETTA 2016. LNCS, vol. 9984, pp. 229–245. Springer, Cham (2016). https://doi.org/10.1007/978-3-319-47677-3_15
2. Ansible - simple IT automation. https://www.ansible.com
3. Boreas scheduler (source code). https://github.com/torgeirl/boreas-scheduler
4. Bravetti, M., Giallorenzo, S., Mauro, J., Talevi, I., Zavattaro, G.: Optimal and automated deployment for microservices. In: Hähnle, R., van der Aalst, W. (eds.) FASE 2019. LNCS, vol. 11424, pp. 351–368. Springer, Cham (2019). https://doi.org/10.1007/978-3-030-16722-6_21

5. Burns, B., Grant, B., Oppenheimer, D., Brewer, E., Wilkes, J.: Borg, Omega, and Kubernetes: Lessons learned from three container-management systems over a decade. Queue **14**, 70–93 (2016)
6. Catan, M., et al.: Aeolus: mastering the complexity of cloud application deployment. In: Lau, K.-K., Lamersdorf, W., Pimentel, E. (eds.) ESOCC 2013. LNCS, vol. 8135, pp. 1–3. Springer, Heidelberg (2013). https://doi.org/10.1007/978-3-642-40651-5_1
7. Di Cosmo, R., Eiche, A., Mauro, J., Zacchiroli, S., Zavattaro, G., Zwolakowski, J.: Automatic deployment of services in the cloud with aeolus blender. In: Barros, A., Grigori, D., Narendra, N.C., Dam, H.K. (eds.) ICSOC 2015. LNCS, vol. 9435, pp. 397–411. Springer, Heidelberg (2015). https://doi.org/10.1007/978-3-662-48616-0_28
8. Di Cosmo, R., et al.: Automated Synthesis and Deployment of Cloud Applications. In: ASE. ACM (2014)
9. Di Cosmo, R., Mauro, J., Zacchiroli, S., Zavattaro, G.: Aeolus: a component model for the cloud. Inf. Comput. **239**, 100–141 (2014)
10. Fazio, M., Celesti, A., Ranjan, R., Liu, C., Chen, L., Villari, M.: Open issues in scheduling microservices in the cloud. IEEE Cloud Comput. **3**(5), 81–88 (2016)
11. Gabbrielli, M., Giallorenzo, S., Guidi, C., Mauro, J., Montesi, F.: Self-reconfiguring microservices. In: Theory and Practice of Formal Methods. Springer, Cham (2016)
12. Garefalakis, P., Karanasos, K., Pietzuch, P., Suresh, A., Rao, S.: Medea: scheduling of long running applications in shared production clusters. In: EuroSys. ACM (2018)
13. de Gouw, S., Mauro, J., Zavattaro, G.: On the modeling of optimal and automatized cloud application deployment. JLAMP **107**, 108–135 (2019)
14. Hightower, K., Burns, B., Beda, J.: Kubernetes: Up & Running: Dive into the Future of Infrastructure. O'Reilly Media, New York (2017)
15. Huang, J., Xiao, C., Wu, W.: RLSK: a job scheduler for federated kubernetes clusters based on reinforcement learning. In: IC2E. IEEE (2020)
16. Johnsen, E.B., Hähnle, R., Schäfer, J., Schlatte, R., Steffen, M.: ABS: a core language for abstract behavioral specification. In: Aichernig, B.K., de Boer, F.S., Bonsangue, M.M. (eds.) FMCO 2010. LNCS, vol. 6957, pp. 142–164. Springer, Heidelberg (2011). https://doi.org/10.1007/978-3-642-25271-6_8
17. Korte, B., Vygen, J.: Combinatorial Optimization: Theory and Algorithms, 5th edn. Springer, Heidelberg (2012). https://doi.org/10.1007/978-3-642-24488-9
18. Managing microservices with the istio service mesh (2017). https://kubernetes.io/blog/2017/05/managing-microservices-with-istio-service-mesh
19. Scheduler algorithm in kubernetes (kubernetes community docs). https://github.com/kubernetes/community/blob/master/contributors/devel/sig-scheduling/scheduler_algorithm.md
20. Extending your Kubernetes Cluster (Kubernetes v1.19 Docs). https://v1-19.docs.kubernetes.io/docs/concepts/extend-kubernetes/extend-cluster
21. Poseidon-Firmament. https://v1-16.docs.kubernetes.io/docs/concepts/extend-kubernetes/poseidon-firmament-alternate-scheduler
22. Linkerd - A different kind of service mesh. https://linkerd.io/2/overview
23. Lascu, T.A., Mauro, J., Zavattaro, G.: Automatic deployment of component-based applications. Sci. Comput. Program. **113**, 261–284 (2015)
24. Lewis, I.: Advanced scheduling in kubernetes 2017. Kubernetes Blog online Posted 2017–03–31 (2017). https://kubernetes.io/blog/2017/03/advanced-scheduling-in-kubernetes

25. Li, D., Wei, Y., Zeng, B.: A dynamic I/O sensing scheduling scheme in Kubernetes. In: HPCC. ACM (2020)
26. Merkel, D.: Docker: lightweight linux containers for consistent development and deployment. Linux J. **2014**(239), 2 (2014)
27. Nginx - a high-performance HTTP server and reverse proxy. https://nginx.com
28. Perron, L.: Operations research and constraint programming at Google. In: Lee, J. (ed.) CP 2011. LNCS, vol. 6876, p. 2. Springer, Heidelberg (2011). https://doi. org/10.1007/978-3-642-23786-7_2
29. Redis - an in-memory database. https://redis.io
30. Song, S., Deng, L., Gong, J., Luo, H.: Gaia scheduler: a kubernetes-based scheduler framework. In: ISPA/IUCC/BDCloud/SocialCom/SustainCom. IEEE (2018)
31. Terraform - an infrastructure as code software tool. https://www.terraform.io
32. Townend, P., et al.: Improving data center efficiency through holistic scheduling in kubernetes. In: SOSE. IEEE (2019)
33. Wang, S., Sheng, Q.Z., Li, X., Mahmood, A., Zhang, Y.: Energy minimization for cloud services with stochastic requests. In: Kafeza, E., Benatallah, B., Martinelli, F., Hacid, H., Bouguettaya, A., Motahari, H. (eds.) ICSOC 2020. LNCS, vol. 12571, pp. 133–148. Springer, Cham (2020). https://doi.org/10.1007/978-3-030-65310-1_11
34. Wei-guo, Z., Xi-lin, M., Jin-zhong, Z.: Research on Kubernetes' resource scheduling scheme. In: ICCNS. ACM (2018)
35. Woods, D.: On infrastructure at scale: a cascading failure of distributed systems. https://medium.com/@daniel.p.woods/on-infrastructure-at-scale-a-cascading-failure-of-distributed-systems-7cff2a3cd2df

Resource Management for TensorFlow Inference

Luciano Baresi, Giovanni Quattrocchi(✉), and Nicholas Rasi

Dipartimento di Elettronica, Informazione e Bioingegneria,
Politecnico di Milano, Milan, Italy
{luciano.baresi,giovanni.quattrocchi,nicholas.rasi}@polimi.it

Abstract. TensorFlow, a popular machine learning (ML) platform, allows users to transparently exploit both GPUs and CPUs to run their applications. Since GPUs are optimized for compute-intensive workloads (e.g., matrix calculus), they help boost executions, but introduce resource heterogeneity. TensorFlow neither provides efficient heterogeneous resource management nor allows for the enforcement of user-defined constraints on the execution time. Most of the works address these issues in the context of creating models on existing data sets (*training* phase), and only focus on scheduling algorithms. This paper focuses on the *inference* phase, that is, on the application of created models to predict the outcome on new data interactively, and presents a comprehensive resource management solution called *ROMA (Resource Constrained ML Applications)*. ROMA is an extension of TensorFlow that (a) provides means to easily deploy multiple TensorFlow models in containers using Kubernetes b) allows users to set constraints on response times, (c) schedules the execution of requests on GPUs and CPUs using heuristics, and (d) dynamically refines the CPU core allocation by exploiting control theory. The assessment conducted on four real-world benchmark applications compares *ROMA* against four different systems and demonstrates a significant reduction (>75%) in constraint violations and 24% saved resources on average.

1 Introduction

TensorFlow [1] is one of the most used machine learning (ML) framework in industry [10] and shares similar functionality with other solutions such as PyTorch [19] or MXNet [5]. While TensorFlow supports different types of ML applications, this paper focuses on *supervised learning* ones because of the two phases that characterize their lifecycle: *training* and *inference*. In the former case, algorithms like logistic regression, decision trees, and deep neural networks are used to create prediction models starting from known input-output pairs

This work has been partially supported by the SISMA national research project, which has been funded by the MIUR under the PRIN 2017 program (Contract 201752ENYB) and by the European Commission grant no. 825480 (H2020), SODALITE.

H. Hacid et al. (Eds.): ICSOC 2021, LNCS 13121, pp. 238–253, 2021.
https://doi.org/10.1007/978-3-030-91431-8_15

(e.g., pictures and contained objects), called training set. In the latter case, generated prediction models are used as oracles to infer the result on new, unknown inputs. The first phase makes these applications batch ones, while the second phase requires that these applications be *interactive*.

Both phases are characterized by highly parallel operations (e.g., matrix calculus) that can exploit multi-core architectures. TensorFlow eases the use of multi-core CPUs and also of GPUs, which provide hundreds of cores and very fast executions. Oftentimes, these applications are executed in the cloud, where virtual machines (VMs) equipped with GPUs and dedicated execution frameworks can easily be rented from many cloud providers.

TensorFlow (similarly to other ML frameworks) does not allow users to define constraints on response times (Service Level Agreements or SLA) for these applications, and resource management is driven by user experience or by simple default policies that do not take actual application needs into account. Training would call for deadlines, that is, constraints on the maximum span of batch processing [21], while inference calls for average response times, computed on a number of subsequent invocations over a predefined time window.

Several approaches in the literature focus on the resource management of ML training [3,12], while the inference phase calls for new studies and approaches. Existing solutions applied to interactive web applications [2,7] cannot be reused since they do not consider the heterogeneity introduced by GPUs but only different types of virtual machines. CPUs and GPUs are interdependent resources while different VMs are not. GPUs are faster than CPUs but they also use CPUs to load and write data, and to be activated. Moreover, they have different scaling capabilities: CPUs can precisely be scaled by allocating fractions of cores to single applications; GPUs can only be time-shared among applications. While faster GPUs alone are usually not enough to serve realistic workloads, the coordinated use of CPUs and GPUSs becomes mandatory to offer reasonable execution times.

On the other hand, solutions that combine the management of CPUs and GPUs target the training phase (or long-lasting processing), they focus on scheduling and loadbalancing algorithms, and do not consider dynamic resource provisioning [17,18]. Finally, in inference mode the distributed heterogeneous execution of multiple concurrent ML applications is still not completely supported in TensorFlow (as in other similar tools) and users are required to manually configure their deployments.

This paper presents *ROMA*, an extension of TensorFlow that helps the deployment and oversees the inference phases of multiple concurrent ML applications deployed onto a shared cluster of nodes that offer both CPUs and GPUs. *ROMA* manages containerized TensorFlow models, automates their deployment using Kubernetes[1], a well known container orchestrator, and allows users to define SLAs as constraint on the response time. *ROMA* enacts the control at three different levels. A centralized component exploits heuristics to prioritize the scheduling of application requests on GPUs or CPUs according to their needs.

---

[1] https://kubernetes.io.

Distributed control-theoretical planners allocate the amount of CPUs needed to each application by considering the boost introduced by GPUs. An intermediate level handles resource contentions that could happen when the system saturates.

The evaluation based on four real-world applications shows that $ROMA$: i) enables the distributed concurrent execution of multiple applications on heterogeneous resources ii) minimizes the number of SLA violations (reduction >75%) compared to static and rule-based solutions, and a simplified control-theoretic approach, and iii) optimizes the use of cluster resources by avoiding unneeded allocations (24% resource saving on average).

The rest of the paper is organized as follows. Section 2 introduces $ROMA$, its architecture and deployment model. Section 3 presents how the schedulers work, and Sect. 4 explains the employed control-theoretical planners. Section 5 shows the empirical evaluation we carried out to assess $ROMA$. Section 6 discusses the related work and Sect. 7 concludes the paper.

2   ROMA

$ROMA$[2] is a comprehensive resource management solution that eases the deployment and operations of multiple interactive ML applications. $ROMA$ can be useful to both users interested in running their ML applications and service providers. In the former case, $ROMA$ helps the user manage resources efficiently and meet set response times. In the latter case, $ROMA$ allows the service provider to allocate fewer resources to each application and offer an higher level solution to users (ML as-a-service).

$ROMA$ is an extension of TensorFlow but it can be easily integrated onto other ML platforms. TensorFlow, as other similar frameworks, does not provide any dedicated support to distribute the inference of new results on computed trained models, neither it takes into account concurrent executions specifically. An extension, called *TensorFlow Serving*[3] (*TF Serving* for brevity) permits users to expose a trained model by means of a built-in web server and a dedicated REST API but the distributed deployment is not supported. $ROMA$ wraps TF Serving instances into containers using *Docker*[4]. Docker also provides means to allocate and share CPU cores among multiple processes through CPU quotas. GPUs can be mounted on Docker containers by using external tools, as the NVIDIA Container Toolkit[5].

The deployment of TF Serving containers is enacted using *Kubernetes*. Kubernetes manages *Pods*, that are, groups of co-located containers and volumes, which bind ephemeral containers to persistent data stores. *Deployments* manage the deployment of pods, along with the number of needed replicas, and how they can be upgraded and configured. *Services* bring communication among related pods by adding shared networking, load-balancing, and external access.

---

[2] Source code is available at https://github.com/deib-polimi/ROMA.
[3] https://www.tensorflow.org/tfx/guide/serving.
[4] https://www.docker.com.
[5] https://github.com/NVIDIA/nvidia-docker.

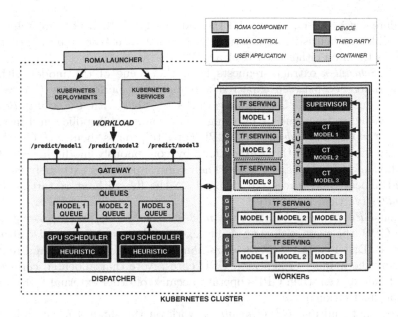

Fig. 1. *ROMA.*

Kubernetes also offers dedicated plugins for AMD and NVIDIA boards (the NVIDIA Container Toolkit is then required) to exploit GPUs [15], but a single GPU cannot be associated with more than one container, and fractions of GPUs cannot be requested (they can only be allocated as complete units).

2.1 Architecture

Figure 1 shows the architecture of *ROMA* while managing three ML models. *ROMA* uses a centralized node, called *dispatcher*, and multiple distributed nodes, called *workers*. *Dispatcher* allows users to add trained models (applications), receives inference (execution) requests, and uses schedulers to distribute these executions on *workers' devices*. Each *worker* provides one or more *devices*, that is, at least one CPU and zero or more GPUs.

ROMA deploys *model executables*, that are containers wrapping a TF Serving instance loaded with one or more models, as Kubernetes pods into *workers*. For each managed model, multiple *model executables* (i.e., replicas) can be deployed onto different *workers* to handle intense workloads. Each *model executable* can be instructed to process a request on CPUs or GPUs. Moreover, *model executables* are deployed onto *workers* along with a dedicated control theory-based controller (*CT Controller*) in charge of the fine-grained allocation of CPU cores.

Gateway accommodates requests in dedicated execution queues, one for each application (i.e., trained model). Requests are kept in the queues waiting for execution, that is, waiting for a GPU or CPU to become available. Requests are removed from the queues and assigned for execution to *model executables* by two different schedulers, one for GPUs and one for CPUs. The two schedulers exploit different heuristics to prioritize requests and instruct *model executables* to process them on either a GPU or a CPU.

GPU Scheduler extracts requests from the queue of the model with the greatest difference between expected and measured performance (see Sect. 3) to boost executions. *CPU Scheduler* works together with *CT Controllers*. It removes requests from queues by using a fair round-robin policy and instructs the proper *model executables* to use CPU cores to process them. *CT Controllers* accelerate or decelerate these executions by continuously modifying the CPU cores allocated to *model executables*. Their control period is extremely fast (i.e., 1 s) and allocated resources are changed on the fly, without restarting *model executables* (vertical scalability).

When *GPU Scheduler* instructs a *model executable* to process a request by using a GPU, the average time needed to execute that *model executable* abruptly decreases[6]. Distributed *CT Controllers* handle this sudden change and react by decreasing the number of allocated CPU cores. Note that allocated cores could not be lowered even when GPUs operate because of other external factors (e.g., workload fluctuations).

Given that multiple *CT Controllers* work on the same *worker* node, their combined resource demand can be greater than the actual capacity of the node: a *Supervisor* deployed onto each *worker* oversees demands and manage contentions. Collected data on resource demand, contention, and execution times can then be used to deploy new *model executables* and new *workers*, but this is out of the scope of this paper. Both schedulers and supervisors exploit lightweight heuristics to be reactive and manage incoming requests properly.

In the case of extremely high workloads, the *dispatcher* can easily be replicated to accommodate a higher level of parallelism without any changes to the underlying control strategies. In this case, clients connect either directly to one of the available replicas or to an additional load balancer that in turn distributes the traffic to the *dispatchers*. Then, each *dispatcher* can work independently of the others by only scheduling the traffic portion it receives. Local *CT Controllers* just need to be informed of the amount of requests executed by the GPUs without any additional knowledge on the deployment of the other components. *Workers* can be managed by a single designated *dispatcher* or shared among multiple ones. In the latter case, the multiple schedulers would not interfere with one another since their algorithms only use application-level performance data that are locally measured by each *dispatcher*.

2.2 Deployment

As soon as a user submits a trained model, along with its SLA, *ROMA Launcher* generates or updates required Kubernetes *deployments* and *services* to let the system deploy and manage the *model executables*.

---

[6] This average execution time is computed by considering the different executions of the same *model executable* over a given time window.

ROMA uses two strategies to deploy *model executables*. The user can set the number of to-be-deployed replicas for each model. Replicas can also be added and removed dynamically according to application needs. The placement of *model executables* can either balance their number on the different nodes or deploy them onto the same *worker* until a predefined number of replicas is reached. Note that *ROMA* does not allow one to deploy multiple replicas of the same model on the same *worker* node for the same device. If *model executables* need more resources on the fly, *CT Controllers* takes care of it without creating new replicas.

To exploit the different *devices*, each *model executable* is bounded to a specific *device*. In particular, given m models selected to be deployed onto a worker node, *ROMA* provisions: (i) m *model executable* containing one model each, and binds them to the node's CPU(s), (ii) one *model executable*, containing all models, for each GPU, and (iii) one container that includes the *CT Controllers* of all models, the *Supervisor*, and one actuator implemented as a Kubernetes volume. This means that since we assume that the worker depicted in Fig. 1 comes with two GPUs, and it manages three models, *ROMA* deploys six containers in total.

This deployment allows *ROMA* to exploit the means provided by Kubernetes for using GPUs on each model and also to exploit the CPUs when needed. As already said, the *Supervisor* and models' *CT Controllers* manage CPU cores. As for CPUs *ROMA* deploys a different container for each model because resources can be allocated to them independently. Since GPUs cannot be shared among multiple containers, nor can their cores be allocated to different models, a single container per GPU with all models is enough. The *GPU Scheduler* is in charge of electing the model that can exploit the GPU to serve the next inference request (this is done by calling an internal, model-specific TensorFlow Serving endpoint). At each control step, *ROMA* uses an actuator based on *Docker out of Docker (DooD)* to provide on-the-fly reconfiguration of running containers. DooD is a volume that provides means to launch Docker commands (e.g., to re-configure a container) within another container[7].

3   Schedulers and Supervisors

The goal of *ROMA* is to fulfill constraint over the response time. While in the following we constrain the *average* response time, more conservative metrics (e.g., high percentiles) would only require a stricter set-point and more used resources, and would provide additional tail-latency guarantees. However, our evaluation (see Sect. 5) shows that even by only constraining the *average*

---

[7] In December 2020, the Kubernetes team announced that the Docker runtime will be considered deprecated in future versions [14]. Docker will not be removed from Kubernetes at least until late 2021. While the evaluation of *ROMA* in Sect. 5 is based on the described Docker-dependent implementation, we are already developing a version of *ROMA* that does not require Docker and that supports other container runtimes as, for example, *containerd* [6].

response time, $ROMA$ provides a lower maximum response time than other competitor approaches (e.g., rule-based).

Given a model m, the average response time computed over a given time window w can be formulated as follows.

$$\tau_{R_m} = \frac{\sum_{g=1}^{G}(\tau_{Q_g} + \tau_{P_g}) + \sum_{c=1}^{C}(\tau_{Q_c} + \tau_{P_c})}{G + C} \tag{1}$$

where G and C are the numbers of requests executed on the GPUs and CPUs respectively in w, τ_{Q_i} is the time spent by a request i in the queue, while τ_{P_i} is

---

Algorithm 1. GPU Scheduling

```
1: function FREEGPU(gpu)
2:      ε = []
3:      M ← getModels()
4:      for m ∈ M do
5:          q ← m.getQueue()
6:          T_E ← []
7:          for n ← 0, n < q.length, n++ do
8:              req ← q[n]
9:              τ_Q = now() − req.getTimeIn()
10:             T_E.append(τ_Q + n * τ_PG_m)
11:         end for
12:         comp ← m.getCompletedRequests()
13:         T_R ← []
14:         for req ∈ comp do
15:             T_R.append(req.getRT())
16:         end for
17:         τ_R_m ← avg(T_R)
18:         τ_E_m ← avg(T_E)
19:         τ_W_m = β * τ_E_m + (1 − β) * τ_R_m
20:         τ°_R_m ← α * τ_SLA_m
21:         if τ_W_m ≤ τ°_R_m then
22:             ε_m ← 0
23:         else
24:             ε_m ← (τ_W_m − τ°_R_m)/τ°_R_m
25:         end if
26:         ε.append(ε_m)
27:     end for
28:     m_S ← M[ε.indexOf(max(ε))]
29:     req ← m_S.getQueue().pop()
30:     gpu.execute(req)
31: end function
```

Algorithm 2. Supervisor

```
1: cs = getControllers()
2: U_C ← []
3: for c ∈ cs do
4:     u_C ← c.nextAllocation()
5:     U_C.append(u_C)
6: end for
7: AC ← MC − GC
8: η ← AC/sum(U_C)
9: for c ← 0, c < cs.length, c++ do
10:    u_C ← U_C[c]
11:    if η ≤ 1 then
12:        u'_C ← u_C * η
13:    else if η > 1 then
14:        u'_C ← (1 − γ) * u_C * +η * γ * u_C
15:    end if
16:    cs[c].updateStateAndActuate(u'_C)
17: end for
```

---

the time spent by a GPU or a CPU to process request i. An SLA on τ_{R_m} can state that:

$$\tau_{R_m} <= \alpha \cdot \tau_{SLA_m} = \tau^{\circ}_{R_m} \tag{2}$$

where τ_{SLA_m} is the threshold on the response time defined in the SLA for model m and α is a parameter, which ranges between 0 and 1, that defines the set point $\tau^{\circ}_{R_m}$ for model m. If $\alpha = 1$ then the set point matches τ_{SLA_m}; lower values are more conservative and let the system tolerate more imprecision.

As already said, $ROMA$ distributes the processing of requests to the different *devices* in the cluster by means of the two dedicated schedulers. Their goal is to select both which request to execute next and on which *device*. The rationale is that *GPU Scheduler* always selects the request of the model with the "highest" needs (see below). To complement GPUs, requests are also scheduled for processing onto CPUs by means of a round-robin policy where the (non-empty) queues to serve are selected randomly. Note that *CPU Scheduler* could find queues empty if the GPUs are fast enough to process all the workload alone.

GPU Scheduler is activated in an event-based fashion. Function *freeGPU* (Algorithm 1) is executed as soon as a GPU (parameter *gpu*) becomes free, that is, at system startup and when a GPU completes the execution of a request. In particular, we designed a heuristic that, for each model m, takes into account a weighted average (τ_{W_m}) of measured response times (τ_{R_m}) and of the estimated response times of the requests that are in the queues waiting to be processed (τ_{E_m}). The estimation is computed by using the accumulated queue time of each request (τ_Q in Eq. 1) and the profiled processing time on GPUs τ_{PG_m}. Parameter β, which ranges in interval $[0, 1]$, defines the weight associated with τ_{R_m} and τ_{E_m}. A higher value of β gives more importance to requests in the queue and makes the system more responsive to workload bursts. Given the computed averaged response time τ_{W_m}, the distance from the set point $\tau_{R_m}^{\circ}$ is computed as ϵ_m (lines 21–25). The selected model m_S is the one with the highest ϵ_m. The first request in queue m_S is the one that is processed by *gpu* using the proper *model executable* (lines 28–30).

The actual allocation of CPU cores is managed by the *CT Controllers* associated with the different *model executables*. For this reason, *CPU Scheduler* dispatches requests to CPU *devices* using a round robin policy. *CPU Scheduler* repeatedly removes a request from a randomly selected queue and schedules it for CPU execution on a randomly selected *model executable*. This way the load sent by *CPU Scheduler* to each *model executable* is homogeneous and the burden of managing CPU allocation is handled locally by *CT Controllers*. Each *worker* is associated with a *Supervisor* in charge of refining the resource allocation computed by *CT Controllers* in case of contention. At each control step (1 s), a *CT Controller* computes the amount of CPU cores u_C (core allocation demand) needed by its *model executable*, which embeds model m, to meet set response time $\tau_{R_m}^{\circ}$ (as described in Sect. 4). Each *CT Controller* computes its u_C independently of the others, that is, they do not communicate.

Supervisors use the heuristic shown in Algorithm 2 to compute a feasible core allocation u_C' for each *CT Controller* deployed on a *worker*. First, all the core allocation demands u_C are gathered in a vector $\mathcal{U}_C$ (line 1–6). Being MC the total number of cores provided by the *worker*, and GC the number of CPU cores statically allocated to support GPU execution, the difference between MC and GC is the actual amount of cores that can be allocated (AC) to *model executables* (line 7) in a given *worker*. As mentioned before, GPUs and CPUs are interdependent since the former consume the processing power of the latter to load data in memory and to be activated. Note that if GC is set to 0, GPUs will slow down requests running on CPUs. This is seen by *CT Controller* as another disturbance that is naturally mitigated by the control logic (described in Sect. 4). Moreover, η is the ratio between AC and the sum of all demanded cores, that is, the sum of all u_C (line 8). Given η, each u_C' is computed as follows. If η is less than 1, the actual demand cannot be fulfilled since demanded cores are more that available ones (under provisioning). Each u'_C is then computed by multiplying each u_C by η (line 12). If η is equal to 1, the amount of demanded cores matches available ones (AC), and $u'_C = u_C$. If η is greater than 1, available cores are over provisioned. However, we introduce parameter γ to maximize resource utilization (line 14). The default value $(\gamma = 0)$ implies that $u'_C = u_C$. If γ is between 0 and 1, we allocate more cores and obtain more responsive models. $\gamma = 1$ means that all AC cores are always used. Finally, the state of each CT $Controller$ is updated using u'_C and computed core allocation is actuated.

4   Controllers

To design the CT $Controller$ we need a dynamic model[8] for the relationship between the CPU and GPU allocation (u_C, u_G) and the response time τ_R; u_C and u_G jointly modify the output rate r_o from the queue, the input rate r_i being an exogenous disturbance. CT $Controllers$ do not require any knowledge of the application structure (i.e., of the operations to execute on input data) and the same dynamic model is general enough to support different kinds of compute- and GPU-intensive interactive applications (e.g., machine learning inference, scientific calculus, graph-based computations), with proper profiling. This is possible because the proposed controllers are grey-box, that is, their model does not include all aspects of the system but just the ones that describe its physics. The employed fast feedback-loop (control period equals to 1 s) is in charge of correcting the imperfections of the model at runtime. Here we represent the compound of the above in a simplified manner (yet adequate, as the reported tests will show) as an additive perturbation, and we set:

$$\begin{cases} \tau_R(t) = \tau_Q(t) + \tau_P(t) \\ \tau_Q(t) = \frac{\ell(t-\tau_Q(t))}{r_o(t)} \\ \frac{d\ell(t)}{dt} = r_i(t) - r_o(t) \\ r_o(t) = r_{on}\big(u_C(t), u_G(t)\big) + d_o(t) \\ \tau_P(t) = \tau_{Pn}\big(u_C(t), u_G(t)\big) + d_P(t) \end{cases} \tag{3}$$

where τ_Q the time spent on the queue, τ_P is the processing time downstream of the queue depending on (u_P, u_G) through a nominal relationship $\tau_{Pn}(\cdot, \cdot)$ with an additive disturbance d_P, and $r_{on}(\cdot, \cdot)$ is the $(u_C, u_G) \to r_o$ relationship in some "nominal" condition, and $d_o(t)$ the combined effect of all the disturbances.

Model (3) explains the physics of the system, but is not suitable as is for control design owing to the contextual presence of a differential equation and an implicit one with delay. It however evidences that under the above assumptions, response time control boils down to queue length control. From Eq. (3) one notices that (i) at steady state r_o has to balance r_i but this can happen for any ℓ, hence (ii) a steady-state variation of τ_R is obtained by $transiently$ causing an

---

[8] To avoid ambiguities, in this section a $dynamic$ $model$ is a mathematical representation of the controlled system, that is, of the ML application.

input/output rate imbalance via u_C and/or u_G, and then restoring the balance once the desired τ_R is achieved as the new queue length, divided – mind the balance – by the through rate, gives the necessary τ_Q, hence τ_R.

$$\begin{cases} \frac{d\ell(t)}{dt} = r_i(t) - r_o(t) \\ r_o(t) = \mu_C u_c(t) + \mu_G u_G(t) \\ \tau_R(t) = \frac{\ell(t)}{r_o(t)} \end{cases} \qquad (4)$$

where the gains μ_C and μ_G account for the processing speed of CPUs and GPUs, respectively, and the delay is considered negligible with respect to the control time scale. Linearised in the vicinity of an operating point described by nominal values of the throughput and the required waiting time, $\bar{r}_o$ and $\bar{\tau}_R$ to name them,

Overall, therefore, the compound of the above gives rise to the continuous-time transfer function description:

$$\Delta\tau_R(s) = G_{\tau_R C}(s)\Delta u_C(s) + G_{\tau_R G}(s)\Delta u_G(s) \qquad (5)$$

where uppercase letters denote the Laplace transform of the corresponding lowercase variables and:

$$G_{\tau_R C}(s) = -\frac{\mu_C}{\bar{r}_o}\frac{1 + s\bar{\tau}_R}{s}, \quad G_{\tau_R G}(s) = -\frac{\mu_G}{\bar{r}_o}\frac{1 + s\bar{\tau}_R}{s} \qquad (6)$$

where s is the Laplace transform complex variable. Transforming (6) to discrete time, we conclude that a physically grounded $\mathcal{Z}$-transform model (denoting by z the corresponding complex variable, i.e., the one-step advance operator) takes the form:

$$\Delta\tau_R(z) = G^*_{\tau_R C}(z)\Delta u_C(z) + G^*_{\tau_R G}(z)\Delta u_G(z) \qquad (7)$$

where

$$G^*_{\tau_R C}(z) = -k_C\frac{z - b}{z - 1}, \quad G^*_{\tau_R G}(z) = -k_G\frac{z - b}{z - 1} \qquad (8)$$

Parameters k_C, k_G, and b can be obtained online by profiling the applications of interest and fitting measured responses to those of the dynamic model. In this work we assume that when a GPU takes part of the work —which is represented as a step-like behaviour of u_G— the CPU attempts to restore the required τ_R so as to free the GPU as soon as possible. This means requiring that the closed-loop transfer function from u_G to τ_R has a zero in $z = 1$. The said transfer function then becomes:

$$F_o(z) = \frac{z - 1}{z - p} \qquad (9)$$

where parameter $p \in [0, 1]$ governs the required response speed: $p \to 0$ means faster response, $p \to 1$ slower. This gives controller

$$G_c(z) = \frac{(k_C - 1)z^2 + (2 - k_C p - k_C b)z + k_G bp - 1}{k_C(z - 1)(z - b)} \tag{10}$$

i.e., a real PID. To further reduce computational complexity, we however decided to employ a PI controller, that is,

$$G_c(z) = K\frac{z - a}{z - 1} \tag{11}$$

and prescribe the closed-loop poles to coincide in $z = q$, where q is interpreted as p above. This is achieved by setting:

$$K = \frac{4(a - 1)(b - 1)}{k(b - a)^2}, \quad a = \frac{(2 - b)q - b}{q - 2b + 1} \tag{12}$$

while the presence of integral action ensures zero steady-state errors.

5   Evaluation

This section describes the experiments we carried out to evaluate the feasibility and benefits of *ROMA*.

To run the experiments, we deployed *ROMA* on a cluster of three virtual machines on Microsoft Azure: one VM of type $HB60rs$ with a CPU with 60 cores and 240 GB of memory for the *dispatcher*, and two VMs, as *worker* nodes, of type $NV6$ equipped with a NVIDIA Tesla $M60$ GPU and a CPU with 6 cores and 56 GB of memory. We also used an additional instance of type $HB60rs$ for generating the client workload.

The experiments exploited four existing ML applications: *Skyline Extraction* [9], *ResNet* [11], *GoogLeNet* [20], and *VGG16* [22]. The first application uses a combination of computer-vision algorithms to extrapolate the horizon skyline from a set of images and the others perform classification tasks. In particular, *ResNet* exploits a residual neural network, while *GoogLeNet* (*G.Net*) and *VGG16* employ two different deep convolutional neural networks. All these four models were trained and then used in inference mode with companion sample images.

ROMA ($\alpha = 0.8$, $\beta = 0.5$ and $\gamma = 0$) was set to use a static deployment strategy and we deployed all applications onto the two *worker* nodes. We statically reserved $GC = 0$ cores for the GPUs, to say that the additional disturbances introduced by the usage of CPUs for loading and operating GPUs are handled by *CT Controllers*. These controllers were manually tuned: $K = 0.15$ and $a = 0.11$.

We compared *ROMA* against the four exemplar systems we implemented by using a different heuristic for the *GPU Scheduler* and/or another type of controllers instead of *CT Controllers*. All these systems used a round robin scheduler (RR) for GPUs. In addition, system *RR+rules* used a rule-based controller that allocated 1 additional CPU core to a *model executable* if the response time is greater than or equal to $0.8 * SLA$. If the response time is equal to or less than

Table 1. SLA and workloads.

Test	Apps	SLA	Workload
2-Apps	Skyline	0.38	20-20-80-80-20-20-20-20
	G.Net	0.45	20-20-20-20-70-70-20-20
2-Apps	ResNet	0.54	40-30-20-40-30-20-30-30
	VGG16	0.56	20-30-40-20-40-40-30-30
AllApps	Skyline	0.38	10-10-10-10-30-30-30-10
	G.Net	0.45	10-30-30-30-10-10-10-10
	ResNet	0.54	10-20-30-10-20-30-10-20
	VGG16	0.56	10-30-20-10-30-20-10-20

Table 2. Comparison.

Test	System	τ_R	τ_{R_M}	τ_{R_σ}	V	Res
2-Apps G.Net Skyline	ROMA	0.168	0.245	0.031	0	748
	RR+CT	0.193	0.358	0.053	0	793
	RR+rules	0.185	0.638	0.075	10	1165
	RR+max	0.152	0.191	0.014	0	3600
	RR+min	0.278	1.053	0.182	40	600
2-Apps ResNet VGG16	ROMA	0.266	0.553	0.068	10	1633
	RR+CT	0.446	0.949	0.117	70	1750
	RR+rules	0.701	3.829	0.528	120	1691
	RR+max	0.337	0.711	0.092	40	3600
	RR+min	1.537	4.423	0.464	180	600
AllApps	ROMA	0.167	0.427	0.022	0	1767
	RR+CT	0.325	1.372	0.130	90	2018
	RR+rules	0.409	1.913	0.158	140	1973
	RR+max	0.208	0.453	0.052	0	3600
	RR+min	1.032	6.828	0.414	170	600

$0.2 * SLA$ it de-allocated a core. The control period was set to 15 s. System *RR+CT* used the same *CT Controllers* as *ROMA* for managing CPU resources. The control period was set to 1 s. System *RR+max* statically allocated all cores (6 per *worker*) fairly distributed to applications. System *RR / min* statically allocated a minimum amount of cores (1 per *worker*) equally distributed to applications.

We tested the systems by running two concurrent applications at a time (test *2-Apps*): i) *GoogLeNet* and *Skyline Extraction* and ii) *ResNet* and *VGG16*. We repeated each test 3 times for a total of 60 executions (5 systems, 4 applications, and 3 executions). Table 1 shows the SLAs (in seconds) and workloads (in incoming requests per second) used in the experiments. Each experiment lasted 300 s and the workload of each application was changed with a different step (shown in column *Workload*) every 37 s (8 times). Table 2 shows the *average* (τ_R) and *maximum* response times (τ_{R_M}) in seconds along with the standard deviation (τ_{R_σ}), the number of SLA violations (V), and the number of allocated CPU resources (Res) measured as *cores * seconds*.

With the first application pair, *ROMA* produced 0 violations and a resource allocation equal to 748 (where the lower means the better). *RR+rules* allocated 1.5 times the resources used by *ROMA* without avoiding SLA violations and obtained longer response times. *RR+CT* performed similarly to *ROMA*, but *ROMA* allocated GPUs in a smarter way (i.e., lower average and maximum response times) and thus relying on CPUs less frequently, which means saving a greater amount of resources. The allocation of all cores makes *RR+max* the fastest system, but by using more than 5 times the CPU resources utilized by *ROMA*. Finally, *RR+min* consumed fewer resources than the other systems at the cost of obtaining 40 SLA violations.

With the second application pair, *ROMA* obtained 10 SLA violations and a resource allocation of 1633 *cores * seconds*. Once again *ROMA* was able to

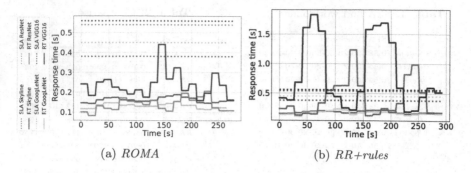

(a) *ROMA*   (b) *RR+rules*

Fig. 2. System experiments - *All Apps*.

outperform the other systems showing a better balance between violations and resource usage, and lower average and maximum response times. Given the presence of *VGG16*, the use of GPUs was fundamental to make the system serve the incoming workload. Results show that a round robin scheduling of GPUs was not sufficient to avoid SLA violations even if all the CPU cores were always allocated statically (*RR+max* produced 40 violations). Compared to *ROMA*, *RR+rules* showed a higher response time and 120 SLA violations and an allocation of almost the same amount of CPU resources. Even with a smarter allocation of CPUs (*RR+CT*) the obtained response time was almost double the one measured with *ROMA* and the number of SLA violations were 70. *RR+min* violated the *SLAs* 180 times and also presented an average response time greater than 1.5 s (almost three times greater than set SLAs).

As final experiment, we ran the four applications concurrently (test *All Apps*) for a total of 60 additional executions (4 applications, 5 systems, 3 repetitions each). Table 2 presents obtained results and the charts of Fig. 2 show the response times obtained with *ROMA* and with *RR+rules* (the best competitor) using the workloads and SLAs reported in Table 1. *ROMA* was able to always keep the response time under the SLAs (0 violations), with an overall average response time equals to 0.167 s, a maximum response time of 0.427 s, and allocated 1767 *cores * seconds*. In contrast, *RR+rules* frequently violated the SLAs while executing *VGG16* and *ResNet*, and resulted in slower executions (average and maximum response times equal to 0.409 and 1.913 s, respectively). *RR+CT* obtained 90 violations and higher response times than *ROMA*, while *RR+max* obtained 0 violations but allocated 3600 *cores * seconds*. The combined use of the heuristic that favors executions on GPUs for resource-hungry applications and its control theory-based CPU allocation made *ROMA* not only faster but also able to exploit fewer resources than all the other systems (except w.r.t. *RR+min* that violated the SLA 170 times).

6   Related Work

Several solutions deal with the management of heterogeneous resources at the node level but not GPUs. For example, the solution presented by Lakew et al. [16] exploits control theory to provision multiple resources dynamically to satisfy SLAs. Similarly to *ROMA*, they exploit containers and can reconfigure resources dynamically. Farokhi et al. [8] present a fuzzy control approach that coordinates the autoscaling of CPU cores and memory. They show that the coordinated control of multiple resources outperforms the performance of the same system with independent controllers.

These approaches manage complementary resources: CPUs uses memory (and also disks) for completing a task, while *ROMA* exploits competing resources since a request can be executed on either CPUs or GPUs. This means that *ROMA* must consider both scheduling and resource provisioning while aforementioned works focus only on the latter.

Different approaches focus on the management on GPUs and CPUs. For example, Khadil et al. [13] present OSched, a resource-aware scheduler for OpenCL jobs that aims to maximize the throughput of the hosting infrastructure. Chen et al. [4] propose a solution for improving the performance of MapReduce applications by scheduling map and reduce tasks on CPUs and GPUs using heuristics. They compared their approach with CPU-only and GPU-only versions of the system obtaining an improvement between 20% and 110%.

Compared to these works, *ROMA* is different from both the control and application domain point of views. First, the mentioned approaches focus on the scheduling of computing tasks on GPUs and CPUs, while *ROMA* combines both scheduling and fine-grained resource allocation in a comprehensive solution. *ROMA*'s scheduling heuristics cooperate with control-theoretical planners in order to minimize constraint violations while optimizing resource usage. Second, existing solutions focus on the management of GPUs in the context of long-lasting compute intensive applications (e.g., machine learning training jobs), while *ROMA* focus on interactive ML applications. To the best of our knowledge *ROMA* is the first solution that provides an architecture, a deployment model and a comprehensive resource management approach for ML inference.

7   Conclusions and Future Work

The paper presents *ROMA*, an extension of TensorFlow that eases the management and operation of ML applications executed on a cluster of heterogeneous resources (GPUs and CPUs) in inference mode. *ROMA* allows users to constrain applications execution times and exploits scheduling heuristics and control-theory based resource provision to run them efficiently. The assessment of the work uses four real-world applications and shows promising results.

References

1. Abadi, M., et al.: TensorFlow: a system for large-scale machine learning. In: 12th Symposium on Operating Systems Design and Implementation, pp. 265–283. USENIX (2016)
2. Baresi, L., Guinea, S., Leva, A., Quattrocchi, G.: A discrete-time feedback controller for containerized cloud applications. In: Proceedings of the 2016 24th International Symposium on Foundations of Software Engineering, pp. 217–228. ACM (2016)
3. Baresi, L., Leva, A., Quattrocchi, G.: Fine-grained dynamic resource allocation for big-data applications. IEEE Trans. Softw. Eng. **47**(8), 1668–1682 (2021)
4. Chen, L., Huo, X., Agrawal, G.: Accelerating MapReduce on a coupled CPU-GPU architecture. In: Hollingsworth, J.K. (ed.) SC Conference on High Performance Computing Networking, Storage and Analysis, pp. 1–11. IEEE/ACM (2012)
5. Chen, T., Li, M., et al.: MXNet: a Flexible and Efficient Machine Learning Library for Heterogeneous Distributed Systems. arXiv (2015)
6. Containerd: an industry-standard container runtime with an emphasis on simplicity, robustness and portability (2021). https://containerd.io
7. Ding, J., Cao, R., Saravanan, I., Morris, N., Stewart, C.: Characterizing service level objectives for cloud services: realities and myths. In: 2019 IEEE International Conference on Autonomic Computing (ICAC), pp. 200–206. IEEE (2019)
8. Farokhi, S., Lakew, E.B., Klein, C., Brandic, I., Elmroth, E.: Coordinating CPU and memory elasticity controllers to meet service response time constraints. In: 2015 International Conference on Cloud and Autonomic Computing, pp. 69–80 (2015)
9. Fedorov, R., Camerada, A., et al.: Estimating snow cover from publicly available images. IEEE Trans. Multimed. **18**(6), 1187–1200 (2016)
10. Forbes: TensorFlow Turns 5 - Five Reasons Why it is the Most Popular ML Framework. http://tiny.cc/Forbes-TF (2020)
11. He, K., Zhang, X., et al.: Deep residual learning for image recognition. In: Proceedings of the IEEE Conference on Computer Vision and Pattern Recognition, pp. 770–778 (2016)
12. Jahani, A., Lattuada, M., Ciavotta, M., Ardagna, D., Amaldi, E., Zhang, L.: Optimizing on-demand GPUs in the cloud for deep learning applications training. In: 2019 4th International Conference on Computing, Communications and Security (ICCCS), pp. 1–8 (2019)
13. Khalid, Y.N., Aleem, M., Prodan, R., Iqbal, M.A., Islam, M.A.: E-OSched: a load balancing scheduler for heterogeneous multicores. J. Supercomput. **74**(10), 5399–5431 (2018)
14. Kubernetes: Don't Panic: Kubernetes and Docker (2020). https://kubernetes.io/blog/2020/12/02/dont-panic-kubernetes-and-docker
15. Kubernetes: Schedule GPUs (2020). https://kubernetes.io/docs/tasks/manage-gpus/scheduling-gpus/
16. Lakew, E., Papadopoulos, A., Maggio, M., Klein, C., Elmroth, E.: KPI-agnostic control for fine-grained vertical elasticity. In: Proceedings of the 17th IEEE/ACM International Symposium on Cluster, Cloud and Grid Computing, pp. 589–598. IEEE (2017)
17. Mittal, S., Vetter, J.S.: A survey of CPU-GPU heterogeneous computing techniques. ACM Comput. Surv. **47**(4), 69:1–69:35 (2015)

18. Nozal, R., Bosque, J.L., Beivide, R.: EngineCL: usability and performance in heterogeneous computing. Future Gener. Comput. Syst. **107**, 522–537 (2020)
19. Paszke, A., et al.: PyTorch: an imperative style, high-performance deep learning library. Adv. Neural Inf. Proc. Syst. **32**, 8024–8035 (2019)
20. Szegedy, C., et al.: Going deeper with convolutions. In: Proceedings of the IEEE Conference on Computer Vision and Pattern Recognition, pp. 1–9 (2015)
21. Verma, A., Cherkasova, L., et al.: Deadline-based workload management for MapReduce environments: pieces of the performance puzzle. In: 2012 IEEE Network Operations and Management Symposium, pp. 900–905. IEEE (2012)
22. Zhang, X., Zou, J., He, K., Sun, J.: Accelerating very deep convolutional networks for classification and detection. IEEE Trans. Pattern Anal. Mach. Intell. **38**(10), 1943–1955 (2015)

Applications and Miscellanea

Representation Learning Based Query Decomposition for Batch Shortest Path Processing in Road Networks

Niu Chen[1], An Liu[1(✉)], Guanfeng Liu[2], Jiajie Xu[1], and Lei Zhao[1]

[1] School of Computer Science and Technology, Soochow University, Suzhou, China
nchen@stu.suda.edu.cn, {anliu,xujj,zhaol}@suda.edu.cn
[2] Department of Computing, Macquarie University, Sydney, Australia
guanfeng.liu@mq.edu.au

Abstract. Shortest path query in road networks is of great importance in various location-based services (LBSs). As the number of the query grows, servers face a lot of pressure because queries are typically processed at the server-side. Processing a larger number of simultaneous queries efficiently has become an important research topic in recent years. A direct solution is to deploy more servers to cope with a large number of concurrent queries, however, this is resource-inefficient. To solve this problem, batch shortest path (BSP) processing algorithms have been proposed to answer a set of queries together using shareable computation. However, existing batch algorithms either assume the batch queries are processed in advance or just use simple heuristics to decompose the batch queries, which results in poor query efficiency. In this paper, we design a deep learning approach to decompose the queries to improve the performance of batch shortest path processing algorithms. Specifically, we first propose a deep learning model to learn the representation of queries, thus supporting accurate and efficient query similarity computation and decomposition. After that, we propose a batch shortest path processing algorithm that provides an approximate solution with a high cache hit ratio and low time consumption. Experiments on a large real-world data set show that our method achieves better results than the state-of-the-art methods.

Keywords: Batch shortest path processing · Representation learning · Query decomposition

1 Introduction

With the development of map-based applications and the proliferation of GPS-enabled mobile technologies, many navigation software and car-hailing software have emerged in recent years, such as Google Map, Didi, and Uber. These software process different types of queries every day, e.g., finding the nearest restaurant, finding the shortest path to a destination. The most basic and important

H. Hacid et al. (Eds.): ICSOC 2021, LNCS 13121, pp. 257–272, 2021.
https://doi.org/10.1007/978-3-030-91431-8_16

type of query among them is the shortest path query. Given an origin and a destination in a road network, the shortest path query returns the path from the origin to the destination that minimizes the cost between them.

Finding the shortest path between two vertexes is a fundamental research problem and is the basis of many applications, such as road network routing [17], knowledge graph question answering [26], and social network analysis [6,13,14]. The most used algorithms are Dijkstra's algorithm [2] and A* algorithm [5], but they are inefficient due to some unnecessary node visits. Therefore, a bunch of index-based algorithms [1,3,9,10,19,20,27] have been proposed recently to further reduce query cost. Although these algorithms can effectively improve the efficiency of shortest path queries, they still have an obvious limitation: it costs them a lot to maintain the index. These index-based algorithms need to construct or update the index when the traffic condition changes. Such drawback becomes much worse in dynamic road networks, where traffic condition is unstable and the accident happens randomly.

Further, all the aforementioned algorithms only target at improving the efficiency of answering a single shortest path query. They process queries one by one and do not consider how to share computation among multiple concurrent queries. It is clear that the sub-path of a shortest path is still a shortest path. Therefore, if a shortest path corresponding to a previous query is $\langle v_1, v_2, \cdots, v_6, v_7 \rangle$ and the current query's answer is $\langle v_2, \cdots, v_7 \rangle$, then the two queries can share the same path $\langle v_2, \cdots, v_7 \rangle$ to avoid duplicate calculation. Based on this observation, some algorithms, such as [21], try to introduce caching technique to shortest path query processing. In particular, they store some shortest paths in a cache so that all subsequent queries whose origin and destination lie on the cached paths can be answered directly. However, the cache has to be updated frequently due to low hit ratio when queries come randomly. If the concurrent queries can be decomposed with similar queries issued together, cache hit ratio can be improved and cache refresh can be reduced.

Another type of solutions, namely batch shortest path processing algorithm [8,15,18,24], processes a group of queries together to improve the query efficiency. They adopt the *path coherence* [19] property of road networks to utilize shared computation. *Path coherence* is a property where the shortest paths originated from spatially close set of locations S and terminated at another spatially close set of locations T are likely to share a common path. Therefore, batch shortest path processing algorithms attempt to decompose coherent queries into several batches, in which the queries have a high probability to share the computation, and answer each batch within a single run, so as to minimize total query cost. However, existing batch algorithms perform query decomposition simply based on some heuristics such as the spatial closeness of origins and destinations, leading to low query efficiency.

Clearly, a good query decomposition is indispensable to both cache-based algorithms and batch shortest path processing algorithms. Therefore, in this paper, we propose a deep learning based query decomposition approach to enhance the possibility of share computation and the performance of shortest path algorithms. The major contributions of this paper are as follows:

- We propose a deep learning approach to automatically learn the representation of a shortest path query, which is the fundamental research problem of query decomposition. The approach can learn more information from queries than existing heuristics-based methods, and thus improves the effectiveness of query decomposition.
- Based on the decomposed queries, we propose an efficient batch shortest path processing algorithm to obtain an approximate shortest path. The efficiency comes from a grid-based cache structure which can make full use of previous computation results.
- We conduct extensive experiments on real-world road networks with real query dataset. The results demonstrate that our approach outperforms existing methods in terms of efficiency and effectiveness.

The remainder of this paper is organized as follows: In Sect. 2, we discuss the work related to shortest path querying. Some definitions and preliminaries are given in Sect. 3. Section 4 formulates a model for query representation. Section 5 presents the detailed description of the batch shortest path processing algorithm. The experimental results are presented in Sect. 6. Finally, Sect. 7 concludes the paper.

2   Related Work

The problem of finding the shortest path from an origin to a destination on a graph has been extensively studied in the literature. Dijkstra's algorithm is the most well-known approach for computing a single source shortest path with a non-negative edge cost. But Dijkstra expands the search space until the destination is reached, which costs much time. There are lots of speed-up techniques proposed for shortest path querying during the past several decades [1,3–5,7,9,10,16,19,20,22,27]. However, those algorithms only target improving the efficiency of answering a single shortest path query. They do not consider how to share computation among multiple queries. Several techniques have been proposed to address this issue.

The batch shortest path processing algorithms adopt the *path coherence* phenomenon in road networks to utilize shared computation. [15] first develops an efficient clustering technique to group path queries based on similarities of Q-lines. They find a common shortest path with respect to each group of path queries and then compute the approximate shortest path for each path query based on the common shortest path of the group. [18] uses the clustering technique to divide the queries into batches and proposes a group-based solution that efficiently computes the shortest path of all the queries in a single pass. Global Cache algorithm [21] uses a cache to store the most beneficial paths so that all the sub-path queries of the cached paths can be answered directly. [24] introduces a generalized A* algorithm to deal with a batch of queries with the same origin or destination. The state-of-the-art method [8] first uses heuristics to decompose the query set, then uses a cache-based algorithm that takes advantage of the previously decomposed query sets for efficient query answering.

The existing batch shortest path processing algorithms are mainly divided into two parts. The first part is to decompose the query set into different sub-query sets and the second part is to use a batch processing algorithm to solve those queries in each sub-query set. The result of query decomposition directly affects the efficiency of the batch processing algorithm. Therefore, a good query decomposition is very important to the batch shortest path processing algorithm.

There are still some major limitations of the existing batch shortest path processing algorithms. Firstly, query decomposition is determined based on simple heuristics such as the spatial closeness of query origins and destinations or the angle between a reference line and the line between the origin and the destination, which cannot generate a beneficial decomposition result sometimes. Secondly, the most used batch processing algorithm is the cache-based algorithm, which requires the origin and destination of the shortest path query to exactly "hit" the cached paths to reuse the previous calculation. However, it is obvious that queries with close origins or destinations can also share computations.

3   Definitions and Problem Statement

In this section, we present some definitions that are essential to understand the problem to be addressed.

Road Network. A road network is a directed graph $G = (V, E)$, where V is a vertex set of locations and $E \subseteq V \times V$ is an edge set of road segments. A vertex v represents a road junction or a road end, which has a spatial coordinate $(v.lon, v.lat)$ reflecting its longitude and latitude. An edge $e = (u, v) \subseteq E$ represents a directed road segment and is associated with a non-negative numerical weight $w(u, v)$ that represents the cost to travel from vertex u to vertex v.

Trajectory. A raw trajectory is a sequence of GPS points, and each point is denoted as $\langle [x_i, y_i], t_i \rangle$, where $g[i] = [x_i, y_i]$ denotes the spatial position and t_i denotes the timestamp. Since trajectory points should be on a road network, we align trajectories to road segments using existing map-matching algorithm and then use the sequences of vertexes to represent trajectories. We use the timestamp of the GPS point closest to the vertex to represent the timestamp of the vertex. Then a trajectory on a road network can be denoted as $T = \langle \langle v_1, t_1 \rangle, \cdots, \langle v_n, t_n \rangle \rangle$. We regard each trajectory as the shortest path from the origin vertex to the destination vertex.

Query. A Query consists of three parts: an origin vertex, a destination vertex, and a departure time, which denoted as $q = \langle o, d, t \rangle$.

Shortest Path Query Set. Given an origin vertex set O and a destination vertex set D, a shortest path query set is denoted as $Q = \{q_i\}$, where $q_i = \langle o_j, d_k, t_i \rangle (o_j \in O, d_k \in D)$ is a shortest path query. The size of Q satisfies: $max(|O|, |D|) \leq |Q| \leq |O| \times |D|$.

Query Representation Learning. Given a collection of queries, a representation $code \in \mathbb{R}^n$ (n is the dimension of a Euclidean space) is learnt for each query so that the representation can reflect the shortest path of the query for computing query similarity.

Query Similarity. Given two shortest path queries q_i, q_j and their corresponding representations $code_i$, $code_j$, the similarity $sim(q_i, q_j)$ between q_i and q_j is defined as the similarity $d(code_i, code_j)$ between $code_i$ and $code_j$, where $d(code_i, code_j)$ represents the distance between $code_i$ and $code_j$.

Shortest Path Query Decomposition Problem. Given a shortest path query set Q and a cost function C, the problem is to decompose Q into several query subset $\hat{Q} = \{Q_i\}$, such that $Q_i \subseteq Q, \cup Q_i = Q, Q_i \cap Q_j = \phi$, and $\sum_{Q_i \in \hat{Q}} C(Q_i)$ is minimum.

4 Query Representation Learning

In this section, we propose a deep learning model to learn the representations of shortest path queries. The similarity of queries is the foundation for query decomposition. Although some works can calculate the similarity of trajectories, such as [12,25], they cannot calculate the similarity of queries.

4.1 Model Overview

Figure 1 shows the architecture of our proposed model, which contains two modules. The first part, denoted as $\mathcal{M}_Q$, represents the query encoding model, aiming to extract the hidden representation vector from the query. Here, a query consists of an origin vertex o, a destination vertex d, and the departure time t. We use road vertex embedding and time slot embedding to convert them into fixed-length vectors. Then, we concatenate the vectors into a vector and use a Multilayer Perceptron model (MLP) to encode the vector into a hidden representation $code$. In particular, we feed the triple queries (anchor query, near query, and far query) into the model to obtain the corresponding hidden representations and use $tripleloss$ to evaluate the difference between them. The second part, denoted as $\mathcal{M}_T$, represents the trajectory encoding model, aiming to extract the spatio-temporal representation for a given trajectory. Specifically, for each element $y_k = \langle v_k, t_k \rangle$ in trajectory, we use the same method to get its vectors and concatenate them into a fixed-length vector. Finally, we obtain a sequence of concatenated representations and use an LSTM model to embed it into a fixed-length vector $stcode$.

Besides, we design an auxiliary task, aiming to bind anchor query to anchor trajectory when training the model. In particular, for each input, we use $\mathcal{M}_Q$ and $\mathcal{M}_T$ to learn the spatial-temporal information in the query and trajectory and encode them into $code$ and $stcode$ respectively. Then we bind $code$ and $stcode$ by minimizing their distance, which is denoted as $auxiliaryloss$. In the prediction phase, we only use $\mathcal{M}_Q$ to encode the anchor query and get the representation of the query for query decomposition.

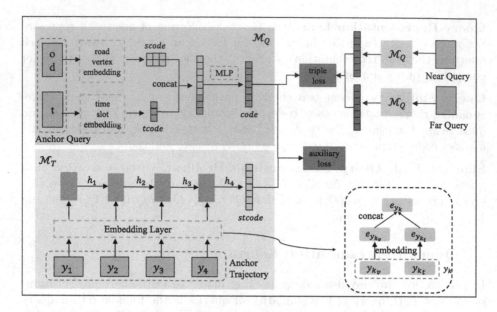

Fig. 1. The architecture of our model

4.2   Training Sample Construction

Our model requires both near query and far query to supervise the learning. We use the method in [23] to construct training input. First, we divide the original trajectory evenly into k segments and average the trajectory points of each segment as the representative point, to obtain a new trajectory of uniform length k. Given a original trajectory $T = \{p_1, p_2, \cdots, p_l\}$ of l GPS points, its simplified trajectory T' is

$$T' = \left\{ \frac{1}{c_1} \sum_{i=1}^{c_1} p_i, \frac{1}{c_2} \sum_{i=c_1+1}^{c_1+c_2} p_i, \cdots, \frac{1}{c_k} \sum_{i=1+l-c_k}^{l} p_i \right\} \tag{1}$$

Here, $p_i = (lat_i, lon_i)$ represents a point with latitude and longitude and $\sum_{i=1}^{k} c_i = l$ with $c_i \in \left[\lfloor \frac{l}{k} \rfloor, \lfloor \frac{l}{k} \rfloor + 1 \right]$. A trajectory is then represented as a $2k$-dimensional vector, in the form of $(T'.lat_1, T'.lon_1, \cdots, T'.lat_k, T'.lon_k)$.

Given a trajectory set $\mathcal{T}$, we simplify all the trajectories in $\mathcal{T}$ and index them using a $2k$-dimensional k-d tree. Note, each point in the k-d tree corresponds to the simplified trajectory of a trajectory in $\mathcal{T}$. When we construct training inputs, we select a trajectory in $\mathcal{T}$ as an *anchor input* I_a, and locate its k nearest neighbors with the help of k-d tree. Among those k returned neighbors, we randomly select one as *near input* I_{ne}. We then randomly sample another point in the k-d tree as *far input* I_f to complete the construction of one triplet training sample. We find the original trajectories T_a, T_{ne}, and T_f corresponding to I_a, I_{ne}, and I_f in $\mathcal{T}$. Then we extract the queries q_a, q_{ne}, and q_f from T_a, T_{ne}, and T_f. So, the input of our model can be formalized as $\langle q_a, q_{ne}, q_f, T_a \rangle$.

4.3   Model Representation

In our model, we consider the spatial-temporal information of the trajectory and embeds it into the vector space.

Road Vertex Embedding. Each road vertex is identified by a unique id, while the input of any machine learning method is usually a vector. One possible solution is to use one-hot encoding to transform each road vertex id into a $|E|$-dimensional vector. However, one-hot representation is too sparse and the distance between any two one-hot codes is the same, so the distance between different road vertexes cannot be distinguished. To address this issue, we design a fully connected neural network to embed one-hot codes into dense vectors. Formally, the process is represented by the formula:

$$\left[D_1, D_2, \cdots, D_{|E|}\right]^\top = \left[O_1, O_2, \cdots, O_{|E|}\right]^\top \mathbf{W}_v \tag{2}$$

where $O_i \in \{0,1\}^{|E|}$ represents the one-hot code of the i-th road vertex, D_i denotes the corresponding dense vector and W_v is the weight matrix of the fully connected neural network.

Considering that each road vertex has influences on its linked road vertexes, adjacent road vertexes should have similar representations. We try to use the unsupervised graph embedding techniques *node2vec* to generate the initial representation for each road vertex. Let $\mathbf{W}_i^0$ be the embedding of the i-th road vertex, we can thereby use the matrix $\mathbf{W}_v^0 = [\mathbf{W}_1^0, \cdots, \mathbf{W}_{|E|}^0]$ to initialize the value of $\mathbf{W}_v$.

Time Slot Embedding. The query departure time t is a timestamp, we need to extract the temporal features from t. We treat the timestamp as a word and turn it into a token in a sequence. First, we normalize the timestamps by converting them into discrete time slots. Given a base timestamp t_0 and a unit time Δt, we can project timestamp t into a particular time slot t_s as below.

$$t_s = \lfloor \frac{t - t_0}{\Delta t} \rfloor \tag{3}$$

Finally, the skip-gram algorithm is employed to derive the embedding sequence with temporal information.

$$\frac{1}{N} \sum_{t=1}^{N} \sum_{-c \leq j \leq c, j \neq 0} \log \mathbb{P}\left(w_{t+j} \mid w_t\right) \tag{4}$$

where w_{t+j} stands for the neighboring slot of w_t if current slot representation w_t is given.

4.4 Loss Function

The representation is represented by $code \in \mathbb{R}^d$. It embeds a query q into a d-dimensional Euclidean space. Here we want to ensure that an anchor query q_a is closer to its near query q_{ne} than it is to any far query q_f. Thus we use triple loss to guide network training

$$tripleloss = \sum_i^N [||code_i^a - code_i^{ne}||_2^2 - ||code_i^a - code_i^f||_2^2 + \alpha]_+ \qquad (5)$$

where α is a margin that is enforced between near query and far query, $||code_i^a - code_i^{ne}||_2$ is the euclidean distance between $code_i^a$ and $code_i^{ne}$. We use the Euclidean metric

$$auxiliaryloss = \sqrt{\sum_j (code[j] - stcode[j])^2} \qquad (6)$$

to evaluate the distance between $code$ and $stcode$. Finally, we use the weighted sum of $tripleloss$ and $auxiliaryloss$ as the final loss, the loss is computed as

$$loss = w \times auxiliaryloss + (1 - w) \times tripleloss \qquad (7)$$

where w is a tuning parameter.

5 Query Decomposition and Batch Processing

In this section, we present a batch shortest path processing algorithm, which can benefit from the decomposition results. We combine Local Cache [8] with Region-to-Region [8] batch algorithm. It is suitable to answer both long queries and short queries.

5.1 Query Decomposition

It is usually unrealistic to achieve the optimal decomposition result because the actual cost $C(Q)$ cannot be obtained until the shortest path search finishes. So we aim to decompose Q as fast as possible using query similarity while achieving a more beneficial decomposition result than the existing heuristic approaches.

We use the generated data to train the model and use the model to learn the representations of queries. After getting the representations of those queries, we will decompose query set Q into different subsets $\{Q_i\}$ use K-Means. We use the cosine similarity to measure the similarity of two query representations:

$$sim(q_i, q_j) = \frac{code_i \cdot code_j}{||code_i|| ||code_j||} \qquad (8)$$

where $code_i$ and $code_j$ is the representation of q_i and q_j, respectively. Similar queries will be clustered into the same group, and the batch algorithm proposed in Sect. 5.2 will be used to find the shortest paths in each group.

5.2   Batch Processing

Cache Structure and Query Processing. The shortest path caching technique makes use of the sub-path property of the shortest path: any sub-paths of a cached path can be answered directly. Although a lot of improvements have been made, the existing works still have a low cache hit ratio. In order to improve the hit ratio, we extend the shortest path caching technique in [8], which uses a super vertex to represent several nearby vertexes. Specifically, we first partition the space into grids of equal size, as shown in Fig. 2(c). We aim to build cache using grid id rather than using vertex id in query answering. In this way, a higher hit ratio can be achieved.

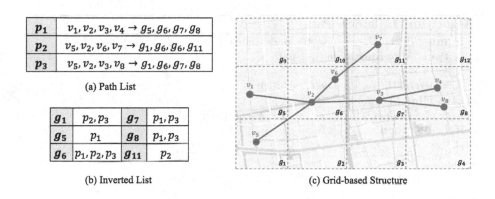

p_1	$v_1, v_2, v_3, v_4 \rightarrow g_5, g_6, g_7, g_8$
p_2	$v_5, v_2, v_6, v_7 \rightarrow g_1, g_6, g_6, g_{11}$
p_3	$v_5, v_2, v_3, v_8 \rightarrow g_1, g_6, g_7, g_8$

(a) Path List

g_1	p_2, p_3	g_7	p_1, p_3
g_5	p_1	g_8	p_1, p_3
g_6	p_1, p_2, p_3	g_{11}	p_2

(b) Inverted List

(c) Grid-based Structure

Fig. 2. Cache structure

The cache structure is the foundation for the case-based algorithm. We build an inverted list from grid id to its cached paths. When constructing the cache, we not only save the id of the vertex but also save the id of the grid where the vertex is located. For example, we have three cached paths p_1, p_2, p_3 as shown in Fig. 2(a). Path p_1 consists of four vertexes, namely v_1, v_2, v_3, v_4 and the grid id of each vertex is g_5, g_6, g_7, g_8. When path p_1 is inserted into the cache, we add its path number p_1 to the inverted list of the grids g_5, g_6, g_7, g_8 respectively. When a new query $q(o, d, t)$ arrives, we first get the gird id of o and d. Assume the id of the grid where o is located is g_o and d is g_d. Then, we check whether there exists the same path number in g_o's and g_d's inverted lists. If there is no identical path id, we process it using $A*$ directly and cache it as long as the current cache size does not exceed the cache limit.

If they have the same path id, we retrieve the path from the cache use Algorithm 1. We first calculate the grid id of origin vertex o and destination vertex d (line 2), namely g_o and g_d respectively, and find the common path p^* from cache (line 3). Each common path contains the path composed of grid id p^*_{grid} and the path composed of vertex id p^*_{vertex}, as shown in Fig. 2(a). Then, we get the positions of g_o and g_d in p^*_{grid} respectively (line 4). After that, we intercept a path in p^*_{vertex} according to the positions of g_o and g_d (line 5–8). This path connects the two regions where the origin vertex o and the destination vertex d are located. Finally, we computes the approximate shortest path for the query based on the common shortest path (line 9). Suppose now there is a new query $q(v_5, v_4)$, we can get the grid id of the origin vertex and destination vertex to be g_1 and g_8. The inverted lists of g_1 and g_8 contain the same path number p_3 and the positions of g_1 and g_8 in p_3 are 0 and 3 respectively. So we intercept the vertexes at positions 0 to 3 from the path p_3, which is v_5, v_2, v_3, v_8. Then we calculate the remaining part using A* directly. Finally, we can get the approximate shortest path $p(v_5, v_4) = sp(v_5, v_5) + sp(v_5, v_8) + sp(v_8, v_4) = (v_5, v_2, v_3, v_8, v_4)$, where $sp(,)$ represents the shortest path between two vertexes.

Algorithm 1: Retrieve Path

    input   : Cache C, origin vertex o, destination vertex d
    output: Approximate shortest path p

1   $p \leftarrow \phi$;
2   $g_o = getGridId(o)$, $g_d = getGridId(d)$;
3   $p^* \leftarrow C(g_o) \bigcap C(g_d)$;
4   $I_o = p^*_{grid}.indexOf(g_o)$, $I_d = p^*_{grid}.indexOf(g_d)$;
5   **if** $I_o < I_d$ **then**
6 | $p = p^*_{vertex}[I_o : I_d]$;
7   **else**
8 | $p = reverse(p^*_{vertex}[I_o : I_d])$;
9   $p \leftarrow sp(s, p[0]) + p + sp(p[end], t)$;
10 **return** p

Batch Query Answering. Suppose the queries come in several batches B. When the first batch B_1 comes, we decompose it and create caches to answer its queries. When B_i comes, the caches are destroyed and new caches are created by the coming batch. Note that since we have considered the shortest path between a source region and its corresponding destination region in the cache, this path may not be the best path for every source-destination point pairs. Thus some path queries may result in a slightly larger path than the optimal shortest path.

6 Experiments

In this section, we evaluate the performance of our proposed algorithms over a real-world road network and a taxi trajectory dataset. The deep learning model was implemented in PyTorch and the batch shortest path processing algorithms were all implemented in Julia, and tested on a CentOS Server with two Xeon E5-2650 CPUs and four GTX 1080 Ti GPUs.

6.1   Experiment Setting

Dataset. We obtain the road network of Beijing from *OpenStreetMap*, which consists of 44840 intersections and 75576 roads. We use a Beijing Taxi Trajectory Dataset [11] in our experimental study. The dataset consists of one-month trajectory data of near 8000 taxis in Beijing, China during May 2009. We aligned the GPS points in trajectories with road networks, then used the sequence of road vertex to represent a trajectory, as introduced in Sect. 3. The origin vertex and destination vertex in the sequence are regarded as a shortest path query.

Hyper Parameters Setting. We split the dataset into the training set, validation set, and test set in the ratio 5:1:4. We set the length of simplified trajectory T', the dimension of road vertex embedding and time slot embedding, the dimension of final query representation, and the loss weight w to 5, 256, 256, 0.4, respectively. The default cell size in the experiments is $100\,\mathrm{m} \times 100\,\mathrm{m}$ and we decompose the query set into 3 sub-sets use K-Means.

Baselines. Our representation method is denoted as Representation Learning Decomposition (RLD). RLD-V represents only road vertex embedding is used for query representation and RLD-T represents only time slot embedding is used for query representation. We consider the following baselines:

- Global Cache(GC) [21]: Global Cache uses the entire query set to build the cache directly without query decomposition.
- Zigzag Decomposition(ZZD) [8]: Zigzag Decomposition first decomposes the queries into several 1-N subsets based on angle/distance thresholds and then merges the similar subsets into larger sets.
- Search Space Estimation Decomposition(SSE) [8]: This method calculates the similarity of the query based on the estimated search space and then decomposes the queries based on query similarity. SSE has its distance sorted version SSE-S and random version SSE-R.

Our batch processing algorithm is denoted as Grid-based Local Cache (GLC). It is compared with Local Cache (LC) [8] and Region-to-Region (R2R) [8].

We generate queries with the size of 10K, 100K, 500K, and 1M from the test set. We use the first 20% queries in each query set to construct the cache, and we use it as the size limit of each local cache. We analyze the effectiveness of our method from three aspects: hit ratio, answering time and average error. The hit ratio is computed as $R_h = \sum h_i/|Q_i|$, where $|h_i|$ is the number of query hit by each cache. The error is computed as $\epsilon = \sum |d_i^* - d_i|/d_i$, where d_i is the actual distance and d_i^* is the approximate distance. The average error is computed on all the approximate queries, excluding the accurate ones.

6.2   Experimental Results

Effectiveness of Query Decomposition. Figure 3 shows the experimental results of the cache hit ratio under different decomposition methods. As shown in Fig. 3(a) and Fig. 3(b), the hit ratio increases as the query size becomes larger, regardless of whether we use GLC or LC. The hit ratio of ZZD is always the lowest because it decomposes the query set into too many subsets. The RLD performs better than all heuristics methods because deep learning can learn more spatial information than heuristic methods to have better decomposition results. Comparing Fig. 3(a) and Fig. 3(b), we can see that GLC gets a higher hit ratio than LC in all test sizes. In summary, our decomposition method can improve the efficiency of the cache-based batch shortest path processing algorithm.

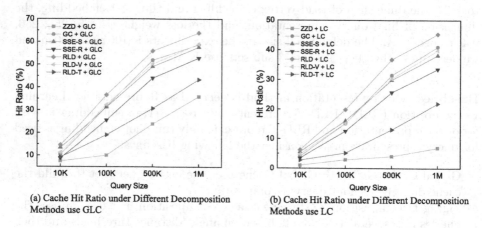

(a) Cache Hit Ratio under Different Decomposition Methods use GLC

(b) Cache Hit Ratio under Different Decomposition Methods use LC

Fig. 3. Cache hit ratio under different decomposition methods

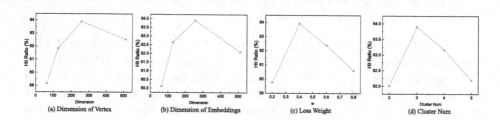

(a) Dimension of Vertex   (b) Dimension of Embeddings   (c) Loss Weight   (d) Cluster Num

Fig. 4. Parameter effect

We also did ablation experiments to see the effect of different components of the model on performance. As we can see from Fig. 3(a) and Fig. 3(b), RLD-V has a higher hit ratio than RLD-T. This shows that the model considers more spatial information when making decisions. If two kinds of information are considered, the best result will be obtained.

Since the decomposition results are consistent with different values of related parameters, we assess the effect of these parameters on the cache hit ratio use the 1M query set. Figure 4(a) shows the hit ratios under different dimensions of learned representation, it can be seen that it is optimal when the value is 256, and gradually decreases after that. As can be seen from Fig. 4(b)(c)(d), the hit ratio is the best when the cluster number is equal to 3, the loss weight w is equal to 0.4, and the dimension of road vertex and time slot embedding is 256.

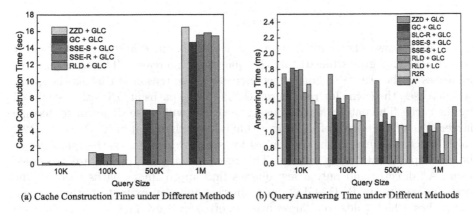

(a) Cache Construction Time under Different Methods   (b) Query Answering Time under Different Methods

Fig. 5. Results of different BSP algorithms

Effectiveness of Batch Processing. The cache construction time is shown in Fig. 5(a) and the query answering time is shown in Fig. 5(b). Naturally, all of the cache construction time increases as the query size grows. When the query size is 10K, the A* performs best. The main reason is that the cache-based algorithms need time to check whether the query hits the caches and cache the path, but the caches that take time to build are not used by the subsequent queries due to the low hit ratio. RLD+GLC performs the best, except in the query size is 10K, its answering time is 45% faster than that of A*. The time complexity of RLD is $O(n)$. The time complexity of the heuristics methods is $O(n \log n)$, although they use a quadtree to speed up the process. RLD+GLC has a lower time complexity and improves the cache hit ratio, which makes for a faster answering time. The query answering time becomes faster as the query size grows. The reason is that a larger number of queries are answered by the cache.

Table 1. Average error and cache size

	Average error (%)		Cache size (MB)
	RLD+GLC	R2R	RLD+GLC
10K	1.9	1.07	0.86
100K	6.6	1.58	7.1
500K	12	2.63	36
1M	14.6	3.41	72

Table 1 shows the average error and cache size in different sizes of query sets. Cache size grows linearly as the query size increases. The average error increases as the size of the query set increases. The reason is that as the query set increases, the cache hit rate increases, and more paths are directly calculated by the cache. The path calculated using the cache will cause the error to become larger. The average error of R2R algorithm is lower than that of RLD+GLC. R2R takes strict measures in the decomposition stage, which makes the query set to be decomposed into many subsets. This means that most queries are processed using A* directly and only a few queries find approximate paths through the previous results. In RLD+GLC, more queries find approximate paths through the caches, which leads to a larger average error. But even so, our experimental result shows the deviation of the path returned by RLD+GLC from the optimal path is only about 14.6% in the average case. On the contrary, the answering time of RLD+GLC is better than that of R2R algorithm, as shown in Fig. 5(b). Besides, we provide RLD+LC for accurate calculation, which also has a better answering time than A*.

7   Conclusion

We study the problem of batch processing of shortest path queries in this paper. To solve the problem of the low cache hit ratio of existing works, we use a deep learning method to learn the representation of the query and decompose the query set into different sub-sets based on the learned representation. Moreover, we design a batch shortest path processing algorithm that takes advantage of the previously decomposed sub-query sets for efficient query answering. The performance of the methods is investigated through extensive experiments on a real-world dataset.

Acknowledgements. This work was supported by the National Natural Science Foundation of China (Grant Nos. 61572336, 61632016, 62072323), the Natural Science Foundation of Jiangsu Province (Grant Nos. BK20211307, BK20191420), the Major Program of the Natural Science Foundation of Jiangsu Higher Education Institutions of China (Grant Nos. 18KJA520010, 19KJA610002), and the Collaborative Innovation Center of Novel Software Technology and Industrialization.

References

1. Akiba, T., Iwata, Y., Yoshida, Y.: Fast exact shortest-path distance queries on large networks by pruned landmark labeling. In: SIGMOD 2013, pp. 349–360. ACM (2013)
2. Dijkstra, E.W.: A note on two problems in connexion with graphs. Numerische Mathematik **1**, 269–271 (1959)
3. Fu, A.W., Wu, H., Cheng, J., Wong, R.C.: IS-LABEL: an independent-set based labeling scheme for point-to-point distance querying. PVLDB **6**(6), 457–468 (2013)
4. Goldberg, A.V., Harrelson, C.: Computing the shortest path: a search meets graph theory. In: SODA 2005, pp. 156–165. SIAM (2005)
5. Hart, P.E., Nilsson, N.J., Raphael, B.: A formal basis for the heuristic determination of minimum cost paths. IEEE Trans. Syst. Sci. Cybern. **4**(2), 100–107 (1968)
6. Jo, Y., Jang, M., Jung, H., Kim, S.: A high-performance graph engine for efficient social network analysis. In: WWW 2018, pp. 61–62. ACM (2018)
7. Li, L., Wang, S., Zhou, X.: Time-dependent hop labeling on road network. In: ICDE 2019, pp. 902–913. IEEE (2019)
8. Li, L., Zhang, M., Hua, W., Zhou, X.: Fast query decomposition for batch shortest path processing in road networks. In: ICDE 2020, pp. 1189–1200. IEEE (2020)
9. Li, L., Zheng, K., Wang, S., Hua, W., Zhou, X.: Go slow to go fast: minimal on-road time route scheduling with parking facilities using historical trajectory. VLDB J. **27**(3), 321–345 (2018)
10. Li, Y., Leong Hou U, Yiu, M.L., Kou, N.M.: An experimental study on hub labeling based shortest path algorithms. PVLDB **11**(4), 445–457 (2017)
11. Lian, J., Zhang, L.: One-month Beijing taxi GPS trajectory dataset with taxi ids and vehicle status. In: DATA@SenSys 2018, pp. 3–4. ACM (2018)
12. Liu, A., Zheng, K., Li, L., Liu, G., Zhao, L., Zhou, X.: Efficient secure similarity computation on encrypted trajectory data. In: ICDE 2015, pp. 66–77. IEEE (2015)
13. Liu, G., et al.: MCS-GPM: multi-constrained simulation based graph pattern matching in contextual social graphs. IEEE TKDE. **30**(6), 1050–1064 (2018)
14. Liu, G., et al.: Multi-constrained graph pattern matching in large-scale contextual social graphs. In: ICDE 2015, pp. 351–362. IEEE (2015)
15. Mahmud, H., Amin, A.M., Ali, M.E., Hashem, T., Nutanong, S., et al.: A group based approach for path queries in road networks. In: Nascimento, M.A. (ed.) SSTD 2013. LNCS, vol. 8098, pp. 367–385. Springer, Heidelberg (2013). https://doi.org/10.1007/978-3-642-40235-7_21
16. Ouyang, D., Qin, L., Chang, L., Lin, X., Zhang, Y., Zhu, Q.: When hierarchy meets 2-hop-labeling: efficient shortest distance queries on road networks. In: SIGMOD 2018, pp. 709–724. ACM (2018)
17. Pedersen, S.A., Yang, B., Jensen, C.S.: Anytime stochastic routing with hybrid learning. PVLDB **13**(9), 1555–1567 (2020)
18. Reza, R.M., Ali, M.E., Hashem, T.: Group processing of simultaneous shortest path queries in road networks. In: MDM 2015, pp. 128–133. IEEE (2015)
19. Samet, H., Sankaranarayanan, J., Alborzi, H.: Scalable network distance browsing in spatial databases. In: SIGMOD 2008, pp. 43–54. ACM (2008)
20. Sankaranarayanan, J., Samet, H., Alborzi, H.: Path oracles for spatial networks. PVLDB **2**(1), 1210–1221 (2009)
21. Thomsen, J.R., Yiu, M.L., Jensen, C.S.: Effective caching of shortest paths for location-based services. In: SIGMOD 2012, pp. 313–324. ACM (2012)

22. Wagner, D., Willhalm, T., Zaroliagis, C.D.: Geometric containers for efficient shortest-path computation. ACM J. Exp. Algorithmics **10** (2005)
23. Zhang, H., et al.: Trajectory similarity learning with auxiliary supervision and optimal matching. In: IJCAI 2020, pp. 3209–3215 (2020)
24. Zhang, M., Li, L., Hua, W., Zhou, X.: Batch processing of shortest path queries in road networks. In: Chang, L., Gan, J., Cao, X. (eds.) ADC 2019. LNCS, vol. 11393, pp. 3–16. Springer, Cham (2019). https://doi.org/10.1007/978-3-030-12079-5_1
25. Zhang, Y., Liu, A., Liu, G., Li, Z., Li, Q.: Deep representation learning of activity trajectory similarity computation. In: ICWS 2019, pp. 312–319. IEEE (2019)
26. Zhao, C., Xiong, C., Qian, X., Boyd-Graber, J.L.: Complex factoid question answering with a free-text knowledge graph. In: WWW 2020, pp. 1205–1216. ACM (2020)
27. Zheng, B., Su, H., Hua, W., Zheng, K., Zhou, X., Li, G.: Efficient clue-based route search on road networks. IEEE TKDE **29**(9), 1846–1859 (2017)

An Adaptive Charging Scheduling for Electric Vehicles Using Multiagent Reinforcement Learning

Xian-Long Lee[1], Hong-Tzer Yang[1]([✉]), Wenjun Tang[2], Adel N. Toosi[3], and Edward Lam[4]

[1] Department of Electrical Engineering, National Cheng Kung University, Tainan City, Taiwan
xllee@mail.ee.ncku.edu.tw, htyang@mail.ncku.edu.tw
[2] Smart Grid and Renewable Energy Lab, Tsinghua-Berkeley Shenzhen Institute, Shenzhen 518055, China
monikatang@sz.tsinghua.edu.cn
[3] Department of Software Systems and Cybersecurity, Faculty of Information Technology, Monash University, Clayton, VIC 3800, Australia
adel.n.toosi@monash.edu
[4] Department of Data Science and Artificial Intelligence, Faculty of Information Technology, Monash University, Clayton, VIC 3800, Australia
edward.lam@monash.edu

Abstract. Scheduling when, where, and under what conditions to recharge an electric vehicle poses unique challenges absent in internal combustion vehicles. Charging scheduling of an electric vehicle for time- and cost-efficiency depends on many variables in a dynamic environment, such as the time-of-use price and the availability of charging piles at a charging station. This paper presents an adaptive charging scheduling strategy that accounts for the uncertainty in the charging price and the availability of charging stations. We consider the charging scheduling of an electric vehicle in consideration of these variables. We develop a Multiagent Rainbow Deep Q Network with Imparting Preference where the two agents select a charging station and determine the charging quantity. An imparting preference technique is introduced to share experience and learn the charging scheduling strategy for the vehicle en route. Real-world data is used to simulate the vehicle and to learn the charging scheduling. The performance of the model is compared against two reinforcement learning-based benchmarks and a human-imitative charging scheduling strategy on four scenarios. Results indicate that the proposed model outperforms the existing approaches in terms of charging time, cost, and state-of-charge reserve assurance indices.

Keywords: Electric vehicle · Adaptive charging scheduling · Reinforcement learning · Multi-agent systems

© Springer Nature Switzerland AG 2021
H. Hacid et al. (Eds.): ICSOC 2021, LNCS 13121, pp. 273–286, 2021.
https://doi.org/10.1007/978-3-030-91431-8_17

1   Introduction

The production and sale of electric vehicles (EVs) have grown considerably in recent years. This growth is mainly driven by stringent regulations on greenhouse gas emissions that cannot be met by internal combustion vehicles [3]. Despite their phenomenal growth, unresolved issues hinder their widespread adoption. Like the fuel price for conventional vehicles, the charging price for EVs varies in time and differs at each Charging Station (CS) due to the time-of-use (ToU) electricity price and other factors. In contrast, the duration of recharging an EV compared to conventional vehicles sometimes renders EVs impractical. Charging its battery can require 20 to 30 min for fast charging and can make a CS unavailable to incoming vehicles [14]. Therefore, drivers of EVs must manage time- and cost-efficient charging plans to meet their requirements (e.g., minimizing charging cost or the queuing time) and the characteristics of their EVs.

These issues raise a practical challenge to scheduling recharges en route. To formulate the problem, we consider concepts from the *Internet of Things* and *Edge Computing* [9]. Communication technologies, such as fifth-generation (5G) cellular networks, have promoted the role of vehicles to an intelligent platform that can provide a wide range of services. Connected vehicles display a variety of applications on Edge Computing architectures [13]. Owing to the benefits of these advanced technologies, we propose a charging scheduling service that has the potential to use the in-vehicle infotainment system to display recommendations for charging an EV. The charging scheduling service receives data from sensors on an EV and from nearby CSs to provide recommendations on charging schedules in real-time. In particular, we aim to address the following questions: 1) how can the EV select CSs and determine charging schedules that meet the driver's requirements given limited data from nearby CSs; and 2) how much energy to recharge at each CS in order to avoid excessive charging times while maintaining best practice guidelines on State-of-Charge (SoC), which require EVs to maintain a minimum SoC of 20% [15].

In this paper, we propose a multi-objective problem to solve the challenges described above. Utilizing a Reinforcement Learning (RL) approach, the proposed charging scheduling model provides an adaptive charging scheduling for the EV en route. The RL agent receives data from its sensors and makes charging decisions in real-time. The advantage of using RL to make charging decisions is that the agent is trained to maximize their long-term objectives without supervision. The agent can avoid recharging when the charging cost or waiting time is suboptimal in order to recharge in optimal circumstances. However, it is challenging for a single RL agent to tackle the multi-objective problem as the single agent faces a high-dimensional action space. We design a **M**ultiagent **R**ainbow **D**eep Q Network (DQN) with **I**mparting Preference model (**MRDI**) to address the charging scheduling problem. Rainbow DQN [4] is applied as the base agents to construct the proposed multiagent model. The proposed MRDI model is designed with two agents to make charging decisions based on estimates of an optimal charging price and occupancy rate while considering charging times, and charging quantity while en route. In summary, the key contributions of this paper are as follows:

- *Adaptive Charging Scheduling*: The proposed charging scheduling estimates the state of the environment and provides an optimal charging decision. Furthermore, the system computes the least amount of energy to recharge and maintains a minimal SoC in the battery upon arrival at the destination. The charging scheduling adapts to the dynamic CS environment and makes charging decisions only when necessary.
- *Multiagent structure with Imparting Preference*: The proposed MRDI model is developed with two Rainbow DQN agents. The agents work on different tasks while jointly learning to perform a cooperative objective. We adopt the imparting preference technique to share experience between the two agents. As a result, it enhances the performance of the model to generate the charging scheduling. The schedule considers cost and time efficiency while considering charging times and a minimum amount of energy.
- *Real Data Simulation and Evaluation*: We employ realistic CS and EV data to simulate four practical scenarios of an EV driven along the routes. The experiment is compared with three baselines methods to explore the physical indications behind the charging decisions. The results demonstrates that the proposed MRDI model achieves better charging scheduling compared to the baselines in the four scenarios.

The rest of the paper is organized as follows: In Sect. 2, we give an overview of the related work on the charging scheduling problem. In Sect. 3, we describe our proposed charging scheduling method. We report experimental results in Sect. 4. Section 5 concludes the paper.

2   Related Work

An increasing number of studies have been conducted regarding the optimization of CS charging scheduling problems for a fleet of EVs. Zhou et al. [19] proposed a charging scheduling model to minimize the charging cost while enduring a few uncertainties, i.e., intermittent prediction of renewable generations and indeterminacy of EV arrival time. Li et al. [5] proposed a model-free approach and formulate an EV charging scheduling problem that tackles the uncertainty in the arrival and departure times. However, these studies do not focus on the charging scheduling problem from the perspective of the EV.

We focus on the charging scheduling problem from the EV's point-of-view to search through nearby CSs. Prior work have explored the optimization of EV charging scheduling considering cost, charging time, and waiting time. Yang et al. [17] formulated the EV charging time optimization problem by receiving global CS information while en route. The EV's waiting time at CSs is minimized, but they do not consider the charging price at the CSs. Yang et al. [16] proposed a charging scheduling that considers the dynamic charging price of CSs while the EV drives along a planned route. However, the charging scheduling neglects the uncertainty of charging slots. Cao et al. [1] proposed a centralized system that allows the EV to reserve a charging pile and resolves the occupancy rate problem from the CSs. However, EVs in this study must connect to a centralized system to communicate.

Considering that individual drivers tend to charge their EVs at their convenience, a centralized system could be impractical in realistic scenarios.

While en route, the EV is presumed to encounter different CSs, which forms a dynamic environment to determine the charging schedule. The adaptive charging scheduling aims to build a service that suggests and selects a preferable CS to charge in the near future. A stochastic optimization problem is of interest, in which some information is previously unknown, but can be obtained in the query time. RL has proven to be an effective technique for handling dynamic environments in various domains [7,12,18]. RL has been used to optimize the charging cost of a fleet of EVs based on the perspective of CS. Da Silva et al. [2] proposed a Multiagent Multiobjective RL method that minimizes the energy cost for recharging. The RL model adapts by changing the charging decisions whenever a new EV arrives at the CS. Panayiotou et al. [8] devised a charging scheduling by applying the RL model considering the price, charging times, and distance while driving in a planned route. However, these approaches do not consider the occupancy rate of each CS and assume that the EV can charge upon arrival. These studies demonstrate that RL is feasible and applicable to the charging scheduling problem.

3   The Charging Scheduling Model

This section presents the charging scheduling problem while en route. We reduce our charging scheduling problem to a discrete-time stochastic control process. Then, we formulate the charging scheduling problem into a Markov Decision Process (MDP), which is then subsequently solved using RL. Finally, we demonstrate how the proposed MRDI structure is developed based on the Rainbow DQN agents with imparting preference. The agents are designed with a shared objective and produce decisions corresponding to the charging schedule.

3.1   Problem Description

Building an effective charging schedule in a dynamic environment poses many challenges. Figure 1 illustrates the problem framework. The driver anticipates that they will encounter CSs en route. It is challenging to determine the charging schedule under diverse CS information within a certain radius. Following charging preferences, the driver is searching for a suitable CS based on a few factors, e.g., time- and cost-efficiency. We consider the charging scheduling to take charging decisions only when necessary to avoid superfluous charging times. The charging quantity associated with each charging decision must also be optimized to prevent charging excessively. Furthermore, the current best practice for recharging a battery stipulates that it must hold between 20% and 80% SoC [15]. When the EV arrives at the destination, its SoC must maintain enough energy to accommodate a future trip. The proposed charging scheduling problem focuses on multiple considerations when taking charging decisions en route, i.e., selecting optimal CSs based on time-efficient and cost-efficient indices, charging quantity, charging times, and battery constraints.

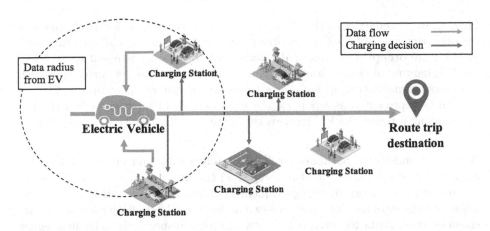

Fig. 1. An illustration of the charging scheduling problem.

3.2 MDP Problem Formulation

We decompose the charging scheduling problem into two individual tasks that are jointly considered in a practical charging scheduling. We thus formulate the charging scheduling problem as a multiagent MDP. A multiagent MDP is a tuple $\langle \mathcal{S}, \mathcal{A}^i, \mathcal{P}^i, \mathcal{R}^i, \gamma \rangle$, which comprises of a set of states $\mathcal{S}$, action space $\mathcal{A}^i$, the transition probabilities of $\mathcal{P}^i$, and the reward function of $\mathcal{R}^i$. i denotes the index of the agents and $\gamma \in (0,1]$ represents the discount rate. $\mathcal{S}$ is the state space of the joint environment. The agents observe the state and interact with the environment by taking actions from their action space $\mathcal{A}^i$. $\mathcal{P}^i$ comprises probabilities of transferring from the current state to the next state. $\mathcal{R}^i$ is the reward received by the agents when taking the actions.

Typically, the objective of an RL model is to maximize the sum of rewards over a sequence of time steps. At each time step $t \in T$, agent i observes the state s_t and chooses the actions that produce the next state s_{t+1} according to the transition probability $p^i(s_{t+1}|s_t, a_t^i)$, where $s_t, s_{t+1} \in \mathcal{S}$, and $a_t^i \in \mathcal{A}^i$. The agents choose actions according to their policy $\pi^i(a_t^i|s_t)$ where $s_t \in \mathcal{S}$ and $a_t^i \in \mathcal{A}^i$. The state s_t generates reward values $r_t^i(s_t, a_t^i, s_{t+1}) \in \mathcal{R}^i$, reflecting by the actions a_t^i at state s_t. Through the sequence, the agents aim to maximize their cumulative reward $r_t^i(s_t, a_t^i, s_{t+1})$ by following a policy π^i. The expected cumulative reward function is $\mathbb{E}_{a^i \sim \pi^i, s \sim T}[\sum_{t=1}^{T} \gamma^t r_t^i(s_t, a_t^i, s_{t+1})]$.

State: In each time step, the EV expects to encounter CSs within a defined radius. The EV will drive to its destination over the time interval $t = 1, 2, \ldots, T$. Let soc_t be the SoC of the EV at time step t. The energy consumption e_t denotes the energy consumption between the previous time step and the current time step t and is calculated by $e_t = (soc_t - soc_{t-1}) * b_{cap}$, where b_{cap} is the battery capacity. In each time step, the EV collects data from up to ten of the nearest CSs within a certain radius. The EV collects the charging price $\lambda_{z,t}$, where $z =$

$\{1, 2, ..., 10\}$ is the index of the CS at time t. Other than the price, $occ_{z,t}$ denotes the occupancy rate of the CS z at time t where $occ_{z,t} \in [0, 1]$. If all charging piles at CS z are occupied at time t, the occupancy rate $occ_{z,t}$ is equal to 1. All of the CS charging prices $\lambda_{z,t}$ and occupancy rate $occ_{z,t}$ values are normalized with min-max normalization, where the values represent the range from 0 to 1. Each CS can be represented as a pair $cs_{z,t} = (\lambda_{z,t}, occ_{z,t})$. In summary when the EV drives along a route, the EV receives the state $s_t = [(\lambda, occ)_{z,t}, (soc_t, e_t)] \in \mathcal{S}$.

Action: Consider the optimal charging scheduling while en route, the EV owner requires two decisions at each time step t: 1) the decision to select a CS and 2) the quantity of energy to charge sequentially. While two decisions need to be made, we separate the decisions into two actions. In the multiagent settings, we consider two agents to carry out the two actions respectively. The first agent has 11 discrete actions to choose from regarding selecting an index z of the CS to charge where $a_t^1 = \{0, 1, 2, ..., 10\}$ and $a_t^1 = 0$ represents the decision of not selecting any CS at the current time step. The second agent has to determine a charging quantity at each time step. The second action set $a_t^2 = \{0, 1, ..., 9\}$ contains 10 discrete actions. The action a_t^2 can be interpreted as a charging ratio of the quantities, and action 0 means no charging. We calculate the charging amount with a charging scale function

$$q(a_t^2) = \frac{a_t^2(soc_{upper} - soc_t)}{9}, \tag{1}$$

where soc_{upper} is an upper bound of the battery's SoC. It charges at different quantities based on the current SoC.

Transition Probability: The transition probability $p^i(s_{t+1}|s_t, a_t^i)$ is affected by the charging decisions and energy consumption while en route. Initially, the model interacts with the environment, in which the transition from state s_t to state s_{t+1} is controlled by action a_t. The state-action pairs are stored to learn to estimate the optimal policy, which approaches the optimal charging scheduling decision through the episodes.

Reward: We evaluate the two decisions in terms of selecting an optimal CS and charging quantity through the time series. The search for an optimal CS $cs_{z,t}$ aims to emphasize minimizing the price $\lambda_{z,t}$ and occupancy rate $occ_{z,t}$. To balance between the price and occupancy rate, we consider a trade-off parameter ξ to calculate weighing between the price and occupancy. The first reward function is presented as follows:

$$r_t^1 = \frac{\xi}{(\lambda_{z,t})^\eta} + \frac{(1 - \xi)}{(occ_{z,t})^\eta}, \tag{2}$$

where η is an amplification factor and acts as the incentive to amplify the differences in rewards. By powering the values of price and occupancy rate, the optimal selections separate from other decisions through the sequence. As a result, the reward is amplified for the agent to learn the optimal decision of price and occupancy rate. Subsequently, the decision regarding the charging amount must not charge above an upper bound soc_{upper} of the SoC. The constraint to regulate the charging amount can be expressed as $soc_t + q(a_t^2) \leq soc_{upper}$. The charging amount aims to charge as least amount as possible. Also, it is impractical to take charging decisions frequently. We define a frequent charging penalty coefficient ζ where $\zeta \in (0, 1]$ to discourage the second agent from charging excessively. On the other hand, the φ reward apprises the agent when it is possibly better not to charge frequently en route. The second reward function for the charging quantity can be denoted as follows:

$$r_{t=1,...,T-1}^2 = \begin{cases} \frac{\zeta}{q(a_t^2)}, & a_t^2 = \{1, ..., 9\} \\ \varphi, & a_t^2 = 0 \end{cases} \tag{3}$$

where $t = 1, 2, ..., T - 1$. Conditionally, we improve the reward function for the agent to be aware of the rule when the episode ends, that is, to save sufficient energy at the end of the time step $T - 1$. The parameters α and β inform the second agent to follow the rule of an assurance threshold. At the end of the time horizon, the current SoC compares with an assurance threshold parameter δ. The second agent's reward, on the evaluation of the charging amount, is promoted if the SoC fulfills the constraint. And discouraged if the SoC violates the restriction. The adjusted reward function is shown as follows:

$$r_{T-1}^2 = \begin{cases} r_{T-1}^2 + \alpha, & soc_{T-1} \geq \delta \\ r_{T-1}^2 - \beta, & soc_{T-1} < \delta \end{cases} \tag{4}$$

3.3 Multiagent Framework

In this section, we present our MRDI model approach to challenge the charging scheduling problem. Hessel et al. [4] introduced the Rainbow DQN model and achieved state-of-the-art performance on Atari games. The Rainbow DQN is best constructed from multiple improvements from the original DQN model [6]. The Rainbow DQN combines the DQN algorithm as a base model with Double DQN, dueling DQN, prioritized experience replay, distributional reinforcement learning, n-step learning, and noisy network for exploration. The proposed MRDI model assembles two Rainbow DQN agents. In the multiagent setting, the complexity grows exponentially with the action-space dimension for a single agent to explore. We consider two agents to observe the same state and take two actions simultaneously for the charging scheduling problem. The actions jointly optimize the charging scheduling decisions and provide a practical solution. The first agent's experience is imparted to the second agent, improving the overall charging scheduling objective. The second agent aims to choose a decisive charging quantity that is related to the preferred CS. Also, it assists the second agent to reduce excessive charging amounts.

Shared Objective and Impart Preferences. On exploring with adequate iteration training, the MRDI model gains sufficient historical experience and estimates to approach the optimal charging scheduling, namely, the ideal selection of a CS and charging quantity. However, it seems ambiguous if one agent takes a *No* action, but the other agent chooses solution action, i.e., $a_t^1 = 0$ with $a_t^2 \neq 0$ or vice versa. We introduce an imparting preference technique to transfer the preference with an *AND* logical gate. If both the two actions chooses a *Yes* action, i.e., $a_t^1 \neq 0$ *AND* $a_t^2 \neq 0$, we interpret this action as a logical true state. We use the normalization factors ν^1, ν^2 to normalize the rewards r_t^1, r_t^2. The discount factor $\psi \in (0, 1]$ is to discourage impractical decisions from the two agents. As a result, both agents learn to perform charging decisions simultaneously and avoid impractical choices. The calculated reward of r_t^2 in each time step is defined as:

$$r_t^2 = \begin{cases} \psi(\nu^1 r_t^1 + \nu^2 r_t^2), & a_t^1 \wedge a_t^2 = 0 \\ \nu^1 r_t^1 + \nu^2 r_t^2, & a_t^1 \wedge a_t^2 = 1 \end{cases} \tag{5}$$

Multiagent Rainbow DQN with Imparting Preference. The proposed MRDI model is constructed based on the Rainbow DQN [4] agents with the imparting preference technique. Algorithm 1 describes our MRDI framework. Given a set of states S received by the EV, T is the time slot while en route, a batch size N to sample from the Prioritized replay buffers $(\mathcal{B}_1, \mathcal{B}_2)$, and Rainbow agents $(\mathcal{I}_1, \mathcal{I}_2)$. In the training stage, the MRDI model starts from performing through the time series T in episode E. For each time slot, the Rainbow agents perform actions based on the current state and compute the rewards sequentially (line 6–8). Afterward, the MRDI model imparts the first agent's reward to the second agent, while the model discounts the ambiguous decisions from the second reward (line 9). The transitions $(s_t, a_t^1, r_t^1, s_{t+1})$ and $(s_t, a_t^2, r_t^2, s_{t+1})$ are stored in the Prioritized replay buffers $(\mathcal{B}_1, \mathcal{B}_2)$ to perform mini-batch training on the model. Instead of sampling from the buffer uniformly, the Prioritized Replay samples important transitions more frequently, therefore, learn more efficiently. The n-step learning technique, introduced by [10], is adopted to sample forwardly with multiple steps of reward instead of a single reward value. The number of steps n is a hyper-parameter that often leads to faster learning [11]. In conclusion, the proposed model determines the charging scheduling for the EV while en route. Unlike Atari games, the charging scheduling problem does not consider finding the *shortest* paths from all states to a goal state. The problem is required to explore through the time slots in each episode. As a result, the complexity of the proposed model is $O(n^2)$ based on the route's length.

4   Performance Evaluation and Experiments

We conducted experiments in a realistic simulator by applying real-world data from historical CSs and vehicle driving data. We used driving records from public transportation data to derive EV energy consumption. We developed a distributed environment of CSs from historical data. We discuss the design of the realistic simulator in the next section.

Algorithm 1: MRDI

Input: episode number E; each episode's step number T; state $s_1, s_2, ..., s_T$;
      batch to train N

1   Initialize Rainbow agents $(\mathcal{I}_1, \mathcal{I}_2)$, Prioritized replay buffer $(\mathcal{B}_1, \mathcal{B}_2)$
2   **for** *episode* $= 1, 2, ..., E$ **do**
3   Initialize state
4   **for** $t = 1, 2, ..., T$ **do**
5   **while** *not terminal* **do**
6   agents chooses a_t^1 and a_t^2 based on its state s_t
7   process and compute action a_t^2 (Equation 1)
8   compute rewards r_t^1, r_t^2 (Equation 2, 3, 4)
9   Imparting preference and compute r_t^1 and r_t^2 (Equation 5)
10   Obtain next state s_{t+1}
11   Compute N-step learning reward and store transitions
                 $(s_t, a_t^1, r_t^1, s_{t+1})$ and $(s_t, a_t^2, r_t^2, s_{t+1})$ in $\mathcal{B}_1$, $\mathcal{B}_2$ respectively
12   **if** *size of* $\mathcal{B}_1, \mathcal{B}_2 \geq N$ **then**
13   Sample mini-batches from prioritized buffer $\mathcal{B}_1, \mathcal{B}_2$
14   Compute N-step learning loss and update agents $\mathcal{I}_1, \mathcal{I}_2$
                 respectively
15   **end**
16   **end**
17   **end**
18 **end**

4.1   Simulation Setup

EV Driving Records: We derive driving records along regular routes using historical data from the New York MTA Bus Time[®][1]. The timestamp records, inferred route id, and distance are used to generate the driving records of a particular route for a vehicle. We assume that the driver begins driving the EV from 10 AM and arrives at the destination at 6 PM. We assume that the length of each time step is $t = 5$ minutes and the total time horizon is $T = 96$. The velocity is calculated with the average velocity function $\bar{v} = \Delta x / \Delta t$, where Δx is the resultant displacement and Δt is the period. Furthermore, we consider the Tesla Model 3 as the chosen EV. We referenced the velocity and power consumption graph on ABetterRouteplanner.com,[2] which provides the power consumption (kW) at various constant speeds (m/s). We used the yellow dots from the velocity and power consumption figure in the reference (the median data) and built a quadratic function $(\Delta p = 2(\Delta \bar{v})^2 / 125 - \Delta \bar{v} / 250 + 3)$ to estimate the velocity-power consumption en route. We calculate the energy consumption in kilowatt-hour (kWh) in each time interval Δt by

$$\Delta energy_{(kwh)} = \frac{\Delta p_{(kW)} * \Delta t_{(s)}}{3600}.$$

---

[1] http://web.mta.info/developers/MTA-Bus-Time-historical-data.html.
[2] https://forum.abetterrouteplanner.com/blogs/entry/22-tesla-model-3-performance-vs-rwd-consumption-real-driving-data-from-233-cars/.

Data Preprocessing for Charging Stations: We designed a simulated environment with randomly distributed CSs in each time step. The dataset[3] includes the historical data of the EV charging sessions for each charging pile. We sampled charging piles from the data to construct samples of CSs with different sizes. The occupancy rate of each CS is calculated from the charging sessions in the dataset. By organizing the charging sessions hourly, we divide the sessions by the total sessions in the day. The occupancy rate from a particular CS varied by the hour and is simulated and calculated by

$$occ_{z,t}^{hour} = \frac{\sum_0^n cp_{z,t}}{\sum_0^{23} \sum_0^n cp_{z,t}},$$

where $cp_{z,t}$ represents the charging session counts and n is the total number of charging piles within the CS z at time t. Additionally, we referenced commercial charging prices from open charging data.[4] The samples of CSs are paired with one charging price randomly. In different time steps, the ToU price rates are calculated with the charging price based on the time step in semi-peak or peak periods. We referenced the ToU price rates, semi-peak, and peak periods from Taiwan Power Company data.[5] We set the peak periods from 10 AM to 12 PM and 1 PM to 5 PM. The semi-peak periods are from 12 PM to 1 PM and 5 PM to 6 PM. As a result, the charging prices are calculated by

$$\lambda_{z,t} = \begin{cases} \lambda_{z,t} * 1.55, & t = 1, ..., 24 \\ \lambda_{z,t} * 1.002, & t = 25, ..., 36 \\ \lambda_{z,t} * 1.55, & t = 37, ..., 84 \\ \lambda_{z,t} * 1.002, & t = 85, ..., 96 \end{cases}$$

4.2   Results and Analysis

Experimental Settings: We considered four practical scenarios to demonstrate different driving behaviors for the simulation. The trade-off parameter ξ was tested and observed for two different situations. In the cost-efficiency scenario ($\xi = 0.9$), the EV driver prefers charging at an optimal price when searching for the charging schedule. Furthermore, the parameter is set to 0.1 to search for a low occupancy rate, which is significantly more promising for the EV driver who wants to charge instantly without waiting in line. Other than the trade-off parameters, we analyzed more extreme scenarios by setting different assurance threshold parameters δ and initial SoC $soc_{t=1}$ values at the beginning of the time series. The assurance threshold and initial SoC significantly affect the charging times and amount of the charging scheduling. Table 1 presents the settings of the four scenarios that demonstrate different driving behaviors. The trade-off parameter reflects the driver's decision of selecting the CS based on the cost or time. And the assurance threshold and initial SoC present a different application usage of the EV.

---

[3] https://data.dundeecity.gov.uk/dataset/ev-charging-data.

[4] https://openchargemap.org/site.

[5] https://www.taipower.com.tw/en/page.aspx?mid=317.

Table 1. Driving behaviors for four scenarios

Description	Trade-off ξ	Assurance threshold δ	Initial SoC $soc_{t=1}$
Cost-efficient (CE)	0.9	0.4	0.9
Time-efficient (TE)	0.1	0.4	0.9
Intensive Charging (IC)	0.9	0.7	0.9
Low Initial SoC (LIS)	0.9	0.4	0.5

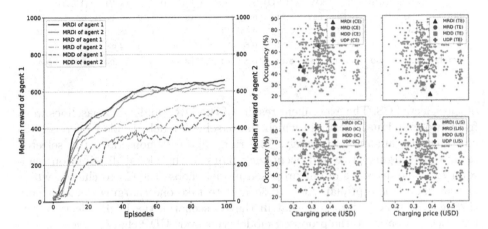

Fig. 2. Performance comparison of the baseline models with the proposed model. (**Left**) Median cumulative rewards comparison with two baseline RL models. (**Right**) The cost/occupancy decisions among 4 driving scenarios in the global distribution of charging stations' cost/occupancy. Each gray dot represents a cost/occupancy pair of a single charging station.

Performance Comparison: We compare our MRDI model with three other baselines. (**i**) Multiagent Rainbow DQN (MRD): The same multiagent Rainbow DQN model without imparting preference. We evaluate the performance without experience sharing to measure the improvements in the results of the charging scheduling. (**ii**) Multiagent Double DQN (MDD): The multiagent Double DQN model without imparting preference. We construct another multiagent RL model to analyze the learning performance with our model. (**iii**) Upon Depletion Charging Policy (UDP): We design the charging scheduling that imitates human charging behavior. Like fueling conventional vehicles, drivers intend to fill up the gas tank if the fuel is almost depleted. We emulate this fueling behavior by charging the EV when the SoC is near 20% left of the battery. The driver will search for the most affordable charging price or the lowest occupancy rate among the CSs available in the current time step.

Figure 2 summarizes the learning performance of our proposed model and baseline models. The left figure represents the median cumulative rewards of the RL models. Our proposed model can impart the preference empirically from the first agent to the second agent, in which the second agent receives the preference

Table 2. Charging scheduling comparisons of 4 different charging scenarios with different baseline models. The bracket indicates the total charging times through the time series. The underlined text symbolizes that the method did not fulfill the requirements. CE, TE, IC, and LIS stands for Cost-Efficient, Time-Efficient, Intensive Charging, and Low Initial SoC scenarios respectively. The C.A. stands for the charged amount in the scenarios.

	CE			TE			IC			LIS		
	C.A. (kWh)	Cost (USD)	SoC	C.A. (kWh)	Cost (USD)	SoC	C.A. (kWh)	Cost (USD)	SoC	C.A. (kWh)	Cost (USD)	SoC
MRD	11.88	3.08	0.50	14.17	5.71	0.54	14.88	3.85	0.79	17.49(2)	4.53	0.54
MDD	12.57	3.26	0.52	14.21	6.5	0.54	13.05	3.41	<u>0.61</u>	18.04(2)	5.01	0.45
UDP	19.66	6.70	0.88	19.66	7.31	0.88	18.78(2)	5.34	0.83	22.68	5.87	0.52
MRDI	**10.8**	**2.59**	**0.48**	**13.58**	**5.05**	**0.53**	**14.73**	**3.81**	**0.76**	**17.04**	**4.41**	**0.43**

of the selected CS. The experiment results of the MRD and MDD baselines work from two individual agents, in which the baseline models decide to choose CSs and charging amounts separately. The right figure demonstrates the selected results of charging price and occupancy pairs in the global distribution environment. The decisions of our proposed model choose the CS to charge, which is near the global optimal. Also, it decides to take one charging decision only through the time series. Note that in the IC scenario, the UDP selects a better price compared to the proposed model. However, UDP charges two times to fulfill the required assurance amount, and the total charging cost is higher than our proposed model.

Table 2 presents a comparison of the optimal charging schedule against the other three baseline models. We compare the charged amount (C.A.), cost, and the SoC at time T. Our charging scheduling aims to charge the least amount of energy that guarantees the EV to arrive at the end of time steps. In the three scenarios, CE, IC, and LIS aim at cost-efficient charging, in which the objective is to minimize the charging cost. Furthermore, the SoC results are much near the threshold value, in which the charging scheduling charges enough amount only when arriving at the destination.

Our experiments present a charging schedule recommendation for the EV en route to a destination. It is designed to accommodate a diverse selection of CSs in every time step, whereas other work only consider a few CSs for the EV to select en route [17]. The experimental results in [17] indicate that the proposed method requires visiting the CSs multiple times, whereas our model requires one charging time to the destination. In [16], the proposed algorithm aims at the EV route optimization problem in a planned region. The problem considers fully charging the battery when the EV returns to the starting point. It considers the charging cost of both regular charging and fast charging. It is unfair to compare the performance of charging cost since our experiment considers only fast charging en route. Our proposed model evaluates the destination and provides the charging decision with adequate quantity when necessary. It guarantees that the EV has efficient energy without considering any further charging when the EV arrives at the destination.

5   Conclusion

In this paper, we propose a Reinforcement Learning model named Multiagent Rainbow DQN with Imparting Preference. Leveraging concepts from Edge Computing, the model provides an adaptive charging scheduling service to EV drivers. The model manages two tasks by recommending suitable charging stations and determining a proper charging plan that respects battery constraints and arrival energy guarantees. Imparting experience sharing is embedded within the agents to balance the coupling effects between the two tasks. This technique increases the learning efficiency and thus enhances the performance of the scheme. Utilizing real-world data, we compare our proposed approach against three benchmarks (an idiomatic behavior of EV driver and two other RL-based models) in the experiments. The results show that our model outperforms the benchmarks in terms of charging cost, total charging times, and total charged amount. The overall performance demonstrate the robustness and practicability of our proposed method for efficient charging scheduling. In future work, the simulation can be extended to consider multiple routes or different routines, such as weekdays and weekends. We will further investigate the generalization and performance of the EV charging scheduling behavior across several routes. We aim to develop the model to operate in a highly realistic environment that considers multiple routes, which improves the generalization of the model's charging schedule recommendations. Another future avenue might investigate the charging scheduling for two-way EV charging and consider the case for Vehicle-to-Grid (V2G).

References

1. Cao, Y., Wang, T., Kaiwartya, O., Min, G., Ahmad, N., Abdullah, A.H.: An EV charging management system concerning drivers' trip duration and mobility uncertainty. IEEE Trans. Syst. Man Cybern.: Syst. **48**(4), 596–607 (2016)
2. Da Silva, F.L., Nishida, C.E., Roijers, D.M., Costa, A.H.R.: Coordination of electric vehicle charging through multiagent reinforcement learning. IEEE Trans. Smart Grid **11**(3), 2347–2356 (2019)
3. Greenblatt, J.B., Saxena, S.: Autonomous taxis could greatly reduce greenhouse-gas emissions of us light-duty vehicles. Nat. Clim. Chang. **5**(9), 860–863 (2015)
4. Hessel, M., et al.: Rainbow: combining improvements in deep reinforcement learning. arXiv preprint arXiv:1710.02298 (2017)
5. Li, H., Wan, Z., He, H.: Constrained EV charging scheduling based on safe deep reinforcement learning. IEEE Trans. Smart Grid **11**(3), 2427–2439 (2019)
6. Mnih, V., et al.: Human-level control through deep reinforcement learning. Nature **518**(7540), 529–533 (2015)
7. Na, J., Zhang, H., Deng, X., Zhang, B., Ye, Z.: Accelerate personalized IoT service provision by cloud-aided edge reinforcement learning: a case study on smart lighting. In: Kafeza, E., Benatallah, B., Martinelli, F., Hacid, H., Bouguettaya, A., Motahari, H. (eds.) ICSOC 2020. LNCS, vol. 12571, pp. 69–84. Springer, Cham (2020). https://doi.org/10.1007/978-3-030-65310-1_6

8. Panayiotou, T., Chatzis, S.P., Panayiotou, C., Ellinas, G.: Charging policies for PHEVs used for service delivery: a reinforcement learning approach. In: 2018 21st International Conference on Intelligent Transportation Systems (ITSC), pp. 1514–1521. IEEE (2018)

9. Shi, W., Cao, J., Zhang, Q., Li, Y., Xu, L.: Edge computing: vision and challenges. IEEE Internet Things J. **3**(5), 637–646 (2016). https://doi.org/10.1109/JIOT.2016.2579198

10. Sutton, R.S.: Learning to predict by the methods of temporal differences. Mach. Learn. **3**(1), 9–44 (1988)

11. Sutton, R.S., Barto, A.G., et al.: Introduction to Reinforcement Learning, vol. 135. MIT Press, Cambridge (1998)

12. Valogianni, K., Ketter, W., Collins, J.: Smart charging of electric vehicles using reinforcement learning. In: Proceedings of the 15th AAAI Conference on Trading Agent Design and Analysis, pp. 41–48 (2013)

13. Wang, H., et al.: Architectural design alternatives based on cloud/edge/fog computing for connected vehicles. IEEE Commun. Surv. Tutor. **22**(4), 2349–2377 (2020)

14. Winkler, T., Komarnicki, P., Mueller, G., Heideck, G., Heuer, M., Styczynski, Z.A.: Electric vehicle charging stations in Magdeburg. In: 2009 IEEE Vehicle Power and Propulsion Conference, pp. 60–65. IEEE (2009)

15. Woody, M., Arbabzadeh, M., Lewis, G.M., Keoleian, G.A., Stefanopoulou, A.: Strategies to limit degradation and maximize Li-ion battery service lifetime-critical review and guidance for stakeholders. J. Energy Storage **28**, 101231 (2020)

16. Yang, H., Yang, S., Xu, Y., Cao, E., Lai, M., Dong, Z.: Electric vehicle route optimization considering time-of-use electricity price by learnable partheno-genetic algorithm. IEEE Trans. Smart Grid **6**(2), 657–666 (2015)

17. Yang, S.N., Cheng, W.S., Hsu, Y.C., Gan, C.H., Lin, Y.B.: Charge scheduling of electric vehicles in highways. Math. Comput. Model. **57**(11–12), 2873–2882 (2013)

18. Zhang, F., Yang, Q., An, D.: CDDPG: a deep-reinforcement-learning-based approach for electric vehicle charging control. IEEE Internet Things J. **8**(5), 3075–3087 (2021). https://doi.org/10.1109/JIOT.2020.3015204

19. Zhou, Y., Yau, D.K., You, P., Cheng, P.: Optimal-cost scheduling of electrical vehicle charging under uncertainty. IEEE Trans. Smart Grid **9**(5), 4547–4554 (2017)

Locating False Data Injection Attacks on Smart Grids Using D-FACTS Devices

Beibei Li[1]([✉])(iD), Qingyun Du[1](iD), Jiarui Song[1](iD), Aohan Li[2](iD),
and Xiaoxia Ma[1](iD)

[1] School of Cyber Science and Engineering, Sichuan University, Chengdu, China
libeibei@scu.edu.cn, {duqingyun,jiaruisong,maxiaoxia}@stu.scu.edu.cn
[2] Department of Electrical Engineering, Tokyo University of Science, Tokyo, Japan
aohanli@ee.kagu.tus.ac.jp

Abstract. In the context of Industry 4.0, the high-profile false data injection (FDI) attacks are posing increasing cyber threats to the reliability of smart grids. Recent studies have investigated the possibilities of detecting FDI attacks on smart grids by using the distributed flexible AC transmission system (D-FACTS) devices. However, few studies focus on further locating such cyber threats using D-FACTS devices. To meet this gap, we systematically explored such a topic and propose a graph theory based scheme to locate FDI attacks by employing D-FACTS devices, where both single-bus FDI attacks and multiple-bus FDI attacks are considered. Numerical results on the standard IEEE 14-bus system demonstrated that the proposed scheme can achieve 100% accuracy when locating any single-bus FDI attacks and most of the independent multiple-bus FDI attacks. Future potential solutions are also discussed to some special cases of multiple-bus FDI attacks that the proposed scheme cannot well handle.

Keywords: Industry 4.0 · Smart grids · D-FACTS devices · Graph theory · Location of false data injection (FDI) attacks

1 Introduction

The Industry 4.0 framework requires more interaction and connections among equipment, products, and operators. As the key element to Industry 4.0, the power grid is rapidly evolving to the smart grid. Next-generation smart grid networking technologies are required to provide high reliability and low latency

This work was supported in part by the National Key Research and Development Program of China (No. 2020YFB1805400); in part by the National Natural Science Foundation of China (No. 62002248); in part by the China Postdoctoral Science Foundation (No. 2019TQ0217 and No. 2020M673277); in part by the Provincial Key Research and Development Program of Sichuan (No. 20ZDYF3145); in part by the Fundamental Research Funds for the Central Universities; in part by the China International Postdoctoral Exchange Fellowship Program (Talent-Introduction).

© Springer Nature Switzerland AG 2021
H. Hacid et al. (Eds.): ICSOC 2021, LNCS 13121, pp. 287–301, 2021.
https://doi.org/10.1007/978-3-030-91431-8_18

synchrophasor communications. However, the communication capabilities of the intelligent sensor, the measurement device, and the control center exposed the adverse vulnerability to attackers in the context of Industry 4.0 [6]. At the same time, the damage caused by networking attacks not only affects the information system operations, but also destroys the security of the physical system due to their high integration. Serious consequences may include grid paralysis or large-scale power outages [10].

In recent years, there have been frequent incidents of penetrating into the power grid to destroy it through cyber attacks. In December 2015, the Ukrainian grid suffered a malicious cyberattack and caused a large-scale power outage. The attacker also cleared the root record on the control center, which delayed the recovery of the power grid [12]. In 2019, Venezuela had encountered a national power outage. The official representative said that the accident was caused by malicious attacks against the hydropower power center [4]. Such incidents demonstrate that the safety of the power grid is much likely to remain ongoing targets of interest shortly. In this case, it is very important to ensure the network security of the smart grid to enhance social stability and national security.

Since the security and stability of smart grids are usually supported by reliable state estimation (SE), SE tends to be main target of the network attacks. Liu et al. first proposed false data injection (FDI) attacks in 2009 [14]. In essence, the FDI attack is designed to escape the bad data detection (BDD) in the state estimation. Attackers need to acquire knowledge of the power grid connections and configurations and inject pre-constructed data into the measurement data to tamper with the SE and cause the grid failure. The recent work has illustrated the possibility of achieving FDI detection by disturbing the impedance of the power grid using the distributed flexible AC transmission system (D-FACTS) devices. Morrow *et al.* first proposed to achieve topology perturbation using D-FACTS devices to detect injected false data in the power grid [16]. Lately, Li *et al.* proposed a framework to detect FDI attacks on smart grids by using the D-FACTS [11]. While some research has been carried out on using D-FACTS devices to detect FDI attacks, few studies have investigated their feasibility of location. To meet this gap, we propose a location scheme using D-FACTS devices to locate both single-bus FDI attacks and multiple-bus FDI attacks. The main contributions of this paper are three-fold:

- First, we propose a graph theory based FDI location scheme for smart grids by using D-FACTS devices, and prove that when the *unknown branches* cover at least a spanning tree of the power grid graph, any single-bus FDI attacks on smart grids can be accurately located.
- Second, an algorithm is designed to locate multiple-bus FDI attacks, given the results of FDI detection, by which the locations of the independent multiple-bus FDI attacks can be accurately identified in most cases.
- Third, we notice that in occasional special cases, locating multiple-bus FDI attacks using D-FACTS devices is not always easy. The location accuracy for multiple-bus FDI attacks decreases, as the growing interconnections of

attacked multiple buses and the increasing number of *leaf buses* (with a degree equalling one).

The remaining of this paper is organized as follows. Section 2 reviews state-of-the-art solutions to detecting and locating FDI attacks on smart grids. Section 3 presents our system model and the threat model considered. The proposed location scheme for two types of FDI attacks is elaborated in Sect. 4, followed by the numerical results in Sect. 5. We conclude this paper in Sect. 6.

2 Related Work

2.1 False Data Injection Detection Using D-FACTS

A successful FDI attack is based upon the knowledge of power grid measurement, the admittance of the power line, and topology configurations of the grid for state estimation [2,3]. Therefore, it is possible to proactively change the configuration of the grid system, so that the information required by the FDI attackers is inaccurate and the attack will be detected by BDD. Morrow *et al.* pioneered the idea of using distributed flexible AC transmission system (D-FACTS) devices to achieve topology perturbation in 2012 [16]. Moving target defense (MTD) in the power system is a promising defense strategy to detect false data injection (FDI) attacks against state estimation using distributed flexible AC transmission system (D-FACTS) devices. Based on this, Rahman *et al.* proposed the MTD to enhance the state estimation of the power system in 2014, one of which is to disturb the admittance of the power line by using D-FACTS devices [18]. In 2017, Tian *et al.* proposed a hidden MTD method to prevent attackers from calculating the changes in the system [21]. In 2018, Salehghaffari *et al.* proposed an optimal defense strategy by applying perturbations to the impedance of transmission lines by D-FACTS devices and monitoring their effects on the system [19]. In 2019, Lakshminarayana *et al.* showed that the coordinated cyber and physical FDI attack can be detected by using game theory methods to optimize the deployment of D-FACTS equipment [8]. In 2020, Li *et al.* explored the relationship between the minimum efforts and the injected data and proved that as long as the deployment of D-FACTS devices covers at least a spanning tree can detect the existence of all these FDI attacks [11]. In 2021, Zhang *et al.* revealed the correlation between the MTD design and FDI detection and optimize MTD's performance in terms of detecting FDI attacks. Furthermore, a heuristic algorithm is developed to compute a near-optimal solution for the deployment of D-FACTS devices[23]. In the same year, Liu *et al.* investigated a depth-first-search-based D-FACTS placement algorithm to guarantee the MTD hiddenness while maximizing the rank of its composite matrix, i.e., an indicator of the MTD effectiveness, and covering all necessary buses[13].

2.2 Location of False Data Injection Attacks

However, there is an increasing need for research in the stage to take the location of FDI attacks into account. Because the system operators must take action and respond to attacks after the attack. Some researchers regard the attack locational problem as another task after attack detection. For example, in 2017, MohammadPourfard *et al.* used several statistical methods to obtain measurement features in the attack detection phase, using conventional outlier detection algorithms to achieve location [15]. Another part of studies can be located while detecting the FDI attack. In 2018, Shi *et al.* trained fourteen extreme learning machines (ELM) to calculated whether the bus was attacked [20]. However, when faced with a large-scale power system, the method is too cumbersome. In 2019, Li *et al.* used matrix separation to detect the FDI attack and achieved the location of the FDI by analyzing the sparse attack matrix [9]. Its accuracy depends on the matrix decomposition algorithm. In 2020, Wang *et al.* designed an approach based on deep Learning-based Locational Detection architecture (DLLD) to detect the exact locations of FDIA in real-time [22]. In 2021, Mukherjee developed a deep neural network model with conventional bad data detection (BDD) to identify the locations. This model in association with traditional bad data detection algorithms is capable of detecting the exact locations of both structured as well as unstructured FDI attacks [17]. However, the machine learning method involves considerable analyses of global power grid data, which will cause huge computation costs.

3   System Model and Threat Model

3.1   System Model

Security state estimation has real-time demand. For computational speed and simplicity, the DC linear power flow is used to approximate the AC model in the research and application of power system [1]. Thus, our system model is discussed on the DC power flow model.

DC State Estimation. In the DC model, the voltage magnitudes of all buses in the power grid are approximately equal to 1 p.u. And only is the voltage phase angle considered as the state variable while ignoring the impedance of the transmission line. Based on the above assumptions, the measurement data and system states are related by

$$\mathbf{z} = \mathbf{Hx} + e, \tag{1}$$

where $\mathbf{x} \in \mathbb{R}^{n \times 1}$ indicates system state vector composed of bus voltage phase angles. The active power injections on each bus and active power flow on each branch consists measurement, which is $\mathbf{z} \in \mathbb{R}^{m \times 1}$. $e \in \mathbb{R}^{m \times 1}$ is measurement error vector which follows the Gaussian distribution with zero mean and covariance $\mathbf{W} \in \mathbb{R}^{m \times m}$, a diagonal matrix. $\mathbf{H} \in \mathbb{R}^{m \times n}$ is a Jacobian matrix imply connection information and configuration of the grid. The form of the $\mathbf{H}$ is given by

$$\mathbf{H} = \begin{bmatrix} \mathbf{A}^{\mathsf{T}} \mathbf{D} \mathbf{A} \\ \mathbf{D} \mathbf{A} \\ -\mathbf{D} \mathbf{A} \end{bmatrix}, \tag{2}$$

where $\mathbf{A} \in \mathbb{R}^{l \times n}$ indicates the branch-bus connection matrix, l indicates the number of branches. $\mathbf{D} \in \mathbb{R}^{l \times l}$ denotes the diagonal matrix of admittance. Since the impedance of the power line is ignored in the DC model, its value is negative susceptance.

Based on the Eq. (1), weighted least squares (WLS) is used to solve estimated state vector:

$$\hat{\mathbf{x}} = \left(\mathbf{H}^\mathbf{T}\mathbf{W}^{-1}\mathbf{H}\right)^{-1}\mathbf{H}^\mathbf{T}\mathbf{W}^{-1}\mathbf{z}. \tag{3}$$

Thus, the estimated measurement data $\hat{\mathbf{z}}$ is given by

$$\hat{\mathbf{z}} = \mathbf{H}\hat{\mathbf{x}}. \tag{4}$$

Bad Data Detection. State estimation uses BDD to ensure the integrity and accuracy of the data. Existing BDD methods typically use hypothesis testing to detect bad measurement data by observing the maximum normalization residuals. Measurement residual $\mathbf{r} \in \mathbb{R}^{m \times 1}$ is the difference between measurement and estimated measurement, which can be shown as below:

$$\mathbf{r} = \mathbf{z} - \hat{\mathbf{z}}. \tag{5}$$

The hypothesis testing is expressed as

$$\begin{cases} \text{Null hypothesis } \mathbf{H}_0 : \|\mathbf{r}\| > \tau \\ \text{Alternative hypothesis } \mathbf{H}_1 : \|\mathbf{r}\| <= \tau \end{cases} \tag{6}$$

$\|\cdot\|$ represents the Frobenius norm. This mechanism compares the number of measurement residual to a predefined threshold τ. If $\|\mathbf{r}\| > \tau$, the null hypothesis is accepted, indicating that there is abnormal data in the measurement, and the BDD will alarm; otherwise (i.e., $\|\mathbf{r}\| < \tau$), null hypothesis are rejected, and the measurement is considered as normal data by BDD. The value of τ can be determined by a chi-squared test with a significance level of α, where $\|\mathbf{z} - \mathbf{H}\hat{\mathbf{x}}\|^2 \sim \mathcal{X}^2(v)$ and $v = m - n$ is the degree of freedom [1].

3.2   Attack Model

To build an FDI attack, an attacker needs to design an attack vector $\mathbf{a} \in \mathbb{R}^{m \times 1}$, and makes up a malicious measurement vector $\mathbf{z_a} = \mathbf{z} + \mathbf{a}$. Liu *et al.* proposed, assuming the original measurement can pass the BDD, if $\mathbf{a}$ is a linear combination of the column of $\mathbf{H}$, the malicious vector $\mathbf{z_a}$ can also can pass the BDD, a successful FDI constructed [14]. The estimated states vector $\hat{\mathbf{x}}_\mathbf{a}$ with reference to Eq. (3) is satisfied $\hat{\mathbf{x}}_\mathbf{a} = \hat{\mathbf{x}} + \mathbf{c}$. Now, the measurement residual norm is

$$\begin{aligned} \|\mathbf{r_a}\| &= \|\mathbf{z_a} - \mathbf{H}\hat{\mathbf{x}}_\mathbf{a}\| \\ &= \|\mathbf{z} + \mathbf{a} - \mathbf{H}(\hat{\mathbf{x}} + \mathbf{c})\| \\ &= \|\mathbf{z} - \mathbf{H}\hat{\mathbf{x}} + (\mathbf{a} - \mathbf{Hc})\| \\ &= \|\mathbf{z} - \mathbf{H}\hat{\mathbf{x}}\| \leq \tau \end{aligned} \tag{7}$$

Since $\mathbf{r_a} = \mathbf{r}$, the BDD detector can't detect abnormal data, and the FDI attack successfully bypasses the BDD in the state estimation.

4   The Proposed Location Scheme

In this paper, we consider two types of FDI attack location. The estimated state vector is injected offset c. Then, the FDI can be classified according to the number of buses affected:

Single-Bus FDI Attacks. Such FDI attacks only targets the voltage phases of a specific single bus, such as, $c = (0, 0, \theta_a, 0, \ldots)^T$.

Multiple-Bus FDI Attacks. This type of FDI attack can build attacks on multiple buses at the same time and independently, such as, $c = (0, \theta_{a1}, 0, \ldots, \theta_{an}, 0, \ldots)^T$.

4.1   Rational of Detecting FDI Using D-FACTS

The pre-relevant work has detected FDI attack by using the D-FACTS device to change the impedance of the power line [8,11,21]. The D-FACTS devices attach directly to transmission lines, which can be used to dynamically control effective line impedance and power flow to manage the congestion in the power system [5]. Assuming that the D-FACTS device is activated, the line admittance has changed as follows:

$$D' = D + \Delta D. \tag{8}$$

Consequently, the Jacobian matrix are altered by:

$$H' = \begin{bmatrix} A^T D' A \\ D' A \\ -D' A \end{bmatrix} = \begin{bmatrix} A^T (D + \Delta D) A \\ (D + \Delta D) A \\ -(D + \Delta D) A \end{bmatrix} = H + \Delta H. \tag{9}$$

The measurement z, the injected measurement z_a, the estimated state vector $\hat{x}$ and the injected estimated state vector $\hat{x}_a$ will change, and the updated value is: z', z'_a, $\hat{x}'$, $\hat{x}'_a$. Re-conducting state estimation algorithm, the measurement residual will change as follows:

$$\begin{aligned} \|r'_a\| &= \|z'_a - H'\hat{x}'_a\| \\ &= \|z' + a - H'(\hat{x}' + \Delta x)\|, \\ &= \|z' - H'\hat{x}' + a - H'\Delta x\| \end{aligned} \tag{10}$$

Δx is an injected offset on system state vector after the D-FACTS device is activated. Now $a - H'\Delta x = Hc - H'\Delta x \neq 0$, the resulting offset is sufficiently large to trigger the BDD, so the FDI attack can be detected. Li *et al.* analyzes the minimum efforts required for D-FACTS devices to detect the FDI attack, and draw the following statement [11]:

Statement 1. *D-FACTS devices deployed on a branch is able to help detect the existence of effective FDI attacks targeted on either end bus(es) of this branch, as long as the injected phase angle difference between the two end buses is larger than the tolerance threshold c_{th}.*

Accordingly, a theorem is further proved that the minimum branch of the D-FACTS device needs to be deployed for successfully detecting FDI attacks.

Theorem 1. *The D-FACTS is feasible to detect effective FDI attacks, if and only if the branches deployed with D-FACTS devices cover at least a spanning tree of the power grid graph.*

Based on Statement 1 and Theorem 1, we can further analyze the location of the FDI attack using D-FACTS devices.

For convenience, this section is now defined on buses and lines in the power grid topology [11].

Definition 1. *A branch is termed as a known branch if its susceptance (or admittance) is unalterable and can be known to the attackers; otherwise, it is termed as an unknown branch. A bus is termed as a protected bus if it is connected to at least one unknown branch; and an unprotected bus otherwise.*

Definition 2. *If a protected bus is only connected to an unknown branch, it is called a leaf bus; otherwise it is called a branch bus.*

According to Statement 1, the D-FACTS device can detect FDI attacks for either end bus of the branch it deployed, so the location of the FDI attack can be determined in two buses. However, if we want to determine which end bus of the transmission line is injected, further analyses are required. This section uses the topology map of the grid and graph theory to feature the location of single-bus FDI attacks and multiple-bus FDI attacks.

4.2 Location of Single-Bus FDI Attacks

Based on Statement 1 and Theorem 1, it can be given to the Corollary 1 and proof.

Corollary 1. *If the unknown branches cover at least a spanning tree of the power grid graph, the targeted bus of the single-bus FDI attacks can be accurately located.*

Proof. Assume that there is $n-1$ branch deployed D-FACTS device in the power grid, those branches and the buses connected to them constitute a spanning tree; at this time, all buses in the power grid is *protected bus*. Now divide all buses of this spanning tree into two categories, a bus with degree equal to 1 term as *leaf bus*, a bus with degree greater than 1 term as branch bus. Because the number of buses in the actual power grid is numerous, this section only considers the number of buses greater than two. Therefore, according to the nature of the topology, the *protected bus* connected to the *leaf bus* must be a branch bus. Assuming that the *leaf bus* is n_l, the branch bus connected to it is n_b, and the *unknown branch* between them is $k_l = (n_l, n_b)$. When the attacker is only attack $k_l = (n_l, n_b)$, it will trigger D-FACTS device alarm of k_l. For the control center's defender, he will suspect to n_l and n_b. But only k_l alerts in all unknown transmission lines connected to n_b, so n_b can be excluded and defender can successfully locate to n_l. When the attacker is only attacking n_b, assume that the collection of the connected branch is L_b. Now, all branch of the L_b will alert, the control center will suspect that all buses are connected to n_b. If the other end of the branch in L_b is the *leaf bus*, it can be excluded; if the other end of the branch in L_b is the branch bus, only one branch connect to it has an alert, so it can be excluded and successfully locate to the n_h.

For example, in Fig. 1 an attacker attacked bus 3, and an FDI alert can be observed on the branch k_{34}, which means that there is an FDI attack in bus 3 or 4. However, since the alert is not triggered on the k_{24}, it can be concluded that bus 3 is the target of the FDI attack. In the case of single-bus attack, the FDI alert can only be observed from an unknown transmission line. Then, by observing whether the FDI alert is triggered on all *unknown branch* connected to the bus, it can be eliminated one by one. Therefore, the goal of the FDI attack can be inferred. Accordingly, the location of single-bus FDI attacks can achieve 100% accuracy by using D-FACTS devices.

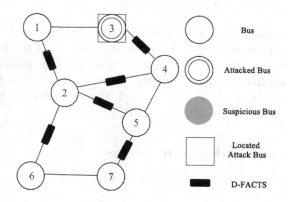

Fig. 1. Location of single-bus FDI attacks.

4.3   Location of Multiple-Bus FDI Attacks

Since the location of this paper only needs to be implemented with the branch deployed with D-FACTS, all discussions in this section only consider branches of the spanning tree deployed with D-FACTS. For the convenience of description, we make the following definition.

Definition 3. *If both ends of an unknown branch are attacked buses, then the branch called attacked branch.*

Algorithm 1. Location algorithm of multiple-bus FDI attacks

Input: $\mathcal{N}$, $\mathcal{L}$, $\mathcal{L}_a$
Output: $\mathcal{S}_p$, $\mathcal{S}_n$, $\mathcal{S}_l$

1: **for** each $k_{mn} \in \mathcal{L}_a$ **do**
2:     put b_m and b_n in the set $\mathcal{S}_p$;
3:     **for** each $p_n \in \mathcal{S}_p$ **do**
4:         **if** p_n connected to $k \notin \mathcal{L}_a$ **then**
5:             exclude p_n from $\mathcal{S}_p$;
6:         **while** locate the p_n with Statement 2 **do**
7:             put the p_n in $\mathcal{S}_l$;
8:             exclude p_n from $\mathcal{S}_p$;
9:         **end**
10:     **end**
11: **end**
12: **return** $\mathcal{S}_p$, $\mathcal{S}_n$, $\mathcal{S}_l$

We consider a power grid network consisting of a set $\mathcal{N} = \{b_1, b_2, ..., b_n\}$ of buses and a set $\mathcal{L}$ of branches. $k_{mn} = (b_m, b_n) \in \mathcal{L}$ is the branch connecting bus b_m and bus b_n. Assume that the set of normal buses is $\mathcal{S}_n$, the set of Located attack buses is $\mathcal{S}_l$, and the set of branch that observes an FDI alert is $\mathcal{L}_a$.

Based on the analysis of single-bus FDI attacks location, we can find that when there is a branch that observes an FDI alert, two buses of both ends may be attacked. We name these buses as possible buses and got a set of them, say $\mathcal{S}_p = \{p_1, p_2, ..., p_n\}$. The location process is to determine that $p_n \in \mathcal{S}_n$ or $p_n \in \mathcal{S}_l$. Since in D-FACTS deployed spinning tree, if a branch does not observed alert, its two end buses can be determined to be normal. Therefore, if a p_n connected to a branch without alert, then $p_n \in \mathcal{S}_n$. At this time, if a $p_{n1} \in \mathcal{S}_p$ is determined to be a normal bus, the another bus $p_{n2} \in \mathcal{S}_p$ connected to it must be an attacked bus, i.e., $p_{n2} \in \mathcal{S}_l$. Thus, we can get Statement 2.

Statement 2. *Only when at least one adjacent bus of a possible bus is connected with branch without alert, it can be judged as a located attacked bus.*

The remaining p_n are called suspicious buses. In the perspective of the system defender, it may be an attacked bus, or it is possible to be a normal bus. The location process can be summarized as Algorithm 1.

As shown in Fig. 2(a), the attacker targets bus 3 and bus 7, respectively. FDI alerts can be observed on branch k_{57} and k_{34}, and bus 3, bus 4, bus 5, and bus 7 are possible attacked buses. However, since the transmission line k_{24} and k_{25} do not observe alert, bus 5 and bus 4 can be excluded. Therefore, it can be concluded that bus 3 and bus 7 are the target of the attack. Such that we find out the attacked buses. In most cases, due to the restricted ability of the attacker, the attacked buses are less and unconnected. In most instances, we can achieve 100% location accuracy.

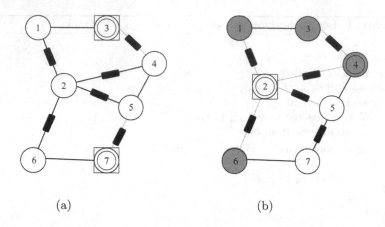

(a)   (b)

Fig. 2. Location of multiple-bus FDI attacks.

4.4   Discussions on Some Special Cases

However, as the attack buses become more concentrated, there will appear inaccurate judgment and suspicious buses. As shown in Fig. 2(b), it is assumed that the FDI attack is targeted in bus 2 and bus 4. Therefore, branch k_{12}, k_{24}, k_{25}, k_{26} and k_{34} will trigger the FDI alert. Since the alert is observed on the branch k_{25}, not the trigger on the k_{57}, it can be easily concluded: bus 2 is the target of the FDI attack. However, bus1, bus 3, bus 4, and bus 6 will be suspected. Since they are not connected to any normal bus, it cannot be accurate conclusions.

Based on Algorithm 1 we can derive that if neighbors of an attacked bus are *leaf bus* or also attacked buses, it will not be accurately located from the system defender's perspective. And it will eventually become a suspicious bus. At the same time, due to the degree of its adjacent *leaf bus* is 1, there is no more information to determine whether the *leaf bus* is attacked. Then this leaf bus will also become a suspicious bus. That is, if the attacker's target is concentrated in one area, the number of attack branches will increase. With increasing of *attacked branch*, the number of connections between attacked buses and normal buses decreases. This will make it difficult to confirm the located attack bus, and lead to more suspected buses. At the same time, as the number of *leaf buses* connected to attacked buses increases, the number of suspicious buses will grow. Thus, we have the Statement 3.

Statement 3. *The number of attacked branches is directly proportional to the number of suspicious buses and inversely proportional to the number of located attacked buses. The number of leaf buses connected to attacked buses is proportional to the number of suspicious buses.*

The future potential solutions will continue to improve the location accuracy of some special cases of multiple-bus FDI attacks based on Statement 3.

5   Simulation Results

In this section, we conduct simulation experiments on the IEEE-14 bus system to verify our findings. The grid topology and the deployment of D-FACTS devices are shown in Fig. 3. All the simulations are conducted in MATLAB and the power grid data (i.e., topological information, power grid parameters, and measurements) is from MATPOWER. By analyzing the minimum efforts required for D-FACTS devices of each power line, we can get D-FACTS deployment of IEEE-14 bus system in Fig. 3 based on the minimum spanning tree algorithm (Kruskal's algorithm [7] in our simulation).

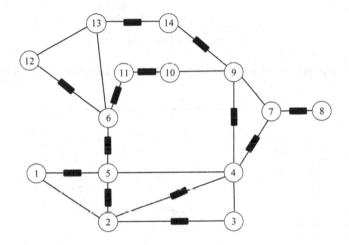

Fig. 3. The D-FACTS devices deployment on IEEE-14 bus system.

First, we simulated the FDI attacks with the number of attacked buses ranging from 1 to 5. For each case, we traverse the situation of the attacked buses' distribution in the IEEE-14 bus system. Then we simulate the location process for each situation to count the number of located attack buses and suspicious buses. The located attack bus here has been verified to be located correctly. Afterward the number of located attack buses and suspicious buses after location in all distributions is grouped according to the number of *attacked branch*, and the average and standard deviation of each group of data are calculated. Finally, the average and standard deviation are drawn into a graph in the form of the errorbar.

As shown in Fig. 4 and Fig. 5, for each I-shaped pattern, the dot in the middle represents the average of this set of data, and the two horizontal lines above and below represent the standard deviation of this set of data. From Fig. 4, we can see that in the case of a multiple-bus FDI attack, as the number of *attacked branches* in the grid increases, the number of located attack buses will decrease. In the case of single-bus FDI attacks location, the standard deviation of this

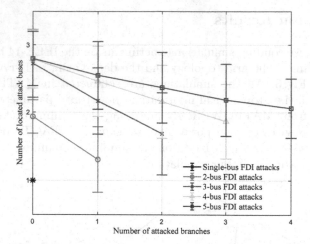

Fig. 4. The number of located attack buses with different number of *attacked branches*.

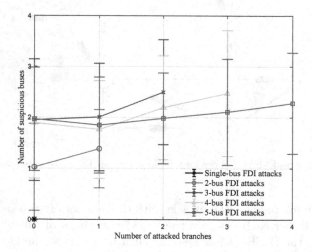

Fig. 5. The number of suspicious buses with different number of *attacked branches*.

group of data is 0, which means that the number of located attack buses is always 1 in each situation, and we can accurately locate this attacked bus. As shown in Fig. 5, as the number of *attacked branches* in the power grid increases, the number of suspicious buses will increase accordingly in the case of multiple-bus FDI attacks. For single-bus FDI attacks location, the standard deviation of this group of data is still 0, and the account of the suspicious buses is always 0. Prove once again that we have accurately located single-bus FDI attacks and there are no other suspicious buses.

However, the standard deviation of the number of suspicious buses in Fig. 5 is larger than the one in Fig. 4, indicating that the number of doubts fluctuates under the same account of *attacked branches*. It can be found by comparison that in addition to the number of *attacked branches*, there may have more factors affecting the number of suspicious buses. Therefore, we perform simulation experiments in the 3-bus FDI attacks to count the number of suspicious buses with the different number of *leaf buses* connected to the attacked buses. The experimental results are shown in Fig. 6. As we can see from the figure, the number of suspicious buses is always increasing as the number of *leaf buses* connected to the attacked buses increases. Prove that the number of *leaf buses* connected to attacked buses is proportional to the number of suspicious buses. While we can see the standard difference of each group of data is smaller than the one in Fig. 5, this shows that under the same number of *attacked branches* and *leaf buses* connected to attacked buses, the number of suspicious buses tends to stabilize, but may still be affected by the connection structure of different attacked buses.

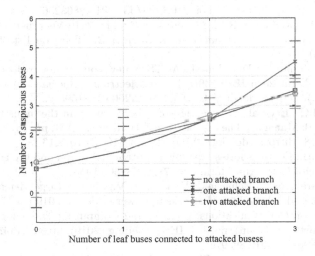

Fig. 6. The number of suspicious buses with different number of *leaf buses* connected to attacked buses.

6   Conclusion

In this paper, we have recalled the method in detecting FDI attacks using D-FACTS devices, and proposed a graph theory based scheme for locating both single-bus FDI attacks and multiple-bus FDI attacks on smart grids using D-FACTS devices. We proved that the proposed scheme can achieve 100% accuracy in locating single-bus FDI attacks, if the *unknown branches* cover at least a spanning tree of the power grid graph. In addition, an algorithm was also proposed to locate multiple-bus FDI attacks on smart grids. We proposed an algorithm to locate multiple-bus FDI attacks based on the given results of FDI detection. However, we notice that locating multiple-bus FDI attacks using D-FACTS devices is not perfect when attack buses are connected to each other. Extensive simulation experiments on the standard IEEE-14 bus system fully demonstrated our findings. Extending these findings to more real-world power systems will be one important research direction.

References

1. Abur, A., Gómez Expósito, A.: Power system state estimation: theory and implementation. Power Engineering, Marcel Dekker, New York, NY (2004). OCLC: ocm55070738
2. Ashok, A., Govindarasu, M., Ajjarapu, V.: Online detection of stealthy false data injection attacks in power system state estimation. IEEE Trans. Smart Grid, p. 1 (2016). https://doi.org/10.1109/TSG.2016.2596298
3. Deng, R., Liang, H.: False data injection attacks with limited susceptance information and new countermeasures in smart grid. IEEE Trans. Industr. Inf. **15**(3), 1619–1628 (2019). https://doi.org/10.1109/TII.2018.2863256
4. Devanny, J., Goldoni, L.R.F., Medeiros, B.P.: The 2019 Venezuelan blackout and the consequences of cyber uncertainty. Revista Brasileira de Estudos de Defesa **7**(2) (2020)
5. Divan, D., Johal, H.: Distributed FACTS-A new concept for realizing grid power flow control. In: 2005 IEEE 36th Power Electronics Specialists Conference, pp. 8–14 (2005). https://doi.org/10.1109/PESC.2005.1581595
6. Ervural, B.C., Ervural, B.: Overview of cyber security in the industry 4.0 era. In: Industry 4.0: Managing The Digital Transformation. SSAM, pp. 267–284. Springer, Cham (2018). https://doi.org/10.1007/978-3-319-57870-5_16
7. Kruskal, J.B.: On the shortest spanning subtree of a graph and the traveling salesman problem. Proc. Am. Math. Soc. **7**(1), 48–50 (1956)
8. Lakshminarayana, S., Belmega, E.V., Poor, H.V.: Moving-target defense for detecting coordinated cyber-physical attacks in power grids. In: 2019 IEEE International Conference on Communications, Control, and Computing Technologies for Smart Grids (SmartGridComm), pp. 1–7. IEEE, Beijing (2019). https://doi.org/10.1109/SmartGridComm.2019.8909767
9. Li, B., Ding, T., Huang, C., Zhao, J., Yang, Y., Chen, Y.: Detecting false data injection attacks against power system state estimation with fast go-decomposition approach. IEEE Trans. Industr. Inf. **15**(5), 2892–2904 (2019). https://doi.org/10.1109/TII.2018.2875529
10. Li, B., Wu, Y., Song, J., Lu, R., Li, T., Zhao, L.: DeepFed: federated deep learning for intrusion detection in industrial cyber-physical systems. IEEE Trans. Industr. Inf. **17**(8), 5615–5624 (2020)
11. Li, B., Xiao, G., Lu, R., Deng, R., Bao, H.: On feasibility and limitations of detecting false data injection attacks on power grid state estimation using D-FACTS devices. IEEE Trans. Industr. Inf. **16**(2), 854–864 (2020). https://doi.org/10.1109/TII.2019.2922215
12. Liang, G., Weller, S.R., Zhao, J., Luo, F., Dong, Z.Y.: The 2015 Ukraine blackout: implications for false data injection attacks. IEEE Trans. Power Syst. **32**(4), 3317–3318 (2017). https://doi.org/10.1109/TPWRS.2016.2631891

13. Liu, B., Wu, H.: Optimal planning and operation of hidden moving target defense for maximal detection effectiveness. IEEE Trans. Smart Grid (2021). https://doi.org/10.1109/TSG.2021.3076824

14. Liu, Y., Ning, P., Reiter, M.K.: False data injection attacks against state estimation in electric power grids. ACM Trans. Inf. Syst. Secur. **14**(1), 1–33 (2011). https://doi.org/10.1145/1952982.1952995

15. Mohammadpourfard, M., Sami, A., Seifi, A.R.: A statistical unsupervised method against false data injection attacks: a visualization-based approach. Expert Syst. Appl. **84**, 242–261 (2017). https://doi.org/10.1016/j.eswa.2017.05.013

16. Morrow, K.L., Heine, E., Rogers, K.M., Bobba, R.B., Overbye, T.J.: Topology perturbation for detecting malicious data injection. In: Proceedings of the 2012 45th Hawaii International Conference on System Sciences, HICSS 2012, pp. 2104–2113. IEEE Computer Society (2012). https://doi.org/10.1109/HICSS.2012.594

17. Mukherjee, D., Chakraborty, S., Ghosh, S.: Deep learning-based multilabel classification for locational detection of false data injection attack in smart grids. Electr. Eng., 1–24 (2021). https://doi.org/10.1007/s00202-021-01278-6

18. Rahman, M.A., Al-Shaer, E., Bobba, R.B.: Moving target defense for hardening the security of the power system state estimation. In: Proceedings of the First ACM Workshop on Moving Target Defense, pp. 59–68 (2014)

19. Salehghaffari, H., Khorrami, F.: Resilient power grid state estimation under false data injection attacks. In: 2018 IEEE Power Energy Society Innovative Smart Grid Technologies Conference (ISGT), pp. 1–5 (2018). https://doi.org/10.1109/ISGT.2018.8403396

20. Shi, W., Wang, Y., Jin, Q., Ma, J.: PDL: an efficient prediction-based false data injection attack detection and location in smart grid. In: 2018 IEEE 42nd Annual Computer Software and Applications Conference (COMPSAC), vol. 2, pp. 676–681 (2018). https://doi.org/10.1109/COMPSAC.2018.10317

21. Tian, J., Tan, R., Guan, X., Liu, T.: Hidden moving target defense in smart grids. In: Proceedings of the 2nd Workshop on Cyber-Physical Security and Resilience in Smart Grids, CPSR-SG 2017, pp. 21–26. Association for Computing Machinery, New York (2017). https://doi.org/10.1145/3055386.3055388

22. Wang, S., Bi, S., Zhang, Y.J.A.: Locational detection of the false data injection attack in a smart grid: a multilabel classification approach. IEEE Internet Things J. **7**(9), 8218–8227 (2020). https://doi.org/10.1109/JIOT.2020.2983911

23. Zhang, Z., Deng, R., Cheng, P., Chow, M.Y.: Strategic protection against FDI attacks with moving target defense in power grids. IEEE Trans. Control Netw. Syst. (2021). https://doi.org/10.1109/TCNS.2021.3100411

Privacy-Preserving Worker Recruitment Under Variety Requirement in Spatial Crowdsourcing

Zhixiang Zhang[1], An Liu[1(✉)], Shushu Liu[2], Zhixu Li[3], and Lei Zhao[1]

[1] School of Computer Science and Technology, Soochow University, Suzhou, China
20194227024@stu.suda.edu.cn, {anliu,zhaol}@suda.edu.cn
[2] Department of Communication and Networking, Aalto University, Espoo, Finland
liu.shushu@aalto.fi
[3] School of Computer Science and Technology, Fudan University, Shanghai, China
zhixuli@fudan.edu.cn

Abstract. With the rapid growth of spatial crowdsourcing applications, more and more people are benefiting from it. The idea of spatial crowdsourcing is recruiting a set of workers to finish the spatial tasks. Existing worker recruitment mechanisms do not consider the variety requirement, which is easy to meet if the Spatial Crowdsourcing (SC) platform has full knowledge of the data of each worker. Since the SC platform is not fully trusted, workers are concerned about the privacy of their data. To prevent information leaks, workers' data needs to be specially processed before it can be sent to untrusted platforms for task assignment. The data specially processed by existing privacy-preserving processing methods cannot be used directly to complete such variety tasks with high quality. To solve this problem, we propose a new variety optimization method based on the classical local differential privacy (LDP) mechanism. It can efficiently select the sets of workers with variety of categorical attributes while providing privacy protection for workers. In addition, we also propose a two-step LDP perturbation protocol that can improve the optimization result in the case of uneven distribution of worker attributes. Extensive experiments on synthetic and real datasets show that our methods can efficiently select variety worker subset with better task quality than baseline and close to optimal selection results.

Keywords: Privacy-preserving · Local differential privacy · Spatial crowdsourcing

1 Introduction

Spatial Crowdsourcing (SC) has grown rapidly in recent years, bringing convenience to many aspects of people's lives [12]. In this paradigm, an SC platform recruits a set of workers and asks them to complete a set of tasks through some kind of incentives. To realize global optimization during worker recruitment,

© Springer Nature Switzerland AG 2021
H. Hacid et al. (Eds.): ICSOC 2021, LNCS 13121, pp. 302–316, 2021.
https://doi.org/10.1007/978-3-030-91431-8_19

workers are required to submit their own information to the SC platform. For example, workers need to send their real-time positions to the SC platform so that every task can be assigned to its nearby worker while optimizing some global objectives such as maximizing the total number of assigned tasks.

Existing mechanisms [6,18] of worker recruitment do not consider the variety requirement, i.e., the recruited workers should be different from each other in terms of some attributes. However, the variety requirement is important for many practical SC applications, as the variety of workers will affect the quality of task completion. For example, in a data sensing task where workers are asked to collect some kind of information in an urban area, the variety requirement means the recruited workers should come from different sub-areas of the urban area, making the sensed data as complete as possible. Moreover, the variety requirement implies the number of workers in different sub-areas should be as equal as possible. This is because if most recruited workers come from a same sub-area, the final sensed data will be determined by this sub-area and thus cannot reflect the feature of the whole area. Therefore, the mechanisms of worker recruitment should consider the variety requirement in order to ensure the quality of task completion.

Worker recruitment under the variety requirement is easy to meet if the SC platform has full knowledge of the data of each worker. Unfortunately, the SC platform is not fully trusted and privacy is thus a big concern of most workers. Though there has been a lot of work focusing on privacy-preserving worker recruitment [8–11,15–17], the techniques are designed largely for the protection of workers' location. The challenge in these work is to calculate the distances between workers and tasks over disguised locations. Methods based on encryption [15–17] apply homomorphic encryption schemes which allow the distance between two encrypted locations to be calculated directly without requiring access to the decrpytion key. Privacy is guaranteed at the expense of huge computation cost. On the other hand, methods based on differential privacy [9–11] achieve privacy protection via adding noise to locations, and allow the distance to be calculated efficiently while keeping the error within a preset range. However, these methods cannot be applied to the problem of worker recruitment under the variety requirement. As shown in Fig. 1, the goal of privacy-preserving worker recruitment with the variety guarantee is to select a subset of workers with maximum variety based on the disguised data of workers. As will be shown later, the variety of a set of workers involves complicated calculations that cannot be supported efficiently by homomorphic encryption. The direct use of differential privacy will reduce the utility of data significantly, which makes it hard for the SC platform to effectively determine a set of workers with maximized variety.

In this paper, we study the problem of privacy-preserving worker recruitment under the variety requirement and propose a solution based on local differential privacy (LDP) [4]. First we analyze the classical LDP data perturbation mechanism and compute the hidden distribution of the workers' perturbed data based on the LDP perturbation probabilities. To better measure variety, we choose entropy as evaluation metric. Based on the hidden distribution and evaluation

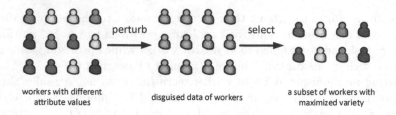

workers with different   disguised data of workers   a subset of workers with
attribute values   maximized variety

Fig. 1. Privacy-preserving worker recruitment under the variety requirement.

metric, we generalize an optimization problem with entropy as the objective function and LDP requirement as the constraints. Therefore, the optimal solution allows the selection of a subset of maximized variety workers with high probability on the LDP perturbed data. After that, in order to solve this optimization problem efficiently, we propose a gradient-based optimization method based on the convex property of entropy function. The time complexity of the method is $O(kd^2)$, where k is the number of selected workers and d is the size of the domain of the attribute values the workers have. Lastly, since the optimization method does not work well on uneven distributions, we propose a novel two-step LDP perturbation protocol to filter the workers with high proportion attributes by an additional round of perturbation. By doing this, the variety requirement can still be meet even under the influence of uneven distributions. We prove that the two-step perturbation protocol satisfies the LDP requirements. Our contribution is summarized as follows:

- To our best knowledge, we are the first to consider the variety requirement in privacy-preserving worker recruitment. We generalize the variety worker recruitment problem to an optimization problem under LDP constraints and propose an efficient method to solve this optimization problem.
- We propose a novel two-step perturbation protocol. Through a round of filtering, this protocol can improve the variety maximization effect in the case of uneven distribution of workers. We prove that the protocol satisfies the LDP requirements.
- We have conducted extensive experiments on synthetic and real datasets. The experimental results show that our method can effectively solve the LDP variety problem and is significantly better than baseline and close to the optimal solution.

In the rest of this paper, we review related work in Sect. 2. The problem is defined in Sect. 3 and the solution is presented in Sect. 4. Section 5 shows the experimental results. The paper is summarized in Sect. 6.

2 Related Work

We investigated the existing privacy protection mechanisms for spatial crowd-sourcing, which fall into two main categories, LDP based methods and Encryption based methods.

LDP Based Methods. Local differential privacy (LDP) is an extension of differential privacy (DP) [5], which allows local data privacy protection. Therefore, it is widely used for privacy protection in spatial crowdsourcing. To improve the utility, a new privacy protection concept Geo-Indistinguishability (GI) [2] is proposed on top of LDP. [3] proposed a perturbation method satisfying GI. It applied linear optimization to determine the perturbation probability between different locations, which can effectively improve the utility of geolocation data. [10] proposed an efficient private task planning solution framework via using GI to provide privacy protection. [11] applied GI to the hierarchically well-separated tree index to protect worker location privacy. It should be noted that the privacy protection of GI is not equivalent to that of LDP because the requirements of LDP are more stringent, but the proposed GI linear optimization method is inspiring for our LDP approach.

Encryption Based Methods. These methods use special encryption to process worker data and perform specific operations on the data. In [15], the authors used homomorphic encryption to protect workers' bids during the proposed secure reverse auction process. And [16] uses attribute-based encryption to build secure channels and ensure that task locations was delivered securely and accurately by untrusted servers. [17] generalized workers' private location data to travel cost and protected it in a k-anonymity manner via bitwise XOR homomorphic cipher system. Encryption methods for worker data cannot satisfy the computation of variety requirements, because computing the variety of a subset of workers is more complex.

3 Problem Definition

Workers and Attributes. We assume that there is a set $W = \{w_1, w_2, \ldots, w_n\}$ of n workers. Each worker w_i has an attribute value v_i. The attribute value owned by the worker is in the domain d. We use $[d]$ to denote the set $\{1, 2, 3, \ldots, d\}$, and we assume without loss of generality that the input domain is $[d]$. We use the set $T = \{t_1, t_2, t_3, \ldots, t_d\}$ to represent the distribution of worker attributes. For a given attribute value $j \in [d]$, t_j denotes the number of workers who have attribute j. Clearly we have $t_j \in [0, n]$ and $\sum_j^{[d]} t_j = n$.

Variety of Worker Attributes. We use entropy as the variety evaluation metric for the distribution of worker attributes. For a worker set $W = \{w_1, w_2, \ldots, w_n\}$ of n workers whose attribute distribution is $T = \{t_1, t_2, t_3, \ldots, t_d\}$, its variety is denoted as

$$E(W) = -\sum_i^{[d]} \frac{t_i}{n} \log \frac{t_i}{n}. \tag{1}$$

The higher the value of $E(W)$, the greater the variety of W.

Differential Privacy. An algorithm A with input domain D satisfies ϵ-local differential privacy (ϵ-LDP), where $\epsilon \geq 0$, if and only if for any input $v_1, v_2 \in D$, we have

$$\forall z \in Range(A) : \Pr[A(v_1) = z] \leq e^{\epsilon} \Pr[A(v_2) = z],$$

where $Range(A)$ denotes the set of all possible outputs of the algorithm A. $\epsilon \geq 0$ is known as the privacy budget, and smaller ϵ means a higher degree of privacy protection, but also a lower utility of data. If an algorithm A_i satisfies ϵ_i-LDP for $i = 1, 2, \cdots, m$, then their sequential combination $(A_1, A_2, \cdots, A_m)$ satisfies $(\sum_i^m \epsilon_i)$-LDP.

Variety Worker Recruitment. Given an algorithm A satisfying ϵ-LDP with input domain $[d]$ and output domain $[m]$. There is a worker set W of n workers whose attributes are distributed as $T = \{t_1, t_2, \ldots, t_d\}$. The attribute of worker w_i is $v_i \in [d]$. v_i is perturbed by algorithm A and the output is $o_i \in [m]$. Counting the output results of all workers yields the perturbation output distribution $C = \{c_1, c_2, \ldots, c_m\}$, where c_j denotes the number of workers whose perturbation output is $j \in [m]$.

Now the goal is to determine a solution that selects a worker subset W_k of size k from W, such that the selected workers are not biased towards a particular attribute, which means maximizing the variety $E(W_k)$ of the attribute distribution of these k selected workers. We denote this solution by $X = \{x_1, x_2, \ldots, x_m\}$, where x_j denotes the number of selected workers whose perturbation output is j, we have $x_j \in [0, c_j]$ and $\sum_j^{[m]} x_j = k$.

There are two main challenges to this problem:

1. Due to the strong privacy protection of the LDP, the crowdsourcing platform has very little knowledge about the true attribute of a particular worker. The platform cannot infer the true attributes of workers with high confidence based on the output after LDP perturbation, and thus it is also difficult to determine the true worker attribute distribution of the selected subset of workers based on the distribution of the perturbed output.
2. The true distribution of worker attributes has a large impact on the variety of the selected subset. If the true distribution of workers' attributes is uniform, i.e., the number of workers with various attributes is equal, then a randomly selected subset of workers is sufficient to satisfy the variety requirement. However, when the distribution of worker attributes is uneven, in order to maximize the variety of the selected worker subset, we should select more workers with less attribute distribution and select fewer workers with more attribute distribution. And this is difficult on the data perturbed by LDP.

4 Our Method

In this section, we first present our algorithm for maximizing the variety of selected subsets of workers in Sect. 4.1, and then we present the LDP mechanism for adding invalid perturbations and the two-step LDP perturbation mechanism that combines this method in Sect. 4.2.

4.1   Maximize Hidden Distribution Variety

We analyze the classical LDP perturbation methods for categorical attributes and the corresponding frequency estimation methods, and then propose a solution for the variety problem. For illustration, Generalized Random Response (GRR) [7] is used as an example, and other LDP methods are also applicable.

For the GRR method, a worker w_i with attribute $v_i \in [d]$ sends the true value v_i with probability p and sends a randomly selected $v' \in [d] - \{v_i\}$ with probability $1 - p$. The input domain is $[d]$, and the output domain is also $[d]$. The perturbation probability function is formally defined as

$$\Pr[GRR(i) = j] = \begin{cases} p = \frac{e^\epsilon}{e^\epsilon + d - 1}, & \text{if } i = j \\ q = \frac{1}{e^\epsilon + d - 1}, & \text{if } i \neq j \end{cases} \tag{2}$$

This satisfies ϵ-LDP since $\frac{p}{q} = e^\epsilon$. For subsequent illustration, we use a matrix P to represent the perturbation probabilities, where $p_{ij} = \Pr[GRR(i) = j]$, indicating the probability of perturbing attribute i to attribute j. Suppose the number of workers is n, and the true attribute distribution of workers is $T = \{t_1, t_2, \ldots, t_d\}$, t_i represents the number of workers whose true attribute is $i \in [d]$. The platform collects the perturbed attributes of the workers and obtains perturbation output distribution $C = \{c_1, c_2, \ldots, c_d\}$, where c_j denotes the number of workers whose perturbation output is $j \in [d]$. The platform can estimate the frequency, i.e., the true attribute distribution of workers. We use $T' = \{t'_1, t'_2, \ldots, t'_d\}$ to denote the estimation of the true distribution, where $t'_i = (c_i - nq)/(p - q)$. The existing work [13] proves that t'_i is the unbiased estimation of t_i. Although it is not possible to obtain T directly, we can use T' instead of T in the subsequent calculation. Also, to avoid negative values in T' and to reduce the variance of the estimation, we make some adjustments to T' using the estimation method proposed in [14].

Next we analyze the hidden distribution in the perturbation output of the true attribute of workers. We define a hidden distribution matrix M, where

$$M = \begin{bmatrix} m_{11} & \cdots & m_{1d} \\ \vdots & \ddots & \vdots \\ m_{d1} & \cdots & m_{dd} \end{bmatrix} = \begin{bmatrix} t'_1 & & \\ & \ddots & \\ & & t'_d \end{bmatrix} \begin{bmatrix} p_{11} & \cdots & p_{1d} \\ \vdots & \ddots & \vdots \\ p_{d1} & \cdots & p_{dd} \end{bmatrix} \tag{3}$$

m_{ij} denotes the number of workers with true attribute i and perturbation output j, since $m_{ij} = t'_i p_{ij}$. We call M the hidden distribution matrix because the ith column in M represents the hidden true attribute distribution of workers whose perturbation output is i. Taking $T = \{20, 40, 60\}$ as an example, we assume that the privacy budget of GRR is $\ln 2$, which means that $p_{ij} = \frac{1}{2}$, if $i = j$, otherwise $p_{ij} = \frac{1}{4}$. We have

$$\begin{bmatrix} 20 & & \\ & 40 & \\ & & 60 \end{bmatrix} \begin{bmatrix} \frac{1}{2} & \frac{1}{4} & \frac{1}{4} \\ \frac{1}{4} & \frac{1}{2} & \frac{1}{4} \\ \frac{1}{4} & \frac{1}{4} & \frac{1}{2} \end{bmatrix} = \begin{bmatrix} 10 & 5 & 5 \\ 10 & 20 & 10 \\ 15 & 15 & 30 \end{bmatrix}$$

For the first column $\{10, 10, 15\}$, it represents that there are 10 workers with real attribute value 1 and perturbation output value 1, 10 workers with real attribute value 2 and perturbation output value 1, and 15 workers with real attribute value 3 and perturbation output value 1. For these $10 + 10 + 15 = 35$ workers with perturbation output value of 1, the hidden true attribute distribution is $\{10, 10, 15\}$.

With the hidden distributions corresponding to different perturbation outputs, we can calculate the hidden true attribute distribution for a worker subset W_k. Suppose the platform needs to select k workers, where $X = \{x_1, x_2, \ldots, x_d\}$ workers are selected for each of the different perturbation outputs. We calculate the hidden true attribute distribution H of these k selected workers by the following

$$
H = \begin{bmatrix} h_1 \\ \vdots \\ h_d \end{bmatrix} = \begin{bmatrix} \frac{m_{11}}{sum(1)} & \cdots & \frac{m_{1d}}{sum(d)} \\ \vdots & \ddots & \vdots \\ \frac{m_{d1}}{sum(1)} & \cdots & \frac{m_{dd}}{sum(d)} \end{bmatrix} \begin{bmatrix} x_1 \\ \vdots \\ x_d \end{bmatrix} \tag{4}
$$

where $sum(i) = \sum_j^{[d]} m_{ji}$. From the previous, the hidden true distribution of workers with perturbation output i is $\{m_{1i}, m_{2i}, \ldots, m_{di}\}$. Obviously, if x_i workers are randomly selected from those with perturbation output i, their hidden true attribute distribution is $\{\frac{m_{1i}}{sum(i)} x_i, \frac{m_{2i}}{sum(i)} x_i, \cdots, \frac{m_{di}}{sum(i)} x_i\}$. The hidden true attribute distributions of the k selected workers H are obtained by summing up the hidden true attribute distributions of the workers selected with different perturbation outputs, where h_i denotes the number of workers with hidden true attribute i in the selected subset of workers.

The goal of the variety task is to maximize the true attribute distribution of the selected worker subset W_k, i.e., to maximize the hidden true attribute distribution H. We therefore summarize it as an optimization problem as follows

$$
\max \quad E(W_k) = -\sum_i^{[d]} \frac{h_i}{k} \log \frac{h_i}{k}
$$

$$
s.t. \quad \begin{cases} \sum_i^{[d]} x_i = k \\ 0 \le x_i \le c_i, \, i \in [d] \end{cases}
$$

Since the solution $X = \{x_1, x_2, \ldots, x_d\}$ are integers and the objective function is convex, we design an iterative algorithm based on the gradient of the objective function. According to Eq. 4, we have

$$
E(W_k) = -\sum_i^{[d]} \frac{h_i}{k} \log \frac{h_i}{k} = -\sum_i^{[d]} \frac{\sum_j^{[d]} \frac{m_{ij}}{sum(j)} x_j}{k} \log \frac{\sum_j^{[d]} \frac{m_{ij}}{sum(j)} x_j}{k} \tag{5}
$$

We denote the gradient of the objective function as $G = \{g_1, g_2, \cdots, g_d\}$, where $g_i = \frac{\partial E(W_k)}{\partial x_i}$, and then calculate it by the following

$$
g_i = \frac{\partial E(W_k)}{\partial x_i} = -\sum_j^{[d]} \frac{m_{ij}}{sum(j)k} \log \frac{h_i}{k} + \frac{m_{ij}}{sum(j)k} \tag{6}
$$

Optimization methods using gradients have a wide range of applications, such as stochastic gradient descent (SGD) for training neural networks. Based on a similar idea, we can keep adjusting the integer solution X according to the gradient until it converges to the optimal solution, since the objective function $E(W_k)$ is a convex entropy function. The specific algorithm is shown in Algorithm 1. First, line 1 takes a random feasible integer solution for X. Then lines 2–9 calculate the gradient G and find the smallest one g_l in it, $l \in [d]$, let $x_l = x_l - 1$, then calculate the gradient again, find the largest one g_h, $h \in [d]$, let $x_h = x_h + 1$. Keep repeating lines 2–9 until X converges. At this point X is the worker selection scheme that maximizes the variety of the hidden true attribute distribution of the selected workers. Each iteration increases the variety of the hidden distribution of the result and the value of X changes by only 1 in each iteration, so that at most k iterations are needed to obtain the optimal solution, since $\sum_i^{[d]} x_i = k$. The time complexity of computing the gradient G is $O(d^2)$. Therefore, the total time complexity of Algorithm 1 is $O(kd^2)$.

Algorithm 1. Maximize hidden distribution variety

Input: The hidden distribution matrix M, perturbation output distribution C
Output: The solution X
1: Select a random integer solution $X = \{x_1, x_2, \ldots, x_d\}$
2: **while** X does not converge **do**
3:     Calculate the gradient $G = \{g_1, g_2, \cdots, g_d\}$ according to equation 6
4:     find the smallest one g_l in G
5:     $x_l = x_l - 1$
6:     Calculate the gradient G
7:     find the largest one g_h in G
8:     $x_h = x_h + 1$
9: **end while**
10: **return** X

4.2   Two-Step LDP Perturbation Protocol

We analyze the classical LDP perturbation mechanism and design a variety maximization scheme based on its hidden distribution. Through some experiments we find that the largest factor affecting the variety of the selected workers' true attribute distribution is the original true attribute distribution of all workers. We still take the true attribute distribution $T = \{20, 40, 60\}$ mentioned in the previous section as an example, the hidden distribution of different perturbation output values is $\{10, 10, 15\}$, $\{5, 20, 15\}$ and $\{5, 10, 30\}$. If a worker is randomly selected from workers with different perturbation outputs, the probability that this worker has true attribute value 3 is $\frac{15}{10+10+15} = 0.43$, $\frac{15}{5+20+15} = 0.5$ and $\frac{30}{5+10+30} = 0.67$, respectively. This means that the minimum percentage of workers with true attribute value 3 among the selected workers is 0.43, regardless of the optimal selection. One of the main reasons for this is the high proportion of workers with attribute value 3, which is $\frac{60}{20+40+60} = 0.5$, so the proportion of workers with real attribute value 3 in different hidden distribution is inevitably high as well. This high proportion is detrimental to achieve attribute variety, since our goal is to preserve an equal selection of different attributes even they are unevenly distributed.

To address this issue, i.e., to reduce the impact of high proportional attributes in the original attribute distribution on the variety of attributes in the hidden distribution, we propose to add an invalid perturbation value to the set of LDP perturbation outputs. In addition to the original set of perturbed outputs $[d]$, there is a certain probability that the worker's true attribute is perturbed to an invalid value v_{in}, and workers whose output is v_{in} will not be used as candidate workers. Attribute with high proportion have a high probability to be perturbed into the invalid value v_{in}, so that fewer workers with common attribute will enter the candidate worker set, which is beneficial for variety optimization. Conversely, the probability that an attribute with low proportion is perturbed to the invalid value v_{in} should be low, so that more workers with rare attribute will enter the candidate worker set. We have designed a new LDP perturbation mechanism ϕ based on this idea.

We predetermine an invalid value perturbation probability p_{in}, which is the probability that the attribute with the highest proportion is perturbed to an invalid value. The attribute with the lowest proportion should have a smaller probability of being perturbed to the invalid value. The minimum probability is $\frac{p_{in}}{e^\epsilon}$ as limited by the LDP condition. We make the probability of different attributes being perturbed to the invalid value proportional to their proportion, which can be calculated by the following

$$\Pr[\phi(i) = v_{in}] = \frac{p_{in}}{e^\epsilon} + \frac{t_i - t_{min}}{t_{max} - t_{min}}(p_{in} - \frac{p_{in}}{e^\epsilon}) \tag{7}$$

where t_{max} denotes the maximum value of the number of workers with different attributes and t_{min} denotes the minimum value.

Before determining the probability of perturbation for other values, we propose a concept of proportional perturbation error, which is defined as

$$PE(P,T) = \sum_{i,j\in[d]} \frac{t_i}{n} p_{ij}|t_i - t_j|\alpha_i \tag{8}$$

where α_i is the weight related to the number of workers t_i. For the convenience of calculation, we take $\alpha_i = \frac{1}{t_i}$ in the later experiments. The error arises when attribute i is perturbed to j, $j \neq i$. Since we care about the effect of attribute proportion, we use the absolute value $|t_i - t_j|$ as a measure of the difference between attribute i and attribute j.

We can then determine the perturbation probabilities through a linear programming problem. We have

$$\min \sum_{i,j \in [d]} \frac{t_i}{n} p_{ij} |t_i - t_j| \alpha_i$$

$$s.t. \begin{cases} p_{iz} \leq e^{\epsilon} p_{jz}, & i,j,z \in [d] \\ \sum_{j}^{[d]} p_{ij} + \Pr[\phi(i) = v_{in}] = 1, & i \in [d] \\ p_{ij} \geq 0, & i,j \in [d] \end{cases}$$

It is clear that the perturbation mechanism ϕ generated by the above linear programming satisfies the e^{ϵ}-LDP. This linear programming problem can be solved efficiently using existing tools such as matlab.

For the example distribution $T = \{20, 40, 60\}$, we assume $p_{in} = 0.6$ and then obtain a different perturbation matrix containing an invalid perturbation value by linear programming. And we calculate the hidden distribution matrix by

$$\begin{bmatrix} 20 & & \\ & 40 & \\ & & 60 \end{bmatrix} \begin{bmatrix} 0.26 & 0.40 & 0.04 & 0.30 \\ 0.13 & 0.38 & 0.04 & 0.45 \\ 0.13 & 0.20 & 0.07 & 0.60 \end{bmatrix} = \begin{bmatrix} 5.2 & 8 & 0.8 & 6 \\ 5.2 & 15.2 & 1.6 & 18 \\ 7.8 & 12 & 4.2 & 36 \end{bmatrix}$$

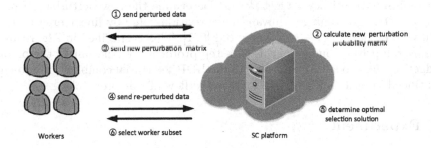

Fig. 2. Workflow of our solution.

This perturbation matrix still satisfies $\ln 2$-LDP because the ratio of any two probability values in any column is at most 2. In the first three columns, p_{ij} still indicates the probability of perturbing attribute i to attribute j. The last column are the probability of perturbing attribute i to the invalid value v_{in}, we denote this as $p_{id+1} = \Pr[\phi(i) = v_{in}]$. Similar to the previous hidden distribution matrix, the first three columns are the hidden distributions of the different perturbation outputs. The last column $\{6, 18, 36\}$ is the numbers of invalid workers who do not participate in the optimization, for example, there are 60 workers with true attribute value 3, and the probability that attribute 3 is perturbed to the invalid value is 0.6. Therefore $60 \times 0.6 = 36$ of these workers will not participate in the subsequent variety optimization. This hidden distribution is better in terms of variety than the previous unprocessed hidden distribution. Because the minimum proportion of workers with true attribute value 3 in the hidden distribution is now $\frac{12}{8+15.2+12} = 0.34 < 0.43$. This example therefore illustrates how adding an invalid perturbation value can effectively reduce the impact of high proportional attributes.

Algorithm 2. Two-step LDP perturb protocol

1: Workers send perturbed attributes with privacy budget βe.
2: The SC platform estimates the true distribution of workers and calculates the perturbation probability containing the invalid value with privacy budget $(1 - \beta)e$ by the linear programming approach.
3: The SC platform sends the new perturbation probability matrix to all workers.
4: Workers re-perturb their attributes and send the results.
5: The SC platform determines the optimal selection solution using Algorithm 1 on valid worker data.
6: The SC platform selects the worker subset.

Before linear optimization we need to know the true attribute distribution T of the workers, which can be obtained by frequency estimation of the LDP mechanism. We therefore propose a two-step LDP protocol: (1) perturbing the worker attributes and estimating their true distributions using the classical LDP mechanism with privacy budget βe. (2) Determine the new perturbation probability matrix containing an invalid perturbation value by linear programming with privacy budget $(1 - \beta)e$, where $\beta \in [0, 1]$. This is specified in Algorithm 2. The overall privacy budget of this two-step protocol is e (the sum of the privacy budgets of the two steps) according to the LDP sequential combination property mentioned in Sect. 3. Figure 2 illustrates the flow of this protocol.

5 Experiment

5.1 Experimental Setup

Datasets. We conducted experiments on two synthetic datasets EDS, NDS and one real dataset TDS. Synthetic dataset EDS is exponentially distributed and NDS is normally distributed, where the number of workers is 5000 and the number of attribute values is [5, 15]. The real dataset TDS is the census data extracted from the Integrated Public Use Microdata Series [1], which contains data from the 2010 China census for up to 15 randomly selected attributes. For the privacy budget ϵ, it is known from relevant research that a privacy budget less than 1 can provide reliable privacy protection, so the privacy budget of our experiment is taken as $\{0.2, 0.4, 0.6, 0.8, 1.0\}$.

Baselines. Since no previous work has studied the variety problem based on LDP perturbation, we then chose the random selection method and the optimal selection method without considering privacy as the comparison methods.

- RS: The random selection method selects a completely random subset of workers from the perturbed candidate workers. The random method can achieve good results when the true distribution of workers is even.
- OS: The optimal method for selecting workers without considering privacy. The best selection solution can be determined without considering privacy. Although the best result cannot be guaranteed under privacy protection, we still use it as a comparison method that can reflect the degree of variety.
- VM: Our proposed method for selecting the subset of workers using Algorithm 1.
- INVM: Our proposed two-step method of first adding an invalid perturbation value and then selecting the subset of workers using Algorithm 2.

For the variety evaluation metric, we choose entropy defined by Eq. 1.

5.2   Experimental Results

For the default parameters, the total number of workers $n = 5000$, the number of selected workers $k = 250$, the number of attributes $d = 10$, the differential privacy $\epsilon = 1.0$ and $\beta = 0.5$ and $p_{in} = 0.4$ in the INVM method.

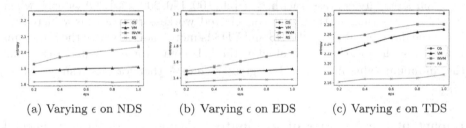

(a) Varying ϵ on NDS   (b) Varying ϵ on EDS   (c) Varying ϵ on TDS

Fig. 3. Results of varying ϵ

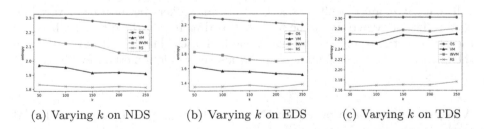

(a) Varying k on NDS   (b) Varying k on EDS   (c) Varying k on TDS

Fig. 4. Results of varying k

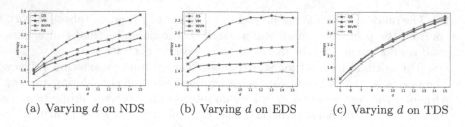

(a) Varying d on NDS   (b) Varying d on EDS   (c) Varying d on TDS

Fig. 5. Results of varying d

Impact of Privacy Budget. Figure 3 shows the experimental results on three datasets with different privacy budgets $\epsilon = \{0.2, 0.4, 0.6, 0.8, 1.0\}$. From the results, the variety of our methods VM and INVM outperforms the random selection method on all three data sets. And the INVM method outperforms the VM method, thus showing that adding invalid perturbation value does effectively improve variety. Obviously the larger the ϵ, the higher the data utility, so it can be seen that the variety increases with increasing ϵ on all data sets.

Impact of the Number of Selected Workers. Figure 4 shows the experimental results on three datasets with $k = \{50, 100, 150, 200, 250\}$. Obviously, when $min(T)$ is less than $\frac{k}{d}$, the variety of selected workers decreases as k increases. Since the data distribution of NDS and EDS is more uneven, where the minimum value is less than $\frac{k}{d}$, the results of all methods become worse as k increases, while the minimum value in TDS is still greater than $\frac{k}{d}$ therefore its results change less.

Impact of the Number of Attributes. Figure 5 shows the experimental results on three datasets with $d = [5, 15]$. The increase in d means that more distributions of attributes have to be considered when selecting workers, which will make it more difficult to select variety of workers because more variables need to be considered. It can be seen that as d increases, the difference between the other methods and the optimal value increases. The INVM method is still the closest to the optimum and outperforms the random method by about 50% or more.

Analysis of the Parameters of INVM. The main parameters in the INVM method are p_{in} and β. The values of the parameters are analyzed experimentally in Fig. 6.

p_{in} represents the probability of invalid perturbation of the attribute with the highest proportion. If p_{in} is too low then the undesirable effects of high proportion attributes cannot be eliminated, and if p_{in} is too high then most workers will become invalid workers who do not participate in the selection, which will also cause a decrease in variety. Experiments show that $p_{in} = 0.5$ works best for NDS, $p_{in} = 0.3$ works best for EDS and TDS.

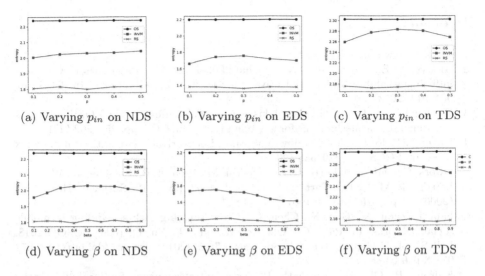

(a) Varying p_{in} on NDS   (b) Varying p_{in} on EDS   (c) Varying p_{in} on TDS

(d) Varying β on NDS   (e) Varying β on EDS   (f) Varying β on TDS

Fig. 6. Results of varying p_{in} and β

β is the parameter that regulates the INVM two-step LDP privacy budget. If β is large, the privacy budget of the first part is large and the privacy budget of the second part is small, which means that the true distribution of workers is estimated accurately in the first step while the invalid perturbation in the second step will be less accurate. Experiments show that $\beta = 0.5$ works best for NDS, $\beta = 0.3$ works best for EDS and $\beta = 0.5$ works best for TDS.

6   Conclusion

In this paper we generalize the variety worker recruitment problem to a LDP optimization problem and explore an efficient method to solve this optimization problem by maximizing the variety of worker attributes under LDP privacy protection. We further propose a novel two-step LDP protocol, which can improve the variety maximization result in the case of uneven distribution of workers by filtering workers through an additional round of LDP perturbations. Extensive experiments on synthetic and real datasets show that our methods can effectively solve the LDP variety problem and is notably better than baseline and close to the optimal solution.

Acknowledgements. This work was supported by the National Natural Science Foundation of China (Grant Nos. 61572336, 61632016, 62072323), the Natural Science Foundation of Jiangsu Province (Grant Nos. BK20211307, BK20191420), the Major Program of the Natural Science Foundation of Jiangsu Higher Education Institutions of China (Grant Nos. 18KJA520010, 19KJA610002), and the Collaborative Innovation Center of Novel Software Technology and Industrialization.

References

1. https://www.ipums.org
2. Andrés, M.E., Bordenabe, N.E., Chatzikokolakis, K., Palamidessi, C.: Geo-indistinguishability: differential privacy for location-based systems. In: CCS, pp. 901–914 (2013)
3. Bordenabe, N.E., Chatzikokolakis, K., Palamidessi, C.: Optimal geo-indistinguishable mechanisms for location privacy. In: CCS, pp. 251–262 (2014)
4. Duchi, J.C., Jordan, M.I., Wainwright, M.J.: Local privacy and statistical minimax rates. In: FOCS, pp. 429–438 (2013)
5. Dwork, C.: Differential privacy. In: Bugliesi, M., Preneel, B., Sassone, V., Wegener, I. (eds.) ICALP 2006, Part II. LNCS, vol. 4052, pp. 1–12. Springer, Heidelberg (2006). https://doi.org/10.1007/11787006_1
6. Fan, J., Zhou, X., Gao, X., Chen, G.: Crowdsourcing task scheduling in mobile social networks. In: Pahl, C., Vukovic, M., Yin, J., Yu, Q. (eds.) ICSOC 2018. LNCS, vol. 11236, pp. 317–331. Springer, Cham (2018). https://doi.org/10.1007/978-3-030-03596-9_22
7. Kairouz, P., Oh, S., Viswanath, P.: Extremal mechanisms for local differential privacy. J. Mach. Learn. Res. 17, 17:1-17:51 (2016)
8. Liu, A., et al.: Privacy-preserving task assignment in spatial crowdsourcing. J. Comput. Sci. Technol. 32(5), 905–918 (2017)
9. Liu, A., et al.: Differential private collaborative web services QoS prediction. World Wide Web 22(6), 2697–2720 (2019)
10. Tao, Q., Tong, Y., Li, S., Zeng, Y., Zhou, Z., Xu, K.: A differentially private task planning framework for spatial crowdsourcing. In: MDM, pp. 9–18 (2021)
11. Tao, Q., Tong, Y., Zhou, Z., Shi, Y., Chen, L., Xu, K.: Differentially private online task assignment in spatial crowdsourcing: a tree-based approach. In: ICDE, pp. 517–528 (2020)
12. Tong, Y., Zhou, Z., Zeng, Y., Chen, L., Shahabi, C.: Spatial crowdsourcing: a survey. VLDB J. 29(1), 217–250 (2020)
13. Wang, T., Blocki, J., Li, N., Jha, S.: Locally differentially private protocols for frequency estimation. In: USENIX, pp. 729–745 (2017)
14. Wang, T., Lopuhaä-Zwakenberg, M., Li, Z., Skoric, B., Li, N.: Locally differentially private frequency estimation with consistency. In: NDSS (2020)
15. Xiao, M., et al.: SRA: secure reverse auction for task assignment in spatial crowd-sourcing. IEEE Trans. Knowl. Data Eng. 32(4), 782–796 (2020)
16. Yuan, D., Li, Q., Li, G., Wang, Q., Ren, K.: Priradar: a privacy-preserving frame-work for spatial crowdsourcing. IEEE Trans. Inf. Forensics Secur. 15, 299–314 (2020)
17. Zhai, D., et al.: Towards secure and truthful task assignment in spatial crowdsourc-ing. World Wide Web 22(5), 2017–2040 (2019)
18. Zhao, Y., Zheng, K., Cui, Y., Su, H., Zhu, F., Zhou, X.: Predictive task assignment in spatial crowdsourcing: a data-driven approach. In: ICDE, pp. 13–24 (2020)

T2L2: A Tiny Three Linear Layers Model for Service Mashup Creation

Minyi Liu, Yeqi Zhu, Hanchuan Xu, Zhiying Tu, and Zhongjie Wang$^{(\boxtimes)}$

Faculty of Computing, Harbin Institute of Technology, Harbin, China
1173710229@stu.hit.edu.cn, {liumy,xhc,tzy_hit,rainy}@hit.edu.cn

Abstract. Mashup creation is a classic problem in service computing and can be solved using service recommendation approaches. There are many service recommendation studies and have achieved remarkable results. However, there is a growing tendency for these studies to use multiplex data and more complicated models to improve the performance of recommendations, especially after the emergence of deep learning. This trend has led to a heavy reliance on computational resources and an increased cost of data acquisition, which limits the practical use of these methods, but the performance gains are still very limited. In this paper, we improve recommendation performance by rethinking the characteristics of the data in the mashup creation scenario, i.e. representation heterogeneity between services and mashup, rather than the use of multiplex data and more complicated models. To achieve this, we propose a Tiny Three Linear Layers (T2L2) model. T2L2 is a tiny model with three linear layers requiring only requires functional descriptions of services and mashups as input. The first two linear layers are used to align the representation space of services and mashups. The last linear layer is used to calculate the matching scores of services and mashups. Extensive experiments conducted on a real-world dataset from ProgrammableWeb show that T2L2 outperforms existing state-of-the-art methods in commonly-used evaluation metrics with a significant reduction in model complexity and required data.

Keywords: Mashup creation · Service recommendation · Model complexity

1 Introduction

With the rapid development of new technologies such as cloud, edge, and mobile computing, the number and diversity of available services are dramatically exploding, and services have become increasingly important to people's daily work and life. The increasing number and diversity of services bring significant challenges to effective service management and reuse. Consequently, selecting suitable services for creating new mashups has become a common but still challenging issue.

© Springer Nature Switzerland AG 2021
H. Hacid et al. (Eds.): ICSOC 2021, LNCS 13121, pp. 317–331, 2021.
https://doi.org/10.1007/978-3-030-91431-8_20

Keywords [8] and TF-IDF [27] are the first generation approaches used to match services to satisfy mashup creation. However, these approaches have poor performance and are difficult to use in the practical scenarios. Researchers have started to improve the performance of service recommendations for mashup creation in different directions. Their improvement efforts can be divided into two categories:

(1) **Multiplex Data**: This kind of effort improves the approach's performance by introducing more types and larger amounts of data. For example, Karthikeyan et al. [11] use domain ontologies to extend keywords-based approaches to match high-level concepts between services and mashups. [3,5,30] introduce a wider variety of additional information, including the invocation history between services and mashups, the quality of the services (QoS), the tags of the services and mashups, users' feedback, etc. **While the use of more data can indeed lead to improvements in recommendation performance, the limitations of these approaches are clear: obtaining additional complementary data in the real world is not an easy task.** For example, there is a lack of suitable domain ontologies, and the construction of ontologies requires a huge manual annotation cost, and invocation relations are not accessible (e.g., mobile application).

(2) **More complicated models:** This kind of effort improves the approach's performance by introducing complicated models to extract better feature representation of services and mashups. For example, [12,31] introduce topic models to obtain semantic features of services and mashups. With the development of deep learning, many studies [4,9,14] are using deep neural networks (DNNs) to learn better feature representations or to fine-tune pre-trained models [6,7] trained on a large scale of external data. Complicated models increase performance but also bring two unavoidable problems: **1) Complicated models that simply combine different information with more modules cause a difficulty to explain the exact role of the different modules in the model. 2) Complicated models lead to a dramatic increase in the number of parameters and thus in demand for computational resources, limiting real-world application scenarios (e.g., edge scenarios).** For example, some models have billions of parameters for fine-tuning on pre-trained models.

In this paper, we improve recommendation performance by rethinking the characteristics of the data in the mashup creation scenario, rather than use multiplex data and more complicated models. To achieve this, we propose a tiny three linear layers based model called T2L2, which is simple and easy to interpret model and aims to obtain better performance with as little data as possible. T2L2 only requires functional descriptions of services and mashups as input, and **the main idea of T2L2 is to get performance improvements by aligning the representation spaces between mashups and services.** The difference in representation space is the result of services and mashups aim at different user groups, and their descriptions contain many domain vocabularies. Mashups are aimed at non-expert users, and their descriptions will focus more on describing their functions using business-oriented language. Services are aimed at developers so their descriptions focus on their performance and input/output format in a technical-oriented language style. For example, *Tweeplers*[1] is a mashup whose description is *"tweeplers displays currently trending users on Twitter. With this mashup, you can discover latest news as well as you will get idea about whom to follow on twitter..."*. While its component service *Twitter*[2] has a more technical-sound description *"The Twitter micro-blogging service includes two RESTful APIs. The Twitter REST API methods allow developers to access core Twitter data ... The API presently supports the following data formats: XML, JSON, and the RSS and Atom syndication formats, with some methods only accepting a subset of these formats"*.

As shown in Fig. 1, T2L2 addresses the differences in the representation space of services and mashups through two linear layers. The first linear layer, called the transformation function, is used to migrate the representation of the mashups to the aligned representation space. While the second linear layer is used to generate message for the propagation function, which can migrate the representation of the services to the aligned representation space. By learning these two functions, the services and mashups can be placed in the same representation space, resulting in a better performance.

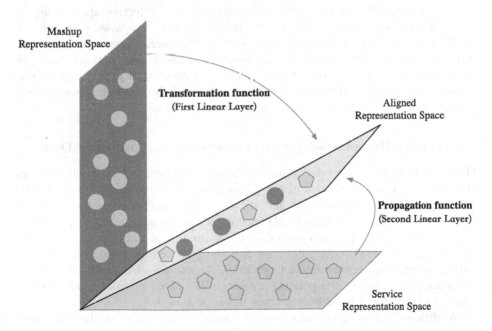

Fig. 1. Illustration of representation space aligning

---

[1] https://www.programmableweb.com/mashup/tweeplers.
[2] https://www.programmableweb.com/api/twitter.

The main contributions of this paper are summarized as follows:

1. We propose a method to eliminate representation heterogeneity between services and mashups by aligning them to the same representation space.
2. We propose a deep learning model called T2L2, which consists of three simple linear layers and only requires the description of services and mashups as input.
3. We conduct extensive experiments on the real-world dataset ProgrammableWeb, which shows that T2L2 significantly outperforms several state-of-the-art approaches.

The remainder of this paper is organized as follows: In Sect. 2, we introduce the related work. In Sect. 3, we describe relevant details of the T2L2 model. In Sect. 4, we give the details of the experiment settings. In Sect. 5, we present the experiment results. In the final section, we present the conclusion.

2   Related Work

The use of service recommendation techniques to create new mashups that satisfy the requirements of users has become a research hotspot. Many academic and industrial organizations have proposed a great deal of effective approaches on service recommendation. At first the recommendations were based on keywords [8,27] from the service categories and names. However, these approaches are suffering from a poor performance because of the insufficient understanding of the semantics. To address this issue, researchers have started to take more kinds of data into account. Based on the complexity and the data they used, their improvement efforts can be mainly categorized as follows:

2.1   Service Recommendation Approaches Using Multiplex Data

Multiplex data such as service descriptions, user preferences, and quality of service (QoS) are required to address the semantics shortness problem. Works [1,11,20] annotate requirements and services with domain ontologies and use these ontologies to match high-level concepts or calculate their semantic similarities. However, such approaches are difficult to use in real-world scenarios due to the lack of suitable domain ontologies and the huge cost of manual annotation during the ontology construction. Chen et al. [4] propose a framework for service recommendation whose components are extendable, for example, its embedding layer can be adapted for different kinds of input data.

Additionally, historical usages are also helpful with following the real-world constraints. To make full use of the historical usage data, some works apply graph techniques to deal with the problem. For example, works [16,23] design recommendation algorithms based on the feature learned on a knowledge graph. Graph-based approaches usually work in conjunction with collaborative filtering (CF). For example, Chen et al. [5,30] propose a neighborhood integrated matrix factorization approach to predict the QoS of candidate services. Chang et al. [3]

design a graph-based matrix factorization approach to predict QoS, and then use the QoS to select the services. Besides, graph is also applied to find similar users or services. For example, Maardji et al. [15] propose a frequent pair mining method for mashup development. Qi et al. [18] adopt a hybrid random walk to compute the similarities between users or services, and a CF model is designed for service recommendation. [13,28] build a heterogeneous information network using various information of services and mashups to measure the similarity between mashups, and then use the user-based CF to rank candidate services.

It is worthy of recognition that the performance have been improved after more data were introduced, but it is not satisfying and have the space to be improved; for example, Chen et al.'s approach [4] that can adopt multiple type of data for input, whose $F1@5$ does not exceed 20% on the ProgrammableWeb dataset.

2.2 Service Recommendation Approaches with Complicated Structure

Besides introducing more data, constructing a more complicated model to extract better feature representation of services and mashups is also a common method. For example, [12] uses topic model to explore the semantic relationships between mashups and services. [31] refactors the descriptions by using Author-Topic Model [19] to eliminate the gaps between mashups and services. Li et al. [12] add the invocation relations between requirements and service to a latent Dirichlet allocation (LDA) model to enable the topic model learn the relationship between services and requirements. Jain et al. [10] combines topic model, CF-based matrix factorization, and QoS-based ranking together to recommend satisfying services for mashup creation. Samanta et al. [21] also apply topic models, along with neighbor interaction probabilities to calculate similarity scores between services and requirements, and then multiply these scores to rank candidate services.

With the great success of deep learning models in the NLP and pre-trained language models (PLMs), some researchers start using PLMs and deep learning to deal with the service recommendation problem. For example, Bai et al. [2] designed a stacked denoising autoencoders (SADE) to extract features for recommendation. Xiong et al. [29] integrates the invocation relations between services and requirements as well as their description similarity into a deep neural network. Chen et al.'s extendable framework [4] is a preference-based neural collaborative filtering [9] recommendation model, which use multi-layer perception to capture the non-linear user-item relationships and obtain abstract data representation from sparse vectors. [14] utilize the powerful representation learning abilities provided by deep learning to extract textual features and features from various types of interactions between mashups and services. These models are more complicated than others and some models require a great number of data for pre-training. However, the experimental results show that the improvement of performance from the PLMs and deep learning is still limited, possibly due to the inability of existing models to directly adapt to service recommendation and negative transfer [24].

Although the complicated model is an improvement over the original methods, the current SOTA approach [14] still has an $F1@5$ value below **40%** on the ProgrammableWeb dataset.

3   Tiny Three Linear Layers Based Model

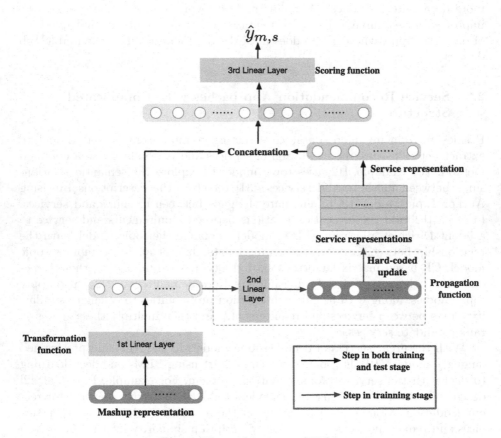

Fig. 2. The architecture of T2L2

As shown in Fig. 2, the proposed T2L2 model consists of three linear layers. The first linear layer called transformation function, which active projection the representation of the mashups to the aligned representation space. The second linear layer is a part of propagation function, which propagate information from aligned representation space to service representation space to make service passive migration to aligned representation space. It should be note the propagation function only used in training stage. The last linear layer called scoring function, which give a score to a given mashup and service.

During the training stage, the input of T2L2 model is a mashup m that is satisfied by a set of component services $C_m^+ = \{s_1, s_2, \ldots, s_n\}$. While in the inference stage, the input of T2L2 model is a mashup m, and the output is a set of recommended component services $\hat{C}_m = \{\hat{s}_1, \hat{s}_2, \ldots, \hat{s}_m\}$. T2L2 maintains a set of service representations $S \in \mathcal{R}^{N \times d_s}$ that are initialized by a PLM, where N is the number of services and d_s is the dimension of service representation. For each mashup m we also use the pre-trained model to obtain its representation $\mathbf{v}_m \in \mathcal{R}^{d_m}$, where d_m is the dimension of mashup representation. **It is important to note that the PLM is only used to obtain the initial representation vector and T2L2 does not need to do fine-tune on the PLM.**

3.1   Transformation Function

As we state in Sect. 1, a key problem in real-world mashup creation is to aligning services and mashups representation to same vector space. Transformation function f_t can be learned to active project the mashup representations into the aligned representation space.

In this paper, we use a linear layer to implement the transformation function f_t:

$$\mathbf{v}_m^a - f_t(\mathbf{v}_m) - W_t \cdot \mathbf{v}_m + \mathbf{b}_t \tag{1}$$

where $W_t \in \mathcal{R}^{d_m \times d_s}$ is a trainable weight matrix and $\mathbf{b}_t \in \mathcal{R}^{d_s}$ is bias. $\mathbf{v}_m^a$ denotes the aligned mashup representation.

3.2   Propagation Function

Propagation function only used in the training stage and consists of two sub-functions: propagation message generation and service representation update.

Propagation message generation function f_p is implemented by the second linear layer:

$$\mathbf{g}_m = f_p(\mathbf{v}_m^a) = W_p \cdot \mathbf{v}_m^a + \mathbf{b}_p \tag{2}$$

where $W_p \in \mathcal{R}^{d_s \times d_s}$ is a trainable weight matrix and $\mathbf{b}_p \in \mathcal{R}^{d_s}$ is bias. $\mathbf{g}_m$ denotes the generate propagation representation.

The service representation update function uses the generated propagation information $\mathbf{g}_m$ to update the relevant service representation so that the service representation space migrates to the aligned representation space:

$$S_i = \sigma(S_i + \mathbf{g}_m) \quad \forall i \in C_m^+ \tag{3}$$

where σ is an activation function, we use *sigmod* function in this paper. As the service representation update function is a hard-coded algorithm, no additional trainable parameters are introduced.

3.3 Scoring Function

The scoring function is used to give a score $\hat{y}_{m,s}$ based on the given aligned mashup representation $\mathbf{v}_m^a$ and service representation S_s to indicate the probability of mashup m invoking service s. Services with a high score will be recommended for mashup m creation:

$$\hat{y}_{m,s} = W_s \cdot [\mathbf{v}_m^a; S_s] + \mathbf{b}_s \tag{4}$$

where $W_s \in \mathcal{R}^{2d_s \times 1}$ is a trainable parameters and $\mathbf{b}_s \in \mathcal{R}^1$ is bias.

3.4 Loss Function

For a given mashup r with component services $C_m^+ = \{s_1, s_2, \ldots, s_n\}$, we minimize the following loss function:

$$\mathcal{L}_1 = - \sum_{s \in C_m^+ \cup C_m^-} y_{m,s}^t \log \hat{y}_{m,s}^t + (1 - y_{m,s}^t) \log(1 - \hat{y}_{m,s}^t) \tag{5}$$

where $y_{m,s}^t \in \{0, 1\}$ denotes whether s is a component service of m, and C^- denotes a set of negative samples with services that are not component services of m. Usually, a mashup is created using a limited number of services, but the number of candidate services is much larger than the number of services required. So it is not appropriate to use all unselected services as negative samples, and we select negative samples of number $|C^-| = 6|C^+|$ by **random sampling**.

3.5 Model Complexity

In this section, we use floating point operations (FLOPs) to measure model's time complexity and use the number of model parameters maintained by T2L2 to denote the space complexity [22]. The FLOPs of linear layer can be calculated as follows:

$$FLOPs = (2d_{in} - 1) \times d_{out} \tag{6}$$

where d_{in} and d_{out} are the input and output dimension of the linear layer. So that the time complexity of T2L2 during training stage can be calculated as:

Time: $(2d_m - 1) \times d_s + (2d_s - 1) \times d_s + (2(d_s + d_s) - 1) \times 1 \backsim \mathcal{O}(d_m d_s + d_s^2)$ (7)

For each linear layer the number of trainable parameters is:

$$NumLinearParameters = d_{in} \times d_{out} + d_{out} \tag{8}$$

Then the total trainable parameters number of T2L2 is $d_m d_s + d_s^2 + 4d_s + 1$. T2L2 also need to maintain a set of service representations of size $N \times d_s$, so the space complexity of T2L2 is:

Space: $d_m d_s + d_s^2 + 4d_s + 1 + N \times d_s \backsim \mathcal{O}(d_m d_s + d_s^2 + N d_s)$ (9)

4 Experiment Settings

4.1 Dataset and Metrics

We evaluate the proposed T2L2 model on real-world ProgrammableWeb dataset, which are also the dataset used in existing mashup creation studies.

ProgrammableWeb: The dataset is the largest online Web service registry. We collected a total of 23,520 APIs and 7,947 mashups, on Oct 10, 2020. The mashups and services without functional description, the services that have not been invoked, and the mashups with fewer than two component services were removed. The experimental dataset contains 3,379 mashups, whose functional descriptions are used as requirements, and 720 APIs. Table 1 displays some statistical information of the dataset. We randomly select 2, 700 mashups as the training set and the remaining 680 mashups are used as the test set.

Table 1. Some statistical information of the dataset

Description	Count
Percent of mashup invokes no more than 5 services	91.2%
Percent of mashup invokes no more than 15 services	99.5%
Percent of mashup invokes no more than 30 services	99.9%
Number of mashup	3379
Number of service	720
Average number of service invoked by a mashup	3.16

We adopted the following evaluation metrics to measure the recommendation performance:

$$Precision@N = \frac{1}{|M|} \sum_{m \in M} \frac{|\hat{C}_m \cap C_m|}{|\hat{C}_m|} \tag{10}$$

$$Recall@N = \frac{1}{|M|} \sum_{m \in M} \frac{|\hat{C}_m \cap C_m|}{|C_m|} \tag{11}$$

$$F1@N = \frac{1}{|M|} \sum_{m \in M} \frac{|\hat{C}_m \cap C_m|}{|C_m| + |\hat{C}_m|} \tag{12}$$

where M is the set of mashups in the test set and $|M|$ denotes the size of M. For mashup m, $\hat{C}_m$ is the recommended services, while C_m is its actual component services.

There are 91.2% mashups whose componential services are no more than 5, and almost all mashups (99.9%) invoke no more than 30 services. Therefore, we choose 5, 10, 15, 20, 25, and 30 as N, respectively to evaluate the performance of the approaches on this dataset comprehensively.

4.2   Implementation Details

We use *bert-base-uncased* provided by Transformers [25] to obtain mashup representation with the dimension d_m set to 768, and it should be noted that we do not do fine-tune on *bert-base-uncased*. Service representations S are initialized by a $128d$ Word2Vec [17] word embedding trained on *text8*[3]. We use the two different pre-trained language models to reflect the representation gap between requirement and service.

We do not use dropout and batch size is set to 200. We use Adam optimizer with the learning rate set to 0.0001. We conduct 5 independent experiments for each approach to prevent serendipity, and early-stop is applied to avoid overfitting. All the results reported are average results.

4.3   Baselines

To evaluate the effectiveness of model, we select six state-of-the-art service recommendation approaches:

1. AFUP [10]: This approach first leverages probabilistic topic models to compute relevance between a service and a given requirement. description. And then use collaborative filtering to estimate the probability of a service being used by existing similar requirements. Finally, the multiplies these two term based on Baye's theorem to rank candidates service.
2. SFTN [21]: This approach extends AFUP by using hierarchical dirichlet process (HDP) and probabilistic matrix factorization (PMF) to tackle cold start issues and usage history.
3. PNCF [4]: This approach uses multi-layer perceptron to capture the nonlinear user-item relationships and obtain abstract data representation from sparse vectors. However, text features were not considered in their original version, so we constructed two variants: PNCF-HDP using HDP adopted in SFTN to obtain text features, and PNCF-Deep using a pre-trained language model to obtain text features.
4. MISR [14]: This approach proposes a deep neural network that can captures multiplex interactions between services and requirements to extract hidden structures and features for better recommendation performance.
5. MTFM++ [26]: This approach proposes a neural framework based on multi-model fusion and multi-task learning, which exploits a semantic component to generate representations of requirements and introduces a feature interaction component to model the feature interaction between mashups and services.

It should be noted that most baselines do not provide official code and we can only reproduce them as described in their papers. In some cases we were not able to reproduce the results they reported, possibly due to different ways of dividing the dataset and missing important parameter values. In these cases, we chose to directly compare the results reported in [14].

---

[3] http://mattmahoney.net/dc/text8.zip.

5   Results

5.1   Overview

Table 2. Performance comparison of different approaches.

Metric	N	MISR	PNCF-Deep	SFTN	AFUP	MTFM++	PNCF-HDP	T2L2 (our)
F1@N	5	0.361	0.311	0.249	0.181	0.305	0.161	**0.601**
	10	0.258	0.228	0.19	0.136	0.198	0.12	**0.471**
	15	0.203	0.181	0.15	0.109	0.148	0.102	**0.351**
	20	0.168	0.151	0.125	0.092	0.121	0.092	**0.277**
	25	0.145	0.131	0.108	0.08	0.104	0.08	**0.229**
Recall@N	5	0.541	0.469	0.366	0.268	0.592	0.245	**0.764**
	10	0.627	0.557	0.453	0.323	0.649	0.298	**0.962**
	15	0.675	0.607	0.492	0.358	0.682	0.344	**0.988**
	20	0.708	0.639	0.519	0.382	0.712	0.387	**0.993**
	25	0.734	0.672	0.546	0.403	0.737	0.408	**0.997**
Precision@N	5	0.287	0.248	0.203	0.145	0.206	0.128	**0.495**
	10	0.17	0.15	0.126	0.089	0.117	0.0784	**0.312**
	15	0.124	0.111	0.092	0.066	0.083	0.0615	**0.213**
	20	0.098	0.088	0.073	0.053	0.066	0.052	**0.161**
	25	0.082	0.074	0.062	0.045	0.056	0.044	**0.129**

Table 2 shows the performance comparison of different approaches, showing that the T2L2 outperforms all the six baselines across all evaluation metrics.

The AFUP, PNCF-HDP and SFTN performed the worst of all the baselines with the $F1@5$ below 25%, which is caused by the following two main reasons: 1) They use a topic model to extract service/mashup representation from the description text, which ignores the order of words and further leads to lost semantic information; 2) Rough handling of service historical usage information.

The PNCF-Deep, MTFM++ and MISR perform better than the other baselines because they use PLMs to obtain better representations of the services/mashup and do fine-tune on these PLMs. In addition, Table 3 summarises the information used by the different approach. While MTFM++ uses the most information, its performance is worse than MISR and PNCF-Deep, suggesting that simply using more data does not necessarily lead to better results. MISR performs the best of all the benchmark methods because it takes into account multiple types of interactions between services and requirements.

T2L2 requires less information than the baselines, while its performance is significantly better than all baselines. For example, all baselines require description of mashups/APIs and mashup-API graph, while T2L2 only needs description of mashups and APIs, and MISR (MTFM++) additionally requires the tags (tags and QoS) of the service. Compared to the best performing baseline approach MISR, T2L2 improves the $Precision@5$, $Recall@5$ and $F1@5$ metrics by **20.8%**, **22.3%** and **24.0%**, respectively. The performance improvements mainly

Table 3. The information used in different approaches.

	MISR	PNCF-Deep	SFTN	AFUP	MTFM++	PNCF-HDP	T2L2
Description	✓	✓	✓	✓	✓	✓	✓
Tag	✓				✓		
QoS					✓		
Mashup–API graph	✓	✓	✓	✓	✓	✓	

benefit from transformation function and propagation function that allow the acquisition of better representation of services and requirements in same vector space.

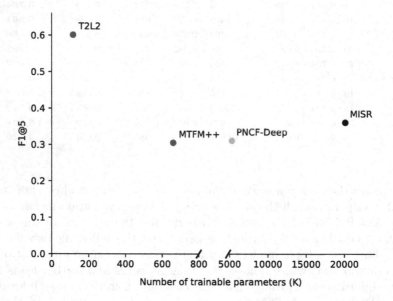

Fig. 3. Comparison of $F1@5$ and the number of trainable parameters within DL-based models

Figure 3 is the comparison of $F1@5$ and the number of trainable parameters among DL-based approaches. The x-axis and y-axis represent the number of trainable parameters and the $F1@5$, respectively. T2L2 locates at the top-left corner and it is distinctly separated, which means that T2L2 has the fewest parameters while keeping the best performance within the DL methods.

Comparing with the MTFM++, PNCF-Deep, and MISR that have 660K, 5100K, 20100K trainable parameters, respectively, T2L2 has 115K parameters because the only trainable parameters in T2L2 are the weights of three linear layers, however, the other methods need to train or fine-tune both the weights in the structure and the features from networks or texts.

5.2   Ablation Study

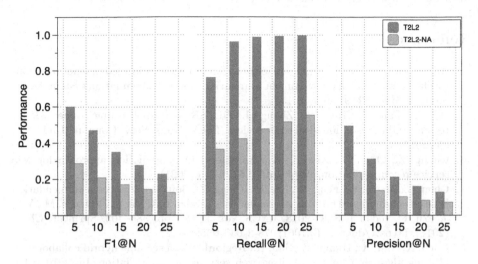

Fig. 4. Performance comparison of T2L2 and its variant T2L2-NA

In this section we design an ablation study in order to demonstrate that the performance improvement of T2L2 comes from aligning the service representation and the mashup representation. We designed a variant of T2L2 called T2L2-NA, which turns off the transformation function and propagation function.

The comparison between T2L2 and T2L2-NA is shown in Fig. 4. T2L2 significant outperforms T2L2-NA on all evaluation metrics and the $F1@5$ value of T2L2-NA is 28.8% close to PNCF-Deep and MTFM++, indicating that the performance improvements do come from the transformation and propagation functions rather than from using a larger PLM (Bert) to extract the mashup representation.

6   Conclusion

In this paper, we propose a tiny three linear layer based model called T2L2 for mashup creation. Unlike traditional approaches, which improve recommendation performance by using complicated models or introducing new data, T2L2 dramatically improves recommendation performance by eliminating representation gaps between mashups and service through transformation and propagation functions without introducing new data and using simple models. Experiments on a real-world dataset demonstrated that the proposed approach significantly outperforms several state-of-the-art approaches regarding three evaluation metrics.

Acknowledgement. The research in this paper is partially supported by the National Key Research and Development Program of China (No. 2018YFB1402500) and the National Natural Science Foundation of China (61772155, 61832004).

References

1. Al-Hassan, M., Lu, H., Lu, J.: A semantic enhanced hybrid recommendation approach: a case study of e-government tourism service recommendation system. Decis. Support Syst. **72**, 97–109 (2015)
2. Bai, B., Fan, Y., Tan, W., Zhang, J.: DLTSR: a deep learning framework for recommendations of long-tail web services. IEEE Trans. Serv. Comput. **13**(1), 73–85 (2017)
3. Chang, Z., Ding, D., Xia, Y.: A graph-based QoS prediction approach for web service recommendation. Appl. Intell. **51**, 1–15 (2021)
4. Chen, L., Zheng, A., Feng, Y., Xie, F., Zheng, Z.: Software service recommendation base on collaborative filtering neural network model. In: Pahl, C., Vukovic, M., Yin, J., Yu, Q. (eds.) ICSOC 2018. LNCS, vol. 11236, pp. 388–403. Springer, Cham (2018). https://doi.org/10.1007/978-3-030-03596-9_28
5. Chen, X., Liu, X., Huang, Z., Sun, H.: RegionKNN: a scalable hybrid collaborative filtering algorithm for personalized web service recommendation. In: 2010 IEEE International Conference on Web Services, pp. 9–16. IEEE (2010)
6. Church, K.W.: Word2vec. Nat. Lang. Eng. **23**(1), 155–162 (2017)
7. Devlin, J., Chang, M.W., Lee, K., Toutanova, K.: Bert: pre-training of deep bidirectional transformers for language understanding. arXiv preprint arXiv:1810.04805 (2018)
8. He, Q., et al.: Efficient keyword search for building service-based systems based on dynamic programming. In: Maximilien, M., Vallecillo, A., Wang, J., Oriol, M. (eds.) ICSOC 2017. LNCS, vol. 10601, pp. 462–470. Springer, Cham (2017). https://doi.org/10.1007/978-3-319-69035-3_33
9. He, X., Liao, L., Zhang, H., Nie, L., Hu, X., Chua, T.S.: Neural collaborative filtering. In: Proceedings of the 26th International Conference on World Wide Web, pp. 173–182 (2017)
10. Jain, A., Liu, X., Yu, Q.: Aggregating functionality, use history, and popularity of APIs to recommend mashup creation. In: Barros, A., Grigori, D., Narendra, N.C., Dam, H.K. (eds.) ICSOC 2015. LNCS, vol. 9435, pp. 188–202. Springer, Heidelberg (2015). https://doi.org/10.1007/978-3-662-48616-0_12
11. Karthikeyan, N., RS, R.K., et al.: Fuzzy service conceptual ontology system for cloud service recommendation. Comput. Electr. Eng. **69**, 435–446 (2018)
12. Li, C., Zhang, R., Huai, J., Sun, H.: A novel approach for API recommendation in mashup development. In: 2014 IEEE International Conference on Web Services, pp. 289–296. IEEE (2014)
13. Liang, T., Chen, L., Wu, J., Dong, H., Bouguettaya, A.: Meta-path based service recommendation in heterogeneous information networks. In: Sheng, Q.Z., Stroulia, E., Tata, S., Bhiri, S. (eds.) ICSOC 2016. LNCS, vol. 9936, pp. 371–386. Springer, Cham (2016). https://doi.org/10.1007/978-3-319-46295-0_23
14. Ma, Y., Geng, X., Wang, J.: A deep neural network with multiplex interactions for cold-start service recommendation. IEEE Trans. Eng. Manag. **68**(1), 105–119 (2021)

15. Maaradji, A., Hacid, H., Skraba, R., Vakali, A.: Social web mashups full completion via frequent sequence mining. In: 2011 IEEE World Congress on Services, pp. 9–16. IEEE (2011)
16. Mezni, H., Benslimane, D., Bellatreche, L.: Context-aware service recommendation based on knowledge graph embedding. IEEE Trans. Knowl. Data Eng. (2021)
17. Mikolov, T., Chen, K., Corrado, G., Dean, J.: Efficient estimation of word representations in vector space (2013)
18. Qi, L., Zhou, Z., Yu, J., Liu, Q.: Data-sparsity tolerant web service recommendation approach based on improved collaborative filtering. IEICE Trans. Inf. Syst. **100**(9), 2092–2099 (2017)
19. Rosen-Zvi, M., Griffiths, T., Steyvers, M., Smyth, P.: The author-topic model for authors and documents. arXiv preprint arXiv:1207.4169 (2012)
20. Rupasingha, R.A., Paik, I.: Alleviating sparsity by specificity-aware ontology-based clustering for improving web service recommendation. IEEJ Trans. Electr. Electron. Eng. **14**(10), 1507–1517 (2019)
21. Samanta, P., Liu, X.: Recommending services for new mashups through service factors and top-k neighbors. In: 2017 IEEE International Conference on Web Services (ICWS), pp. 381–388 (2017). https://doi.org/10.1109/ICWS.2017.128
22. Szegedy, C., et al.: Going deeper with convolutions (2014)
23. Wang, H., Wang, Z., Hu, S., Xu, X., Chen, S., Tu, Z.: DUSKG: a fine-grained knowledge graph for effective personalized service recommendation. Future Gener. Comput. Syst. **100**, 600–617 (2019)
24. Wang, Z., Dai, Z., Póczos, B., Carbonell, J.: Characterizing and avoiding negative transfer. In: Proceedings of the IEEE/CVF Conference on Computer Vision and Pattern Recognition, pp. 11293–11302 (2019)
25. Wolf, T., et al.: Transformers: state-of-the-art natural language processing. In: 2020 Conference on Empirical Methods in Natural Language Processing: System Demonstrations, pp. 38–45. ACL (2020)
26. Wu, H., Duan, Y., Yue, K., Zhang, L.: Mashup-oriented web API recommendation via multi-model fusion and multi-task learning. IEEE Trans. Serv. Comput. (2021). https://doi.org/10.1109/TSC.2021.3098756
27. Xia, B., Fan, Y., Tan, W., Huang, K., Zhang, J., Wu, C.: Category-aware API clustering and distributed recommendation for automatic mashup creation. IEEE Trans. Serv. Comput. **8**(5), 674–687 (2014)
28. Xie, F., Wang, J., Xiong, R., Zhang, N., Ma, Y., He, K.: An integrated service recommendation approach for service-based system development. Expert Syst. Appl. **123**, 178–194 (2019)
29. Xiong, R., Wang, J., Zhang, N., Ma, Y.: Deep hybrid collaborative filtering for web service recommendation. Expert syst. Appl. **110**, 191–205 (2018)
30. Zheng, Z., Ma, H., Lyu, M.R., King, I.: Collaborative web service QoS prediction via neighborhood integrated matrix factorization. IEEE Trans. Serv. Comput. **6**(3), 289–299 (2012)
31. Zhong, Y., Fan, Y., Tan, W., Zhang, J.: Web service recommendation with reconstructed profile from mashup descriptions. IEEE Trans. Autom. Sci. Eng. **15**(2), 468–478 (2016)

Internet-of-Things, Crowdsourced, Social, and Conversational Services

Energy-Aware Placement of Device-to-Device Mediation Services in IoT Systems

Abdessalam Elhabbash[1](✉)(iD) and Yehia Elkhatib[2](iD)

[1] School of Computing and Communications, Lancaster University, Lancaster, UK
a.elhabbash@lancaster.ac.uk
[2] School of Computing Science, University of Glasgow, Glasgow, UK
yehia.elkhatib@glasgow.ac.uk

Abstract. Internet-of-Things (IoT) systems are becoming increasingly complex, heterogeneous and pervasive, integrating a variety of physical devices, virtual services, and communication protocols. Such heterogeneity presents an obstacle especially for interactions between devices of different systems that encounter each other at run time. Mediation services have been proposed to facilitate such direct communication by translating between messaging protocols, interfacing different middlewares, etc. However, the decision of where to place a mediation service within an IoT topology has repercussions and is in some cases critical for satisfying system objectives. In this paper, we propose an integer linear programming solution to optimize the placement decision specifically in terms of energy consumption. Our solution takes into account the energy consumed by each interaction at each device along the data transfer paths. Through simulations that use topologies of real-world IoT systems, we show the effect of our approach on energy consumption, messaging delay, and placement decision time. Our algorithm outperforms a state-of-the-art solution in terms of reducing energy consumption by almost a third in large-scale typologies. We also demonstrate the feasibility of our approach in terms of overhead.

Keywords: Energy consumption · Internet of Things · Cyber physical systems · Mediator · Middlebox · Sustainable computing

1 Introduction

The Internet of Things (IoT) and Cyber-Physical System (CPS) paradigms connect a variety to devices in order to form a system that is capable of monitoring and controlling its environment. The benefits of this paradigm span across several areas such as smart cities [24], smart buildings [25] and environmental monitoring [26], among others. These tangible benefits have given rise to the production of vast numbers of IoT devices with an expected growth from 8.74 billion in 2020 to more than 25.4 billion by 2030 [1].

Interoperability between IoT devices is a major challenge when using device-to-device (D2D) communication. IoT industry producers tend to develop their

© Springer Nature Switzerland AG 2021
H. Hacid et al. (Eds.): ICSOC 2021, LNCS 13121, pp. 335–350, 2021.
https://doi.org/10.1007/978-3-030-91431-8_21

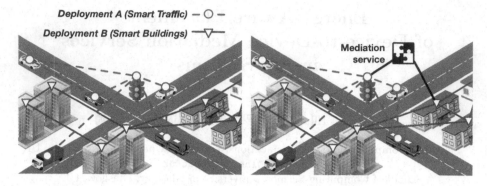

Fig. 1. An example of IoT and CPS deployments sharing the same environment but not being able to intercommunicate due to heterogeneity arising from the use of different communication protocols, service semantics, message formats, middleware software, etc. Deploying a mediation service (see figure on the right) enables interoperation between different deployments.

own APIs and protocols to enable connectivity of their devices given the constraints of their service [33]. This has created a large space of highly heterogeneous devices. However, the difference of APIs, messaging models and message formats complicates direct interaction. For example, the CoAP [32] protocol adopts a client-server messaging model and a maximum message size of 1152 bytes whereas MQTT [7] adopts a publish-subscribe model of messages upto ≈260 Mbytes. Therefore, a device that uses CoAP protocol will not be able to interoperate with another that uses MQTT (see illustration in Fig. 1).

Consider for example the case of a fire fighting emergency team in a smart building. In this scenario, the rescue crew may need to install their equipment in the site and interact with the smart building network to collect situational awareness data. It may not be attainable or convenient to adopt a cloud-based architecture in this case due to unavailability or high delays. In this case, direct interaction is required to interconnect the rescue equipment with the building devices and, thus, a mediator is inevitably necessary.

A solution to cope with the heterogeneity issue is to employ a middlebox to bridge between devices and abstract their functional semantics. The middlebox will reside somewhere in the network as a mediation service and translates between the messaging models of different protocols. Examples include network intent mediation [15], the FIESTA-IoT directory service [31], and the (Data eXchange Mediator Synthesizer) DeXMS framework [9].

However, a notable question that the literature on mediation services does not answer is *where* to place the mediator in the network. This question has not yet been thoroughly tackled by the IoT community, though a method for optimizing the end-to-end delay between the interacting devices has recently been proposed [12]. We argue that energy consumption is a substantial factor to consider in such cases for two reasons. First, efficient energy consumption is crucial to maintain device functionality for the longest period of time possible, especially that some IoT devices have non-rechargeable power sources. Second, efficient energy consumption contributes to the principle of designing sustainable computing solutions.

In this paper, we develop a method that utilizes the network structure to compute the placement of mediation services in order to minimize the energy consumed by the interactions between IoT devices. Our method formulates the placement problem as an integer linear programming (ILP) problem and produces the optimal placement given the interaction load and bandwidth constraints. In this sense, the proposed method is adaptive as it allows placement recalculation whenever the data size and/or available bandwidth change. We compare our proposed method to the delay-optimizing method in recent literature [12] and with a naïve baseline method of random placement. The results show that our adaptive method achieves minimal energy consumption for different IoT network topologies.

Overall, this paper makes the following contributions:

- We formulate the placement of a mediation service as an ILP problem (Sect. 3.1);
- We provide an energy-aware solution to the placement problem (Sect. 3.2); and
- We carry out extensive experiments using the topologies of 4 real-world IoT deployments from different domains, comparing our approach to the state-of-the-art (Sect. 4.5).

2   Related Work

2.1   The Need for Mediation in IoT Systems

A fundamental challenge in designing IoT systems is to choose a communication protocol to be used by all device types regardless of function (sensing, actuating, processing, etc..), manufacturer, or computational capability [14]. A number of protocols have been proposed to enable such D2D communication. A prominent solution is the OASIS standard MQTT [7]: a simple and lightweight protocol that adopts a publish-subscribe paradigm and runs on top of TCP. MQTT defines a small message header, making it preferable for resource constrained networks. An alternative proposed by the IETF is CoAP [32], which follows a client-server paradigm, is based on the Representational State Transfer (REST) architecture, and runs on top of UDP. Other solutions include HTTP, AMQP [3], XMPP [2], among others.

Despite these attempts to standardize communication protocols, different IoT vendors still use varying messaging protocols [14,27], which hampers IoT engineers from building more complex systems (*e.g.,* [16,28]). As such, mediation between devices of different vendors is a common approach. Additionally, IoT systems designed by different teams of engineers are likely to use different protocols. To resolve this, mediation is typically used to act as a bridge between different protocols. For instance, the DeX framework [9] is a recent contribution to support mediation between different IoT protocols. However, little work has been done on how to optimize the placement of mediators in the network considering network and application constraints. A recent proposal [12], which we use as a baseline in our experiments, aims to do this while optimizing for delay-sensitive applications.

2.2 Virtual Network Function Placement

A related research topic is the placement of Virtual Network Functions (VNF) in order to optimize for certain objectives while meeting the system's functional requirements. Although the problem is similar at a high level, the solutions proposed in the literature (*e.g.*, [4,11,36,37]) are not suitable as they optimize placement for different objectives such as link utilization and the size of the network forwarding table. A recent example [13] that is more pertinent to our problem presents an ILP-based model for the placement of virtual security functions (VSFs). The model considers server CPU capacities, VSF processing requirements, and network link capacities to calculate the optimal placement for minimizing energy consumption.

2.3 Energy-Aware IoT

Optimizing energy consumption has been a long sought after goal in IoT systems. This problem has been tackled from different perspectives, such as switching to low-power communication technologies (*e.g.*, [29,35]), being selective about what data to aggregate/process/drop and where (*e.g.*, [5,18,22]), forecasting overall energy consumption [19], and so on.

Some proposals attempt to minimize the energy consumption of application servers within an IoT system (*e.g.*, [6]) and, as such, optimize for application metrics such as request satisfaction. However, none has tackled the challenge taking into consideration where to place mediation services and how this affects the energy consumption of D2D communication.

3   Energy-Aware Placement

In this section, we present the system model and formulate the energy-aware mediator placement problem as an integer linear programming problem.

3.1   System Model

We consider an IoT system with a set of things $T = \{t_1, t_2, \ldots, t_m\}$, a set of access points $AP = \{ap_1, ap_2, \ldots, ap_k\}$, a set of nodes $N = \{n_1, n_2, \ldots, n_p\}$, and a gateway GW. The set of things includes sensors that read environmental data, actuators that effect actions, and external equipment that can be integrated into the network (*e.g.*, rescue teams equipment). The set of nodes consists of static machines that host mediation services to enable heterogeneous things to interact. The access points are hubs that connect the things and nodes to the gateway. In normal cases, the gateway connects the IoT system to the cloud where communication between devices occurs. However, when direct communication is required, which is the focus of this paper, the communication between things and nodes is always directed through the Gateway. Figure 2 shows an typical topology of where things and nodes are located.

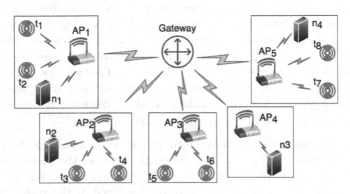

Fig. 2. Typical topology of an IoT system.

We assume that a location attribute $l = \{x, y, z\}$ is associated with each of the things, nodes, access points and the gateway where x, y and z are the coordinates of the location. We also assume that each of the things has a protocol attribute $p(t_i)$ that specifies the messaging protocol that defines the rules and formats of the messages exchanged with other things. The communication between the system things is represented as a set of interactions that occur during the lifetime of the system. We denote an interaction as i_j^{ab} where an interaction j involves things a and b. Each interaction involves sending messages of size $m(i_j)$ for a number of times $f(i_j)$.

The system is represented as a weighted graph $G = (V, E)$ where V and E denote sets of vertices and edges, respectively. Each vertex $v_i \in V$ represents a thing, node, access point or gateway. Each edge $e_{ij} \in E$ represents a link between two vertices and has a weight w_{ij} that indicates the available link bandwidth.

3.2   Problem Formulation

The energy-aware mediator placement problem can be formally stated as follows: *Given a set of things, nodes, interactions and links, deploy the mediation service on a node so that the total energy consumed by the interactions is minimized provided that the bandwidth consumed on each link is constrained by the link's available bandwidth.* In the following we present how the end-to-end energy consumption is calculated and develop the objective function and constraints.

Links. In order to calculate the energy consumption of an interaction, we need to consider the energy consumed for transmitting and receiving data on each link that connects each pair of devices (thing, node, access point or gateway) along the interaction path. Consider the example given in Fig. 2. For an interaction that involves t_1 and t_5 where the mediation service is deployed on n_1, data will traverse the links $t_1 \rightarrow AP_1$, $AP_1 \rightarrow n_1$, $n_1 \rightarrow AP_1$, $AP_1 \rightarrow GW$, $GW_1 \rightarrow AP_3$, $AP_3 \rightarrow t_5$ (notation: $sender \rightarrow receiver$). On the link $t_1 \rightarrow AP_1$, energy consumed at t_1 to send the interaction messages from t_1 to AP_1 and energy is also consumed at AP_1 to received those messages; and so on for the other links. These links are grouped into a first-leg group of the interaction and a second-leg group where the first-leg includes links from the sending thing to the node hosting the mediation service and the second-leg includes links from the hosting node to the receiving thing. This grouping is important because the messaging protocol (and hence the message size) is different in the two legs. On the first-leg the used messaging protocol is the messaging protocol used by the sending thing ($p(t_1)$ in the above example) and on the second-leg the used messaging protocol is that of the receiving device ($p(t_5)$ in the above example).

Energy Consumed Per Interaction. In order to calculate the consumed energy, we denote $\epsilon^T(d_u)$ and $\epsilon^R(d_u)$ for each device in the system, where the former refers to the transmission energy per bit and the latter refers to the receiving energy per bit of device d_u. Note that each of the transmitting and receiving devices can be a thing, node, access point or gateway. Now, in order to calculate the energy consumed for an interaction i_j^{ab}, we calculate the energy consumed by each leg of the interaction using Eqs. 1, 2, and 3 where $m(i_j(p(t_a)))$ and $m(i_j(p(t_b)))$ are the message sizes of the messaging protocol of the sender and receiver things, respectively, and $\epsilon(i_j^{ab})$ is the energy consumed by the interaction.

$$\epsilon(first - leg_j) = (\sum(\epsilon^T(d_u)) + \sum(\epsilon^R(d_v))) \times m(i_j(p(t_a))) \times f(i_j) \qquad (1)$$

$$\epsilon(second - leg_j) = (\sum(\epsilon^T(d_u)) + \sum(\epsilon^R(d_v))) \times m(i_j(p(t_b))) \times f(i_j) \qquad (2)$$

$$\epsilon(i_j^{ab}) = \epsilon(first - leg_j) + \epsilon(second - leg_j) \qquad (3)$$

Objective Function. Next, we calculate the total energy that is consumed by all the interactions so that we utilize it to reason about the selection of a node to host the mediator. Given a number of interactions n that occur in the system, the total consumed energy is calculated using Eq. 4 which sums up the energy consumed by each interaction.

$$\epsilon_{total} = \sum_{r=1}^{n} \epsilon(i_r^{ab}) \qquad (4)$$

Note that we do not include the processing energy consumption of the generation of the mediator nor the mediation because we assume these will be the same regardless of the where the mediation service is deployed.

Mediator Host Selection Constraints. Given an interaction, the following two constraints must be satisfied for any mediation deployment to be acceptable:

- *Bandwidth constraint.* Given a host node and an interaction i_j^{ab}, the interaction will consume $m(i_j) \times f(i_j)$ bandwidth on every link along the interaction path from the source thing a to the destination thing b. The consumed bandwidth must be less than or equal to the available bandwidth on each of the links along the path. Algorithm 1 describes how this constraint is checked: it takes as input a potential hosting node, a graph representing the topology and lists of things and interactions. It returns *True* if the bandwidth constraint is satisfied. It starts by extracting all the edges. Then, for each link, the algorithm accumulates the bandwidth that would be consumed by each interaction and checks if the total is less than the link bandwidth.

Algorithm 1. Check Bandwidth constraint

Input: A list of Things T, hosting node n_p, Interactions I, Graph G
Output: True: if the consumed bandwidth is less then the available, False: otherwise
1: **For** each edge e_i in G
2:   **For** each interaction i_j^{ab} in I
3:     Find a path leg_1 from t_a to n_p using the Breadth First search
4:     Find a path leg_2 from n_p to t_b using the Breadth First search
5:     **For** link (edge) el_m in $leg_1 \cup leg_2$
6:       **If** $el_m == e_i$
7:         $bandwidthUsed \mathrel{+}= m(i_j) \times f(i_j)$
8:       **EndIf**
9:     **EndFor**
10:    **If** $bandwidthUsed > bandwidth(e_i)$
11:      **return** False
12:    **EndIf**
13: **EndFor**
14: **EndFor**
15: **return** *True*

- *Allocation constraint.* For each interaction i_j^{ab}, there is a set of nodes N that can host the mediation service of that interaction. However, for each interaction i_j^{ab}, we should only select one node to host the mediation service. We denote the selection of a node n_j to host the mediation service y_j^{ab}, the following constraint must be satisfied:

$$\sum_{n \in N} y_j^{ab} = 1 \tag{5}$$

Based on this modeling, the mediator placement problem is formalized below with $w_{n_p}^{ab}$ being the bandwidth of the path from t_a to t_b when the mediator is hosted on node n_p.

$$
\begin{aligned}
\text{minimize} \quad & \epsilon_{total} \\
\text{subject to} \quad & \forall i_j^{ab} \; \forall n_p \sum m(i_j) \times f(i_j) \leq w_{n_p}^{ab} \\
& \sum_{n \in N} y_j^{ab} = 1
\end{aligned}
\tag{6}
$$

4   Evaluation

To assess the efficiency and efficacy of our energy-aware placement algorithm, we run a set of rigorous experiments of mediator service placement in various contexts based on real-world IoT scenarios (Sect. 4.2). We compare our algorithm against three baselines: a naïve algorithm, a state-of-the-art one for delay optimization [12] (Sect. 4.3) and a state-of-the-art one for bandwidth optimization. We inspect the ability to improve different system performance metrics and the associated overhead (Sect. 4.4).

4.1   Experimental Setup

The experiments are conducted on a PC with Intel Pentium D 3.0 GHz, 1 GB RAM, running Linux Ubuntu v18. We used Java SE v1.8.0 to implement the placement algorithms and simulate the IoT infrastructure. We generate the parameters values as follows:

- Interactions are generated by randomly selecting two different things provided they have different messaging protocols so that a mediation service is required. The size and frequency of messages are generated randomly from the ranges [0, 100] and [0, 1000] respectively.
- Interface bandwidths of things, access points, and gateways are generated from the ranges [11, 54], [11, 54], [54, 450] Mbps respectively according to the specification in [21].
- The values of energy per bit transmitted/received are generated from the ranges [5, 20] mJ/bit [34] and [13.97, 1902.11] nJ/bit [20].
- The locations of the system elements are generated within the Euclidean space of range [0, 0]–[1000, 1000] in meters.

4.2   IoT Contexts

We use 4 real-world IoT deployments as evaluation contexts. These were chosen to represent different scales and structures of IoT systems, as summarized in Table 1.

Table 1. A summary of the IoT deployments used for evaluation.

Name	#Things	#Nodes	Ref.	Use
AirPollution	14	6	[8]	Monitor city-wide air quality
SmartSantander	1,570	23	[30]	Monitor various issues such as noise, ambient temperature, light intensity, vehicle activity, Carbon Monoxide levels, etc.
Sphere	1,500	500	[17]	Healthcare provision in residential environments
MassiveIrrigation	15,000	1,000	[23]	Manage freshwater distribution for precision irrigation of agricultural crops

4.3   Baseline Placement Algorithms

- **Random** – In this naïve algorithm, a node to host the mediation service is selected at random from the list of potential hosting nodes, excluding those that violate bandwidth/allocation constraints.
- **Delay-optimized** – The algorithm proposed in [12] is, as discussed, the only contribution so far to address the mediation placement problem in IoT systems. The algorithm defines an objective function that aims to find a placement that minimizes the delay between interacting things. Delay is calculated as the sum of the transmission and propagation delays. The algorithm uses the absolute locations of things and nodes in the deployment environment to compute the propagation delay as the distance that data travel divided by the wave propagation speed. In other words, the algorithm makes no attempt to consider the network topology. In order to make a fair comparison with this algorithm, we modify the way distance is calculated to include the total distance between the sending thing and the receiving thing through the hosting node, access points and the gateway.
- **Bandwidth-optimized** – This algorithm determines placement such that the overall bandwidth consumed by D2D interactions is minimized. The algorithm calculates the bandwidth that interactions will consume on every link along the interaction path. It then sums up all the estimated bandwidth consumption on each link for each placement and solves the objective function to find the optimal placement.

4.4   Evaluation Criteria

The three algorithms are compared in terms of the following criteria:

- **Energy consumption** – The total energy consumed to deliver messages between things. We focus on transmitting and receiving messages, and ignore the energy of mediation assuming the latter is the same on all nodes.
- **Delay** – The end-to-end time delivery time between sender and receiver.
- **Execution time** – The time taken by the algorithm to find a placement of the mediation service.

4.5   Results

We presents our findings and draw comparison between the four algorithms.

Energy Consumption. The average values of energy consumption per interaction are depicted in Fig. 3. The plots indicate that significant amounts of energy could be saved using our placement algorithm. This per-interaction improvement ranges between 12.9% in the case of a small topology like the air pollution

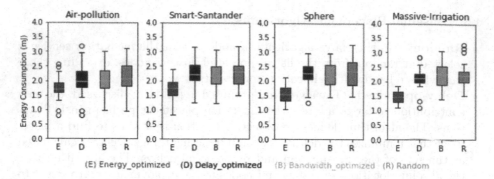

Fig. 3. The average energy consumed on message sending between source and destination, including intermediaries, at 250 interactions.

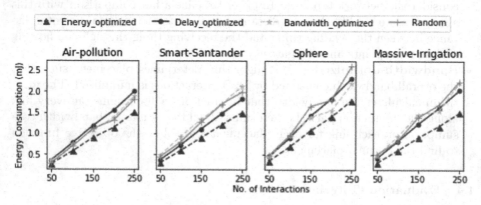

Fig. 4. The average energy of messaging for varied scales of interaction.

scenario, to 31.6% for large deployments such as the massive irrigation one. Energy consumption for the other placement algorithms is, overall, not better than the random placement strategy. To further determine the scalability of the algorithms, we plot the energy consumption versus the number of interactions in Fig. 4. Our algorithm improves energy consumption for different levels of interaction. In addition, energy consumption grows as the number of interactions grow, which is due to demand for more traffic. Energy consumption increases linearly with the number of interactions, but with a steeper slope for all but our algorithm.

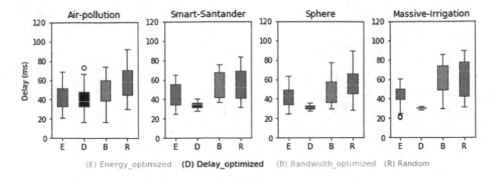

Fig. 5. The average end-to-end delay of message exchange at 250 interactions.

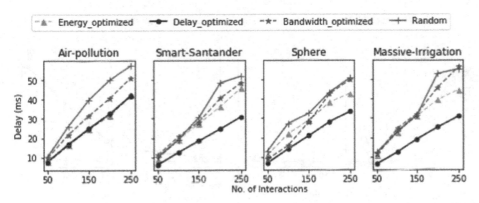

Fig. 6. The average end-to-end delay of message exchange for varied number of inter-actions.

Delay. Figure 5 exhibits the average end-to-end messaging delay for each topology. The delay-optimized algorithm clearly achieves lower levels of delay than the alternatives. The amount of delay reduction is in the order of 3% in the case of small topology to 30.6% in the case of large topology – compared to the energy-optimized algorithm. Figure 6 plots the delay at different interaction intensities. Unsurprisingly, the delay-optimized algorithm improves the delay for varied number of interactions. The effect of the scale of the topology is also evident as the slope of the linear relationship between increased traffic and delay: the larger the topology, the longer the delays.

Execution Time. The plots in Fig. 7 portray the overhead in terms of execution time of each placement algorithm. All three non-trivial algorithms require very equivalent execution times. This is due to their similar levels of complexity, as all their run times scale with the number of device interfaces and interactions involved in the deployment. The last strategy requires the least due to it being a naïve one. With respect to scalability (Fig. 8), a linear trend with the increase

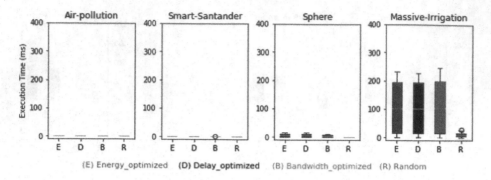

Fig. 7. The execution times to find the optimal placement at 250 interactions.

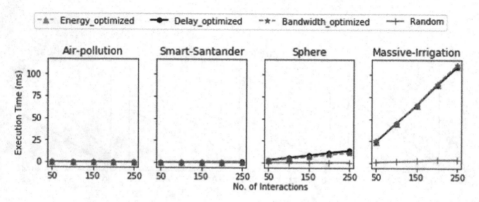

Fig. 8. The overhead in terms of average time taken by each algorithm to find the optimal placement.

of the number of interactions is again observed for all algorithms. This indicates that the energy-optimized algorithm is able to find the energy-optimal placement in a practicably acceptable runtime.

5   Discussion

We now reflect on the implications of our findings, and lay groundwork for future work.

Trade-Off and Limitation – There is a clear advantage in terms of energy consumption at the expense of modest algorithm execution times and reversion to average messaging delays. In terms of making IoT deployments more sustainable and long-living, the latter overheads are deemed acceptable especially for large IoT deployments. The obvious limitation is that our approach is geared towards reducing energy consumption and not other metrics such as end-to-end delay. We aim to address this in future work (see point below).

Multi-objective Optimization – The results presented in the previous section show that our proposed approach achieves lower energy consumption, but sometimes at the expense of higher end-to-end delay. Future work could build on both this and the delay-optimize alternative by defining the placement problem as a multi-objective optimization problem. Additionally, this can be extended by including other non-functional service objectives such as load balance, reliability, etc.. Simultaneous optimization of multiple objective functions would require defining weights for each of the objectives of interest.

Adaptive Placement – The inherent dynamism of IoT environments, arising from different factors (such as node mobility, usage patterns, failures, ephemeral nature), make adaptive placement a crucial operational procedure. One of the advantages of the presented approach is its reactive quality, through recalculation of the objective function. This adaptive capability can be further enhanced to provide proactive adaptation by utilizing techniques for change prediction.

Practicability – In the design of our optimization algorithm, there is an assumption that the scale of interactions between devices, and the volume of exchanged traffic is known beforehand. This is an unreasonable assumption for most real deployments. Instead, interaction frequency and volume could be estimated by analyzing historical data. This issue is similar to that of workload estimation in the cloud, (*e.g.,* [10]) a field that can inform interaction estimation.

6 Conclusion

We propose an approach for placement of mediation services in an IoT system. The approach targets environments where IoT devices need to directly interact to exchange data. The approach is based on two key ideas. First, we formulate the placement problem as an integer linear programming problem taking into account the topology of the infrastructure. The proposed algorithm takes into consideration the energy consumed by each interaction along the path between source and destination things. Second, the approach devices an adaptive placement of the mediation services whereby recalculating the placement based on environmental changes. We demonstrate the feasibility of our approach through a methodology of quantitative evaluation, comparing our approach to base-lines from the literature. The results show that our approach provides a systematic way of finding a placement that minimizes energy consumption with a nominal computational overhead. This novel contribution has strong implications in IoT and CPS environments with direct device-to-device interactions and where minimizing energy consumption is needed for sustainable deployments.

Acknowledgments. This work was supported by the Adaptive Brokerage for the Cloud (ABC) project, UK EPSRC grant EP/R010889/1.

References

1. Number of Internet of Things (IoT) connected devices worldwide from 2019 to 2030. https://www.statista.com/statistics/1183457/iot-connected-devices-worldwide/. Accessed 08 Apr 2021
2. Extensible messaging and presence protocol (XMPP): Core. RFC 3920, IETF (2004). https://tools.ietf.org/html/rfc3920
3. Advanced message queuing protocol version 1.0. Standard, OASIS (2012). http://docs.oasis-open.org/amqp/core/v1.0/os/amqp-core-overview-v1.0-os.html
4. Afrin, M., Jin, J., Rahman, A.: Energy-delay co-optimization of resource allocation for robotic services in cloudlet infrastructure. In: Pahl, C., Vukovic, M., Yin, J., Yu, Q. (eds.) ICSOC 2018. LNCS, vol. 11236, pp. 295–303. Springer, Cham (2018). https://doi.org/10.1007/978-3-030-03596-9_20
5. Azar, J., Makhoul, A., Barhamgi, M., Couturier, R.: An energy efficient IoT data compression approach for edge machine learning. Future Gener. Comput. Syst. **96**, 168–175 (2019). https://doi.org/10.1016/j.future.2019.02.005
6. Badri, H., Bahreini, T., Grosu, D., Yang, K.: Energy-aware application placement in mobile edge computing: a stochastic optimization approach. IEEE Trans. Parallel Distrib. Syst. **31**(4), 909–922 (2020). https://doi.org/10.1109/TPDS.2019.2950937
7. Banks, A., Gupta, R.: MQTT version 3.1.1. Standard, OASIS (2014). http://docs.oasis-open.org/mqtt/mqtt/v3.1.1/os/mqtt-v3.1.1-os.html
8. Basford, P.J., Bulot, F.M.J., Apetroaie-Cristea, M., Cox, S.J., Ossont, S.J.: LoRaWAN for smart city IoT deployments: a long term evaluation. Sensors **20**(3), 648 (2020). https://doi.org/10.3390/s20030648
9. Bouloukakis, G., Georgantas, N., Ntumba, P., Issarny, V.: Automated synthesis of mediators for middleware-layer protocol interoperability in the IoT. Future Gener. Comput. Syst. **101**, 1271–1294 (2019). https://doi.org/10.1016/j.future.2019.05.064
10. Calzarossa, M.C., Massari, L., Tessera, D.: Workload characterization: a survey revisited. ACM Comput. Surv. **48**(3), 1–43 (2016). https://doi.org/10.1145/2856127
11. Chen, X.: Energy efficient NFV resource allocation in edge computing environment. In: International Conference on Computing, Networking and Communications (ICNC), pp. 477–481 (2020). https://doi.org/10.1109/ICNC47757.2020.9049765
12. Chio, A., Bouloukakis, G., Hsu, C.H., Mehrotra, S., Venkatasubramanian, N.: Adaptive mediation for data exchange in IoT systems. In: Workshop on Adaptive and Reflexive Middleware, pp. 1–6. ACM (2019). https://doi.org/10.1145/3366612.3368122
13. Demirci, S., Sagiroglu, S., Demirci, M.: Energy-efficient virtual security function placement in NFV-enabled networks. Sustain. Comput.: Inform. Syst. **30**, 100494 (2021). https://doi.org/10.1016/j.suscom.2020.100494
14. Dizdarević, J., Carpio, F., Jukan, A., Masip-Bruin, X.: A survey of communication protocols for internet of things and related challenges of fog and cloud computing integration. ACM Comput. Surv. **51**(6), 1–29 (2019). https://doi.org/10.1145/3292674
15. Elhabbash, A., Blair, G.S., Tyson, G., Elkhatib, Y.: Adaptive service deployment using in-network mediation. In: International Conference on Network and Service Management (CNSM), pp. 170–176 (November 2018)

16. Elhabbash, A., Nundloll, V., Elkhatib, Y., Blair, G.S., Sanz Marco, V.: An ontolog-ical architecture for principled and automated system of systems composition. In: International Symposium on Software Engineering for Adaptive and Self-Managing Systems (SEAMS) (July 2020). https://doi.org/10.1145/3387939.3391602

17. Fafoutis, X., Elsts, A., Piechocki, R., Craddock, I.: Experiences and lessons learned from making IoT sensing platforms for large-scale deployments. IEEE Access **6**, 3140–3148 (2018). https://doi.org/10.1109/ACCESS.2017.2787418

18. Fitzgerald, E., Pióro, M., Tomaszwski, A.: Energy-optimal data aggregation and dissemination for the Internet of Things. IEEE Internet Things J. **5**(2), 955–969 (2018). https://doi.org/10.1109/JIOT.2018.2803792

19. Han, T., Muhammad, K., Hussain, T., Lloret, J., Baik, S.W.: An efficient deep learning framework for intelligent energy management in IoT networks. IEEE Internet Things J. **8**(5), 3170–3179 (2021). https://doi.org/10.1109/JIOT.2020.3013306

20. Hoque, M.A., Siekkinen, M., Nurminen, J.K.: Energy efficient multimedia stream-ing to mobile devices - a survey. IEEE Commun. Surv. Tutor. **16**(1), 579–597 (2014). https://doi.org/10.1109/SURV.2012.111412.00051

21. Intel: Different Wi-Fi protocols and data rates. https://www.intel.com/content/www/us/en/support/articles/000005725/wireless/legacy-intel-wireless-products.html. Accessed 30 Apr 2021

22. Jalali, F., Khodadustan, S., Gray, C., Hinton, K., Suits, F.: Greening IoT with fog: a survey. In: International Conference on Edge Computing, pp. 25–31 (2017). https://doi.org/10.1109/IEEE.EDGE.2017.13

23. Kamienski, C., et al.: Smart water management platform: IoT-based precision irrigation for agriculture. Sensors **19**(2), 276 (2019). https://doi.org/10.3390/s19020276

24. Kim, T., Ramos, C., Mohammed, S.: Smart city and IoT. Future Gener. Comput. Syst. **76**, 159–162 (2017). https://doi.org/10.1016/j.future.2017.03.034

25. Minoli, D., Sohraby, K., Occhiogrosso, B.: IoT considerations, requirements, and architectures for smart buildings-energy optimization and next-generation building management systems. IEEE Internet Things J. **4**(1), 269–283 (2017). https://doi.org/10.1109/JIOT.2017.2647881

26. Montori, F., Bedogni, L., Bononi, L.: A collaborative Internet of Things architec-ture for smart cities and environmental monitoring. IEEE Internet Things J. **5**(2), 592–605 (2018). https://doi.org/10.1109/JIOT.2017.2720855

27. Naik, N.: Choice of effective messaging protocols for IoT systems: MQTT, CoAP, AMQP and HTTP. In: International Systems Engineering Symposium, pp. 1–7 (2017). https://doi.org/10.1109/SysEng.2017.8088251

28. Nundloll, V., Elkhatib, Y., Elhabbash, A., Blair, G.S.: An ontological framework for opportunistic composition of IoT systems. In: International Conference on Infor-matics, IoT, and Enabling Technologies (ICIoT), pp. 614–621. IEEE (February 2020)

29. Qin, H., Cao, B., He, J., Xiao, X., Chen, W., Peng, Y.: Cross-interface scheduling toward energy-efficient device-to-gateway communications in IoT. IEEE Internet Things J. **7**(3), 2247–2262 (2020). https://doi.org/10.1109/JIOT.2019.2958612

30. Sanchez, L., et al.: SmartSantander: IoT experimentation over a smart city testbed. Comput. Netw. **61**, 217–238 (2014). https://doi.org/10.1016/j.bjp.2013.12.020. Special issue on Future Internet Testbeds - Part I

31. Serrano, M., Gyrard, A., Tragos, E., Nguyen, H.: FIESTAIoT project: federated interoperable semantic IoT/cloud testbeds and applications. In: The Web Confer-ence, pp. 425–426 (2018). https://doi.org/10.1145/3184558.3186199

32. Shelby, Z., Hartke, K., Bormann, C.: The constrained application protocol (CoAP). RFC 7252, IETF (2014). https://www.rfc-editor.org/rfc/rfc7252.txt

33. Sinche, S., et al.: A survey of IoT management protocols and frameworks. IEEE Commun. Surv. Tutor. **22**(2), 1168–1190 (2020). https://doi.org/10.1109/COMST. 2019.2943087

34. Sun, L., Sheshadri, R.K., Zheng, W., Koutsonikolas, D.: Modeling WiFi active power/energy consumption in smartphones. In: International Conference on Distributed Computing Systems, pp. 41–51 (2014). https://doi.org/10.1109/ICDCS. 2014.13

35. Wilhelmsson, L.R., Lopez, M.M., Sundman, D.: NB-WiFi: IEEE 802.11 and Bluetooth low energy combined for efficient support of IoT. In: Wireless Communications and Networking Conference, pp. 1–6 (2017). https://doi.org/10.1109/WCNC. 2017.7925808

36. Xu, Z., Zhang, X., Yu, S., Zhang, J.: Energy-efficient virtual network function placement in telecom networks. In: International Conference on Communications (2018). https://doi.org/10.1109/ICC.2018.8422879

37. Zong, Y., et al.: Location-aware energy efficient virtual network embedding in software-defined optical data center networks. J. Opt. Commun. Netw. **10**(7), 58–70 (2018). https://doi.org/10.1364/JOCN.10.000B58

Fairness-Aware Crowdsourcing of IoT Energy Services

Abdallah Lakhdari$^{(\boxtimes)}$ and Athman Bouguettaya

School of Computer Science, University of Sydney, Sydney, Australia
{abdallah.lakhdari,athman.bouguettaya}@sydney.edu.au

Abstract. We propose a Novel Fairness-Aware framework for Crowdsourcing Energy Services (FACES) to efficiently provision crowdsourced IoT energy services. Typically, efficient resource provisioning might incur an unfair resource sharing for some requests. FACES, however, maximizes the utilization of the available energy services by maximizing fairness across all requests. We conduct a set of preliminary experiments to assess the effectiveness of the proposed framework against traditional fairness-aware resource allocation algorithms. Results demonstrate that the IoT energy utilization of FACES is better than FCFS and similar to Max-min fair scheduling. Experiments also show that better fairness is achieved among the provisioned requests using FACES compared to FCFS and Max-min fair scheduling.

Keywords: Service provisioning · Crowdsourcing · IoT energy · Fairness

1 Introduction

The proliferation of the Internet of things (IoT) may give rise to a self-sustained crowdsourced IoT ecosystem [2]. The augmented capabilities of IoT devices such as sensing and computing resources may be leveraged for peer-to-peer sharing. People can exchange a wide range of IoT services such as computing offloading, hotspot proxies, *energy sharing*, etc. These crowdsourced IoT services present a convenient, cost-effective, and sometimes the only possible solution for a resource-constrained device [11]. For instance, a passenger's smartphone with low battery power may elect to receive energy from nearby wearables *using Wifi* [22]. The focus of this paper is on crowdsourcing IoT energy services.

The concept of *wireless energy crowdsharing* has been recently introduced to provide IoT users with power access, anywhere anytime, through crowdsourcing [4,16,22]. We leverage the service paradigm to unlock the full potential of IoT energy crowdsourcing. We define *an IoT Energy Service* as the abstraction of energy wireless delivery from an IoT device (i.e., *provider*) to another device (i.e., *consumer*) [17]. Crowdsourcing IoT energy services has the potential of creating a *green* service exchange environment by *recycling* the unused IoT energy or relying on *renewable* energy sources. For example, an IoT device may share

© Springer Nature Switzerland AG 2021
H. Hacid et al. (Eds.): ICSOC 2021, LNCS 13121, pp. 351–367, 2021.
https://doi.org/10.1007/978-3-030-91431-8_22

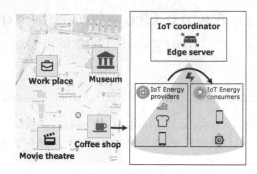

Fig. 1. Crowdsourcing IoT energy services

its spare energy with another IoT device in its vicinity. Another example, a smart shoe may harvest energy from the physical activity of its wearer [7,9]. Additionally, wireless charging allows energy crowdsharing to be a *convenient* alternative as the devices do not need to be tethered to a power point, nor use power banks. Crowdsourcing energy services can be deployed through already existing wireless power transfer technologies such as *Energous*[1] that can deliver up to 3 W power within a 5-meter distance to multiple receivers.

The crowdsourced IoT energy ecosystem is a *dynamic* environment that consists of providers and consumers congregating and moving across *microcells* boundaries. A microcell is any confined area in a smart city where people may gather (e.g., coffee shops, restaurants, museums, libraries), see Fig. 1. The deployment of the energy crowdsharing ecosystem depends on the willingness of the IoT device owners to participate. Indeed, providers may share their energy *altruistically* to contribute to a *green* IoT environment. They may also be motivated by *egotistic* purposes where participants are encouraged to share energy through a set of *incentives* [28]. We assume that the IoT coordinator provides incentives to encourage energy sharing in the form of credits. These would be used to receive more energy when the providers act as consumers in the future [1,28]. The IoT coordinator is assumed to be deployed one hop away from the energy providers and consumers (e.g., router at the edge) to minimize the communication overhead and latency while advertising energy services and requests. The participation of IoT users in the energy crowdsharing ecosystem depends on the security and trust of the deployed ecosystem. Novel security modules and new privacy-preserving trust models have been developed for crowdsourced IoT environments. These aspects are outside the scope of this paper. Our primary focus in this work is on fairness-aware crowdsourcing of IoT energy services.

We propose a fairness-aware service provisioning framework to cater for *multiple* energy requests in a crowdsourced IoT market. *The under-provision of energy requests may demotivate consumers to participate in the crowdsourced IoT energy market.* In this paper, we focus on the notion of *fairness* in provisioning IoT energy services to satisfy the maximum number of energy requests.

---

[1] https://www.energous.com/.

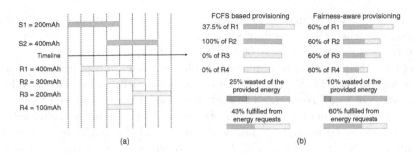

Fig. 2. (a) Time constraints of energy services and requests (b) Energy provisioning

Sometimes, in a crowdsourced IoT environment, the available energy services in a microcell may not satisfy all existing requests. It is challenging to satisfy consumers by fulfilling only parts of their energy requirements. An efficient scheduler, in traditional resource allocation algorithms, aims at maximizing the throughput (i.e., the amount of resource utilization in a unit of time) [10]. In some embedded systems, the scheduler must also ensure meeting deadlines of multiple requests [6]. Typically, maximizing the throughput and meeting requests' deadlines might incur an unfair resource sharing for some requests (e.g., starvation of long requests in a short job first scheduler). In a crowdsourced IoT energy market, however, we claim that *if more energy requests are satisfied with respect to their time intervals (i.e., fairness), more energy would be consumed.* We transform the fairness-aware service provisioning problem into an optimization problem, i.e., maximizing the utilization of the available energy services by maximizing fairness across all requests. The contributions of this paper are:

- A formulation of the IoT energy services provisioning problem as a time-constrained optimization problem.
- A fairness model to accommodate multiple IoT energy requests in the crowdsourced IoT environment.
- A spatio-temporal framework for fairness-aware crowdsourcing of IoT energy services (FACES).
- An experimental analysis with two implementations of the proposed fairness-aware energy crowdsourcing framework.

2   Motivating Scenario

We will use the following scenario: Six IoT users staying at a coffee shop. Two users are willing to provide their energy services S_1 and S_2. The other four IoT users are requesting energy from their neighboring IoT devices R_1, R_2, R_3, and R_4. The advertisement of services and requests includes various information, e.g., the start time, the end time, the location of the IoT device, and the provided or requested energy amount. Figure 2 (a) illustrates the available services and requests by their timelines. It also shows the amounts of provided and requested

IoT energy. It is challenging to allocate energy and fulfill multiple requests' requirements when there are limited energy services. For example, in Fig. 2 the available energy represents only 60% of the total requested energy.

Figure 2 (b) presents the outcome of different allocation plans for the available energy to R_1, R_2, R_3, and R_4. Our goal is to fairly and efficiently allocate energy services to all requests. The first allocation plan follows the FCFS (i.e., First Come First Served) scheduling strategy. Each request is provided with energy according to its arrival (i.e., start time) and the available energy at its time interval. For example, in Fig. 2 (a) R_1 receives energy from S_1. However, when R_2 arrives, it receives energy only from S_2. Even S_1 is also within its time interval, S_1 has been already reserved by R_1. Scheduling strategies such as FCFS and priority-based schedulers may not be a good fit to provision crowdsourced IoT energy. These strategies fulfill the requirements of each energy request independently and sequentially based on their arrival time. Services may fulfill the requirements of an energy request without being fully utilized, which affects the energy allocation efficiency. For example, all the requirements of R_2 have been fulfilled. On the other hand, R_3 and R_4 did not receive any energy. The FCFS-based scheduling could fulfill only 43% of the total amount of the requested energy and wasted 25% of the total available IoT energy.

The coordinator aggregates the provided energy by all services based on their time intervals. The aggregated energy is then shared among all requests according to their time constraints. The second energy allocation plan in Fig. 2 (b) is a good illustration of the effect of a fairness-aware provisioning plan. Allocating 60% of the requirement to each energy request maximizes the consumption of the available energy to 90% (i.e., 10% wastage). The limited provided energy and the time constraints of requests represent critical challenges for efficient and fairness-aware provisioning of IoT energy services. We reformulate our service provisioning problem as *a multi-objective time-constrained optimization problem*, i.e., *(i) maximizing the allocated energy provided by the available services, and (ii) maximizing the fairness for each request with respect to its time constraints.*

3   Preliminaries

We first adopt the definitions of IoT energy services and requests in [16]. We then introduce the concept of fairness among energy requests based on their allocated energy. This work considers a provisioning framework for stationary services and requests to focus only on the temporal constraints in allocating energy to multiple requests in a microcell within a predefined time interval. The goal is to ensure fairness over a predefined time while maximizing green energy provision. In the future, we will extend the framework to fit into a dynamic crowdsourced market by dealing with moving services and requests.

Definition 1. An energy service CES is a tuple $< Eid, Eownerid, F, Q >$ where:

- *Eid* is a unique service ID,
- *Eownerid* is a unique ID for the owner of the IoT device,

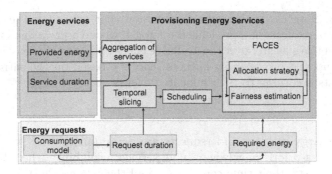

Fig. 3. FACES framework

- F is the set of CES functionalities offered by an IoT device D.
- Q is a tuple of $< q_1, q_2, ..., q_n >$ where each q_i denotes a QoS property.

Definition 2. Crowdsourced IoT energy Quality of Service (QoS) Attributes allow users to distinguish among crowdsourced IoT energy services. QoS parameters are defined as a tuple $< l, St, Et, DEC, I, Tsr, Rel_i >$ [17] where:

- l is the location of the provider.
- St represents the start time of a crowdsourced IoT energy service.
- Et represents the end time of a crowdsourced IoT energy service respectively.
- DEC is the deliverable energy capacity.
- I is the intensity of the wirelessly transferred current.
- Tsr represents the transmission success rate.
- Rel_i represents the reliability QoS

The spatio-temporal features of the IoT energy services (i.e., l, St and Et) are defined based on the pattern of time spent in regularly visited places e.g., coffee shops using their daily activity model in a smart city [8]. DEC and Rel_i are estimated based on the energy usage model of the IoT device. I and Tsr are defined based on the specifications of the provided energy services.

Definition 3. Crowdsourced IoT Energy request is defined as a tuple $R =< t_s, t_e, l, RE >$ where:

- St refers to the timestamp when the energy request is launched.
- Et represents the end time of the period of time, an energy consumer may wait for charging.
- l refers to the location of the energy service consumer. We assume that a consumer's location is fixed after launching the request.
- RE represents the required amount of energy. We also assume that the required energy is estimated based on an energy consumption model of the IoT device.

Definition 4. Fairness is defined as a function that quantifies the *satisfaction* among a set of requests in a predefined microcell within a predefined time frame. The function takes as an input the available energy AE and the existing requests R and outputs the provisioning fairness score Fp based on the satisfaction Sf of all requests according to their allocated energy Al.

Assumptions

- All IoT energy services and requests are deterministic and stationary, i.e., there is an a-priori knowledge about service availability, their QoS values, energy requests, their time constraints, and their demands [16].
- The IoT coordinator (at the edge) is responsible for *batching* the energy requests from all consumers in a microcell *over a predefined period of time*.
- The IoT coordinator is also responsible for *aggregating* all available energy from all providers in a microcell *over a predefined period of time*.
- The energy services may deliver energy to *multiple* consumers at the same time without any loss.

4   Provisioning Energy Services

Figure 3 presents the building blocks of our proposed framework. The framework takes as input, the advertised services and the energy requests. Service providers use the previously defined energy service model to advertise their wireless energy services [16]. We assume that energy consumers define their energy requirements and their charging waiting time (i.e., request duration) based on predefined consumption models.

In a microcell C, the fairness-aware service provisioning framework is executed at the level of the IoT coordinator in the edge (i.e., a router within the microcell C). Given a set of crowdsourced IoT energy services in the microcell C, $S = \{S_1, S_2, \ldots S_n\}$ and a set of all existing requests within the same time interval W, $R = \{R_1, R_2, \ldots R_m\}$. The IoT coordinator aims at minimizing the wastage Wsg while provisioning the aggregated energy to all existing requests within the time window W by performing the following steps:

Temporal Slicing. The goal of the temporal slicing module is *to segment* the requests time intervals and define the overlapping parts. We follow the temporal chunking of energy services in [16] to define the time slices of the time window W. We define all the possible timestamps where a preemptive scheduler may switch to another request. Each timestamp is either the start time or the end time of existing requests. We divide the time window W into several time slices based on these timestamps. The time slots represent the arrival time of a new request or the exit time of an existing request (i.e., vertical dotted lines in Fig. 4 (a)) [16]. For example, S_2 in Fig. 4 may be *temporally* chunked into four *parts of services* S_iP_j (i.e., part i of service j) as follows: $< S_2P_1, S_2P_2, S_2P_3, S_2P_4 >$. Similarly, R_1 in Fig. 4 may be *temporally* chunked into three *parts of requests*

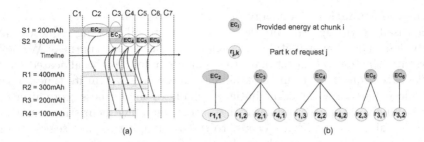

Fig. 4. (a) Chunking crowdsourced IoT energy services and requests (b) The bipartite graph representation of the time-constrained allocation problem

R_iP_j as follows: $< R_1P_1,\ R_1P_2,\ R_1P_3 >$. At each chunk, a part of service S_iP_k may provision a part of a request R_iP_j within the same chunk. For example, in Fig. 4 (b), S_1P_2 provides energy to R_1P_1 since they are within the same chunk. Each request R_i may be provisioned by a *composition* of parts of services S_iP_k where a part of service delivers energy to a part of the request at each chunk [17]. After scheduling the requests, it is more challenging to provide energy to multiple requests in a fair way.

Aggregation of Services. The framework starts by *aggregating* all the available services within the time window W. Energy services are composed according to their spatio-temporal features. We use the framework of composing crowdsourced IoT energy services proposed by Lakhdari et al. [17]. The composition considers the time interval of each service to define a composite energy service that includes all the available services. The IoT coordinator defines a sequence of time intervals and the available energy at each time interval. If two or more energy services overlap within a time interval, the IoT coordinator sums the provided energy by all services available at that time interval.

$$AggE = \sum_i DEC_i\ \forall CES_i \in agt.$$

agt represents the composite energy service resulting of the spatio-temporal composition of available services S. $AggE$ is a QoS of the composite energy service agt. $AggE$ denotes the total energy provided by the aggregated services.

Scheduling. The scheduling module takes the segmented requests and starts by planing the provision for only the non overlapping segments for each request. The allocated energy amount Al_k to a request R_k can only be provided from the available energy within its time interval $[St_k, Et_k]$. $[S_k, E_k]$ represents the time interval when a request R_k may receive energy. Av_k represents the available energy within the time interval $[S_k, E_k]$. For example, in Fig. 4 the IoT coordinator provides energy to R_4 only from the available energy within the time chunks C_3 and C_4 .

Fairness Estimation. In energy provisioning, the fairness score Fp is calculated based on the sparsity in allocating energy to all existing requests. Intuitively, less allocation sparsity among requests reflects more fairness. We define a sparsity function Sf to estimate the sparsity based on the allocated energy Al_k to each request R_k from the available energy Av_k within its time interval. The fairness estimation module initially calculates the fairness score after only provisioning the non-overlapping requests segments. The heuristic cannot estimate the fairness and allocate energy to the overlapping request segments only if there is a prior knowledge about the allocated energy to the non-overlapping segments.

Allocation Algorithm. The allocation algorithm aims at minimizing the wastage of the aggregated energy and maximize the fairness among requests. We transform the problem of fairness-aware energy provisioning into a time-constrained resource allocation problem as follows:

$$Minimize \quad wsg = AggE - \sum_{i=1}^{n} Al_i$$

$$Maximize \quad Fp = sf(Al_i), \forall R_i \in R$$

$$Subject\ to \quad [St_i, Et_i] = [S_i, E_i], \forall R_i \in R$$

$$Where \quad \forall R_i \in R$$

$[St_i, Et_i]$ *is the interval of the request* R_i

$[S_i, E_i]$ *is the interval when* R_i *may receive energy*

The algorithm aims at solving the said *multi-objective optimization* by efficiently provisioning the overlapping segments of requests. Next, the *fairness estimation module* recalculates the fairness score at each optimization step. In the following, we explain the fairness concept for energy requests in a crowdsourced IoT energy market as we present the building blocks of the heuristic-based allocation algorithm.

5   Fairness-Aware Crowdsourcing of Energy Services (FACES)

In a framework for provisioning energy services, there is a dual need to, on the one hand, maximize energy use from a consumer perspective and, on the other hand, maximize the provisioning of energy from the providers' point of view. We propose a scheme whereby energy requests from all consumers in a microcell (over a predefined time frame) are batched while all available energy from all providers in a microcell is aggregated. Figure 5 presents a batched set of energy services and requests from 5:00 to 6:30. A global view of all available services and requests within a predefined time interval allows the IoT coordinator to aggregate the provided energy by *composing* all services based on their availability time intervals [17]. The coordinator aims to efficiently and fairly share the aggregated energy among all the existing requests according to their time constraints.

5.1 Fairness Estimation

Fairness-aware provisioning does not necessarily imply an equal allocation of the available energy to all requests. In a crowdsourced IoT energy market, distributive fairness [19] is defined by equally provisioning requests according to their *features* (i.e., requirements and time constraints). Provisioning IoT energy services fairly aims to *satisfy* more consumers rather than maximizing the energy allocation for some requests. Typically in resource allocation problems, when the resources are limited, consumers will not be satisfied by an efficient allocation of available resources to all requests [21]. However, in a crowdsourced IoT environment, fairness-aware provisioning of energy services is claimed to increase the utilization of the available energy services. We rely on the satisfaction of energy consumers to monitor the fairness of our service provisioning framework.

Satisfaction: We first define a satisfaction score Sf for energy consumers. Intuitively, the amount of the acquired energy is directly proportional to the satisfaction of consumers. However, consumers already realize the limited availability of energy services in the crowdsourced IoT energy market. In this work, we consider an *altruistic* behavior of energy consumers. Consumers' goal is both to maximize their allocated energy and to contribute selflessly to fair provisioning. They may adjust their satisfaction score based on the market (i.e., available energy services and existing requests).

Definition 5. The satisfaction Sf_i of an energy consumer toward a request R_i reflects their perception of the allocated energy Al_i to their request. We quantify Sf_i score for a request R_i based on the allocated energy Al_i and the available energy in the crowdsourced market as follows:

$$Sf_i = \begin{cases} \frac{Al_i}{RE_i} \times \frac{\sum_{i=1}^{n} Al_i}{\sum_{j=1}^{m} DEC_j}, & \text{if } Al_i \leq RE_i \\ 1, & \text{otherwise} \end{cases}$$

Where $\sum_{i=1}^{n} RE_i$ represents all the requested energy in the crowdsourced market by the set of all existing requests $R_i \in ExR$. $\sum_{j=1}^{m} DEC_j$ represents all the energy in the market provided by the available energy services $S_j \in AvS$

Fairness Score: We define a global fairness metric for energy services provisioning Fp based on the satisfaction of all consumers. We measure the global fairness of the service provisioning framework by estimating the overall proximity score among the satisfaction scores of all consumers [3]. An unfair provisioning plan is reflected by *sparse* satisfaction scores among consumers (i.e., some requests have high satisfaction score than others). Contrarily, less sparse satisfaction scores reflect higher proximity among all requests.

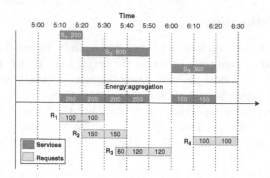

Fig. 5. Example of batched energy services and requests

Definition 6. The *global fairness* Fp is a metric to quantify the sparsity of the satisfaction scores among all requests in the crowdsourced IoT energy market. We capture the global fairness Fp using the *information entropy* [24]. The information entropy measures the disorder degree of all requests $R_i \in ExR$ based on their satisfaction scoreSf_i as follows:

$$Fp(ExR) = -\sum Sf_i \log_2 Sf_i$$

5.2   Heuristic-Based Fairness-Aware Allocation Algorithm

We propose a heuristic-based allocation strategy, i.e., Fairness-Aware Crowd-sourcing of Energy Services (FACES), which extends the traditional resource allocation strategies by optimizing the energy allocation for *overlapping* requests. Our proposed heuristic does not only consider the allocated time for each request. It also considers sharing the available energy when two or multiple requests are overlapping. For example, at the time segment [5:20, 5:30] in Fig. 5 when R_1 and R_2 overlap, FACES divides the available energy at that time segment (200 mAh) between R_1 and R_2. Algorithm 1 presents the pseudocode of the heuristic-based fairness-aware provisioning. First, the energy services are aggregated by the IoT coordinator (Line 2). Next, the time interval is chunked based on the arrival time of energy requests (Lines 3–9). the provisioning framework starts by the non overlapping requests. Then, for each chunk containing overlapping requests, the available energy at that chunk would be equally split among those chunks (Lines 10–13). Finally, all the allocated energy is aggregated per request (Lines 14–17). Provisioning overlapping requests simultaneously improves fairness among requests (i.e., $\sigma = 8.03$) and minimizes the wastage of the available energy, i.e., 10% of the available energy. An optimal fairness-aware provisioning plan will maximize the consumption of the available aggregated energy.

The complexity of the proposed fairness algorithm can be estimated based on the number of available requests and the number of chunks C and the number of overlapping requests at each chunk. The runtime complexity of FACES is O(Cn). If we consider n as the number of available partial requests within a chunk.

Algorithm 1. Heuristic-based fairness-aware energy allocation

---

Input: C, $S = \{S_1, S_2, \ldots S_n\}$, $W < St, Et >$, $R = \{R_1, R_2, \ldots R_m\}$.
Output: $Al = \{Al_1, Al_2, \ldots Al_m\}$.
    // Aggregating energy services
1: **for** $S_i \in S$ **do**
2:    $AggE = \sum_i DEC_i \; \forall CES_i \in agt$
    // Chunking energy requests
3: $Chunk_0.st \leftarrow W.St$
4: **for** $int \; t = W.St$ to $W.Et$ **do**
5:    **if** ($\forall \; R_i \in R$ and $t = R_i.st$ or $t = R_i.et$) **then**
6:        $Chunk_i.et \leftarrow t$
    // create new chunk
7:    **if** $t \neq W.Et$ **then**
8:        $Chunk_{i+1}.st \leftarrow t$
9:        $t \leftarrow t + 1$
10: **for** $R_i \in R$ **do**
    // Chunk-based provisioning
11:    **for** $Ch \in Chunk$ **do**
    // First, provision non-overlapping requests
    // Second, provision overlapping requests per chunk
    // $Ch_p r$ is the set of partial requests within a chunk
    // $Ch_A E$ is the available energy within a chunk
12:        **for** $Pr \in Ch_p r$ **do**
13:            $pr \leftarrow Ch_A E / |Ch_p r|$
14:        **While**($pr_i \in R_i$)
15:        $Al_i \leftarrow Al_i \cup \{pr_i\}$
16:        **End While**
17:    $Al \leftarrow Al \cup \{Al_i\}$
18: **return** Al

5.3 Assessment of Allocation Strategies

Table 1 presents different allocation plans for the aggregated energy to accommodate R_1, R_2, R_3, and R_4 (see Fig. 5). We calculate the amount of energy (i.e., capacity) each request can receive energy according to different allocation strategies. The first allocation plan follows the FCFS (First Come First Served) scheduling strategy. Each request is provided with energy according to its arrival (i.e., start time). Contrarily, the Round Robin (RR) is a preemptive scheduler that allocates a fixed time interval for each request. In our example, we consider 10 min as a fixed time interval. RR reduces the provision wastage compared to FCFS. A Preemptive implementation of FCFS (P-FCFS) extends the FCFS strategy by considering overlapping requests. FCFS, RR, and P-FCFS strategies are runtime efficient schedulers that consider only one request at a time. Their goal is to allocate time to each request *efficiently*. We evaluate the outcome of the different energy allocation strategies based on the energy *wastage* and *fairness* among requests. We define energy wastage as the amount of lost energy

Table 1. Allocation strategy effect on the energy provisioning

	Algorithms' results (%)			
Request (Capacity)	FCFS	RR	P-FCFS	FACES
R1 (200 mAh)	100	50	100	100
R2 (300 mAh)	0	100	50	83
R3 (180 mAh)	100	67	67	85
R4 (100 mAh)	100	100	100	100
Provision wastage	48.72	26.93	20.52	10
Provision unfairness	43.30	21.60	21.60	8.03

that could not be utilized to fulfill the capacity of all requests. For example, the Round Robin algorithm in Table 1 exhibits 26.93% wastage. For a simplistic illustration of fairness, we use the standard deviation σ to estimate the fairness. Intuitively, a better fairness is reflected by a lower value of σ. In the example illustrated by Fig. 5, P-FCFS provides more fairness compared to FCFS because the provision sparsity of P-FCFS ($\sigma = 21.60$) is less than the one of FCFS.

6   Experiments

We conduct a set of preliminary experiments to evaluate the proposed theoretical concepts of fairness-aware provisioning of crowdsourced energy services. We essentially assess the *effectiveness* of different fairness strategies on maximizing the utilization of the available energy within a microcell. We measure the ratio of the consumed energy over the available energy across different microcells. We monitor the changes in the fairness score and the energy utilization ratio while varying the number of energy requests. We implement two variants of the proposed approach(FACES) and compare them with traditional resource allocation algorithms, namely, FCFS, P-FCFS, and Max-min fair scheduling [26].

6.1   Dataset and Experiment Environment

We create a crowdsourced IoT environment scenario close to reality. We mimic the energy sharing behavior of the crowd within microcells by utilizing a dataset published by IBM for a coffee shop chain with three branches in New York city[2]. The dataset consists of transaction records of customers purchases in each coffee shop for one month. Each coffee shop consists of, on average, 560 transnational records per day and 16,500 transaction record in total. We use the IBM dataset to simulate the spatio-temporal features of energy services and requests. The dataset contains information about the crowd's behavior in coffee shops. People may check-in, rate, and recommend these venues. In our experiment, we only

---

[2] https://ibm.co/2O7IvxJ.

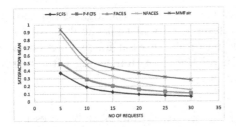

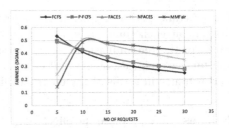

Fig. 6. The mean score of consumers satisfaction.

Fig. 7. The standard deviation score of consumers satisfaction.

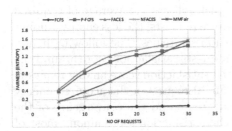

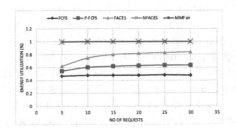

Fig. 8. The Entropy score of consumers satisfaction.

Fig. 9. The energy utilization ratio

focus on people's check-ins information. We extract the crowd size for each coffee shop at each hour (*hour*) of the day (*weekday*). We assume these people as IoT users. They may offer energy services from their wearables while staying in the coffee shop. We define spatio-temporal features of energy services by generating customers' check-in and check-out timestamps to confined areas using the previously extracted data from their transactions. For example, the start time *st* of an energy service from an IoT user is the time of their check-ins into a coffee shop. Energy request time *R.st* and duration *R.et* are also generated from check-in and check-out times of customers. *To the best of our knowledge, it is challenging to find a dataset about the wireless energy transfer among human-centric IoT devices.* We use a random uniform distribution to generate the energy amount for each request and the amount of provided energy for each service.

6.2 Effectiveness

We implement two variants of the FACES framework, namely, FACES and NFACES. FACES considers only one request at a time, similar to FCFS and P-FCFS. NFACES, however, considers multiple requests at a time similar to max-min fair scheduler [26]. FACES and NFACES chunk the requests before provisioning. The chunks are defined based on the overlapping between requests [17]. We implemented a modified version of the Max-min scheduler to consider the temporal constraints of energy requests. For each chunk, if there is more than one request, max-min fair scheduling is performed. Contrarily, to the max-min fair scheduler, NFACES privileges the partial requests with the highest required amount at each chunk. The remaining available energy at that chunk is reallocated to the remaining requests in descending order. In what follows, we assess the fairness metrics, sigma and entropy for all the algorithms along with their performance in terms of the energy utilization.

Fairness. We evaluate the effectiveness of the proposed framework by assessing the effect of the fairness-aware allocation strategy on energy utilization. We first investigate fairness through different metrics, namely, the mean, standard deviation, and entropy satisfaction score for existing requests. Figure 6 illustrates the change of the satisfaction mean value which reflects the average of acquired energy amount per request. Intuitively, the more requests, the less energy amount to acquire per request for all the five allocation strategies. The following figure, Fig. 7 presents the dispersion of the energy requests satisfaction score around the mean. This metric reflects the variation of the satisfaction score among requests. With a larger number of requests (more than 10 requests), the acquired energy decreases significantly, which explains the decrease and the convergence of the standard deviation due to the decrease of the satisfaction score among most of the requests.

The information entropy captures the multi-modal dispersion and irregularities in the distribution of the satisfaction score of energy consumers (see Fig. 8). We leverage the information entropy to monitor the fairness in provisioning energy requests. A lower value of entropy means better fairness in the allocated energy. It is worth mentioning that the entropy metric could capture the small variations in the satisfaction score when the number of requests is larger. These variations cannot be noticed only with a fairness metric based on the standard deviation (see Fig. 7). In Fig. 8 FCFS exhibits a near zero score for the entropy, which can be explained by the fact that most of the requests satisfaction score is equal to zero. NFACES, however, demonstrates a better performance behavior in terms of fair provisioning for energy requests. With a larger number of requests, the entropy values for NFACES are lower than those of P-FCFS and Max-min fair scheduler.

Energy Utilization. The fourth experiment compares the Energy Utilization (See Fig. 9). The goal of proposing a fairness-aware provisioning framework is to leverage fairness as a driver to increase the utilization of the available energy services in a crowdsourced IoT environment by increasing the participation of energy consumers. Energy utilization is the ratio of the amount of the allocated energy services over the total amount of available energy services. Overall, all the energy allocation techniques converge after 15 requests. FACES exhibits the best performance behavior among the three algorithms that consider only one request at a time (i.e., FCFS, P-FCFS, and FACES). The energy utilization ratio is significantly higher with NFACES and Max-min fair scheduler, an expected behavior by these two strategies as a result of considering overlapping requests, i.e., more than one request at a time.

In conclusion, this set of preliminary experiments confirms our claim that fairness-aware allocation strategies would better utilize the available energy in a crowdsourced IoT environment. It is worth mentioning that NFACES exhibits far better fairness behavior compared to Max-min fair scheduler, nonetheless the same performance in terms of the energy utilization.

7   Related Work

Service computing is a key enabler for wireless energy sharing. *Service composition* is expected to play a vital role in the crowdsourced IoT environment. A single IoT energy service may not fulfill the requirement of a consumer due to the limited resources of IoT devices [13]. Several service composition techniques have been proposed. Mainly, the service composition techniques can be categorized into a functionality-based composition or QoS-based composition. For example, Tan et al. [25] proposed a data-driven composition approach that uses Petri-nets to meet the application's functional requirements. Wang et al. [27] address the problem of service functionalities constraints by introducing a pre-processing technique and a graph search-based algorithm to compose services.

Service selection and composition also play an important role in emerging fields such as cloud computing, IoT-based smart systems [5,23]. In IoT, services are mainly composed according to their spatio-temporal features [12]. They also must fulfill consumer preferences (QoS). For example, Lakhdari et al. design and implement a spatio-temporal service composition framework for crowdsourced IoT services [15]. User preferences are used to define the spatial and temporal composability models, Neiat et al. proposed a spatio-temporal service composition framework to describe and compose region services like WiFi hotspots [20]. Existing energy service composition frameworks mainly consist of the real-time discovery and selection of nearby energy services [14]. The focus of these composition techniques was only on the spatio-temporal composability [17] and addressing the challenges related to the energy fluctuation and the mobility of the available services [18].

The current work adds a new contribution to the field of energy crowd sharing. Indeed, existing service composition techniques address the challenges related to one single consumer at a time. Our proposed approach considers provisioning multiple consumers in a predefined time and space. To the best of our knowledge, the work is among the first attempts to address fairness challenges in a crowdsourcing IoT energy services.

8   Conclusion

We proposed a fairness-aware framework for provisioning IoT energy services in a crowdsourced IoT environment. We introduced the concept of *fairness* to efficiently provision available IoT energy services and accommodate multiple energy requests in a microcell within a predefined time frame. The under-provision of energy requests may demotivate consumers to participate in the crowdsourced

IoT energy market. We investigated different allocation strategies to provision energy services, namely, FCFS, P-FCFS, and Round Robin. We defined a fairness model based on the satisfaction of consumers. Our goal is to leverage the fairness as a means to maximize the utilization of the available energy services. We designed and develop a fairness-aware scheduling framework to provision IoT energy services. We conducted a set of preliminary experiments to assess the effectiveness of the proposed framework.

Acknowledgment. This research was partly made possible by DP160103595 and LE180100158 grants from the Australian Research Council. The statements made herein are solely the responsibility of the authors.

References

1. Abusafia, A., Bouguettaya, A.: Reliability model for incentive-driven iot energy services. arXiv preprint arXiv:2011.06159 (2020)
2. Atzori, L., Iera, A., Morabito, G.: The internet of things: a survey. Comput. Netw. **54**(15), 2787–2805 (2010)
3. Basık, F., Gedik, B., Ferhatosmanoglu, H., Wu, K.L.: Fair task allocation in crowdsourced delivery. IEEE Trans. Serv. Comput. **14**, 1040–1053 (2018)
4. Bulut, E., Hernandez, S., Dhungana, A., Szymanski, B.K.: Is crowdcharging possible? In: 2018 IEEE ICCCN (2018)
5. Chaki, D., Bouguettaya, A.: Fine-grained conflict detection of iot services. In: 2020 IEEE International Conference on Services Computing (SCC), pp. 321–328. IEEE (2020)
6. Cheng, T.E., et al.: A concise survey of scheduling with time-dependent processing times. European Journal of Operational Research **152**(1), 1–13 (2004)
7. Choi, Y.M., Lee, M.G., Jeon, Y.: Wearable biomechanical energy harvesting technologies. Energies **10**(10), 1483 (2017)
8. Do, T.M.T., Gatica-Perez, D.: The places of our lives: visiting patterns and automatic labeling from longitudinal smartphone data. IEEE Trans. Mobile Comput. **13**(3), 638–648 (2013)
9. Gorlatova, M.: Movers and shakers: kinetic energy harvesting for the internet of things. In: ACM SIGMETRICS Performance Evaluation Review, vol. 42, pp. 407–419. ACM (2014)
10. Graham, R.L., Lawler, E.L., Lenstra, J.K., Kan, A.R.: Optimization and approximation in deterministic sequencing and scheduling: a survey. In: Annals of Discrete Mathematics, vol. 5, pp. 287–326. Elsevier (1979)
11. Habak, K., Ammar, M., Harras, K.A., Zegura, E.: Femto clouds: Leveraging mobile devices to provide cloud service at the edge. In: CLOUD. pp. 9–16. IEEE (2015)
12. Hamdi, A., Shaban, K., Erradi, A., Mohamed, A., Rumi, S.K., Salim, F.D.: Spatiotemporal data mining: a survey on challenges and open problems. Artif. Intell. Rev. pp. 1–48 (2021)
13. Lakhdari, A., Abusafia, A., Bouguettaya, A.: Crowdsharing wireless energy services. In: 2020 IEEE CIC, pp. 18–24. IEEE, USA (2020)
14. Lakhdari, A., Bouguettaya, A.: Fluid composition of intermittent IOT energy services. In: SCC, pp. 329–336. IEEE (2020)
15. Lakhdari, A., Bouguettaya, A.: Proactive composition of mobile iot energy services. In: ICWS. IEEE (2021)

16. Lakhdari, A., Bouguettaya, A., Neiat, A.G.: Crowdsourcing energy as a service. In: Pahl, C., Vukovic, M., Yin, J., Yu, Q. (eds.) ICSOC 2018. LNCS, vol. 11236, pp. 342–351. Springer, Cham (2018). https://doi.org/10.1007/978-3-030-03596-9_24

17. Lakhdari, A., Bouguettaya, A., Mistry, S., Neiat, A.G.: Composing energy services in a crowdsourced iot environment. IEEE TSC (2020)

18. Lakhdari, A., Bouguettaya, A., Mistry, S., Neiat, A.G.: Elastic composition of crowdsourced IOT energy services. In: Mobiquitous. EAI (2020). arxiv.org/abs/2011.06771

19. Leventhal, G.S.: What should be done with equity theory? In: Social exchange, pp. 27–55. Springer (1980)

20. Neiat, A.G.: Crowdsourced coverage as a service: two-level composition of sensor cloud services. IEEE TKDE **29**(7), 1384–1397 (2017)

21. Radunovic, B., Le Boudec, J.Y.: A unified framework for max-min and min-max fairness with applications. IEEE/ACM Trans. Netw. **15**(5), 1073–1083 (2007)

22. Raptis, T.P.: Online social network information can influence wireless crowd charging. In: IEEE DCOSS (2019)

23. Shahzaad, B., Bouguettaya, A., Mistry, S., Neiat, A.G.: Resilient composition of drone services for delivery. Future Gen. Comput. Syst. **115**, 335–350 (2021)

24. Shannon, C.E.: A mathematical theory of communication. Bell Syst. Tech. J. **27**(3), 379–423 (1948)

25. Tan, W., Fan, Y., Zhou, M., Tian, Z.: Data-driven service composition in enterprise SOA solutions: a petri net approach. IEEE Trans. Autom. Sci. Eng. **7**(3), 686–694 (2010)

26. Tassiulas, L., Sarkar, S.: Maxmin fair scheduling in wireless networks. In: Joint Conference of the IEEE Computer and Communications Societies INFOCOM. vol. 2, pp. 763–772. IEEE (2002)

27. Wang, P., Ding, Z., Jiang, C., Zhou, M.: Constraint-aware approach to web service composition. IEEE Trans. Syst. Man Cybern. Syst. **44**(6), 770–784 (2014)

28. Wu, H., et al.: Revenue-driven service provisioning for resource sharing in mobile cloud computing. In: Maximilien, M., Vallecillo, A., Wang, J., Oriol, M. (eds.) ICSOC 2017. LNCS, vol. 10601, pp. 625–640. Springer, Cham (2017). https://doi.org/10.1007/978-3-319-69035-3_46

Dynamic Conflict Resolution of IoT Services in Smart Homes

Dipankar Chaki$^{(\boxtimes)}$ and Athman Bouguettaya

School of Computer Science, University of Sydney, Sydney, Australia
{dipankar.chaki,athman.bouguettaya}@sydney.edu.au

Abstract. We propose a novel conflict resolution framework for IoT services in multi-resident smart homes. The proposed framework employs a preference extraction model based on a temporal proximity strategy. We design a preference aggregation model using a matrix factorization-based approach (i.e., singular value decomposition). The concepts of current resident item matrix and ideal resident item matrix are introduced as key criteria to cater to the conflict resolution framework. Finally, a set of experiments on real-world datasets are conducted to show the effectiveness of the proposed approach.

Keywords: IoT service · Multi-resident smart home · Preference extraction · Preference aggregation · Conflict resolution

1 Introduction

Internet of Things (IoT) is the umbrella term covering everyday objects (a.k.a. things) that are connected to the Internet. These are usually equipped with ubiquitous intelligence [18]. IoT technologies are the key enablers of many cutting-edge applications such as smart cities, smart campuses, smart grids, and intelligent transport systems. A particular application domain of IoT is *smart homes*. A smart home is defined as a home that is fitted with IoT devices. These IoT devices are attached to everyday "things" to monitor usage patterns. The purpose of a smart home is to provide its residents with *convenience* and *efficiency* [11].

The concept of IoT is congruent with the *service paradigm* [1]. Each "thing" has a set of *functional* and *non-functional* (a.k.a. quality of service) properties. In this regard, we leverage the service paradigm as a framework to define the functional and non-functional properties of smart home devices as *IoT services* [4]. For instance, a light bulb in a smart home is regarded as a light service. The functional property of the light service is to provide illumination. Examples of non-functional properties include luminous intensity, color, connectivity.

In a multi-occupant smart home, different residents may have different service requirements, leading to IoT service conflicts [5]. For example, a resident may prefer the light to be "on" while watching TV, and another resident may prefer the light to be "off". Therefore, an *IoT service conflict* occurs since the light service cannot satisfy multiple residents' requirements at the same time

© Springer Nature Switzerland AG 2021
H. Hacid et al. (Eds.): ICSOC 2021, LNCS 13121, pp. 368–384, 2021.
https://doi.org/10.1007/978-3-030-91431-8_23

and location. In this context, *detecting* and *resolving* conflicts is paramount to provide residents with a higher level of convenience and satisfaction.

Residents usually communicate *face-to-face* when co-located in a home. They can exchange their opinion and decide the appropriate state of shared services through this face-to-face communication. For example, family members may decide to watch a television channel by discussing with each other. Although this communication enables them to discuss their interest in television shows, it is cumbersome to find a show that would be agreeable to all in a world of thousands of available channels. This negotiation may lead to *tension* and *stress* [24]. In addition to the ability of humans to resolve conflict, technologies may enable them to resolve conflict automatically [25]. Some works focus on conflict resolution considering *preference aggregation* strategies, and they estimate preferences from previous service usage history [2,5,9]. They did not take into account the rationality of *interactions* and the *fairness* of the residents. Hence, these aggregation strategies, which are unlikely to find out the best resolution that most residents can accept, may lead to unsatisfying service provision.

We propose a novel conflict resolution approach that integrates *current service requirements* (i.e., interactions) with *preferences* from previous service usages. Integrating interactions with preference is challenging due to the *dynamic nature* of the residents' *desires* and *requirements*. For example, residents may have different requirements at different times on different days. This is why we design a *preference extraction* model using the concept of *temporal proximity*. We further design a *preference aggregation* model using a matrix factorization-based approach, namely, *Singular Value Decomposition (SVD)*. When the residents' preferences conflict heavily, we smooth their preferences by low-rank matrix factorization to ensure fairness. The concept of *current resident item matrix* and *ideal resident item matrix* are introduced to cater to the conflict resolution framework. The contribution of this paper is threefold:

- A novel preference extraction model using the temporal proximity concept that estimates preference scores based on previous service usage records.
- A novel preference aggregation model using SVD technique, current resident item matrix, ideal resident item matrix that integrates current requirements and previous preferences to find out the best item for conflict resolution.
- Experimental evaluation is conducted on real-world datasets to exhibit the effectiveness of the proposed framework.

2   Motivation Scenario

We consider the following motivating scenario to demonstrate the significance of our work. Suppose three residents (R1, R2, R3) want to watch TV between 20:00 and 20:30 in the living room. However, they have different channel requirements. R1, R2, R3 want to watch channels Ch3, Ch2, and Ch5, respectively (Fig. 1).

A conflict occurs since the TV cannot telecast more than one channel simultaneously (assuming the TV does not have multi-screen/split-screen features). Note that, channel is a functional property of a TV service. In this case, action may be taken to eliminate the conflict. The system may: (i) select a channel based on priorities (i.e., residents' can be prioritized based on age and/or role in a family) [19], (ii) adopt the use first strategy (i.e., whoever wants to use the TV first, only his/her preferred channel will be telecast) [15], (iii) randomly pick a channel, (iv) inform users that they should explicitly resolve the conflict. However, the best choice according to these selections may still leave some residents feeling dissatisfied and slighted. Moreover, unresolved or inadequately resolved conflicts tend to result in tension, which may trigger or intensify posterior conflicts. The objective of conflict resolution is to offer a smoother and more pleasant user experience. In this regard, there is a need to have a methodology that incorporates residents' intentions (i.e., current requirements) and preferences (i.e., prior interactions). We aim to maximize residents' satisfaction by providing services that may be preferred by the majority of them. Prior interactions uncover information such as hidden patterns, correlations, habits, and preferences.

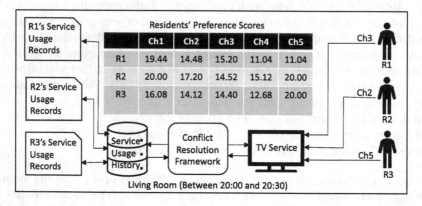

Fig. 1. Residents' current requirements and preferences from previous usage.

Let us assume, we know the preference scores of each channel of the residents (table in Fig. 1). The preference scores are calculated based on the residents' prior service interactions. The procedures of computing preference scores are showed in the proposed framework (Sect. 4.2.1). Preference aggregation methods such as *average (AVG)*, *least-misery (LM)*, and *most-pleasure (MP)* can be used to select the preferred channel [2,9]. However, these methods cannot always generate a fair solution for each member in a group, leading to low satisfaction.

Table 1. Results of preference aggregation methods

Methods	Ch1	Ch2	Ch3	Ch4	Ch5
AVG	18.51	15.27	14.71	12.95	17.01
LM	16.08	14.12	15.20	11.04	11.04
MP	20.00	17.20	15.20	15.12	20.00

We apply these methods to the preference table mentioned in Fig. 1 and get the results (Table 1). The AVG method selects the channels with the highest average ratings, Ch1 and Ch5 (if we consider the top two items). LM method selects Ch1 and Ch3 whereas MP method selects Ch1 and Ch5. We observe that both AVG and MP selects Ch5. Though R2 and R3 have a high preference for Ch5, R1 has a relatively low preference score. Ch5 is an unfair recommendation for R1. Note that, all the methods select Ch1 which is not a suitable selection, because none of the residents requests this channel in the current situation.

Hence, conflict resolution is situation-specific and dynamic. There is a need for a conflict resolution framework that integrates current requirements with previous usage patterns to extract preferences. The objective of conflict resolution is to enhance the residents' overall satisfaction when a conflict occurs.

3   Preliminaries and Problem Formulation

We represent the notion of *IoT service*, *IoT service event* and *IoT service request* to explain the concept of *IoT service conflict*. The definitions of IoT service, IoT service event and IoT service request have been adopted from [6].

An *IoT Service (S)*, is a tuple of $\langle S_{id}, S_{name}, F, Q \rangle$ where:

- S_{id} represents the unique service identifier (ID).
- S_{name} is the name of the service.
- F is a set of $\{f_1, f_2, ..., f_n\}$ where each f_i is a functional attribute of a service. The purpose of having a service is considered as the function of a service.
- Q is a set of $\{q_1, q_2, ..., q_m\}$ where q_j is a non-functional attribute of a service.

An *IoT Service Event (SE)* records the service state along with its user, execution time and location during the service manifestation (i.e., turn on, turn off, increase, decrease, open, close). An *IoT Service Event Sequences (SES)* is a set of $\{SE_1, SE_2, SE_3, ...SE_k\}$ where each SE_i is a service event. Occupants usually interact with IoT services for various household chores and the *previous* interactions are recorded as IoT service event sequences. An IoT service event is a tuple of $\langle SE_{id}, \{S_{id}, F, Q\}, T, L, U \rangle$ where:

- SE_{id} is the unique service event ID.
- S_{id} is a unique ID of the enacted service. F is a set of functional attributes. Q is a set of non-functional attributes.
- T is the time interval of the service consumption. T is a tuple of $\langle SET_s, SET_e \rangle$ where SET_s and SET_e represent the start time and end time of the service.
- L is the service event location and U is user who consumed the service.

An *IoT Service Request (SR)*, is an instantiation of a service and it represents a resident's *current* service requirement. An *IoT Service Request Sequences (SRS)* is a set of $\{SR_1, SR_2, SR_3, \ldots\ldots SR_n\}$ where each SR_i is an IoT service request. Residents' current service requirements are recorded as IoT service request sequences. An IoT Service Request (SR) is a tuple of $\langle SR_{id}, \{S_{id}, F, Q\}, \{SRT_s, SRT_e\}, L, U \rangle$ where:

- SR_{id} is the unique service request ID.
- S_{id} is a unique ID of the requested service. F is a functional attribute and Q is a non-functional attribute of the requested service.
- $\{SRT_s, SRT_e\}$ represent the requested service's start time and end time.
- L is the location of the service and U is the user of the service.

3.1   Formal Problem Statement

An IoT service (S) is associated with a set of functional and non-functional properties. An IoT service event (SE) illustrates a resident's previous service usage, in conjunction with time and location. IoT service event sequences (SES) record all the history of service events and preferences can be estimated from these previous events. An IoT service request (SR) captures a resident's current service usage requirement. Multiple residents' requirements are stored in service request sequences (SRS). A conflict may emerge since different residents may have different service requirements. Consequently, a conflict resolution (Res) technique is required to maximize the satisfaction of the residents. Given this information, the paper aims to identify a function $F(S, SRS, SES)$, where $Res \approx F(S, SRS, SES)$. In other words, our goal is to resolve conflict using service-related, current requirement-related and previous usage-related data.

4   Conflict Resolution Framework

The proposed conflict resolution framework has 4 modules: (i) service event sequences (a.k.a., service usage history), (ii) service request sequences, (iii) conflict detection, and (iv) conflict resolution (Fig. 2). Service usage history and service request sequences modules are described in Sect. 3. In this section, we thoroughly describe conflict detection and conflict resolution modules.

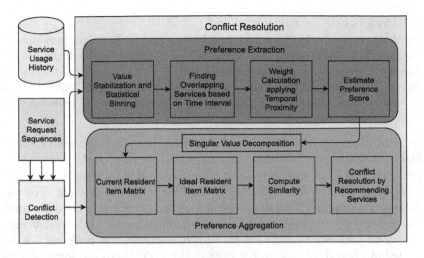

Fig. 2. IoT service conflict resolution framework.

4.1   Conflict Detection

Conflict detection is the pre-requisite of conflict resolution. An *IoT service conflict* occurs when a service cannot satisfy the requirements of multiple users at the same time and location. Conflicts are defined considering the current requirements of occupants, and these requirements are generated from the IoT service requests. Given two service requests (SR_i, SR_j), the following conditions have to be satisfied to be considered as a conflict situation.

- $L_{S_i} \simeq L_{S_j}$, meaning, two services (S_i, S_j) are executed at the same location.
- $(SRT_{s_i}, SRT_{e_i}) \cap (SRT_{s_j}, SRT_{e_j})) \neq \emptyset$, denoting that two service requests (SR_i, SR_j) are invoked at the same time and there is a temporal overlap.
- $U_{S_i} \neq U_{S_j}$, meaning, these two requests are invoked by two different users.
- $\exists Q_k \in S.Q : S_i.Q_k \neq S_j.Q_k$; there exist at least one property which is different between $S_i.Q$ and $S_j.Q$.

We adopt the conflict detection algorithm proposed in [6]. This component is not the core of our contributions; however, it produces the input for the conflict resolution module, which holds the present work's core contributions.

4.2   Conflict Resolution

Conflict resolution is conducted in two phases: (i) preference extraction and (ii) preference aggregation. Phase 1 mines previous service usage records and extracts occupants' preferences. Phase 2 aggregates all the occupants' preferences and selects the service that may give relatively high satisfaction to them.

4.2.1   Preference Extraction

In this phase, we estimate users' preferences for a service based on previous usage records. Conflict detection module outputs the name of the conflicting services and the overlapping time-period where a conflict occurs. These are the inputs of this phase along with previous service usage history. It extracts residents' service usage patterns from the previous history. Then it computes the preference score of frequently used services.

Value Stabilization and Statistical Binning. Some service event (SE) data need to go through some pre-processing steps such as *value stabilization* and *statistical binning* [17]. Several values are advertised within a short period of time for some service attributes, where only the final value is relevant. For example, browsing through TV channels before settling down at a final channel. In this work, we only consider the final settled down value while measuring the service usage preference of the residents. We compute the preference score of each attribute based on categorical values. However, there are some attributes that have numerical values. Therefore, we apply a statistical method called data binning. It takes the continuous numerical values and puts them into multiple categories. We use a dynamic programming approach to get the optimal bin [17].

Finding Overlapping Service Events. This step scans the previous history to find out all the overlapping service events (algorithm 1). The input of this algorithm is the previous service usage dataset (DB) and the conflicting time-period. All the previous events that have overlap with the given conflicting time interval are the output of this algorithm. For example, a conflict related to a TV service occurs in the living room between 20:00 and 20:30. This component searches all the TV service events which previously occurred, either partially or fully, between 20:00 and 20:30 in the living room; stores them into a list (OSE). This list contains the overlapping service events along with their timestamps.

Algorithm 1. Overlapping Service Events

Input: DB, $[s, e]$ // conflicting time-period $[s, e]$
Output: OSE // overlapping service events along with time interval
1: $TM = \emptyset, OSE = \emptyset$
    // Finding overlapping service events
2: **for each** se_i in DB **do**
3:     **for each** s_j in se_i **do**
4:         **if** $s_j.L == se_i.L$ **then**
5:             **if** $s_j.SET_s$ or $s_j.SET_e$ falls between $[s, e]$ **then**
6:                 $TM \leftarrow addTimeInterval(s_j.SET_s, s_j.SET_e)$
7:                 $OSE \leftarrow insert(s_j, TM)$
8:             **end if**
9:         **end if**
10:    **end for**
11: **end for**
12: **return** OSE

Weight Calculation Applying Temporal Proximity Technique. We use temporal proximity strategy to find out weight of the relevant events. Temporal proximity technique for evaluating the distance between time-interval data is adopted from [23]. For each service event, SE_i, we use a function f_i with respect to t to map the temporal aspect of SE_i. Event start time and end time are represented with $SE_{i_{st}}$ and $SE_{i_{et}}$, respectively. f_i is formalized in Equation (1).

$$f_i(t) = \begin{cases} 1, & t \in [SE_{i_{st}}, SE_{i_{et}}] \\ 0, & otherwise \end{cases} \tag{1}$$

We generate a set of functions $f_1, f_2, ... f_n$ corresponding to the service event instances (SE). Equation (2) calculates the temporal proximity $(temp_{prox})$ for all the overlapping events.

$$temp_{prox} = \frac{\int_{t_1}^{t_{2n}} \sum_{i=1}^{n} f_i(t)dt}{(t_{2n} - t_1).n} \tag{2}$$

Here, t_1 and t_{2n} are the first and last time information of overlapped events from OSE, and n is the number of instances. Consider the following two events of watching TV from a resident, R1. One Sunday, they watched TV between 20:00 and 21:00; another Sunday, they watched TV between 20:45 and 21:45. Using Eq. 2, the temporal proximity of these two events can be calculated as $((20:45 - 20:00)+(21:00 - 20:45) * 2 + (21:45 - 21:00))/((21:45 - 20:00) * 2 = 0.57$. Consider another scenario where a resident, R2, watched TV between 18:00 and 19:00. Another day, they watched TV between 18:10 and 19:10. The temporal proximity of these two events can be calculated as $((18:10 - 18:00) + (19:00 - 18:10) * 2 + (19:00 - 19:10))/((19:10 - 18:00) * 2) = 0.86$. Thus the latter case has more weight while calculating the preference score of watching TV service.

Estimate Preference Score. We mine out the frequent service usage records and calculate the preference score for each resident. For example, if a resident watched Discovery 6 times and Fox 4 times between 20:00 and 20:30 (fractional overlapping time is also considered while calculating frequency) on the last 10 days, then, the frequency of each channel for this resident would be $\langle \{Fox, 4\}, \{Discovery, 6\} \rangle$. Frequency (F) is formally defined in Eq. 3 and 4 [20].

$$S = (s_1, s_2, ..., s_n) : s_i \in A \tag{3}$$

$$F(a) = \sum_{i=1}^{n} [s_i = a] \tag{4}$$

where the sequence S contains elements of the set A. The frequency value $F(a)$ for an element a is defined as the number of its occurrences in the sequence S. Then, we compute the preference score (PS) for each element (a) by multiplying the frequency value and temporal proximity as follows:

$$PS = \sum_{i=1}^{n} (temp_{prox}(a) \times F(a)) \tag{5}$$

Let us consider the motivation scenario again. A conflict related to a TV service occurs between 20:00 and 20:30. We calculate the preference score of each resident for each TV channel from the previous usage record. Suppose in the last 100 days, Resident, R1, watched channel, Ch1, 19 times (frequency $= 19$) at the same time period between 20:00 and 20:30 (i.e., temporal proximity $= 1$). One time (frequency $= 1$), they watched Ch1 at the time period which partially overlaps with the current conflicting period (assume, temporal proximity $= 0.44$). Then, R1's preference score for Ch1 becomes $(19 * 1) + (1 * 0.44) = 19.44$.

4.2.2   Preference Aggregation

In this phase, we use the example from the motivation scenario 1 to illustrate preference aggregation methodology. We first create a Historical Resident Item Matrix (H) considering the highest preference score of each resident in a group. Then, we do Singular Value Decomposition (SVD) on the H matrix and construct a Current Resident Item Matrix (CRIM). CRIM deduces the features of the ideal item in latent factor space by incorporating the current requests (current requests are also represented in a matrix) [10]. After that, we define an Ideal Resident Item Matrix (IRIM) based on CRIM and represent the ideal item of the conflicting group in preference space. Finally, we can resolve conflicts by offering the ideal items (in this case, TV channels) that are more likely to be accepted by the residents.

Current Resident Item Matrix. At first, we introduce the notion of the *item set* of each group into latent space, and then we represent the current resident item matrix. Given a group of residents $G = (R_1, R_2, ..., R_{|G|})$, their item set($IS$) would be $IS = (I_1, I_2, ..., I_{|IS|}) = \bigcup_{i=1}^{|G|} \bigcup_{j=1}^{|N|}$. Here, IS represents the group's item set and each item belongs to at least one of the resident's item sets. For example, if we pick 3 items with the highest preference scores from Ch1 to Ch5 (see motivation scenario) for each resident, then, group's item set would be, $IS = (I_1 \cup I_2 \cup I_3) = \{Ch1, Ch2, Ch3, Ch5\}$ where $I_1 = (Ch1, Ch3, Ch2)$, $I_2 = (Ch1, Ch5, Ch2)$, $I_3 = (Ch5, Ch1, Ch2)$. The union operation on I_1, I_2, I_3 gives $\{Ch1, Ch2, Ch3, Ch5\}$. We create the H matrix using IS as follows:

$$H = (PS(i,j))_{|G| \times |IS|} \tag{6}$$

where $(PS(i,j))_{|G| \times |IS|}$ is the preference score of resident R_i to the $j - th$ item. For the example of the motivation scenario 1, using Eq. 6, we get:

$$H = \begin{bmatrix} 19.44 & 14.48 & 15.20 & 11.04 \\ 20.00 & 17.20 & 14.52 & 20.00 \\ 16.08 & 14.12 & 14.40 & 20.00 \end{bmatrix}$$

Preference scores of Ch1, Ch2, Ch3, and Ch5 are represented in the 1st, 2nd, 3rd and 4th columns, respectively. Ch4 is not considered since it does not belong to any resident's top-3 item list. We apply singular value decomposition (SVD) to the H matrix to produce a set of vectors corresponding to features in the matrix. We compute SVD of matrix H as follows:

$$H_{|G| \times |IS|} = A_{|G| \times |G|} D_{|G| \times |IS|} V_{|IS| \times |IS|}^T \qquad (7)$$

where A is the resident-feature matrix, D is the diagonal weight matrix, and V is the item-feature matrix. Additionally, dimentionality reduction can be achieved by low-rank matrix approximation as follows:

$$\tilde{H} = A_{|G| \times |w|} D_{|w| \times |w|} V_{|IS| \times |w|}^T$$
$$= \tilde{A} \tilde{D} \tilde{V}^T \qquad (8)$$

where $w = min\left\{ w | \frac{\sum_{k=1}^{w} D(k,k)}{\sum_{k=1}^{|G|} D(k,k)} > \alpha \right\}$, w denotes the significant features' number. Parameter α controls the degree of denoising or smoothness. When α is smaller, the smoothness becomes heavier. This process is required when there is a significant variance in the residents' preferences. We apply Eq. 7 to our running example and get the singular value decomposition of $H = ADV^T$ as:

$$A = \begin{bmatrix} -0.5278 & -0.8206 & 0.2194 \\ -0.6320 & 0.2068 & -0.7469 \\ -0.5675 & 0.5328 & 0.6277 \end{bmatrix}$$

$$D = \begin{bmatrix} 57.1127 & 0 & 0 & 0 \\ 0 & 6.8771 & 0 & 0 \\ 0 & 0 & 1.8235 & 0 \end{bmatrix}$$

$$V = \begin{bmatrix} -0.5607 & -0.4724 & -0.3176 & 0.6013 \\ -0.4644 & -0.1166 & -0.4422 & -0.7584 \\ -0.4442 & -0.2614 & 0.8385 & -0.1767 \\ -0.5221 & 0.8336 & 0.0211 & 0.1792 \end{bmatrix}$$

where $A(i,k)$ measures the preference of resident R_i to feature F_k, $D_{k,k}$ denotes the feature's importance, and the preference of item I_j to feature F_k is measured by $V_{j,k}$. For the running example, we set $\alpha = 0.97$ in Eq. 8 to denoise D to $D(1:2, 1:2)$, and we get:

$$\tilde{A} = \begin{bmatrix} -0.5278 & -0.8206 \\ -0.6320 & 0.2068 \\ -0.5675 & 0.5328 \end{bmatrix} \quad \tilde{D} = \begin{bmatrix} 57.1127 & 0 \\ 0 & 6.8771 \end{bmatrix} \quad \tilde{V} = \begin{bmatrix} -0.5607 & -0.4724 \\ -0.4644 & -0.1166 \\ -0.4442 & -0.2614 \\ -0.5221 & 0.8336 \end{bmatrix}$$

Integrating the residents' preferences in the decomposed latent space with current service requests (SR) is defined as the current resident item matrix (CRIM). We formally define CRIM for each group as:

$$CRIM = \frac{1}{|G|} \sum_{i=1}^{|G|} \sum_{j=1}^{|IS|} SR_j^i \tilde{V}(IS_j^i, 1 : w) \qquad (9)$$

where IS_j^i is the position of R_i's preferred item S_j^i in item set IS. Applying Eq. 9 to the running example[1], we get current resident item matrix as:

---

[1] R1 requests Ch3, R2 requests Ch2, R3 requests Ch5. In the $\tilde{V}$ matrix, row1, row2, row3, and row4 represent Ch1, Ch2, Ch3, and Ch5, respectively.

$$CRIM = ((1.00, 0.00, 0.00).\tilde{V}([3, 2, 4], 1 : 2) + (1.00, 0.00, 0.00).\tilde{V}([2, 3, 4], 1 : 2)$$
$$+ (1.00, 0.00, 0.00).\tilde{V}([4, 2, 3], 1 : 2))/3$$
$$= ((-0.4442, -0.2614) + (-0.4644, -0.1166) + (-0.5221, 0.8336))/3$$
$$= (-0.48, 0.15)$$

Ideal Resident Item Matrix. Given CRIM, if we want to resolve conflict (i.e., provide group-oriented optimal services), we have to figure out the most similar items to CRIM. To find similar items, we project CRIM to the first matrix H by matrix multiplication. Thus, we define ideal resident item matrix ($IRIM$) as:

$$IRIM = \tilde{A} \times \tilde{D} \times CRIM^T \tag{10}$$

$IRIM$ is the prototype of aggregated preferences in preference space and can be considered as ideal items. When a decision is made considering conflicting requirements, each element in $IRIM$ implies to what degree this resident's preference can be considered or expressed in a particular conflicting situation. Consequently, we tend to select candidate items whose preference scores are very close to the given group's $IRIM$ scores for group-oriented service. We compute the ideal resident item distance ($IRID$) to measure the similarity between the currently requested item (RI_j) and $IRIM$. We define $IRID(RI_j, IRIM)$ as:

$$IRID(RI_j, IRIM) = ||H(1 : |G|, RI_j) - IRIM||_2 \tag{11}$$

We can then choose the most preferred items with the lowest $IRID$ values as the final selections for conflict resolution considering residents are more likely to agree on the items similar to the aggregated unitary preference. Applying Eq. 10 to the running example, we get ideal resident item matrix as follows:

$$IRIM = \tilde{A} \times \tilde{D} \times CRIM^T = \begin{bmatrix} -0.5278 & -0.8206 \\ -0.6320 & 0.2068 \\ -0.5675 & 0.5328 \end{bmatrix} \times \begin{bmatrix} 57.11 & 0 \\ 0 & 6.88 \end{bmatrix} \times \begin{bmatrix} -0.48 \\ 0.15 \end{bmatrix}$$
$$= (13.623, 17.539, 16.107)^T$$

$IRIM$ is the ideal item of unitary preference in preference space for this conflicting group. The estimated items from three residents, which are more similar to $IRIM$'s corresponding elements, are better. By using Eq. 11, we get $IRID$ as:

$$IRID(RI_1, IRIM) = ||H(1 : |G|, RI_1) - IRIM||_2$$
$$= ||(19.44, 20.00, 16.08) - (13.62, 17.53, 16.10)||_2 = 6.32$$
$$IRID(RI_2, IRIM) = 2.19 \qquad IRID(RI_3, IRIM) = 3.81$$
$$IRID(RI_4, IRIM) = 4.93 \qquad IRID(RI_5, IRIM) = 5.28$$

$IRID(RI_2, IRIM)$ and $IRID(RI_3, IRIM)$ are the lowest, which means Ch2 and Ch3 are similar to the ideal resident item matrix. In other words, Ch2, Ch3 are closer to the best choice of residents. If we pick Ch2 and Ch3 as conflict resolutions, it's more likely that each resident has a relatively high satisfaction.

5   Experimental Results and Discussion

5.1   Experimental Data

We use a dataset collected from the Center for Advanced Studies in Adaptive Systems (CASAS) to evaluate the proposed conflict resolution framework [7]. We use four individual residents' service interaction records (labels HH102, HH104, HH105, HH106) and merge them to mimic the environment of multi-resident smart homes. We select these labels as they contain activities of a similar period (between June 15, 2011, and August 14, 2011). Descriptions of dataset attributes are displayed in Table 2. The dataset has "Watch_TV" activity label, however, the channel information is missing. Hence, we augment the dataset by randomly assigning channel values based on a uniform distribution. We use another dataset, namely CAMRa2011, which has 145096 ratings for 7740 movies. It has the rating records of 602 residents from 290 households [2]. Among these 290 households, 272 households have 2 residents, 14 households have 3 residents, and 4 households have 4 residents. The rating scale is [1–100]. We consider the rating score as the preference score and each movie as a TV channel to evaluate our proposed framework. Since this dataset does not have any timestamps, we randomly generate the timestamp records based on a uniform distribution.

Table 2. Description of the dataset attributes

Attributes	Description
Date	The service execution date
Time	The service execution time
Sensor	Name of the sensors such as motion sensors, light switch, light sensors, door sensors, temperature sensors
Status	ON, when the service starts, and OFF, when the service stops

5.2   Experimental Setup

In the experiments, we mainly evaluate the *preference aggregation* model. We did not find any relevant work to compare the *preference extraction* model. This paper is the first attempt to extract preferences from prior service interactions, aiming to compute preference scores for the purpose of conflict resolution. The evaluation of preference aggregation is not affected by preference extraction since all the aggregating strategies are implemented in the same settings of preference scores. The α parameter in SVD is set as 0.97 without special illustration.

5.2.1   Experimental Methods

We select three state-of-the-art preference aggregation methods used on group recommendation as baselines. They are average (AVG) strategy, least-misery (LM) strategy, and most-pleasure (MP) strategy.

5.2.2 Metrics

We recommend items for conflict resolution. Here, items refer to the values of service attributes. Two widely used group recommendation metrics are utilized for the evaluation of the proposed model. We calculate the average value of all our results on these metrics in all the conducted experiments.

Satisfaction Gain (SG). SG metric measures the satisfaction of a group to a list of recommended items [21]. $SG = \frac{1}{|G|}\sum_{j=1}^{|G|}\sum_{k=1}^{|L|} PS(j,k)$, where $|G|$ represents the group, $|L|$ denotes the recommended items, $PS(j,k)$ is the preference score of each member on item (I_k) and I_k is an adopted item. Adopted items refer to the items that have been used more than 60% times by the residents.

Harmonic (H). H metric estimates the equity of the recommended items to the group, $H = |G|/(\sum_{j=1}^{|G|} \frac{1}{\sum_{k=1}^{|L|} R(j,k)})$. If the value of harmonic metric is high, it can be said that the recommendation is fair to all members [3].

5.3 Experimental Results

5.3.1 Efficiency Results

The efficiency results are illustrated by comparing different methods and their running times. The average running times (in seconds) of each method on CASAS and CAMRa2011 datasets are displayed in Table 3. These time records do not include the runtime of the preference extraction step; they include the runtime of the preference aggregation step and conflict resolution step. AVG, LM, and MP are very efficient in terms of runtime. For each group, they directly calculate item scores from the preference table. AVG, LM, and MP methods require more time on CAMRa2011 dataset than on CASAS dataset since items are denser on CAMRa2011. Our approach takes a long time on both datasets than these methods because we compute matrix approximation for all the candidate items for each conflict situation.

Table 3. Efficiency results (average running time in seconds)

Datasets	AVG	LM	MP	Our approach
CASAS	1.05	1.39	1.26	2.52
CAMRa2011	1.53	2.24	2.34	4.36

5.3.2 Effectiveness Results

The performances of various conflict resolution strategies are evaluated in this part. The results on two metrics concerning the number of residents are shown in Fig. 3 and Fig. 4.

On SG metric, our approach performs better than other existing approaches with all sizes of groups (Fig. 3(a) and Fig. 4(a)). AVG does not always perform best because only the adopted items are considered during the computation of SG values. Items with high preference scores are defined as adopted items, meaning those items are frequently used previously. Some items will not be accepted by all the members even though they have high preference scores by other members. In this regard, AVG may lose some gains. Figure 3(b) and Fig. 4(b) report the results of different methods based on harmonic metric. Harmonic metric decreases when the group size becomes larger, denoting low fairness in larger groups. Almost all methods perform better on CAMRa2011 dataset than CASAS dataset. However, their performances worsen when the number of residents increases because it is more difficult to aggregate preferences in larger groups.

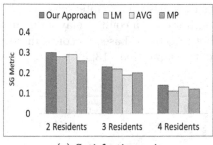

(a) Satisfaction gain

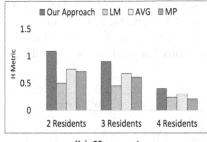

(b) Harmonic

Fig. 3. Effectiveness results on CASAS dataset.

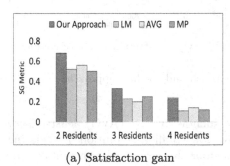

(a) Satisfaction gain

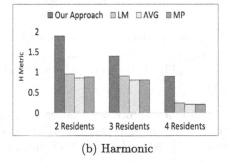

(b) Harmonic

Fig. 4. Effectiveness results on CAMRa2011 dataset.

Finally, we conduct another set of experiments to compare our approach with an existing approach, namely, Use First (UF) proposed in [15]. For this experiment, we consider TV channel data to measure satisfaction between residents. We undertake this experiment considering conflicts between 2 residents, 3 residents, and 4 residents, respectively. Figure 5 refers that the satisfaction score decreases as the number of residents increases. More residents mean more service requirements, thus creates more service conflicts—the greater number of conflicts, the lesser satisfaction scores. On one hand, in the UF approach, the user who starts watching TV first will be enjoying the TV without considering other residents' preferences. On the other hand, our approach is preemptive. Thus, it resolves conflict by selecting the TV channel that suits most users.

6   Related Work

The concepts of conflict detection and resolution are surveyed in the relevant literature. Conflicts are categorized based on three criteria: (i) source, (ii) intervenience, and (iii) solvability. Different types of sources are responsible for conflict occurrence [12]. A conflict may occur when many users try to use a resource-defined as a *resource-level conflict* [14]. A conflict may happen when several applications utilize a resource simultaneously-regarded as an *application-level conflict* [14]. A conflict may arise due to conflicting policies for a given context, known as a *policy-level conflict* [16]. Conflicts may arise due to intervenience [22]. Conflict is common in multi-occupant homes, however, a conflict may happen in single-occupant homes. For instance, a conflict may occur based on contradictory intentions like saving energy and comfort at the same time [13].

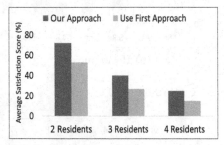

(a) Avg. satisfaction between residents   (b) Avg. satisfaction vs no. of conflicts

Fig. 5. Comparison between our approach and use first approach.

Some preference aggregation strategies such as average (AVG), least-misery (LM), and most-pleasure (MP) are used for conflict resolution in existing research [2,8,9]. However, they did not consider the service requirements of the present situation. Thus, fairness and interactions are ignored in these works. Consequently, they can not always generate a fair solution for each resident in a conflicting situation, leading to low satisfaction. Hence, there is a need for a framework that ensures fairness by integrating current interactions with preferences extracted from the past usage patterns. We use both previous usage data and current interaction data to build the conflict resolution framework.

7   Conclusion and Future Work

We propose a novel approach for conflict resolution of IoT services by combining current interactions and historical interactions. The proposed preference estimation model is developed based on the temporal proximity strategy. The framework employs a preference aggregation model based on singular value decomposition. The effectiveness of the proposed approach is tested with other existing approaches. In our future work, we will improve the conflict resolution framework by utilizing not only preferences, but also other contextual information related to the residents. Factors such as interpersonal relationship can play a vital role for conflict resolution. Meanwhile, we will test our solutions in more complicated scenarios, e.g., more experimental settings on even larger datasets.

Acknowledgement. This research was partly made possible by DP160103595 and LE180100158 grants from the Australian Research Council. The statements made herein are solely the responsibility of the authors.

References

1. Bouguettaya, A., Singh, M., Huhns, M., Sheng, Q.Z., et al.: A service computing manifesto: the next 10 years. Commun. ACM **60**(4), 64–72 (2017)
2. Cao, D., He, X., et al.: Attentive group recommendation. In: 41st International ACM SIGIR Conference on R&D in Information Retrieval, pp. 645–654 (2018)
3. Carvalho, L.A.M.C., et al.: Users' satisfaction in recommendation systems: an approach based on noncooperative games. In: ICWWW, pp. 951–958 (2013)
4. Chaki, D., Bouguettaya, A.: Fine-grained conflict detection of IoT services. In: 2020 IEEE International Conference on Services Computing (SCC), pp. 321–328 (2020)
5. Chaki, D., Bouguettaya, A.: Adaptive priority-based conflict resolution of IoT services. arXiv preprint arXiv:2107.08348 (2021)
6. Chaki, D., Bouguettaya, A., Mistry, S.: A conflict detection framework for IoT services in multi-resident smart homes. In: 2020 IEEE ICWS, pp. 224–231 (2020)
7. Cook, D.J., Crandall, A.S., Thomas, B.L., Krishnan, N.C.: Casas: a smart home in a box. Computer **46**(7), 62–69 (2012)
8. Fattah, S.M.M., Bouguettaya, A., Mistry, S.: A CP-net based qualitative composition approach for an IaaS provider. In: Hacid, H., Cellary, W., Wang, H., Paik, H.-Y., Zhou, R. (eds.) WISE 2018. LNCS, vol. 11234, pp. 151–166. Springer, Cham (2018). https://doi.org/10.1007/978-3-030-02925-8_11
9. Guo, L., Yin, H., Wang, Q., Cui, B., Huang, Z., Cui, L.: Group recommendation with latent voting mechanism. In: 2020 IEEE ICDE, pp. 121–132. IEEE (2020)
10. Hasan, H.M., et al.: A novel approach to extract important keywords from documents applying latent semantic analysis. In: 2018 KST, pp. 117–122. IEEE (2018)
11. Huang, B., Bouguettaya, A., Neiat, A.G.: Convenience-based periodic composition of IoT services. In: Pahl, C., Vukovic, M., Yin, J., Yu, Q. (eds.) ICSOC 2018. LNCS, vol. 11236, pp. 660–678. Springer, Cham (2018). https://doi.org/10.1007/978-3-030-03596-9_48
12. Ibrhim, H., Hassan, H., Nabil, E.: A conflicts' classification for IoT-based services: a comparative survey. PeerJ Comput. Sci. **7**, e480 (2021)
13. Lakhdari, A., Bouguettaya, A.: Fluid composition of intermittent IoT energy services. In: 2020 IEEE SCC, pp. 329–336. IEEE (2020)
14. Lalanda, P., Hadj, R.B., Hamon, C., Vega, G.: Conflict management in service-oriented pervasive platforms. In: 2017 IEEE SCC. IEEE (2017)
15. Lee, Y.H., Lin, F.J.: Situation awareness and conflict resolution in smart home with multiple users. In: 2019 IEEE 5th WF-IoT, pp. 852–857. IEEE (2019)
16. Miandashti, F.J., Izadi, M., et al.: An empirical approach to modeling user-system interaction conflicts in smart homes. IEEE THMS **50**(6), 573–583 (2020)

17. Mishra, P., Gudla, S.K., et al.: Alternate action recommender system using recurrent patterns of smart home users. In: 17th ACCNC, pp. 1–6. IEEE (2020)
18. Nauman, A., Qadri, Y.A., Amjad, M., Zikria, Y.B., Afzal, M.K., Kim, S.W.: Multimedia internet of things: a comprehensive survey. IEEE Access **8**, 8202–8250 (2020)
19. Nurgaliyev, K., et al.: Improved multi-user interaction in a smart environment through a preference-based conflict resolution. In: ICIE, pp. 100–107. IEEE (2017)
20. Roushan, T., Chaki, D., et al.: University course advising: overcoming the challenges using decision support system. In: 16th ICCIT, pp. 13–18. IEEE (2014)
21. Shahabi, C., Chen, Y.S.: An adaptive recommendation system without explicit acquisition of user relevance feedback. Dist. Parallel Databases **14**(2), 173–192 (2003)
22. Shahzaad, B., Bouguettaya, A., Mistry, S.: A game-theoretic drone-as-a-service composition for delivery. In: 2020 IEEE ICWS, pp. 449–453. IEEE (2020)
23. Shao, W., Salim, F.D., Song, A., Bouguettaya, A.: Clustering big spatiotemporal-interval data. IEEE Trans. Big Data **2**(3), 190–203 (2016)
24. Shin, C., Dey, A.K., Woo, W.: Mixed-initiative conflict resolution for context-aware applications. In: Proceedings of the 10th ICUC, pp. 262–271 (2008)
25. Xiao, D., et al.: A3ID: an automatic and interpretable implicit interference detection method for smart home via knowledge graph. IEEE IoT J. **7**(3), 2197–2211 (2019)

Migration-Based Service Allocation Optimization in Dynamic IoT Networks

Mengyu Sun[1]($\boxtimes$), Zhangbing Zhou[1,2]($\boxtimes$), Xiao Xue[3], and Walid Gaaloul[2]

[1] China University of Geosciences (Beijing), Beijing 100083, China
zbzhou@cugb.edu.cn
[2] TELECOM SudParis, Évry 91000, France
[3] Tianjin University, Tianjin 300350, China

Abstract. Considering the resource-hungry and capability-constraint of *Internet of Things* (*IoT*) nodes, their functionalities, which are encapsulated as containerized *IoT* services, are composed to satisfy user requests. *IoT* nodes are usually duty-cycled and energy-awareness. Therefore, *IoT* service allocation to respective *IoT* nodes should be re-calibrated on-demand through migrating certain *IoT* services from their hosted *IoT* nodes to the others, in order to satisfy the functionally diversity of requests. To solve this problem, this paper proposes a *Distributed Migration-based Service Allocation* (*DMSA*) mechanism in dynamic *IoT* networks, where a game-theoretic approach is adopted to achieve the Nash equilibrium of *IoT* service allocation optimization. Extensive experiments are conducted, and evaluation results demonstrate that our *DMSA* performs better than the state of art's techniques in reducing the response latency of requests and improving the resource utilization efficiency.

1 Introduction

The wide-deployment of *Internet of Things* (*IoT*) networks enables the request-enactment at the network edge through the functional collaboration of *IoT* nodes [1]. Leveraging the micro-service architecture, the functionalities of *IoT* nodes are encapsulated as containerized *IoT* services, and their collaboration is achieved through the composition of functionally compatible and geographically contiguous *IoT* services. Considering the resource-hungry and capability-constraint of typical *IoT* nodes, few services can be hosted by single *IoT* node, and appropriate *IoT* services should be deployed on-demand upon certain *IoT* nodes, in order to satisfy functionally diverse requests issued at a certain time duration. To prolong the network lifetime, an *IoT* node may change its state from *working* to *sleep* when its remaining resources are scarce. In this dynamic *IoT* network, the allocation of *IoT* services may be re-calibrated on-demand through migrating containerized *IoT* services from their hosted *IoT* nodes to the others. Consequently, certain requests can be satisfied properly, and the network resources should be utilized in an optimized manner.

Service allocation in dynamic *IoT* networks has been attracting wide attention, where on-demand resource re-scheduling is concerned for improving energy

© Springer Nature Switzerland AG 2021
H. Hacid et al. (Eds.): ICSOC 2021, LNCS 13121, pp. 385–399, 2021.
https://doi.org/10.1007/978-3-030-91431-8_24

efficiency and supporting latency-sensitive requests. Computational tasks are configured on the network edge or IoT nodes for optimizing task allocation in static networks through techniques like greedy-based algorithms, heuristic algorithms and reinforcement learning algorithms. These works aim to reduce large-scale data transmission on the backbone network from end devices to the remote cloud through reasonably scheduling and managing resources. However, they may hardly be adopted in dynamic IoT networks, since the network topology change due to the state switch of IoT nodes between *working* and *sleep* is not considered. Some techniques guarantee service availability through augmenting temporary work period to reduce unnecessary latency caused by excess waiting-time of non-working states [2]. They make some optimization of the node activation mode for timely responding services, but they inevitably increase the energy consumption burden of nodes and thus reduce the network lifetime. In [3], authors complement and dispatch mobile devices to alleviate resource limitations in IoT networks for completing multi-user offloading. All tasks are regarded as simple computational tasks, and they do not consider the diversity of functionalities provided by heterogeneous IoT nodes. Therefore, how to re-calibrate service allocation upon energy-aware and duty-cycle IoT nodes remains a challenge.

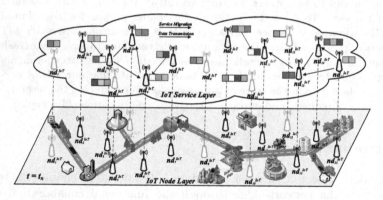

Fig. 1. The dynamic IoT network framework includes two layers: (i) the IoT node layer contains IoT nodes stayed in the *working* or *sleep* state at t_n time slot, and (ii) the IoT service layer includes containerized IoT services, which are migrated from hosting IoT nodes to the others on-demand, and composed to satisfy certain requests.

To address this challenge, we propose a migration-based service allocation mechanism for achieving requests processing with optimized latency and energy consumption as shown in Fig. 1. Our contributions are summarized as follows:

- We construct a dynamic IoT network framework, where energy-aware and duty-cycle IoT nodes are switched over time and frequent topology variations are constructed. IoT services hosted by lightweight containers upon collaborative IoT nodes are composed to satisfy requests.
- The service allocation in dynamic IoT networks is formulated as a multi-objective optimization problem, which is solved by our proposed Distributed

*M*igration-based *S*ervice *A*llocation (*DMSA*) mechanism, where a Nash equilibrium solution is derived to minimize the request latency and achieve the energy efficiency of the network.

– Extensive experiments are conducted, and evaluation results demonstrate that our *DMSA* outperforms the state of art's techniques in reducing the response latency of service requests and improving the resource utilization efficiency of *IoT* networks.

This paper is organized as follows. Section 2 presents relevant concepts and network environment, Sect. 3 introduces computation, transmission and migration models. Section 4 formulates a service allocation game and finds a Nash equilibrium solution. Section 5 evaluates the proposed mechanism experimentally. Section 6 reviews relevant techniques, and Sect. 7 concludes this work.

2 Preliminaries

2.1 Concept Definition

Definition 1 (IoT Node). *An IoT node nd^{IoT} = (*wkt, C^{wrk}, eng, f, bdw, stg, SEV, N^{cnt}*), where* wkt *is the working state,* C^{wrk} *is a set of working cycles,* eng *is the remaining energy,* f *is the computational capability,* bdw *is the bandwidth capability,* stg *is the storage capability, of* nd^{IoT}*,* SEV *is a set of services configured, and* N^{cnt} *is the maximum of instantiated containers for hosting services, by* nd^{IoT}*.*

Definition 2 (IoT Service). *An IoT service sev^{IoT} = (*dpt, ds, cyc, bdw, stg, ND^{IoT}*), where* dpt *is the brief text description,* ds *is the datasize,* cyc *is the required number of CPU cycles,* bdw *is the required bandwidth,* stg *is the required storage, of* sev^{IoT}*, and* ND^{IoT} *is a set of IoT nodes hosting* sev^{IoT}*.*

Definition 3 (Service Request). *A service request* srq = *(SEV^{srq}, lgD), where* SEV^{srq} *is a finite set of IoT services, and* lgD *is the logical dependency relations, contained by* srq*.*

2.2 Dynamic IoT Networks

An *IoT* node in dynamic *IoT* networks is duty-cycled, which works periodically and has two possible states: *working* state and *sleep* state. An *IoT* node in *working* state can implement computation, transmission and migration works, while those *IoT* nodes with *sleep* state turn off all of their functional modules except a timer to wake itself up. Assume that the *working/sleep* state switching which is also called the working cycle, of each *IoT* node, is determined once the network is deployed. For simplicity, we assume that each *IoT* node is in *working* state within a continuous temporal period which is enough for processing at least one successful computation, transmission or migration.

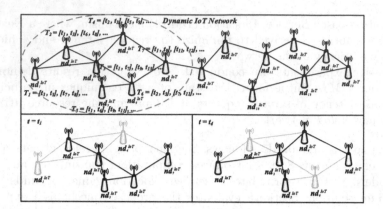

Fig. 2. The working cycle of each IoT node is represented, and hence, the network topology is changed continuously with the transformation of IoT nodes working state at different time slots ($e.g.$, $t = t_1$ and $t = t_4$ as shown in this figure).

Therefore, network topology is frequently changed in terms of the working state switching of IoT nodes, where at each moment t, there exists a dynamic IoT network which contains a set of IoT nodes with $working$ state. Hence, the network topology is evolved as time slot $T = \{t_0, t_1, \ldots, t_n, t_{n+1}, \ldots\}$ shown as Fig. 2. The initial service placement scheme is implemented, and this is not the focus of our research. The service allocation can be adjusted and scheduled by migrating certain IoT services from one IoT node to other required IoT node for efficiently accommodating service requests. Similar to many studies of computational scheduling [4], our problem is considered in a quasi-static scenario where service requests remain unchanged during the service allocation process.

3   System Model

3.1   Computation Model

The computation process represents the residence and execution for completing a certain sev_i^{IoT} on an IoT node nd_j^{IoT}. A binary variable P_i^m is denoted for representing service placement decision, where $P_i^m = 1$, if the sev_i^{IoT} is placed on nd_j^{IoT}, and $P_i^m = 0$, otherwise.

Note that f_j is the computational capacity of the IoT node, cyc_i refers to the required CPU cycles for implementing the IoT service sev_i^{IoT}, and hence, the computation latency is computed as follows:

$$L_{cmp}(sev_i^{IoT}, nd_j^{IoT}) = \frac{cyc_i}{f_j} \tag{1}$$

The power consumption of an IoT node is modelled as $P = \kappa f^2$, where κ is the effective switched capacitance depending on chip architecture. The energy consumption for executing an IoT service is computed as follows:

$$E_{cmp}(sev_i^{IoT}, nd_j^{IoT}) = L_{cmp}(sev_i^{IoT}, nd_j^{IoT}) \times P = cyc_i \times \kappa f_j^2 \tag{2}$$

3.2 Transmission Model

The transmission overhead is produced through sending and receiving data packages in the process of instantiating adjacent IoT services on physically contiguous IoT nodes. A binary variable $T_i^{j,j'}$ for transmission model is denoted, where $T_i^{j,j'} = 1$, if the data is transmitted from nd_j^{IoT} to $nd_{j'}^{IoT}$, otherwise, $T_i^{j,j'} = 0$.

The transmission latency and corresponding transmission energy consumption between sender and receiver IoT nodes for uploading service sev_i^{IoT} with data size $ds_i^{jj'}$ are represented as follows:

$$L_{trs}(sev_i^{IoT}, nd_j^{IoT}) = \frac{ds_i^{jj'}}{\gamma_{jj'}} = \frac{ds_i^{jj'}}{W \log(1 + \frac{p_j g_{jj'}}{N_0})} \tag{3}$$

$$E_{trs}(sev_i^{IoT}, nd_j^{IoT}) = p_j \times \frac{ds_i^{jj'}}{\gamma_{jj'}} = \frac{p_j \times ds_i^{jj'}}{W \log(1 + \frac{p_j g_{jj'}}{N_0})} \tag{4}$$

where the $\gamma_{jj'}$ is denoted as the transmission rate, W refers to the bandwidth of the link, $g_{jj'}$ represents the channel gain, between sender and receiver IoT nodes nd_j^{IoT} and $nd_{j'}^{IoT}$, p_j is the transmission power, and N_0 is the noise power.

3.3 Service Migration Model

Service migration represents the process of migrating container that encapsulates certain IoT service from a source IoT node to another destination IoT node, where physical properties of the destination IoT node planing to host the service should be satisfied. The service migration conditions can be expressed as follows:

$$bdw_i \leq R(bdw_{j'}) \ \& \ stg_i \leq R(stg_{j'}) \ \& \ |S_{j'}^{sev}| \leq N_{j'}^{cnt} \tag{5}$$

where Eq. (5) indicates the remaining bandwidth, remaining storage and hosting capacity, of the destination IoT node, should exceed the resources occupied by the IoT service.

We define a binary variable for service migration, where $M_i^{j,j'} = 1$, if the sev_i^{IoT} is migrated from nd_j^{IoT} to $nd_{j'}^{IoT}$, and $M_i^{j,j'} = 0$, otherwise. We further compute migration latency and energy consumption from the source IoT node to the destination IoT node shown as follows:

$$L_{mgt}(sev_i^{IoT}, nd_j^{IoT}) = \frac{stg_i}{\gamma_{jj'}} \tag{6}$$

$$E_{mgt}(sev_i^{IoT}, nd_j^{IoT}) = p_j \times \frac{stg_i}{\gamma_{jj'}} \tag{7}$$

4 Migration-Based Service Allocation Game

4.1 Problem Formulation

The service allocation decision for each IoT service sev_i^{IoT} is denoted as $a_i \in \{0, 1, \ldots, m\}$. Specifically, we have $a_i = 0$ if sev_i^{IoT} is instantiated on an initially placed IoT node, $P_i^j = 1$ and $M_i^{j,j'} = 0$. The $a_i > 0$ if sev_i^{IoT} is migrated from an IoT node to another IoT node, $P_i^j = 0$ and $M_i^{j,j'} = 1$. The $T_i^{j,j'}$ is determined by the following: (i) if no requirement of data transmission between IoT nodes nd_j^{IoT} and $nd_{j'}^{IoT}$, there is $T_i^{j,j'} = 0$; and (ii) if a certain amount of datasize is transmitted between IoT nodes nd_j^{IoT} and $nd_{j'}^{IoT}$, there is $T_i^{j,j'} = 1$. Therefore, there are four $Conditions$ including: ($Condition1$) $P_i^j = 1$, $T_i^{j,j'} = 0$, $M_i^{j,j'} = 0$; ($Condition2$) $P_i^j = 1$, $T_i^{j,j'} = 1$, $M_i^{j,j'} = 0$; ($Condition3$) $P_i^j = 0$, $T_i^{j,j'} = 0$, $M_i^{j,j'} = 1$; ($Condition4$) $P_i^j = 0$, $T_i^{j,j'} = 1$, $M_i^{j,j'} = 1$. The consumed latency and energy of executing sev_i^{IoT} are specified as follows:

$$Z^L(a_i) = \begin{cases} \frac{cyc_i}{f_j}, (a_i = 0, Condition1) \\ \frac{cyc_i}{f_j} + \frac{ds_i^{jj'}}{\gamma_{jj'}}, (a_i = 0, Condition2) \\ \frac{stg_i}{\gamma_{jj'}} + \frac{cyc_i}{f_{j'}}, (a_i > 0, Condition3) \\ \frac{ds_i^{jj'}}{\gamma_{jj'}} + \frac{stg_i}{\gamma_{jj'}} + \frac{cyc_i}{f_{j'}}, (a_i > 0, Condition4) \end{cases} \tag{8}$$

$$Z^E(a_i) = \begin{cases} cyc_i \times \kappa f_j^2, (a_i = 0, Condition1) \\ cyc_i \times \kappa f_j^2 + p_j \times \frac{ds_i^{jj'}}{\gamma_{jj'}}, (a_i = 0, Condition2) \\ p_j \times \frac{stg_i}{\gamma_{jj'}} + cyc_i \times \kappa f_{j'}^2, (a_i > 0, Condition3) \\ p_j \times \frac{ds_i^{jj'}}{\gamma_{jj'}} + p_j \times \frac{stg_i}{\gamma_{jj'}} + cyc_i \times \kappa f_{j'}^2, (a_i > 0, Condition4) \end{cases} \tag{9}$$

We denote $d \in D = \{L, E\}$ that is concerned from two dimensions for evaluating system overhead. The consumed latency and energy are normalized as efficacy factors denoted as $f^d(a_i)$ between 0 and 1 avoiding the operation of different magnitudes, which is computed as follows:

$$f^d(a_i) = \begin{cases} \frac{Z_{init}^d - Z^d(a_i)}{Z_{init}^d - Z_{min}^d}, (Z_{init}^d \neq Z_{min}^d) \\ 1, (Z_{init}^d = Z_{min}^d) \end{cases} \tag{10}$$

where Z_{init}^d and Z_{min}^d describe the consumed latency (or energy) on initial placed IoT node and the minimum latency (or energy) for all possible service allocation decisions, respectively. Leveraging linear weighted sum method, service allocation decision a_i is evaluated through considering both two dimensions, which is presented as $Z(a_i) = \sum_{d \in D} w^d \cdot f^d(a_i)$, and w^d is the weighting of $Z^d(a_i)$.

Given a service allocation decision profile $\mathbf{a} = (a_1, \ldots, a_n)$ of all service components, the service allocation problem can be modelled as a constrained optimization problem, which is formally expressed as follows:

$$min \sum_{i=1}^{n} Z(a_i) \quad \text{subject to Equation (5)} \tag{11}$$

4.2   Game Formulation

To find a decision profile that optimizes service allocation and achieves service requests in an overhead-efficient manner, a decentralized game-theoretic solution is proposed leveraging the intelligence of individuals. We denote $a_{-i} = (a_1, \ldots, a_{i-1}, a_{i+1}, \ldots, a_n)$ to represent service allocation decisions except i-th service. For the rest services' decisions a_{-i}, sev_i^{IoT} expects to select an optimal decision, for minimizing system overhead, shown as $min_{a_i \in \{0,\ldots,m\}} Z(a_i)$. We formulate this service allocation problem as a game $\Upsilon = (\mathcal{N}, \{\mathcal{A}_i\}_{i \in n}, \{Z(a_i)\}_{i \in n})$, where $\mathcal{N}$ is the set of players, $\mathcal{A}_i$ is the finite set of service allocation decisions, and $Z(a_i)$ is the system overhead function of decision $a_i \in \mathcal{A}_i$. We make efforts to research whether the game admits at least one Nash equilibrium solution.

Definition 4 (Nash equilibrium). *A service allocation decision profile $a^* = (a_1^*, \ldots, a_n^*)$ is a Nash equilibrium solution if no players can further reduce its system overhead by unilaterally changing its allocation decision, i.e. $Z_{a_{-i}^*}(a_i^*) \geq Z_{a_{-i}^*}(a_i), \forall i \in n, a_i \in \mathcal{A}_i$.*

4.3   Nash Equilibrium Existence Analysis

We discuss the existence of Nash equilibrium solution for the service allocation game, where the problem is proved as a potential game [5] defined as follows:

Definition 5 (Potential Game). *A game is a potential game if it exists a potential function $\psi(a)$, for each $i \in n$, $a_i, a_i' \in \mathcal{A}_i$ and $a_{-i} \in \Pi_{i \neq s} \mathcal{A}_s$, there is $Z_{a_{-i}}(a_i) < Z_{a_{-i}}(a_i') \Rightarrow \psi_{a_{-i}}(a_i) < \psi_{a_{-i}}(a_i')$.*

There is at least one Nash equilibrium solution in the potential game [5]. To conclude our service allocation game as a potential game, a property is shown:

Lemma 1. *Given a service allocation decision profile $a = (a_1, \ldots, a_n)$, for each service consumed system overhead $Z^d(a_i)$ thereinto $i \in n$, and available resource R_j^d of IoT node nd_j^{IoT}, a_i can be allocated to nd_j^{IoT} (denoted as $\rho_{a_i} = j$) if all the services that have been allocated on the same nd_j^{IoT}, they satisfy: $\xi_i^d(a) \triangleq \sum_{k \in \mathcal{N} \setminus \{i\}: \rho_{a_k} = j} Z^d(a_k) \leq T_i^d$ and $T_i^d = R_j^d - Z_{init}^d + f^d(a_i) \cdot (Z_{init}^d - Z_{min}^d)$.*

Proof. If a service sev_i^{IoT} is allocated to nd_j^{IoT}, available resource constraints are followed, for each $d \in D$, there is

$$\sum_{k\in\mathcal{N}:\rho_{a_k}=j} Z^d(a_k) = \sum_{k\in\mathcal{N}\backslash\{i\}:\rho_{a_k}=j} Z^d(a_k) + Z^d(a_i) \leq R_j^d$$

$$\Longrightarrow \sum_{k\in\mathcal{N}\backslash\{i\}:\rho_{a_k}=j} Z^d(a_k) \leq R_j^d - Z^d(a_i)$$

$$\Longrightarrow \sum_{k\in\mathcal{N}\backslash\{i\}:\rho_{a_k}=j} Z^d(a_k) \leq R_j^d - (Z_{init}^d - f^d(a_i)\cdot(Z_{init}^d - Z_{min}^d)) \tag{12}$$

$$\overset{i.e,}{\Longrightarrow} T_i = \sum_{d\in D} w^d \cdot \left(R_j^d - Z_{init}^d + f^d(a_i)\cdot(Z_{init}^d - Z_{min}^d)\right)$$

According to Lemma 1, we know that when a service is allocated on a certain IoT node, it is indispensable for the selected IoT node that has enough available resources. Based on Lemma 1, we show that the service allocation game is indeed a potential game, and a potential function is defined as follows:

$$\psi_{a_{-i}}(a_i) = -\sum_{i\in n}\sum_{d\in D} w^d \cdot f^d(a_i)\cdot T_i \cdot I_{\{a_i=0\}} +$$
$$\frac{1}{2}\sum_{i\in n}\sum_{j\neq i}\sum_{d\in D} w^d \cdot f^d(a_i)\cdot w^d \cdot f^d(a_j)\cdot I_{\{a_i=a_j\}}\cdot I_{\{a_i>0\}} \tag{13}$$

where $I_{\{...\}}$ is a boolean function, it is valued to 1 when the condition is true, otherwise the value of $I_{\{...\}}$ is set to 0.

Theorem 1. *The service allocation game is a potential game with the potential function as given by Eq. (13), and hence there is at least one Nash equilibrium solution.*

Proof. For each sev_i^{IoT}, two service allocation decisions a_i and a_i' are compared, we suppose that they fulfill $Z_{a_{-i}}(a_i) < Z_{a_{-i}}(a_i')$. According to the Definition 5, the potential function should be proven as $\psi_{a_{-i}}(a_i) < \psi_{a_{-i}}(a_i')$. There are the following three cases: (i) $a_i > 0$, $a_i' > 0$; (ii) $a_i = 0$, $a_i' > 0$; (iii) $a_i > 0$, $a_i' = 0$.

For case (i) $a_i > 0$, $a_i' > 0$, given $Z_{a_{-i}}(a_i) < Z_{a_{-i}}(a_i')$, there is

$$\sum_{d\in D} w^d \cdot f^d(a_i) < \sum_{d\in D} w^d \cdot f^d(a_i')$$
$$\Longrightarrow \sum_{k\neq i}\sum_{d\in D} w^d \cdot f^d(a_k)\cdot I_{\{a_k=a_i\}} < \sum_{k\neq i}\sum_{d\in D} w^d \cdot f^d(a_k)\cdot I_{\{a_k=a_i'\}} \tag{14}$$

We then know that:

$$\psi_{a_{-i}}(a_i) - \psi_{a_{-i}}(a_i') = \frac{1}{2} \sum_{d \in D} w^d \cdot f^d(a_i) \cdot \sum_{k \neq i} \sum_{d \in D} w^d \cdot f^d(a_k) \cdot I_{\{a_k = a_i\}}$$

$$- \frac{1}{2} \sum_{d \in D} w^d \cdot f^d(a_i) \cdot \sum_{k \neq i} \sum_{d \in D} w^d \cdot f^d(a_k) \cdot I_{\{a_k = a_i'\}}$$

$$= \frac{1}{2} \sum_{d \in D} w^d \cdot f^d(a_i) \cdot \sum_{k \neq i} \sum_{d \in D} [w^d \cdot f^d(a_k) \cdot I_{\{a_k = a_i\}} - w^d \cdot f^d(a_k) \cdot I_{\{a_k = a_i'\}}] < 0$$

$$\tag{15}$$

For case (ii) and case (iii), given $Z_{a_{-i}}(a_i) < Z_{a_{-i}}(a_i')$, we can also know that $\psi_{a_{-i}}(a_i) < \psi_{a_{-i}}(a_i')$, due to the space limitation, the specific proof processes are omitted. We can further infer that the service allocation game is a potential game and it implies that a Nash equilibrium is guaranteed in the game.

4.4   Distributed Migration-Based Service Allocation Algorithm

We develop a *DMSA* algorithm to find a Nash equilibrium solution of service allocation game. Given a set of *IoT* nodes with certain working cycles and initial service placement in dynamic *IoT* network, service allocation is implemented in a distributed fashion through scheduling and migrating *IoT* services upon *IoT* nodes. As presented by Algorithm 1, for each service in service requests, the latency upon different *IoT* nodes with *working* state in current network topology is estimated according to Eq. (8) (lines 1–3). When the required latency does not exceed the working cycle boundary of an *IoT* node, the *IoT* node is added to the candidate set CDT_i that can be selected to allocate certain service (lines 4–6). The decision profile is initialized through selecting a candidate *IoT* node randomly (line 8). Then, the total system overhead $\varepsilon_{a(s)}(nd_j^{IoT})$ for a certain *IoT* node nd_j^{IoT} in the current iteration s ($s = 1, 2, \ldots$) is updated (line 10). The service allocation system updates constantly, and based on the finite improvement property, each service can improve its benefit update from the current allocation decision a_i to a better decision a_i' in the iteration process. For each required service, the system overhead is updated under $a'(s)$ with the change from a_i to a_i' (lines 13–16), according to three cases as follows:

$$\mu_{a'(s)}(nd_j^{IoT}) = \begin{cases} \varepsilon_{a(s)}(nd_j^{IoT}) + \sum_{d \in D} w^d \cdot f^d(a_i), (\rho_{a_i'} = j) \\ \varepsilon_{a(s)}(nd_j^{IoT}) - \sum_{d \in D} w^d \cdot f^d(a_i), (\rho_{a_i} = j) \\ \varepsilon_{a(s)}(nd_j^{IoT}), (otherwise) \end{cases} \tag{16}$$

When the non-optimal decision is replaced, $\mu_{a'(s)}(nd_j^{IoT})$ is updated accordingly. The optimal service allocation decision that achieves the lowest system overhead for sev_i^{IoT} is found in corresponding CDT_i (line 17). If current decision a_i and optimal decision a_i' are different, sev_i^{IoT} will send a message for contenting decision update opportunity and the i-th service sev_i^{IoT} is inserted into opportunity set OPT (lines 18–19). Items in OPT compete in constant

---

Algorithm 1. *DMSA*: Distributed Migration-based Service Allocation

---

Require: $\mathcal{M}$: the set of IoT nodes; C^{wrk}: the working cycle for each IoT node; SEV^{srq}: the set of required IoT services; t: the moment in dynamic IoT network.
Ensure: X_{opt} : an optimal service allocation decision.

1: **for** each $sev_i^{IoT} \in SEV^{srq}$ **do**
2:    **for** $wkt_j = working$ **do**
3:       $Z_L(a_i) \leftarrow$ computed by Equation (8)
4:       **if** $[t, t + Z^L(a_i)] \subseteq C_j^{wrk}$ **then**
5:          $CDT_i = CDT_i \cup \{nd_j^{IoT}\}$
6:       **end if**
7:    **end for**
8:    $\rho_{init}(sev_i^{IoT}) = Random(CDT_i)$
9: **end for**
10: $\varepsilon_{a(s)}(nd_j^{IoT}) \triangleq \sum_{d \in D} \sum_{\rho_{a_i} = j} w^d \cdot f^d(a_i)$
11: $upd = 1$
12: **while** $upd = 1$ **do**
13:    **for** each $sev_i^{IoT} \in SEV^{srq}$ **do**
14:       **for** $nd_j^{IoT} \in CDT_i$ **do**
15:          $\mu_{a'(s)}(nd_j^{IoT}) \leftarrow$ computed by Equation (16)
16:       **end for**
17:       $a_i' \leftarrow$ find the optimal decision from CDT_i
18:       **if** $a_i \neq a_i'$ **then**
19:          $OPT = OPT \cup \{a_i'\}$
20:          **if** $i = Random(OPT)$ **then**
21:             $a_i = a_i'$
22:             **if** $\rho_{a_i}.SEV \cap \{sev_i^{IoT}\} = \emptyset$ **then**
23:                $\bigcup \{sev_i^{IoT} \to \rho_{a_i}\}$
24:             **end if**
25:             $OPT = OPT - \{a_i'\}$
26:          **end if**
27:       **end if**
28:       **if** $OPT = \emptyset$ **then**
29:          $upd = 0$
30:       **end if**
31:    **end for**
32: **end while**
33: $X_{opt} = (\rho_{a_1}, \ldots, \rho_{a_i}, \ldots, \rho_{a_n})$

---

iteration process, and only one service wins and obtains the opportunity to update its service allocation decision (lines *20–21*). If sev_i^{IoT} is not pre-placed on nd_j^{IoT}, sev_i^{IoT} needs to be migrated for completing optimal service allocation (lines *22–24*). Those services that do not win the opportunity cannot update their decisions, and the iteration process is stopped until no service would like to update their decisions (lines *28–30*). The optimal service allocation decision profile as a solution is found by scheduling each required IoT service upon an appropriate IoT node (line *33*).

5   Implementation and Evaluation

A prototype is implemented and network environment is constructed based on the *EdgeSim* (available at https://github.com/search?q=EdgeSim). We consider a dynamic network environment served by *M IoT* nodes, where each *IoT* node is heterogeneous and is initially configured by different types of services. Services are encapsulated by containers and the maximum number of containers is limited. The working cycle of each *IoT* node is randomly specified by one or several contiguous time slots. Specifically, service requests are generated based on a typical business process model which is publicly accessible in [6]. The parameter settings are presented at Table 1.

Table 1. Parameter settings in our experiments.

Parameter	Value	Parameter	Value
M	20–100	f_j	200–500 MHz
ds_i	1–10 MB	W	20 MHz
cyc_i	50–200 M	p_j	0.2 W
N^{cnt}	2–6	$g_{jj'}$	20^{-4}
κ	10^{-11}	N_0	10^{-8} mW

In order to verify the effectiveness and efficientness, we compare our *DMSA* mechanism with the following three state-of-the-art techniques:

- *Random-Migration Service Allocation (RMSA)* approach: An *IoT* service is migrated from a source *IoT* node to a random *IoT* node that can cover the time duration of the service and corresponding constraints are satisfied.
- *Genetic Algorithm-based Service Allocation (GASA)* approach [7]: An *IoT* services allocation solution is optimized based on the genetic algorithm, where *IoT* services are migrated from initial placed *IoT* node to the allocated *IoT* node in terms of allocation decisions.
- *Non-Migration Benchmark Service Allocation (NMBSA)* approach [4]: A benchmark service allocation game is optimized by implementing *IoT* services on a current optimal *IoT* node based on the initial placement without considering migrating services to other *IoT* nodes.

5.1   Experimental Results

Parameter Performance Comparison.

- *Number of IoT Nodes:* Fig. 3(a) and 3(b) show the comparison for the average energy consumption and the average latency of *DMSA*, *RMSA*, *GASA* and *NMBSA* with *IoT* nodes ranging from *20* to *100*, when *50* requests

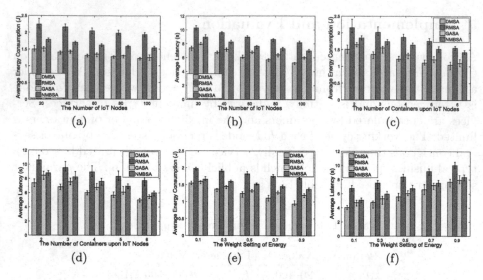

Fig. 3. Comparison for (a) average energy consumption, (b) average latency, by different number of *IoT* nodes, (c) average energy consumption, and (d) average latency, by different number of containers upon *IoT* nodes, (e) average energy consumption, and (f) average latency, by different energy-latency weighting.

are executed. To control the effect of other parameters, the number of containers upon *IoT* nodes and the energy-latency weighting are set to fixed values. These two figures show that our *DMSA* outperforms the other three approaches both on average energy consumption and average latency. In addition, with the increasing number of *IoT* nodes, available *IoT* nodes at *working* state alleviate certain number of service migration to some extent, and thus optimizing energy consumption and latency for processing service requests. When the number of *IoT* nodes reaches a certain level (*e.g.* the number of *IoT* nodes is set to *60* in our experiment), the average energy consumption and the average latency are gradually stabilized, since more service requests can be satisfied through local computation and transmission.

– *Number of Containers upon IoT Nodes:* Fig. 3(c) and 3(d) show the comparison for the average energy consumption and the average latency of four algorithms by different number of containers upon *IoT* nodes. In the dimension of energy consumption, it can be observed that our *DMSA* helps to save more energy of *IoT* nodes, and thus extending the network lifecycle. The maximum and minimum of energy consumption are labelled in the figures to record the performance fluctuating, and the average energy consumption decreases with the increasing number of containers hosted by each *IoT* node. Besides, our *DMSA* performs better than other three approaches in terms of average latency on account of the faster response of service requests. Similarly, the average latency presents a downward tendency when the number of containers upon *IoT* nodes increases. This is due to the fact that a larger number of hosted containers means an *IoT* node can configure more functional services, where both service migration and data transmission between different *IoT* nodes are optimized in the process of completing task-dependent service requests.

- *Energy-Latency Weighting:* Fig. 3(e) and 3(f) show the comparison for the average energy consumption and the average latency of *DMSA*, *RMSA*, *GASA* and *NMBSA* by different energy-latency weightings, where the energy weighting is set ranging from *0.1* to *0.9* with the increment of *0.2*. The number of *IoT* nodes is set to *60* and each of them hosts *4* containers. Other parameters are set according to Table 1. Figure 3(e) shows that, these four algorithms, regardless of which one, the lines about average energy consumption are decreasing, when the energy weighting of the objective function is increasing. Besides, our *DMSA* performs better than other three algorithms due to saving more energy. In contrary, more response latency is consumed with the increasing energy weighting as shown by Fig. 3(f). A larger energy weighting inevitably causes relatively long-time latency, since the emphasis on energy-efficient optimization brings certain compromise of response latency when optimal service allocation decision is selected.

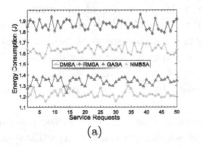 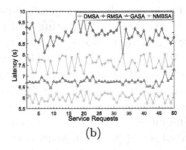

(a)   (b)

Fig. 4. Comparison for (a) energy consumption and (b) latency, of algorithms *DMSA*, *RMSA*, *GASA* and *NMBSA*, when algorithms are executed for achieving *50* requests.

Algorithm Performance Comparison. There are *50* service requests implemented for evaluating the algorithm performance. The number of *IoT* nodes in the network is set to *60*, each of them host various number of containers ranging from *2* to *6*. The weighting between energy consumption and latency is set to *0.5*. The comparison for energy consumption and latency of four algorithms including *DMSA*, *RMSA*, *GASA* and *NMBSA* are demonstrated as Fig. 4(a) and 4(b), respectively. The figures demonstrate that the optimization effect of our *DMSA* is more pronounced compared to other approaches, both in terms of energy consumption and latency. This is due to our *DMSA* is optimized through the mutual game between multiple services to generate approving service allocation decisions for enabling each service find a close-to-optimal solution. *RMSA* causes a relatively large deviation because of random migration without adequately measuring the quality of service migration destination. Although the *GASA* optimizes migration destination to some extent by the heuristic algorithm, however, as a result of the limitations of the genetic algorithm, the algorithm ability of exploring new solution space is restricted and it is easy to converge to the local optimal solution. The service migration of *NMBSA* is not considered during the implementation of service requests, so for *IoT* services placed on those *IoT* nodes at *sleep* state, normal service execution is broken, inevitably increases the energy consumption and respond latency of service requests.

6   Related Works and Comparison

Service allocation has investigated in dynamic network environments, where the sleeping/waking up and arriving/leaving behaviours of physical facilities (*e.g.* *IoT* nodes) are inevitable, which increases the complexity of network resource optimization. For a typical *IoT* model, Yu *et al.* present a minimum active time slot augmentation approach in duty-cycle wireless sensor networks for timely responding through changing established node working cycles [2]. The approach is not the fist-class citizen since the network load-balancing is disturbed by compromising the energy consumption for accelerating task processing. The mobile edge computing is proposed for offloading computational tasks [3], through planning path of mobile nodes and scheduling network resource from global perspective to complement resource limitations. In [8], Wang *et al.* extend service framework through migrating tasks from remote cloud to the network edge, where an meta reinforcement learning method is proposed to adapt dynamic task offloading environment. These existing works focus mainly on dispatching computational tasks, where a large amount of data transmission is inevitably generated, and migrating services to supply physically contiguous facilities is not considered.

The emergence of virtualization technology brings a novel fashion to share the resource of physical devices, by loading service provision and utilization of resource into lightweight virtual machines (or containers) instead of completely occupancy. Tang *et al.* implement a container migration manager prototype system [9], where a deep reinforcement learning mechanism is developed to find the optimal decision-making. In [10], authors propose an energy-efficient container migration scheme based on best-fit container placement technique for solving the overload problem in *IoT*-resource constrained network. However, current researches mainly focus on optimizing service migration to support single-structure requests, and pay little attention to complete optimal service compositions.

Consequently, we propose a migration-based service allocation mechanism to optimize efficient service allocation. Service availability and energy efficiency of *IoT* nodes is considered, *IoT* services are migrated on-demand to schedule network resources, for instantiating delay-sensitive service compositions.

7   Conclusion

This paper proposes a migration-based service allocation mechanism in dynamic *IoT* networks through migrating containerized *IoT* services from source *IoT* node to required destination, in order to re-calibrate network resource for supporting optimized service composition. A game-theoretic approach is adopted to reduce this problem as a potential game, and our *DMSA* algorithm is developed to search a Nash equilibrium solution. Evaluation results show that our approach outperforms the state-of-art's techniques for achieving close-to-optimal service allocation in terms of energy consumption and response latency.

Acknowledgment. This work was supported by the National Key R&D Program of China (Funding No. 2018YFB1402803), and by the National Natural Science Foundation of China under Grant 61772479 and 42050103.

References

1. Na, J., Zhang, H., Deng, X., Zhang, B., Ye, Z.: Accelerate personalized IoT service provision by cloud-aided edge reinforcement learning: a case study on smart lighting. In: Kafeza, E., Benatallah, B., Martinelli, F., Hacid, H., Bouguettaya, A., Motahari, H. (eds.) ICSOC 2020. LNCS, vol. 12571, pp. 69–84. Springer, Cham (2020). https://doi.org/10.1007/978-3-030-65310-1_6
2. Chen, Q., Gao, H., Cheng, S., Fang, X., Cai, Z., Li, J.: Centralized and distributed delay-bounded scheduling algorithms for multicast in duty-cycled wireless sensor networks. IEEE/ACM Trans. Netw. **25**(6), 3573–3586 (2017)
3. Gao, M., et al.: Computation offloading with instantaneous load billing for mobile edge computing. IEEE Trans. Serv. Comput. (2020). https://doi.org/10.1109/TSC.2020.2996764
4. He, Q., et al.: A game-theoretical approach for user allocation in edge computing environment. IEEE Trans. Parallel Distrib. Syst. **31**(3), 515–529 (2020)
5. Monderer, D., Shapley, L.S.: Potential games. Games Econom. Behav. **14**(1), 124–143 (1996)
6. Halima, R.B., Kallel, S., Gaaloul, W., Jmaiel, M.: Optimal cost for time-aware cloud resource allocation in business process. In: IEEE International Conference on Services Computing, pp. 314–321 (2015)
7. Wu, Q., Ishikawa, F., Zhu, Q., Xia, Y.: Energy and migration cost-aware dynamic virtual machine consolidation in heterogeneous cloud datacenters. IEEE Trans. Serv. Comput. **12**(4), 550–563 (2019)
8. Wang, J., Hu, J., Min, G., Zomaya, A.Y., Georgalas, N.: Fast adaptive task offloading in edge computing based on meta reinforcement learning. IEEE Trans. Parallel Distrib. Syst. **32**(1), 242–253 (2021)
9. Tang, Z., Zhou, X., Zhang, F., Jia, W., Zhao, W.: Migration modeling and learning algorithms for containers in fog computing. IEEE Trans. Serv. Comput. **12**(5), 712–725 (2019)
10. Chhikara, P., Tekchandani, R., Kumar, N., Obaidat, M.S.: An efficient container management scheme for resource constrained intelligent IoT devices. IEEE Internet Things J. (2020). https://doi.org/10.1109/JIOT.2020.3037181

Automated Paraphrase Generation with Over-Generation and Pruning Services

Auday Berro[1(✉)], Marcos Baez[1(✉)], Boualem Benatallah[1,2(✉)],
Khalid Benabdeslem[1(✉)], and Mohammad-Ali Yaghub Zade Fard[2(✉)]

[1] Université Claude Bernard Lyon 1, LIRIS UMR5205, Villeurbanne, France
{auday.berro,marcos-antonio.baez-gonzalez,
khalid.benabdeslem}@univ-lyon1.fr
[2] University of New South Wales, Sydney, Australia
{m.yaghoubzadehfard,b.benatallah}@unsw.edu.au

Abstract. Conversational services are emerging as a new paradigm for accessing information by simply uttering questions in natural language, posing a whole new set of challenges to the design and engineering of information systems. Training conversational services to deal with the nuances of natural language often requires collecting a high-quality and diverse set of training samples (i.e., paraphrases). Traditional approaches such as hiring an expert or crowdsourcing involve data collection processes that are often costly and time-consuming. Automated paraphrase generation is a promising cost-effective and scalable approach to generating training samples. Current automatic techniques, however, tend to specialise in specific types of lexical or syntactic variations. As a result, generated paraphrases may not perform well in relevant quality aspects such as diversity and semantic relatedness. In this paper, we follow an approach inspired by services integration to address these issues and generate paraphrases in English that are semantically relevant and diverse. We propose an **extensible** and **reusable** pipeline that combines automatic paraphrasing techniques in a two-step process that first focus on i) leveraging the strengths of multiple techniques to generate the most diverse (and possibly noisy) set of paraphrases, to then ii) address common quality issues in a separate step. Through empirical evaluations we show the benefits of the two-step process design and of combining techniques for more balancing relevance and diversity.

1 Introduction

Conversational services such as chatbots and Question/Answering (Q&A) systems are emerging as the new frontier for human-machine natural language interactions [22]. Over the last few years, thousands of domain-specific bots have been used in a variety of significant cases: office tasks, IT, healthcare, sports, e-commerce, education, and e-government services. Users can obtain responses by uttering requests in natural language, e.g., *"which company makes the iPod"* instead of browsing a Website or reading a document. The design and engineering of such services pose a whole new set of challenges [39], now concerned with how to interpret and deliver natural experiences in human language.

© Springer Nature Switzerland AG 2021
H. Hacid et al. (Eds.): ICSOC 2021, LNCS 13121, pp. 400–414, 2021.
https://doi.org/10.1007/978-3-030-91431-8_25

This shift in the interaction paradigm introduces crucial gaps in the engineering of conversational services. Especially in rapid deployment situations (e.g., the COVID-19 crisis), fast acquisition of training data is a major roadblock to their fast deployment. Requiring the acquisition of large, high-quality training samples in such situations can lead to chatbots with low-quality comprehension and less natural interaction styles [10]. However, it is essential to have a linguistically diverse utterance set to train such systems on how to interpret different variations of the same user utterance. A user request can be expressed in many different ways. For our previous example, another user may ask *"who manufactures the iPod?"*. Failing to correctly identify and process such nuances of natural language (i.e., intent matching) can have a negative impact on the effectiveness of the conversational services and, ultimately, on the user experience [20].

In this context, *paraphrasing* is an important natural language processing task that aims to reformulate a given natural language utterance into its many possible variations to generate additional training data [21]. Relying on experts to provide and annotate utterance paraphrases at scale can be costly, which has motivated research into other *utterance acquisition methods* [38]. These approaches fall into three main methods: i) *bot usage*, referring to those relying on deployed prototypes to collect utterances directly from users, ii) *crowdsourcing*, as those leveraging *crowdsourcing* to collect paraphrases at scale with non experts and iii) *automated approaches*, to those that generate paraphrases systematically. All the approaches involve trade-offs between relevant quality metrics, such as diversity, naturalness, correctness, and operational costs [38].

Automated paraphrasing offers a promising direction to address the challenge of fast acquisition of training paraphrasing sets. As we will see, current techniques focus on introducing specific *lexical* variations (e.g., synonyms substitutions) or *syntactic* variations (structural changes) on the input sentence while still maintaining semantic similarity to the original sentence [28]. Thus, important quality dimensions for assessing these techniques are semantic *relevance* and *diversity* of the resulting paraphrases [38]. While quality is a much involved concept [38], in this work we focus on these dimensions as they dictate to what extent a conversational service will interpret a relevant user request under its plausible expressions. Existing techniques, however, still fall behind in terms of quality, with the literature pointing to models often failing to produce sufficiently diverse and semantically related paraphrases [21,35].

In this paper, we follow an approach inspired by services integration to address the key challenge of automatically generating paraphrases *in English* that are semantically relevant and diverse. We propose an extensible and reusable pipeline that unifies, integrates and extends various paraphrasing services, enabling the definition of paraphrase generation pipelines. In doing so, the pipeline contributes with the design and evaluation of a two-step process, including: i) paraphrase *candidate over-generation*, leveraging specialised techniques that can be combined to generate a large number of diverse but (potentially) noisy candidate paraphrases, and ii) *candidate selection*, with services that can be incorporated to discard semantically irrelevant paraphrases and duplicates, thus filtering out low quality paraphrases. The rationale behind decoupling this process in two steps is that we can focus first on generating the most diverse possible set of candidate paraphrases by combining the variations introduced by different specialised paraphrasing services (e.g., the lexical diversity in the weak supervision technique, with the syntactical diversity of T5), to then have a dedicated step addressing the challenge of ensuring the semantic relevance of the outcome. Through an empirical evaluation we show the benefits of our pipeline approach to paraphrase generation, with combinations of paraphrasing services and automatic candidate selection leading to more balanced performance on relevance and diversity metrics. The resulting pipeline framework offers a Web interface, a Python SDK and REST APIs, that pushes paraphrasing as a service.

2   Problem Statement

We frame the problem in the context of fast acquisition of utterance paraphrase sets for training the ability of conversational AI systems to interpret natural language user requests (i.e., intent recognition task). Given an input utterance x, we can define paraphrasing as the problem of generating a set of k utterance paraphrases $Y = \{y_1, y_2, ..., y_k\}$ so that each $y \in Y$ is generated by introducing *variations* of x while keeping the same meaning [3]. Thus, the goal is to produce a *diverse* set Y while preserving *semantic* equivalence to x.

Broadly speaking, automatic paraphrasing techniques rely on approaches that aim at introducing *lexical* and *syntactic* variations. The quality of these techniques is commonly measured[1] in terms of the semantic *relevance*, denoting the extent to which the output paraphrases are similar in meaning to the input utterance, and *diversity*, as the breath and variety of paraphrases in the resulting corpus [38]. The literature on automatic paraphrasing (see Sect. 6) has seen the development of a myriad of specialised techniques, but that still struggle in addressing and balancing these important quality aspects [21,35]. For example, the diversity of a technique might be limited by the types of variations it specialises for (e.g., only lexical), and the relevance by the noise introduced in the generation process (e.g., semantically irrelevant paraphrases).

In this paper we explore, through design and empirical evaluations, an approach to paraphrase generation that aims at addressing the above limitations. The proposed automated paraphrase generation pipeline (see next section) contributes with the design and evaluation of the following key design decisions:

- Reusing and combining existing paraphrasing techniques so as to benefit from the diversity of variations in the state of the art
- Turning the generation in a two-step process that incorporates automated quality control, so as to address quality issues in automatic techniques.

---

[1] Quality aspects such as fluidity, grammatical correctness, and other dimensions explored especially in the context of crowdsourcing [38], are not addressed in this work.

3   Automated Paraphrasing Pipeline

In our approach we see existing techniques as *services* that provide the building blocks for defining paraphrase generation data-flow pipelines. The idea is that by combining services we can leverage the variations introduced by specialised techniques and produce better results. As seen in Fig. 1, the paraphrasing pipeline defines a two-step process that takes an input sentence and generates a list of semantically relevant and diverse paraphrases as output, by performing *candidate over-generation* and *candidate selection*. We organise the pipeline in these two steps to make sure the process can leverage services that both expand on paraphrase candidates while also pruning low quality ones from the final list.

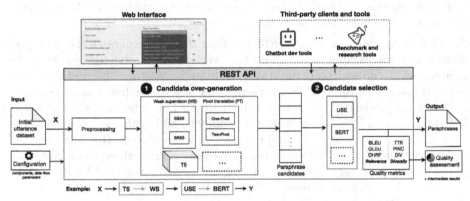

Fig. 1. Automated paraphrase generation pipeline architecture

The proposed framework supports *handcrafted* pipelines, i.e., the definition of data-flow pipelines as combinations of services. An expert can design the pipeline by selecting the services to be combined, their configuration parameters and the specific data-flow these services will describe. These complex pipelines are supported by leveraging a programmatic interface in Python, and can be enacted from a command-line client, a Web interface and REST API. To support developers, we also provide a ready-to-use pool of predefined pipelines that mirror combinations of techniques proposed in the literature. To support researchers, the pipeline comes with built-in automatic metrics (see next section) that facilitate benchmarks and ablation studies. The community can also contribute with new over-generation and candidate selection techniques by extending the current pool of services. The code and documentation is available as open source.[2] In the following the introduce the two main steps in the paraphrase generation pipeline and the type of services supported.

3.1   Candidate Over-Generation Services

Candidate over-generation refers to the use of services that can be combined to expand on the input sentence to incrementally generate a larger and more

---

[2] https://github.com/AudayBerro/automatedParaphrase.

diverse set of paraphrase candidates. The services we currently support were implemented by taking existing techniques and models, extending them to offer higher flexibility, as well as offer sensible defaults based on experimentation.

Weak Supervision. It is a learning approach that automatically creates its own training data through the use of noisy data [6,24]. We rely on weak supervision to generate candidate paraphrases from the input utterances by replacing individual words with their synonyms. To do so, we begin by performing part-of-speech (POS) tagging to identify tokens (verbs and nouns) to be replaced using *SpaCy* [11], to then select relevant synonyms from *NLTK-Wordnet*.[3] Unlike previous work [20], we adopted two complementary strategies, discussed next, for synonym selection and replacement so as to balance relatedness of the generated candidates and exploration of diverse paraphrases.

Select Best Synonym Sentence (SBSS): This strategy generates the best possible candidate paraphrases by selecting variants with the highest semantic relatedness. To do so, the paraphrase candidate is generated by replacing each selected token with the WordNet synonym that has the highest cosine similarity respecting a predefined interval threshold $[\alpha, \beta]$. Let τ be the selected token, $\mathbb{S} = \{s_1, s_2, ..., s_N\}$ its list of WordNet synonyms and ψ the selected synonym. $\forall s \in \mathbb{S} : \psi = argmax[\cos(\vec{\tau}, \vec{s})]$ and $\alpha \leq \psi \leq \beta$, where $\vec{\tau}, \vec{s}$ are the *USE* sentence embeddings using τ and s respectively. This will generate three candidate paraphrases for each sentence, one by replacing all the tokens marked VERB, one by replacing all the tokens marked NOUN and the last by replacing all the tokens marked as VERB and NOUN at the same time.

Semantically Relevant Synonym Sentences (SRSS): This strategy follows a more exploratory approach, by relaxing the selection to include *all* synonyms above the threshold α. To do so, following the *POS tagging* phase, each selected token is replaced by the Wordnet synonyms that have a cosine similarity greater than a threshold α. Let τ be the selected token, $\mathbb{S} = \{s_1, s_2, ..., s_N\}$ its list of Wordnet synonyms. $\forall s \in \mathbb{S} : if \cos(\vec{\tau}, \vec{s}) \geq \alpha \Rightarrow$ generate a candidate by replacing τ with s. For each sentence, three different lists of paraphrases will be generated, one by replacing the token marked VERB, the other by replacing the token marked NOUN and the last by replacing the token marked VERB or NOUN.

Pivot Translation. The intuition behind pivot translation is that two sentences that have the same foreign translation can be assumed to have the same meaning. Thus, paraphrases can be obtained by translating a sentence in source language S into a foreign language F and then back-translating it into S. In this component, we leverage multiple pivot languages and multiple translation engines to generate more candidate paraphrases per input sentence. Below we elaborate on two important dimensions of pivot translation:

Paraphrase System: A paraphrase system can be defined as a triple (MT_i, PL, MT_j) where a Machine Translation Engine MT_i translates a source sentence S into a pivot language PL and then Machine Translation Engine MT_j

---

[3] NLTK: https://www.nltk.org/ and Wordnet: https://wordnet.princeton.edu/.

translates the result back into S, thus generating the paraphrase [40]. When one language is used as pivot, it is called a *single-pivot* paraphrase system, and a *multi-pivot* paraphrase when it is made up of a set of single-pivot systems, each generating one candidate paraphrase. In practical terms, it is preferable to have different MTs in order to maximise the chances of getting more diverse paraphrase options [40], since each engine has its own architecture and was trained differently. In this service, we adopted a multi-pivot system as default. In terms of implementation, the pivot translation service supports online NMT services,[4] such as Google Translate, Deepl and MyMemory. The pipeline is also shipped with pre-trained NMTs like the Huggingface Marian Machine Translator [13,32]. The type of machine translator is a parameter of the pivot translation service.

Pivot-Language Level and Selection: We informed the pivot selection on the work by Zhao et al. [40], but observed in our trial runs that languages with similar grammatical structure would lead to paraphrases very similar to the source sentence, thus hurting diversity. We thus selected as sensible defaults pivot languages that are not close to the source, i.e., given the source language in English, the system selects pivot languages such as Chinese and Arabic, instead of French and Spanish. Our observation aligns with the recent work by [8] recommending the pivot languages with unrelated grammar so as to improve diversity.

This service also supports different pivot-language levels, i.e., the number of intermediate pivot languages chained to generate the paraphrases. The pipeline can be set to work with a i) *single-level* pivot, including one intermediate language (e.g., *English* → *Italian* → *English*), and a ii) *two-level* pivot, with two intermediate pivot languages (e.g., *English* → *Arabic* → *German* → *English*).

Language-Based Models (T5). Transformers are a type of neural network architecture developed to perform *Sequence Transduction*, meaning any task that transforms an input sequence to an output sequence (e.g., machine translation, text summarization). Introduced by Vaswani et al. [29], the idea is to use the *attention mechanism* to eliminate the need for Recurrent Neural Networks (RNN), and their known issues, e.g., challenges in handling long-term dependencies and the sequential nature of RNN preventing parallelisation. We include a paraphrasing service based on T5 [23], a transformer implemented by Google to perform sequence transduction. By default T5 does not perform paraphrasing, so we fine-tuned it on the Quora Question Pairs dataset [25] and Para-NMT datsets [31] to generate paraphrases, following the work of Goutham[5]. For each given input sentence the T5 model will generate a list of candidate paraphrases.

3.2 Candidate Selection Services

The use of automatic paraphrasing techniques and the emphasis on diversity in the over-generation phase can lead to potential quality issues that must be addressed. We mentioned that generated paraphrases can be semantically different from the

---

[4] Available at https://translate.google.com/, https://www.deepl.com/translator and https://mymemory.translated.net/.

[5] Paraphrase any question with T5 (2020), https://git.io/JEYQM.

input phrase (e.g., selecting wrong synonyms for the context), and duplicated paraphrases formed (e.g., techniques generating to very similar paraphrases). Hence, given a pool of noisy candidate paraphrases at this stage, the objective of the candidate selection services is to address specific issues to ensure higher quality outcomes by removing irrelevant and duplicates paraphrases. We currently support services adapted from Parikh et al. [20] that perform filtering of semantically unrelated paraphrases and de-duplication.

Let v be a vector representation of the initial utterance sentence and P its set of N-paraphrases $P = \{p_1, p_2, ..., p_N\}$. To discard irrelevant and duplicate paraphrase, we first obtain the embedding representation of v and $\forall p \in P$, and then compute the semantic similarity between the v embedding and each paraphrases embedding. We use cosine similarity for the semantic similarity, with values ranging from -1 (exact opposite) to 1 (identical) with intermediate values indicating the degree of (dis)similarity. On the cosine similarity score, we define a lower and upper thresholds for selecting semantically relevant paraphrases, borrowing the values defined by [20]. The candidate selection services then perform the following:

Filtering Out Irrelevant Paraphrases. Semantically irrelevant candidates are discarded evaluating the cosine similarity between the vector representations of the input utterance and each candidate paraphrase. We first compute the cosine similarity of the USE [7] embeddings and, in a second pass, using the cosine similarity of the BERT [4] embeddings. If the cosine score is below 0.5, for any of the two embedding models, we consider the candidate paraphrase not to be semantically related and it is filtered out. The reason for using two different models is that some semantically irrelevant candidates are not identified when filtering with USE or BERT. As we confirmed experimentally, a combination of both models achieves better performance.

Filtering Out Duplicates. Duplicate paraphrases are discarded using cosine similarity between the vector representation of the input utterance and each generated paraphrase using BERT embeddings. If the cosine score is above 0.95, we consider the candidate paraphrase to be a duplicate and it is filtered out.

We should note that to make BERT work with sentence embeddings, we tested various *pooling strategies* [34] but observed that the concatenation of the last four layers of each token embedding vector to be the most suitable for the semantic similarity task. USE already supports sentence embeddings.

4 Experimental Setup

The goal of the evaluation is to assess our approach that considers automatic paraphrase generation as a pipeline that combines specialised services in a two-step process. In this section, we describe the experimental setup for how we: (a) Investigate whether there are gains in terms of *relevance* and *diversity* of resulting paraphrases when organising the generation process in over-generation and candidate selection steps; (b) Explore the benefits of combining existing paraphrase generation techniques for *relevance* and *diversity*.

Dataset. We run our experiments on two relevant datasets. We used the *GraphQuestions* dataset [27], a benchmark paraphrasing corpora for Q&A that contains 5,166 pairs of crowdsourced paraphrases questions with their answers in English. We chose this dataset as it is representative of the type of source sentences for our paraphrasing task. For our experiments, we selected a random sample of 237 questions. We also selected the *WebQuestions* dataset [2], a Q&A dataset that uses Freebase as the knowledge base. This dataset was created by crawling questions through the Google Suggest API to then crowdsource answers on Amazon Mechanical Turk. In our experiment, we use the *devtest* dataset, containing 189 questions. Notice that we only use the *questions* for paraphrasing.

Experimental Procedure. To test the impact of our approach, we selected configurations of the pipeline based on two dimensions: (i) *process design*, with over-generation only (OG) and over-generation with candidate selection (CS) as alternatives, and (ii) *service combination*, with individual and combined services as alternatives. We used as baseline services those reported in Sect. 3.[6]

To assess the impact of the process design, we first run pipeline configurations with the individual services: weak supervision (WS), pivot translation (PT) and T5, and for each, we generated paraphrases with the two process design alternatives (OG, CS). We leveraged the evaluation metrics (presented below) to assess the impact of candidate selection on the resulting paraphrases. The results from these metrics were complemented with qualitative observations of the generated paraphrases of each configuration, for a small random sample of 20 sentences.[7]

Next, to assess the benefits of combining automatic paraphrasing techniques, we run the pipelines configurations that combined the services and compared them to the individual services. We created the sequences WS → PT and WS → T5 to combine observed properties of the underlying services. These pipelines used the same configurations for the underlying services as the individual service pipelines. The resulting paraphrased were evaluated using our reference metrics.

Evaluation Metrics. The pipeline configurations were evaluated using automatic evaluation metrics commonly used in assessing paraphrase quality [37]

To capture the **relevance** of the generated paraphrases to the input utterance, we use two different metrics. This includes the *Bi-Lingual Evaluation Understudy* (BLEU) [19], a widely adopted metric that measures the similarity between two given sentences. It considers the exact match between the reference sentence and the generated paraphrase by counting overlapping n-grams. In our tests we consider $n = 2, 3, 4$. We also incorporate *Google's BLEU* (GLEU) [33], which measures sentence-level similarity by recording first all sub-sequences of 1, 2, 3 and 4 tokens in output and target sequence (n-grams), to then calculate precision and recall based on matching n-grams. The GLEU score is then the minimum of precision and recall. For these metrics, the score for a list of resulting paraphrases is computed as the average of the individual sentence scores.

---

[6] Services configured with their default values, listed here https://bit.ly/3fHFNgB.

[7] Notice that the goal of the qualitative observation was to characterise the limitations and strengths of the techniques and not to provide a full human evaluation.

We assess the **diversity** of the generated paraphrases with n-grams metrics that capture diversity at *corpus* level, i.e., of all the candidate paraphrases for a reference sentence, and at *sentence* level, i.e., between a single candidate and the reference sentence. The *Type-Token Ration* (TTR) calculates lexical diversity at corpus level, as the rate of unique words in a candidate paraphrase to the total number of words in the candidates set. Then, *Paraphrase In N-gram Changes* (PINC) [5], computes diversity at sentence level as the percentage of n-grams that appear in the candidate sentence but not in the reference sentence. The PINC score for the candidate paraphrase set is computed as the mean of the sentence scores. *Diversity* (DIV) [14] computes diversity at corpus level by calculating n-grams changes between all the pairs in the candidate paraphrases set, rewarding the unique n-grams between each two candidates pairs. In our evaluation, the score for each experimental condition is the mean of the metric scores of all reference sentences in the given dataset.

5 Results

5.1 Impact of Two-Step Process Design

The performance of the baseline configuration pipelines for process designs with and without candidate selection is illustrated in Table 1. To properly dissect the impact of candidate selection, we start by separately analysing the impact of filtering out duplicates and semantically irrelevant paraphrases.

Table 1. Performance of over-generation services for a process design with over-generation only (OG), and over-generation and candidate selection services (CS), after removing irrelevant paraphrases ($\star$) and removing duplicates ($\dagger$)

Metric	GraphQuestions						WebQuestions					
	WS		PT		T5		WS		PT		T5	
Relevance	OG	CS*	OG	CS*	OG	CS*	OG	CS*	OG	CS*	OG	CS*
BLEU$_2$	0.494	0.497	0.451	0.511	0.403	0.407	0.572	0.577	0.350	0.446	0.406	0.411
BLEU$_3$	0.377	0.380	0.368	0.416	0.319	0.323	0.487	0.491	0.292	0.370	0.319	0.322
GLEU	0.409	0.412	0.389	0.444	0.338	0.342	0.474	0.479	0.275	0.365	0.320	0.324
Diversity	OG	CS†	OG	CS†	OG	CS†	OG	CS†	OG	CS†	OG	CS†
TTR	0.223	0.233	0.312	0.589	0.281	0.422	0.255	0.307	0.314	0.421	0.304	0.426
PINC	0.539	0.546	0.568	0.771	0.587	0.653	0.469	0.478	0.684	0.845	0.642	0.718
DIV	0.611	0.614	0.733	0.724	0.732	0.704	0.532	0.552	0.830	0.849	0.775	0.770

As seen in the table, for all over-generation services in both datasets, removing *irrelevant paraphrases* contributes to higher scores in the BLEU and GLEU metrics (CS*), indicating more relevant paraphrases as a result. Similarly, removing *duplicates* (CS†) has the effect of higher diversity, in terms of more diverse vocabulary in the resulting paraphrase corpus (TTR), as well as when comparing the generated paraphrases at a sentence level (PINC). However, this does not affect the overall (lexical and syntactical) diversity at the corpus level (DIV).

Weak Supervision	Pivot Translation	T5
Duplicate which company make the ipod	What company makes iPod? Which company makes the iPod?	Which company makes iPod? What company makes the iPod?
Relevant which company **produce** the ipod ? which company **build** the ipod which company **develop** the ipod	Which company **manufactures** ipods? **What** company **manufactures** the ipod? Which company **does** the ipod? **What** <u>kind of</u> company does an iPod?	Which company *sells* the iPod? Which company makes the iPod <u>Touch</u>? *Who makes iPod, <u>and what brand is it from</u>?* What are the <u>famous</u> companies that make iPods?
Irrelevant which company **attain** the ipod which **companionship establish** the ipod	What company does the iPod **do**? What company does the iPod **make**?	Which company makes **iPhones**? Which company creates **iPad**?

Fig. 2. Example paraphrases generated for the input sentence "which company makes the ipod?", highlighting type of variations introduced.

A close inspection of the generated paraphrases, and those filtered out, gave us insights into the strengths and limitations of the candidate selection services. The duplicate filtering is effective in removing paraphrases that result from simple lexical permutations, contractions, switching plural and singular, adding and removing articles, simple wh-question substitution, single synonym substitution in long sentences, among other basic variations. In turn, the filtering of semantically irrelevant paraphrases is good at removing those that result from significant variations of the input sentence (e.g., "What is the reason that 9/11 attacks occurred?" as a paraphrase for "find terrorist organizations involved in September 11 attacks") but less effective in identifying semantic differences resulting from subtle changes, such as replacing a word with the wrong synonym. This limitation also includes cases where important entities and concepts are replaced by synonyms (e.g., "who wrote twilight[name of book]?" as "who wrote dusk").

The above tells us that current techniques indeed suffer from quality issues, and that by designing a process that ensures candidate selection we can have higher quality paraphrases. However, there is still room for improving and developing better candidate selection services.

5.2 Characterising Over-Generation Services

The results in Table 2 helps us draw comparisons between the performance of the over-generation services (WS, PT, T5) after candidate selection[8]. For both datasets, we can see WS leading with higher scores for the relevance metrics (BLEU, GLEU) compared to PT and T5. This can be attributed to the word-level substitutions performed by WS, which introduce variations that are still close to the input sentence. For the same reason, this service can only provide lexical diversity, limiting the diversity and the characteristic of the resulting paraphrases (see Fig. 2). In terms of the type of mistakes introduced by WS, we observed the selection of wrong synonyms (due to the lack of sentence-level context) as the main reason leading to irrelevant paraphrases.

---

[8] For a qualitative comparison of the paraphrases generated by the various techniques, refer to our Appendix at https://bit.ly/3go11zU.

Table 2. Performance of pipelines featuring individual and combined over-generation services. Bold values denote best result compared to individual services, and italics second best. Gray denotes best result among individual services.

Metric	GRAPHQUESTIONS					WEBQUESTIONS				
	WS	PT	T5	WS-PT	WS-T5	WS	PT	T5	WS-PT	WS-T5
BLEU$_2$	0.490	0.275	0.294	*0.356*	*0.458*	0.580	0.216	0.267	*0.372*	*0.446*
BLEU$_3$	0.372	0.210	0.227	*0.263*	*0.344*	0.493	0.181	0.209	*0.309*	*0.369*
GLEU	0.405	0.224	0.235	*0.282*	*0.374*	0.482	0.150	0.190	*0.286*	*0.356*
TTR	0.233	0.488	0.423	*0.308*	*0.248*	0.309	0.479	0.428	*0.329*	*0.323*
PINC	0.541	0.525	0.650	**0.676**	*0.576*	0.471	0.612	0.713	**0.680**	*0.616*
DIV	0.612	0.448	0.697	**0.789**	*0.656*	0.547	0.481	0.759	**0.783**	*0.722*

On the other hand, PT scored the lowest on the relevance metrics and on all but one of the diversity metrics (TTR). The higher score on TTR (only) tells us that PT can lead to a richer vocabulary but an overall lower diversity at a corpus level. However, our observations of the resulting paraphrases showed that it can offer not only lexical but also syntactic diversity by introducing grammatical variations in the sentences. Among the limitations, we observed a higher percentage of duplicate paraphrases compared to the other services, due to the back-translation process generating paraphrases very similar to the original sentence for some language pairs. We also observed substitution of wrong synonyms and the meaning of questions getting lost in the translation process.

T5 shows a solid performance, coming second in terms of relevance metrics but featuring the highest sentence and corpus level diversity scores. A close inspection of the resulting paraphrases revealed the different ways T5 contributes to diversity (see Fig. 2 for illustrative examples). It introduces lexical diversity by replacing words with synonyms, although these tend to be fewer but context-aware and therefore significantly less noisy than WS. We also observed the richest syntactic diversity in terms of grammatical changes, summarisation of sentences (e.g., "Who makes iPod"), generalisation and extrapolation ("..and what brand is it from?"), and adding details (e.g., "iPod" with "iPod Touch"). In terms of frequent types of mistakes, the higher diversity introduced candidate sentences that, while on the same topic, are semantically different from the original.

5.3 Combining Over-Generation Services

The comparison of pipeline configurations featuring individual and combined over-generation services is shown in Table 2. For both datasets, we can see that the configurations with combined services yield the most balanced performances, improving on the weaknesses of their individual services while achieving results comparable to the best performing one. In the case of WS → PT, this resulted into paraphrases that showed improved scores in relevance metrics (BLEU, GLEU) compared to PT and on diversity metrics compared to WS and even PT (PINC, DIV). We can observe a similar trend with WS → T5.

We should note that this balanced performance was obtained with a simple combination of the over-generation services, without optimising the parameters to better combine the characteristics of each service. Tuning parameters to better leverage synergies could result in better performances.

6 Related Work

Crowdsourcing is a widely used approach to paraphrase generation [30]. In a crowdsourced process, an initial utterance, usually provided by an expert or generated using generative models or grammars [26,30], is presented as a starting point, and workers are asked to paraphrase the expression to new variations. It is a popular strategy as it can help scale the paraphrases generation efforts while reducing the costs, compared to hiring experts [15]. However, the generated paraphrases may suffer from various quality problems (e.g., cheating, semantic errors, spelling and linguistic errors, task misunderstanding) [36]. Thus, quality control in this context is an important step, typically requiring quality control tasks run with the crowd or involving experts. The costs of running such a crowdsourcing process can still be significant, depending on the configuration of the process and the task design [38].

Automated Paraphrases Generation. The literature on automated paraphrases generation covers a wide range of approaches, including probabilistic, hand-written rules and formal grammar models [9], data-driven techniques [17], machine translation techniques [12,18], and recently approaches that take advantage of contextual representations models a.k.a embeddings, BERT [7] and USE [4]. Here we provide an overview of the most prominent approaches.

Recent work has focused on approaches based on Machine Translation (MT) techniques. This includes the Rule-based Machine Translation (RBMT), Statistical Machine Translation (SMT) and Neural Machine Translation (NMT) [12,18]. SMT relies on statistical analysis of bilingual text corpora to generate paraphrases. It treats translation as a machine learning problem, applying a learning algorithm to a large parallel corpus, parallel text or bitext so that the learner is then able to translate previously unseen sentences [16]. NMT is another prominent MT approach. In its conventional form, the so called encoder-decoder approach, it encodes a whole input sentence into a fixed-length vector from which a translation will be decoded [1], enabling a sentence to be paraphrased into new variations [38]. In this work, we take these existing automatic paraphrasing techniques as the foundation, adopting three prominent techniques to conceptualise, develop and evaluate a pipeline approach to automatic paraphrase generation.

The closest to the approach presented in this paper is the work by Parikh et al. [20]. They proposed an ensemble of techniques and automatic filtering algorithms in the context of the generation of question utterances from documents. Their approach takes a document, applies extractive summarisation to identify key sentences to then apply automatic paraphrasing. For the paraphrasing, they combine the *output* of four over-generation techniques *running in parallel* that were selected for their problem so as to produce *larger number* of candidate paraphrases. They then propose a novel candidate selection algorithm that assesses the semantic relatedness of each resulting paraphrase to the source sentence by computing the cosine similarity between the vector representations of the sentences (USE and BERT). While this approach is very valuable and informs our approach, we differ and contribute in distinct ways. (i) We propose a framework that supports the definition, enactment and evaluation of automatic paraphrasing pipelines, whereas [20] leverage a specific configuration of techniques applicable to a specific problem and system. (ii) We provide and support an extensible and configurable pool of services, instead of a static set of techniques. We do adopt two general techniques (WS and PT), also present among the four in [20], but implemented them with higher configurability. We propose synonym and replacement strategies for WS, and support different paraphrasing systems, pivot language level and selection for PT. Unlike [20], we also include a language model based technique (T5). (iii) We add a layer of composition on top of a pool of available techniques. The combination of techniques allows developers and researchers to *chain* or *merge* the outcomes of techniques so maximise diversity by leveraging the variations introduced by specialised techniques – thus not limited to a specific configuration or set of techniques. A separate quality control step, while currently based on the algorithms by Parikh et al. [20], is designed to incorporate a broader set of candidate selection services. (iv) In addition to these design contributions, we also offer empirical evidence supporting these design decisions, and a framework for the exploration, development and evaluation of paraphrasing pipelines and services.

Thus, our proposed framework conceptualises the automatic paraphrase generation process in a two step, adds service composition on top of an evolving pool of services, and supports the definition, enactment and evaluation of automatic paraphrasing pipelines.

7   Discussion and Concluding Remarks

In this paper we proposed a data-flow pipeline that unifies, integrates and extends various paraphrasing services, in a two-step process. The experiments provided empirical evidence in support for the pipeline design. The two-step process enables us to first focus on leveraging the good properties of over-generation techniques to generate the most diverse set of paraphrases – even if, as we have seen, they might provide noisy output. Thus, in considering candidate selection as a whole separate problem, we are able to redirect the efforts towards solving specific quality issues, such as duplicates and semantically irrelevant paraphrases. We showed that this approach can indeed increase the relevance and diversity of the outcomes. However, we also pointed out limitations in, among others, detecting semantic changes from subtle variations. This calls for a deeper investigation into specific issues arising from automatic paraphrase generation and development of more effective candidate selection techniques to address them.

Combining over-generation services was successful in producing more balanced results. We have seen that individual techniques have different strengths, introducing distinct types of variations. We observed that combining over-generation services could lead to paraphrases with a better balance of relevance and diversity compared to using individual services. These observations were obtained even without optimising the pipelines to create better synergies between techniques.

As part of our ongoing efforts, we are integrating more over-generation and selection services, experimenting with novel pipelines, and exploring the integration of crowdsourcing for candidate generation and selection.

References

1. Bahdanau, D., Cho, K., Bengio, Y.: Neural machine translation by jointly learning to align and translate. arXiv preprint arXiv:1409.0473 (2014)
2. Berant, J., Chou, A., Frostig, R., Liang, P.: Semantic parsing on freebase from question-answer pairs. In: Proceedings of EMNLP, pp. 1533–1544 (2013)
3. Cao, Y., Wan, X.: DivGAN: towards diverse paraphrase generation via diversified generative adversarial network. In: EMNLP, pp. 2411–2421 (2020)
4. Cer, D., Yang, Y., Kong, S.Y., Hua, N., Limtiaco, N., et al.: Universal sentence encoder. arXiv preprint arXiv:1803.11175 (2018)
5. Chen, D., Dolan, W.B.: Collecting highly parallel data for paraphrase evaluation. In: Proceedings of HLT, pp. 190–200 (2011)
6. Dehghani, M., Zamani, H., Severyn, A., Kamps, J., Croft, W.B.: Neural ranking models with weak supervision. In: Proceedings of ACM SIGIR, pp. 65–74 (2017)
7. Devlin, J., Chang, M.W., Lee, K., Toutanova, K.: BERT: pre-training of deep bidirectional transformers for language understanding. arXiv:1810.04805 (2018)
8. Federmann, C., Elachqar, O., Quirk, C.: Multilingual whispers: generating paraphrases with translation. In: Proceedings of W-NUT, pp. 17–26 (2019)
9. Fujita, A., Furihata, K., Inui, K., Matsumoto, Y., Takeuchi, K.: Paraphrasing of japanese light-verb constructions based on lexical conceptual structure. In: Proceedings of MWE: Integrating Processing, pp. 9–16 (2004)
10. Höhn, S., Bongard-Blanchy, K., et al.: Heuristic evaluation of COVID-19 chatbots. In: Følstad, A. (ed.) CONVERSATIONS 2020. LNCS, vol. 12604, pp. 131–144. Springer, Cham (2021). https://doi.org/10.1007/978-3-030-68288-0_9
11. Honnibal, M., Montani, I., Van Landeghem, S., Boyd, A.: spaCy: Industrial-Strength Natural Language Processing in Python (2020). https://doi.org/10.5281/zenodo.1212303
12. Huang, S., Wu, Y., Wei, F., Luan, Z.: Dictionary-guided editing networks for paraphrase generation. In: Proceedings of AAAI, vol. 33, pp. 6546–6553 (2019)
13. Junczys-Dowmunt, M., Grundkiewicz, R., Dwojak, T., et al.: Marian: fast neural machine translation in C++. arXiv preprint arXiv:1804.00344 (2018)
14. Kang, Y., Zhang, Y., Kummerfeld, J.K., Tang, L., Mars, J.: Data collection for dialogue system: a startup perspective. In: Proceedings of HLT, vol. 3, pp. 33–40 (2018)
15. Lee, W., et al.: Effective quality assurance for data labels through crowdsourcing and domain expert collaboration. In: EDBT, pp. 646–649 (2018)
16. Lopez, A.: Statistical machine translation. CSUR 40(3), 1–49 (2008)
17. Madnani, N., Dorr, B.J.: Generating phrasal and sentential paraphrases: a survey of data-driven methods. Comput. Linguist. 36(3), 341–387 (2010)
18. Mallinson, J., Sennrich, R., Lapata, M.: Paraphrasing revisited with neural machine translation. In: Proceedings of EACL: Volume 1, Long Papers, pp. 881–893 (2017)

19. Papineni, K., Roukos, S., Ward, T., Zhu, W.J.: BLEU: a method for automatic evaluation of machine translation. In: Proceedings of ACL, pp. 311–318 (2002)
20. Parikh, S., Vohra, Q., Tiwari, M.: Automated utterance generation. arXiv preprint arXiv:2004.03484 (2020)
21. Park, S., Hwang, S.W., Chen, F., Choo, J., Ha, J.W., et al.: Paraphrase diversification using counterfactual debiasing. In: AAAI, vol. 33, pp. 6883–6891 (2019)
22. Piccolo, L.S.G., Mensio, M., Alani, H., et al.: Chasing the chatbots. In: Bodrunova, S.S. (ed.) INSCI 2018. LNCS, vol. 11551, pp. 157–169. Springer, Cham (2019). https://doi.org/10.1007/978-3-030-17705-8_14
23. Raffel, C., Shazeer, N., Roberts, A., et al.: Exploring the limits of transfer learning with a unified text-to-text transformer. arXiv preprint arXiv:1910.10683 (2019)
24. Ratner, A., Bach, S.H., Ehrenberg, H., Fries, J., Wu, S., Ré, C.: Snorkel: rapid training data creation with weak supervision. In: VLDB, vol. 11, p. 269 (2017)
25. Shankar, I., Nikhil, D., Kornel, C.: First quora dataset release: question pairs (2017). https://www.quora.com/q/quoradata/First-Quora-Dataset-Release-Question-Pairs
26. Su, Y., Awadallah, A.H., Khabsa, M., Pantel, P., Gamon, M., Encarnacion, M.: Building natural language interfaces to web APIs. In: CIKM, pp. 177–186 (2017)
27. Su, Y., et al.: On generating characteristic-rich question sets for QA evaluation. In: EMNLP, pp. 562–572 (2016)
28. Thompson, B., Post, M.: Paraphrase generation as zero-shot multilingual translation: disentangling semantic similarity from lexical and syntactic diversity. arXiv preprint arXiv:2008.04935 (2020)
29. Vaswani, A., et al.: Attention is all you need. arXiv preprint arXiv:1706.03762 (2017)
30. Wang, W.Y., Bohus, D., Kamar, E., Horvitz, E.: Crowdsourcing the acquisition of natural language corpora: Methods and observations. In: 2012 IEEE Spoken Language Technology Workshop (SLT), pp. 73–78. IEEE (2012)
31. Wieting, J., Gimpel, K.: ParaNMT-50M: pushing the limits of paraphrastic sentence embeddings with millions of machine translations. arXiv:1711.05732 (2017)
32. Wolf, T., et al.: Transformers: state-of-the-art natural language processing. In: EMNLP 2020 System Demonstration, pp. 38–45 (2020)
33. Wu, Y., Schuster, M., Chen, Z., Le, Q.V., Norouzi, M., et al.: Google's neural machine translation system: bridging the gap between human and machine translation. arXiv preprint arXiv:1609.08144 (2016)
34. Xiao, H.: BERT-as-service (2018). https://github.com/hanxiao/bert-as-service
35. Xu, Q., Zhang, J., Qu, L., Xie, L., Nock, R.: D-PAGE: diverse paraphrase generation. arXiv preprint arXiv:1808.04364 (2018)
36. Yaghoub-Zadeh-Fard, M.A., Benatallah, B., Barukh, M.C., Zamanirad, S.: A study of incorrect paraphrases in crowdsourced user utterances. In: Proceedings of NAACL-HLT, vol. 1, pp. 295–306 (2019)
37. Yaghoub-Zadeh-Fard, M.A., Benatallah, B., Casati, F., Barukh, M.C., Zamanirad, S.: Dynamic word recommendation to obtain diverse crowdsourced paraphrases of user utterances. In: Proceedings of IUI, pp. 55–66 (2020)
38. Yaghoub-Zadeh-Fard, M.A., Benatallah, B., Casati, F., Barukh, M.C., Zamanirad, S.: User utterance acquisition for training task-oriented bots: a review of challenges, techniques and opportunities. IEEE Internet Comput. 24, 30–38 (2020)
39. Yang, Q., Steinfeld, A., Rosé, C., Zimmerman, J.: Re-examining whether, why, and how human-AI interaction is uniquely difficult to design. In: CHI, pp. 1–13 (2020)
40. Zhao, S., Wang, H., Lan, X., Liu, T.: Leveraging multiple MT engines for paraphrase generation. In: Proceedings of Coling, pp. 1326–1334 (2010)

Privacy-Aware Identity Cloning Detection Based on Deep Forest

Ahmed Alharbi, Hai Dong$^{(\boxtimes)}$, Xun Yi, and Prabath Abeysekara

School of Computing Technologies, Centre for Cyber Security Research
and Innovation, RMIT University, Melbourne, Australia
{s3633361,s3693452}@student.rmit.edu.au, {hai.dong,xun.yi}@rmit.edu.au

Abstract. We propose a novel method to detect identity cloning of
social-sensor cloud service providers to prevent the detrimental outcomes
caused by identity deception. This approach leverages non-privacy-
sensitive user profile data gathered from social networks and a powerful
deep learning model to perform cloned identity detection. We evaluated
the proposed method against the state-of-the-art identity cloning detection techniques and the other popular identity deception detection models atop a real-world dataset. The results show that our method significantly outperforms these techniques/models in terms of Precision and
F1-score.

Keywords: Social-sensor cloud service provider · Identity cloning
detection · Non-privacy-sensitive user features · Deep learning

1 Introduction

Social sensing is a model that enables multiple *social-sensors*, such as humans,
smart phones and smart glasses, to gather data [25]. This sensed data, often
referred to as *social-sensor data*, can take various forms and be hosted on *social-
sensor clouds* (i.e. social networks, e.g. Twitter and Facebook) [2,3]. Examples for such social-sensor data include Facebook status messages and Twitter
posts. Social-sensor clouds are an important open medium that allows social-
sensors/social media users to express their views on issues and events [2]. Critical information can be posted, especially descriptions and pictures of accidents
or public activities [25]. Social-sensor clouds currently play an important role
in special events (e.g. sports, crimes, etc.). Thousands or even millions of posts
can be published by social-sensors (in text and/or in images), over social-sensor
clouds. This large amount of information can be summarised as *social-sensor
cloud services* (SocSen services) [2,3]. The special events can be represented
from various points of view, such as where, when and what, by using the *functional* and *non-functional* properties of SocSen services [1].

The proliferation of social-sensor clouds has drawn plenty of attackers in the
recent past. These attackers often seek to exploit the identities of *SocSen service
providers* (i.e. social media information providers) and deceive users in a variety of

© Springer Nature Switzerland AG 2021
H. Hacid et al. (Eds.): ICSOC 2021, LNCS 13121, pp. 415–430, 2021.
https://doi.org/10.1007/978-3-030-91431-8_26

ways. One such method of exploiting SocSen service providers' identities is identity cloning in which an attacker registers a fake profile using the SocSen service provider's identity information. Instances of identity cloning can be divided into two types: single-site and cross-site identity cloning [7]. The former applies to cases in which an intruder establishes a cloned persona of a SocSen service provider in the same social-sensor cloud whereas the latter refers to cases where an intruder steals a SocSen service provider's identity from another cloud. Here, we primarily focus on single-site identity cloning detection. Many identity cloning related crimes have occurred in the past few years. For instance, it has been reported that the Facebook Chief Executive Officer - Mark Zuckerberg's Facebook account has been cloned and used in financial fraud[1]. In another well-known incident, the cloned Twitter account of Russian President Vladimir Putin has attracted over 1 million followers[2].

The majority of social-sensor clouds does not support automatic detection of identity cloning. For example, Twitter and Instagram, at present, investigate identity cloning reports after obtaining a valid identity cloning report from end-users. Automated methods to detect identity cloning are currently unavailable on these platforms[3,4]. Meanwhile, the majority of existing research on cloned identity detection uses *both* privacy-sensitive and non-privacy-sensitive user profile attributes. Due to privacy limitations, third-party applications cannot access privacy-sensitive user profile attributes such as the user's full name, date of birth, or personal images available in social-sensor clouds through Application Programming Interfaces (APIs) or other means. As a result, most current techniques [13,19,20] for detecting cloned identities are potentially less applicable to third-party applications. Suppose an intruder uses a cloned account to log into the web or application of a third-party. Then, by using current techniques, this third-party will have difficulty determining with certainty whether or not the account is cloned. In contrast, non-privacy-sensitive user profile attributes, such as the user's screen name, profile definition, and so on, are often readily available to third-party applications and can be directly accessed from the APIs exposed by social networking platforms. Hence, there is an apparent need and potential for exploring approaches to detect identity cloning by utilizing only non-privacy-sensitive user profile attributes.

Moreover, the majority of current techniques detect cloned accounts using simple feature similarity [13,15,19,20]. Simple feature similarity is typically calculated using human-defined metrics such as TF-IDF-based cosine similarity or Jaro-Winkler distance [13,15,18]. *These metrics are incapable of encapsulating the semantics of a wide variety of literal strings* and focus only on character distance or word frequency. For example, the above metrics cannot quantify the

---

[1] https://www.nytimes.com/2018/04/25/technology/fake-mark-zuckerberg-facebook. html.

[2] https://www.abc.net.au/news/2018-11-29/twitter-suspends-account-imperson ating-vladimir-putin/10569064.

[3] https://help.twitter.com/en/rules-and-policies/twitter-impersonation-policy.

[4] https://help.instagram.com/446663175382270.

semantics of the terms *king* and *man* as a gender-based relationship. In such a setting, deep learning (DL), as an emerging technology, has demonstrated its overwhelming performance on executing big data processing and analytics tasks in diverse fields [22]. Nevertheless, to the best of our knowledge, using deep learning techniques to detect identity cloning remains to be explored. Therefore, we intend to fill this gap by investigating how DL could potentially be applied in the domain of identity cloning.

Though some DL models are powerful, they are not directly applicable/suitable for our application on detecting identity cloning. The reasons are two-folds. Firstly, most of the DL models require a large amount of training data. This is required to effectively learn a representation of a phenomenon associated with the underlying training dataset. Secondly, most DL models such as Deep Neural Networks (DNNs) have many hyperparameters that need to be fine-tuned as the learning performance of most DNNs depends on how well their hyperparameters are configured. This can often be a tedious and time consuming task [29]. In contrast, deep forest (DF) has a comparatively smaller number of hyperparameters that need tuning. Furthermore, the ability of DF to adaptively adjust the number of cascade levels required seems particularly an enticing feature by which the model complexity can be automatically determined. This enables DF to perform better on smaller data [29]. DF has also been shown to achieve competitive performance compared to DNNs in a variety of tasks [29].

To address the limitations in existing identity cloning approaches outlined above, we formalize the identity cloning detection task as a classification problem using multiple representations of two accounts (account pair) as input. We propose a novel approach for SocSen service provider identity cloning detection based on non-privacy-sensitive user information and a DF framework. Our main contributions can be summarized as follows:

- We propose a novel SocSen service provider identity cloning detection method for third-party applications by utilizing only non-privacy-sensitive user profile attributes accessible through social-sensor cloud APIs.
- We design multi-faceted representations to capture non-privacy-sensitive account features for effective identity cloning detection.
- We employ an effective DL model for cloned identify prediction. This is the first exploration on the application of DL in this problem setting.
- We conducted extensive experiments using a real-world dataset. The experimental results show that our method produces higher precision and F1-score compared to the state-of-the-art identity cloning detection techniques, the other machine learning-based techniques and the variants of our proposed method.

The rest of the paper is structured as follows. Section 2 reviews state-of-the-art identity cloning detection techniques. Section 3 presents the details of our proposed solution. Section 4 describes the evaluation of our proposed solution and discusses the results obtained. Section 5 concludes the paper.

2   Related Work

A significant number of techniques had been proposed in the current literature to detect spammers or fake accounts on social networks [6]. The most commonly used techniques employ behavioural profiles of users that includes features such as writing style, accounts followed, etc., to classify users as trustworthy or untrustworthy [21,27]. However, the aforementioned features used in behavioural profiles cannot detect cloned accounts accurately because an attacker attempting to clone the identities can imitate those features. This demands finding features that are able to accurately characterize account pairs to detect cloned identities. Meanwhile, other works make use of trust relationships that exist between users in social networks to detect identity cloning. The main assumption of these methods is that a fake/spammer account cannot build an arbitrary number of trusted connections with legitimate accounts in social networks [4,21]. This assumption might not hold true in the context of identity cloning since attackers can attempt to imitate the profiles of legitimate. As a result, cloned accounts can build trust connections with legitimate accounts easier than other types of fake identities.

A few approaches have been proposed in the context of social media to detect identity cloning [5,6]. Kontaxis et al. [20] proposed a technique that can be used by social medial users to determine if they have been a victim of identity cloning. Devmane and Rana [13] devised a method to detect identity cloning in both single-site and cross-site contexts. To detect cloned profiles, the aforementioned approach searches for similar user-profiles and then computes a similarity index. Jin et al. [18], in the meantime, analysed and characterised identity cloning attacks' behaviours. They introduced two schemes for detecting suspicious profiles based on profile similarity. Kamhoua et al. [19] overcame identity cloning attacks by comparing user profiles across different social networks. They determined profile similarity using a hybrid string-matching similarity algorithm. Goga et al. [15] proposed a method for detecting impersonation attacks. The proposed method determines whether two accounts are being used by the same person or an imposter. It first compares the behaviour and reputations of impersonation accounts and then detects impersonation attacks using a binary classifier trained using a Support Vector Machine (SVM).

The majority of existing research [13,19,20] detects identity cloning using both privacy-sensitive and non-privacy-sensitive user profile attributes. Many third-party applications and websites authenticate users from their social networking profiles. They are unable to access privacy-sensitive user profile attributes through social network APIs. Therefore, prior approaches may not be applicable to these third parties. In addition, the majority of the existing approaches [13,15,18–20] are built on simple feature similarity models or classic machine learning models. DL technologies have shown their superior performance on processing and analyzing big data in many application domains [22]. To the best of our knowledge, there has been no attempt of applying DL technologies for identity cloning detection.

3 Methodology

In this section, we present a detailed overview of the proposed approach and its key components.

3.1 Overview

The proposed methodology is presented in Fig. 1, which consists of four major components, namely, 1) graph construction (GC) which aims to build an undirected graph from a given collection of social media accounts to identify the pairs of similar accounts; 2) an account pair feature representation, which extracts two categories of non-privacy-sensitive user features for each paired account; 3) a multi-view account representation, which constructs a representation for each account in an account pair from multiple non-privacy-sensitive perspectives; 4) a DF based prediction model, which predicts whether or not each account pair are an account and its replica using a concatenated representation of the account pair feature and multi-view account representations. We discuss these four components in detail in the following sections.

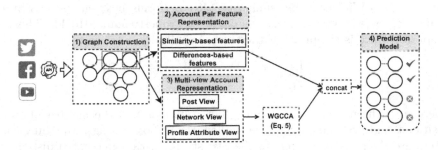

Fig. 1. The workflow of our proposed methodology

3.2 Graph Construction

Given a set of social media accounts and their profile information, we aim to construct an undirected graph, where each pair of mutually connected nodes indicate the possibility that an account is the clone of the other. A cloned account is more likely to share the same screen name or username with the original account. Therefore, this graph connects nodes based on the screen name and username similarity. We connect two nodes with an edge only if the similarity score of the screen names or usernames of the two corresponding accounts is over a threshold δ. This graph can locate almost all possible account pairs (i.e. a cloned account and its victim) in the dataset while generating fewer false positives with an appropriate δ value. We elaborate as well as make recommendations on the process of determining an appropriate value of δ in the forthcoming experiments.

3.3   Account Pair Feature Representation

Once the undirected graph is constructed, we then extract non-privacy-sensitive user features for each pair of connected accounts. The extracted features consist of two categories of non-privacy-sensitive user features in the form of 1) similarity-based features and 2) difference -based features that can differentiate a cloned account from a legitimate account. We describe each of these feature(s) in detail in the following subsections.

Similarity-Based Features: These features are used to analyse the textual similarity between the non-privacy-sensitive attributes of the profiles that belong to a pair of accounts, such as username, screen name, description and location. Each feature is assigned a value from the range $[0, 1]$. For example, when the username similarity feature is 1, this indicates the pair of accounts compared has 100% textual similarity on the corresponding feature. In contrast, 0 indicates that the pair of accounts does not have any textual similarity on the given feature. We introduce the semantics of calculating the aforementioned textual similarity in more detail below.

Username, Screen Name and Location Similarity: Previous studies have shown that the Jaro-Winkler string similarity (JS) performs best on the attributes' named values (e.g., username, screen name, or property name) [10,11]. Thus, we adopt JS, which is computed as the textual similarity between two strings as:

$$JS = \begin{cases} \frac{1}{3} \cdot \frac{m}{|S1|} + \frac{m}{|S2|} + \frac{m-t}{|m|} & if : m > 0 \\ 0 & : otherwise \end{cases} \quad (1)$$

where m is the number of matching characters, t is half the number of transpositions, and $|S1|$ and $|S2|$ are the lengths of both strings. Matching characters are the same characters in the two strings with a maximum distance of $w = \frac{max(|S1|,|S2|)}{2}$. JS uses a prefix scale p, which provides a more specific result when the two strings have a common prefix up to a specified maximum length l.

$$Jaro - Winkler = JS + p + l * (1 - JS) \quad (2)$$

Description Similarity: Users usually provide a short textual description of themselves in their social media profiles, which commonly shows their associations to organizations, occupations and interests. Therefore, we calculate the description similarity of the account pair. We first pre-process the textual description by converting to lowercase, removing stop words and punctuation marks. We then use term frequency-inverse document frequency (TF-IDF) to convert the text description into vectors. We then used the cosine similarity to find the similarity between two account descriptions as:

$$\cos(\theta) = \frac{\mathbf{A} \cdot \mathbf{B}}{||\mathbf{A}|| \cdot ||\mathbf{B}||} \quad (3)$$

where $\mathbf{A}$ and $\mathbf{B}$ are the TF-IDF scores of two accounts.

Table 1. account pair feature representation and their descriptions

Feature category	No.	Features	Description
Similarity-based features	1	Username similarity	Username similarity between the account pair
	2	Screen name similarity	Screen name similarity between the account pair
	3	Location similarity	Location similarity between the account pair
	4	Description similarity	Description similarity between the account pair
	5	Followers Ratio	The ratio of the number of followers between the account pair.
Differences-based features	6	Followers differences	The number of followers difference between the account pair
	7	Friends differences	The number of friends difference between the account pair
	8	Tweets differences	The number of tweets difference between the account pair
	9	Favorite differences	The number of favorite difference between the account pair
	10	Account age differences	The account age difference between the account pair

Differences-Based Features: These features are used to analyse the differences between the general profile attributes (e.g. the post count, friends count, etc.) that characterize individual accounts. We assume that the differences between the general profile attributes of a cloned account and its victim account will be higher than the other account pair. For example, a higher degree of differences between the number of tweets can indicate an avatar form of a pair of cloned and victim accounts.

Altogether, an account pair feature representation consists of 10 features across the two aforementioned categories, which are summarized in Table 1.

3.4 Multi-view Account Representation

Our objective is to construct a multi-view account representation for each account in the account pair by joining multiple views that correspond to the account's non-privacy-sensitive profile attributes. We utilise the post, network, and profile attribute views associated with the user account. These views can accurately reflect a user account, which attackers are highly likely to mimic. Then, a single embedding is learned from these views using weighted generalized canonical correlation analysis (wGCCA) [17]. Each view is discussed in detail in the following subsections.

Post View: We obtain the pre-trained language representation for each account in the account pair to generate the post view. We use the Sentence-BERT (SBERT) [23] to obtain the user posts' vector-space representations. SBERT is an adjustment of the pre-trained bidirectional encoder representations from the transformers network (BERT) [12]. These pre-trained models are extremely efficient at extracting the text representation associated with any given task such as question answering, classification, etc. [12]. SBERT generates semantically meaningful sentence representations using Siamese and Triplet network structures. Similar to BERT models, SBERT models are also based on transformer networks [12]. Additionally, SBERT performs a pooling operation on the output of BERT in order to obtain a sentence representation with a fixed length. Typically, the sentence representation is computed by calculating the mean of all output vectors. We collect n posts that are publicly accessible for a given user account u, denoted as

$T = (t_1, ..., t_n)$. Each post $t_i (i \in 1, .., n)$ is represented by the language representation that is pre-trained. Each post t_i is tokenized into a single word w_i and then marked with special tokens called [CLS] and [SEP] to indicate the start and the end of a sentence, respectively. Then, a set of tokenized words is passed through BERT to embed fixed-sized sentences. Then, in the pooling layer, the t representations are generated using mean aggregation. The mean aggregation is known to perform better than max aggregation or CLS aggregation [23]. Each post's output is 768 dimensions, which is BERT's default setting. Finally, we aggregate all posts representation for the user account by computing the mean of all the posts' representation T.

Network View: A network of accounts is a collection of users who interact in a variety of ways, such as friending, retweeting, and so on, within a social network, which can be represented as a graph. If one of the users in the social network interacts (i.e. follow, retweet, etc.) with another, an edge between them will appear in the graph. We consider two types of interaction networks: follower and friend networks. In the follower network, two users will be connected when a user follows a specific user (e.g. a friend or celebrity). In the friend network, two users will be connected when a user gets followed by another user. Inspired by the graph representation's success, we use the Node2Vec [16] to learn the network representation, or, in other words, the network view of an account. Node2vec is a widely used unsupervised graph representational learning technique. It utilises a biased random walk method to maximise the log-probability between a node's neighbours, or in other words, accounts with an edge between them.

Profile Attribute View: We obtain 12 non-privacy-sensitive user attributes to create an attribute vector to construct the profile attribute view of an account. These non-privacy-sensitive user attributes can be used to categorise an account's actions and credibility. For instance, the number of tweets may indicate a user's activity, while the number of followers may indicate a user's credibility. Table 2 shows the 12 non-privacy-sensitive user attributes.

3.4.1   Embedding Learning Model

The proposed views in the previous section can include some helpful information that can be used to detect cloned accounts. Using each view separately can cause a loss of valuable knowledge in comparison to using them in tandem. A simple and naive technique is to concatenate all the proposed views together. However, this concatenation might cause over-fitting on small training datasets because of the resulting larger account representation or possibility of the resulting model ignoring the meaningful knowledge contained in the proposed views, as each view has unique statistical properties. Therefore, we employ generalized canonical correlation analysis (GCCA) which is a technique to learn single embedding from multiple views. GCCA has many variants, for example, [9,24,26]. In our proposed approach, we use Carroll [9]'s GCCA as it is based on a computationally simple and efficient eigenequation. The GCCA objective can be formulated as follows:

Table 2. Features that profile attribute view contains and their descriptions

No.	Features	Description
1	Friend (following) count	The number of accounts that the user follows
2	Follower count	The number of followers that the account has
3	Favorite count	The number of tweets liked by the account
4	Tweet count	The number of tweets (including retweets) posted by the account
5	List count	The number of public lists of which the account is a member
6	Account age	The account's lifetime to date, measured in months from the date of registration
7	Profile background	A binary value indicating whether or not the account has changed the background or theme of their profile
8	Profile image	A binary value indicating whether the account has not uploaded a profile image and instead uses the default image
9	Has profile description	A binary value indicating whether or not the account has added a description to their profile
10	Profile URL	A binary value indicating whether or not the account has added a URL to their profile
11	Screen name length	The length of the screen name of the account
12	Description length	The length of the description of the account

$$arg \min_{G_i, U_i} \sum_i \parallel G - X_i U_i \parallel_F^2 \qquad s.t. G'G = I \tag{4}$$

where $X_i \in \mathbb{R}^{n \times d_i}$ corresponds to the data matrix of the ith view, $G \in \mathbb{R}^{n \times k}$ contains all learned account embedding and $U_i \in \mathbb{R}^{d_i \times k}$ maps from the latent space to the observed view i. However, each view might have more or less knowl edge for detecting identity cloning. As a result, we employ weighted GCCA (wGCCA). wGCCA adds weight w_i for each view i in Eq. 4 as follows:

$$arg \min_{G_i, U_i} w_i \sum_i \parallel G - X_i U_i \parallel_F^2 \ s.t. G'G = I, w_i \geq 0 \tag{5}$$

where w_i represents the weight of a view and this weight shows the view's importance. The columns of G are the eigenvectors of $\sum_i w_i X_i (X_i'X_i)^{-1} X_i'$ and the solution for $U_i = (X_i'X_i)^{-1} X_i'G$.

3.5 Prediction Model

The final accounts pair representation A_i is the concatenation of the account pair feature representation and the multi-view account representation.

$$y = classifier(concat(F, wgcca)) \tag{6}$$

where F is represented as a feature vector $F (\in \mathbb{R}^{10})$ where each feature F_i in F is indicative of an augmented feature derived based on the similarity or difference of a non-privacy-sensitive user profile feature and $wgcca$ is the embeddings learned from the multi-view account representation.

We employ DF to learn whether or not the account pair contains a cloned account and its corresponding victim account. The DF is a decision tree ensemble framework that can perform well even with relatively fewer data, and more

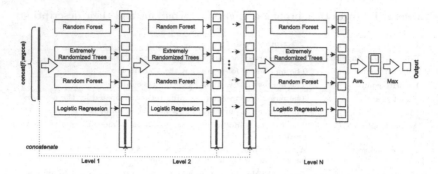

Fig. 2. The architecture of the proposed deep forest model

importantly, has much fewer hyperparameters. The DF employs a cascade structure where each level of the cascade takes in a feature vector concatenated by its previous level and outputs its generating result to the next level of the cascade [29].

Diversity is highly recommended for ensemble construction [28]. Therefore, the proposed DF model uses two types of random forests (RF), extremely randomized trees (ERT) and logistic regression (LR). Figure 2 shows the overall architecture of the proposed DF, which is of self-adapting depth with multiple levels. The RF model is an ensemble classifier which utilizes multiple decision trees at training time and uses averaging to get better prediction performance [8]. The ERT is similar to the RF model; however, they differ in the way splits are computed. The RF splits on trees while the ERT splits randomly [14].

In the first level of the DF architecture, each model will take the $concat(F, wgcca)$ feature vector as an input and produce a class vector as output. This class vector is then concatenated with the $concat(F, wgcca)$ feature vector to be fed into the next level of the cascade. Herein, we aim to predict a binary value y indicating whether an account pair contains a cloned account and its victim. Therefore, each of the four models (2 RFs, ERT, LR) produces a binary output. Thus, the input of the next level of the cascade is composed of $8 (= 2 \times 4)$ augmented features. k-fold cross-validation ($k = 5$) is applied to generate the class vector. This will result in $k - 1$ class vectors that are then averaged to produce the final class vector as augmented features for the next level of the cascade. After expanding one more level, the prediction performance of the whole cascade is estimated by the validation set. The cascade growth is automatically terminated if there is no significant increase in the performance of class prediction. Therefore, the number of cascade levels is said to be self-determined [29].

4   Evaluation

A set of experiments was performed to evaluate and analyse the effectiveness of our proposed solution against existing state-of-the-art identity cloning detection approaches. In addition, we also evaluated several candidate machine learning models to assess their performance in this particular problem context and justify the use of DF as the cloned identity predictor. All machine learning models were run for 10 rounds with different random permutations of the data. The results were presented as an average computed across the all rounds of experiments, together with standard deviation.

4.1 Dataset

To the best of our knowledge, there are no readily available and publicly accessible datasets for evaluating identity cloning detection in the context of social networks. Most existing works, albeit limited, have used simulated data to evaluate their proposed techniques. We, therefore, developed a dataset via authorised non-privacy sensitive user profile attributes fetched out of Twitter APIs[5] in order to evaluate our proposed method. We collected 4,030 public Twitter accounts (2,015 cloned accounts and their corresponding victim accounts) from[6]. We also randomly collected 20,152 public Twitter accounts to add noises to the dataset. Finally, we have 35,122 public Twitter accounts in total. The resulting dataset was randomly split with an 80:20 training-to-split ratio in order to derive training and test datasets.

4.2 Other Approaches Evaluated

We compared and evaluated our proposed approach against the following existing state-of-the-art identity cloning detection approaches [6] and variants of the proposed approach.

Basic Profile Similarity (BPS) [18]: This technique determines the degree to which a given user profile and its suspected cloned account share public attributes and common friends.

Devmane and Rana [13]: This technique compares names, education, profile photos, places lived, birthdate, workplace, gender, photos added to the profile, and number of friends/connections.

Goga et al. [15]: This method compares profile similarity, social neighbourhood overlap, time overlap accounts, and account differences. It then trains an SVM classifier using a linear kernel to determine whether or not a given account has been impersonated.

Kamhoua et al. [19]: This method compares friend list similarity and calculates attribute similarity using a modified similarity metric called Fuzzy-Sim. To calculate the attribute similarity, it considers the following attributes: name, education, city, age, workplace, gender, and friend list. We used the same threshold values recommended by the original work (0.565 and 0.575) for the Fuzzy-Sim.

---

[5] https://developer.twitter.com/en/docs.

[6] https://impersonation.mpi-sws.org/.

Table 3. Hyperparameter values used for the candidate machine learning and DL algorithms

Model	Parameter
ADA	Estimators = 50
CNN	10 layers, filters = 64, kernel size = 2, pool size = 2
DNN	5 layers (250, 200, 50, 1)
KNN	Neighbors = 5
MLP	Solver = adam, activation = relu
RF	Estimators = 50

Zheng et al. [27]: This is a typical model for detecting spammers. It makes use of 18 features, some of which are profile-related, such as the number of followers, and others of which are content-related, such as the average number of hashtags. It then trains an SVM classifier using a Radial Basis Function (RBF) kernel to determine whether an account belongs to a spammer or not.

GC ($\delta = 0.8$): This is a variant of our proposed solution that only feeds the results of the graph construction into the DF model.

Account: This is also a variant of our proposed solution that only feeds the account pair feature representation into the DF model.

WGCCA: This is also a variant of our proposed solution that only feeds the multi-view account representation into the DF model.

We further compared our proposed DF model against the following machine learning and DL models in order to justify the use of the DF as the identity cloning predictor. These models are broadly applied in the context of social media identity deception detection [6]. These models are, namely, Adaboost (ADA), Convolutional Neural Network (CNN), Deep Neural Network (DNN), K nearest neighbours (KNN), LR, Multi-layer Perceptron (MLP) and RF. In addition, we compared the proposed DF model with the other types of DF models (RF-based DF (DF_{RF}), ERT-based DF (DF_{ERT}) and LR-based DF (DF_{LR})) to further justify the performance of the model.

4.3 Hyperparameter Tuning

All the hyperparameters of the supervised machine learning models were properly tuned to obtain their optimal performance. Table 3 shows the hyperparameter values used for the machine learning configured and (or) tuned the parameters as recommended in their respective original works. We also only used the non-privacy-sensitive user attributes provisioned by Twitter APIs. For our proposed solution, we find the optimal δ value of the GC is 0.8 according to the experimental results. We used 'paraphrase-distilroberta-base-v1'[7] as the pre-trained

---

[7] https://huggingface.co/sentence-transformers/paraphrase-distilroberta-base-v1.

Table 4. Comparison with the state of the art identity cloning approaches. Standard deviation (σ) is provided to the KPIs of our proposed solution and Goga et al.'s algorithm that were evaluated over 10 iterations.

Model	Precision (σ)	Recall (σ)	F1-score (σ)
BSP [18]	76.8	75.1	76.9
Devmane and Rana [13]	66.3	68.1	67.2
Goga et al. [15]	65.4 (1.1)	**85.9 (1.5)**	74.3 (0.7)
Kamhoua et al. [19]	68.2	70.1	69.1
Zheng et al. [27]	68.15	73.34	70.64
Our proposed solution	**90.08 (3.42)**	77.95 (1.69)	**83.52 (0.94)**

model for SBERT. This pre-trained model was trained on millions of paraphrase sentences. SBERT by default uses 768 as the dimension of its post representation. The default dimension of the Node2vec for both the follower and friend network is 128. We also used the probability of moving away from source node $q = 2$, the probability of returning to source node $p = 0.5$, the number of random walks per root node $n = 10$ and the maximum length of a random walk as 15. All the profile attribute views were normalized to $[0, 1]$. The weights w of the wGCCA were set as $[0.25, 0.5, 0.5, 0.25]$ via experiments.

4.4 Results and Discussion

Overall performance: The performance comparison results are shown in Table 4. Our proposed solution yielded the best amongst the models compared against Precision and F1-Score. BSP [18] achieved the second best performance against Precision and F1-Score. Meanwhile, Goga et al. [15]'s proposed technique yielded the best-performing result on Recall. BSB [18] only employs profile attribute similarities and shared friends between account pairs. Goga et al. [15]'s proposed technique compares an account pair using only a traditional similarity technique and does not consider a filtering method for the account pair similar to our GC. The methods introduced by Kamhoua et al. [19] and Devmane and Rana [13] use a simple method to calculate profile attribute similarity. These techniques do not take into account the impact of the account's posts and the account's network information representation. Zheng et al. [27]'s proposed technique only takes into account a subset of features that compares spammer behaviour patterns. The obtained results indicate that our proposed solution is more suitable to a setting where only the non-privacy-sensitive user profile attributes are used for identity cloning detection in social media.

The comparison of results among the proposed DF model as well as other machine learning and DL models revealed that our DF model significantly outperformed all the other candidate models (see Table 5). We attribute this superior performance to two reasons. First, our DF model generates an ensemble of its base learners (i.e. RF, ERT, and LR) with a cascading structure where each cascade is an ensemble of the aforementioned base learners. Consequently, such a behaviour encourages diversity thereby improving its generalization performance eventually contributing to the significant increase in performance of our proposed solution. Further, the ability of DF to adaptively determine the best model complexity required for the problem context at hand also allows generating comparatively simpler models compared to the other approaches such as DNNs. This also helps improve the generalization performance of DF [29].

Table 5. Comparison with the baseline machine and DL models evaluated as the predictor of our proposed solution. Each KPI is presented as an average over 10 iterations together with standard deviation (σ).

Model	Precision (σ)	Recall (σ)	F1-score (σ)
ADA	84.63 (1.49)	78.15 (1.49)	81.26 (0)
CNN	83.54 (0.41)	77.67 (1.87)	80.49 (1.20)
DNN	85.66 (2.38)	76.68 (2.12)	80.88 (0.42)
KNN	78.30 (1.49)	78.52 (0)	78.41 (1.49)
LR	84.64 (0)	78.15 (1.49)	81.27 (1.49)
MLP	86.55 (3.81)	72.55 (3.69)	78.83 (2.37)
RF	83.84 (0.27)	78.56 (0.12)	81.12 (0.12)
DF_{RF}	84.16 (0.49)	**78.82 (0.25)**	81.41 (0.34)
DF_{ERT}	83.98 (0.16)	78.44 (0.25)	81.11 (0.06)
DF_{LR}	80.42 (0.433)	77.64 (1.32)	79.01 (0.77)
DF	**90.08 (3.42)**	77.95 (1.69)	**83.52 (0.94)**

5   Conclusion and Future Work

We propose a novel SocSen service provider identity cloning detection approach based on non-privacy-sensitive user attributes. In the proposed approach, an undirected graph is first constructed to identify the pairs of similar SocSen service providers' identities. We then extract an account pair feature representation. Afterwards, we also extract a multi-view account representation for each account. Then, these two representations are concatenated and fed into a DF classifier to predict whether or not a given account pair contains a cloned account. Our proposed solution was evaluated on a real-world Twitter dataset against other state-of-the-art cloned identity detection techniques and machine learning models. The results show that the proposed approach significantly outperformed the other models.

In the future, we plan to develop more effective identity cloning detection techniques and conduct experiments on large-scale datasets.

References

1. Aamir, T., Dong, H., Bouguettaya, A.: Social-sensor composition for tapestry scenes. IEEE Trans. Serv. Comput. (2020)
2. Aamir, T., Bouguettaya, A., Dong, H., et al.: Social-sensor cloud service selection. In: Proceedings of IEEE ICWS, pp. 508–515 (2017)
3. Aamir, T., Bouguettaya, A., Dong, H., Mistry, S., Erradi, A.: Social-sensor cloud service for scene reconstruction. In: Maximilien, M., Vallecillo, A., Wang, J., Oriol, M. (eds.) ICSOC 2017. LNCS, vol. 10601, pp. 37–52. Springer, Cham (2017). https://doi.org/10.1007/978-3-319-69035-3_3
4. Al-Qurishi, M., Al-Rakhami, M., Alamri, A., et al.: Sybil defense techniques in online social networks: a survey. IEEE Access 5, 1200–1219 (2017)
5. Alharbi, A., Dong, H., Yi, X., Abeysekara, P.: NPS-AntiClone: identity cloning detection based on non-privacy-sensitive user profile data. In: Proceedings of IEEE ICWS (2021)
6. Alharbi, A., Dong, H., Yi, X., et al.: Social media identity deception detection: a survey. CSUR 54(3), 1–35 (2021)
7. Bilge, L., Strufe, T., Balzarotti, D., Kirda, E.: All your contacts are belong to us: automated identity theft attacks on social networks. In: Proceedings of WWW, pp. 551–560 (2009)
8. Breiman, L.: Random forests. Mach. Learn. 45(1), 5–32 (2001)
9. Carroll, J.D.: Generalization of canonical correlation analysis to three or more sets of variables. In: Proceedings of APA Convention, pp. 227–228 (1968)
10. Christen, P.: Data Matching: Concepts and Techniques for Record Linkage, Entity Resolution, and Duplicate Detection. Springer, Heidelberg (2012). https://doi.org/10.1007/978-3-642-31164-2
11. Cohen, W.W., Ravikumar, P., Fienberg, S.E.: A comparison of string distance metrics for name-matching tasks. In: Proceedings of IIWeb, pp. 73–78 (2003)
12. Devlin, J., Chang, M.W., Lee, K., Toutanova, K.: BERT: pre-training of deep bidirectional transformers for language understanding. arXiv:1810.04805 (2018)
13. Devmane, M., Rana, N.: Detection and prevention of profile cloning in online social networks. In: Proceedings of ICRAIE, pp. 1–5 (2014)
14. Geurts, P., Ernst, D., Wehenkel, L.: Extremely randomized trees. Mach. Learn. 63(1), 3–42 (2006)
15. Goga, O., Venkatadri, G., Gummadi, K.P.: The Doppelgänger bot attack: exploring identity impersonation in online social networks. In: Proceedings of IMC, pp. 141–153 (2015)
16. Grover, A., Leskovec, J.: Node2Vec: scalable feature learning for networks. In: Proceedings of SIGKDD, pp. 855–864 (2016)
17. Hotelling, H.: Relations between two sets of variates. In: Breakthroughs in Statistics, pp. 162–190 (1992)
18. Jin, L., Takabi, H., Joshi, J.B.: Towards active detection of identity clone attacks on online social networks. In: Proceedings of CODASPY, pp. 27–38 (2011)
19. Kamhoua, G.A., Pissinou, N., Iyengar, S., et al.: Preventing colluding identity clone attacks in online social networks. In: Proceedings of ICDCSW, pp. 187–192 (2017)
20. Kontaxis, G., Polakis, I., Ioannidis, S. Markatos, E.P.: Detecting social network profile cloning. In: Proceedings of PERCOM Workshops, pp. 295–300 (2011)
21. Masood, F., Almogren, A., Abbas, A., et al.: Spammer detection and fake user identification on social networks. IEEE Access 7, 68140–68152 (2019)

22. Najafabadi, M.M., Villanustre, F., Khoshgoftaar, T.M., Seliya, N., Wald, R., Muharemagic, E.: Deep learning applications and challenges in big data analytics. J. Big Data **2**(1), 1–21 (2015). https://doi.org/10.1186/s40537-014-0007-7
23. Reimers, N., Gurevych, I.: Sentence-BERT: sentence embeddings using Siamese BERT-networks. In: Proceedings of EMNLP-IJCNLP (2019)
24. Robinson, P.M.: Generalized canonical analysis for time series. JMVA **3**(2), 141–160 (1973)
25. Rosi, A., Mamei, M., Zambonelli, F., et al.: Social sensors and pervasive services: approaches and perspectives. In: Proceedings of PERCOM Workshops, pp. 525–530 (2011)
26. Tenenhaus, A., Tenenhaus, M.: Regularized generalized canonical correlation analysis. Psychometrika **76**(2), 257 (2011)
27. Zheng, X., Zeng, Z., Chen, Z., et al.: Detecting spammers on social networks. Neurocomputing **159**, 27–34 (2015)
28. Zhou, Z.H.: Ensemble Methods: Foundations and Algorithms. CRC Press, Boca Raton (2012)
29. Zhou, Z.H., Feng, J.: Deep forest: towards an alternative to deep neural networks. In: Proceedings of IJCAI, pp. 3553–3559 (2017)

Multiple Agents Reinforcement Learning Based Influence Maximization in Social Network Services

Yiming Liu, Waichau Sze, Xiaofeng Gao$^{(\boxtimes)}$, and Guihai Chen

MoE Key Lab of Artificial Intelligence, Department of Computer Science
and Engineering, Shanghai Jiao Tong University, Shanghai 200240, China
{lucien,siweizhou14,gaoxiaofeng,chen-gh}@sjtu.edu.cn

Abstract. Influence Maximization (IM), an NP combinatorial optimization problem, has been broadly studied in the past decades. Existing algorithms for IM are still limited by accuracy, scalability and generalization. Moreover, they solve the influence overlapping problem implicitly. This paper proposes Multiple Agents Influence Maximization (MAIM) scheme, a novel Machine Learning based method for IM problem. We focus on explicitly solving the influence overlapping hidden in IM. MAIM first generates a list of sorted nodes as seed candidates in a descending order of overall influence, and drops those with serious influence overlapping based on multiple reinforcement learning (RL) agents in different rounds. We make full use of the characteristics of RL agents: continuous interaction with the environment, quick decision on whether a node should be accepted or dropped and better generalization. We also propose Memory Separated Deep Q-Network to improve training efficiency. Experiments on eight real-world social networks validate the effectiveness and efficiency of our algorithm compared to state-of-the-art algorithms.

Keywords: Social network services · Influence maximization · Influence overlapping · Reinforcement learning · Deep Q-Network

1 Introduction

The dramatically rapid development of social network services makes information dissemination faster and wider, and has a huge practical importance in viral marketing [2]. *Influence Maximization (IM)* was proposed to serve for those services. IM was firstly abstracted as an algorithmic problem by Kempe et al. [6]. In IM, a social network is represented as a graph $G = (V, E)$, where V is the set of nodes in graph G, and E is the set of edges. A diffusion model M illustrates how influence spreads through the network and converts abstract connections between people into definite edge lengths between nodes, such as *Independent Cascade (IC)* model, *Linear Threshold (LT)* model. The objective of IM is to find a set S of k seed nodes to influence nodes in the social network as many as possible. It is *NP-hard* under IC and LT models.

© Springer Nature Switzerland AG 2021
H. Hacid et al. (Eds.): ICSOC 2021, LNCS 13121, pp. 431–445, 2021.
https://doi.org/10.1007/978-3-030-91431-8_27

The IM problem has been well studied and triggered many researches in-depth. Traditional IM algorithms are often based on simulations, and adopt a greedy algorithm according to the submodularity of influence function $\sigma_{G,M}(\cdot)$, but always suffer from unbearable computational efficiency problem. Proxy-based methods such as shortest path [7] use a proxy model instead of running a heavy MC simulation to estimate the influence spread, which can improve practical efficiency. Nevertheless, they lack theoretical guarantees and may give unstable results. *Sketched-based methods* such as IMM [14], SSA [12] were proposed to devise theoretically efficient solutions that guarantee a certain approximation ratio, but they have weak generalization capacity. Some learning-based methods aims to learn a group of parameters and use them to calculate the marginal gain, such as DISCO [9]. However, the training process may cost much time and the models may perform unpleasantly in generalization. Moreover, all the previous methods consider and tackle the *influence overlapping* problem implicitly, as is shown and explained in Fig. 1.

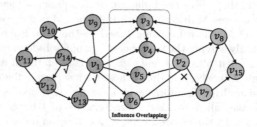

Fig. 1. The illustration of IM and influence overlapping problem in a directed graph with $k = 2$. Here we only consider a single-round activation. We should choose two nodes v_1 and v_{14} to maximize the neighbors. First, obviously, we choose v_1 in our seed set because it is the most influential node with 7 neighbors. v_2 is the second most influential node with 6 neighbors, but we drop it because it has 4 same neighbors (v_3, v_4, v_5, v_6) as v_1. If we select v_2 as the seed, most of its influence would be wasted, and it could not activate as many inactivated nodes as v_{14} could.

To tackle the above problem, we implement a Reinforcement Learning (RL) Framework to explicitly solve influence overlapping hiding in IM problem. We design **M**ultiple **A**gents **I**nfluence **M**aximization algorithm, a novel machine learning based method for IM problem. MAIM simulates pseudo submodularity to hold a approximation ratio bound and drop nodes with severe overlapping problems. First it neglects submodularity, and sorts the nodes by their individual Overall Influence. And then, based on the characteristics of RL agents that can continuously interact with the environment, it estimates approximate influence overlapping, and decides whether a node should be accepted or dropped in this order with the help of multiple RL agents. Our method is also distinguished with simulation-based methods, as we consider each candidate node only once. If this candidate suffers an unbearable influence overlapping, we will just drop it without reconsideration. Our contributions can be summarized as follows:

- We introduce RL to better solve the potential influence overlapping in IM problem explicitly. Our model adopts a series of Deep Q-Network as agents in the seed node selecting an dropping process. To the best of our knowledge, it is the first time that influence overlapping is explicitly considered.
- We propose Memory Separated Deep Q-Network (MSDQN), to boost and stabilize the training process of multiple agents, and theoretically prove the lower bound of approximation ratio for MAIM under ideal circumstances.
- Experiments based on eight real-world social networks demonstrate that MAIM overperforms the state-of-the-art models on influence spread and effectiveness.

2   Related Works

In 2003, Kempe et al. [6] proposed GeneralGreedy method, the first *simulation-based* approach to solve IM problem. This model originated from basic Monte-Carlo (MC) simulation. Leskovec et al. [8] proposed CELF to decrease simulations wasted by "lazy-forward" strategy. Following this direction, other algorithms like CELF++, NewGreedy and MixedGreedy were proposed in the next decade [4,5]. Although they performed well in optimizing MC simulations, generality and accuracy, and maintained a bounded approximation ratio, their computational cost were still too heavy and infeasible in practical usage.

To improve algorithm scalability in modern huge social network, some *proxy-based* approaches were specifically designed for certain diffusion models. In proxy-based solutions, ranking methods such as DEGDIS [3], provided efficient approaches to estimate spread of nodes' influence. However, two critical drawbacks existed among proxy-based methods. i) Due to the structure of the proxy model, their influence estimation might diverge from actual influence spread; ii) all those ranking proxies ignored the existence of influence overlappings [10].

Recently, algorithms including StaticGreedy [4] and TIM+ [15] were proposed to guarantee both scalability and accuracy in the IM problem. Together with IMM [14], SSA [12], RIS [3], etc., they could be classified as sketched-based approach [10]. In order to reduce the MC simulations needed in seed selections, those methods pre-computed several snapshots based on specific diffusion models, and used those sketches to evaluate influence spread among nodes. However, this quick estimation was actually at the expense of computation and memory cost in an unbalanced way, as a result of putting too much pressure on memory when analyzing huge networks.

Many researchers are also trying to apply Machine Learning methods in IM problem such as SCSS [1] and DISCO [9]. Those methods aims to learn a group of parameters and use them to calculate the marginal gain, showing machine learning a potential approach for IM problem. Moreover, Reinforcement Learning methods have been used in IM problem, such as a LinUCB-based bandit algorithm [16] focusing on regret bound, NSQ to solve competitive IM problem and IMGER [17] focusing on graph embedding. However, most of the training process of ML-based methods may cost much time and the models performs unpleasantly in generalization.

3 Preliminaries

3.1 Problem Statement

In this paper, we use Independent Cascade (IC) as the diffusion model M. The definition of IC model and IM problem is shown as follows:

Definition 1. (Independent Cascade Model) *Given a graph G and a user u, when node u becomes active, it has a single chance of activating each currently inactive neighbor v. The activation attempt succeeds with probability $p_{u,v}$.*

Definition 2. (Influence Maximization) *Given a graph $G = (V, E)$, an information diffusion model M, a positive integer k, the influence maximization problem aims to select a set S ($S \subseteq V$) with k nodes under the diffusion model M, to maximize influence spread $\sigma_{G,M}(S)$. The problem can be modeled as:*

$$\text{argmax}_{S \subseteq V, |S|=k} \, \sigma_{G,M}(S) \tag{1}$$

Note that our approach aims to solve the IM problem by tackle the *influence overlapping* problem explicitly. Here we formally define influence overlapping.

Definition 3. (Influence Overlapping) *Given a node v, it has potential to activate a set of nodes called P. However, most of nodes in P have been activated by previous active nodes, denoted as set A. If we choose v into the seed set, its influence would be wasted, namely there are few newly activated nodes by v. This is the influence overlapping problem for v with overlapping ratio $\beta = \frac{|A|}{|P|}$.*

3.2 Submodularity: The Starting Point

Kempe [6] proved that influence spread function under IC Model has two properties: submodularity and monotonicity. Here we define submodularity:

Definition 4. (Submodularity) *An influence spread function $\sigma(\cdot)$ is submodular iff $\sigma(S \cup \{v\}) - \sigma(S) \geq \sigma(S^* \cup \{v\}) - \sigma(S^*)$ for any $S \subseteq S^* \subseteq V$ and $v \in V \backslash S^*$.*

Let X denote a possible influence spread process in an IC model, $\sigma_X(S)$ be the influence of S under X and $R(v, X)$ as the set of nodes with a path activated to node v under X. Now, we can get

$$\sigma_X(S) = |\cup_{v \in S} R(v, X)| \tag{2}$$

Similarly, the *Overall Influence* of a node u under X can be represented as:

$$O_{u,X} = |R(u, X)| \tag{3}$$

Due to the existence of submodularity, influence overlapping happens between seed nodes. To illustrate the situation with better clarity, we introduce two new concepts: *Wasted Influence W* and *Valued Influence V*:

$$W_{u,S,X} = |\cup_{v \in S} R(v, X) \cap R(u, X)|, V_{u,S,X} = O_{u,X} - W_{u,S,X} \tag{4}$$

Under the influence spread process X and the current seed set S, for a node u, the Overall Influence $O_{u,S,X}$ is influence spread of a node ignoring influence overlapping, irrelevant to S. The Wasted Influence $W_{u,S,X}$ is the influence spread wasted of node u due to influence overlapping, and the Valued Influence $V_{u,S,X}$ could be obtained according to $O_{u,S,X}$ and $W_{u,S,X}$, equivalent to a individual node u's marginal gain.

4 Methodologies

4.1 MAIM Algorithm

To tackle the above difficulties, and explicitly consider influence overlapping problem, we design Multiple Agents Influence Maximization (MAIM) scheme, to provide an alternative to reduce the cost of adding a new node to the seed set. The overall structure of our model is shown in Fig. 2.

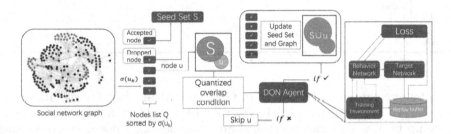

Fig. 2. The illustration of MAIM model. First, it constructs a node list by the individual Overall Influence in a descending order. Next, based on different relax factors, multiple DQN agents are trained in order to detect the influence overlapping problem among candidate nodes. Particularly, in node list Q, from up to down, the agents will drop the nodes that have strong influence but suffer serious influences overlapping with the seed set. Meanwhile, if a node is accepted as a seed by the agents, its influence spread will be recorded on the graph.

Different from previous methods that strictly hold submodularity, MAIM ignores submodularity and sort all the nodes in a descending order by Overall Influence. With the help of multiple reinforcement agents, it can estimate approximate influence overlapping, and decide whether a node should be accepted or dropped. The entire MAIM algorithm could be divided into two stages:

Stage 1: Preparation. First, the model calculates the Overall Influence of each individual node, sorts nodes by Overall Influences in the descending order and returns the largest Overall Influence. This stage only runs once.

Stage 2: Dropping. Algorithm 1 shows the whole process of dropping stage. This stage runs on the basis of preparation stage and a series of Deep Q-learning agents trained by Memory Separated Deep Q-Network (MSDQN) in Algorithm 3.

Algorithm 1: DROPPING_ADVANCED $(SOT, O_{max}, k, \lambda)$

Input: Sorted node list SOT, Largest Overall influence O_{max}, Seed size k, Relax factors $\lambda_0, \lambda_1, ... \lambda_j$

Output: Seed Set S

1 $step \leftarrow 1$, $i \leftarrow 0$
2 $\lambda \leftarrow \lambda_0$ The tightest Relax factor
3 **for** v in V **do**
4 | $G.v.hit = 0$ ▷ Times node v get activated
5 **while** $|S| \leq k$ **do**
6 | $G^- \leftarrow$ DeepCopy(G) ▷ Duplicate Graph G
7 | $u \leftarrow SOT[step]$
8 | $u_f \leftarrow$ Collision(G^-, u)
9 | $Action \leftarrow A_\lambda(G^-, u_f)$ ▷ If accept, G^- is updated
10 | $step \leftarrow step + 1$
11 | **if** $Action$ is $accepted$ **then**
12 | | $S \leftarrow S \cup \{u\}$
13 | | $G \leftarrow G^-$ ▷ Update the graph
14 | **else**
15 | | **if** $u.O \leq O_{max} \cdot \lambda$ or $step = |SOT|$ **then**
16 | | | $i \leftarrow i + 1$
17 | | | Switch to agent $A_{\lambda_{i+1}}$ with looser relax factor
18 | | | $step \leftarrow 1$, Restart and check nodes not in S
19 | | **else**
20 | | | Skip node u
21 **return** S

After preparation stage, nodes in G are sorted by their Overall Influence. However, an influential node will be less valuable if its Overall Influence is mostly made up by Wasted Influence. Therefore, when adding a node, we are looking for higher marginal gain, namely higher Valued influence:

$$V_{u,S} = \sigma(S \cup u) - \sigma(S) = \sum_{Outcomes\ X} Prob[X] \cdot V_{u,S,X} \tag{5}$$

Nevertheless, estimating the accurate Valued Influence requires heavy Monte-Carlo simulations where the model traverses all the left nodes in each round. To tackle this problem, we explicitly consider the influence overlapping problem.

As we have mentioned, a series of agents with different relax factors are trained for dropping stage. In Algorithm 1, the model starts with the strictest agent and with relax factor λ_0, denoted as A_{λ_0} (Line 4). With the help of trained RL Agents, it only accepts node u such that $V_u/O_u \geq \lambda$, where $\lambda \in (0, 1)$ is the relax factor (Line 6–13). Agents should be switched when Overall influence of current node is already lower than $\lambda_0 \cdot O_{max}$ or when the node list is went over and $|S| < k$ (Line 15–20). In those situations, the model switches to a looser agent A_{λ_1}, such that $0 < \lambda_0 < \lambda_1 < 1$. The model starts with the strictest agent with relax factor λ_0, denoted as A_{λ_0}, and switches to a looser agent A_{λ_1} when the current agent A_{λ_0} is "useless", instead of traversing all the nodes in the list. And so on, it will continue the switching until $|S| = k$. This strategy also helps to build an ideal theoretical lower bound of approximation ratio for the algorithm, and we will discuss it in Sect. 4.3.

Collision Algorithm in Algorithm 1 (Line 8) inspects and records the degree of influence overlapping between a node u and current seed set S, which serves as an evidence of dropping. It performs in two stages. First, on G, it simulates influence spread by node u and records the total times that each node w is activated during the activation in an IC model. $G.w.hit$ record the times node w has been activated. This process runs H times where H denotes the running episode (Line 1–3). After that, we check nodes activated by influence spread of u and classify them into three states: T (Touched), I (Influenced) and C (Collided). Note that $\alpha \in (0,1)$ is a hyperparameter here. If the times that a node is activated is larger than H, it means that other nodes also have high chances to activate it, so we classify it into C. A large C serves as an evidence for high Wasted Influence. Reversely, a large T is an evidence for high Valued Influence since the nodes are hardly touched before (Line 4–10).

Algorithm 2: COLLISION (G, u)

Input: Social network G, Node u
Output: T (Touched), I (Influenced) and C (Collided)
1   **for** $i \leftarrow 1$ **to** H **do**
2   **for** each w activated by u's influence spread **do**
3       $G.w.hit \leftarrow G.w.hit +1$

4   **foreach** w activated by u's influence spread **do**
5   **if** $G.w.hit > H$ **then**
6       $C \leftarrow C +1$
7   **else if** $G.w.hit \in [\alpha \cdot H, H]$ **then**
8       $I \leftarrow I + 1$
9   **else if** $G.w.hit \in [0, \alpha \cdot H)$ **then**
10       $T \leftarrow T + 1$

11   **return** $[\frac{C}{H}, \frac{I}{H}, \frac{T}{H}]$

4.2 Q-Learning

To decide whether a node should be accepted or dropped, we train a series of model-free RL agents to help. They are trained to learn evaluation function Q, the long-term gain from taking actions.

First, we clarify the formulation of the RL framework with top priority:

- **State:** A State (S, u) consists of two components: current seed set S and current node u waiting for consideration.
- **Action:** $Action \in \{0, 1\}$ is defined as either accepting current node and add it into seed set (denoted as 0) or dropping it (denoted as 1).
- **Rewards:** The reward function $r(S, u)$ at State (S, u) for accepting a node u is used to evaluate the transition reward of an action. It is defined as:

$$r(S, u) = (\sigma(S \cup u) - \sigma(S)) - \lambda \cdot \sigma(u) \qquad (6)$$

It indicts whether a serious influence overlapping will take place if we add current node to the seed set. λ is the relax factor indicting how strict we are for influence overlapping. The reward for dropping a node is 0.

- **Policy:** The agent will always make the decision to maximize Q value, the long time benefit:

$$\pi(u \mid S) = \arg\max_{0,1} Q(u_f, a; \theta) \tag{7}$$

Algorithm 3: TRAINING-MSDQN(G, SOT, λ_k)

Input: Social network G, Sorted nodes SOT, Relax factor λ
Output: Trained θ

1   Initialize Replay Buffer D with capacity N, function Q with parameter set θ and $\hat{Q}$ with parameter set $\hat{\theta}$

2   **for** *episode* ← *1 to M* **do**

3   **for** t ← *1 to T* **do**

4       $G^- \leftarrow$ DeepCopy(G)   ▷ Duplicate Graph G

5       $u \leftarrow SOT[t]$

6       $u_f \leftarrow$ Collision(G^-,u)

7       $a_t \leftarrow \begin{cases} x \in \{0,1\} \text{ randomly} & \text{w.p. } \epsilon \\ \arg\max_{0,1} Q(u_f, a; \theta) & \text{otherwise} \end{cases}$

8   **if** *Action is accept* **then**

9         $S \leftarrow S \cup \{u\}$

10        $G \leftarrow G^-$ ▷ Update the graph

11   **else**

12   Skip node u

13       $r_t \leftarrow \sigma(S \cup u) - \sigma(S) - \lambda \cdot \sigma(u)$

14       $v_f \leftarrow$ Collision(G, $SOT[t+1]$)

15   Save $\{u_f, a_t, r_t, v_f\}$ into D_A or D_D

16   Mix D_A and D_D as D

17   From D sample random batch B

18   Update θ by SGD over Equation 9

19   Every C turns, $\hat{\theta} \leftarrow \theta$

20   **return** θ

In DQN, Mnih designed a new module called Replay Buffer [11] to save actions and rewards in buffer D as $[state, action, reward, nextstate]$ tuple and apply random sampling to generate training batch. Unfortunately, original Replay Buffer does not fit our training requirement. At the beginning of training, since the agent is quite tolerant and the seed set is empty, it will accept most nodes into the seed set, and the replay buffer will be full of acceptance records with positive reward and only a few negative dropping records generated by random actions with regard to ϵ (Line 7). Similarly, due to serious overlapping problem and the strict agent, replay buffer will be filled with droppings records at the end of node list. This happens in each episode and makes training uncontrollable. To solve this problem, we design **M**emory **S**eperated **D**eep **Q**-Network (MSDQN) to balance the training process. We separate the memory buffer into dropping buffer D_D and acceptance buffer D_A, shown in Fig. 3. MSDQN prevents agent from a misconception that dropping is better than acceptance overall and vice versa, and makes the training more efficient and stable.

In each step, we use standard (1-step) Q-learning to update parameters, in which $v = Q[t+1]$, and we learn previous parameters in order to minimize the loss of samples in B:

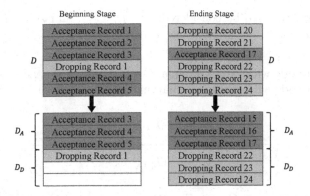

Fig. 3. Replay buffer in MSDQN (D_D and D_A). Assume the size of replay buffer D is 6. I.e., in the beginning stage, even if we have 5 acceptance records, we only add the 3 latest records in D_A, because the space in D_A is only 3. Similarly, in the ending stage, we discard dropping record 20 and 21, because the size of D_D is only 3.

$$L_t(\theta_t) = E_{(u_f, a_t, r_t, v_f)}[(r_t + \gamma \cdot \arg\max_{0,1} Q(v_f; \hat{\theta}_t) - Q(u_f, a_t; \theta_t))^2] \quad (8)$$

where $L_t(\theta_t)$ is the loss function. Next, we can update θ_t in step t by SGD method, we can calculate the gradient of Eq. 8 as:

$$\frac{\partial L_i(\theta_i)}{\partial \theta_i} = E_{(u_f, a_t, r_t, v_f)}[(r_t + \gamma \cdot \arg\max_{0,1} Q(v_f; \ddot{\theta}_t) - Q(u_f, a_t; \theta_t))\nabla_{\theta_t} Q(u_f, a_t; \theta_t)] \quad (9)$$

In the algorithm structure, we also install two sub-networks: behavior network Q and target network $\hat{Q}$. By "freezing" the target network in a period of time, we improve the stability of the learning algorithm [11]. The algorithm terminates when $|S| = k$.

4.3 Approximation Ratio Analysis

Assumption 1. *If Deep Q-Network agents are well trained and provides correct judgement, for each node u_i that is accepted in the seed set, $\Lambda_{u_i} = V_{u_i}/O_{u_i} \geq \lambda$.*

Theorem 1. *The approximation ratio of MAIM will be at least $(1 - 1/e^{\lambda^*})$, where λ^* is the relax factor for the loosest agent we used in seed selection.*

Proof. We call the seed set generate by Greedy method [6] as S^G, the seed set generated by MAIM as S^D and the optimal seed set as S^*. Assume the initial relax factor is λ_0 and seed set size is k. Obviously, both Greedy and MAIM method will choose the node with largest Overall influence as the first node, so it is clear that: $\sigma(S_1^D) \geq \lambda_0 \cdot \sigma(S_1^G)$. For simplicity, we assume that k nodes have already been selected by A_{λ_0}. Then, if the $(k+1)^{th}$ node is also found, we set v_i, the ith node in the list, as u_{k+1}^D, the $(k+1)^{th}$ seed found by MAIM, and set v_j, the jth node in the list, as u_{k+1}^G, the $(k+1)^{th}$ seed found by Greedy method.

There are three cases to be considered: $i \leq j$, $i > j$, and A_{λ_0} fails to accept a new node and switch to a looser relax factor.

(1) For the case: $[\, i \leq j \,]$
In this case, a node with larger or equal Overall influence is accepted by MAIM instead of the node with maximum marginal gain.

$$\frac{V_{u_{k+1}^D,S}}{V_{u_{k+1}^G,S}} = \frac{\frac{V_{u_{k+1}^D,S}}{O_{u_{k+1}^D}} \cdot O_{u_{k+1}^D}}{\frac{V_{u_{k+1}^G,S}}{O_{u_{k+1}^G}} \cdot O_{u_{k+1}^G}} = \frac{\Lambda_{u_{k+1}^D} \cdot O_{u_{k+1}^D}}{\Lambda_{u_{k+1}^G} \cdot O_{u_{k+1}^G}} \tag{10}$$

It's obvious that $O_{u_{k+1}^D} \geq O_{u_{k+1}^G}$, since they are sorted by Overall Influence in the list. According to Assumption 1, we have $\Lambda_{u_{k+1}^D} \geq \lambda_0$ and $\Lambda_{u_{k+1}^G} \leq 1$. Therefore,

$$\frac{V_{u_{k+1}^D,S}}{V_{u_{k+1}^G,S}} \geq \frac{\Lambda_{u_{k+1}^D}}{\Lambda_{u_{k+1}^G}} \geq \lambda_0 \tag{11}$$

(2) For the case: $[\, i > j \,]$
In this case, a node with less Overall Influence is accepted by MAIM while the node with maximum marginal gain is ignored. In MAIM, $O_{u_{k+1}^D} \geq \lambda_0 \cdot O_{max}$. Furthermore, based on the Assumption 1, we have $\Lambda_{u_{k+1}^G} \leq \lambda_0$ or u_{k+1}^G shouldn't be dropped. Inversely, $\Lambda_{u_{k+1}^D} \geq \lambda_0$ since u_{k+1}^D is accepted. Now we can get:

$$\frac{O_{u_{k+1}^D}}{O_{u_{k+1}^G}} \geq \frac{O_{u_{k+1}^G}}{O_{max}} \cdot \frac{O_{u_{k+1}^D}}{O_{u_{k+1}^G}} = \frac{O_{u_{k+1}^D}}{O_{max}} \geq \lambda_0 \tag{12}$$

which means,

$$\frac{V_{u_{k+1}^D,S}}{V_{u_{k+1}^G,S}} = \frac{\Lambda_{u_{k+1}^D} \cdot O_{u_{k+1}^D}}{\Lambda_{u_{k+1}^G} \cdot O_{u_{k+1}^G}} \geq \lambda_0 \tag{13}$$

(3) For the case: [**Switch to a looser relax factor**]
If there's no node left satisfying $O_{u_{k+1}^D} \geq \lambda_0 \cdot O_{max}$, we have to switch to an agent trained with looser relax factor until a new node is accepted. Assume a new node is found with λ_p, then we go back to either case 1 or case 2 and we can prove that: $\frac{V_{u_{k+1}^D,S}}{V_{u_{k+1}^G,S}} \geq \lambda_p$ This process may happen several times in the iteration. Assume λ^* is the loosest relax factor we use, assume we replace all the λ_0 and λ_p in previous part by λ^*.

Based on those three cases, we have:

$$\sigma(S_k^D + \{u_{k+1}^D\}) - \sigma(S_k^D) \geq \lambda^*(\sigma(S_k^D + \{u_{k+1}^G\}) - \sigma(S_k^D)) \tag{14}$$

Assume $S^* = \{u_0^*, .., u_{k-1}^*\}$ is the optimal seed set, which brings largest influence spread. Since the IC model is both monotone and submodular, we have:

$$\sigma(S^* \cup S_k^D) = \sigma(S^* \cup S_k^D) - \sigma(\{u_0^*, .., u_{k-1}^*\} \cup S_k^D) + \sigma(\{u_0^*, .., u_{k-1}^*\} \cup S_k^D)$$

$$= \sigma(S_k^D) + \sum_{j=1}^{k}(\sigma(S_k^D \cup \{u_0^*, ..., u_j^*\}) - \sigma(S_k^D \cup \{u_0^*, ..., u_{j-1}^*\}))$$

$$\leq \sigma(S_k^D) + \sum_{u \in S^*} \sigma(S_k^D \cup \{u\}) - \sigma(S_k^D)$$

$$(15)$$

u_{k+1}^G is chosen to maximize the marginal gain in choosing the $(k+1)$th node. Note that the marginal gain by adding u_{k+1}^G in the seed set is larger than or equal to that gaining by adding the seed node in S^*. Based on this fact and Eq. 14, we can further write the inequality as:

$$\sigma(S_k^D) + \sum_{u \in S^*} \sigma(S_k^D \cup \{u\}) - \sigma(S_k^D) \leq \sigma(S_k^D) + k(\sigma(S_k^D \cup \{u_{k+1}^G\}) - \sigma(S_k^D)))$$

$$\leq \sigma(S_k^D) + \frac{k}{\lambda^*}(\sigma(S_k^D \cup \{u_{k+1}^D\}) - \sigma(S_k^D))) \leq \sigma(S_k^D) + \frac{k}{\lambda^*}(\sigma(S_{k+1}^D) - \sigma(S_k^D)))$$

$$(16)$$

By setting $a_k = \sigma(S^*) - \sigma(S_k^D)$, it is straight forward to derive that $a_{k+1} \leq a_k - \frac{\lambda^*}{k}a_k$, which leads to $a_k \leq (1 - \frac{\lambda^*}{k})^k a_0$. Combine it with the common inequality $1 - x \leq e^{-x}$ where $x \in (0, 1)$ and $a_0 \leq \sigma(S^*)$, we will have:

$$\sigma(S_k^D) \geq (1 - 1/e^{\lambda^*})\sigma(S^*)$$

In conclusion, the lower bound of approximation ratio is $(1 - 1/e^{\lambda^*})$, if reinforcement agents are perfectly trained. Even if the approximation ratio is ideal, our model still achieves better influence spread and reduces simulation time and memory cost in large scale social networks, as is shown in Sect. 5.

5   Experiments

5.1   Experiment Setup

Datasets. During the experiments, we use eight real-life datasets from websites, as is shown in Table 1. Two of them, *HEP* and *PHY*, are academic collaborations extracted from different sections in arXiv, which also serves as data in Chen's study [3]. Others could be found at Stanford Large Network Dataset Collection website. Note that W is the edge weight, denoting the probability that an active node can activate each of its inactivated neighbor.

Baselines. We select six baselines in total. *Random* randomly selects nodes in the network. *Naive Greedy* sorts all nodes by individual influence spread individually and accept first k nodes as seeds. *DEGDIS* [3] is proxy-based algorithm

Table 1. Eight datasets used in experiment

Dataset	Nodes	Edges	Directed?	W	Dataset	Nodes	Edges	Directed?	W
HEP	15 K	58 K	Directed	0.1	Wiki-topcats	1.8 M	28.5 M	Directed	0.001
PHY	37 K	37 K	Directed	0.1	Wiki-topcats	2.4 M	5 M	Directed	0.001
Cit-HepPh	34 K	421 K	Directed	0.01	Gemsec-deezer	143 K	846 K	Undirected	0.01
Cit-HepTh	27 K	352 K	Directed	0.01	Com-Amazon	335 K	925 K	Undirected	0.01

introduced by Chen et al., which consider nodes with high discounted-degree is influential. It works well on IC Model and has time complexity $o(klog(n) + m)$. *CELF* [8] is a kind of well-accepted simulation-based algorithm. In the experiment, we choose r = 300 in order to make run time receivable. *TIM+* [15] is sketched-based algorithmn. Here we set ϵ (a hyperparameter in TIM+) as 0.1 unless otherwise specified. *TSIM* [13] is a state-of-the-art algorithm which applies discount-degree descending technology and lazy-forward technology in order to balance accuracy and time cost.

We implement multiple algorithms on eight large networks extracted from real life, on a machine with an Intel(R) Core(TM) i7-8700 K, 3.7 GHz CPU and 32 GB memory. All the experiments are based on Independent Cascade (IC) Model. In MAIM, we set $H = 10$ and $\alpha = 0.5$ in Algorithm 2. In Algorithm 3, two agents networks are trained with $\lambda_0 = 0.5$ and $\lambda_1 = 0.4$. In the agents, both Behavior Network Q and Target Network $\hat{Q}$ have two dense (fully connected) layers. Agents are only leveraged to detect serious influence overlapping, and it shows outstanding robustness. We use multiple agents trained in *HEP* with $W = 0.05$. We set training episode $M = 15$ and seed set size $k = 50$. **This process only costs 40 min. The whole experiments are based on the multiple agents we trained in this stage, which is time-saving.**

5.2 Experiment Results

Naive Greedy v.s. MAIM. The MAIM without dropping stage is technically the same as Naive Greedy. To show the good generalization capacity of agents, we not only test its performance on trained network, but also test it on a totally different network *PHY*. From Fig. 4, we can find that estimating pseudo submodularity, dropping stage can help to predict the possible overlapping problem in seed selection process and improve the performance of influence spread.

Spread Comparison. We run tests on eight large scale social networks. The size of seed sets are selected ranging from 10 to 50. From Fig. 5, it is obvious that MAIM outperforms all the comparision algorithms on *Cit-HepTh*, *Cit-HepPh*, *WikiTalk*, *Wiki-topcats*, *Gemsec-deezer* on influence spread. We can find that CELF was finished only on three of the networks, since we set a upper bound for running time as 10,000 s. TIM+ is a quite efficient and influential algorithm, among all the data sets except *Gemsec-deezer*, it performs only 2% to 3% worse than MAIM. However, its high efficiency and influence spread are at a cost of unbearable memory consumption.

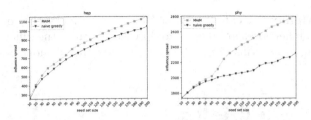

Fig. 4. Naive vs MAIM ($W = 0.1$)

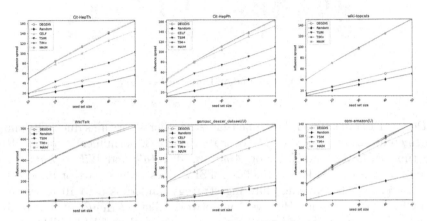

Fig. 5. Multiple algo on different large social networks

On *Cit-HepTh*, MAIM performs 15.07%, 63.75% and 125.27% better than CELF, TSIM and DRGDIS with seed size $k = 50$. In terms of *Cit-HepPh*, MAIM is 6.90%, 47.7% and 89.4% better than CELF, TSIM and DRGDIS with seed size $k = 50$. Since those two networks are relatively small, both CELF and TSIM finish the whole seed selection.

On huge networks like *Wiki-topcats* and *WikiTalk*, TSIM fails to finish the whole seed selection within 10,000 s, and the memory cost of TIM+ is too heavy and exceeds 32 GB. To tackle this problem, we relax ϵ to 0.5. By this way, TIM+ keeps the same influence spread with MAIM but with heavy memory cost. MAIM is 152.26% and 140.32% better than TSIM and DEGDIS on influence spread with $k = 30$. TSIM and DegreeDiscount do a great job, and this is because *Wiki-topcats* is a graph with very high average degree, and algorithms related to degree-discount descending technology will perform better.

On undirected networks like *Gemsec-deezer*, MAIM performs sightly better than TIM+ and TSIM on influence spread, and 25.58% and 266.10% better than CELF and Degree Discount. On *Com-amazon*, a huge undirected network, MAIM performs worse than other algorithms. It is 8.96% and 9.28% worse than TSIM and TIM+. We guess it is because agents of MAIM was trained in a small directed network and fail to fully handle a large undirected network. Furthermore, the improvement of MAIM tends to increase with growth of seed size.

Time and Memory Cost. Running time and memory cost of selecting 50 nodes on all the networks are represented in Fig. 6. Since the difference between them is too large, we utilize $\log_{10}$ to present time and memory cost.

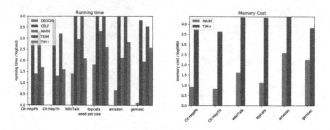

Fig. 6. Time and memory cost

Degree Discount spends less time than any other algorithms due to its simple implementation, but this doesn't cover its drawback on influence spread. Running times of CELF and TSIM on *Amazon*, *WikiTalk* and *Wiki-topcats* exceed 10,000 s, and are recorded as 10,000+. TSIM does reduce part of unnecessary computation by its two-stage filtering strategy, and runs 5 to 10 times faster than CELF most of times. However, on networks like *Cit-HepPh*, it fails to filter enough candidate nodes and runs even more slowly than CELF. TIM+ shows both high influence spread and good efficiency during the experiment. However, its memory cost is too heavy, as is shown in Fig. 6. We can see the memory cost of TIM+ is thousand times heavier than MAIM.

6   Conclusion

In this paper, we introduce MAIM, a novel machine-learning based IM method. Instead of keeping strict submordularity, MAIM estimates influence overlapping and drops nodes by multiple RL agents in different rounds. We also propose MSDQN to guarantee agents' training speed and generalization. Moreover, we also theoretically prove the ideal lower bound of approximation ratio is $(1 - 1/e^{\lambda^*})$ with well trained agents. This algorithm is hundreds of times faster Greedy algorithm, use hundreds times less memory than TIM+ and has stronger robustness to large network size and seed set size. In conclusion, MAIM's memory cost and influence spread fluctuation is less sensitive to network size, seed size and edge weight, which makes it practical on large scale social network services.

Acknowledgements. This work was supported by the National Key R&D Program of China [2020YFB1707903]; the National Natural Science Foundation of China [61872238, 61972254], Shanghai Municipal Science and Technology Major Project [2021SHZDZX0102], the Tencent Marketing Solution Rhino-Bird Focused Research Program [FR202001], and the CCF-Tencent Open Fund [RAGR20200105].

References

1. Ali, K., Wang, C., Chen, Y.: A novel nested Q-learning method to tackle time-constrained competitive influence maximization. IEEE Access **7**, 6337–6352 (2019)
2. Banerjee, S., Jenamani, M., Pratihar, D.K.: A survey on influence maximization in a social network. Knowl. Inf. Syst. **62**(9), 3417–3455 (2020). https://doi.org/10.1007/s10115-020-01461-4
3. Chen, W., Wang, Y., Yang, S.: Efficient influence maximization in social networks. In: International Conference on Knowledge Discovery and Data Mining (SIGKDD), pp. 199–208 (2009)
4. Cheng, S., Shen, H., Huang, J., Zhang, G., Cheng, X.: Staticgreedy: solving the scalability-accuracy dilemma in influence maximization. In: The Conference on Information and Knowledge Management (CIKM), pp. 509–518 (2013)
5. Goyal, A., Lu, W., Lakshmanan, L.V.: Celf++: optimizing the greedy algorithm for influence maximization in social networks. In: International Conference on World Wide Web (WWW), pp. 47–48 (2011)
6. Kempe, D., Kleinberg, J., Tardos, É.: Maximizing the spread of influence through a social network. In: International Conference on Knowledge Discovery and Data Mining (SIGKDD), pp. 137–146 (2003)
7. Kimura, M., Saito, K.: Tractable models for information diffusion in social networks. In: Fürnkranz, J., Scheffer, T., Spiliopoulou, M. (eds.) PKDD 2006. LNCS (LNAI), vol. 4213, pp. 259–271. Springer, Heidelberg (2006). https://doi.org/10.1007/11871637_27
8. Leskovec, J., Krause, A., Guestrin, C., Faloutsos, C., Vanbriesen, J.M., Glance, N.S.: Cost-effective outbreak detection in networks. In: International Conference on Knowledge Discovery and Data Mining (SICKDD) (2007)
9. Li, H., Xu, M., Bhowmick, S.S., Sun, C., Jiang, Z., Cui, J.: Disco: influence maximization meets network embedding and deep learning. arXiv preprint arXiv:1906.07378 (2019)
10. Li, Y., Fan, J., Wang, Y., Tan, K.L.: Influence maximization on social graphs: a survey. IEEE Trans. Knowl. Data Eng. (TKDE) **30**(10), 1852–1872 (2018)
11. Mnih, V., et al.: Human-level control through deep reinforcement learning. Nature **518**(7540), 529–533 (2015)
12. Nguyen, H.T., Thai, M.T., Dinh, T.N.: Stop-and-stare: Optimal sampling algorithms for viral marketing in billion-scale networks. In: International Conference on Management of Data (SIGMOD), pp. 695–710 (2016)
13. Qiu, L., Gu, C., Zhang, S., Tian, X., Mingjv, Z.: TSIM: a two-stage selection algorithm for influence maximization in social networks. IEEE Access **8**, 12084–12095 (2020)
14. Tang, Y., Shi, Y., Xiao, X.: Influence maximization in near-linear time: a martingale approach. In: Proceedings of the 2015 ACM SIGMOD International Conference on Management of Data, pp. 1539–1554 (2015)
15. Tang, Y., Xiao, X., Shi, Y.: Influence maximization: near-optimal time complexity meets practical efficiency. In: International Conference on Management of Data (SIGMOD), pp. 75–86 (2014)
16. Vaswani, S., Kveton, B., Wen, Z., Ghavamzadeh, M., Lakshmanan, L.V., Schmidt, M.: Model-independent online learning for influence maximization. In: International Conference on Machine Learning (ICML), pp. 3530–3539. PMLR (2017)
17. Wang, C., Liu, Y., Gao, X., Chen, G.: Reinforcement learning model for influence maximization in social networks. In: International Conference on Database Systems for Advanced Applications (DASFAA) (2021)

Service Composition
and Recommendation

On the Scalability of Compositions of Service-Oriented Applications

Nicolás Pozas and Francisco Durán[✉]

ITIS Software, University of Málaga, Málaga, Spain
pozas91@uma.es, duran@lcc.uma.es

Abstract. One of the current challenges in the context of service-oriented applications is the generation of composition plans for applications that optimize their QoS attributes by taking advantage of the resources offered by different providers, and generate them as efficiently as possible. Scalability is indeed a major issue, and the problem becomes a real challenge for applications with big numbers of services. In this work, we propose a divide-and-conquer algorithm that exploits the architecture of applications, to reduce the size of the search space. With it, we are able to recompose the solution for the global problem, with a significant gain in execution time. A variant of the algorithm—in which, when a sub-problem cannot be further divided without loosing information, a solver is used to find the optimal solution for it—allows us to trade execution time and precision. We report on the extensive experimentation carried out, where applications with up to 2 000 services are considered, and which includes a comparison with the results delivered by GA solvers.

1 Introduction

Nowadays, web services, micro-services and IoT services are being widely employed in many fields and play an important role in practical applications. Awareness of the quality of service (QoS) in these environments aims at obtaining a deployment plan using available resources with an optimal composition that satisfies user requirements. In large-scale scenarios, like those we typically found in micro-services or IoT applications, for a given request, the composition can have a significant number of alternatives.

Research Problem. The complexity of QoS-aware services composition lies in many factors that must simultaneously be accounted for. First, services combine their input and outputs as dictated by the architecture of the application, which has a direct impact on its quality attributes. This becomes more complicated when, in addition to sequential patterns, the architecture includes conditional, iterative or parallel patterns. The second factor is the optimization problem: the result combination must achieve the best overall QoS. The bigger the search space the more expensive the resolution of the optimization problem, and how the computation time grows becomes key for scalability. For example, an application with 100 components and 4 alternative providers for each component,

© Springer Nature Switzerland AG 2021
H. Hacid et al. (Eds.): ICSOC 2021, LNCS 13121, pp. 449–463, 2021.
https://doi.org/10.1007/978-3-030-91431-8_28

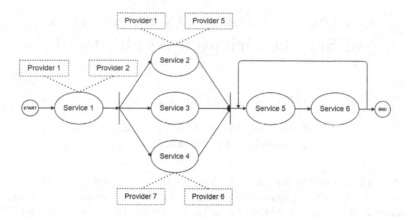

Fig. 1. Sample typical application composition

has 4^{100} = 1.606938e + 60 possible combinations, and although this number may be reduced by applying structural constraints (components that need to be deployed at the same provider or that cannot be hosted by some providers), the amount of alternatives to be analysed is too high when only a few of them will satisfy the user's requirements.

In composition problems, one can find different approaches to how to work with compositions. One of them is to see each service as an abstract service (e.g., a search service) for which a concrete service (e.g., Algolia, CloudSearch, etc.), with specific metrics for the QoS attributes, must be selected. An alternative problem is to see services as specific services, that need to be deployed on specific providers (PaaS services by different providers, different virtual machines by different providers, a local linux box, an Arduino device, etc.), which again offer specific QoS metrics. Although they both pose a very similar problem, we will focus on the second one throughout this work. The specific problem we address is exemplified by the application depicted in Fig. 1. In it, we can see the architecture of an application in which Service 1 can be deployed in both Provider 1 and Provider 2, Service 2 can be deployed in Provider 1 and Provider 5, etc.

There is a certain consensus on the use of genetic algorithms (GA) as the best option for the composition problem. In general, GA-based solutions are able to find a good-enough solution rather quickly, although it may take a longer time to find an optimal solution for huge search spaces like the ones at hand. Figure 2 shows results on some experiments that illustrate how GA-based solutions behave when the size of the composition grows.[1] Fig. 2a shows the average execution time of finding an appropriate deployment for applications with up to 1 000 services and different numbers of providers when no timeout is given.[2]

---

[1] The GA solver used in this paper is implemented using the Jenetics library (https://jenetics.io/). The hyper-parameters used in our experiments can be found in Appendix A. The Jenetics library offers two stop conditions: a hard timeout can be given, but also a convergence criteria can be provided so that the evolution stops when the fitness is deemed as converged.

[2] Each of the experiments in this paper has been executed 10 times, and averages are shown to make the graphs smoother.

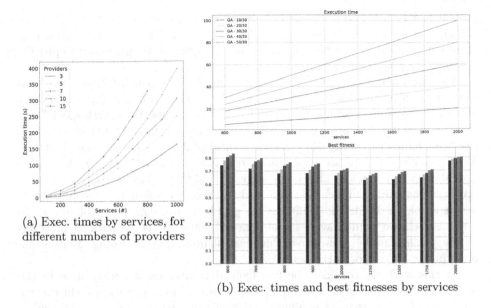

(a) Exec. times by services, for different numbers of providers

(b) Exec. times and best fitnesses by services

Fig. 2. Scalability of the solution based on genetic algorithms

We can observe that the execution time increases exponentially as the number of services grows. We can also observe how the time, as the search space size, grows with the number of providers. Of course, by setting a timeout, we will stop the algorithm before a local optimum is reached. But there is a tradeoff between the time and the quality of the found solution. First, it would not make sense to have a fix timeout, since then the bigger the search space the worst the quality of the solution. To overcome this problem, let us consider a timeout that depends on the number of services. In Fig. 2b, e.g., GA - 20/30 represents the function with slope 20 and shift 30. The charts in this figure illustrate how this timeout is related to the quality of the solution. We can see at the top of Fig. 2b different functions defining the timeouts used, and the corresponding best fitnesses of the corresponding solutions at its bottom. Please note the colour correspondence between an execution time and its best fitness. Although we will explain our fitness function in the coming sections, we can observe in these charts that the smaller the timeout, the bigger the lost in the precision of the solution. Indeed, setting a timeout too low may lead to unacceptable solutions.

Contribution of the Paper. The main goal of this paper is to improve the scalability of the current solutions, and reduce the execution time to solve them without losing the quality of the global composition. To do this, we propose exploiting the information that the architecture of the application at hand has to offer us. We propose a divide-and-conquer (D&C) algorithm that allows us to de-compose the global problem into sub-problems. Our claim is that given any of these sub-problems, in most cases they can be solved in isolation using the desired composition algorithm—either based on exact methods, GA, ant colonies, or recursively invoking our D&C algorithm. The resolution of each of these sub-problems will return a composition, which will then be used to provide a global composition to return it to the user.

To grasp an idea of the reduction in the complexity of the solution, let us consider an application with 10 services, where each service can have 2 providers, not necessary the same providers for each service. In this case, the search space has a total of $2^{10} = 1\,024$ possible combinations. If we pass from 10 to 20 services, with the same number of providers, we have a total of $2^{20} = 1\,048\,576$ combinations. Now, assume we have an application with 2\,000 services with 15 alternative providers each of them. This gives a total of $15^{2\,000}$ possible combinations, a nowhere negligible number that can lead to excessive resource consumption. If we were able to divide the 2\,000-services problem into, e.g., 200 problems of 10 services each, we would have a search space of $200 * 15^{10}$ combinations, a significantly smaller number. Of course, this must be done without losing information, or losing as little information as possible.

In this work we consider the two QoS attributes most widely used in the related literature, namely cost and response time, and application architectures made up of the four most common architectural patterns, namely sequential, iterative, conditional and parallel. Although different solvers can be invoked to solve base-case sub-problems, all results presented in this paper use a GA-based solver for sub-problems of size greater than 1, to facilitate presentation and comparison. Single-service sub-problems are solved using an exhaustive method.

Outline. The organization of the rest of the paper is as follows: Sect. 2 reviews some related work. Section 3 introduces some basic notation and terminology to better understand our proposal. Section 4 presents in detail the proposed solution. Section 5 shows some experimental results. Finally, Sect. 6 presents some conclusions, discusses on some limitations of our approach, and presents some open lines for future improvement.

2   Some Related Work

The problem of deployment-plan discovery has been approached from different perspectives by different authors. We can find different alternative solutions for composition in the existing literature, among which the most prominent ones propose the use of exact methods [8], ant colonies [11] or genetic algorithms [2]. In [4], Deshpande and Sharm propose the use of a machine-learning classifier to choose between these three alternative solutions depending on the complexity of the problem. Although the decision depends on multiple factors, in general, for problems with few services, the classifier recommended the exact methods, while for more complex problems the classifier recommended the use of the solution based on genetic algorithms. Indeed, genetic algorithms are widely accepted to solve composition problems, since they obtain good-enough results in the shortest possible time. However, even though they are the best current alternative, they present serious scalability problems.

In [3], Cardoso et al. propose some aggregation functions to calculate the value of the QoS attributes for some specific patterns within an architecture, and to be able to calculate the global value of these attributes. Different authors, e.g., [1,2,10] have proposed to use genetic algorithms to solve the composition problem on architectures that use the same patterns used in [3]. Although these solutions tackle the general problem from different perspectives, they are not concerned about the scalability of the problem, solve the problem as a whole, and all the cases they consider are rather small, with applications of 10–15 services in the most complicated cases.

In [7], a constraints-based approach is used to remove user-specified constraints that may be redundant, reducing the complexity of the composition plan and improving it. Several authors [5,6,9] have tried to reduce the search space by minimizing the services within the composition plan. Although the problem and the solution are very different, they focus, like us, on the complexity of the problem for applications with huge numbers of services.

These papers have contributed to the solution of the problem, and have tried to, in one way or another, finding a composition plan in the most efficient way possible. However, in most cases, architectures mentioned in these papers tend to be small, with few services or a relatively small search space.

3   Preliminaries

This section presents some preliminaries on the problem at hand and the proposed solution. Specifically, we present the fitness function and architectural patterns that we consider, the application encoding, and the normalization used.

3.1   Fitness Function and Architectural Patterns

When we talk about genetic algorithms, the notion of fitness function comes to mind. Fitness functions is the method used to evaluate the individuals in a population, granting them a score that allows us to compare the individuals with each other. We are not going to go into this area, as it is not the goal of our work, but it is necessary to show the fitness function we have used for our experiments, since this is the function we use as *criterion to compare alternative solutions*. Equation 1 shows the usual fitness function in this type of problems.

$$f_i = W_c \times (1 - C_i) + W_t \times (1 - R_i) \tag{1}$$

In Eq. (1), C_i and R_i are the aggregated costs and the response times, respectively, for a particular solution. Both measures are to be minimized. Then, W_c and W_t are weights that indicate the user's preferences for cost and response time attributes, respectively. For example, if we want both attributes to have the same relevance within the composition, they should both take value 0.5. This fitness function is defined in the range of $[0, 1]$, and we will take the individual (composition) with the highest f_i value.

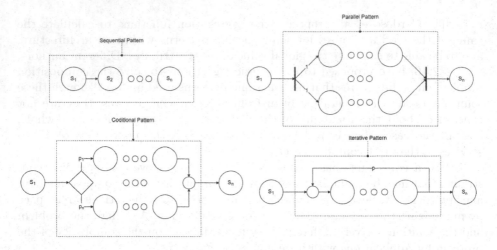

Fig. 3. Architectural patterns considered

Table 1. Aggregation functions

QoS Attr.	Sequential	Conditional	Parallel	Iterative
Time (T)	$\sum_{i=1}^{n} T(t_i)$	$\sum_{i=1}^{n} p_i * T(t_i)$	$Max\{T(t_i)_{i \in \{1...n\}}\}$	$T(t)/(1-p)$
Cost (C)	$\sum_{i=1}^{n} C(t_i)$	$\sum_{i=1}^{n} p_i * C(t_i)$	$\sum_{i=1}^{n} C(t_i)$	$C(t)/(1-p)$

The architectural patterns that we consider are shown in Fig. 3. Table 1 then shows the aggregation functions used to calculate the cost and response time taking into account the different architectural patterns—as proposed in [3]. Note that in the architectural patterns, probabilities represent the likelihood of executing a branch or another in a conditional pattern, or making another iteration on the loop of services or getting out of it. Note also that these probabilities are also used in the aggregation functions. As usual, these probabilities can be learnt from actual executions of the application or being estimated by architectural experts.

Sequential. In this pattern, each component must wait for the previous component to perform its task. That is, the output from a component is the input of the next component in the sequence. The goal is for each component to carry out its work as efficiently as possible, since the provider that offers us the highest quality in isolation will be the best provider globally (for accumulative QoS attributes).

Conditional. This pattern has several branches, each of which has a probability p_i, with $0 \leq p_i \leq 1$ and $\sum_{i=0}^{n} p_i = 1$, to be selected. Thus, to calculate the fitness function of each branch, we simply have to calculate the value for that branch, and multiply it by its probability.

Parallel. In a parallel structure, all branches are executed concurrently. The services being executed in parallel must synchronize once completed, and,

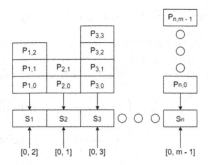

Fig. 4. Encoding of an application as chromosomes

therefore, its response time is given by the response time of the slowest branch. As we will see below, this is key, since, in this pattern, faster services may relax its response-time requirement in favour of improving other attributes. E.g., we may have cases in which we decide to take a cheaper provider for a service because a faster, more-expensive one is possibly not going to improve the global fitness value.

Iterative. This pattern represents a loop that have a probability p of repeating its execution, where $0 < p < 1$. Notice that $p = 0$ would mean that the body of the loop will never execute, and $p = 1$ an infinite loop.

As we will see below, the same architectural patterns shown in Table 1 for the aggregation of functions, will serve as guide to carry out the decomposition of the architecture in our proposal.

3.2 Application Encoding

A GA needs, in addition to a fitness function, a chromosome representation of the problem at hand. In the case of a composition problem, we must provide an encoding of the application (or fragment of the considered application at each step of the process).

Figure 4 depicts a graphic representation of this encoding, where $S_1...S_n$ are chromosomes that represent the services, and $P_{i,0}...P_{i,m_i}$ represent the providers available for a particular service S_i. An application is then represented as a genotype of n chromosomes, each one representing a service. Each of these chromosomes has a single gene, a value $x \in \mathbb{Z}$ in the range $[0, m_i - 1]$, for chromosome i, where x will be the selected provider, and m_i is the total number of providers available for that service i.

Notice that with this encoding, chromosomes can have different sizes, since each service may have a different number of providers. If all services had the same number of providers, it would have been possible to use a single chromosome with n genes. Notice also that this encoding does not have information about the architecture of the application that we are going to solve. The architecture, however, is available for the calculation of the fitness function. While finding the optimal composition, the genetic algorithm must have the necessary information on how services are connected to each other.

3.3   A Word on Normalization and Re-Scaling

For all attributes to have the same relevance in the composition, independently of their scale, they are normalized. Our procedure implements two ways to scale or normalize data using the usual *scaling* and *normalizing* functions:

$$scaling(x_i, \vec{x}, minimize) = \begin{cases} 1 - \dfrac{x_i}{max(\vec{x})}, & \text{if minimize is } True \\ \dfrac{x_i}{max(\vec{x})}, & \text{otherwise} \end{cases} \tag{2}$$

$$normalize(x_i, \vec{x}, minimize) = \begin{cases} \dfrac{max(\vec{x}) - x_i}{max(\vec{x}) - min(\vec{x})}, & \text{if minimize is } True \\ \dfrac{x_i - min(\vec{x})}{max(\vec{x}) - min(\vec{x})}, & \text{otherwise} \end{cases} \tag{3}$$

where, $\vec{x}$ is the list of values to scale, x_i is a specific value within that list, and, respectively, $max(\vec{x}) \neq 0$, and $(max(\vec{x}) - min(\vec{x})) \neq 0$.

Both functions transform the values of numeric variables so that the transformed data ranges between 0 and 1. The difference is that, when re-scaling we are just changing the range of your data, whilst when normalizing we also change the shape of the distribution of the data. For example, values $[6, 7, 8, 8, 5]$ are re-scaled as $[0.75, 0.875, 1.0, 1.0, 0.625]$ and normalized as $[0.33, 0.66, 1.0, 1.0, 0.0]$.

In the literature, some authors propose normalizing and others re-scaling. Since, depending on the input data, one transformation may work better than the other, we leave the choice of which one to use to the user. However, in the experiments presented in the rest of the paper, to normalize the QoS attributes of the architecture, we have taken the maximum and minimum value for each provider QoS attribute and calculated the fitness function score of this deployment as the maximum and minimum reference. Although this deployment may be impossible, we only need these values as a reference to normalize.

4   Divide, When Possible, and Conquer

As already explained, our algorithm proceeds by breaking down the problem of finding the optimal composition for an application by breaking it into subproblems with fewer services. This section presents the details of the algorithm and provides some details on its complexity.

4.1   Decomposing Architectures

We have seen that by decomposing an architecture into sub-architectures with fewer services, we get an execution time gain. However, each pattern has its own features and aggregation functions, and they cannot be handled in the same way without information lost. Of course, if our problem has only one service, we directly solve the assignment by taking the best provider. Assuming a description

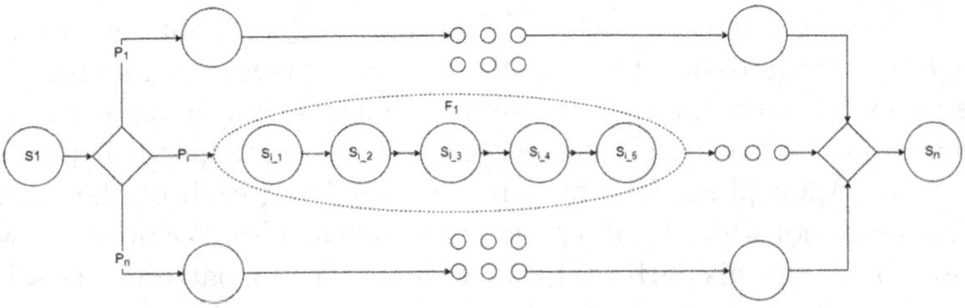

Fig. 5. Conditional architecture decomposition

of the architecture of our service-based application, using a tree-like representation like in BPEL-WS or BPMN, we proceed recursively depending on the type of operator at the root of the subproblem being considered. In the following, we explain the way to decompose and recompose each of these patterns.

Sequential Pattern. Since the values of all the considered QoS attributes get added in the sequential pattern, we can split any sequence, independently solve the subproblems, and then get the total cost and response time just by summing them. Whenever a part of the problem is solved, we get a piece of the composition that is stored in memory to compose the complete composition, the number of generations that have been made to solve each part, and the number of sub-architectures generated.

The algorithm proceeds by solving the subproblem corresponding to the first service in the sequence, and, recursively, the rest of the architecture. Therefore, each sub-architecture will be solved in isolation, and the sub-architecture get replaced by a *fake* service with the corresponding QoS attributes. The re-composition process will then combine these partial solutions into a solution to the original global architecture.

The complexity of solving the composition of a sequence of subproblems is linear with respect to the number of subproblems.

Iterative Pattern. The decomposition of this pattern is quite similar to the sequential pattern. Since an iterative pattern can be seen as a sequential pattern that has an associated probability p of repeating itself, the same method is applied on the pattern, returning a result to the composition problem. The value of this composition will be multiplied by the probability associated to the pattern to complete the re-composition.

Conditional Pattern. We can work with conditional sub-architectures like a sequential pattern in which each component (or branch) has an associated probability that needs to be considered for the decomposition. Each branch is solved on its own. For example, Fig. 5 shows an example in which we see that to solve one of the branches of a conditional sub-architecture, we proceed recursively, by solving, in this case, the corresponding sequential sub-architecture.

The complexity of solving the composition of a conditional pattern is therefore linear with respect to the number of its branches.

Parallel Pattern. As we can see in Table 1, the aggregation function for the response time attribute for the parallel pattern takes the maximum of the response times of its branches. This basically means that changes can be made at different points of the architecture, initially unrelated, which may provide a better composition plan. This prevents from solving each of the branches in isolation, if we do not want to miss precision in our results. We propose two alternative ways to handle this pattern. In the first case, these patterns are solved as a whole, without attempting their decomposition. That is, when a sub-architecture is reached with a parallel operator at its top, an external solver is invoked—in our experiments, a GA solver. As we will see in the coming sections, this will lead to a potentially better solution. However, since we may have a big problem to solve, we will have to trade time and precision. In the second alternative, given a parallel architecture, we solve the optimization problem for each branch, fix the best one, and then we solve the problem without considering the response times for the rest of the branches. In this way, we may be loosing some good combinations, since we may be missing suboptimal local solutions that might lead to optimal global ones. However, giving n branches, the complexity of this solution is linear, since we have to solve $2n - 1$ problems. With this solution the speed up is dramatic, as we will see in Sect. 5, where some experimental results comparing these two alternatives are provided.

Nested Patterns. Any architecture of interest will present patterns nested inside other patterns. In the above examples we have seen how once a subproblem is solved, the sub-architecture is replaced by an equivalent component with corresponding QoS values and size. Indeed, throughout the paper we have talked about 'components' as something abstract, avoiding only referring to services. In our work, we treat both services and sub-architectures uniformly, what allows us to proceed recursively.

4.2 Divide-and-Conquer Algorithm

As already explained, the procedure is implemented by a recursive algorithm following the standard divide-and-conquer strategy. Every architecture is seem as a tree with one of the above patterns at the top. Depending on this pattern the problem is decomposed as already explained. The algorithm proceeds by dividing the problem until a subproblem of size one is found. The only exception is the parallel pattern, for which, as we have just seem, the algorithm may proceed by either invoking the GA solver or by computing a number of alternative problems. Once all the subproblems are solved, the solution is composed and its fitness function calculated.

The complexity of the algorithm depends on the alternative chosen to solve parallel patterns. If the external solver is invoked, the complexity of the algorithm is given by the complexity of the solver. The execution time will greatly depend on the position of the parallel patterns in the specific application. With the second alternative the algorithm is linear.

5   Experiments

This section presents results on some experiments conducted to illustrate the performance of our D&C algorithm. The analysis has been carried out on randomly generated architectures. The procedure to generate architectures takes as argument the number of services to have in the generated application, a flag that indicates whether all services have the same providers or not, the number of alternative providers each service will have, and the probabilities of picking each of the architectural patterns. If we choose to have different providers for each service, we need to provide the total number of providers in the application's catalog, and the minimum and maximum number of providers that a service can have. This will randomly pick providers for each service in that range within the catalog. Providers, and their QoS attributes, have also been generated randomly. The generation procedure creates architectures of all kinds in a completely random way. In all the experiments presented here the patterns in the generated problems were equiprobable

In what follows, we will show results of the composition of random problems using the GA solver and our D&C algorithm, both handling parallel patterns by invoking the same GA solver (D&C-parallels) and by the decomposition strategy explained in Sect. 4 (D&C).

As pointed out in the introduction, our GA solver is implemented using the Jenetics library, and the hyper-parameters used in our experiments can be found in Appendix A. As also highlighted in Sect. 1, the quality of the solution provided by the GA-solver depends on the stopping conditions. Let us begin by comparing the execution time and quality of the solutions provided GA solver on the global problem and the D&C-parallels algorithm. As we did for Fig. 2b, the execution of the GA-solver is limited by a timeout defined by some slope and shift values. Since problems with parallel patterns are solved by invoking the same solver, their execution is limited using the same function.

Figure 6 compares execution times and best fitnesses of the GA solver on the global problem and the D&C-parallels algorithm on problems of up to 2 000 services. In both cases, timeouts are given by functions with slopes/shifts of 10/30, 20/30, 30/30, 40/30 and 50/30. Whilst for the GA case the execution time is dictated by the timeout function, applied on the global problem, for the D&C algorithm the timeout is applied only on subproblems with a parallel pattern at top. Observe that even though the D&C-parallels is around a 20–25% faster, it always provides better best fitness values.

Figure 7 includes in the comparison the execution of the GA and D&C-parallels solutions with no timeouts, and the D&C algorithm with the alternative way of handling parallel patterns explained in Sect. 4. First, notice that the GA solver with no timeout takes a significant amount of time, much bigger than the rest of the alternatives. Although the execution times for the D&C-parallels with no timeout is smaller, it is however still quite big. These curves are interesting though. The results for GA - no timeout gives a good reference for the best fitness values, which are shown in the chart at the bottom. Even though as already said, all problems where solved 10 times, and averages are shown, the

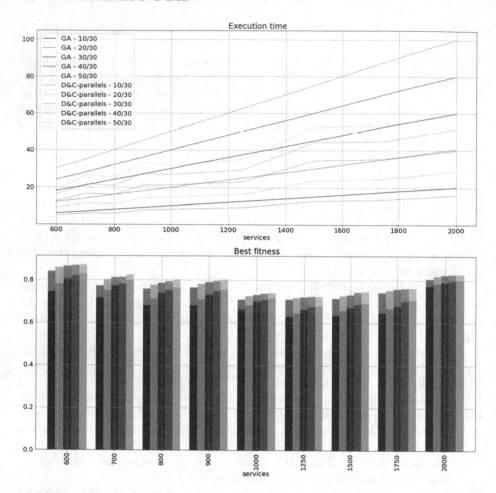

Fig. 6. Genetic algorithm vs. D&C, with and without stopping on parallels, with slope/shift timeouts (between 7 and 12 providers out of 15 for each service)

execution times for the D&C-parallels - no timeout show a significant variability. It is due to the impact on the execution time that has the position at which the parallel patterns are located. If the pattern is found high in the tree structure, the problem to be solved using the GA-solver takes a significant amount of time. In this case, we only show results for the D&C-parallels and GA with timeouts given by slopes/shifts 30/30 and 40/30, just to have then as a reference. The interesting part, of course, is on the values obtained for the D&C algorithm. The D&C algorithm executes at a time very close to zero, insignificant if compared to the times shown by any of the other solvers.

Let us focus now on the chart in the lower part of Fig. 7. Taking the best fitness of the GA - no timeout execution as a reference, there are several observations we may take from the chart: (1) the D&C-parallels - no timeout algorithm

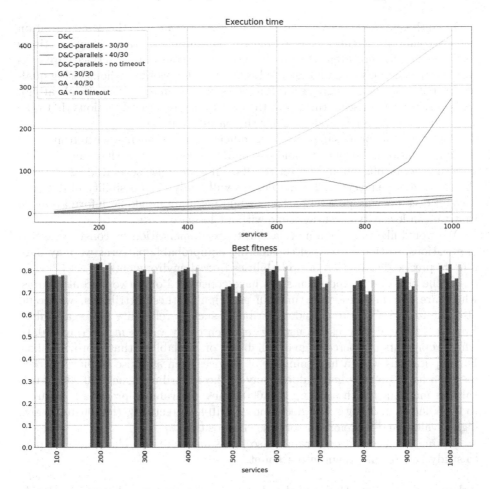

Fig. 7. Genetic algorithm vs. D&C, with and without stopping on parallels, and with and without timeouts (between 7 and 12 providers out of 15 for each service)

gets the same fitness values as the GA - no timeout in all cases, which means that it is not loosing quality, even though it runs faster, (2) the D&C algorithm shows almost as good values as these in almost all cases, i.e., low precision lost even though its small execution time, and (3) the D&C algorithm is better than the GA with timeouts, which are also behind the results for the D&C algorithm with timeouts.

6   Conclusions

This papers presents a divide-and-conquer algorithm for the generation of deployment plans that allows decomposing huge architectures to improve scaling issues without loosing precision.

Even though the D&C algorithms execution times include the de-composition and re-composition time of the different sub-problems, its execution times remains close to zero even when architectures of thousands of services are considered. In general, we claim that the D&C algorithm works without losing quality for patterns whose aggregation functions are summative (or multiplicative). However, as we have seen, this is not the case for aggregation functions that take a maximum or minimum value, as for the parallel pattern.

Although the proposal presents significant improvements with respect to existing solutions, we plan to address many pending issues that may lead to a more general solution and better results. First, we have several ideas to make the solver more efficient and versatile. We will study the possibility of different ways of decomposing parallel patterns while maintaining global information, so that we can lower its execution time without losing quality.

We would like to make a more accurate experimentation by considering real applications, so that instead of considering equiprobable patterns we may have a more precise distribution of probabilities in real environments.

In the performed experiments, we have considered only two QoS attributes, which are cost and response time. In addition to these attributes, we would also like to find a way to consider attributes such as reliability and availability. However, these attributes are usually represented by values in the range $[0, 1]$, which represents the percentage of reliability or availability that a provider has. For applications with a huge number of services such as those we have worked on, even having a very high value of any of these attributes such a 0.999, if this value is multiplied with itself up to 1 000 times, the value is practically reduced to 0. Whereas in doing so, in decomposed sub-architectures, these usually give higher values and therefore distort the composition.

Taking into account constraints also poses an interesting challenge. We plan to study how to take them into account.

Acknowledgements. This work has been partially supported by projects UMA-CEIATECH-09 (Andalucía TECH/J. Andalucía/FEDER), UMA18-FEDERJA-180 (J. Andalucía/FEDER), PGC2018-094905-B-I00 (Spanish MINECO/FEDER).

A   GA settings

Hyper-parameters. The hyper-parameters with which experiments in this paper have been performed are as follows:

- Population: 100.
- Probability to mutate any chromosome: 13%.
- Crossover probability: 70%, which can affect a total of 5 different chromosomes at once (Multi-point crossover of 5 used).
- Survivor selector: Elitist of 2 individuals. This feature assumes some risk, as it is possible to drag individuals which are local minimums during the GA execution.

– OffSpring selector: The individuals chosen to create offspring will use the *RouletteWheelSelector* method, meaning that the probability that an individual will be chosen to generate offspring will be $P(i) = \frac{f_i}{\sum_{j=0}^{N-1} f_j}$, where N is the total population.

References

1. Ai, L.: QoS-aware web service composition using genetic algorithms. Ph.D. thesis, Queensland University of Technology (2011)
2. Canfora, G., Di Penta, M., Esposito, R., Villani, M.L.: An approach for QoS-aware service composition based on genetic algorithms. In: 7th Annual Conference on Genetic and Evolutionary Computation (GECCO), pp. 1069–1075. Association for Computing Machinery (2005). https://doi.org/10.1145/1068009.1068189
3. Cardoso, J., Sheth, A., Miller, J., Arnold, J., Kochut, K.: Quality of service for workflows and web service processes. J. Web Semant. **1**(3), 281–308 (2004). https://doi.org/10.1016/j.websem.2004.03.001
4. Deshpande, N., Sharma, N., et al.: Composition algorithm adaptation in service oriented systems. In: Muccini, H. (ed.) ECSA 2020. CCIS, vol. 1269, pp. 170–179. Springer, Cham (2020). https://doi.org/10.1007/978-3-030-59155-7_13
5. Fan, S.-L., Ding, F., Guo, C.-H., Yang, Y.-B.: Supervised web service composition integrating multi-objective QoS optimization and service quantity minimization. In: Jin, H., Wang, Q., Zhang, L.-J. (eds.) ICWS 2018. LNCS, vol. 10966, pp. 215–230. Springer, Cham (2018). https://doi.org/10.1007/978-3-319-94289-6_14
6. Fan, S.-L., Peng, K.-Y., Yang, Y.-B.: Large-scale QoS-aware service composition integrating chained dynamic programming and hybrid pruning. In: Jin, H., Wang, Q., Zhang, L.-J. (eds.) ICWS 2018. LNCS, vol. 10966, pp. 196–211. Springer, Cham (2018). https://doi.org/10.1007/978-3-319-94289-6_13
7. Wu, Z., Lin, P., Huang, P., Peng, H., He, Y., Chen, J.: A user constraint awareness approach for QoS-based service composition. In: Miller, J., Stroulia, E., Lee, K., Zhang, L.-J. (eds.) ICWS 2019. LNCS, vol. 11512, pp. 48–62. Springer, Cham (2019). https://doi.org/10.1007/978-3-030-23499-7_4
8. Yu, T., Zhang, Y., Lin, K.J.: Efficient algorithms for web services selection with end-to-end QoS constraints. ACM Trans. Web **1**(1), 6-es (2007). https://doi.org/10.1145/1232722.1232728
9. Zeng, L., Benatallah, B., Ngu, A.H.H., Dumas, M., Kalagnanam, J., Chang, H.: QoS-aware middleware for web services composition. IEEE Trans. Software Eng. **30**, 311–327 (2004). https://doi.org/10.1109/TSE.2004.11
10. Zhang, M., Liu, L., Liu, S.: Genetic algorithm based QoS-aware service composition in multi-cloud. In: IEEE Conference on Collaboration and Internet Computing (CIC), pp. 113–118 (2015). https://doi.org/10.1109/CIC.2015.23
11. Zhang, W., Chang, C., Feng, T., Jiang, H.: QoS-based dynamic web service composition with ant colony optimization. In: IEEE 34th Annual Computer Software and Applications Conference, pp. 493–502 (2010). https://doi.org/10.1109/COMPSAC.2010.76

ServiceBERT: A Pre-trained Model for Web Service Tagging and Recommendation

Xin Wang[1], Pingyi Zhou[2], Yasheng Wang[2], Xiao Liu[3], Jin Liu[1(✉)], and Hao Wu[4]

[1] School of Computer Science, Wuhan University, Wuhan, China
{xinwang0920,jinliu}@whu.edu.cn
[2] Noah's Ark Lab, Huawei, Shenzhen, China
{zhoupingyi,wangyasheng}@huawei.com
[3] School of Information Technology, Deakin University, Geelong, Australia
xiao.liu@deakin.edu.au
[4] School of Information Science and Engineering, Yunnan University, Kunming, China
haowu@ynu.edu.cn

Abstract. Pre-trained models have shown their significant values on a number of natural language processing (NLP) tasks. However, there is still a lack of corresponding work in the field of service computing to effectively utilize the rich knowledge accumulated in the Web service ecosystem. In this paper, we propose ServiceBERT, which learns domain knowledge of Web service ecosystem aiming to support service intelligence tasks, such as Web API tagging and Mashup-oriented API recommendation. The ServiceBERT is developed with the Transformer-based neural architecture. In addition to using the objective of masked language modeling (MLM), we also introduce the replaced token detection (RTD) objective for efficiently learning pre-trained model. Finally, we also implement the contrastive learning to learn noise-invariant representations at the sentence level in pre-training stage. Comprehensive experiments on two service-related tasks successfully demonstrate the better performance of ServiceBERT through the comparison with a variety of representative methods.

Keywords: Pre-trained model · Web service ecosystem · Domain knowledge · Web API · Contrastive learning

1 Introduction

With the flourishing development of service computing, an increasing number of accessible Web services are developed to automatically and interactively connect business processes between heterogeneous applications [13,21]. The rapid growth of Web services provides a backbone for the formation of a Web service ecosystem (a logical collection of Web services) [1]. According to the data from

© Springer Nature Switzerland AG 2021
H. Hacid et al. (Eds.): ICSOC 2021, LNCS 13121, pp. 464–478, 2021.
https://doi.org/10.1007/978-3-030-91431-8_29

ProgrammableWeb[1], which is the largest online API registry, the number of Web APIs was about 12,000 in 2015 [27], and this number has grown to 24,145 by May 1, 2021. The rapid growth of Web APIs makes it extremely difficult for software developers to effectively search and select the most suitable Web APIs satisfying their requirements [17,29]. Especially for those newly created APIs, there are often no tags. Many existing works [19,20,26] attempt to automatically assign appropriate tags to Web APIs (namely **Web API tagging task**), thereby effectively promoting the discovery of Web APIs and greatly reducing the search space of Web APIs. Nevertheless, in the face of a large number of complex business scenarios, it becomes increasingly impossible for individual Web API to meet the full user requirements. As a result, Mashup has become a promising technology by combining multiple APIs with different functionalities to meet user requirements. Recommending suitable APIs according to the Mashup development requirements has attracted more and more attention [21]. Numerous existing works [15,25,30] have been proposed to recommend appropriate Web APIs for Mashup developments (namely **Mashup-oriented API recommendation task**).

However, despite that these methods work well when applied to respective tasks, we argue that they still suffer from two following major limitations:

1. **Limitation 1:** These methods often need to design task-specific model architectures and cannot be directly utilized on other service-related tasks. This limits the generality of these methods.
2. **Limitation 2:** These methods are difficult to make full use of the rich domain knowledge accumulated in the Web service ecosystem, such as *API news, SDKs, Libraries, Frameworks, Source Codes and Changelogs, etc.*

In recent years, pre-trained models have received widespread attentions. The model is first pre-trained on large unsupervised data, then it can be fine-tuned using only one additional output layer to produce excellent results on a wide range of downstream tasks without the need of designing task-specific model architectures. Many pre-trained models such as ELMo [11], BERT [5], RoBERTa [10] and GPT [12] have achieved significant performance improvements on various natural language processing (NLP) tasks. These pre-trained models can learn effective contextual representations from large amounts of unlabeled data optimized by self-supervised objectives.

So far, Web service ecosystem still lacks a pre-trained model suitable for service discovery and recommendation. How to leverage domain knowledge of Web service ecosystem to promote the development of service-related tasks is still a challenging issue. Inspired by the success of pre-trained models in NLP, we propose ServiceBERT, a pre-trained model for Web service tagging and recommendation. Specifically, we firstly crawl all important information about Web services from the ProgrammableWeb as the corpora for pre-training. Afterwards, in addition to employing the objective of masked language modeling (MLM) [5], we also introduce the replaced token detection (RTD) [4] objective for efficient

---

[1] https://www.programmableweb.com/.

learning of pre-trained model. Finally, we introduce contrastive learning (CL) in pre-training process to learn noise-invariant representations at the sentence-level without requiring specialized architectures or a memory bank.

The main contributions of this paper can be summarized as follows:

- We propose a new pre-trained model, named ServiceBERT. To the best of our knowledge, this is the first pre-trained model in the field of service computing. It can make full use of the rich domain knowledge accumulated in the Web service ecosystem, and can act on numerous downstream tasks without the need of designing specific model architectures.
- We introduce a replaced token detection objective to detect replaced tokens for efficient learning of the model. In addition, we also introduce contrastive learning at the pre-training stage to learn noise-invariant representations at the sentence-level by contrasting positive pairs against negative pairs.
- We conduct comprehensive experiments on two service-related downstream tasks, which successfully demonstrate that ServiceBERT can obtain significant improvements over representative methods.

The remainder of this paper is organized as follows. Section 2 reviews some recent related works. Section 3 presents the details of ServiceBERT. Section 4 demonstrates the experimental results. Finally, Sect. 5 concludes our paper and points out the future work.

2   Related Work

In this section, we first introduce some studies about pre-trained models and contrastive learning, then we review some related works about Web service tagging and recommendation.

2.1   Pre-trained Model

A pre-trained model is usually first pre-trained on large-scale unlabeled data, aiming to provide excellent model initialization to obtain satisfactory performance for downstream tasks [22]. BERT [5] and GPT [12] are two early representative works in the field of pre-training language models. GPT uses a left-to-right Transformer [18] and performs well on lots of natural language generation (NLG) tasks. BERT exploits a bidirectional Transformer and performs well on various natural language understanding (NLU) tasks. In the pre-training process, different pre-training objectives are designed to speed up the efficiency of pre-training. For instance, GPT adopts the Causal Language Modeling (CLM) objective, which predicts the target token according to the input context tokens. BERT utilizes the Masked Language Modeling (MLM) objective, which predicts the masked tokens in a randomly masked token sequence given surrounding contexts. ELECTRA [4] presents the objective of Replaced Token Detection (RTD), which predicts whether each token in the corrupted input was replaced by a generator sample or not to efficiently train the model.

2.2   Contrastive Learning

Recently, contrastive learning has received increasing attentions due to its great success in various computer vision tasks [3]. Some researchers use the spatial/geometric transformations (such as cropping and resizing, rotation [9] and cutout [6]) or the appearance transformations (such as color distortion [16], Gaussian blur, etc.) of the same image to make the image agree with each other. The key of contrastive learning is to augment positive samples through data augmentation. Then, the positive pairs and negative pairs are contrasted to learn noise invariant representations of samples during the training process. For textual data, the way of data augmentation is different from that of images. EDA [23] presents four simple but powerful operations for textual data: synonym replacement, random insertion, random swap, and random deletion. CERT [7] regards the reverse-translated sentence and the original sentence as a pair of positive examples. CLEAR [24] exploits various data augmentation strategies to generate positive pairs, including word and span deletion, reordering, and substitution.

2.3   Web API Tagging and Recommendation

Accurate Web service tagging can greatly reduce the search space, thus effectively promoting the discovery of Web services. Wang et al. [20] proposed a spatial and sequential combined method for Web service classification. They integrated the Graph Convolutional Network (GCN) with Bidirectional Long Short-Term Memory (Bi-LSTM) to capture the Web service representations. Yang et al. [26] proposed ServeNeT to automatically abstract low-level representation of both service name and service description to high-level merged features for Web service classification. Cao et al. [2] proposed a topical attention based Bi-LSTM for Web API classification, They utilized the offline training to obtain the topic vector of Web service and performs the topic attention strengthening processing for feature representations. Wang et al. [19] presented a dual-graph convolutional network combining functional description documents and Mashup-API co-invocation patterns for Web service classification.

In order to help developers quickly select appropriate Web APIs covering multiple functions for mashup development, researchers have contributed a lot of effort. Shi et al. [15] presented a tag attention-based neural network for API recommendation. They fuse tags and description documents together, and then jointly learn representations of APIs and Mashups through two siamese LSTM networks. Xiong et al. [25] proposed a deep learning based hybrid method for Web API recommendation by combining collaborative filtering and textual content. Zhong et al. [30] jointly modeled Mashup descriptions and used APIs using author topic model (ATM) to reconstruct service profiles for Mashup-oriented API recommendation. Shi et al. [14] proposed a text expansion and deep model-based approach for service recommendation by expanding the description of services at sentence level based on a probabilistic topic model.

3   ServiceBERT

In this section, we describe the details about ServiceBERT, including the model architecture, pre-training objectives and the contrastive learning framework.

3.1   Model Architecture

We follow BERT and utilize the multi-layer bidirectional Transformer [18] as the model backbone. Given a Web service document $w = \{w_1, w_2, ..., w_{|w|}\}$, the input of the pre-trained model is defined as $x = \{[CLS], w, [SEP]\}$, where [CLS] is a special token in front of every input example, the final hidden state corresponding to this token is used as the aggregate sequence representation. The [SEP] is also a special token that marks the end of the previous sequence.

The embedding of each token in x is the sum of corresponding token and position embeddings. We utilize L-layer bidirectional Transformer [18] to encode the input vectors into contextual representations $H_l = \text{Transformer}_l(H_{l-1}), l \in [1, L]$. The output of each Transformer layer is drived as follows:

$$S_l = \text{LN}(\text{MHA}(H_{l-1}) + H_{l-1}) \tag{1}$$

$$H_l = \text{LN}(\text{FFN}(S_l) + S_l) \tag{2}$$

where MHA denotes a multi-headed self-attention operator, LN represents a layer normalization, and FFN is a two layer feed forward network.

The process of a multi-headed self-attention (MHA) in the l-th Transformer layer is drived by:

$$Q_i = H_{l-1}W_i^Q, \quad K_i = H_{l-1}W_i^K, \quad V_i = H_{l-1}W_i^V \tag{3}$$

$$head_i = \text{Softmax}(\frac{Q_i K_i^{\text{T}}}{\sqrt{d_k}})V_i \tag{4}$$

$$\check{S}_l = \text{Concat}(head_1, head_2, ..., head_n)W_l^O \tag{5}$$

The query (Q), key (K) and value (V) matrices are computed by projecting the output H_{l-1} of previous layer using three learnable weight matrices $W_i^Q, W_i^K, W_i^V \in \mathbb{R}^{d_h \times d_k}$, respectively. d_h denotes the hidden size and d_k refers to the dimension of a head. n is the number of heads and $W_l^O \in \mathbb{R}^{d_h \times d_h}$. $\check{S}_l$ is the output of a multi-headed self-attention in the l-th Transformer layer after concatenating of all heads.

3.2   Pre-training Data

We train ServiceBERT with Web service data crawled from the largest online API registry, ProgrammableWeb, which contains 128,536 samples across different types of information, including Web API, Mashup, API news, SDK, Library, Changelog, Framework, Glossary and Sample Source Code. Table 1 shows the basic statistics of the pre-training data, and each sample is an individual description document. We use a set of constraints and rules to filter the data. For instance, (1) each document shorter than 10 tokens is removed. (2) We truncated each *API news* document into many sequence of block size (512). (3) We concatenate all *Changelogs* into one sequence and then phase it into many subsequences of block size because they are all very short. (4) For other samples, we discard the tokens that exceed the block size, and pad samples whose lengths are less than the block size.

Table 1. Statistics of the pre-training data.

Item type	Statistics
Web API documents	22,144
Mashup documents	6,438
API news	12,089
SDKs	19,381
Libraries	1,665
Sample Source Code	12,377
Changelogs	50,737
Frameworks	554
Glossaries	161
All	128,536

3.3 Pre-training Objectives

To train ServiceBERT, we adopt two pre-training objectives. The first one is the masked language modeling (MLM) objective, which has been proved effective in many existing works. The second one is replaced token detection (RTD) objective, which is used to detect whether the token generated by the generator is consistent with the original token. Figure 1 illustrates the examples of these two pre-training objectives.

Masked Language Modeling (MLM). Given a input sequence x, we randomly select 15% of tokens from the sequence. We replace 80% of them with [MASK] tokens, 10% with random tokens, and the remaining 10% unchanged, which is following the same setting as [5]. Finally, the MLM loss function is defined as follows:

$$\mathcal{L}_{\mathrm{MLM}} = -\sum_{i}^{V}\sum^{M} y_i^{\mathrm{MLM}} \ln p_i^{\mathrm{MLM}} \tag{6}$$

where M represents a random set of masked tokens, V denotes the vocabulary size, y_i^{MLM} is the label of the masked token i and p_i^{MLM} denotes the predicted result of the token i.

Replaced Token Detection (RTD). We adopt a random simpler as the generator G to generate a new token according to the masked token. Then a discriminator (ServiceBERT) is trained to determine whether the generated token is the original one or not. The RTD loss function is drived by the following equations:

$$\hat{i} \sim G(i) \quad \text{for} \quad i \in M \tag{7}$$

$$\mathcal{L}_{\text{RTD}} = -\sum_{\hat{i}} [y_{\hat{i}}^{\text{RTD}} \ln p_{\hat{i}}^{\text{RTD}} + (1 - y_{\hat{i}}^{\text{RTD}}) \ln(1 - p_{\hat{i}}^{\text{RTD}})] \tag{8}$$

where $\hat{i}$ refers to the new token generated by the masked token $i \in M$. $y_{\hat{i}}^{\text{RTD}}$ denotes the label of the new token ($\hat{i}$) indicating whether it is consistent with the original token (i). $p_{\hat{i}}^{\text{RTD}}$ represents the predicted result, original or replaced.

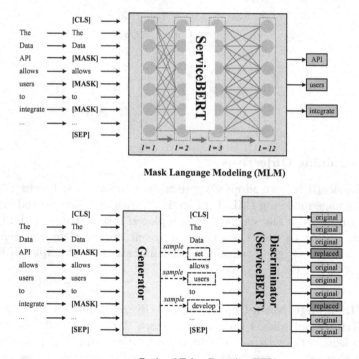

Mask Language Modeling (MLM)

Replaced Token Detection (RTD)

Fig. 1. Examples of two pre-training objectives: mask language modeling (MLM) and replaced token detection (RTD). The generator is a language model, which can be any model that produces an output distribution over tokens. The discriminator is the targeted pre-trained model, which is trained via detecting plausible alternatives tokens sampled from the generator. The generator is thrown away during the fine-tuning stage.

3.4   Contrastive Learning in ServiceBERT

Inspired by the success of contrastive learning in computer vision, we introduce the contrastive learning to learn noise-invariant representations at the sentence-level by contrasting positive pairs against negative pairs. Figure 2 illustrates the structure of our contrastive learning framework, which consists of three stages:

- Firstly, we need to generate the positive pairs. For a given sequence (x_i) in the pre-training data, we randomly choose and perform a data augmentation strategy, including synonym replacement, random insertion, random swap, and random deletion [23]. Then we achieve the augmented sequence (x_i^+). Then we exploit a random mask operator to mask different tokens with different random seeds. $x_i = \text{MASK}(x_i, seed_1)$ and $x_i^+ = \text{MASK}(x_i^+, seed_2)$. The sample x_i and its noisy sample x_i^+ are a pair of positive samples.
- Secondly, we input all these samples into ServiceBERT to obtain the final representations. Next, we adopt the feature vectors of their [CLS] tokens $h_{[CLS]}$ as final representations of sequences. Then, an extra neural network (MLP) layer $f(.)$ acting on $h_{[CLS]}$. Through the nonlinear transformation, more information can be maintained in $h_{[CLS]}$ [3]. $\boldsymbol{v}_i = f(\text{ServiceBERT}(x_i))$, $\boldsymbol{v}_i^+ = f(\text{ServiceBERT}(x_i^+))$.

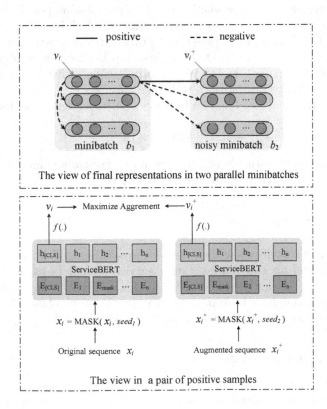

Fig. 2. Our contrastive learning framework.

- For an input x_i with representation v_i, we apply the *in-batch* and the *cross-batch* negative sampling. In this way, we can obtain a set $\mathbf{X}^-$ of $2N - 2$ negative samples for each x_i. We denote the set of representations for samples in $\mathbf{X}^-$ as $\mathbf{V}^- = \{v_1^-, \dots, v_{2N-2}^-\}$. We use the contrastive learning to maximize the representation similarity between positive samples, and minimize the representation similarity between negative samples. The noise contrastive learning loss for a positive pair (x_i, x_i^+) in two parallel minibatch is defined as:

$$l(x_i, x_i^+) = -\ln \frac{\exp(v_i \cdot v_i^+)}{\exp(v_i \cdot v_i^+) + \sum_{k=1}^{2N-2} \exp(v_i \cdot v_k^-)}, \tag{9}$$

where the similarity of a pair of samples is defined by the dot product of their representations as: $v_i \cdot v_i^+$. We calculate the loss for the same pair twice with order switched, i.e., (x_i, x_i^+) changes to (x_i^+, x_i) as the dot product with negative samples for x_i and x_i^+ are *different*. The final contrastive loss is defined as follows:

$$\mathcal{L}_{\mathrm{CL}} = \sum_i^N \left[l(x_i, x_i^+) + l(x_i^+, x_i) \right], \tag{10}$$

We let ServiceBERT judge whether a pair of samples are positive or negative, so that it can learn a more even decision boundary, which is useful for matching-related task. In addition, most pre-training objectives in pre-trained models are token-level, such MLM and RTD. There is a gap between these objectives and sentence-level downstream tasks. We introduce contrastive learning to better learn sentence-level representations to bridge this gap.

Overview, the final loss function in ServiceBERT is defined as follows:

$$\mathcal{L} = \mathcal{L}_{\mathrm{MLM}} + \mathcal{L}_{\mathrm{RTD}} + \mathcal{L}_{\mathrm{CL}} + \lambda \|\Theta\|^2 \tag{11}$$

where Θ contains all learnable parameters in our pre-trained model. λ is the L_2 regularization coefficient using to prevent overfitting.

4   Experiments

In this section, we firstly show the details of pre-training. Then we evaluate our pre-trained model on two representative service-related tasks, including Web API tagging and Mashup-oriented API recommendation. Many methods using different information have been proposed to solve these two tasks. In this paper, we explore the use of textual information for these two tasks.

4.1   Pre-training Settings

ServiceBERT is trained adopting the Transformer encoder architecture with 12 layers, 12 self-attention heads and 768 dimensional hidden size same as BERT-base. We train ServiceBERT using 8 NVIDIA Tesla V100 with 32GB memory.

We set the length of input sequences to 512 containing special tokens. We set the following hyper-parameters to train the model: batch size is 96 and the learning rate is 1e-4. An Adam optimizer is adopted to optimize the parameters of the model. To accelerate the training process, we use parameters of BERT-base to initialize our model. Finally, we train ServiceBERT for 30 epochs and evaluate it on downstream tasks. We conduct all experiments using the deep learning library PyTorch[2].

4.2 Evaluation Metrics

We evaluate our proposed model versus other methods in terms of two commonly used metrics: Recall@N ($N \in \{3, 5, 10\}$) and NDCG@N ($N \in \{3, 5, 10\}$). For both of these metrics, bigger values indicate better performance.

Recall@N concentrates on the number of items both in the recommendation list and the GroundTruth:

$$\text{Recall@N} = \frac{|\{\text{GroundTruth}\} \cap \{\text{Top-N items}\}|}{|\{\text{GroundTruth}\}|} \tag{12}$$

DCG@N will assign more weights to high ranking items. One of the commonly used descriptions is:

$$\text{DCG@N} = \sum_{i=1}^{N} \frac{2^{rel(i)} - 1}{log_2(i+1)} \tag{13}$$

Here, $rel(i)$ denotes whether a candidate item in the GroundTruth or not. If it is true, $rel(i) = 1$; otherwise, $rel(i) = 0$. NDCG@N is obtained by normalizing DCG@N with the ideal DCG: $\text{NDCG@N} = \frac{\text{DCG@N}}{\text{IDCG@N}}$, where IDCG@N is pre-calculated by GroundTruth.

4.3 Web API Tagging Task

Web API tagging task is to automatically assign tags for Web APIs, effectively promoting the discovery of Web services. We collect a Web API dataset (until May 1 2021) from ProgrammableWeb. The problem of data imbalance is widespread in the web service ecosystem, so we remove tags that are used less than 50 times, which is a common practice. We remove Web APIs whose description document length is less than 20. Finally, the dataset contains 20,958 Web APIs and 276 tags. The number of tags in each Web API is 3.15 in average. We randomly select 90% of APIs for training, and the remaining 10% of APIs for testing. We adopt Recall and NDCG as our evaluation metrics and report results of representative methods in the Table 2. We use the binary cross entropy as the loss function to optimize all models. For the methods in the first group, we remove stop words, punctuations, and restore all words to their root forms using

---

[2] https://pytorch.org/.

the NLTK toolkit[3], which are common operators effectively improving performance in literature [21, 26]. We exploit 300-dimensional GloVe[4] word vectors for word embedding.

Figure 3 shows the process of fine-tuning ServiceBERT on Web API tagging task. Specifically, we input the description document of each Web API into ServiceBERT, and use the final hidden state of [CLS] token as the aggregate sequence representation. Then we input it into an extra MLP layer to obtain the probability distribution on all candidate tags.

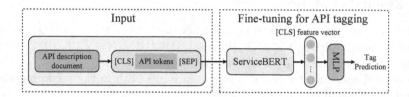

Fig. 3. The process of fine-tuning on the Web API tagging task.

Table 2. Results on API tagging task.

Methods	Recall			NDCG		
	Top-3	Top-5	Top-10	Top-3	Top-5	Top-10
BLSTM-Att	0.4712	0.5676	0.6846	0.5084	0.5656	0.6196
LAB-BiLSTM	0.4895	0.5803	0.6925	0.5229	0.5767	0.6291
WSC-GCN	0.5247	0.6012	0.7285	0.5531	0.5978	0.6591
SSWC	0.5598	0.6479	0.7412	0.5771	0.6039	0.6723
ServeNet	0.5701	0.6588	0.7532	0.6042	0.6433	0.7035
BERT-base	0.6090	0.7068	0.7830	0.6524	0.7126	0.7497
ServiceBERT	**0.6207**	**0.7256**	**0.8056**	**0.6655**	**0.7301**	**0.7688**

BLSTM-Att [8] proposes a hierarchical attention network at word-level and sentence-level to capture service description features. **LAB-BiLSTM** [2] incorporates topic modeling into the Bi-LSTM to learn representation of Web service. **WSC-GCN** [28] uses the graph convolutional neural network to learn Web APIs representations by capturing word relationships. **ServeNet** [26] adopts the stacked 2-D CNN and Bi-LSTM for feature extraction of service description. **SSWC** [20] uses a spatial and sequential combined method for Web service classification. The second group is the results of pre-trained models. We use **BERT-base** to fine-tune on Web service dataset. We can see that **ServiceBERT** that incorporates domain knowledge of Web services for pre-training outperforms all other methods, which demonstrates the effectiveness of our pre-trained model.

---

[3] http://www.nltk.org/.

[4] https://nlp.stanford.edu/projects/glove/.

4.4   Mashup-Oriented API Recommendation Task

Mashup-oriented API recommendation task is to recommend appropriate Web APIs to developers for Mashup creations. Many Web APIs are not involved in Mashup developments, we only care about the Web APIs invoked at least one time, so many Web APIs are removed from the candidate set. We do the same data preprocessing the same as Web API tagging task. The refined dataset contains 5,413 Mashups and 1,193 candidate Web APIs.

Figure 4 shows the process of fine-tuning ServiceBERT on Mashup-oriented API recommendation task. We input the descriptions of APIs and Mashups into ServiceBERT, and use their final hidden state of [CLS] token as feature vectors of them, respectively. Then we calculate dot product of feature vectors as the relevance score of them. The experimental results are shown in Table 3.

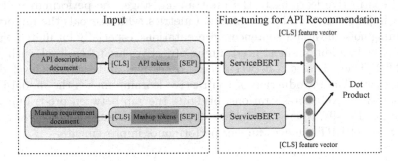

Fig. 4. The process of fine-tuning on the Mashup-oriented API recommendation task.

Table 3. Results on API recommendation task.

Methods	Recall			NDCG		
	Top-3	Top-5	Top-10	Top-3	Top-5	Top-10
SPR	0.3627	0.4326	0.5098	0.3098	0.3477	0.3890
DHSR	0.3840	0.4587	0.5355	0.3385	0.3733	0.4010
TA-BLSTM	0.4018	0.4729	0.5687	0.3671	0.4012	0.4309
FC-LSTM	0.4211	0.4874	0.5786	0.3725	0.4153	0.4527
BERT-base	0.4822	0.5592	0.6543	0.4461	0.4822	0.5165
ServiceBERT	**0.5270**	**0.5968**	**0.6770**	**0.4816**	**0.5149**	**0.5450**

SPR [30] jointly models Mashup descriptions and used APIs using author topic model (ATM) to reconstruct service profiles for API recommendation. **DHSR** [25] integrates collaborative filtering with textual content within a deep neural network for API recommendation. **TA-BLSTM** [15] trains a tag attention-aware long short-term memory network to learn representations for descriptions. **FC-LSTM** [14] proposes a functional and contextual attention-based method for API recommendation. Results show that our **ServiceBERT** achieves better performance than other methods, which proves the effectiveness of our model.

4.5   Ablation Study

In order to understand how each designed component contributes to the overall performance gain of our model, we perform an ablation study on the API recommendation task as shown in Table 4. In (2), ServiceBERT(domain) refers to that we continue to train the BERT-base using Web service data listed in Table 1. In (3), we introduce the RTD objective into the pre-training process. In (4), we introduce the contrastive learning to learn noise-invariant representations at the sentence-level. In (5), we combine all designed components.

From the results reported in Table 4, we can have some observations. Compared with (1), the introduction of Web service domain data brings significant performance improvement as shown in (2). In (3), by integrating RTD objective into the pre-training process, the performance is further improved. In(4), when adding contrastive learning to the pre-training stage, the performance obtains further improvements on both evaluation metrics, which reveals the importance of learning noise-invariant sentence representations, especially for matching task in this case. In addition, most pre-training objectives are token-level, such MLM and RTD. There is a gap between these objectives and sentence-level downstream tasks. The introduction of contrastive learning makes the model better learn sentence-level representations, bridging the gap between pre-training and fine-tuning. Finally, when we combine all proposed designs into the pre-training stage, ServiceBERT achieves further performance improvements.

Table 4. Ablation study on Mashup-oriented API recommendation task.

Methods	Recall			NDCG		
	Top-3	Top-5	Top-10	Top-3	Top-5	Top-10
(1) BERT-base	0.4822	0.5592	0.6543	0.4461	0.4822	0.5165
(2) ServiceBERT (domain)	0.5034	0.5742	0.6637	0.4613	0.4934	0.5247
(3) ServiceBERT (domain+RTD)	0.5081	0.5797	0.6684	0.4689	0.4977	0.5303
(4) ServiceBERT (domain+CL)	0.5203	0.5886	0.6721	0.4753	0.5078	0.5379
(5) ServiceBERT (All)	**0.5270**	**0.5968**	**0.6770**	**0.4816**	**0.5149**	**0.5450**

5   Conclusion

This paper presented a novel pre-trained model for Web API tagging and recommendation, called ServiceBERT. Specifically, we incorporate rich knowledge of Web service ecosystem crawled from ProgrammableWeb into the pre-training process, so as to enable effective learning of the model on domain knowledge. In addition to employing the objective of masked language modeling (MLM), we also introduce the replaced token detection objective for efficient learning of the pre-trained model. Finally, we also introduce contrastive learning to learn noise-invariant representations at the sentence-level by contrasting positive pairs against negative pairs. Comprehensive experiments on two service-related tasks have successfully demonstrated the overall performance improvement of ServiceBERT over a variety of representative methods for API tagging and API recommendation.

Acknowledgment. This work is supported by the National Natural Science Foundation of China under Grants 61972290 and the National Key R&D Program of China under Grant 2018YFC1604000. This work is also supported by the National Natural Science Foundation of China (61962061) and partially supported by the Yunnan Provincial Foundation for Leaders of Disciplines in Science and Technology (202005AC160005).

References

1. Barros, A.P., Dumas, M.: The rise of web service ecosystems. Science and Engineering Faculty (2006)
2. Cao, Y., Liu, J., Cao, B., Shi, M., Wen, Y., Peng, Z.: Web services classification with topical attention based BI-LSTM. In: International Conference on Collaborative Computing: Networking, Applications and Worksharing, pp. 394–407 (2019)
3. Chen, T., Kornblith, S., Norouzi, M., Hinton, G.: A simple framework for contrastive learning of visual representations. In: ICML 2020: 37th International Conference on Machine Learning, vol. 1, pp. 1597–1607 (2020)
4. Clark, K., Luong, M.T., Le, Q.V., Manning, C.D.: ELECTRA: pre-training text encoders as discriminators rather than generators. In: ICLR 2020 : Eighth International Conference on Learning Representations (2020)
5. Devlin, J., Chang, M.W., Lee, K., Toutanova, K.N.: BERT: pre-training of deep bidirectional transformers for language understanding. In: Proceedings of the 2019 Conference of the North American Chapter of the Association for Computational Linguistics: Human Language Technologies, Volume 1 (Long and Short Papers), pp. 4171–4186 (2018)
6. Devries, T., Taylor, G.W.: Improved regularization of convolutional neural networks with cutout. arXiv preprint arXiv:1708.04552 (2017)
7. Fang, H., Xie, P.: CERT: contrastive self-supervised learning for language understanding. arXiv preprint arXiv:2005.12766 (2020)
8. Fletcher, K.K.: An attention model for mashup tag recommendation. In: International Conference on Services Computing, pp. 50–64 (2020)
9. Gidaris, S., Singh, P., Komodakis, N.: Unsupervised representation learning by predicting image rotations. In: International Conference on Learning Representations (2018)
10. Liu, Y., et al.: RoBERTa: a robustly optimized BERT pretraining approach. arXiv preprint arXiv:1907.11692 (2019)
11. Peters, M.E., et al.: Deep contextualized word representations. In: Proceedings of the 2018 Conference of the North American Chapter of the Association for Computational Linguistics: Human Language Technologies, Volume 1 (Long Papers), vol. 1, pp. 2227–2237 (2018)
12. Radford, A., Narasimhan, K., Salimans, T., Sutskever, I.: Improving language understanding by generative pre-training (2018)
13. Saied, M.A., Raelijohn, E., Batot, E., Famelis, M., Sahraoui, H.A.: Towards assisting developers in API usage by automated recovery of complex temporal patterns. Inf. Softw. Technol. **119**(119), 106213 (2020)

14. Shi, M., Tang, Y., Liu, J.: Functional and contextual attention-based LSTM for service recommendation in mashup creation. IEEE Trans. Parallel Distrib. Syst. **30**(5), 1077–1090 (2019)
15. Shi, M., Tang, Y., Liu, J.: TA-BLSTM: tag attention-based bidirectional long short-term memory for service recommendation in mashup creation. In: 2019 International Joint Conference on Neural Networks (IJCNN), pp. 1–8 (2019)
16. Szegedy, C., et al.: Going deeper with convolutions. In: 2015 IEEE Conference on Computer Vision and Pattern Recognition (CVPR), pp. 1–9 (2015)
17. Uddin, G., Khomh, F., Roy, C.K.: Mining API usage scenarios from stack overflow. Inf. Softw. Technol. **122**(122), 106277 (2020)
18. Vaswani, A., et al.: Attention is all you need. In: Proceedings of the 31st International Conference on Neural Information Processing Systems, vol. 30, pp. 5998–6008 (2017)
19. Wang, X., Liu, J., Liu, X., Cui, X., Wu, H.: A novel dual-graph convolutional network based web service classification framework. In: 2020 IEEE International Conference on Web Services (ICWS), pp. 281–288 (2020)
20. Wang, X., Liu, J., Liu, X., Cui, X., Wu, H.: A spatial and sequential combined method for web service classification. In: APWeb-WAIM 2020 : Proceedings of the 4th Asia-Pacific and Web-Age Information Management International Joint Conference on Web and Big Data, pp. 764–778 (2020)
21. Wang, X., Liu, X., Liu, J., Chen, X., Wu, H.: A novel knowledge graph embedding based API recommendation method for mashup development. World Wide Web **24**(3), 869–894 (2021)
22. Wang, X., et al.: SYNCOBERT: syntax-guided multi-modal contrastive pre-training for code representation. arXiv: Computation and Language (2021)
23. Wei, J.W., Zou, K.: Eda: easy data augmentation techniques for boosting performance on text classification tasks. In: Proceedings of the 2019 Conference on Empirical Methods in Natural Language Processing and the 9th International Joint Conference on Natural Language Processing (EMNLP-IJCNLP), pp. 6381–6387 (2019)
24. Wu, Z., Wang, S., Gu, J., Khabsa, M., Sun, F., Ma, H.: CLEAR: contrastive learning for sentence representation. arXiv preprint arXiv:2012.15466 (2020)
25. Xiong, R., Wang, J., Zhang, N., Ma, Y.: Deep hybrid collaborative filtering for web service recommendation. Expert Syst. Appl. **110**, 191–205 (2018)
26. Yang, Y., et al.: ServeNet: a deep neural network for web services classification. In: 2020 IEEE International Conference on Web Services (ICWS), pp. 168–175 (2020)
27. Yao, L., Wang, X., Sheng, Q.Z., Benatallah, B., Huang, C.: Mashup recommendation by regularizing matrix factorization with API co-invocations. IEEE Trans. Serv. Comput. **14**, 502–515 (2021)
28. Ye, H., Cao, B., Chen, J., Liu, J., Wen, Y., Chen, J.: A web services classification method based on GCN. In: 2019 IEEE International Conference on Parallel and Distributed Processing with Applications, Big Data and Cloud Computing, Sustainable Computing and Communications, Social Computing and Networking (ISPA/BDCloud/SocialCom/SustainCom), pp. 1107–1114 (2019)
29. Yuan, W., Nguyen, H.H., Jiang, L., Chen, Y., Zhao, J., Yu, H.: API recommendation for event-driven android application development. Inf. Softw. Technol. **107**, 30–47 (2019)
30. Zhong, Y., Fan, Y., Tan, W., Zhang, J.: Web service recommendation with reconstructed profile from mashup descriptions. IEEE Trans. Autom. Sci. Eng. **15**(2), 468–478 (2018)

Top-k Dynamic Service Composition in Skyway Networks

Babar Shahzaad[(✉)] and Athman Bouguettaya

The University of Sydney, Sydney, NSW 2000, Australia
{babar.shahzaad,athman.bouguettaya}@sydney.edu.au

Abstract. We propose a novel top-k service composition framework for drone services under a dynamic environment. We develop a system model for formal modeling of drone services in a skyway network. The composition process is accomplished in two phases, i.e., computing top-k compositions and extending and ranking top-k compositions using probabilistic wait and recharge times under congestion conditions. We propose a top-k composition algorithm to compute the best service composition plan meeting user's requirements. A set of experiments with a real dataset is conducted to demonstrate the effectiveness of the proposed approach.

Keywords: Drone delivery · Drone service · Service composition · Top-k · Skyway network

1 Introduction

Drones have gained significant attention in recent years due to their potential benefits for a multitude of civilian applications [1]. The use of drones will play a paramount role in enabling new services in various domains such as disaster management, remote sensing, and delivery of goods [2]. Drones provide safe, contactless, and more resilient alternatives to deliver goods in remote locations [3]. Many start-up companies such as FlyTrex and large companies such as Amazon and Google are investing in the use of drones for delivery services [4].

The *service paradigm* [5] offers a powerful mechanism to abstract the capabilities of a drone *as drone services*. As any other service, a drone service is defined by its *functional* and *non-functional* properties [6]. In this instance, the functional property represents the *transport of a package* from a node (e.g., warehouse rooftop) to another node (e.g., customer's building rooftop) in a *skyway* network. The non-functional (i.e., *Quality of Service* (QoS)) properties of a drone service represent such attributes as the payload capacity, flight range, battery capacity, etc. A *skyway network* is defined as a set of connected nodes representing take-off and landing stations [7]. Each node may concurrently act as a recharging station. The transport/delivery of a package by a drone along a line segment that directly connects two nodes represents an atomic service abstraction. An instantiation of this service abstraction is the transport of a

© Springer Nature Switzerland AG 2021
H. Hacid et al. (Eds.): ICSOC 2021, LNCS 13121, pp. 479–495, 2021.
https://doi.org/10.1007/978-3-030-91431-8_30

package by a specific drone between two named nodes that are connected by a direct segment, operating under a set of requirements/constraints.

A single drone service may not guarantee the direct delivery of a package from a warehouse to a customer's desired location due to flight range limitations, flight regulations, battery life, etc. Therefore, drone service *composition* is required to ensure successful package delivery. An optimal drone service composition is defined as the selection of the best drone services in a skyway network from a given source to a destination [8]. The composition of services creates a value-added service [9–11]. We compose drone services to deliver packages while considering customer's QoS requirements. We assume that no handover of packages occurs among drones at intermediate stations as each drone has its own delivery plan, i.e., the same drone delivers a package from source to destination.

A key challenge in drone service composition is the uncertainty in congestion behaviour at recharging stations. This uncertainty is caused by the stochastic arrival of drones at particular stations. The arrival of a drone is greatly influenced by the payload weight, drone speed, and weather conditions [12]. For example, several drones may be scheduled to arrive at a certain recharging station. If drones arrive earlier or later than the scheduled time, this may cause congestion at this station. A congested station is defined as a recharging station where all pads are occupied and the drone may have to wait for the availability of pads [13]. Each drone that operates in a multi-drone environment has its own delivery plan. Therefore, an accurate prediction of congestion at stations may not be possible for long-term periods [14]. This uncertainty in congestion behaviour makes the composition problem significantly complex compared to a static skyway network where all drone services are deterministic.

The existing drone service composition approaches do not consider the uncertainty in congestion behaviour at recharging stations [15, 16]. We propose a *top-k drone service composition framework* that can effectively deal with the uncertain nature of the environment. We assume that drones are partially recharged at intermediate recharging stations. This assumption helps drones delivering packages faster. First, we compute *top-k drone service compositions* based on the service time of each drone service without considering congestion conditions. Then, we rank the compositions based on the shortest service time to support the faster package delivery from a given source to a destination. For example, top-3 compositions are computed and ranked in ascending order based on the service time for each composition. We consider the probabilistic availability of pads to estimate the waiting and recharging times at each station under congestion conditions. Then, we compute a new delivery time for each composition in top-k compositions which is a sum of service time, waiting time, and recharging time for each drone service. We rerank the compositions using the new delivery times and select the best service composition plan. Finally, we compare the results of top-k composition approach with exhaustive drone service composition approach to analyze its performance in terms of execution time, delivery time, and delivery cost. We summarize the main contributions of this paper as follows:

- Designing a system model for the provisioning of drone services.
- Proposing a top-k drone service composition framework under recharging constraints.
- Developing a heuristic-based approach for the composition of drone services and ranking the drone service composition.
- Conducting experiments using a real drone dataset to demonstrate the performance of the proposed composition approach.

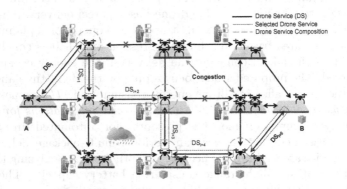

Fig. 1. Drone service composition for package delivery in a skyway network

2 Motivating Scenario

Drones can be used for safe and contactless delivery of packages such as parcel, mail, medication, and meal. Let multiple delivery service providers offer package delivery services using drones in Texas, USA. Suppose Robert requests a fast package delivery service using a drone from *San Marcos* to *San Antonio* (92 km). The flight range of a typical delivery drone varies from 3 to 33 km [13]. The weather conditions, the payload weight, and the drone speed influence the drone's flight range. Therefore, multiple times of recharge is required to meet the delivery request. In this regard, it is of paramount importance to avoid bad weather and congestion conditions at the recharging stations.

We construct a skyway network following the drone flying regulations such as avoiding flying in restricted areas (e.g., airport and military). The skyway network is divided into predefined skyway segments where each segment is a skyway path between two nodes. The nodes are the rooftops of the buildings which are assumed to be a *recharging station* and/or a *delivery target*. Each recharging station has a fixed set of pads for drones to land and recharge. Each skyway segment is a *drone service* which is served by a drone. The nodes in the skyway network are considered as hubs where dynamic congestion of drones occurs, i.e., all recharging pads are occupied. An optimal drone service composition avoids hub nodes and provides fast and cost-efficient delivery. Figure 1 depicts a drone service composition scenario for package delivery from point A to point B.

3   Related Work

The existing research on drone-based deliveries can be divided into two categories: (1) Data-driven Approaches (2) Service-driven Approaches.

Data-driven Approaches. Data-driven approaches focus on point-to-point deliveries using drones [17]. A parcel delivery system using drones is designed considering the impact of payload on the energy consumption of the drones [18]. The energy consumption of the drone is approximated as a linear function of the payload weight to schedule a reliable drone-based parcel delivery. It is assumed that the flying speed of drones is fixed. Strategic and operational planning is proposed for a given area based on a linear regression model. It is concluded that 60% of flight paths fail to complete the delivery if the energy consumption is not considered. The proposed study focuses only on the flight time and payload weight as the factors affecting drone energy consumption. *The proposed system does not consider the congestion conditions at recharging stations for drones.*

An energy consumption model is presented for automated drone delivery in [19]. It is assumed that drones can perform multi-package deliveries in a predefined service area. The drone fleet size is optimized by analyzing the impact of payload weight and flight range considering battery capacity. They explore the relationship between four variables (working period, drone speed, demand density of service area, and battery capacity) to minimize the total costs of the drone delivery system. The study indicated that the long hours of operation would benefit both service providers and customers. They found that drone deliveries are more cost-effective in areas with high demand densities. *This study does not take into account the recharging requirements of drones and the impact of congestion conditions on drone deliveries.*

A drone routing problem in a distribution network is studied considering the wind effects on power consumption [20]. It is assumed that the drone speed, wind speed, and wind direction remain constant during the delivery operation. It is also assumed that the payload weight of a drone remains fixed during a trip. As all influencing factors are deterministic, energy consumption becomes a constant number. All the deliveries are time-constrained, which requires the completion of the delivery operation in a given time window. Thus, energy constraints are ultimately transformed into generalized resource constraints. *The proposed approach does not consider the real-world changing weather and congestion conditions at recharging stations in the drone delivery network.*

A modular optimization method is proposed for the drone delivery system in [21]. The proposed method is beneficial in increasing the readiness of the drone fleet and decreasing the overall drone fleet size. A module in the proposed system lends more flexibility in drone operations with its interchangeable components: propellers, replaceable batteries, carriers, and motors. A forward-looking strategy is applied to enhance the performance of drone-based delivery. The modular delivery drones are compared to non-modular delivery drones using the proposed approach. The simulation results demonstrate that the modular optimization method is more efficient at reducing the power consumption and delivery time of a drone. *The proposed model does not consider the weather conditions and congestion conditions caused by other drones in the same delivery system.*

Service-driven Approaches. Service-driven approaches ensure *congruent* and *effective provisioning* of drone-based deliveries [16,22–24]. There is a paucity of literature focusing on service-driven approaches that consider drone-based deliveries in complex and dynamic environments. A formal drone service model is designed considering the spatio-temporal features of the drone services in [16]. The spatio-temporal features represent the location and time of the drone service. A formal QoS model is also designed to incorporate the non-functional properties of a drone service. The QoS properties include the service flight time and the delivery cost of a drone service. A heuristic-based algorithm is developed to select and compose the right drone services taking into account the QoS properties. *The proposed approach focuses only on the deterministic properties of services which is not realistic.*

A prototype for drone service provision is presented that includes a drone, a controller, and a client [23]. Each drone is embedded with a server to answer the service requests of clients made through a smartphone application. The simulation experiments are performed to analyze the factors that affect drone service delivery. The main factors include the number of drones, frequency of client requests, and relative localization of control stations. In addition, the scheduling strategies for distributing the service load among different drones are found more effective compared to a simple queue strategy. *However, the different recharging requirements of drones and uncertain wind conditions are not considered.*

A deterministic drone service composition approach is proposed to incorporate the recharging constraints at stations in [22]. The drone service selection and composition problem is formulated as a multi-armed bandit tree exploration problem. A skyline approach is proposed to reduce the search space for optimal selection of candidate drone services. A lookahead heuristic-based algorithm is presented for the selection and composition of optimal services. *However, the uncertain weather conditions over different skyway segments and dynamic recharging constraints are not considered in the proposed composition approach.*

A drone service system is presented to provide long-distance delivery services considering refueling and maintenance of drones in [24]. The objective of this system is to minimize the travel distance of a drone and the number of landing depots during the delivery operation. An ant colony algorithm with the A* algorithm is proposed to solve the problem of long-distance delivery services. *The proposed system does not take into account the factors affecting the flight range of a drone such as a payload and wind conditions.* Additionally, the congestion conditions at recharging stations are not considered in the proposed system. To the best of our knowledge, this paper is the first attempt to present a top-k drone service composition that considers congestion conditions at recharging stations.

4   Drone Service System Model

We propose a drone service system model for the provisioning of drone delivery services. The proposed model consists of four components: (1) Skyway Network,

(2) Drone Service Model, (3) No-Congestion Drone Service Model, and (4) Congestion Drone Service Model.

4.1 Skyway Network

We describe our multi-drone skyway network in which drone services operate to deliver packages. Let D is a set of drones where $D = \{d_1, d_2, \ldots, d_n\}$. The skyway network is modelled as an undirected graph $G = (N, E)$. N is a set of nodes, each of which represents a delivery target (i.e., customer's location) or recharging station. E is a set of edges, each of which represents a skyway segment *drone service* joining a pair of nodes. Each node has a *fixed number of recharging pads*. B is a set of battery capacities for all drones in D. The battery consumption and cost to travel from a node i to j are represented by b_{ij} and c_{ij} respectively. The battery consumption of the drone increases as the payload weight and the travelling distance increase.

4.2 Drone Service Model

The drone service, drone service query, and drone service composition problem are defined as follows.

Definition 1: Drone Service (DS). A drone service is a tuple of $< DS\_id, DS_f, DS_q >$, where

- $DS.id$ is a unique drone service ID,
- DS_f represents the delivery function of a drone over a skyway segment. The location and time of a drone service are tuples of $< loc_s, loc_e >$ and $< t_s, t_e >$, where
- loc_s and loc_e represent the start location and the end location of a drone service,
- t_s and t_e represent the start time and the end time of a drone service,
- DS_q is a tuple of $< q_1, q_2, \ldots, q_n >$, where each q_i represents a quality parameter of a drone service, e.g., flight range and payload capacity.

Definition 2: Drone Service Query (DSQ). A drone service query is defined as a service request for package delivery from a source location (i.e., warehouse rooftop) to a destination location (customer's building rooftop). A drone service query is a tuple $< \zeta, \xi, qt_s, w >$, where ζ is the source, ξ is the destination, qt_s is the query start time, and w is the weight of the package.

Definition 3: Drone Service Composition Problem. Given a set of drone services $S_{DS} = \{DS_1, DS_2, ..., DS_n\}$ and drone service query $< \zeta, \xi, qt_s, w >$, the drone service composition problem is to compose the services for delivering a package from the source to the destination in minimum time.

4.3   No-Congestion Drone Service Model

We propose a no-congestion model for drone services where the congestion conditions at recharging stations are ignored. We assume that a recharging pad is *always available* when a drone reaches a station, i.e., the recharging pads at each station are infinite. We use this assumption to compute *top-k compositions* that consider only the service time of a drone service to select a service in the composition process. This is motivated by the fact that the service time is *always higher* than the recharging time when a partial recharge policy is followed. The delivery time for a customer C_n ($n \in N$) is the sum of service times for each component drone service. Figure 2 represents top-K compositions in a no-congestion drone service model. The total delivery time for each composition is calculated by adding the sum of deterministic service times for all component drone services. For example, the service time for a drone service from node 1 to node 2 is 30 min. The total delivery time is the sum of services leading from source node 1 to destination node 12 which is 95 min in case of *service composition 1*.

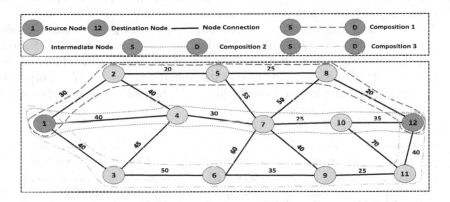

Fig. 2. Top-k compositions in no-congestion drone service model

4.4   Congestion Drone Service Model

Congestion is a natural phenomenon in a resource-constrained dynamic network [25]. The effect of congestion is primarily that the waiting time on a congested recharging station increases as more drones approach the same congested station. In a deterministic skyway network, each drone service has perfect knowledge of all other incoming and outgoing drones at a particular station and their scheduled arrival times. Each drone service then chooses the recharging station with the lowest waiting time. In this regard, the delivery time for a customer C_n ($n \in N$) can simply be modelled as follows:

$$T_n = S_n + R_n + W_n \tag{1}$$

where T_n is the deterministic delivery time, S_n is the service time of all component drone services in the skyway path from source to destination, and R_n and W_n are the sums of recharging and waiting times at each intermediate station, respectively.

In a dynamic skyway network, the drones do not have perfect knowledge about the availability of pads at a recharging station. Therefore, we consider the likelihood of pad's availability at a recharging station, i.e., probability of availability. We compute the delivery time considering the probabilities of the pad's availability and its duration of availability for recharging. We use the following equation to calculate the delivery time for a customer C_n $(n \in N)$:

$$T_n = S_n + \sum_{i=0}^{n} Pr_i * (R_i + W_i) \qquad (2)$$

where T_n is the stochastic delivery time, S_n is the service time of all component drone services in the skyway path from source to destination, R_i and W_i are the recharging and waiting times at a station i, and Pr_i is the probability of recharging and waiting times for a station i.

The probabilistic availability of recharging stations varies with time. Therefore, we compute probabilities incrementally for neighbour recharging stations corresponding to the current station during the delivery operation. This process continues until the package is delivered to its desired destination. We incorporate the recharging and waiting times with their probabilities in precomputed top-k compositions as shown in Fig. 3.

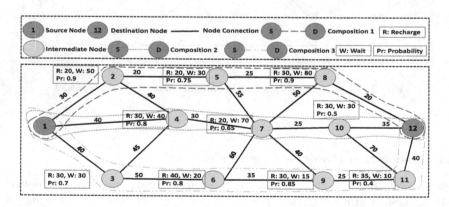

Fig. 3. Extended top-k composition in congestion drone service model

5   Top-k Drone Service Composition Framework

A single drone service usually cannot satisfy a user's end-to-end delivery require-ments. We often need to use drone service composition, which aggregates a set of drone services in order to serve a long-distance delivery request. In this paper, we propose a top-k drone service composition approach to support long-distance package deliveries using drones. We initially compute and rank top-k compo-sitions considering service times of each component drone service. The service time represents the time to travel from one end to another end of a drone service.

In real-world situations, drone service compositions are influenced by the stochastic arrival of drones at intermediate stations and the changes in weather conditions. As a result, the established composition plans may become non-optimal. We, therefore, consider uncertainties involved in weather and congestion conditions at stations to provide an efficient and reliable drone service compo-sition. We use the probabilistic arrival of drones at recharging stations that are a part of the top-k compositions. In addition, we also compute their effects on waiting and recharging times. As the congestion conditions are time-variant, we compute probabilities at each recharging station incrementally. We then cal-culate the stochastic delivery time using Eq. 2 in the congestion drone service model to incorporate the effects of dynamic congestion conditions in top-k com-positions. We rerank the extended composition plans based on the delivery times with higher probabilities.

5.1   Algorithm

This section describes the top-k drone service composition algorithm for drone-based delivery services. The drone service composition process is accomplished in two phases. In the first phase, we compute, select, and rank top-k compositions considering the delivery time in no-congestion drone service model. In the second phase, we incorporate dynamism in top-k compositions considering congestion conditions described in congestion drone service model and rerank the extended composition plans. The details of the algorithm are described in Algorithm 1.

In Algorithm 1, the output $DSComp$ is a set of top-k drone service com-position plans from a source location to a destination location. The input is the skyway network represented by graph G, the set of delivery drones D, the source ζ, the destination ξ, the package weight w, the query start time qt_s, and the number of top compositions to be selected k. Each skyway segment drone service in graph G is served by a drone selected from the drone set D. We consider the start location, end location, and the distance between the two ends of each skyway segment drone service in graph G. We create empty lists for $DSComp, DSBase, topKComp, T_{DSComp}$, and T_{DSBase} (Lines 1–5). We use the *Block Nested Loop (BNL)* [26] algorithm to select an optimal set of drones from

---

Algorithm 1. Top-k Drone Service Composition

Input: G, D, ζ, ξ, w, qt_s, k
Output: $DSComp$
 1: $DSComp \leftarrow \phi$
 2: $DSBase \leftarrow \phi$
 3: $topKComp \leftarrow \phi$
 4: $T_{DSComp} \leftarrow \phi$
 5: $T_{DSBase} \leftarrow \phi$
 6: $d_{sel} \leftarrow$ block_nested_loop (D, w)
    Phase 1. Initial top-k compositions
 7: $topKComp, T_{DSBase} \leftarrow$ base_comps $(G, \zeta, \xi, k, d_{sel}, w)$
 8: $DSBase \leftarrow$ rank_comps $(topKComp, T_{DSBase})$
    Phase 2. Extend top-k compositions considering congestion conditions
 9: **for** $DS_i \in DSBase$ **do**
10:    $curTime \leftarrow qt_s$
11:    $T_i \leftarrow 0$
12:    **for** $ds_j \in DS_i$ **do**
13:       $Pr_j, W_j, R_j \leftarrow$ probability_wait_recharge $(ds_j.loc_e, curTime)$
14:       $T_i \leftarrow T_i + S_j + Pr_j * (R_j + W_j)$
15:       $curTime \leftarrow curTime + T_i$
16:    **end for**
17:    T_{DSComp}.append(T_i)
18: **end for**
19: $DSComp \leftarrow$ rank_comps $(DSBase, T_{DSComp})$
20: **return** $DSComp$

---

a large set of delivery drones D given the payload weight (Line 6). Algorithm 2 provides the details of the BNL algorithm. Multiple drone service providers offer package delivery services. Each provider has several drones with different quality attributes. The BNL approach supports the selection of an optimal drone set determined to be a good fit for the delivery request. First, we filter the large set of delivery drones D based on the package weight w to select the candidate drones in Algorithm 2 (Lines 2–6). Then, we select a set of non-dominated drones based on the best QoS properties for each candidate drone. We use the negative and positive parameters to select drones, such as recharging time and travel distance, respectively (Lines 8–9). We obtain the better and worse values of quality parameters for each drone using Algorithm 3. The range of a drone is of paramount importance to serve long-distance areas. Therefore, we prefer the flight range parameter for selecting a drone from the optimal drone set to serve the delivery request in Algorithm 2 (Line 31).

Algorithm 2. block_nested_loop (D, w)

1:   $candidateDrone \leftarrow \phi$
2: **for** each $drone \in D$ **do**
3:    **if** $drone.pl \geq w$ **then**
4:      $candidateDrone$.append($drone$)
5:    **end if**
6: **end for**
7:   $rows \leftarrow candidateDrone.to\_dict()$
8:   $to\_min \leftarrow$ negative parameters, e.g., recharging time
9:   $to\_max \leftarrow$ positive parameters, e.g., travel distance
10:   $to\_sel \leftarrow$ important parameter for drone selection, e.g., range
11:   $selDrone \leftarrow candidateDrone[0]$
12: **for** each $drone \in candidateDrone[1 : n]$ **do**
13:    $is\_dominated \leftarrow False$
14:    $to\_drop \leftarrow set()$
15:    **for** each $q_i \in selDrone$ **do**
16:      $better, worse \leftarrow$ count_diff $(rows[drone.q_i], rows[q_i], to\_min, to\_max)$
17:      **if** $worse > 0$ and $better = 0$ **then**
18:        $is\_dominated \leftarrow True$
19:        break
20:      **end if**
21:      **if** $better > 0$ and $worse = 0$ **then**
22:        to_drop.add(q_i)
23:      **end if**
24:      **if** $is\_dominated$ **then**
25:        continue
26:      **end if**
27:      $selDrone \leftarrow selDrone$.difference($to\_drop$)
28:      $selDrone$.add($drone$)
29:    **end for**
30: **end for**
31: **return** $selDrone[to\_sel]$

In phase 1, we compute top-k compositions and their delivery times using the selected drone and payload weight. Each drone service composition constitutes a skyway path based on the shortest delivery time leading the package w from the source ζ to the destination ξ (Line 7). We perform a straightforward ranking of compositions considering the respective delivery times (Line 8). In phase 2, we calculate the wait and recharge times and their corresponding probabilities at certain timestamps using a black-box approach for each component service and its intermediate station. We repeat the process for all top-k compositions and estimate the updated times considering weather and congestion conditions (Lines 9–18). We rerank the composition plans based on their extended delivery times and finally return a list of top-k drone service compositions (Lines 19–20). The reranking is essential as an initial optimal composition plan may become non-optimal due to changing weather and congestion conditions.

Algorithm 3. count_diff (*paramA, paramB, to_min, to_max*)

1: *better* ← 0, *worse* ← 0
2: **for each** $f \in to\_min$ **do**
3:     *better* ← *better* + (*paramA*[*f*] < *paramB*[*f*])
4:     *worse* ← *worse* + (*paramA*[*f*] > *paramB*[*f*])
5: **end for**
6: **for each** $f \in to\_max$ **do**
7:     *better* ← *better* + (*paramA*[*f*] > *paramB*[*f*])
8:     *worse* ← *worse* + (*paramA*[*f*] < *paramB*[*f*])
9: **end for**
10: **return** *better, worse*

---

6   Performance Evaluation

We evaluate the performance of our proposed drone service composition approach using the following evaluation settings:

- **Performance Metrics:** The delivery time and cost are paramount in drone delivery services. We use the drone travelling distance as a function of delivery cost. Therefore, we use (1) *execution time*, (2) *delivery time*, and (3) *distance travelled* as performance metrics. The execution time is used to evaluate the runtime complexity of the algorithms.
- **Baseline:** To evaluate our proposed approach, we compare the top-k drone service composition algorithm with an exhaustive drone service composition approach. The exhaustive composition approach takes exponential time for the increasing number of nodes.

6.1   Experiment Settings with Real-World Datasets

We develop a top-k drone service composition framework for delivery services to evaluate the performance of our proposed approach. The modules of the framework are shown in Fig. 4. We build a skyway network using the NetworkX python library, where each node can be a delivery target or a recharging station. We model multiple drone services from different drone service providers operating in the same network. The drone set consists of quality parameters of each drone operating in the skyway network, e.g., flight range and payload capacity. The experiments are conducted for an average of 50% times the total number of nodes. For example, if there are 40 nodes in the network, the experiment is performed 20 times. We select a random source and a random destination point for each experiment. The delivery request module is used for initiating drone-based delivery services. The Block Nested Loop implements Algorithm 2 which is used to select the right drone. We use a real urban road network dataset for the Tokyo city, including data for coordinates, nodes, and length of each edge between two nodes [27]. We extract a sub-network of 5000 connected nodes to construct a skyway network. We augment a dataset for different types of drones considering the payload, speed, flight range, recharging time, and battery capacity. The experimental variables are described in Table 1.

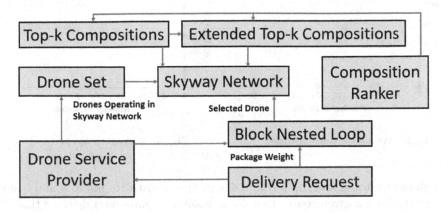

Fig. 4. Top-k drone service composition framework for delivery services

Table 1. Experimental variables

Variable	Values
Drone model	DJI M200 V2
Maximum payload capacity	1.45 Kg
Maximum drone flight time	24 min
Maximum drone flight range	32.4 km
Maximum drone speed	81 km/h
Recharging time from 0% to 100%	2.24 h
Maximum nodes in the skyway network	40
No. of pads at each recharging station	3
Experiment run the total number of nodes	50%

6.2 Results and Discussion

The proposed top-k approach performs the composition of the right drone services to deliver the package faster. We rank the top-k compositions and select the best composition plan for comparison with the baseline approach. For example, the top-3 compositions in the results show the best extended composition plan among 3 compositions with the least delivery time that is computed after incorporating the probabilistic recharging and waiting times. A similar approach is

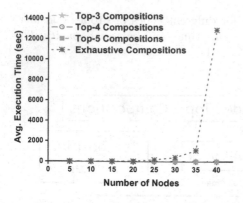

Fig. 5. Average execution time

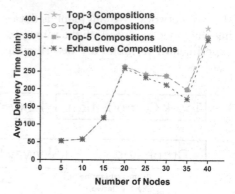

Fig. 6. Average delivery time

considered for top-4 and top-5 compositions that constitute initial 4 and 5 skyway paths from a given source to a destination with minimum delivery time.

Average Execution Time. The time complexity is an important parameter to evaluate the performance of an algorithm. The exhaustive composition approach is computationally expensive compared to the proposed top-k composition approach. The execution time increases as the number of possible drone service compositions increase. The average execution times for exhaustive, top-3, top-4, and top-5 compositions are presented in Fig. 5. The execution times for all top-k compositions are approximately similar because of avoiding exhaustive drone service compositions. As expected, the average execution time for the exhaustive grows exponentially for an increasing number of nodes. The experiments indicate that when the nodes are above 40, the results' trends are similar. As a result, we set the maximum number of nodes at 40. It shows that the use of the baseline approach is not practical in real-world scenarios for large-scale problems because of its exhaustive nature. We observe that our proposed approach outperforms the exhaustive composition approach to compute an optimal composition plan.

Average Delivery Time. The delivery time of a drone is a summation of recharging, waiting, and service times. The delivery time is mainly affected by the occupancy of certain recharging stations for long periods of time. Figure 6 shows the delivery times of exhaustive, top-3, top-4, and top-5 compositions. The exhaustive approach always computes all possible drone service compositions, which in turn provides exact solutions. The top-k compositions provide delivery solutions close to the exhaustive composition approach. We observe that the delivery time is 5% higher for the top-3 compositions and 4% higher for the top-4 and top-5 compositions compared to the exhaustive composition approach. This increase in delivery time is because the top-k compositions do not initially anticipate the arrival of other drones and congestion conditions at recharging stations. However, the top-k composition approach is significantly faster than the exhaustive composition approach, as shown in Fig. 5.

Average Distance Travelled. The cost of drone-based delivery services is estimated to be $0.1 for a 2 kg package delivery within a range of 10 km [28]. We define the cost function of the drone delivery as its travelling distance. Due to the uncertain nature of the environment, the initially attractive services may lead to congested stations. The average distances travelled by exhaustive, top-3, top-4, and top-5 compositions are shown in Fig. 7. The least distance services selected by the top-k composition approach may result in higher delivery time because of the uncertainty involved in the composition process. We observe that the distance travelled by the exhaustive composition approach is slightly higher than our proposed top-k composition approach. This is because the exhaustive composition approach always selects the optimal delivery time services. It shows that the delivery cost for the top-k composition approach is slightly less than the exhaustive composition approach.

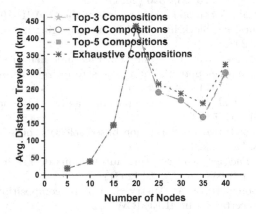

Fig. 7. Average distance travelled

7   Conclusion

We propose a novel framework for drone service composition considering the stochastic congestion constraints at recharging stations. A Block Nested Loop algorithm is used for the selection of the right drone at the source location. The proposed approach initially computes top-k compositions with minimum service times from the source to the destination. Then, we incorporate the probabilistic impact of recharging time and waiting time at stations. We rank the top-k compositions based on their delivery times and select the best composition plan. We run a set of experiments to evaluate the efficiency of our approach compared to the exhaustive composition approach. The experimental results prove that the proposed approach is computationally efficient and cost-effective to deliver the packages compared to the exhaustive composition approach. Moreover, our proposed approach is a practical solution for real-world scenarios of drone delivery services due to its stable and computationally efficient solutions. In future, we plan to include other types of environmental uncertainties such as temperature and their impact on drone delivery.

Acknowledgment. This research was partly made possible by DP160103595 and LE180100158 grants from the Australian Research Council. The statements made herein are solely the responsibility of the authors.

References

1. Shakhatreh, H., et al.: Unmanned aerial vehicles (UAVS): a survey on civil applications and key research challenges. IEEE Access **7**, 48572–48634 (2019)
2. Shahzaad, B., et al.: Resilient composition of drone services for delivery. Future Gener. Comput. Syst. **115**, 335–350 (2021)
3. Chamola, V., et al.: A comprehensive review of the COVID-19 pandemic and the role of IoT, drones, AI, blockchain, and 5G in managing its impact. IEEE Access **8**, 90225–90265 (2020)
4. Aurambout, J.P., Gkoumas, K., Ciuffo, B.: Last mile delivery by drones: an estimation of viable market potential and access to citizens across European cities. Eur. Transp. Res. Rev. **11**, 1–21 (2019)
5. Bouguettaya, A., et al.: A service computing manifesto: the next 10 years. Commun. ACM **60**(4), 64–72 (2017)
6. Alkouz, B., Bouguettaya, A.: Formation-based selection of drone swarm services. In: Mobiquitous. EAI (2020)
7. Lee, W., et al.: Package delivery using autonomous drones in skyways. In: Proceedings UbiComp/ISWC, pp. 48–50 (2021)
8. Shahzaad, B., Bouguettaya, A., Mistry, S.: Robust composition of drone delivery services under uncertainty. In: IEEE ICWS (2021)
9. Lakhdari, A., et al.: Elastic composition of crowdsourced IoT energy services. In: Mobiquitous. EAI (2020)
10. Chaki, D., Bouguettaya, A.: Adaptive priority-based conflict resolution of IoT services. arXiv preprint arXiv:2107.08348 (2021)
11. Lakhdari, A., Bouguettaya, A.: Proactive composition of mobile IoT energy services. In: IEEE ICWS (2021)
12. Alkouz, B., Bouguettaya, A.: Provider-centric allocation of drone swarm services. In: IEEE ICWS (2021)
13. Kim, J., et al.: CBDN: cloud-based drone navigation for efficient battery charging in drone networks. Trans. Intell. Transp. Syst. **20**, 1–18 (2018)
14. Shahzaad, B., Bouguettaya, A., Mistry, S.: A game-theoretic drone-as-a-service composition for delivery. In: IEEE ICWS, pp. 449–453 (2020)
15. Alkouz, B., Bouguettaya, A., Mistry, S.: Swarm-based drone-as-a-service (SDAAS) for delivery. In: IEEE ICWS, pp. 441–448 (2020)
16. Shahzaad, B., et al.: Composing drone-as-a-service (DAAS) for delivery. In: IEEE ICWS, pp. 28–32, Milan (2019)

17. Dorling, K., et al.: Vehicle routing problems for drone delivery. Trans. Syst. Man Cybern. **47**(1), 70–85 (2017)
18. Torabbeigi, M., Lim, G.J., Kim, S.J.: Drone delivery scheduling optimization considering payload-induced battery consumption rates. J. Intell. Robot. Syst. **97**(3), 471–487 (2020)
19. Choi, Y., Schonfeld, P.M.: Optimization of multi-package drone deliveries considering battery capacity. In: 96th Annual Meeting of the Transportation Research Board, pp. 8–12, Washington (2017)
20. Radzki, G., Thibbotuwawa, A., Bocewicz, G.: Uavs flight routes optimization in changing weather conditions - constraint programming approach. Appl. Comput. Sci. **15**(3), 5–20 (2019)
21. Lee, J.: Optimization of a modular drone delivery system. In: IEEE SysCon, pp. 1–8 (2017)
22. Shahzaad, B., Bouguettaya, A., Mistry, S., Neiat, AGi.: Constraint-aware drone-as-a-service composition. In: Yangui, S., Bouassida Rodriguez, I., Drira, K., Tari, Z. (eds.) ICSOC 2019. LNCS, vol. 11895, pp. 369–382. Springer, Cham (2019). https://doi.org/10.1007/978-3-030-33702-5_28
23. Alwateer, M., Loke, S.W., Rahayu, W.: Drone services: An investigation via prototyping and simulation. In: IEEE WF-IoT, pp. 367–370 (2018)
24. Shao, J., et al.: A novel service system for long-distance drone delivery using the "ant colony+a*" algorithm. IEEE Syst. J. **15**, 1–12 (2020)
25. Fotouhi, Z., et al.: A general model for EV drivers' charging behavior. IEEE Trans. Veh. Technol. **68**(8), 7368–7382 (2019)
26. Hsu, W.T., et al.: Skyline travel routes: exploring skyline for trip planning. In: IEEE MDM, vol. 2, pp. 31–36, QLD (2014)
27. Karduni, A., Kermanshah, A., Derrible, S.: A protocol to convert spatial polyline data to network formats and applications to world urban road networks. Sci. Data **3**(1), 160046 (2016)
28. D'Andrea, R.: Guest editorial can drones deliver? Trans. Autom. Sci. Eng. **11**(3), 647–648 (2014)

Cloud/edge Computing

Graph-Based Data Deduplication
in Mobile Edge Computing Environment

Ruikun Luo[1], Hai Jin[1], Qiang He[2], Song Wu[1($\boxtimes$)], Zilai Zeng[1], and Xiaoyu Xia[3]

[1] National Engineering Research Center for Big Data Technology and System
Services Computing Technology and System Lab, Cluster and Grid Computing Lab
Huazhong University of Science and Technology, Wuhan, China
{rkluo,hjin,wusong,zilaizeng}@hust.edu.cn
[2] Swinburne University of Technology, Hawthorn, Australia
qhe@swin.edu.au
[3] Deakin University, Burwood, Australia
xiaoyu.xia@deakin.edu.au

Abstract. *Mobile edge computing* (MEC) extends cloud computing by deploying edge servers with computing and storage resources at base stations within users' geographic proximity. The networked edge servers in an area constitute an *edge storage system* (ESS), where edge servers cooperate to provide services for the users in the area. However, the potential of ESSs is challenged by edge servers' constrained storage resources due to their limited physical sizes. A straightforward method to tackle this challenge is to reduce data redundancy in the ESS. The unique characteristics and constraints in the MEC environment, e.g., edge servers' geographic coverage and distribution, render conventional data deduplication techniques designed for cloud storage systems obsolete. In this paper, we make the first attempt to study this novel *Edge Data Deduplication* (EDDE) problem. First, we model it as a constrained optimization problem with the aim to maximize data deduplication ratio under latency constraint by taking advantage of the collaboration between edge servers. Then, we prove that the EDDE problem is $\mathcal{NP}$-hard and propose an approach named EDDE-O for solving the EDDE problem optimally based on integer programming. To accommodate large-scale EDDE scenarios, we propose a $ln\alpha + 1$-approximation algorithm, namely EDDE-A, to find sub-optimal EDDE solutions efficiently. The results of extensive experiments conducted on a widely-used dataset demonstrate that EDDE-O and EDDE-A can solve the EDDE problem effectively and efficiently, outperforming four representative approaches significantly.

Keywords: Mobile edge computing · Edge data storage · Data deduplication · Integer programming · Approximation algorithm

1 Introduction

In recent years, the world has witnessed an exponential growth of network traffic produced by mobile and *internet-of-things* (IoT) services [12]. The transmission

© Springer Nature Switzerland AG 2021
H. Hacid et al. (Eds.): ICSOC 2021, LNCS 13121, pp. 499–515, 2021.
https://doi.org/10.1007/978-3-030-91431-8_31

of massive mobile and IoT data incurs heavy network traffic and consumes excessive network resources. In the meantime, the cloud computing paradigm is failing to fulfill various services' demand for low latency [5]. To tackle these challenges, *mobile edge computing* (MEC) as a new computing paradigm has emerged, which extends the cloud's computing and storage capabilities to the network edge in close proximity to mobile and IoT devices.

In the MEC environment, edge servers with computing and storage resources are deployed at base stations. The networked edge servers in an area constitute an *edge storage system* (ESS). Service providers like Facebook and YouTube can cache popular data on edge servers to enable low-latency data retrieval for their users [13,15]. Data produced by mobile and IoT devices can also be stored on the edge storage system to be shared or processed in real time. However, unlike cloud servers, edge servers' storage resources are highly constrained due to their limited physical sizes [5]. This unique *capacity constraint* sets an upper bound on the performance of an ESS and the services deployed on the system. It is a major challenge that service providers have never encountered before in the cloud computing environment. Many approaches have been proposed in recent years to explore the potentials of ESSs under this constraint [6,14,19].

Reducing data redundancy in the ESS is an effective way to alleviate the capacity constraint. Shared by various application vendors, as well as mobile and IoT devices, an ESS is often subject to data redundancy. For example, the real-time communication between vehicles and edge servers can lead to a large number of duplicate video frames on the same or different edge servers in an ESS. Reducing data redundancy in the ESS by removing duplicate data can effectively save on the storage resources on the system. A similar problem named data deduplication has been investigated intensively in the context of cloud storage systems with the aim to maximize data redundancy reduction [11, 18]. However, this *cloud data deduplication* (CDDE) problem is fundamentally different from the *edge data deduplication* (EDDE) problem. To reduce data redundancy, most CDDE approaches first split the data stored on all the storage nodes in the system into multiple fine-grained chunks of a specific size, e.g., 4KB and 8KB. Then, they identify and remove duplicate data chunks across all those storage nodes. A user requesting a data can, from a metadata server, retrieve the locations of all the required data chunks for building the data. In the MEC environment, a user can only access its nearby edge servers directly, i.e., edge servers that cover the user [5]. This *proximity constraint* disables all the CDDE approaches because they commonly assume that a user can access any of the storage nodes in the system. In addition, the extra time taken to build a data from data chunks undermines MEC's pursuit of low data retrieval latency. Thus, unlike CDDE that reduces data redundancy at the data chunk level, EDDE aims to reduce data redundancy at the file level by removing duplicate data across edge servers in the system.

In recent years, researchers are beginning to investigate data deduplication in the MEC environment [8,9]. However, existing studies have followed the same idea and design as CDDE approaches. Making the same assumptions as CDDE approaches, the approaches proposed in [8,9] cannot solve the EDDE problem in the real-world MEC environment for the same reasons discussed above. In addition, these approaches have failed to leverage the ability of edge servers to communicate and transmit data over the edge server network connecting the edge servers in the ESS, which has been widely acknowledged as a promising way to enable collaboration among edge servers [6,16,19]. To serve a user's data request, the requested data can be delivered to the user from an edge server multiple hops away over the edge server network under the latency constraint. Thus, an EDDE approach is urgently needed that reduces data redundancy in an ESS at the file level under the proximity constraint and the latency constraint.

This paper makes the first attempt to study the *Edge Data Deduplication* (EDDE) problem in realistic MEC environments, with the aim to maximize data deduplication ratio while fulfilling the proximity constraint and the latency constraint. Its major contributions include:

- We motivate the EDDE problem and present its fundamental differences from the traditional data deduplication problem in cloud storage systems.
- We formulate the EDDE problem as a constrained optimization problem and prove that it is $\mathcal{NP}$-hard.
- We propose an optimal approach named EDDE-O for solving small-scale EDDE problems based on integer programming, and an approximation approach named EDDE-A for solving large-scale EDDE problems efficiently with a proven $\ln\alpha + 1$-approximation ratio.

We comprehensively evaluate the effectiveness and efficiency of EDDE-O and EDDE-A against four representative approaches through experiments conducted on a real-world dataset.

The remainder of this paper is organized as follows. Section 2 motivates the EDDE problem with an example. Section 3 formulates the EDDE problem and theoretically analyze its $\mathcal{NP}$-hardness. Section 4 presents EDDE-O and EDDE-A in detail. Section 5 shows the experimental results of EDDE-O and EDDE-A. Section 6 reviews the related work. Section 7 summarizes this paper and points out the future work.

2 Motivating Example

Video streaming services accounted for 75% of the total internet traffic in 2017, and this proportion is expected to increase to 82% by 2022 [10]. This emphasizes the importance of data deduplication for ESSs. Figure 1(a) presents an ESS comprised of 13 edge servers $\{s_1, s_2, ..., s_{13}\}$ deployed in a specific area, e.g., Melbourne CBD. Assuming that a popular video d^1 is stored on edge servers s_1, s_2, s_4, s_5, s_{11}, and s_{13} to serve the users within the area marked by the yellow line. This area is referred to as the *data coverage* hereafter. In this example, we assume that the application-specific latency constraint is two hops - the

---

[1] Multiple data can be deduplicated individually and independently.

video can be delivered to a user from an edge server within two hops over the edge server network. In real-world EDDE scenarios, the latency constraint is application-specific and and the communication latency between edge servers may not always be the same. To study the EDDE problem in a generic manner, the latency constraint is measured by the number of hops over the edge server network, similar to [6,16]. Our approaches can easily handle latency constraints measured in milliseconds easily.

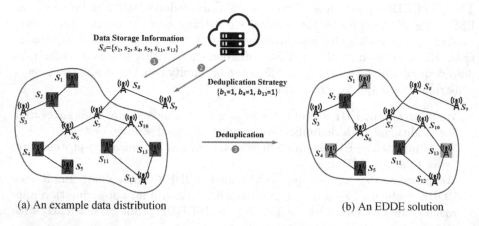

(a) An example data distribution   (b) An EDDE solution

Fig. 1. Example EDDE scenario. In this example, data replicas are removed from s_1, s_4, and s_{13}. The data coverages before and after deduplication, as shown in (a) and (b), respectively, are the same.

As shown in Fig. 1(a), from the perspective of the edge infrastructure provider, e.g., T-Mobile or Amazon, this ESS does not need all the six video replicas to serve all the users within the data coverage. Some video replicas can be removed to save on system storage resources. Based on the data storage information collected from the system, an EDDE strategy can be formulated that indicates which video replicas can be removed. It will be sent to the edge servers for implementation. This process is *edge data deduplication* (EDDE). The latency constraint must not be violated - the system must still be able to deliver the video to all the users within the data coverage within 2 hops. For example, if we retain only one video replica on the system, say the one on s_1, and remove all the other video replicas, most of the users in the original data coverage will not able to retrieve the video within 2 hops. Specifically, the video can be delivered to serve only the users covered by s_1, s_2, s_3, and s_6. This EDDE solution is apparently not feasible. Figure 1(b) presents another EDDE solution that removes the data replicas on edge servers s_1, s_4, and s_{13} while keeping those on s_2, s_5, and s_{11}. As presented in Fig. 1(b), this solution offers the same data coverage as Fig. 1(a). The users within the data coverage can retrieve the video under the latency constraint. Compared with Fig. 1, the EDDE solution stores only three video replicas in the ESS, 50% fewer than Fig. 1(a). Apparently, EDDE can save on system storage resources significantly. In the real world, the sizes of ESSs may be much larger, and there may be many possible EDDE solutions. Finding the optimal EDDE solution can save on the most system storage resources but may not be easy. An effective and efficient EDDE approach is needed.

3 Problem Statement

In this section, we formulate the EDDE problem and prove its hardness theoretically.

3.1 Problem Formulation

Let us model the n connected edge servers in an ESS as an undirected graph $G(S, E)$, where each edge server $s_i \in S$ is represented by a vertex in G and the link between two edge servers s_i and s_j is represented by an edge $e_{i,j}$ in G.

Let $S_d \subseteq S$ denote the set of edge servers where data d is stored and a_i is the binary variable indicating whether d is stored on edge server s_i:

$$a_i = \begin{cases} 0 & \text{if } d \text{ is not stored on } s_i, \ s_i \in S \\ 1 & \text{if } d \text{ is stored on } s_i, \ s_i \in S \end{cases} \tag{1}$$

$$S_d = \{s_i | \ a_i = 1, s_i \in S\} \tag{2}$$

Let h denote the latency constraint, representing the maximum number of hops that data can be delivered from an edge server to a user over G. It is application-specific. A low h value indicates that a low latency is required. Let $N(s_i)$ denote the set of s_i' neighbor edge servers, i.e., those within h hops over G, and $\hat{S}_d$ ($S_d \subseteq \hat{S}_d \subseteq S$) denote the set of edge servers[2] that can retrieve d from S_d under the latency constraint:

$$N(s_i) = \{s_j | \ h_{ij} \leq h, s_j \in S\} \tag{3}$$

$$\hat{S}_d = \{N(s_i) \mid s_i \in S_d\} \tag{4}$$

Equation (3) is employed to identify s_i's neighbor edge servers when h is measured by the number of hops. If the latency constraint is measured in milliseconds, say 20 ms, Eq. (3) can be replaced with $N(s_i) = \{s_j | \ latency_i^j \leq 20, s_j \in S\}$, where $latency_i^j$ is the communication latency between s_i and s_j.

To represent an EDDE strategy B, let binary variable b_i denote whether d is removed from edge server $s_i \in S_d$ by B (Table 1):

$$b_i = \begin{cases} 0 & d \text{ not removed from } s_i, \ s_i \in S_d \\ 1 & d \text{ removed from } s_i, \ s_i \in S_d \end{cases} \tag{5}$$

---

[2] The edge server covering a user will retrieve a data from other edge servers if it does not have the data requested by the user. Thus, we refer to edge servers instead of users here for ease of exposition.

Table 1. Summary of notations

Notation	Description
a_i	Binary variable representing whether s_i has d
B	EDDE strategy
b_i	EDDE decision representing whether d is removed from s_i
d	Data to be deduplicated
E	Set of connections between edge servers
G	Graph representing connected edge servers in ESS
h_{ij}	Minimum hops from s_i to s_j
h	Latency constraint
$N(s_i)$	Set of neighbor edge servers of s_i under latency constraint
n	Number of edge servers in ESS
R	Deduplication ratio
S	Set of edge servers in ESS
S_d	Set of edge servers with d before deduplication
S_{d+}	Set of edge servers with d after deduplication
S_{d-}	Set of edge servers not with d after deduplication
$\hat{S}_d$	set of edge servers covered by S_d under latency constraint
$\hat{S}_{d+}$	Set of edge servers covered by S_{d+} under latency constraint
s_i	ith edge server in ESS

Let $S_{d+} \subseteq S_d$ denote the set of edge servers with d after d is deduplicated from S_d:

$$S_{d+} = \{s_i|\ b_i = 0, s_i \in S_d\} \tag{6}$$

Similar to S_{d+}, we employ $S_{d-} \subseteq S_d$ ($S_{d+} \cup S_{d-} = S_d$) to denote the set of edge servers where d is removed.

As illustrated and discussed in Sect. 2, over-deduplication will reduce the coverage area of S_d and stop some users from being able to retrieve d under the latency constraint. To ensure the same data coverage, the users that could retrieve data before data deduplication must also be able to retrieve it after data deduplication. This *coverage constraint* is defined below:

$$\hat{S}_d = \hat{S}_{d+} \tag{7}$$

The deduplication ratio produced by an EDDE strategy B, denoted by R, is calculated as follows:

$$R = 1 - \frac{\sum_{i=1}^{n} b_i}{\sum_{i=1}^{n} a_i} \tag{8}$$

The optimization objective of the EDDE problem, i.e., to maximize the data deduplication ratio under the latency constraint (3) and the coverage constraint

(7), can be expressed as follows:

$$\text{maximize } R \tag{9}$$

3.2   Problem Hardness

In this section, we prove the $\mathcal{NP}$-hardness of the EDDE problem by reducing it from the classical $\mathcal{NP}$-hard *uncapacitated facility location* (UFL) problem [3]. Given a weighted bipartite graph $G < F, C, E, W >$, where F represents the candidate locations for opening facilities, C represents the clients that need to be served by facilities, E represents the connections from clients to facilities, and W is the connection cost matrix from C to F. The UFL problem aims to find a set of locations, denoted as $F' \subseteq F$, for opening facilities with the minimum overall cost, including the cost of opening all the facilities in F' and the cost of connecting clients to F', while ensuring that all clients can be served. Let $cost(f)$ denote the cost of opening up a facility f. The formulation of this UFL problem can be expressed as follows:

$$\min\Big(\sum_{f \in F'} cost(f) + \sum_{c \in C, f \in F'} x_{c,f} w_{c,f} \Big) \tag{10}$$

$$s.t. \qquad \sum_{f \in F'} w_{c,f} x_{c,f} \geq 1 \tag{11}$$

$$x_{c,f} \in \{0, 1\} \tag{12}$$

where $x_{c,f}$ is the connection decision from client c to opened facility f and $w_{c,f}$ is the cost of connecting client c to facility f.

Now we reduce the EDDE problem to the UFL problem: 1) removing edge servers not in S_d and the corresponding edges; 2) connecting each edge server and its neighbor servers within h hops; 3) setting the same cost of storing d on individual edge servers. This reduced EDDE problem can now be equally converted to minimize the storage cost, i.e., the cost of storing d in the system, while ensuring that all the edge servers can retrieve d within 1 hop. Since the cost of each edge is 0, the objective to maximize the data deduplication ratio in the EDDE problem is equivalent to selecting the fewest edge servers in S_d to minimize the storage cost, the same as Objective (10) in the UFL problem. Moreover, Constraint (7) is converted to cover all the edge servers in the reduced EDDE problem, equivalent to Constraint (11). Constraint (12) denotes whether client c can connect to the opened facility f. Thus, it is obvious that constraint (12) is equal to constraint (1).

In conclusion, any solution that satisfies the UFL problem can be reduced to the corresponding EDDE problem after the above discussion in polynomial time. Thus, the EDDE problem is $\mathcal{NP}$-hard.

4   EDDE Approaches

In this section, two approaches are proposed to solve the different scales of EDDE problem correspondingly.

4.1 Optimal Approach

The optimal solution to the EDDE problem must maximize the data deduplication ratio while fulfilling the same data coverage before and after deduplication under the latency constraint. As introduced in Sect. 3.1, S_d donates the set of edge servers that have data d before deduplication, and $b_i \in \{0,1\}$ denotes whether d is removed from $s_i \in S_d$. Thus, this EDDE problem can be modeled as a *constrained optimization problem* (COP) as follows:

$$\max \left(1 - \sum_{s_i \in S_d} b_i / |S_d|\right) \tag{13}$$

$$h_{i,j} \leq h, \forall s_i \in S_d, s_j \in N(S_d) \tag{14a}$$

$$\cup_{\{b_i = 0 | s_i \in S_d\}} N(s_i) = N(S_d) \tag{14b}$$

where constraint (14a) ensures the latency constraint and Constraint (14b) ensures the coverage constraint.

EDDE-O can be implemented by employing some classic integer programming solvers such as CPLEX[3] and Gurobi[4] for solving the COP presented above. The solution is an assignment of 0 or 1 to each b_i, where $s_i \in S_d$, that maximizes the data deduplication ratio (13) while fulfilling the latency constraint (14a) and the coverage constraint (14b). According to the solution, the data replicas are removed from the edge servers whose corresponding b_i values are 1.

4.2 Approximation Approach

Due to the $\mathcal{NP}$-hardness of the EDDE problem proven in Sect. 3.2, it is unrealistic to find the optimal solutions of large-scale EDDE problems. In such scenarios, it takes EDDE-O a lot of time to explore the possible solutions and find the optimal one. This can easily incur a significant delay in the implementation of edge data deduplication and lower the utilization of ESSs. Thus, this section introduces EDDE-A, an efficient approximation approach for finding sub-optimal solutions to large-scale EDDE problems efficiently. The pseudo-code of EDDE-A is presented in Algorithm 1.

In this algorithm, it first initializes the value of S_{d-}, S'_{d-}, the former for saving the EDDE solution and the latter for saving the set of candidate edge servers (Line 2). Then, it sets $R', R = 0$ to record the new deduplication ratio and the final deduplication ratio, respectively (Line 3). Next, the neighbor edge servers of $s_i(s_i \in S_d)$ can be obtained based on the latency constraint h, i.e., Eq. (3). Then, the algorithm sorts the edge servers in S_d by the number of their neighbor edge servers within h hops (Line 7). For all edge servers with the fewest neighbors, the algorithm obtains the one, denoted as s_{max}, with maximum $distance(s_j)$, i.e., the total distance from s_j to each of its neighbor edge servers in $N(s_j)$ (Lines

---

[3] https://www.ibm.com/analytics/cplex-optimizer.
[4] https://www.gurobi.com/products/gurobi-optimizer/.

Algorithm 1. EDDE-A

Input: $G(S, E)$, S_d, h
Output: EDDE solution S_{d-};
1: **Initialization:**
2: $S_{d-}, S'_{d-} \leftarrow \emptyset$
3: $R', R \leftarrow 0$
4: **End of initialization**
5: **while** $\hat{S}_{d+} \neq \hat{S}_d$ **do**
6:    identify s_i's neighbor edge servers $N(s_i)$ with Eq. 3, for every $s_i \in S_d$
7:    sort edge servers in S_d by $|N(s_i)|$ high to low;
8:    **for** $s_j \in \arg\min_{s_i \in S_d} |N(s_i)|$ **do**
9:       **for** each edge server $s_k \in N(s_j)$ **do**
10:          $distance(s_j, N(s_j)) \leftarrow distance(s_j, N(s_j)) + d_{k,j}$
11:       **end for**
12:    **end for**
13:    $s_{max} \leftarrow \arg\max\{distance(s_j, N(s_j)), s_j \in \arg\min_{s_i \in S_d} |N(s_i)| \}$
14:    $S'_{d-} \leftarrow S'_{d-} \cup \{s_{max}\}$
15:    $S_d \leftarrow S_d - s_{max}$
16:    calculate R' with Eq. 8
17:    **if** $R' > R$ **then**
18:       $R \leftarrow R'$
19:       $S_{d-} \leftarrow S'_{d-}$
20:    **end if**
21: **end while**
22: **return** S_{d-}

8–13). After that, s_{max} can be included into the set of candidate edge servers S'_{d-} and removed from S_d (Lines 14–15). Then, the new data deduplication ratio R' obtained by including s_{max} in S_{d-} can be calculated with Eq.(8) (Line 16). It will then be compared with the current data deduplication ratio R. If it is higher, it will replace R and S_{d-} is updated accordingly (Lines 18–21). The above process iterates until the coverage constraint is fulfilled, i.e., the set of edge servers covered by S_{d+} is equal to the set of edge servers covered by S_d (Line 5). Finally, S_{d-} is returned as the final EDDE solution. According to S_{d-}, an EDDE strategy B can be formulated by setting the corresponding $b_i = 1$ (if $\exists s_i \in S_{d-}$) or $b_i = 0$ otherwise.

Approximation Ratio. Now we analyze the approximation ratio and time complexity of EDDE-A theoretically. Let $S'_{d-}(t)$ denote the set of candidate edge servers obtained by EDDE-A in the tth iteration. According to Algorithm 1, whether an edge server s_j is included in S'_{d-} depends on $|N(s_j)|$, i.e., the number of its neighbor edge servers, and $distance(s_j, N(s_j))$, i.e., their distance from s_j. Thus, let us define $\beta_t = |N(S'_{d-}(t))|/|S'_{d-}(t)|$ to represent the average number of neighbor edge servers covered by each selected edge server in the tth iteration. Let S^*_{d-} denote the optimal EDDE solution found by EDDE-O.

Compared with S_{d-}^*, the EDDE solution obtained by EDDE-A, denoted with S_{d-}, will not be able to remove more data replicas:

$$\frac{1}{\beta_t} \leq \frac{|S_{d-}'(1)|}{|N(S_{d-}'(t))|} \leq \frac{|S_{d-}'(t)|}{|N(S_{d-}'(t))|} \leq \frac{|S_{d-}^*|}{|N(S_{d-}'(t))|} \tag{15}$$

Let $|S_{d-}|$ denote the number of data replicas removed by EDDE-A. After the final iteration of Algorithm 1, the number of data replicas removed by EDDE-A follows:

$$|S_{d-}| \leq \frac{1}{\beta_1}(|N(S_{d-}'(1))| - |N(S_{d-}'(0))|) + \frac{1}{\beta_2}(|N(S_{d-}'(2))| - |N(S_{d-}'(1))|)$$
$$+ ... + \frac{1}{\beta_\alpha}(|N(S_{d-}'(t))| - |N(S_{d-}'(t-1))|) \tag{16}$$

Based on Eq. (15) and Eq. (16), we can infer the following:

$$|S_{d-}| \leq \frac{|N(S_{d-}'(1))| - |N(S_{d-}'(0))|}{|N(S_{d-}'(1))|}|S_{d-}^*| + \frac{|N(S_{d-}'(2))| - |N(S_{d-}'(1))|}{|N(S_{d-}'(2))|}|S_{d-}^*|$$
$$+ ... + \frac{|N(S_{d-}'(t))| - |N(S_{d-}'(t-1))|}{|N(S_{d-}'(t))|}|S_{d-}^*| \tag{17}$$

Let α denote the maximum number of iteration, i.e., $\alpha = |S_d|$. Based on mathematical induction, we can obtain Eq. (18):

$$|S_{d-}| \leq (\ln \alpha + 1)|S_{d-}^*| \tag{18}$$

Based on Eq. (18), we can find the approximation ratio of EDDE-A as follows:

$$\frac{R}{R^*} = \frac{|S_{d-}|/|S_d|}{|S_{d-}^*|/|S_d|} \leq \frac{(\ln \alpha + 1)|S_{d-}^*|}{|S_{d-}^*|} \leq \ln \alpha + 1 \tag{19}$$

Therefore, the approximation ratio of EDDE-A is $\ln \alpha + 1$.

Computation Complexity. Given an EDDE scenario with n edge servers $S = \{s_1, s_2, ..., s_n\}$, Algorithm 1 takes at most $O(n)$ time to find the edge servers with minimum $|N(s_i)|$ in Line 6. Then, in Lines 7–12, the algorithm selects an edge server from these edge servers based on their distance from their neighbor edge servers. The distance calculation in Line 8–9 takes $O(n^2)$ time in the worst case because the maximum number of edge servers in any $N(s_j)$ $(s_j \in S_d)$ is $n - 1$. Thus, the overall computation complexity of EDDE-A is $O(n^2)$.

5   Evaluation

In this section, the experiments are conducted to comprehensively evaluate our proposed two approaches, i.e., EDDE-O and EDDE-A.

5.1 Experimental Settings

Dataset. To evaluate the approaches realistically, we conduct the experiments on a widely-used real-world dataset[5] [7], which contains 1,464 edge servers with their geographic coordinates in Melbourne, Australia.

Competing Approaches. EDDE-O and EDDE-A are evaluated against the following four approaches:

- **Random:** This approach randomly removes data replicas from edge servers, one after another, until no more data replicas can be removed without violating the latency constraint or the coverage constraint.
- **Greedy:** This greedy-based approach always removes data replicas from edge servers with the fewest neighbor edge servers, one after another, until no more data replicas can be removed without violating the latency constraint or the coverage constraint.
- **EF-dedup** [9]: This approach originates from [9] and is adapted in the context of EDDE to remove data replicas instead of duplicate data chunks. It first creates $|S_d|$ clusters, each comprised of the neighbor edge servers of an edge server in S_d within h hops. Then, it removes data replicas within those clusters until there is one data replica within each of the clusters.
- **TSC21** [14]: The *edge data caching* (EDC) problem studied in [14] is slightly similar to the EDDE problem. This approach finds edge servers for storing data replicas, aiming to minimize the number of data replicas for fulfilling the latency constraint under the capacity constraint.

Parameter Settings. A set of small-scale experiments (Set #1) and a set of large-scale experiments (Set #2) are conducted. The parameter settings in the experiments are summarized in Table 2. All the experiments are conducted on a machine equipped with Intel Core i5-8400 processor (8 cores, 8 threads) and 8 GB RAM, running Windows-10. When the value of each of the following four setting parameters varies, the experiments are repeated for 200 times and the averaged value is reported.

- **Data redundancy rate (θ):** This parameter is the redundancy of data d in the ESS. Studies find that the redundancy of IoT data, e.g., multimedia and traffic video sequences is generally up to 70% [17,20]. Thus, the value of θ varies from 30% to 80% in both Set #1 and Set #2.
- **Number of edge servers (n):** This parameter decides the scale of the ESS, increasing from 10 to 30 in steps of 5 in Set#1.2, from 50 to 250 in steps of 50 in Set #2.2.
- **Edge server density (ds):** Defined as $ds = |E|/n$, this parameter is the density of the graph that represents the edge servers in the ESS. It varies from 1.0 to 2.5 in steps of 0.3 in Set #1.3, from 2.0 to 5.0 in steps of 0.6 in Set #2.3.

---

[5] https://github.com/swinedge/eua-dataset.

- **Latency constraint** (h): This parameter enforces the latency constraint, increasing from 1 to 5 in steps of 1 in both Set #1 and Set #2.

Table 2. Parameter settings

	θ	n	ds	h
Set # 1.1	30%, 40%, ..., 80%	20	1.0	1
Set # 1.2	60%	10, 15, ..., 30	1.0	1
Set # 1.3	60%	20	1.0, 1.3, ..., 2.5	1
Set # 1.4	60%	20	1.0	1, 2, ..., 5
Set # 2.1	30%, 40%, ..., 80%	150	2.0	1
Set # 2.2	60%	50, 100, ...,250	2.0	1
Set # 2.3	60%	150	2.0, 2.6, ..., 5.0	1
Set # 2.4	60%	150	2.0	1, 2, ..., 5

Performance Metrics

- **Data deduplication ratio** (R), calculated with (8), the higher the better.
- **Computation time,** measured by the CPU computation time that taken to find the EDDE solution by an approach, the lower the better.

5.2   Experimental Results

Effectiveness. Figures 2 and 3 show the effectiveness of the approaches in Set #1 and Set #2, respectively. Figure 2 shows that EDDE-O and EDDE-A achieve the highest and the second highest data deduplication ratios among all six approaches. Second to only EDDE-O with an average performance gap of only 8.68% across all the experiments in Set #1, EDDE-A outperforms EF-dedup, Greedy, TSC21, and Random by an average of 7.82%, 10.33%, 16.24%, and 24.87% in maximizing the data deduplication ratio. Figure 3 demonstrates EDDE-A's superior performance in maximizing data deduplication ratios in Set #2, which is 9.47%, 16.71%, 20.34%, and 32.03% higher on average than EF-dedup, Greedy, TSC21, and Random, respectively.

Figures 2(a) and 3(a) demonstrate the impact of data redundancy (θ) on data deduplication ratio in Set #1.1 and Set #2.1. Given a fixed number of edge servers in the ESS, a larger θ grows the number of data replicas on the ESS and the *data density* measured by the ratio of edge servers in the system with data replicas. This immediately increases the number of data replicas that can be removed without violating the latency constraint or the coverage constraint. For example, if any adjacent edge servers have duplicate data, one of them can be removed. Thus, the data deduplication ratios achieved by all approaches

increases. Figures 2(b) and 3(b) demonstrate the impact of the number of edge
servers (n) on data deduplication ratio in Set #1.2 and Set #2.2. Given a fixed
data redundancy rate, a larger n will further distribute data replicas across the
edge servers in the ESS. This decreases the data density in the system, making
it harder to remove data replicas without violating some constraints, i.e., the
latency constraint and the coverage constraint. For example, data replicas are
less likely to be found on adjacent edge servers. Thus, the data deduplication
ratios of all approaches decrease when n increases, opposite to the impact of θ
shown in Figs. 2(a) and 3(a). Figures 2(c) and 3(c) depict the results in Set #1.3
and Set #2.3 where edge server density ds varies. When the edge server density ds increases, the data deduplication ratios produced by the six approaches
increase. A larger ds connects each individual edge server to connect to more
other edge servers in the system. The data stored on an edge server can be
delivered to users over the edge server network under the latency constraint.
This indicates the importance of leveraging edge servers' ability to communicate
and collaborate. Figures 2(d) and 3(d) show the impact of latency constraint
(h) on data deduplication ratio in Set #1.4 and Set #2.4. As h increases, the
latency constraint is relaxed. Users can retrieve data from edge servers further
away. This reduces the number of data replicas needed in the system to accommodate all the users within the data coverage. Thus, more data replicas can
be removed, and the average deduplication ratios produced by all approaches
increase accordingly.

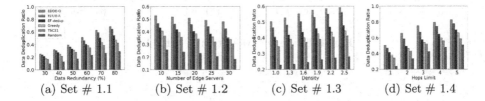

(a) Set # 1.1   (b) Set # 1.2   (c) Set # 1.3   (d) Set # 1.4

Fig. 2. Effectiveness evaluation in Set #1

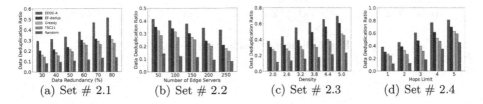

(a) Set # 2.1   (b) Set # 2.2   (c) Set # 2.3   (d) Set # 2.4

Fig. 3. Effectiveness evaluation in Set #1

Efficiency. Figures 4 and 5 demonstrate the efficiency of all approaches in Set #1 and Set #2, respectively. Figure 4 illustrates the high computation time obtained by EDDE-O in Set #1 that renders those of other approaches negligible. This high computational overheads validate the EDDE's $\mathcal{NP}$-hardness proved in Sect. 3.2. This tells us that EDDE-O is indeed not suitable for solving large-scale EDDE scenarios. Compared with EDDE-O, EDDE-A is much more efficient in solving large-scale EDDE problems. In Set #1, it takes only 1.27 ms on average to find a solution, only 0.16% of what EDDE-O takes. Please note that EDDE-O is excluded from Set #2 because it cannot find a solution within a reasonable amount of time in such large-scale EDDE scenarios. In Fig. 5, EDDE-A always takes more computation time for finding an EDDE solution than the other four competing approaches, specifically, 14.67 ms, 19.72 ms, 24.29 ms, and 28.43 ms more than EF-dedup, Greedy, TSC21, and Random, respectively. Overall, EDDE-A scales with θ and n, taking no more than 125 ms to find a solution in Set #2. Given its outstanding advantages in maximizing data deduplication ratios over EF-dedup, Greedy, TSC21, and Random, its extra computational overhead is worthwhile in most large-scale EDDE scenarios.

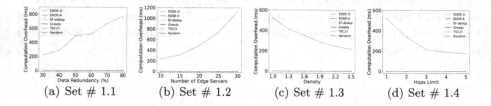

(a) Set # 1.1   (b) Set # 1.2   (c) Set # 1.3   (d) Set # 1.4

Fig. 4. Efficiency evaluation in Set #1

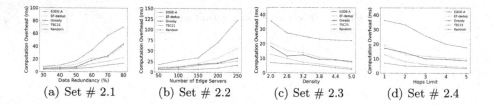

(a) Set # 2.1   (b) Set # 2.2   (c) Set # 2.3   (d) Set # 2.4

Fig. 5. Efficiency evaluation in Set #1

6   Releated Work

A large amount of data are being produced by mobile and IoT devices at the network edge, e.g., images, video frames, and locality data [12]. It has become a trend for application vendors to cache popular data on edge servers to reduce the cost and latency incurred by transmitting data from the cloud to the network edge [16]. However, the constrained storage resources on edge servers are a major challenge to explore the potentials of edge storage systems comprised of networked edge servers [6,14,19]. Reducing data redundancy within an edge storage system can save up to 70% storage resources overall [8,17]. This can be achieved through data deduplication.

Cloud Data Deduplication. (CDDE) has been extensively studied for cloud storage systems [4,11,18]. To name a few, Dubnicki et al. [4] proposed a CDDE approach capable of deduplicating data at the data chunk level across multiple data centers based on an improved distributed hash table. Yan et al. [18] proposed a novel data deduplication approach named Z-Dedup. Z-Dedup can monitor and remove redundancy at chunk-level in compressed back-up data by exploiting some invariant information contained in the metadata compressed data. Unlike most data deduplication studies that focus on back-up data, Meister et al. [11] proposed to deduplicate data for online file systems in HPC centers with chunking strategies specifically designed based on HPC applications' data characteristics. Based on research on data deduplication, cloud service providers like Amazon and Microsoft have offered and deployed data deduplication services for their cloud storage servers [1,2].

However, specifically designed for conventional cloud storage systems, these *cloud data deduplication* (CDDE) techniques are not suitable to directly employ in edge storage systems due to the unique characteristics of the MEC environment, particularly, edge servers' geographic distribution, limited coverage, and constrained resources. In recent years, researchers are starting to investigate data deduplication in edge storage systems [8,9]. Specifically, Li et al. [9] formulated the data deduplication problem at the network edge as a clustering optimization problem. They proposed an approximate algorithm for partitioning edge servers into disjoint clusters so that CDDE approaches can be employed to deduplicate data within individual clusters. In their subsequent study [8], another approximation algorithm was proposed to take data popularity into account. However, these studies have followed the same idea of CDDE and failed to consider the unique characteristics that differ edge storage systems from cloud storage systems fundamentally, in particular, the capacity constraint, proximity constraint, and latency constraint discussed in Sect. 1 and widely acknowledged in state-of-the-art studies of MEC [5,7,16]. To facilitate EDDE, this paper makes the first attempt to motivate, model, and solve the EDDE problem with consideration of the unique characteristics of the MEC environment.

7 Conclusion and Future Work

In this paper, we formulated the *novel edge data deduplication* (EDDE) problem in the MEC environment as a constrained optimization problem. We proved that it is $\mathcal{NP}$-hard and proposed two EDDE approaches. The first one is named EDDE-O and finds optimal solutions to small-scale EDDE problems based on integer programming. The other one is named EDDE-A and finds approximate solutions to large-scale EDDE problems efficiently. The results of extensive experiments conducted on a widely-used real-world dataset demonstrate that EDDE-O and EDDE-A can solve the EDDE problem effectively and efficiently, outperforming four representative approaches significantly.

This research has first motivated the importance to deduplicate redundancy in ESSs by fully exploring the characteristic of the MEC environment. As for further works, we will attempt to devise lightweight mechanisms for detecting data duplication and dynamic data deduplication.

Acknowledgement. We thank the anonymous reviewers for their helpful feedback. This work is supported by National Science Foundation of China under grant No.62032008.

References

1. https://docs.aws.amazon.com/fsx/latest/windowsguide/using-data-dedup.html
2. https://docs.microsoft.com/en-us/windows-server/storage/data-deduplication/overview
3. Chudak, F.A., Shmoys, D.B.: Improved approximation algorithms for the uncapacitated facility location problem. SIAM J. Comput. **33**(1), 1–25 (2003)
4. Dubnicki, C., et al.: Hydrastor: a scalable secondary storage. In: Proceedings of 7th USENIX Conference on File and Storage Technologies, vol. 9, pp. 197–210 (2009)
5. He, Q., et al.: A game-theoretical approach for user allocation in edge computing environment. IEEE Trans. Parallel Distrib. Syst. **31**(3), 515–529 (2019)
6. He, Q., et al.: A game-theoretical approach for mitigating edge DDoS attack. IEEE Trans. Dependable Secure Comput. 1 (2021). https://doi.org/10.1109/TDSC.2021.3055559
7. Lai, P., et al.: Optimal edge user allocation in edge computing with variable sized vector bin packing. In: Pahl, C., Vukovic, M., Yin, J., Yu, Q. (eds.) ICSOC 2018. LNCS, vol. 11236, pp. 230–245. Springer, Cham (2018). https://doi.org/10.1007/978-3-030-03596-9_15
8. Li, S., Lan, T.: Hotdedup: managing hot data storage at network edge through optimal distributed deduplication. In: Proceedings of 39th IEEE Conference on Computer Communications, pp. 247–256 (2020)
9. Li, S., Lan, T., Balasubramanian, B., Ra, M.R., Lee, H.W., Panta, R.: Ef-dedup: enabling collaborative data deduplication at the network edge. In: Proceedings of 39th IEEE International Conference on Distributed Computing Systems, pp. 986–996. IEEE (2019)
10. Li, T., Braud, T., Li, Y., Hui, P.: Lifecycle-aware online video caching. IEEE Trans. Mob. Comput. **20**, 2624–2636 (2020)
11. Meister, D., Kaiser, J., Brinkmann, A., Cortes, T., Kuhn, M., Kunkel, J.: A study on data deduplication in HPC storage systems. In: Proceedings of International Conference on High Performance Computing, Networking, Storage and Analysis, pp. 1–11 (2012)
12. Shinkuma, R., Nishio, T., Inagaki, Y., Oki, E.: Data assessment and prioritization in mobile networks for real-time prediction of spatial information using machine learning. EURASIP J. Wirel. Commun. Netw. **2020**(1), 1–19 (2020). https://doi.org/10.1186/s13638-020-01709-1

13. Xia, X., et al.: Budgeted data caching based on k-median in mobile edge computing. In: Proceedings of 27th IEEE International Conference on Web Services, pp. 197–206. IEEE (2020)
14. Xia, X., Chen, F., Grundy, J., Abdelrazek, M., Jin, H., He, Q.: Constrained app data caching over edge server graphs in edge computing environment. IEEE Trans. Serv. Comput. 1 (2021). https://doi.org/10.1109/TSC.2021.3062017
15. Xia, X., et al.: Graph-based optimal data caching in edge computing. In: Proceedings of 17th International Conference on Service-Oriented Computing, pp. 477–493 (2019)
16. Xia, X., Chen, F., He, Q., Grundy, J.C., Abdelrazek, M., Jin, H.: Cost-effective app data distribution in edge computing. IEEE Trans. Parallel Distrib. Syst. **32**(1), 31–44 (2020)
17. Yan, H., Li, X., Wang, Y., Jia, C.: Centralized duplicate removal video storage system with privacy preservation in IoT. Sensors **18**(6), 1814 (2018)
18. Yan, Z., Jiang, H., Tan, Y., Skelton, S., Luo, H.: Z-dedup: a case for deduplicating compressed contents in cloud. In: Proceedings of 33rd IEEE International Parallel and Distributed Processing Symposium, pp. 386–395 (2019)
19. Yuan, L., et al.: Coopedge: a decentralized blockchain-based platform for cooperative edge computing. In: Proceedings of the 30th Web Conference (2021)
20. Zhang, Y., Wu, Y., Yang, G.: Droplet: a distributed solution of data deduplication. In: Proceedings of 13th ACM/IEEE International Conference on Grid Computing, pp. 114–121 (2012)

IaaS Signature Change Detection with Performance Noise

Sheik Mohammad Mostakim Fattah[(⊠)] and Athman Bouguettaya

School of Computer Science, University of Sydney, Sydney, Australia
{sheik.fattah,athman.bouguettaya}@sydney.edu.au

Abstract. We propose a novel framework to detect changes in the performance behavior of an IaaS service. The proposed framework leverages the concept of the IaaS signature to represent an IaaS service's long-term performance behavior. A new type of performance signature called categorical IaaS signature is introduced to represent the performance behavior more accurately. A novel performance noise model is proposed to accurately identify IaaS performance noise and accurate changes in the performance behavior of an IaaS service. A set of experiments based on real-world datasets is carried out to evaluate the effectiveness of the proposed framework.

Keywords: IaaS performance · Performance signatures · Change detection · Performance noise

1 Introduction

Infrastructure-as-a-Service (IaaS) models offer various computational resources such as CPU, memory, storage, and network are offered as Virtual Machines (VMs) [3]. Large organizations tend to utilize IaaS cloud services on a *long-term basis* (e.g., 1–3 years). Most leading IaaS cloud providers such as Amazon, Google, and Microsoft offer significant discounts on long-term subscriptions. Selecting a service for a long-term period is a key decision for many consumers. Committing to a service for a long-term period that may perform poorly, may cause loss of revenue. Therefore, it is important for a consumer to know the performance of an IaaS service.

IaaS providers typically reveal *limited* performance information in their advertisements due to *market competition* and *business secrecy* [16]. For example, most IaaS advertisements do not contain actual vCPU (virtual CPU) speed, memory bandwidth, or VM startup time information. The performance of a VM may change over time due to the dynamic nature of the cloud [9]. Therefore, advertised performance information may not reflect the true service performance for a certain time.

An effective way to deal with the limited performance information is to leverage free trials [15]. Most IaaS providers promote *free short-term trials* and invite potential consumers to test their application in the cloud. Therefore, a consumer may run its application workload on different IaaS cloud services and compare

© Springer Nature Switzerland AG 2021
H. Hacid et al. (Eds.): ICSOC 2021, LNCS 13121, pp. 516–530, 2021.
https://doi.org/10.1007/978-3-030-91431-8_32

their performance. Free trial experiences, however, do not provide sufficient information to make a long-term commitment [6]. The performance of IaaS services changes *periodically* due to the multi-tenant nature of the cloud [9]. The observed performance in a trial in one month may change if the trial is performed in a different month. Therefore, making a long-term commitment based on only short trials may lead to a poor selection.

IaaS performance signatures provide an effective alternative to deal with the unknown service performance variability for the long-term selection [6,11]. The performance signature of an IaaS service represents its *expected* performance behavior over a long period of time. For instance, a signature of a VM may indicate that its response time is expected to increase by 10% in January than the response time in December. A consumer's trial experience of a service and its corresponding signature can be utilized together to make a better selection for the long-term period. A signature-based IaaS selection approach is proposed that generates IaaS signatures using the experience of past trial users over different periods of a year [6]. However, most existing selection approaches do not consider the long-term changes in IaaS performance behavior where the signature may need to be re-evaluated periodically. *The focus of this work is to detect changes in long-term IaaS performance behavior.*

An IaaS service's performance behavior may change over time due to a number of reasons [4,11]. For instance, a provider may upgrade its infrastructure or change its multi-tenant management policy resulting in the change of service performance [10]. Therefore, detecting the change of IaaS performance is important to ensure that its signature reflects the *current* performance behavior of the service. *We focus on the detection of changes in IaaS performance behavior as represented by its signature.* In this case, the IaaS performance signature may need to be updated to be representative of the new performance profile of the service.

There are two key challenges in IaaS performance Signature change detection. The first challenge is detecting the point in time where the signature needs to be re-evaluated. A change may occur at any point in time. Therefore, it is required to identify change points in time where there is a high probability of performance change occurrence. This is typically known as the *Change Point Detection* problem [1]. The second challenge is to differentiate between the *noise* and *true changes* in performance. Noise typically indicates the irregular or anomalous behavior in service performance that may not be the long-term performance changes [12]. For instance, a major power failure may impact the service performance at a time without necessarily indicating a long-term performance change. Noise in IaaS performance is very common due to the dynamic nature of the cloud.

To the best of our knowledge, existing research has not given enough attention to the long-term IaaS performance change detection problem [6]. An IaaS performance change detection framework is proposed that utilizes an ECA model to detect changes in IaaS performance [5]. However, it does not consider noise in IaaS performance during the change detection. Therefore, *the focus of this paper is to distinguish the true changes in IaaS performance from the changes that are caused by performance noise.*

Noise in signal processing generally represents the unwanted disturbance in electrical signals, which is usually generated during the capture, storage, transmission, processing, or conversion of the signal. In the case of IaaS cloud, noise can be generated from co-tenants, system upgrade, or temporary service disruptions [14]. *We propose a novel framework to detect changes in IaaS performance signature by accurately detecting noise and true changes in IaaS performance.* The proposed framework introduces a new type of IaaS performance signature called *categorical IaaS signature*. The categorical IaaS signature models performance behavior more *accurately* than the *general IaaS signature* introduced in [6] as the general IaaS signature does not consider the effect of different categories of workloads, i.e., CPU-intensive, I/O-intensive, and memory-intensive on IaaS performance. The proposed framework utilizes a heuristic-based approach to determine noise in IaaS performance. In this approach, the categorical signature and the general signature are utilized to define performance noise bandwidth. The performance noise bandwidth is updated over time to detect performance changes more accurately. The key contributions are summarized as follows:

- A new type of IaaS performance signature called Categorical IaaS Signature that models an IaaS service's long-term performance behavior based on different categories of workloads.
- A novel performance noise model that defines the noise bandwidth based on the categorical and general IaaS signatures.
- A performance change detection model that leverages the proposed performance noise model to detect changes in IaaS performance.

2 IaaS Performance Signatures

We overview the general and categorical IaaS performance signatures, their representations, and generation techniques.

2.1 General IaaS Performance Signatures

The general IaaS performance signature is first introduced in [6]. The general signature of an IaaS service is represented based on its *relative* performance changes over time, i.e., how much a service's performance may increase or decrease in one time compared to another time. For example, the general signature of a VM may inform that its response time is expected to increase by 5% on weekend nights than regular weekdays. The general signature mainly focuses on the effect of seasonality on IaaS performance. It assumes that the effect of different types of workload on the observed performance is not substantial compared to the effect of seasonal performance variability. Therefore, this signature is called general signature as it considers all types of workloads equally. Note that the signature does not tell the exact performance of a service. Therefore, a consumer is unable

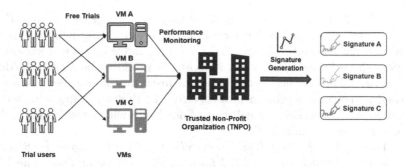

Fig. 1. IaaS performance signature generation

to select a service based on only its signature. Instead, the consumer needs to perform the trial with its application workloads and utilize the trial experience and the IaaS signature to estimate the long-term service performance [6].

Definition 1. *General IaaS Performance Signature: An IaaS performance signature is a temporal representation of relative performance changes of an IaaS service over a long period.*

The general IaaS performance signature is represented by a set of QoS parameters that are relevant to the service. The *relevant* QoS attributes are defined by the most important QoS attributes to measure the performance of a particular type of IaaS service [6]. For example, data read/write throughput and disk latency are the key QoS attributes for virtual storage services.

We denote the general signature of a service as $S = \{S_1, S_2, ... S_n\}$, where n is the number of QoS attributes in the signature. Each S_i corresponds to a QoS attribute. Each S_i denotes a time series for t period which is represented as $S_i = \{s_{i1}, s_{i2}, ... s_{it}\}$. Here, s_{it} is the relative performance of the provider at the time t for a particular QoS attribute. We use the following representation to denote a signature:

$$S = \begin{bmatrix} s_{11} & s_{12} & .. & s_{1t} \\ s_{21} & s_{22} & .. & s_{2t} \\ s_{31} & s_{13} & .. & s_{3t} \\ .. & .. & ... & \\ s_{n1} & s_{n2} & .. & s_{nt} \end{bmatrix} \quad (1)$$

where each row corresponds to the QoS signature of S_i and each column represents a timestamp t. From the Eq. 1, we see that a signature may include several QoS attributes. However, we describe the proposed approach using only one QoS attribute in this work, i.e., throughput of an IaaS service for simplicity. However, the proposed approach is applicable for more than one QoS attribute of IaaS performance signatures.

2.2 General IaaS Performance Signature Generation

It is important to note that, the past trial users may not want to share their experience publicly to protect their privacy, security, and the conflict of interests with the provider [17]. However, they may share their trial experience with a *Trusted Non-Profit Organization* (TNPO) for a limited period to help new consumers in the selection [2]. Examples of such TNPOs are available in public sectors where privacy-sensitive information about individuals needs to be shared to deliver better services. For instance, health research institutes often collect data about individual patients to improve health services. TNPOs are responsible for data *integration* and *distribution* of collective knowledge without revealing individual's privacy-sensitive information.

We Assume that the Past Trial Users Who Have Utilized Some IaaS Services Share Their Experience with a TNPO for a Limited Period of Time. The TNPO generates IaaS performance signatures based on the aggregated experience of past trial users and deletes the users' data afterward. Let us assume that there are three IaaS providers (A, B, and C) who offer three VMs (VM_a, VM_b, and VM_c) with similar configurations (e.g., resource capacity, location) for free short-term trials as shown in Fig. 1. There are past users who utilized the VMs to find the performance over different periods of time. The trial users do not want to share their trial experience publicly. However, each trial user shares its experience with a TNPO for a short period. The TNPO generates the signature to identify the long-term performance variability of each VM. The TNPO has to delete users' experience once the signatures are computed. A signature provides an aggregated view of a VM's long-term performance variability. It is not possible to derive individual trial experience from the signature. As a result, *the TNPO does not violate the privacy of past trial users.*

We create IaaS performance signatures in a way that requires less detailed performance information about the service performance and the past trial users and yet useful enough to make a long-term selection. Let us assume that k number of past trial users share their observed trial performance Q_k over the period T for a service. Here, Q_k refers to the performance observed by the kth consumer for the QoS attribute Q over the period T. We denote Q_k as $Q_k = \{q_{1k}, q_{2k}, .., q_{tk}\}$. The following steps are performed to generate the signature for the QoS attribute Q:

1. For a QoS attribute Q, the performance observed by the trial users is collected over time T.
2. At each timestamp $t \in T$, the average performance observed by k number of consumers is measured for Q. The average performance is denoted by $\overline{Q_k}$.

The value of $s_n t$ at any t represents the average QoS performance compare to any other time t' in Eq. 1. This representation of the signature offers two benefits. First, the use of signature becomes easier once a consumer has utilized free trials based on its workloads. The performance for any other time can be found by comparing the ratio between the trial month and other times. Second, signatures can be stored and updated easily over time as it does not require storing detailed information about consumers' trial.

2.3   Categorical IaaS Performance Signatures

In this subsection, we introduce a new type of signature called categorical IaaS performance signature. For simplicity, we refer to the categorical IaaS performance signature as the categorical signature and the general IaaS performance signature as the general signature. The motivation behind creating the categorical signature is to produce a more accurate signature that captures the effect of different types of workloads on IaaS performance behavior. The performance of an IaaS service may depend on the workload it runs [7]. Therefore, IaaS providers often advertise CPU-intensive, memory-intensive, or network-intensive VMs. For instance, Amazon EC2 offers a wide range of compute-optimized, storage-optimized, and memory-optimized instances.

IaaS workloads can be categorized based on several workload parameters such as resource requirements, request arrival rates, and workload distribution. Without loss of generality, we only consider resource requirements as workload parameters for categorization in this work. Therefore, workload categories will be CPU-intensive, memory-intensive, and I/O intensive. The proposed workload categorization is applicable for any other workload parameters. Let us assume there are N_c types of workload based on resource requirements of consumer requests. Therefore, we create N_c number of categorical signatures. A categorical signature is represented as:

$$S_c = \begin{bmatrix} s_{11} & s_{12} & \cdots & s_{1t} \\ s_{21} & s_{22} & \cdots & s_{2t} \\ s_{31} & s_{13} & \cdots & s_{3t} \\ \cdots & \cdots & \cdots \\ s_{n1} & s_{n2} & \cdots & s_{nt} \end{bmatrix} \tag{2}$$

where S_c represents the signature for c categories of workloads. Here, c is one of the categories in N_c. Rest of the attributes of Eq. 2 are same as the general signature in Eq. 1.

2.4   Categorical IaaS Performance Signature Generation

The key difference between the categorical signature generation and the general signature generation is the consideration of different workload categories. First, we define a set of categories (C) based on the resource requirements where $C = \{1, 2, 3, ... N_c\}$. For each category, we define the criteria that determine the category of each request (workload). Let us assume that a consumer's request has R number of attributes where each attribute denotes a resource in the VM such as vCPU, storage, or memory. For each attribute (a), we define a minimum resource requirement M_a. If a request has more than M_a amount of resource requirement for the attribute a, we consider that request as a-intensive request. For example, if a request has 80% of CPU usage requests, then we consider that request as a CPU-intensive request. According to this approach, a request can be in multiple categories of workloads. The minimum resource requirement for each attribute is defined experimentally by the TNPO for each cloud provider, i.e., the different threshold is considered as the minimum resource requirement for

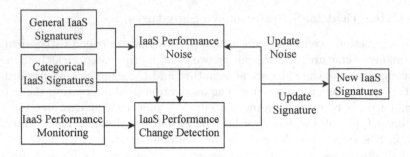

Fig. 2. IaaS performance change detection framework

each category to find the most effective threshold. Once we define the category for each workload, we create the categorical signature as follows:

1. For a QoS attribute Q, the performance observed by the trial users is collected over time T.
2. For each category a at each trial length δT, we identify k number of a-intensive requests. The average performance $(\overline{Q_k})$ is measured for each QoS attribute.

We computed the average performance of a QoS attribute to obtain the IaaS signature. The signature should reflect performance behavior of the service for all types of workloads. However, the performance of a service may depend on its workload. Therefore, we introduced the categorical signature to represent signature for similar categories of workloads. It is not practical to define signature for every workload. Therefore, we utilized the average performance as it is a good approximation of the performance behavior. We improve the accuracy of the signature by adjusting the noise bandwidth over time.

3   Proposed Change Detection Framework

In this section, we discuss the proposed change detection framework as shown in Fig. 2. The proposed framework consists of two key components: a) IaaS performance noise and b) IaaS performance change detection. The performance noise is initially defined by the general signature and the categorical signature. The performance noise is then updated dynamically based on the observed performance of the free trial users. The change detection framework utilizes the knowledge of IaaS performance noise and the categorical IaaS signature to detect changes in the categorical signature based on the observed performance by the free trial users. The change detection framework updates the knowledge about the performance noise based on the observed performance over time.

3.1   IaaS Performance Noise

A key step in identifying changes in IaaS performance is to accurately determine the noise in IaaS performance. We define the noise in IaaS performance as the

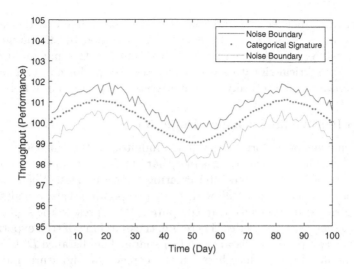

Fig. 3. IaaS performance noise bandwidth

deviation from the expected performance behavior as represented by the signature of an IaaS service. The key challenge in defining the performance noise is to determine the amount of performance fluctuation from the expected performance behavior. A boundary must be defined, which will determine whether the observed performance fluctuations can be considered as the noise or a permanent change in the performance behavior. In signal processing, image processing, and other domains, there are many approaches to define and detect different types of noises such as White noise, Gaussian noise, and Salt and pepper noise. *To the best of our knowledge, there is no definitive way of defining noise in the case of IaaS performance behavior.* Therefore, we propose a heuristic-based approach using the general signature and the categorical signature to define the initial performance noise boundary of an IaaS service. We call it *IaaS performance noise bandwidth*. The noise bandwidth is updated over time based on the observed performance behavior of an IaaS service. The performance noise bandwidth is defined as follows:

Definition 2. *IaaS Performance Noise Bandwidth: The surrounding area created by the acceptable fluctuation from the expected performance of an IaaS service is the IaaS performance noise bandwidth of that service.*

The amount of acceptable fluctuation is initially defined by the general signature and the categorical signature as shown in Fig. 3. The distance between the general signature and the categorical signature D is computed for each timestamp by the following equation:

$$D = dist(S, S_c) = \forall (S_i, S_{ci})\ abs(S_i, S_{ci}) \qquad (3)$$

where S is the general signature, S_c is the categorical signature, S_i is the value of the general signature at ith timestamp, and S_{ci} is the value of the categorical signature at ith timestamp. The dist function is computed based on the absolute distance between S_i and S_{ci}. D is then considered as the acceptable deviation from the expected performance as represented by the categorical signature. Therefore, any observed performance that has the maximum deviation D from the categorical signature is considered noisy performance. The data for Fig. 3 are obtained synthetically to demonstrate the performance noise.

3.2 IaaS Performance Change Detection

Detecting changes in performance requires monitoring the current performance behavior of an IaaS service. We assume that the TNPO continues to monitor the experience of free trial users after creating the signatures. When most of the users' experience does not *match* with the corresponding categorical signature, the existing signature needs to be re-computed. We represent the signatures and the trial experience as time series. Therefore, the matching of trial experience and signature has two parts: a) distance and b) shape. The distance D' is computed based on the absolute distance between the categorical signature and the trial experience for a given trial period T using the following equation:

$$D' = \forall_{i \in T} \, abs(S_{ci}, E_i) \tag{4}$$

where S_{ci} and E_i are the value of the categorical signature and observed performance at timestamp i. We utilize the pearson correlation coefficient to measure the shape based similarity using the following equation:

$$S(E, S_c)^{PCC} = \frac{\sum_{i=1}^{T}(S_{ci} - \bar{S})(E_i - \bar{E})}{\sqrt{(S_{ci} - \bar{S}_c)^2}\sqrt{(E_i - \bar{E})^2}} \tag{5}$$

where $\bar{E}$ and $\bar{S}_c$ are the average of E and S_c in period T. When the observed performance of a user has a distance from the categorical signature within the performance noise bandwidth, and the shape of the observed performance is similar to the categorical signature, we assume that there is no change in performance. We identify the following cases during the matching based on the shape and the distance:

1. Case 1: Most of the users' observed performance is within the noise bandwidth, and the shape of the performance is similar to the corresponding categorical signatures. In this case, no action is taken.
2. Case 2: Most of the users' observed performance is outside the noise bandwidth, and the shape of the performance is not similar to the corresponding categorical signatures. In this case, signatures are required to be recomputed.
3. Case 3: Most of the users' observed performance is within the noise bandwidth, and the shape of the performance is not similar to the corresponding signatures. In this case, we reduce the size of the performance noise bandwidth.
4. Case 4: Most of the users' observed performance is outside but adjacent to the noise bandwidth, and the performance shape is similar to the corresponding categorical signatures. In this case, we increase the size of the performance noise bandwidth.

Let us assume that the noise bandwidth at timestamp t is defined by d^+ and d^- where d^+ is the distance from the categorical signature to the noise boundary on the upper side of the Y-axis, and d^- is the distance from the categorical signature to the noise boundary on the downside of Y-axis. Therefore, we need to measure whether the observed performance d is in between d^+ and d^- at each timestamp. The first two cases are straightforward. We define a threshold Th. When Th percentage of the users' observed performance matches with case 1 or case 2, we either take no action or update the signature. The value of T_h is set experimentally. In case 3, if T_h percentage of users' performance is within the noise bandwidth and their shape does not match then we reduce the performance noise bandwidth. We experimentally define a similarity threshold T_s, which determines the minimum acceptable similarity between observed performance and the categorical signature. After reducing the bandwidth, we apply the change detection process again for each user's observed performance. In case 4, we increase the size of the noise bandwidth based on the observed performance and apply the change detection process again. We define a threshold δd, which determines how much noise bandwidth needs to be increased or decreased in cases 3 and 4. Value of δd is set based on trials on the experiment.

4   Experiment

A series of experiments are conducted to evaluate the proposed change detection approach. We identify two key attributes: a) average delay and b) ability to detect changes or detection accuracy to evaluate the proposed approach. The proposed approach is compared with the existing IaaS performance changed detection approach proposed in [5].

4.1   Experiment Setup

The focus of this paper is to detect changes in IaaS performance behavior to keep the signature up to date. To evaluate the proposed framework's ability to detect changes, we require an environment where a set of consumers performs free trials on different services based on their workloads over different periods and observe service performance over a long period of time. We then require a scenario where service performance changes and impacts the experience of the trial users. Finding such real-world workload-performance dataset is challenging. To the best of our knowledge, there is no existing long-term workload-performance datasets of IaaS services available publicly. Therefore, we leverage existing short-term available datasets to synthesize datasets for our experiments. We use the Eucalyptus IaaS workload to generate the trial workloads of different consumers[1]. It contains six workload traces of a production cloud environment. We select a trace that contains 34 days of workloads of a large company with 50,000 to 100,000 employees. We partition the data into 360 parts and consider each partition

---

[1] https://www.cs.ucsb.edu/~rich/workload/.

Table 1. Experiment variables

Variable name	Values
Total provisioning period	360 days
Trial length of each consumer	30 days
Total number of IaaS performance signatures	5
Total number of Consumers	18
Similarity thresholds	.6 to 0.9
Anomaly thresholds	60% to 90%

an average workload of day to create a 1-year workload data. The long-term performance of 5 IaaS providers is generated from the benchmark results published SPEC Cloud IaaS 2016 [6]. We augment the workload traces with the performance data to generate a long-term workload-performance dataset of five IaaS providers. We create the signature of each provider using the approach in Sect. 2.2. The experiment variables are shown in Table 1. We conduct the experiments by changing the signatures randomly to create new signatures. We have developed the experiment using Matlab on a computer with Intel Core i7 (2.80 GHz and 8 Gb ram). *We have made our dataset and source code publicly available to make this experiment reproducible*[2]

We identify the following two key variable in the experiment that drives the performance of the proposed approach:

- Similarity Threshold: The similarity threshold indicates the minimum similarity between the shape of the observed performance in the trial of a consumer and the corresponding signature. The similarity threshold is utilized to determine shape-based similarity.
- Anomaly Threshold: The proposed change detection framework relies on the trial experience of the majority of the users. Based on the observation of the majority of the users, we either confirm change on update performance noise. The anomaly threshold defines the minimum number of users that are considered as the majority of the users.

4.2   Evaluation and Discussion

We evaluate the proposed approach in terms of the average delay to detect signature changes and its ability to detect true changes in signature. The expectation is to reduce the average delay to detect the change in performance and increase the accuracy of detecting changes. Here, accuracy refers to the true positives, i.e., how many changes the proposed approach is able to detect. Figure 4 depicts the results of experiments. Figure 4(a) and (b) show the average delay in detecting changes. Figure 4(a) shows the average delay for different similarity thresholds.

---

[2] https://github.com/sm-fattah/IaaS-Signature-Change-Detection-Experiment.

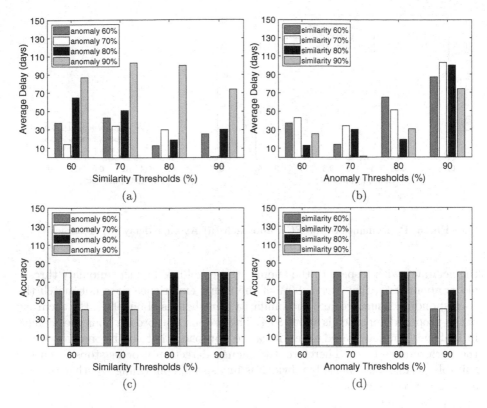

Fig. 4. (a) Average delay for variable similarity thresholds (b) Average delay for variable anomaly thresholds (c) Accuracy for variable similarity thresholds (d) Accuracy for variable anomaly thresholds

There is no trend visible that indicates that there is a linear relationship between the similarity threshold and average change detection delay. The figure shows that the average delay is minimum when the similarity threshold is about 90%. However, the average also depends on the anomaly threshold. When the anomaly threshold is about 70%, the average delay is minimum in most cases in Fig. 4(a). Similarly, Fig. 4(b) shows the average delay for different anomaly thresholds. It also shows no common trend in the average detection delay based on the anomaly threshold. The average delay is minimum when the anomaly threshold is about 70%, and the similarity threshold is about 80%.

The average delay is not the only attribute to measure the performance. We consider the accuracy of the proposed approach in terms of its ability to identify true changes correctly. Figure 4(c) and (d) show the accuracy of the proposed approach. In Fig. 4(c), the accuracy is illustrated with respect to the different similarity thresholds. The accuracy of the proposed approach is about 80% when the similarity threshold is 90%. The effect of different anomaly thresholds is not very substantial on the accuracy according to the figure. Figure 4(d) illustrates

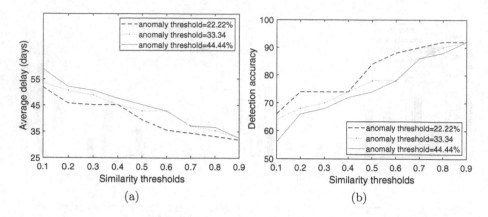

Fig. 5. Performance of the ECA approach (a) Average delay (b) Accuracy

the accuracy with respect to the anomaly threshold. When the anomaly threshold is about 90%, that means 90% of the users' experience does not match the corresponding signature, and the similarity threshold is about 90%, the accuracy of the proposed approach is about 80%. The proposed approach finds the changes in IaaS performance based on an iterative approach that conditionally updates the performance noise. Therefore, the change detection process stops when the suitable performance noise bandwidth is measured, confirming whether there is a change in the signature.

4.3 Comparison with Existing Work

We have implemented the proposed ECA approach in [5] and applied it to our dataset. The result of the ECA approach is illustrated in Fig. 5. Figure 5(a) shows the average delay for different similarity thresholds and anomaly thresholds in the ECA approach. The average delay in this approach can be 55 days to 35 days, depending on the similarity and anomaly thresholds. The average delay in our approach can be from 2 days to 110 days, depending on the similarity and the anomaly thresholds. Choosing the right similarity and anomaly threshold provides a better result than the ECA approach in terms of average change detection delay. The detection accuracy in Fig. 5 shows that the ECA approach provides accuracy from 60% to 90%, depending on the similarity and the anomaly threshold. The proposed approach in this work has an accuracy of about 60% to 80%. However, it does not produce any false positives where the proposed ECA approach in [5] produces a significant number of false positives.

5   Related Work

Performance is one of the most important criteria during cloud service selection [9]. The performance of IaaS services has been studied in numerous studies [6,8,10,15]. An IaaS cloud service's performance is typically measured for different applications based on short-trials in IaaS cloud [6,15]. Most existing approaches do not consider the long-term performance variability of IaaS cloud services. IaaS performance has been extensively studied in [10]. The study suggests that cloud performance is a "moving target" and requires re-evaluation periodically. A signature-based IaaS cloud service selection approach is proposed in [6]. The proposed approach represents the long-term IaaS performance variability using the concept of the IaaS performance signature. The performance signature of an IaaS service is generated from the experience of the past trial users who share their data with a trusted third party. The trusted third party analyzes the periodic performance behavior of an IaaS service to generate its corresponding performance signature. However, the proposed work does not consider the changes in the signature over a long period of time or the effect of different types of workload in the performance of an IaaS service [6].

To the best of our knowledge, there is no prior work that addresses the long-term IaaS performance change detection problem [6]. The proposed approach in [5] mainly focuses on the change point detection (CPD) in IaaS performance. The CPD is a pre-requisite of IaaS performance change detection [1]. In the CPD problem, the distribution of data before and after the change is often considered known. The proposed work in [5] introduces an ECA model to detect change points in IaaS performance behavior. The ECA approach is an effective CPD technique. Other change point detection techniques include Bayesian change point detection, Shapelet, Model fitting, and Gaussian process. The work in [5] utilizes the CUSUM control chart to detect changes in IaaS performance. CUSUM relies on the mean and standard deviation of a time series to detect changes. However, CUSUM is unable to differentiate between noise and change in IaaS performance [13]. Change detection in time series data is usually performed using different similarity measure techniques. However, most of these approaches do not consider the noise that may appear in the data. Therefore, we introduce a change detection framework that identifies noise in IaaS performance by leveraging the concept of categorical signature and noise bandwidth.

6 Conclusion

We propose a novel framework to detect long-term changes in IaaS performance behavior. The long-term performance behavior of an IaaS is represented by its performance signature. A new type of IaaS performance signature called categorical IaaS performance signature is introduced to capture the effect of different types of workload in the IaaS signature. The proposed framework introduces a signature change detection approach with performance noise. The key challenge in performance change detection is to differentiate between noise and accurate changes in IaaS performance. We introduce a new IaaS performance noise model to identify performance change accurately. The experiment results show that the proposed framework detects changes in IaaS performance effectively. We aim to investigate IaaS performance noise in more detail to develop more accurate change detection approaches in future work.

Acknowledgement. This research was partly made possible by DP160103595 and LE180100158 grants from the Australian Research Council. The statements made herein are solely the responsibility of the authors.

References

1. Aminikhanghahi, S., Cook, D.J.: A survey of methods for time series change point detection. Knowl. Inf. Syst. **51**(2), 339–367 (2016). https://doi.org/10.1007/s10115-016-0987-z
2. van den Braak, S.W., Choenni, S., Meijer, R., Zuiderwijk, A.: Trusted third parties for secure and privacy-preserving data integration and sharing in the public sector. In: DGO, pp. 135–144. ACM (2012)
3. Chaisiri, S., Lee, B.S., Niyato, D.: Optimization of resource provisioning cost in cloud computing. IEEE TSC **5**(2), 164–177 (2012)
4. Chaki, D., Bouguettaya, A.: Fine-grained conflict detection of IoT services. In: SCC. IEEE (2020, to be published)
5. Fattah, S.M.M., Bouguettaya, A.: Event-based detection of changes in IaaS performance signatures. In: SCC, pp. 210–217. IEEE (2020)
6. Fattah, S.M.M., Bouguettaya, A., Mistry, S.: Signature-based selection of IaaS cloud services. In: 2020 IEEE International Conference on Web Services (ICWS), pp. 50–57. IEEE (2020)
7. Feitelson, D.G.: Workload modeling for performance evaluation. In: Calzarossa, M.C., Tucci, S. (eds.) Performance 2002. LNCS, vol. 2459, pp. 114–141. Springer, Heidelberg (2002). https://doi.org/10.1007/3-540-45798-4_6
8. Iosup, A., Prodan, R., Epema, D.: IaaS cloud benchmarking: approaches, challenges, and experience. In: Li, X., Qiu, J. (eds.) Cloud Computing for Data-Intensive Applications, pp. 83–104. Springer, New York (2014). https://doi.org/10.1007/978-1-4939-1905-5_4
9. Iosup, A., Yigitbasi, N., Epema, D.: On the performance variability of production cloud services. In: CCGrid, pp. 104–113. IEEE (2011)
10. Leitner, P., Cito, J.: Patterns in the chaos–a study of performance variation and predictability in public IaaS clouds. ACM TOIT **16**(3), 15 (2016)
11. Mi, N., Cherkasova, L., Ozonat, K., Symons, J., Smirni, E.: Analysis of application performance and its change via representative application signatures. In: NOMS, pp. 216–223. IEEE (2008)
12. Moens, V., Zénon, A.: Learning and forgetting using reinforced Bayesian change detection. PLoS Comput. Biol. **15**(4), e1006713 (2019)
13. Page, E.: Cumulative sum charts. Technometrics **3**(1), 1–9 (1961)
14. Varadarajan, V., Kooburat, T., Farley, B., Ristenpart, T., Swift, M.M.: Resource-freeing attacks: improve your cloud performance (at your neighbor's expense). In: Proceedings of the 2012 ACM Conference on Computer and Communications Security, pp. 281–292. ACM (2012)
15. Wang, W., et al.: Testing cloud applications under cloud-uncertainty performance effects. In: ICST, pp. 81–92. IEEE (2018)
16. Wenmin, L., Wanchun, D., Xiangfeng, L., Chen, J.: A history record-based service optimization method for QoS-aware service composition. In: ICWS, pp. 666–673. IEEE (2011)
17. Zhu, J., He, P., Zheng, Z., Lyu, M.R.: A privacy-preserving QoS prediction framework for web service recommendation. In: ICWS, pp. 241–248. IEEE (2015)

WattEdge: A Holistic Approach for Empirical Energy Measurements in Edge Computing

Mohammad S. Aslanpour[1,2]([⊠]), Adel N. Toosi[1], Raj Gaire[2],
and Muhammad Aamir Cheema[1]

[1] Department of Software Systems and Cybersecurity, Faculty of Information
Technology, Monash University, Clayton, Australia
mohammad.aslanpour@monash.edu
[2] CSIRO's DATA61, Canberra, Australia

Abstract. Of the main challenges to keep the edge computing dream alive is to efficiently manage the energy consumption of highly resource-limited nodes. Past studies have limited or often simplistic focus on energy consumption factors considering computation or communication-only solutions, questioned by either costly hardware instrumentation or inaccurate software-specific limitations. With this gap in mind and the wide adoption of single-board computers (SBCs) such as Raspberry Pis in edge, in this paper, we propose a novel holistic and accurate energy measurement approach in edge computing. Exploring a *Test and Learn* strategy, (1) we firstly perform a comprehensive analysis of identifying factors affecting energy consumption of edge nodes; (2) we develop and utilize WattEdge, a standard framework to evaluate the identified factors; (3) we conduct extensive empirical experiments on Raspberry Pis to thoroughly and uniformly assess the significance of each factor, thereby proposing an all-inclusive energy model. Wattedge is able to measure energy consumption factors such as CPU, memory, storage, a combination of them, connectivity, bandwidth usage, and communication protocols, as well as energy sources such as batteries. The results specifically warn us of the necessity of considering previously underestimated factors such as connectivity. A Smart Agriculture use case is implemented to validate the performance of the energy model, demonstrating a 95% accuracy.

Keywords: Edge computing · Energy consumption · Measurement · Raspberry Pi · Internet of Things (IoT) · Performance evaluation

1 Introduction

With the ever-increasing growth of the Internet of Things (IoT), Cisco believes that "the number of connected devices will exceed three times the global population by 2023 [1]." Edge (or Fog) Computing can bring the compute, storage and network resources closer to IoT devices to address low latency requirements of IoT applications [5]. Low power and small sized devices are intended to bring those capabilities at the edge. Recently, Single-Board Computers (SBCs) have attracted

© Springer Nature Switzerland AG 2021
H. Hacid et al. (Eds.): ICSOC 2021, LNCS 13121, pp. 531–547, 2021.
https://doi.org/10.1007/978-3-030-91431-8_33

special attention and are entitled to realize the presumed edge nodes [22]. SBCs such as Raspberry Pis (Pis) or Odroids are highly power-constraint [12].

The problem of efficient energy utilization for ultra low power edge nodes appears urgent [4,20,21,24]. On the demand side, this is urgent because while edge nodes struggle with their energy management for running heavy tasks (e.g., AI tasks) [13,15,16], they are also expected to share their resources with peers [6,19], known as task offloading. On the supply side also, the challenge of harvesting energy from the environment (solar, wind, or thermoelectric) became a challenging issue. This, however, does not exclude line-powered edge platforms from pressing environmental and economical side effects of high energy usage.

Given the exponential growth of IoT, a myriad of connected devices in industry, including agriculture, automobile, telecommunication, etc., will co-exist in the near future which will increase energy consumption and the demand for power supply. Such concerns warn the importance of intelligence about the energy consumption of IoT and its underlying platforms, so that optimization actions become feasible. Basically, this intelligence cannot be achieved without the knowledge of the major energy consumers and their impact on these platforms.

The key questions to optimise the energy consumption on the edge devices is *what are the factors contributing to energy consumption? How significant each factor could be?* And more essentially, *how to develop a practical holistic approach for accurate estimation and measurements of these factors?* With the current state of the art literature [7,14,22,23], however, answering these questions appears difficult since each work only measures an in-comprehensive list of factors. Moreover, accumulating partial measurements from different studies such as [3,8,11] that employ dissimilar system under tests, cannot guarantee a reliable outcome. More critically, they either perform software-based measurements that present a restricted coverage to specific applications, or perform hardware-based measurements that require costly hardware instrumentation [16]. Rigorous countermeasures are required to first identify potential factors. Also, the significance of each factor needs to be assessed under a similar setting and for a reasonable duration so that accurate and reliable energy models can be built [4,12,20,24].

Motivated by this gap in knowledge, we believe that a systematic and thorough study is required to identify energy consumption factors and the degree at which these factors affect energy consumption. To achieve this, the following key contributions are made:

- Identifying potential factors impacting energy consumption of edge nodes;
- Proposing *WattEdge*, a standard framework for measuring energy consumption of SBCs; *WattEdge* does not require costly hardware instrumentation such as sensors, shunt, analog-to-digital converter, etc.
- Empirically evaluating various edge-related energy consumption factors using *WattEdge*, supplemented by an all-inclusive energy model; and
- Validating the model's performance in Smart Agriculture domain using a practical application and demonstrating a 95% accuracy.

The remainder of this paper is structured as follows. Section 2 discusses our proposed holistic approach to identify major energy consumption factors for edge nodes. Then, we propose "*WattEdge*", a standard framework for our empirical experiments in Sect. 3. In Sect. 4, the factors are empirically studied under the same settings to provide the basis for (a) accurate comparison, (b) acquiring the significance thereof, and (c) an energy model. In Sect. 5, we validate the energy model generated by *WattEdge* using a practical application in Smart Agriculture domain on a cluster of Raspberry Pis Finally, we discuss the key findings of this research in Sect. 6 and conclude in Sect. 7.

2   Related Work and Energy Consumption Factors

Identifying potential factors impacting energy consumption of edge computing devices, the literature on measuring and modelling the energy consumption factors of edge computing is thoroughly reviewed. Our study uncovers nine factors impacting the energy consumption of the edge nodes. A summary of the degree at which those factors are considered in related work is provided in Fig. 1 (numbers in Fig. 1 correspond to references).

To begin with, a baseline for measurements is considered as an essential factor. Hence, measuring energy consumption when the device is in idle state ① seems unavoidable as perceived by several studies [8, 10, 22, 23, 25]. Edge nodes host the IoT applications, demanding them to utilize computational resources. Among them, of course, CPU ② is fairly dominant [14], but other resources such as memory ③ and storage ④ are also worth considering for two reasons: firstly, edge nodes are highly power-constrained and hence sensitive to minor factors; secondly, cer-

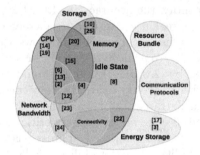

Fig. 1.   Related work on energy measurement and modelling: red=major, yellow=moderate and gray=minor effort. (Color figure online)

tain IoT applications (e.g. AI applications) heavily rely on such resources. To the best of our knowledge, only one work considers the memory [20], and none paid attention to the storage in edge. Hence, we also included cloud-specific efforts [10,25] in Fig. 1. Despite individual CPU, memory and storage, the energy usage due to a bundle of resources ⑤ is a matter of concern as well which is neglected to a large extent. However, calculating energy consumption for individual resources and then accumulating them may not give an accurate estimation, as their combination also alters the energy usage.

Connectivity is critical for edge nodes [18], where short-range connectivity means ⑥ such as WiFi, Bluetooth, ZigBee, USB, HDMI, VNC, etc. play essential role in Edge-IoT domain. Therefore, their effects on energy consumption have to be considered. Notably, WiFi as a widely-used means of connectivity has already gained a lot of attention [4,12,23,24]. By connectivity, the communication comes into the play. The degree at which communication influences energy consumption may vary which makes it worthy of consideration [2]. Industrial IoT (IIoT) applications tend to send and receive continuous messages containing single-data points such as temperature and humidity, for instance, while images sent by Traffic Control Cameras in a Smart City application utilize much more network bandwidth [5]. Considering this, the network bandwidth utilization ⑦ and its impact on energy usage under different levels of data transmission must be investigated [12,23,24]. Communications rely on underlying protocols ⑧ that function in either a request/reply (e.g., HTTP or CoAP) or a publish/subscribe (e.g., MQTT or DDS) fashion, whose impact is missed in the related work.

On the supply side, however, it is essential to understand the energy supply limitations. Edge nodes have to rely on only limited capacity batteries or renewable energy sources harvested locally, other than or along with the grid. Given that, the estimation of energy consumption would be practical only when the behaviours of energy source and storage ⑨ such as battery are well understood.

Our proposed approach differs from the existing solutions as specified in the following. Firstly, the works mentioned above tend to consider a selective list of factors from only one [2,6] to four [10,17]. In contrast, our approach holistically covers the nine identified factors to provide a fine-grained measurement. Secondly, the accuracy in [4,6,24,25] is doubted by not validating the proposal using real use cases or by merely relying on simulations; hence, in addition to extensive empirical studies, we validate our proposal in a realistic scenario. Thirdly, to achieve reasonable accuracy, cutting-edge hardware instrumentation used by [2,3,6,10,13,20,24] would not always be feasible due to its complexity and cost. We try to avoid this by encouraging a lightweight and low-cost Test and Learn strategy. Moreover, the lightness of the proposed framework for resource-limited edge nodes appears critical, which is compromised in [11,15,19,20,22]. Finally, our proposed approach is accompanied with a framework for reproducibility and extensibility, similar to [8] which provides an open-source framework, while [2,6,11,17,19–21,24] lack such features.

3   WattEdge: The Evaluation Framework

The *WattEdge* framework, open-sourced on GitHub[1], is designed and implemented on a real SBC-based testbed to measure the significance of all identified factors (see Fig. 2). In brief (see Fig. 2), ① an SBC edge node is prepared. ② Simultaneously, a Stress Worker and System Monitor Agent on the main edge node and ③ a Power Monitor Agent on the secondary Pi is invoked. ④ The Stress Worker invokes the Stress Function ⑤ which triggers stress tools. ⑥ Supplementary services and scripts are executed on the edge nodes. Finally, ⑦ the Logger function collects and reports the monitored data.

Edge Device: Emerging in 2012, Raspberry Pis have gained the momentum in the race of IoT devices [4]. They are recently employed as a perfect option for adopting edge computing, whether as standalone or even clusters of edge nodes [22]. In Pi family, we find Raspberry Pi 3 Model B+ to be one of the most utilized ones [3,6,17,22]. This Pi features a 1.4Ghz Quad-Core Processor, a 1GB LPDDR2 SDRAM, a 40-pin GPIO header, 5v USB power adaptor

---

[1] https://github.com/aslanpour/wattedge.

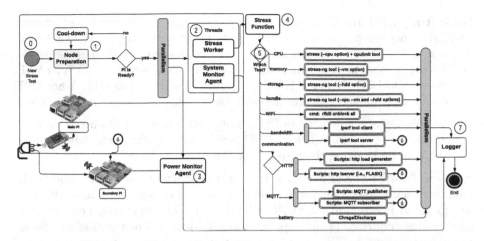

Fig. 2. *WattEdge*: The proposed edge energy measurement framework.

with a 1200 mA current, and connectivity options such as WiFi, Bluetooth, HDMI, and USB, all in an ARM architecture standing on a Raspberry Pi OS platform. Comparative quad-core SBCs include: AML-S805X-AC (La Frite),[2] UDOO BOLT V8,[3] ASUS Tinker Board,[4] and Odroid-C2.[5] To obtain sufficiently accurate measurements: (a) Pis are configured headless; (b) connectivity ports such as USB and HDMI are disabled; (c) communication means such as WiFi and Bluetooth are turned off (unless specified otherwise); (d) Pis are not re-positioned to avoid environmental conditions; (e) reasonable cool-down times are considered between each test; (f) tests last long enough and are repeated several times, and average and standard errors are reported for reliability; (g) certain tests are conducted at night to minimize network interference; and (h) the Raspberry Pi OS is updated with minimal installations.

Testbed: Two Pis are needed to emulate edge nodes (see Fig. 2). The main Pi runs the stress test program, i.e., Stress Worker, and the System Monitor Agent in concurrent threads. While stressing the Pi, a fine-grained monitoring agent continuously monitors and logs the whole system under test (e.g., CPU usage). To obtain accurate measurements, a hardware-level approach is adopted by employing a USB power meter model UM25C, which is highly accurate as shown in [22]. The meter reports the power and energy data in millisecond granularity via Bluetooth connection. Obtaining these measurements demands Bluetooth connection which influences the actual energy consumed on the Pi under test. Hence, the Power Monitor Agent, collecting the power and energy data, lives on a secondary Pi and is invoked remotely. The agent is connected to the power meter and reads the measurements during the stress tests.

---

[2] https://libre.computer/products/boards/aml-s805x-ac/.
[3] https://www.udoo.org/docs-bolt/Introduction/Introduction.html.
[4] https://www.asus.com/au/Single-Board-Computer/Tinker-Board/.
[5] https://wiki.odroid.com/odroid-c2/odroid-c2.

Node Preparation: ① prepares the edge node for a new stress test wherein no interference exists. Actions include disabling services such as MQTT broker which may have been employed for certain tests, disconnecting the Pi's battery and freeing up the memory, cache and swap. Disabling interfaces such as WiFi and Bluetooth, USB chip, and HDMI output are confirmed as well. A hot CPU can significantly influence the results, so a reasonable cool-down time is imposed.

Stress Worker: ② is written in Python and lives on a thread on the main Pi. It can run the specified test, e.g., CPU stress, for specific levels depending on the test plan by invoking the Stress Function.

System Monitor Agent: ② is run on a concurrent thread. It collects the monitored data every single second and, at the end of test, saves it on the storage (a 32GB micro SanDisk SDHC UHS-I card). The lightness, i.e., low overhead, will be confirmed in our empirical studies. Measured metrics include: timestamp, battery charge, CPU (usage, temperature, frequency, context switching and interrupts), memory usage, disk (usage, I/O read/writes) and bandwidth (packet sent/received). The *psutils* python module is employed to measure those metrics, except for the battery charge level which is measured by the *pijuice* module. The data is kept in memory until the end of test to avoid disk operations.

Power Monitor Agent: ③ is remotely invoked on the secondary Pi by Stress Worker. It gets connected to the power meter through Bluetooth and reads the power and energy data such as the wattage, current, volts, watt-hours etc. The data is finally saved on a local file.

Stress Function: ④ executes the specified test to stress a resource by ⑤ evaluating the test plan. It interacts with the secondary Pi depending on the test plan to run required services as well ⑥. Such interactions happen for running *iperf* server/client, HTTP server/client or MQTT publisher/subscriber.

Logger: ⑦ collects, merges and stores the data monitored by the two monitors.

4   Empirical Study

We use *WattEdge* to empirically analyze the 9 identified factors with a *Test and Learn* strategy. Note that all tests are conducted for 15 min and repeated 3 times, and average and standard errors are reported. We believe that 15 min is large enough for the purpose of building energy model and provides stable results. In reporting energy consumption results, we present all the y-axes at the same range, i.e., 0-1000 mWh for the sake of easy comparison. We firstly obtain energy usage in idle state as a baseline for drawing an analogy between the impact of different factors. Then, each factor is analyzed by first reporting the overall energy consumption of that stress test, then subtracting already identified factors to obtain the actual energy consumption of the investigated factor.

Idle State Stress. To establish a baseline, a series of non-stress tests are performed wherein the Pi is idle. The measurements are labeled as "idle" in figures. The energy consumption, denoted as E_{idle}, was measured as a total of 179.33 mWh on average. The average CPU usage was observed at 1.56%, confirming the lightness of *WattEdge*.

CPU Stress. The Stress Function employs the widely used *stress* tool to stress test the CPU [9] at full capacity and meanwhile it runs the *cpulimit* tool to throttle the usage at certain percentages (see Fig. 3). Results show increasing energy usage, starting from 179 to 699 mWh (see Fig. 3). The upward slope appears constant for CPU usages up to 50% while it gradually reaches a flat plateau for usages above 70%. The reason for such behavior was found in the CPU temperature. The temperature throttling for Pi 3 is capped at $60C°$ upon which the CPU frequency is reduced automatically to avoid overheating. CPU usage below 70% never reached this threshold. This also warns us that (a) the long-running benchmark tests are more reliable and the accuracy of performance evaluations that last for only a few seconds/minutes as in [4] is questionable; and (b) the CPU frequency tends to be driven by the temperature in certain IoT use cases such as Smart Farming wherein devices are exposed to the sunshine.

Energy Model: By fitting the collected data to a linear regression, we can model the energy consumption driven by CPU usage as follows: $E_{cpu}(u) = (22.9u + 107.6) \times t$ where E_{cpu} stands for energy consumption in mW due to the CPU usage percentage u and t is the duration of the experiment in hours (if 15 min, $t = 0.25$). Given the interference of power management mechanism on the device, for a pure CPU-dominant model, we use a sub-model as $\widehat{E_{cpu}}(u) = (26.9u+24.6) \times t$, measured by only considering CPU usages below 70% that gives the R^2 value of 99.7%. With the pure CPU model, a total energy model (E) is modelled as $E = E_{idle} + \widehat{E_{cpu}}$.

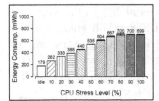 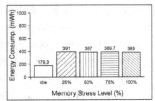 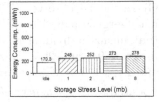

Fig. 3. CPU stress   **Fig. 4.** Memory stress   **Fig. 5.** Storage stress

Memory Stress. To stress test the memory, the advanced version of *stress* tool, *stress-ng*, is employed. This allows the workers to stress on specific percentage of unused memory. A sample command is: *stress-ng --vm 1 --vm-bytes 25% −t 900s*. That is, spawning 1 worker spinning on 25% of unused memory. Four different tests stressing on 25, 50, 75 and 100% of unused memory are performed.

The true impact of memory load on energy consumption appears rather similar for all memory loads (Fig. 4). Noticeably, a slight increase in energy consumption for lower memory loads is observed. This is due to the overhead on CPU context switching and interrupts. Technically, the *stress-ng* tool is continuously calling *mmap(2)/munamp(2)* and writing to the allocated memory. If the allocated memory is smaller (e.g., the 25% stress), the writing process is finished sooner and since the experiment lasts for minutes, this happens more often. Such context switching and interrupts appeared to be less for memory stress on higher loads. Further analysis shows an average 26% CPU usage in all memory experiments. The sole CPU stress at 26% constitutes for the energy consumption of 369 mWh, which is 5% lower than the average energy consumption of 388 mWh obtained in memory experiment. In other words, the memory can impose 11% more energy consumption (added to the idle) when under load which appears serious for highly power-constrained edge devices, while neglected in related works.

Energy Model: A memory-bound energy usage, $E_{memory}(m)$, here is equivalent to $E_{idle} \times \frac{m}{100}$, where m is the memory impact and for a Pi 3 B+ $m = 11$. Memory impact should be involved in the $\widehat{E_{cpu}}$ sub-model when the edge node is executing both CPU- and memory-bound IoT applications. This leads to an aggregated formula as: $E(u, m) = E_{idle} + \widehat{E_{cpu}}(u) + E_{memory}(m)$.

Storage Stress. The aim of this stress is to evaluate if there exists any difference in energy consumption of (a) read and write, as well as (b) combined operations on storage and to what extent. This is evaluated using *stress-ng* tool. Observations for storage stress in terms of individual read and write operations for 15 min confirm that write operations (264 mWh) consume more energy than reads (235 mWh). A 11% difference in energy usage between read and write operations is seen. The main dichotomy in their performance can be attributed to the 79% more context switching occurrences by write operations. The question, however, is whether the increased energy usage is only due to the disk operations or the impact of memory and CPU, i.e., over-fitting? If so, how much? Given the 5% observed CPU usage, we ran a CPU stress at 5% to measure the net energy usage. The *WattEdge* framework reported 218 mWh energy usage that means individual read and write operations can impose an extra energy usage of 9% and 26%. This gives an energy model as: $E_{storage^r} = E_{idle} \times 9\%$ and $E_{storage^w} = E_{idle} \times 26\%$, respectively. Having that, the $E_{total}(u, m)$ can be updated to $E_{total}(u, m) = E_{idle} + \widehat{E_{cpu}}(u) + E_{memory}(m) + E_{storage^r} + E_{storage^w}$.

In practice, the read and write operations are highly likely to exist simultaneously, whose energy usage pattern may be different. We ran the storage stress by continuously writing, reading and removing files of different sizes of 1, 2, 4, and 8 MB (the experiments at KB scale are done by [10]). Simplistically, such file sizes can resemble media files, ranging from image, to voice and video streams. Figure 5 confirms that combined operations' energy usage will always be higher than that of read-only operations (i.e., 235 mWh) and also higher (file sizes > 2M) than write-only operations (i.e., 264 mWh). The CPU usage again remains similar to individual operations ($u = 5\%$, equivalent to 218 mWh energy usage). At maximum, combined operations showed 278 mWh energy usage. Excluding the impact of CPU (218 mWh) and memory (20 mWh), the net value increases due to storage is $278 - 218 - 20 = 40 mWh$, equivalent to 22% imposed energy usage (added to the idle state) only due to combined storage operations which is considerable. We also evaluated larger file sizes, but the usage would not increase much further due to the SD card and CPU performance used in our testbed.

Energy Model: Involving CPU usage along with combined read and write operations of storage, i.e., $E_{storage^{rw}}$ (at high intensity), we can estimate that $E_{storage^{rw}} = E_{idle} \times 22\%$. More precisely, the energy usage observed in Fig. 5 shows a linear pattern that can be formulated as: $E_{storage^{rw}}(l) = (42.2l - 17.9) \times t$, where l stands for stress level: $l = \{1, 2, 4, 8\}$, and the accuracy is approximated at $R^2 = 92\%$. This insight leads the total energy model to $E(u, m, l) = E_{idle} + \widehat{E_{cpu}}(u) + E_{memory}(m) + \left[[E_{storage^r} + E_{storage^w}] \vee [E_{storage^{rw}}(l)]\right]$.

Resources Bundle Stress. The *stress-ng* tool is able to stress all resources simultaneously. Four different levels of stress are imposed to the edge devices. The stress levels for CPU and memory are considered at 25%, 50%, 75% and 100% while the storage is undergoing simultaneous read and write operations at the size of 1, 2, 4, and 8 MB. This also could be deemed a realistic application which is not necessarily single-resource-bound.

Observations are shown in Fig. 6. The energy usage presents a considerable increase over the idle mode. The slight decrease for the fourth level, compared to the third level, once again has the root in the energy management mechanism on Pi devices. In this series, the mechanism is automatically activated for all levels, but at different points. It is also important to note that this mechanism was not activated for CPU usages below 70% in CPU-only stress while in combined resources this happened for even 25% stress. The exact impact of resource bundle needs further investigations. Take 25% stress as an example. According to the obtained energy model, we expect a total energy usage of $E(53.85, m, 1) = E_{idle} + \widehat{E_{cpu}}(53.85) + E_{memory}(m) + E_{storage^{rw}}(1) = 179.33 + 368.6 + 20 + 6.83 = 574.76$. This estimation is less than the observed energy usage in Fig. 6 (i.e., 627 mWh). Analysing all four stress levels, an average extra usage of 8.4% for a resource bundle energy usage is obtained which may have the root in increased context switching due to resource (CPU, memory and storage operation) interference which causes this overhead.

Energy Model: The revised energy model, considering the impact of resource bundle energy usage, i.e., E_{bundle}, can be equal to a constant (i.e., β, here $\beta = 8.4$) value which is added to the total expected energy usage. This gives $E_{bundle}(u, m, l, \beta) = \left(\widehat{E_{cpu}}(u) + E_{memory}(m) + E_{storage}(l)\right) \times \left(\frac{\beta}{100}\right)$. The following aggregated formula including the impact of resource bundle is hence gained: $E(u, m, l, \beta) = E_{idle} + \widehat{E_{cpu}}(u) + E_{memory}(m) + E_{storage}(l) + E_{bundle}(u, m, l, \beta)$.

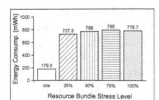

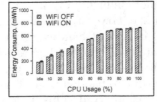

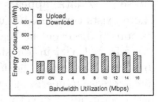

Fig. 6. Resources bundle stress

Fig. 7. Connectivity stress (no comm.)

Fig. 8. Bandwidth utilization stress

Connectivity Stress. In the literature [12,13], WiFi and Ethernet connectivity have gained more attraction due to highly adaptability to IoT domain. However, the limitations of employing the Ethernet in many wide-area IoT use cases makes it less worthy of consideration [18]. We redo experiments on CPU tests wherein WiFi is enabled, but no data transmission is occurred. The results for when WiFi is off is used as a baseline for comparison. This study is essential since idle state for edge nodes is highly likely, yet the consequences are left unattended, particularly for connectivity impacts [13,14,17,19].

Results in Fig. 7 reveal that the WiFi connectivity impact exists most of the times even though insignificant overall. In details, the lower the resource utilization, the higher the impact of the idle WiFi activities will be. Activities can be seen as responding to the beacon signals sent by a router or peers. A slight CPU temperature increase due to such activities was also reported by the System Monitor Agent. Precisely, an extra energy usage of between 0 and 17.38% for idle state is observed. Not a linear trend is seen, hence the average impact of WiFi enabled is considered here (7.82%). Further investigation is conducted for connectivity means such as Bluetooth, USB, HDMI and VNC which unexpectedly showed 18, 128, 6 and 18% extra energy usage, respectively. This and WiFi observations means that connectivity, at least for investigated means, can impose a sum of 178% extra energy usage.

Energy Model: A constant c representing the influence of connectivity, i.e., sum of WiFi-enabled (but idle), Bluetooth,USB, HDMI and VNC, can be involved as $E_{connectivity}(c) = E_{idle} \times (\frac{c}{100})$. This finding leads the aggregated energy model to the following: $E(u, m, l, \beta, c) = E_{idle} + \widehat{E_{cpu}}(u) + E_{memory}(m) + E_{storage}(l) + E_{bundle}(u, m, l, \beta) + E_{connectivity}(c)$.

Network Bandwidth Stress. Communications between edge nodes can be categorized in upload and download actions, regardless of the data type. However, one cannot ignore the importance of data transfer rate. To study it, an *iperf3* client is invoked on the main Pi and an *iperf3* server is invoked on the secondary Pi. Then, the client sends data in TCP mode at different rates to the server: {2, 4, 6, 8, 10, 12, 14, and 16 Mbps}. *WattEdge* measures the upload impact on energy usage. Similarly, the opposite roles are given to the Pis also to measure the impact of download operations.

Results, in Fig. 8, show the energy consumption due to upload and download at particular transmission rates. It is obvious that the more the bandwidth is utilized, the more the energy is consumed. Moreover, the upload (generating and sending data) appears more influential than the download (receiving data). There exists certain CPU usage, however, which needs to be taken into consideration to discover the real impact of bandwidth utilization. The CPU usage grows from 1.53% in idle state to 5% for the highest bandwidth utilization, i.e., 16 Mbps. Excluding the idle state and CPU usage, a maximum of 58% and 26% increase in energy usage due to bandwidth utilisation for upload and download operations, respectively, is observed. This understanding will help making a reasonable decision for establishing or preventing communication in edge.

Energy Model: The bandwidth net effect, excluding CPU, is involved in the E_{total}, as the CPU effect is independently considered by E_{cpu}. It presents a linear pattern which in Pi 3 B+ is measured as: $E_{bandwidth^u}(r) = (14.8r + 173) \times t$ for upload with $R^2 = 99\%$ and $E_{bandwidth^d}(r) = (-0.9r + 172.2) \times t$ for download with $R^2 = 92\%$, respectively, where $r = \{2, 4, 6, 8, 10, 12, 14, 16\}$ stands for the rate of data transmission in Mbps. This eliminates the need for calculating the connectivity solely, i.e., $E_{connectivity}(c)$ as WiFi is under use. Involving bandwidth in E, we have: $E(u, m, l, \beta, r) = E_{idle} + \widehat{E_{cpu}}(u) + E_{memory}(m) + E_{storage}(l) + E_{bundle}(u, m, l, \beta) + [E_{bandwidth^u}(r) \vee E_{bandwidth^d}(r)]$.

Communication Protocols Stress. In practice, as we observed in storage analyses, the communication operations as upload and download are expected to co-exist. Hence, this study evaluates the energy consumption due to communication protocol families: request/reply and publish/subscribe in a full cycle of transmission. The *WattEdge* picks up the most popular ones from each category in IoT domain, i.e., *HTTP* and *MQTT*, respectively. The test scenario for HTTP is to send simple HTTP GET requests from a client to a server which is a Python Flask HTTP server echoing the message. For MQTT, a publisher sends messages to a subscriber on another node through a Mosquitto MQTT broker. The subscriber receives messages and publishes its response to the original publisher, similar to the HTTP study design for consistency. Note that in the request/reply family only client and server live and consume the energy while in the publish/subscribe there are publisher, subscriber and broker. The *WattEdge* framework comprehends such differences and assigns each role to the main Pi and the auxiliaries on the secondary Pi, depending on the test plan.

Tools such as *Jmeter* can be used as a client generating the load. Jmeter, however, is unreasonably heavy for SBCs such as Pi 3 B+. Since we aim at both considering the client and server impact of protocols, the *WattEdge* framework benefits from a lightweight customized python script for load generations. For the MQTT load test, the *paho* Python module is employed which efficiently generates and publishes messages with imposing negligible overhead. The load generator will concurrently send 10 to 90 requests/messages per second (in 9 tests) to the server in HTTP tests and to the subscriber in MQTT tests. This is the maximum load a Pi 3B+ could generate according to our configurations.

HTTP: The difference between client and server's impact appears insignificant (Fig. 9). Energy consumption increases from 179 mWh in idle mode to 192 mWh in WiFi-enabled and to 443 and 430 mWh for maximum client and server stress, respectively. To reveal the net value for energy usage, we exclude the idle state and CPU usage obtained by the System Monitor Agent. More CPU usage was seen for the client than server. The net value is as 22% and 35% additional energy usage due to the HTTP client (E_{http^c}) and server (E_{http^s}), respectively, at maximum. The range of energy usage for different rates of concurrently, e.g., 10–90, is narrow and no linear pattern with a reasonable accuracy is observed. Hence, an average energy usage satisfies the inclusion of this factor which is observed at 18% (cl) and 30% (se) energy usage for client, $E_{http^c}(cl) = E_{idle} \times \frac{cl}{100}$, and server, $E_{http^s}(se) = E_{idle} \times \frac{se}{100}$, respectively. The cl and se stands for client and server's impact which for Pi 3 B+ will be 18 and 30, respectively.

MQTT: The energy usage depends on three entities: publisher, broker and subscriber. Figure 10 shows that the MQTT mechanism adds to the energy usage, but insignificant differences exist between entities. The slight difference is seen, mostly for heavy loads (e.g., 80 and 90 messages), where the subscriber was dominant and the broker consumed relatively less energy than others. Excluding the idle state and CPU usage (observed at < 5% for entities), the net energy usage for publisher (E_{mqtt^p}), subscriber (E_{mqtt^s}) and broker (E_{mqtt^b}) at maximum load is measured as 28, 32 and 23% additional energy usage, respectively. Similar to HTTP, the range of energy usage is narrow, and the interest of simplicity, an average energy usage of 23 (pu), 26 (su) and 22% (br) for publisher, subscriber and broker is considered. This gives the following formulas: $E_{mqtt^p}(pu) = E_{idle} \times \frac{pu}{100}$, $E_{mqtt^s}(su) = E_{idle} \times \frac{su}{100}$ and $E_{mqtt^b}(br) = E_{idle} \times \frac{br}{100}$.

HTTP vs. MQTT: Overall, entities in HTTP consume much more CPU and energy than in MQTT. However, excluding CPU usage, the MQTT is imposing further energy usage. It should not be neglected that a third-party entity as broker exists in MQTT scenario whose energy usage must be considered. With this in mind, if we exclude the broker, the energy usage for both HTTP and MQTT becomes comparable. Moreover, this considerable usage due to communication raises the following question: "Is the task or data offloading, which requires communication between nodes, in edge computing always affordable?" With this insight, the total energy usage can consider finer-grained measurements based on entities performance in each protocol as follows:

$$E(u, m, l, \beta, cl, se, pu, su, br) = E_{idle} + \widehat{E_{cpu}}(u) + E_{memory}(m) + E_{storage}(l) +$$

$$E_{bundle}(u, m, l, \beta) + \left[\left[E_{http^c}(cl) + E_{http^s}(se) \right] \vee \left[E_{mqtt^p}(pu) + E_{mqtt^s}(su) + E_{mqtt^b}(br) \right] \right].$$

Energy Sources Stress. With the widespread usage of the Lithium-ion batteries as energy storage, *WattEdge* employs a PiJuice HAT (i.e., Hardware Attached on Top–HAT) installed on the Pi to supply battery power. The PiJuice HAT features an on-board 1820mAh battery, original battery from Motorola Droid 2 (A955), and communicates with the Pi through GPIO Pins. A remotely controlled 5V Single Channel Relay Module handles the connection and disconnection of the charger.

The studies on the battery are to find out two behaviors: charging and discharging. For the former, we keep charging the battery from 10% to 98% and babysit the powering behavior. Figure 11 shows energy usage during three hours. Starting from 10% charge, the PiJuice software asked the battery to get higher wattage. The wattage is reduced by reaching at the moderate charge level around 30–50%, increased at charge levels between 50–80% and then gradually decreased the powering until fully charged (163 min). After that, the incoming wattage is significantly reduced. This is evidencing that the battery software system considerably influences the powering which is worth considering.

On the discharge side, we are concerned about the efficiency of batteries. Hence, we drained a certain amount of the battery storage and measured how much energy it needs to obtain same amount of energy again. This revealed that the battery is returning 20% less energy. This is due to the internal resistance of the batteries. Also, the aging issue in Lithium-ion batteries deteriorates performance and increases internal resistance, all warning us of the energy sources considerations as well as energy consumers.

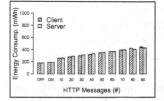
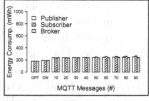
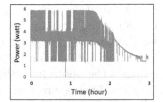

Fig. 9. HTTP communication stress

Fig. 10. MQTT communication stress

Fig. 11. Energy sources: battery charging

The Test and Learn strategy provides us with an understanding of energy consumption factors in a practical measurement including: (1) *idle* state; (2) *computation* such as CPU, memory, storage and resource bundle (the storage is ignored for non-data-intensive applications); (3) *connectivity* if connectivity means are enabled; and (4) *communication* if data need to be transferred between the edge nodes using connectivity technology e.g. Wifi. For communication, if merely data transmission is of interest, bandwidth usage is included, otherwise only communication factors are included where specific protocols such as http or mqtt are used. If one wants to use the proposed model in practice, parameters of the model such as u, m, l, β, c, r, cl, se, pu, su, and br should be set based on the specifications of the edge nodes and running applications. In the next section, we validate the proposed energy model for an edge platform hosting a real-world application from agricultural domain.

5 Validation

An edge computing platform for Smart Agriculture—A Bird Deterrent System— is practically implemented, that under the hood is a cluster of Pis. In this use case, a bird deterrent device utilizing motion and camera sensors is equipped with a Pi to act as an edge node (see Fig. 12). The edge nodes reside in a local network and are connected to each other using a wireless router. The IoT application works as fol-

Fig. 12. A pest bird deterrent application's workflow

lows (Fig. 12): (1) a motion sensor continuously senses the environment. (2) If a motion is perceived, the camera sensor is activated to take a photo. A trigger is pulled to call an object detection application on the device, for processing. (3)

We utilized a YOLO[6] (Real-Time Object Detection) function running as a web service using Flask (Python web framework) deployed on Docker containers for such processing. (4) If a bird is detected in the image, the deterrent device is activated for a certain time duration.

In a cluster of nodes, we assume nodes can share resources for computation offloading (scheduling the YOLO object detection container on peers) to save energy since fake owls are intended to be powered by batteries and solar panels. The edge nodes form a Kubernetes (K3s) cluster (see Fig. 13). Given the event-driven nature of the application, a Serverless platform, OpenFaaS, is employed for deploying the core YOLO object detection function. Upon a photo taken by the camera, the function's endpoint is triggered and a request is sent to OpenFaaS gateway on the master node. The gateway invokes the function, and requests the photo from the Pi, generating the task.

Experiments are conducted in (A) local execution and (B) computation offloading scenarios to validate the energy model. We deploy the System Monitor Agent of *WattEdge* on each Pi to monitor the actual energy consumption. Using profiling, we obtain parameters that the energy model requires, i.e., u and l for estimations. Then we compare the energy consumption estimated by our energy model to the actual usage measured by the *WattEdge*. A Poisson distribution is used to generate task. Two Pis are involved in experiments: Worker 1 (task generator in both scenarios and task executor in scenario A) and Worker 2 (idle in scenario A and task executor in scenario B). A Master node (OpenFaaS gateway) also exists that is not involved in task generation and executions and only performs orchestration. Thus we do not discuss its energy consumption. The monitor reads energy consumption from the USB Meter locally. Hence, for accuracy, we include the Bluetooth-related energy usage in the model. Also, for consistency, our experiments last for 15 min and are repeated 3 times.

(A) For local execution, the actual energy usage of Worker 1 for the duration of test is reported at 573 by the USB Meter (see Fig. 13). This scenario involves computation: CPU (u), memory (m), storage (l) and resource bundle (β). Since the energy data is read locally, the Bluetooth connection energy usage (c) is considered in connectivity. In terms of communication, although Worker 1 is both task generator and executor, it still needs communication with Master node. This communication in Kubernetes is based on a request/reply protocol, so the client (cl) and server (se) roles must be considered for Worker 1. Hence, the

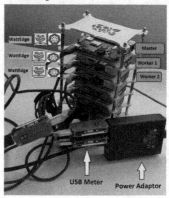

Fig. 13. A cluster of Pis with Kubernetes, OpenFaaS and WattEdge.

total energy usage will be $E(u, m, l, c, cl, se)$. The variables such as $u = 41.43$ and $l = 1$ are obtained through profiling and constants are already known for

---

[6] https://pjreddie.com/darknet/yolo/.

Pi 3 (see Sect. 4). These two variables and other constants are used to estimate energy consumption using our proposed energy model. The estimation using the energy model results in total of 612.64 mWh which demonstrates 93% accuracy compared to the actual energy consumption. Using the same method for Worker 2, which was almost idle in this scenario, an accuracy of 91% is observed.

(B) For offloading execution, the actual energy consumption of Worker 1 is reported at 316 mWh (less than previous scenario). Applying the energy model on the observed CPU utilization, storage and constant values, and comparing the estimated value with the actual one, a 97% and 98% accuracy in energy consumption estimation is obtained for Worker 1 and 2, respectively.

6   Discussion

Our findings show the significance of various factors in energy consumption of power constrained edge devices.

- Major factors: Connectivity prompts to be a major factor, neglected to a large extent by the literature. Confirming findings from previous studies (see Fig. 1), our findings pinpoint that the CPU and idle state are also major energy consumption factors.
- Moderate factors: Communication protocols and resource bundle are found to be moderate factors. The request/reply protocols are shown to be more power hungry compared to publish/subscribe models. The network bandwidth utilization and energy sources factors have moderate impact on the energy consumption.
- Minor factors: Impact of the memory and storage utilization appeared to be less significant.

We believe that the novel Test and Learn strategy in *WattEdge* significantly contributes to the literature by providing an accurate, low-cost, lightweight, fine-grained/holistic, and extensible framework. The *WattEdge* approach provides accurate enough measurements missed in software-based approaches while avoiding high-cost hardware instrumentation in hardware-based solutions. The high accuracy was ensured by running a diverse workflow (CPU-, memory- and storage-intensive as well as communication). The energy model developed based on *WattEdge* framework measurements. Two use cases were evaluated to validate the accuracy of energy models. An average accuracy of 95% are obtained in validation tests. The *WattEdge* framework is designed to be sufficiently lightweight as in practice it would not consume CPU usage of more than 1% as observed in our empirical studies. It is sufficiently fine-grained to allow a realistic and accurate measurement of a wide range of energy consumption factors: CPU, memory, storage etc. Finally, while the obtained power model is dependent on Pis, the *WattEdge* framework can be applied to other SCBs such as NVIDIA Jetson or Odroid [6] to obtain hardware-specific power models. In other words, SBCs considerably feature the same potential power factors but in different capacities. The modular design of *WattEdge* allows simple extensions for such resources. Besides, edge candidates other than SBCs can extrapolate the *WattEdge* idea.

7   Conclusions and Future Work

In this work, we conducted a comprehensive review to identify factors impacting energy consumption of edge devices first. Then, a framework called *WattEdge* was proposed to evaluate energy consumption of edge devices through a 9-step assessment using identified factors. These factors include: node's idle state, CPU, memory, storage, resource bundle, connectivity, network bandwidth, communication protocols and energy storage. *WattEdge* was implemented on a real SBC-based edge computing testbed while several empirical experiments were conducted. Based on the empirical analysis, an evolutionary all-inclusive energy model was developed. Our findings confirms that, in addition to major energy consumption factors such as CPU and idle state, connectivity uses significant energy in edge devices. This highlights the need for low power connection technologies and energy efficient communication protocols for the edge. Using real-world application in the smart agricultural domain, we validated our proposed energy model demonstrating a 95% accuracy of the model. In future, we will extend *WattEdge* to support a wider range of edge computing's requirements. This involves the study of: (a) renewable energy sources such as solar, (b) connectivity means such as Lora, and (c) communications protocols such as DDS.

References

1. Cisco Annual Internet Report (2018–2023) White Paper. Technical report (2020). https://www.cisco.com/c/en/us/solutions/collateral/executive-perspectives/annual-internet-report/white-paper-c11-741490.html
2. Ardito, L., Torchiano, M.: Creating and evaluating a software power model for linux single board computers. In: Proceedings of the 6th International Workshop on Green and Sustainable Software, pp. 1–8. GREENS '18, Association for Computing Machinery, New York, NY, USA (2018). https://doi.org/10.1145/3194078.3194079
3. Asaad, M., Ahmad, F., Alam, M.S., Rafat, Y.: IoT Enabled monitoring of an optimized electric vehicle's battery system. Mob. Netw. Appl. **23**(4), 994–1005 (2018)
4. Bekaroo, G., Santokhee, A.: Power consumption of the Raspberry Pi: a comparative analysis. In: 2016 IEEE International Conference on Emerging Technologies and Innovative Business Practices for the Transformation of Societies (EmergiTech), pp. 361–366 (2016)
5. Bouguettaya, A., et al.: An Internet of Things Service Roadmap. Communications of the ACM (2021)
6. Cabaccan, C.N., Reidj, F., Cruz, G.: Power characterization of Raspberry Pi agricultural sensor nodes using arduino based voltmeter. In: 3rd International Conference on Computer and Communication Systems, pp. 349–352 (2018)
7. Dizdarević, J., Carpio, F., Jukan, A., Masip-Bruin, X.: A survey of communication protocols for internet of things and related challenges of fog and cloud computing integration. ACM Comput. Surv. (CSUR) **51**(6), 1–29 (2019)
8. Fieni, G., Rouvoy, R., Seinturier, L.: SmartWatts: Self-Calibrating Software-Defined Power Meter for Containers. arXiv preprint arXiv:2001.02505 (2020)
9. Hoque, S., De Brito, M.S., Willner, A., Keil, O., Magedanz, T.: Towards container orchestration in fog computing infrastructures. In: 2017 IEEE 41st Annual Computer Software and Applications Conference (COMPSAC), vol. 2, pp. 294–299 (2017)

10. Hylick, A., Sohan, R., Rice, A., Jones, B.: An analysis of hard drive energy consumption. In: 2008 IEEE International Symposium on Modeling, Analysis and Simulation of Computers and Telecommunication Systems, pp. 1–10 (2008)
11. Jiang, Q., Lee, Y.C., Zomaya, A.Y.: The power of ARM64 in public clouds. In: 2020 20th IEEE/ACM International Symposium on Cluster, Cloud and Internet Computing (CCGRID), pp. 459–468 (2020)
12. Kaup, F., Gottschling, P., Hausheer, D.: PowerPi: measuring and modeling the power consumption of the Raspberry Pi. In: 39th Annual IEEE Conference on Local Computer Networks, pp. 236–243 (2014)
13. Kaup, F., Hacker, S., Mentzendorff, E., Meurisch, C., Hausheer, D.: Energy models for NFV and service provisioning on fog nodes. In: NOMS 2018–2018 IEEE/IFIP Network Operations and Management Symposium, pp. 1–7 (2018)
14. Kecskemeti, G., Hajji, W., Tso, F.P.: Modelling low power compute clusters for cloud simulation. In: 2017 25th Euromicro International Conference on Parallel, Distributed and Network-based Processing (PDP), pp. 39–45 (2017). https://doi.org/10.1109/PDP.2017.33
15. LeBeane, M., Ryoo, J.H., Panda, R., John, L.K.: Watt watcher: fine-grained power estimation for emerging workloads. In: 2015 27th International Symposium on Computer Architecture and High Performance Computing (SBAC-PAD), pp. 106–113 (2015)
16. McCullough, J.C., Agarwal, Y., Chandrashekar, J., Kuppuswamy, S., Snoeren, A.C., Gupta, R.K.: Evaluating the effectiveness of model-based power characterization. In: USENIX Annual Technical Conferences, vol. 20 (2011)
17. Mudaliar, M.D., Sivakumar, N.: IoT based real time energy monitoring system using Raspberry Pi. Internet Things 12, 100292 (2020)
18. Orsini, G., Posdorfer, W., Lamersdorf, W.: Saving bandwidth and energy of mobile and IoT devices with link predictions. Journal of Ambient Intelligence and Humanized Computing (2020)
19. Paniego, J.M., et al.: Unified power modeling design for various Raspberry Pi generations analyzing different statistical methods. In: Pesado, P., Arroyo, M. (eds.) CACIC 2019. CCIS, vol. 1184, pp. 53–65. Springer, Cham (2020). https://doi.org/10.1007/978-3-030-48325-8_4
20. Rashti, M., Sabin, G., Vansickle, D., Norris, B.: WattProf: a flexible platform for fine-grained HPC power profiling. In: 2015 IEEE International Conference on Cluster Computing, pp. 698–705 (2015)
21. Rieger, F., Bockisch, C.: Survey of approaches for assessing software energy consumption. In: Proceedings of the 2nd ACM SIGPLAN International Workshop on Comprehension of Complex Systems, pp. 19–24. CoCoS 2017, Association for Computing Machinery, New York, NY, USA (2017)
22. Sagkriotis, S., Anagnostopoulos, C., Pezaros, D.P.: Energy usage profiling for virtualized single board computer clusters. In: 2019 IEEE Symposium on Computers and Communications (ISCC), pp. 1–6 (2019)
23. Serrano, P., Garcia-Saavedra, A., Bianchi, G., Banchs, A., Azcorra, A.: Per-frame energy consumption in 802.11 devices and its implication on modeling and design. IEEE/ACM Trans. Netw. 23(4), 1243–1256 (2015)
24. Toldov, V., Igual-Pérez, R., Vyas, R., Boé, A., Clavier, L., Mitton, N.: Experimental evaluation of interference impact on the energy consumption in Wireless Sensor Networks. In: 2016 IEEE 17th International Symposium on A World of Wireless, Mobile and Multimedia Networks (WoWMoM), pp. 1–6 (2016)
25. Zedlewski, J., Sobti, S., Garg, N., Zheng, F., Krishnamurthy, A., Wang, R.Y.: Modeling hard-disk power consumption. FAST 3, 217–230 (2003)

Improving Load Balancing for Modern Data Centers Through Resource Equivalence Classes

Kaiyue Duan[1], Yusen Li[1(✉)], Trent G. Marbach[2], Gang Wang[1], and Xiaoguang Liu[1]

[1] College of CS, Nankai University, Tianjin, China
{duanky,liyusen,wgzwp,liuxg}@nbjl.nankai.edu.cn
[2] Department of Mathematics, Ryerson University, Toronto, Canada

Abstract. Load balancing is one of the most significant concerns for data center (DC) management, and the basic method is reassigning applications from overloaded servers to underloaded servers. However, to ensure the service availability, during the reassignment of an application, some resources (i.e., *transient resources*) are consumed simultaneously on its initial server and its target server, which imposes a challenge for load balancing. The latest research has proposed a concept called resource equivalence class (REC: a set of resource configurations such that a latency-critical (LC) application running with any one of them can meet the QoS target). In this paper, we use the REC to improve the load balancing for a DC where multiple LC applications have already been co-located on servers with the service availability and QoS requirements. We formulate the proposed load rebalancing problem as a multi-objective constrained programming model. To solve the proposed problem, we propose to use a machine learning-based classification model to construct the RECs for applications, and we develop a local search (LS) algorithm to approximate the optimal solution. We evaluate the proposed algorithm via simulated experiments using real LC applications. To our knowledge, it is the first time to use REC for improving load balancing.

Keywords: Load rebalancing · Resource equivalence class · Local search

1 Introduction

The load balancing in DC management has been brought to the forefront with the booming development of cloud computing. Load balancing is one of the most significant concerns for DC management in that it is beneficial to reduce services' response time and makespan [22,26], to avoid network bottlenecks [9,20],

This work is supported by State Key Lab of Computer Architecture, ICT, CAS, under Grant No. CARCHB202013; NSFC (U1833114, 61872201); Science and Technology Development Plan of Tianjin (18ZXZNGX00140, 18ZXZNGX00200, 20JCZDJC00610).

H. Hacid et al. (Eds.): ICSOC 2021, LNCS 13121, pp. 548–562, 2021.
https://doi.org/10.1007/978-3-030-91431-8_34

to boost energy-efficiency [24, 26], availability [26], throughput [19, 22], and scalability [13]. Modern cloud service providers have deployed various load balancers in their data centers to meet load balancing requirements at different levels [1].

The basic method to achieve load balance is through judiciously reassigning tasks from overloaded servers to underloaded ones. To avoid service interrupt, when we reassign an application from its initial server to a target server, a copy of that application is constructed on the target server and begins to consume resources on that server; then the requests (i.e., workload) are redirected from that application to the newly constructed copy; finally, the original application is terminated. During the reassignment, some resources (i.e., transient resources) are consumed simultaneously on the initial and the target server.

The transient resource imposes a challenge for load balancing because an application might not be reassigned to its target server if the capacities for transient resources are insufficient. Furthermore, co-located applications will contend for shared resources and thus may suffer from performance interference. To minimize the impact of performance interference, partitioning shared resources for co-located LC applications is necessary [7, 11, 23, 28, 30–32, 38–40]. In this case, achieving load balance is more challenging because we must partition sufficient resources for LC applications to meet their QoS targets.

Previous works [7, 32] proposed the REC: the set of all resource configurations such that an LC application running with any one of these configurations can meet the QoS target. For example, configuration ⟨2 cores, 16 LLC ways⟩ (LLC: last level cache) and ⟨4 cores, 4 LLC ways⟩ may both satisfy an LC application's QoS target, and so would both be included in its REC. Using the RECs can facilitate the load balancing in two ways: (a) simply adjust the configurations of LC applications may lead to a more balanced load among servers; and (b) LC applications can switch to a configuration with lower demands for transient resources, and thereby make the reassignment operation easier.

Despite the advantages of utilizing the REC as mentioned above, using the REC imposes several challenges for load balancing. First, the REC of an LC application is difficult to construct, because it varies for different workloads while measuring all the resource configurations for every possible workload is impractical. Second, when the REC is considered, the search space for the load balancing problem is dramatically expanded and the complexity is greatly increased. Third, using the REC to improve load balancing may increase the total resource usage of a DC, so we need to trade-off between load balancing and cost-efficiency.

In this paper, we use the REC to improve load balancing in DCs with co-located LC applications. The main contributions are as follows. First, we formulate the proposed problem as a multi-objective constrained programming model, which jointly improves the load balancing and cost-efficiency for a DC while maintaining the service availability and QoS guarantee for LC applications. Second, we propose using a machine learning-based approach to construct the REC for each LC application and design an efficient LS algorithm to approximate the optimal solution of the proposed problem. Third, we conduct extensive experiments to evaluate the effectiveness of the proposed solution. The results show that using the REC improves load balancing and cost-efficiency for DCs.

Table 1. Configuration of the platform

Cores and LLC	8 Xeon E5-2609 v4 cores, 20 MB 20-way set-associative
Memory and storage	56 GB DDR4, 2TB HDD and 2 × 128 GB SSD
OS and virtualization	Centos 7, kernel 5.8.10, Linux Container 1.0.11

2 Motivation

Resource Equivalence Classes. We consider the REC for five real-world LC applications from the TailBench suite [21]. They are Sphinx, Img-dnn, Moses, Xapian, and Masstree, and are used for speech recognition, handwriting recognition, machine translation, search engine, key-value database respectively.

Figure 1 displays the REC of Img-dnn and Xapian running on a server (specification listed in Table 1) under various resource configurations (cores and LLC ways) and workload (measured in requests per seconds, RPS), where the x-axis and y-axis respectively denote the number of LLC ways and cores, and the color of the grid denotes the tail latency (i.e., the 95th percentile of response delays, which is measured in milliseconds). As shown in the color bar, darker colors indicate lower delays, and the colored cells represent the configurations that satisfy the QoS target, constituting the REC of an application, while the white cells are the configurations that violate the QoS target. The QoS target (the number on the rightmost side of each color bar) is the tail latency of an application running under the maximum workload (denoted by maxRPS) using all cores and LLC ways, exceeding the maximum workload will cause a significant increase of latency. The REC of other LC applications is omitted due to the length limit.

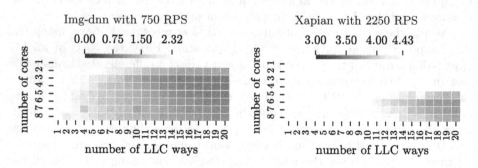

Fig. 1. The REC of each application under given RPS

We have several observations from the results in Fig. 1. First, the RECs vary across applications. This is because the properties, such as the functionality, resource demand, and contention features, vary across applications. Second, a higher workload results in a smaller REC (i.e., with fewer valid resource configurations). This is because a higher workload generally requires more resources, which reduces the number of configurations that meet the QoS target.

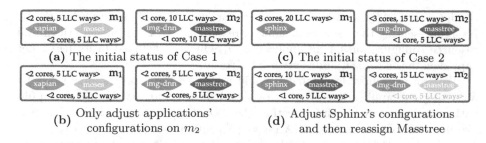

(a) The initial status of Case 1   (c) The initial status of Case 2

(b) Only adjust applications' configurations on m_2

(d) Adjust Sphinx's configurations and then reassign Masstree

Fig. 2. Using the REC makes the reassignment operation easier

How RECs Improve Load Balancing. We use two examples to show how RECs improve load balancing. The first example is shown in Fig. 2(a) and (b), there are two servers m_1 and m_2 with identical configurations as shown in Table 1. Initially (Fig. 2(a)) Xapian and Moses are co-located on server m_1 and have the same resource configuration ⟨2 cores, 5 LLC ways⟩, while img-dnn and masstree are co-located on server m_2 and have the same resource configuration ⟨1 core, 10 LLC ways⟩. Suppose we can swap Xapian with Img-dnn (or swap Moses with Masstree), the load of m_1 and m_2 would be balanced. However, performing such a swap is unacceptable because it will violate the transient resource capacity of m_2 for LLC. The previous load rebalancing methods do not use RECs, and they may fail in reassigning applications in this case. If the REC is used, we can switch the configuration of img-dnn and Masstree to ⟨2 cores, 5 LLC ways⟩, as shown in Fig. 2(b), the load of m_1 and m_2 becomes balanced. In this case, load balancing is improved by changing the configurations according to the REC.

The second example is shown in Fig. 2(c) and (d), sphinx runs on m_1 with resource configuration ⟨8 cores, 20 LLC ways⟩, while Img-dnn and Masstree are co-located on m_2, with resource configurations ⟨3 cores, 15 LLC ways⟩ and ⟨1 core, 5 LLC ways⟩ respectively. Transient resource constraint prevents us from reassigning any application between m_1 and m_2 because m_1 does not have any available cores and LLC ways to accommodate new applications. Therefore, the previous load rebalancing methods fail in reassigning applications in this case. If the REC is used, we can switch the configuration of Sphinx to ⟨2 cores, 10 LLC ways⟩. If so, there is enough capacity on m_1 for accommodating Masstree, and the load between m_1 and m_2 becomes more balanced after reassigning Masstree to m_1 (in Fig. 2(d)). The resources used by Masstree on m_2 will be returned after the reassignments are completed. In this case, we reduce the demand for transient resources by using different configurations and thus facilitate the reassignment.

3   Problem Formulation

In this section, we formally define the load rebalancing problem that uses REC to achieve a more balanced load among servers. Let S and A respectively denote a set of servers (with identical specifications) and a set of LC applications. Each application $a \in A$ has a given workload (i.e., RPS) and is deployed on its initial server s_a^* ($s_a^* \in S$), and we use the set P_a to denote its REC, where each resource configuration $p \in P_a$ is represented by a vector, with the rth element (denoted by $p[r]$) representing the resource demand of resource $r \in R$. Let p_a^* denote the initial resource configuration for an application a, which is included in its REC. Let cap_s^r denote the capacity of a server s for resource r.

We aim to achieve load rebalance and minimize the total resource usage by adjusting the applications' resource configurations and reassigning the applications among servers while meeting the QoS target and service availability. We define two matrices $X_{A,S}$ ($X_{A,S} = \{X_{a,s} | a \in A, s \in S\}$) and $X_{A,P}$ ($X_{A,P} = \{X_{a,p} | a \in A, p \in P_a\}$) to respectively denote the assignment of applications to servers and the configuration of applications: $X_{a,s} = 1$ (binary) indicates application a is assigned to server s; $X_{a,p} = 1$ (binary) indicates application a selects the configuration p.

We define the load of a server s for resource r (denoted by U_s^r) as the total resource demand of resource r of all applications on server s, and use $\bar{u}_r$ to quantify the *ideal* usage of resource r per server.

$$U_s^r = \sum_{\forall a \in A} \sum_{\forall p \in P_a} X_{a,s} \cdot X_{a,p} \cdot p[r], \qquad \bar{u}_r = \frac{\sum\limits_{\forall a \in A} \sum\limits_{\forall p \in P_a} X_{a,p} \cdot p[r]}{\sum\limits_{\forall s \in S} \text{cap}_s^r}.$$

If it were possible to perfectly reassign applications and partition resources, then we would have $U_s^r = \bar{u}_r$ for all servers s. Based on the above definitions, the objective function of the load balancing problem is defined as

$$\min \omega \overbrace{\sum_{\forall r \in R} \sum_{s \in S} (|U_s^r - \bar{u}_r|)}^{\text{load imbalance}} + (1-\omega) \overbrace{\sum_{\forall r \in R} \sum_{s \in S} U_s^r}^{\text{resource usage}}, \tag{1}$$

where the first item denotes the load imbalance, the second one denotes the total resource usage, and the weight ω adjusts the importance of the two objectives.

We have several hard constraints. The *single configuration constraint*: each application should be assigned one configuration from its REC.

$$\sum_{\forall p \in P_a} X_{a,p} = 1.$$

During each reassignment operation, transient resources such as cores, LLC, and memory are consumed simultaneously on the applications' initial servers and their target servers. The transient resources used by applications are not returned to their initial servers until the reassignments are physically complete in the DC. Therefore, we develop the *transient resource constraint*: there should be enough transient resource capacity to accommodate an application a on its initial server s_a^* and its target server, which is defined as

$$\overbrace{\sum_{\substack{a \in A \\ s_a^* = s}} \sum_{\forall p \in P_a} (1 - X_{a,s}) \cdot p_a^*[r] + X_{a,s} \cdot X_{a,p} \cdot p[r]}^{\text{part1}} + \overbrace{\sum_{\substack{a \in A \\ s_a^* \neq s}} \sum_{\forall p \in P_a} X_{a,s} \cdot X_{a,p} \cdot p[r]}^{\text{part2}} \leq \text{cap}_s^r.$$

This constraint calculates the resource usage of server s as follows. If s is the initial server of a, then the constraint is dominated by part 1: if a is placed on s, then we take one of its resource configurations p into account; otherwise, we take its initial configuration p_a^* into account. If s is not the initial server of a, then the constraint is dominated by part 2, where the p is taken into account.

Note that all configuration adjustments and reassignments are theoretically simulated rather than physically operated. We cannot adjust the initial configurations of applications because of service availability. In addition, the objective function represents a final state where all reassignments and configuration adjustments are supposed to be physically complete, and all the transient resources on initial servers are released. The $\overline{u}_r$ varies as we change configurations.

4 Solution

In this section, we complete two tasks: construct the RECs for applications and compute the optimal solution for the problem.

Construct the REC. As shown in Fig. 1, the REC varies with workloads. Therefore, measuring the tail latency for all resource configurations under every workload to construct the REC is implausible due to the large profiling overhead.

To address this issue, we train an XGBoost binary classifier [2] for each type of application, which predicts if a given resource configuration can make an application running under a fixed RPS meet its QoS target. The input features include a resource configuration and a given RPS; the output is a binary label indicating whether the given QoS target is satisfied. Based on the classifier, we enumerate all possible configurations and RPSs to predict their QoS results, and then filter the inputs that violate QoS target out to construct the RECs.

Search for the Optimal Solution. The load rebalancing problem is $\mathcal{NP}$-hard [3,5,12]. Thus, we design an LS algorithm to approximate the optimal solution within a time limit. The workflow of the LS is presented in Algorithm 1. The $X_{A,P}$ and $X_{A,S}$ follow their definitions in Sect. 3, and are initialized by applications' initial configuration and server. The weighted cost Ω is denoted by $f(X_{A,P}, X_{A,S})$, i.e., the value of objective function. The Quick_Shrinking adjusts applications' configurations, Quick_Balancing reassigns applications on the overloaded servers to the underloaded ones, and Greedy_Reassign creates subproblems and iteratively reduces the cost by optimally solving them.

Algorithm 1: Local Search

1: $(X_{A,P}, X_{A,S}) \leftarrow$ initial solution pair of configuration and assignment
2: $\Omega \leftarrow f(X_{A,P}, X_{A,S})$
3: Quick_Shrinking$(X_{A,P}, X_{A,S}, A)$
4: Quick_Balancing$(X_{A,P}, X_{A,S}, S)$
5: Greedy_Reassign$(X_{A,P}, X_{A,S}, S)$

The details of Quick_Shrinking are presented in Algorithm 2. We sort all servers in descending order according to the product of the server's usage for each resource (line 1). Then, we set each application's current resource configuration to the configuration p^- that has the minimal product of demands for all resources (line 5). If any constraint is violated or the weighted cost Ω is increased, we roll back to a backup pair $(X^*_{A,P}, X^*_{A,S})$; otherwise, we accept the $(X_{A,P}, X_{A,S})$.

Algorithm 2: Quick_Shrinking$(X_{A,P}, X_{A,S}, S)$

1: Sort all servers in S in descending order according to $\prod_{\forall r \in R} U^r_s$
2: **for** each server s in S **do**
3:      **for** each application a on s **do**
4:          $\Omega \leftarrow f(X_{A,P}, X_{A,S}), (X^*_{A,P}, X^*_{A,S}) \leftarrow (X_{A,S}, X_{A,P})$
5:          $p^- \leftarrow \arg\min_{p \in P_a} \prod_{\forall r \in R} p[r]$
6:          try to set the resource configuration of a to p^- without any violations
7:          if Ω is increased, revert to $(X^*_{A,P}, X^*_{A,S})$; otherwise, use $(X_{A,P}, X_{A,S})$

Algorithm 3: Quick_Balancing$(X_{A,P}, X_{A,S}, S)$

1: Sort all servers in S in descending order according to $\prod_{\forall r \in R} U^r_s$
2: **for** each i in $\{0, \dots, K\}$ **do**
3:      **for** each application a on s_i **do**
4:          **for** each j in $\{K, \dots, 0\}$ **do**
5:              $\Omega \leftarrow f(X_{A,P}, X_{A,S}), (X^*_{A,P}, X^*_{A,S}) \leftarrow (X_{A,S}, X_{A,P})$
6:              try to shift a to s_j without any violations
7:              if Ω is increased, then revert; otherwise use $(X_{A,P}, X_{A,S})$, **break**

The details of Quick_Balancing are presented in Algorithm 3. We first sort all servers in descending order. Next, we try to shift applications from the top K (a parameter) overloaded servers to the top K underloaded servers, satisfying all constraints (lines 2–7). If the weighted cost Ω is reduced after shifting applications, we accept the $(X_{A,P}, X_{A,S})$ and continue to next application; otherwise, we revert to $(X^*_{A,P}, X^*_{A,S})$. The parameter K leads to a trade-off between performance and efficiency. A larger K corresponds to a larger problem scale, which aids in reducing the weighted cost since more servers are involved. However, the computational overhead increases as K grows. So the K should be carefully set.

Algorithm 4: Greedy_Reassignment$(X_{A,P}, X_{A,S}, S)$

1: **repeat**
2:      $S' \leftarrow$ a set of $K/10$ randomly selected servers
3:      Sort all servers in S' in descending order according to $\prod_{\forall r \in R} U^r_s$
4:      **for** each i in $\{0, \dots, |S'| - 1\}$ **do**
5:          **for** each application a on s_i in the set S' **do**
6:              **for** each j in $\{|S'| - 1, \dots, 0\}$ **do**
7:                  $\Omega \leftarrow f(X_{A,P}, X_{A,S}), (X^*_{A,P}, X^*_{A,S}) \leftarrow (X_{A,S}, X_{A,P})$
8:                  flag $\leftarrow$ Super_Shift$(X_{A,P}, X_{A,S}, a, s_j, \Omega)$
9:                  if flag=**false**, then revert; otherwise, use $(X_{A,P}, X_{A,S})$, **break**
10: **until** time limit

The details of Greedy_Reassignment are presented in Algorithm 4. We first create each subproblem by randomly selecting a smaller set of servers (denoted by S'). Then we sort servers in S' in descending order, shifting applications on the overloaded servers to the underloaded ones via Super_Shift (lines 4–9). Based on the return value of Super_Shift, we either accept $(X_{A,P}, X_{A,S})$ and continue to next application or revert to $(X_{A,P}^*, X_{A,S}^*)$.

The Super_Shift method is presented in Algorithm 5. Given an application a and a target server s, we try to directly shift a to s (line 1). If s cannot accommodate a or the weighted cost Ω is not reduced, we adjust the resource configuration of a to reduce its resources demand (lines 4–5). After that, if the Ω is reduced, then return **true**. Or if s can accommodate a with the new resource configuration, we try to shift a to s again (line 7). Finally, if the Ω is reduced, then return **true**; otherwise, return **false** (line 8).

Algorithm 5: Super_Shift$(X_{A,P}, X_{A,S}, a, s, \Omega)$

1: **if** shifting a to s succeeds and Ω is reduced **then**
2: return **true**
3: **else**
4: **for** each resource configuration p in P_a **do**
5:   try to set the configuration of a to p
6:   **if** Ω is reduced, return **true**
7:   try to shift a to s without any violations
8:   **if** Ω is reduced, return **true**; otherwise, return **false**

Time Complexity. Let $|A|/|S|$ denote the number of applications on each server, and let $|P|$ denote the number of resource configurations of each application. Let T denote the number of calls of Algorithm 4. The complexity of Quick_Shrinking, Quick_Balancing, Super_Shift, and Greedy_Reassign approximate $\mathcal{O}(|S|\log|S| + |A||P|)$, $\mathcal{O}(K^2|A|/|S| + |S|\log|S|)$, $\mathcal{O}(|P|)$, and $\mathcal{O}(T(K\log(K/10)/10 + K^2|A||P|/100|S|))$ respectively.

5 Evaluations

5.1 Experimental Settings and Implementation

We consider a DC with homogeneous servers whose specifications are listed in Table 1 and there are three types of transient resources: CPU cores, memory, and LLC, where memory is not included in the REC (since the memory allocation of each application is set to a maximum value). We adopt the Linux's *cpuset* [10] and Intel's CAT [27] to partition cores and LLC ways among the colocated applications. In simulated experiments, the demands and capacities for each resource are min-max normalized to (0,1]. We assume load imbalance and resource usage are equally important, i.e., the parameter ω is set to 0.5.

We use five types of LC applications mentioned in Sect. 2. The QoS target of each application is determined as described in Sect. 2. For each application,

Table 2. Information of synthetic scenarios

	C_1	C_2	C_3	C_4	C_5	C_6	C_7	C_8
Application workload	Small	Small	Small	Small	Large	Large	Large	Large
Balancing level	Good	Bad	Good	Bad	Good	Gad	Good	Gad
Server load	Light	Light	Heavy	Heavy	Light	Light	Heavy	Heavy
Imbalance cost	282.83	367.89	173.71	196.2	286.55	355.9	221.13	240.46
Usage cost	696.13	696.13	883.88	883.88	580.5	580.5	747.13	747.13

we follow the steps below to collect enough samples: first, we randomly select various resource configurations and loads, and then run that application under the selected configurations and loads to measure the tail latencies, and finally determine if the QoS target is met and output the label. Given that the samples have fewer features, the main parameters of the XGBoost model such as the number of boosting rounds, the boosting learning rate, and the maximum tree depth for base learners are respectively set to 150, 0.15, and 2 for avoiding the over-fitting and achieving good performance. Other parameters are set to the default. We use 70% of the samples for training and the rest for testing.

For the proposed LS algorithm, we find that $K = 50$ work well for most of the problem input scenarios. If the number of servers is smaller than 100, K is set as the smaller value between $|S|$ (the number of servers) and 20.

We simulate two application workload patterns: large and small. For the small (resp. large) workload pattern, the RPS of an application is randomly selected from (0, maxRPS/2] (resp. [maxRPS/2, maxRPS]). We simulate two load balancing patterns: roughly-balanced (good) and poorly-balanced (bad). To generate a roughly-balanced load distribution pattern, we use the Worst-Fit method to place as many applications on each server as possible. The poorly-balanced pattern is generated based on the roughly-balanced pattern by randomly reassigning applications from a part of the servers to the other servers. We simulate two server load patterns: light and heavy. To generate the former (resp. latter), we randomly delete 30% (resp. 10%) of the applications from each server.

We simulate 8 different input scenarios with different resource demand patterns, load balancing patterns, and server workload patterns (as shown in Table 2). By default, we simulate 1000 servers for each scenario and the corresponding applications, whose resource configurations and RPSs are generated according to the related patterns. We also list the initial cost of load imbalance and resource usage for these scenarios with 1000 servers. For each experiment in this section, we repeat 5 times for each algorithm and compute the average result, and the time limit is set to 5 min. The numbers displayed in Fig. 3 and Fig. 4 indicate the optimal weighted cost achieved by the baseline algorithms and LS.

5.2 Baseline Algorithms

We compare the proposed LS algorithm with two baselines. The first baseline is a greedy algorithm (denoted by Greedy), which focuses on only adjusting applications' resource configurations to reduce the weighted cost without reassigning any applications. In detail, we first invoke the `Global_Resource_Shrink` method (Algorithm 3) to reduce the demands of all applications for resources. Next, we iterate for multiple rounds: in each round, we randomly select a server s, and try to change the resource configuration of each application on s by selecting the resource configuration that maximizes the reduction in the weighted cost.

The second baseline (denoted by NLS[1]) is the state-of-the-art algorithm for the machine reassignment problem [33] (which is similar to the proposed problem) without considering REC, which is ranked first among other load rebalancing methods [15]. The NLS adopts the large process reassignment, sorting-based swap method, and multiple restarts to reassign processes among servers iteratively. The large process reassignment method reassigns the process with the largest resource demand to a server with low resource usage, and reassign other processes from that server to other servers. To escape from the local optima and improve the quality of the solution, the NLS adopts a noisy strategy with various random seeds, restarting multiple times according to the seeds.

5.3 Results

Accuracy of the Classification Model. The sample sizes of the classifiers of Sphinx, Img-dnn, Moses, Xapian, and Masstree are 480, 2410, 3214, 2408, and 3040, respectively. The AUCs of these classifier respectively are 0.94, 0.98, 0.96, 0.96, and 0.97; and the F1-scores respectively are 0.94, 0.98, 0.95, 0.97, and 0.96. The overhead for these classifiers respectively are 202 ms, 258 ms, 262 ms, 256 ms, and 261 ms. For each application, our classifier has high AUC and f1 scores, indicating that our model can efficiently and accurately predict whether an application meets its QoS target under a given configuration and RPS.

Overall Performance. Figure 3 shows the weighted cost produced by LS and the two baselines for different scenarios, where darker (resp. light) colors denote the resource usage (resp. load imbalance) cost. We have several observations.

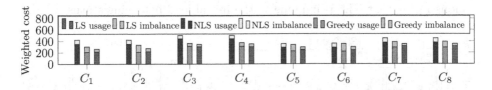

Fig. 3. The load imbalance cost and resource usage cost produced by the algorithms

First, LS outperforms NLS and Greedy for all scenarios, with an average advantage of 26% and 11% respectively, confirming that jointly use REC and reassignment scheme is much better than using one of them alone. The maximum advantage of LS over NLS and Greedy is 38% (on C_1) and 18% (on C_2) respectively, indicating that LS is best suited for scenarios with small application

---

[1] https://github.com/harisgavranovic/roadef-challenge2012-S41.

workload and light server load because these scenarios contain fewer applications, and instances' RECs have more resource configurations, causing easier reassignments of applications and more flexible adjustments of configurations. These factors make the two baselines work well, but LS benefits more from them.

Second, in terms of load imbalance cost, LS achieves the lowest ones for these scenarios, comparing with the two baselines, because it jointly uses the REC and reassignment to improve the load balancing; NLS outperforms Greedy for all scenarios, indicating that only adjusting the resource configuration to achieve load balancing is not a good choice. In terms of resource usage cost, Greedy outperforms LS for all scenarios because of its functionality; NLS does not consider the REC, therefore, it cannot reduce the resource usage cost.

Third, Greedy and LS produce relatively higher weighted costs when scenarios contain applications with large workloads (C_5 to C_8 vs. C_1 to C_4). The reason is that applications with large workloads need more resources to meet the QoS target, causing a high resource usage cost. Moreover, the three algorithms produce higher weighted cost when handling scenarios with heavy server load (C_3, C_4, C_7, and C_8 vs. C_1, C_2, C_5, and C_6), because these scenarios contain more applications than others, leading to higher resource usage costs.

Fourth, interestingly, NLS produces higher weighted costs when handling scenarios with small application workload (C_1 to C_4 vs. C_5 to C_8), because these scenarios initially have higher resource usage costs than others (according to Table 2), and the NLS is incapable of adjusting applications' configurations to reduce the resource usage cost. Furthermore, for the scenarios that contain applications with a large workload and servers with a heavy load (C_7 and C_8), the NLS produces the highest imbalance cost because the remaining capacity of each server is stringent, hindering NLS from reassigning applications.

Fifth, the Greedy and LS both produce slightly lower weighted costs when handling the roughly-balanced scenarios (C_1, C_3, C_5, and C_7 vs. C_2, C_4, C_6, and C_8), because when the initial load among servers is roughly-balanced, Greedy and LS are likely to produce lower load imbalance costs. The NLS produces almost the same weighted costs on the roughly/poorly balanced scenarios, demonstrating that NLS is immune to the initial load balancing status.

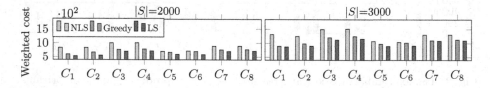

Fig. 4. The weighted cost by the three algorithms as the problem scale grows

Scalability. We investigate how the algorithms perform as the problem scale grows. We simulate 2000 and 3000 servers and let each algorithm run for 10 min to ensure that they can converge. The results are displayed in Fig. 4.

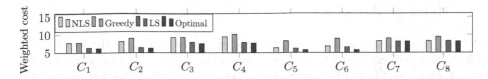

Fig. 5. Comparing the weighted cost produced by the algorithms with the optimal one

In addition to the phenomena mentioned in the Overall Performance experiment, we observe that the weighted cost produced by each algorithm increases as the problem scale grows. The reason is twofold: first, achieving load balancing for a larger DC is more difficult because the search space is exponentially growing as the number of servers increases; second, the resource usage grows as the number of applications increases, causing a higher initial weighted cost. Although the LS outperforms the two baselines for all scenarios, its advantage slightly decreases as the problem scale grows. We attribute this to that finding the optimal solution to a larger problem scale efficiently is more difficult.

Compared to the Optimal Solution. Since the load rebalancing problem is $\mathcal{NP}$-hard, it is implausible to optimally solve the proposed problem within an acceptable time limit. To evaluate the optimality of the LS, we consider a small problem scale with 20 servers. We use the optimization solver Gurobi [17] to compute the optimal solution. The results are plotted in Fig. 5, where the Optimal denotes the Gurobi solver. We observe that the weighted cost produced by LS is close to the optimal solution generated by Gurobi, with an average gap of 4% for all scenarios, demonstrating that LS can find near-optimal solutions efficiently. Again, using the configuration adjustments or reassignments alone cannot produce near-optimal solutions, hence we need to jointly use the two schemes to facilitate load balancing.

Overhead. Figure 6 shows the real-time weighted cost produced by each algorithm during the running period of 5 min for scenario C_3. We observe that all the algorithms converge in 5 min. The NLS has the fastest converging speed (in 2 min) but achieves the highest weighted cost. The Greedy converges as fast as LS (in 3 min), but produces a higher imbalance cost than that of LS, indicating that reassigning applications is necessary to further improve the load balancing. There is a trade-off between overhead and performance: the NLS is more computationally efficient while the LS is more powerful.

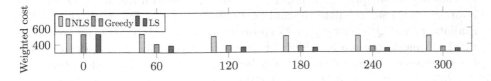

Fig. 6. The weighted cost changes over time (s)

6   Related Work

Recent studies have pointed out that resource partitioning is the key to minimize the performance interference between co-located microservices in DCs [7,11,23,28,30–32,38–40]. Specifically, Chen et al. [7] and Patel et al. [32] use REC to find the optimal resource configurations. Chen et al. [7] designed an online resource-wheel-based partition algorithm (i.e., PARTIES) and co-located multiple LC applications with batch jobs. Patel et al. [32] implemented a Bayesian Optimization-based partition algorithm, which improved PARTIES in terms of maximizing the throughput of batch jobs. Nishtala et al. [28] proposed using a deep reinforcement learning framework and it outperformed PARTIES in terms of saving energy. However, these works did not consider the load balancing.

Well-designed load balancing strategies are beneficial to reduce services' response time and makespan [22,26], to boost energy-efficiency [24,26], availability [26], throughput[19,22], and scalability [13]. Generally, there are two categories of load balancing algorithms: *static* [36] and *dynamic* [8]. The static schemes require the load balancer to make a set of assumptions on the tasks and servers according to prior knowledge, and most of them are deemed as offline scheduling methods such as Round Robin [35] and Randomized Algorithm [4]. The dynamic schemes apply profiling technology to measure real-time performance metrics (e.g., Cycles per instruction, CPI), yielding better balancing status but at the cost of the efficiency and simplicity of design and implementation. The representative ones such as Central Queue [16], average imbalance level based on multi-resources [37], Honey Bee Algorithm [22], and Throttled Algorithm [29].

The proposed problem naturally is the load rebalancing problem, which is proved to be $\mathcal{NP}$-hard [3,5,12]. The latest proposed machine reassignment problem [33] also considered improving load rebalancing for DCs, where a group of processes has already been placed on a group of machines and a balancer needs to re-schedule processes to machines under hard constraints for minimizing a weighted cost. The researchers proposed various methods, such as mixed-integer programming and constraint programming [25], variable neighborhood search [6], large neighborhood search [18], hybrid search [14], genetic algorithm [34] and efficient LS algorithms [15]. Unfortunately, these methods neither use REC to improve load rebalancing nor optimize resource efficiency at the same time.

7   Conclusions

In this paper, we present a novel multi-objective optimization problem that improves the load rebalancing and cost-efficiency for a DC with the service availability and QoS guarantees. We propose jointly using the REC and reassignment scheme to optimally achieve the two objectives. The results demonstrate the effectiveness, optimality, and scalability of the proposed solution. However, due to the hardware limitation, we consider only partitioning two resources (the cores and LLC) among the colocated applications, while other shared resources, e.g., memory bandwidth, are not partitioned. We would like to claim that the impact is insignificant because the LC applications are basically CPU intensive and partitioning LLC is deemed as an indirect way to mitigate the competition for memory bandwidth. Furthermore, we do not evaluate the proposed algorithm on real DCs. Moreover, the proposed algorithm is suitable for some dedicated DCs, e.g., search engines DCs, where most applications will run for a long time.

References

1. Elastic load balancing. https://aws.amazon.com/elasticloadbalancing/
2. XGBoost documentation. https://xgboost.readthedocs.io/en/latest/
3. Aggarwal, G., Motwani, R., Zhu, A.: The load rebalancing problem. In: SPAA 2003, pp. 258–265 (2003)
4. Azar, Y., Cohen, I.R., Panigrahi, D.: Randomized algorithms for online vector load balancing. In: ACM SIAM, pp. 980–991 (2018)
5. Belikovetsky, S., Tamir, T.: Load rebalancing games in dynamic systems with migration costs. TCS **622**, 16–33 (2016)
6. Butelle, F., et al.: Fast machine reassignment. Ann. Oper. Res. **242**(1), 133–160 (2015). https://doi.org/10.1007/s10479-015-2082-3
7. Chen, S., Delimitrou, C., Martínez, J.F.: Parties: QoS-aware resource partitioning for multiple interactive services. In: ASPLOS 2019, pp. 107–120 (2019)
8. Cybenko, G.: Dynamic load balancing for distributed memory multiprocessors. J. Parallel Distrib. Comput. **7**(2), 279–301 (1989)
9. Dean, J., Barroso, L.A.: The tail at scale. Commun. ACM **56**(2), 74–80 (2013)
10. Derr, S., Jackson, P., Lameter, C., Menage, P., Seto, H.: CPUSETS (2004). https://www.kernel.org/doc/Documentation/cgroup-v1/cpusets.txt
11. El-Sayed, N., Mukkara, A., Tsai, P.A., Kasture, H., Ma, X., et al.: KPart: a hybrid cache partitioning-sharing technique for commodity multicores. In: HPCA-24, pp. 104–117 (2018)
12. Fang, J., Zhang, R., Fu, T.Z.J., Zhang, Z., Zhou, A., et al.: Distributed stream rebalance for stateful operator under workload variance. TPDS **29**(10), 2223–2240 (2018)
13. Fardbastani, M.A., Sharif, M.: Scalable complex event processing using adaptive load balancing. J. Syst. Softw. **149**, 305–317 (2019)
14. Gabay, M., Zaourar, S.: Vector bin packing with heterogeneous bins: application to the machine reassignment problem. Ann. Oper. Res. **242**(1), 161–194 (2016)
15. Gavranović, H., Buljubašić, M.: An efficient local search with noising strategy for google machine reassignment problem. Ann. Oper. Res. **242**(1), 19–31 (2016)
16. Grosu, D., Chronopoulos, A.T.: Noncooperative load balancing in distributed systems. J. Parallel Distrib. Comput. **65**(9), 1022–1034 (2005)
17. Gurobi Optimization, L.: Gurobi Optimization, LLC (2018). http://www.gurobi.com
18. Jaśkowski, W., Szubert, M., Gawron, P.: A hybrid MIP-based large neighborhood search heuristic for solving the machine reassignment problem. Ann. Oper. Res. **242**(1), 33–62 (2015). https://doi.org/10.1007/s10479-014-1780-6
19. Jin, H., Yang, G., Yu, B., Yoo, C.: TALON: tenant throughput allocation through traffic load-balancing in virtualized software-defined networks. In: ICOIN, pp. 233–238 (2019)
20. Kapoor, R., Porter, G., Tewari, M., Voelker, G.M., Vahdat, A.: Chronos: predictable low latency for data center applications. In: SoCC 2012 (2012)

21. Kasture, H., Sanchez, D.: TailBench: a benchmark suite and evaluation methodology for latency-critical applications. In: IISWC, pp. 1–10 (2016)
22. Dhinesh, B.L., Krishna, P.V.: Honey bee behavior inspired load balancing of tasks in cloud computing environments. Appl. Soft Comput. **13**(5), 2292–2303 (2013)
23. Lo, D., Cheng, L., Govindaraju, R., Ranganathan, P., Kozyrakis, C.: Heracles: improving resource efficiency at scale. In: ISCA 2015, pp. 450–462 (2015)
24. Mekala, M.S., Viswanathan, P.: Energy-efficient virtual machine selection based on resource ranking and utilization factor approach in cloud computing for IoT. Comput. Electr. Eng. **73**, 227–244 (2019)
25. Mrad, M., Gharbi, A., Haouari, M., Kharbeche, M.: An optimization-based heuristic for the machine reassignment problem. Ann. Oper. Res. **242**(1), 115–132 (2015). https://doi.org/10.1007/s10479-015-2002-6
26. Nashaat, H., Ashry, N., Rizk, R.: Smart elastic scheduling algorithm for virtual machine migration in cloud computing. J. Supercomput. **75**(7), 3842–3865 (2019). https://doi.org/10.1007/s11227-019-02748-2
27. Nguyen, K.T.: Introduction to cache allocation technology in the Intel® Xeon® processor E5 v4 Family (2016). https://software.intel.com/content/www/us/en/develop/articles/introduction-to-cache-allocation-technology.html
28. Nishtala, R., Petrucci, V., Carpenter, P., Själander, M.: Twig: multi-agent task management for colocated latency-critical cloud services. In: HPCA-26, pp. 167–179 (2020)
29. Mahitha, O., Suma, V.: Deadlock avoidance through efficient load balancing to control disaster in cloud environment. In: ICCCNT, pp. 1–6 (2013)
30. Park, J., Park, S., Baek, W.: CoPart: coordinated partitioning of last-level cache and memory bandwidth for fairness-aware workload consolidation on commodity servers. In: EuroSys 2019, pp. 1–16 (2019)
31. Park, J., Park, S., Han, M., Hyun, J., Baek, W.: HyPart: a hybrid technique for practical memory bandwidth partitioning on commodity servers. In: PACT 2018, pp. 1–14 (2018)
32. Patel, T., Tiwari, D.: CLITE: efficient and QoS-aware co-location of multiple latency-critical jobs for warehouse scale computers. In: HPCA-26, pp. 193–206 (2020)
33. roadef.org: ROADEF/EURO challenge 2012: machine reassignment (2012). http://www.roadef.org/challenge/2012/en/
34. Sabar, N.R., Song, A., Zhang, M.: A variable local search based memetic algorithm for the load balancing problem in cloud computing. In: Squillero, G., Burelli, P. (eds.) EvoApplications 2016. LNCS, vol. 9597, pp. 267–282. Springer, Cham (2016). https://doi.org/10.1007/978-3-319-31204-0_18
35. Samal, P., Mishra, P.: Analysis of variants in round robin algorithms for load balancing in cloud computing. IJCSIT **4**(3), 416–419 (2013)
36. Tantawi, A.N., Towsley, D.: Optimal static load balancing in distributed computer systems. J. ACM **32**(2), 445–465 (1985)
37. Tian, W., Zhao, Y., Zhong, Y., Xu, M., Jing, C.: A dynamic and integrated load-balancing scheduling algorithm for cloud datacenters. In: CCIS, pp. 311–315 (2011)
38. Wang, X., Chen, S., Setter, J., Martínez, J.F.: SWAP: effective fine-grain management of shared last-level caches with minimum hardware support. In: HPCA-23, pp. 121–132 (2017)
39. Xiang, Y., Wang, X., Huang, Z., Wang, Z., Luo, Y., et al.: DCAPS: dynamic cache allocation with partial sharing. In: EuroSys 2018, pp. 1–15 (2018)
40. Zhu, H., Erez, M.: Dirigent: enforcing QoS for latency-critical tasks on shared multicore systems. In: ASPLOS 2016, pp. 33–47 (2016)

Computation Offloading and Resource Management for Energy and Cost Trade-Offs with Deep Reinforcement Learning in Mobile Edge Computing

Ruichao Mo[1], Xiaolong Xu[1,2](✉), Xuyun Zhang[3], Lianyong Qi[4], and Qi Liu[1,2]

[1] School of Computer and Software, Nanjing University of Information Science and Technology, Nanjing 210044, China
xlxu@ieee.org, qi.liu@nuist.edu.cn
[2] Engineering Research Center of Digital Forensics, Ministry of Education, Nanjing University of Information Science and Technology, Nanjing, China
[3] Department of Computing, Macquarie University, Sydney, NSW 2109, Australia
xuyun.zhang@mq.edu.au
[4] School of Information Science and Engineering, Qufu Normal University, Rizhao 276826, China

Abstract. Mobile edge computing, as a formidable paradigm, sinks the computing and communication resources from the centralized cloud to the edge of networks near to users, which meets the growing demands of mobile applications. However, owing to the mobility of mobile devices and the stochastic edge environment, it is difficult to obtain the prior knowledge of the remaining computing, communication resources and the queuing status of mobile devices and edge servers, how to achieve effective computation offloading and resource management to achieve the trade-offs between completion delay and energy consumption without knowing the prior knowledge of the dynamic edge environment is still facing a great challenge. For addressing this challenge, a computation offloading and resource management method, named PCORA, is proposed for the dynamic mobile edge computing environment. Technically, considering the time-varying characteristics of the network and the dynamic resource requests, the dynamic computation offloading and resource management problem is constructed as a Markov decision process (MDP). Then, the proximal policy optimization (PPO) is employed to obtain the optimal computation offloading and resource management strategy to optimize the completion delay and energy consumption. Finally, comprehensive experimental results are analyzed to illustrate the effectiveness of PCORA.

Keywords: Mobile edge computing · Computation offloading · Resource management · PPO

H. Hacid et al. (Eds.): ICSOC 2021, LNCS 13121, pp. 563–577, 2021.
https://doi.org/10.1007/978-3-030-91431-8_35

1   Introduction

With the rapid development of 5G, the ubiquitous mobile devices like smart phones, tablets, and wearable devices are driving the advancements of the Internet of Things (IoT) [1]. Meanwhile, the emergence of various mobile applications is also advancing the employment of the IoT in real life. As the complexity of mobile applications continues to increase, in particular, computing-intensive applications such as virtual reality (VR), augmented reality (AR) and speech recognition, the local computing demand for mobile devices is increasing rapidly [2]. However, the computing resources possessed by the mobile device cannot meet the demand of the computing-intensive application. Moreover, the execution of the application locally will bring huge energy consumption. Therefore, the implementation of computation-intensive applications on mobile devices with limited computing resources and limited battery life faces great challenges [3].

Currently, mobile edge computing is a split-new computing paradigm that brings computing resources from remote cloud data centers to the edge of networks [4]. The computing tasks of the computation-intensive applications are offloaded to edge servers, which ensures ultra-low completion delay of computation tasks, and provides high quality and reliable services for the mobile users. The offloading of computing tasks to the edge servers significantly supplements the computing resources of the mobile devices and reduces the energy consumption of mobile devices, but there are still some problems that need to be addressed during the computation offloading and resource management under a dynamic edge environment for the mobile devices [5]. On one hand, as the computing demands of the mobile devices increase sharply, unreasonable computing offloading and resource management strategies will cause the queuing delay of computing tasks to be extended without limit, which in turn leads to performance degradation [6]. On the other hand, the information of the edge environment (e.g., the number of mobile devices, the queuing status of local or edge servers, etc.) is constantly changing, mobile devices need to continuously realize computation offloading and resource management decisions based on changing edge environment, which is inefficient and highly complex. Therefore, how to implement computation offloading and resource management to realize the trade-off between completion delay and energy consumption without knowing the prior knowledge of the edge environment is still facing great challenges.

Reinforcement Learning (RL), as an important branch of artificial intelligence, is a method of learning how to get the maximum reward through the continuous trial and error of the agent in the interaction with the environment, which can solve complex optimization problems [7]. Moreover, with the rapid development of RL, the combination of RL and deep neural network (DNN) gives rise to deep reinforcement learning (DRL) [8]. The emergence of DRL allows high-dimensional state space and action space of the environment to be represented, which improves the performance of RL to solve complex optimization problems [9]. By utilizing DRL, the agent obtains computing offloading and resource management decisions by observing the state of the current mobile edge computing environment, thereby ensuring the quality of service (QoS) for users.

However, how to achieve effective computation offloading and resource management when the queuing status of mobile devices and edge servers is unknown, thus ensuring the trade-off between the completion delay and the energy consumption is a huge challenge [10].

To address this challenge, a proximal policy optimization (PPO)-based computation offloading and resource management method (PCORA) that considers the queuing delay under the dynamic edge network is discussed in this paper. Specifically, the key contributions of this paper are listed as the following:

- The dynamic computation offloading and resource management problem considering the queuing delay of the task is established as a Markov decision process (MDP).
- The Proximal Policy Optimization (PPO) [11] is leveraged to realize dynamic computation offloading and resource management without knowing the prior knowledge of the edge environment, which in turn realizes the joint optimization of average queuing delay, average completion delay, and average energy consumption.
- Comprehensive simulation experiments are implemented to evaluate PCORA. A large number of numerical results are analyzed to illustrate the performance of PCORA.

The rest of this paper is structured as follows. Initially, the related work is discussed in Sect. 2. Subsequently, the system model and problem formulation are described in Sect. 3. Then, the design of PCORA is described in Section. Furthermore, experimental evaluation is described in Sect. 5. Eventually, conclusion and future work of this paper are drawn in Sect. 6.

2   Related Work

Nowadays, with the rapid growth of the number of the mobile devices, the demand for computing resources at the edge is raising [12]. Mobile edge computing has emerged as a computing paradigm to achieve efficient execution of end-user computing demands [13]. However, how to implement edge systems for efficient computing offloading and resource management for end-users is facing great challenges.

In [14], Chen et al. established computation offloading as an optimization problem to reduce costs while meeting performance requirements with a stochastic optimization-based algorithm. Chen et al. [15] studied the task offloading problem of edge computing based on software-defined network (SDN) to minimize delay and save the battery life of user devices.

However, the environment of the edge system is constantly changing, it is difficult to obtain accurate network environment information such as communication and computing resources. Therefore, the optimization algorithms discussed above may not be effective in actual mobile edge computing environments.

To cope with the challenges of computation offloading caused by the different states of the edge servers, Huang et al. [16] proposed a DRL-based method to solve the problem of joint task offloading and resource allocation for each user, realizing optimizing energy consumption and delay. Tong *et al.* [17] considered the mobility of mobile users and proposed an adaptive computation offloading algorithm, optimizing the average delay and energy consumption. Dai *et al.* [18] leveraged DRL to implement computation offloading that takes into account wireless channel status, and computing resources, thereby minimizing the energy consumption.

In the above research, DRL is leveraged to implement the computation offloading and resource allocation under dynamic edge networks, but these studies lacked analysis of queuing delays for tasks performed locally or on the edge. Furthermore, the completion delay of the tasks and energy consumption as important indicators also need to be considered jointly. Therefore, a dynamic computation offloading and resource management algorithm based on PPO is proposed in this paper.

3   System Model and Problem Formulation

3.1   System Overview

We consider a wireless network with D mobile devices and N edge servers, represented by $\mathcal{D} = \{1, 2, ...d, ..., D\}$ and $\mathcal{N} = \{1, 2, ...n, ..., N\}$, repectively. In time slot $t \in \mathcal{T}$, mobile device d generates M tasks to be executed, denoted by $\mathcal{M}_d = \{1, 2, ..., m, ..., M\}$. Meanwhile, a binary computation offloading is considered, that is, the task can only be performed locally or on the edge server. Furthermore, assuming that the edge server has a better computing performance than the mobile devices so that the tasks that can not be satisfied locally will be offloaded to the edge for effectively processing.

As illustrated in Fig. 1, the computing task generated by d within t will make the offloading decisions. The mobile device will make the offloading decisions for the tasks generated in t. Let an indicator variable $x_{d,n}^m(t) \in \{0, n\}$ represent the offloading strategy of the task m, $x_{d,n}^m(t) = 0$ represents the tasks generated by d will be performed locally. Otherwise, $x_{d,n}^m(t) = n$ represents that the task generated by d will be offloaded to the edge server n for processing. Furthermore, the tasks will be sent to the waiting queue of the local or edge server according to the offloading decisions, and the tasks will be executed in a First-In, First-Out (FIFO) order.

3.2   Communication Model

Assuming that the computation offloading among the mobile devices and edge servers is realized through the wireless network. Therefore, the data transmission rate is interfered by the transmission power, the interference, and the bandwidth of the communication channel. Meanwhile, we considered the mutual interference

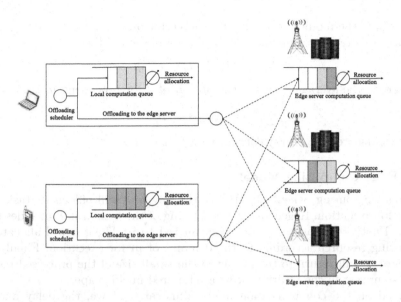

Fig. 1. An illustration of computation offloading and resource management in mobile edge computing.

caused by other devices during the transmission. Therefore, the data transmission rate between d and n is measured by

$$R_{d,n}(t) = w_{d,n}(t) \cdot \log_2(1 + \frac{P_{d,n} \cdot G_{d,n}}{I_{d,n}}), \tag{1}$$

where $w_{d,n}(t)$ is the bandwidth between d and n. Besides, $P_{d,n}$ represents the transmission power. $G_{d,n}$ denotes the wireless channel gain, $I_{d,n}$ represents the average interference power.

3.3 Local Computing Model

In the time slot $t \in \mathcal{T}$, if $x_{d,n}^m(t) = 0$, the task $m \in \mathcal{M}_d(t)$ will be put in the computation queue at the local device d. When the computation queue at the local device is empty, the queueing delay of the task m is 0. Otherwise, let $WL_d(t)$ denote the total computation workload queued on the mobile device d within t. Therefore, the queuing delay of m is measured by

$$Q_{d,m}^{queue}(t) = \frac{WL_d(t)}{f_d^l(t)}, \tag{2}$$

where $f_d^l(t)$ represents the computing capacity within t.

Meanwhile, the execution delay of m is measured by

$$P_{d,m}^{exe}(t) = \frac{C_m}{f_d^l(t)}, \tag{3}$$

where C_m is the required computing resource for m.

Furthermore, the completion delay of m is measured by

$$TL(t) = Q_{d,m}^{queue}(t) + P_{d,m}^{exe}(t). \tag{4}$$

Besides, the average energy consumption of d for processing m is measured by

$$EL(t) = \varphi_d \cdot C_m \cdot f_d^l(t)^2, \tag{5}$$

where φ_d denotes the energy consumption factor of d.

3.4 Edge Computing Model

For edge computing, when $x_{d,n}^m(t) = n$, the device d will offload its task m to $n \in \mathcal{N}$ for execution. In general, the processing of the task m in n includes three stages. Firstly, the task m will be transmitted to n. Then, n will allocate the computing resource according to the demand of m for execution. Finally, the results of m will return to the n, due to the small size of the processed results, the system cost in the return process are ignored in this paper.

Based on the communication model illustrated above, the delay and the energy consumption for offloading m is measured, respectively, by

$$T_{n,m}^{trans}(t) = C_m \cdot R_{d,n}(t)^{-1}, \tag{6}$$

and

$$E_{n,m}^{trans}(t) = P_{d,n} \cdot T_{n,m}^{trans}(t). \tag{7}$$

Furthermore, we consider the scenario that the task will be sent to the computation queue on the edge server waiting to be executing. Same to the local device, when the computation queue on n is empty, the queuing delay of m will be 0. Otherwise, the queuing delay of m on n is calculated by

$$Q_{n,m}^{queue}(t) = \frac{WE_n(t)}{f_n^e(t)}, \tag{8}$$

where $WE_n(t)$ denotes the total computation workload of the computation queue on n. Besides, $f_n^e(t)$ represents CPU computing capability which n allocates to m.

The average execution delay of m and average energy consumption of n are calculated, respectively, by

$$P_{n,m}^{exe}(t) = \frac{C_m}{f_n^e(t)}, \tag{9}$$

and

$$E_{n,m}^{exe}(t) = \beta_n \cdot C_m \cdot f_n^e(t)^2. \tag{10}$$

where β_n denotes the energy consumption factor of n within t.

Then, we calculate the completion delay of m and energy consumption of n, respectively, by

$$TS(t) = Q_{n,m}^{queue}(t) + P_{n,m}^{exe}(t), \tag{11}$$

and

$$ES(t) = E_{n,m}^{trans}(t) + E_{n,m}^{exe}(t). \tag{12}$$

3.5   Problem Formulation

In the time slot t, the N mobile devices in the edge system generate tasks that need to be executed, it can either offload them to the edge server or perform them locally. Thus, for any task of the N devices, the average completion delay is calculated by

$$ACT(t) = \frac{1}{D} \cdot \frac{1}{M} \cdot \left\{ \sum_{d \in \mathcal{D}} \sum_{m \in \mathcal{M}_d(t)} \left(1 - \left\lceil \frac{x_{d,n}^m(t)}{N} \right\rceil \right) \cdot TL(t) + \left\lceil \frac{x_{d,n}^m(t)}{N} \right\rceil \cdot TS(t) \right\}$$

(13)

where $\lceil \bullet \rceil$ is the ceiling function.

Furthermore, the average enerage consumption for any task of the N devices within time slot t is measured by

$$AET(t) = \frac{1}{D} \cdot \frac{1}{M} \cdot \left\{ \sum_{d \in \mathcal{D}} \sum_{m \in \mathcal{M}_d(t)} \left(1 - \left\lceil \frac{x_{d,n}^m(t)}{N} \right\rceil \right) \cdot EL(t) + \left\lceil \frac{x_{d,n}^m(t)}{N} \right\rceil \cdot ES(t) \right\}.$$

(14)

The objective of the dynamic computation offloading and resource management problem is to optimize the average completion delay and average energy consumption within t, which is erected as the following optimization problem:

$$\min ACT(t), \ AET(t). \tag{15}$$

$$s.t. \ 0 \leq f_d^l(t) \leq F_d^l, \ \forall d \in \mathcal{D}, \tag{16a}$$

$$0 \leq f_n^e(t) \leq F_n^e, \ \forall n \in \mathcal{N}, \tag{16b}$$

$$0 \leq w_{d,n}(t) \leq W_n, \ \forall d \in \mathcal{D}, \ \forall n \in \mathcal{N}, \tag{16c}$$

$$x_{d,n}^m(t) \in \{0, n\}, \forall m \in \mathcal{M}_d(t). \tag{16d}$$

Constraints (16a) and (16b) indicate that the number of computing resources allocated by d and edge server n within t cannot exceed the total number of computing resources owned by d and n. Moreover, constraint (16c) represents that the communication resource allocated to the d cannot exceed the total communication resources. Constraint (16d) indicates that the offloading strategy of the task m of the device d is either locally or to edge servers n.

4   The Design of PCORA

In this section, a computation offloading and resource management method, named PCORA, is proposed. Specifically, the objective of PCORA is to optimize the average completion delay and average energy consumption.

Generally, considering the time-varying characteristics of task queues in both mobile devices and edge servers, the dynamic computation offloading and resource management problem is constructed as a Markov decision process (MDP). Then, the proximal policy optimization (PPO) is employed to obtain the optimal computation offloading and resource management strategy, thereby optimizing the completion delay and energy consumption. The structure of the PCORA is illustrated in Fig. 2.

4.1   MDP Model

The problem to be solved in this paper is established as a MDP, which is represented as a 3-tuple $< S, A, R >$. S is the state space of the environment, and A represents the action. Besides, the $R(A|S)$ indicates the immediate reward earned by executing A.

State. The state $s(t) \in S$ of the mobile edge computing system environment observed by the mobile device d within t is denoted as

$$s(t) \triangleq < M(t), DQ(t), SQ(t), DC(t), SC(t), SR(t) >, \tag{17}$$

where $M(t) = \{m_1(t), m_2(t), ..., m_D(t)\}$ represents the task set generated by the mobile devices within t. The $DQ(t) = \{dq_1(t), dq_2(t), ..., dq_D(t)\}$ and $SQ(t) = \{sq_1(t), sq_2(t), ..., sq_N(t)\}$ are the queuing status of the mobile devices and edge servers within t, respectively. $DC(t) = \{dc_1(t), dc_2(t), ..., dc_D(t)\}$ and $sc(t) = \{sc_1(t), sc_2(t), ..., sc_N(t)\}$ indicate the remaining computing resources of the mobile devices and edge servers, respectively. Besides, $SR(t) = \{sr_1(t), sr_2(t), ..., sr_N(t) \}$ represents the remaining communication resources of the edge servers within t.

Action. Based on the observations of the system state within t, the agent takes appropriate actions to ensure that the immediate reward is maximized. Generally, mobile devices make computation offloading and resource management decisions by observing the state of the system environment within t, thereby ensuring that the completion delay and energy consumption of tasks are minimized. The action $a(t)$ of the edge system is denoted as

$$a(t) \triangleq < x(t), f^l(t), f^e(t), w(t) >, \tag{18}$$

where $x(t) = \{x_{1,1}^1(t), x_{1,1}^2(t), ..., x_{d,n}^m(t), ..., x_{D,N}^M(t)\}$ represents the offloading decision of the task generated by mobile device within t. $f^l(t) = \{ f_1^l(t), ..., f_d^l(t), ..., f_D^l(t) \}$ and $f^e(t) = \{f_1^e(t), ..., f_n^e(t), ..., f_N^e(t)\}$ represent the computing resource management strategy within t. Besides, $w(t)$ represents the communication resource allcation strategy in the t. When a task is executed locally, the local device will allocate computing resources for the task, instead of allocating computing resources of the edge server and communication resources.

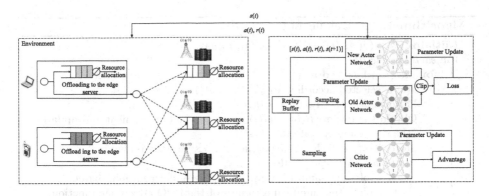

Fig. 2. The structure of the PCORA.

Reward Function. At the beginning of t, d will get an immediate reward $R_t(a(t)|s(t)) \in \mathcal{R}$ after taking action $a(t)$ according to $s(t)$. In this paper, the objective of the problem to be solved is to minimize completion delay and energy consumption. Thus, the immediate reward is denoted as

$$R_t(a(t)|s(t)) = -E\left[ACT(t) + AET(t)\right]. \tag{19}$$

Furthermore, the cumulative reward of $\mathcal{T}$ time slot is measured by

$$\mathcal{R} = \lim_{\mathcal{T} \to \infty} \frac{1}{\mathcal{T}} \sum_{t=1}^{T} \lambda_t R_t(a(t)|s(t)), \tag{20}$$

where $\lambda_t \in [0,1]$ is the discount factor.

4.2 PPO-based Computation Offloading and Resource Management Algorithm

PPO is an upgrade version of the trust region policy optimization (TRPO). The main feature of TRPO is that when the policy parameters are updated in each episode, the policy is optimized in a better direction, to avoid problems such as oscillation when the policy gradient descent and worse performance of the policy. Compared with TRPO, PPO only needs the first-order optimization to maintain the data efficiency and reliability of TRPO, but it can greatly simplify the complexity of implementation. Therefore, PPO is utilized to implement PCORA.

In the training step, the objective function of PPO is denoted as

$$L(\theta) = \tilde{E}(t)(\tilde{A}(t)), \tag{21}$$

where $\tilde{A}(t)$ represents the estimate of the advantage function within t. $\tilde{A}(t)$ is denoted as

$$\tilde{A}(t) = \min(r_t(\theta)\tilde{A}(t), clip(r_t(\theta), 1 - \varepsilon, 1 + \varepsilon)\tilde{A}(t)), \tag{22}$$

Algorithm 1: The training of the PCORA.

Initialize $\pi_\theta^{new}(a(t)|s(t))$, $\pi_\theta^{old}(a(t)|s(t))$, replay buffer;
for *each episode* do
    for *each $t = 1$ to T* do
        $a(t)$ is selected according to $\pi_\theta^{old}(a(t)|s(t))$;
        Perform $a(t)$ based on Eq.(19) ;
        Obtain the reward $R_t(a(t)|s(t))$ given by the environment and update
          the environment state to $s(t+1)$;
        Store $< s(t), a(t), R_t(a(t)|s(t)), s(t+1) >$ into the replay buffer ;
        for *each update episode* do
            K tuples are sampled from the replay buffer as a mini-batch;
            Calculate the empirical estimate of the PPO advantage function
              $\tilde{A}(t)$;
            Calculate the empirical average of the PPO advantage function
              $\tilde{E}(\tilde{A}(t))$;
            Calculate the derivative of L with respect to θ;
            Update actor network parameters through gradient ascent $\theta_{old} = \theta_{new}$;
        end
    end
end

---

where $r_t(\theta)$ represents the probability ratio between the old and new policy.

$$r_t(\theta) = \frac{\pi_\theta^{new}(a(t)|s(t))}{\pi_\theta^{old}(a(t)|s(t))}. \tag{23}$$

In (21), when $\tilde{A}_t > 0$, the larger the advantage function means that the policy is updating in a better direction, and the clip item will cut off this part of the change. Otherwise, when $\tilde{A}_t < 0$, the smaller the advantage function, it is considered that the policy is updated in the worse direction. Meanwhile, the clip function will retain the minimum degradation effect, and will not ignore the degradation of the PPO advantage function due to the reduction of the policy update ratio. Compared with other policy gradient algorithms without the clip, PPO with the clip ensures the stability of the algorithm during policy updates. The pseudocode for training the PCORA is shown in Algorithm 1.

5   Experimental Evaluation

5.1   Parameter Settings

We implement PCORA and analyze its performance in this section. The PCORA is implemented on a server with Intel Core i5-10600K 4.10 GHz, NVIDIA GeForce GTX 3090, 64 GB RAM, and Manjaro 5.9.16-1. Besides, we consider an edge network with $N = 10$ edge servers, $D= \{5, 10, 15, 20, 25, 30\}$ devices.

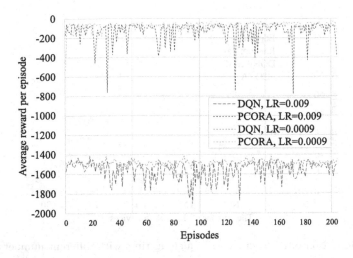

Fig. 3. Comparison of converagence performance with different learning rate.

The computation capabilities of mobile device F_d^l and edge server F_n^e are 1Ghz and 5Ghz, respectively. The bandwidth $w_{d,n}$ is set as [1,4] Gb. In addition, the batchsize is set as 128. The number of training episode is set as 10000, and the capacity of the replay buffer is set as 2000. The discount factor λ_t is set as 0.99, and the ε is set as 0.2 [11].

5.2 Comparison Algorithms

To illustrate the performance of PCORA, four algorithms are selected in this paper for comparison.

- *Local computing* [18]: The computing task will be processed locally, and the local device will randonmly allocate the computing resources for the task.
- *Edge computing*: The computing tasks are randomly offloaded to any edge server for processing. The edge network will randomly allocate communication resources for the task, and the edge server will allocate computing resources for the task in a randomly manner.
- *Random-based* [15]: The computing tasks first randomly generate offloading decisions. When the offloading strategy of the computing task is executed locally, the local device will also allocate computing resources according to the size of the task. Otherwise, the edge will randomly allocate communication resource for the task, and edge server will randomly allocate computing resources.
- *DQN-based* [13]: In the DQN-based algorithm, the DQN agent interacts with the edge environment to produce computation offloading and resource allocation decisions within t. Besides, the rewards obtained after the DQN agent performs the action are utilized to train the agent, which is composed of task completion delay and energy consumption.

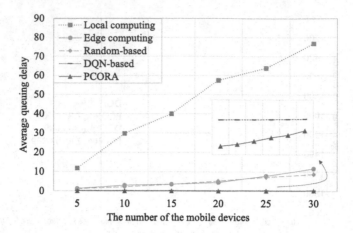

Fig. 4. Comparison of the average task queuing time with different number of mobile devices.

5.3 Performance Evaluation

Coveragence Analysis. Figure 3 shows the convergence performance of PCORA and DQN with different learning rates. When the learning rate is set to 0.009 and 0.0009 respectively, the reward value of POCRA and DQN gradually begins to converge after training. As shown in the figure, the performance of DQN and PCORA is better than that of 0.009 when the learning rate is 0.0009. In addition, although PCORA has a large oscillation in the training process, the reward obtained by PCORA for implementing computation offloading and resource management is better than that of *DQN-based* on the whole.

Comparison of Average Queuing Delay. To implement the dynamic analysis of the network environment of the edge, the queuing delay of the tasks on the local device or the edge device after offloading is evaluated. Figure 4 illustrates the performance of average queuing delay with the different number of mobile devices. It can be seen from the experimental results that as the number of mobile devices increases, the average queuing delay of tasks gradually increases. Compared with the other algorithms, the strategy found by PCORA makes the tasks queuing delay of the task generated by the mobile device significantly shorter than other methods in the case of mobile devices of different scales.

Comparison of Average Completion Delay. Furthermore, the average completion delay is calculated by averaging the completion delay of all computing tasks in an episode. Figure 5 illustrates the results of the average completion delay of PCORA and four comparison algorithms with different amount of mobile devices, the average completion delay raises as the amount of mobile devices increases. Moreover, the PCORA achieves the shortest average completion delay

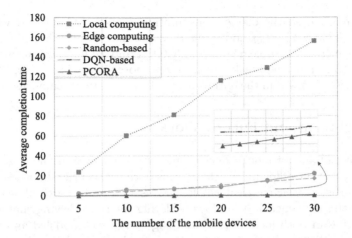

Fig. 5. Comparison of the average completion delay with different number of mobile devices.

compared to the comparison algorithms. PCORA performs better performance on average completion delay because PCORA guarantees the shortest queuing delay of tasks, and PCORA performs reasonable computing and communication resource management for the tasks, thereby ensuring the shortest average completion delay.

Comparison of Average Energy Consumption. Finally, the average energy consumption for processing the tasks is evaluated. In Fig. 6, with the increase in the number of mobile devices, the number of resources allocated to the devices

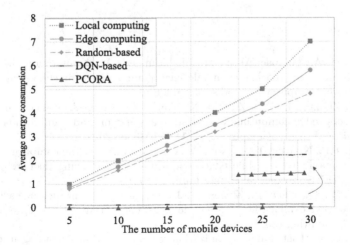

Fig. 6. Comparison of the average energy consumption with different number of mobile devices.

is also increasing, so the energy consumption is rising. Compared with *Local computing*, *Edge computing*, and *Random-based*, the computation offloading and resource management implemented by PCORA and *DQN-based* make the average energy consumption of task execution rise more slowly. Moreover, PCORA is better than *DQN-based* in the optimization of the energy consumption indicator.

6   Conclusion and Future Work

Due to the mobility of mobile devices and the stochastic of the edge environment, computation offloading without considering the prior knowledge of the edge system is still facing great challenges, as well as resource allocation. For addressing this challenge, a scenario considering the time-varying characteristics of task queues in both local devices and edge servers is modeled and the computation offloading problem is constructed as a MDP. Furthermore, we propose the PCORA which is based on PPO to obtain optimal offloading and resource allocation decision to optimize the cost. Fianlly, comprehensive experiments are implemented to illustrate the performance of PCORA.

Regarding future work, we will further optimize PCORA so that it can be deployed in scenarios with a large number of mobile devices. Moreover, we will also consider using historical data for queueing delay prediction to further optimize the decision performance of computation offloading.

Acknowledgment. This research is supported by the Natural Science Foundation of Jiangsu Province of China under grant No.BK20211284, the Financial and Science Technology Plan Project of Xinjiang Production and Construction Corps under grant No.2020DB005. Besides, this reserach is supported by the National Natural Science Foundation of China under grant No.61872219. Dr. Xuyn Zhang is the recipient of an ARC DECRA (project No.DE210101458) funded by the Australian Government.

References

1. Shakarami, A., Ghobaei-Arani, M., Shahidinejad, A.: A survey on the computation offloading approaches in mobile edge computing: a machine learning-based perspective. Computer Networks, p. 107496 (2020)
2. Rui, L., Zhang, M., Gao, Z., Qiu, X., Wang, Z., Xiong, A.: Service migration in multi-access edge computing: a joint state adaptation and reinforcement learning mechanism. J. Netw. Comput. Appl. **183**, 103058 (2021)
3. Truong, T.P., Nguyen, T.-V., Noh, W., Cho, S., et al.: Partial computation offloading in noma-assisted mobile edge computing systems using deep reinforcement learning. IEEE Internet of Things Journal (2021)
4. Cui, G., He, Q., Chen, F., Zhang, Y., Jin, H., Yang, Y.: Interference-aware game-theoretic device allocation for mobile edge computing. IEEE Transactions on Mobile Computing (2021)
5. Lin, R., et al.: Distributed optimization for computation offloading in edge computing. IEEE Trans. Wireless Commun. **19**(12), 8179–8194 (2020)

6. Yang, B., Cao, X., Bassey, J., Li, X., Qian, L.: Computation offloading in multi-access edge computing: a multi-task learning approach. IEEE Transactions on Mobile Computing (2020)
7. Mnih, V., et al.: Human-level control through deep reinforcement learning. Nature **518**(7540), 529–533 (2015)
8. Shakarami, A., Shahidinejad, A., Ghobaei-Arani, M.: An autonomous computation offloading strategy in mobile edge computing: a deep learning-based hybrid approach. J. Netw. Comput. Appl. **178**, 102974 (2021)
9. Li, Y.: Deep reinforcement learning: An overview. arXiv preprint arXiv:1701.07274 (2017)
10. Li, C., et al.: Dynamic offloading for multiuser muti-cap mec networks: a deep reinforcement learning approach. IEEE Trans. Veh. Technol. **70**(3), 2922–2927 (2021)
11. Schulman, J., Wolski, F., Dhariwal, P., Radford, A., Klimov, O.: Proximal policy optimization algorithms. arXiv preprint arXiv:1707.06347 (2017)
12. Hou, X., et al.: Reliable computation offloading for edge-computing-enabled software-defined iov. IEEE Internet Things J. **7**(8), 7097–7111 (2020)
13. Chen, Z., Wang, X.: Decentralized computation offloading for multi-user mobile edge computing: a deep reinforcement learning approach. EURASIP J. Wireless Commun. Network. **2020**(1), 1–21 (2020)
14. Chen, Y., Zhang, N., Zhang, Y., Chen, X.: Dynamic computation offloading in edge computing for internet of things. IEEE Internet Things J. **6**(3), 4242–4251 (2018)
15. Chen, M., Hao, Y.: Task offloading for mobile edge computing in software defined ultra-dense network. IEEE J. Selected Areas Commun. **36**(3), 587–597 (2018)
16. Huang, L., Feng, X., Qian, L., Wu, Y.: Deep reinforcement learning-based task offloading and resource allocation for mobile edge computing. In: Meng, L., Zhang, Y. (eds.) MLICOM 2018. LNICST, vol. 251, pp. 33–42. Springer, Cham (2018). https://doi.org/10.1007/978-3-030-00557-3_4
17. Tong, Z., Deng, X., Ye, F., Basodi, S., Xiao, X., Pan, Y.: Adaptive computation offloading and resource allocation strategy in a mobile edge computing environment. Inform. Sci. **537**, 116–131 (2020)
18. Dai, Y., Zhang, K., Maharjan, S., Zhang, Y.: Edge intelligence for energy-efficient computation offloading and resource allocation in 5g beyond. IEEE Trans. Veh. Technol. **69**(10), 12175–12186 (2020)

Deep Reinforcement Learning Based Task Offloading Strategy Under Dynamic Pricing in Edge Computing

Bing Shi[1,2(✉)], Feiyang Chen[1], and Xing Tang[1]

[1] School of Computer Science and Artificial Intelligence, Wuhan University of Technology, Wuhan 430000, China
bingshi@whut.edu.cn

[2] Shenzhen Research Institute of Wuhan University of Technology, Shenzhen 518000, China

Abstract. Mobile edge computing has become a new paradigm for efficient computing, which allows users to offload computing tasks to edge servers to accomplish the tasks. However, in the real world, users usually keep moving, and the edge servers may dynamically change the offered service prices in order to maximize their own profits. At this moment, we need a highly efficient task offloading strategy for users. In this paper, we design a task offloading strategy when users are on the movement and edge servers dynamically change the service prices based on the deep reinforcement learning algorithm, which is named as DUTO. Furthermore, we run extensive experiments to evaluate our offloading strategy against four benchmark offloading strategies. The experimental results show that DUTO task offloading strategy can effectively improve the long-term profits of users in the dynamic environment with different experimental settings.

Keywords: Mobile edge computing · Dynamic pricing · Task offloading · Deep reinforcement learning

1 Introduction

According to the Cisco report [1], mobile devices (such as smart phones, mobile sensors) are becoming increasingly popular in current life. However, the limited computing power, storage resource and battery capacity of mobile devices cannot meet the low latency and high computing intensity requirements of mobile applications. At this moment, mobile edge computing [2], as a new and efficient computing paradigm, is proposed to solve these problems.

In the mobile edge computing, how users with mobile devices offloading computing tasks is one of the key issues. Specifically, edge servers are usually run by self-interested enterprises, and they may provide paid services to users to make profits. At this moment, they may dynamically change the prices according to the computing environment to make more profits (e.g., when there exist sufficient computing resource, the edge server may decrease the price to encourage more users to perform the task offloading to increase the profit). The dynamic pricing may affect users' task offloading decisions. For example,

© Springer Nature Switzerland AG 2021
H. Hacid et al. (Eds.): ICSOC 2021, LNCS 13121, pp. 578–594, 2021.
https://doi.org/10.1007/978-3-030-91431-8_36

when the price of the edge server is low, users will offload as many tasks as possible to the edge server, which causes server resources to be consumed quickly. In contrast, when the price of the edge server is high, users may give up offloading tasks. Furthermore, users may keep moving, and therefore they may be covered by different edge servers during their movements, which will affect their offloading decisions. In this paper, we will analyze how users offload tasks to edge servers when they are on the movement and the service prices are dynamically changed. To the best of our knowledge, we are the first to consider dynamic pricing of edge server in the user's task offloading strategy.

Specifically, we consider the scenario where users are on the movement and edge servers dynamically change the prices, and propose an efficient task offloading strategy to maximize the long-term profits of users[1]. Users' offloading decisions at the current time are affected by the decisions at the last time, and edge servers' prices and users' task offloading decisions are affected by each other. Therefore, this is a sequential decision problem. We model the task offloading problem as a Markov decision process and use reinforcement learning to address it. Since edge servers' prices at the current time are affected by users' offloading decisions at the last time, we assume that edge servers will also adopt reinforcement learning to determine the prices to maximize their own profits. Furthermore, we run extensive experiments to evaluate our task offloading strategy against four typical strategies. In the experiment, we show how the dynamic pricing can affect users' task offloading decisions. Furthermore, the experimental results show that in the environment with dynamic pricing and moving users, our task offloading strategy can outperform four benchmarks strategies.

The structure of this paper is as follows. In Sect. 2, we discuss the related work. In Sect. 3, we introduce the basic settings. In Sect. 4, we describe how to use a deep reinforcement learning algorithm to design the task offloading strategy. We evaluate the task offloading strategy in Sect. 5. Finally, we conclude in Sect. 6.

2 Related Work

In recent years, edge computing has been widely studied, such as the research about the security of edge computing [3], edge server collaboration [4], data integrity on edge computing [5] and so on. How users offloading tasks is one of the most important issues among them [6]. There exist plenty of works analyzing the task offloading problem in the edge computing. Some works focus on minimizing the time delay in offloading tasks. For example, Peng *et al.* [7] model the task offloading problem as an online multidimensional integer linear programming problem, and propose a decentralized reactive approach to solve it. Zhao *et al.* [8] propose a cross-edge computation offloading framework for partitionable applications based on Lyapunov optimization. Cao *et al.* [9] propose a multi-agent deep reinforcement learning scheme for edge servers to cooperate with each other. Du *et al.* [10] propose an online algorithm based on Lyapunov optimization to solve the task offloading problem.

There also exist some works focusing on minimizing the energy consumption during the task offloading. Shen *et al.* [11] propose a dynamic task offloading approach in the

---

[1] In the task offloading, the profit of user is defined as the difference between the cost of local execution and the cost of offloading to edge server for execution, i.e. the saved cost.

edge computing based on the reinforcement learning algorithm. Chen *et al.* [12] use centralized and distributed greedy scheduling algorithms to minimize energy consumption. Fang *et al.* [13] propose a joint optimization method for task offloading and content caching based on traffic flow prediction.

Some works focus on maximizing the profits of edge servers or minimize the costs of users during the task offloading. Li *et al.* [14] propose an optimization framework based on reinforcement learning to minimize the total costs of all users. Zhang *et al.* [15] define the process of vehicle computing offloading as a Stackelberg game and propose a distributed algorithm to solve it. Du *et al.* [16] model computational task offloading as a random optimization problem with multiple optimization goals, and propose an online joint task offloading and resource allocation algorithm. Xia *et al.* [17] model the edge data caching problem as a constrained optimization problem, and use Lyapunov optimization to minimize the system costs.

However, these works usually assume that users with mobile devices are stationary [11, 19, 20]. In the real world, users may change their positions over time, which make users are covered by different edge servers. Furthermore, these works usually consider that edge servers adopt static service prices and ignore the fact that edge servers may change their prices to maximize the profits. In this paper, we will consider these factors when designing the task offloading strategy.

3   Basic Settings

In this section, we describe the basic settings, which include the task offloading process for users, profits and costs of users and edge servers. The notations used in this paper are shown in Table 1.

Table 1. Notations

Notation	Description
N	The number of edge servers
M	The number of users
T	The number of time periods
L_n	The position of edge server n
Rad	The service coverage radius of edge server
F	The task processing capacity of edge server
p_n^t	The resource price of edge server n at time period t
l_m^t	The position of user m at time period t
OT_m^t	Computing tasks of user m at time period t

(continued)

Table 1. (*continued*)

Notation	Description
$o_{m,n}^t$	The task offloading decision of user m at time period t, which chooses whether to offload to server n
$\tau o_{m,n}^t$	The total time required for OT_m^t to be offloaded to server n for processing
$uo_{m,n}^t$	The profit of user m when OT_m^t is offloaded to server n
cl_m^t	The cost of user m when OT_m^t is executed locally
$co_{m,n}^t$	The cost of user m when OT_m^t is offloaded to server n for processing
$us_{m,n}^t$	The profit of server n when OT_m^t is offloaded to server n for processing
$cs_{m,n}^t$	The cost of server n when OT_m^t is offloaded to server n for processing

3.1 Task Offloading Process

In the edge computing environment, edge servers will first set prices for resources. If the user accepts the price and makes a payment, the task will be offloaded to an edge server. Otherwise, the user will not offload the task but execute the task locally.

In this process, we assume that the user is on the movement. At this moment, the user may be covered by different edge servers, and the option for offloading is changing. As shown in Fig. 1(a), at time period t, user 2 is covered by edge servers 1 and 2. At this time, the user can choose to offload the computing task to server 1, 2 or execute it locally. At time period $t + 1$, as shown in Fig. 1(b), user 2 is only within the service range of server 2. At this time, the user can only choose to offload the take to service 2 or execute it locally.

Furthermore, edge servers may dynamically change the resource prices in order to maximize their own profits. This means that even if the user is covered by the same edge servers, user may change its offloading decision because of the changed resource price. For example, in Fig. 1(a), user 3 can offload the task to server 2 where the resource price is set to $1. In Fig. 1(b), user 3 may choose to offload the task to server 3, where the price is set to $0.8.

Note that in the task offloading process, the user's offloading decision will affect remaining resource capacity of edge server, which will affect the server's resource price at the next time period. At the same time, the server's resource price will affect the user's task offloading decision. Therefore, the server's dynamic pricing strategy and the user's offloading strategy will be affected by each other.

In this process, we assume that there are N edge servers and M users. Two-dimensional Euclidean Coordinates are used to represent the positions of the edge servers, where the position of edge server n is denoted as $L_n = (X_n, Y_n)$. The service coverage radius of edge server is denoted as Rad. The task processing capacity of edge server is denoted as F. The set of edge servers is defined as $E = \{e_1, \cdots, e_N\}$ where $e_n = (L_n, Rad, F)$.

At the same time, considering that the user is moving, we divide the entire time into several time periods, $1, 2, \cdots, T$. The set of users is defined as $U = \{u_1, \cdots, u_M\}$. Then

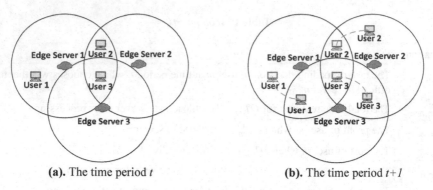

(a). The time period t　　　　　　　**(b).** The time period $t+1$

Fig. 1. Users' movement over time

the moving trajectory of the user m can be expressed as $l_m^t = (x_m^t, y_m^t)$, where (x_m^t, y_m^t) is the position of user m at time period t. Therefore, we can calculate the distance between the user and edge server as $dis_{m,n}^t = \sqrt{(X_n - x_m^t)^2 + (Y_n - y_m^t)^2}$. For the computing task of user m at time period t, we define it as a two-tuple: $OT_m^t = (d_m^t, f_m^t)$, where d_m^t is the size of data to be transferred when OT_m^t is offloaded to edge server, f_m^t is the computing resources required to complete OT_m^t, such as the number of CPU cycles required. We use $o_{m,n}^t \in \{0, 1\}$ to represent the offloading decision of user m at time period t. If $o_{m,n}^t = 1$, it means that user m chooses to offload OT_m^t to edge server n. If $o_{m,n}^t = 0$, it means that user m executes OT_m^t locally.

3.2　Task Offloading Settings

For computing task, users can choose local execution or offload tasks to edge servers. In the local execution, we assume that all mobile devices have same task processing capability ϕ, which is quantified by CPU frequency. At the same time, we set P_d as the data transmission power of mobile device.

At time period t, the energy required to execute OT_m^t locally is:

$$el_m^t = P_l \cdot \frac{f_m^t}{\phi} \tag{1}$$

In general, the power consumption of CPU can be modeled as a super-linear function of its own frequency [23], which is: $P_l = \kappa_u(\phi)^\zeta$, where κ_u and ζ are model parameters according to the chip structure of mobile device CPU.

At time period t, when computing task is offloaded to edge server, the channel power gain between edge server n and user m can be modeled as $h_{m,n}^t = h_0/(dis_{m,n}^t)^2$, where h_0 is the received power when reference distance d_0 is 1 m [22]. Therefore, we can calculate the transmission rate when user m transmits the data of OT_m^t to edge server n, which is $v_{m,n}^t(t) = B\log_2(1 + P_d \cdot h_{m,n}^t/\sigma^2)$, where B is the bandwidth of transmission channel between mobile device and edge server, σ^2 is the noise power between the mobile device and edge server [9, 23]. Therefore, the wireless transmission energy consumed when

OT_m^t is offloaded to edge server n is:

$$eo_{m,n}^t = P_d \cdot \frac{d_m^t}{v_{m,n}^t} \tag{2}$$

When edge server processes computing tasks, it consumes a certain amount of energy. We set the power consumption of edge server as: $P_s = \kappa_s(F)^{\zeta'}$, where κ_s and ζ' are model parameters according to the chip structure of edge server CPU. Therefore, when OT_m^t is offloaded to edge server n, the energy consumption of edge server n is:

$$es_{m,n}^t = P_s \cdot \frac{f_m^t}{F} \tag{3}$$

Finally, the total time it takes for OT_m^t to be offloaded to edge server n is:

$$\tau o_{m,n}^t = \frac{d_m^t}{v_{m,n}^t} + \frac{f_m^t}{F} \tag{4}$$

3.3 User's Profit

We set the unit energy consumption cost of mobile device as c_u. At time period t, the resource price of edge server n is denoted as p_n^t. If OT_m^t is executed locally, the cost of user m is $cl_m^t = c_u \cdot el_m^t$. When OT_m^t is offloaded to edge server for processing, the cost of user m is:

$$co_{m,n}^t = c_u \cdot eo_{m,n}^t + p_n^t \cdot \tau o_{m,n}^t \tag{5}$$

where $c_u \cdot eo_{m,n}^t$ is cost of energy, $p_n^t \cdot \tau o_{m,n}^t$ is the price charged by the edge server.

When OT_m^t is offloaded to edge server n for processing, the profit of user m is defined as the difference between the cost of local execution and the cost of offloading to edge server n, i.e. the saved cost:

$$uo_{m,n}^t = cl_m^t - co_{m,n}^t \tag{6}$$

Note that when OT_m^t is executed locally, the profit of user m is 0.

3.4 Edge Server's Profit

When OT_m^t is offloaded to edge server n for processing, the cost incurred by edge server is:

$$cs_{m,n}^t = c_s \cdot es_{m,n}^t \tag{7}$$

where c_s is the unit energy consumption cost of the edge server.

When OT_m^t is offloaded to edge server n for processing, the profit of edge server n is the payment received from user minus the cost:

$$us_{m,n}^t = p_n^t \cdot \tau o_{m,n}^t - cs_{m,n}^t \tag{8}$$

4 Deep Reinforcement Learning Based Task Offloading Strategy

As we have discussed in the above, the task offloading decisions made by users will affect the resource prices of edge servers, which will affect the task offloading decisions of users at the next time period. Therefore, the problem of user task offloading under the dynamic resource prices of edge servers is a sequential decision-making problem. We model this problem as a Markov decision process (MDP). Furthermore, this problem involves a huge state space and a discrete action space, and therefore we adopt a typical deep reinforcement learning DQN to solve it.

4.1 Markov Decision Process

As we have discussed in the above, we model the task offloading problem in the dynamic environment as a Markov decision process. MDP is defined as a tuple $< S, A, T, r, \gamma >$, where S is a set of states, A is a set of actions, T is a transition probability function, r is the immediate reward made in the process and γ is a discount factor that decreases the impact of the past rewards. In the following, we describe these notations in details. The state $s_t \in S$ is defined as:

$$s_t = (rc_t, d_t, f_t, (x_t, y_t), p_t), s_t \in S, t \in T \tag{9}$$

In the state s_t, $rc_t = (rc_1^t, \cdots, rc_N^t)$, where rc_n^t is the remaining loading capacity of edge server n at time period t, $d_t = (d_1^t, \cdots, d_M^t)$, where d_m^t is the data size that needs to be transmitted when OT_m^t is offloaded to edge server at time period t, $f_t = (f_1^t, \cdots, f_M^t)$, where f_m^t is the computing resources required to process OT_m^t at time period t, $(x_t, y_t) = \{(x_1^t, y_1^t), \cdots, (x_M^t, y_M^t)\}$, where (x_m^t, y_m^t) is the coordinates of user m at time period t, and $p_t = (p_1^t, \cdots, p_N^t)$, where p_n^t is the unit price of computing resource of edge server n at time period t. The task offloading action $a_t \in A$ is:

$$a_t = \left(a_t^1, \cdots, a_t^M \right), a_t \in A, t \in T \tag{10}$$

where a_t^m indicates the offloading decision of user m for OT_m^t at time period t, which means whether OT_m^t is executed locally on the mobile device or offloaded to one of edge servers for processing. The immediate reward r_t made by users is:

$$r_t = \sum_{m=1}^{m=M} uo_{m,n}^t \tag{11}$$

where $uo_{m,n}^t$ is the profit made by user m when OT_m^t is offloaded to edge server n for execution. The transition probability function is defined as $T(s_t, a_t, s_{t+1}) = Pr(s_{t+1}|s_t, a_t)$ where $s_t, s_{t+1} \in S$ and $a_t \in A$.

4.2 Task Offloading Strategy Under Dynamic Pricing

In the task offloading process, we can see that the server prices will affect users' offloading decisions. Therefore, a dynamic pricing strategy for edge servers is needed. In the following, we first introduce the dynamic pricing strategy of edge servers.

Dynamic Pricing Strategy

The servers' resource prices will affect users' offloading decisions. At the same time, the users' offloading decisions will affect the load of servers, which will affect the servers' resource prices at the next time period. Edge servers need to adapt their prices efficiently to maximize their own profits. Therefore, how edge servers dynamically adapting their prices is also a sequential decision problem, which can be modeled as a MDP as well. It is defined as a tuple $< S', A', T', r', \gamma' >$, where S' is a set of states, A' is a set of actions, T' is a transition probability function, r' is the immediate reward and γ' is a discount factor that decreases the impact of the past rewards. In the following, we describe these notations in details. The state $s_t' \in S'$ is defined as:

$$s_t' = (rc_t, lr_{t-1}, c_{t-1}, p_{t-1}, num_{t-1}), s_t' \in S', t \in T \tag{12}$$

In the state s_t', $rc_t = \left(rc_1^t, \cdots, rc_N^t\right)$, where rc_n^t is the remaining loading capacity.

of edge server n at time period t, $lr_{t-1} = \left(lr_1^{t-1}, \cdots, lr_N^{t-1}\right)$, where lr_n^{t-1} is the profit obtained by edge server n at time period $t-1$, $c_{t-1} = \left(c_1^{t-1}, \cdots, c_N^{t-1}\right)$, where c_n^{t-1} is the cost of edge server n at time period $t-1$, $p_{t-1} = \left(p_1^{t-1}, \cdots, p_N^{t-1}\right)$, where p_n^{t-1} is the resource price set by edge server n at time period $t-1$, and $num_{t-1} = (num_1^{t-1}, \cdots, num_N^{t-1})$, where num_n^{t-1} is the number of tasks offloaded to edge server n at time period $t-1$. The dynamic pricing action $a_t' \in A'$ is defined as:

$$a_t' = \left(a_t^{1'}, \cdots, a_t^{N'}\right), a_t' \in A', t \in T \tag{13}$$

where $a_t^{n'}$ is the resource price set by edge server n at time period t. The immediate reward r_t' made by edge servers is:

$$r_t' = \sum_{n=1}^{n=N} us_{m,n}^t \tag{14}$$

where $us_{m,n}^t$ is the profit made by edge server n at time period t when OT_m^t is offloaded. The transition probability function defined as $T'\left(s_t', a_t', s_{t+1}'\right) = Pr\left(s_{t+1}' \middle| s_t', a_t'\right)$ where $s_t', s_{t+1}' \in S'$ and $a_t' \in A'$.

The server's resource price can be regarded as a continuous value. Therefore, we use a typical deep reinforcement learning algorithm DDPG to design a dynamic pricing strategy for server resources, which is named as DESRP. DESRP dynamic pricing strategy is described in Algorithm 1.

Algorithm 1: DDPG based Edge Server Resource Pricing (DESRP) Strategy

Input:	The set of edge servers E; The set of users U
Output:	The resource pricing strategy π'
1:	Initialize the experience pool D';
2:	Initialize Critic network $Q(s, a|\theta^Q)$ and Actor network $\mu(s|\theta^\mu)$ with θ^Q, θ^μ;
3:	Initialize the target network Q' and μ', and set the weight $\theta^{Q'} \leftarrow \theta^Q, \theta^{\mu'} \leftarrow \theta^\mu$;
4:	**for** $i = 1$ to Maximum number of iterations **do**
5:	Initialize the initial state s_1' and the random process δ;
6:	**for** $t = 1, 2, \ldots, T$ **do**
7:	The edge servers $(e_1, \cdots, e_N)$ observe the state s_t' and select the action $a_t' = \mu(s_t' \mid \theta^\mu) + \delta_t$ according to the current strategy and the exploration noise, and execute it to get the reward r_t' and enter the next state s_{t+1}';
8:	Store the state transition tuple $(s_t', a_t', r_t', s_{t+1}')$ into D';
9:	Randomly select a set of samples $(s_k', a_k', r_k', s_{k+1}')$ from D' for training;
10:	Set $Y_k' = r_k' + \gamma Q'(s_{t+1}', \mu'(s_{t+1}' \mid \theta^{\mu'}) \mid \theta^{Q'})$;
11:	By minimizing the number of losses: $$L = \frac{1}{X} \sum_k (Y_k' - Q(s_k', a_k' \mid \theta^Q))^2 \text{ update Critic;}$$
12:	Use the sample policy gradient to update the Actor policy: $$\nabla_{\theta^\mu} J \approx \frac{1}{X} \sum_k \nabla_{a'} Q(s', a'|\theta^Q) \mid_{s'=s_k', a'=\mu(s_k')} \nabla_{\theta^\mu} \mu(s' \mid \theta^\mu) \mid_{s'=s_k'};$$
13:	Update the target network: $$\theta^{Q'} \leftarrow v\theta^Q + (1-v)\theta^{Q'}, \quad \theta^{\mu'} \leftarrow v\theta^\mu + (1-v)\theta^{\mu'}$$
14:	Set $s_t' = s_{t+1}'$;
15:	**end for**
16:	**end for**

Task Offloading Strategy

We now describe how to design a task offloading strategy when users are on the movement and edge servers use DESRP strategy to set price.

As we have discussed previously, the task offloading process is a Markov decision process, and we intend to use a deep reinforcement learning algorithm to solve it. Since this problem involves a huge state space and a discrete action space, we use DQN algorithm to design the task offloading strategy under dynamic pricing.

Users intend to maximize their long-term profits. At time period t, the users' accumulative reward R_t (i.e. the long-term profit) is:

$$R_t = r_t + \gamma r_{t+1} + \gamma^2 r_{t+2} + \cdots + \gamma^{T-t} r_T = \sum_{k=t}^{T} \gamma^{k-t} r_k \tag{15}$$

where γ is the discount factor. When users know that under all possible actions a_{t+1}, the optimal value of the next state s_{t+1} is $Q^*(s_{t+1}, a_{t+1})$, and then the optimal offloading strategy can be obtained by choosing action a' to maximize the expected value $r_t + \gamma Q^*(s_{t+1}, a_{t+1})$. The optimal action value function is $Q^*(s_t, a_t) = E_{s_{t+1}}[r_t + \gamma Q^*(s_{t+1}, a_{t+1}) \mid s_t, a_t]$.

However, given the huge state and action space, we have to use a function approximator to estimate the action value function, which is $Q(s_t, a_t; \theta) \approx Q^*(s_t, a_t)$. In the task offloading strategy based on DQN algorithm, Q network is a neural network function approximator with weight θ. By continuously adjusting parameter θ_i during iteration to train Q network, we use the approximate target value of parameter θ_i^- in the previous iteration $y_t = r_t + \gamma \max_a Q(s_t, a_t; \theta_i^-)$ to replace the optimal target value $r_t + \gamma \max_a Q^*(s_t, a_t)$.

Therefore, the loss function $L_i(\theta_i)$ that changes in each iteration can be obtained:

$$L_i(\theta_i) = E\left[(y_t - Q(s_t, a_t; \theta_i))^2\right] + E\left[V_{s_{t+1}}[y_t]\right] \tag{16}$$

We keep parameter θ_i^- in the previous iteration unchanged, and then minimize the loss function $L_i(\theta_i)$ in the iteration i. The last part of $L_i(\theta_i)$ is the variance of optimization target, which does not depend on parameter θ_i currently being optimized. Therefore, this part can be ignored. Finally, $L_i(\theta_i)$ is differentiated according to weight, and the gradient of task offloading strategy is:

$$\nabla_{\theta_i} L(\theta_i) = E[(r_t + \gamma \max_a Q(s_{t+1}, a_{t+1}, \theta_i^-) - Q(s_t, a_t; \theta_i))\nabla_{\theta_i} Q(s_t, a_t; \theta_i)] \tag{17}$$

The task offloading strategy in the dynamic pricing environment, which is called DUTO, as shown in Algorithm 2. In Algorithm 2, lines 1–3 represent the initialization of the experience pool D and two neural networks (Q, Q'). Line 7 indicates that after edge servers change the prices, users observe the environment and get state s_t, and then generate and execute the offloading action a_t according to $\mathcal{E}$ –greedy strategy. Users get reward r_t and enter the next state s_{t+1}. Lines 8–12 indicate that users store the state transition tuple (s_t, a_t, r_t, s_{t+1}) into the experience pool D, randomly take out a certain number of samples for training. Users constantly update Q network, and then update the target network every J generation. Line 13 means algorithm enters the next state.

Algorithm 2: DQN-based User Task Offloading (DUTO) Strategy

Input:	The set of edge servers E; The set of users U
Output:	The task offloading strategy π
1:	Initialize the experience pool D;
2:	Initialize the action value function Q with parameter θ;
3:	Initialize the target action value function Q' with parameter $\theta^- = \theta$;
4:	**for** $i = 1$ to Maximum number of iterations **do**
5:	Initialize the initial state s_1;
6:	**for** $t = 1,2,\dots,T$ **do**
7:	The users observe the environment and obtain the state s_t and select the action a_t, and then execute it according to $\mathcal{E}$ –greedy strategy, and obtain the reward r_t and enter the next state s_{t+1};
8:	Store the state transition tuple (s_t, a_t, r_t, s_{t+1}) into D;
9:	Randomly select a set of samples (s_k, a_k, r_k, s_{k+1}) from D for training;
10:	**if** training is not over: $y_k = r_k + \gamma \max\limits_{a_{k+1}} Q(s_{k+1}, a_{k+1}; \theta)$;
	else: $y_k = r_k$;
11:	Perform gradient descent on $(y_k - Q(s_k, a_k; \theta))^2$ according to the parameter θ of the neural network;
12:	Update the neural network parameters every J generation, set $Q' = Q$;
13:	Set $s_t = s_{t+1}$;
14:	**end for**
15:	**end for**

5 Experimental Evaluation

5.1 Experimental Settings

In this section, we run simulation to experimentally evaluate our strategy. In the experimental environment, the area size is set to 200 m × 200 m. For users, considering that the Random Waypoint (RWP) [24] model is widely used in the simulation of mobile networks, we use RWP model to generate the movement trajectory of users. We assume that OT_m^t of user m follows a Poisson distribution [25], which is $d_m^t \sim P(5), f_m^t \sim P(5)$. At the same time, we assume that the unit energy consumption cost c_u is 8, the mobile device transmission power P_d is 500 mw, the mobile device CPU chip model parameters κ_u and ζ are 10^{-27} and 3 respectively, and the computing power ϕ of mobile devices is 0.5 GHz.

For edge servers, we assume that coordinates of edge servers in the environment are $L_1 = (50, 150)$, $L_2 = (150, 150)$, $L_3 = (50, 50)$ and $L_4 = (150, 50)$, the edge server CPU chip model parameters κ_s and ζ' are 10^{-29} and 3 respectively, and the unit energy consumption cost c_s is 4.

For the edge computing environment, the entire time is divided into 100 time periods, i.e. $T = 100$. We assume that the received power h_0 is -30 dB when reference distance is 1 m, the channel bandwidth B is 20 MHz, and the noise power σ^2 between the mobile device and the edge server is -60 dBm/Hz. The experimental parameters are shown in Table 2.

Table 2. Experimental parameters

Parameter	Description
$N = 4$	Number of edge servers
$\kappa_s = 10^{-29}, \zeta' = 3$	Edge server CPU chip model parameter
$c_s = 4$	Edge server unit energy consumption cost
$T = 100$	Total time period
$d_m^t \sim P(5)$	Data size of OT_m^t
$f_m^t \sim P(5)$	Computing resources required for OT_m^t
$\phi = 0.5$ GHz	Computing power of mobile devices
$\kappa_u = 10^{-27}, \zeta = 3$	Mobile device CPU chip model parameter
$P_d = 500$ mw	Mobile device transmission power
$c_u = 8$	Unit energy consumption cost of mobile device
$h_0 = -30$ dB	The received power when the reference distance is 1 m
$B = 20$ MHz	Channel bandwidth
$\sigma^2 = -60$ dBm/Hz	Noise power between mobile device and edge server

We now introduce the benchmark approaches used in the evaluation. In the realistic edge computing environment, the Nearest Offloading strategy (*NO*, users choose to offload each computing task to the nearest edge server) and the Greedy Offloading strategy (*GO*, users choose the edge server that can generate the most profit to offload) are often used, and they are also widely used as benchmark approaches in the related work, such as [9, 18, 26, 27]. In addition to evaluating against *NO* and *GO*, we also evaluate our strategy against two state of the art approaches. One is an online user allocation strategy based on mobility-aware and migration-enabled (*MobMig*), where the user selects the edge server with the aim at maximizing the profit. When the edge server is overloaded, it may migrate computing tasks [21]. The other is a dynamic task offloading strategy based on SARSA (*DOM*), where users use games to choose edge servers that maximize the profits of users [11]. Note that we need to analyze the performance of these benchmark approaches when the edge servers dynamically change prices based on DESRP pricing strategy. Therefore, we first need to train the pricing strategy against the above benchmark approaches respectively.

In this paper, we intend to maximize the long-term profits of users and analyze the impact of dynamic pricing on users' offloading decisions. Therefore, we consider the following four metrics for evaluation, which are total profits of users, total costs of users, total profits of edge servers and total costs of edge servers.

5.2 Experimental Analysis

In each experiment, users' trajectory is different when RWP model is adopted. The initial prices of the edge servers are dynamically set when DESRP dynamic pricing strategy is adopted. Therefore, we repeat the experiments for 10000 times to show the average performance of our algorithm.

Firstly, we show how the dynamical pricing can affect users' task offloading decisions. For illustrative purpose, we set $M = 6$, $Rad = 100$ m, $F = 3$ GHz, and the experimental results are shown in Fig. 2. We find that when the price of edge server is decreased, more users will be attracted to offload tasks. For example, we choose time step 17–19 and 49–51 to show the dynamics of the price. Figure 2(a) shows the price changes of each server under different task offloading strategy. Note that *MobMig* strategy will migrate tasks, which may cause the prices to fluctuate greatly. *NO* strategy will select the nearest server to offload tasks, making the server's load unbalanced, and will also cause the server's price to fluctuate greatly. When step = 18, we can see that the price of server 4 in *DUTO* is lower, our strategy will select server 4 while users with *MobMig* and *NO* strategies select server 1. Although users with *DOM* and *GO* strategies will also choose server 4, the price of server 4 under *DUTO* strategy is lower. Therefore, the total profits of users are higher than other four strategies, as shown in Fig. 2(b). Furthermore, we find that when step = 50, the price of each server in *DUTO* is relatively high, but the total profits of users are still the highest. This is because *DUTO* strategy will reserve server capacity in advance for high-value offloading tasks through continuous learning, so as to avoid these tasks being discarded, which improve users' profits, as shown in Fig. 2(b).

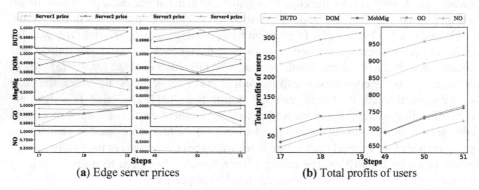

(a) Edge server prices   (b) Total profits of users

Fig. 2. The impacts of dynamic pricing on task offloading with step 17–19 and 49–51

We now run experiment with different number of users when $Rad = 100$ m and $F = 3$ GHz. The experimental results are shown in Fig. 3. We find that *DUTO* strategy can outperform other strategies. When the number of users increases, *DUTO* can perform better (e.g. when $M = 6$, *DUTO* is 5.59% higher than *DOM*, 13.20% higher than *MobMig*, 16.78% higher than *GO*, and 21.09% higher than *NO* in terms of the total profits of users). This is because by sensing the prices and capacities of edge servers, *DUTO* can make reasonable offloading decisions in the dynamic environment. In terms of total costs of users, *DUTO* always outperforms *MobMig*, *GO* and *NO* (e.g. when $M = 6$, *DUTO* is 47.38% lower than *MobMig*, 44.49% lower than *GO* and 44.59% lower than *NO*). This is because *DUTO* can make reasonable decisions in the dynamic environment. When the price is too high, users will give up offloading and do the local execution, reducing the costs of users.

In terms of the total profits of edge servers, with the increased number of users, we find that the edge servers make less profits when users adopt *DUTO* strategy. This is because when users use *DUTO* strategy, DESRP dynamic pricing strategy cannot take advantage on users to make more profits. At the same time, in terms of the total costs of edge servers, with the increased number of users, *DUTO* can help edge servers to reduce the costs. This is because *DUTO* can make effective decisions with respect to the dynamic prices of edge servers. When edge server increases its price, resulting in fewer tasks offloaded, and thus reduces the cost.

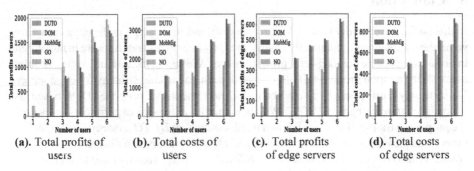

(a). Total profits of users   (b). Total costs of users   (c). Total profits of edge servers   (d). Total costs of edge servers

Fig. 3. Experimental results with different number of users when $Rad = 100$ m and $F = 3$ GHz

Furthermore, in addition to analyzing the impact of dynamic pricing on task offloading decisions, we run experiments with different values of coverage radius *Rad* and task processing capacity F for edge servers, in order to analyze how different characteristics of edge servers can affect the task offloading strategy. Because of the page limits, for illustrative purpose, we show the results of the key evaluation metric (the average value of total profits of users and its standard deviation) with 6 users in Table 3. We find that our strategy can still outperform other strategies. Furthermore, we find that when F increases, edge server can provide more computing resources, resulting in more tasks offloaded, which can increase users' profits. When *Rad* increases, users' profits may not increase. This is because when the coverage radius is not changed too much, i.e. $Rad = 80$ m compared with $Rad = 100$ m, the number of users covered by each edge server is not changed too much. Therefore, edge servers that users can choose to offload the tasks are roughly the same, which may result in similar users' profits.

Table 3. The experimental results with different *Rad* and *F* when $M = 6$

Strategy	$Rad = 80$ m, $F = 2$ GHz		$Rad = 80$ m, $F = 3$ GHz		$Rad = 100$ m, $F = 2$ GHz		$Rad = 100$ m, $F = 3$ GHz	
	Users' profits	Std	Users' profits	Std	Users' profits	Std	Users' profits	Std
DUTO	1580.3	9.4	1854.8	8.5	1573.7	9.1	1938.3	14.4
DOM	1558.1	6.6	1810.2	13.3	1411.4	6.7	1867.4	10.6
MobMig	1314.3	2.9	1741.0	3.4	1300.8	6.3	1743.9	7.4
GO	1202.1	1.6	1688.6	1.8	1203.5	3.4	1688.6	3.5
NO	1122.1	1.8	1628.5	1.3	1122.2	2.9	1628.5	1.6

6   Conclusion

In this paper, we consider how to design a task offloading strategy in the edge computing when the edge servers dynamically change the resource prices and users are in movement, in order to maximize the long-term profits of users. We model the task offloading problem as an MDP. We then propose a DDPG based dynamical pricing strategy for edge servers. Under this dynamic pricing strategy and users' movements, we propose a DQN based task offloading strategy, named *DUTO*. We also conduct extensive experiments to evaluate the proposed strategy. The experimental results show that *DUTO* strategy can outperform other strategies in terms of users' profits, and *DUTO* strategy can also reduce the users' costs. We also run the experiments with different coverage radiuses and task processing capabilities of edge servers. We find that by improving task processing capabilities of edge servers, users' profits are increased. The experimental analysis can provide useful insights for designing the practical task offloading strategy.

Acknowledgement. This paper was funded by the Humanity and Social Science Youth Research Foundation of Ministry of Education (Grant No. 19YJC790111), the Philosophy and Social Science Post-Foundation of Ministry of Education (Grand No. 18JHQ060) and Shenzhen Fundamental Research Program (Grant No. JCYJ20190809175613332).

References

1. Cisco v, Cisco Annual Internet Report (2018–2023). White Paper (2020). https://www.cisco.com/c/en/us/solutions/collateral/executive-perspectives/annual-internet-report/white-paper-c11-741490.html
2. Hu, Y.C., Patel, M., Sabella, D., et al.: Mobile edge computing-a key technology towards 5G. ETSI White Paper **11**(11), 1–16 (2015)
3. He, Q., Wang, C., Gui, G., et al.: A game-theoretical approach for mitigating edge DDoS attack. IEEE Trans. Dependable Secure Comput. **1**(1), 1–16 (2021)
4. Yuan, L., He, Q., Tan, S., et al.: Coopedge: a decentralized blockchain-based platform for cooperative edge computing. In: The 30th Web Conference, pp. 2245–2257 (2021)
5. Li, B., He, Q., et al.: Auditing cache data integrity in the edge computing environment. IEEE Trans. Parallel Distrib. Syst. **32**(5), 1210–1223 (2021)

6. Lin, H., Zeadally, S., Chen, Z., et al.: A survey on computation offloading modeling for edge computing. J. Netw. Comput. Appl. **169**(1), 1–25 (2020)
7. Peng, Q., Xia, Y., Wang, Y., et al.: A decentralized reactive approach to online task offloading in mobile edge computing environments. In: The 18th International Conference on Service-Oriented Computing, pp. 232–247 (2020)
8. Zhao, H., Deng, S., Zhang, C., et al.: A mobility-aware cross-edge computation offloading framework for partitionable applications. In: 2019 IEEE International Conference on Web Services, pp. 193–200 (2019)
9. Cao, Z., Zhou, P., Li, R., et al.: Multiagent deep reinforcement learning for joint multichannel access and task offloading of mobile edge computing in industry 4.0. IEEE Internet Things J. **7**(7), 6201–6213 (2020)
10. Du, W., Lei, Q., et al.: Multiple energy harvesting devices enabled joint computation offloading and dynamic resource allocation for mobile edge computing systems. In: 2019 IEEE International Conference on Web Services, pp. 154–158 (2019)
11. Shen, B., Xu, X., Dai, F., et al.: Dynamic task offloading with minority game for internet of vehicles in cloud-edge computing. In: 2020 IEEE International Conference on Web Services, pp. 372–379 (2020)
12. Chen, W., et al.: Multi-user multi-task computation offloading in green mobile edge cloud computing. IEEE Trans. Serv. Comput. **12**(5), 726–738 (2018)
13. Fang, Z., Xu, X., Dai, F.F., et al.: Computation offloading and content caching with traffic flow prediction for internet of vehicles in edge computing. In: 2020 IEEE International Conference on Web Services, pp. 380–388 (2020)
14. Li, J., Gao, H., Lv, T., et al.: Deep reinforcement learning based computation offloading and resource allocation for MEC. In: 2018 IEEE Wireless Communications and Networking Conference, pp. 1–6 (2018)
15. Zhang, K., et al.: Optimal delay constrained offloading for vehicular edge computing networks. In: 2017 IEEE International Conference on Communications, pp. 1–6 (2017)
16. Du, W., Lei, T., He, Q., et al.: Service capacity enhanced task offloading and resource allocation in multi-server edge computing environment. In: 2019 IEEE International Conference on Web Services, pp. 83–90 (2019)
17. Xia, X., Chen, F.F., He, Q., et al.: Online collaborative data caching in edge computing. IEEE Trans. Parallel Distrib. Syst. **32**(2), 281–294 (2021)
18. Chen, X., Zhang, H., Wu, C., Mao, S., Ji, Y., Bennis, M.: Optimized computation offloading performance in virtual edge computing systems via deep reinforcement learning. IEEE Internet Things J. **6**(3), 4005–4018 (2019)
19. Cao, H., Cai, J.: Distributed multiuser computation offloading for cloudlet-based mobile cloud computing: a game-theoretic machine learning approach. IEEE Trans. Veh. Technol. **67**(1), 752–764 (2018)
20. Huang, L., Bi, S., et al.: Deep reinforcement learning for online computation offloading in wireless powered mobile edge computing networks. IEEE Trans. Mob. Comput. **19**(11), 2581–2593 (2019)
21. Peng, Q., Xia, Y., Feng, Z., et al.: Mobility-aware and migration-enabled online edge user allocation in mobile edge computing. In: 2019 IEEE International Conference on Web Services, pp. 91–98 (2019)
22. Du, Y., Yang, K., et al.: Joint resources and workflow scheduling in uav-enabled wirelessly-powered MEC for IoT systems. IEEE Trans. Veh. Technol. **68**(10), 10187–10200 (2019)
23. Lyu, X., Tian, H., et al.: Energy-efficient admission of delay-sensitive tasks for mobile edge computing. IEEE Trans. Commun. **66**(6), 2603–2616 (2018)
24. Johnson, D.B., Maltz, D.A.: Dynamic source routing in ad hoc wireless networks. In: Mobile Computing, pp. 153–181 (1996)

25. Zaitoun, T.A., Issa, M.B., et al.: Evaluation and enhancement of the edgecloudsim using poisson interarrival time and load capacity. In: The 8th International Conference on Computer Science and Information Technology, pp. 7–12 (2018)
26. Zhang, X., Zhang, J., Liu, Z., et al.: MDP-based task offloading for vehicular edge computing under certain and uncertain transition probabilities. IEEE Trans. Veh. Technol. **69**(3), 3296–3309 (2020)
27. Xu, X., Li, Y., Huang, T., et al.: An energy-aware computation offloading method for smart edge computing in wireless metropolitan area networks. J. Netw. Comput. Appl. **133**(1), 75–85 (2019)

Vision Papers

BRIBOT: Towards a Service-Based Methodology for Bridging Business Processes and IoT Big Data

Volker Gruhn[1], Yanbo Han[2(✉)], Marc Hesenius[1], Manfred Reichert[3], Guiling Wang[2], Jian Yu[4], and Liang Zhang[5]

[1] Institute for Software Engineering, University of Duisburg-Essen, Schützenbahn 70, 45127 Essen, Germany
{volker.gruhn,marc.hesenius}@uni-due.de
[2] Beijing Key Laboratory on Integration and Analysis of Large-scale Stream Data, North China University of Technology, No.5 Jinyuanzhuang Road, Shijingshan District, Beijing 100144, China
{yhan,wangguiling}@ict.ac.cn
[3] Institute of Databases and Information Systems, Ulm University, Ulm, Germany
manfred.reichert@uni-ulm.de
[4] Department of Computer Science, Auckland University of Technology, Auckland 1142, New Zealand
jian.yu@aut.ac.nz
[5] School of Computer Science, Fudan University, Shanghai Key Laboratory of Data Science, Shanghai Institute of Intelligent Electronics and Systems, Shanghai, China
lzhang@fudan.edu.cn

Abstract. We envisage that BPM and IoT Big Data will be the two pillars of next-generation Process-Aware Information Systems (PAIS). While IoT enables BPM to perceive and react to realtime events in the physical world, BPM can equip IoT with a well-developed modelling and implementation platform. However, the integration of BPM and IoT is facing paradigm misalignment challenges including *mismatch of programming mechanisms, mismatch of resource management mechanisms, and mismatch of adaptation mechanisms*. In this paper, we present the vision and architectural solution of the recently funded NSFC-DFG cooperation research project BRIBOT, which aims to develop novel service-based approaches and techniques for these challenges. The paper presents the BRIBOT methodology that comprises four parts: abstraction and servitization of IoT data, resource space that handles service and data assets, modelling and transformation of IoT and business events, and IoT-event-driven process awareness and adaptation.

Keywords: Internet of Things (IoT) · IoT Big Data · IoT Services · Business Process Management (BPM) · Process-Aware Information Systems (PAIS)

H. Hacid et al. (Eds.): ICSOC 2021, LNCS 13121, pp. 597–611, 2021.
https://doi.org/10.1007/978-3-030-91431-8_37

1   Introduction

The Internet of Things (IoT) has gained huge momentum and is becoming the new infrastructure for next-generation distributed computer systems. IoT enables the inter-connectivity of sensors, actuators, everyday electronics and vehicles, and heralds a new era in which people, physical objects and virtual objects are naturally integrated and can interact with each other in a convenient and efficient way [1,2]. Meanwhile, Business Process Management (BPM), as the cornerstone for modern Process-Aware Information Systems (PAIS), has established itself as a powerful technology in the design, analysis, configuration, enactment, and evolution of cooperative processes [3]. BPM and related technologies have been widely used in retailing, logistics, manufacturing, and many other service industries for decades.

We anticipate that by integrating IoT capabilities to sense realtime situations of the physical environment, traditional PAIS will potentially have enhanced situation-awareness and become more proactive, leading to increased usability and a wider range of possible applications. The ever growing amount of data generated by IoT, which holds great economic potential for future applications, can also be better leveraged and handled by means of BPM, as the latter gives domain experts direct control over business processes.

However, the integration of BPM and IoT is facing paradigm misalignment challenges. For example, IoT-enabled PAIS require programming mechanisms for creating situation-awareness that the traditional predefined process models of BPM cannot cope with [4]. The mismatch between the volume and velocity of IoT Big Data with the structured data models of traditional BPM poses challenges as well [5]. Furthermore, IoT applications may be highly dynamic and change on short notice (e.g. due to the mobility of users and systems), whereas existing approaches to business process modelling follow a more static approach.

The joint research project "Service-based Abstraction and Programming Mechanisms for Bridging Business Processes and IoT Big Data (BRIBOT)" aims to tackle these challenges. In particular, service-based technologies can be a major enabler in the given context. With service-based modelling and transformation serving as the core foundation, the project aims to make breakthroughs in the abstraction and servitization of IoT data, accretion and management of service and data assets, modelling and transformation of IoT events, and IoT-service-enabled process awareness and adaptation. In order to promote discussions and interests within the service community to BPM and IoT integration, we report the BRIBOT methodology in this paper.

2   Motivation and Vision

In this section, we first discuss the main challenges of integrating IoT and BPM that motivate the proposal of the project, and then we present the vision and goal that BRIBOT aims to achieve.

As discussed in Sect. 1, IoT can upgrade traditional BPM to *proactive BPM* systems with realtime situation-awareness capability. However, we argue that several *paradigm alignment* issues must be resolved in the first place to enable the smooth integration of BPM and IoT. We have identified three major paradigm mismatch issues:

1) **Mismatch of programming mechanisms**

Sensors are one of the major components of an IoT system, and event streams generated by sensors flow continuously in the system, which necessitates proper abstraction and related programming mechanisms to define and manage event streams. Although events are also a key concept in the traditional BPM systems (for example message and error events in BPMN), they are, in general, asynchronous and discrete, and are thus not appropriate for modelling event streams. Some early works on extending BPMN with elements for modelling IoT event steams have been carried out. For example, Appel et al. [6,7] encapsulated IoT event streams into Stream Processing Units (SPU), a special type of BPMN tasks. Yousfi et al. [8] proposed uBPMN, which introduces additional task stereotypes for, e.g., audio and video streams. While some IoT event stream models have been proposed, how to *program* such models is still a research issue to be further investigated.

On the other hand, an IoT environment is in general not structured and highly dynamic. Unstructuredness is the principal characteristic of the IoT as most of the communication between loosely-coupled objects is accomplished in an ad-hoc and situative manner [4,9]. IoT devices exist in the physical world and, thus, they have geographical/spatial properties. Furthermore, IoT devices are highly dynamic, e.g., they can move in space or change their states over time. Traditional BPM approaches with monolithic process models have trouble dealing with such situation as both orchestration and choreography, which are the two main mechanisms of BPM for organizing and coordinating business flows, require knowledge about the structure and interactions of participating processes. Moreover, the traditional process modelling methods are geared towards routine and deterministic processes, whereas PAIS running in an IoT environment are expected to be *situation-aware* [4] and make decisions upon the occurrence of non-routine and non-deterministic events. Such characteristics require a programming mechanism that is situation-aware, which can be considered as a new challenge to the traditional BPM systems.

2) **Mismatch of resource management mechanisms**

Due to the huge complex network introduced by IoT, more sophisticated resource management mechanisms become necessary than the traditional batch or centralized cloud-based services utilized by BPM systems. The recently flourishing research area of "Edge computing" (or "Fog computing") conveniently meets this demand with a paradigm bringing resource management and processing closer to the location where it is needed to improve response times and to save bandwidth [10]. To cater for the IoT environment, it becomes necessary for BPM systems to optimise the execution of business processes through rationalizing stream-batch data processing, data placement and caching, and task scheduling strategies in the collaborative cloud and edge environment [11,12].

The exploding number of IoT objects/resources poses additional challenges to resource discovery and selection of BPM processes. Such over-choice issue becomes even more apparent with the rapidly expanding IoT network. Recommender systems as an effective method to deal with the exploding information recently are gaining increasing attentions by the community due to the advances in deep learning [13,14]. The dynamic nature of IoT, together with its huge size, requires improved recommendation mechanisms, which then will be an effective tool to bridge BPM process tasks with IoT resources.

3) **Mismatch of adaptation mechanisms**

In the highly dynamic IoT environment, PAIS are required to react to changing environmental conditions and business requirements more frequently and in a more agile manner. Reichert et al. [15], and Song et al. [16] have studied many issues and proposed practical solutions to process adaptation that enable either static adaptation or dynamic adaptation. However, when integrating IoT into BPM, another big gap hardly noticed so far concerns the long-tail business process adaptation requirements induced by scarce yet significant asynchronous events due to the five V's of IoT Big Data (volume in size, variety in type, velocity in time, veracity in quality, and value sparsity [17]). No matter what technologies are employed, these long-tailed events can be the blind-spot for IoT Big Data enabled BPM approaches, making it difficult to react to these events timely, effectively, and efficiently.

Bearing the above challenges in mind, BRIBOT aims to investigate mechanisms for the modelling, automatic provisioning and execution of next-generation PAIS that accommodate IoT streaming data and events. BRIBOT adopts the Everything-as-a-Service (XaaS) model and abstracts IoT physical things and digital data sources, IoT Big Data processing capabilities (including data acquisition, transformation, integration, query, storage, analysis, and visualization both at the edge and the cloud), and application logic in terms of services. As illustrated by Fig. 1, the supposed effect of BRIBOT is that the BPM modellers and power users (power users are the business users who have the skills and knowledge to use the advanced features) can 'see', 'bind', and 'control' certain IoT data and service assets at both modelling and run time. For BPM modellers, they can navigate and select suitable service assets and visualize data assets at modelling time. For power users, at run time, they can 1) navigate, select and bind IoT business events to business process elements; 2) monitor the physical environment continuously and track the data provenance of business events; 3) respond to IoT events and control the IoT resources.

3   Methodology and Approaches

An overview of the BRIBOT methodology is shown in Fig. 2. From the bottom up, at the IoT resource layer, physical sensor devices, IoT gateways and IoT applications continuously sense the physical environment and produce raw data

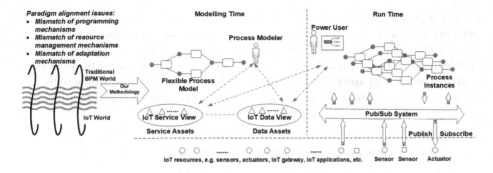

Fig. 1. Supposed effect of BRIBOT

streams. Raw sensor data are then aggregated, linked and abstracted as higher-level business events that can be bound to business process elements.

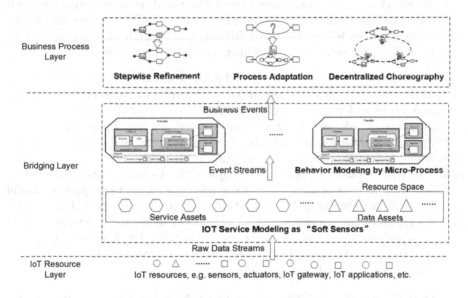

Fig. 2. BRIBOT methodology overview

At the middle bridging layer, raw event streams are modelled as IoT services and transformed to service events that can be utilized by micro processes. This layer hosts two communities: a service space and a data space. It further hosts IoT-aware micro processes that transform service events into business events, which can then be used and interpreted at the business process level [18].

At the business process layer, three types of process awareness/adaptation are considered: 1) **stepwise refinement**. This type of flexibility leaves the over-all business process model structure untouched, and allows for refinement at task level, while keeping consistency with the overall business process logic. 2) **process adaptation**. This type of flexibility allows ad hoc adjustments of business process at runtime through user-enabled decision-making and replacement, and enables late-binding/spontaneous reaction of certain model elements. 3) **decentralized choreography**. In case of cross-domain collaboration or cloud-edge topologies, decentralized choreography could be enabled to coordinate process segments and sub-processes through IoT business events.

3.1   Abstraction and Servitization of IoT Data

In this section, we introduce the notion of *IoT Service*, which is a service-based abstraction model for bridging IoT Big Data. As shown in Fig. 2, IoT Service is at the bottom of the bridging layer that interfaces with the IoT resource layer. It maps raw IoT data to service events, sets up links to the data space, and supports formalized event calculus. Based on service behavior patterns, more coarse-grained IoT services can be formed.

In recent years, some researchers have investigated on related open research problems of IoT services for both enhancing event based IoT systems and bridging the gap between IoT systems and BPM (e.g., [19–21]). In this paper, three fundamental requirements have been identified for IoT service:

- We treat various physical devices, including sensors, tags and actuators, as 'IoT objects'. IoT services correspond to their twin representation in the digital world and provide capabilities to access them. We also denote such IoT services as 'soft-sensors' or 'software-defined sensors'. The communication protocols and data formats need to be adapted in the first place so that the physical devices can be accessed in a uniform manner.
- IoT services should encapsulate the capabilities to read/write attributes of IoT objects as well as to manage their lifecycles. The *micro process* model needs to be adopted here. We will introduce it in detail in Sect. 3.3.
- IoT services should provide the necessary functionality to process raw sensor data as well as to generate events for the upper layer. By doing so, a large volume of raw data streams with low value density is transformed to meaningful information to be used by micro processes.

To satisfy the aforementioned requirements, we define five characteristics for IoT services:

- **calculable**. Although raw IoT data may appear in massive volume, the value density is often low, thus raw data need to be processed and further analyzed, e.g. filtered, aggregated or mined in order to generate events being of interest to the upper layer of BRIBOT. IoT services should be able to describe event streams and compound events, to recognize and detect meaningful events from raw data streams, to define, learn and validate complex event processing rules, and to reason on the behaviors of the IoT objects.
- **composable**. The upper layer often needs events that are interrelated with multiple cross-organizational IoT objects instead of a single IoT object; thus,

IoT services are designed to be composable into larger-granularity IoT services that encapsulate read/write and lifecyle management operations for a collection of interrelated IoT objects.

- **bindable**. After generating IoT service, the mapping needs to be established between the IoT service and the business process model elements, either at modelling time or later during execution. With IoT services, the business process instances could read service events or write control commands from/to IoT devices and/or IoT applications. Both the mapping relationship at modelling time, and the association between service events and process elements during execution lifecycle of IoT services and business processes are covered. Such mapping needs to be considered when deploying, instantiating, starting, stopping, resuming, and completing services and the associated business processes. We call this process for building up such mapping relationship both at modelling time and run time as *binding process*, and call this capability *bindable*.

- **fault-tolerant**. Most IoT devices such as wearable devices and internet of vehicles are highly dynamic, and some devices are deployed in harsh environments. Although the underlying technological framework such as wireless sensor network (WSN) copes with issues related to network failures, power shortage or node failures, the data collected from sensors are prone to be damaged due to the IoT environment's intrinsic issues such as sensor errors, exceptional events from the open real-world scenarios, and IoT objects joining and leaving. Therefore, IoT services need to be fault-tolerant to ensure the quality of output events.

- **proactive**. Proactivity refers to the ability to mitigate or eliminate undesired future events, or to identify and take advantage of future opportunities, by applying prediction and automated decision making techniques [22]. The growing availability of IoT Big Data as well as the development in predictive data analysis open the door for IoT services to become proactive, i.e., on one side to sense the IoT situation based on IoT services such that specific services can be dynamically selected and bound to the predefined elements of a business process instance according to its IoT physical environment; and on the other to predict and output events and to make decisions before these events actually occur.

Based on the above analysis, a high-level design of IoT Services is shown in Fig. 3. For each IoT object, an IoT service with standard operation APIs for accessing its attributes and generating service events is generated. The input and output of service operations are specified by subscriptions and advertisements of event streams. For example, the input of a service operation that continuously reads the temperature of a room is specified by a subscription to "temperature" topic for a certain room with the associated subscription parameters. Except for such standard operations, other event processing logic such as event filtering, event aggregation and learning-based event prediction can be encapsulated in specific operation APIs.

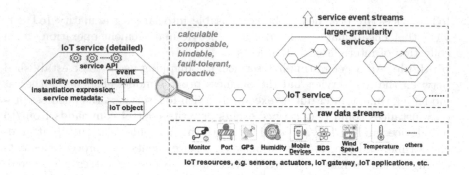

Fig. 3. IoT Services ("Soft Sensors")

Specifically, an IoT service has properties such as *validity condition, instantiation expression*, and *service metadata* to describe the conditions when an IoT service becomes instantiated and alive, the input and output, the stream processing logic, and service properties, e.g., the location and quality of an IoT object.

3.2 Resource Space

This section gives a detailed description to *Resource Space*, which corresponds to a community for managing, sharing, and recommending resources in BRIBOT. As shown in Fig. 2, the bridging layer hosts the resource space.

Four fundamental requirements need to be met by the resource space:

- To meet the needs of process modellers, power users, and the IoT physical environment, the resource space is designed to organize and manage the cross-organizational BRIBOT resources, including IoT data sources, IoT objects and IoT services as well as other services, processes and the associated stream and batch data.
- The resource management mechanisms need to support an optimised scheduling in the collaborative cloud and edge environment. To schedule a huge number of IoT objects and services as well as a huge volume of data, a distributed and/or decentralized resource management architecture is needed to optimise the execution performance of business processes.
- To manage the complexity of the resources, the resource space shall be designed to facilitate power users to manage resources at different levels with the zoom-in/zoom-out operations to link different pieces of resources and history elements while exploring the data provenance of business events.
- The resource space is designed in a way that shall facilitate power users to discover and choose appropriate resources from a dynamic and large community hosting tens of millions of objects.

To satisfy the above requirements, we define three characteristics the resource space needs to have:

- **optimised scheduling.** IoT objects, the associated stream and batch data, and the tasks/services can be allocated to the locations specified by either the power user or the system including the cloud and the edge. Resource scheduling methods are designed to achieve specific optimisation goals for business processes under different business or environmental constraints.
- **manageable and customizable.** In order to improve the use of various resources in a dynamic IoT environment, resource management and customization mechanisms are designed to provide different resource views to different users in diverse IoT situations.
- **dynamic resource recommendation.** To support power users in discovering and choosing the proper objects within the potentially huge and dynamic IoT environment, a recommender system is needed that adapts to both temporal and spatial changes.

A high-level design for dynamic service recommendation based on the resource space is illustrated by Fig. 4. First, the process modeller defines a placeholder with certain functional requirements which is sent to the service registry. Second, some essential services are selected based on the functional requirements and the descriptions/tags of the services from the service registry. At the same time, some supplemental services are recommended according to the topological and organization model of the services network. Third, the essential and candidate services are matched and ranked based on the IoT situation generated by the IoT services. Fourth, the placeholder is realized with one or multiple services at run time.

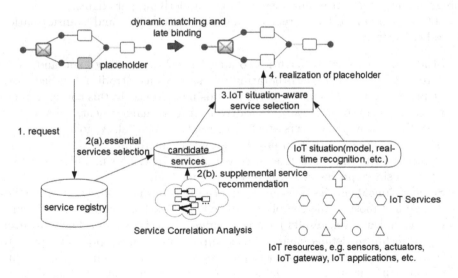

Fig. 4. Dynamic service recommendation based on resource space

Although a lot of works have been reported on personalized, context-aware or situation-aware service organization, discovery and recommendation [23–25], there is still a lack of effective approaches to address the dynamic and large-scale nature of the service space in an IoT environment. For example, how to apply the recently proposed complex network models to build the topological and temporal evolutionary model of services and evaluate their effectiveness, and how to discover and rank the available services based on the advances in deep learning research are worth further investigation.

3.3 Event Modelling and Transformation

In this section, we give insights into *Event Modelling and Transformation*. The latter is a key programming mechanism in the bridging layer in Fig. 2 to encapsulate event streams into business events of interest to the business process, consume and utilize IoT business events at business process level, and better control the interactions with the real world.

IoT and business processes are located at different levels in PAIS. IoT focuses on processing event streams continuously, while contemporary business processes focus on a rather high level of abstraction, e.g., the status of (black-box) business activities. As discussed in Sect. 2, although events handlers in the traditional BPM systems can match discrete IoT events, flow logic of BPM only captures sequential logic, whereas IoT event processing heavily relies on strict timed semantics. The particular challenge is how to effectively and efficiently integrate the two different concepts and how to cope with naturally occurring programming mechanism mismatches in the underlying paradigms.

Three fundamental requirements for event modelling and transformation have been identified:

- Study the coordination facilities to adapt synchronous flow logic and asynchronous IoT event by incorporating IoT services as introduced in Sect. 3.1.
- Define suitable modelling elements for business events. In this context, micro processes pick up the idea of data-driven process management, enhancing it with the concepts of objects and object relations [26–28]. As IoT objects can be easily mapped onto such objects, adopting micro processes as modelling elements for business events as well as building blocks for modularizing IoT-aware business processes seems to be very natural.
- Some technical entities must be integrated into business processes, nevertheless. While most of the complexity of IoT applications should be dealt with on a technical level, results naturally influence decisions on a business level. Thus, technical details having direct impact on business processes need to be incorporated into the business process models. For example, data quality of different sensors or external services may influence business decisions or machine learning algorithms. The latter are commonly employed to analyze IoT data, but return a probabilistic result, which, in turn, requires appropriate processing on a business level.

With these requirements in mind, we define the following characteristics for suitable *Event Modelling and Transformation*:

- **micro process enabled.** The modelling and transformation of event stream into business events is based on micro processes. We propose IoT-aware micro processes and their lightweight coupling to form the overall multi-object business processes. By integrating IoT-aware micro processes and related information, the real-world aware execution, monitoring, mining, and decision support for business processes becomes possible. Moreover, due to the object-centric approach of micro processes, the black-box nature of process activities can be broken [26].
- **technical dependency sensitive.** IoT solutions consist of several technical entities (e.g. sensors, web services, algorithms, etc.) introducing constraints to the business processes that must be obeyed or handled (e.g. probabilities in machine learning).
- **automatically executable.** Solely defining business process models would require manual implementation and thus not remedy the problems described before, but introduce potential inconsistencies between model and implementation. Automatisms are thus required to transform IoT-enabled business process models into executable entities, i.e., business process instances. We envision a system which can receive business process models and convert them into the necessary software components.

To design a solution meeting these requirements, we argue that such systems require a hybrid activity-/object-centric process modelling approach combining the advantages of activity-centric process models (e.g. BPMN models) with the ones of object-centric micro processes. This approach shall include patterns, methods and algorithms for mapping multiple IoT-aware micro processes to a process model in such a way that neither the modelled object behaviors nor the semantic relations between the micro processes contradict to the overall business process logic. At runtime, the IoT-aware micro process instances involved in the enactment of a business process instance should be allowed to run asynchronously and concurrently as far as possible on one hand, while on the other their execution needs to be coordinated at certain points taking their semantic relationships into account.

3.4 Process Awareness and Adaptation

Once event modeling and transformation have converged IoT events into business messages, business processes can deal with them in reaction to environmental events. Some of these messages are consumed directly by business processes following the prescribed models; others require further treatments via the close work of BPM with the event modeling and transformation layer to handle unpredictable situations. The latter one needs process adaptation support in BPM.

Process adaptation is a persistent topic in BPM. As introduced in Sect. 2, many issues and proposed practical solutions to process adaptation have been studied [15,16]. However, there is one scenario that neither [15] nor [16] has touched, i.e., the *long-tailed events* that need the tight interaction of event processing and business process management. Long-tailed events are a kind of short-lived events that occur with low frequency and unpredictable moments. Nevertheless, such events might be important for the business process. For example, during COVID-19, many regulations and policies must be adjusted frequently due to fast-changing situations like family isolation, community closure, resident-pass system, and social distance in public places. As a result, the business cannot operate normally according to the established process model. The limp in dealing with long-tailed events in BPM is rooted in the paradigm mismatch between IoT event processing and BPM. On the one hand, IoT can perceive events in due course, but it is still lagging off behind the semantics of business messages required by BPM; on the other hand, BPM focuses on the automation and compliance enforcement for the modeling and execution of business processes, which is challenging to deal with transient events effectively.

Generally, long-tailed events can hardly be automatically identified by standard process/data mining techniques due to the rarity of indicators in the event streams. In particular, due to the nature of long-tailed events, events captured at the IoT layer need to be further analyzed and verified at the business process management layer or inspired by business practitioners and then fed back to the event modeling and transformation layer for further justification. In other words, the identification of long-tailed events usually needs tight collaboration of bridging layer and the business process level in Fig. 2. Take the logistics during the COVID-19 period as an example. The events about complaints on delayed delivery creep away from traditional mining algorithms (lack of sufficient support) and deep learning techniques (shortage of annotated training data). However, business managers could awake traits of clues in their study of daily logs. Like *canaries in the mine*, these managers can discover meaningful clues with their practical experience or professional intuition. As a result, they can provide additional business activities or specify new criteria to help the filters capture meaningful events iteratively. For example, business managers can ascribe that these delays come from personal problems (such as sudden damage to the delivery vehicle) or the strict inspection system for outsiders (delivery workers) entering the destination community. Feeding these supplementary judgments again into the event modeling and transformation layer can help identify transient yet meaningful events.

Similarly, we cannot expect to deal with long-tailed events from BPM alone. It is beyond the capability of traditional BPM and deviates from BPM practice. Moreover, facing the long-tailed events, the whole PAIS might paralyze due to economic problems (events being too many in types and rare in emergence) or logical problems (making the process model fall into details and lose performance and maintainability). Still, it is unwisely to feed IoT events directly to BPM that PAIS cannot catch up with the pace of changes because of inconstant policies. In a word, in tackling long-tailed events, we have to develop effective solutions by the close collaboration of the bridging layer and the business process layer.

With such challenges in mind, we identify four fundamental requirements for process adaptation in the new context:

- characterizing long-tailed events precisely and studying their impact on necessary business process adaptations.
- developing a practical technology for identifying long-tailed events in time.
- innovating process adaptation techniques to leverage PAIS' resilience.
- improving quality-guaranty and business governance to embrace ad-hoc adaptation of business processes.

To satisfy these requirements, we define the following characteristics for process adaptation:

- **less invasive.** Our goal is to reuse the business process model as much as possible in a low code manner and let business personnel rather than IT technicians respond to the long-tailed change requirements of the business model based on business events.
- **verification support.** Any adjustments on the business process model, especially those adjustments on collaborative processes, should be tested to avoid violating the business nature.

We aim to adapt the classic PAIS framework [15] and exploit annotation facilities in the BPMN standard to adjust process behaviors according to situations detected by IoT. More specifically, we plan to define an annotation language to describe new capabilities, constraints, and KPI claims in response to certain IoT events at the design stage. At the run-time stage, we plan to use a low-code paradigm to enhance the process engine by adding corresponding handlers to interpret formatted annotations, which changes the original process variables to interfere with the execution of process instances. We also plan to study the feasibility of extending current controllability verification algorithms [29] to handle panorama KPIs in the setting of collaborative processes.

4   Concluding Remarks

With the convergence of design time and run time, cyber and physical objects, as well as ad hoc and regulatory decision-making, the modelling and execution of services also need to evolve. New application requirements and emerging challenges drive forward the service-oriented methodologies. The paper reports our undergoing efforts in applying service-based approaches to bridge BPM and IoT Big Data. With this, we hope to stir more interests and discussion on the related issues such as servitization of IoT data, and service-based triggering of BPM adaptation in particular.

Acknowledgements. This work is supported by Projects of International Cooperation and Exchanges NSFC (Grant No. 62061136006), Deutsche Forschungsgemeinschaft DFG (Grant No. 449721677).

References

1. Stankovic, J.A.: Research directions for the Internet of Things. IEEE Internet Things J. **1**(1), 3–9 (2014). https://doi.org/10.1109/JIOT.2014.2312291
2. Stoyanova, M., Nikoloudakis, Y., Panagiotakis, S., Pallis, E., Markakis, E.K.: A survey on the Internet of Things (IoT) forensics: challenges, approaches, and open issues. IEEE Commun. Surv. Tutorials **22**(2), 1191–1221 (2020). https://doi.org/10.1109/COMST.2019.2962586
3. Weske, M.: Business Process Management: Concepts, Languages. Springer, Architectures (2019)
4. Janiesch, C., et al.: The Internet of Things meets business process management: a manifesto. IEEE Syst. Man Cybern. Mag. **6**(4), 34–44 (2020)
5. Kolajo, T., Daramola, O., Adebiyi, A.: Big data stream analysis: a systematic literature review. J. Big Data **6**(1), 1–30 (2019). https://doi.org/10.1186/s40537-019-0210-7
6. Appel, S., Kleber, P., Frischbier, S., Freudenreich, T., Buchmann, A.: Modeling and execution of event stream processing in business processes. Inform. Syst. **46**, 140–156 (2014). https://doi.org/10.1016/j.is.2014.04.002
7. Appel, S., Frischbier, S., Freudenreich, T., Buchmann, A.: Event stream processing units in business processes. In: Daniel, F., Wang, J., Weber, B. (eds.) Business Process Management, pp. 187–202. Springer, Berlin Heidelberg (2013). https://doi.org/10.1007/978-3-642-40176-3_15
8. Yousfi, A., Bauer, C., Saidi, R., Dey, A.K.: uBPMN: A BPMN extension for modeling ubiquitous business processes. Inform. Softw. Technol. **74**, 55–68 (2016). https://doi.org/10.1016/j.infsof.2016.02.002
9. Leotta, F., Marrella, A., Mecella, M.: IoT for BPMers. Challenges, case studies and successful applications. In: Hildebrandt, T., van Dongen, B.F., Röglinger, M., Mendling, J. (eds.) BPM 2019. LNCS, vol. 11675, pp. 16–22. Springer, Cham (2019). https://doi.org/10.1007/978-3-030-26619-6_3
10. Shi, W., Cao, J., Zhang, Q., Li, Y., Xu, L.: Edge computing: vision and challenges. IEEE Internet Things J. **3**(5), 637–646 (2016)
11. Rejiba, Z., Masip-Bruin, X., Marín-Tordera, E.: A survey on mobility-induced service migration in the fog, edge, and related computing paradigms. ACM Comput. Surv. (CSUR) **52**(5), 1–33 (2019)
12. Chen, W., Paik, I., Li, Z.: Cost-aware streaming workflow allocation on geo-distributed data centers. IEEE Trans. Comput. **66**(2), 256–271 (2017). https://doi.org/10.1109/TC.2016.2595579
13. Botangen, K.A., Yu, J., Sheng, Q.Z., Han, Y., Yongchareon, S.: Geographic-aware collaborative filtering for web service recommendation. Expert Syst. Appl. **151**, 113347 (2020)
14. Wang, X., He, X., Chua, T.S.: Learning and reasoning on graph for recommendation. In: Proceedings of the 13th International Conference on Web Search and Data Mining, pp. 890–893 (2020)
15. Reichert, M., Weber, B.: Enabling Flexibility in Process-Aware Information Systems: Challenges, Methods, Technologies. Springer Science & Business Media (2012). https://doi.org/10.1007/978-3-642-30409-5
16. Song, W., Jacobsen, H.: Static and dynamic process change. IEEE Trans. Serv. Comput. **11**(1), 215–231 (2018). https://doi.org/10.1109/TSC.2016.2536025
17. Gudivada, V.N., Baeza-Yates, R., Raghavan, V.V.: Big data: promises and problems. Computer **48**(03), 20–23 (2015)

18. Andrews, K., Steinau, S., Reichert, M.: Enabling runtime flexibility in data-centric and data-driven process execution engines. Inform. Syst. **101**, 101447 (2021). https://doi.org/10.1016/j.is.2019.101447

19. Zhang, Z., Liu, C., Li, X., Han, Y.: A service-based declarative approach for capturing events from multiple sensor streams. In: Pahl, C., Vukovic, M., Yin, J., Yu, Q. (eds.) ICSOC 2018. LNCS, vol. 11236, pp. 255–263. Springer, Cham (2018). https://doi.org/10.1007/978-3-030-03596-9_17

20. Zhang, Y., Chen, J.L., Cheng, B.: Integrating events into SOA for IoT services. IEEE Commun. Mag. **55**(9), 180–186 (2017). https://doi.org/10.1109/MCOM. 2017.1600359

21. Arellanes, D., Lau, K.K.: Evaluating IoT service composition mechanisms for the scalability of IoT systems. Future Gener. Comput. Syst. **108**, 827–848 (2020). https://doi.org/10.1016/j.future.2020.02.073

22. Engel, Y., Etzion, O.: Towards proactive event-driven computing. In: Proceedings of the 5th ACM International Conference on Distributed Event-Based System, pp. 125–136. DEBS '11, Association for Computing Machinery, New York, NY, USA (2011). https://doi.org/10.1145/2002259.2002279

23. Liu, Q., Ma, H., Chen, E., Xiong, H.: A survey of context-aware mobile recommendations. Int. J. Inform. Technol. Decis. Making **12**(01), 139–172 (2013). https://doi.org/10.1142/S0219622013500077

24. Chang, C.K., Jiang, H.Y., Ming, H., Oyama, K.: Situ: a situation-theoretic approach to context-aware service evolution. IEEE Trans. Serv. Comput. **2**(3), 261–275 (2009). https://doi.org/10.1109/TSC.2009.21

25. Hirmer, P., et al.: Situation recognition and handling based on executing situation templates and situation-aware workflows. Computing **99**(2), 163–181 (2016). https://doi.org/10.1007/s00607-016-0522-9

26. Künzle, V., Weber, B., Reichert, M.: Object-aware business processes: fundamental requirements and their support in existing approaches. Int. J. Inform. Syst. Model. Des. **2**(2), 19–46 (2011)

27. Künzle, V., Reichert, M.: PHILharmonicFlows: towards a framework for object-aware process management. J. Softw. Maintenance Evol. Res. Pract. **23**(4), 205–244 (2011). https://doi.org/10.1002/smr.524

28. Andrews, K., Steinau, S., Reichert, M.: Engineering a highly scalable object-aware process management engine using distributed microservices. In: Panetto, H., Debruyne, C., Proper, H.A., Ardagna, C.A., Roman, D., Meersman, R. (eds.) OTM 2018. LNCS, vol. 11230, pp. 80–97. Springer, Cham (2018). https://doi.org/ 10.1007/978-3-030-02671-4_5

29. Eder, J., Franceschetti, M.: Time and business process management: Problems, achievements, challenges. In: 27th International Symposium on Temporal Representation and Reasoning, pp. 25–32 (2020)

Cross-Silo Process Mining
with Federated Learning

Asjad Khan[✉], Aditya Ghose, and Hoa Dam

University of Wollongong, Wollongong, Australia
maak458@uowmail.edu.au, {aditya,hoa}@uow.edu.au

Abstract. Process analytics techniques such as process discovery play
an important role in mining event data and providing organizations with
insights about the behaviour of their deployed processes. In many practical settings, process log data is often geographically dispersed, may
contain information that may be deemed sensitive and may be subject
to compliance obligations that prevent this data from being transmitted
to sites distinct to the site where the data was generated. Traditional process mining techniques operate by assuming that all relevant available
process data is available in a single repository. However, anonymising,
giving control access and safely transferring sensitive data across organi-
zation/site boundaries while preserving priacy guarantees is non-trivial.
In this paper, we lay out the first steps for a federated future for process
analytics where organizations routinely collaborate to learn and mine
geographically dispersed process-related data.

Keywords: Distributed process discovery · Business process mining ·
Privacy-preserving process mining

1 Introduction

Modern organizations routinely deploy process analytics, including process discovery techniques on their process data, both to gain insight into the reality of
their operational processes and also to identify process improvement opportunities [2]. However, in many practical settings, process log data is geographically
dispersed and can contain information that may be deemed sensitive. Traditional
process mining techniques operate by assuming that all relevant available process data has been curated into a central site for analysis. However, anonymising,
giving control access and safely transferring sensitive data across organizations is
non-trivial. Moreover, organizations face legal constraints, risk of data breaches
(or hacks) along with data integration challenges, preventing them from building
a centralised data warehouse [8]. This leads to a scenario where event-log data is
present in organizational silos and distributed among several custodians, none of
whom are allowed to share/transfer their sensitive data directly with each other
[18]. Mining process data in such cross-silo settings can prove to be invaluable
for providing relevant operational support to organizations if privacy guarantees
can be offered [14].

© Springer Nature Switzerland AG 2021
H. Hacid et al. (Eds.): ICSOC 2021, LNCS 13121, pp. 612–626, 2021.
https://doi.org/10.1007/978-3-030-91431-8_38

Consider a scenario from the field of medical research involving impediments to data migration. Here a number of different hospitals wish to jointly mine their process logs for the purpose of medical research, but are faced with regulatory and legislative compliance hurdles that prevent clinical process histories being shared across health jurisdictions (hospitals, health districts, national boundaries, etc.). Hospitals are therefore restricted from ever pooling their data or revealing it to each other leading to small dataset available for knowledge extraction. This negatively impacts the confidence with which clinicians might deploy the results thus obtained. Our inability to migrate clinical process data also implies that we miss out on the opportunities for extracting higher-impact insights that might have been possible if data from multiple health jurisdictions could have been analysed in juxtaposition [19]. Here a solution is needed that enables the hospitals to compute the desired data mining algorithm on the union of their databases, without ever pooling or revealing their data.

Federated learning (FL) has recently gained popularity, in the machine learning and data science research communities [17,21] as it enables collaborative learning without centralising the training data [26]. In this paper, we explore the potential of *federated learning paradigm* for building secure distributed process analytics solutions. We present a case study where we highlight the benefits of FL and demonstrate its usefulness in settings where organisations might be unwilling to share the sensitive data directly, but might still have a shared incentive in analyzing the disparate log sources to jointly mine process models, such that it leads to the collective benefit (e.g. mining of best practices across industry). Overall, we envision a federated future for process analytics where organizations routinely collaborate to learn and mine geographically dispersed process-related data.

Contributions: We identify the problem of FL based secure distributed process mining as an important research direction. We present a practical *process discovery* algorithm designed to work under the cross-silo Federated Learning paradigm where we perform computation at the edge. Our approach allows organizations to collaborate under the coordination of a central server, while keeping the sensitive process data localized. Our method incorporates various privacy-preserving protocols and mechanisms to ensure end-to-end privacy while the distributed mining process is executed.

2 Preliminaries

2.1 Process Mining

Process Mining allows for the analysis of business processes based on event logs (which are generated by most of today's information systems) in order to extract knowledge and insights. Such insights can allow analysts to analyse and under the behaviour and actual performance of deployed processes.

Process Discovery algorithms can extract a business process model from an event log, which captures the control-flow relations between tasks recorded in the event log [23]. Process Discovery algorithms take as input event logs which contain information about the start or completion of process steps, sometimes coupled together with related context data (e.g. actors and resources). Several process discovery algorithms have been proposed in the literature. For a survey we refer the reader to recent survey by Augusto et al. [2].

2.2 Federated Learning and Analytics

Federated Learning is a collaborative learning approach where a family of algorithms have been proposed, aimed at addressing characteristics, constraints, and challenges unique to secure distributed training of machine learning (ML) models where privacy is a major concern. Kairouz et al. [16] define Federated Learning as *"a machine learning setting where multiple entities (clients) collaborate in solving a machine learning problem, under the coordination of a central server or service provider. Each client's raw data is stored locally and not exchanged or transferred; instead, focused updates intended for immediate aggregation are used to achieve the learning objective"*. Federated Learning assumes that the participating nodes are capable of training models locally and are responsible for transmitting model characteristics (e.g., parameters, gradients). In federated learning, our goal is to collaboratively learn a shared global consensus model by a loose federation of participating nodes, which are coordinated by a central server, such that the final model can generalize over test dataset $\mathcal{D}_{\text{test}}$ without compromising the privacy of data in individual datasets [16,26].

A related but independent line of research known as *Federated Analytics* has a similar goal of moving computations closer to data, where local computations are performed over individual data, while only revealing the resulting insights (aggregated results) from each analysis [21]. This allows us to perform analysis of decentralized raw data and answer basic questions of statistical nature about the data. e.g. computing counts or rates. An application of such methods is the discovery of heavy hitters in a population of user-generated data stream or discovering frequently-taken actions on mobile phone app [26].

2.3 Differential Privacy

Differential Privacy provides us with a formal privacy notion for datasets that are released publicly or might come in contact with potentially malicious adversaries [20]. It is considered as the *de facto* standard for ensuring privacy in a variety of domains. The definition proposed by Dwork et al. [11] offers a mathematically rigorous gold standard for ensuring privacy protection when analyzing datasets like process logs(or results of a randomized algorithm) that might contain sensitive or private information. We modify the definition slightly for event logs:

Definition 1: Differential Privacy (adapted from [11]). A randomized mechanism $\mathcal{M} : \mathcal{D} \to \mathcal{R}$ with a domain $\mathcal{D}(e.g.,,$ possible event logs) and range $\mathcal{R}(e.g.,$ all possible trained models) satisfies $(\epsilon, \delta)-$ differential privacy if for any two adjacent process logs $l, l' \in \mathcal{D}$ and for any subset of outputs $S \subseteq \mathcal{R}$ it holds that $\Pr[\mathcal{M}(d) \in S] \leq e^{\epsilon} \Pr[\mathcal{M}(d') \in S] + \delta$

Two process log l and l' are defined to be adjacent if l' can be constructed by adding or removing a single instance(entry) from the log l. By bounding the potential worst-case information loss, the above definition provides us with a strong formal privacy guarantee. Formally, under the (ε, δ)-differential privacy definition, we measure Differential Privacy properties of our method by epsilon and delta values. Epsilon(ϵ) is the privacy loss parameter in differential privacy and is inversely proportional to the amount of noise added. i.e. Lower values of ε imply stronger privacy guarantees. A Differentially private mechanism typically involves using a randomized mechanim that perturbs the input dataset, intermediate calculations, or the outputs of a function, using a calculated quantity of noise (usually at the cost of utility) [9]. Such a mechanism is considered private if it hides the isolated contribution of any single individual in the databases. i.e. removing a single entry will not result in much difference in the output distribution [1, 11].

Definition 2 (Global Sensitivity [10]). For a real-valued query function $q : \mathcal{D} \to \mathbb{R}$, where $\mathcal{D}$ denotes the set of all possible datasets, the global sensitivity of q, denoted by Δ, is defined as

$$\Delta = \max_{\mathcal{D}_1 \sim \mathcal{D}_2} |q(\mathcal{D}_1) - q(\mathcal{D}_2)|$$

2.4 Secure Multi-Party Computation

Secure Multi-party security models involves multiple parties, collaborating to compute a common function of interest, without revealing their private inputs to other parties [13]. The protocol is considered secure if, at the end of the computation, parties learn nothing but the final result and no other information. Secure Aggregation is a class of Secure Multi-Party Computation algorithms wherein a group of mutually distrustful parties $u \in \mathcal{U}$ each hold a private value x_u and collaborate to compute the aggregate value(such as sum $\sum_{u \in \mathcal{U}} x_u$) without revealing to one another any information about their private values except what is learnable from the aggregate value itself [5, 7]. Secure aggregation in a federated learning setting presents its own unique set of challenges, which several recent works have tried to tackle [6, 22].

3   Case Study: Cross-Silo Automated Process Discovery

In Privacy-Preserving Distributed Process Discovery, our goal is to discover a global process model by privately mining multiple distributed process log independently and share only the resulting insights from each analysis. i.e. mining a differentially private process model, without ever pooling the data to a central site, in a way that reveals nothing but the final discovery process model to the participating organizations.

Challenges and Considerations: To develop a secure protocol for process discovery, where privacy is paramount, we have to consider a number of data, communication and privacy-related challenges. We briefly explain these challenges here:

Privacy is a first-order concern in our cross-silo federated learning setting [20,25]. The primary challenge is to protect data privacy by ensuring that there is no information leakage of individual entries held in the private databases of the participants. We also want to prevent individual participants from inferring and reconstructing private information from collective or intermediate results shared during protocol execution. Additionally, there is the challenge of collusion, where multiple participants might collaborate to reconstruct the sensitive data held by other participants. Second, no single participating client might own data which is a representative sample of the overall distribution. i.e. Participants might hold unbalanced distributions which means data points contributed by each individual may be highly skewed in terms of modalities, dimensionality and characteristics [17,25]. Lastly, if connected via internet, communication is often the primary bottleneck with low-throughput and high-latency connections. This requires techniques that can minimize the number of rounds of communication and reliably communicate the relevant frequency or aggregated statistics in an efficient fault-tolerant way.

We note that a solution that addresses all the constraints, and open challenges associated with designing a distributed Privacy-Preserving Protocol is not possible. Rather the characteristics of any proposed solution would be often a trade-off between privacy, efficiency and computational/communication complexity, where we try to ensure 'correctness' of the final mined model to a sufficient extent.

Problem Definition: Formally, the problem setting is described as follows: We are given a set of n participating clients nodes (or data owners) $\{\mathcal{F}_1, \ldots \mathcal{F}_N\}$, each with access to i.i.d or non.i.i.d event log data $\{\mathcal{E}_1, \ldots \mathcal{E}_N\}$. A typical process discovery algorithm would consolidate the logs $\mathcal{E} = \mathcal{E}_1 \cup \ldots \cup \mathcal{E}_N$ to discover a global model $\mathcal{M}_{global}$. Our goal is to discover a federated process model $\mathcal{M}_{FED}$ in a cross-silo setting, wherein each participating clients keeps its share of the data $\mathcal{E}_i = \{\mathbf{x}_1^i \cdots \mathbf{x}_{l_i}^i\}$ secure locally and private from server S. Our goal is to systematically address privacy concerns by building a Mechanism $M(x)$ that offers privacy guarantees while maintaining sufficient utility (measured by precision, recall and generalization).i.e. we want the utility of $\mathcal{M}_{FED}$ as close to $\mathcal{M}_{global}$. i.e. $|\mathcal{M}_{FED} - \mathcal{M}_{global}| < \delta$, where δ measures the accuracy loss.

Threat Model: To ensure our proposed protocol provides the required privacy properties, we first define the threat model which specifies the assumptions we are allowed to make. We consider the *honest-yet-curious* threat model (sometimes also referred to as the *semi-honest* threat model in literature) [25]. We consider the cross-silo federated learning setting where we assume each party faithfully follows the specified security protocol. i.e. Parties follows the protocol honestly without tampering, performing the necessary specified computations and communicating honest results to the co-ordinating server. Second, we assume that both participating clients and server are *honest-yet-curious* whereby they are able to passively observe intermediate results, and perform arbitrary processing on them to infer sensitive information about other participating contributors. Furthermore, participants involved in the computation can potentially collude by pooling their views together. Lastly, we assume the communication channel is secure. i.e. no participant can see observe data that is not directly communicated to it.

We note that ensuring privacy in case of public release of the final mined model is not within the scope of this work, rather our focus is on preserving privacy in the scenario of inter-organizational collaboration.

3.1   Method

In this section explain the technical workings and key execution steps protocol of our protocol. To designing our solution, we consider the computations involved for process discovery, the flow of information containing intermediate results during the process and the threat model (e.g. the actors involved in the computations and their roles). Federated Learning setting assumes that computation occurs in a distributed fashion across a number of interconnected nodes. i.e. We assume a hub-and-spoke topology, where hub represents a central organising server that orchestrates the mining process(but never sees the raw process data) and spokes connecting to the participating nodes [26].

We have designed our privacy preserving protocol for the task of *automated process discovery* in cross-silo setting where we assume the availability of a trusted aggregator(co-ordinating server), responsible for orchestrating the complete mining protocol. The server in this scenario has two roles. Firstly, it acts a central access point for all communication by routing messages between different parties and secondly, it computes the aggregation results in between various phases during protocol execution and acts as a custodian of intermediate results(or data structures) needed for computing the final shared process model. During execution each participant in the collaboration agrees on the function to be computed in a particular phase. Then each participant subsequently computes and returns a collection of relevant local statistics. The participating nodes communicate by message passing and a shared *Global process model* is mined(in a centrally differentially private way) under the coordination of a honest-but-curious server.

During execution, we address the privacy concerns, such that it becomes hard for a malicious party/adversary (under the described threat model) to potentially compromise the privacy of the individual client data by inferring specific details contained in the process logs. i.e. prevent any adversary from identifying information or linking items of interest to specific participants. To address the privacy concerns (defined under the threat model) and prevent many of the systematic privacy risks, we design our protocol by composing a number of privacy-preserving technologies such as *secure aggregation (SA)*, *Secure Union*, and *differential privacy* into an end-to-end solution that offers strong (worst-case) privacy properties. Federated Learning, follows the principle of focused collection and data minimization where, during protocol execution, focused statistics are shared with the server(stored ephemerally) and raw data never leaves the participating node's device [25]. Cryptographic secure aggregation on the other hand allows us the server to just learn aggregate function of the individual client contributions. Secure Aggregation, additionally protects the clients data from the trusted server that may have access to the memory of aggregator instances [4]. Lastly to obtain precise privacy guarantees, we integrated secure aggregation (SA) prototcol with a differential privacy mechanism such that the final result can satisfy the desired differential privacy properties for federated learning [15].

We have designed our solution by building upon the Heuristic miner algorithm [23] which works well in practical settings where event logs may contain noise and non-trivial constructs with a low degree of block structuredness [2]. We first provide a high-level summary of the mining process:

1. **Exchange Task List:** The mining process is initialized by a trusted server which is responsible for orchestrating the whole process of mining the distributed logs. The first step involves, constructing a set of all tasks appearing in the log using a secure set union protocol. Based on this task list, the server then initializes a *Direct successor matrix* (also known as a dependency matrix) and two *loop count matrices*(representing loops of length one and length two) with elements having an initial null value. The three initialized matrices are then broadcasted to each of the participants.

2. **Mining Global Direct Successor Matrix:** In the first phase our goal is to mine a *Global Dependency Graph*. This is done by each participant analyzing their own individual event log and populating the three matrices obtained from the previous step. To safely compute the sum of the an individual resulting matrices from each participant, we treat the problem as secure multi-party computation (MPC), where an aggregation protocol [6] is used to protect the values of the original matrices contributed by each of the participant.

3. **Generate loop count matrices:** Step 2 is repeated for mining *loop count matrices*, representing loops for length one and length two matrices.

4. **Compute Dependency Graph/Causal-Net:** In this step, the orchestrating server, receives the contributions of all participants and performs the merge of each of the three matrices. This results in a *Global Successor Matrix* and a *Global loop Count* Matrices to which the server applies various predefined frequency thresholds. To further protect the individual contributions, under the differential privacy model, server adds calibrated Gaussian noise to the resulting matrices. Collectively the three matrices are then used as input to generate a dependency graph. The dependency graph is translated to an aggregated causal-net(c-net) by the co-ordinating serer and distributed back to the participating clients for the next round of computations.

5. **Mining AND/OR Splits and Long-Term Dependencies:** In the second phase, Causal-net(C-net) and local logs are used by each participant as input to mine split/join relations. Similarly, in the last phase, we mine long-distance

dependency relations. To ensure differential privacy guarantees where individual inputs are statistically indistinguishable, each participant employs the secure aggregation protocol while the server perturbs the final values using a differential privacy mechanism.

3.2   Protocol Phase Details

We now discuss the three major mining phases that lead to process discovery in detail : *i) mining dependency graph, ii) mining AND/OR Splits* and *(iii) mining long term dependencies*. In each individual phase, the protocol executes in multiple rounds, and returns a shared process model. We provide the details of each phase below:

Phase I - Mining Dependency Graph: In the first phase, our goal is to mine a *dependency graph*(representing causal dependencies between tasks) from independent distributed logs of each participant. The *dependency graph* has been defined by Weijters et al. [24] as follows:

Definition 3: Dependency Graph [24]. The dependency graph is defined as $DG = \{(a, b) \mid (a \in E \land b \in a\square) \lor (b \in E \land a \in \square b)\}$. where E is the finite set of activities, for which events are recorded in the event log, $\square b$ denotes the activities preceding b, and $a\square$ consists of the activities succeeding a.

In order to build the *dependency graph*, we need to collect local statistics that capture dependency relations in each individual process log. This is done by constructing a *'direct successor'* frequency matrix(also known as dependency matrix) M_{ds} of dimension $n \times n$ that captures the dependency measures for each activity in the process log.

The starting point of Phase-I, is identifying a set of all common tasks appearing in process logs [24]. The mining process, therefore begins by computing a global *set of shared tasks* T. i.e. $T = \{t \mid \exists_{\sigma \in W+}[t \in \sigma]\}$ is a set containing all tasks appearing in all process logs of all the sites involved in the computation. To securely compute this list, we rely on the *secure union* algorithm proposed by Clifton et al. [7]. During execution, each site encrypts its local task list and adds them to the global task list. After removing dublicates, each site decrypts every item to get the union of items. Using this task list, the server constructs the structure of three matrices where first column and row represents are the task names. Each entry of these matrices is then intialized with a null value.

To populate these matrices, each participant $u \in \mathcal{U}$ receives a copy of *direct successor matrix*, with values initialized by the server. A frequency-based metric is used to capture the extent of dependency relation between two events A and B (represented by $a \Rightarrow_W b$). Each participant then populates the matrix by computing elements $M_{a,b}$(where a and b are two activities present in event log) of the matrix using the following definition [24]:

$$a \Rightarrow_W b = \left(\frac{|a >_W b| - |b >_W a|}{|a >_W b| + |b >_W a| + 1} \right)$$

The frequency metrics indicate the certainty level of a dependency relationship between two events a and b (high values indicate a strong relation). Following the FL paradigm, each party performs computations based on their private process logs and just shares the results of their site with the co-ordinating server.

Federated Mining via Secure Aggregation: Our next step involves aggregating locally-computed dependency matrices which will result in a *global dependency matrix* (where each entry represents an average of all the individual contributed values). To merge the matrices while limiting the amount of information that can be inferred during the mining process, we securely compute the sum of the local dependency matrices in a distributed manner by treating the problem as a special case of *Secure Multi-party Computation*. Specifically, we rely on *Secure Aggregation*, a Secure Multi-Party Computation protocol that uses encryption to hide the intermediate results (contribution) of individual participants from the co-ordinating server while only revealing the aggregate of input values at the end. The protocol allows us to mitigate the privacy concerns by analysing the multiple process logs separately and sharing only the resulting metrics (e.g. frequency statistics) from each analysis in a decentralised setting. In our collaborative federated learning setting, the co-ordinating server only learns participant's inputs in aggregate. To make the security notion concrete, in the context of secure multiparty computation protocol of *secure aggregation*, we consider the Real-Ideal Paradigm which is used in security literature to judge the security of a proposed protocol [12]. Formally, we define the security in the honest-yet curious MPC setting as follows [12]:

Definition 4 [12]. Let π be a protocol and $\mathcal{F}$ be a functionality. Let C be the set of parties that are corrupted, and let Sim denote a simulator algorithm. We define the following distributions of random variables:

- $\text{Real}_\pi(\kappa, C; x_1, \ldots, x_n)$: run the protocol with security parameter κ, where each party P_i runs the protocol honestly using private input x_i. Let V_i denote the final view of party P_i, and let y_i denote the final output of party P_i

- $\text{Ideal}_{\mathcal{F},\text{sim}}(\kappa, C; x_1, \ldots, x_n)$: Compute $(y_1, \ldots, y_n) \leftarrow \mathcal{F}(x_1, \ldots, x_n)$ Output $\text{Sim}(C, \{(x_i, y_i) \mid i \in C\}), (y_1, \ldots, y_n)$

Here the view of a participant is its privately held event long and messages received during the execution of protocol, while the view of an adversary consists of the combined views of all colluding parties [12]. Considering the real-ideal paradigm, a protocol is considered secure against semi-honest adversaries if the colluding parties in the real world have views that are indistinguishable from their views in the ideal world.

Definition 5 [12]. A protocol π securely realizes $\mathcal{F}$ in the presence of semi-honest adversaries if there exists a simulator Sim such that, for every subset of corrupt parties C and all inputs $x_1, \ldots, x_n$, the distributions $\text{Real}_\pi(\kappa, C; x_1, \ldots, x_n)$ and $\text{Ideal}_{\mathcal{F},\text{Sim}}(\kappa, C; x_1, \ldots, x_n)$ are indistinguishable (in κ).

Several secure aggregations protocols exist and we specifically picked the one proposed by Bonawitz et al. [6]. Their proposed protocol is considered state-of-the art and is tailored to work in a cross-siloed federated learning setting (under our threat model) where we deal with high-dimensional vectors. The protocol is also robust from a communication point of view, as it can recover from failure during protocol execution if participants drop out. It consists of *four rounds* and is run in a synchronous network between a *single server* S and a set of n participating organizations. The server acts as a coordinator and *aggregates* inputs from n parties $U_1, \ldots, U_n$ each holding their locally generated direct successor matrix, $M_{ds(1)}, \ldots, M_{ds(n)}$. The goal of the protocol is to compute $\sum_{u \in \mathcal{U}} M_{ds(u)}$ in a secure fashion, providing a guarantee that the server only learns a sum of the clients' inputs containing contributions from each participating client organizations. To illustrate the workings of the protocol we explain the steps for the *direct successor* matrix case:

We assume that the elements $M_{a,b}$ of $M_{ds(u)}$ and $\sum_{u \in \mathcal{U}} M_{ds(u)}$ are in $\mathbb{Z}_R$ for some R. The process initiates by grouping the participating clients into pairs that agree on a matched pair of input perturbations(exchanged over a secure channel). Formally, we refer to these perturbations as *one-time masks* which consist of random matrices $S_{u,v}$ of size $n \times n$ with elements selected uniformly from $[0, R)^k$. Each participating client computes the direct successor matrix, along with masking matrix and sends y_u to the server. The server computes $\sum_{u \in \mathcal{U}} y_u$ where the *paired masks* will be canceled out, when their matrices are added together, but their actual original direct successor matrix(contributed by each organisation) will not be revealed [6].

$$z = \sum_{u \in \mathcal{U}} y_u$$

$$= \sum_{u \in \mathcal{U}} \left(M_{ds(u)} + \sum_{v \in \mathcal{U}:u<v} s_{u,v} - \sum_{v \in \mathcal{U}:u>v} s_{v,u} \right)$$

$$= \sum_{u \in \mathcal{U}} M_{ds(u)} \pmod{R}$$

The relatively simple approach of masking with *one time pads* works well in an ideal environment. However, in practice we face several privacy and communication efficiency issues. To mitigate these, Bonawitz et al. [6] have proposed several modifications, which we will describe here:

Firstly, the $O\left(kn^2\right)$ communication overhead can be reduced by having the participants agreeing on common seeds instead of $S_{u,v}$ using a cryptographically secure pseudorandom generator (PRG). Here each participant generates Diffie-Hellman secret key and public keys(to reach a key agreement) which are signed and sent to the server [6]. The server broadcasts these keys to all participants which allows participants to agree on a secret and for server to maintain a consistent view of each user state.

Secondly, there might occur cases where participating organizations might dropout in the middle of protocol execution which poses privacy risks. To solve this Bonawitz et al. [6] propose a (t, n)- threshold secret sharing scheme where each participant computes t-out-of-n secret shares for their Diffie-Hellman secret using a (t, n) - threshold scheme and sending it to all users. This makes it possible for a server to recover pairwise seeds even if some clients dropout, so long as some of the active participants respond with the shares of dropped keys. Lastly, to protect individual data in scenarios of high latency connection where users might appear dropped out and server can learn M_{ds} . To counter this threat, a double masking structure is used, where participants cryptographically upload individually mined *masked* matrices and the co-ordinating server accumulates a sum of the masked individual contributions [6]. We note that another added benefit of double masking approach is that it protects us from a compromised server.

$$y_u = M_{ds(u)} + \mathbf{PRG}\,(b_u)$$
$$+ \sum_{v \in \mathcal{U}:u<v} \mathbf{PRG}\,(s_{u,v})$$
$$- \sum_{v \in \mathcal{U}:u>v} \mathbf{PRG}\,(s_{v,u}) \quad (\mathrm{mod}\ R)$$

In the unmasking round, participants reveal sufficient cryptographic secrets, allowing the server to reveal the sum. For dropped users at least t shares of $s_{u,v}$ are required while t shares of b_u for all active users are sufficient for server to subtract off the remaining masks. We refer the reader to [6] for a more detailed description of the above Secure Aggregation protocol.

Using the described secure aggregation primitive, the server is able to privately combine outputs of local dependency matrices, by computing element-wise averages, resulting in a *Global Dependency Matrix*. Note that, in some scenarios, it might make sense to take a weighted average. e.g. in case of intra-organization Process discovery where each individual contribution is highly unbalanced. Next, same steps will be repeated for securely computing matrices M_{L1} and M_{L2} representing length-one loops and length-two loops respectively. Global loop count matrices are securely computed in a manner similar to the Global dependency matrix. Elements of these matrices are computed by applying using following equations [24]:

$$a \Rightarrow_W a = \left(\frac{|a >_W a|}{|a >_W a| + 1} \right)$$

$$a \Rightarrow_W^2 b = \left(\frac{|a >>_W b| + |b >>_W a|}{|a >>_W b| + |b >>_W a| + 1} \right)$$

Pruning Using Thresholds: After the server computes the aggregates, we select a frequency based metric approach where we apply three kinds of thresholds to select the strongest connections between events. We can apply *threshold parameters* to get rid of uncertain dependency relations(possibly caused by noise in the dataset) and retain values of dependency measure which represent an acceptable(strong) dependency relation. Heuristic Miner provides, threshold parameters such as Dependency threshold, length one-two threshold and length n threshold which help in deciding if a dependency relation is incorporated in the final dependency graph, exists or not. After applying these thresholds, the server is able to take the *global dependency matrix* and construct a *dependency graph*. This completes the four-round interactive protocol.

Generating a Differentially Private Dependency Graph: Secure aggregation protocol protects the computation inputs from exposure to the server, however does not formally guarantee that the final result of distributed computation, if shared with participants, would not leak any information about an individual in a sensitive process log. i.e. we want to prevent any participant from being able to reconstruct the private data of another participant by exploiting the global shared matrix. Additionally, there is also the risk of collusion, where multiple parties can collaborate to reconstruct the private data of another client by exploiting the final output (global dependency matrix).

To address these challenges, we rely on client-level differential privacy [15] as a second defence mecahnism, which offers information theoretic guarantees and a relatively simple approach for achieving the desired level of privacy. Formally, let us consider a scenario where we want to publish in a differentially private way the output of a function f (e.g. aggregation function that computes the global dependency model). Differential privacy offers a standard privacy-preserving solution, whereby sufficient Gaussian noise(enough to mask the contribution of a single participant) is added to the output value of f, in order to prevent any leakage about a single individual and mitigate any privacy risks. Formally we describe it as follows [1,11] :

Definition 6. Given any function $f : \mathbb{N}^{|X|} \to \mathbb{R}^k$, the mechanism is a Laplace Mechanism $\mathcal{M}$ if:

$$\mathcal{M}(x) = f(x) + \eta$$

where $x \in X$ and η is a vector of independent and identically distributed random variables drawn from $\text{Lap}(\Delta f/\varepsilon)$.

Definition 7. For a function $f : D \to R^k$, sensitivity of f is

$$\Delta f = \max_{D,D'} \| f(D) - f(D') \,|$$

for all D, D' differing in at most one element. The global sensitivity of a function is determined the maximum change in output when the input differs in a single entry [1].

Following the above definitions, our goal here is to share in a differentially private way, the output of our mining function f, that computes the dependency graph. To achieve differential privacy, orchestrating server would serve as the trusted implementer of a differential mechanism, whereby each entry of the output *global dependency matrix* is perturbed using noise drawn from the symmetric Laplacian distribution with scale $\lambda = \frac{\Delta}{\epsilon}$. The zero-mean Laplacian distribution has a symmetric probability density function $f(x)$ with a scale parameter λ defined as [11]:

$$f(x) = \frac{1}{2\lambda} e^{-\frac{|x|}{\lambda}}$$

We ensure that noise is enough to hide any single client's contributions. The dependency graph can be easily transformed the into a causal net (A, I, O) where A is a finite set of activities, $I : A \rightarrow \mathcal{P}(\mathcal{P}(A))$ is the input pattern function and $O : A \rightarrow \mathcal{P}(\mathcal{P}(A))$ is the output pattern function [23]. The server broadcasts the resulting differentially-private causal-net to the participants. This concludes the Phase-I of our protocol.

Phase II-III: Mining Split/Join Relations and Long Term Dependencies. In Phase II, our goal is to mine, for each task in the dependency graph, the different split and join patterns. First, each participant receives a copy of causal-net(equivalent of dependency graph) mined in the previous step. Using local event log, each participating client mines statistics about the ordering of the tasks. This is done by using the following equation which computes a control-flow metric for each activity in the process log while considering its corresponding two elements in the input or output set [23]:

$$a \Rightarrow_W b \wedge c = \left(\frac{|b >_W c| + |c >_W b|}{|a >_W b| + |a >_W c| + 1} \right)$$

The value obtained from applying this definition determines if activities b and c are for example in an AND-relation or in a XOR-relation with respect to activity a.

Similar to Phase-II, we now mine long-term dependency relations that identifies instances in which a task a depends indirectly on another task b for execution. Such relations characterize the split or join decision point, which is determined by decisions made elsewhere in the process. Follow equation, lets us determine the frequency-based metric used to determine these relationships [24]:

$$a \Rightarrow_W^l b = \left(\frac{2 \left(|a >>>_W b| \right)}{|a| + |b| + 1} \right) - \left(\frac{2 \, Abs(|a| - |b|)}{|a| + |b| + 1} \right)$$

Much of the intuition behind the algorithm and privacy guarantees we presented in the previous section applies to Phase II and Phase III. The individual entries are protected by utilizing secure aggregation protocol discussed in the previous section and the final output is perturbed by introducing privacy-preserving noise (using any of the well-known DP mechanisms) before broadcasting the final results.

Noise Calibration: Using any differential privacy techniques is a trade-off between utility and privacy. To achieve optimal utility, we have to ensure that the injected noise is carefully calibrated [10]. We perform two additional steps where we carefully chose the noise distribution to add just add enough noise that achieves differential privacy while ensuring highest possible utility. First, we employ an algorithmic noise calibration strategy which allows us to calibrate the noise of our Gaussian perturbation mechanism, to the match the sensitivity of a given function f. Here we employ numerical evaluations of the Gaussian cumulative density function (CDF) to obtain the optimal variance which results in ϵ-differential privacy [3]. In the second step, we perform post-processing which denoises the output using an adaptive estimation technique allowing us to improve the accuracy of each shared individual entry [3].

This concludes the protocol execution steps. The server may finally apply a pre-defined *relative to best* and *positive observation* threshold to ensure there are no disconnected activities and broadcast the final global process model.

4   Conclusion

Distributed data mining and machine learning is a longstanding goal pursued by many research communities (including cryptography, databases, and machine learning) [16]. We believe that FL holds significant potential for enabling disruptive innovations in developing privacy-preserving process analytics solutions. FL based solutions would disrupt the traditional cloud computing model and enable organizations to create a data alliance where mining private data would be a common practice. Our case study demonstrates how the promise of FL can be turned into practical process analytic methods that can combine knowledge learned from non-co-located data. Our proposed approach is also illustrative of a general-purpose methodology that will allow future researchers to develop federated learning, based, privacy-preserving solutions capable of solving many of the existing key process mining problems in distributed settings, where privacy is a major concern.

References

1. Acs, G., Castelluccia, C.: Dream: Differentially private smart metering. arXiv preprint arXiv:1201.2531 (2012)
2. Augusto, A., et al.: Automated discovery of process models from event logs: review and benchmark. IEEE Trans. Knowl. Data Eng. **31**(4), 686–705 (2018)
3. Balle, B., Wang, Y.X.: Improving the gaussian mechanism for differential privacy: analytical calibration and optimal denoising. In: International Conference on Machine Learning, pp. 394–403. PMLR (2018)
4. Bonawitz, K., et al.: Towards federated learning at scale: System design. arXiv preprint arXiv:1902.01046 (2019)
5. Bonawitz, K., et al.: Practical secure aggregation for federated learning on user-held data. arXiv preprint arXiv:1611.04482 (2016)
6. Bonawitz, K., et al.: Practical secure aggregation for privacy-preserving machine learning. In: proceedings of the 2017 ACM SIGSAC Conference on Computer and Communications Security, pp. 1175–1191 (2017)
7. Clifton, C., Kantarcioglu, M., Vaidya, J., Lin, X., Zhu, M.Y.: Tools for privacy preserving distributed data mining. ACM Sigkdd Explorations Newsletter **4**(2), 28–34 (2002)
8. Dunkl, R., Fröschl, K.A., Grossmann, W., Rinderle-Ma, S.: Assessing medical treatment compliance based on formal process modeling. In: Holzinger, A., Simonic, K.-M. (eds.) USAB 2011. LNCS, vol. 7058, pp. 533–546. Springer, Heidelberg (2011). https://doi.org/10.1007/978-3-642-25364-5_37

9. Dwork, C., Kenthapadi, K., McSherry, F., Mironov, I., Naor, M.: Our data, ourselves: privacy via distributed noise generation. In: Vaudenay, S. (ed.) EUROCRYPT 2006. LNCS, vol. 4004, pp. 486–503. Springer, Heidelberg (2006). https://doi.org/10.1007/11761679_29
10. Dwork, C., McSherry, F., Nissim, K., Smith, A.: Calibrating noise to sensitivity in private data analysis. In: Halevi, S., Rabin, T. (eds.) TCC 2006. LNCS, vol. 3876, pp. 265–284. Springer, Heidelberg (2006). https://doi.org/10.1007/11681878_14
11. Dwork, C., Roth, A., et al.: The algorithmic foundations of differential privacy. Found. Trends Theor. Comput. Sci. 9(3–4), 211–407 (2014)
12. Evans, D., Kolesnikov, V., Rosulek, M.: A pragmatic introduction to secure multiparty computation. Foundations and Trends® in Privacy and Security, vol. 2, no. 2–3 (2017)
13. Goldreich, O., Micali, S., Wigderson, A.: How to play any mental game, or a completeness theorem for protocols with honest majority. In: Providing Sound Foundations for Cryptography: On the Work of Shafi Goldwasser and Silvio Micali, pp. 307–328 (2019)
14. Jensen, P.B., Jensen, L.J., Brunak, S.: Mining electronic health records: towards better research applications and clinical care. Nat. Rev. Genet. 13(6), 395–405 (2012)
15. Kairouz, P., Liu, Z., Steinke, T.: The distributed discrete gaussian mechanism for federated learning with secure aggregation. arXiv preprint arXiv:2102.06387 (2021)
16. Kairouz, P., et al.: Advances and open problems in federated learning. arXiv preprint arXiv:1912.04977 (2019)
17. Konečný, J., McMahan, H.B., Ramage, D., Richtárik, P.: Federated optimization: Distributed machine learning for on-device intelligence. arXiv preprint arXiv:1610.02527 (2016)
18. Lang, M., Bürkle, T., Laumann, S., Prokosch, H.U.: Process mining for clinical workflows: challenges and current limitations. In: MIE, vol. 136, pp. 229–234 (2008)
19. Lenz, R., Reichert, M.: It support for healthcare processes-premises, challenges, perspectives. Data Knowl. Eng. 61(1), 39–58 (2007)
20. McSherry, F., Talwar, K.: Mechanism design via differential privacy. In: 48th Annual IEEE Symposium on Foundations of Computer Science (FOCS'07), pp. 94–103. IEEE (2007)
21. Ramage, D.: Federated analytics: Collaborative data science without data collection (2020). https://ai.googleblog.com/2020/05/federated-analytics-collaborative-data.html
22. So, J., Güler, B., Avestimehr, A.S.: Turbo-aggregate: breaking the quadratic aggregation barrier in secure federated learning. IEEE J. Selected Areas Inform. Theor. 2(1), 479–489 (2021)
23. Weijters, A., van Der Aalst, W.M., De Medeiros, A.A.: Process mining with the heuristics miner-algorithm. Technische Universiteit Eindhoven, Technical report, WP, vol. 166, pp. 1–34 (2006)
24. Weijters, A., Ribeiro, J.T.S.: Flexible heuristics miner (fhm). In: 2011 IEEE Symposium on Computational Intelligence and Data Mining (CIDM), pp. 310–317. IEEE (2011)
25. Yang, Q., Liu, Y., Chen, T., Tong, Y.: Federated machine learning: concept and applications. ACM Transactions on Intelligent Systems and Technology (TIST) 10(2), 1–19 (2019)
26. Zhu, W., Kairouz, P., McMahan, B., Sun, H., Li, W.: Federated heavy hitters discovery with differential privacy. In: International Conference on Artificial Intelligence and Statistics, pp. 3837–3847. PMLR (2020)

Application-Platform Co-design
for Serverless Data Processing

Sebastian Werner[✉] and Stefan Tai

Information Systems Engineering, Technische Universität Berlin, Berlin, Germany
{sw,st}@ise.tu-berlin.de

Abstract. "Application-platform co-design" refers to the phenomenon of new platforms being created in response to changing application needs, followed by application design and development changing due to the emergence (and the specifics, limitations) of the new platforms, therefore creating, again, new application and platform requirements. This continuous process of application and platform (re-)design describes an engineering and management responsibility to constantly evaluate any given platform for application fit and platform-specific application design, and to consider a new or evolutionary platform development project due to evolving and changing application needs.

In this paper, we study this phenomenon in the context of serverless computing and (big) data processing needs, and thus, for application-platform co-design for serverless data processing (SDP). We present an analysis of the state-of-the-art of function-as-a-service (FaaS) platforms, which reveals several configuration, deployment, execution, and measurement differences between popular platforms happening at-speed. These differences indicate already ongoing platform (re-)design processes resulting in more specialized serverless platforms and new, platform-specific challenges for application design. We discuss data processing needs of applications using the serverless model and present common initial (and undesirable) workaround solutions on the application level, giving additional argument to the creation of new SDP platforms. We present critical SDP requirements and possible new platform augmentations, but identify the need for engineering methods and tooling to better guide application-platform co-design. We argue to pay appropriate attention to the phenomenon of continuous application-platform co-design to better anticipate and to control future platform and application developments.

Keywords: Platform design and development · Platform-specific application design and development · Co-design · Serverless computing · Serverless data processing

1 Introduction

Traditionally, new software platforms were created in response to new application demands, such as specific elasticity or big data processing requirements. Once a new platform is in place, application design and development on top of

© Springer Nature Switzerland AG 2021
H. Hacid et al. (Eds.): ICSOC 2021, LNCS 13121, pp. 627–640, 2021.
https://doi.org/10.1007/978-3-030-91431-8_39

the platform has to take the platform features, specifics, and constraints into account. Often, the impact of a new platform on application design and development is significant. And in turn, new application requirements are created as a result, which, again, may suggest the development of a new (variant of the) software platform.

Notably, the advent of NoSQL database systems serves as an example for this phenomenon of application-platform co-design. Originally initiated by data processing and concurrency needs of large enterprises, system designs like, Google's GFS [8] and Amazon's DynamoDB [6] fueled an explosion of numerous (ca. over 250) new, NoSQL data storage platforms over the last decades. Today, a developer can choose between a magnitude of managed and self-managed data storage systems that can meet almost every niche application requirement. But each platform, however, may provide different data consistency guarantees, shifting data synchronization or conflict resolution, for example, from the platform to the application as a new application responsibility.

Analogously, the way we run applications on cloud platforms has been evolving significantly and at-speed, too. Web services can be deployed on elasticity managed VMs, with sophisticated container orchestration platforms such as Kubernetes, or using tiny micro-VMs in a serverless setting. Modern cloud platforms, thus, already support a plethora of ways a developer can deploy, scale, and run web-serving applications.

The same application-platform co-design phenomenon can be observed, too, within the field of serverless computing. With serverless computing, the basic idea is to free application developers from responsibilities related to elasticity, deployment, and monitoring, that is, from almost any operational task. Current serverless platforms, specifically Function-as-a-Service (FaaS) offerings, have rapidly changed and improved since their early introduction in 2014. The initial one-size-fits-all model suggested with serverless computing has already, almost in the background, started to shift, and several variants of serverless platforms serving different application needs than just simple web-serving tasks have emerged [11,27].

Specifically, distributed data processing [5,7,22] shows to benefit from the serverless computing model and its extreme scalability, low operational overhead, work-based billing model, and overall simplicity. Moreover, classical data processing frameworks, e.g., Apache Spark, Hive, and Apache Flink, require data analysts to deploy, configure, and operate clusters of servers and thus require developer responsibility for operational tasks that can impose considerable and potential disastrous entry barriers [29] to anyone that needs to analyze data. Serverless data processing frameworks, such as Lithops [23] and Pywren [12] aim to reduce such entry barriers by providing data processing APIs with similar abstractions to classical frameworks without upfront cluster management needs.

Be it NoSQL stores, cloud platforms, FaaS offerings, or data processing solutions, the continuous cycle of application-platform co-design has led and is still leading to an abundance of platforms, some of which differ only in details, and some of which differ significantly. This introduces the continuous need to question the application fit of any given platform, to design applications in a platform-specific manner, or, to develop a new general-purpose or application-specific platform (variant). As a consequence, software engineering requires increasing attention to be paid to the diverse phenomena of application-platform co-design.

In this paper, we study and discuss application-platform co-design for serverless data processing. Based on an analysis of the current state of serverless platforms, we highlight areas where current platforms are already differentiating themselves from each other. Further, we discuss data processing needs of applications using the serverless computing model and present common initial, but undesirable workaround solutions on the application level, giving additional argument to the creation of new serverless data processing (SDP) platforms. We present critical SDP requirements and possible new platform augmentations, but identify the need for engineering methods and tooling to better guide application-platform co-design. We argue to pay appropriate attention to the phenomenon of continuous application-platform co-design.

2   Serverless Computing Platforms

Let us first take a closer look at the current state of serverless computing platforms. In this section, we specifically compare the popular FaaS offerings of the four major cloud providers Amazon, Google, Microsoft and IBM, and highlight both similarities and differences.

Cloud-based FaaS offerings, the most widely adopted form of serverless computing, ask developers only to define applications through arbitrary function code and triggering event definitions. The cloud provider is responsible for deploying, running, and scaling these functions in response to arriving events. For all cloud providers, developers can select from a set of predefined runtime environments and only manage few additional configurations, such as setting memory limits, maximum concurrency and environment variables. Thus, all current FaaS offerings enable almost operations free delivery of stateless serverless applications. However, current offerings still lack support for state management, hardware acceleration and suitable programming abstractions [18, 25] to support any cloud-based application, although platform vendors already started to differentiate themselves by addressing these and other open serverless challenges [13].

At first sight, from a developer perspective, all platforms provide a similar programming interface and execution model. Thus, in theory, the choice of a specific serverless computing platform should not significantly affect the application design. However, taking a closer look, the available configuration space, runtime isolation, platform limitations and auxiliary services can differ substantially between the different platforms, and thus, careful developer consideration is a must.

Table 1. Configuration, deployment, execution, and measurement differences in FaaS

		AWS	GCF	ICF	ACF	Source
Configuration	min. Mem. [MB]	128	128	128	N.A.	Docs
	max. Mem. [MB]	10240	8192	2048	14336	Docs
	Memory Space [#]	10112	7	1920	14336	Docs
	Timeout [s]	900	540	60	600	Docs
	vCPU Cores [#]	6	1	?	4	Docs
	CPU [GHz]	2.5	4.8	?	2.4	Docs
	max Concurrency [#]	1000+	1000	1000+	VM*100	Docs
Deployment	Trigger [#]	8	6	3+	4+	Docs
	Supported Runtimes [#]	15+	13	8+	7	Docs
	Dependency management	Layers	Files	Docker/Files	Files	Docs
	max. Size [MB]	250	500	48	−1	Docs
	Host controllable	No	No	No	Yes	Docs
Execution	Isolation	firecracker	gVisor	VM+runc	VM	Docs
	Event scheduling	Push-based	Unknown	Push-based	Pull-based	[2]
	Local storage [MB]	512	0	0	143360	Docs
	Network Storage [Y/N]	Yes	No	No	Yes	Docs
	Private networking [Y/N]	Yes	Yes	No	Yes	Docs
	Function networking [Y/N]	Unsupported	Unsupported	Unsupported	Yes	Docs
	Tracing [Y/N]	Yes	Yes	No	No	[4]
	Function Metrics [Y/N]	Yes	Yes	Yes	Yes	[4]
	Cloud Logs [Y/N]	Yes	Yes	Yes	Yes	[4]
	Billing Interval [time]	1 ms	100 ms	100 ms	100 ms-1 h	Docs
	Threads [#]	1024	unknown	1024	varies	Docs
	Connections [#]	1024	unknown	1024	600	Docs
	Payload Size [MB]	6	10		100	Docs
	Rate limit	10 × 1000 /s	100 MB/s	84/s	unmanaged	Docs
Meas.	Configiruation Chages [ms]	996	36630	22	521100	[16]
	Cold Start Variance [ms]	9	4900	10528	83691	[17]
	Cold default throughput [trps]	120	120	120	5	[17]

Further, larger applications built as serverless systems do not consist of a single function but a composition of functions and other services. The available platform services for function composition and orchestration differ significantly.

2.1   Platform Comparison

Table 1 provides a comparative overview of the serverless computing platforms from Amazon (AWS), Google (GCF), IBM (ICF) and Microsoft (ACF). We compare these platforms along four general categories: First, configuration options – all exposed "tuning knobs" a developer can control; second, deployment options – e.g., available runtimes and deployment environments; and third, execution criteria – important criteria for function execution and existing limits. Finally, we also provide some basic metrics and measurements that indicate platform qualities such as performance or elasticity.

Configuration reveals two principle models: AWS, GCF, and ICF expose developers to a singular, highly sensitive performance-related sizing parameter.

On the other end, AWS offers over 10.000 unique settings to control performance. GCF, in contrast, presents only seven options. This singular parameter affects multiple resource sizes simultaneously, e.g., memory, network bandwidth, available threads. Hiding many complex resource configurations behind a singular value leads to the need for sizing tools. With Azure, however, the ability to select from different VM offerings as a back-end for serverless workloads exists and so, the sizing problem is different.

Deployment options are similar for all platforms under comparison. While the number of selectable runtimes differs, the most common programming languages are supported by all platforms. A major difference, however, relates to dependency management. The limited allowance for deployment package sizes (between 50-500MB) and the management of dependency versions has led some platform provides to offer more advanced features for dependency management. Among them, AWS allows developers to build shareable layers that multiple functions can reuse. IBM's OpenWhisk opened the runtime API to enable developers to define complete docker images with all dependencies built-in to address this issue.

Execution in serverless computing platforms is based on three main factors: Function isolation, assignment of invocations (execution guarantees), and invocation triggering.

For isolation, AWS uses firecracker [1], a KVM based micro-VM. Thus, each function is strongly isolated while removing comparably long startup times of classical VMs. Google uses gVisor, a form of OS-level isolation that shares common roots with AWS firecracker but is also used for other Google services and thus is less specialized. ICF and Azure use a VM per user to isolate functions. Thus, functions might interfere with the execution of other functions of the same user while not interfering with functions of other users. Here, the scaling of functions depends on the time it takes to launch new VMs per customer.

Besides isolation, the assignment of events to functions is different between these platforms. For AWS, GCF and ICF, we see a pull-based approach: free hosts will pull available events. Azure, on the other hand, uses a push-based approach, which can impact elasticity.

Lastly, all platforms offer means to trigger functions synchronously and asynchronously. However, the number of available options to trigger functions can differ. For instance, AWS provides triggers for most database services. At the same time, other platforms such as ACF or ICF give developers only a few endpoints to trigger functions synchronously or asynchronously.

2.2 Vendor Directions

The comparison shows that the current landscape of serverless platforms shares a common programming and operations model, while at the same time, revealing notable differences with respect to limitations and configurable resources between platforms.

Some recent platform (re-)design efforts taken by cloud providers further include introductions of additional platform services and features to overcome identified shortcomings. For example, Microsoft recently introduced durable functions, a programming model to store function states after execution. Similarly, Amazon recently added the Elastic File System (EFS) for Lambda, thus enabling functions to persist data across multiple executions, multiple function-deployments and between parallel invocations.

Vendors are constantly differentiating their offerings and as a consequence, the initial common programming model shared between multiple platforms diverges into diverse, different models, making it nearly impossible to switch platforms later on. Moreover, the larger serverless research and practitioners' community has started to propose novel changes for FaaS platforms as well, addressing some of the most commonly identified serverless shortcomings [10], again resulting in diverse platform developments.

3   Serverless Data Processing

Let us now look into modern applications' data processing needs and how these translate into serverless data processing (SDP) requirements.

3.1   System Requirements

We conducted a series of experiments related to serverless computing and (big) data processing, initially presented in 2018 [29] and continued with [15–17] and [28]. From these lessons learned, we define the following serverless data processing system (platform and application) requirements:

1. **Scaleable**: A serverless data processing system should use the scalability potential of a serverless platform and adapt the resource demands of each computation to the task. Further, the system should have comparable performance characteristics as conventional data processing solutions (such as an Apache Spark Cluster) of similar cost and size.
2. **Fully-Serverless**: The serverless data processing system should be fully serverless, that is, the serverless data processing system should be able to scale down to zero if no resources are needed. Thus, the system should not incur costs or management tasks if idle (an exception can be made for storing input data). Further, the analyst should not know the inner workings of the used services, such as avoiding cold-starts or selecting the optimal size of AWS S3 files for Lambda.
3. **Self-Contained**: The system should be self-contained. Specifically, the system should handle deployment, re-execution of faulty invocations or re-configuration of wrongly sized execution environments.
4. **Tuneable**: The system should allow developers to define high-level objectives for each computation, such as low cost or fast computation time. The system should drive all configurations and executions based on these high-level tunables.

5. **Integratable**: Modern data processing applications need to combine multiple tools, programs and algorithms for pre/post-processing to appropriately integrate with all relevant business processes. Thus, the system should allow for arbitrary, yet performance-aware pre/post-processing integration.

Serverless data processing platforms should be as versatile as conventional data processing solutions such as Apache Spark or Apache Flink. However, not all use-cases will benefit equally from the properties of serverless data processing [10]. We observe that SDP is most useful for ad-hoc analytics [28], tasks such as data cleaning, data inspections, as well as IoT scenarios such as predictive maintenance or troubleshooting. Similarly, exploratory data analytics relevant in pre-processing of machine learning [24] can benefit well from the ad-hoc processing capabilities of SDP. Further, tasks that only require infrequent processing, such as indexing for data lakes, also benefit from the fast deployment and redeployment of processing resources in the serverless model.

3.2   Common Application Workarounds

Multiple SDP frameworks have emerged in the last four years [5,12,22,23]. Naturally, the complexity of available programming interfaces has increased and different options exist to address the serverless data processing requirements identified above.

The most common trend, however, still present in all SDP frameworks, is the use of workarounds to overcome known platform limitations.

Serverless job orchestration involves the generation of invocations for each task in a processing job, waiting on the completion of these invocations and the collection or redistribution of task results. Each of these steps can be addressed in different ways. A driver can generate events asynchronously (the most common approach), thus, only submitting tasks to the serverless platform. In that case, the driver now has to query the platform repeatedly to observe each task. This design forces an extensive network and request overhead to enable drivers to observe functions in real-time.

Alternatively, each invocation can be performed synchronously, removing the need to constantly poll for results but, in turn, limiting the maximum number of concurrent invocations a single driver can manage. Most platforms require that each synchronous invocation contains a single event and thus requires a driver to open as many connections as functions should run in parallel. With this strategy, it is virtually impossible to reach the scalability potential of state of the art serverless platforms.

A third option is to use a platform-specific orchestration mechanism, such as a workflow engine, for example, AWS Step-Functions. However, current platform-specific orchestration mechanisms are all geared for orchestrating a flow of events through a tree of different functions rather than facilitating a highly parallel execution of few functions. On top of that, each mechanism increases management and configuration overhead and makes migration to other platforms far more work-intensive.

A fourth strategy that we see is to spawn functions without specific instructions. Instead, each function connects to an external service to pull tasks from a shared task queue [5]. This approach removes the need to observe the completion of functions through the serverless platform and can use a lightweight mechanisms to launch many functions in parallel. However, at the cost of introducing new external dependencies that are difficult to maintain, to scale and that typically are not serverless, fundamental requirements of serverless data processing may be broken.

Serverless state management in serverless data processing is divided into two major sub-problems, intermediate storage and data access. Essentially, both intermediate data storage, data ingestion and saving results involve an external state management system. Here, frameworks commonly use an object store such as Amazon's S3 or a managed message queue system. However, these systems introduce latency and network overhead for each computation. As an added complication, each function has to manage the connection to the storage regardless of the selected back end, thus, introducing added overhead per function and many more sources for errors to occur. It is further unclear if the selected storage-backends are well suited to transport the type of ephemeral data efficiently.

Serverless uniformity also creates a challenge for framework designers. In most cases, a framework will deploy one function per task or sometimes even a single function for all tasks in a processing job. Thus, the sizing of that function must always fit the largest part of a task to ensure that a computation does not run out of memory or takes too long. Consequently, serverless processing systems either struggle with processing skew or otherwise heterogeneous data or waste a significant amount of resources. The fact that platforms do not allow applications to implement custom failure recovery mechanisms, such as temporary increasing resource limits, to address these issues means that application developers need to find other solutions.

Additionally, we observe that the cold-start of functions is impacted by both memory size selection and deployment package size [21]. Thus, the design of current SDP frameworks must take both runtime size and sizing into account to address cold-start issues. Therefore, it should come as no surprise that most of these frameworks target AWS Lambda, as it is the most flexible platform in terms of runtime environments, deployment sizes, and memory sizes. However, it remains to be seen if platform improvements can be equally or even better provided for Azure, Google or IBM SDP platforms.

Serverless support eco-system describes the problem of selecting appropriate services to augment missing features in the serverless compute platform. Most frameworks rely on one or more additional cloud-based infrastructure services to fully support each processing step. Thus, selecting a suitable service can often impact the overall performance, manageability and cost of a framework. These auxiliary services often differ significantly between vendors, making the portability of these frameworks problematic as well. Moreover, are these auxiliary services are rarely designed for serverless workloads and serverless data processing workloads. In particular, the usage for orchestration or data transfer is often inefficiently supported or could easily break if vendors decide to change service properties without serverless workloads in mind. Consequently, the design of serverless data processing systems is strongly dependent on the selected cloud platform and the composition of available auxiliary services and serverless computing resources.

3.3   Next Steps

Current SDP applications, unsurprisingly, already utilize existing FaaS platforms and SDP frameworks quite well. However, as discussed above, there are many specifics and platform and programming model limitations that quickly lead to potentially significant design inefficiencies and platform lock-in. Applications need to adapt to platform evolution and welcome desirable innovations, such as higher-level programming abstractions. While early SDP frameworks only supported bare-bone map-reduce, the more recent frameworks start to support higher-level APIs and query languages. Nevertheless, the prominent presence of many workarounds as described above, and the use of auxiliary services that were never intended to serve as a backbone to highly parallel computations, creates a significant risk regarding the usage of current SDP frameworks.

4   Towards Guided Co-design

We expect serverless platforms and current serverless data processing applications to continue to evolve to fully support all serverless data processing requirements. To this end, we envision current limitations and workarounds to be replaced by solutions that require new platform augmentations. At the same time, we see the need for new engineering methods and tooling to better guide platform and application re-design and evolution.

4.1   New Platform Augmentations

We can identify function orchestration, intermediate data transfer, and straggling executions as the most pressing issues in the SDP context requiring new platform augmentations. In the following, we revisit the undesirable workarounds presented in Sect. 3.2 and discuss how platform augmentations, or the selection of new platform features, can remove these issues while remaining true to the serverless data processing model.

Our discussion and recommendations are based on own prior and other related work, including both exploratory FaaS studies [15, 19, 30], benchmarks [16, 21] and technical platform papers [1] as well as emerging open-source developments [11], SDP prototype developments [29] and exploratory SDP studies [28].

For **serverless job orchestration**, the different approaches discussed all can introduce undesirable inefficiencies. Each of the presented workarounds thus introduces a possible adaption cause.

Based on benchmarks performed in previous work [17], it appears that AWS is the most suitable platform for using synchronous executions. Alternatively, we can augment existing platforms to address the issue of spawning and observing multiple function invocations simultaneously. For example, platforms can introduce new means to batch invocations with a callback on completion to allow frameworks to spawn thousands of functions without the need to manage each invocation individually. Thus, this immediately removes the need to create complicated management structures around existing platform APIs from a developer perspective. This would also allow for more predictive scheduling and reduce overly aggressive polling of APIs for these types of use-cases from a platform perspective.

For **serverless state management** several proposals to address the intermediate storage problem are already emerging. Klimov et al. [14], for example, propose flash-based storage that can be used by serverless analytics in place of the currently used object storage for intermediate data. However, platforms could aid function developers by offering an intermediate storage layer on each worker to address intermediate storage needs on a platform level. These could hold data for a short time, thus allowing functions to batch read, write to external data sources, or even reuse data for intermediate computations. Further, platforms could address the problem of redundant connection to the selected storage back-end by integrating connection pooling on the worker level.

Serverless uniformity can in part be addressed on the application level by chaining the deployment strategy of current frameworks. Instead of deploying a function with only one configuration, frameworks could deploy functions in multiple sizes and switch the invocations to larger deployments in case of skewed data. However, not all platforms allow flexible sizing of deployment packages, and thus, developers risk oversizing and overpaying with this strategy. Here, platforms can offer more flexible sizing options, integrate sizing aid at runtime or enable other mechanisms to adjust deployments in case of errors.

Furthermore, the programming interface of functions could be extended to include other life-cycle related events such as function termination and function-creating to allow frameworks to group some common tasks on the start and end of a function life-cycle instead of every single execution, thus reducing the risk of timeouts during IO operations. Also, we foresee new serverless platforms that are breaking even more with the initial one-size-fits-all model of serverless computing to address specific application requirements, such as the support of computation accelerators [20], edge-computing infrastructure and optimized systems for parallel computing.

4.2   Understanding Co-design

As discussed in general in the introduction and as exemplified for serverless data processing, software platforms will continue to evolve or be newly created in response to changing application demands. These platforms continue to push the envelope of what applications can do and thus again present new demands that motivate platform changes and, ultimately, again lead to new platforms.

This phenomenon of application platform co-design takes place both consciously and unconsciously between platform and application developers. Understanding this phenomenon better enables application developers to anticipate platform changes as well as new platforms, and thus allows for better management of coming changes. Similarly, application developers can take control of the application-platform co-design cycle and influence new platform developments directly.

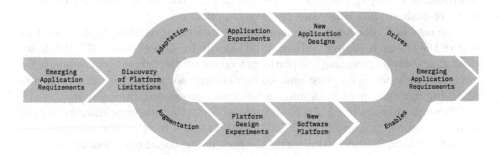

Fig. 1. Conceptual view of application platform co-design cycle

Figure 1 illustrates the continuous nature of application platform co-design. Newly emerging application demands and requirements drive the discovery of software platform limitations, for example, native state management in serverless computing. Once a limitation is known, application developers start to use workarounds, as described in Sect. 3.2. These workarounds often create a demand for new application designs and, in turn, new application requirements, in the case of SDP, for example, the trend towards higher-level language support. However, at some point these emerging application designs will benefit more from new platforms that turn workarounds into supported platform features. Thus, new platform developments may be initiated, and new platforms emerge.

For the platform route in Fig. 1, in a first step, we need to identify the application requirements that are better addressed through platform support. As described earlier, requirements such as the SDP requirements [29], must be defined first. For later validation and to help with the identification of platform-driven limitations, experimental measurements and application [9, 28]- and platform benchmarks [3, 17, 26] to evaluate against these requirements are needed. Based on the results, developers can either adapt their applications using the benchmarking results as a guide when designing necessary workarounds, or developers can start to implement new prototypical features in the platform and adapt the application to utilize these features accordingly. By reusing or extending the application and platform benchmarks, we can evaluate if the changes lead to significant improvements for the application use case. By iteratively applying these steps, we ultimately create a new platform adapted to the specific application needs or new applications that are adapted to current platform limitations.

5   Conclusion

In this paper, we described the application platform co-design phenomena and illustrated it for serverless computing platforms and serverless data processing, in particular. More specifically, we discussed concrete challenges and needs in an SDP context and how these are initially addressed through application workarounds, but may lead to new platform features and designs, resulting in a continuously changing platform landscape and the continuous need for developers to re-evaluate platforms and re-design applications.

The new SDP platform augmentations discussed have been implemented as part of the research project SMILE at TU Berlin for OpenWhisk [27]. While we are still actively augmenting the platform to meet all the defined requirements for serverless data processing systems, we can already see significant improvements regarding function invocation management and processing throughput.

Through projects like SMILE and related work and observations, we expect more and more undesirable application workarounds to be eventually replaced by new platform features, confirming the continuous co-design phenomenon, but at the same time making clear, how little engineering support and understanding for such continuous co-design process exists to-date. The duality of application and platform (re-)design challenges, the option to address identified limitations either on the application or the platform level, the continuous nature of both, and the need to study in depth fine-granular technical platform details, presents a larger challenge that demands new methods and tooling to better cope with application-platform co-design. We believe that application platform co-design awareness is critical to modern engineering needs such as SDP, and that appropriate methods and tooling should become an important piece of any developers tool-belt. Platforms will not stop evolving, and simultaneously, the choice of what software to use or adapt will grow, correspondingly.

References

1. Agache, A., et al.: Firecracker: lightweight virtualization for serverless applications. In: 17th Symposium on Networked Systems Design and Implementation, pp. 419–434, NSDI 2020, USENIX Association, February 2020
2. Barcelona-Pons, D., García-López, P.: Benchmarking parallelism in FaaS platforms. Futur. Gener. Comput. Syst. **124**, 268–284 (2021). https://doi.org/10.1016/j.future.2021.06.005
3. Bermbach, D., Wittern, E., Tai, S.: Cloud Service Benchmarking: Measuring Quality of Cloud Services from a Client Perspective. Springer, Heidelberg (2017). https://doi.org/10.1007/978-3-319-55483-9
4. Borges, M.C., Werner, S., Kilic, A.: Faaster troubleshooting - evaluating distributed tracing approaches for serverless applications. In: 2021 IEEE International Conference on Cloud Engineering (IC2E), IC2E 2021. IEEE (2021)

5. Carver, B., Zhang, J., Wang, A., Cheng, Y.: In search of a fast and efficient serverless dag engine. In: 2019 IEEE/ACM Fourth International Parallel Data Systems Workshop (PDSW), pp. 1–10, PDSW 2019 (2019). https://doi.org/10.1109/PDSW49588.2019.00005

6. DeCandia, G., et al.: Dynamo: Amazon's highly available key-value store. In: Proceedings of Twenty-First ACM SIGOPS Symposium on Operating Systems Principles, pp. 205–220, SOSP 2007. Association for Computing Machinery (2007). https://doi.org/10.1145/1294261.1294281

7. Fouladi, S., et al.: From laptop to lambda: outsourcing everyday jobs to thousands of transient functional containers. In: 2019 USENIX Annual Technical Conference, pp. 475–488, USENIX 2019. USENIX, July 2019

8. Ghemawat, S., Gobioff, H., Leung, S.T.: The google file system. In: Proceedings of the Nineteenth ACM Symposium on Operating Systems Principles, pp. 29–43 (2003)

9. Grambow, M., Pfandzelter, T., Burchard, L., Schubert, C., Zhao, M., Bermbach, D.: Befaas: an application-centric benchmarking framework for FaaS platforms (2021). https://arxiv.org/abs/2102.12770

10. Hellerstein, J.M., et al.: Serverless computing: one step forward, two steps back. In: CIDR 2019, 9th Biennial Conference on Innovative Data Systems Research. CIDR, January 2019. http://arxiv.org/abs/1812.03651

11. Hunhoff, E., Irshad, S., Thurimella, V., Tariq, A., Rozner, E.: Proactive serverless function resource management. In: Proceedings of the 2020 Sixth International Workshop on Serverless Computing, pp. 61–66, WoSC 2020. Association for Computing Machinery (2020). https://doi.org/10.1145/3429880.3430102

12. Jonas, E., Pu, Q., Venkataraman, S., Stoica, I., Recht, B.: Occupy the cloud: distributed computing for the 99 Cloud Computing, pp. 445–451, SoCC 2017. ACM (2017). https://doi.org/10.1145/3127479.3128601

13. Jonas, E., et al.: Cloud programming simplified: a Berkeley view on serverless computing, February 2019. http://arxiv.org/abs/1812.03651

14. Klimovic, A., Wang, Y., Kozyrakis, C., Stuedi, P., Pfefferle, J., Trivedi, A.: Understanding ephemeral storage for serverless analytics. In: USENIX Annual Technical Conference, pp. 789–794. ATC 2018. USENIX, July 2018

15. Kuhlenkamp, J., Werner, S.: Benchmarking FaaS platforms: call for community participation. In: Proceedings of the 3rd International Workshop on Serverless Computing, pp. 189–194, WoSC 2018. IEEE, December 2018. https://doi.org/10.1109/UCC-Companion.2018.00055

16. Kuhlenkamp, J., Werner, S., Borges, M.C., El Tal, K., Tai, S.: An evaluation of FaaS platforms as a foundation for serverless big data processing. In: Conference on Utility and Cloud Computing, pp. 1–9, UCC 2019. ACM (2019). https://doi.org/10.1145/3344341.3368796

17. Kuhlenkamp, J., Werner, S., Borges, M.C., Ernst, D.: All but one: Faas platform elasticity revisited. SIGAPP Appl. Comput. Rev. 20(3), 5–19 (9 2020). https://doi.org/10.1145/3429204.3429205

18. Kuhlenkamp, J., Werner, S., Tai, S.: The IFS and buts of less is more: a serverless computing reality check. In: 2020 IEEE International Conference on Cloud Engineering (IC2E), pp. 154–161, IC2E 2020. IEEE (2020). https://doi.org/10.1109/IC2E48712.2020.00023

19. Leitner, P., Wittern, E., Spillner, J., Hummer, W.: A mixed-method empirical study of function-as-a-service software development in industrial practice. J. Syst. Softw. 149, 340–359 (2018). https://doi.org/10.1016/j.jss.2018.12.013

20. López, P.G., Slominski, A., Behrendt, M., Metzler, B.: Serverless predictions: 2021–2030 (2021), https://arxiv.org/abs/2104.03075
21. Manner, J., Endreß, M., Heckel, T., Wirtz, G.: Cold start influencing factors in function as a service. In: Proceedings of the 3rd International Workshop on Serverless Computing, pp. 181–188, WoSC 2018. IEEE, December 2018. https://doi.org/10.1109/UCC-Companion.2018.00054
22. Müller, I., Marroquín, R., Alonso, G.: Lambada: interactive data analytics on cold data using serverless cloud infrastructure. In: Proceedings of the 2020 ACM SIGMOD International Conference on Management of Data, pp. 115–130, SIGMOD 2020. ACM (2020). https://doi.org/10.1145/3318464.3389758
23. Sampe, J., Garcia-Lopez, P., Sanchez-Artigas, M., Vernik, G., Roca-Llaberia, P., Arjona, A.: Toward multicloud access transparency in serverless computing. IEEE Softw. **38**(1), 68–74 (2021). https://doi.org/10.1109/MS.2020.3029994
24. Schifferer, B., et al.: GPU accelerated feature engineering and training for recommender systems. In: Proceedings of the Recommender Systems Challenge 2020, pp. 16–23. ACM, Virtual Event Brazil, September 2020. https://doi.org/10.1145/3415959.3415996
25. Schleier-Smith, J., et al.: What serverless computing is and should become: The next phase of cloud computing. Commun. ACM **64**(5), 76–84 (2021). https://doi.org/10.1145/3406011
26. Shahrad, M., Balkind, J., Wentzlaff, D.: Architectural implications of function-as-a-service computing. In: Proceedings of the 52nd International Symposium on Microarchitecture, pp. 1063–1075, MICRO'52,.ACM (2019). https://doi.org/10.1145/3352460.3358296
27. Werner, S.: SMILE: Supporting MIgration to ServerLess Environments. https://ise-smile.github.io/ (2020). Accessed 7 Oct 2021
28. Werner, S., Girke, R., Kuhlenkamp, J.: An evaluation of serverless data processing frameworks. In: Proceedings of the 2020 Sixth International Workshop on Serverless Computing, pp. 19–24, WoSC 2020. ACM (2020). https://doi.org/10.1145/3429880.3430095
29. Werner, S., Kuhlenkamp, J., Klems, M., Müller, J., Tai, S.: Serverless big data processing using matrix multiplication as example. In: Proceedings of the IEEE International Conference on Big Data, pp. 358–365, Big Data 2018. IEEE, December 2018. https://doi.org/10.1109/BigData.2018.8622362
30. Werner, S., et al.: Diminuendo! tactics in support of FaaS migrations. In: Paasivaara, M., Kruchten, P. (eds.) Agile Processes in Software Engineering and Extreme Programming - Workshops, pp. 125–132. Springer, Cham (2020). https://doi.org/10.1007/978-3-030-58858-8_13

Short Papers

A Reinforcement Learning Approach for Re-allocating Drone Swarm Services

Balsam Alkouz[(✉)] and Athman Bouguettaya

University of Sydney, NSW, Sydney, Australia
{balsam.alkouz,athman.bouguettaya}@sydney.edu.au

Abstract. We propose a novel framework for the re-allocation of drone swarms for delivery services known as Swarm-based Drone-as-a-Service (SDaaS). The re-allocation framework ensures maximum profit to drone swarm providers while meeting the time requirement of service consumers. The constraints in the delivery environment (e.g., limited recharging pads) are taken into consideration. We utilize reinforcement learning (RL) to select the best allocation and scheduling of drone swarms given a set of requests from multiple consumers. We conduct a set of experiments to evaluate and compare the efficiency of the proposed approach considering the provider's profit and run-time efficiency.

Keywords: Drones swarm · Service composition · Swarm re-allocation · Homogeneous swarms · Provider-centric · Congestion-aware

1 Introduction

Swarm-based Drone-as-a-Service (SDaaS) is a concept that describes services offered by swarms of drones [1]. The SDaaS notion is an augmentation on the Drone-as-a-Service (DaaS) concept that describes services offered by single drones [2]. It offers added capabilities to cover services a single drone is not capable of achieving. Examples of these services include search and rescue [3], sky shows and entertainment [4], and delivery of goods [5]. Our focus is on the use of drone swarms in delivery. An increasing dependency on drone delivery is perceived especially during pandemics, as they are contact-less and fast. Therefore, robust and effective deliveries of multiple/heavier packages are needed. Such deliveries are only possible using a swarm of drones as flight regulations only allow the use of small drones (payload<2.5 kg) to deliver in the city[1]. In addition, swarms of drones in delivery are capable of covering longer trips by distributing the payload over several drones decreasing the rate of battery consumption [1]. Swarm-based drone deliveries operating in a city are assumed to be flying within line of sight segments in a skyway network [6]. The skyway network nodes are assumed to be building rooftops equipped with recharging pads that a

---

[1] https://www.faa.gov/uas/advanced_operations/package_delivery_drone.

© Springer Nature Switzerland AG 2021
H. Hacid et al. (Eds.): ICSOC 2021, LNCS 13121, pp. 643–651, 2021.
https://doi.org/10.1007/978-3-030-91431-8_40

swarm may land on to extend its flight range [7]. We formally define an SDaaS as a swarm carrying packages and travelling in a skyway segment frome node A to node B. The composition of optimal segments between a source node and a destination node would result in an optimal composite SDaaS service. An SDaaS service maps to the key components of service computing, i.e. functional and non-functional attributes [8]. The function of an SDaaS is the successful delivery of packages by a swarm between two nodes. The non-functional attributes or the Quality of Services (QoS) include the delivery time, cost, etc.

Three main steps are involved in a successful SDaaS delivery. First, an optimal swarm members allocation approach is essential to serve multiple consumers requests in a day. Second, an optimal path composition method is required to optimize the QoS. Third, a failure-recovery solution is necessary in case of uncertainties. In this paper, we focus on the first step, with respect to the composition, to optimally allocate swarms to consumers requests from a provider point of view. The last step, i.e. failure recovery, is the future extension of this work. An optimal allocation is key in assuring that a provider owned drones are optimally *utilized* and *re-utilized* within a day. Therefore, fulfilling as many consumers requests as possible and increasing a provider profit.

There are several challenges in the swarms allocation problem. First, a provider owns a *limited set of drones* that needs to be utilized maximally. Second, the delivery time of consumers requests may overlap as they need to be delivered within *strict time windows*. Hence, requests that maximize the providers profit need to be allocated. Third, the requests need to be served in a way that optimizes the *re-utilization* of drones. Hence, within a time window, a swarm may be reused if its round trip time to the first request is smaller than the time window. This problem is challenging since the allocation of any swarm is highly dependent on the availability of other drones because they are *re-allocatable*. In addition, each swarm is bounded by a *Round Trip Time* from the source to the destination and back to the destination. This means that the allocation of any request highly *affects the allocation of other requests in the same time-window and other windows* as the provider owns a limited set of drones. We propose to allocate *any* available drones to *multiple time-constrained* requests, and *re-utilize* the drones multiple times within a time window to *maximize a providers profit*. We summarize our main contributions as following:

- A modified A* congestion-aware algorithm to compose SDaaS services.
- An RL SDaaS allocation algorithm to maximize providers profit.

2   Related Work

A robotic swarm is a set of robots that collectively solve a problem to achieve a common goal. In delivery, majority of literature refer to swarms of drones as multiple single independent drones managed to deliver multiple independent deliveries [9]. However, we refer to a swarm as a set of drones carrying multiple packages for a single delivery operation. In this regard, a sequential and parallel delivery services composition using a swarm of drones was proposed [1]. While drone swarms in delivery represent a major advancement, developing *swarm allocation* methods is essential to unlock their full potential and obtain teamwork benefit [10].

Multi-Robot Task Allocation (MRTA) addresses the assignment of set of tasks to a set of robots [11]. The robots need to be optimally allocated to tasks to optimize the overall team performance [12]. Multi Robot Task Scheduling (MRTS) deals with the scheduling of the tasks to minimize the overall cost, make it be: time, money, or energy. Most multi-robot systems deal with MRTA and MRTS as two different steps. However, the decoupling of these steps leads to partial observability and lack of full insights [11]. In addition, to the best of our knowledge, most work done in MRTA does not deal with the *multiple reallocations* of the robots in a *time-constrained* environment. Hence, we propose to couple the MRTA and MTRS problems and deal with multiple re-allocations of drone swarms in a time-constrained environment using a *service-oriented approach*.

The service paradigm is a key enabler of drone deliveries in a skyway network. It ensures congruent and effective provisioning of drone-based deliveries [13]. Previous works discuss the optimal composition of services, i.e. composing the best path from the source to the destination [1]. In a different application, a reinforcement learning approach to compose moving WiFi hotspot services was proposed [14]. Majority of the existing work uses deep reinforcement learning for services composition and not allocation [15]. Hence, this work is the first that deals with the *re-allocation* of SDaaS services to optimize the QoS. This work takes into consideration the optimal *SDaaS composition* and challenges due to the simultaneous use of the skyway network by multiple swarms.

3   Swarm-Based Drone-as-a-Service Model

In this section, we present a swarm-based drone delivery service model. We abstract a swarm carrying packages and travelling in a skyway segment between two nodes as a service (Fig. 1).

Definition 1: Swarm-based Drone-as-a-Service (SDaaS). An SDaaS is defined as a set of drones, carrying packages and travelling in a skyway segment. It is represented as a tuple of $< SDaaS\_id, S, F >$, where

- $SDaaS\_id$ is a unique service identifier
- S is the swarm travelling in SDaaS. S consists of D which is the set of drones forming S, a tuple of D is presented as $< d_1, d_2, .., d_m >$. S also contains the properties including the current battery levels of every d in D $< b_1, b_2, .., b_m >$, the payloads every d in D is carrying $< p_1, p_2, .., p_m >$, and the current node n the swarm S is at.
- F describes the delivery function of a swarm on a skyway segment between two nodes, A and B. F consists of the segment distance *dist*, travel time *tt*, charging time *ct*, and waiting time *wt* when recharging pads are not enough to serve D simultaneously in node B.

Definition 2: SDaaS Request. A request is a tuple of $< R\_id, \beta, P, T >$, where

- R_id is the request unique identifier.
- β is the request destination node.
- P are the weights of the packages requested, where P is $< p_1, p_2, .., p_m >$.
- T is the time window of the expected delivery, it is represented as a tuple of the window start and end times $< st, et >$.

4   SDaaS Members Re-allocation Framework

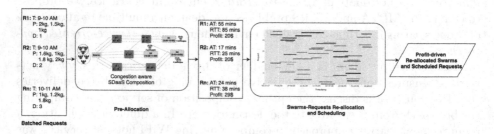

Fig. 1. SDaaS members re-allocation framework

The SDaaS members allocation and scheduling framework composes of two main modules. In the first module, the composition of SDaaS services for every received request is performed. The output of the first module is the maximum time taken for the packages to arrive at the destination (AT), the maximum round trip time back to the source (RTT), and the profit if the request is served. In the second module, the AT, RTT, and profit are used to allocate and re-allocate the provider owned drones to the most profitable requests and schedule them in a way that serves as many requests as possible.

4.1   SDaaS Pre-allocation

The pre-allocation module mainly consists of the SDaaS optimal composition of all requests to their respective destinations. The optimal path that reduces the delivery time is composed. The intermediate nodes contain different numbers of recharging pads. The composition should consider the optimal selection of nodes that would reduce the charging times. In addition, contention may occur at a node if two swarms serving different requests take the same path at a time causing *congestion* [16]. We assume that the weight of the packages do not exceed a drones payload capacity. We also assume that a drone may carry a single package at a time. The swarm is assumed to serve one request in a single trip. Therefore, the size of a swarm, serving a request, is equivalent to the number of packages in the request. A request is assumed to have a maximum capacity of m packages. The goal of this module is to compute the maximum time a swarm would take to serve a request (AT) and come back to the source (RTT). The RTT is the maximum possible time of a trip with the existence of other swarms in the network at the same time. Hence, the composition is considered congestion-aware. The composed path is an optimal path in terms of delivery time that a swarm may take while considering the probability of having other swarms utilizing the charging pads, i.e. congestion. Hence, we propose a modified congestion-aware A* approach for SDaaS composition. The AT of the packages at the destination and the RTT is key in scheduling the requests to serve as many requests as possible. We assume that the environment is deterministic, i.e. we know the availability of recharging pads considering other providers using the network.

The composition is initiated with a set of swarm drones (S_D), fully charged at the source. The swarm is assumed to be static [17], i.e. it traverses the network without splitting midway. While the drone is not at the destination and back at the source, the algorithm computes the likelihood for the swarm to reach the dest/src nodes using Dijkstra's shortest path without stopping at intermediate nodes. The likelihood of reaching is computed based on the payload of all the drones and the energy consumption rate over the distance travelled. If the swarm is capable of reaching the dest/src directly, it traverses the network and the RTT gets updated with the travel time tt. Otherwise, if the swarm is not capable of reaching the dest/src node directly, it selects the optimal neighbouring node. An optimal neighbor is a neighbouring node with the least travel time tt and node time nt. The nt is dependant on the number of available recharging pads at a node. The nt composes of the charging times ct and the waiting times wt due to sequential charging in case the number of pads is less than the size of the swarm. We assume that a node may be used by a maximum of two swarms at a time. At every node, we consider the potential of congestion to compute the maximum possible AT and RTT. We assume that each drone is occupied by all the other drones owned by the provider P_D if they are less than the maximum swarm size m. Otherwise, we assume a station is used by another swarm of size m. We compute the node time considering the number of available recharging pads under congestion. When the best neighbour is selected, the swarm traverses to the node and charges fully. The swarm attempts again to reach the dest/src directly. The process continues until the swarm is at the dest/src. The RTT is updated to include the charging time back at the source. The profit is computed using the number of drones utilized to serve a request S_D and the RTT of the trip.

4.2 SDaaS Allocation and Scheduling

The composed services from Subsect. 4.1 are used to allocate drones to the most profitable requests for the provider. There might be instances where aggregated less profitable requests result in a better total profit than few high profit requests. Hence, the allocation and scheduling algorithm needs to maximize the total profit per day. These allocated requests need to be scheduled in the timeline efficiently to serve as many possible requests. The allocation and scheduling should take in consideration the limited number of provider owned drones. At a time t a provider may serve a maximum of N packages at a time. Therefore, we propose a reinforcement learning allocation and scheduling algorithm.

Reinforcement Learning Based Allocation. The proposed framework aims to allocate the provider owned drones P_D to the consumers requests R in the best possible manner, i.e. maximize profit. This imposes the maximum utilization of drones and scheduling the request in the best possible timings to be able to re-allocate the drones over and over again. We leverage *Reinforcement Learning (RL)* to find, allocate, and schedule the requests. In RL, an *agent* learns about an *environment's* behaviour through *explorations*. RL is capable of discovering the best set of requests to be allocated and schedule them at the most optimal time to facilitate the re-use of drones. The main reason for our choice of RL is its *ability to discover the "cumulative" optimal set of requests* to be allocated. The RL does that by assigning rewards for every action the agent invokes. In our work, the actions are the service requests and time slots that a swarm can get allocated to. The agent's role is to pick the next service request and allocation time that would maximize the overall reward. Therefore, the agent should not only consider the current requests to make the selection but also future requests and available drones. The *environment* that the agent interacts with in this solution is designed to be problem specific. The environment checks for requests validity, overlapping allocations, drones' availability, and time inter-dependencies and permits only valid actions to be taken by the agent.

We define the agent's *actions* as a tuple of request ID and time slot $< R_{id}, AT_w >$. The time slot represents the arrival time within the consumer specified delivery time window $< R_{st}, R_{et} >$. The agent at every step takes an action, i.e. adds a specific request to the environment at a certain time window. The environment checks the validity of allocating the request by looking at the overlapped allocated requests and the availability of the provider owned drones. The *state* is updated at every step with the total accumulated profit of the allocated requests. We implement a *Q-learning* algorithm that seeks to find the best action to take given the current state [18].

5   Experiments

In this section, we evaluate the performance in terms of total profit gained and the execution time of the proposed algorithm. A brute force baseline is time and memory extensive and is not feasible as described earlier. Therefore, we compare the proposed RL allocation method to the First Come First Served (FCFS) algorithm [19]. In the FCFS approach, the first request received gets allocated first. If a request can't be allocated due to the limited number of drones being occupied at a time window, the request does not get allocated and the next arriving request gets checked and allocated.

An urban road network dataset from the city of london is used to mimic the arrangement of a skyway network [20]. The dataset consists of nodes representing intersections and segments connecting those nodes. For the experiments, we

extracted a sub-network consisting of 129 connected nodes. Each node is allocated with different number of recharging pads randomly. A source node is then
selected and r service requests are generated with different destination nodes. For
each request, we synthesize maximum 5 packages payload and a maximum weight
of 1.4 kg. The drone model is assumed to be the DJI phantom 3. All the power
consumption computation is based on this model, the distance travelled, and
payload carried. We used the congestion-aware SDaaS composition algorithm to
compute the AT, RTT, and profit for each request given the recharging pads constraints. These requests are assigned to different time windows randomly. Each
time window is assumed to be one hour. Hence, the AT of the package should
lie within this hour. The experiments were run on 7th Gen Intel® Core™ i7-
7700HQ Processor (2.8 GHz), 16 GB RAM, 64-bit Windows OS PC.

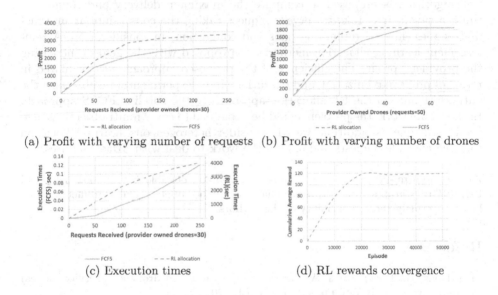

(a) Profit with varying number of requests (b) Profit with varying number of drones

(c) Execution times   (d) RL rewards convergence

Fig. 2. Proposed method effectiveness

In the first experiment, we study the effect of varying the number of received
requests a day on the profit. We assume the provider owns a fixed set of 30
drones. As shown in Fig. 2a, the RL allocation outperforms the FCFS. This
is because of its ability to learn the optimal allocation and scheduling of the
requests to maximize the profit. The FCFS is performing worse than RL because
allocating services in an FCFS manner does not consider any order in terms of
most profitable request and round trip times. Therefore, the non-optimal set of
requests gets allocated at non-optimal time windows.

The same behaviour is noted with varying the number of provider owned
drones for a set of 50 requests as shown in Fig. 2b. The RL allocation converges
to the maximum possible profit earlier by serving all the 50 requests. This performance of the RL allocation method comes with the cost of execution. Figure 2c

shows the execution times varying the number of requests received a day. The left y-axis represents the execution times of the FCFS. The right y-axis represents the execution time for the RL based algorithm. Since the number of state-action pairs in RL only increase in one dimension and converges at almost the 20000 episode (Fig. 2d), the execution time does not increase significantly. We assume the requests are received in batch a day earlier, hence, the learning could occur overnight.

6   Conclusion

We proposed a provider-centric re-allocation of drone swarm services known as, Swarm-based Drone-as-a-Service (SDaaS). A congestion-aware SDaaS composition algorithm is proposed to compute the maximum delivery and round trip times a swarm may take to serve a request taking the constraints at intermediate nodes (limited recharging pads and congestion) in consideration. A reinforcement learning allocation method was proposed with the goal of increasing the provider's profit. The efficiency of the proposed approach was evaluated in terms of profit maximization and execution time. Experimental results show the outperformance of the RL allocation approach to the baseline FCFS approach. In the future work, the problem could be expanded to cover multi-objectives, e.g. profit and time. In addition, we will consider heterogeneous swarms allocation to serve multiple requests and extend the work to deal with SDaaS failures.

Acknowledgment. This research was partly made possible by DP160103595 and LE180100158 grants from the Australian Research Council. The statements made herein are solely the responsibility of the authors.

References

1. Alkouz, B., Bouguettaya, A., Mistry, S.: Swarm-based drone-as-a-service (sdaas) for delivery. In: ICWS, pp. 441–448. IEEE (2020)
2. Hamdi, A., Salim, F.D., Kim, D.Y., Neiat, A.G., Bouguettaya, A.: Drone-as-a-service composition under uncertainty. IEEE TSC (2021)
3. Cardona, G.A., Calderon, J.M.: Robot swarm navigation and victim detection using rendezvous consensus in search and rescue operations. Appl. Sci. 9(8), 1702 (2019)
4. Waibel, M., Keays, B., Augugliaro, F.: Drone shows: Creative potential and best practices. Technical report, ETH Zurich (2017)
5. Alkouz, B., Bouguettaya, A.: Formation-based selection of drone swarm services. In: EAI Mobiquitous Conference (2020)
6. Lee, W., Alkouz, B., Shahzaad, B., Bouguettaya, A.: Package delivery using autonomous drones in skyways. In: Proceedings of the UbiComp/ISWC, pp. 48–50 (2021)
7. Shahzaad, B., Bouguettaya, A., Mistry, S.: A game-theoretic drone-as-a-service composition for delivery. In: ICWS, pp. 449–453. IEEE (2020)
8. Shahzaad, B., Bouguettaya, A., Mistry, S.: Robust composition of drone delivery services under uncertainty. In: ICWS. IEEE (2021)

9. Kuru, K., Ansell, D., et al.: Analysis and optimization of unmanned aerial vehicle swarms in logistics: An intelligent delivery platform. IEEE Access **7**, 15804–15831 (2019)
10. Gigliotta, O.: Equal but different: task allocation in homogeneous communicating robots. Neurocomputing **272**, 3–9 (2018)
11. Elfakharany, A., Yusof, R., Ismail, Z.: Towards multi robot task allocation and navigation using deep reinforcement learning. In: Journal of Physics (2020)
12. Khamis, A., Hussein, A., Elmogy, A.: Multi-robot task allocation: a review of the state-of-the-art. Cooperative Robot. Sens. Netw. **2015**, 31–51 (2015)
13. Shahzaad, B., Bouguettaya, A., Mistry, S., Neiat, A.G.: Resilient composition of drone services for delivery. FGCS **115**, 335–350 (2021)
14. Gharineiat, A., Bouguettaya, A., Ba-hutair, M.N.: A deep reinforcement learning approach for composing moving IoT services. IEEE TSC (2021)
15. Wang, H., Zhou, X., Zhou, X., Liu, W., Li, W., Bouguettaya, A.: Adaptive service composition based on reinforcement learning. In: Maglio, P.P., Weske, M., Yang, J., Fantinato, M. (eds.) ICSOC 2010. LNCS, vol. 6470, pp. 92–107. Springer, Heidelberg (2010). https://doi.org/10.1007/978-3-642-17358-5_7
16. Alkouz, B., Bouguettaya, A.: Provider-centric allocation of drone swarm services. In: ICWS. IEEE (2021)
17. Akram, R.N., Markantonakis, K., et al.: Security, privacy and safety evaluation of dynamic and static fleets of drones. In: IEEE/AIAA 36th DASC (2017)
18. Watkins, C.J., Dayan, P.: Q-learning. Mach. Learn. **8**(3–4), 279–292 (1992)
19. Tanenbaum, A.S., Bos, H.: Modern operating systems. Pearson (2015)
20. Karduni, A., Kermanshah, A., Derrible, S.: A protocol to convert spatial polyline data to network formats and apps to world urban road nets. Sci. Data **3**(1), 1–7 (2016)

TAGen: Generating Trigger-Action Rules for Smart Homes by Mining Event Traces

Liwei Liu[1,2], Wei Chen[1,2(✉)], Lu Liu[1,2], Kangkang Zhang[1,2], Jun Wei[1,2,3], and Yan Yang[1,2]

[1] Institute of Software, Chinese Academy of Sciences, Beijing, China
{liuliwei19,wchen,liulu20,zhangkangkang19,wj,yy}@otcaix.iscas.ac.cn
[2] University of Chinese Academy of Sciences, Beijing, China
[3] State Key Laboratory of Computer Sciences, Beijing, China

Abstract. A smart home facilities human daily lives by orchestrating IoT devices through trigger-action (TA) rules. However, creating TA rules is challenging for novice users as (1) it requires comprehensive domain knowledge, (2) the created rules often deviate from user intents, and (3) errors are usually inevitable. To address these challenges, this paper proposes TAGen, an approach to automating TA rule generations by mining historical event traces. TAGen augments events and event traces with contextual information based on a deep understanding of a smart home system. It synthesizes TA rules by identifying frequent event pairs, inferring potential conditions, and heuristically filtering and ranking rule candidates. We implement a prototype and evaluate it with a preliminary experiment, and the experimental results show that TAGen effectively generates TA rules aligned with user behaviors.

Keywords: Smart home · Trigger-action rules · IoT device · Event trace

1 Introduction

A smart home (SH) is a complex system making people's daily lives convenient and comfortable with intelligence techniques, whose one essential capability is orchestrating Internet of Things (IoT) smart devices. In particular, an SH exploits trigger-action (TA) rules [12] to automate IoT devices, i.e., lighting, switches, and locks, to behave in alignment with occupants' intents.

TA rules are presented in the form of "IF a `trigger occurs`, THEN `do an action`." In this way, actions are automatically performed when triggering events occur and some specific conditions (if they exist) are satisfied. An occupant can develop TA rules with tools like IFTTT[1] and Zapier[2] to orchestrate smart home devices. For instance, *"IF the smart lock changes to on THEN turns on the living*

---

[1] https://ifttt.com/.
[2] https://www.zapier.com/.

© Springer Nature Switzerland AG 2021
H. Hacid et al. (Eds.): ICSOC 2021, LNCS 13121, pp. 652–662, 2021.
https://doi.org/10.1007/978-3-030-91431-8_41

room lamp" is a TA rule automating the action *"turning on the lamp"* when the event *"the smart lock changes to on"* occurs.

However, creating a TA rule is not simple, requiring end-users comprehensively regarding multiple factors of humans, devices, and physical environmental contexts (contexts for short hereafter). Furthermore, end-users often cannot accurately specify their potential intents and do not know their actual demands, resulting in bugs [3] and inconsistencies between user mental models and TA rules [8]. In consequence, developing proper TA rules from scratch is still thorny for novice occupants.

This paper proposes **TAGen** to mitigate the gap between user intents and smart home TA rules. TAGen generates TA rules aligning with occupants' intents by mining event traces of a smart home. Occupants usually operate smart home devices regularly, which reflect their actual intents and daily routines, and hence it is viable to generate TA rules by identifying the regularities.

The contributions of this work are summarized as follows.

1. We propose a set of definitions and formalize the problem based on a deep understanding of a smart home system.
2. We propose an approach to generating TA rules by synthesizing triggers, actions and conditions obtained from smart home event traces.
3. We prototype TAGen and integrates it into a popular open-source smart home system Home Assistant[3] (HA).

2 Related Work and Problem Analysis

2.1 Related Work

Two ways are popular in generating TA rules, i.e., trigger action programming (TAP) and data mining-based TA rule generation.

Some work facilitates end-users developing, debugging, and understanding TA rules. AutoTap [15] translates properties to LTL (linear temporal logic) specifications and automatically synthesizes compliant TA rules. Like scratch programming, Block Rule Composer [9] creates rules with visual blocks. Zhao et al. [16] implemented user interfaces that visualize differences between TA rules in syntax, behaviors, and properties, helping users understand how a TA rule modification changes an ultimate behavior.

The other way to generate TA rules is by learning from historical smart home event logs [2]. The approaches focus on activity recognition and behavior pattern discovery through mining frequent/periodic/temporal patterns and casual relations from event logs. PCMiner [7] discovers periodic composite IoT services from event sequences by employing significance and proximity strategies to make filtering. CoPMiner [4] mines temporal relations among smart home appliances from endpoint sequences transformed from interval-based event sequences. Trace2TAP [14] applies symbolic reasoning and SAT solving to synthesize a comprehensive set of TA rule candidates automatically.

---

[3] https://www.home-assistant.io/.

Similar to mining TA rules, process mining extracts insight in processes from event logs [11]. An event log is viewed as a set of traces containing all the activities of a particular process instance [10]. Heuristics Miner generates process models from event logs and is robust to deal with noises [13]. Fuzzy Miner is configurable to generate multiple models at different levels of detail for dealing with unstructured processes [5].

2.2 Problem Analysis

On the one hand, EUD (end-user development) based TAP is of low effectiveness. (1) Writing TA rules requires much domain knowledge, e.g., how to use rule development tools and how IoT devices and sensors work [6]. (2) End users cannot handle complex scenarios and often create buggy rules [8]. (3) End users do not exactly know their actual requirements and daily routines, let alone mapping them to TA rules. On the other hand, limitations exist in data mining-based TA rule generations. (1) Devices are orchestrated with multiple relations, e.g., temporal relations, causal relations, and associations due to user habits; the conditions under which devices collaborate are complex, such as various physical environment contexts and temporal properties. Nevertheless, contemporary work only considers one or part of relations and conditions. (2) The other approaches usually mine high-level activity patterns from sensor data. However, there are gaps between transforming such activities into fine-grained executable TA rule scripts.

Therefore, we are motivated to propose TAGen, an approach to generating fine-grained executable TA rules based on smart home event trace mining.

3   Definitions and TA Rule Template

We showcase an exemplary scenario of a user's daily routine at the beginning.

An Example Scenario. *On workdays, Jason usually comes back home around 18 o'clock. When he enters his house, he will turn on the living room air conditioner if he feels hot and then closes the living room window within one minute if the window is open at that moment. He usually sits on the couch and turns on the TV and the lamp in his living room around 19 o'clock every day.*

3.1   Definitions

The above scenario is user-driven in an ordinary home. In other words, the user is a central controller that manually operates home devices according to his perception of surroundings (e.g., temperature), habits (e.g., watching TV), and other intents. In essence, a smart home system replaces the role of an occupant in an ordinary home. To control target devices as if the user acts on them directly, the smart home should deduce user intents from multiple aspects, such as environmental contexts and user states and behaviors perceived by sensors.

Smart home devices are of two types, i.e., *sensors* and *actuators*. Sensors perceive contexts, e.g., physical environmental contexts, human activities and states, and physical object state changes. Unlike sensors, an actuator is a smart device capable of changing the environmental context or providing some services.

We propose a set of definitions based on our understanding of a smart home.

Definition 1 (A smart home) *is defined as* $\mathcal{SH} =< \mathcal{D}, \mathcal{L}, \mathcal{C} >$, *where*

- $\mathcal{D} = \{d_1, d_2, \cdots, d_n\}$ denotes a set of IoT devices in $\mathcal{SH}$, and each device is either a sensor or an actuator.
- $\mathcal{L} = \{l_1, l_2, \cdots, l_m\}$ is a set of zones constituting $\mathcal{SH}$, e.g., a living room.
- $\mathcal{C} = \{Env, Dev, Act\}$ denotes three types of contexts, i.e., environmental contexts (Env), device states (Dev), and occupant activities and states (Act).

Definition 2 (An actuator) *is defined as* $d_a =< id, l, P, A, S, \Delta, \Theta >$, *where*

- id is a unique identity of d_a, and $d_a \in \mathcal{SH}.\mathcal{D}$.
- $l \in \mathcal{SH}.\mathcal{L}$ is the location of d_a.
- P is a set of properties of d_a, e.g., the color of a lamp.
- $A = \{a_1, a_2, \cdots, a_i\}$ is a set of operations offered by d_a, and there are two basic ones, i.e., *switch on* and *switch off*.
- $S = \{s_o, s_f, S'\}$ is the state set of d_a, s_o, s_f are two default states representing *on* and *off*, and S' is the set of other states.
- $\Delta : S \times A \mapsto S$ denotes state transitions, e.g., $\delta_1 : a_1 \times s_1 \mapsto s_2$ is a transition from s_1 to s_2 after an operation a_1, where $s_1, s_2 \in S$ and $a_1 \subset A$.
- Θ is a set of associations between d_a's operations and their effects on contexts, including physical environment contexts and device states. For example, $\theta_1 : a_1 \mapsto< temp, increase >$ is an association specifying d_a's operation a_1 *increases* the *temperature*, where $temp \in \mathcal{SH}.\mathcal{C}$.

Definition 3 (A sensor) *is defined as* $d_s =< id, l, c >$, *where*

- id is a unique identity of d_s, and $d_s \in \mathcal{SH}.\mathcal{D}$.
- $l \in \mathcal{H}.\mathcal{L}$ is the location of the device d_s.
- c is the context d_s perceives, $c \in \mathcal{SH}.\mathcal{C}$.

A smart home is an event-driven system. Events in the smart home $\mathcal{SH}$ are of two types according to their sources and semantics. (1) An actuator d_a fires an *operation event* when an act changes its state, e.g., an event *lamp-switching-on*. (2) A sensor outputs a *state-change event* when perceiving a target object's state change. Therefore, we define an event as the following.

Definition 4 (An event) *is defined as* $e =< type, d, desc >$, *where*

- $type \in \{operation, statechange\}$ is the type of e.
- d is the source device of e, from which we can obtain other information, e.g., where e happens.

– *desc* describes what the event *e* is, in terms of a *subject-predicate* phrase, e.g., "*TV turns on*", "*someone enters*", "*window opens*".

Definition 5 (An event trace) *is defined as* $\mathcal{R} =< t_s, t_e, E >$, *where*

– t_s and t_e are the beginning and the end time of event trace $\mathcal{R}$.
– $E =< e_1, e_2, \cdots >$ is a temporal sequence of event occurrences.

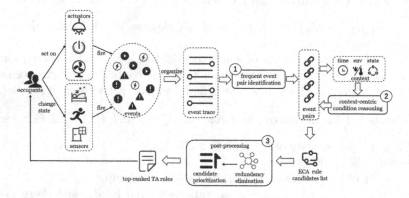

Fig. 1. The overview of TAGen's workflow.

Therefore, we can construct event traces for each person and handle them separately by identifying and clustering multiple users' events. Notably, we construct an event trace per day, but the time unit of a trace can be varied.

3.2   Rule Template

In general, a TA rule comprises three parts, i.e., an event, an action and conditions, and thus, we propose **a TA rule template**:

IF *e* happens, WHILE [*con*], THEN act *a* [within t_i],

e is a triggering event. *a* is an action on a device. t_i restricts the max time span between *e* and *a*. *con* is a boolean expression representing conditions. Note that the elements in square brackets are optional.

Unlike prior work creating a workflow, we concentrate on TA rules containing only one trigger and one action. It is because TA rules are fundamental building blocks, and the event-driven mechanism can chain a set of TA rules naturally. In the example scenario, the event *entering the living room* triggers the action *switching on the AC* that triggers the following action *closing the window*.

4   Methodology

As Fig. 1 shows, TAGen works in three steps, i.e., (1) identifies frequent event pairs, (2) infers rule conditions, and (3) post-processes TA rule candidates. This section elaborates on the details of each step.

4.1 Identify Frequent Event Pairs

We enumerate combinations of every two events and measure their co-occurrence frequency in event traces. Intuitively, the more frequently two events co-occur, the more likely they can be the trigger and action of a TA rule.

Valid Event Pair Enumeration. An enumerated event pair is valid only if,

1. Two events often co-occur within a short period. One action happening right after one trigger event implies a temporal relation between them, and otherwise not. We use the number of other events occurring between the two events as a relative threshold ($T_{interval}$).
2. The first event as a trigger is an *operation event* or a *state-change event*. The second event as an action must be an *operation event* implying an action on a device. A TA rule usually specifies that an occupant acts on an actuator right after changing his own state or other physical object's state.
3. Two paired events relate to different devices because we concentrate on TA rules that can orchestrate multiple devices.

Measure Event Co-occurrence Frequency. For a valid event pair, TAGen measures their co-occurrence frequency in a set of event traces $\mathcal{R} = \{R_1, R_2, \cdots\}$. An event pair is considered frequent only if the *support* and *confidence* of its co-occurrence are not less than the thresholds sup_{min} and con_{min}, respectively.

- *Support* measures how frequently an event pair co-occurs with Eq. 1; $NumOfTrace(e_1, e_2)$ is the number of traces containing the event pair at least once, and $NumOfTrace(\mathcal{R})$ is the total number of event traces.
- *Confidence* measures the possibility of e_2 happening after e_1 with Eq. 2, where $Num(e_1, e_2)$ denotes the total number of e_2 occurring after e_1, and $Num(e_1)$ is the total occurrences of e_1.

$$sup(e_1, e_2) = \frac{NumOfTrace(e_1, e_2)}{NumOfTrace(\mathcal{R})} \tag{1}$$

$$con(e_1, e_2) = \frac{Num(e_1, e_2)}{Num(e_1)} \tag{2}$$

This step outputs a set of frequent event pairs, and in each of which, the two events are a trigger and an action, respectively.

4.2 Infer TA Rule Conditions

Recall the example scenario, a TA rule must approximate conditions influencing an occupant's decision from several aspects, such as environmental contexts (e.g., *temperature*), device states (e.g., *a window is open*), and time intervals (e.g., *within one minute*).

Environmental Contextual Condition. The physical environmental context is a critical factor for an occupant to make a decision. We represent a contextual condition as $c \diamond \hat{c}$, where c is the perceived context value relating to an action act on an actuator, $\hat{c}$ is the boundary value of c, and $\diamond$ is an operator denoting a logical relation, e.g., "==", "$\geq$", etc. For example, we infer the operator $\diamond$ is "$\geq$" and set $\hat{c}$ with the minimum perceived value of $temperature$ before the action "*turning AC on*" occurrences.

Device State Condition. Device states influence whether performing an action. For instance, when an occupant feels hot, he will switch on an AC only if the other similar actuator, e.g., a fan, is off, at the moment.

According to the pre-defined smart home model, S^{t-} records the states of all devices before time t. Thus, given an event pair (e_1, e_2), we get the states before event e_2. We notice that, in general, most devices (excluding sensors) in a smart home are *off* at a certain time, and only the *non-off* devices more likely influence the subsequent action. Therefore, Eq. 3 measures the possibility ($p(d, s|e_2)$) of whether a device d in a state s is a condition of the action derived from e_2, where $|d, s|$ is the times of device d in state s when the event pair occur, and $|e_1, e_2|$ is the total occurrences of the event pair. We consider (d, s) as a condition if $p(d, s|e_2)$ exceeds a threshold T_{state}.

$$p(d, s|e_2) = \frac{|d, s|}{|e_1, e_2|} \tag{3}$$

Temporal Restriction. A temporal restriction limits the max time span between a trigger and an action, e.g., "*closing the window*" should be performed "*within in one minute*" once the trigger "*turning on the AC*" occurs. For an event pair $< e_1, e_2 >$ occurring n times, $SD(e_1, e_2)$ is the standard deviation of their time interval. The smaller $SD(e_1, e_2)$ is, the more regular the temporal restriction is. We set T_{span} with a sum of the max perceived time interval $max(x)$ and $SD(e_1, e_2)$, as the time span threshold.

Finally, a candidate rule is synthesized with an event pair and inferred conditions based on the rule template.

4.3   Post-process Rule Candidates

TAGen first removes redundant candidate rules whose effects are similar. Then, it prioritizes the remaining rules and recommends the top K rules to end-users. Note that the value of K is configurable, and we set it with 20 as default.

Filter Redundant Candidate Rules. TAGen constructs a directed graph (DG) whose vertexes are triggers and actions of obtained candidate rules, and each directed edge goes from a trigger to an action along with conditions on it. Within DG, a redundancy exists if (1) there are two or more paths from a trigger to an action, and (2) conditions in the paths are equal or similar.

Rank Candidate Rules. TAGen ranks the filtered candidates by regarding their diversity and significance. It clusters the candidates in groups and each of which contains candidates with the same actions. TAGen prioritizes the candidates within each group according to the action occurrences they can automate and chooses the top one as a recommendation. Finally, TAGen ranks all recommended rules in descending order by their *confidence* in original event traces and outputs the top 20 TA rules.

4.4 Prototype Implementation

We implement a prototype and integrate it into HA. HA provides an environment for users to customize TA rules in the form of YAML-based scripts. Specifically, we implement the front-end of TAGen based on a Python Web framework Flask, where the top 20 candidate rules are listed in default. Once a recommended rule is confirmed, TAGen generates a YAML-based HA automation script by synthesizing its trigger, conditions, and action. Finally, a user can find a generated rule in the automation card of HA and enable (or disable) it with the offered switch.

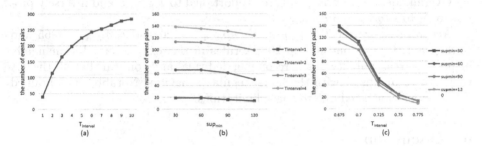

Fig. 2. (a) The effect of $T_{interval}$ on identified event pairs, (b) The effects of thresholds sup_{min}, $T_{interval}$ on identified event pairs, (c) The effects of thresholds con_{min}, sup_{min} on identified event pairs

5 Evaluation

We evaluate TAGen's performance in TA rule recommendation with a public dataset [1]. Notably, the dataset is augmented with some physical environment context data (temperature and humidity) of another publicly available dataset provided CASAS[4]. In particular, we analyze the impact of threshold settings, i.e., $T_{interval}$, sup_{min}, con_{min}, on TAGen's performance.

Maximum Interval. We set sup_{min} with 50 and con_{min} with 0.65 in respective and increase $T_{interval}$ from 1 to 10 for analyzing the effect of $T_{interval}$ on identified event pairs. Figure 2(a) depicts the changes of identified event pairs along with the increase of $T_{interval}$. The identified event pairs significantly increase when $T_{interval}$ increases from 1 to 4 and then increase more gently, indicating that most frequent event pairs contain events happening very closely. The

---

[4] http://casas.wsu.edu/datasets/.

event pairs with larger intervals would be filtered out at last due to their low co-occurring frequencies. Therefore, it is reasonable to set $T_{interval}$ in [1,4].

Minimum Support. Figure 2(b) shows the effects of $T_{interval}$ and sup_{min} on identified event pairs in the condition of $con_{min} = 0.7$. It is obvious that no matter what $T_{interval}$ is, sup_{min} has little effect on the number of identified event pairs. Therefore, we set sup_{min} with $\{30, 60, 90, 120\}$ in this experiment.

Minimum Confidence. We vary con_{min}, sup_{min} with $T_{interval} = 3$. Figure 2(c) shows the results. We vary sup_{min} and con_{min} to analyze their impact on the identified event pairs. We observe that the number of event pairs decreases drastically when setting con_{min} with a value around 0.700. It is also seen that no matter what value sup_{min} is, the number of event pairs will be less than 20 when con_{min} approaches 0.800. Therefore, we set con_{min} in the range of [0.65,0.8] to get a more reasonable number of events pairs.

Overall, identified event pairs are proportional to $T_{interval}$ and inversely proportional to sup_{min} and con_{min}.

Accordingly, we set $T_{interval} = 2$, $sup_{min} = 120$ and $con_{min} = 0.65$ and configure TAGen to output top 20 TA rules in this experiment. We manually inspect the reasonability of the recommended rules and confirm that all the TA rules are in alignment with the users' regular behaviors. Notably, the obtained TA rules are not listed due to space limitations.

6   Discussion

Although our preliminary experiment reveals that TAGen is capable of mining TA rules from event traces, some limitations still exist.

(1) The parameter settings would affect TAGen's performance, and thus setting reasonable values may be specific to different users and scenarios. We will explore adaptive parameter configuration algorithm in future work.
(2) TAGen currently only processes event logs in single-user environment, and its applicability in multi-user environment needs to be verified.
(3) TAGen's robustness in handling noises in event traces should be concerned and evaluated. In future work, we will evaluate TAGen with much more datasets and compare it with other techniques extensively.

7   Conclusion

Automated TA rule generation helps end-users customize smart home device orchestrations in alignment with their daily lives and intents. This paper systematically proposes an approach TAGen to generate TA rules by mining smart home historical event traces. TAGen synthesizes TA rule candidates with identified frequent event pairs and inferred conditions based on a general rule template. It filters out redundant rule candidates and ranks the remaining ones heuristically. We implement a prototype and perform preliminary evaluations.

Acknowledgment. This work is partially supported by National Key R&D Program of China under Project 2017YFA0700603, National Natural Science Foundation of China (61732019, U20A6003).

References

1. Alemdar, H., Ertan, H., et al.: Aras human activity datasets in multiple homes with multiple residents. In: 2013 7th International Conference on Pervasive Computing Technologies for Healthcare and Workshops, pp. 232–235 (2013)
2. Antić, M., Papp, I., Ivanović, S., Matić, M.: Learning from smart home data: Methods and challenges of data acquisition and analysis in smart home solutions. IEEE Consum. Electron. Mag. **9**(3), 64–71 (2020)
3. Brackenbury, W., Deora, A., Ritchey, J., Vallee, J., He, W., et al.: How users interpret bugs in trigger-action programming. In: Proceedings of the 2019 CHI Conference on Human Factors in Computing Systems, pp. 552. ACM (2019)
4. Chen, Y.-C., Chen, C.-C., Peng, W.-C., Lee, W.-C.: Mining correlation patterns among appliances in smart home environment. In: Tseng, V.S., Ho, T.B., Zhou, Z.-H., Chen, A.L.P., Kao, H.-Y. (eds.) PAKDD 2014. LNCS (LNAI), vol. 8444, pp. 222–233. Springer, Cham (2014). https://doi.org/10.1007/978-3-319-06605-9_19
5. Günther, C.W., van der Aalst, W.M.P.: Fuzzy mining – adaptive process simplification based on multi-perspective metrics. In: Alonso, G., Dadam, P., Rosemann, M. (eds.) BPM 2007. LNCS, vol. 4714, pp. 328–343. Springer, Heidelberg (2007). https://doi.org/10.1007/978-3-540-75183-0_24
6. He, W., Martinez, J., Padhi, R., Zhang, L., Ur, B.: When smart devices are stupid: negative experiences using home smart devices. In: 2019 IEEE Security and Privacy Workshops (SPW), pp. 150–155. IEEE (2019)
7. Huang, B., Bouguettaya, A., Neiat, A.G.: Convenience-based periodic composition of IoT services. In: Pahl, C., Vukovic, M., Yin, J., Yu, Q. (eds.) ICSOC 2018. LNCS, vol. 11236, pp. 660–678. Springer, Cham (2018). https://doi.org/10.1007/978-3-030-03596-9_48
8. Huang, J., Cakmak, M.: Supporting mental model accuracy in trigger-action programming. In: Proceedings of the 2015 ACM International Joint Conference on Pervasive and Ubiquitous Computing, pp. 215–225. Association for Computing Machinery, New York (2015)
9. Mattioli, A., Paternò, F.: A visual environment for end-user creation of IoT customization rules with recommendation support. In: Proceedings of the International Conference on Advanced Visual Interfaces, AVI 2020. Association for Computing Machinery (2020)
10. Rojas, E., Munoz-Gama, J., Sepúlveda, M., Capurro, D.: Process mining in healthcare: a literature review. J. Biomed. Inform. **61**, 224–236 (2016)
11. Tax, N., Sidorova, N., Haakma, R., van der Aalst, W.M.P.: Event abstraction for process mining using supervised learning techniques. In: Bi, Y., Kapoor, S., Bhatia, R. (eds.) IntelliSys 2016. LNNS, vol. 15, pp. 251–269. Springer, Cham (2018). https://doi.org/10.1007/978-3-319-56994-9_18
12. Ur, B., et al.: Trigger-action programming in the wild: an analysis of 200,000 IFTTT recipes. In: Proceedings of the 2016 CHI Conference on Human Factors in Computing Systems, pp. 3227–3231. ACM (2016)
13. Weijters, A., van Der Aalst, W.M., et al.: Process mining with the heuristics miner-algorithm. Technische Universiteit Eindhoven, Technical report, WP 166, 1–34 (2006)

14. Zhang, L., He, W., Morkved, O., Zhao, V., Ur, B.: Trace2TAP: synthesizing trigger-action programs from traces of behavior. Proc. ACM Interact. Mob. Wearable Ubiquitous Technol. 4(3), 1–26 (2020)
15. Zhang, L., He, W., et al.: AutoTap: synthesizing and repairing trigger-action programs using LTL properties. In: Proceedings of the 41st International Conference on Software Engineering, pp. 281–291. IEEE Press (2019)
16. Zhao, V., et al.: Visualizing differences to improve end-user understanding of trigger-action programs, CHI EA 2020, pp. 1–10. Association for Computing Machinery (2020)

Joint Optimization of UAV Trajectory and Task Scheduling in SAGIN: Delay Driven

Hongyue Kang[1], Xiaolin Chang[1($\boxtimes$)], Jelena Mišić[2], Vojislav B. Mišić[2], and Junchao Fan[1]

[1] Beijing Key Laboratory of Security and Privacy in Intelligent Transportation, Beijing Jiaotong University, Beijing, People's Republic of China
{19112051,xlchang,20120468}@bjtu.edu.cn
[2] Ryerson University, Toronto, ON, Canada
{jmisic,vmisic}@ryerson.ca

Abstract. This paper aims to study a computation task scheduling problem in the space-air-ground integrated network (SAGIN). The prior works on this problem usually assume that an unmanned aerial vehicle (UAV) is static or has a fixed flying trajectory. In this paper, we allow a UAV to plan its own trajectory and to have a certain coverage area. Our objective is to design a policy that minimizes the maximum task processing delay by joint optimization of task scheduling and UAV trajectory. We first formulate this nonconvex optimization problem as a Constrained Markov Decision Process (CMDP) under the constraints of UAV energy capacity and mobility space. Then, we design a Deep Deterministic Policy Gradient (DDPG)-based reinforcement learning algorithm to learn the optimal task offloading ratio and UAV trajectory. Our work is evaluated from three aspects: (1) SAGIN network architecture vs. single layer network; (2) DDPG-based algorithm vs. Deep Q Network-based algorithm; (3) optimized UAV trajectory vs. fixed UAV position. Experiment results validate that the optimized UAV trajectory can achieve a lower task processing delay than fixed UAV position .

Keywords: LEO · RL · SAGIN · Task offloading · UAV trajectory optimization

1 Introduction

The space-air-ground integrated network (SAGIN) emerges to provide high-rate, seamless and reliable transmission, which is conceived to become the next generation wireless communication network [1]. A typical SAGIN has three layers: ground layer, aerial layer and space layer. IoT devices are restricted by ground infrastructure and have limited computing capacity. Therefore, there is a need to exploit aerial/space to alleviate terrestrial computation pressure. Low Earth Orbit (LEO) satellites in the space layer can provide wide coverage for remote areas and have been devoted to the commercialization, such as SpaceX [2] and OneWeb [3]. But they are limited by large satellite-terrestrial delay. Unmanned Aerial Vehicles (UAVs) in the aerial layer can move flexibly to provide temporary coverage enhancement. Moreover, UAVs are low cost and can be deployed

© Springer Nature Switzerland AG 2021
H. Hacid et al. (Eds.): ICSOC 2021, LNCS 13121, pp. 663–671, 2021.
https://doi.org/10.1007/978-3-030-91431-8_42

quickly to relieve the booming traffic demands of terrestrial networks. However, UAVs are constrained by energy supply and cannot provide service for a long time [4]. Satellites, UAVs and IoT in different layers can complement each other to provide seamless and fast service for IoT devices, which is the origin of SAGIN [5].

Researches have been conducted on the computation task scheduling problem in SAGIN [6, 7]. But they usually ignored UAV mobility or merely assumed fixed UAV trajectory. Actually, during the UAV flight, users can join or exit the network dynamically because of new tasks arrival and/or the completion of old tasks. According to these dynamics, the UAV should adjust its position to serve more users [7]. Studies have shown that UAV trajectory optimization can improve the transmit power of IoT devices and enhance the network reliability [8]. Therefore, it is necessary to consider UAV trajectory optimization in the computation task scheduling of SAGIN.

In this paper, we endeavor to minimize the maximum task processing delay for IoT devices by joint optimization of task scheduling and UAV trajectory in SAGIN. In our scenario, IoT devices generate tasks and then decide to compute locally or upload part of tasks to the UAV. Similar to previous studies [6, 7], a flying UAV provides edge computing service for IoT devices and a LEO satellite as a cloud center offers ubiquitous access. Considering UAV mobility, each UAV is assumed to have a certain coverage range and can only provide service to the IoT devices within its coverage area [9]. Therefore, there may be the situation where tasks are not completed at a UAV and the IoT device is out of the range. In that case, the UAV must transmit the remaining tasks to the LEO satellite to make sure that the tasks are finished and can be returned to IoT devices [10]. During the process, there are two decisions to make. The first is that IoT devices should decide how many tasks need to be offloaded to the UAV. The second is that the UAV needs to adjust its speed and angle to optimize its trajectory.

Considering the limitations of UAV energy capacity and mobility space, we formulate the delay-oriented task scheduling and UAV trajectory optimization problem as a Constrained Markov Decision Process (CMDP) [11]. Since the UAV action space is continuous, a Deep Deterministic Policy Gradient (DDPG)-based reinforcement learning algorithm is designed to address the CMDP [12]. To evaluate the advantages of the proposed algorithm, we compare our algorithm with a Deep Q Network (DQN)-based algorithm. The results indicate that our algorithm behaves better than DQN-based algorithm in terms of task processing delay.

The rest of the paper is organized as follows. In Sect. 2, we describe the considered SAGIN network architecture and introduce the computation, transmission, and energy consumption models. The optimization problem is formulated in Sect. 3. Section 4 describes the designed algorithm. The performance evaluation is presented in Sect. 5. Section 6 concludes the paper.

2 System Model

Figure 1 illustrates a SAGIN architecture including three layers, the ground layer with N IoT devices, the aerial layer with a UAV and the space layer with a LEO satellite.

In the ground layer, IoT devices are located in the areas where there is no cellular coverage. Due to the lack of ground infrastructure, the IoT devices can offload a portion of the tasks to the UAV and execute the remaining tasks locally. The UAV in the aerial layer can serve as an edge node to provide edge computing service for IoT devices. However, the UAV is moving and has its coverage limit. When the IoT device in service is out of the UAV coverage and becomes disconnected due to UAV mobility, the UAV will offload the remaining tasks to the LEO satellite, ensuring that the processing results can return to IoT devices. Moreover, given that the UAV energy capacity is limited, all tasks must be finished within the allowed energy.

Fig. 1. An overview of the SAGIN architecture

In this paper, we aim to minimize the maximum task processing delay for IoT devices by task scheduling and UAV trajectory optimization. We consider a discrete time-slotted system $\Gamma = \{1, 2, \cdots, t\}$ with equal length time slots. The computation task, transmission, and energy consumption models are presented in the following. The notations and default settings of variables can be found in Table 1.

Table 1. Notations and default settings of variables

Notation	Definition
cyc	The CPU cycles required to process each unit byte
P_{com}	The power consumption for UAV processing tasks
M_u	Weight of the uav
t_{fly}	The time of UAV flying
$f_{UAV} \; f_{IoT} \; f_{LEO}$	UAV, IoT, LEO process unit cpu-cycle frequency
$rate_u(t)$	The wireless transmission rate of the IoT-UAV link
$rate_l(t)$	The wireless transmission rate of the UAV-LEO link
P_l	Transmission power of UAV-LEO link
d_S	The propagation delay of uav-leo link
$r_n(t)$	The ratio of IoT offloading to UAV
t_{cov}	UAV coverage time
$task_n(t)$	The task size produced by IoT device n in time slot t
$delay_{all}(t)$	The delay for all offloaded tasks processed at UAV in time slot t

(1) Computation Task Model

We now present the processing delays in local computing, UAV computing and LEO computing, respectively.

1) The delay for computing locally is $delay_{loc}(t) = (1 - r_n(t)) \cdot task_n(t) \cdot cyc/f_{IoT}$.

2) Considering the UAV coverage time, the actual delay of task computing at the UAV is

$$delay_{UAV}(t) = \begin{cases} r_n(t) \cdot task_n(t) \cdot cyc/f_{UAV}, & delay_{all} \leq t_{cov} \\ t_{cov}, & else \end{cases}$$

3) The remaining task size that needs to run at the LEO satellite is

$$task_{LEO}(t) = \begin{cases} 0, & delay_{all} \leq t_{cov} \\ r_n(t)task_n(t) \cdot cyc - t_{cov}f_{UAV}, & else \end{cases}$$

Namely, the delay for computing at LEO satellite is $delay_{LEO}(t) = task_{LEO}(t)/f_{LEO}$.

(2) Transmission Model

We now present the transmission delays on the IoT-UAV link and the UAV-LEO link, respectively.

1) The delay for transmitting tasks from IoT devices to the UAV in time slot t is given by $delay_{IU}(t) = r_n(t)task_n(t)/rate_u(t)$.

2) The transmission delay from the UAV to the LEO satellite is given by $delay_{UL}(t) = task_{LEO}(t)/rate_l(t) + d_S$.

(3) Energy Consumption Model

The UAV energy consumption consists of flying energy, computing energy and transmission energy. Note that we ignore the energy consumption for hovering.

1) The energy consumed to fly is $e_{fly}(t) = M_u||v(t)||^2 t_{fly}/2$.

2) The energy consumption for computing is denoted by $e_{com}(t) = P_{com} \cdot delay_{UAV}(t)$.

3) The energy consumption for transmission is denoted by $e_{trans}(t) = P_l \cdot delay_{UL}(t)$.

The cumulative energy consumption is $e_{t+1} = e_t - e_{fly}(t) - e_{com}(t) - e_{trans}(t)$.

3 Problem Formulation

This paper focuses on minimizing the maximum processing delay by optimizing UAV trajectory and task scheduling, while satisfying the UAV energy capacity and mobility space constraints. Let $delay_{off}(t) = delay_{UAV}(t) + delay_{LEO}(t) + delay_{IU}(t) + delay_{UL}(t)$. Based on the models in Sect. 2, the optimization problem in SAGIN can be formulated as $P1$.

$$P1: \quad \min \sum_{t=1}^{T} \sum_{n=1}^{N} \beta_n(t) \max\left[delay_{loc}(t), delay_{off}(t)\right] \tag{1a}$$

$$s.t. \ \beta_n(t) \in \{0, 1\}, \forall t \in \{1, 2, \cdots, T\}, n \in \{1, 2, \cdots, N\} \tag{1b}$$

$$\sum_{n=1}^{N} \beta_n(t) = 1, \forall t, \tag{1c}$$

$$(x_{n,t}, y_{n,t}) \in [0, L], \tag{1d}$$

$$(x_{uav,t}, y_{uav,t}) \in [0, L], \tag{1e}$$

$$0 \le r_n(t) \le 1, \forall n, t, \tag{1f}$$

$$flag_n(t) \in \{0, 1\}, \forall n, t, \tag{1g}$$

$$\sum_{t=1}^{T} \sum_{n=1}^{N} \left(e_{fly,n}(t) + e_{com,n}(t) + e_{trans,n}(t)\right) \le e_{total}, \forall n, \tag{1h}$$

$$\sum_{t=1}^{T} \sum_{n=1}^{N} \beta_n(t) \cdot task_n(t) = task_{all} \tag{1i}$$

Equation (1a) is the objective that minimizes the maximum delay for processing all tasks over T time slots. Equation (1b) and Eq. (1c) restrict that only one IoT task can be processed in a time slot. Equation (1d) and Eq. (1e) limit the locations of the UAV and IoT devices. Equation (1f) constrains the range of task offloading ratio. Equation (1g) expresses whether there is a blockage between the UAV and IoT devices, and Eq. (1h) restricts the energy capacity. Equation (1i) represents all tasks must be completed over T time slots.

The states, actions, reward, and policy in an MDP can be formulated as follows.

1) *State*: In time slot t, $s_t = (UAV_{loc}(t), IoT_n(t), Task_n(t), flag_n(t)), n \in N$ is used to describe the system state, where $s_t \in S$. $UAV_{loc}(t)$ indicates the location of the UAV, $IoT_n(t)$ represents the location of IoT device n, $Task_n(t)$ denotes the task size produced by IoT device n, and $flag_n(t)$ is to indicate whether the signal between the UAV and IoT device n is blocked by obstacles in time slot t.

2) *Action*: $a_t = (\theta(t), v(t), R(t))$, $a_t \in A$. $\theta(t)$, $v(t)$ and $R(t)$ represent UAV flight angle, UAV flight speed, and task offloading ratio in time slot t, respectively.

3) *Reward function*: The reward function is defined as $R(s_t, a_t) = -delay(t)$, where the processing delay turns to max $\sum_{t=1}^{T} \sum_{n=1}^{N} \beta_n(t) \max[delay_{loc}(t), delay_{offload}]$.

4 Algorithm

In order to train DNN effectively, state normalization is adopted to preprocess the observed states. To minimize the maximum task processing delay, DDPG-based joint optimization scheme is shown in Algorithm 1. It is noted that the training phase is run for N_{ep} episodes with each episode N_{ex} steps. The algorithm includes two parts: the network environment initialization (line 1) and the deep RL algorithm (lines 2–15).

As introduced above, the state needs to be normalized first (line 5) and then is fed to actor network. The actor produces a with observation s by $A(s|\theta_a)$ and the noise is added to ensure sufficient exploration (line 6). Each interaction with the environment is stored as a tuple (line 8) and a set of data is extracted from the buffer in the learning phase (line 9). During the process of training, the parameters of actor and critic networks are updated iteratively (lines 10–12). And target networks are updated by line 13 to avoid divergence of the learning algorithm.

5 Experiment Results

This section conducts extensive simulations to evaluate the proposed SAGIN scheme. The simulation is implemented via Python 3.8 and Pytorch open-source machine learning library. The training of DNNs is conducted with an Intel(R) Core (TM) i5-9400F CPU @ 2.90 GHz. The default detailed parameters are referred to [13].

Our work is evaluated from two aspects: network architecture evaluation and algorithm evaluation. First, the task processing delay under different offloading mechanisms is presented in Fig. 2, where local-only, UAV-only and LEO-only mean that all tasks are only allowed to be computed by IoT devices, the UAV and the LEO satellite, respectively. SAGIN represents the tasks are offloaded according to the scheme in Sect. 2. From it, we can see the proposed offloading approach can achieve the lowest delay because of the learnt optimal offloading policy.

Algorithm 1 DDPG-based joint optimization of task scheduling and UAV trajectory algorithm

Input: Episode times N_{ep}, exploration times N_{ex}, actor learning rate η_a,

critic learning rate η_c, parameter of state normalization $\lambda_x, \lambda_y, \lambda_{task}$

Output: Learned actor $A(s;\theta_a)$ and critic $C(s,a;\theta_c)$

1   **Initialization:**

    Initialize actor network $A(s|\theta_a)$ and critic network $C(s,a|\theta_c)$ randomly with θ_a and θ_c

    Initialize target actor network A' and target critic network C' with $\theta_a' \leftarrow \theta_a$ and $\theta_c' \leftarrow \theta_c$

2   **for** $i = 1$ to N_{ep} **do**

3   Obtain initial observed state s_1

4   **for** $j = 1$ to N_{ex} **do**

5   Normalize state s_t to s_t' by state normalization

6   Get action a_t by $a_t = A(s;\theta_a) + noise$

7   Execute action a_t, obtain reward r_t and new state s_{t+1}

8   Save $\{s_t, a_t, r_{t+1}, s_{t+1}\}$ to the memory

9   Sample a batch size of data from memory

10   Obtain y_i by Eq. (6)

11   Update critic network by Eq. (5)

12   Update actor network by Eq. (7)

13   Update the target networks $\theta_a' \leftarrow \tau\theta_a + (1-\tau)\theta_a'$, $\theta_c' \leftarrow \tau\theta_c + (1-\tau)\theta_c'$

14   **end for**

15   **end for**

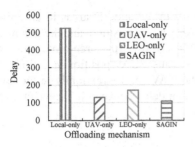

Fig. 2. Delay under different offloading mechanisms

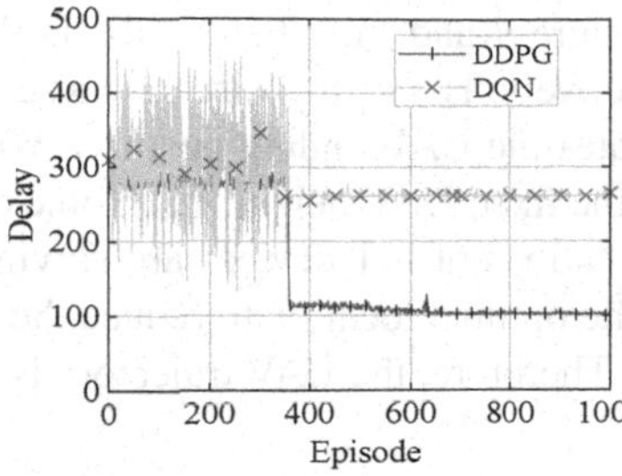

Fig. 3. Delay under different RL algorithms

Next, we present the task processing delay under different reinforcement learning algorithms (DDPG and DQN algorithms). From Fig. 3, we can see DDPG behaves better than DQN in terms of reducing task processing delay in SAGIN. Because of the discrete action space, DQN may miss the optimal policy. However, DDPG explores a continuous action space and takes an accurate action, which can find the optimal policy.

In Figs. 4, 5 and 6, we investigate the impact of bandwidth, UAV computing capability, and energy capacity on the task processing delay. We can see that the delay with optimized UAV trajectory is less than that with fixed UAV position under different bandwidths, UAV computing capabilities and energy capacities. From Fig. 6, we can see that the delay with optimized UAV trajectory reduces from 10 to 50 kJ and then remains stable after 50 kJ, which is because the UAV cannot deal with all the tasks when its battery capacity is low. If the battery capacity is large enough, the UAV can handle all the tasks within the battery capacity.

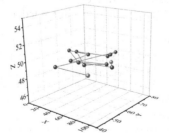

Fig. 4. Delay under different bandwidths

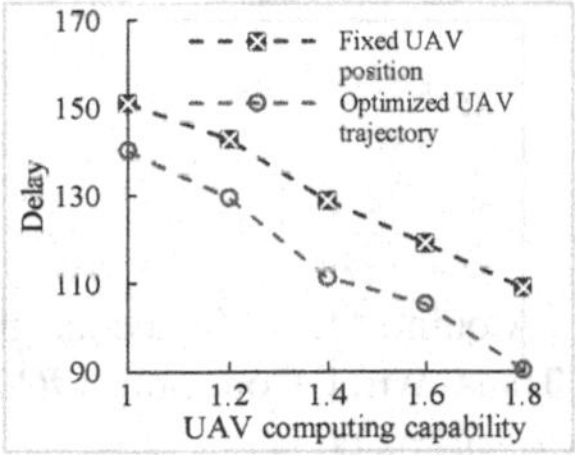

Fig. 5. Delay under different UAV computing capabilities

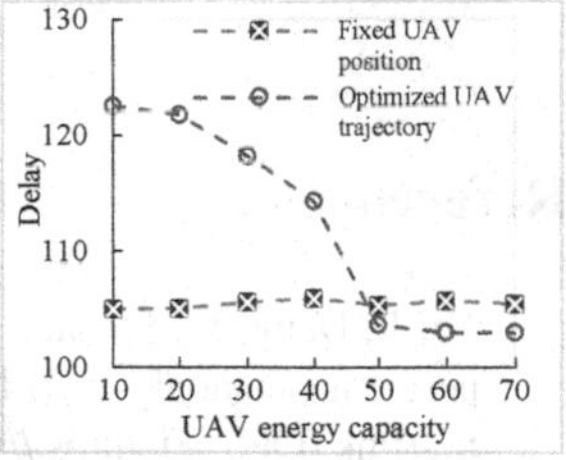

Fig. 6. Delay under different energy capacities

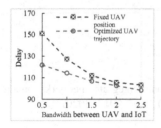

Fig. 7. 3D UAV trajectory

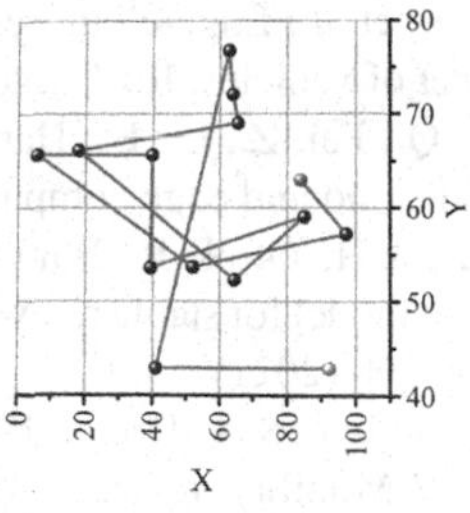

Fig. 8. 2D UAV trajectory

Figure 7 and Fig. 8 show the UAV trajectory in 3D and 2D areas in an episode, respectively. The yellow circle represents the UAV starting position, and the green circle indicates the UAV ending position. We set a $100 \times 100 \times 100$ three-dimension space with the fixed UAV height. Each blue circle represents a UAV position variation. Since the locations of IoT devices are varying, and the UAV can fly randomly in the area to find the optimal location to reduce the transmission delay between IoT devices and the UAV. Therefore, the UAV trajectory is irregular.

6 Conclusion

In this paper, a novel SAGIN network architecture is described, in which IoT devices generate tasks and decide to compute locally or upload a portion of the tasks to the UAV. Different from other researches, our UAV is flexible and can plan its trajectory in order to reduce the task processing delay. In addition, the LEO satellite as a standby to deal with the tasks that the UAV cannot finish within the limited time. We aim to find a policy to minimize the maximum task processing delay by joint optimization of task scheduling and UAV trajectory. We formulate the optimization problem as a CMDP. To capture the continuous action of the UAV, a DDPG-based RL algorithm is adopted to solve the CMDP. The experiment results indicate that the delay with optimized UAV trajectory is lower than that with fixed UAV position.

Acknowledgment. The work of H. Kang, X. Chang and J. Fan was supported by the National Natural Science Foundation of China under Grant No. U1836105 and the Fundamental Research Funds for the Central Universities 2020YJS042. The work of J. Mišić and V. B. Mišić was supported by Natural Science and Engineering Research Council (NSERC) of Canada through their respective Discovery Grants.

References

1. Ye, J., Dang, S., Shihada, B., Alouini, M.-S.: Space-air-ground integrated networks: outage performance analysis. IEEE Trans. Wirel. Commun. **19**(12), 7897–7912 (2020)
2. Starlink (Online). https://www.starlink.com/
3. OneWeb (Online). https://oneweb.world/
4. Cao, X., Yang, B., Yuen, C., Han, Z.: HAP-reserved communications in space-air-ground integrated networks. IEEE Trans. Veh. Technol (2021). (Early Access)
5. Cao, B., et al.: Edge-cloud resource scheduling in space-air-ground integrated networks for internet of vehicles. IEEE Internet Things J. **8**(11), 9164–9176 (2021)
6. Tang, Q., Fei, Z., Li, B., Han, Z.: Computation offloading in LEO satellite networks with hybrid cloud and edge computing. IEEE Internet Things J. **8**(11), 9164–9176 (2021)
7. Abualola, H., Otrok, H., Barada, H.R., Al-Qutayri, M., Al-Hammadi, Y.: Matching game theoretical model for stable relay selection in a UAV-assisted internet of vehicles. Veh. Commun. **27**, 100290 (2021)
8. Hadiwardoyo, S.A., Dricot, J.M., Calafate, C.T., Cano, J.-C., Hernández-Orallo, E., Manzoni, P.: UAV Mobility model for dynamic UAV-to-car communications in 3D environments. Ad Hoc Netw. **107**, 102193 (2020)

9. Shakoor, S., Kaleem, Z., Do, D.-T., Dobre, O.A., Jamalipour, A.: Joint optimization of UAV 3-D placement and path-loss factor for energy-efficient maximal coverage. IEEE Internet Things J. **8**(12), 9776–9786 (2021)

10. Yu, S., Gong, X., Shi, Q., Wang, X., Chen, X.: EC-SAGINs: edge computing-enhanced space-air-ground integrated networks for internet of vehicles. CoRR abs/2101.06056 (2021)

11. Satija, H., Amortila, P., Pineau, J.: Constrained markov decision processes via backward value functions. In: ICML 2020, pp. 8502–8511 (2020)

12. Silver, D., Lever, G., Heess, N., Degris,T., Wierstra, D., Riedmiller, M.A.: Deterministic policy gradient algorithms. In: ICML 2014, pp. 387–395 (2014)

13. Cheng, X., et al.: Space/aerial-assisted computing offloading for IoT applications: a learning-based approach. IEEE J. Sel. Areas Commun. **37**(5), 1117–1129 (2019)

Weaving Open Services with Runtime Models for Continuous Smart Cities KPIs Assessment

Martina De Sanctis[1]([✉])[iD], Ludovico Iovino[1][iD], Maria Teresa Rossi[1][iD], and Manuel Wimmer[2][iD]

[1] Gran Sasso Science Institute, L'Aquila, Italy
{martina.desanctis,ludovico.iovino,mariateresa.rossi}@gssi.it
[2] CDL-MINT, Johannes Kepler University, Linz, Austria
manuel.wimmer@jku.at

Abstract. The automatic Key Performance Indicators (KPIs) assessment for smart cities is challenging, since the input parameters needed for the KPIs calculations are highly dynamic and change with different frequencies. Moreover, they are provided by heterogeneous data sources (e.g., IoT infrastructures, Web Services, open repositories), with different access protocol. Open services are widely adopted in this area on top of open data, IoT, and cloud services. However, KPIs assessment frameworks based on smart city models are currently decoupled from open services. This limits the possibility of having runtime up-to-date data for KPIs assessment and synchronized reports. Thus, this paper presents a generic service-oriented middleware that connects open services and runtime models, applied to a model-based KPIs assessment framework for smart cities. It enables a continuous monitoring of the KPIs' input parameters provided by open services, automating the data acquisition process and the continuous KPIs evaluation. Experiment shows how the evolved framework enables a continuous KPIs evaluation, by drastically decreasing (∼88%) the latency compared to its baseline.

Keywords: Models@run.time · Continuous monitoring · Smart cities assessment

1 Introduction

The Smart Cities (SCs) ecosystem is an ideal ground for service-based applications, where the role of Service-Oriented Architecture (SOA) is to enable the integration between city services to realize innovative services and applications (e.g., [1,2]). Particularly, we focus on the smart governance [3] process within SCs, concerning the use of technology in processing information and supporting *smart decision making*. Specifically, it exploits Key Performance Indicators (KPIs) assessment to measure qualitative metrics over cities to support their smart and sustainable growth[1]. For instance, the International Telecommunication Union (ITU) defined a list of all the KPIs for Smart Sustainable Cities, along with its collection methodology [4]. The KPIs assessment

---

[1] https://bit.ly/3ekdT9D.

© Springer Nature Switzerland AG 2021
H. Hacid et al. (Eds.): ICSOC 2021, LNCS 13121, pp. 672–681, 2021.
https://doi.org/10.1007/978-3-030-91431-8_43

process involves different tasks, e.g., retrieving input data, calculating indicators, and reporting evaluation results. Traditional approaches, e.g., manual or spreadsheet-based approaches[2], envisage a significant human contribution to perform such operations, with expensive and repetitive activities requiring resources and time to be performed.

Enabling *automation* in the KPIs assessment to both the retrieval of input data and calculation of KPIs, is not trivial, since the input parameters needed for the calculations may come from different types of data sources (e.g., IoT infrastructure, open data repositories or statistics elaborated by public entities) in different formats. Moreover, the values of the input parameters can change periodically (e.g., hourly), and thus, the KPIs assessment process has to be synchronized and re-assessed accordingly.

On the one hand, Web services and APIs, i.e., the most common way to specify open services in the SC domain, are widely adopted to build new applications on top of open data, IoT, and cloud services. On the other hand, model-based approaches are exploited in the SC domain, i.e., to represent complex systems through abstract models [5]. However, despite the huge availability of SC services and models, they are currently not well-connected, which would be required to reach the notion of a digital twin [6]. Moreover, the currently available frameworks for the KPIs calculation are mainly online spreadsheets[3], which are far from being automated, and Web-based applications (see, e.g., [7]) only providing a fixed set of predefined KPIs. In our previous work [8], we presented a flexible and automated model-based approach for KPIs assessment in SCs. However, the research efforts in [8] have focused on the definition of the model-based artifacts of the framework, while ignoring the relationship with the independent and heterogeneous data sources providing KPIs input parameters and the constant synchronization with them. Thus, in [8] the input parameters values have to be manually retrieved and updated in the models.

With these premises, we developed a generic service-oriented middleware that connects open services and runtime models. Specifically, we evolve the architecture in [9] of our approach in a service-oriented fashion, by means of the message-oriented middleware enabling: (i) continuous monitoring of KPIs input parameters from heterogeneous sources available as (open) services, and (ii) runtime models evolution with up-to-date input parameters for the SC modeling artifacts, in accordance with the real-world SCs evolution reflected by the open services. In other words, *we provide a generic solution for monitoring runtime model parameters from open services for SCs models*. Thus, we turn SC models into digital twins, by weaving open services and the runtime models, allowing the automated information flow from the system to the model [6].

The rest of the paper is organized as follows: background and motivation for this work are discussed in Sect. 2. Section 3 presents the proposed approach. Evaluation results of the implemented prototype are reported in Sect. 4. Finally, Sect. 5 discusses the related work and draws conclusions and future directions.

---

[2] https://bit.ly/37EFR9r.
[3] https://bit.ly/3dT1zwV.

2   Background and Motivation

In this section, we describe the assessment process realized by the smart cities KPIs modeling framework from [8], its limitations, and the challenges we aim to address.

2.1   A Smart Cities KPIs Assessment Framework

Figure 1 depicts the overall KPIs evaluation approach consisting in four main phases, each with dedicated input and output elements. The assessment of a SC starts from the *SC Modeling* phase, during which the city under evaluation is modeled, by means of MDE techniques. In the *SC Model*, SCs are designed in terms of their stakeholders (e.g., municipality), infrastructures (e.g., IoT infrastructures), data sources (e.g., open data, IoT services) and data types. This way, the *SC Model* provides the *input parameters* needed to calculate the KPIs of interest, as we will see in the following. In the *KPIs Definition* phase, by following *KPIs Guidelines/Documentation* (e.g., [4,7]), the user models or select the relevant KPIs for the SC under evaluation (e.g., Air Pollution KPI, Travel Time Index KPI). In the *KPIs Model* given as output, the calculation formulae of the selected KPIs are defined by using a textual Domain-Specific Language (DSL) [10]. The designed *SC Model* and *KPIs Model*, are the inputs for an evaluation engine that executes the *KPIs Assessment* over the candidate SC. The assessment phase returns an *Evaluated KPIs Model* reporting the KPIs concrete values resulted from the assessment. The *Evaluated KPIs Model*, in turn, is the input of the *KPIs Visualization* phase during which *Dashboard*s representing the KPIs status are generated, through code generation.

In the following, we give a trivial but concrete example of a KPI evaluated for a smart city, as done in [8]. Specifically, we consider the KPI *Air Pollution (AP)* that measures the air quality based on the values reported for specific pollutants [4]. It is based on the *Air Quality Index (AQI)* formula, calculated as in (1), where p refers to the pollutant (e.g., $PM2.5$) whereas the *legal limit* is established by the law:

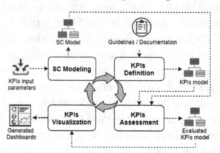

Fig. 1. KPIs assessment: process overview.

$$AQI_p = (measured\ concentration_p / legal\ limit) \times 100 \qquad (1)$$

The worst AQI_p (i.e., the greater) determines the *Air Pollution AP* KPI, which is evaluated w.r.t. five evaluation classes, i.e., Excellent, Good, Discrete, Bad, Terrible. To calculate the AP KPI we need, as *input parameters*, the measured concentrations of the required pollutants. These values are provided by the *SC Model* together with the data sources from which they have been collected, e.g., the Breezometer open API[4]. An

---

[4] https://www.breezometer.com/.

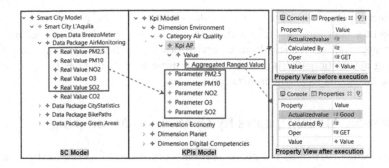

Fig. 2. Excerpts of the smart city model designing the city of *L'Aquila*.

excerpt of the *SC model* of the smart city of *L'Aquila* is depicted in Fig. 2. It shows the tree-view of the model as shown in the Eclipse Modeling Framework (EMF)[5], on top of which the assessment framework has been designed. Figure 2 also shows an excerpt of the tree-view of the *KPIs Model* where the AP KPI formula is nested into the `Aggregated Ranged Value`. The corresponding textual representation through the provided DSL [8] can be found in our online repository[6]. It is important to notice that, in the KPI definition, the names of the parameters whose values are provided by the *SC Model* must conform. This match will be executed by the evaluation engine during the assessment. Figure 2 eventually shows the *Property View* reporting the AP KPI *Actualized Value before* and *after* the assessment, i.e., Good.

2.2 Limitation and Challenges

In the selected framework, the KPIs assessment process envisages the involvement of the users (e.g., KPIs experts) not only in the initial design of the required models but also in the manual retrieving of the KPIs input parameters. This means that the user has to manually fill the *SC model* every time the KPIs input parameters change, and then trigger the re-execution of the KPIs assessment process. These manual tasks are time-consuming and error-prone. Moreover, some KPIs input parameters are highly dynamic, since they change with very different frequencies (e.g., monthly, hourly). For instance, data about pollutants concentrations can be collected every hour or even minutes. Lastly, KPIs input parameters are provided by a multitude of heterogeneous sources, such as IoT sensors, social media, open data, usually available and accessible as (open) APIs and services. Given the discussion above, we can identify the following challenges: **(C1)** The framework must guarantee a *continuous and possibly automated monitoring* of KPIs parameters sources, i.e., services, and runtime update of the models using these parameters. **(C2)** The framework must provide *real-time evaluated KPIs*, i.e., as much

---

[5] https://bit.ly/3lc1GHG.

[6] https://github.com/iovinoludovico/runtime-kpi-assessment.

up-to-date as possible w.r.t. the current status of the smart city, given that KPIs support and affect the decision-making processes in smart cities. For these reasons, we believe that our approach can benefit from a service-oriented continuous monitoring feature, providing automatic gathering of data and runtime models updates (i.e., *SC models*), enabling the dashboards synchronization.

3 Runtime Model Updates by Continuous Monitoring

The architecture [9] behind our previous framework [8] was focused on the assessment phase, thus keeping the gathering of data and the consequent models update as manual tasks. To address the challenges discussed above and overcome the current limitations of the framework, we refactored and extended its architecture by adding a *message-oriented middleware* enabling continuous monitoring of KPIs data sources and runtime update of models in the KPIs assessment for SCs, as shown in Fig. 3. This extension evolves the manual and standalone framework into an automatic and service-oriented one, where heterogeneous data sources continuously feed the assessment process.

In the *front-end*, we have the KPIs Modeling Editor (implemented with Xtext[7]) devoted to the selection and definition of the relevant KPIs for the SC under evaluation, through custom textual DSLs. The Smart City Modeling Editor [11] (implemented with Sirius [12]), instead, helps users to model the SC under evaluation through the exploitation of graphical functionalities [11]. Lastly, the graphical Dashboard, obtained through model to code transformations (and visualized with Picto[8]) allows the interpretation of the KPIs assessment results.

In the *back-end*, the Requests Manager handles: (i) KPIs assessment requests to the Evaluation Engine (modeled with the Epsilon Object Language[9]) that is responsible for performing the SC evaluation; (ii) visualization requests from the Evaluation Engine to the Dashboard component. In particular, the Dashboard Synchronizer converts the KPIs model instantiated after the assessment in an HTML file, which is in sync with source files of the Dashboard. The synchronizer has its own listener that every time the model changes the HTML file is reloaded, updating the views. The Requests Manager also handles requests to the Models Manager to gather or store the models needed in the KPIs assessment process. The models manager handles the persistence of models in the SC Models Repository and the KPIs Models Repository.

---

[7] https://www.eclipse.org/Xtext/.

[8] https://bit.ly/3l8jL9s.

[9] https://www.eclipse.org/epsilon/doc/eol/.

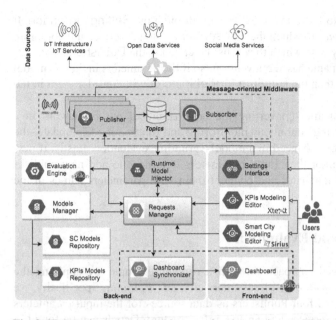

Fig. 3. The service-oriented architecture for the continuous KPIs assessment of SCs. The arrows shape the data-flow among components. White and blurred grey components show the architecture from [9], where the blurred grey ones required modifications for this work. In grey, instead, the newly integrated components.

We now describe the new components and the *message-oriented middleware*. The Publishers and the Subscriber implement the classic publish/subscribe communication pattern based on Topics. The type of topics are the types of parameters the SC can handle in the evaluation, e.g., pollutants, travel time, and so on. Specifically, the Publisher components can be multiple, considering the multiple data sources. They send calls to data sources, e.g., open services, to gather the input parameters needed for the KPIs calculations. Each publisher prepares the data, before publishing changed parameters on the assigned topic. These components are interfaces implemented, in turn, by specific Java classes.

The topics are published as MQTT [13] messages with a specific structure, namely $lat/\{latitude\}/long/\{longitude\}/parameter$, allowing multi-city evaluation. Latitude and longitude are the GPS coordinate of the smart city under evaluation. This way we can provide multiple publishers as types of data gatherer for different cities, by matching the smart cities coordinates. Then, the subscriber is able to distinguish which data intercept, by using the latitude and longitude of the smart city under evaluation. The Subscriber is devoted to the synchronization of the models with the data sources. It receives changed parameters through the subscription to the corresponding topic and actions can be triggered, as specified in the following. The Runtime Model Injector is invoked by the Subscriber, when it receives new data from the topics, and devoted to the retrieving of the SC models that need to be synchronised. It checks if the input parameters in the models are in line with the ones received by the Subscriber by querying the model. It is also in charge of SC models *update*, that is the operation of filling the models with the received up-to-date data, through EOL queries. Furthermore, the Runtime Model Injector interacts with the Requests Manager to trigger the KPIs assessment process due to changed input parameters, requesting the last saved SC models. The overall monitoring process is enabled by the user that is responsible for setting up the continuous monitoring features, only for the dynamic parameters with the *runtime* attribute set to TRUE in the SC model, through the Settings Interface. It is used for defining the *topics* to which the Subscriber has to subscribe, and configure the APIs and the frequency with which they must be called in the Publishers. This setting is provided through a name based convention, so if the parameters in the SC model are included in the topics, then the Runtime Model Injector will consider them in the process.

It is worth noting that after converting the architecture of our framework in a service-oriented one, enabling continuous monitoring and runtime models update, the assessment approach can be enhanced in a models@runtime evaluation. Lastly, if new KPIs are modeled, to monitor their input parameters it suffices to add new publishers according to provided templates and connect them with parameters names in the *SC Model*.

4   Implementation and Evaluation

We demonstrate the evolved approach through a running example, by applying the extended evaluation framework over a real smart city, i.e., *L'Aquila*. Specifically, we consider 6 *dynamic* KPIs and four Publishers as data sources for the input parameters of these KPIs, i.e., 3 open services and an IoT infrastructure. Details can be found in our online repository[10]. We experimentally assess the service-based continuous KPIs assessment and compare it with its previous version where the KPIs parameters continuous monitoring and runtime models update were not available.

Research Question (RQ). We aim to answer the following RQ: What is the impact of KPIs input *data retrieving*, *models update* and *evaluation engine execution* tasks on the latency? How does the presented approach compare with its baseline [9] w.r.t. the impact to latency of these tasks?

Experiment Setup. To answer to **RQ**, we have conducted an experiment by comparing the *baseline framework* proposed in [9], requiring manual data retrieving and models filling, with the fully *automated framework*, enabling continuous monitoring and runtime models update presented in this paper. We consider one subject smart city and 6 dynamic KPIs. For this experiment, the framework run on a Macbook Pro 2019, 2,3 GHz 8-Core Intel Core i9 processor, 32 GB 2667 MHz DDR4 RAM and 2TB SSD of storage. This laptop runs the Mosquitto client, all the publishers, the subscriber and the evaluation engine. We run the experiment for 6 h. Anytime (and only when) the *SC Model* is not up to date, the subscriber updates the parameters in the model with the new received values and it runs the evaluation engine that triggers the dashboard's update. All these activities have been automatically monitored and measured in a log.

Results for RQ. Table 1 shows to which extent the *data retrieving*, *SC Model update* and *evaluation engine* execution contribute to the framework latency, in both the Automated and Baseline *Exp*s. Specifically, Table 1 reports the average execution time for each of the three phases in milliseconds (ms), for both *Exp*s. As expected, each of the three phases requires quite more time in the Baseline *Exp*, where the data retrieving

---

[10] https://github.com/iovinoludovico/runtime-kpi-assessment.

and model update (performed manually) are the most time consuming ones. Moreover, the latency in the Baseline Exp could also depend from communication issues among the users involved in the monitoring of data sources and update of the models. The evaluation engine execution also contributes more to the latency in the Baseline Exp, since it has to be manually launched anytime changes are applied in the *SC Model* due to the evolution of the KPIs input parameters.

Table 1. Latency contributed by the three phases.

Approach	Data retrieving	SC model update	Evaluation engine
Baseline	14.929,89 ms	18.668,28 ms	6.605,22 ms
Automated	525,89 ms	2,96 ms	138,82 ms

Discussion. Current limitations concern the generalizability and scalability of the approach. Although it has been applied on a single smart city to evaluate 6 KPIs, it uses techniques (e.g., PubSub pattern, open APIs) that can be generalized and extended to more complex systems, as long as there are accessible data sources to get real input parameters for *dynamic* KPIs to be measured on real smart cities. Indeed, PubSub is known to offer better scalability w.r.t. traditional client-server, by means of parallel operation and message caching. Of course, the message-oriented middleware might add a network latency delay. However, keeping the data retrieving and update of models as manual tasks is impractical, considering the huge number of identified KPIs.

5   Related Work, Conclusion, and Future Work

Several SCs architectures can be found in the literature [14]. Matar *et al.* [15] present an approach for designing smart city's ecosystems, by means of a reference architecture (RA), *SmartCityRA*, by exploiting model-driven architecture techniques. Voronin *et al.* [16], propose an RA for designing a smart city context through the use of Big Data. However, both approaches [15,16] do not support SCs evaluation.

The currently available *frameworks for the KPIs calculation* are still far from being automated. Manual and online spreadsheets are not appropriate for dynamic data retrieving. Among Web-based framework, Bosch *et al.* [7] select a set of KPIs to assess SCs to measure their smartness and to visualize them with graphical representations. However, the tool does neither envisage automatic calculation nor retrieving of data. Moustaka *et al.* [17] present a framework to support maturity benchmarking of SCs. However, it lacks continuous monitoring and automatic injection of data.

Run-time monitoring (RM) and *models@runtime* [18] have been widely exploited in model-based systems and applications. Hili *et al.* [19] propose an architecture supporting RM of executions of models of real-time and embedded systems. In their case studies they connect the code generated from a model with a range of external tools for different purposes (e.g., run-time verification). While they apply RM on model artifacts, we monitor heterogeneous third-party data sources, to dynamically update model artifacts (i.e., the *SC Model*). Other approaches exploiting RM are proposed in the IoT context, to support the management of its inherent heterogeneity, as done, for instance, in Chen *et al.* [20]. Differently, we aim to apply continuous monitoring both to IoT architectures and to other data sources (e.g., Open services), with diverse architectures and access protocols. This further increases heterogeneity beyond that inherent in IoT architectures. In service-based systems, Johng *et al.* [2] propose a continuous service monitoring framework to control changes in services by detecting SLA's violations, to facilitate collaborations among DevOps software teams. Differently, our framework is not just a notification system but integrates a complete SC assessment.

Nevertheless, despite the availability of numerous smart cities services, and the wide use of models@runtime and service-based technologies, to the best of our knowledge, it does not exist a service-oriented framework for the continuous evaluation of SCs.

In conclusion, we presented a service-oriented architecture for a model-based KPIs assessment framework supporting decision-making processes in SCs, and providing a robust and fully automated platform. As future work, we aim to integrate time-series databases [21] enabling temporal models to support the storing of historical values. This way, we may store the history of the input parameters and time-based analysis of the KPIs result, which can be used to visualize the evolution of the smart city and its performance over time. Lastly, we aim to deploy the framework online as a Web application. This way, the framework would become itself a smart city service provider.

Acknowledgements. This work was partially supported by the Centre for Urban Informatics and Modelling (CUIM) and the PON Cultural Heritage-AIM1880573, National Projects at GSSI, and by the Austrian Federal Ministry for Digital and Economic Affairs and the National Foundation for Research, Technology and Development (CDG).

References

1. Bucchiarone, A., De Sanctis, M., Marconi, A.: ATLAS: a world-wide travel assistant exploiting service-based adaptive technologies. In: Maximilien, M., Vallecillo, A., Wang, J., Oriol, M. (eds.) ICSOC 2017. LNCS, vol. 10601, pp. 561–570. Springer, Cham (2017). https://doi.org/10.1007/978-3-319-69035-3_41

2. Johng, H., Kalia, A.K., Xiao, J., Vuković, M., Chung, L.: Harmonia: a continuous service monitoring framework using DevOps and service mesh in a complementary manner. In: Yangui, S., Bouassida Rodriguez, I., Drira, K., Tari, Z. (eds.) ICSOC 2019. LNCS, vol. 11895, pp. 151–168. Springer, Cham (2019). https://doi.org/10.1007/978-3-030-33702-5_12

3. Mutiara, D., Yuniarti, S., Pratama, B.: Smart governance for smart city. In: IOP Conference Series: Earth and Environmental Science, vol. 126, pp. 12–73 (2018)

4. International Telecommunication Union, Collection Methodology for Key Performance Indicators for Smart Sustainable Cities (2017). https://bit.ly/3vFsfqW

5. Rosique, F., Losilla, F., Pastor, J.A.: A domain specific language for smart cities. In: Proceedings of the 4th International Electronic Conference on Sensors and Applications (2018)

6. Bordeleau, F., Combemale, B., Eramo, R., van den Brand, M., Wimmer, M.: Towards model-driven digital twin engineering: current opportunities and future challenges. In: Babur, Ö., Denil, J., Vogel-Heuser, B. (eds.) ICSMM 2020. CCIS, vol. 1262, pp. 43–54. Springer, Cham (2020). https://doi.org/10.1007/978-3-030-58167-1_4

7. Bosch, P., Jongeneel, S., Rovers, V., Neumann, H.-M., Airaksinen, M., Huovila, A.: Citykeys indicators for smart city projects and smart cities (2017). https://bit.ly/3tr9WEt

8. De Sanctis, M., Iovino, L., Rossi, M.T., Wimmer, M.: MIKADO - a smart city KPIs assessment modeling framework. Softw. Syst. Model. (2021). https://doi.org/10.1007/s10270-021-00907-9

9. De Sanctis, M., Iovino, L., Rossi, M.T., Wimmer, M.: A flexible architecture for key performance indicators assessment in smart cities. In: Jansen, A., Malavolta, I., Muccini, H., Ozkaya, I., Zimmermann, O. (eds.) ECSA 2020. LNCS, vol. 12292, pp. 118–135. Springer, Cham (2020). https://doi.org/10.1007/978-3-030-58923-3_8

10. Kolovos, D.S., Paige, R.F., Kelly, T., Polack, F.A.: Requirements for domain-specific languages. In: Proceedings of the Workshop on Domain-Specific Program Development (2006)

11. Basciani, F., Rossi, M.T., De Sanctis, M.: Supporting smart cities modeling with graphical and textual editors. In: 1st International Workshop on Modeling Smart Cities, in STAF 2020 Workshop Proceedings. CEUR-WS.org (2020)

12. Viyović, V., Maksimović, M., Perisić, B.: Sirius: a rapid development of DSM graphical editor. In: Proceedings of the International Conference on Intelligent Engineering Systems, pp. 233–238 (2014)

13. Light, R.A.: Mosquitto: server and client implementation of the MQTT protocol. J. Open Source Softw. **2**(13), 265 (2017)

14. da Silva, W.M., Alvaro, A., Tomas, G.H.R.P., Afonso, R.A., Dias, K.L., Garcia, V.C.: Smart cities software architectures: a survey. In: Proceedings of the 28th Annual ACM Symposium on Applied Computing (SAC), pp. 1722–1727. ACM (2013)

15. Abu-Matar, M., Mizouni, R.: Variability modeling for smart city reference architectures. In: IEEE International Smart Cities Conference, pp. 1–8 (2018)

16. Voronin, D., Shevchenko, V., Chengar, O., Mashchenko, E.: Conceptual big data processing model for the tasks of smart cities environmental monitoring. In: Alexandrov, D.A., Boukhanovsky, A.V., Chugunov, A.V., Kabanov, Y., Koltsova, O., Musabirov, I. (eds.) DTGS 2019. CCIS, vol. 1038, pp. 212–222. Springer, Cham (2019). https://doi.org/10.1007/978-3-030-37858-5_17

17. Moustaka, V., Maitis, A., Vakali, A., Anthopoulos, L.: CityDNA dynamics: a model for smart city maturity and performance benchmarking. In: Proceedings of the 6th International Workshop: Web Intelligence and Smart Cities (2020)

18. Bencomo, N., Götz, S., Song, H.: Models@run.time: a guided tour of the state of the art and research challenges. Softw. Syst. Model. **18**(5), 3049–3082 (2019). https://doi.org/10.1007/s10270-018-00712-x

19. Hili, N., Bagherzadeh, M., Jahed, K., Dingel, J.: A model-based architecture for interactive run-time monitoring. Softw. Syst. Model. **19**(4), 959–981 (2020). https://doi.org/10.1007/s10270-020-00780-y

20. Chen, X., Li, A., Zeng, X., Guo, W., Huang, G.: Runtime model based approach to IoT application development. Front. Comp. Sci. **9**(4), 540–553 (2015). https://doi.org/10.1007/s11704-015-4362-0

21. Mazak, A., Wolny, S., Gómez, A., Cabot, J., Wimmer, M.: Temporal models on time series databases. J. Object Technol. **19**, 3:1 (2020)

A Structure Alignment Deep Graph Model for Mashup Recommendation

Eduardo Lima and Xumin Liu[✉]

Rochester Institute of Technology, Rochester, NY 14623, USA
xmlics@rit.edu

Abstract. In this paper, we propose a novel approach to recommend services for a given mashup development task. We model service data as a heterogeneous service graph which includes multiple types of nodes and edges to capture rich information extracted from the data. We extend the design of the graph convolutional networks to learn optimal graph embeddings based on a novel structure alignment framework leveraging the latent heterogeneous graph structural features. We then design a ranking mechanism to recommend those services so that their links to the mashup can best fit the latent graph structural features. Both the embedding learning and ranking process make the use of meta-paths to incorporate prior domain knowledge into recommendation. A comprehensive experimental study is conducted on a real-world data set and the result indicates that our approach can significantly outperform the existing solutions.

Keywords: Graph convolutional neural networks · Mashup recommendation · Service recommendation

1 Introduction

As software reuse has been one of the major driving forces for the development of web services, it is important to efficiently discover relevant services for a given software development task, i.e., developing service mashup. However, identifying the most suitable APIs from a large pool of candidates for mashup construction poses some fundamental challenges. For example, a popular web service repository, ProgrammableWeb[1], lists $24,147$ public services, but the support for service search is either keyword-based or category/tag-based, which is limited. Finding the relevant services from such a large service pool can be quite time consuming and error prone. Inspired by the tremendous success of current recommender systems, such as Netflix movie recommendation and Amazon product recommendation, mashup recommendation, which is to recommend services for a given mashup development task (usually described in free-form text), has received significant attention in service computing communities [2,7]. Mashup recommendation has a great potential of promoting the usage of web

---

[1] https://www.programmableweb.com.

© Springer Nature Switzerland AG 2021
H. Hacid et al. (Eds.): ICSOC 2021, LNCS 13121, pp. 682–690, 2021.
https://doi.org/10.1007/978-3-030-91431-8_44

services as it significantly simplifies the work of finding relevant services for a given development task and improves the discovery result.

The majority of mashup recommendation solutions rely on textual descriptions of services and mashups [4,6]. Some of them also consider the usage of services by mashups and use either collaborative filtering or generative process to make recommendation [1,3,7,13]. Some recent approaches take a step on capturing and utilizing links between services, i.e., forming service graphs where services are connected through their features, e.g., categories or mashups. Such relational information is then incorporated into the recommendation process [9,11]. They also leverage the current deep learning techniques to learn the representations of mashups, services, and their relationships for recommendation. However, most of the modeled service graphs are either homogeneous where all the nodes have the same type, i.e., services, or only the direct relations between them, i.e., linked by the same mashup, are leveraged. This could cause the ignorance of some important but latent knowledge, such as indirect inter-service relationship derived from connectivity between different types of entities (such as mashup, providers, tags, categories) and interesting structural patterns that can be leveraged into the recommendation.

In this paper, we propose to model a heterogeneous service graph among services and their features, similar to Heterogeneous Information Networks (HIN) [8], to capture more latent knowledge that can contribute to the recommendation results. Such a graph consists of different types of nodes, such as services, mashups, tags, and categories, and multiple types of edges, such as those between services and their tags, those between services and mashups (if a service is used in a mashup), and so on. Through this design, the graph can not only capture the information directly obtained from the data (*e.g.*, node and edge features) and the connectivity between nodes, but also the latent information derived from meta-paths [8], which has been shown to be effective in representation learning of graph data. With such a graph, the recommendation of APIs for mashups is performed by maximizing the alignment of the recommendation result to the inherent graph structural features learned from the graph. The major technical contributions of this paper are summarized as follows.

1. We propose a deep graph learning model based on graph convolutions on a heterogeneous graph to learn embeddings that encode graph structural latent features for mashup recommendation.
2. We propose a ranking method to evaluate how well a recommendation result can preserve the current graph structural features based on the embeddings of services and mashups.
3. We conduct a comprehensive experimental study using ProgrammableWeb data, a real world dataset, to evaluate the performance of the proposed approach.

The rest of this paper is structured as follows. Section 2 introduces related work. Section 3 presents the methodology of our proposed model. Section 4 presents the experimental settings, evaluation process and performance comparison in our experiments. Section 5 presents our conclusions.

2   Related Work

The early efforts recommend services based on the similarities between candidate services and the mashup being developed. [4] uses Relational Topic Model (RTM) to derive latent links between a service and a mashup based on the textual descriptions and tags. [10] proposes a category-based service recommendation approach to ensure the diversity of recommendation results. Services are clustered into categories first based on their functionality and the recommendation is distributed to the matching service categories to select service in each category. LDA is used to model service functional features and compute the relevance of a service to the mashup. [6] builds a hierarchical structure of topics that defines semantics to compute the matching score between a service and a natural language query. Some later efforts incorporate the usage history of services by mashup into the recommendation process. [13] uses Probabilistic Matrix Factorization (PMF) to recommend services based on both service profiles and service co-invocation history. The limitations of these work lie in the fact that they don't go beyond textual descriptions and usage history of services, failing to leverage more information from service data, including those related to relationships other than being invoked by the same mashups.

Some recent works leverage the current graph mining and deep learning technique into service recommendation. [11] generates a service network consisting of services and their attributes, where edges are only between services if they are used by a same mashup. It proposed a deep representation learning model to recommend services based on the GAT2VEC where the loss function is linked to both network connectivity and service features. [14] modeled mobile app interactions as a knowledge graph consisting of entity-relation-entity triplets with multiple relations. The recommendation is performed through learning the embeddings of nodes and predicting the matching scores by the final representations of users and apps. Our approach is different as the proposed heterogeneous service graph is more comprehensive and challenging to process compared to the homogeneous graphs.

3   Deep Graph Model Based Mashup Recommendation

Figure 1 shows the overall process of mashup recommendation. It takes a new mashup description as the input from user and feeds that to the structural alignment neural network. The model takes a heterogeneous service graph, generated from the data collected from public service repository, such as ProgrammableWeb, as well as candidate meta-paths, to train the optimal node embeddings for services, mashups, and their features through graph convolutional layers. A multivariate Gaussian is used to initialize the first layer for the embeddings. The embeddings are used to compute the scores of a service for the given mashup description and rank them, where the model uses a learned transformation for each meta-path to generate the intermediate scores. A final score for each service is then generated considering all the selected meta-paths

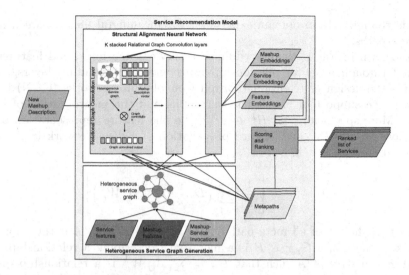

Fig. 1. Structure alignment service recommendation framework

and all pairs of nodes from the corresponding paths. The ranked list of services will be returned to the user as the output of this recommendation process.

Heterogeneous Service Graph Generation. The first step is to extract features related to services and mashups and transform them to a heterogeneous service graph. The key difference between heterogeneous graphs and homogeneous graphs is that the former has multiple types of nodes and edges while in the latter, nodes are in the same type and so do the edges. In a heterogeneous service graph, nodes can be services, mashups, categories, terms, and tags.

To generate the service graph, we map each service to a service node, each mashup to a mashup node, each tag to a tag node, and each category to a category node. For term nodes, we use the standard Natural Language Processing (NLP) tools, such as tokenization, stop-word removal, PoS tagging, and lemmatization to process textual descriptions of services and mashups. Edges are created between different nodes if there is such a connection is observed in the data.

Structural Alignment Neural Network. To go beyond the current mashup recommendation solutions that rely on service-mashup relationships, the proposed structural alignment neural network allows to incorporate more types of relationships into the learning by taking the heterogeneous service network as part of the input. It also allows domain knowledge to be included to improve the recommendation result, where domain knowledge is encoded as meta-paths. A *meta-path* p a type of paths that follow a specified sequence of node types. For example, a meta-path $p = TM \rightarrow M \rightarrow S$ refers to those paths that start with a term node, followed by a mashup node, and ends with a service node. It can link a given term to the APIs that compose mashups with corresponding description terms in TM. For another example, the meta-path $p = S \rightarrow M \rightarrow S$ links those services that are both used in the same Mashup M. Therefore, we can encode the input from domain experts on the meaningful links between nodes as meta-paths.

As shown in Fig. 1, the embeddings of services, mashups, and features are learned through a set of relationship-aware graph convolution layers, which extends the design of traditional Graph Convolution Networks (GCN) in two aspects: the support of heterogeneous graphs and the incorporation of meta-paths. More specifically, let $H^k \in \mathbb{R}^{N \times d}$ be the feature representation of the k-th layer in a GCN. The forward propagation of a deep network layer in the proposed network is defined as:

$$H^{k+1} = \sigma \left[\frac{1}{|P|} \sum_{r \in P} \left(\tilde{D}^{-\frac{1}{2}} \tilde{A} \tilde{D}^{-\frac{1}{2}} H^k W_r^k \right) \right] \tag{1}$$

where P is the set of all meta-paths, $\tilde{A} = A + I \in \mathbb{R}^{N \times N}$, A is the adjacency matrix of the graph G, $r \in P$ is a meta-path describing a relationship, $\tilde{D}$ is the degree matrix of $\tilde{A}$ such that $D_{ii} = \sum_i \tilde{A}_{ij}$, W_r^k is a relationship-specific learnable weight matrix, and σ is an activation function, e.g. Rectified Linear Unit (ReLU). The meta-paths in P determine the types of relations in the service network that will be evaluated for the propagation. We use $|P|$ (the cardinality of P) to normalize vector values and avoid numeric representation overflow. The output of this model contains the embeddings for all entities including services, mashups, and features, which will be used later to compute service scores.

The loss function for neural network training can be defined as the mean squared error of the difference between the predicted connectivity $\hat{y}$ and the actual connectivity y, for all nodes.

$$J = \frac{1}{|V|} \sum_{v_l \in V} (y - \hat{y})^2 \tag{2}$$

V is the set of all vertices. $|V|$ is the vertex set cardinality. y is the normalized node degree calculated from the training data, i.e., the in-degree of a node divided by M where M is a hyper-parameter used to set the maximum allowed vertex degree. $\hat{y}$ is the predicted normalized node degree.

Once the embeddings are learned through the network, the relevance scores for services for a given mashup description is computed as the bi-linear transformations W_r from the learned node embeddings for each meta-path r and then be aggregated, as shown in Formula 3.

$$score(v_l) = \sum_r \frac{1}{|V_r|} \sum_{l,m \in V_r} 1_Q \cdot h(v_l)^T \cdot W_r \cdot h(v_m) \tag{3}$$

where 1_Q is the indicator function for the set of vertices that is part of the query set Q, $h \in \mathbb{R}^d$ is a vertex embedding generated by our model, $W_r \in \mathbb{R}^{d \times d}$ is the relationship-specific learned weight matrix, and v_l, v_m are vertices from V_r which are the vertices from meta-path r. Since the scores are correlated with the connectivity, a higher score means that recommending the service to the given mashup will yield better alignment with the original graph structure.

Notice that for each relationship described by the meta-path r, we go over all possible pairs of vertices from the paths that follows the meta-path definition. In another word, each path from the meta-path r is broken down into a sequence of vertex pairs. We introduce a simple normalization factor for the meta-path-specific sub-score, $\frac{1}{|V_r|}$, to prevent the score from increasing with the number of available paths. As meta-paths deliver the domain knowledge on meaningful relations among services, using meta-paths can guide the selection of potentially good paths, which are used as evidence when learning matrices W_r to maximize the objective that is correlated to the service recommendation.

4   An Experimental Study

We conducted a set of experiments to evaluate the performance of the proposed mashup recommendation approach, using the data collected from one of the largest public web service repositories, ProgrammableWeb [7]. We only chose those APIs that were used in at least one mashup, which results in 1,350 APIs. Based on a thorough analysis, we selected three meta-paths in the experiments: F-S (Feature $\rightarrow$ API), F-M-S (Feature $\rightarrow$ Mashup $\rightarrow$ API), and F-S-M-S (Feature $\rightarrow$ API $\rightarrow$ Mashup $\rightarrow$ API). The experiments were carried out on a computer with 8-core Intel i7 3.60 GHz CPU, 32 GBs of RAM and Nvidia GeForce GTX 2070 Super GPU, running Ubuntu Linux 20.4 LTS. We compared the performance to the following recent works and used standard metrics, including precision, recall, and F1 score.

- PASREC [5], a collaborative filtering model that uses multiple relationships mined from a service heterogeneous information network;
- HDP-PMF [7], a probabilistic matrix factorization approach that uses HDP to discover latent representations of services;
- HINGAN [12], a deep generative adversarial network model that models service relations using meta-paths in a heterogeneous graph;
- DSASR (our proposed model), a deep structural alignment learning model that models relationships as meta-paths in a heterogeneous service graph.

Evaluation Metrics. We evaluated our recommendation approach using a training-test split, a typical setting for deep learning models, where the testing split consisted of all mashups with at least 4 services in their composition, with a train/test ratio of 90–10. The following evaluation metrics were used to measure the recommendation performance: Precision@K, Recall@K, and F1-measure@K:

$$Precision@K = \frac{1}{|V|} \sum_{l \in V} \frac{|recommended(l) \cap actual(l)|}{|recommended(l)|} \tag{4}$$

$$Recall@K = \frac{1}{|V|} \sum_{l \in V} \frac{|recommended(l) \cap actual(l)|}{|actual(l)|} \tag{5}$$

$$F1@K = 2 \frac{Precision@K \cdot Recall@K}{Precision@K + Recall@K} \tag{6}$$

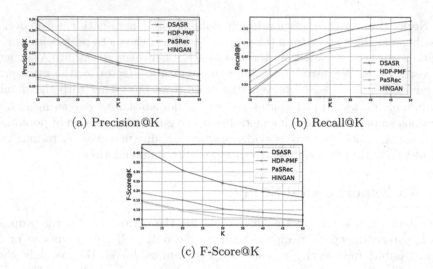

(a) Precision@K   (b) Recall@K

(c) F-Score@K

Fig. 2. Performance comparison

where V is the set of mashups in the testing split, $|V|$ is the the cardinality of V, $recommended(l)$ is the recommended service list and $actual(l)$ is the actual ground-truth service list.

Performance Comparison. Figures 2(a)–(c) present the results of our experiments, respectively for the Precision@K, Recall@K and F-Score@K. With the Precision@K metric, the performance of all the approaches decreases with K as the actual number of services in a mashup is typically less than 10. Our approach, DSASR, is about 16% better than the second best one, which is HDP-PMF, when K is 10. It is also consistently the best with the various values of K. The two other deep learning based techniques, HINGAN and PaSRec, perform the worst. Regarding Recall@K metric, the deep learning based technique superiority became clear when K is small and DSASR performed significantly better than PaSRec and HINGAN. As for F-score@K, where both precision and recall are considered, the performance of all the approaches change in a steady and similar way, which shows this metrics is more stable and reliable than the other two. Our DSASR model was still the best performing one, outperforming other approaches by a large margin.

5   Conclusion

We propose a deep graph learning architecture that is trained to learn the structure of a graph as part of its representation learning objective. We show empirical results in a real-world dataset that suggests that our approach are at least as good as the state-of-the-art recommendation models with very significant improvement of 91% improvement of F-1@10, making the task closer for adoption in real-world setting. We model the API data as a heterogeneous graph and leverage meta-paths to extract rich and human-interpretable relationships while allowing multiple relationships to be incorporated seamlessly. By ranking the services that better align with the original graph structure, we are able to outperform current state-of-the art models. For future work, we plan to incorporate other graph neighborhood normalization techniques into the objective function to further enhance performance.

References

1. Gao, Z., et al.: SeCo-LDA: mining service co-occurrence topics for recommendation. In: IEEE International Conference on Web Services, pp. 25–32 (2016)
2. He, Q., et al.: Efficient keyword search for building service-based systems based on dynamic programming. In: Maximilien, M., Vallecillo, A., Wang, J., Oriol, M. (eds.) ICSOC 2017. LNCS, vol. 10601, pp. 462–470. Springer, Cham (2017). https://doi.org/10.1007/978-3-319-69035-3_33
3. Jain, A., Liu, X., Yu, Q.: Aggregating functionality, use history, and popularity of APIs to recommend mashup creation. In: Barros, A., Grigori, D., Narendra, N.C., Dam, H.K. (eds.) ICSOC 2015. LNCS, vol. 9435, pp. 188–202. Springer, Heidelberg (2015). https://doi.org/10.1007/978-3-662-48616-0_12
4. Li, C., Zhang, R., Huai, J., Sun, H.: A novel approach for API recommendation in mashup development. In: 2014 IEEE International Conference on Web Services, pp. 289–296 (2014)
5. Liang, T., Chen, L., Wu, J., Dong, H., Bouguettaya, A.: Meta-path based service recommendation in heterogeneous information networks In: Sheng, Q.Z., Stroulia, E., Tata, S., Bhiri, S. (eds.) ICSOC 2016. LNCS, vol. 9936, pp. 371–386. Springer, Cham (2016). https://doi.org/10.1007/978-3-319-46295-0_23
6. Lin, C., Kalia, A., Xiao, J., Vukovic, M., Anerousis, N.: NL2API: a framework for bootstrapping service recommendation using natural language queries. In: 2018 IEEE ICWS, pp. 235–242. IEEE (2018)
7. Samanta, P., Liu, X.: Recommending services for new mashups through service factors and top-k neighbors. In: 2017 IEEE ICWS, pp. 381–388. IEEE (2017)
8. Sun, Y., Han, J.: Mining heterogeneous information networks: a structural analysis approach. ACM SIGKDD Explor. Newsl. **14**(2), 20–28 (2013)
9. Wei, C., Fan, Y., Zhang, J., Lin, H.: A-HSG: Neural attentive service recommendation based on high-order social graph. In: 2020 IEEE ICWS, pp. 338–346. IEEE (2020)
10. Xia, B., Fan, Y., Tan, W., Huang, K., Zhang, J., Wu, C.: Category-aware API clustering and distributed recommendation for automatic mashup creation. IEEE Trans. Serv. Comput. **8**(5), 674–687 (2014)
11. Xiao, Y., et al.: Structure reinforcing and attribute weakening network based API recommendation approach for mashup creation. In: 2020 IEEE International Conference on Web Services (ICWS), pp. 541–548. IEEE (2020)
12. Xie, F., Li, S., Chen, L., Xu, Y., Zheng, Z.: Generative adversarial network based service recommendation in heterogeneous information networks. In: 2019 IEEE International Conference on Web Services (ICWS), pp. 265–272. IEEE (2019)

13. Yao, L., Wang, X., Sheng, Q.Z., Ruan, W., Zhang, W.: Service recommendation for mashup composition with implicit correlation regularization. In: IEEE International Conference on Web Services, pp. 217–224 (2015)
14. Zhang, M., Zhao, J., Dong, H., Deng, K., Liu, Y.: A knowledge graph based approach for mobile application recommendation. In: Kafeza, E., Benatallah, B., Martinelli, F., Hacid, H., Bouguettaya, A., Motahari, H. (eds.) ICSOC 2020. LNCS, vol. 12571, pp. 355–369. Springer, Cham (2020). https://doi.org/10.1007/978-3-030-65310-1_25

CSSR: A Context-Aware Sequential Software Service Recommendation Model

Mingwei Zhang[1], Jiayuan Liu[1], Weipu Zhang[1], Ke Deng[2(✉)], Hai Dong[2], and Ying Liu[1]

[1] Software College, Northeastern University, Shenyang, China
{zhangmw,liuy}@swc.neu.edu.cn, {2071295,1871164}@stu.neu.edu.cn
[2] School of Computing Technologies, RMIT University, Melbourne, Australia
{Ke.Deng,Hai.Dong}@rmit.edu.au

Abstract. We propose a novel software service recommendation model to help users find their suitable repositories in GitHub. Our model first designs a novel context-induced repository graph embedding method to leverage rich contextual information of repositories to alleviate the difficulties caused by the data sparsity issue. It then leverages sequence information of user-repository interactions for the first time in the software service recommendation field. Specifically, a deep-learning based sequential recommendation technique is adopted to capture the dynamics of user preferences. Comprehensive experiments have been conducted on a large dataset collected from GitHub against a list of existing methods. The results illustrate the superiority of our method in various aspects.

Keywords: Recommender system · Service recommendation · Sequential recommendation · Software services · GitHub repository

1 Introduction

With the development of emerging computing areas such as cloud computing, big data, and Internet of Things, the Web-based services available on the Internet have increased rapidly in both quantity and type. Following [1], software service is specifically defined as *services which contain code under open-source licenses for others to use and modify freely*, such as open-source projects or repositories on social coding sites (e.g., GitHub, Bitbucket, SourceForge). Users can build their Web services, applications, or even scientific experiment systems quickly by exploiting functional code modules in massive software services [9].

As a representative software service hosting platform, GitHub is widely known to developers from all over the world, who find it easier and quicker to build up their complex applications from particular repositories. As of January 2020, GitHub reports having over 40 million users and more than 100 million repositories [3], making it the largest host of software services in the world. The large number of repositories has undoubtedly increased the difficulty of selecting the most suitable ones to fulfill users' application development. Therefore, software service recommendation has become of practical importance. Sun et al. [10]

© Springer Nature Switzerland AG 2021
H. Hacid et al. (Eds.): ICSOC 2021, LNCS 13121, pp. 691–699, 2021.
https://doi.org/10.1007/978-3-030-91431-8_45

proposed an approach to recommend repositories considering both user behaviors and repository features. Shao et al. [9] designed a novel cross-platform recommender system, *paper2repo*. It recommended relevant repositories on GitHub that match a given paper, by integrating text encoding and constrained graph convolutional networks. LRMF [5] is a pairwise regularization framework for GitHub open source repository recommendation based on matrix factorization, focusing mainly on exploiting user language preference. PNCF [1] is the state-of-the-art repository recommender model, which combined deep learning with collaborative filtering to enhance recommendation effectiveness, and also focused on language preference.

The above methods proposed effective strategies to make software service recommendation. However, they suffer from the following two common issues. First, *the well-known data sparsity problem is not addressed*. Although the number of users and repositories on GitHub can be very large, the interactions between users and repositories are highly sparse, i.e., most users typically interact with a few repositories. Second, *user preferences may exhibit dynamic characteristics*. For instance, users' preferences may drift over time due to the continuous evolution of software technology and the influence of other users.

To address the two aforementioned issues, a novel recommendation model named CSSR (Context-aware Sequential Software Service Recommendation) is proposed in this paper with two unique traits. Firstly, we leverage more comprehensive contextual information of repositories (i.e., topics, general description, *README*) compared with the state-of-the-art recommendation methods [1,5]. It can model the similarity between repositories more precisely to make better recommendation when the interaction data is sparse. Secondly, users on GitHub interact with repositories in a chronological order. The temporal information of user interaction behaviors can help to model users' dynamic interests. For example, it is reasonable to assume that a user is most likely to access the repositories which are relevant to the repositories the user has interacted with recently. Therefore, we adopt sequential user-repository interactions to capture the dynamics of user preferences. More specifically, CSSR first explores contextual information to construct a repository graph upon which the latent vector of each repository can be derived through the graph embedding. Then, the repository sequences of users are fed into a GRU model, where the latent vector of each repository is applied to identify the appropriate repositories and recommend them to users. We have conducted comprehensive experiments to compare CSSR with the state-of-the-art methods on a large real-world dataset crawled from GitHub[1]. The experimental results show that CSSR achieves at least 16.16%, 22.05% and 11.35% improvements over the best baseline in terms of Hit Rate, Mean Reciprocal Rank and Normalized Discounted Cumulative Gain respectively, and the performance boost is more significant in the situation of high level of data sparsity.

---

[1] The dataset and source code are released on https://github.com/JiaYuan6/CSSR.

2   Problem Formulation

Each user has interacted with a sequence of repositories ordered by time on GitHub. The repositories may be created by a user directly or forked from other users. Each repository has contextual information.

Let $\mathcal{U} = \{u_1, u_2, ..., u_{|\mathcal{U}|}\}$ and $\mathcal{R} = \{r_1, r_2, ..., r_{|\mathcal{R}|}\}$ be sets of users and repositories, with $|\mathcal{U}|$ and $|\mathcal{R}|$ being the sizes, respectively. Each user u can be associated with a sequence of repositories $\mathcal{R}^u = \{r_1^u, r_2^u, ..., r_{|\mathcal{R}^u|}^u\}$ by sorting interaction records in a chronological order, where r_t^u represents the repository that user u interacted with at time step t. $\mathcal{R}_{t_1:t_2}^u (t_1 < t_2)$ refers to the subsequence from interaction $r_{t_1}^u$ to $r_{t_2}^u$. We learn how to recommend the next repository for each user based on the recent repository subsequence of length L the user interacted with, where L is a hyperparameter. For each user u at time step t, we will have a training data record where the features are $R_{t-L:t-1}^u$ and the label is r_t^u. For all users from $t = 1$ to $t_{cur} - 1$ (t_{cur} denotes the current time step and $t_{cur} - 1$ is greater than L), we will obtain a training data set. Based on it, the research problem investigated in this study is to (1) represent user preferences and repositories, and (2) develop a prediction model to identify and recommend the preferable repositories to users. The objective is to optimize the performance by addressing the data sparsity issue and the dynamics of user preferences along with time.

3   Methodology

3.1   Context-Induced Repository Graph Construction

First, a repository graph is constructed where the text-based contextual information is exploited. On GitHub, developers usually tag their repositories with topics using words or phrases. The topics are suggested by a topic extraction framework, called *repo-topix*, which was developed by GitHub considering many engineering problems. We utilize the topics tagged by users with the suggestion of *repo-topix* directly rather than extracting the similar information using topic modeling like in existing studies. However, some repositories may not be tagged with such information explicitly or tagged incompletely. We then, for each repository, exploit its general description and *README* to derive and complete its topics by techniques such as keyword matching against the explicitly-tagged topics. In addition, the programming language of a repository can also be used as a special kind of topic-like information. This is because users are more likely to find source codes with languages they have used before.

Let $\mathcal{T} = \{t_1, t_2, ..., t_{|\mathcal{T}|}\}$ be the set of topics of repositories $\mathcal{R} = \{r_1, r_2, ..., r_{|\mathcal{R}|}\}$. Each repository r has a repository topic vector $\mathcal{RT} = \{rt_1, rt_2, ..., rt_{|\mathcal{T}|}\}$, where $rt_k = 1$ if r has t_k (either directly tagged by developers or derived from description, *README*); otherwise $rt_k = 0$.

Given any two repositories r_p and r_q, $\mathcal{RT}_p = \{rt_{p \cdot 1}, rt_{p \cdot 2}, ..., rt_{p \cdot |\mathcal{T}|}\}$ and $\mathcal{RT}_q = \{rt_{q \cdot 1}, rt_{q \cdot 2}, ..., rt_{q \cdot |\mathcal{T}|}\}$ are their corresponding repository topic vectors.

The similarity between r_p and r_q is measured using cosine distance between $\mathcal{RT}_p$ and $\mathcal{RT}_q$ as follows:

$$s_{p,q} = \frac{\mathcal{RT}_p \cdot \mathcal{RT}_q}{\|\mathcal{RT}_p\|\|\mathcal{RT}_q\|} = \frac{\sum_{i=1}^{|\mathcal{T}|} rt_{p \cdot i} \times rt_{q \cdot i}}{\sqrt{\sum_{i=1}^{|\mathcal{T}|} rt_{p \cdot i}^2} \sqrt{\sum_{i=1}^{|\mathcal{T}|} rt_{q \cdot i}^2}} \tag{1}$$

The similarity ranges from 0 (meaning that two repositories don't have any same topic) to 1 (meaning two repositories have the exactly same set of topics). We further define a hyperparameter in our model, i.e., the edge keeping threshold $\varepsilon \in (0, 1)$, which is used to help generate an effectual and simple graph. With the threshold, the similarity between r_p and r_q is refined as follows:

$$s_{p,q} = \begin{cases} 0, & p = q \\ s_{p,q}, & (p \neq q) \wedge (s_{p,q} \geq \varepsilon) \\ 0, & (p \neq q) \wedge (s_{p,q} < \varepsilon) \end{cases} \tag{2}$$

After calculating the similarity of any two repositories, we can get a similarity matrix $\mathcal{S} = \{s_1, s_2, ..., s_{|\mathcal{R}|}\} \in \mathbb{R}^{|\mathcal{R}| \times |\mathcal{R}|}$, where $s_r = \{s_{r,1}, s_{r,2}, ..., s_{r,|\mathcal{R}|}\}$. We represent each repository r as a vertex v_r. So, there are $\{v_1, v_2, \cdots, v_{|\mathcal{R}|}\}$ vertices; and there is a link between two vertices v_p and v_q only if similarity $s_{p,q}$ is greater than 0. By this way, we obtain a homogeneous graph where the contextual similarity between repositories has been captured. The graph is called *context-induced repository graph*.

3.2   Context-Induced Repository Graph Embedding

For nodes in a graph, graph embedding automates the process of extracting low-dimensional node feature vectors. It has been proved very useful in many downstream tasks, such as classification, link prediction and recommendation. Various graph embedding models have been proposed. For embedding the context-induced repository graph $\mathcal{G}$, we adopt Structural Deep Network Embedding model (SDNE) [11], which is a representative embedding model for homogeneous graphs.

3.3   Sequential Repository Recommendation

The framework of our proposed model (CSSR) highlights the sequential repository recommendation component as illustrated in Fig. 1. Recall, in a training data record, the features are $R_{t-L:t-1}^u$ and the label is r_t^u. More specifically, $R_{t-L:t-1}^u$ includes L repositories, i.e., $r_{t-L}^u, \cdots, r_{t-1}^u$. Correspondingly, the sequential recommendation component consists of L GRU (Gated Recurrent Unit) [2] blocks as shown in Fig. 1. The input of GRU block $t - i$ ($1 \leq i \leq L$) is a nonlinear transformed vector $\hat{r}_{t-i}^u$ of the combined feature vector of repository r_{t-i}^u. The repository combined feature vector is derived from graph embeddings as discussed in Sect. 3.2. It is coupled with a list of other repository features relevant to repository recommendation (e.g., the number of watches, stars and forks). The output of the last GRU block is the inferred repository $\hat{y}^{u^{(t)}}$ which will be compared against the ground truth (i.e., r_t^u, the label of the training record), and the GRU parameters will be learned.

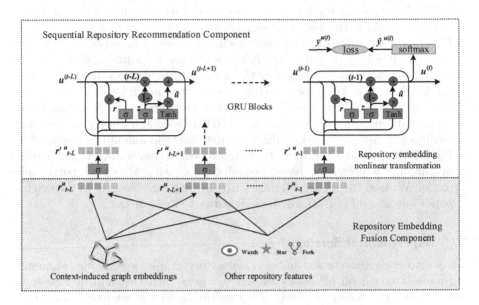

Fig. 1. The framework of the proposed CSSR model.

4 Experiments and Evaluation

4.1 Dataset Description

We evaluate the proposed method on a large dataset crawled from GitHub. We use GitHub REST API to create calls to obtain the data in JSON format and store them in MongoDB. A user is considered to prefer a repository if the user forked it. This means the user produced a personal copy of someone else's repository so that she can contribute to it or use it as the starting point for her own. All the repositories that a user created or forked are listed in her Web page in a chronological order. We randomly select users who forked more than 5 repositories. For each selected user, we crawl the information of all her forked repositories (e.g. topics, programming languages, *README*). Such information is used to construct context-induced repository graph. We eliminate repositories forked by fewer than 5 users. There are 2,616 users, 3,126 repositories, and 21,924 interactions in the dataset after preprocessing. The data sparsity is 0.268%.

4.2 Baseline Methods

Next, we compare CSSR against the following baseline methods.

- **Pop** simply recommends top ranked repositories based on popularity in training data.
- **Item-KNN** [8] recommends a user the repositories similar to the previously forked repositories by the user based on cosine similarity.
- **BPR** [7] is a classic method for non-sequential recommendation, which optimizes a Matrix Factorization model using a pairwise ranking loss.
- **FFM** [6] is the representative recommendation model based on factorization machine. It groups features into fields, and learns the interactions between users and repositories to complete the user-repository implicit rating matrix.
- **GRU4Rec** [4] is a representative sequential recommendation model, which also utilizes GRU to model user action sequences. We feed randomly-generated repository embeddings into GRU blocks, and obtain the best performance by using Xavier initializer against other random number generators.
- **PNCF** [1] is the state-of-the-art GitHub repository recommendation method by building a preference-based neural collaborative filtering recommender model. We feed the model not only with the language features in the original paper but also all our utilized topic features to make it fair.

4.3   Experimental Settings

For constructing the context-induced repository graph, we conduct stemming and lemmatization on all topics tagged by users with the help of *repo-topix*, and extract 4,015 topics. The edge keeping threshold ε is set to 0.3, which can generate a reasonable number of edges. The final constructed graph contains 3,126 repositories with 168,039 edges between them.

The hyperparameters are learned from the validation dataset and set as follows. The size of initial repository embedding is 140. The size of user embedding is 64. $L = 4$ means that the recent 4 interacted repositories are considered to infer recommendations. The learning rate is 0.009. The maximum number of epoch is 100 during the model training. All the experimental results of our model are achieved by using the above hyperparameter configuration settings if no specific situations are provided. The optimal hyperparameters of each baseline method are set based on the experiment reports of the relevant research papers. We implement our CSSR model in Tensorflow.

4.4   Performance Comparison

The experimental results of of CSSR and all the baselines are reported in Table 1. We have the following observations. (1) In most cases, the state-of-the-art baseline PNCF achieves the best performance than the other baseline methods. (2) The proposed CSSR consistently achieves better performance on all the metrics at different N values compared with all the baselines by at least 10%. Specifically, it improves the performance slightly more on the metric MRR than on HR and NDCG. It achieves slightly more performance improvement when $N = 10$ than other N values. (3) All the baselines except GRU4Rec are sequential-information free models. However, GRU4Rec doesn't outperform the other baselines by just using randomly-initialized repository embeddings. Compared with GRU4Rec, the significant improvement of CSSR validates the importance of the context-induced repository graph embedding component in our model.

4.5 Impact of Data Sparsity

We compare CSSR and all the baselines at different levels of data sparsity. The aim is to evaluate the solution applied in CSSR for mitigating the issue of sparse data. Since each user has at least 3 repositories and a repository has at least one user, we delete at most 14,081 interactions in our dataset to simulate different

Table 1. The performance comparison (The method with the best performance is starred and the method with the second-best performance is boldfaced; columns "KNN" and "GRU" denote the baseline "Item-KNN" and "GRU4Rec" respectively; column "Improv." denotes the improvement ratio of CSSR relative to the best baseline).

top-N	Metrics	Pop	KNN	BPR	FFM	GRU	PNCF	CSSR	Improv.
5	HR (%)	1.566	2.467	3.103	2.709	3.086	**3.231**	**3.769***	16.65%
	MRR (%)	0.662	1.421	1.646	1.428	1.288	**1.705**	**2.085***	22.29%
	NDCG (%)	0.886	1.923	2.003	1.746	1.712	**2.079**	**2.497***	20.11%
10	HR (%)	2.428	3.955	4.713	3.926	4.414	**4.962**	**6.077***	22.47%
	MRR (%)	0.762	1.628	1.857	1.586	1.448	**1.926**	**2.378***	23.47%
	NDCG (%)	1.151	2.599	2.519	2.136	2.099	**2.629**	**3.206***	21.95%
15	HR (%)	4.855	5.090	**6.206**	5.300	5.781	6.115	**7.308***	17.76%
	MRR (%)	0.962	1.723	1.975	1.694	1.576	**2.018**	**2.472***	22.50%
	NDCG (%)	1.803	**3.064**	2.915	2.499	2.501	2.935	**3.523***	14.98%
20	HR (%)	5.834	5.991	**7.384**	6.203	6.680	7.269	**8.577***	16.16%
	MRR (%)	1.016	1.774	2.042	1.745	1.620	**2.082**	**2.541***	22.05%
	NDCG (%)	2.032	**3.444**	3.194	2.712	2.685	3.206	**3.835***	11.35%

Table 2. The performance comparison at different sparsity levels.

Ratio (Sparsity)	Metrics	Pop	KNN	BPR	FFM	GRU	PNCF	CSSR	Improv.
ALL (0.096%)	HR (%)	**2.346**	1.006	2.194	1.735	1.904	2.250	**3.369***	43.61%
	MRR (%)	0.741	0.402	0.748	**0.927**	0.711	0.772	**1.457***	57.17%
	NDCG (%)	1.103	0.543	1.085	1.116	0.989	**1.119**	**1.881***	68.09%
Half (0.182%)	HR (%)	2.747	2.709	3.403	2.624	3.633	**3.640**	**4.648***	27.69%
	MRR (%)	0.924	0.872	1.434	1.067	1.323	**1.511**	**1.922***	27.20%
	NDCG (%)	1.350	1.538	1.893	1.429	1.853	**2.004**	**2.487***	24.10%
No (0.268%)	HR (%)	2.428	3.955	4.713	3.926	4.414	**4.962**	**6.077***	22.47%
	MRR (%)	0.762	1.628	1.857	1.586	1.448	**1.926**	**2.378***	23.47%
	NDCG (%)	1.151	2.599	2.519	2.136	2.099	**2.629**	**3.206***	21.95%

settings of sparsity. Table 2 shows the performance of all the methods at three levels of sparsity, i.e., deleting all/half of/none of the 14081 interactions respectively. We set $N = 10$, and adopt all repositories in the training set that a user has interacted with to train the model in the first two sparsity levels, i.e., the repository sequence length L is not fixed. From Table 2, we have the following observations. (1) The performance of all the methods gets worse and worse when the data sparsity changes from 0.268% to 0.182% and then to 0.096%. (2) Compared with all the baselines except Pop, the impact of data sparsity on CSSR is much weaker. CSSR can have much more stable performance than the other methods except Pop, and achieve more significant improvements against the best baseline in the sparser data set. (3) Although the impact of data sparsity on Pop is weaker than CSSR, the performance of Pop is very poor among baselines. In short, our model achieves the best performance and demonstrates robustness in the situation of data sparsity.

5   Conclusion

This paper presented a context-aware sequential software service recommendation model—CSSR. It can recommend repositories on GitHub matching users' interests. CSSR is a joint model that incorporates a graph embedding technique into a GRU formulation to generate latent vectors of users and repositories. Specifically, graph embedding technique is leveraged to exploit rich repository contextual information to alleviate the data sparsity problem. The context-aware latent vectors of repositories are then fed into a GRU model, which captures the dynamics of user preference and eventually recommend repositories to users. The results of extensive experiments show that our method can significantly outperform the existing state-of-the-art repository recommender models in various aspects.

Acknowledgement. This work is partially supported by Australian Research Council Linkage Project (No.LP180100750) and Discovery Project (No.DP210100743).

References

1. Chen, L., Zheng, A., Feng, Y., Xie, F., Zheng, Z.: Software service recommendation base on collaborative filtering neural network model. In: Pahl, C., Vukovic, M., Yin, J., Yu, Q. (eds.) ICSOC 2018. LNCS, vol. 11236, pp. 388–403. Springer, Cham (2018). https://doi.org/10.1007/978-3-030-03596-9_28
2. Cho, K., van Merrienboer, B., Bahdanau, D., Bengio, Y.: On the properties of neural machine translation: encoder-decoder approaches. In: Proceedings of SSST@EMNLP, pp. 103–111. Association for Computational Linguistics (2014)
3. GitHub: The state of the octoverse (2020). https://octoverse.github.com/
4. Hidasi, B., Karatzoglou, A., Baltrunas, L., Tikk, D.: Session-based recommendations with recurrent neural networks. In: Proceedings of ICLR, pp. 1–10 (2016)
5. Jiang, J., Cheng, P., Wang, W.: Open source repository recommendation in social coding. In: Proceedings of SIGIR, pp. 1173–1176. ACM (2017)

6. Juan, Y., Zhuang, Y., Chin, W., Lin, C.: Field-aware factorization machines for CTR prediction. In: Proceedings of RecSys, pp. 43–50. ACM (2016)
7. Rendle, S., Freudenthaler, C., Gantner, Z., Schmidt-Thieme, L.: BPR: Bayesian personalized ranking from implicit feedback. In: Proceedings of UAI, pp. 452–461. AUAI Press (2009)
8. Sarwar, B.M., Karypis, G., Konstan, J.A., Riedl, J.: Item-based collaborative filtering recommendation algorithms. In: Proceedings of WWW, pp. 285–295. ACM (2001)
9. Shao, H., et al.: paper2repo: GitHub repository recommendation for academic papers. In: Proceedings of WWW, pp. 629–639. ACM/IW3C2 (2020)
10. Sun, X., Xu, W., Xia, X., Chen, X., Li, B.: Personalized project recommendation on GitHub. Sci. China Inf. Sci. **61**(5), 1–14 (2018)
11. Wang, D., Cui, P., Zhu, W.: Structural deep network embedding. In: Proceedings of KDD, pp. 1225–1234. ACM (2016)

LogLAB: Attention-Based Labeling of Log Data Anomalies via Weak Supervision

Thorsten Wittkopp[✉], Philipp Wiesner[✉], Dominik Scheinert[✉],
and Alexander Acker[✉]

Technische Universität Berlin, DOS, TU-Berlin, Berlin, Germany
{t.wittkopp,wiesner,dominik.scheinert,alexander.acker}@tu-berlin.de

Abstract. With increasing scale and complexity of cloud operations, automated detection of anomalies in monitoring data such as logs will be an essential part of managing future IT infrastructures. However, many methods based on artificial intelligence, such as supervised deep learning models, require large amounts of labeled training data to perform well. In practice, this data is rarely available because labeling log data is expensive, time-consuming, and requires a deep understanding of the underlying system. We present LogLAB, a novel modeling approach for automated labeling of log messages without requiring manual work by experts. Our method relies on estimated failure time windows provided by monitoring systems to produce precise labeled datasets in retrospect. It is based on the attention mechanism and uses a custom objective function for weak supervision deep learning techniques that accounts for imbalanced data. Our evaluation shows that LogLAB consistently outperforms nine benchmark approaches across three different datasets and maintains an F1-score of more than 0.98 even at large failure time windows.

Keywords: Anomaly labeling · AIOps · Log analysis

1 Introduction

As more and more companies outsource their IT services to the cloud, the number of servers and interconnected devices is continuously increasing. In the meantime, modern abstraction layers are driving the creation of large multilayered systems while adding technical complexity under the hood. This aggravates the operation and maintenance of systems and services and, therefore, poses new challenges for cloud operators. To maintain control over complexity, monitoring becomes an integral part of cloud infrastructure operations. However, in today's systems the amount of monitoring data is often growing to an extent that cannot be analyzed manually.

The area of artificial intelligence for IT operations (AIOps) is intended to support cloud operators to ensure operational efficiency as well as dependability and serviceability [5]. A core component of any AIOps system is the detection of anomalies in monitoring data such as metrics, logs, or traces. Log data are one

H. Hacid et al. (Eds.): ICSOC 2021, LNCS 13121, pp. 700–707, 2021.
https://doi.org/10.1007/978-3-030-91431-8_46

of the most important resources for troubleshooting because they record events during the execution of service applications. However, even though most types of log messages come with a severity level, these do not necessarily reflect the status of the overall system. Therefore, recent research utilizes deep learning models to analyze log data and perform anomaly detection [2,16,29]. One of the main obstacles in log anomaly detection is the lack of labeled log data [25]. Labeling data is costly and time-consuming, as experts need to analyze every single log message and investigate which messages reflect their corresponding errors. Since supervised models that train on large volumes of labeled data show significant performance in log anomaly detection [27,29], it is important to automate the labeling process to gain a strong accelerator for log anomaly detection [19].

To address this problem, we propose LogLAB, an attention-based model for binary labeling of anomalies in log data via weak supervision. It relies only on rough estimates of when an error has occurred - information that can often be derived from other monitoring systems [23]. Specifically, the contributions of this paper are:

- A problem description for how to label anomalies in log data using monitoring information and weak supervision including a method solving this.
- A custom objective function for weak supervision deep learning techniques that takes class-imbalanced data into account.
- An extensive evaluation of ten different approaches solving the defined problem, including LogLAB and its implementation[1].

The remainder of this paper is structured as follows. Section 2 surveys the related work. Section 3 provided a problem description and explains our approach LogLAB. Section 4 evaluates LogLAB in comparison to nine other approaches. Section 5 concludes the paper.

2 Related Work

We discuss works for text classification, anomaly detection and PU learning.

Text-Based Classification. Many established methods are discussed in [10]. The PCA algorithm [9] is for instance often employed for dimensionality reduction right before the actual classification procedure. Random forests [7] are another technique and a suitable tool due to their ensemble learning design. Logistic regression [8] belongs to the classic statistical methods [4]. Other publications utilize the Rocchio algorithm that is compared against kNN in [22]. In another work [21], the authors design a pipeline involving the Rocchio algorithm.

Log Anomaly Detection. The experience report for anomaly detection on system logs [6] discusses additional methods. Invariant Miners [13] retrieve structured logs using log parsing, further group log messages according to log parameter relationships, and mine invariants from the groups to perform actual anomaly

---

[1] https://github.com/dos-group/LogLAB.

detection on logs. Decision Trees [18] are another solution often employed in classification problem scenarios. SVMs are evaluated in [14] for document classification and anomaly detection. The authors of [20] propose a boosting-based system and thus ensemble learning method that shows good performance. Deep Learning methods are also more and more used in the realm of log anomaly detection. DeepLog [2] utilizes an LSTM and thus interprets a log as a sequences of templates to performs anomaly detection per log message. More recent works [26–28] also make use of deep learning.

PU Learning. A problem setting also discussed in other works. For instance, the authors in [12] utilize the EM algorithm together with naive Bayesian classification. A more conservative variant of this method is proposed in [3] where the set of reliable negative instances is iteratively pruned using a binary classifier, which ultimately leads to improved final prediction results due to the few but high quality negative instances. An ensemble learning method for PU learning is proposed in [15]. The authors motivate bagging SVM, i.e. the aggregation of multiple SVM classifiers in order to answer sources of instability often encountered in PU learning situations.

3   Automated Log Labeling

3.1   Problem Description

Log messages can describe failures that occur during runtime, such as the crash of a service. We refer to such log messages as 'abnormal'. Modern monitoring solutions raise alerts when a system runs into an abnormality or outages occur by observing metrics, hardware component failures, workload deployment failures and other failure scenarios [23]. Therefore, we assume that in an IT operation center failure time windows of services and systems are roughly known. We use this information in retrospect to identify and label abnormal log messages.

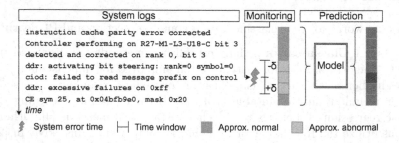

Fig. 1. We use rough estimates for failure times provided by monitoring systems in order to identify and label abnormal log messages via weak supervision. (Color figure online)

Figure 1 provides an example for the described problem. It displays the log of a system with one abnormal log event (colored in red). We utilize monitoring information to estimate time windows of the length $2 * \delta$ in which we suspect abnormal log events. The model's task is to identify the abnormal log messages in the time window and classify all others as normal.

We describe the log labeling as a weak supervision learning problem with inaccurate labels as defined by Zhou et al. [30]. Thereby, label inaccuracy stems from the imprecision of the failure time windows. We assign inaccurate labels for all log events, depending on whether they are in the failure time windows or not. Further, we utilize PU learning [11,12] which is short for learning from positive and unlabeled data. Thereby, the underlying log data is divided into two classes, positive $\mathcal{P}$ and unlabeled $\mathcal{U}$, where $\mathcal{U}$ consists of all log messages that occur in the aforementioned failure time windows and $\mathcal{P}$ of the remaining log messages.

3.2 LogLAB

For the labeling of logs, we design a processing and modeling pipeline illustrated in Fig. 2. The individual steps are as follows:

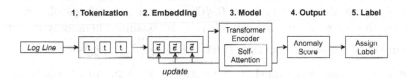

Fig. 2. High level log message labeling pipeline.

First, we convert the content c_i of each log message l_i into a sequence of tokens t_i by splitting on the symbols . , : / and whitespaces. Subsequently, we clean the resulting sequence of tokens by replacing certain tokens with place-holders. Thereby placeholder tokens for hexadecimal values '[HEX]' and any number greater or equal 10 '[NUM]' are introduced. Finally, we prefix the sequence of transformed tokens with a special token '[CLS]' which serves as a numerical summary of the whole log message. An exemplary log message: `time.c: Detected 3591.142 MHz` is thus transformed into a sequence of tokens: ['[CLS]', 'time', 'c', 'Detected', '[NUM]', '[NUM]', 'MHz'].

Since these sequences can vary in length, we truncate them to a fixed size and pad smaller sequences with '[PAD]' tokens. For each token w_j of the token sequence t_i, an embedding $\vec{e}_i(j)$ is obtained. The truncated sequences of embeddings $\vec{e_i}$ serves as the input for the model.

The model computes an output embedding, for each input sequence $\vec{e_i}'$, which summarizes the log message by utilizing the embeddings of all tokens. This output embedding is encoded in the embedding of the '[CLS]' token which is also modified during training. For this purpose, we utilize the transformer architecture [1] with additional self-attention [24]. During the training process, the model is supposed to learn the meanings of the log messages, thereby getting an intuition of what is normal and abnormal. Finally, this model outputs a vector (embedding) for each input sequence $\vec{e}_i'$. We denote the output of the model as $z_i = \Phi(\vec{e}_i'; \Theta)$ and use it throughout the remaining steps. Thereby the anomaly score is calculated by the length of the output vector $\|z_i\|$. Anomaly scores close to 0 represent normal log messages, whereby large vectors indicate an abnormal log message. The computed anomaly score is used to assign a label $\widehat{y}_i$ to the log message l_i, i.e. either normal or abnormal.

3.3 Objective Function

To label the log data, the model must be trained in a way that it is capable to handle the problem of weak supervision with inaccurate labels. Thus, the objective function must assign log anomaly scores to log messages that occur in class $\mathcal{P}$ and $\mathcal{U}$. Log messages that occur only in $\mathcal{U}$ are likely abnormal and must therefore have higher anomaly scores. In addition, the loss function must be able to handle large amounts of incorrectly labeled log messages, since the class $\mathcal{U}$ can increase quickly for large δ. The objective function consist of two parts. The first part minimize the errors of samples from class $\mathcal{P}$, from which the calculated anomaly scores should be close to 0. The second part of the objective must minimize the errors of samples from class $\mathcal{U}$, by pushing them away from 0. The structure of the objective function is defined as $\frac{1}{m} \sum\limits_{i=1}^{m} ((1 - \tilde{y}_i) * a(z_i) + (\tilde{y}_i) * b(z_i)$,

where $\tilde{y}_i$ is the inaccurate label, z_i the output vector and m the batch size. The function '$a()$' becomes 0 if the sample is from class $\mathcal{U}$, while the second function '$b()$' becomes 0 if the sample is from class $\mathcal{P}$. For a we choose $a(z_i) = \|z_i\|^2$ and for b we choose $b(z_i) = \frac{q^2}{\|z_i\|}$ to minimize the error. Thereby a calculates the squared error of the length of the output for samples from class $\mathcal{P}$. In contrast, we increase the error for all small anomaly scores when the log message is of class $\mathcal{U}$. Thereby q is a numerator between 0 and 1 that represents the relation of the number of samples in $\mathcal{P}$ and $\mathcal{U}$. To ensure that q is representing the relation of $\mathcal{P}$ and $\mathcal{U}$ and remains in the boundaries of 0 to 1, we model q as a limited function $f(x) = \frac{x}{x+1}$, with $\lim\limits_{x \to \infty} f(x) = 1$, that is provided with the relation of $\mathcal{P}$ and $\mathcal{U}$:

$q = f(\frac{|\mathcal{P}|}{|\mathcal{U}|}) = \frac{\frac{|\mathcal{P}|}{|\mathcal{U}|}}{(\frac{|\mathcal{P}|}{|\mathcal{U}|}+1)} = \frac{|\mathcal{P}|}{|\mathcal{P}|+|\mathcal{U}|}$. Thus the total loss function can be expressed

as: $\frac{1}{m} \sum\limits_{i=1}^{n} \left((1 - \tilde{y}_i) * \|z_i\|^2 + (\tilde{y}_i) * \frac{(\frac{|\mathcal{P}|}{|\mathcal{P}|+|\mathcal{U}|})^2}{\|z_i\|} \right)$.

4   Evaluation

To obtain a significant and wide benchmark, we compare LogLAB to several state of the art text-classification and anomaly detection approaches presented in a recent text-classification survey [10] as well as in an established survey for anomaly detection in system logs [6]. Namely, we choose PCA, Invariant Miners, Deeplog, Decision Trees, Random Forests, SVMs, Logistic Regression, the Rocchio algorithm, and boosting approaches as benchmark methods. Thereby we measure the deviation from the ground truth y_i and the calculated labels $\widehat{y}_i$.

4.1   Experimental Setup

We evaluate all methods on three labeled log datasets recorded at different large-scale computer systems[17]. The *BGL* dataset contains 4 747 963 log messages of which 7.3 % are abnormal and records a period of 214 days, with on average 0.25 log messages per second. We selected the first 5 M log messages from the *Thunderbird* dataset of which 4.5 % are abnormal. They account for a period of 9 days, with on average 6.4 log messages per second. Again, we selected the first 5 M log messages from the *Spirit* dataset of which 15.3 % are abnormal. They cover a period of 48 days, with on average 1.2 log messages per second.

We create our evaluation datasets with inaccurate labels by including all abnormal log events as well as their surrounding events within a time window $2*\delta$ in $\mathcal{U}$; all remaining log events are in $\mathcal{P}$. Thereby we investigate the performance at three different time windows: $\pm 1000\,ms$ (2s), $\pm 5000\,ms$ (10s) and $\pm 15000\,ms$ (30s). The amount of samples in $\mathcal{U}$ is changing for BGL: $0.39M$, $0.44M$ and $0.47M$, Thunderbird: $1.42M$, $2.36M$ and $2.90M$ and Spirit: $1.00M$, $2.33M$ and $3.26M$ regarding the respective time window δ.

Each sequence of tokens t_i is truncated to have a length of 20 for *Thunderbird*, 16 for *Spirit*, and 12 for *BGL*. The dimensionality d of our embeddings is set to 128. For the training of our LogLAB model, we use a hidden dimensionality of 256, a batch size of 1024, a total of 8 epochs, and a dropout rate of 10%. We use the Adam optimizer with a learning rate of 10^{-4} and a weight decay of $5 \cdot 10^{-5}$.

4.2   Results

Table 1. Evaluation results: F1-scores above 0.99 and 0.98 are highlighted in blue and cyan, respectively.

| Dataset | Metric | Learning $\mathcal{P}$ | | | Learning $\mathcal{P}$ and $\mathcal{U}$ | | | | | | |
		PCA	Invariant Miners	Deeplog	Decision Tree	Random Forest	SVM	Logistic Regr.	Boost	Rocchio	LogLAB
					$\delta = \pm 1000ms$						
BGL	F1-Score	0.5963	0.5102	0.7759	0.9974	0.9830	0.9840	0.9976	0.9908	0.7096	0.9977
TBird	F1-Score	0.3048	0.1824	0.0880	0.3242	0.3144	0.3235	0.3242	0.3361	0.3440	0.9995
Spirit	F1-Score	0.8043	0.5807	0.9926	0.9967	0.9604	0.9857	0.9962	0.9968	0.9971	0.9997
					$\delta = \pm 5000ms$						
BGL	F1-Score	0.5930	0.5112	0.7755	0.9874	0.9646	0.9680	0.9875	0.9795	0.8054	0.9949
TBird	F1-Score	0.3053	0.1936	0.0651	0.2669	0.2415	0.2439	0.2678	0.2869	0.3146	0.9995
Spirit	F1-Score	0.7691	0.5740	0.9929	0.6513	0.5453	0.5584	0.6560	0.5830	0.9946	0.9980
					$\delta = \pm 15000ms$						
BGL	F1-Score	0.5879	0.5130	0.7760	0.9753	0.9483	0.9523	0.9767	0.9762	0.7898	0.9902
TBird	F1-Score	0.3025	0.1933	0.1113	0.1341	0.1248	0.1348	0.1350	0.1476	0.2241	0.9995
Spirit	F1-Score	0.4958	0.4254	0.8236	0.4909	0.4735	0.4836	0.4917	0.4887	0.5192	0.9825

To compare LogLAB to our baselines, we assess the prediction performance $\tilde{y}_i \sim y_i$ in terms of F1-score metrics. The F1-scores are presented in Table 1. As expected, with increasing δ and thus growing size of $\mathcal{U}$, the performance across all approaches tends to decrease. For $\delta = \pm 1000\,ms$ this was apparently easy to achieve for most of the methods. An exception is the Thunderbird dataset, which is characterized by a large $\mathcal{U}$ class: No baseline manages to achieve an F1-score higher than 0.35, except LogLAB. For $\delta = \pm 5000\,ms$ we notice that the performance degradation previously observed for most approaches on the Thunderbird dataset now also start to manifest on the Spirit dataset. The biggest gap in performance becomes evident at the largest observed time window of $\delta = \pm 15000\,ms$. For the dataset BGL, we notice a considerable drop in F1-scores of other approaches to 0.97, while LogLAB maintains its high performance.

5   Conclusion

This paper presents LogLAB, a novel model for labeling large amounts of log data, such that the usually required need of time-consuming manual labeling through experts is automated. It relies only on rough estimates of failure time windows provided by monitoring systems to generate labeled datasets in retrospect. LogLAB is based on the attention mechanism and uses a custom objective function for weak supervision deep learning techniques that accounts for imbalanced data and deals with inaccurate labels. We evaluated LogLAB on three different datasets in comparison to nine benchmark approaches. LogLAB outperforms other approaches across all experiments and shows a performance of more than 0.98 F1-score, even for large amount of inaccurate labels. As further work we consider to enhance the labeling process by iteratively moving log messages from $\mathcal{U}$ to $\mathcal{P}$ during training, which have significantly lower anomaly scores, calculated by the model. Likewise, this method can be extended by adding other sources for estimating the time windows and therefore improve the training basis.

References

1. Devlin, J., Chang, M., Lee, K., Toutanova, K.: BERT: pre-training of deep bidirectional transformers for language understanding. In: Burstein, J., Doran, C., Solorio, T. (eds.) NAACL-HLT. Association for Computational Linguistics (2019)
2. Du, M., Li, F., Zheng, G., Srikumar, V.: Deeplog: anomaly detection and diagnosis from system logs through deep learning. In: SIGSAC (2017)
3. Fusilier, D.H., Montes-y Gómez, M., Rosso, P., Cabrera, R.G.: Detecting positive and negative deceptive opinions using PU-learning. Inf. Process. Manag. **51**, 433–443 (2015)
4. Genkin, A., Lewis, D.D., Madigan, D.: Large-scale bayesian logistic regression for text categorization. Technometrics **49**(3), 291–304 (2007)
5. Gulenko, A., Acker, A., Kao, O., Liu, F.: Ai-governance and levels of automation for aiops-supported system administration. In: ICCCN. IEEE (2020)
6. He, S., Zhu, J., He, P., Lyu, M.R.: Experience report: system log analysis for anomaly detection. In: ISSRE. IEEE (2016)

7. Ho, T.K.: Random decision forests. In: ICDAR. IEEE (1995)
8. Hosmer Jr., D.W., Lemeshow, S., Sturdivant, R.X.: Applied Logistic Regression, vol. 398. Wiley, Hoboken (2013)
9. Jolliffe, I.: Principal component analysis. Encyclopedia of statistics in behavioral science (2005)
10. Kowsari, K., Jafari Meimandi, K., Heidarysafa, M., Mendu, S., Barnes, L., Brown, D.: Text classification algorithms: a survey. Information 10(4), 150 (2019)
11. Liu, B., Dai, Y., Li, X., Lee, W.S., Yu, P.S.: Building text classifiers using positive and unlabeled examples. In: ICDM. IEEE (2003)
12. Liu, B., Lee, W.S., Yu, P.S., Li, X.: Partially supervised classification of text documents. In: ICML, Sydney, NSW (2002)
13. Lou, J.G., Fu, Q., Yang, S., Xu, Y., Li, J.: Mining invariants from console logs for system problem detection. In: USENIX Annual Technical Conference (2010)
14. Manevitz, L.M., Yousef, M.: One-class SVMs for document classification. J. Mach. Learn. Res. 2(Dec), 139–154 (2001)
15. Mordelet, F., Vert, J.P.: A bagging SVM to learn from positive and unlabeled examples. Pattern Recognit. Lett. 37, 201–209 (2014)
16. Nedelkoski, S., Bogatinovski, J., Acker, A., Cardoso, J., Kao, O.: Self-attentive classification-based anomaly detection in unstructured logs. In: ICDM (2020)
17. Oliner, A., Stearley, J.: What supercomputers say: a study of five system logs. In: DSN (2007)
18. Quinlan, J.R.: Induction of decision trees. Mach. Learn. 1(1), 81–106 (1986)
19. Ratner, A.J., De Sa, C.M., Wu, S., Selsam, D., Ré, C.: Data programming: creating large training sets, quickly. NIPS 29, 3567–3575 (2016)
20. Schapire, R.E., Singer, Y.: Boostexter: a boosting-based system for text categorization. Mach. Learn. 39, 135–168 (2000)
21. Selvi, S.T., Karthikeyan, P., Vincent, A., Abinaya, V., Neeraja, G., Deepika, R.: Text categorization using rocchio algorithm and random forest algorithm. In: ICoAC. IEEE (2017)
22. Sowmya, B., Srinivasa, K., et al.: Large scale multi-label text classification of a hierarchical dataset using rocchio algorithm. In: CSITSS. IEEE (2016)
23. Sukhwani, H., Matias, R., Trivedi, K.S., Rindos, A.: Monitoring and mitigating software aging on IBM cloud controller system. In: ISSREW. IEEE (2017)
24. Vaswani, A., et al.: Attention is all you need. In: Guyon, I., et al. (eds.) NeurIPS (2017)
25. Wittkopp, T., Acker, A., et al.: Decentralized federated learning preserves model and data privacy. In: Hacid, H. (ed.) ICSOC 2020. LNCS, vol. 12632, pp. 176–187. Springer, Cham (2021). https://doi.org/10.1007/978-3-030-76352-7_20
26. Wittkopp, T., et al.: A2log: attentive augmented log anomaly detection. In: HICSS (2022)
27. Yang, L., et al.: Semi-supervised log-based anomaly detection via probabilistic label estimation. In: ICSE. IEEE (2021)
28. Yang, R., Qu, D., Gao, Y., Qian, Y., Tang, Y.: NLSALog: an anomaly detection framework for log sequence in security management. IEEE Access 7, 181152–181164 (2019)
29. Zhang, X., et al.: Robust log-based anomaly detection on unstable log data. In: ESEC/FSE (2019)
30. Zhou, Z.H.: A brief introduction to weakly supervised learning. Natl. Sci. Rev. 5(1), 44–53 (2018)

LogDP: Combining Dependency and Proximity for Log-Based Anomaly Detection

Yongzheng Xie[1], Hongyu Zhang[2][(✉)], Bo Zhang[2], Muhammad Ali Babar[1], and Sha Lu[3]

[1] CREST - The Centre for Research on Engineering Software Technologies, The University of Adelaide, Adelaide, Australia
{yongzheng.xie,ali.babar}@adelaide.edu.au
[2] The University of Newcastle, Callaghan, NSW, Australia
hongyu.zhang@newcastle.edu.au, c3288930@uon.edu.au
[3] University of South Australia, Adelaide, Australia
sha.lu@mymail.unisa.edu.au

Abstract. Log analysis is an important technique that engineers use for troubleshooting faults of large-scale service-oriented systems. In this study, we propose a novel semi-supervised log-based anomaly detection approach, LogDP, which utilizes the dependency relationships among log events and proximity among log sequences to detect the anomalies in massive unlabeled log data. LogDP divides log events into dependent and independent events, then learns the normal patterns of dependent events based on the dependencies among events and the normal patterns of independent events based on the deviation of values from a historic mean. Events violating any normal pattern are identified as anomalies. By combining dependency and proximity, LogDP is able to achieve high detection accuracy. Extensive experiments have been conducted on real-world datasets, and the results show that LogDP outperforms six state-of-the-art methods.

Keywords: Log analysis · Log-based anomaly detection · Dependency-based anomaly detection · System operation and maintenance

1 Introduction

Modern software-intensive systems, including service-oriented systems, have become increasingly large and complex. While these systems provide users with rich services, they also bring new challenges to system operation and maintenance. One of the challenges is to identify faults and discover potential risks by analyzing a massive amount of log data. Logs are composed of semi-structured texts, i.e., log messages. Log analysis is one of the main techniques that engineers use for troubleshooting faults and capturing potential risks. When a fault occurs, checking system logs helps to efficiently detect and locate the fault. However,

© Springer Nature Switzerland AG 2021
H. Hacid et al. (Eds.): ICSOC 2021, LNCS 13121, pp. 708–716, 2021.
https://doi.org/10.1007/978-3-030-91431-8_47

with the increase in scale and complexity, manual identification of abnormal logs from massive log data has become infeasible.

During the past decade, many automated log analysis approaches, including supervised, semi-supervised, and unsupervised approaches, have been proposed to detect system anomalies reflected by logs [1–6]. Although supervised approaches show promising results, the scarcity of labeled anomalous log data is a daunting issue. In contrast, unsupervised and semi-supervised approaches have a significant advantage in that no labeled anomalous data are needed. However, the existing unsupervised and semi-supervised approaches [1,3,4,7–9] have low accuracy.

In this paper, we propose a log anomaly detection method, LogDP, which simultaneously utilizes both dependency and proximity among log sequences to detect anomalous log sequences. LogDP first discovers the normal patterns for logs, then identifies the log sequences that violate these patterns as anomalies. There are two types of normal patterns, dependency patterns (DPs) and proximity patterns (PPs). DPs are related to the events that have dependency relationships with other events, and PPs are for the events that are independent of other events. To find the DP of an event, LogDP trains a predictive model to predict this event using some other events as predictors. Here, we name the log event to be predicted as the *focused event*, and the predictor events as the *related events* of the focused event. To find the PP of an event, a mean prediction model is trained to use the mean value of the event as the expected value of the event. When detecting anomalies, given a log sequence, its expected values on all log events are predicted using the learned models, and the differences between the observed values and expected values are calculated, named *pattern deviations*, which indicate the degree of the log sequence deviating from their corresponding normal dependency. If any pattern deviations are beyond normal ranges, i.e., the normal patterns are violated, the log sequence is flagged as an anomaly.

In summary, our main contributions in this work are as follows:

- We propose LogDP, a novel log-based anomaly detection method, which utilizes dependency among log events and proximity among log sequences at the same time. To our best knowledge, we are the first to introduce the dependency-based anomaly detection techniques in the field of log analysis.
- We experimentally demonstrate the effectiveness of the proposed method on seven settings of three widely-used log datasets. The empirical experiments show that the proposed approach can outperform the state-of-the-art unsupervised and semi-supervised log-based anomaly detection methods.

2   The LogDP Method

In this section, we first explain log preprocessing, and then present the LogDP method. The LogDP method consists of two phases, the training phase and the test phase. In the training phase, for each log event, LogDP trains an expected value prediction model and produces the corresponding threshold. In the test phase, the trained prediction modes and thresholds are used to determine if a log sequence is an anomaly or not.

(a) A snippet of log parsing.   (b) An event count matrix.

Fig. 1. Log preprocessing.

2.1 Log Preprocessing

Logs are usually semi-structured texts, which are used to record the status of systems. Each log message consists of a constant part (log event) and a variable part (log parameter). Log parsers [10–12] can parse log messages into log events, which are the templates of the log messages. Figure 1a shows a snippet of raw logs and the results after they are parsed.

Log messages can be grouped into log sequences (i.e., series of log events that record specific execution flows) according to sessions or time windows. Session-based log partition often utilizes certain log identifiers to generate log sequences. When using time windows to partition logs, two types of strategies are usually used, i.e., fixed window and sliding window. Fixed window strategy uses a pre-defined window size, e.g., 1 h, to produce log sequences, while sliding windows strategy generates log sequences using overlapping between two consecutive fixed windows. For each log sequence, the occurrences of the events are counted, resulting in an Event Count Matrix (ECM). For example, an ECM is shown in Fig. 1b, where c_{ij} indicates the number of occurrences of $event_j$ in $sequence_i$, namely $instance_{ij}$.

The notation used in this paper is as follows. We use a boldfaced upper case letter, e.g. $\mathbf{X}$ to denote a matrix; a boldfaced lower case letter, e.g. $\mathbf{e}$, for a vector; a lower case letter, e.g. c, for a scalar. We have reserved $\mathbf{X} \in \mathbb{R}^{n \times m}$ for an ECM with n log sequences and m log events. $\mathbf{E} = \{E_1, \cdots, E_m\}$ represents the set of log events of $\mathbf{X}$ and E is a log event, i.e., $E \in \mathbf{E}$. A log sequence is denoted as $\mathbf{c} = \{c_1, \cdots, c_m\}$, where c is a log instance, i.e., the occurrences count of an event in $\mathbf{c}$. The log instance of event E_j in sequence $\mathbf{c}_i$ is represented as c_{ij}.

2.2 The Training Phase of LogDP

The workflow of the training phase of the LogDP method is presented in Fig. 2. The inputs of the training phase are a training set $\mathbf{X}^{train}$ and a validation set $\mathbf{X}^{val}$, both of which only contain normal log sequences. $\mathbf{X}^{train}$ is used to train expected value prediction models, and $\mathbf{X}^{val}$ is used to obtain the thresholds. The training phase is composed of two steps, related event selection and prediction model training. In the related event selection step, for each event, named focused event, its related event is selected to be used as predictors to predict the focused event. In the prediction model training step, two different prediction models are trained according to if Markov blanket (MB) is found for the focused event. If

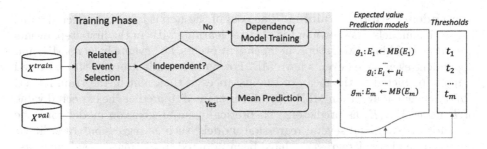

Fig. 2. The workflow of the training phase of the LogDP method

the focused event is not independent, i.e., it has MB, a Multi-Layer Perceptron (MLP) regressor is trained to embody the dependency relationship between the focused event and its MB. If the focused event is independent, i.e., it has not MB found, a mean prediction model is trained. That is, DPs are learned for dependent events using the dependency-based technique, and PPs are for independent events using the proximity-based technique. After training the expected value prediction models, $\mathbf{X}^{val}$ is input to obtain the corresponding thresholds. The outputs of the training phase include a set of prediction models and their corresponding thresholds.

Related Event Selection. In this step, we aim to identify the related events for a focused event, which are later used as predictors in a predictive model to predict the value of a focused (independent) event. We follow [13] to adopt a causal feature selection technique, MBs, in the step to achieve a good prediction accuracy and efficiency. MBs are defined in the context of a Bayesian Network (BN) [14]. A BN is a type of probabilistic graphical model used to represent and infer the dependency among variables. In the context of log analysis, variables correspond to log events. A BN can be denoted as a pair of (G, P), where G is a Directed Acyclic Graph (DAG) showing the structure of the BN, and P is the joint probability of the nodes in G. Specifically, $G = (\mathbf{E}, \mathbf{A})$, where $\mathbf{E}$ is the set of nodes representing the random variables in the domain under consideration, and $\mathbf{A} \subseteq \mathbf{E} \times \mathbf{E}$ is the set of arcs representing the dependency among the nodes. $E_1 \in \mathbf{E}$ is known as a parent of $E_2 \in \mathbf{E}$ (or E_2 is a child of E_1) if there exists an arc $E_1 \rightarrow E_2$. For any variable $E \in \mathbf{E}$ in a BN, its MB contains all the children, parents, and spouses (other parents of the children) of E, denoted as $MB(E)$. Given $MB(E)$, E is conditionally independent of all other variables in $\mathbf{E}$, i.e.,

$$P(E|MB(E)) = P(E|MB(E), \mathbf{S}) \tag{1}$$

where $\mathbf{S} = \mathbf{E} \setminus (\{E\} \cup MB(E))$.

According to Eq. 1, $MB(E)$ represents the information needed to estimate the probability of E by making E irrelevant to the remaining variables, which makes $MB(E)$ is the minimal set of relevant variables to obtain the complete dependency of E. The study in [13] has shown that using MBs as related variables could achieve better performance than other choices of related events.

Dependency Model Training. The goal of the step is to train expected value prediction models. As shown in Fig. 2, after learning MBs in the first step, events are categorized into two groups, independent events, i.e., events have no MB, and dependent events, i.e., events have MB. For an independent event, the expected value is predicted as the mean of the instances of the event in the training set. For a dependent event, an MLP regressor is trained to predict the expected value of E using $MB(E)$ as predictors. Theoretically, any regression model could be used for the step, and several regression models, such as regression trees, linear regression and SVM regressors, have been adopted in exiting dependency-base anomaly detection techniques. We chose MLP as the dependency model because it could deal with more complex data distribution and shows better performance than other regression models in our experiments.

In LogDP, we consider both dependent and independent log events in anomaly detection because it is common that some anomalous messages are printed to system logs only when anomalies occur. These anomalous log messages usually have no dependency on other log events. If this case is not included in the anomaly detection, a lot of anomalies could be missed. As these anomalous events only occur when anomalies happen, they are unlikely presented in normal log sequences, which is the reason that LogDP detects them by examining the deviation from the mean of values of normal sequences.

To obtain the threshold, a validation set $\mathbf{X}^{val}$ with normal log sequences is input into the learned expected value prediction models to get the expected value of the validation set, i.e., $\hat{\mathbf{X}}^{val}$. The deviation matrix of $\mathbf{X}^{val}$ are calculated as $\mathbf{D} = |\mathbf{X}^{val} - \hat{\mathbf{X}}^{val}|$. Then, for each event, its threshold is calculated as the maximum value of the deviations of the event, i.e., $t_i = maximum(\mathbf{D}_{*i})$, where $\mathbf{D}_{*i}$ is the j-th column of $\mathbf{D}$.

2.3   The Test Phase of LogDP

The goal of the test phase is to use the learned models and thresholds to detect anomalies. Given a log sequence $\mathbf{c} = \{c_i, \cdots, c_m\}$, the expected value of each instance $c_i \in \mathbf{c}$ is predicted by corresponding prediction model. Then, the deviation is calculated as $\delta = |c_i - \hat{c}_i|$. If $\delta > t_i$, then $\mathbf{c}$ is flagged as an anomaly. $\mathbf{c}$ is considered to be normal only if it follows all the normal patterns.

3   Evaluation

Datasets. Three public log datasets, HDFS, BGL and Spirit, are used in our experiments, which are available from [15]. From the three datasets, we generate seven datasets using different log grouping strategies. The HDFS is generated using session, and BGL and Spirit are generated using 1-hour logs, 100 logs, and 20 logs windows. The names of the datasets of BGL and Spirit are denoted as Dataset-Window, e.g., BGL-100logs as shown in Table 1.

For LogDP, the first 2/3 sequences of the training set are used for training, and the remaining 1/3 sequences are used as a validation set.

Table 1. Overview of datasets used in the experiments.

Datasets	# Evt	Window	Training set			Test set		
			# Seq	# Anom.	%Anom.	# Seq	# Anom.	%Anom.
HDFS	29	Session	287,530	8,419	2.93%	287,531	8,419	2.93%
BGL	980	1 h	3,673	495	13.48%	1,481	170	11.48%
		100 logs	37,707	4,009	10.63%	9,426	816	8.66%
		20 logs	188,539	17,252	9.15%	47,134	3,005	6.38%
Spirit	1,229	1 h	1,751	1,213	69.27%	585	225	38.46%
		100 logs	79,999	20,598	25.75%	19,999	429	2.15%
		20 logs	399,999	82,002	20.50%	99,999	498	0.50%

#Evt: number of events; #Seq: number of sequences; #Anom.: number of anomalies; %Anom.: percentage of anomalies.

Benchmark Methods. Six state-of-the-art log-based anomaly detection methods are selected as the benchmark methods, including three proximity-based methods, PCA [7], OneClassSVM [8] (OCSVM), LogCluster [9]; a sequential-based methods, DeepLog [4]; and two invariant relation-based methods, Invariant Mining [1] (IM) and ADR [3]. The description of the benchmark methods can be found in Sect. 4.

Experimental Results. The experimental results (in precision, recall and F1) of LogDP and benchmark methods are presented in Table 2. The best results are in boldface. Overall, LogDP produces superior results comparing to benchmark methods. Out of 7 datasets, LogDP achieves all the best results in F1; five best results in precision; two best results in recall.

As for different strategies of log partitioning, i.e., session (for HDFS) or time window (for BGL and Spirit), LogDP performs well with both strategies. In contrast, as IM, ADR and DeepLog are designed to be more suitable for session-based log partitioning, they yield good results on the HDFS dataset but relatively poor results on other datasets. Compared to the benchmark methods based on proximity-based anomaly detection techniques, i.e., PCA, OCSVM and LogCluster, LogDP produces significantly better results on all datasets except for the precision of PCA on the HDFS dataset. In summary, the experiments have shown the superior performance of LogDP on different datasets with different log partition strategies.

4 Related Work

Log-based anomaly detection has been intensively studied in recent decades. In terms of the techniques used for anomaly detection, the existing approach can be roughly categorized into proximity-based, sequential-based, and relation-based approaches. Proximity-based methods, such as PCA (Principal Component Analysis) [7] and LogCluster [9], cast a log event sequence, as a point in a

Table 2. Experimental results of LogDP and benchmark methods.

Dataset	Metrics	LogDP	PCA	OCSVM	LogCluster	DeepLog	IM	ADR
HDFS-session	F1	**0.987**	0.790	0.068	0.800	0.945	0.943	0.974
	Precision	0.979	**0.980**	0.035	0.870	0.958	0.893	0.951
	Recall	0.995	0.670	0.940	0.740	0.933	**1.000**	**1.000**
BGL-1hour	F1	**0.789**	0.170	0.393	0.147	0.596	0.490	0.547
	Precision	**0.935**	0.352	0.383	0.009	0.474	0.343	0.377
	Recall	0.682	0.112	0.403	0.394	0.802	0.859	**1.000**
BGL-100logs	F1	**0.539**	0.130	0.132	0.243	0.378	0.387	0.250
	Precision	**0.858**	0.440	0.075	0.147	0.321	0.324	0.143
	Recall	0.393	0.076	0.556	0.705	0.461	0.482	**0.987**
BGL-20logs	F1	**0.460**	0.237	0.168	0.226	0.224	0.203	0.204
	Precision	**0.985**	0.447	0.094	0.129	0.126	0.163	0.114
	Recall	0.300	0.162	0.744	0.884	0.981	0.269	**0.988**
Spirit-1hour	F1	**0.821**	0.187	0.601	0.367	0.582	0.387	0.792
	Precision	**0.697**	0.312	0.742	0.324	0.412	0.678	0.656
	Recall	**1.000**	0.133	0.505	0.422	0.991	0.271	**1.000**
Spirit-100logs	F1	**0.575**	0.111	0.003	0.110	0.153	0.107	0.445
	Precision	**0.405**	0.094	0.002	0.152	0.087	0.057	0.287
	Recall	0.993	0.135	0.023	0.086	0.643	0.993	**0.994**
Spirit-20logs	F1	**0.905**	0.095	0.009	0.173	0.135	0.032	0.558
	Precision	**0.835**	0.051	0.005	0.150	0.191	0.016	0.387
	Recall	0.988	0.639	0.057	0.205	0.104	0.974	**0.999**

feature space and utilize distances or density metrics to evaluate the proximity of the log sequence with others. The sequences far from the others are flagged as anomalies. Sequential-based methods, such as DeepLog [4] and LogAnomaly [5], use sequences of the log events to train models and try to predict future events. The log sequences that do not comply with the predicted sequential patterns are identified as anomalies. Relation-based methods such as Invariants Mining [1] and ADR [3], try to find meaningful relations among the log events and use the relations to detect anomalies. As a relation-based method, LogDP is more flexible than the existing ones. Existing relation-based methods [1,3] are based on the invariant relationships among log events. Invariant relations refer to the linear relationships among log events that are related to the program workflows. However, there are two limitations in the existing invariant relation-based methods: (1) the mined relations are sensitive to data noise; (2) the mined relations are restricted to linear relations among the events. In contrast, LogDP utilizes the probabilistic relationships among log events, which makes it less sensitive to data noise. LogDP also adopts MLP regressors as dependency models, which can deal with both linear and non-linear relationships.

5 Conclusion

We have proposed a log-based anomaly detection method, LogDP, which utilizes the deviations from normal patterns to effectively detect anomalous log sequences. LogDP divides log events into two types, dependent events and independent events. For dependent events, the normal patterns are learned from the probabilistic relationship among an event and its MB, i.e., the dependency among events. For independent events, the normal patterns are obtained from the mean prediction models, i.e., the proximity among sequences. The log sequences that violate any normal pattern are identified as anomalies. Our experimental results show that LogDP outperforms the state-of-the-art benchmark methods. Our source code and experimental data are available at: https://github.com/ilwoof/LogDP.

Acknowledgments. This research was supported by an Australian Government Research Training Program (RTP) Scholarship, and by the Australian Research Council's Discovery Projects funding scheme (project DP200102940). The work was also supported with super-computing resources provided by the Phoenix High Powered Computing (HPC) service at the University of Adelaide.

References

1. Lou, J.G., Fu, Q., Yang, S., Xu, Y., Li, J.: Mining invariants from console logs for system problem detection. In: USENIX Annual Technical Conference (2010)
2. He, S., Zhu, J., He, P., Lyu, M.: Experience report: system log analysis for anomaly detection. In: ISSRE, pp. 207–218. IEEE (2016)
3. Zhang, B., Zhang, H., Moscato, P., Zhang, A.: Anomaly detection via mining numerical workflow relations from logs. In: SRDS. IEEE (2020)
4. Du, M., Li, F., Zheng, G., Srikumar, V.: Deeplog: anomaly detection and diagnosis from system logs through deep learning. In: CCS (2017)
5. Meng, W., et al.: Loganomaly: unsupervised detection of sequential and quantitative anomalies in unstructured logs. In: IJCAI 2019, pp. 4739–4745 (2019)
6. Le, V.H., Zhang, H.: Log-based anomaly detection without log parsing. In: Proceedings of the 2021 IEEE/ACM Automated Software Engineering Conference, ASE (2021)
7. Xu, W., Huang, L., Fox, A., Patterson, D., Jordan, M.I.: Detecting large-scale system problems by mining console logs. In: SOSP, pp. 117–132 (2009)
8. Schölkopf, B., Platt, J.C., Shawe-Taylor, J., Smola, A.J., Williamson, R.C.: Estimating the support of a high-dimensional distribution. Neural Comput. **13**(7), 1443–1471 (2001)
9. Lin, Q., Zhang, H., Lou, J., Zhang, Yu., Chen, X.: Log clustering based problem identification for online service systems. In: ICSE-C. IEEE (2016)
10. He, P., Zhu, J., Zheng, Z., Lyu, M.: Drain: an online log parsing approach with fixed depth tree. In: ICWS. IEEE (2017)
11. Du, M., Li, F.: Spell: streaming parsing of system event logs. In: IEEE ICDM, pp. 859–864. IEEE (2016)
12. Dai, H., Li, H., Chen, C., Shang, W., Chen, T.: Logram: efficient log parsing using n-gram dictionaries. IEEE Trans. Softw. Eng. (2020)

13. Lu, S., Liu, L., Li, J., Le, T.D., Liu, J.: Lopad: a local prediction approach to anomaly detection. In: Advances in Knowledge Discovery and Data Mining (2020)
14. Pearl, J.: Causality: Models, Reasoning and Inference. Springer, Heidelberg (2000)
15. He, S., Zhu, J., He, P., Lyu, M.R.: Loghub: a large collection of system log datasets towards automated log analytics. arXiv e-prints (2020)

MMA-Net:
A MultiModal-Attention-Based Deep Neural Network for Web Services Classification

Jing Zhang[1], Changran Lei[1], Yilong Yang[1,2(✉)], Borui Wang[1], and Yang Chen[1]

[1] College of Software, Beihang University, Beijing, China
{zhang_jing,yilongyang}@buaa.edu.cn
[2] State Key Laboratory of Software Development Environment, Beijing, China

Abstract. Recently, machine learning has been widely used for services classification that plays a crucial role in services discovery, selection, and composition. The current methods mostly rely on only one data modality (e.g. services description) for web services classification but fail to fully exploit other readily available data modalities (e.g. services names, and URL). In this paper, a novel *MultiModal-Attention-based deep neural network (MMA-Net)* is proposed to facilitate the web services classification task via effective feature learning from multiple readily available data modalities. Specifically, a new multimodal feature learning module is introduced to achieve effective message passing and information exchanging among multiple modalities. We conduct experiments on the real-world web services dataset using various evaluation metrics, and the results show that our framework achieves the state-of-the-art results.

Keywords: Deep learning · Web services · Services classification · Multimodal learning · Attention

1 Introduction

Web services provide a unified, loosely coupled integration for the reuse of heterogeneous software components [23]. A large number of web services in the common services library are very high-value resources [21]. The commonly used services repositories specify publication specifications for services publishers. The key to use services in software development is to find the required services in the repository, which is the primary concern in services discovery [5].

The most common and practical search method for services discovery is keyword-based search [2,6]. Recently, several machine learning-based web services classification methods [9,12,18,22] are proposed to automatically predict

Electronic supplementary material The online version of this chapter (https://doi.org/10.1007/978-3-030-91431-8_48) contains supplementary material, which is available to authorized users.

and recommend services keywords, which have achieved promising results, especially the deep learning-based methods. These methods generally take the services descriptions as input and the services tags as output and develop a machine learning model to achieve the automatic services classification.

Conventional machine learning methods (e.g., Naive Bayes [14], SVM[27], C4.5 [13], and LDA-SVM) have been widely used to predict the tags of services [8, 9,12,18] on 7 or 10 categories. Recently, deep neural networks [11] have also been applied to services classification in many studies [20,22,26,28], which can classify more categories with higher accuracy. However, most of the current methods merely rely on a single data modality without considering some other readily available data sources provided by the API sharing platform.

In the machine learning community, a well-defined problem named multimodal machine learning [1] aims at building models that process and relate information from multiple modalities. Motivated by multimodal learning, in the context of web services classification, we define different input types to the model as different data modalities, such as services description, name, and the URL that links to the web services. These modalities are closely related since they are pointing towards the same services but may contain complementary information due to their different views of descriptions. A recent work [22] proposes a simple sum-fusion method to merge features of two different modalities (e.g., services names and services descriptions) extracted by BERT [3]. Though the fusion method improves the performance compared to its single modality counterpart, the shared and complementary information between different modalities is not well exploited due to its simplicity. Motivated by a recently proposed popular language model, transformer[25], the cross-attention-based methods [15] have been proposed and achieved promising results among the multimodal fusion methods. However, they are originally designed for vision and language tasks. Thus, their performance in the context of web services classification is unknown. Moreover, most of the cross-attention-based methods are only designed and evaluated for two different modalities. Thus, how to excavate both consensus and complementary information from more than two modalities is still a challenging task in both multimodal machine learning and web services classification.

In this paper, we take three different data modalities into account, and propose a new MultiModal-Attention-based deep neural network (MMA-Net) for web services classification, which improves the performance by a newly proposed multimodal feature learning module which flexibly exchange and fuse information from multimodal data.

The contributions of this paper are summarized as follows:

- We for the first time propose to excavate knowledge from three different data modalities, namely services name, services description, and services URL, to enhance the performance of the web services classification task.
- A novel MultiModal-Attention-based deep neural network (MMA-Net) is proposed for web services classification, which fully exploits multiple data modalities by flexibly exchanging and fusing information and can be easily extended to more data modalities.

– Experiments are conducted on a public 50-category web services benchmark[1] with multiple evaluation metrics. The results show that the proposed method outperforms the state-of-the-art web services classification methods.

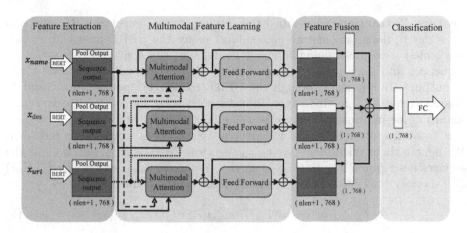

Fig. 1. Overview of the MMA-Net model architecture.

2 MMA-Net

In this section, we introduce the details of the MultiModal-Attention Network (MMA-Net). Suppose the web services dataset is $\mathcal{D} = \{(\boldsymbol{x}_i, \boldsymbol{y}_i)\}_{i=1}^{N}$ with N labeled training data, where $\boldsymbol{x}_i$ denotes the input web services text data (e.g. services name, services description, and services URL) while $\boldsymbol{y}_i$ indicates the corresponding class label of $\boldsymbol{x}_i$. We denote the number of classes as K, then we encode the label of a web service as a one-hot vector as $\boldsymbol{y}_i = [y_i^1, ..., y_i^K] \in \{0, 1\}^K$. The goal of our MMA-Net model is to correctly classify the web services based on the designed model and the training data.

The overview of the proposed *MMA-Net* framework is shown in Fig. 1, which is consisted of four modules: 1) feature embedding module, 2) attention-based multimodal feature learning module, 3) feature fusion module, and 4) classification module. The proposed model takes the services name (denoted by $\boldsymbol{x}_{name}$), services URL (denoted by $\boldsymbol{x}_{url}$), and the services description (denoted by $\boldsymbol{x}_{des}$) as inputs. The feature extraction module uses a pre-trained BERT model [3] to embed different inputs into high-quality feature vectors, respectively. After extracting individual features, the multimodal feature learning module exchanges and integrates multimodal features through a multimodal attention mechanism. The feature fusion module then fuses the three individual features

---

[1] http://www.programmableweb.com.

after information exchanging as the final joint feature representations. Then the classification results are obtained by feeding the fused features into a classification module.

Feature Extraction. We embed the services names, services URL, and services descriptions into feature embeddings using the BERT model [3], which is a widely used pre-training language model that can convert string-type text sequences into high-quality feature vectors. A sentence will obtain two types of outputs after passing through the BERT model: 1) "pool output", and 2) "sequence output". In this paper, in order to ensure the comprehensive representation for multimodal feature learning, we will concatenate "pool output" and "sequence output" as the feature representation of every single modality. We denote the services name as x_{name}, services URL as x_{url}, and x_{des} as the services description. The features of services name (F_{name}), services URL (F_{url}) and services description (F_{des}) of one services can be defined as,

$$F_{modal} = concat(F_{bert}^{pool}(x_{modal}), F_{bert}^{seq}(x_{modal})), \tag{1}$$

where $modal \in \{name, url, des\}$ indicates different modalities, $F_{bert}^{pool}(\cdot)$ and $F_{bert}^{seq}(\cdot)$ represent the "pool output" and "sequence output" produced by the BERT model, respectively.

Attention-Based Multimodal Feature Learning. To achieve effective feature fusion, we introduce a novel multimodal-attention module.

The key idea of our multimodal-attention is motivated by the attention mechanism in transformer [17]. In self-attention, the features are split into query (Q), key (K), and value (V). Q is then multiplied by the affinity matrix produced by the inner-product of K and V. The affinity matrix characterizes the similarities between pairs of tokens in a sentence. To achieve cross-modal message passing, a recently proposed cross-attention method [15] exchanges key-value pairs between two different modalities. However, when data from multiple modalities are presented, the pair-wise exchanging strategy is computationally costly with $O(M^2)$ complexity (where M is the number of data modalities). By contrast, we propose to fuse the keys and values from different modalities, respectively, to obtain the joint key-value pair that serves as a multimodal dictionary for the queries from each individual modality. In this way, the complexity becomes $O(M)$. Moreover, compared to the cross-attention-based methods, the joint key-value pairs proposed in our method allow the learning of more flexible attention maps that enhance the feature learning for each modality.

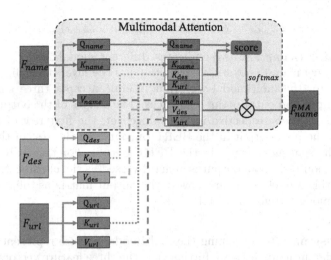

Fig. 2. Illustration of the multimodal feature learning module for F_{name}. Note that other data modalities (F_{des} and F_{url}) are processed by following a similar procedure.

The details of the Multimodel Attention module are shown in Fig. 2. F_{name} is divided into Q_{name}, K_{name}, and V_{name}. F_{des} and F_{url} are processed in the same way. In the attention-based method, this operation is usually achieved through a set of linear transformation networks (e.g. $\mathcal{F}_{linear}^{name}(\cdot)$, $\mathcal{F}_{linear}^{des}(\cdot)$, $\mathcal{F}_{linear}^{url}(\cdot)$). The feature transformations are obtained through:

$$Q_{modal}, K_{modal}, V_{modal} = \mathcal{F}_{linear}^{modal}(F_{modal}), \tag{2}$$

where $modal \in \{name, url, des\}$ indicates different modalities. Then, the K and V of different modalities are concatenated as K_{multi} and V_{multi} to realize the exchange of information between the modalities as follows,

$$K_{multi} = concat(K_{name}, K_{des}, K_{url}), \tag{3}$$

$$V_{multi} = concat(V_{name}, V_{des}, V_{url}). \tag{4}$$

The attention map is then obtained as follows,

$$\hat{F}_{modal}^{MA} = \frac{softmax(Q_{modal} \cdot (K_{multi})^T) \cdot V_{multi}}{\sqrt{d_K}}, \tag{5}$$

where $modal \in \{name, url, des\}$ indicates different modalities, the $softmax(\cdot)$ function normalises all elements of the vector between 0 and 1 with the sum of all elements as 1, and d_K is the second dimension of K for normalization.

A feed forward network is added after the multimodal-attention module. Specifically, the feed forward neural network is a multilayer perceptron (MLP), which is also known as fully connected layer, a type of classic deep neural network layers. For easier optimization, the shortcut connections are added to the cross-attention module and the feed forward network. The specific forms of shortcut connections and feed forward neural networks are as follows,

$$F_{modal}^{MA} = \mathcal{F}_{fw}(Norm(\hat{F}_{modal}^{MA} + F_{modal})), \tag{6}$$

where $modal \in \{name, url, des\}$ indicates different modalities, $\mathcal{F}_{fw}$ represents the feed forward neural network, and $Norm(\cdot)$ is the layer normalization.

To sum up, the multimodal-attention module accepts three single modal features as input and outputs three matrices. The shapes of the output matrices are the same as their respective inputs. Moreover, the first row of the matrix is similar to the pool output in the BERT output, and the rest of the rows are similar to the sequence output in the BERT output. For the BERT model in the classification task, pool output is generally used as the classification feature. Inspired by this, we select the first row in the output matrix as the final features of the multimodal-attention module.

Feature Fusion. After obtaining the multimodal feature representations produced by different modalities, we further fuse the three feature vectors output by the multimodal-attention module into one single vector. The result after feature merging f_{fuse} can be defined as:

$$F_{fuse} = F_{name}^{MA}[1,:] + F_{des}^{MA}[1,:] + F_{url}^{MA}[1,:], \tag{7}$$

where $[1,:]$ is the slicing operator to extract the first row of the matrix.

Classification Module. The task of the classifier layer is to obtain the final classification results. In our model, we use a fully connected neural network that converts high-level feature information into classification prediction. To train the model, a standard classification loss function $\mathcal{L}_{cls}$ is defined on all the training data pairs $(\boldsymbol{x}, \boldsymbol{y}) \sim \mathcal{D}$ as follows,

$$\mathcal{L}_{cls} = \mathbb{E}_{(\boldsymbol{x},\boldsymbol{y})\sim\mathcal{D}}L_{cross\_entropy}(\mathcal{F}_C(F_{fuse}), \boldsymbol{y}), \tag{8}$$

where the standard cross-entropy loss $L_{cross\_entropy}$ is used in our method.

3   Evaluation

3.1   Implementation Details

Network Hyper-Parameters. We choose the pre-trained BERT model named ($bert\_en\_uncased\_L-12\_H-768\_A-12$) from Tensorflow Hub[2], which transforms each word of services description and services name into a 768-dimension vector. For multimodal cross attention, we set the parameter rate to 0.7, the number of heads to 1, and the number of layers to 1. To avoid over-fitting, we add a dropout layer between every two layers of *MMA-Net* with drop probability (rate) 0.1.

---

[2] https://tfhub.dev/tensorflow.

Training Hyper-Parameters. In *MMA-Net*, the Adam optimizer is used for training with the learning rate = 2e-5, beta1 = 0.9, beta2 = 0.999, epsilon = 1e-6, and weight decay = 0.01. The total epoch number is 20 with batch size as 64.

3.2   Web Services Dataset

For a fair comparison with previous methods, we use the publicly released web services dataset proposed by [22] and follow the same setting as [22]. Specifically, the web services data were crawled from the API sharing platform website through crawlers. The dataset contains 15,340 pieces of services data, a total of 401 categories. Each services data contains 20 fields, includes title, description, URL, etc. In this paper, we select the title (i.e., services name), description (i.e., services description), and URL as input, and the primary category fields as the services classification ground-truth label. By following [22], the dataset is preprocessed by removing the small size categories. The final web services dataset contains 50 categories with 10943 services samples.

3.3   Evaluation Protocols

We choose Top-N accuracy as our primary evaluation metrics, which is commonly used in multi-class classification problems. For the calculation of the top-N accuracy, the number of correct labels counts when the top-N predicted labels contain the ground-truth target category label. We use the commonly adopted top-1 and top-5 accuracy for evaluation. In addition, we also evaluate using F1-score and AUC score, both of which take data imbalance into account.

3.4   Compared Methods

We compare our method with both conventional machine learning methods and deep learning models for services classification on the services dataset. Our experiments show that the modern deep learning-based methods outperform the conventional machine learning methods.

For the deep learning-based methods, we compare our method with: 1) Convolutional neural network (CNN) [19] is a special feedforward neural network with convolutional operations. 2) Long short-term memory (LSTM) [7], which is a special type of recurrent neural network (RNN) [24]. 3) Combination methods of CNN and RNN [10]. 4) BI-LSTM [4], which is an improved LSTM. 5) CARL-Net [16] uses the attention mechanism. 6) ServeNet [22] combines different deep learning models. Among these methods, CARL-Net and ServeNet [22] achieve the state-of-the-art performance on web services classification.

Table 1. Comparison with deep learning-based methods.

Model	Top-5	Top-1	AUC	F1
CNN [19]	58.46	27.60	0.36	0.24
LSTM [7]	80.10	51.18	0.48	0.41
Recurrent-CNN [10]	84.29	60.02	0.57	0.54
BI-LSTM [4]	86.70	60.45	0.68	0.58
CARL-Net [16]	89.00	**71.50**	0.86	0.69
ServeNet [22] (w/two modalities)	91.58	69.95	0.83	0.65
ServeNet [22] (w/three modalities)	91.93	70.06	0.85	0.69
Cross-attention (w/two modalities)	89.53	67.62	0.77	0.59
Cross-attention (w/three modalities)	89.69	68.83	0.79	0.62
MMA-Net (w/two modalities)	92.54	70.18	0.88	0.74
MMA-Net (w/three modalities)	**94.18**	70.82	**0.90**	**0.77**

3.5   Experimental Results and Discussion

The experimental results are shown in Table 1. It can be observed that the proposed method achieves the best performance on top-5 accuracy (94.18%), F1 (0.77), AUC (0.9), and comparable top-1 accuracy, compared to the state-of-the-art CARL-Net and ServeNet [22], as well as the cross-attention-based multi-modality feature learning method. We analyze the results from the following perspectives.

Discussion on the Deep Learning-Based Methods: For the deep learning methods, the key to the natural language processing model is to summarize and encode the context information into a unified feature vector or matrix. However, due to the serious phenomenon of gradient vanishing and exploding in RNN-based models, it is still very hard for LSTM to capture the long-term dependencies in long sequences with multi-layer structures. Thus, the attention-based model, such as BERT is more successful in processing long sequences of texts. Here, CARL-Net, ServeNet [22], and our method all rely on the BERT pre-trained model, and the results are much better than the RNN-based methods.

Comparison with the Cross-Attention-Based Methods: Cross-attention is generally calculated between two different modalities. We implement the cross-attention method with both two and three modalities and show the results in Table 1. It is obvious that our method outperforms cross-attention in both settings of two modalities and three modalities.

Comparison with CARL-Net: In addition, when comparing with the state-of-the-art method CARL-Net, the top-1 accuracy between CARL-Net and our method is comparable. However, our method significantly outperforms CARL-Net on top-5 accuracy, F1 score, and AUC results. We argue that top-5 accuracy is more important than top-1 accuracy in some scenarios since one web service generally corresponds to multiple tags, rather than a single one. In addition, since the services classification data are generally imbalanced the F1 score and AUC score for evaluating the performance on the imbalanced data are also essential.

Comparison with ServeNet: To make a fair comparison, we have reproduced and adapted the ServeNet [22] so that it can also use three modalities of data as input. At the same time, two modal data are also tested in our proposed model. The experimental results show that the proposed model is optimal in both three modalities and two modalities. Also, it is easy to observe that our proposed model performs significantly better when using three modalities than when using two modalities, which shows the validity of the multimodal learning strategy.

Ablation Study: We have conducted ablation Study by comparing our full method with the variants of our method that removes Multimodal Feature Learning (i.e., MFL) and Feature Fusion (i.e., Fusion), respectively. The results (%) are shown in Table 2, which verify that both of the proposed modules contribute to the improved performance.

Table 2. Ablations on comparison between our full method and its variants.

Model	Top-5 Accuracy	Top-1 Accuracy
Ours (Full)	**94.18**	**70.82**
Ours (w/o MFL)	87.57	68.31
Ours (w/o Fusion)	92.86	69.41

4   Conclusion and Future Work

In this paper, we introduce a novel deep-learning-based services classification method, named MMA-Net. By observing that more than one data sources (e.g. services description, services name, and services URL) are generally readily available in many web services data, we propose the multimodal fusion strategy for improving the classification results. Specifically, we propose a new multimodal-attention mechanism for effective information exchange and fusion between different modalities. We evaluate our method by comparing it with the state-of-the-art traditional machine learning and deep learning-based methods. The experimental results show that our method outperforms or is comparable to existing methods on different evaluation metrics. Moreover, our method is flexible and can be extended by involving more modalities with limited computational cost, which will be left to our future work.

Acknowledgment. This work was supported by the National Natural Science Foundation of China under Grant No. 62006012 and No. 61732019, and the Opening Project of Shanghai Trusted Industrial Control Platform No. KH54327801.

References

1. Baltrusaitis, T., Ahuja, C., Morency, L.: Multimodal machine learning: a survey and taxonomy. IEEE Trans. Pattern Anal. Mach. Intell. **41**(2), 423–443 (2018)
2. Cheng, B., Zhao, S., Li, C., Chen, J.: MISDA: web services discovery approach based on mining interface semantics. In: IEEE International Conference on Web Services (ICWS 2016), pp. 332–339, June 2016
3. Devlin, J., Chang, M., Lee, K., Toutanova, K.: BERT: pre-training of deep bidirectional transformers for language understanding. In: Burstein, J., Doran, C., Solorio, T. (eds.) Proceedings of the 2019 Conference of the North American Chapter of the Association for Computational Linguistics: Human Language Technologies, NAACL-HLT 2019, Minneapolis, MN, USA, 2–7 June 2019, vol. 1 (Long and Short Papers), pp. 4171–4186. Association for Computational Linguistics (2019)
4. Graves, A., Mohamed, A.R., Hinton, G.: Speech recognition with deep recurrent neural networks. In: 2013 IEEE International Conference on Acoustics, Speech and Signal Processing, pp. 6645–6649. IEEE (2013)
5. Hajlaoui, J.E., Omri, M.N., Benslimane, D., Barhamgi, M.: QoS based framework for configurable IaaS cloud services discovery. In: 2017 IEEE International Conference on Web Services (ICWS 2017), pp. 460–467, June 2017
6. Hasselmeyer, P.: On service discovery process types. In: Proceedings of the 3th International Conference Service-Oriented Computing (ICSOC 2005), pp. 144–156, December 2005
7. Hochreiter, S., Schmidhuber, J.: Long short-term memory. Neural Comput. **9**(8), 1735–1780 (1997)
8. Kapitsaki, G.M.: Annotating web service sections with combined classification. In: 2014 IEEE International Conference on Web Services, pp. 622–629 (2014)
9. Katakis, I., Meditskos, G., Tsoumakas, G., Bassiliades, N., Vlahavas: On the combination of textual and semantic descriptions for automated semantic web service classification. In: Proceedings of IFIP International Conference on Artificial Intelligence Applications and Innovations (AIAI 2009), pp. 95–104, April 2009
10. Lai, S., Xu, L., Liu, K., Zhao, J.: Recurrent convolutional neural networks for text classification. In: Twenty-Ninth AAAI Conference on Artificial Intelligence (2015)
11. LeCun, Y., Bengio, Y., Hinton, G.: Deep learning. Nature **521**(7553), 436 (2015)
12. Liu, X., Agarwal, S., Ding, C.C., Yu, Q.: An LDA-SVM active learning framework for web service classification. In: Reiff-Marganiec, S. (ed.) IEEE International Conference on Web Services, ICWS 2016, San Francisco, CA, USA, 27 June–2 July 2016, pp. 49–56. IEEE Computer Society (2016)
13. Maliah, S., Shani, G.: MDP-based cost sensitive classification using decision trees. In: Proceedings of the Thirty-Second Conference on Artificial Intelligence (AAAI 2018), February 2018
14. Su, J., Shirab, J.S., Matwin, S.: Large scale text classification using semisupervised multinomial Naive Bayes. In: Proceedings of the 28th International Conference on Machine Learning, (ICML 2011), pp. 97–104, June 2011

15. Tan, H., Bansal, M.: LXMERT: learning cross-modality encoder representations from transformers. In: Proceedings of the 2019 Conference on Empirical Methods in Natural Language Processing and the 9th International Joint Conference on Natural Language Processing (EMNLP-IJCNLP), pp. 5100–5111 (2019)

16. Tang, B., Yan, M., Zhang, N., Xu, L., Ren, H.: Co-attentive representation learning for web services classification. Expert Syst. Appl. **180**, 115070 (2021)

17. Vaswani, A., et al.: Attention is all you need. In: Guyon, I., et al. (eds.) Advances in Neural Information Processing Systems 30: Annual Conference on Neural Information Processing Systems 2017, Long Beach, CA, USA, 4–9 December 2017, pp. 5998–6008 (2017)

18. Wang, H., Shi, Y., Zhou, X., Zhou, Q., Shao, S., Bouguettaya, A.: Web service classification using support vector machine. In: Proceedings of IEEE International Conference on Tools with Artificial Intelligence (ICTAI 2010), pp. 3–6, October 2010

19. Wang, S., Huang, M., Deng, Z.: Densely connected CNN with multi-scale feature attention for text classification. In: Proceedings of the Twenty-Seventh International Joint Conference on Artificial Intelligence, (IJCAI 2018), pp. 4468–4474, July 2018

20. Wang, X., Liu, J., Liu, X., Cui, X., Wu, H.: A novel dual-graph convolutional network based web service classification framework. In: 2020 IEEE International Conference on Web Services (ICWS) (2020)

21. Yang, Y., et al.: Medshare: a novel hybrid cloud for medical resource sharing among autonomous healthcare providers. IEEE Access **6**, 46949–46961 (2018)

22. Yang, Y., Qamar, N., Liu, P., Grolinger, K., Liao, Z.: Servenet: a deep neural network for web services classification. In: 2020 IEEE International Conference on Web Services (ICWS) (2020)

23. Yang, Y., Zu, Q., Liu, P., Ouyang, D., Li, X.: MicroShare: privacy preserved medical resource sharing through microservice architecture. Int. J. Biol. Sci. **14**(8), 907 (2018)

24. Zaremba, W., Sutskever, I., Vinyals, O.: Recurrent neural network regularization. Eprint Arxiv (2014)

25. Zhang, C., Yang, Z., He, X., Deng, L.: Multimodal intelligence: representation learning, information fusion, and applications. IEEE J. Sel. Top. Signal Process. **14**(3), 478–493 (2020)

26. Zhang, J., Chen, Y., Yang, Y., Lei, C., Wang, D.: ServeNet-LT: a normalized multi-head deep neural network for long-tailed web services. In: 2021 IEEE International Conference on Web Services (ICWS 2021) (2021)

27. Zhang, P., Shu, S., Zhou, M.: An online fault detection model and strategies based on SVM-grid in clouds. IEEE/CAA J. Automatica Sinica **5**(2), 445–456 (2018)

28. Zou, G., Qin, Z., He, Q., Wang, P., Zhang, B., Gan, Y.: Deepwsc: a novel framework with deep neural network for web service clustering. In: 2019 IEEE International Conference on Web Services (ICWS), pp. 434–436 (2019)

Incentive Mechanism for Spatial Crowdsourcing Cooperation: A Fair Revenue Allocation Method

Xiaowei Wang[1], An Liu[1(✉)], Shushu Liu[2], Junhua Fang[1], and Jiajie Xu[1]

[1] School of Computer Science and Technology, Soochow University, Suzhou, China
20195223023@stu.suda.edu.cn, {anliu,jhfang,xujj}@suda.edu.cn
[2] Department of Communication and Networking, Aalto University, Espoo, Finland
liu.shushu@aalto.fi

Abstract. With the development of intelligent mobile devices, spatial crowdsourcing (SC) has become popular recently, and SC platforms cooperation has attracted people's attention, which can enlarge the whole social-economic benefits. The way to encourage platforms to take part in cooperation is essential. A viable method is to make each platform in cooperation get higher revenue via allocating the revenue generated by cooperation. However, the current work lack studies on the revenue allocation in SC platform cooperation. In this paper, based on cooperative game theory, we propose some ideal properties that the revenue allocation method should satisfy. Then, based on Shapley value, we propose a fair revenue allocation method named SRA, measured by the marginal contribution of each platform. Given the exponential complexity of the method, we propose an efficient approximation method, Coalition-based Shapley value Revenue Allocation (CSRA). Extensive experimental results verify the effectiveness and efficiency of our algorithms.

Keywords: Spatial crowdsourcing · Incentive mechanism · Shapley value · Revenue allocation

1 Introduction

Spatial crowdsourcing (SC) is a new resource allocation model that integrates the power of the masses to accomplish some complex tasks with spatial and temporal features [5,7]. As a new form of employment, SC has provided a large number of jobs for society and driven the development of related industries. It has a wide range of daily applications, including ride-hailing services (e.g., Uber and Didi Chuxing), citizen sensing services (e.g., OpenStreet Map), and food delivery services (e.g., Eleme and Meituan).

SC realizes rational resources allocation by means of task assignment (a.k.a. supply-demand matching) conducted by platforms. In particular, an SC platform arranges tasks to suitable workers with different optimization objectives such as maximizing the total number of assigned tasks or minimizing the total travel cost of the allocated workers. This *traditional task assignment* occurs within each

© Springer Nature Switzerland AG 2021
H. Hacid et al. (Eds.): ICSOC 2021, LNCS 13121, pp. 728–735, 2021.
https://doi.org/10.1007/978-3-030-91431-8_49

platform [3–5]. In the real world, however, the distribution of tasks and workers in a platform is usually uneven, leading to an imbalance between supply (workers) and demand (tasks). As a result, some tasks are unable to be completed due to the lack of workers or some workers have nothing to do due to the lack of tasks [2]. Through *sharing tasks and workers from multiple platforms in a cooperative manner, and delegating the tasks that cannot be completed or that are costly to complete to other platforms' workers (cooperative task-worker matching)*, the platforms can reduce the negative effects of the uneven distribution. This multi-platform cooperation model enables tasks to be completed at a much lower cost (e.g., the travel distance of workers) and are expected to accomplish tasks that would otherwise be impossible due to the lack of workers, thus increasing the benefits (e.g., profit, task completion ratio).

There are two key problems needed to be addressed in this multi-platform cooperation mode: 1) how to assign tasks and workers across platforms, and 2) how to distribute the revenue generated by the cooperation fairly. For the first problem, Cheng et al. [2] propose a real-time cross online matching method (COM) that permits a platform to "borrow" idle workers from other platforms for finishing the tasks, while the second key problem remains to be researched. In this paper, we propose an effective revenue allocation method and two efficient approximate methods for the second problem.

In this paper, we first propose some natural properties based on cooperative game theory that the revenue allocation method should satisfy. Then, we propose a fair revenue allocation method called Shapley value-based Revenue Allocation (SRA), which quantifies the marginal contribution of each platform when joining the cooperation in different orders and allocates the revenue based on the contribution of each platform. Considering that calculating the marginal contribution of each platform in all possible orders will result in exponential complexity, we then propose an efficient approximation algorithm.

The paper is organized as follows. Section 2 provides the preliminaries. Section 3 shows the details of the revenue allocation method SRA. Section 4 describes in detail our approximate method. Section 5 presents the experimental results and discussions. Finally, we conclude this paper in Sect. 6.

2 Preliminaries

In this section, we provide some definitions that will be used throughout the paper and then formally state our problem.

Definition 1 (Spatial Task). A spatial task (task for short) t is defined as a tuple $t = (t.ts, t.plat, t.ori, t.des, t.price)$. More specifically, the task t is published on platform $t.plat$ at time $t.ts$, and a worker must travel from an origin location $t.ori$ to a destination location $t.des$ to complete it. After the task t is completed, the platform $t.plat$ can gain profit $t.price$.

Definition 2 (Worker). A worker w is a tuple $w = (w.ts, w.plat, w.loc, w.r)$ where the $w.plat$ represents the platform the worker belongs to, $w.loc$ means the current location at time $w.ts$, and $w.r$ is the working radius, that is, worker w is willing to perform a task if and only if the distance (e.g., Euclidean distance) between worker and task is not larger than working radius $w.r$.

Definition 3 (Cooperative Task Assignment). Given a platform set $N = \{1, 2, \cdots, n\}$, and each platform i has its own task set $T_i = \{t_{i1}, t_{i2}, \cdots\}$ and worker set $W_i = \{w_{i1}, w_{i2}, \cdots\}$. Each platform in the coalition N realizes cross-platform task-worker matching in a specific task assignment method by sharing workers W_i and tasks T_i.

Each platform sends all tasks and workers data to the central server, and the central server implements cross-platform task assignment. It should be pointed out that this centralized approach is not necessary, and distributed solutions can also work.

Problem Statement (Revenue Allocation Problem). Given the revenue $v(N)$ gained by the platform set N, the problem of revenue allocation is to explore a reasonable and effective revenue allocation method based on the contribution of each platform so that all platforms are willing to continue to participate in cooperation.

3   Shapley Value-Based Revenue Allocation Method

In this section, we will introduce a precise Shapley value-based Revenue Allocation method (SRA) to encourage platforms to take part in cooperation. We regard that SC platforms' cooperation as a cooperative game, and we use the Shapley value to allocate the revenue gained by cooperation. Considering a set of platforms N and a function $v(\cdot)$ that maps each subset $S \subseteq N$ of platforms to real numbers, modeling the revenue of cooperation when platforms in S participate in it. The Shapley value is one way to fairly quantify the total contribution of each platform to the result $v(N)$ of the cooperative game, and it satisfies a set of desirable properties:

1) Group Rationality: All total revenue $v(N)$ obtained by the coalition N should be distributed to the participating platforms.
2) Individual Rationality: The revenue of the platform participating in the cooperation should be greater than that of the platform not participating in the cooperation.
3) Symmetry: If for platform i and j and any subset $S \subseteq N - \{i, j\}$, We have $v(S \cup \{i\}) = v(S \cup \{j\})$, then we think the contribution of these two platforms is the same, and they should get the same profit.
4) Dummy Player: For any subset $S \subseteq N - \{i\}$, if $v(S) = v(S \cup \{i\})$, it means that the platform i did not make any contribution, and then it won't be allocated any profit from coalition revenue.

For a given platform i, the Shapley value can be computed as follows:

$$\varphi_i = \sum_{S \subseteq N} \frac{(|S| - 1)!(|N| - |S|)!}{|N|!} [v(S) - v(S - \{i\})] \tag{1}$$

where φ_i represents the contribution of platform i, and it is also the revenue allocated to the platform i. The Shapley value for player i defined above can be interpreted as the average marginal contribution of platform i to all possible coalition S that can be formed without it. The specific method of revenue distribution is shown in the Algorithm 1.

Algorithm 1: Shapley value-based Revenue Allocation (SRA)

Input: platform set N, task set T, worker set W
Output: platform revenue set $\{\varphi_1, \varphi_2, \cdots, \varphi_n\}$
1 Initialize $\varphi_i = 0$, for $i = 1, \cdots, n$;
2 Initialize $v(S) = 0$, for all nonempty subset $S \subset N$;
3 **foreach** *nonempty subset $S \subset N$* **do**
4 $\quad$ $v(S) = TaskAssignment(S, T_S, W_S)$;
5 $\quad$ **foreach** *platform $i \in S$* **do**
6 $\quad\quad$ $\varphi_i = \varphi_i + \frac{(|S|-1)!(|N|-|S|)!}{|N|!}[v(S) - v(S - \{i\})]$;
7 $\quad$ **end**
8 **end**
9 **Return**: $\{\varphi_1, \varphi_2, \cdots, \varphi_n\}$;

Algorithm Details. The input of SRA is the platform set N, the task set T, worker set W. The output is the revenue set of each platform $\{\varphi_1, \varphi_2, \cdots, \varphi_n\}$. Firstly, initialize platform revenue $\varphi_i = 0$ and each coalition revenue $v(S) = 0$ (Lines 1–2). For each nonempty subset $S \subseteq N$, use a specific task assignment method to get the corresponding revenue $v(S)$ (Lines 3–4). After that, we calculate the revenue of each platform according to Eq. 1 (Lines 5–6), and return the revenue set (Line 9).

Complexity Analysis. The Algorithm 1 consists of two parts: calculating revenue and distributing revenue. The first part mainly uses a specific task assignment method to calculate all the revenue, and the computational complexity varies with different task assignment methods, and take the greedy task assignment method as an example, the computational complexity is $O(|T| \times |W| \times 2^n)$ since it needs to compute all non-empty subsets of set N. The second part uses Eq. 1 to allocate the revenue fairly, and its computational complexity is $O(n \times 2^n)$. Therefore, the total computational complexity is $O(2^n \times (|T| \times |W| + n))$. The space complexity is $O(|T| + |W| + n)$.

4   Approximate Shapley Value-Based Revenue Allocation

In order to calculate the Shapley value accurately, it is necessary to calculate all possible subsets of N, and the computational complexity is exponentially large in the size of the platform number. In addition, the computation of $v(S)$ for each $S \subseteq N$ involves a process of assigning tasks, and take the greedy task assignment as an example as before, its time complexity is $O(|T_S| \times |W_S|)$. As a result, it is impossible to accurately distribute the revenue according to the Shapley value in a limited time. In this section, we discuss an approximation method for efficiently estimating the Shapley value.

Algorithm 2: Coalition-based Shapley value Revenue Allocation

---

Input: N, T, W, t

Output: each platform's revenue $\{\varphi_1, \varphi_2, \cdots, \varphi_n\}$

1 Initialize $\varphi_i = 0$ for $i = 1, \cdots, n$;

2 Divide N into t coalitions $C = \{C_1, \cdots, C_t\}$ randomly and uniformly;

3 Initialize $\varphi_{C_i} = 0$ for $i = 1, \cdots, t$;

4 **foreach** $S \subseteq C$ **do**

5 $\quad$ $v(S) = TaskAssignment(S, T_S, W_S)$;

6 $\quad$ **foreach** $C_i \in S$ **do**

7 $\quad\quad$ $\varphi_{C_i} = \varphi_{C_i} + \frac{(|S|-1)!(|C|-|S|)!}{|C|!}[v(S) - v(S - \{C_i\})]$;

8 $\quad$ **end**

9 **end**

10 **foreach** *coalition* C_i **do**

11 $\quad$ **foreach** $S \subset C_i$ **do**

12 $\quad\quad$ $v(S) = TaskAssignment(S, T_S, W_S)$;

13 $\quad\quad$ **foreach** *platform* $i \in S$ **do**

14 $\quad\quad\quad$ $\varphi_i = \varphi_i + \frac{(|S|-1)!(|C_i|-|S|)!}{|C_i|!}[\varphi_{C_i} - v(S - \{i\})]$;

15 $\quad\quad$ **end**

16 $\quad$ **end**

17 **end**

18 **Return**: $\{\varphi_1, \varphi_2, \cdots, \varphi_n\}$;

Basic Idea. We propose an improvement in the exponential calculation of the Shapley value. Each platform participates in the cooperation in the form of individuals in the original calculation method. We assume that they participate in cooperation in the form of a particular coalition. That is, they form t coalitions firstly, and then these coalitions participate in the cooperation. We allocate the revenue $v(N)$ among coalitions, and then we distribute the revenue to platforms within the same coalition so that we reduce the number of task assignment needed to calculate revenue allocation from 2^n to $2^t + t \times 2^{n/t}$, described with more detail in Algorithm 2.

Algorithm Details. The input is the set of platforms N, the set of tasks T, the set of workers W, the number of coalitions t and the output is the revenue of each platform $\{\varphi_1, \cdots, \varphi_n\}$. First, we initialize the platform revenue $\varphi_i = 0$, and then divide platforms uniformly into t coalitions $C = \{C_1, \cdots, C_t\}$ and initialize the coalition revenue $\varphi_{C_i} = 0$ (Lines 1–3). For each non-empty set $S \subset C$, we calculate its revenue and update the revenue of each coalition $C_i \in S$ (Lines 4–7). And then, we continue to distribute the revenue from each coalition among platforms. In a similar way, we first calculate the revenue of all non-empty sets $v(S), S \subseteq C_i$ (Lines 10–12), then we allocate revenue to each platform $i \in S$ (Lines 13–14). Finally, we return the set of platforms' revenue $\{\varphi_1, \cdots, \varphi_n\}$ (Line 18).

Complexity Analysis. The algorithm can be divided into two parts: allocation of revenues to coalitions (Lines 4–9) and allocation of revenues to platforms (Lines 10–17). The computational complexity of the first part is $O(2^t \times (|T| \times |W| + t))$ and that of the second part is $O(t \times 2^{n/t} \times (max(|T_{C_i}| \times |W_{C_i}|) + n/t)$. Considering the complexity, we suggest that t is set to $[\sqrt{n}]$.

5 Experiment

In this section, we evaluate our proposed algorithms' effectiveness and efficiency by conducting a series of experiments on a real dataset and reporting the experimental results.

5.1 Experimental Setup

We conduct our experiments using a real DiDi dataset [1], which provides taxi order tasks, which are used to simulate our problem. The taxi order dataset was collected from Chengdu in November 2016, and wherein each task is associated with a release time, an end time, a start GPS point, an end GPS point, and the reward for the task. Since these tasks come from one platform, we randomly divide them into several platforms to accommodate our problems and generate several workers for each platform. In total, the dataset provides taxi order data in the area of Chengdu (with latitude from $30.653°$ to $30.728°$ and longitude from $104.042°$ to $104.130°$), which includes 67714 tasks and 6770 workers each day on average. We use the data of the first 20 days to train the learning model and carry out the simulation experiment based on the data of the 21st day. Table 1 shows our experimental setting, where the default values of all parameters are in bold. Here, $|N|$ is the number of platforms, $|T|$ ($|W|$) is the average number of tasks (workers) of each platform.

Table 1. Experiment parameters

Parameters	Values
$|N|$	2, 3, **4**, 5, 6
$|T|$	2 k, 4 k, **6 k**, 8 k, 10 k
$|W|$	200, 400, **600**, 800, 1000
r	0.5, **1.0**, 1.5, 2.0
Task value	**real**

We propose a baseline approximation algorithm: Weighted Average (WA) to compare with our methods, in which the revenue is distributed by considering the proportion of tasks and workers of each platform, and the calculation is as follows:

$$\varphi_i = (a \times \frac{|T_i|}{|T|} + b \times \frac{|W_i|}{|W|}) \times v(N) \qquad (2)$$

where, a and b describe the importance of the number tasks and the workers respectively, and they meet the requirements $a + b = 1$, and we set $a = b = 0.5$. We evaluate our methods regarding efficiency and effectiveness according to the time-consuming and error (using Mean Absolute Percentage Error index) of estimation accuracy and revenue allocation in two task assignment methods, real-time online Greedy method and TGOA-OP [6]. It should be noted that in this experiment, we only consider the dynamic appearance of tasks. All methods can be summarized as follows:

- **SRA:** Calculate the revenue of each platform according to Algorithm 1.
- **WA:** Calculate the revenue according to the proportion of workers and tasks of each platform.
- **CSRA:** The platform set is divided into several coalitions, and then the revenue is calculated according to Algorithm 2.

5.2   Experimental Result

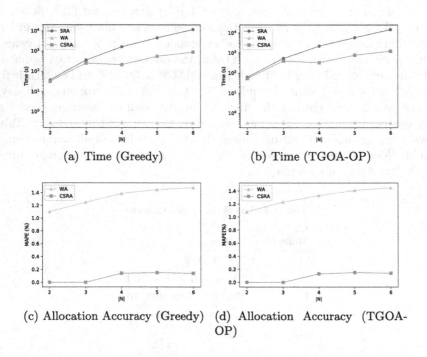

(a) Time (Greedy)

(b) Time (TGOA-OP)

(c) Allocation Accuracy (Greedy)

(d) Allocation Accuracy (TGOA-OP)

Fig. 1. Effect vs $|N|$

Effect of $|N|$. In Figures 1(a) and 1(b), the time consumption of SRA increases exponentially in both two task assignment methods as expected and makes the enormous time cost, followed by CSRA. As for CSRA, the value of t varies with the $|N|$ as we suggested before. When $|N|$ increases from 3 to 4, the value of

t changes to 2, resulting in the time consumption of CSRA does not change as before. The time consumption of the WA method is the smallest among all methods, and it is relatively fixed. As for revenue allocation accuracy, shown in Figs. 1(c) and 1(d), the CSRA method has the highest accuracy, and the WA method has the lowest accuracy. It should be noted that when $|N| = 2$ or 3, the value of t in the CSRA method is 1, the CSRA method is completely consistent with the SRA method, so the error MAPE is 0.

6   Conclusion

In this paper, we present the importance of revenue allocation for platforms' cooperation and propose a Shapley value-based Revenue Allocation (SRA), which can achieve fair revenue allocation in the cooperation scenario of SC platforms. Then, considering the exponential complexity of the SRA method, We propose an approximation methods CSRA, for efficient revenue allocation, and extensive experimental results verify the effectiveness and efficiency of our approach.

Acknowledgements. This work was supported by the National Natural Science Foundation of China (Grant Nos. 61572336, 61632016, 62072323), the Natural Science Foundation of Jiangsu Province (Grant Nos. BK20211307, BK20191420), the Major Program of the Natural Science Foundation of Jiangsu Higher Education Institutions of China (Grant Nos. 18KJA520010, 19KJA610002), and the Collaborative Innovation Center of Novel Software Technology and Industrialization.

References

1. Gaia of didi. https://outreach.didichuxing.com/research/opendata/en/
2. Cheng, Y., Li, B., Zhou, X., Yuan, Y., Wang, G., Chen, L.: Real-time cross online matching in spatial crowdsourcing. In: ICDE, pp. 1–12. IEEE (2020)
3. Fan, J., Zhou, X., Gao, X., Chen, G.: Crowdsourcing task scheduling in mobile social networks. In: Pahl, C., Vukovic, M., Yin, J., Yu, Q. (eds.) ICSOC 2018. LNCS, vol. 11236, pp. 317–331. Springer, Cham (2018). https://doi.org/10.1007/978-3-030-03596-9_22
4. Liu, C., Gao, X., Wu, F., Chen, G.: QITA: quality inference based task assignment in mobile crowdsensing. In: Pahl, C., Vukovic, M., Yin, J., Yu, Q. (eds.) ICSOC 2018. LNCS, vol. 11236, pp. 363–370. Springer, Cham (2018). https://doi.org/10.1007/978-3-030-03596-9_26
5. Qu, Y., et al.: Posted pricing for chance constrained robust crowdsensing. IEEE Trans. Mob. Comput. **19**(1), 188–199 (2020)
6. Tong, Y., Zeng, Y., Ding, B., Wang, L., Chen, L.: Two-sided online micro-task assignment in spatial crowdsourcing. IEEE Trans. Knowl. Data Eng. **33**(5), 2295–2309 (2021)
7. Tong, Y., Zhou, Z., Zeng, Y., Chen, L., Shahabi, C.: Spatial crowdsourcing: a survey. VLDB J. **29**(1), 217–250 (2019). https://doi.org/10.1007/s00778-019-00568-7

Sprelog: Log-Based Anomaly Detection with Self-matching Networks and Pre-trained Models

Haitian Yang[1,2(✉)], Xuan Zhao[3], Degang Sun[2(✉)], Yan Wang[1], and Weiqing Huang[1,2]

[1] Institute of Information Engineering, Chinese Academy of Sciences, Beijing, China
{yanghaitian,sundegang,wangyan,huangweiqing}@iie.ac.cn
[2] School of Cyber Security, University of Chinese Academy of Sciences, Beijing, China
[3] York University, Ontario, Canada
xuanzhao@eecs.yorku.ca

Abstract. With the development of software systems, log has become more and more important in system maintenance. During the past few years, log-based anomaly detection has attracted much attention. We propose a novel log-based anomaly detection model, called Sprelog, which captures "inconsistent" information during the evolution of log messages by exploring word-word interactions features. Firstly, we compute the interactive information of each word-word pair in the input log sequence, constructing self-matching attention vectors. Next, we use these self-matching attention vectors to manage the log sequence and construct the representation vectors. Hence, the log sequence can be matched word-by-word, adapting to the evolution of log messages. In addition, we combine pre-trained models in our proposed network to generate the higher-level semantic component information. More importantly, we use a low-rank bi-linear pooling approach to connect inconsistent and compositional information, thus our model can reduce potential information redundancy without weakening the discriminative ability. Experiment results on publicly available datasets demonstrate that our model significantly outperforms extant baselines on standard evaluation metrics, including precision, recall, F1 score and accuracy.

Keywords: Log analysis · Anomaly detection · Self-matching networks · Pre-trained models

1 Introduction

With the continuous development of software systems, the scale of systems becomes larger and larger, hence it is almost impossible to detect system anomalies manually. During the past decade, we witness the introduction of many automated log-based approaches [1,2]. These methods often apply useful information from logs to detect system anomalies. We observe that some methods

© Springer Nature Switzerland AG 2021
H. Hacid et al. (Eds.): ICSOC 2021, LNCS 13121, pp. 736–743, 2021.
https://doi.org/10.1007/978-3-030-91431-8_50

adopt data mining and machine learning techniques to analyze log data and detect the occurrence of system anomalies. For example, Xu, et al. [2] treated the log-based anomaly detection task as an unsupervised learning problem and utilized Principal Component Analysis (PCA) to detect anomalies.

However, most of these log-based anomaly detection approaches are not sufficiently robust in the real-world implementation. Therefore, in this paper, we propose a method named Sprelog - a novel log-based anomaly detection approach, which can achieve accurate and robust anomaly detection on real-world, ever-changing, and noisy log data. More importantly, we evaluate the proposed approach using the public log data collected from Hadoop. Specially, we reorganize the injection ratios of the Hadoop log data to evaluate the effectiveness of the proposed approach. Our experimental results demonstrate that when we increase the injection rate from 5% to 20%, the F1-score merely decreases from 0.97 to 0.94. Hence, the experiment not only shows that our approach can effectively detect anomalies of the online service system with the ever-changing and noisy log data, but also, more importatnly, very robust.

We summarize the main contributions of this paper as follows:

(1) We aim to solve the task of unstable log anomaly detection. Specifically, we adopt a self-matching network that captures "inconsistent" information during the evolution of log messages by exploring word-word interaction features. This self-matching network assists our method to manage both the instability during the evolution of log messages and the noise in the log data.

(2) We adopt two semantic representations, the local static-based word embedding (word2vec [3] or glove [4]) and the global dynamic word embedding (ReBERTa [5]). Also, we apply the low-rank bi-linear pooling approach to integrate these two semantic representations effectively.

(3) We have evaluated Sprelog using two public datasets. The results confirmed the effectiveness of our approach.

2   The Proposed Model

2.1   Task Description

In this research, the log-based anomaly detection task can be described as a tuple of three elements (S, I, y), where $S = [s^1, s^2, \ldots, s^g]$ represents the log event whose length is g. I denotes the current log message task ID and $y \in Y$ conveys the anomaly detection status of the log. More detailed, Y={Yes, No} which Yes represents that log is normal, and No means that the log is abnormal. Generally, the function of our model Sprelog is to assign a label to each task ID based on the conditional probability $Pr(y|S, I)$ according to the given set of $\{S, I\}$ to solve the log-based anomaly detection task.

2.2   Overview of the Proposed Model

In this section, we describe our proposed model in detail. Model architecture is depicted in Fig. 1. First, we process the unstructured original log data into the structured log events by log parsing, and then convert each word of log events into a vector by word embedding. Then, to transform log events into fixed-dimensional log sequence semantic vectors, we combine word-to-word interactions vectorization with Roberta-based semantic feature vectorization. Finally, to further synthesize the vectorized log event sequences, we use Low-rank Bi-linear Pooling to integrate the log sequence information for the log-based anomaly detection task.

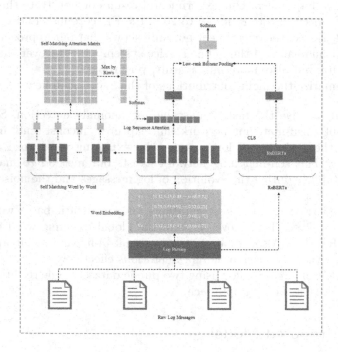

Fig. 1. Overview of our proposed Sprelog model.

2.3   The Representation of the Local Semantic Log Sequence

In this section, we acquire the representation of the local semantic information. Firstly, we construct word-to-word interactions features from parsed logs. Secondly, we combine the word information with the log sequence local semantic information via our self-matching networks [6]. After the above-mentioned steps, we fix the number of the word-to-word interactions vector of the whole log sequence.

It is worth noting that the self-matching network can generate a attended feature vector for the input log sequence: $f_a = S \cdot a$, where $a \in R^n$ is the self-matched attention vector. Literature [7] provides study to demonstrate the effectiveness of semantic incongruity as a predictor for log-based anomaly detection. Hence, attention vector a can be designed to capture log sequence incongruity.

In this paper inspired came from "co-attention" network proposed by Lu et al. to address the Visual Question Answering (VQA) task [8]. They introduce an affinity matrix C to attend input picture feature map V and text question representation Q. C is calculated by:

$$C = \tanh\left(Q \cdot W_a \cdot V\right) \tag{1}$$

where W_a contains attention weights.

A joint activation approach (e.g. maximize by rows and columns) is adopted to adjust attention weights for V and Q simultaneously. We modify this approach by introducing a weight matrix between word-to-word pair to improve the ability of capturing joint information of words.

Given a word pair (e_i, e_j), the the joint feature vector $w_{i,j}$ is computed:

$$w_{i,j} = \tanh\left(\mathbf{e}_i \cdot \mathbf{M}_{i,j} \cdot \mathbf{e}_j^{\mathrm{T}}\right) \tag{2}$$

where e_i and e_j are word embeddings for i and j [9], $w_{i,j} \in R$ measuring the joint information between word i and word j , and $M_{i,j} \in R^{k \times k}$ is a parameter matrix.

The self-matching information matrix W based on all joint information $w_{i,j}$, $i.j \in (1, 2, \ldots, n)$ is computed:

$$\mathbf{W} = \begin{pmatrix} w_{1,1} & w_{1,2} & \cdots & w_{1,n} \\ w_{2,1} & w_{2,2} & \cdots & w_{2,n} \\ \vdots & \vdots & \ddots & \vdots \\ w_{n,1} & w_{2,2} & \cdots & w_{n,n} \end{pmatrix} \tag{3}$$

A maximization activation approach is applied to calculate the self-matched attention vector a. We first calculate an intermediate vector $m \in R^n$, by maximizing elements in W by rows.

$$m_i = \max\left(w_{i,1}, w_{i,2}, \ldots, w_{i,n}\right), \forall i \in (1, 2, \cdots, n) \tag{4}$$

Then, we input m into a standard softmax function to calculate a: $a = softmax(m)$. Softmax function is adopted for the purpose of normalization.

2.4   The Representation of the Global Semantic Log Sequence

In this section, we use Reberta to obtain global semantic features in log sequence. Specifically, the Reberta applied contains token embeddings, segment embeddings, position embeddings, and Transformer with multi-head attention [5] as the encoder layer to obtain H-dimensional encoded log sequence containing contextual information. To achieve these representations, we first use $S = [s^1, s^2, \ldots, S^g]$ to represent the log event whose length is g. In the pre-trained method Reberta, we obtain global contextual log sequence representation f_l by applying the fixed-dimensional output vector as the semantic representation of the entire log event. The output vector is symbolized as the [cls]. The detailed equation is demonstrated as follows:

$$f_l = Reberta_{cls}(S) \tag{5}$$

2.5 Low-Rank Bilinear Pooling

After the previous steps, two log sequences feature vectors are acquired: f_a generated by the self-matching network and f_l generated by the Reberta encoder. Here, we concatenate these two feature vectors for the final prediction. We employ a Low-rank Bilinear Pooling (LRBP) method based on Hadamard product to reduce the dimension of the final input vector to control the potential information redundancy without reducing feature vector's discriminative power [10].

In this work, we follow the concept of LRBP to pool information from two input feature vectors: $f_a \in R^k$ and $f_l \in R^d$. The final projection feature vector for the input log sequence is calculated:

$$f = U^T \cdot f_a \circ V^T \cdot f_l + g \tag{6}$$

where $\circ$ represents the Hadamard product, $f \in R^c$, $U \in R^{k \times c}$, and $V \in R^{d \times c}$ are parameters that need to be learned. $g \in R^c$ is bias, c, k and d are hyperparameters.

f is the final feature vector for the inputted log sequence. We input f into a standard softmax classification layer to make the log-based anomaly detection prediction:

$$p_i = softmax(W_f \cdot f + b) \tag{7}$$

where $p_i \in R^2$ represents whether the input log event sequence is normal or not, and $W_f \in R^{2 \times c}$, $b \in R^2$ are parameters to be learned.

2.6 Training Objective

The lost function of this Log-Based Anomaly Detection classification task is a standard cross-entropy:

$$J(\theta) = - \sum_{i=1}^{N} [y_i \cdot \log p_i + (1 - y_i) \cdot \log (1 - p_i)] + \lambda \cdot R \tag{8}$$

where N is the size of training dataset, y_i is the true label for log sequence i. $\theta = \{M_{i,j}, U, V, g, W_f, b\}$ are model parameters. $R = \|\theta\|_{L2}$ regularization term, λ is a hyperparameter measuring the weight of regularization term.

3   Experimental Setup

3.1   Dataset and Hyper Parameters

We evaluate our proposed Sprelog on two datasets, including the original HDFS datasets [11] and the synthetic unstable HDFS datasets. To prepare for the synthetic datasets, we randomly collect 51,000 log sequences from the original HDFS datasets consisting of 50,000 normal and 1,000 anomaly sequences. We inject the unstable log data into it and create two testing sets: NewTesting 1 and 2, which contain injected unstable log events and unstable log sequences, respectively. The details of the two datasets are show Table 1:

Table 1. The synthetic HDFS datasets

Set	Unstable event	Unstable seq.	Normal	Anomaly	Total
Training	No	No	6,000	6,000	12,000
NewTesting1	Yes	No	50,000	1,000	51,000
NewTesting2	No	Yes	50,000	1,000	51,000

We fix all the hyper-parameters applied to our model. Specifically, We train our networks by stochastic gradient descent with the learning rate of 0.1, the momentum of 0.9, the weight decay of 0.0005, the dropout ratio of 0.5, and the gradient clipping of 0.1. The training batch size for all datasets is tuned amongst 64, 128, 256. The L2 regularization is set to 10^{-5} for the original HDFS datasets, and 10^{-3} for synthetic unstable HDFS datasets.

3.2   Results and Analysis

To analyze the effectiveness of our model, we take some current competitive methods as baselines on the above two datasets to compare the performance of Sprelog with other models. The results are demonstrated as follows.

Table 2. Experiment results on synthetic HDFS dataset of untable log sequences (the NewTesting1 set)

Injection ratio	Metric	LR [10]	SVM [12]	IM [13]	PCA [11]	LogAnomaly [14]	PLELog [15]	LogRobust [7]	Sprelog
5%	Precision	0.25	0.36	0.78	0.90	0.97	0.91	1.00	0.99
	Recall	0.92	0.96	0.56	0.66	0.89	0.78	0.91	**0.95**
	F1-score	0.39	0.53	0.65	0.76	0.93	0.84	0.95	**0.97**
10%	Precision	0.18	0.11	0.88	0.90	0.86	0.82	0.89	**0.92**
	Recall	0.95	0.89	0.40	0.64	0.94	0.89	1.00	0.96
	F1-score	0.30	0.20	0.56	0.74	0.90	0.85	0.94	0.94
15%	Precision	0.08	0.11	0.84	0.82	0.82	0.78	0.86	**0.90**
	Recall	0.85	0.90	0.41	0.42	0.97	0.85	0.99	0.99
	F1-score	0.14	0.20	0.55	0.55	0.89	0.81	0.92	**0.94**
20%	Precision	0.06	0.09	0.82	0.82	0.92	0.78	0.99	0.96
	Recall	0.87	0.89	0.43	0.41	0.88	0.75	0.81	**0.92**
	F1-score	0.11	0.16	0.56	0.54	0.90	0.76	0.89	**0.94**

(1) Experiments on the Synthetic HDFS Dataset

Our work focuses on the anomaly detection problem in unstable logs. To further prove that the model proposed in this paper can effectively solve the anomaly detection issue in unstable logs, we conduct two groups of experiments. First, for the unstable log events, our model is trained on the original HDFS log datasets and tested on the synthetic unstable log event datasets (NewTesting1). The comparison results on the NewTesting1 set are shown in Table 2. We can note that as the proportion of unstable log injection increases, the performance of the five baselines continues to decline. The f1 value of our model Sprelog is around 0.94 based on different injection rates, which strongly proves that our method has high robustness and can effectively solve the anomaly detection issue in unstable logs. The main reason is that, during the log presentation process, our model applies the pre-trained model and semantic vectors, projecting the logs into higher dimensions, thus higher-level semantic information can be obtained.

Next, we conduct another group of experiments on the unstable log data. Specifically, our model is trained on the original HDFS log datasets and tested on the synthetic unstable log sequence datasets (NewTesting2). The experimental results are shown in Table 3.

Table 3. Experiment results on synthetic HDFS dataset of untable log sequences (the NewTesting2 set)

Injection ratio	Metric	LR [10]	SVM [12]	IM [13]	PCA [11]	LogAnomaly [14]	PLELog [15]	LogRobust [7]	Sprelog
5%	Precision	0.97	0.94	0.03	0.95	0.98	0.93	0.99	0.98
	Recall	0.85	0.98	0.84	0.65	0.92	0.81	0.93	**0.96**
	F1-score	0.96	0.96	0.06	0.77	0.95	0.87	0.96	**0.97**
10%	Precision	0.44	0.77	0.03	0.96	0.92	0.96	0.94	**0.96**
	Recall	0.93	0.97	0.97	0.63	0.96	0.76	0.99	0.97
	F1-score	0.61	0.86	0.06	0.76	0.92	0.82	0.96	0.96
15%	Precision	0.09	0.21	0.02	0.83	0.95	0.83	0.98	0.98
	Recall	0.88	0.93	0.97	0.39	0.92	0.74	0.91	**0.95**
	F1-score	0.17	0.33	0.04	0.53	0.93	0.78	0.94	**0.96**
20%	Precision	0.07	0.07	0.01	0.87	0.90	0.76	0.92	**0.95**
	Recall	0.82	0.86	0.98	0.37	0.96	0.68	0.97	**0.98**
	F1-score	0.12	0.14	0.03	0.52	0.93	0.72	0.95	**0.96**

We can observe that LogAnomaly [14], LogRobust [7], and our proposed Sprelog are semantic-based models. When the injection ratio of log sequences increases, these models performance reduces slower compared to other methods. In particular, our proposed method Sprelog still remain significant performance, when the injection ratio of log sequences increases, log sequences suffer from missed, duplicated, or shuffled problems. The f1 value of the model Sprelog is basically around 0.96. The reason is that our model uses a self-matching network in the log sequence representation. The self-matching network explores the contextual information embedded in the log sequence and learns the different importance of log events through the attention mechanism. Therefore, it makes our model robust to small changes in the sequence.

4 Conclusion

Engineers can use logs (for example, system log messages) to investigate the anomalies. However, due to the continuous evolution of log statements and the emergence of processing log noise, the current log anomaly analysis model are not robust enough. To overcome this issue, we propose a new log-based anomaly detection method - Sprelog. Which can capture the inconsistency in the evolution of log sequences and higher-level semantic component information. Experiment results on publicly available datasets, our proposed Sprelog model achieves state-out-of-art performance, outperforming the most advanced log-based anomaly detection models that exist. In the future, our research group would like to improve the computing speed of Sprelog to further level up the performance of our solution.

References

1. He, P., Zhu, J., He, S., Li, J., Lyu, M.R.: Towards automated log parsing for large-scale log data analysis. IEEE Trans. Dependable Secure Comput. **15**(6), 931–944 (2017)
2. Xu, W., Huang, L., Fox, A., Patterson, D., Jordan, M.I.: Detecting large-scale system problems by mining console logs. In: Proceedings of the ACM SIGOPS 22nd Symposium on Operating Systems Principles, pp. 117–132 (2009)
3. Mikolov, T., Sutskever, I., Chen, K., Corrado, G.S., Dean, J.: Distributed representations of words and phrases and their compositionality. In: Advances in Neural Information Processing Systems, pp. 3111–3119 (2013)
4. Pennington, J., Socher, R., Manning, C.D.: Glove: global vectors for word representation. In: EMNLP, pp. 1532–1543 (2014)
5. Liu, Y., Ott, M., Goyal, N., Du, J., Joshi, M., et al.: Roberta: a robustly optimized Bert pretraining approach. Corr abs/1907.11692 (2019)
6. Park, C., Song, H., Lee, C.: S3-net: SRU-based sentence and self-matching networks for machine reading comprehension. TALLIP **19**(3), 1–14 (2020)
7. Zhang, X., Li, Z., Chen, J., He, X., et al.: Robust log-based anomaly detection on unstable log data, pp. 807–817, August 2019
8. Lu, J., Yang, J., Batra, D., Parikh, D.: Hierarchical question-image co-attention for visual question answering. In NIPS, pp. 289–297 (2016)
9. Tay, Y., Tuan, L.A., Hui, S., Su, J.: Reasoning with sarcasm by reading in-between. pp. 1010–1020, January 2018
10. Kim, J.H., On, K., Kim, J., Ha, J.W., Zhang, B.T.: Hadamard product for low-rank bilinear pooling. arXiv:1610.04325 (2016)
11. Xu, W., Huang, L., Fox, A., Patterson, D., Jordan, M.: Detecting large-scale system problems by mining console logs, pp. 37–46, January 2010
12. Zhang, Y., Sivasubramaniam, A.: Failure prediction in ibm bluegene/l event logs. In: ISPA, pp. 1–5 (2008)
13. Lou, J.G., Fu, Q., Yang, S., Xu, Y., Li, J.: Mining invariants from console logs for system problem detection (2010)
14. Meng, W., Liu, Y., Zhu, Y., et al.: Loganomaly: unsupervised detection of sequential and quantitative anomalies in unstructured logs. In: IJCAI, vol. 19, pp. 4739–4745 (2019)
15. Yang, L., Chen, J., Wang, Z.: Semi-supervised log-based anomaly detection via probabilistic label estimation. In: ICSE, pp. 1448–1460. IEEE (2021)

Cloud/Edge/Fog Computing and Internet-of-Things

Service Allocation/Placement in Multi-Access Edge Computing with Workload Fluctuations

Subrat Prasad Panda[✉], Kaustabha Ray, and Ansuman Banerjee

Advanced Computing and Microelectronics Unit, Indian Statistical Institute,
Kolkata, India
{kaustabha_r,ansuman}@isical.ac.in

Abstract. In this paper, we present a load variation aware adaptive stochastic method for user service request allocation and service placement in Multi-Access Edge Computing (MEC). Simulation based experimental results on the benchmark EUA dataset show that our approach can better handle workload fluctuations as compared to state of the art.

Keywords: Edge computing · Service allocation · Stochastic optimization

1 Introduction

In Multi-Access Edge Computing (MEC), a service allocation policy determines which service requests from which mobile user is provisioned by which MEC server [3], while a placement policy determines the service containers to be deployed on each MEC server [3]. MEC servers have capacity constraints and thus cannot host or execute all service containers simultaneously. Deciding which services to host at which server is difficult apriori, considering the spatial and temporal diversity of user service requests, mobility of users, latency constraints of application services and varying resource footprints for service execution. In the event that a service request cannot be allocated on any edge server, either due to absence of the required service container or lack of resources for execution, it is allocated to a cloud server with additional user perceived latencies.

This paper presents a joint optimization approach for user request allocation and container placement considering runtime load variations of service execution arising due to heterogeneous service invocations and their consequent resource demands, and edge server capacity constraints. A challenge for allocation is in deriving an estimate of the amount of resources that may need to be allocated to each container at runtime for execution. This is often difficult to learn or predict based on past usage records, due to the dynamic nature of the services, the invocation patterns and the resulting execution variations. In this paper, we propose a novel stochastic optimization model for the joint service allocation and placement problem. We use random variables to model the resource requirements of service requests, thereby effectively representing their stochastic nature

H. Hacid et al. (Eds.): ICSOC 2021, LNCS 13121, pp. 747–755, 2021.
https://doi.org/10.1007/978-3-030-91431-8_51

and solve a stochastic programming formulation to generate optimal solutions through determinization. Our formulation thus entails a more accurate estimate of resource variability and yields a better allocation any time when executed on user service requests. Our provisioning model is fully dynamic, wherein we execute the allocator whenever the existing allocation needs to be revisited. We consider an event driven dynamic approach - our algorithm is executed whenever: (a) users move in/out of coverage zones of edge servers, (b) users or edge servers become inactive, or (c) new service requests are placed. We propose a simple caching based heuristic solution on top of our basic model for real-time dynamic execution of the algorithm. The ability to model both resource and environment variations is a novelty that distinguishes our work from others.

We present experimental results on the EUA dataset, a real-world MEC benchmark. We compare our results with state-of-the-art approaches that do not consider workload fluctuations to show that our framework fares better in terms of lesser runtime overflows and more user onboarding on the edge servers.

2   Problem Formulation

Our stochastic constraint model for the user server allocation and placement problem considers the parameters memory, CPU, bandwidth as random variables. Further, we assume that even the distributions of these variables are unknown, we only have information about their expected mean and variance. We formulate stochastic constraints and present solutions that satisfy the constraints probabilistically, as is usually done in stochastic programming. We discuss our approach in detail in the following section. We have the following in our context:

- A set of edge services $S = \{s_1, s_2, \ldots, s_p\}$, a set of users $U = \{u_1, u_2, \ldots, u_n\}$.
- A set of edge servers $E = \{e_1, e_2, \ldots, e_m\}$.
- A set $R = \{r_1, r_2, \ldots, r_k\}$ of service requests from users in U for services $\in S$. Each request r_i is owned by an user $u(r_i) \in U$ for some service in S.
- For each server, we have memory capacity Q_e, CPU compute capacity C_e, uplink bandwidth capacity $B_e^\uparrow$ and downlink bandwidth capacity $B_e^\downarrow$.
- For each request $r_i \in R$, we have a set of parameters modeled as:
    - Memory: random variable s_{r_i} with mean $\mu_s^{r_i}$ and variance $(\sigma_s^{r_i})^2$
    - CPU: random variable (c_{r_i}) with mean $\mu_{r_i}^c$ and variance $(\sigma_{r_i}^c)^2$
    - Uplink bandwidth: random variable $(b_{r_i}^\uparrow)$ with mean $\mu_{r_i}^{b^\uparrow}$, variance $(\sigma_{r_i}^{b^\uparrow})^2$
    - Downlink: random variable $(b_{r_i}^\downarrow)$ with mean $\mu_{r_i}^{b^\downarrow}$, variance $(\sigma_{r_i}^{b^\downarrow})^2$

Further, as part of our stochastic formulation, we have a bound on each parameter $Q_e, C_e, B_e^\uparrow$ and $B_e^\downarrow$ to be satisfied with probability $\geq 1 - \alpha$, where α is the overflow probability. The essential idea is to place containers and onboard users on the edge servers, while satisfying capacity constraints on the server parameters probabilistically. To develop the stochastic model, we first discuss a simple integer programming model below based on the one in [6], considering all users are covered by all edge servers for simplicity. We later dispense with this requirement in a later subsection when we present our formulation.

Let E_c represent the cloud server. Let $E_u \subseteq E$ denote the set of edge servers covering user $u \in U$. An user can be under the coverage area of multiple edge servers. The set $S_e \subseteq S$ denotes the services at server $e \in E$. Each edge server can host a number of services from S having different resource requirements. Requests from user $u \in U$ under the coverage of a server $e \in E$ can be allocated provided that the service container can be hosted at the edge server with the required memory, computation and bandwidth resources available. The cloud server E_c hosts all available services. In the case that an user is not allocated to any edge server due to resource constraints, we allocate the user to E_c.

2.1   A Simple Optimization Model

We first present a standard Integer Linear Programming (ILP) formulation for allocation and placement. The ILP formulation below attempts to minimize the number of users sent to the cloud server. We use a binary $(0/1)$ decision variable v_{ij} for the ILP formulation, where $v_{ij} = 1$ denotes service request r_i is onboarded on some edge server $e_j \in E$. Let $R_e \subseteq R$ denote the set of requests allocated to edge server $e \in E$. Thus, for each request r_k in R_e, we have $v_{ke} = 1$.

Objective:

$$Maximise: \sum_{r_i \in R, e_j \in E} v_{ij} \tag{1}$$

Subject To:

$$\sum_{r_k \in R_e} c_{r_k} \le C_e \quad (2) \sum_{r_k \in R_e} s_{r_k} \le Q_e \quad (3) \sum_{r_k \in R_e} b_{r_k}^\uparrow \le B_e^\uparrow \tag{4}$$

$$\sum_{r_k \in R_e} b_{r_k}^\downarrow \le B_e^\downarrow \ (5) \ \forall e \in E, R_e \cap R_{e'} = \phi \text{ where } e, e' \in E \text{ and } e \ne e' \ (6)$$

Equation 1 is the optimization objective. Any feasible allocation needs to restrict each user to be allocated to only 1 edge server, expressed by Eq. 6. Equations 2, 3, 4 and 5 ensure that the combined requirements of the requests allocated to any edge server satisfy memory, CPU, uplink, downlink capacities.

2.2   Stochastic Optimization Model

The constraints involve random variables c_{r_k}, s_{r_k}, $b_{r_k}^\uparrow$, $b_{r_k}^\downarrow$ and cannot be directly solved by ILP solvers. To deal with the randomness of resource elements, we formulate probabilistic capacity constraints with bounding values to express the requirement that the capacity constraints at each edge server for each of the parameters have to be satisfied with a certain probability. This is in sharp contrast to allocation and placement methods that treat these as constants, and formulate optimization models to satisfy cumulative resource bounds on the same for each edge server. To this end, we define an overflow probability α between

0 and 1. Consequently, the probability $1 - \alpha$ represents the probability of the event where the allocation strategy of users to the edge server does not overflow, hence total resource utilization by the services are within the edge server resource capacity. The probabilistic version of resource constraints are as below. $\forall e \in E$, we have:

$$P\left[\sum_{r_k \in R_e} c_{r_k} \leq C_e\right] \geq 1 - \alpha \quad (7) \quad P\left[\sum_{r_k \subset R_e} s_{r_k} \leq Q_e\right] \geq 1 - \alpha, \quad (8)$$

$$P\left[\sum_{r_k \in R_e} b^\uparrow_{r_k} \leq B^\uparrow_e\right] \geq 1 - \alpha \quad (9) \quad P\left[\sum_{r_k \in R_e} b^\downarrow_{r_k} \leq B^\downarrow_e\right] \geq 1 - \alpha \quad (10)$$

Determinization: A standard approach for solving such optimization problems is to transform the probabilistic constraints into equivalent deterministic ones. By doing so, the original linear stochastic constraint may no longer remain linear after the transformation. As in [4], we transform the probabilistic constraints to their deterministic equivalents, thereby making them solvable by standard solvers. We assume that the probabilistic distribution of the resource parameters is unknown. In this case, we use the Chebyshev's inequality [1] for analysis.

Consider a random variable X with mean μ and variance $\sigma^2 (\neq 0)$ and t be a positive real number. The one-sided Chebyshev's inequality (Cantelli's inequality) can be stated as: $P[\frac{X-\mu}{\sigma} > t] \leq \frac{1}{1+t^2}$.

As discussed, the resource requirements $s_{r_i}, c_{r_i}, b^\uparrow_{r_i}$ and $b^\downarrow_{r_i}$ of any service request $r_i \in R$ requested by any user $u \in U$ follows an unknown distribution with mean $\mu^s_{r_i}, \mu^c_{r_i}, \mu^{b^\uparrow}_{r_i}, \mu^{b^\downarrow}_{r_i}$ and standard deviation $\sigma^s_{r_i}, \sigma^c_{r_i}, \sigma^{b^\uparrow}_{r_i}, \sigma^{b^\downarrow}_{r_i}$ respectively. Let $X^c_e = \sum_{r_k \in R_e} c_{r_k}$. Observe that X^c_e is a random variable, denoting the aggregate memory demand at an edge server, following an unknown distribution with mean as $\eta^c_e = \sum_{r_k \in R_e} \mu^c_{r_k}$ and variance as $(\gamma^c_e)^2 = \sum_{r_k \in R_e} (\sigma^c_{r_k})^2$.

Now, $P[X^c_e \leq C_e] \geq 1 - \alpha \implies$
$$P\left[\frac{X^c_e - \eta^c_e}{\gamma^c_e} \leq \frac{C_e - \eta^c_e}{\gamma^c_e}\right] \geq 1 - \alpha \implies P\left[\frac{X^c_e - \eta^c_e}{\gamma^c_e} > \frac{C_e - \eta^c_e}{\gamma^c_e}\right] \leq \alpha$$

Using one-sided Chebyshev's inequality with $t = \frac{C_e - \eta^c_e}{\gamma^c_e}$

$$\implies P\left[\frac{X^c_e - \eta^c_e}{\gamma^c_e} > \frac{C_e - \eta^c_e}{\gamma^c_e}\right] \leq \frac{1}{1+(\frac{C_e - \eta^c_e}{\gamma^c_e})^2} \leq \alpha \implies \eta^c_e + \gamma^c_e \sqrt{\frac{1-\alpha}{\alpha}} \leq C_e,$$

Thus, the transformed deterministic constraint formulation of Eq. 7 is:

$$\eta^c_e + \gamma^c_e \sqrt{\frac{1-\alpha}{\alpha}} \leq C_e, \; \forall e \in E, \; 0 \leq \alpha \leq 1 \tag{11}$$

Similarly, the transformations for Eq. 8, 9 and 10 $\forall e \in E, \; 0 \leq \alpha \leq 1$ are:

$$\eta^r_e + \gamma^r_e \sqrt{\frac{1-\alpha}{\alpha}} \leq Q_e \; (12) \quad \eta^{b^\uparrow}_e + \gamma^{b^\uparrow}_e \sqrt{\frac{1-\alpha}{\alpha}} \leq B^\uparrow_e \; (13) \quad \eta^{b^\downarrow}_e + \gamma^{b^\downarrow}_e \sqrt{\frac{1-\alpha}{\alpha}} \leq B^\downarrow_e \; (14)$$

Finally, using the determinized constraints obtained above, and using $K = \sqrt{\frac{1-\alpha}{\alpha}}$, the ILP formulation to maximize the number of users allocated on the edge can be formulated as discussed below. We define the following:

$$x_{ji} = \begin{cases} 1, & \text{If the service } s_i \text{ is placed at edge server } e_j \\ 0, & \text{Otherwise} \end{cases}$$

$$y_{ji} = \begin{cases} 1, & \text{If service request } r_i \in R \text{ is allocated to edge server } e_j \\ 0, & \text{Otherwise} \end{cases}$$

Objective:

$$Maximise \sum_{r_i \in R, e_j \in E} y_{ji} \tag{15}$$

Subject To:

– Integer Constraints:

$$x_{ji} \in \{0, 1\} : e_j \in E, s_i \in S \quad (16) \quad y_{ji} \in \{0, 1\} : e_j \in E \cup \{E_c\}, r_i \in R \quad (17)$$

– Coverage Constraint:

$$y_{ji} = 0, \ \forall r_i \in R, \ e_j \notin E_{u(r_i)} \tag{18}$$

$u(r_i)$ is the owner of request r_i and $E_{u(r_i)}$ is the set of servers covering $u(r_i)$.

– Service Placement Constraint:

$$y_{ji} \leq x_{ji}, \ \forall e_j \in E, \ r_i \in R \tag{19}$$

– Memory Constraint:

$$\sum_{r_i \in R_e} x_{ji} \mu_{r_i}^s + K \sqrt{\sum_{r_i \in R_e} x_{ji} (\sigma_{r_i}^s)^2} \leq Q_e, \forall e \in E \tag{20}$$

– Computation Load Constraint:

$$\sum_{r_i \in R_e} y_{ji} \mu_{r_i}^c + K \sqrt{\sum_{r_i \in R_e} y_{ji} (\sigma_{r_i}^c)^2} \leq C_e, \forall e \in E \tag{21}$$

– Bandwidth Constraint $\forall e \in E$:

$$\sum_{r_i \in R_e} y_{ji} \mu_{r_i}^{b^\uparrow} + K \sqrt{\sum_{r_i \in R_e} y_{ji} (\sigma_{r_i}^{b^\uparrow})^2} \leq B_e^\uparrow \tag{22}$$

$$\sum_{r_i \in R_e} y_{ji} \mu_{r_i}^{b^\downarrow} + K \sqrt{\sum_{r_i \in R_e} y_{ji} (\sigma_{r_i}^{b^\downarrow})^2} \leq B_e^\downarrow \tag{23}$$

– User-Server Mapping:

$$\sum_{e_j \in E_u \cup E_c} y_{ji} = 1, \forall r_i \in R \tag{24}$$

The integer program formulation aims to maximize the number of users allocated to the edge, as in Eq. 15 along with other constraints. Users should only be allocated to an edge server when within the coverage of that edge server, this is expressed in Constraint 18. A service provisioned has to be hosted on the edge server, as expressed in Constraint 19. A single user should not be allocated to more than one edge server, as in Constraint 24. The constraints in Eqs. 20, 21, 22 and 23 are deterministic ones which bound the overflow probability on each server. A solution satisfying all constraints for a given α is an allocation for a set of user requests to a given set of edge servers, such that the overflow probability on the aggregate resource demand of the requests allocated to an edge server is bounded for each of memory, compute, uplink and downlink bandwidth.

2.3   Putting Everything Together

Our allocation and placement scheme is fully dynamic, wherein we execute the above whenever an existing allocation needs to be revisited. In the initial step, we solve the above constraint model for the initial set of user service requests, edge servers and user positions. The allocation produced by the optimization solver is used to set up the binding between servers and user requests, as mandated by the constraint model. Following this, we consider an event driven dynamic approach - our algorithm is executed whenever users move in/out of coverage zones of edge servers, users or edge servers become inactive or new service requests are placed. As and when any of these events happen, the constraint model is recomputed with the changed parameters. To expedite this computation, we consider a simple heuristic approach on top of the constraint model to incorporate real time dynamic execution requirements. The heuristic stores and judiciously reuses the solutions from earlier instances. Whenever any of the above events happen, the integer programming formulation is modified to include equality constraints in the stochastic formulation for users whose parameters do not change. Thus we reuse the existing solution for those users i.e. we keep the user-server binding unchanged for such users. Consider that at time instant t_1, service requests from users u_1 and u_2 are bound to servers e_1 and e_2 respectively. Suppose at time instant t_2, user u_2 moves out of the coverage of e_2. In such a case, we re-execute the constraint model with the new coordinates for u_2, however, our heuristic excludes u_1 from the computation and forces the solution e_1 to u_1 and a new solution for u_2 only is computed. This helps to reduce the search space that the optimization solver needs to examine for generating a solution, thereby effectively reducing the time taken to obtain the solution.

3   Experiments and Results

We use the EUA [5] data-set for edge server and edge user locations. The coverage areas of edge servers are set to values less than 150 m radius. We randomly select several users and include the following randomly: (a) to simulate user movement, assign 20% users with $0m/s$ speed to represent static users, 30% users with speed between $1 - 2$ m/s, the average walking speed of humans, and the remaining 50% users with speed between $10 - 20$ m/s, the average vehicle speed in the city (b) assign an initial direction between $0°$ to $360°$ which follows the random way-point mobility model [5] and (c) remove and add users. The overflow probability α is set to 0.15. We average over 50 repeated experiments. The resources of each server and requirements of service requests are represented as [C, R, BU, BD] and resource availability of each edge server is set to [10 GHz, 20 GB, 15 Mbps, 35 Mbps]. The services requested by users are taken from the zipf distribution [6] which is mapped randomly to one of the five services shown in Table 1 listing some predetermined range of values, representative of widely used services hosted on the edge servers [6], from which the values are generated randomly. For example, if a request is mapped to the Augmented Reality service, the memory requirement value μ_s^r will be assigned randomly from the range 1 to 4. The five services used in this experiment are shown in Table 1. We compare our proposal with algorithms (ILP and ILP approximation) provided in [6]. We use Gurobi as the ILP solver [2]. Whenever an event is registered, our dynamic event-driven algorithm is executed with the updated environmental scenarios. We adapt the ILP and ILP approximation algorithms in [6] to also run in a similar manner since they can also be used in an event-driven context. The time out for all the algorithms is set to 25 s, i.e., whenever an event occurs, the maximum amount of time that each algorithm runs is set as 25 s. The results obtained within the 25 s timeout is utilized as the new allocation. In case of timeouts, we utilize the partial results generated by the ILP solver Gurobi within that time frame. We consider two scenarios for each set of experiments in conjunction with the ILP and approximation approaches: (i) utilize the maximum resource utilization and (ii) utilize the average resource utilization. The maximum value used for the ILP is computed using the maximum value observed among 1000 random samples using mean and variances as given in Table 1. Similarly, the average value is estimated by averaging over 1000 random samples from a normal distribution (to demonstrate our approach in known scenarios). All experiments are conducted on an Intel Core i5-8250U processor with 8 GB RAM.

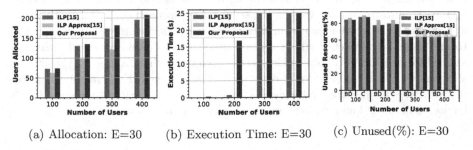

(a) Allocation: E=30   (b) Execution Time: E=30   (c) Unused(%): E=30

Fig. 1. Maximum case with E = 30

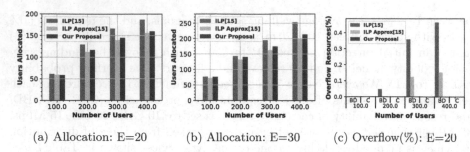

(a) Allocation: E=20   (b) Allocation: E=30   (c) Overflow(%): E=20

Fig. 2. Varying Servers (E) with Average Case

3.1   Results

Figure 1a depicts the number of users allocated with $E = 30$ for resource request sizes. The resource availability of servers is kept fixed at [10 GHz, 20 GBs, 15 Mbps, 30 Mbps] while the number of services is fixed at 5. The maximum case approach in traditional approaches being conservative allocates less number of users, however, our proposal obtains higher number of users allocated to the edge server. Figure 1c represents unused resource percentage on edge servers. Due to less number of users being allocated to edge server in other allocation policies, the unused resource percentage is higher in case of [ILP] and [ILP approx]. Similarly, Figs. 2a and 2b depict the number of users allocated when varying the number of edge servers assuming the average values for resource request sizes. Here, the number of allocations generated by our approach is lower to avoid overflow. As depicted in Fig. 2c, the overflows due to allocation generated by the stochastic approach is negligible. Whenever an overflow does indeed occur, we handle overflow scenarios by re-allocating users involved in the overflow to the cloud server, with additional access latencies. The additional latencies to the cloud is taken as $112ms$, as shown in [7] measured as the real world round-trip latency to a public cloud provider. Figure 3 illustrates the extra latencies incurred due to overflow for the set-up in Fig. 2. In certain cases, the extra latencies are almost negligible as can be seen in the figure. The access latencies vary in other scenarios, however, on an average, the stochastic approach outperforms the other approaches. The stochastic optimization approach performs well in comparison to traditional approaches which do not take into account workload variations and performs especially well in large scale scenarios where a greater variation in the number of allocated users at edge servers is observed. Even in the situations of overflow, the incurred latencies as a result of re-allocating requests to the back-end cloud is lower for our approach as compared to others.

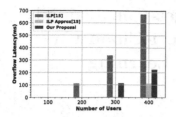

Fig. 3. Extra latencies for overflows with average case, $E = 30$

Table 1. Service parameter values used

Services	Resources							
	Computation		Memory		Uplink Bandwidth		Downlink Bandwidth	
	Mean	Std	Mean	Std	Mean	Std	Mean	Std
Video streaming	0	0	1–4	0–1.3	0	0	1–8.5	0–2.8
Face recognition	0.4–1.6	0–0.5	1–5	0–1.6	1–4	0–1.3	0	0
File compression	0.05–0.2	0–0.06	0.02	0	1–4	0–1.3	0.25–1	0
AR	0.3–1.2	0–0.4	1–10	0–3.3	1–4	0–1.3	0.25–1	0–0.3
ML Inference	0.35–1.4	0–0.6	1–10	0–3.3	0.5–2	0-0.6	0.1	0

4   Conclusion and Future Work

In this paper, we propose a joint service allocation and placement policy which takes into account the stochastic nature of service workloads. We perform extensive experiments on real-world datasets to demonstrate the effectiveness of our approach. As future work, we plan to design a stochastic approximation algorithm which builds on our present proposal.

References

1. Bertsekas, D.P., Tsitsiklis, J.N.: Introduction to probability (2000)
2. Gurobi Optimization, LLC: Gurobi Optimizer Reference Manual (2021). https://www.gurobi.com
3. Lai, P., et al.: Optimal edge user allocation in edge computing with variable sized vector bin packing. In: Pahl, C., Vukovic, M., Yin, J., Yu, Q. (eds.) ICSOC 2018. LNCS, vol. 11236, pp. 230–245. Springer, Cham (2018). https://doi.org/10.1007/978-3-030-03596-9_15
4. Nandi, B.B., Banerjee, A., Ghosh, S.C., Banerjee, N.: Stochastic vm multiplexing for datacenter consolidation. In: SCC, pp. 114–121 (2012)
5. Peng, Q., et al.: Mobility-aware and migration-enabled online edge user allocation in mobile edge computing. In: ICWS, pp. 91–98 (2019)
6. Poularakis, K., Llorca, J., Tulino, A.M., Taylor, I., Tassiulas, L.: Service placement and request routing in mec networks with storage, computation, and communication constraints. IEEE/ACM Trans. Netw. **28**(3), 1047–1060 (2020)
7. Zhang, W., Li, S., Liu, L., Jia, Z., Zhang, Y., Raychaudhuri, D.: Hetero-edge: Orchestration of real-time vision applications on heterogeneous edge clouds. In: IEEE INFOCOM, pp. 1270–1278 (2019)

Location-Aware and Budget-Constrained Service Brokering in Multi-Cloud via Deep Reinforcement Learning

Tao Shi[1]([✉]), Hui Ma[1], Gang Chen[1], and Sven Hartmann[2]

[1] School of Engineering and Computer Science, Victoria University of Wellington,
Wellington, New Zealand
{`tao.shi,hui.ma,aaron.chen`}`@ecs.vuw.ac.nz`
[2] Department of Informatics, Clausthal University of Technology,
Clausthal-Zellerfeld, Germany
`sven.hartmann@tu-clausthal.de`

Abstract. Multi-cloud makes it possible to effectively utilize various cloud services provided by multiple cloud providers at different locations. To process the requests for latency-sensitive applications, cloud brokers must select proper cloud services in multi-cloud to minimize the network latency without running into the risk of over-spending. The problem of location-aware and budget-constrained service brokering in multi-cloud demands a machine learning approach to handle the highly dynamic requests. In this paper, we apply deep reinforcement learning to solve the problem. The proposed algorithm, named DeepBroker, can dynamically and adaptively select virtual machines in multi-cloud for new arriving requests at a global scale. Specifically, DeepBroker trains brokering policies by employing a deep Q-network combined with the newly designed state extractor and action executor. To ensure financial viability, we introduce a penalty-based reward function to prevent over-budget situations. Evaluation based on real-world datasets shows that DeepBroker can significantly outperform several commonly used heuristic-based algorithms in terms of network latency minimization and budget satisfaction.

Keywords: Cloud service brokering · Multi-cloud · Location-aware · Budget-constrained · Deep reinforcement learning

1 Introduction

Gartner forecasts that the worldwide public cloud service revenue will exceed 300 billion U.S. dollars in 2021. In the booming public cloud marketplace, *multi-cloud* has become a popular cloud ecosystem, because it allows cloud users to share the cloud services across multiple cloud providers to achieve high quality of services with low operation cost and also avoid vendor lock-in [9,12]. By providing a single entry point to multiple clouds, *cloud broker* is responsible for the deployment and management of cloud services for cloud applications on behalf of the cloud users [8,11].

© Springer Nature Switzerland AG 2021
H. Hacid et al. (Eds.): ICSOC 2021, LNCS 13121, pp. 756–764, 2021.
https://doi.org/10.1007/978-3-030-91431-8_52

The network latency between cloud users and cloud services in different locations significantly affects the performance of cloud applications [3], especially for latency-sensitive applications, e.g., patient respiratory monitoring and visitor identification [5]. To satisfy cloud users' requirements on low latency, leading cloud providers have established data centers in many geographic locations. Note that the prices of cloud services in different regions can vary substantially. For example, the prices of m6g.large (Linux) from Amazon EC2[1] are $0.077 and $0.1224 per hour in Northern Virginia (USA) and Sao Paulo (Brazil) respectively. This raises the problem to select proper services from multi-cloud data centers for various user requests. In [3,7], this problem is studied to select virtual machines (VMs) to minimize the total cost and network latency between cloud users and selected VMs. Concretely, the two objectives are transformed into a single objective through weighted sum. From the perspective of cloud brokers, the problem formulation fails to satisfy the practical requirements, e.g., the stringent budgetary control to ensure financial viability [10,11]. Therefore, we study the *Location-aware and Budget-constrained Service Brokering in Multi-cloud (LBSBM)* to minimize the network latency within the total budget over a time span such as a billing day.

The *LBSBM* problem is highly challenging because the user requests are highly dynamic in terms of resource requirements and geo-distribution. Recently, Deep Reinforcement Learning (DRL) has been successfully applied to various combinatorial optimization problems with high dynamicity [2,13]. In a DRL system, an agent interacts with an environment by iteratively observing the state of the environment, choosing an action to perform, and obtaining a scalar reward. The goal of the agent is to optimize the expected cumulative reward. For this purpose, the DRL system applies a deep neural network, e.g., deep Q-network (DQN) [6], to capture the optimal action-selection policy.

There are two key advantages of using DRL to solve the *LBSBM* problem. On the one hand, the trained deep neural network, as a model of the service brokering policy, can maximize the overall reward during a long period of system operation. On the other hand, the neural network presents a computationally efficient way to select VMs for handling new arriving user requests.

However, we have two major challenges in applying DRL to the *LBSBM* problem. First, because theoretically cloud brokers can select an unlimited number of VM instances in multi-cloud, a fixed-size description of the system state is difficult to obtain. Second, to meet the budgetary constraint, DRL requires a specific mechanism to prevent the overuse of expensive VMs. The aim of this paper is to tackle these two challenges and propose a new DRL-based algorithm with novel components: a state extractor to extract information for all available *VM types* (determinate amount) and an action executor to identify specific *VM instances* for processing user requests. Moreover, we design a new penalty-based reward function to train the deep neural network so that the brokering policy can generate budget-compliant solutions.

---

[1] https://aws.amazon.com/ec2/pricing/on-demand/.

2   Problem Description

Generally, a broker can select various VMs from multiple cloud providers to satisfy any user request. A set of VM types V is offered by different cloud providers at a set of regions $\mathcal{R}$ covered by multi-cloud data centers. Each type of VM $v \in V$ provides the capacities of CPU G_v and memory M_v. Besides, for each VM type v we use $R_v \subseteq \mathcal{R}$ to denote the set of available regions offered by its cloud provider.

Let N denote the number of requests submitted to the broker during a time period T (e.g., one billing day). Each request i from user location u_i has resource requirements, e.g., CPU g_i and memory m_i, and specifies how long it will use the resource for, denoted by t_i. When request i arrives at time T_i, the broker will instantly assign it to an VM instance. The *VM instance* can be either an idle VM instance or a newly selected VM instance.

As in [3], the following assumptions are made in this paper.

- The same VM instance can be used to process one request or multiple requests sequentially. Each request can only be assigned to a single VM instance that will process the request.
- VM usage is charged on an hourly rate, and the price is determined based on its provider, type, and region.
- Once a VM instance is selected, its configuration cannot be changed during its use.

We also consider the following constraints when request i is assigned to an instance of VM type v.

$$g_i \leqslant G_v, \ m_i \leqslant M_v, \ t_i \leqslant \mathsf{T}_{v,i}, \tag{1}$$

where $\mathsf{T}_{v,i}$ is the leased VM hours of v for request i. The above constraints in Eq. (1) are important to meet the resource demands. In the remaining of this paper, we use *capacity-feasible* VM types to refer to the VM types whose capacities are at least as high as the resource demands.

To process the N requests during time span T, the total cost (TC) and average network latency (ANL) can be calculated as follows:

$$TC = \sum_{v \in V} \sum_{r \in R_v} C_{v,r} x_{v,r}, \ ANL = \frac{1}{N} \sum_{i=1}^{N} \sum_{v \in V} \sum_{r \in R_v} L_{i,r} y_{i,v,r}, \tag{2}$$

where $C_{v,r}$ is the hourly price of VM type $v \in V$ in region $r \in R_v$ and $x_{v,r}$ is the sum of leased hours of VM type v in region r. That is, $x_{v,r}$ is computed by accumulating the hours of corresponding VM instances over T, including the newly selected VM instances as well as the additional hours of selected VM instances. On the other hand, we use the decision variable, $y_{i,v,r} \in \{0, 1\}$, to decide whether request i is assigned to an instance of VM type $v \in V$ in region $r \in R_v$. $L_{i,r}$ is the network latency between user location u_i and region r.

Therefore, the *LBSBM* problem aims at minimizing *ANL*, as defined in Eq. (2), subject to the total budget:

$$TC \leq \sum_{i=1}^{N} b_i, \qquad (3)$$

where b_i is the budget for request i. We use *budget feasible* or *feasible* solutions to refer to the solutions of request assignment during time period T that satisfy the budgetary constraint. Following the recent research in [11] we define b_i in Eq. (4):

$$b_i = C_{i,min}t_i + k \cdot (C_{i,max}t_i - C_{i,min}t_i), \qquad (4)$$

where $C_{i,max}$ and $C_{i,min}$ are the hourly prices of the most expensive VM type and the cheapest capacity-feasible VM type for request i respectively. $k \in [0,1]$ is the budget factor to determine how tight the budgetary control is. The larger k is, the more budget the broker has.

3   DeepBroker: A DRL-Based Algorithm

In the *LBSBM* problem, each state transition occurs whenever a new request arrives from a user. We define the DRL system as follows.

- **State** s_i: The observed state includes the new request i and all the leased VM instances at T_i.
- **Action** a_i: To select a specific instance of capacity-feasible VM types, i.e., an idle VM instance or a newly selected VM instance, for request i.

Figure 1 shows the DQN-based brokering policy, which is composed of State Extractor, Deep Q-Network, and Action Executor. Concretely, State Extractor transforms the information regarding the new user request and currently leased VM instances to a state feature vector as the input of DQN. Afterwards,

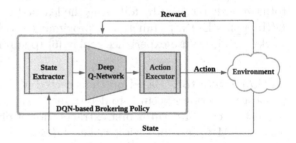

Fig. 1. Training DQN-based brokering policy.

DQN generates Q-values, which decide the VM type as the input of Action Executor. Finally, Action Executor uses the VM type to select a specific VM instance to process the request. *DeepBroker* trains the brokering policy based on request arrival history. Subsequently, the trained brokering policy is commissioned to select VM instances for each new request. In the following, we provide a detailed description for each component of the DQN-based brokering policy.

State Extractor. State Extractor first translates the user location of request i into a latency vector $l_i = [L_{i,r}]_{r \in \mathcal{R}}$ including the network latency between user location u_i and all the regions $\mathcal{R}$ covered by multi-cloud data centers. Next, State Extractor extracts information for each VM type $v \in V$ in region $r \in R_v$. Subject to the resource constraints defined in Eq. (1), State Extractor first checks the CPU and memory capacities of VM type v. If v satisfies the resource demands for request i, State Extractor then checks whether there are certain idle VM instances. If there are several idle VM instances of type v in region r, State Extractor uses the maximum remaining time of these VM instances as the state feature of VM type v in region r, i.e., $mrt_{v,r}$. The rationale behind it is two-fold. On the one hand, the cost for processing request i depends on the remaining time of the assigned idle VM instance. On the other hand, the idle VM instance with $mrt_{v,r}$ has the greatest potential on cost saving for processing request i, because the instance is most likely to process the request without leasing additional VM hours. If VM type v is not capacity-feasible or does not have the corresponding idle VM instances, State Extractor sets its state feature as 0. Finally, State Extractor returns the extracted feature vector $f_i = [l_i, g_i, m_i, t_i, [mrt_{v,r}]_{v \in V, r \in R_v}]$.

DRL for Training DQN. We define the reward function to direct DRL to minimize ANL among all user requests during time span T subject to the budgetary constraint. Suppose that request i is assigned to an instance of VM type v in region r based on action a_i, the corresponding reward is:

$$r_i = -L_{i,r} - \max(0, (C_{v,r}t_i - b_i)). \tag{5}$$

We apply Q-learning to maximise the expected cumulative reward, i.e., the total rewards received by following the learned Q-function from any given state. DRL applies DQNs as function approximators. Following many existing research works [2,13], we use experience replay [6] to stabilize Q-learning.

Action Executor. Based on the selected VM type v in region r, we further propose an Action Executor to determine the specific VM instances for assigning requests. Action Executor first extracts the set of idle instances of the capacity-feasible VM type v in region r, i.e., $idleV_{v,r}$. If $idleV_{v,r}$ is not empty, Action Executor returns the idle VM instance with the maximum remaining time. Otherwise, Action Executor returns a new VM instance of type v in region r for request i.

4   Experiments

Datasets. Based on the latest report regarding the worldwide Infrastructure-as-a-Service public cloud service market share, we have collected the real VM type descriptions and pricing schemes in April 2021 from three leading cloud providers, i.e., Amazon Web Services (AWS)[2], Microsoft Azure[3] and Alibaba Elastic Compute Service (ECS)[4]. 12 different VM types (4 from AWS, 4 from Azure, and 4 from Alibaba) have been included in the experiments. We also consider a total of 8 regions for major AWS, Azure and Alibaba data centers, i.e. Northern Virginia, Dublin, Singapore, Tokyo, Sydney, Northern California, Sao Paulo, and Mumbai. Furthermore, we adopt 36 user locations from 35 countries on 6 continents in the Sprint IP Network[5] to simulate the global user community.

We trace user requests based on the public VM request workload in the Microsoft Azure dataset [1], which contains request arrival time, lifetime, resource requirements in terms of CPU and memory, and subscription information. Because the workload within a subscription is logically related [1], we attach the identical user location to the requests from the same subscription in the dataset. Following [2], we scale down the request arrival rate by 20 for faster training convergence, while retaining the original arrival pattern of the complete workload.

To evaluate the network latency between users and assigned VM instances, we use real-world observations of network latency from Sprint IP backbone network databases (see Footnote 5).

Algorithm Implementation. We implement *DeepBroker* using PyTorch on a server with Intel Core i7-8700 CPU (3.2 GHz and 16 GB of RAM). The built DQN has two fully-connected hidden layers, each with 64 nodes. The input and hidden layers use rectified linear units (ReLUs). We apply MSE as the loss function and Adam [4] as the optimizer. Refer to [13], the initial and minimum ϵ, i.e., the probability that DRL randomly chooses an action, are set as 0.2 and 0.01, respectively. Other algorithm settings include: learning rate α is 0.001, discount factor γ is 1.0, and mini-batch size is 32.

We extract one day's workload with 365 user requests from the Azure dataset for training the DQN-based brokering policy. In training, we implement 4 budget factors, i.e., 0.2, 0.4, 0.6, and 0.8, to simulate different budgetary levels. The one-day workload is trained repeatedly for 100 episodes until the model converges.

Baselines. The greedy heuristic in [3] iteratively assigns each user request to the best possible VM instance in terms of the weighted sum of the normalized cost and network latency. Concretely, the weight for cost ω_1 and the weight for network latency ω_2 are set as different combinations ($\omega_1 + \omega_2 = 1$) to reflect the different preference of the broker. For example, for values of ω_1 close to 1, the broker prefers low-budget solutions, which may result in higher latency. To make the greedy heuristic adaptive to our budget-constrained optimization problem, we tune an appropriate combination of ω_1 and ω_2 based on the training

---

[2] https://aws.amazon.com/ec2/instance-types/.

[3] https://azure.microsoft.com/en-us/services/virtual-machines/.

[4] https://www.alibabacloud.com/product/ecs..

[5] https://www.sprint.net/tools/ip-network-performance.

workload so that ANL is minimized subject to the total budget. For convenience, we denote the baseline algorithm as *Greedy*.

The heuristic in [13] first identifies a set of eligible processors with enough resources that can process the arriving request. Then, it assigns the request to the processor with the highest post-allocation utilization. In multi-cloud environment, the VM instance with the highest post-allocation utilization can be an idle instance or a new instance. We adapt the heuristic to the *LBSBM* problem as follows. If there are idle instances with the highest post-allocation utilization, we assign the user request to the closest one (i.e., with the minimal latency). Otherwise, we select the closest instance of VM type subject to $C_{v,r}t_i \leqslant b_i$ to process request i (i.e., for budget compliance). For convenience, we denote the baseline algorithm as *Consolid*.

Evaluation Results. We evaluate the performance of *DeepBroker* and baselines using a workload of 362 requests on the following day in the Azure dataset. Each experiment is repeated independently for 30 times. The mean and standard deviation of ANL and TC achieved by the competing algorithms under different budget factors are presented in Table 1. For algorithm *Greedy*, the tuned ω_1 and ω_2 based on the training workload are also included in Table 1.

Table 1. Algorithm performance comparison for the *LBSBM* problem under different budget factors (ANL in ms., total budget and TC in USD, the best is bold).

k	Total budget	DeepBroker			Greedy based on [3]					Consolid based on [13]		
		ANL	TC	n	ANL	TC	ω_1	ω_2	n	ANL	TC	n
0.2	178.71	**26.83 ± 0.23**	164.98 ± 4.8	249	124.4 ± 0	182.21 ± 0	1.00	0.00	181	105.73 ± 0	192.39 ± 0	172
0.4	197.68	**26.93 ± 0.3**	162.18 ± 3.61	253	61.83 ± 0	191.75 ± 0	0.95	0.05	221	97.53 ± 0	196.1 ± 0	171
0.6	216.65	**26.86 ± 0.2**	171.65 ± 5.83	245	38.17 ± 0	219.09 ± 0	0.85	0.15	225	73.35 ± 0	221.56 ± 0	172
0.8	235.62	**27.01 ± 0.29**	167.82 ± 6.58	249	26.55 ± 0	237.6 ± 0	0.75	0.25	230	73.35 ± 0	221.56 ± 0	172

Table 1 indicates that only when $k = 0.4$, *Greedy* assigns user requests within the total budget. For 2 out of 4 cases ($k = 0.2$ and 0.6), *Consolid* cannot generate feasible solutions. Without the information or knowledge from the training workload, it is challenging for *Consolid* to meet the budget requirement in the complicated multi-cloud brokering environment. Based on our proposed penalty-based reward function, the brokering policy obtained by *DeepBroker* can effectively prevent the over-budget situations with the lowest TC under all budget factors.

Only considering ANL of the budget feasible solutions, *DeepBroker* achieves 56% less ANL than *Greedy* and 72% less ANL than *Consolid* when $k = 0.4$, and 63% less ANL than *Consolid* when $k = 0.8$. The observed performance differences between *DeepBroker* and the baseline algorithms are all verified through statistical test (Wilcoxon Rank-Sum test) with significance level of 0.05. This reveals the effectiveness of *DeepBroker*, as compared to the heuristic-based optimization algorithms. We also observed that *DeepBroker* has small standard deviation, confirming its stability and reliability for the *LBSBM* problem.

Analysis. We analyse the experimental results by checking the total number of leased VM instances for the test workload. Corresponding results are shown in Table 1 (n columns). With the best performance in terms of ANL, *DeepBroker* always has the biggest n among the competing algorithms. The results are intuitive because using more VM instances means more requests can be processed by the VM instances with shorter network latency. *Greedy* also shows the strong relationship between n and ANL. That is, ANL decreases with the increasing n under different k. However, using more VM instances, i.e., a bigger n, may cause VM instances to become heavily underutilized. We can see TC of *Greedy* increases tremendously with the increase of n. In comparison, *DeepBroker* performs well with respect to both ANL and TC.

It takes less than 30 min to train DQN-based brokering policies until convergence. The policies can select VM instances for arriving requests with trivial computational overhead (within 1 ms), which is highly feasible in practice.

5 Conclusions

The paper studies the *LBSBM* problem, i.e., selecting VMs for arriving user requests to minimize the average network latency of VMs subject to the total budget over a time span. We propose a DRL-based algorithm, named *Deep-Broker*, with the problem-specific state extractor, action executor, and penalty-based reward function to train the DQN-based service brokering policies. The experiments based on the real world datasets show the trained brokering policies significantly outperform several heuristic-based algorithms in terms of both average network latency and budget satisfaction.

References

1. Cortez, E., Bonde, A., Muzio, A., Russinovich, M., Fontoura, M., Bianchini, R.: Resource central: understanding and predicting workloads for improved resource management in large cloud platforms. In: Proceedings of the 26th Symposium on Operating Systems Principles, pp. 153–167 (2017)
2. Du, B., Wu, C., Huang, Z.: Learning resource allocation and pricing for cloud profit maximization. In: Proceedings of the AAAI Conference on Artificial Intelligence, vol. 33, pp. 7570–7577 (2019)
3. Heilig, L., Buyya, R., Voß, S.: Location-aware brokering for consumers in multi-cloud computing environments. J. Netw. Comput. Appl. **95**, 79–93 (2017)
4. Kingma, D.P., Ba, J.: Adam: A method for stochastic optimization. arXiv preprint arXiv:1412.6980 (2014)
5. Mahmud, R., Ramamohanarao, K., Buyya, R.: Latency-aware application module management for fog computing environments. ACM Transactions on Internet Technology (TOIT) **19**(1), 1–21 (2018)
6. Mnih, V., et al.: Human-level control through deep reinforcement learning. Nature **518**(7540), 529–533 (2015)
7. Shi, T., Ma, H., Chen, G.: A genetic-based approach to location-aware cloud service brokering in multi-cloud environment. In: 2019 IEEE International Conference on Services Computing (SCC), pp. 146–153. IEEE (2019)

8. Shi, T., Ma, H., Chen, G.: Divide and conquer: seeding strategies for multi-objective multi-cloud composite applications deployment. In: Proceedings of the 2020 Genetic and Evolutionary Computation Conference Companion, pp. 317–318 (2020)
9. Shi, T., Ma, H., Chen, G.: Seeding-based multi-objective evolutionary algorithms for multi-cloud composite applications deployment. In: 2020 IEEE International Conference on Services Computing (SCC), pp. 240–247. IEEE (2020)
10. Shi, T., Ma, H., Chen, G., Hartmann, S.: Location-aware and budget-constrained application replication and deployment in multi-cloud environment. In: 2020 IEEE International Conference on Web Services (ICWS), pp. 110–117. IEEE (2020)
11. Shi, T., Ma, H., Chen, G., Hartmann, S.: Location-aware and budget-constrained service deployment for composite applications in multi-cloud environment. IEEE Trans. Parallel Distrib. Syst. **31**(8), 1954–1969 (2020)
12. Toosi, A.N., Calheiros, R.N., Buyya, R.: Interconnected cloud computing environments: challenges, taxonomy, and survey. ACM Comput. Surv. (CSUR) **47**(1), 7 (2014)
13. Yi, D., Zhou, X., Wen, Y., Tan, R.: Efficient compute-intensive job allocation in data centers via deep reinforcement learning. IEEE Trans. Parallel Distrib. Syst. **31**(6), 1474–1485 (2020)

Edge Node Placement with Minimum Costs: When User Tolerance on Service Delay Matters

Xiaoyu Zhang, Shixun Huang, Hai Dong$^{(\boxtimes)}$, and Zhifeng Bao

School of Computing Technologies, RMIT University, Melbourne, Australia
xiaoyu.zhang5@student.rmit.edu.au,
{shixun.huang,hai.dong,zhifeng.bao}@rmit.edu.au

Abstract. Edge node placement optimization has been an emerging research area that has drawn extraordinary attention from the disciplines of distributed and services computing. Existing studies, nevertheless, barely focus on overall deployment cost minimization with edge node site selection and server amount optimization, while bearing users' delay tolerance. In this paper, we focus on investigating feasible user delay tolerance-aware edge node site selection and server placement optimization strategies adaptive for real-world large-scale use cases, with the objective of deployment cost minimization. A *Coverage First Search* method is proposed to address this problem in polynomial time. The experiments conducted on a real-world dataset demonstrate the effectiveness of our method.

1 Introduction

Mobile Edge Computing (MEC) is a network architecture accompanying 5G. MEC deploys plenty of small-scale servers (known as edge servers or edge nodes) to network edges in a distributed manner. Users stay closer to those edge nodes in a MEC network, which not only can significantly reduce network latency but also can provide substantial computing resources to mobile users [5].

Problem. In this paper, we study the problem of optimal edge node deployment, aiming to provide qualified and low-latency services to massive mobile users city-wide with minimum cost. There are many factors that should be considered during the edge node deployment. First, the network QoS (Quality of Service) guarantee is the baseline of the deployment. For example, delay, as one of the most important QoS factors, should not exceed users' tolerance [4]. Second, minimizing the deployment cost is always welcome and should never be neglected [1,6]. Third, the resource is finite, but the design of MEC is expected to provide users ample resources, with which goal the MEC should be optimized for higher productivity. [3,7,8]. Thus, the selected edge nodes with "just enough" computation resources allocated is always the ideal case.

Motivation. There is always a trade-off between the edge node deployment cost and the delay experienced by mobile users [5]. That trade-off is highly related

© Springer Nature Switzerland AG 2021
H. Hacid et al. (Eds.): ICSOC 2021, LNCS 13121, pp. 765–772, 2021.
https://doi.org/10.1007/978-3-030-91431-8_53

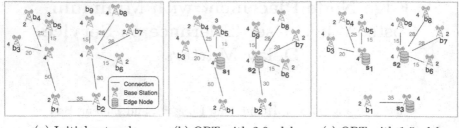

(a) Initial network   (b) OPT with 3.0s delay   (c) OPT with 1.5s delay

Fig. 1. Example of optimal EN deployment under different delay tolerance

to edge node site selection and the corresponding resource allocation. Deploying more edge nodes can potentially reduce the transmission delay by decreasing the average distance between base stations and edge nodes. Also, adding more servers (i.e. computing resources) into edge nodes can cut down the computation delay as edge nodes would have higher computation capacity. However, both cases will inflate the overall deployment cost. Therefore, with users' delay tolerance, it is necessary to find the most cost-efficient edge node deployment strategy such that the overall deployment cost is minimized, as shown in the following example.

Example 1. Figure 1 demonstrates how users' delay tolerance affects the optimal edge node deployment when considering cost-efficiency. Figure 1a shows the initial connections between base stations. Edge nodes will be deployed that co-locate with base stations. Developing an edge node within a base station will introduce a setup cost, while adding servers to an edge node to increase its computing capacity will generate server purchase costs. Given users' delay tolerance threshold and the goal of cost minimization, placing just the right amount of edge nodes accompanying workload-matched server numbers is the ideal case.

With the objective of minimizing the total cost, the optimal edge node deployment strategy will vary under different users' delay tolerance. Figure 1b illustrates the optimal edge node placement in case the users' delay tolerance threshold is 3.0 s, where the most cost-efficient deployment is to develop two edge nodes S_1 and S_2. Adding one more edge node is more expensive than adding more servers to existing nodes. However, when we decrease the delay tolerance threshold to 1.5s, the optimal placement becomes what is shown in Fig. 1c. To satisfy this more rigorous delay tolerance requirement, there are two intuitive options: continuously adding more servers to existing edge nodes to further decline the computation delay, or developing a new edge node to decrease the transmission delay. Figure 1c shows that the optimal solution is to develop a new edge node instead of adding more servers.

To the best of our knowledge, few researchers attempted to address the trade-off between cost and delay while considering the computation resource allocation [2,6]. Existing studies are subject to the following major limitations. First, the *scalability* and *practicability* of existing solutions have not been fully explored for large-scale datasets. in reality, the number of deployed base stations is significant and keeps increasing (e.g., Shanghai in China is projected to have 50 5G base stations per square km[1]). Designing a highly scalable and efficient solution is therefore essential. Second, the issue of delay has not been well addressed. The existing studies ignore the fact that the computation delay is supposed to decrease with more servers placed in edge nodes.

Main Contributions. In this paper, we aim to address the trade-off between the cost and delay by formulating our edge node deployment problem with the objective of minimizing the deployment cost while considering users' delay tolerance. Our deployment plan will not only explore optimal edge node sites but also provide the optimal resource allocation according to the real workload in edge nodes. Our major contributions include:

– We formulate a problem to address the trade-off between the deployment cost, and the transmission and computation delay. We propose a peak-based workload measurement for the robustness of our deployment. Moreover, we define a delay measurement to make it fit in real-world cases (Sect. 2)
– We propose a Coverage First Search (CFS) algorithm to solve the defined problem in polynomial time (Sect. 3).
– We conduct extensive experiments to demonstrate the effectiveness of our method (Sect. 4).

2   Problem Formulation

In this section, we firstly define the MEC network and its components. Then, we define the workload and delay measurement. Finally, we formulate our problem with the goal of minimizing the deployment cost with delay tolerance satisfied.

Preliminaries. Here, we introduce some key concepts to facilitate our illustration across the paper.

MEC Network. The MEC network consists of a set B of base stations (BSs) and a set S of edge nodes (ENs). Elements in both B and S are denoted by a tuple (id, lat, lng, n) where lat, lng and n represent latitude, longitude and number of servers added respectively. Following a widely adopted setting [3,7,8]: ENs are co-located with BSs, we upgrade a BS to an EN by adding servers to it. Multiple servers are allowed to an EN to provide enough computation capacity. Then, we have: (1) $\forall\, b \in B,\ b.n = 0$; (2) $\forall\, s \in S,\ s.n \geq 1$;

EN Setup Cost and Server Cost. We define two kinds of costs: *EN setup cost* and *server cost*. Let p_r denote the setup cost, which is the cost of upgrading a BS to an EN, such as infrastructure renting fee and construction fee. Let p_s denote the server cost, which is the cost for purchasing new servers to ENs. To be more specific, installing a server to a base station will cost $p_r + p_s$, while adding a server to edge node will simply cost p_s.

---

[1] https://techblog.comsoc.org/2020/08/07/5g-base-station-deployments-open-ran-competition-huge-5g-bs-power-problem/.

Connectivity and EN Service Range. We define two BSs b_1 and b_2 are connected if they meet a certain delay threshold which is constrained by transmission delay and computation delay together. We will elaborate these two delays later in this section. Then, the service range of an EN $s \in S$ denoted as $R(s)$ is represented by a set of BSs, that are directly connected with s.

BS Assignment. Give that ENs may have their service range overlapped, we assign base stations to edge nodes based on the following criteria: (1) a BS can be assigned to one EN only; (2) the selected ENs cover all BSs in the network. We assign EN with enough computation capacity to process all incoming tasks from the assigned BSs and will not further offload the task to other ENs. We represent the assignment with a set of key-value pairs $\mathcal{A}$, where the key is the EN, followed by a set of assigned BS as value, e.g. $\mathcal{A}[s_1] = \{b_1, b_2, b_{19}, ...\}$.

Workload Measurement. Most of existing studies measures the workload of a BS or an EN by task's average requesting [7]. However, in real cases, the workload usually fluctuates dramatically during a day [5], so the peak workload is non-negligible in some cases considering the robustness of the network, especially during the rush hour.

We propose a peak metric to measure the workload. We assume that the tasks transmitted in the network are all data-intensive computing tasks, e.g. HD videos, to guarantee that the MEC network is capable of dealing with overwhelming workload. We define the task size of a single task as ξ in bits. Then the peak workload will appear at the time period that has the largest number of coming tasks. We assume the task can be processed as soon as it arrives. We define tasks that have their processing time overlap as concurrent tasks. Let CT denote the number of concurrent tasks and CT_{max} denote the largest number of concurrent tasks that have occurred.

Thus, with the peak metric, we define the workload of a BS b as:

$$W(b) = \xi \cdot CT_{max} \tag{1}$$

Delay Measurement. Since we assume task offloading between ENs is not allowed, there are two major delays: transmission delay for a task to transmit between a BS and an EN and the computation delay for a task to be computed in an EN [5], which are related to the channel's transmission capacity and EN's computation capacity respectively.

Transmission Capacity. We adopt Shannon's channel capacity formula[2] to compute a channel's transmission capacity (denoted as C_{trans}):

$$C_{trans} = \mathcal{B} \log_2 \left(1 + \frac{SP}{N}\right) \tag{2}$$

In this equation, $\mathcal{B}$ represents the channel's bandwidth, SP represents the average received signal power over the channel and N represents the average noise power over the channel. We assume that the signal power is identical to

---

[2] Shannon theorem: http://www.inf.fu-berlin.de/lehre/WS01/19548-U/shannon.html.

all channels. Considering channel noise can be affected by many factors, such as distance, environments and quality of cable[3], we use a very common way in the literature by assuming that the channel noise is only affected by the distance [3,7]. We define the noise as $N = \alpha \cdot d(s, b)$, where $d(s, b)$ denotes the distance between s and b, and α is a coefficient between N and the distance.

Computation Capacity. Adding servers to EN gives it computation capacity. We assume that servers placed to EN have the same computation capacity μ bit/s. Then, for an EN s with $s.n$ servers placed, the computation capacity is:

$$C_{comp} = s.n \cdot \mu \tag{3}$$

Delay. The delay calculation depends on the data size and processing capacity[4]. Since the delay incurred between a BS b and an EN s includes transmission delay and computation delay, we define our delay model as

$$D(b, s) = \frac{W(b)}{C_{trans}} + \frac{W(s)}{C_{comp}} \tag{4}$$

Definition 1 *Qualified EN Placement Plan.* *Given a set of BSs B and a delay threshold θ, select a subset $S \subseteq B$ as ENs such that the following constraints hold: (1) $\forall s \in S$ $b \in \mathcal{A}[s]$, $D(s, b) \leq \theta$; (2) $\bigcup_{s \in S} \mathcal{A}[s] = B \backslash S$; (3) $\forall s_i, s_j \in S, s_i \neq s_j, \mathcal{A}[s_i] \cap \mathcal{A}[s_j] = \emptyset$.*

Intuitively, these constraints indicate that the total delay experienced by the user does not exceed θ, S should serve all $b \in B \backslash S$, and each BS will be assigned to one and only one EN for task offloading, respectively.

Definition 2 *Cost Minimization in MEC Edge Node Placement (CMMENP).* *The CMMENP problem is to find a solution S^* which can minimise the total cost*

$$F(S^*) = \arg \min_{S \subseteq B} \sum_{s \in S} (p_r + s.n \cdot p_s) \tag{5}$$

where $F(S^*)$ denotes the total cost incurred by selecting S^* as ENs, S is a qualified EN placement plan, p_r is the setup cost, and p_s is the server cost.

3   Methodologies

In this section, we will introduce a greedy-based solution: Coverage First Search (CFS), which is an efficient algorithm that aims to provide a solution in polynomial time.

---

[3] Noise: https://documentation.meraki.com/MR/WiFi_Basics_and_Best_Practices.
[4] https://manuals.gfi.com/en/exinda/help/content/exos/how-stuff-works/network-performance-metrics.htm.

Algorithm 1: CFS Algorithm

Input : Base Station set B, Delay threshold θ
Output: Edge Node set S

1 $S= \emptyset$, $\mathcal{A} \leftarrow \emptyset$;   // $\mathcal{A}$: a set of $\langle s : \{b_1, b_2, ...\} \rangle$ for BS assignment
2 **while** $B \neq \emptyset$ **do**
3      $B \leftarrow$ getConnection(B, θ)
4      $b_s \leftarrow \arg\max\{|R(b)| \mid b \in B\}$; $\mathcal{A}[b_s] \leftarrow R(b_s)$
5      $S \leftarrow S \cap b_s$;
6      $B \leftarrow B \setminus b_s$
7   **foreach** $b \in \mathcal{A}[b_s]$ **do**
8          $B \leftarrow B \setminus b$
9 **return** S

In order to improve the computation efficiency, considering the objective of cost minimization, we devise an approximate algorithm, Coverage First Search (CFS). The core idea of CFS is to minimize the number of ENs being deployed, as the construction cost of edge nodes (e.g., EN setup cost) is usually much greater than the cost of a standard server (e.g., server cost) [6]. As shown in Algorithm 1, we will first model the connections between BSs according to the delay threshold θ (line 3). Then, we iteratively pick the BS which has the highest number of connections as the site to construct an EN, and assign it with all its connected BSs in its service range R (line 4). Finally, we remove the EN and its assigned BSs from the input BS set (lines 6–8). We repeat this process until all the BSs in the input set being assigned.

4   Evaluation

We conduct extensive experiments on CFS and random method to evaluate their effectiveness with a real-world large-scale dataset.

4.1   Experiment Settings

Dataset. Our experiments are conducted on the Shanghai Telecom Dataset[5].

Experiment Environment. All experiments are conducted on MacOS (2.5 GHz Daul-Core Intel i7 processor and 16 GB memory). Our methods are implemented in Java.

Parameter Settings. Following [6], we also set the ratio of edge node construction cost and a standard server cost as 4:1 and we set the computing capacity of a standard server as $\mu = 100$ bps. The bandwidth $\mathcal{B}$ is set to 200 Mbps[6]. The Channel signal power SP is set to -35 dBm[7]. The single task size ξ is configured

---

[5] ShanghaiTelecomDataset: http://sguangwang.com/TelecomDataset.html.

[6] https://go.frontier.com/business/internet/200-mbps.

[7] https://www.metageek.com/training/resources/wifi-signal-strength-basics.html.

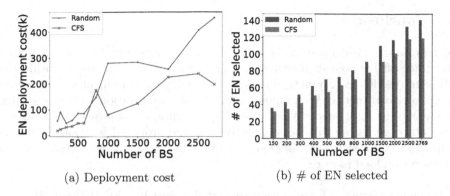

(a) Deployment cost

(b) # of EN selected

Fig. 2. Effectiveness with different BS input scale

to 15 bits[8]. Furthermore, all our experiments are conducted with a default delay threshold $\theta = 14$ s based on the empirical studies depicted in Sect. 4.2.

Evaluation Metrics. The effectiveness metrics include the deployment cost and the number of selected ENs. We measure the effectiveness of CFS and Random on different numbers of BSs.

Methods for Comparison. We compare the performance of the following two methods: a Random method that randomly picks BSs and our proposed CFS method.

4.2 Experimental Results

The deployment cost and the number of selected ENs of the aforementioned candidate solutions on different BS input scales are shown in Fig. 2a and 2b.

As shown in Fig. 2a, compared with Random, CFS shows outstanding cost-saving performance especially when the number of participated BSs is high. The cost growth of CFS is relatively smoother than Random method with the increasing number of BSs, which indicates its higher reliability.

We can observe from Fig. 2b that the numbers of ENs selected by CFS is clearly smaller than that is selected by Random. It shows a steady increasing trend for both random and CFS in terms of the number of EN selected, while we can see obvious fluctuations in terms of the deployment cost in Fig. 2a. Such phenomenon reflects the major limitation of CFS that it is incapable of finding all potentially suitable EN locations and optimizing the assignment between BSs and ENs, which causes the following problem: (1) its selected ENs may not be in the optimal locations. (2) the ENs would require high computation capacity to serve distant BSs. It explains the abnormal cost fluctuations experienced by CFS (e.g. when the number of BSs is 800 in Fig. 2a). Similarly, the Random selection also experiences such issue, as we can see obvious fluctuations for random either.

---

[8] https://www.amaysim.com.au/blog/stuff-made-simple/internet-data-usage-guide.

5   Conclusion

In this paper, we defined an MEC Edge Node Placement Problem to address the trade-off between deployment cost and users' delay tolerance. Within this problem, we defined a practical and delicate delay measurement and propose a peak workload metric. We proposed an approximate solution CFS whose effectiveness is demonstrated via our extensive experiments on a real-world dataset. For future works, we will focus on optimizing the proposed solutions to further improve their effectiveness and exploring their performance with respect to the average workload metric.

Acknowledgments. This research is supported in part by ARC DP200102611.

References

1. Chen, L., Wu, J., Zhou, G., Ma, L.: Quick: Qos-guaranteed efficient cloudlet placement in wireless metropolitan area networks. J. Supercomput. **74**(8), 4037–4059 (2018)
2. Fan, Q., Ansari, N.: Cost aware cloudlet placement for big data processing at the edge. In: ICC, pp. 1–6. IEEE (2017)
3. Guo, Y., Wang, S., Zhou, A., Xu, J., Yuan, J., Hsu, C.: User allocation-aware edge cloud placement in mobile edge computing. Softw. Pract. Exp. **50**(5), 489–502 (2020)
4. Ma, L., Wu, J., Chen, L., Liu, Z.: Fast algorithms for capacitated cloudlet placements. In: CSCWD, pp. 439–444. IEEE (2017)
5. Mao, Y., You, C., Zhang, J., Huang, K., Letaief, K.B.: A survey on mobile edge computing: the communication perspective. IEEE Commun. Surv. Tutorials **19**(4), 2322–2358 (2017)
6. Mondal, S., Das, G., Wong, E.: Ccompassion: a hybrid cloudlet placement framework over passive optical access networks. In: INFOCOM, pp. 216–224. IEEE (2018)
7. Wang, S., Zhao, Y., Xu, J., Yuan, J., Hsu, C.: Edge server placement in mobile edge computing. J. Parallel Distrib. Comput. **127**, 160–168 (2019)
8. Xu, X., et al.: Load-aware edge server placement for mobile edge computing in 5G networks. In: Yangui, S., Bouassida Rodriguez, I., Drira, K., Tari, Z. (eds.) ICSOC 2019. LNCS, vol. 11895, pp. 494–507. Springer, Cham (2019). https://doi.org/10.1007/978-3-030-33702-5_38

Prediction-Awareness Edge User Allocating in Edge Based Intelligent Video Systems Driven by Priority

Liqiang Xu, Gaofeng Zhang, Ensheng Liu, Benzhu Xu, and Liping Zheng[⊠]

School of Computer Science and Information Engineering,
Hefei University of Technology, Hefei, China
zhenglp@hfut.edu.cn

Abstract. Recently, to mitigate tremendous damage caused by various accidents, edge-cutting technologies are utilised to protect lives and properties continuously. Specifically, edge based intelligent video systems have been proved to be an effective tool to monitor and regulate these public security accidents. In these systems, Edge User Allocation (*EUA*) problem focuses on allocating edge resources to various calculating tasks efficiently, which attracts much attention with multiple approaches proposed. However, in these existing approaches, the priorities of tasks and the varieties of these priorities are not fully considered. Furtherly, these tasks' priorities are not immutable, which depends on these previous moving persons in the evacuation process. In this regard, we take these concerns into consideration and formulate a Priority-Awareness Edge User Allocation (*PA-EUA*) problem. Then, we propose our novel prediction-based approaches called *UGP* and *CCGP*. Lastly, three series of extensive experiments are conducted on a widely-used real-world data to evaluate our approaches against four representative approaches, and the results show that our novel approaches dominate the performances.

Keywords: Edge computing · Edge user allocation · Prediction · Priority · RVO

1 Introduction

Recently, the increasing of public accidents occurring lead to massive property losses and casualties. Thus, many edge-cutting technologies are combined with traditional technologies. Specifically, as a traditional technology, video surveillance systems play a vital role in the security area. Therefore, intelligent video systems [7] based on edge computing are widely discussed. Due to the distributed feature of edge computing, data analysis tasks can be processed by multiple edge servers. And to tackle this allocation issue, the Edge User Allocation (*EUA*) problem [4] has recently received great attention.

However, existing *EUA* does not fully consider the priorities of tasks and the varieties of these priorities. Varieties of priorities make different allocation results of tasks at different time spots. To satisfy high-priorities tasks as much

© Springer Nature Switzerland AG 2021
H. Hacid et al. (Eds.): ICSOC 2021, LNCS 13121, pp. 773–780, 2021.
https://doi.org/10.1007/978-3-030-91431-8_54

as possible, tasks of lower priorities should transmit resources for tasks of higher priorities. When transmitting tasks, it may causes high transmission costs. In this regard, the Return Value Optimization (RVO) [1] algorithm is an effective approach and RVO is suitable for our problem, as it can simulate the movement of crowds in an urban area with avoiding collision.

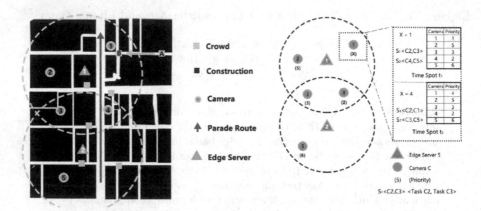

(a) First case: crowds in a parade   (b) Second case: changes of resource

Fig. 1. A motivating example (Color figure online)

A motivating example in considering the priorities of tasks and the varieties includes two cases for tasks allocation. In Fig. 1(a), the first case shows the parade in an urban area (Melbourne CBD area in Australia). Parade follows route (red arrow), and several individuals (blue square) gather to join parade. Specifically, there are five cameras (orange circle) C (the set of cameras c_i) within the range of two edge servers (blue triangle) S (the set of edge servers s_j) respectively. Assuming there are individuals moving from A to B at time spot t_1 and t_2 respectively. When the individuals at position A, task of camera c_1 with a low priority and can not be allocated. As the individuals moving to B at time spot t_2, c_1 has a higher priority than before. Then, task c_1 should be allocated on s_1.

In Fig. 1(b), the changes of resource is shown to demonstrate the allocation details. Tasks c_{i1} and c_{i2} are allocated on s_j, which is described as $s_j < c_{i1}, c_{i2} >$. At time spot t_1, priorities of tasks c_1, c_2, c_3, c_4 and c_5 are 1, 5, 3, 2 and 6. Tasks c_2 and c_3 are allocated in s_1, and c_4 and c_5 are allocated in s_2. At time spot t_2, and the priority of c_1 is increased from 1 to 4. According to the new priorities, we reallocate the c_3's resource to c_1 and c_4's resource to c_3. Finally, c_2 and c_1 are allocated in s_1, and c_3 and c_5 are allocated in s_2.

In this paper, we make the following major contributions: 1) we formulate the PA-EUA problem and prove its NP-hardness; 2) we creatively propose two novel approaches based on prediction to protect crowds. One approach is Unrestricted Greedy Prediction (UGP), which is proposed for the situation without involving transmission costs. Another approach is Cost Controlled Greedy Prediction

($CCGP$), which is proposed for the situation involving transmission costs; 3) we evaluate our approaches and the approaches' performance is superior to representative approaches on a widely-used real-world dataset.

In the following of this paper, Sect. 2 reviews the related work. The PA-EUA problem is formulated in Sect. 3. And the proposed approaches UGP and $CCGP$ are discussed in detail. Finally, we evaluate our approaches in Sects. 4 and 5 concludes this paper.

2   Related Work

Existing works in Edge Computing, Dynamic Allocation, Priority Based and Prediction Approaches are valuable supports for our paper, respectively.

Currently, resource allocating in edge computing has been an important problem due to the general insufficiency of hardware resources. To solve this problem, Xu et al. [8] use a utility-aware resource allocation model to allocate resources. In comparison, edge computing is our background, and ours focuses on task allocation driven by priority.

Considering the dynamic systems, static approaches may not fully applicable. Specifically, Chen et al. [2] discuss the time-varying resource management problem in industrial IoT executed in MEC server. To mitigate the accuracy loss in the IoT applications, those works about dynamic environments inspire us by the variety motivation.

It is effective to integrate the priorities of tasks when performing multi-task allocation. Madej et al. [6] discuss priority-based fair scheduling in edge computing systems, which is valuable support for our paper. Meanwhile, prediction is an effective approach in terms of varieties. As an effective prediction approach, simulation based prediction approaches are also widely used [10] in some scenarios without massive training costs. Therefore, simulation based prediction approaches that driven by priority are considered in this paper.

Considering the related researches, prediction-awareness allocation approaches UGP and $CCGP$ are proposed in a simulation environment to deal with PA-EUA problem.

3   Problem Formulation and Our Approaches

3.1   Problem Definition

In the PA-EUA problem, the priority p_{it} (priorities of camera i's task at time spot t) of each camera's task is decided by the number of individuals in the camera's shooting range. And we use A_t (the set of allocation marks of which tasks occupy resources at time spot t) to mark tasks' allocation situations as shown in Eq. (1). Then we obtain the sum of allocated tasks' priorities at one specific time spot.

Therefore, PA-EUA is formulated as shown in Eq. (2). Its primary goal is to ensure the average of these sums in every time spot of the whole process, which we called Priority Satisfiability (PS). Besides, the secondary objective also needs to be satisfied as needed, which is to minimize the Total Transmission Cost (TTC).

$$\begin{cases} a_{it} = 1, & c_i \quad is \quad allocated \\ a_{it} = 0, & c_i \quad is \quad not \quad allocated \end{cases}$$
$$s.t. \forall c_i \in C, i = 1, 2, ..., n, t = 0, 1, ..., L \tag{1}$$

$$\begin{cases} Max \quad PS(A, P) = \frac{1}{L} \sum_{t=0}^{L} \sum_{i=1}^{n} (a_{it} \times p_{it}) \\ s.t. \forall a_{it} \in A_i, \forall p_{it} \in P_t, i = 1, 2, ..., n, t = 0, 1, ..., L \\ Min \quad TTC(T) = \sum_{t=0}^{L} tran_t, s.t.t = 0, 1, ..., L \end{cases} \tag{2}$$

3.2   Problem Hardness

Theorem 1. *The PA-EUA problem is NP.*

Proof. It is assumed that n video tasks are assigned to m edge servers. Each task can be assigned to at most one edge server. All tasks assigned to an edge server must not require more computing resources than the total computing resources available on the edge server. We can verify all individuals in polynomial time $O(mn)$. Therefore, the PA-EUA problem is NP.

Theorem 2. *The PA-EUA problem is NP-hard.*

Proof. Firstly, the allocation problem at every time spot in the PA-EUA problem is a special case of the EUA problem. Specifically, all tasks need to be check once at every moment, and high-priority tasks need to be prioritized. If the n tasks at a time have the same priority, the PA-EUA problem is equivalent to the EUA problem. As proved by [3], the EUA problem is extended from the BP problem. Since BP problem is a NP-hard problem [4], the EUA problem and the PA-EUA problem also is a NP-hard problem.

3.3   UGP

$$\begin{cases} u_{kt} = 1, u_{kt} \in cov(c_i) \\ u_{kt} = 0, u_{kt} \notin cov(c_i) \end{cases}, p_{it} = \sum_{k=1}^{r} u_{kt} \tag{3}$$
$$s.t. \forall c_i \in C, i = 1, 2, ..., n, t = 0, 1, ..., L$$

$$P_{ave} = (\frac{1}{l} \sum_{t=t-l}^{t} p_{1t}, \frac{1}{l} \sum_{t=t-l}^{t} p_{2t}, ..., \frac{1}{l} \sum_{td=t-l}^{t} p_{nt}) \tag{4}$$
$$s.t.t = t - l, t - l + 1, ..., t$$

As introduced before, UGP focuses on the situation without considering transmission cost and consists of two phases. At each time spot, RVO is used to

---

Algorithm 1: *UGP*

Input: edge servers S, individuals U, cameras' tasks C, prediction period l

Output: PS, TTC, and AM

1 **Phase 1:** Prediction based planing
2 **for** *each time spot $t = 0, 1, ..., L$* **do**
3 $\quad$ Obtain P_t by equation (3)
4 $\quad$ **if** $t == 0$ *or $t \mod l == 0$* **then**
5 $\quad\quad$ Obtain P_{ave} by equation (4) and sort all tasks descendingly according to P_{ave}
6 $\quad\quad$ Greedy allocate sorted tasks to obtain the wth tasks allocation result AM_t at time t, and record it into AM

7 **Phase 2:** Allocating Action
8 **for** *each time spot $t = 0, 1, ..., L$* **do**
9 $\quad$ **if** $t == 0$ *or $(t \mod l) == 0$* **then**
10 $\quad\quad$ Reallocate all tasks according to the wth allocation result in AM_t

11 $\quad$ Obtain P_t by equation (3), and sort all tasks descendingly according to P_t
12 $\quad$ **for** *each task c_i in order of P_t* **do**
13 $\quad\quad$ **if** *LT is allocated on edge servers that cover c_i and $p_{LTt} < p_{it}$* **then**
14 $\quad\quad\quad$ Free LT's resource to allocate c_i

15 $\quad$ *PS increase by all allocated tasks' priorities at this time spot, and TTC is increased by time consuming $tran_t$*

---

update each individual's position. Then, by using positions, we can get priorities P_t for tasks and p_{it} is generated by Eq. (3) (Line 3). When each time passing l, the average priority P_{ave} of each task is calculated by Eq. (4), and P_{ave} is sorted descendingly (Line 5). At the final of each loop, we allocate tasks greedily in the descending order of P_{ave} to obtain allocation result the Allocation Matrix (AM_t), and we record AM_t at the wth entry of AM (Line 6), where w is $\lceil L/l \rceil$. Finally, AM records allocation results of w time spots, which is the basis of next phase. Then, individuals' positions are updated by RVO to generate priorities for tasks. After sorting tasks by P_t (Line 11), we check each task's resource suffering its priority. When checking a task c_i, if all edge servers that cover c_i with resources are occupied by other tasks, and the priority of the Lowest priority Task (LT) in those tasks is lower than c_i's (Line 13). Then, LT's resource is freed and reallocated to c_i to increase PS (Line 14). Besides, at each time spot, the PS increase by all tasks' priorities that occupy resources. And in this step, TTC is increased by consuming time $tran_t$ (Line 15). Finally, PS, TTC and AM are output as results.

3.4   CCGP

As introduced before, $CCGP$ focuses on the situation with considering transmission cost and also has two phases. Based on UGP, we add servers' relationship G (the set to mark each task can be allocated on which edge server) to reduce

TTC. In prediction based planning phase, a new step is added before line 2. In this step, firstly, all s_j cover c_i are recorded into SC_i (the set of edge servers cover task c_i). Then $mark_j$ is increased every time s_j is recorded. Finally, the minimum $mark_j$ is got in SC_i by Eq. (5), and s_j is recorded into CS_i (the set of task c_i can be allocated on which edge server). CS_i make up the tasks and servers' relationship G.

$$\begin{cases} SC_i = SC_i \cup mark_j, s.t.c_i \in cov(s_j), \forall c_i \in C, \forall s_j \in S \\ mark_j = mark_j + 1, s.t.s_j \in CS_i, \forall mark_j \in SC_i \\ CS_i = CS_i \cup s_i, s.t.minimum\{mark_j \in SC_i\} \end{cases} \tag{5}$$

Consequently, in *CCGP*, tasks can only be allocated to corresponding edge servers base on G, while *UGP* does not restrict this (Line 6). And when checking a task c_i in allocation action phase, in *CCGP*, only edge servers recorded in CS_i can allocate c_i, while in *UGP* all edge servers that cover c_i can allocate it (Line 13 to 14). Furthermore, the complexities of *UGP* and *CCGP* are shown as follow:

Theorem 3 *(Complexity). The computing complexity of UGP is $O(n(2L + \frac{L}{l}))$ and CCGP's complexity is $O(n(1 + 2L + \frac{L}{l}))$.*

Proof. For UGP, in the whole time period L, each of the n tasks' priorities P_t is calculated once at each time spot. And when time increase by l, the average priority P_{ave} of each task is calculated once. Then, each task Thus, the complexity of prediction in UGP is $O(n \times L + n \times \frac{L}{l})$. For allocation action phase, in the whole time period L, each of the n tasks' priority is calculated once at each time spot. The complexity of allocation phase is $O(n \times L)$. For CCGP, at the first of CCGP, we added a step traverse and assign C equally to S. So the complexity of prediction in CCGP is $O(n + n \times L + n \times \frac{L}{l})$. For allocation action phase, similar as UGP the complexity of allocation phase is $O(n \times L)$.

Hence, the complexity of UGP is $O(n \times L + n \times \frac{L}{l} + n \times L) = O(n(2L + \frac{L}{l}))$ and the complexity of CCGP is $O(n + n \times L + n \times \frac{L}{l} + n \times L) = O(n(1 + 2L + \frac{L}{l}))$.

4   Experimental Evaluation

4.1   Comparison Approaches and Experiment Settings

Four representative approaches are shown as follow. *RANDOM*: The idle resources of each edge server are randomly assigned to the video tasks within the coverage of the edge server. *GREEDY*: At first, tasks' priorities are sorted descendingly. Then allocate tasks on edge servers according to priorities. *MCF* [5]: It is a heuristic approach for the *EUA* problem, which can find a sub-optimal solution. *TSPP* [9]: This time-series pattern prediction approach is based on *K-MaxSDev* and Time-Series Pattern Generation Algorithm (*TSPG*).

Our experiments are based on the *EUA* Dataset [4], including 125 base stations and 816 individuals within the Melbourne *CBD* area in Australia. And three parameters are changed in experiments respectively. (1) Number of Individuals (*NoI*): To reflect the ability of protect crowds in different approaches under the pressure of *NoI*, we select individuals from 816 real position data. (2) Number of Edge Resources (*NoER*): To reflect the performance under the different extent of resource insufficient, *NoER* is used to determine the number of tasks that edge servers can load. (3) Single Transmission Cost (*STC*): In *PA-EUA*, a goal is to reduce the *TTC*. Since in different network environments, *STC* is different and the transmission costs are influencing available resources on edge servers.

4.2   Experimental Results and Discussion

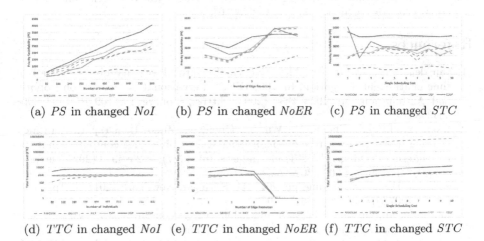

(a) *PS* in changed *NoI*   (b) *PS* in changed *NoER*   (c) *PS* in changed *STC*

(d) *TTC* in changed *NoI*   (e) *TTC* in changed *NoER*   (f) *TTC* in changed *STC*

Fig. 2. Resulted metrics of three experiments

In Fig. 2(a), we only change the *NoI*. *UGP* has the best performance and *CCGP* can deal with the pressure of *NoI* well. In Fig. 2(d), *CCGP* performs close to non-prediction approaches, while *UGP* has under performed. In Fig. 2(b), *UGP* has the best performance and *CCGP* perform well in insufficient situation. In Fig. 2(e), *UGP* has higher costs than most approaches in insufficient situation, i.e. *NoER* less than 4, while *CCGP* has almost the best performance. Besides, when resources are sufficient, all approaches perform close in *PS* and the *TTC* of *UGP* and *CCGP* become 0. In Fig. 2(c). *UGP* and *CCGP* have the two highest performances. And *UGP* performs poorly in *TTC*. In Fig. 2(f), *CCGP* can always keep its *TTC* at better level than *UGP*.

In summary, *UGP* has the best performance of *PS* in most cases, while it performs poorly in *TTC*. And *CCGP* has the second best performance of *PS* in most cases, and it performs much better than *UGP* in *TTC*. Through the experiment based on the three sets above, it is evaluated that our approaches can satisfy two goals well.

5 Conclusion

In public security, the intelligent video system based on edge computing is widely used. However, resources on edge servers can not support all video analysis tasks with varied priorities. Thus, we formulated *PA-EUA* problem based on *EUA* problem and proposed two prediction-based approaches. By comparison with four representative approaches, we evaluated that our approaches' performance. In the future, resource diversity, disaster tolerance, and personal information security will be taken into investigation.

Acknowledgement. This work is supported by the National Natural Science Foundation of China (Grant No. 61972128) and the Fundamental Research Funds for the Central Universities, China (PA2021KCPY0050).

References

1. van den Berg, J., Lin, M., Manocha, D.: Reciprocal velocity obstacles for real-time multi-agent navigation. In: 2008 IEEE International Conference on Robotics and Automation, pp. 1928–1935 (2008). https://doi.org/10.1109/ROBOT.2008.4543489
2. Chen, Y., Liu, Z., Zhang, Y., Wu, Y., Chen, X., Zhao, L.: Deep reinforcement learning-based dynamic resource management for mobile edge computing in industrial internet of things. IEEE Trans. Industr. Inf. **17**(7), 4925–4934 (2021). https://doi.org/10.1109/TII.2020.3028963
3. Johnson, D.S.: Bin Packing, pp. 207–211. Springer, New York (2016). https://doi.org/10.1007/978-1-4939-2864-4-49
4. Lai, P., et al.: Optimal edge user allocation in edge computing with variable sized vector bin packing. In: Pahl, C., Vukovic, M., Yin, J., Yu, Q. (eds.) ICSOC 2018. LNCS, vol. 11236, pp. 230–245. Springer, Cham (2018). https://doi.org/10.1007/978-3-030-03596-9_15
5. Lai, P., et al.: Cost-effective app user allocation in an edge computing environment. IEEE Trans. Cloud Comput. 1 (2020). https://doi.org/10.1109/TCC.2020.3001570
6. Madej, A., Wang, N., Athanasopoulos, N., Ranjan, R., Varghese, B.: Priority-based fair scheduling in edge computing. In: 2020 IEEE 4th International Conference on Fog and Edge Computing (ICFEC), pp. 39–48 (2020). https://doi.org/10.1109/ICFEC50348.2020.00012
7. Wu, D., Bao, R., Li, Z., Wang, H., Zhang, H., Wang, R.: Edge-cloud collaboration enabled video service enhancement: a hybrid human-artificial intelligence scheme. IEEE Trans. Multimed. **23**, 2208–2221 (2021). https://doi.org/10.1109/TMM.2021.3066050
8. Xu, J., Palanisamy, B., Ludwig, H., Wang, Q.: Zenith: utility-aware resource allocation for edge computing. In: 2017 IEEE International Conference on Edge Computing (EDGE), pp. 47–54 (2017). https://doi.org/10.1109/IEEE.EDGE.2017.15
9. Zhang, G., Liu, X., Yang, Y.: Time-series pattern based effective noise generation for privacy protection on cloud. IEEE Trans. Comput. **64**(5), 1456–1469 (2015). https://doi.org/10.1109/TC.2014.2298013
10. Zhang, L., Gao, N., Li, J., Dai, X., Song, B.: Modeling and simulation of subway station emergency evacuation based on improved social force model. In: 2020 IEEE 5th Information Technology and Mechatronics Engineering Conference (ITOEC), pp. 10–14 (2020). https://doi.org/10.1109/ITOEC49072.2020.9141854

Service Deployment with Predictive Ability for Data Stream Processing in a Cloud-Edge Environment

Shouli Zhang[1,2,3(✉)], Chen Liu[2,3], Han Li[2,3], Zhuofeng Zhao[2,3], and Xiaohong Li[1]

[1] Division of Intelligence and Computing, Tianjin University, Tianjin, China
xiaohongli@tju.edu.cn
[2] Beijing Key Laboratory On Integration and Analysis of Large-Scale Stream Data, North China University of Technology, Beijing, China
{liuchen,lihan,ed_zhao}@ncut.edu.cn
[3] Cloud Research Center, North China University of Technology, Beijing, China

Abstract. Runtime IoT data fluctuation brings challenges for optimizing the resource allocation for a data stream processing (DSP) flow in a cloud-edge environment. It can result in extra high latency for a flow. Optimized strategy of dynamic resource allocation is still hard to design to timely dealing with the IoT data fluctuation. In this paper, the above challenge is abstracted and redefined as the service deployment problem. An improved GA optimization algorithm, integrating with the IoT data fluctuation prediction ability, is proposed to handle IoT data fluctuations during the running of a DSP flow. Effectiveness of the proposed approach is evaluated based on the real datasets from a real application.

Keywords: Latency · Service Deployment · Data Prediction · Optimization · Cloud-edge Environment

1 Introduction

Today, many efforts have been made to integrate cloud and edge devices by allowing the computing resources to be shared and comprehensively utilized [1–4]. In this settling, due to fluctuation of IoT data stream in the runtime, it is still challenge to design an optimized strategy of the dynamic resource allocation for a data stream processing (DSP) flow, which is commonly structured as a directed graph whose vertices are IoT data services [5–7], whereas edges represent the data streams between services [8].

Existing works for deploying services in a cloud-edge environment can be divided into two categories: the static off-loading deployment and dynamic deployment [9–15]. In the static offloading literatures, researchers pay attention to decide which and how the computations are offloaded to the edge nodes while meeting partial metrics such as latency, WAN traffic, and so on [9–11]. The limitation of static deployment lies in that they usually assume that the DSP flow is pregiven and static. More recent works deal with dynamic service deployment problem who changing the initial static deployment by

© Springer Nature Switzerland AG 2021
H. Hacid et al. (Eds.): ICSOC 2021, LNCS 13121, pp. 781–789, 2021.
https://doi.org/10.1007/978-3-030-91431-8_55

redeploying services to different edge to cope with events such as load changes, device failures, among other issues [12–15].

Due to the dynamic nature of IoT environment as well as the limited computing capability of edge devices, it still faces several challenges to dynamically allocate adequate resources for a DSP flow for timely processing of the IoT data. Firstly, the data dependencies and data movement between services [16, 17] introduce data overhead. The fluctuation of IoT data streams makes the data overhead continually varied over time. It can result in extra latency and become an important factor in making deployment decision. Secondly, a DSP flow is not always running and keep consuming lots of resources. It may be activated sometime and keep running until no more data to be handled. The task dispatch process of a DSP flow is highly dynamic and random. Most current service deployment methods are not applicable to deal with the data streams arrive dynamically.

In this paper, we abstract and redefine the above challenge as the service deployment problem. We propose a dynamic service deployment approach for a DSP flow. An improved GA service deployment algorithm is proposed to meeting resource constraints and minimizing latency which integrating the IoT data fluctuation prediction ability to handle IoT data fluctuations during the running of a DSP flow.

2   The Definition of Problem

The Definition 1 shows a DSP workflow which is composed of several IoT data services [18]. The goal of the service deployment is to find an optimized strategy to minimize the latency during the execution of a DSP flow in a cloud-edge environment.

Definition1. Data Stream Processing Flow (DSP Flow): A data stream processing flow can be represented a directed acyclic graph of vertex and edges: $G = \langle S, E \rangle$, where $S = \{s_1, s_2, \ldots, s_j \ldots, s_n\}$ is service vertices that processing arriving data stream. An edge $E = \{e_1, e_2, \ldots, e_m \ldots, e_M\}$ represents a set of M links between services. Each edge is represented as $e_m = < s_{sour}^m, s_{dest}^m, \hbar^m >$, where s_{sour}^m represents upstream source service, s_{dest}^m denotes the destination service as the target of the edge e_m, $\hbar^m$ denotes the percentage of data generated by s_{sour}^m that is routed towards s_{dest}^m.

The computing resource contains both the cloud and edge infrastructure that is represented as a graph $\mathcal{G} = \langle R, L \rangle$. $R = \{r_1, r_2, \ldots r_i \ldots, r_m\}$ is the set of computing resources. We use a vector $r_i = \langle CPU\,core, memory \rangle$ to represent the available computation resource or the resource requirement for service. Note that the above vector is apt to be extended if more resource types are required. $L = \{l_{(i,j)}|i, j \in [1, m]\}$ is the set of network links. $l_{(i,j)} = \langle bdw_{(i,j)}, lat_{(i,j)} \rangle$ is the network link between computational resources r_i and r_j where $bdw_{(i,j)}$. is the bandwidth capability, $lat_{(i,j)}$ is the network delay. We consider t delay of a resource to itself to be 0. Besides, we use $f_{r_i} \in \{0, 1\}$ signals whether is a cloud resource.

The external stream data sources who are inputted into a DSP flow can be represented as $EX = \{ex_1, ex_2, \ldots, ex_p \ldots, e_P\}$, each ex_p. is an external data source, λ^{ex_p} is the output data rate of this data source. We distinguish the input and output transmission rates for a service. The input transmission rate $\psi_{s_i}^{in}$. for a service s_i is the sum of the stream rates on all its incoming sources. $\psi_{s_i}^{out}$ represents the output transmission rate of a service.

$$\psi_{s_i}^{in} = \sum_{e_i \in E | s_{sour}^m = \exp_p^m \& s_{dest}^m = s_i} \lambda^{exp} + \sum_{s_j \in S | s_{sour}^m = s_{dest}^m = s_i} \hbar^m * \psi_{s_j}^{out} \tag{1}$$

where $\sum_{e_i \in E | s_{sour}^m = \exp_p^m \& s_{dest}^m = s_i} \lambda^{exp}$ is the total input stream data ces from the extra data source. And $\sum_{s_j \in S | s_{sour}^m = s_{dest}^m = s_i} \hbar^m * \psi_{s_j}^{out}$ is the total data transferred from its upstream services.

The problem of service deployment is defined as follows:

Definition 2. The Service Deployment: The service deployment at time step t can be modeled as a mapping function $A^t : G^t \rightarrow \mathcal{G}^t$. We use $y_{s_i}^{r_m}(t)$ to present the deployment decision of service s_i at time step t, if service s_i is deployed onto edge device r_m, then $y_{s_i}^{r_m}(t) = 1$, otherwise, $y_{s_i}^{r_m}(t) = 0$.

The data processing rate for s_i if it is deployed on r_j is denoted as $\mu(s_i, r_j)$. The reference values of CPU, memory requirements for service s_i on r_j when processing data $Refd_{s_i}$ can be defined as $fcpus_{s_i}$, $fmem_{s_i}$ respectively which can be obtained by profiling it on a reference resource [12]. Thus, one service's CPU (cpu_{s_i}) and memory (mem_{s_i}) requirements needs to process its incoming data stream can be calculated as follows:

$$cpu_{s_i} = \frac{fcpus_{s_i} \times \psi_{s_i}^{in}}{Refd_{s_i}} \tag{2}$$

$$mem_{s_i} = \frac{fmem_{s_i} \times \psi_{s_i}^{in}}{Refd_{s_i}} + lmem_{s_i} \tag{3}$$

Note that the overall memory comprises the memory needed to load itself $lmem_{s_i}$ as well as the memory required for processing the incoming data.

The data transmission rate $V_{s_i \rightarrow s_j}$ is also given, which is the stream rate of the number of events or sensor data passing between services per time unit. With the data transmission rate, the data overhead of a service in a DSP flow can be defined as the multiply of the data transmission rate $V_{s_i \rightarrow s_j}$ with a time interval θ using the time window technique.

The calculation for latency of DSP flow contains two parts: the service execution time $etime_{s_i}$ and stream transfer latency $(\frac{\hbar^m * \psi_{s_j}^{out}}{V_{s_j \rightarrow s_i}} * \theta + lat_{(i,j)})$. Thereby, the latency of a data analysis flow is the aggregate latency of all services, it can be calculated as following:

$$Latency = \sum (y_{s_i}^{r_j}(t) * \frac{\psi_{s_i}^{in}}{\mu(s_i, r_j)}) + \sum (\frac{\hbar^m * \psi_{s_j}^{out}}{V_{s_j \rightarrow s_i}} * \theta + lat_{(i,j)}) \tag{4}$$

The problem of service deployment is to find a mapping that minimizes the latency and respects the resource constraints. That is:

$$min(Latency) \tag{5}$$

Subject to:

$$\forall A_k^t, \langle s_i, r_p \rangle \in A_k^t | s_i \in S^{src} \rightarrow eu \in EU$$
$$| s_i \in S^{snk} \rightarrow Cloud \tag{6}$$

$$\sum y_{s_i}^{r_j}(t) * cpu_{s_i} \leq cpu_{EU} \tag{7}$$

$$\sum y_{s_i}^{r_j}(t) * \text{mem}_{s_i} \leq mem_{EU} \tag{8}$$

$$y_{s_i}^{r_j}(t) \in \{0, 1\}, j = 1, \ldots, m \tag{9}$$

Constraints (6) guarantees that the source services must be placed on edge devices because they directly operate on the sensor streams, while the sink service must be placed on the cloud, because they will output final results to applications. Constraints (7) and (8) make sure that the required computing resources of services are not exceeded the available computing resources of edge devices.

3   The Predictive Service Deployment Approach

We propose a Predictive Service Deployment Approach (PSDA) that incorporates two advanced optimization algorithms to address the above challenges.

Firstly, we use Genetic Algorithm to generate service deployment strategy candidate solutions. The encoding operation aims at representing a feasible joint solution. We use a binary encoding scheme to construct a chromosome. In his paper, the population is denoted by.

Pop_c, which is computed by using the formula (10)

$$Pop_c = \begin{bmatrix} y_{mn} & \cdots & y_{mN} \\ \vdots & \ddots & \vdots \\ y_{mn} & \cdots & y_{MN} \end{bmatrix} \tag{10}$$

where M is the number of edge nodes, N is the number of services that need to be deployed. If the service s_n is deployed on edge node e_m, then $y_{mn} = 1$, else, $y_{mn} = 0$. There is a critical problem that the definition of the fitness function for the evaluation of the chromosomes. The objective function of Eq. (5) can be considered as a fitness function (Fit) of the genetic algorithm.

$$Fit = 1 - \frac{1}{Latency} \tag{11}$$

At the running time, we use the prediction technology to predict future data fluctuations so that we can predict the services whose input data rates will be changed. We can use the predicted value to predict the service's expected resource requirements (Eq. (2) and Eq. (3)).

The data overhead is a typical real-time streaming time-series data obtained over a specific period or since a certain point in time. We use a vector to model the data overhead of service s_i can be modeled as a vector $z_i^t = (x_i^t, y_i^t)$, in which, $y_i^t = (\psi_{s_i}^{in})^t$, and $x_i^t = (\psi_{s_i}^{int-1}, ..., \psi_{s_i}^{int-m}, ..., \psi_{s_i}^{int-k+1}, \sum \psi_{s_j}^{outt}, \sum \psi_{s_j}^{outt-1}, ..., \sum \psi_{s_j}^{outt-m} ..., \sum \psi_{s_j}^{outt-k+1})$. In which, t is the current time window $t(t_a, t_b)$, the length of t is a constant which can be defined as $|t_b - t_a|$. t − m is the mth previous time window, k is a temporal constant.

For the given the time series of incoming data overhead, we use a decomposable time series model with two main model components: trend and seasonality to build the prediction model. They are combined in the following equation:

$$y(t) = \frac{C(t)}{1 + exp(-k(t - b))} + \sum \left(a_n \cos\left(\frac{2\pi nt}{P}\right) + b_n \sin\left(\frac{2\pi nt}{P}\right) \right) + \varepsilon_t \quad (12)$$

Here $\frac{C(t)}{1+exp(-k(t-b))}$ is the trend function which models non-periodic changes in the value of the time series, $C(t)$ is the time-varying capacity, k the growth rate, and b an offset parameter. $\sum(a_n \cos(\frac{2\pi nt}{P}) + b_n \sin(\frac{2\pi nt}{P}))$ represents periodic changes (e.g., weekly and yearly seasonality), we rely on Fourier series to provide a flexible model of periodic effects [19]. In which P is the regular period we expect the time series to have (e.g., P = 365.25 for yearly data or P = 7 for weekly data, when we scale our time variable in days). a_n and b_n are required estimating parameters. The error term ε_t represents any idiosyncratic changes which are not accommodated by the model.

Based on the prediction value, Greedy heuristic can be used to adopt a deployment plan generated by the genetic algorithm at runtime because it provides a feasible low-complex algorithm that adapted to real-time dynamic cloud-edge computing environment. In future time slot t + 1, PSDA finds the services affected by the data stream fluctuation directly or indirectly. Then, for each service affected, it finds the best resource provisioning solution based on the predicted data overhead. Based on the predicted data overhead, we can get each service's input data rate and required computation resources in the future time slot t + 1. Current resource usage of edge nodes can be obtained by using network resource monitoring tools installed in the edge computing network platform. We will remove edge node that does not meet future computation requirements of service. The remaining edge nodes in this list will be used to find the best edge nodes to deploy service with the help of the Minimax with Alpha-Beta pruning algorithm [20].

4   Experiment

4.1   Experiment Setup

Experiment Environment: The experiment environment is composed of a cloud center and several edge devices. Five Acer AR580 F2 rack servers via Citrix XenServer 6.2 are utilized to build a private cloud, each of which own 8 processors (Intel Xeon E5-4607 2.20 GHz), 64 GB RAM and 40 TB storage. Four different types of Raspberry Pis are used as the edge devices in terms of computation capacity. 150 edge devices are selected to build up the edge environment. The edge devices are connected to the cloud with a bandwidth of 100 Mbps.

Experiment Dataset: The dataset in the experiment is real collected from the SGCC in scenario 2. Data streams from 5871 sensors are involved.

We have realized 1322 services abstracts on the cloud. Four different structures of DSP flows are constructed randomly: the DSP flow 1 contained 10 data services, the DSP flow 2 contained 20 data services, the DSP flow 3 contained 30 data services. the DSP flow 4 contained 50 data services. We have created total 100 the DSP flow instances which contains 40 instances of the DSP flow 1, 30 instances of the DSP flow 2, 20 instances of the DSP flow 3 and 10 instances of the DSP flow 4.

We will conduct the following methods for stream processing: *the resource-aware approach (RA), the location-aware approach (LA), and the predictive service deployment approach (PSDA) in this paper.* The main performance metric is the latency of a DSP flow for stream data processing. It can be calculated by the Eq. (4).

4.2 Experiment Results and Evaluation

We first change the input rate of the services: we vary the data stream rate of sensors from 10, 20, 40, 80, 160, 320, 640, 1000 to 2000 (10^4 records/s) for services. Each experiment runs for 50 times.

Figure 1 compares the latency with different service deployment solutions under different input stream rates. It can be seen that the proposed PSDA method also can deliver a shorter latency than other two method (i.e., 45.67% lower than RA on average in four DSP flows, and 41.35% lower than LA).

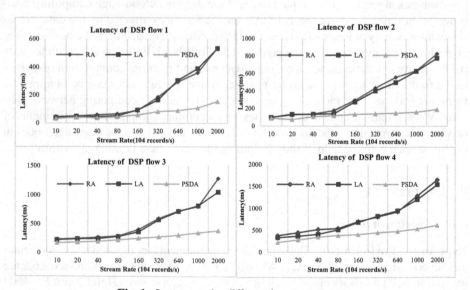

Fig. 1. Latency under different input stream rates

Then, we set a fixed input stream rate of 160×10^4 records/s and change the input stream numbers at system running time from 100, 200, 400, 800, 1600 to 3200. The results of latency evaluation are shown in Fig. 2. As number of data streams inputted to the stream process graphs increases, the proposed PSDA method performs the best among the two methods. It can reduce the average latency by 46.12% compared to the RA, and by 40.85% compared to the LA.

The experiment results prove that the proposed PSDA is more efficient than RA and LA. The reason is that data overhead among services can result in latency due to the cost of moving and storage. The RA and LA both do not consider it when deploying the services. Furthermore, the data overhead continually varied over time due to the fluctuation characteristic of sensor streams. It makes the current deployment strategy may be not the optimal one. The proposed PSDA have integrated the prediction ability of runtime data fluctuations that can predictively offer a satisfactory service deployment solution for current as well as future DSP flow activations.

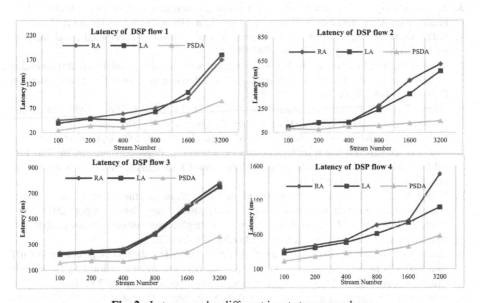

Fig. 2. Latency under different input stream numbers

5 Conclusion

This paper proposed a distinctive problem of dynamically deploying the services in a cloud-edge environment to support the emerging real-time requirement of IoT applications. We define the optimization problem for dynamic deployment of services with data overhead and compute constraints. We have proposed a predictive service deployment approach to adaptively deploy services from cloud onto edge devices by predicting the fluctuation of data overhead. The effectiveness of the proposed approach is demonstrated by examining real cases of State Grid Corporation of China.

Acknowledgement. This work is supported by the Key Program of National Natural Science Foundation of China Research on Big Service Theory and Methods in Big Data Environment (No. 61832004).

References

1. Renart, E.G., Diaz-Montes, J., Parashar, M.: Data-driven stream processing at the edge. In: IEEE International Conference on Fog and Edge Computing, Madrid, Spain, pp. 31–40. IEEE (2017)
2. Zhang, S., Chen, L., Han, Y., et al.: Seamless Integration of Cloud and Edge with a service-based approach. In: 2018 IEEE International Conference on Web Services, San Francisco, CA, USA, pp. 155–162. IEEE (2018)
3. Xu, X., Huang, S., Feagan, L., et al.: EAaaS: edge analytics as a service. In: 2017 IEEE International Conference on Web Services, Honolulu, HI, pp. 349–356. IEEE (2017)
4. Varghese, B., Wang, N., Li, J., et al.: Edge-as-a-service: towards distributed cloud architectures. Adv. Parallel Comput. **32**, 784–793 (2017)
5. Moussa, H., Yen, I.L., Bastani, F.: Service management in the edge cloud for stream processing of IoT data. In: 2020 IEEE 13th International Conference on Cloud Computing, Beijing, China, pp. 91–98. IEEE (2020)
6. Huang, Z., Lin, K.J., Tsai, B.L., et al.: Building edge intelligence for online activity recognition in service-oriented IoT systems. Futur. Gener. Comput. Syst. **87**, 557–567 (2018)
7. Pallewatta, S., Kostakos, V., Buyya, R.: Microservices-based IoT application placement within heterogeneous and resource constrained fog computing environments. In: The 12th IEEE/ACM International Conference on Utility and Cloud Computing, New York, United States, pp. 71–81. ACM (2019)
8. Barika, M., Garg, S., Chan, A., et al.: Scheduling algorithms for efficient execution of stream workflow applications in multicloud environments. IEEE Trans. Serv. Comput. (2019)
9. Veith, A., Assuncao, M., Lefèvre, L.: Latency-aware placement of data stream analytics on edge computing. Service-Orient. Comput.**11236**, 215–229 (2018)
10. Veith, A., Renart, E.G., Balouek-Thomert, D., et al.: Distributed operator placement for IoT data analytics across edge and cloud resources. In: IEEE/ACM International Symposium in Cluster, Cloud, and Grid Computing, Larnaca, Cyprus, pp. 459–468. ACM (2019)
11. Salaht, F.A., Desprez, F., Lebre, A., et al.: Service placement in fog computing using constraint programming. In: 2019 IEEE International Conference on Services Computing, pp. 19–27. IEEE (2019)
12. de Souza, F.R., Da Silva Veith, A., Dias de Assunção, M., Caron, E.: Scalable joint optimization of placement and parallelism of data stream processing applications on cloud-edge infrastructure. In: Kafeza, E., Benatallah, B., Martinelli, F., Hacid, H., Bouguettaya, A., Motahari, H. (eds.) ICSOC 2020. LNCS, vol. 12571, pp. 149–164. Springer, Cham (2020). https://doi.org/10.1007/978-3-030-65310-1_12
13. Maia, A.M., Ghamri-Doudane, Y., Vieira, D., et al.: Dynamic service placement and load distribution in edge computing. In: 16th International Conference on Network and Service Management, Izmir, Turkey, pp. 1–9. IEEE (2020)
14. Gao, X., Huang, X., Bian, S., et al.: PORA: predictive offloading and resource allocation in dynamic fog computing systems. IEEE Internet Things J. **7**(1), 72–87 (2020)
15. Lambert, T., Guyon, D., Ibrahim, S.: Rethinking operators placement of stream data application in the edge. In: Proceedings of the 29th ACM International Conference on Information & Knowledge Management, New York, NY, USA. Association for Computing Machinery, pp. 2101–2104. ACM (2020)

16. Chen, X., Tang, S., Lu, Z., et al.: iDiSC: a new approach to IoT-data-intensive service components deployment in edge-cloud-hybrid system. IEEE Access **99**(1–1) (2019)
17. Mohtadi, A., Gascon-Samson, J.: Poster: dependency-aware operator placement of distributed stream processing IoT applications deployed at the edge. In: 2020 IEEE/ACM Symposium on Edge Computing, San Jose, California, USA, pp. 161–163. ACM (2020)
18. Han, Y., Liu, C., Su, S., et al.: A proactive service model facilitating stream data fusion and correlation. Int. J. Web Serv. Res. **14**(3), 1–16 (2017)
19. Taylor, S.J., Letham, B.: Forecasting at scale. Am. Stat. **72**(1), 37–45 (2018)
20. Barika, M., Garg, S., Zomaya, A., et al.: Online scheduling technique to handle data velocity changes in stream workflows. IEEE Trans. Parallel Distrib. Syst. **99**, 1 (2021)

A Reinforcement Learning-Based Service Model for the Internet of Things

Christian Cabrera[1]([✉]) and Siobhán Clarke[2]

[1] Department of Computer Science and Technology, University of Cambridge, Cambridge, UK
chc79@cam.ac.uk
[2] Distributed Systems Group, School of Computer Science and Statistics, Trinity College Dublin, Dublin, Ireland
Siobhan.Clarke@scss.tcd.ie

Abstract. The Internet of Things (IoT) creates environments where devices and users interact. Service-oriented architectures (SOAs) encapsulate devices' capabilities as IoT services which users can request. SOAs manage the scale of IoT services by placing services descriptions about appropriate services in distributed architectures (e.g., a network of IoT gateways). Such distribution increases the chances of responding to users in an efficient fashion as requests are attended locally. However, dynamic IoT environments can easily outdate the distribution of services descriptions, which in turn impacts SOAs efficiency when the required services descriptions are not in place. Current architectures use pre-defined knowledge to adapt the distribution of services descriptions reactively. However, such human intervention is not always available and may be error-prone in dynamic IoT environments. We propose a reinforcement learning model that IoT gateways use to automatically decide how to distribute services descriptions over time. We evaluate the model in a real IoT testbed and results show that its performance in different scenarios compares favourably against a reactive baseline.

Keywords: Internet of Things · Service oriented computing · Self-adaptive systems · Pervasive computing · Reinforcement learning

1 Introduction

Service-oriented architectures (SOAs) manage IoT devices as IoT services [4]. Users request these services to retrieve and process relevant information [5]. SOAs have proposed storing services descriptions in networks of IoT gateways, enabling efficient responses to requests by placing services' information closer to end users [5,7]. Events in dynamic IoT environments can outdate services distribution, which in turn impacts the efficiency of SOAs when responding to users' requests. The distribution of services descriptions must change accordingly. Otherwise, SOAs will not be able to efficiently respond users' requests. Similarly, new IoT gateways can join and need to determine which services to store. SOAs must self-adapt to respond to users' requests in dynamic IoT environments [4,6].

© Springer Nature Switzerland AG 2021
H. Hacid et al. (Eds.): ICSOC 2021, LNCS 13121, pp. 790–799, 2021.
https://doi.org/10.1007/978-3-030-91431-8_56

Current SOAs self-adapt by reacting to changes in the IoT system (e.g., devices battery levels) [1,8] or the IoT environment [2,3]. Some approaches sense variables in the IoT environment and decide when to trigger adaptive processes based on the values of such variables and predefined thresholds. Other approaches use pre-defined knowledge about events to trigger the adaptation. Reactive approaches tend to experiment with performance degradation before events are identified. Additionally, such approaches are likely to be error-prone, and might not suit IoT environments where predefined knowledge is not available. This paper presents a reinforcement learning-based service model for the IoT, which adapts services distribution based on users' requests. The approach is based on a Q-learning algorithm [12], which works on a network of IoT gateways. Each gateway uses this algorithm to learn from requests that arrive and moves services' descriptions between them accordingly. This algorithm enables new gateways to automatically determine which services to store. Our model is evaluated in an IoT testbed where we explore three different IoT scenarios.

2 Related Work

Different self-adaptive SOAs have been proposed to manage IoT environments. Trendy [2] groups services according to their location. It has a Directory Agent (DA) which updates services status according to requests' behaviour. del Val et al. [10] propose an agent-based approach to discover atomic services. Each agent in the system offers a service and can trigger adaptation processes under two circumstances. First, an agent can change the network topology according to the request's resolution and forwarding. Second, an agent can change the population of agents by cloning itself when there are many requests for its services. Kumar and Satyanarayana [8] propose a self-adaptive model based on semantic annotations, which are used to compute the relevance of web services for user queries. This relevance changes according to historical usage of services. Athanasopoulos [1] proposes a service organisation schema based on service functionalities. Services are organised into hierarchical groups based on their descriptions (i.e., providers' perspective). This structure adapts according to the historical usage (i.e., consumers' perspective) which is used to calculate the similarity between services. Cabrera et al. [3] propose an adaptive service model for smart cities. Such model reactively responds to city events by reorganising services' information in distributed repositories. Events are identified by evaluating the system performance against a threshold, or they are pre-defined by city authorities.

Current self-adaptive SOAs architectures identify changes in the environment or the system to trigger adaptations. Such adaptation is mostly reactive as architectures respond to events after they are identified, which is likely to result in performance degradation. Additionally, system adaptations (e.g., adding a new component) require pre-defined knowledge that requires human intervention. Few architectures [1,8] self-adapt by using historical data (e.g., logs). Even for those that do, such data might not be always available in IoT environments, which makes models that interact and learn from the environment more suitable.

3   Learning-Based Service Model

We consider IoT environments where capabilities are encapsulated as IoT services. A network of IoT gateways stores information about these services in their local repositories. Each gateway is defined as $g_i = \langle R, D \rangle$, where R is the local repository that stores services descriptions, and D is the set of domains that defines the services that g_i manages. Gateways initially configure the network and define D based on contextual information from the IoT environment [5]. R stores services descriptions, which are defined as $s_{desc} = \langle id, I, O, D \rangle$, consisting of a service identifier, input types, output types, and domains. Users can send requests to gateways, and each request is defined as $r = \langle I, O, D \rangle$, consisting of request input types, output types and domains. New IoT gateways can join the network at any time without any service or pre-defined information. They only receive requests and exchange messages with other gateways in the network. The IoT environments recognise repetitive time periods (e.g., days, weeks, etc.), which also have recognised sub-periods (e.g., a day has 24 h). Each gateway models environments' time periods as a discrete variable $T = \langle t_0, t_1, ..., t_m \rangle$, where m is their number of sub-periods. Requests reflect periodic users' behaviour, which means that users are likely to ask for the same service at the same time in a given period. Each gateway stores a request's history as $H = \{\langle t_1, D_1 \rangle, \langle t_2, D_2 \rangle, ..., \langle t_n, D_n \rangle\}$, which captures the set of domains D_i of all received requests at a given time t_i. Similarly, each gateway stores information about other gateways as $G = \{\langle gw_1, D_1 \rangle, \langle gw_2, D_2 \rangle, ..., \langle gw_m, D_m \rangle\}$, which captures the set of domains D_j for the services managed by gateway gw_j.

3.1   Reinforcement Learning Model

Each IoT gateway gw_i implements a reinforcement learning model that decides how to update its local repository according to users' requests. The learning model represents the system performance as an utility function (Eq. 1, encapsulating a set of metrics that measure the service management efficiency in each gateway. These metrics include the rate of solved requests, average search precision, average search response time, average number of hops and percentage of used storage.

$$u(sd)_t = w_1 rsr_t + w_2 asp_t - w_3 v(art_t) - w_4 anh_t - w_5 pus_t \tag{1}$$

Equation 2 defines the reward function used by the reinforcement learning model. It captures the difference between the system utility from state $t - 1$ to state t in a given period. If the utility function increases from one time t_{i-1} to another time t_i, the reward is positive. Otherwise, the reward is negative.

$$r_t = u(sd)_t - u(sd)_{t-1} \tag{2}$$

Figure 1 represents the states that the learning model uses to represent IoT environments periods of time (i.e., T), and its sub-periods (i.e., $t_0, t_1, ..., t_m$). The model can decide to do nothing (i.e., a_0), move services (i.e., a_1), or remove services

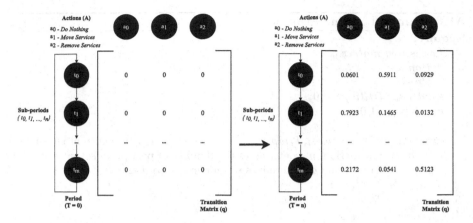

Fig. 1. States and actions in an IoT environment.

(i.e., a_2) to update services repositories at any sub-period t_i. A transition matrix q drives the action selection and stores the reward from the environment. Algorithm 1 shows the Q-learning [9,11] process each gateway executes while solving service requests from users. This algorithm uses a transition matrix q to represent the IoT environment states and gateways actions. It also stores the utility of the last state, the service information received from other gateways, and the current system state. The current time t_i, the time period T (e.g., day identifier), and the memory periods mp are parameters. Memory periods mp determine the number of historical time periods to be considered when calculating the utility (Line 3). This parameter enables the learning algorithm to identify utility degradation even when system has had good performance over a long time. The algorithm starts by calculating the reward based on the current and previous utility values (Line 2 to 4). The first time the algorithm is executed, the Q-matrix is initialised as a zero matrix (Line 6). Otherwise, the Q-matrix is updated using Eq. 3 (Line 8). Then, the algorithm updates the epsilon parameter e if the current period is greater than the decay time parameter dt (Line 9 to 10). The epsilon parameter e defines whether it explores the actions space in the current state, or exploits the accumulated knowledge to select the next action. The decay function balances the exploration versus exploitation trade-off by prioritising the exploitation as time passes as there is more knowledge in the Q-matrix. The decay time parameter dt prioritises exploration at the beginning when there is not enough knowledge in the Q-matrix. The algorithm determines the action to perform based on the epsilon e value (Line 11 to 15). It selects a random action, if a random number r is lower than e (Lines 12 and 13). The algorithm selects the action that generates a higher reward based on the Q-matrix knowledge otherwise (Lines 14 and 15).

$$q[t,a] = (1 - \alpha)q[t,a] + \alpha(r_t + \gamma \max(q[t+1,*]])) \tag{3}$$

$$a(t) = \gamma \max(q[t,*]]) \tag{4}$$

Algorithm 1. Learning Algorithm.

Require:
    Transition matrix q
    Action a
    State s_t
    Double lastUtility $= 0.0$
    Epsilon e $= 1.0$
    received $= [\ ]$

1: **function** Q-LEARNING(t_i, T, mp, te)   ▷ where t_i is the current sub-period, T is the current period, mp determines the number of past periods that the utility function considers, and dt determines when e starts to decay

2:     $u_{t_{i-1}} \leftarrow lastUtility$
3:     $u_{t_i} \leftarrow calculateUtility(t_i, mp)$
4:     $r_{t_i} \leftarrow u_{t_i} - u_{t_{i-1}}$
5:     **if** $t = 0$ **and** $T = 0$ **then**
6:         $s_{t_i} \leftarrow init(q)$
7:     **else**
8:         $s_{t_i} \leftarrow update(q, s_{t_i}, a, r_{t_i}, T, t_i)$
9:         **if** $T > dt$ **then**
10:            $e \leftarrow decayEpsilon(e)$
11:     $r \leftarrow getRandom()$
12:     **if** $r < e$ **then**
13:         $a \leftarrow getRandomAction()$
14:     **else**
15:         $a \leftarrow getMaxAction(q)$
16:     **if** $a = a_0$ **then**
17:         *do nothing*
18:     **if** $a = a_1$ **then**
19:         $RD \leftarrow defineRequiredDomains(t_i, H)$
20:         $destinations \leftarrow getDestinations(RD, G)$
21:         **for each** $gw \in destinations$ **do**
22:            $sendMessage(Adp_{msg}(gw_{id}, RD)$
23:         $localRepository.insert(receivedServices)$
24:         **for each** $service \in receivedServices$ **do**
25:            $received.add(service.id)$
26:     **if** $a = a_2$ **then**
27:         $localRepository.remove(received)$
28:         $received = [\ ]$

If the algorithm selects a_0 (do nothing), then the gateway waits until the next iteration. If the algorithm selects a_1 (move services), the gateway sends a message Adp_{msg} to the destinations asking for services from the required domains RD (Lines 21 and 22). The selected gateways respond with their available services' information, and the gateway inserts those services' descriptions in the local repository (Line 23). If the algorithm selects a_2 (delete services), then the gateway removes the services previously received (Lines 27 to 28).

4 Evaluation

We implemented the learning model[1] in Python 3.5. It was deployed in an IoT testbed of 5 Raspberry Pi3. One board is the consumer and sends requests the other boards, which form a network of IoT gateways. Gateway 1 receives requests, monitors the utility function, and asks for services descriptions to other gateways. We evaluate the proposed approach in three different scenarios.

Scenario 1 represents environments where requests are periodic and do not change over time. Experiments last 8 h with periods of 8 min, for a total of 60 periods. Periods has 4 sub-periods that last 2 min each. Services from known domains are requested between sub-periods 0 and 1, 2 and 3, and 3 and 4 at each period. Services from unknown domains are requested between sub-periods 1 and 2. **Scenario 2** represents environments where requests are periodic and change in the middle of each experiment when a new type of service request emerges. Experiments last 8 h with periods of 8 min, for a total of 60 periods. Periods has 4 sub-periods that last 2 min each. Services from known domains are requested between sub-periods 0 and 1, 2 and 3, and 3 and 4 at each period before period 30. Services from unknown domains are requested between sub-periods 1 and 2 at each period from the beginning of the experiment, and between sub-periods 3 and 4 after period 30 (i.e., emergent unknown service request). **Scenario 3** represents environments where a new gateway joins the network. Gateway 1 starts receiving requests and does not have any pre-defined knowledge or services' information at the beginning. This scenario has the same configuration as scenario 1 regarding periods, sub-periods, and services requests' pattern. We run experiments 10 times for each combination of scenarios and parameters. The memory periods varies from 1 to 5, increasing by 2. The decay time varies from 0% of the experiment time to 100%, increasing by 25%. Decay type can be Boolean or exponential. We use a learning rate (i.e., α) of 0.8, and a discount factor (i.e., γ) of 0.95 as a high value for α speeds up the learning, and a higher value for γ gives future rewards more value [9].

4.1 Results

Figure 2 presents the model performance with different decay types, and parameters in scenario 1. We report the utility mean from the 10 repetitions, with a 95% CI. Results show the utility is higher with a Boolean decay as it changes e from 1 to 0 straight away, and the model selects actions with higher rewards for a longer time. The number of memory periods impacts the utility in an inverse fashion. The model has the best performance with a memory of 1 period as it is more sensitive to performance changes. This sensitivity produces greater positive or lower negative rewards, which reinforce the accumulated knowledge in a more significant fashion. The utility increases with a higher decay time as the learning model exploits more the accumulated knowledge. Figure 3 shows the model performance in scenario 2, where there is an emergent service request.

---

[1] Smart City SD GitLab - https://gitlab.scss.tcd.ie/groups/smartcitySD/subgroups.

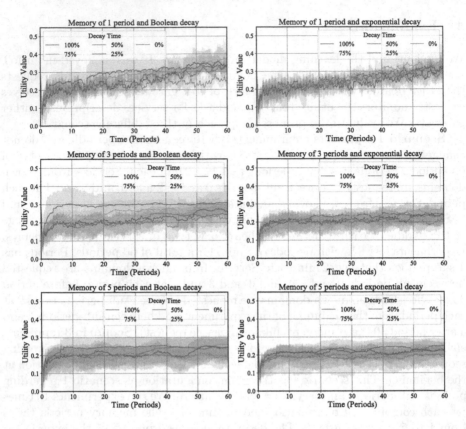

Fig. 2. Scenario 1 - Parameters

This emergent behaviour causes a clear degradation in the performance despite the parameters' values. However, the model manages to recover its performance in most cases. The difference between Boolean and exponential decays is not as clear compared to the first scenario. The highest utility that the model achieves is around 0.25 for both types of decay. The number of memory periods has a similar impact to scenario 1 (i.e., inverse relation). The learning model achieves the best results with a lower number of memory periods. The decay time also has a similar effect as in scenario 1 (i.e., direct relation). The utility increases when the model exploits the accumulated knowledge (e.g., a decay time greater or equal to 50%), even after the new request type emerges.

Figure 4 presents the system performance in scenario 3 when a new gateway joins an IoT environment without any pre-defined knowledge. The model can effectively exploit the resources of the new gateway as it enables the new gateway to learn which services descriptions to manage based on users' requests. Boolean decay offers better performance compared to exponential decay. The system performs better when there is more time to exploit the accumulated knowledge, as in scenario 1. The number of memory periods impacts system performance differently compared to previous scenarios. A lower number of memory periods (e.g., 1) makes the model more sensitive to changes in the environment. The

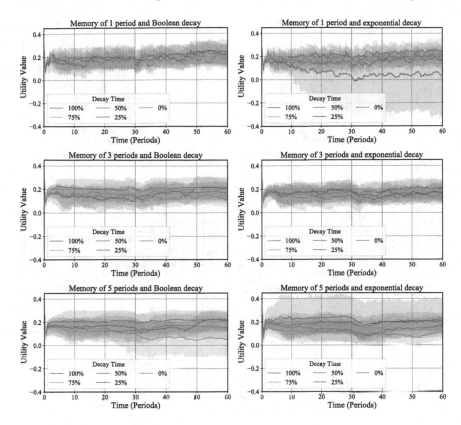

Fig. 3. Scenario 2 - Parameters

utility function degrades to negative values while the model does not have the chance to exploit the accumulated knowledge (i.e., a decay time lower or equal to 50%) when the gateway is new. A higher number of memory periods (i.e., 3 or 5) makes the model less sensitive, so the impact of random decisions is not that high. Results in different scenarios show the model achieves more consistent results with a Boolean decay, 1 period of memory, and 100% of decay time. This configuration is used to compare our model performance with the closest related work which updates repositories in a reactive fashion [3].

Figure 5 shows the behaviour of the reinforcement learning model compared against the baseline in different scenarios. The proposed approach has the best performance in all scenarios as it learns how requests behave and updates the local repositories before changes happen. The baseline has a repetitive behaviour in scenarios 1 and 2 (Figs. 5a and b). First, the utility increases as the baseline addresses requests with the available information. The utility then degrades because requests change and the baseline must identify these changes before updating repositories. The utility increases once changes are identified until a new change in the requests out-dates the services distribution, which again degrades the utility. The baseline cannot do anything in the scenario 3 (Fig. 5c)

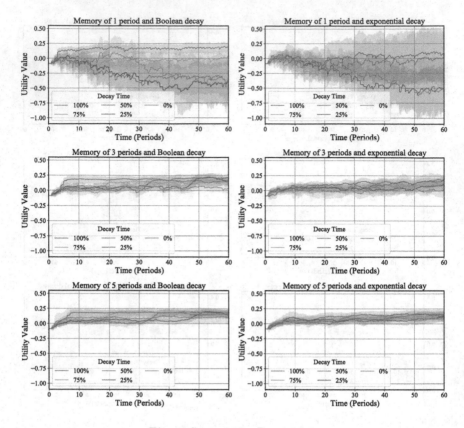

Fig. 4. Scenario 3 - Parameters

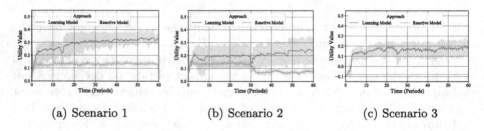

(a) Scenario 1   (b) Scenario 2   (c) Scenario 3

Fig. 5. Baseline comparisons

as it requires pre-defined information that is not available in the new gateway. The learning model accumulates knowledge from requests and updates the gateway repository with relevant information.

5   Conclusions

This paper proposes a reinforcement learning service model for the IoT, which automatically distributes services descriptions to respond to users' dynamic behaviour. The model identifies such behavior from users' requests and updates services repositories accordingly. It avoids human intervention as a Q-learning algorithm accumulates knowledge from the system's interactions with the IoT environment. The algorithm uses such knowledge to decide when and how to re-distribute the services descriptions. We evaluated the model in a real IoT testbed under 3 different scenarios. Results show that the proposed model achieves a better performance than a reactive baseline. Future work will be focused on adaptive architectures that integrate learning models and reactive approaches to address challenges from scenarios with and without repetitive behaviours.

Acknowledgment. This work is supported by Science Foundation Ireland under grant 13/IA/1885. Computational resources have been provided by the TCHPC funded by eINIS.

References

1. Athanasopoulos, D.: Self-adaptive service organization for pragmatics-aware service discovery. In: 2017 IEEE International Conference on Services Computing (SCC), pp. 164–171. IEEE (2017)
2. Butt, T.A., Phillips, I., Guan, L., Oikonomou, G.: Adaptive and context-aware service discovery for the internet of things. In: Balandin, S., Andreev, S., Koucheryavy, Y. (eds.) NEW2AN/ruSMART -2013. LNCS, vol. 8121, pp. 36–47. Springer, Heidelberg (2013). https://doi.org/10.1007/978-3-642-40316-3_4
3. Cabrera, C., Clarke, S.: A self-adaptive service discovery model for smart cities. IEEE Trans. Serv. Comput., 1 (2019). https://ieeexplore.ieee.org/document/88513 03
4. Cabrera, C., Palade, A., Clarke, S.: An evaluation of service discovery protocols in the internet of things. In: Proceedings of the Symposium on Applied Computing, pp. 469–476. ACM (2017)
5. Cabrera, C., White, G., Palade, A., Clarke, S.: The right service at the right place: a service model for smart cities. In: Proceedings of Pervasive Computing Conference, pp. 469–476. IEEE (2018)
6. Fathy, Y., Barnaghi, P., Tafazolli, R.: Large-scale indexing, discovery, and ranking for the internet of things (IoT). ACM Comput. Surv. (CSUR) **51**(2), 29 (2018)
7. Fredj, S.B., Boussard, M., Kofman, D., Noirie, L.: Efficient semantic-based IoT service discovery mechanism for dynamic environments. In: 2014 IEEE 25th Annual International Symposium on Personal, Indoor, and Mobile Radio Communication (PIMRC), pp. 2088–2092. IEEE (2014)
8. Kumar, V.V., Satyanarayana, N.: Self-adaptive semantic classification using domain knowledge and web usage log for web service discovery. Int. J. Appl. Eng. Res. **11**(6), 4618–4622 (2016)
9. Sutton, R.S., Barto, A.G.: Reinforcement Learning, Second Edition: An Introduction. MIT Press (2018). https://books.google.co.uk/books?id=uWV0Dw AAQBAJ
10. del Val, E., Rebollo, M., Botti, V.: Combination of self-organization mechanisms to enhance service discovery in open systems. Info. Sci. **279**, 138–162 (2014)
11. Watkins, C.J., Dayan, P.: Q-learning. Mach. Learn. **8**(3–4), 279–292 (1992)
12. Watkins, C.J.C.H.: Learning from delayed rewards. Ph.D. thesis, University of Cambridge (1989)

Evaluating the Security of Machine Learning Based IoT Device Identification Systems Against Adversarial Examples

Anahita Namvar[1,2(✉)], Chandra Thapa[2], Salil S. Kanhere[1], and Seyit Camtepe[2]

[1] UNSW, Sydney, NSW 2052, Australia
a.namvar@student.unsw.edu.au, salil.kanhere@unsw.edu.au
[2] Data61, Marsfield, NSW 2122, Australia
{chandra.thapa,seyit.camtepe}@data61.csiro.au

Abstract. Machine learning (ML) has been extensively used in Internet of Things (IoT) applications, including traffic profiling, network security, and IoT device identification. However, machine learning models are vulnerable to adversarial examples/attacks leading to misclassification and system malfunction. Though these attacks have been studied in domains such as computer vision, a comprehensive exploration in the IoT context is lacking. This work takes the first step in evaluating the adversarial attacks in this setting and particularly focuses on IoT device identification. To this end, our empirical analyses considering various attack techniques, including Fast Gradient Sign Methods and Jacobian-based Saliency Map, on the real-world IoT device classification dataset demonstrate that the ML-based IoT device classification is vulnerable to these attacks in both white box and black box scenarios. Moreover, these attacks are highly imperceptible in IoT networks and remain stealthy as demonstrated by applying the Kolmogorov-Smirnov goodness-of-fit test and ability to evade one-class Support Vector Machine and Isolation Forest based network intrusion detection systems.

Keywords: Adversarial machine learning · IoT · Security evaluation · Adversarial examples · Gradient based optimization · IoT device classification

1 Introduction

The Internet of Things (IoT) is bringing network connectivity to a wide array of objects ranging from refrigerators, automobiles, watches, light bulbs, and factory machinery. However, along with their wide presence and popularity, their security challenges are also increasing [1]. Thus, IoT device visibility in the network and the ability to identify illegitimate or compromised devices is essential for network administrators. The required visibility is provided by IoT device identification systems.

IoT device identification is typically done by leveraging machine learning (ML) and artificial intelligence (AI) [2]. ML/AI models are capable of profiling IoT devices based on their behaviors in the network, including their network traffic data. Despite their significant usefulness, these ML/AI models are vulnerable to adversarial attacks [3, 4],

© Springer Nature Switzerland AG 2021
H. Hacid et al. (Eds.): ICSOC 2021, LNCS 13121, pp. 800–810, 2021.
https://doi.org/10.1007/978-3-030-91431-8_57

where adversaries aim to fool these models by perturbing normal inputs, such that the manipulations are usually not detected by the system checks. Adversarial ML/AI model attacks have been extensively studied in domains such as deep learning and computer vision [5]. However, a few works consider network-based data (e.g., IoT network traffic), which is structured and time series in nature. Although these works provide some hints on the possibility of adversarial attacks on the IoT device identification systems, it is still unclear about the (detailed) possibility and detectability of adversarial attacks on the IoT device classifiers under both the white box and black box settings.

To this end, this work investigates adversarial attacks on ML/AI-based IoT device classification systems and their detectability in practical network settings. Our studies unveil the severity of security in ML-based IoT device classification systems and motivate further works towards addressing them. We summarize our major contributions in the form of the following research questions:

RQ1: (Possibility Check). Is ML/AI-based IoT device identification system vulnerable to adversarial attacks?

We study adversarial machine learning on IoT device identification based on four ML models, namely logistic regression, feed-forward neural networks, random forest, and decision tree. Our empirical results demonstrate that attacks are successful under both white box and black box attack settings even with minor perturbation (for example $\varepsilon = 0.003$) in popular attacks, namely Fast Gradient Sign Method (FGSM) [6], Basic Iterative Method (BIM) [7], and Jacobian-based Saliency Map Attack (JSMA) [8].

RQ2: (Detectability). Is the adversarial input to the ML/AI-based IoT device classification system detectable?

Our analysis and empirical results demonstrate that the adversarial inputs are highly undetectable. We tested the stealthiness of the adversarial inputs via statistical analysis under nonparametric test, i.e., KS test, and a ML-based intrusion detection system deploying unsupervised one-class SVM and Isolation Forest.

The rest of this paper is organized as follows: Sect. 2 provides background on adversarial examples and attack algorithms, Sect. 3 presents the details of our research methodology, Sect. 4 provides our experiments and results. The relevant related works are overviewed in Sect. 5, and Sect. 6 concludes the paper.

2 Background

In this section, we provide some background on adversarial examples and attack algorithms. An adversarial example is a sample of input data designed to fool a classifier and lead to misclassification. Given an input (train or test) sample x, which is a clean example, the machine learning classifier M can classify it correctly, i.e., $M(x) = y_{\text{True}}$. Szegedy, et al. [9] showed the attacker can run an optimization algorithm to carefully craft change ρ and build adversarial example $\hat{x} = x + \rho$ which is close to x according to some distance metrics, but is classified incorrectly, i.e., $M(\hat{x}) \neq y_{\text{True}}$. In this study, we consider three state-of-the-art adversarial attack models: Goodfellow, et al. [6] proposed FGSM that performs a one-step gradient update along the direction of the sign of gradient for every input in the dataset as follows:

$$X_{\text{adv}} = X + \varepsilon sign(\nabla_x J(X, Y)),$$

where ε is the constant parameter that characterizes the size of perturbation, $\nabla_x J(X, Y)$ is the gradient of loss function with respect to the input X. Kurakin, et al. [7] proposed BIM, which is the straightforward extension of the fast gradient sign method. This method applies adversarial perturbation epsilon with smaller step sizes in multiple iterations and calculates the adversarial example as follows:

$$X_0^{adv} = X, \quad X_{N+1}^{adv} = Clip_{X, \varepsilon} \left\{ X_N^{adv} + \alpha sign\left(\nabla_x J\left(X_N^{adv}, Y_{True} \right) \right) \right\},$$

where J is the loss function of model, N denotes the number of iterations, ε is the maximum permitted perturbation and α is a constant that controls the magnitude of perturbation. The Clip function ensures that the generated adversarial sample is in the range of $[X - \epsilon, X + \epsilon]$. Papernot, et al. [8] proposed JSMA with the aim of minimizing the number of features modified while causing misclassification. JSMA computes the Jacobian matrix of an input sample X, which is defined as:

$$\nabla F(X) = \frac{\partial F(X)}{\partial X} = \left[\frac{\partial F_j(X)}{\partial X_i} \right]_{i \in 1...M, j \in 1...N}$$

According to the Jacobian matrix, the adversarial saliency map is identified. The features are then selected in decreasing order of saliency values, and each is perturbed accordingly by the value of ε (Fig. 1).

3   Methodology

The first step is training an IoT device identification classifier on the original dataset to predict the IoT device class. Then, we assume the attacker has taken over an IoT device (e.g., by deploying malware) and can manipulate traffic sent by that IoT device. The attacker crafts adversarial attacks in two attack scenarios, namely white box and black box. We say the adversarial attack is successful if the adversary can cause the IoT device to be misclassified. Finally, we evaluate the stealthiness of the adversarial attacks.

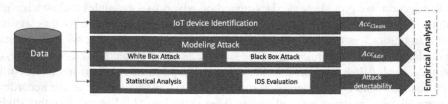

Fig. 1. Methodology

3.1 IoT Device Identification

We set up a multi-class IoT device classifier which will be tested against adversarial attacks in the next step. We use the typical models used in the literature (discussed in related works in Sect. 5), including Feed Forward Neural Network (FF-NN), Logistic Regression (LR), Random Forest (RF), and Decision Tree (DT) for the classification task.

3.2 Modeling Attack

We study the possibility of adversarial attacks on the aforementioned IoT device classification models by manipulating network traffic from an IoT device such that it should be mistaken to be another IoT device in the network. We define two attack scenarios based on attacker knowledge of the following components $\theta = (D, X, f, W)$; where D indicates the dataset $D = \{(x_i, y_i), i = 1, \ldots, n\}$ comprised of n training samples, X represents the feature space, f is the target IoT device classifier that trained in the first step, and W denotes the model parameters.

White Box Scenario. In this scenario, the attacker has complete knowledge of all components: $\theta = (D, X, f, W)$. Implementing the white box attack allows us to test the security of the classifiers in the most extreme setting. The white box attack setup commonly adopted for differentiable classifiers is such that their gradient with respect to the input data can be calculated [10]. Hence, in this scenario, we only attack differentiable classifiers including LR and FF-NN.

Black Box Scenario. In this scenario, the adversary is unaware of the dataset, feature space, target classifier and its architecture used for IoT device identification. We characterize attacker knowledge in black box scenario as $\hat{\theta} = \left(\hat{D}, \hat{X}, \hat{f}, \hat{W}\right)$. The current mainstream method of crafting black box attacks is transferring adversarial examples from a substitute model to the target model [11]. In this attack scenario, we launch white box attack on substitute models of FF-NN and LR, then transfer crafted adversaries to the admitted target models including FF-NN, LR, RF, and DT.

3.3 Attack Stealthiness

A successful stealthy adversarial attack is not perceptible in the network, thus making it difficult to detect. We propose statistical analysis and ML-based intrusion detection system to test the stealthiness of adversarial attacks. We assume the attack is imperceptible in the network if we detect at least one device which has a similar distribution of network traffic as that of the adversarially crafted network traffic. For this purpose, we propose the Two-sample Kolmogorov-Smirnov goodness of fit test (KS-test). Algorithm 1 depicts the detectability checks of the attack using the KS-test. KS-test returns the *p_value*, which is compared with a significance level of α. If *p_value* > α then the adversarial distribution is similar to the original data of at least one other device – this means that the generated adversarial examples are not perceptible in the network. The third method investigates the attack perceptibility by considering an Intrusion Detection System (IDS), which is often deployed in most IoT networks to thwart security attacks. We assume that the attack is not perceptible if adversarial examples can bypass typical ML-based IDS systems.

Algorithm 1. Attack detectability

Input: $X_{adversarial}$, $X_{original}$, significance level α

bution as adversarial data

---

for feature in f : {*list of modified features*}
  for i in devices: {*list of IoT devices in dataset*}
    for j in devices : (check for all including itself)
      $S_1 = X_{adversarial}\ [i]$
      $S_2 = X_{original}\ [j]$
      KS_Test= Ks (S_1, S_2)
      if Ks_{p_value} > significance level α
        output the perturbed feature for device
        i as an imperceptible adversarial data.

---

4 Experimental Results

We implemented our methodology in Python 3.5 on an Intel® Core i5 2.3 GHz CPU, 64 GB of RAM, and running on MAC OS. First, we present an overview of the dataset. Next, we show the performance of ML-based IoT device identification systems in a clean environment. Then we present the vulnerability of these systems to adversarial attacks. Finally, we present the stealthiness of generated adversaries in IoT networks.

4.1 Data

We used a large-scale dataset collected by Sivanathan, et al. [12] in a university campus environment over 6 months[1]. It contains network traffic data from 28 IoT devices, including cameras, lights, plugs, motion sensors, appliances, and health monitors. The authors characterized IoT traffic by features including traffic flow, flow volume, flow duration, sleep time, NTP interval, DNS interval, and domain count.

4.2 IoT Device Identification

We first evaluate the performance of ML-based IoT device classification models in a clean environment. The purpose of this is to have the baseline models trained for assessing the possibility and impact of the adversarial attacks. We trained baseline models of LR, FF-NN, DT, and RF on the training dataset. The multi-class LR is performed using a softmax regression on inputs. The FF-NN is made up of a hierarchy of 3 dense hidden layers including 768, 384, and 200 nodes. The activation function of each node is Rectified Linear Activation (ReLU) and the softmax dense is the output layer.

---

[1] https://iotanalytics.unsw.edu.au.

Table 1. Model performance on test data in clean environment

Classifier	Accuracy score (%)
Logistic Regression (LR)	92.99
Feed Forward Neural Network (FF-NN)	92.07
Random Forest (RF)	99.33
Decision Tree (DT)	99.41

Table 1 presents the classifiers' accuracy on the test dataset. The results show that all classifiers are doing well for IoT device identification problems.

4.3 RQ1: (Possibility Check) is ML/AI-Based IoT Device Identification System Vulnerable to Adversarial Attacks?

White Box Scenario. Here, we evaluate the security of IoT device identification systems explained in Sect. 3.2 against three state-of-the-art adversary threats, i.e., FGSM, BIM, and JSMA, through white box scenario. We use IBM's Adversarial Robustness Toolbox [13] for crafting adversarial examples. Accuracy score is considered as a metric to show the impact of adversarial attacks on the classifiers' performance. Lower accuracy scores imply that the classifiers are more vulnerable to attacks. As described in Sect. 2.3, while generating adversarial examples, the epsilon parameter characterises the maximum admissible perturbation that can be added to the original IoT data. Figure 2 demonstrates the vulnerability of FF-NN and LR-based IoT device classification models against white box adversarial attacks in terms of model accuracy. The accuracy score in both models drops sharply at first relative to the clean environment (i.e., baseline results). For example, a sharp fall of accuracy score at $\epsilon = 0.001$ for JSMA on FF-NN from around 92% to about 70%. This confirms the vulnerability of these models in an adversarial environment. Further increase in attack intensity (indicated by ϵ) has less impact on the performance of the models. For example, after $\epsilon = 0.02$, the change in the models' accuracy under adversarial attack is minimal.

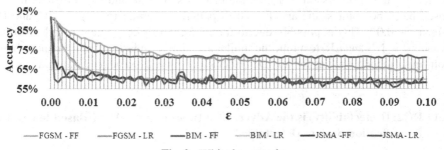

Fig. 2. White box attack

Under FGSM attack, results show that LR is more vulnerable to white box attacks compared to FF-NN since there is a greater drop in the LR model accuracy compared to FF-NN for the same level of perturbation. The possible reason for this can be the simplicity of LR model for adversarial manipulation compare to FF-NN. Under JSMA attack, both FF-NN and LR models present a severe drop in the accuracy even for the lower amount of perturbation compared to FGSM and BIM attacks. In this case, JSMA is more successful than FGSM because, by definition, it perturbs only a small number of selected features to a maximal value. Moreover, the output is relatively susceptible to these selected features than other features. In contrast, FGSM perturbs all features. Besides, FGSM requires a large perturbation and is prone to label leaking [14]. Consequently, the success rate of FGSM is low compare to JSMA.

Black Box Scenario. As described in Sect. 3.2, we generate adversarial attacks in the white box setting and use them to target black box IoT device classifiers including FF-NN, LR, DT, and RF. Figure 3 Part A and Part B show the vulnerability of targeted models against FGSM, BIM, and JSMA black-box attacks where FF-NN and LR are substitute models, respectively. In the figure, Y-axis shows the performance of the models (accuracy score), and X-axis shows the different levels of perturbations. Our results show that the performance of all models drops even with a small amount of perturbation (for example, $\epsilon = 0.001$). In Part A, under adversarial attacks with FGSM and BIM, the attack success pattern (measured in terms of the fall of accuracy with respect to ϵ) for the FF-NN target classifier is comparatively slower than the rest if the perturbation level is less than 0.02. However, DT attains a non-decreasing accuracy pattern (attack success pattern) despite an increase in the perturbation beyond $\epsilon = 0.02$, where the accuracy stays around 78% and 76% for FGSM and BIM, respectively. Similar to the white box scenario and due to the same reasonings, JSMA exhibits a strong ability in attacking FF-NN and LR target classifiers. Also, it is indicated by the more fall in the accuracy for the same level of perturbation than the cases with RT and DT.

Furthermore, FGSM and BIM attacks require larger perturbation for the same level of drop in model accuracy than JSMA. For the black box attack with the LR substitute model, we find a similar pattern of attack success for FGSM, BIM, and JSMA as in their corresponding cases with the FF-NN substitute model (see Fig. 3 Part B). Thus, for black box attack scenarios, our results indicate that a simple and computationally efficient model such as LR effectively generates adversarial attack signals/data in an IoT device identification system. For both the FF-NN substitute and LR substitute model-based black box attack, the attack success pattern is non-decreasing for RF and DT after $\epsilon > 0.02$. This is possibly due to the inability of our gradient-based substitute models (FF_NN and LR) to mimic the similar decision boundaries of non-gradient-based non-linear models such as RF and DT under highly perturbed adversarial samples.

4.4   RQ2: (Detectability) is the Adversarial Input to the ML/AI-Based IoT Device Identification System Detectable?

Statistical Test. As described in Sect. 3.3, a stealthy adversarial attack is not perceptible in the network. We measure the attack perceptibility through KS goodness-of-fit

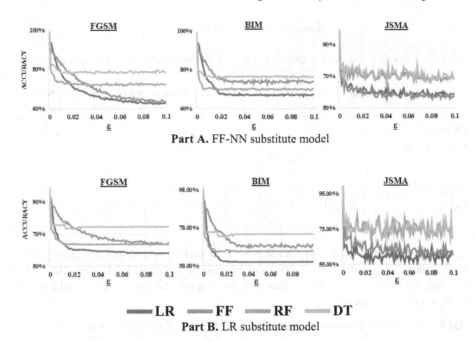

Part A. FF-NN substitute model

$$\blacksquare LR \quad \blacksquare FF \quad \blacksquare RF \quad \blacksquare DT$$

Part B. LR substitute model

Fig. 3. Black box attack

test analysis to compare the distribution similarity between original and adversarial data/examples. To define the KS test statistic, first we specify H_0 hypothesis "H_0: *both adversarial and original samples come from the same distribution*". The KS test returns the P-values of an original signal vs an adversarial one. We set the significance level α to 0.05, which is the most commonly used value [15]. Moreover, Fisher, the father of modern statistics, recommended a significance level of 0.05 as a standard level [16]. We compare P-values to the significance level. Therefore, high confidence, P-value > 0.05, shows that adversarial examples are drawn from the same distribution as the original data. We evaluated the attack perceptibility of all crafted adversaries in this research, and statistical results under the KS test show that all generated attacks are imperceptible in the network for $\epsilon \leq 0.1$. We present our result with $\epsilon = 0.1$ and five devices as an example in Table 2. The table presents KS statistic theory results for black box FGSM attack against LR classifier where the substitute model is FF classifier. The rows show the predicted class label by the LR classifier in FGSM adversarial setting. Columns list all perturbed features in this study. The number of devices that passed the H_0 hypothesis in KS statistical theory is depicted in each cell. Results reveal that for all predicted devices in the adversarial setting, we can find at least one device in a clean environment that has similar distribution for the corresponding perturbed feature. This implies that the adversarial sample is not perceptible in the IoT network with the KS test.

ML-Based Intrusion Detection System. In our experiment, we implemented ML-based IDS systems based on two different anomaly detection models, namely one-class SVM, and isolation forest. Our results are presented in Table 3 and 4. These tables show

Table 2. KS statistical test results

e = 0.1	Number of devices in clean environment that have same distribution as adversarial device					
	Domain count	Sleep time	Flow volume	Flow duration	DNS interval	NTP interval
Device 1	3	6	2	2	4	3
Device 2	5	5	4	3	2	9
Device 3	2	2	3	2	3	5
Device 4	4	7	3	3	2	23
Device 5	3	2	2	2	2	8

the confusion matrix for one-class SVM, and Isolation Forest models, respectively, under the test data. The results show a True positive rate of 8% and 25% for one-class SVM and Isolation Forest, respectively. This confirms the effectiveness of adversarial attacks to bypass the IDS systems.

Table 3. Confusion Matrix for Isolation Forest

Isolation Forest		Predicted class	
		Normal	Attack
Actual class	Normal	TN = 18248	FP = 1777
	Attack	FN = 1503	TP = 496

Table 4. Confusion Matrix for One Class SVM

One class SVM		Predicted class	
		Normal	Attack
Actual class	Normal	TN = 18307	FP = 1718
	Attack	FN = 1824	TP = 175

5 Related Works

In this section, we summarize the relevant related work to machine-learning-based IoT device classification systems. Sivanathan et al. [12] proposed a multi-stage classification framework to classify IoT devices in the network environment. Miettinen, et al. [17] presented IoT SENTINEL, a ML-based system for automatically identifying IoT devices and pinpoint vulnerable devices to limit their communications in a network accordingly. In another work, Long short-term memory with convolutional neural network (LSTM-CNN) cascade models was proposed by Bai, et al. [18] to identify the semantic type of the device with only small training dataset. Siby, et al. [19] proposed the IoT scanner, a system to monitor IoT environment and actively classify streaming IP cameras from non-camera devices. A neural network based approach is proposed by Das, et al. [20] to identify 30 low power IoT devices. In another study, Acar, et al. [21] introduced a novel machine learning based privacy attack in smart home environment for identifying IoT devices.

6 Conclusions

In this paper, we evaluated the possibility of generating adversarial attacks for IoT device identification under the white-box and black-box attack scenarios. We further studied the attack stealthiness by KS statistical test analysis, and IDS system evaluation. Our results demonstrated that adversarial examples are strongly possible, and they lead to the degradation of performance of IoT device identification systems. In addition, these attacks are highly imperceptible in the network for various tests, including statistical analyses. Our results clearly presented the severity of these attacks in IoT device identification systems and motivate further studies to tackle the concerns. Thus, robustness techniques to improve the attack resilience against the adversarial attacks for IoT device identification systems are left as our future work.

References

1. Al-Garadi, M.A., Mohamed, A., Al-Ali, A.K., Du, X., Ali, I., Guizani, M.: A survey of machine and deep learning methods for internet of things (IoT) security. IEEE Commun. Surv. Tutor. **22**(3), 1646–1685 (2020)
2. Cvitić, I., Peraković, D., Periša, M., Gupta, B.: Ensemble machine learning approach for classification of IoT devices in smart home. Int. J. Mach. Learn. Cybern. **12**, 1–24 (2021)
3. Akhtar, N., Mian, A.: Threat of adversarial attacks on deep learning in computer vision: a survey. IEEE Access **6**, 14410 (2018)
4. Yuan, X., He, P., Zhu, Q., Li, X.: Adversarial examples: attacks and defenses for deep learning. IEEE Trans. Neural Netw. Learn. Syst. 30, 2805 (2019)
5. Ren, K., Zheng, T., Qin, Z., Liu, X.: Adversarial attacks and defenses in deep learning. Engineering **6**(3), 346–360 (2020)
6. Goodfellow, I.J., Shlens, J., Szegedy, C.: Explaining and harnessing adversarial examples (2014). In: ICLR 2015 (2014)
7. Kurakin, A., Goodfellow, I., Bengio, S.: Adversarial examples in the physical world (2016)
8. Papernot, N., McDaniel, P., Jha, S., Fredrikson, M., Celik, Z.B., Swami, A.: The limitations of deep learning in adversarial settings. In: IEEE European Symposium on Security and Privacy (EuroS&P), 2016, pp. 372–387. IEEE (2016)
9. Szegedy, C. et al.: Intriguing properties of neural networks. arXiv preprint (2013)
10. Pei, K., Cao, Y., Yang, J., Jana, S.: Deepxplore: automated whitebox testing of deep learning systems. In: Proceedings of the 26th Symposium on Operating Systems Principles, pp. 1–18 (2017)
11. Guo, S., Zhao, J., Li, X., Duan, J., Mu, D., Jing, X.: A black-box attack method against machine-learning-based anomaly network flow detection models. Secur. Commun. Netw. **2021**, 1 (2021)
12. Sivanathan, A., et al.: Classifying IoT devices in smart environments using network traffic characteristics. IEEE Trans. Mob. Comput. (2018)
13. Nicolae, M.-I. et al.: Adversarial robustness toolbox v1.0.0. arXiv preprint arXiv:1807.01069 (2018)
14. Zhang, J., Li, C.: Adversarial examples: Opportunities and challenges. IEEE Trans. Neural Netw. Learn. Syst. **31**(7), 2578–2593 (2019)
15. Chen, H., Fu, C., Zhao, J., Koushanfar, F.: DeepInspect: a black-box Trojan detection and mitigation framework for deep neural networks. In: IJCAI, pp. 4658–4664 (2019)
16. Fisher, R.: Statistical methods and scientific induction. J. Roy. Stat. Soc.: Ser. B (Methodol.) **17**(1), 69–78 (1955)

17. Miettinen, M., Marchal, S., Hafeez, I., Asokan, N., Sadeghi, A.-R., Tarkoma, S.: IoT Sentinel: automated device-type identification for security enforcement in IoT. In: 2017 IEEE 37th International Conference on Distributed Computing Systems (ICDCS), pp. 2177–2184. IEEE (2017)
18. Bai, L., Yao, L., Kanhere, S.S., Wang, X., Yang, Z.: Automatic device classification from network traffic streams of Internet of Things. In: Proceedings-Conference on Local Computer Networks, LCN (2019)
19. Siby, S., Maiti, R.R., Tippenhauer, N.: Iotscanner: detecting and classifying privacy threats in IoT neighborhoods. In: ACM Workshop (2017)
20. Das, R., Gadre, A., Zhang, S., Kumar, S., Moura, J.M.: A deep learning approach to IoT authentication. In: 2018 IEEE International Conference on Communications (ICC), pp. 1–6. IEEE (2018)
21. Acar, A., et al.: Peek-a-Boo: i see your smart home activities, even encrypted!. In: Proceedings of the 13th ACM Conference on Security and Privacy in Wireless and Mobile Networks, pp. 207–218 (2020)

DeepPatterns: Predicting Mobile Apps Usage from Spatio-Temporal and Contextual Features

Basem Suleiman[1]([envelope]) [iD], Kevin Lu[1], Hong Wa Chan[1],
and Muhammad Johan Alibasa[2] [iD]

[1] School of Computer Science, University of Sydney, Sydney, Australia
basem.suleiman@sydney.edu.au, {kelu5219,hcha2938}@uni.sydney.edu.au
[2] School of Computing, Telkom University, Bandung, Indonesia
alibasa@telkomuniversity.ac.id

Abstract. As mobile phones become inseparable from daily activities and lifestyles, users generate a large amount of app usage data. Such data contain patterns that could be useful for accurate mobile application usage prediction which can be used to improve user experience and the performance of smartphones. In this paper, we propose novel enhancements to the state-of-the-art deep learning model, named DeepPatterns model, to improve the performance of the mobile app usage prediction. Our proposed model enhances the contextual awareness of the prediction by adding the Point-of-Interest (PoI) distribution and weather features. Furthermore, we extend the model training by including weekend mobile apps usage data. Finally, we implement a different partitioning method in the training process to tackle the limitations of our smaller dataset size. Our experimental results show that the enhanced model outperformed the state-of-the-art model in the recall, precision, f1-score, and AUC measures ranging from 7% to 11% despite having less than one-tenth of the original dataset.

Keywords: Mobile apps · Usage patterns · Spatio-temporal · Contextual information · Deep learning

1 Introduction

Smart cities utilise sensors to obtain information from the environment and people. In our society nowadays, most people use smartphones that can be applied as sensors since smartphones collect various information such as location, application usage, and others.

These data can be used to predict the next application that will be opened by users. The next application prediction is useful as it can be applied to several smart services, such as recommendation systems, targeted advertising and virtual assistant.

Next-app prediction is a challenging task for two major reasons. Firstly, it is not only a classification problem but also a time-series prediction. App usage

© Springer Nature Switzerland AG 2021
H. Hacid et al. (Eds.): ICSOC 2021, LNCS 13121, pp. 811–818, 2021.
https://doi.org/10.1007/978-3-030-91431-8_58

is highly correlated to the spatial-temporal context and is heavily influenced by both short-term and long-term usage history. This complex relationship could not be well represented by traditional models such as naive Bayes or the hidden Markov model. Secondly, every person has a unique app usage pattern due to reasons such as personal interest, occupation, demographics, and others. A prediction model that predicts well on one user may not predict well on another user. Meanwhile, building a separate model for each user is not computationally effective. These challenges remain until researchers turned to deep learning models which provide a promising framework to solve them.

Currently, DeepApp [10] is the state-of-the-art model in next app prediction. It is a supervised model that applied multi-task learning to learn the relationship among time, location, usage, and app explicitly. In this study, we extend the DeepApp model and propose several novel enhancements to further improve its prediction results. We conduct thorough experiments on a real-world dataset of and found that most of the proposed enhancements can improve performance metrics. The goals of this study are to evaluate the effect of the proposed enhancements on the model's performance and to make significant improvements to the baseline model, the DeepApp [10], with the constraint of smaller dataset size. Both goals contribute to making a better and more efficient next-app prediction model which would improve user experiences. The contributions of our work is threefold:

- We propose novel enhancements to the state-of-the-art deep learning model that improves the prediction of mobile apps usage based on Spatio-temporal and contextual features.
- We develop an enhanced deep learning model, called DeepPatterns, for predicting mobile apps usage patterns.
- We conduct thorough experiments and ablation study to evaluate the effect of our proposed DeepPatterns model and demonstrate how it outperforms the state-of-the-art mobile app usage prediction.

2   Related Work

In the past decades, many studies focused on modelling the relationship between app usage and spatial-temporal context using different techniques so the model could predict the next apps to be used by a user. Qiao et al. [5] utilised a Hidden Markov Model, Wang et al. [9] designed a novel hierarchical Dirichlet process mixture model, Chen et al. [3] built a heterogeneous graph embedding algorithm, Lv et al. [4] designed a rating framework that extracts the semantic information from the spatial data, and Tu et al. [8] used complementing data to make a prediction (posts on social networking websites). Other studies such as Zhao et al. [12], Sarker and Salah [6], Shen et al. [7] and Xia et al. [10] used deep learning methods such as RNN, AppUsage2Vec, DeepApp that increased the model complexity and achieved improved performance. These approaches mainly used temporal, app usage, and location data as input. As in location data, there is a research branch called trajectory data. It focuses on identifying mobility pattern which is also correlated to the app usage behaviour.

Trajectory data could be passively collected via GPS and cellular tower connection when individuals connect their mobile devices to the internet. The immense amount of location data enabled big data analytic of mobility patterns on both individual and population-level [2] which shows that a unique user can be identified by as few as 4 spatial-temporal data points [1].

Additionally, the cellular towers hand-off feature, whereby a user connects to the nearest base station, causes the phenomenon of oscillation. The frequency of oscillation between towers can infer the spatial closeness between the cellular tower [4]. The study discovered individual movement patterns from cell-id trajectories without explicit location information but using their novel sequential pattern mining algorithm. Besides, Yu et al. [11] also showed in their study that PoI is correlated with app usage patterns.

Several of the studies were conducted by using the same dataset in our study. Wang, et al. [9] applied a Bayesian mixture model to predict future app usage of users. It leverages spatial and temporal aspects of the data to aid in the prediction of users that have made minimal requests. Spatially, the PoI distribution of each cellular tower provided context to answer why the user is using the app. Using PoI distribution of each cellular tower is a common theme amongst papers on the same dataset as it is the only source of context whereby GPS offers none. DeepApp model in [10] also stated in the paper that using PoI distribution could be a future work to experiment with.

3   Methodology

Our goal is to predict a set of apps that a user will use in the next time interval given the historical usage and any additional features such as location and weather conditions. Each time interval is 30-min long. We adapt the problem definition in [10] as follows. A user opened WhatsApp and Instagram between 11:00–11:30, denoted as S_1. In the next 30-min interval, during 11:30–12:00, the user opened YouTube and Amazon, denoted as S_2. Subsequently, during 12:00–12:30, user opened WeChat, denoted as S_3. The objective is to predict what apps would be opened by the user in the next 30 min, denoted by S_4.

3.1   Dataset

The study is evaluated using the Tsinghua App Usage Dataset [11] which is procured from China Telecom. It is a collection of user app usage data in a major city in China between 20 and 26 April 2016. The dataset used in this study is a subset of the original dataset mined by China Telecom. It contains 4.2 million records from 871 users and 9,800 base stations. Each record is a network request that contains a timestamp, anonymised user id, mobile application id, category of the mobile application and cellular tower id.

We have 871 users in our dataset with average app usage is 4,789. The usage range is wide from the highest usage request of 1,098,748 to a minimum of 4. For application, it has 1,696 apps, average usage of an app is 2,459, the usage range is also wide, from maximum usage request of 898,308 to minimum of 1. From location wise, we have 6,739 base stations, the mean request from a base station is 4,956 with a maximum of 9,849 and a minimum of 0. From the descriptive statistics, we observed a high variance dataset as some users, applications, and locations have significantly higher observations than others.

3.2 DeepPatterns: A Spatio-Temporal and Contextual-Based Prediction of User's Mobile App Usage

Our proposed enhancements to this problem are: enriching the input, using a different training method, and removing noises. First, we suggest adding PoI distribution as a feature. It is a distribution of the categories of the PoIs under the coverage of a base station. There are 18 categories in total. PoI distribution is a better representation of the spatial information as compared to a discrete base station ID. We also suggest including weather information as an additional feature. Weather information could play a role in app usage behaviour. For instance, users will have different behaviours in sunny vs. rainy days. Since the dataset only contains 7 d' data, seasonality differences could not be analysed. However, between 20 and 27 April 2016, there were few showers during the day which might change user behaviour. This enables us to study the effect of adding weather to the input feature. So, we use all available data for training and testing.

Secondly, we propose to train the model with a different approach to combat the limited amount of data. The DeepApp [10] splits the dataset into training, validation, and test set by day, it used the first 3 d (20, 21, and 22 April 2016) for the training set, the fourth day (24 April 2016) as the validation set and the last day (25 April 2016) as the test set. In our approach, we split the results by user and we use 80% user to train, 10% for validation, and the remaining 10% for testing. The rationale is that there are individuals that have similar behaviours such that the model is better at predicting the app usage of those users. Thirdly, we proposed to remove oscillation from the dataset. In data exploration, we observed a significant amount of oscillation. We believe that removing oscillation can remove the unwanted noise in spatial information, hence improve accuracy.

DeepPatterns: Model Architecture. Our spatio-temporal and contextual-aware prediction model is adapted from the DeepApp [10], and shown in Fig. 1. It consists of three modules. The *Embedding Module* receives the input features and embeds each feature into a dense vector of different dimensions. The embedded vectors are then concatenated into a single vector before passing it to the DeepApp Module. In the *DeepApp Module*, there will be a single layer RNN unit, which can be substituted with any other recurrent neural networks such as GRU and LSTM. The last hidden state would be passed into the *Prediction Module*, which consists of a linear layer to match the expected output dimension and the log-softmax function to calculate the probability of each app being used in the next time interval.

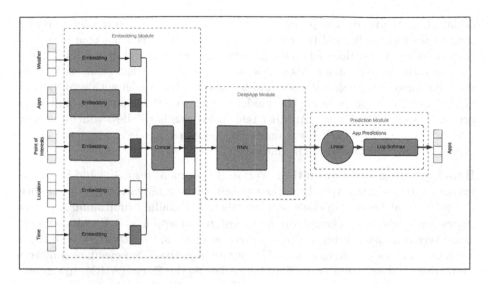

Fig. 1. DeepPatterns: proposed model enhancements

Compared to the original DeepApp model [10], there are two significant changes in our DeepPatterns model. Firstly, location prediction and user prediction were removed from the Prediction Module and only the app prediction is kept. Thus, the loss function only focuses on the binary cross-entropy loss from app prediction. Secondly, with additional features are passed as inputs, the Embedding Module concatenates five dense vectors before passing it to the next module.

Two different partitioning methods are adopted for model training. Therefore, we introduce two different training modes. The implementation of the model can be trained and evaluated in two modes with different settings, defined by the parameter called 'split_mode'. This parameter determines how the training, validation, and test sets are partitioned and imputed into the model. The first mode, the 'temporal' mode, is the one implemented in the original DeepApp implementation [10]. In this setting, each user's pre-processed data is first sorted by date. Subsequently, if only the 5 working days are included in the pre-processed data, the first 3 d serve as the training set, and the remaining 2 d serve as validation and test set. However, if the weekend days are included, our implementation will implicitly use the first 3 weekdays and 1 weekend day as the training set, 1 weekday as the validation set, and the remaining weekday and weekend day as the test set.

The second setting, the 'user' mode, can be selected by setting the 'split_mode' parameter as 'user'. This additional mode is added so that the model can be trained using a subset of users and evaluated and validated on the remaining ones. Namely, it allows the model to be trained on some users' entire data and predicts unseen users' usage data. When set to the 'user' mode, the model implicitly uses all 7 d of data from the users. The proportions of users being assigned to each partition is defined by an additional parameter 'split_ratio' which is a list containing the corresponding proportion of data assigned to the training, validation, and test sets.

The main motivation for this second mode is the assumption that users share some common app usage patterns, and by training the model with a proportion of the users, it is possible for the model to uncover those patterns and make predictions on unseen users. Another reason for this is to allow control on how much data is used for each partition as the 'temporal' mode is restricted by the number of days contained in the dataset.

Benchmarking and Evaluation. Various experiment results would be benchmarked with the DeepApp. Experiments will include all variations of enhancements. Several baseline models will be created, including multinomial logistic regression, multi-layer perceptron, and most recent app usage. Results comparisons were conducted using various evaluation metrics, to show that deep learning recurrent models are more suitable for the objective. Two evaluation metrics were adopted from [10]: Recall@5 and Area Under the Curve (AUC), to evaluate the models. Recall@5, takes the top 5 predictions with the highest probability of being used in the next time interval and compares them with the ground truth. Moreover, Precision@5 and f1@5 are included to take both false positives and false negatives into account.

4   Results

To achieve the best experiment results, we trained our DeepPatterns model with the 'user' mode for the partitioning of our data in the training process. The split proportions were 80–10-10. We used an Adam optimiser and trained for 10 epochs to obtain the model with the best validation metrics. The learning rate is initially set at $1e^{-4}$ and is updated by a scheduler when the loss reaches a plateau. The scheduler updates the learning rate by multiplying the latter with a learning rate decay factor which is set to 0.1 in our optimal setting. Similarly, to the original DeepApp, a dropout layer with a rate of 0.5 is implemented between the embedding layer and extraction modules to prevent overfitting. The optimal model removes the two other tasks (location prediction and user prediction) in the predicting module, which means that the model optimises with the loss of the main app prediction task only. In the Embedding Module where the model learns the best embedding of input features, the embedding size for PoI distribution, base ID, time interval, and app usage are 4, 256, 16, and 512 respectively.

As shown in Table 1, our DeepPatterns model outperforms the original model in all evaluation metrics with improvements ranging from 7% to 11%. The modifications that seem to contribute the most to this increase in performance are the integration of the weekend and the addition of the 'user' mode. These two enhancements allow the model to be trained on more data which helps the latter better capture the usage patterns from different users. The model when set to 'user' mode seems to adapt and predict better on a smaller and scarce dataset. Rather being trained on partial data from all users and predict those same users'

Table 1. Results from different modes that include weekend data

Model	Recall@5	Precision@5	F1-Score@5	AUC
DeepApp model	0.5946	0.5489	0.5580	0.8191
Multinomial logistic regression	0.3172	0.0960	0.1416	0.4342
Multi-layer perceptron	0.2181	0.0579	0.0887	0.4691
Naïve bayes	0.6641	0.6132	0.6329	0.4453
Our DeepPatterns model	0.7050	0.6614	0.6712	0.8925

remaining temporal splits, the model learns from the complete data from some users and predict the remaining unseen users.

Finally, the additional features, PoI and weather data, do not contribute significantly to performance improvements. However, when these two additional features are added, increases in most metrics can be observed in most variants which show that they hypothetically could have a more significant influence on a larger and less scarce dataset.

5   Discussion

Adding related features, using more data to train and training with a different train-test split could significantly improve the performance metrics. The increments in precision score and recall score show that the enhanced model makes fewer false positive and false negative predictions. This is also reflected by an improved F1-score that indicates a balance of precision and recall. In context, the model is less likely to predict apps that would not be used (precision) and are less likely to miss apps that would be actually used (recall). Besides, although the enhancement and experiment results are specific to the DeepApp [10], most of the enhancements focus on improving the input features and training approach. The underlying principles of the enhancement should be invariant to different models, hence these enhancements might be transferable to other studies that are related to app usage prediction.

6   Conclusion

We proposed and elaborated on how we enhanced the spatio-temporal awareness of the model DeepApp by integrating additional contextual information namely PoI distribution of the location and the weather information. We also found that integrating the weekend data, which was excluded in the original DeepApp study, and using a different data partitioning method in the training process could help our model achieve better training efficiency and similar performance to the original model with only a fraction of the original dataset. Through extensive experiments, our enhanced DeepPatterns model demonstrated significant improvements in efficiency and performance compared to the original DeepApp model when trained on smaller dataset size. In the future, we plan to compare the performances of both original and modified models on the larger original dataset, if made accessible, to get a more concrete comparison between our model and the original one. Furthermore, it would be interesting to study how our model would perform on other app usage datasets.

Acknowledgment. We would like to thank Hin Lok, Liu and Kevin Lam for helping out in data analysis needed for this work.

References

1. Bao, X., Gong, N.Z., Hu, B., Shen, Y., Jin, H.: Connect the dots by understanding user status and transitions. In: Proceedings of the 2014 ACM International Joint Conference on Pervasive and Ubiquitous Computing, pp. 361–366 (2014)
2. Chen, C., Ma, J., Susilo, Y., Liu, Y., Wang, M.: The promises of big data and small data for travel behavior (aka human mobility) analysis. Transp. Res. Part C Emerg. Technol. **68**, 285–299 (2016)
3. Chen, X., Wang, Y., He, J., Pan, S., Li, Y., Zhang, P.: Cap: context-aware app usage prediction with heterogeneous graph embedding. Proc. ACM Interact. Mob. Wearable Ubiquit. Technol. **3**(1), 1–25 (2019)
4. Lv, M., Chen, L., Chen, T., Zeng, D., Cao, B.: Discovering individual movement patterns from cell-id trajectory data by exploiting handoff features. Inf. Sci. **474**, 18–32 (2019)
5. Qiao, Y., Zhao, X., Yang, J., Liu, J.: Mobile big-data-driven rating framework: measuring the relationship between human mobility and app usage behavior. IEEE Netw. **30**(3), 14–21 (2016)
6. Sarker, I.H., Salah, K.: Appspred: predicting context-aware smartphone apps using random forest learning. Internet Things **8**, 100106 (2019)
7. Shen, Z., Yang, K., Du, W., Zhao, X., Zou, J.: Deepapp: a deep reinforcement learning framework for mobile application usage prediction. In: Proceedings of the 17th Conference on Embedded Networked Sensor Systems, pp. 153–165 (2019)
8. Tu, Z., Li, Y., Hui, P., Su, L., Jin, D.: Personalized mobile app recommendation by learning user's interest from social media. IEEE Trans. Mob. Comput. **19**(11), 2670–2683 (2019)
9. Wang, H., Li, Y., Zeng, S., Wang, G., Zhang, P., Hui, P., Jin, D.: Modeling spatio-temporal app usage for a large user population. Proc. ACM Interact. Mob. Wearable Ubiquit. Technol. **3**(1), 1–23 (2019)
10. Xia, T., et al.: Deepapp: predicting personalized smartphone app usage via context-aware multi-task learning. ACM Trans. Intell. Syst. Technol. (TIST) **11**(6), 1–12 (2020)
11. Yu, D., Li, Y., Xu, F., Zhang, P., Kostakos, V.: Smartphone app usage prediction using points of interest. Proc. ACM Interact. Mob. Wearable Ubiquit. Technol. **1**(4), 1–21 (2018)
12. Zhao, S., et al.: Appusage2vec: modeling smartphone app usage for prediction. In: IEEE 35th International Conference on Data Engineering (ICDE), pp. 1322–1333. IEEE (2019)

Microservices and APIs

KOSMOS: Vertical and Horizontal Resource Autoscaling for Kubernetes

Luciano Baresi, Davide Yi Xian Hu, Giovanni Quattrocchi(✉),
and Luca Terracciano

Dipartimento di Elettronica, Informazione e Bioingegneria Politecnico di Milano,
Milan, Italy
{luciano.baresi,davide.hu,giovanni.quattrocchi,
luca.terracciano}@polimi.it

Abstract. Cloud applications are increasingly executed onto lightweight containers that can be efficiently managed to cope with highly varying and unpredictable workloads. Kubernetes, the most popular container orchestrator, provides means to automatically scale containerized applications to keep their response time under control. Kubernetes provisions resources using two main components: i) Horizontal Pod Autoscaler (HPA), which controls the amount of containers running for an application, and ii) Vertical Pod Autoscaler (VPA), which oversees the resource allocation of existing containers. These two components have several limitations: they must control different metrics, they use simple threshold-based rules, and the reconfiguration of existing containers requires stopping and restarting them.

To overcome these limitations this paper presents *KOSMOS*, a novel autoscaling solution for Kubernetes. Containers are individually controlled by control-theoretical planners that manage container resources on-the-fly (vertical scaling). A dedicated component is in charge of handling resource contention scenarios among containers deployed in the same node (a physical or virtual machine). Finally, at the cluster-level a heuristic-based controller is in charge of the horizontal scaling of each application.

Keywords: Kubernetes · Containers · Resource provisioning · Control theory

1 Introduction

Containerization is a lightweight virtualization technique that allows operating system (OS) processes to be run and managed independently of one another [9]. Containers are built using different runtime environments (e.g., Docker[1]) that

---

[1] https://docker.com.

This work has been partially supported by the SISMA national research project, which has been funded by the MIUR under the PRIN 2017 program (Contract 201752ENYB) and by the European Commission grant no. 825480 (H2020), SODALITE.

© Springer Nature Switzerland AG 2021
H. Hacid et al. (Eds.): ICSOC 2021, LNCS 13121, pp. 821–829, 2021.
https://doi.org/10.1007/978-3-030-91431-8_59

exploit specific OS features (e.g., namespaces, control groups) to guarantee isolated execution and management. Applications that are executed in containers usually require multiple replicas (i.e., instances of the same container) deployed onto multiple machines to serve intense workloads that cannot be handled by a single executor. These applications are often constrained by requirements on their response time, usually included in Service Level Agreements (SLA). To avoid SLA violations that lead to economic fines and customer dissatisfaction, container resources must be allocated dynamically and precisely so that external factors, such as a highly varying workload and the unstable performance of the underlying cloud infrastructure, do not affect the user-perceived response time.

Since containers live within a single OS, *container orchestrators* are required to properly manage distributed containers running on different host nodes. Kubernetes[2] is by far the most popular container orchestrator [6] and it is also offered as-a-service by all the most important cloud providers. Kubernetes uses an abstraction called *pod*, a bundle composed of a main container and some related components (e.g., volumes, monitoring agents) that is deployed as a single unit[3]. Kubernetes provides two components dedicated to resource allocation: Horizontal Pod Autoscaler (HPA) [3] to scale containers *horizontally* and Vertical Pod Autoscaler(VPA) [5] to scale them *vertically*. *Horizontal scaling* aims to dynamically increase or decrease the number of container replicas that execute a given application; *vertical scaling* dynamically increases or reduces the amount of CPU power and/or memory allocated to a single instance of a container.

Kubernetes autoscaling components are affected by at least three main issues. First, HPA and VPA cannot work together on the same input metric (e.g., the response time). This limitation derives from the fact that the two components are not designed to cooperate, and by working on the same metric they could interfere with one another. Second, VPA does not provide *in-place* vertical scaling but it reconfigures pods in three, less efficient, steps: i) it computes the new resource allocation, ii) it terminates the old containers, iii) it recreates the containers with the new resource allocation. Moreover, VPA can only compute the same reconfiguration for all the running replicas of a container. This means that all the replicas of a pod always have the same amount of resources allocated, no matter their different execution environments (e.g., different types of VMs). Third, they rely on simple rules (e.g., threshold-based heuristics) which could result in sub-optimal performance in non-trivial scenarios.

Few works attempted to overcome the aforementioned limitations. For example, Baresi et al. [8] and Rattihalli et al. [11] present solutions to better exploit vertical scaling in Kubernetes. To do that they update container resources by using directly the underlying Docker runtime (recently deprecated by the Kubernetes team [2]) bypassing the Kubernetes API. Other approaches highlight the potential of combining both horizontal and vertical scaling [7]. Kwan et al. [10]

---

[2] https://kubernetes.io.

[3] In some edge cases a pod can also contain multiple "main" containers. Our solution supports this case, but for simplicity are not considering herein. In the rest of the paper we will use word "container" to refer to the main container of a pod.

state that, when using a combined approach, they obtained a speedup of 49% with respect to using only Kubernetes HPA, but their approach is not integrated with Kubernetes.

This paper presents *KOSMOS*, a comprehensive autoscaling system for Kubernetes. *KOSMOS* is built on top of the API of Kubernetes, it can control multiple concurrent applications simultaneously and it exploits a multi-level control system. At the application level it provides horizontal scaling using a heuristic, at the container level it carries out in-place vertical scaling using control-theoretical planners, and at the node level a dedicated component oversees resource contention among containers that share the same host machine. Moreover, it also provides a resource-aware load balancing system to properly distribute the workload to a set of independently managed container replicas, and a lightweight monitoring mechanism to efficiently feed the controllers with proper metrics. To the best of our knowledge, *KOSMOS* is the first approach that combines three key characteristics: horizontal scaling of containers, in-place vertical scaling of containers, and a seamless integration with the Kubernetes API.

The rest of the paper is organized as follows. Section 2 provides an overview of *KOSMOS*. Section 3 explains the control algorithms employed by our solution. Section 4 surveys some important related work, and Sect. 5 concludes the paper.

2   KOSMOS

To overcome the limitations of state-of-the-art autoscaling systems and to fully exploit the potential of containerization technology, *KOSMOS*[4] was built to provide the following key features.

Kubernetes Integration. Kubernetes is one of the key technology of the modern cloud [6]. *KOSMOS* is an extension of Kubernetes and its additional components are all created using the Kubernetes API.

Fast and Fine-grained Control. Containers unlock the possibility of fast and fine-grained allocation of resources. Containers can be booted in seconds and re-configured in hundreds of milliseconds [12]. Containerization also provides the means to precisely allocate resources to each process (bytes of memory and fractions of cores). *KOSMOS* fully exploits this technology by employing lightweight control-theoretical planners and heuristics that are able to compute precise allocations in constant time for each container. The coordination among the controllers is also lightweight thanks to *KOSMOS*'s multi-level design.

Bi-directional Autoscaling. Unlike VMs that can usually be only scaled horizontally (in public clouds), users can scale containers both horizontally and vertically. Since no existing system provides the two types of scalability in Kubernetes, *KOSMOS* combines horizontal and vertical scaling. Vertical scalability is used to quickly reconfigure existing containers, horizontal scaling is employed only when the efficiency of the system decreases.

---

[4] The source of *KOSMOS* is available at https://github.com/deib-polimi/kosmos.

In-place, Replica-independent Vertical Scaling. In Kubernetes, pods are considered an immutable resource, thus the only way to reconfigure them is to terminate and restart them with a new setting. *KOSMOS* does not require, unlike Kubernetes VPA, to restart containers to actuate a vertical scaling action. To do that, *KOSMOS* exploits an update of Kubernetes (technically, a Kubernetes Enhancement Proposal) that is currently in advanced approval state [1] that allows container resources to be modified at runtime (through a new *patch* endpoint). Moreover, while VPA actions require all the replicas to be reconfigured with the same amount of resources, *KOSMOS* computes a different optimized allocation for each replica.

Resource-Aware Load Balancing. In *KOSMOS* multiple replicas of a container may have different resource allocations, thus policies that evenly distribute the traffic (e.g., the ones adopted in Kubernetes) could be extremely inefficient. Instead, *KOSMOS* adopts a resource-aware heuristic that works in conjunction with vertical and horizontal scaling.

Multiple Applications. Many autoscaling systems focus on single applications, *KOSMOS* is designed to control multiple applications simultaneously. A controller, one for each node, is dedicated to manage resource contention scenarios.

Low Latency Container Monitoring. Since *KOSMOS* aims to fully exploit the speed of containers, the employed monitoring mechanism must not introduce any significant delay. *KOSMOS* provides a per-replica monitoring system of application-level metrics that uses a negligible amount of resources (less than 50 millicores according to our measurements) and that feeds all the control components.

2.1   Architecture

The architecture of *KOSMOS* is an extension of Kubernetes and its components extend some of the key entities of the platform. A Kubernetes cluster is composed of a centralized master node dedicated to the orchestration of a set of distributed worker nodes (i.e., physical or virtual machines). A Kubernetes agent called *Kubelet* is deployed onto each worker node and it used to communicate with the master node.

The master node exposes a so called *API Server* through which Kubernetes *Resources* can be created, read, updated and deleted. Examples of built-in Kubernetes Resources are *pods*, *services* and *nodes*. As mentioned before, a *pod* is a container with some related components that are always deployed as a single unit, a *service* is a logical set of pods (e.g., a set of container replicas) that are exposed with a single interface (e.g., a *loadbalancer*), and a *node* is the representation of a worker node. Kubernetes also supports so-called *Custom Resources* that allow users to enrich the *API Server* with new endpoints dedicated to user-defined types of entities. Kubernetes *Controllers* are components that manage a set of resources using a control loop. Examples of controllers are Kubernetes HPA and VPA.

Figure 1 shows the architecture of *KOSMOS*, the new components are depicted in white, while non-white components are built-in ones. *KOSMOS* defines the following Custom Resources: i) *ServiceLevelAgreement* ii) *PodScale* iii) *PodMetrics*, and iv) *ServiceMetrics*.

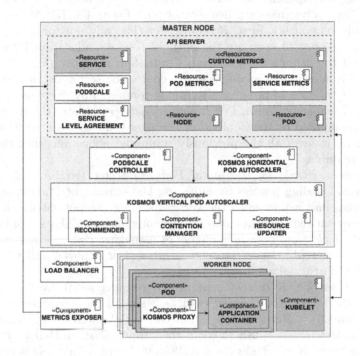

Fig. 1. Architecture of *KOSMOS*.

Resources of type *ServiceLevelAgreement* are defined by users to set a constraint on the response time for a given Kubernetes service. This resource also allows to set the default resource allocation allocated at startup time, the minimum and maximum allocation of CPU cores and memory for each container instance of the service (for vertical scalability), and minimum and maximum number of replicas as bounds for horizontal scaling.

When a resource *ServiceLevelAgreement* is created for a service, an instance of resource *PodScale* is created for each pod that belongs to that service. This kind of resource is used to monitor the current state of the scaling process, embedding all the allocations planned and actuated for a given pod. Thus, a *PodScale* resource that is linked to a pod p, is updated at each vertical scaling action that targets p. A new *PodScale* resource is created (or deleted) when the horizontal autoscaling system scales up (or down) a given service. Resource *PodScale* not only contains the enacted configuration but also the ones that are capped because either desired allocations are too big for the hosting node or for resource contention scenarios. Finally resources *PodMetrics* and *ServiceMetrics* are addition to the built-in *Custom Metrics API*[5] that allows controllers to gather monitoring data of user-defined metrics. Resource *PodMetrics* holds monitoring data at pod-level granularity whereas *ServiceMetrics* at service-level.

KOSMOS employs a set of new Kubernetes Controllers to optimize resource provisioning. Component *KOSMOS Vertical Pod Autoscaler* (KVPA) is in charge of vertically scale each instance of pod. Controller KVPA is composed of three sub-components. First, *Recommender* (logically, one for each container) uses control theory to compute the optimal resource allocation for each container given the defined SLA. Second, *Contention Manager* (logically, one for each node) is in charge of solving resource contention scenarios. In particular, it ensures that the sum of resource allocations computed by *Recommender* never exceeds node capacity. Third, *Pod Resource Updater* actuates the resource allocations as computed by the Contention Manager using in-place vertical scaling. Furthermore, it saves all the previously computed allocations into the proper *PodScale* resource.

Component *KOSMOS Horizontal Pod Autoscaler* (KHPA) takes care of the horizontal scaling process by adjusting the number of Pod replicas. Usually, it comes into action when the vertical scaling can not satisfy the Service Level Agreement requirements. It is implemented as a modular set of heuristics. Finally, *PodScale Controller* is in charge of managing *PodScale* resources when a new *ServiceLevelAgreement* resource is created or removed and when a new pod is created or terminated.

For each service, *KOSMOS* deploys a i) resource-aware loadbalancer that distribute the requests to the pod replicas based on the dynamically allocated resources, and ii) a *Metric Exposer* that collects *PodMetrics*, aggregates them into *ServiceMetrics* and push them to the proper *Custom Metrics* endpoints. Finally, each pod is enriched with a *KOSMOS Proxy*, a lightweight component that, by exploiting the *Monitoring Sidecar* pattern [4], intercepts all the requests incoming to the main container of the pod and propagates the monitoring data to component *Metric Exposer*.

3   Scaling Capabilities

Component KVPA is in charge of vertically scaling each pod given a constraint on the response time. KVPA is composed of three main sub-components: Recommender, Contention Manager and Resource Updater.

The complexity of the whole control loop is linear to the amount of the available pods and given the loose dependency among the computed allocations the algorithm is highly parallelized. While the actual computation of allocation may last hundreds of milliseconds, to actuate the allocations a set of HTTP calls are required. Thus, the control period of KVPA was set to 5 s to accommodate enough time to complete the whole process.

---

[5] Kubernetes distinguishes between Custom Resources and Monitored Resource; herein we omit this distinction for simplicity.

KOSMOS is not limited to only vertical scaling and provides a component *KOSMOS* Horizontal Pod Autoscaler (KHPA) to also scale pods horizontally. Component KHPA is designed to work as a complement of component KVPA. KVPA is considered the main autoscaling component; it is based on a robust theoretical foundation and provides formal guarantees[6]. When KVPA is unable to stabilize the system, or the nodes are poorly utilized, component KHPA comes into play. KHPA works with a larger control period (the default value is set to 5 min) compared to KVPA, to allow KVPA to have enough time to stabilize the control process.

Component KHPA offers three different heuristics to compute the number of replicas needed for each service.

- *PROP.* This heuristic, similar to the one used by Kubernetes HPA, computes the amount of replicas needed by comparing the monitored response time (at the service-level) and the set-point one following the equation: $desiredReplicas = \lceil currentReplicas * \frac{RT}{\alpha * RT^{SLA}} \rceil$. In this case, the monitored response time (RT) refers to the aggregated response time of the service (resource *Service Metrics*). *PROP* is the default heuristic of *KOSMOS*.
- *CONT.* Whenever a contention is detected by component *ContentionManager*, this heuristic is activated and a set of replicas that allows to satisfy the desired allocations are created. This way the load will be distributed across more application instances and a bigger resource pool will be provided to KVPA.
- *UTIL.* This heuristic behaves similarly to the previous one, but instead of looking for resource scenarios it tries to prevent them. This mechanism keeps on watching the resources available on the nodes, and once they fall below a certain percentage, it creates new replicas for the most demanding services.

To avoid frequent, undesired, changes to the amount of replicas, component KHPA employs a *stabilization period,* a time window larger than the control period during which KHPA remains idle waiting for i) new replicas to be scheduled and booted, and for ii) component KVPA to stabilize the system.

4   Related Work

In the literature, one can find multiple works regarding autoscaling systems for containerized applications and/or Kubernetes [8,13].

Knative[7] is a platform that provides a set of Kubernetes components that enrich Kubernetes with serverless capabilities. Compared to *KOSMOS*, Knative has two limitations: i) it does not provide vertical scaling ii) its control algorithm is based on simple threshold based rules as VPA and HPA.

---

[6] An in-depth assessment of the formal guarantees provided by our control-theoretical planners is omitted for lack of space.

[7] https://knative.dev.

Balla et al. [7] presented Libra, an autoscaling system for Kubernetes that provides both vertical and horizontal resource provisioning. Compared to *KOS-MOS*, Libra is not capable of performing in-place vertical scaling, which significantly slow down the adaptation process, and they rely on static loadbalancing policies.

RUBAS [11], similarly to COCOS [8], do not uses the native Kubernetes API but it exploits external components that communicate directly with the low-level container runtime. Finally, compared to *KOSMOS*, RUBAS does not handle horizontal autoscaling and does not exploit application-level metrics (e.g., response time).

5   Conclusions

This paper presents *KOSMOS*, a new autoscaling system that is integrated in Kubernetes and that is able to provide both vertical and horizontal resource allocation. *KOSMOS* exploits control-theory to vertically scale containers and heuristics to solve resource contention scenarios, to horizontally scale containers, and to properly distribute the traffic among different container replicas. In our future work we plan to carry out an extensive empirical evaluation to assess the benefits of *KOSMOS*.

References

1. In-place update of pod resources pull request. https://github.com/kubernetes/enhancements/issues/1287
2. Kubernetes 1.20 changelog. https://github.com/kubernetes/kubernetes/blob/master/CHANGELOG/CHANGELOG-1.20.md
3. Kubernetes HPA. https://kubernetes.io/docs/tasks/run-application/horizontal-pod-autoscale/
4. Kubernetes logging architecture. https://kubernetes.io/docs/concepts/cluster-administration/logging/
5. kubernetes vpa. https://github.com/kubernetes/autoscaler/tree/master/vertical-pod-autoscaler
6. The state of enterprise open source. https://www.redhat.com/en/enterprise-open-source-report/2021
7. Balla, D., Simon, C., Maliosz, M.: Adaptive scaling of kubernetes pods. In: 2020 IEEE/IFIP Network Operations and Management Symposium, pp. 1–5 (2020)
8. Baresi, L., Quattrocchi, G.: COCOS: a scalable architecture for containerized heterogeneous systems. In: IEEE International Conference on Software Architecture, pp. 103–113 (2020)
9. Felter, W., Ferreira, A., Rajamony, R., Rubio, J.: An updated performance comparison of virtual machines and linux containers. In: 2015 IEEE International Symposium on Performance Analysis of Systems and Software (ISPASS), pp. 171–172 (2015)
10. Kwan, A., Wong, J., Jacobsen, H., Muthusamy, V.: Hyscale: hybrid and network scaling of dockerized microservices in cloud data centres. In: 2019 IEEE 39th International Conference on Distributed Computing Systems (ICDCS), pp. 80–90 (2019)

11. Rattihalli, G., Govindaraju, M., Lu, H., Tiwari, D.: Exploring potential for non-disruptive vertical auto scaling and resource estimation in kubernetes. In: 2019 IEEE 12th International Conference on Cloud Computing (CLOUD), pp. 33–40 (2019)

12. Seo, K.T., Hwang, H.S., Moon, I., Kwon, O., jun Kim, B.: Performance comparison analysis of linux container and virtual machine for building cloud, pp. 105–111 (2014)

13. Tang, X., Zhang, F., Li, X., Khan, S.U., Li, Z.: Quantifying cloud elasticity with container-based autoscaling. In: IEEE 15th International Conference on Dependable, Autonomic and Secure Computing, pp. 853–860 (2017)

Pangaea: Semi-automated Monolith Decomposition into Microservices

Simone Staffa, Giovanni Quattrocchi, Alessandro Margara$^{(\boxtimes)}$, and Gianpaolo Cugola

Politecnico di Milano, Milan, Italy
{simone.staffa,giovanni.quattrocchi,alessandro.margara,
gianpaolo.cugola}@mail.polimi.it

Abstract. As microservices become the reference architecture for many practitioners, decomposing an application into microservices remain a challenge. This paper tackles the problem with *Pangaea*, a semi-automatic tool to decompose a software system into microservices. *Pangaea* (i) takes in input a high-level model of the system; (ii) formulates decomposition as an optimization problem, and (iii) outputs a proposed placement of functionalities and data onto microservices, using a visual representation that helps reasoning on the overall architecture. *Pangaea* evaluates design concerns, communication overheads, data management requirements, opportunities and costs of data replication. Our evaluation on a real-world application shows that *Pangaea* consistently delivers more efficient solutions than simple heuristics and state-of-the-art approaches, and provides useful insights to developers.

Keywords: Microservices architectures · Service decomposition · Service modeling · Software architectures

1 Introduction and Motivations

The increasing need to evolve software systems quickly and efficiently made many IT practitioners migrate from monolithic to microservices architectures. Microservices architectures define an application as a composition of independent units. Microservices contain a subset of logically-related application functionalities, and are developed, deployed, and maintained independently from each others. Microservice can be developed using a different technology stacks, they run as independent processes that only interact through network protocols such as HTTP or MQTT, they can be scaled independently, and faults do not make the whole system unresponsive, since there is no single point-of-failure. A key challenge to embrace a microservices approach is how to decompose an application into microservices. Indeed, the adoption of microservices architectures

This work has been partially supported by the SISMA national research project, which has been funded by the MIUR under the PRIN 2017 program (Contract 201752ENYB) and by the European Commission grant no. 825480 (H2020), SODALITE.

encompasses both technical and managerial concerns, which should be carefully considered in the decomposition process. In general, we may classify the desired characteristic of a successful decomposition as organization, communication, and data management aspects.

Organization. Microservices are organized around business capabilities: the decomposition needs to produce microservices that are highly cohesive and include all the data and processing components to implement a given capability.

Communication. Microservices are developed as independent executables that communicate using remote procedure calls or asynchronous propagation of messages. Frequent communication across microservices may increase the overall response time of the application: the decomposition needs to produce microservices that are loosely-coupled.

Data Management. Microservices decentralize data management by design. Each microservice has its local, partial view of the application domain. Data integrity in the presence of concurrent operations and replication is enforced at application level, and may require coordination protocols that are complex, introduce coupling, and may degrade performance. An effective decomposition should be aware of integrity requirements and avoid costly coordination by co-locating related data elements within the same microservice.

In summary, a decomposition always represents a compromise between heterogeneous and conflicting forces. Without any tool to support their reasoning, developers may incorrectly evaluate the possible alternatives, leading to inaccurate decompositions that affect development, operations, and maintenance costs. Given the complexity of this problem, some approaches were presented in the literature to assist engineers in the decomposition process [5,6]. They range from theoretical frameworks that provide principles and guidelines [1,3] to completely automated tools [2,4]. Manual tools still require considerable effort from developers. Automated tools are often limited to specific application types, and generate decompositions that may be inadequate to the developers actual needs. Moving from these premises, this paper introduces *Pangaea* (Sect. 2), a semi-automatic tool to decompose a monolith into microservices. *Pangaea* takes in input a high-level model of the application. It formulates an optimization problem that evaluates design concerns (coupling and cohesion), communication overhead, data management requirements, opportunities and costs of data replication, and searches for the optimal placement of data and operations across a set of microservices. Developers can prioritize certain requirements over the others through a set of parameters in the model. Our evaluation on a real-world application (Sect. 3) shows the effectiveness of *Pangaea* compared to simple heuristics, a manual decomposition, and a state-of-the-art decomposition approach.

2   *Pangaea*

This section presents *Pangaea* in details. Figure 1 overviews its workflow, where developers provide (i) a *system model*, which defines the data entities and operations that build the application, together with their characteristics and mutual

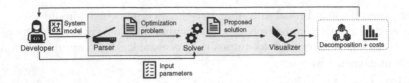

Fig. 1. *Pangaea*: overview of the workflow.

relations; (ii) a set of *input parameters* that configure the tool and steer the decomposition process based on user preferences. Given these inputs *Pangaea* works in three steps: (1) a *parser* translates the system model into an optimization problem; (2) a *solver* outputs a solution to the problem: a possible allocation of data entities and operations onto microservices; (3) a *visualizer* produces a visual representation of the proposed decomposition together with a detailed analysis of the costs it incurs. Developers evaluate the decomposition and decide if accepting it or refining the system model and input parameters.

2.1 System Model

Pangaea builds on an expressive yet easy-to-use modeling framework. Developers model an application in terms of *data entities* and *operations*, both characterized by a set of attributes. They specify data entities and operations as annotations in YAML, using the @Entity and @Operation tags, respectively. Tags can be placed in the source code of the application, as comments next to the definition of the data elements and functionalities they model, or they can be placed in a single or multiple dedicated files.

Data Entities. Data entities are basic elements of data that *Pangaea* treats as atomic units. The concept of data entity is independent of the specific data model and level of granularity, allowing developers to adapt the framework to their needs. For instance, in a relational data model, a data entity can be used to model a single table: *Pangaea* will treat the table as an unbreakable unit and map it to microservices accordingly. Developers may also decide to model multiple related tables as a single data entity or to split a table into multiple data entities. In the first case, *Pangaea* will not distinguish individual tables and will consider them as a whole. In the second case, *Pangaea* will have the opportunity to assign the various parts of the table to different microservices. A data entity e is characterized by the following properties.

Name: a label that uniquely identifies e in the model.

Implementation: an optional string that developers can use to map e to concrete elements in the application (for instance, the database tables e refers to).

Relations: a list of the other data entities e depends on. The use of relations makes *Pangaea* aware of semantic connections between data entities, which it may exploit to increase cohesion and reduce coupling. Developers may also specify the strength of each relation, which can be either *strong* or *weak*. For instance, in the case of relational tables, developers may model foreign key constraints between tables as strong relations.

Replication Overhead: a number indicating the expected overhead of replicating *e* within multiple microservices. Indeed, replication may involve a coordination overhead to keep replicas consistent, which depends on the desired level of consistency and the frequency of updates.

Operations. Operations represent units of execution, which are candidate to become logic functionalities exposed by microservices. Each operation accesses data entities and is associated to a single microservice. In *Pangaea*, an operation *o* is characterized by the following properties.

Name: a label that uniquely identifies *o* in the model.

Entities: the list of data entities accessed by *o*. For each data entity, developers can specify if the access is *read-only* or *read-write*. *Pangaea* interprets accesses as a dependency relation between operations and data entities, and attempts to co-locate on the same microservice an operation and the data entities it accesses. Placing a data entity *e* and an operation *o* that accesses *e* on different microservices incurs a cost in terms of communication (greater for read-write access and lower for read-only access) and it may increase coupling, as it indicates that a microservice is requesting data with remote invocations to another microservice rather than accessing it locally.

Frequency: a number that indicates how frequently *o* is invoked. In the decomposition process, *Pangaea* will prioritize reducing the costs associated to operations that are invoked more frequently.

Integrity: represents the requirements of *o* in terms of data integrity. It can be either *low* or *high*. For instance, integrity may include isolation policies to coordinate concurrent invocations, such that developers may distinguish between a high level of isolation (stronger, but more expensive to enforce, such as serializable isolation) and a low level of isolation (weaker, but less expensive, such as monotonic atomic view isolation). Enforcing integrity requirements is more expensive in distributed settings, that is, when *o* needs to access remote data elements. Accordingly, *Pangaea* will favor decomposition choices that maximize local data access for operations that require (high) integrity.

Forced Entities: list of data entities that need to be located on the same microservice as *o*. For instance, developers may enforce a single microservice being responsible for updating a data entity *e*. Also, developers can use forced entities to encode application-specific concerns such as access control policies.

2.2 Optimization Problem

Pangaea formulates an optimization problem that aims to find an allocation of data entities and operations onto a set of microservices that minimizes three costs: (i) *Coupling cost* is the (design) cost for placing non-related data entities in the same microservice, which decreases cohesion. (ii) *Communication cost* is the overhead of communication across microservices due to dependencies between operations and data entities that are not placed in the same microservice. (iii) *Replication cost* is the overhead of replication. While replication may reduce the communication cost, keeping replicated data entities consistent requires additional coordination and it may result in increased response times. We denote E the set of data entities, O the set of operations, and M a set of microservices. Two decision binary variables x and y encode the placement of operations and data entities onto microservices, respectively:

$$x_{o \in O, m \in M} = 1 \text{ iff } o \text{ is placed on } m, \qquad y_{e \in E, m \in M} = 1 \text{ iff } e \text{ is placed on } m$$

Input Parameters. *Pangaea* takes in input a small number of parameters that guide the decomposition process based on the requirements of developers.

Number of Microservices: is the cardinality of M and indicates the maximum number of microservices that the decomposition can use. The solver may use only a subset of microservices, resulting in a decomposition into fewer microservices.

Organization-Communication Ratio: an integer number α that indicates the importance developers attribute to organization concerns (coupling cost) over communication concerns (communication and replication costs), on a scale between 0 and 100 (default: 50).

Relation Weight: an integer number w_{rel} used to weight the cost of placing on the same microservice two *unrelated* data entities in comparison with the same cost for *weakly* related entities (default: 2).

Access Weight: an integer number w_{acc} that represents the overhead of *read-write* access with respect to *read-only* access to data entities (default: 2).

Integrity Weight: an integer number w_{int} that represents the overhead of enforcing *high* integrity with respect to *low* integrity for operations (default: 2).

Coupling Cost. The coupling cost is the cost associated to placing two unrelated entities on the same microservice, defined for each microservice $m \in M$ as:

$$CPcost_m = \sum_{e1 \in E, e2 \in E} y_{e1,m} \cdot y_{e2,m} \cdot CP_{e1,e2}$$

where $y_{e1,m} \cdot y_{e2,m}$ is 1 if both e_1 and e_2 are placed on m, and 0 otherwise, while $CP_{e1,e2}$ is a measure of the dependencies between e_1 and e_2. A strong dependency leads to a small coupling cost: coupling the two entities in the same microservice is acceptable as it does not decrease the cohesion of the microservice. We compute $CP_{e1,e2}$ based on the *relation* attributes expressed in the system model: it is 0 if e_1 and e_2 are the same entity or if there is a strong relation between them, it is 1 if there is a weak relation, and it equals w_{rel} if they are unrelated.

Communication Cost. The communication cost measures the overhead of placing an operation o and a data entity e accessed by o on two different microservices, defined for each microservice $m \in M$ as:

$$COMMcost_m = \sum_{o \in O, e \in E} x_{o,m} \cdot (1 - y_{e,m}) \cdot COMM_{o,e}$$

where $x_{o,m} \cdot (1 - y_{e,m})$ is 1 if o is placed on m but e is not, and 0 otherwise, while $COMM_{o,e}$ evaluates the weight of communication between e and o, and is defined as: $COMM_{o,e} = acc_{o,e} \cdot int_o \cdot freq_o$ where $acc_{o,e}$ is the *access cost*, which is 0 if o does not access e, 1 if o accesses e in read-only mode and w_{acc} if o accesses e in read-write mode; int_o is the *integrity cost*, which is 1 if o has weak integrity requirements and w_{int} if o has strong integrity requirements; finally, $freq_o$ is the frequency of o, as indicated by the developers in the system model.

Replication Cost. The replication cost is the overhead of replication, defined for each data entity $e \in E$ as:

$$REPLcost_e = \sum_{m \in M} y_{e,m} \cdot REPL_e$$

where the summation indicates that the cost for replicating a data entity is proportional to the number of replicas (the number of microservices that holds a replica of e), while $REPL_e$ is the replication overhead, as indicated by the developers in the system model.

Objective Function. The goal is to minimize the total cost, expressed as the sum of coupling, communication, and replication costs, weighted by the ratio α:

$$TOTcost = \alpha \cdot \sum_{m \in M} CPcost_m + (100 - \alpha) \cdot \left(\sum_{m \in M} COMMcost_m + \sum_{e \in E} REPLcost_e \right)$$

under the constraints that an operation is assigned to a single microservice, while an entity may be replicated to multiple microservices:

$$\forall_{o \in O} \sum_{m \in M} x_{o,m} = 1, \quad \forall_{e \in E} \sum_{m \in M} y_{e,m} \geq 1$$

Notice that the above problem is not linear (the coupling cost requires multiplying y by y, and the communication cost requires multiplying x by y). To linearize the product of any two binary variables a, b, we introduce a new binary variable $c = a \cdot b$. We observe that $c \neq 0 \iff a = b = 1$, which can be expressed with the following linear constraints: $c \leq a, c \leq b, c \leq a + b - 1$.

2.3   Presenting the Output

We conceive *Pangaea* as a decision support tool that should help developers reasoning on the system and evaluate the consequences of a given decomposition choice in terms of design and operational costs. Accordingly, we built a visualizer component that offers a graphical representation of the proposed decomposition as a dynamic Web page. The visualizer shows entities and operations associated to microservices, as well as remote invocations across microservices, labeled with their communication cost. In addition, *Pangaea* outputs a detailed report with the individual contributions to the total cost of the proposed solution. Developers may use the report to evaluate the trade-offs of the solution and to refine their system model or choice of input parameters.

3   Evaluation

We evaluated *Pangaea* on a real-world case study provided by Tutored (https://www.tutored.me/), a tech startup that works in the education sector. The case study consists of a REST API developed with Node.js, Express, and Typescript. Once modelled in *Pangaea*, it includes 45 data entities and 71 operations. The evaluation aims to answer the following research questions: **(RQ1)** How do the decompositions proposed by *Pangaea* compare with alternative ones? **(RQ2)** How do practitioners benefit from the usage of *Pangaea*?

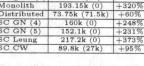

Approach	Cost (comm)	Diff
Manual	140.6k (77.65k)	+206%
Pangaea (4)	52.4k (5.6k)	+14%
Pangaea (5)	45.5k (7k)	-
Monolith	193.15k (0)	+320%
Distributed	73.75k (71.5k)	+60%
SC GN (4)	160k (0)	+248%
SC GN (5)	152.1k (0)	+231%
SC Leung	217.2k (0)	+373%
SC CW	89.8k (27k)	+95%

Fig. 2. Costs with $\alpha = 50$

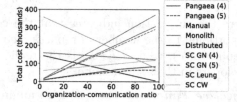

Fig. 3. Total costs by varying α.

To answer RQ1, we compared *Pangaea* with four alternative approaches: (i) a manual decomposition produced at Tutored; (ii) ServiceCutter (SC), a state-of-the-art tool for microservices decomposition that uses a graph clustering approach; (iii) a fully distributed solution (each entity is placed on a separate microservice); (iv) the original monolith. The manual solution was produced by software engineers at Tutored who work on the application. It is based on their knowledge of the domain without the help of any decision support tool. Tutored's software engineers also produced the input system model for *Pangaea*. As the manual solution included four microservices, we evaluated *Pangaea* with two configurations: $|M| = 4$ and $|M| = 5$. All our experiments are performed with the default input parameters presented in Sect. 2, unless otherwise specified. As a solver, we used Gurobi 9, with a maximum timeout of 7 min.

We compare the total cost of each solution using the cost function of *Pangaea*, based on the system model provided by the developers. Figure 2 shows the results in terms of total cost of each solution and the fraction of it that is due to communication (the remaining part being organization). We configure SC with different graph algorithms (Girvan-Newman – GN, Leung, Chinese Whispers – CW). When a tool can be configured with an expected number of microservices, we indicate the number of microservices set as input in parenthesis. *Pangaea* (5) provides the solution with the lower total cost, and *Pangaea* (4), which uses the same number of microservices as the manual decomposition, has a cost that is only 14% higher. Interestingly, the total cost of the manual solution is about 3 times higher, and its communication cost is almost one order of magnitude higher than in *Pangaea*. Our interpretation is that developers tend to be more biased towards organization aspects, such as semantic affinities of data entities. As expected, the monolith solution incurs no communication cost but has a high total cost due to organization concerns (coupling), while the distributed solution results in a high communication cost. In terms of usability, SC provides disparate solutions depending on the selected algorithm, thus it requires developers to understand the details and differences between clustering algorithms. In absolute terms, SC solutions are between 95% and 373% more expensive than *Pangaea*.

Figure 3 shows how the total cost of each solution changes with the organization-communication ratio α. Higher values of α linearly increase the cost of centralized solutions, such as the monolith and SC GN. Conversely, the cost linearly decreases for the distributed solution and SC Leung. The total cost of *Pangaea* is consistently lower than any other solution, the only exception being the distributed solution with low communication cost: however, this is an extreme case that artificially avoids coupling by creating an unrealistically high number of microservices. In conclusion, *Pangaea* solutions are the ones with the lowest total cost with balanced organization-communication ratio and outperform the other approaches even when the ratio changes.

To gether a better insight on the proposed decompositions, we manually analyzed their quality. The analysis offered a strong evidence that alternative approaches could not meet the expectations of developers, leading to decompositions that fall into two extremes: large microservices that cluster many functionalities with low cohesion or very small microservices that require frequent communication and do not justify a separate development and deployment.

To answer **RQ2**, we asked the developers at Tutored to provide an experience report. The time needed to produce the manual decomposition was between 6 and 8 h, against the 2 h needed to annotate the source code for *Pangaea*. In line with our objective, the developers described *Pangaea* as a support tool that can guide users in improving decomposition in an iterative fashion. The most important insights were the ones related to the communication cost, which is much harder to reason about and optimize with respect to organization aspects.

4 Conclusions

This paper introduced *Pangaea*, a semi-automated tool for decomposing a monolith into microservices. *Pangaea* uses a simple model of the application to formulate an optimization problem that balances organization, communication, and data management requirements. It outputs a graphical representation of the proposed decomposition together with detailed information on the costs it incurs. Our evaluation on a real-world application shows that *Pangaea* offers useful insights to developers.

References

1. Balalaie, A., Heydarnoori, A., Jamshidi, P., Tamburri, D.A., Lynn, T.: Microservices migration patterns. Softw. Pract. Experience **48**(11), 2019–2042 (2018)
2. Baresi, L., Garriga, M., Renzis, A.D.: Microservices identification through interface analysis. In: European Conference on Service-Oriented and Cloud Computing ESOCC (2017)
3. Levcovitz, A., Terra, R., Valente, M.T.: Towards a technique for extracting microservices from monolithic enterprise systems (2016)
4. Mazlami, G., Cito, J., Leitner, P.: Extraction of microservices from monolithic software architectures. In: International Conference on Web Services (2017)
5. Selmadji, A., Seriai, A.D., Bouziane, H.L., Oumarou Mahamane, R., Zaragoza, P., Dony, C.: From monolithic architecture style to microservice one based on a semiautomatic approach. In: International Conference on Software Architecture, ICSA (2020)
6. Taibi, D., Systä, K.: From monolithic systems to microservices: a decomposition framework based on process mining. In: International Conference on Cloud Computing and Services Science, CLOSER (2019)

Vertical Scaling of Resource for OpenMP Application

Junfeng Zhao[1]([✉]) [iD], Minjia Zhang[1], and Hongji Yang[2]

[1] Inner Mongolia University, Hohhot, China
cszjf@imu.edu.cn
[2] Leicester University, Leicester, UK
Hongji.Yang@Leicester.ac.uk

Abstract. OpenMP applications have been mostly executed on high-performance devices. As problem size expands and users' demands for performance increase, whether to purchase higher-performance computers has become a problem faced by the organizations. Cloud offers a new way to solve this problem, which can automatically allocate elastic resources to meet different workload demands. In this paper, a vertical elastic solution for OpenMP applications is proposed, which is a combination of exponential smoothing and fuzzy logic control. According to the solution, an elasticity controller ECOMP was implemented, and the experimental verification was conducted from performance and accuracy. The results show that the controller can complete vertical elasticity scaling of resources, shorten the execution time of the program and improve the resource utilisation efficiency.

Keywords: Cloud computing · OpenMP · Resource prediction · Vertical scaling

1 Introduction

OpenMP (Open Multi-Processing) is an application programming interface for writing parallel programs for Shared memory. In accordance with the compilation instruction #pragma added in the source code, the compiler will automatically parallelise the program [1]. OpenMP is widely used in high performance computing because of its advantages of simple use, good portability and high scalability.

In the past, OpenMP application was executed on high-performance infrastructure, which required users to purchase expensive machine clusters and high machine maintenance costs. With the changes of user needs, users also need to purchase higher-performance computers to adapt to the increasing problem scale and performance expectation. This method not only requires a large investment, but also results in a waste of resources when the workload is low.

Elasticity is the ability of a system to dynamically add and remove resources to accommodate real-time load changes [2]. This means that the application's computing resources can vary with requirements without service outages. Elasticity can be divided into horizontal elasticity and vertical elasticity [3]. In general, horizontal elasticity is coarse-grained, and vertical elasticity is fine-grained. Horizontal elasticity applies to

© Springer Nature Switzerland AG 2021
H. Hacid et al. (Eds.): ICSOC 2021, LNCS 13121, pp. 839–849, 2021.
https://doi.org/10.1007/978-3-030-91431-8_61

multi-process parallel programs that can improve performance by adding computational instances, but not to multithreaded parallel programs such as OpenMP. OpenMP application makes use of all available resources of the machine where it is running, but cannot detect or use the VM allocated horizontally. Providing fine-grained resources with vertical elasticity is a key factor in implementing the elastic resource scaling for OpenMP application.

This paper proposes a non-intrusive approach that combines OpenMP application with the vertical elasticity of cloud computing to achieve the elastic scaling of resources during the operation of OpenMP program. In addition, an elasticity controller ECOMP for the scaling of resources of OpenMP application is designed and implemented, which is a middleware that supports the interaction between OpenMP applications and cloud platforms.

The remainder of this paper is structured as follows. Section 2 presents a review of the related work. Section 3 introduces the division strategy of the elasticity domain. The resource prediction model based on Holt exponential smoothing is introduced in Sect. 4. Section 5 explains the design of resource decider based on fuzzy logic in detail. The elasticity controller ECOMP are introduced in Sect. 6, and the analysis of the experimental results is conducted. Finally, the conclusion and future work are introduced in Sect. 7.

2   Related Work

2.1   Elastic Solutions

In the past decade or so, due to the limitation of hypervisor, elastic research has been conducted around horizontal elasticity. The horizontal elasticity is coarse-grained, and the VM configuration needs to be defined before allocation and always remains unchanged, which results in the cloud platform being unable to provide dynamic resource allocation according to the needs of application. Currently, virtual machine hypervisors such as Xen and KVM already support vertical elasticity of resources. With the support of hypervisors, there has been a lot of research dedicated to achieving vertical elasticity of applications. In [4], two vertical self-configuration methods of cloud computing infrastructure are discussed. Elastic VM, a fine-grained vertical scaling architecture, is proposed in [5]. An embedded elasticity controller is proposed in [6]. Embedding the elastic primitives into application source code enables the application to adapt its resources to the changes in runtime requirements or execution flow.

Due to the multithread nature of OpenMP applications and the specific internal structure, the existed elastic solutions cannot be applied for OpenMP application. Elastic solutions for OpenMP applications must consider their internal structure and behavior. OpenMR execution model, a new model based on MapReduce and OpenMP, automatically parallelises the execution of programs through specific compilation instructions [7]. In [8], the authors propose a method for refactoring OpenMP applications into MapReduce program. Galante et al. propose an elasticity support mechanism for OpenMP application, which can dynamically schedule cloud resources according to the internal structure of program and runtime requirements [9].

2.2 Elastic Technology

Lorido-Botran et al. divide the application's elastic scaling technology into five categories [10]. By analysing these categories, it is concluded that control theory has great potential for automatic scaling especially when combined with resource prediction, and time series analysis is highly effective in resource prediction and is the main driving force of proactive scaling technology. Exponential smoothing method is a time series analysis and prediction method developed on the basis of moving average method. It has the advantages of flexibility, simple calculation, and ease of use. Huang et al. present a resource prediction model based on double exponential smoothing to predict the amount of resources required by customers in the future [11]. The scheme in [12] uses double exponential smoothing to predict the future CPU usage of virtual machines, and is supplemented by genetic algorithms to find the optimal virtual machine configuration. In [13], the authors use the ultra-short-term load forecasting method to realise real-time dispatching and security warning of power grid.

The dynamic resource allocation in cloud computing depends on various parameters, which are not interrelated, so a new model that integrates and displays the influence of these parameters in a unified manner is needed. An autonomous resource allocation elasticity controller combining fuzzy logic control and autonomous computing is proposed in [14]. Soodeh et al. use fuzzy logic to design a fuzzy controller, which served as the coordinator of memory and CPU controller to meet the response time requirements of the application program [15].

The existed approach and tools are designed to achieve performance promotion by changing programming model or modifying source code. It is difficult to apply in complex business scenes. Therefore, a non-intrusive elasticity controller is designed to achieve the vertical resource expansion for OpenMP application to reduce the resource idle rate and resource waste.

3 Elasticity Domain Division

In OpenMP, whether a thread group can execute a program in parallel depends on the usage of instructions in program code. During the execution of program, according to the use of the internal instructions of OpenMP program, we can perceive changes in resource requirements in advance and make corresponding elastic actions, which can effectively reduce resource waste.

According to the functions and characteristics of each instruction in the OpenMP 4.5 standard, this paper draws the rules for dividing the elasticity domain of each instruction, as shown in Table 1. There are three scaling states of resources, namely Allocation, Release, and Adjustment. The program resources are adjusted accompanying with the state change of the threads. N_thread is one of the determinants of the scaling of OpenMP application resources. It represents the number of busy threads in each parallel region. "—" means that the elasticity domain is not divided here, so the area code belongs to the previous elasticity domain, and the scaling of resources is adjusted according to the real-time requirements of the program.

Table 1. Correspondence table of start and end tags and resource scaling for main instruction

Instructions/Clauses	Tag	ThreadState (Busy: Active)	Resource scaling	N_{thread}
Parallel	enter_parallel [barr/nbarr]	n:n	Allocation	n
	exit_parallel [barr/nbarr]	1:1	Release	1
For	enter_for [barr/nbarr]	n:n	—	—
	exit_for [barr/nbarr]	n:n	—	—
Single	enter_single [barr]	1:n	Release	1
	exit_single [barr]	n:n	Allocation	n
Single nowait	enter_single [nbarr]	n:n	Adjustment	n
	exit_single [nbarr]	n:n	—	—
Sections	enter_sections [barr/nbarr]	m:n	Adjustment	m
	exit_sections [barr/nbarr]	n:n	Adjustment	n
Parallel for	enter_parallelfor [barr/nbarr]	n:n	Allocation	n
	exit_parallelfor [barr/nbarr]	1:1	Release	1
Parallel sections	enter_parallelsections[barr/nbarr]	m:m	Allocation	m
	exit_parallelsections [barr/nbarr]	1:1	Release	1
Master	enter_master []	n:n	Adjustment	n
	exit_master []	n:n	—	—
Ordered	enter_ordered []	1:n	Release	1
	exit_ordered []	n:n	Allocation	n
Critical	enter_critical [barr]	1:n	Release	1
	exit_critical [barr]	n:n	Allocation	n
Critical nowait	enter_critical [nbarr]	n:n	Adjustment	n
	exit_critical [nbarr]	n:n	—	—

4 Resource Prediction

Exponential smoothing method is a time series analysis prediction method developed on the basis of moving average method. It is suitable for fitting and predicting sequences without obvious trends and seasonal fluctuations. This paper uses Holt non-seasonal smoothing model to complete resource predication for each elastic domain in the process.

The basic idea of the Holt smoothing model is to decompose time series with linear trend, seasonal variation and random fluctuation, and combine them with exponential smoothing method to estimate long-term trend and trend increment respectively, and then establish a predictive model and extrapolate the predicted values. Its prediction formula is:

$$F_{t+m} = a_t + mb_t \tag{1}$$

F_{t+m} represents the prediction value of $t + m$ period, a_t is the stable component of period t, b_t represents the linear component of period t, and m represents the number of periods to be predicted. When the module partition point (instruction/clause) is encountered in the prediction process, t is set to 0 to conduct the prediction of the new stage.

$$a_t = \alpha y_t + (1 - \alpha)(a_{t-1} + b_{t-1}) \tag{2}$$

$$b_t = \beta(a_t - a_{t-1}) + (1 - \beta)b_{t-1} \tag{3}$$

y_t is the observed value of time series in period t, and $\alpha, \beta \in [0, 1]$ are the smoothing factors. Exponential smoothing methods are all based on recursive relationships, which mean that the initial values must be set before usage. The choice of the initial value is not particularly important because the exponential decay law suggests that all exponential smoothing methods have a very short memory capability, and the effect of the initial value becomes negligible only after a few time periods. The most common and reasonable initial value setting method used in this paper is as follows:

$$a_0 = y_1, \; b_0 = \frac{y_5 - y_1}{4} \tag{4}$$

The α, β provided in the Holt smoothing algorithm correspond to the current point level and trend respectively. The parameter values range from 0 to 1, and the influence weight of the recent observations will be smaller when the parameter is close to 0. The determination of these two smoothing factors is very important in exponential smoothing, which has become a factor considered in this paper. It is related to the accuracy of future resource prediction and the method how to measure the prediction accuracy. In order to measure the pros and cons of the prediction method, a variety of metrics have been defined such as Mean Absolute Error (MAE), Mean Absolute Percentage Error (MAPE), Root Mean Square Error (RMSE).

This paper adopts the optimisation method, which is an important branch of mathematics. It mainly studies how to select a scheme to achieve the optimal goal under certain conditions. To establish an optimal value model for parameter determination, we can assign the smoothing parameter $[\alpha, \beta] = [x_1, x_2] = x$. The goal is to minimise the prediction error. The condition is to ensure that the parameter values are within the interval $[0,1]$.

For the solution of the above problems, the Augmented Lagrange Method (ALM) is used to optimise the parameters. Its basic idea is to transform the constraint problem into unconstrained problem, and constantly adjust the penalty factor (M_k) and multiplier vector ($\lambda^{(k)}$) in the iterative process, so as to make the Hesse matrix of the objective function in a positive definite state at all times, and obtain the optimal solution of the problem.

The establishment of the prediction model is divided into four steps. First, the parameters are substituted into the parameter estimation formula (2) (3) to form a parameter estimation model. Second, the initial value calculated by (4) is then substituted into the parameter estimation model. Next, the exponential smoothing values a_t and b_t are calculated each time successively and recursively, and finally the exponential smoothing values are substituted into the prediction formula (1) to calculate the predicted value.

5 Resource Decision

How to accurately determine the degree of impact of different factors on application performance degradation, and how to determine how many resources should be provided to alleviate this performance problem, are the key issues to consider in designing an elasticity resource controller. If the controller cannot solve these problems, it will produce inaccurate resource allocation, resulting in problems such as over-allocation or under-allocation of resources. In order to solve these problems, this paper designs a resource determiner based on fuzzy logic. It uses highly expressive language to perform uncertainty reasoning based on the output of the elasticity domain divider and resource predictor, and completes the decision and allocation of resources in a natural and effective manner.

One of the most typical applications of fuzzy logic is fuzzy control. The calculation process of fuzzy control is roughly divided into four steps: determining input and output variables, fuzziness of input, fuzzy reasoning and certainty of outputs. A multi input single output (MISO) resource decider is designed. The input variables are the predicted value of CPU utilization (U_{CPU}), the number of application threads (N_{thread}), the ratio of the number of threads to the number of CPU cores (T/C). The output variable is the number of CPU cores (cores). U_{CPU} is determined by the resource predictor based on the time series of CPU utilisation observations and the elasticity domain information prediction. In the resource decider, $U_{CPU} = F_{t+1}$. N_{thread} is determined according to the internal structure of the OpenMP program. According to the OpenMP compilation principle and the execution mode of instructions and clauses, we divide the program into different elasticity domains, and then determine the number of threads to start in this area. Fuzzy control uses membership functions (MFs) to define each linguistic term for input and output variables. There are 12 MFs in this study, and we used trapezoidal MF, as is shown in Fig. 1.

Fuzzy reasoning is the process of obtaining fuzzy conclusions based on knowledge base and membership function. The fuzzy knowledge base is based on a set of language rules to determine how to best expand the target system. In order to design fuzzy rules, we designed all possible input scenarios, and invited a number of experts with in-depth knowledge of cloud resource allocation and performance modeling to discuss. The main responsibility of the experts is to determine the reasonable output value according to each prerequisite, and then conduct a collective discussion on the disputed part. We have prepared several questions to extract the required knowledge, such as

$$\text{IF } (U_{cpu} \text{ IS M}) \text{ AND } (T/C \text{ IS L}) \text{ AND } (N_{thread} \text{ IS H}) \text{ THEN } (cores \text{ IS?})$$

In order to reduce the calculation amount of fuzzy relationship synthesis, some redundant rules are merged. At the same time, the average values of the information fed back

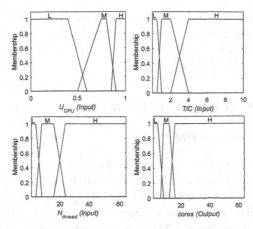

Fig. 1. Membership functions for each linguistic term

Table 2. Fuzzy rule set

Rule number	Rule
RULE 1	IF (U_{cpu} IS H) AND (T/C IS H) THEN (*cores* IS H)
RULE 2	IF (U_{cpu} IS H) AND (T/C IS M) AND (N_{thread} IS H) THEN (*cores* IS H)
RULE 3	IF (U_{cpu} IS H) AND (T/C IS M) AND (N_{thread} IS M) THEN (*cores* IS H)
RULE 4	IF (U_{cpu} IS H) AND (T/C IS M) AND (N_{thread} IS L) THEN (*cores* IS M)
RULE 5	IF (U_{cpu} IS H) AND (T/C IS L) THEN (*cores* IS II)
RULE 6	IF (U_{cpu} IS M) AND (T/C IS H) AND (N_{thread} IS H) THEN (*cores* IS H)
RULE 7	IF (U_{cpu} IS M) AND (T/C IS H) AND (N_{thread} IS M) THEN (*cores* IS M)
RULE 8	IF (U_{cpu} IS M) AND (T/C IS H) AND (N_{thread} IS L) THEN (*cores* IS L)
RULE 9	IF (U_{cpu} IS M) AND (T/C IS M) AND (N_{thread} IS H) THEN (*cores* IS H)
RULE 10	IF (U_{cpu} IS M) AND (T/C IS M) AND (N_{thread} IS M) THEN (*cores* IS M)
RULE 11	IF (U_{cpu} IS M) AND (T/C IS M) AND (N_{thread} IS L) THEN (*cores* IS L)
RULE 12	IF (U_{cpu} IS M) AND (T/C IS L) THEN (*cores* IS M)
RULE 13	IF (U_{cpu} IS L) AND (N_{thread} IS H) THEN (*cores* IS M)
RULE 14	IF (U_{cpu} IS L) AND (N_{thread} IS M) THEN (*cores* IS L)
RULE 15	IF (U_{cpu} IS L) AND (N_{thread} IS L) THEN (*cores* IS L)

by experts are adjusted according to the behavior of the fuzzy controller obtained by monitoring to finally obtain a fuzzy control rule table, as shown in Table 2.

The result of fuzzy inference is a fuzzy set. In actual fuzzy control, there must be a certain output value to control or drive the actuator. Clarification or anti-fuzzification is the process of converting fuzzy conclusions derived from fuzzy reasoning into accurate output. Common clarification methods for continuous domains are the maximum membership method and the center-of-gravity method. In this paper, the center-of-gravity method is used as a method to clarify the fuzzy conclusion, and the final control quantity CPU core number N_{core} is obtained.

6   Tool Implementation and Evaluation

6.1   Elasticity Controller ECOMP

In order to effectively realise the vertical elastic scaling of OpenMP application resources, an autonomic resource controller ECOMP is designed. ECOMP is a middleware that supports the interaction between OpenMP application and the cloud platform, enabling the cloud platform to adapt to OpenMP application with variable workload, allocating appropriate number of CPU cores to application according to the internal structure of OpenMP program and real-time requirements without human intervention, to avoid insufficient and over-provisioned resources. Figure 2 shows the architecture of ECOMP.

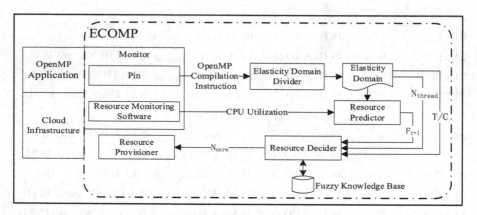

Fig. 2. The architecture of ECOMP

6.2   Experimental Evaluation

To emulate a typical cloud environment and easily perform vertical elasticity, we used Xen Hypervisor. Three OpenMP applications are selected for experimental evaluation, namely Nearest Neighbor (NN), Speckle Reducing Anisotropic Diffusion (SRAD) and Breadth-First Search (BFS), which are all from the parallel computing benchmark test suite Rodinia.

In order to verify whether the elasticity controller ECOMP has improved the performance of the OpenMP application and made full use of resources, this paper compares the execution results of the OpenMP application before and after applying ECOMP, as show in Table 3. Time represents the execution time of the program, Total represents the amount of resources consumed by the execution of the application, and Acc represents the accuracy rate of the resources provided by the cloud platform for the program. The calculation formulas (5) and (6) are shown, where n represents the total number of samples, C_t represents the number of CPU cores of the server at time t, $Count_{Acc}$ represents the CPU utilisation in the interval [0.75, 0.8], which is the value range of U_{CPU} with a membership of 1 for fuzzy set M.

$$Total = \sum_{t=1}^{n} C_t \tag{5}$$

$$Acc = \frac{Count_{Acc}}{n} \tag{6}$$

As can be seen from Table 3, ECOMP can provide an appropriate amount of resources according to the needs of the application to balance the load of the VM, improve the accuracy of resource provision, increase execution speed, and reduce waste of resources. However, the advantages of ECOMP cannot be clearly highlighted for SRAD program with high fluctuation frequency and the relatively stable program BFS. To study what types of programs can benefit more from ECOMP is where we need to improve in the future.

Figure 3 shows the execution results of the NN before and after the application of ECOMP. It can be seen from the figure that the data value of the CPU utilization rate

Table 3. Comparison of raw and elastic results of the experimental evaluation program

	NN		SRAD		BFS	
	Inelastic	Elastic	Inelastic	Elastic	Inelastic	Elastic
Time(s)	684.10	601.39	732.64	677.43	443.09	486.77
Total	272	199	292	350	180	100
Acc	0.2059	0.7833	0.0822	0.9852	0	1.0000

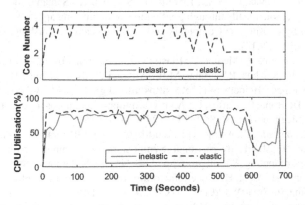

Fig. 3. Comparison of inelastic and elastic results of program NN

is around 80% after using ECOMP, which effectively improves the resource utilization rate.

7 Conclusion and Future Work

With the development of computing technology and the change of user demand, it is worth considering how to deploy OpenMP applications to the cloud platform. Due to the multithread character of OpenMP application, a vertical elasticity solution for OpenMP applications is proposed in this paper, which can infer the number of required processor cores based on the internal structure of OpenMP application and the prediction information of virtual machine resource utilization, and the virtual resources can be dynamically allocated from cloud, so as to realise the automatic scaling of resources for OpenMP application without modifying the source code. In addition, ECOMP, an elasticity controller for OpenMP program is developed. The effectiveness of the proposed elastic solution and elasticity controller is verified through experiments. In the future, we will analyse more OpenMP instructions/clauses to improve module division rules, and consider memory analysis to realise vertical elastic scaling of CPU and memory simultaneously.

Acknowledgments. This work was supported by National Natural Science Foundation of China (No. 61962039) and Inner Mongolia Natural Science Foundation (No. 2019MS06032).

References

1. Lei, H.: Multi-core heterogeneous parallel computing OpenMP 4.5 C/C++. Metallurgical Industry Press, Beijing (2018)
2. Al-Dhuraibi, Y., Paraiso, F., Djarallah, N., Merle, P.: Elasticity in cloud computing: state of the art and research challenges. IEEE Trans. Serv. Comput. **11**(2), 430–447 (2018)
3. Singh, S., Chana, I.: Cloud resource provisioning: survey, status and future research directions. Knowl. Inf. Syst. **49**(3), 1005–1069 (2016)
4. Da Silva Dias, A., Nakamura, L., Estrella, J., Santana, R., Santana, Marcos J.: Providing IaaS resources automatically through prediction and monitoring approaches. In: Proceedings International Symposium on Computers and Communications, Washington, pp. 1–7. IEEE Computer Society (2014)
5. Dawoud, W., Takouna, I., Meinel, C.: Elastic virtual machine for fine-grained cloud resource provisioning. In: Krishna, P.V., Babu, M.R., Ariwa, E. (eds.) ObCom 2011. CCIS, vol. 269, pp. 11–25. Springer, Heidelberg (2012). https://doi.org/10.1007/978-3-642-29219-4_2
6. Galante, G., De Bona, E., Carlos, L.: A programming-level approach for elasticizing parallel scientific applications. J. Syst. Softw. **110**, 239–252 (2015)
7. Wottrich, R., Azevedo, R., Araujo, G.: Cloud-based OpenMP parallelization using a MapReduce runtime. In: IEEE International Symposium on Computer Architecture & High Performance Computing, Washington, pp. 334–341. IEEE Computer Society (2014)
8. Zhao, J., Zhang, M., Yang, H.: Code refactoring from OpenMP to MapReduce model for big data processing. In: SmartWorld/UIC/ATC/SCALCOM/IOP/SCI 2019, Washington, pp. 930–935. IEEE Computer Society (2019)

9. Galante, G., Luis C.E.: Bona: supporting elasticity in OpenMP applications. In: 22nd Euromicro International Conference on Parallel, Distributed, and Network-Based Processing, Washington, pp. 188–195. IEEE Computer Society (2014)
10. Lorido-Botran, T., Miguel-Alonso, J., Lozano, J.: A review of auto-scaling techniques for elastic applications in cloud environments. J. Grid Comput. **12**(4), 559–592 (2014)
11. Huang, J., Li, C., Yu, J.: Resource prediction based on double exponential smoothing in cloud computing. In: 2nd International Conference on Consumer Electronics, Communications and Networks, pp. 2056–2060, Washington. IEEE Computer Society (2012)
12. Mi, H., Wang, H., Yin, G., Zhou, Y., Shi, D., Yuan, L.: Online self-reconfiguration with performance guarantee for energy-efficient large-scale cloud computing data centers. In: IEEE International Conference on Services Computing, Washington, pp. 514–521. IEEE Computer Society (2010)
13. Zhang, M., Zhang,Y., Chen, X.: Algorithm for distribution network state estimation with Holt-Winter-based ultra-short-term load forecasting. J. Lanzhou Univ. Technol. **42**(2), 92–96 (2016)
14. Bhardwaj, T., Sharma, S.: Fuzzy logic-based elasticity controller for autonomic resource provisioning in parallel scientific applications: a cloud computing perspective. Comput. Electr. Eng. **70**, 1049–1073 (2016)
15. Farokhi, S., Lakew, E., Klein, C., Brandic, I., Elmroth, E.: Coordinating CPU and memory elasticity controllers to meet service response time constraints. In: International Conference on Cloud and Autonomic Computing, Washington, pp. 69–80. IEEE Computer Society (2010)

A Decision Model for Selecting Patterns and Strategies to Decompose Applications into Microservices

Muhammad Waseem[1], Peng Liang[1(✉)], Gastón Márquez[2], Mojtaba Shahin[3], Arif Ali Khan[4], and Aakash Ahmad[5]

[1] School of Computer Science, Wuhan University, Wuhan, China
{m.waseem,liangp}@whu.edu.cn
[2] Department of Electronics and Informatics,
Federico Santa María Technical University, Concepción, Chile
[3] Faculty of Information Technology, Monash University, Melbourne, Australia
[4] Faculty of Information Technology, University of Jyvaskyla, Jyvaskyla, Finland
[5] College of Computer Science and Engineering, University of Ha'il,
Ha'il, Saudi Arabia

Abstract. Microservices Architecture (MSA) style is a promising design approach to develop software applications consisting of multiple small and independently deployable services. Over the past few years, researchers and practitioners have proposed many MSA patterns and strategies covering various aspects of microservices design, such as application decomposition. However, selecting appropriate patterns and strategies can entail various challenges for practitioners. To this end, this study proposes a decision model for selecting patterns and strategies to decompose applications into microservices. We used peer-reviewed and grey literature to collect the patterns, strategies, and quality attributes for creating this decision model.

Keywords: Microservices system · Microservices architecture · Decision model · Microservices pattern · Quality attribute

1 Introduction

Microservices Architecture (MSA) inspired by Service-Oriented Architecture (SOA) has gained immense popularity in the past few years [1]. With MSA, an application is designed as a set of business-driven microservices that can be developed, deployed, tested, and scaled independently [15]. Organizations adopt MSA due to better availability, scalability, productivity, performance, fault-tolerance, and cloud support compared with SOA or monolithic applications. It is argued that MSA can also help build autonomous development teams [15].

Microservices systems entail a significant degree of complexity at the design phase and runtime configurations from an architecture perspective [12]. Haselbock et al. [7] identified several design areas for microservices systems, such

© Springer Nature Switzerland AG 2021
H. Hacid et al. (Eds.): ICSOC 2021, LNCS 13121, pp. 850–858, 2021.
https://doi.org/10.1007/978-3-030-91431-8_62

as application decomposition, microservices security, and communication. On the other hand, literature reviews (e.g., [17]), existing practices (e.g., [19]), and exploratory studies (e.g., [18]) indicate several challenges related to the design areas mentioned in [7], for instance, clearly defining the boundaries of microservices, addressing their security concerns, and managing the communication between a large number of microservices.

Both academia and industry have presented reusable solutions for microservices systems in the form of patterns and strategies. These patterns and strategies are currently distributed across different publications (e.g., scientific and grey literature). The practitioners need to navigate pattern to pattern (and strategy) until a suitable combination of patterns (and strategies) that can address the challenges is found. Moreover, the practitioners cannot find a holistic view of the patterns and strategies for a trade-off analysis (e.g., patterns influence Quality Attributes (QAs)). According to the recent studies (e.g., [17–19]), most of the design, development, monitoring and testing challenges are raised when application is decomposed into microservices. To this end, we present a **decision model** that assists practitioners in selecting appropriate patterns and strategies for decomposing applications into microservices. Decision models are a structured way of exploring the problem and solution space to achieve the design goal [10]. The proposed decision model has been developed based on a mini multivocal literature review through reviewing the scientific and grey literature.

Paper Organization: Section 2 describes decision models and modeling nations; Sect. 3 presents the details of the application decomposition decision model; Sect. 4 discusses the threats to validity; Sect. 5 presents related work; Sect. 6 concludes this work with future research directions.

2   Modeling Decision Model

The decision models in software architecture are used to map elements of the problem space to elements of the solution space [10]. The problem space represents functional and non-functional requirements, whereas the solution space represents design elements [10]. To create decision models for microservices systems, we represent the problem space as a set of QAs and the solution space as a set of microservices patterns and strategies. We developed the decision model for application decomposition because most of the design, development, monitoring, testing, and deployment challenges in microservices systems are rooted in this area [17–19]. We collected required patterns, strategies, QAs, and impact of patterns on QAs for creating the decision model based on a mini multivocal literature review.

Figure 1 presents the notations used in the decision model presented in this paper. We used *Inclusive*, *Exclusive*, and *Parallel* gateways of Business Process Model and Notation (BPMN) for indicating the decision flow. An MSA design area is represented through *grey box*. A *circle* is used to denote the start of a decision process. An *Inclusive gateway* is used to trigger more than one outgoing

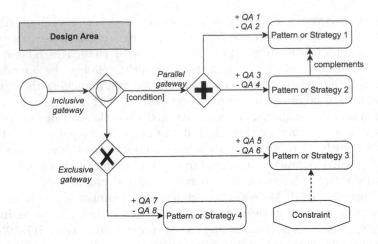

Fig. 1. Notations used in the decision models

paths within a decision process. An *Exclusive gateway* is used to trigger one of the outgoing paths. In contrast, A *Parallel gateway* represents the multiple parallel outgoing paths within a decision process. We used *rounded rectangle* to represent the patterns and strategies belong to an MSA design area. A *double-headed* arrow shows a "complements" relationship between two patterns or strategies. An *octagon and dashed* arrow is used to represent the constraints of each pattern or strategy. Finally, plus (+) and minus (−) signs indicate the positive and negative impact of each pattern or strategy on the QAs.

3   Application Decomposition Decision Model

Monolithic applications need to be decomposed into small, independent, and loosely coupled microservices to achieve the benefits (e.g., improved scalability, independent deployment). There are several ways to break down an application into microservices. The patterns and strategies collected (see Table 1) are used to create the application decomposition decision model (see Fig. 2). The decision process for application decomposition into microservices is based on the team size and impact of patterns and strategies on QAs. If the application needs to be decomposed into microservices for the team of 5–9 people to increase *Availability, Scalability, Cohesion, Deployment, Performance,* and *Maintainability,* we can use one among five illustrated patterns (see Fig. 2). In the following, we further explain the other conditions, impact on QAs, and constraints for each pattern.

To increase *Flexibility, Granularity, Reliability, Reusability, Security, Functional suitability,* and *Portability,* **Decomposed by subdomains** pattern can be used. This pattern guides practitioners in defining each microservice responsibility, boundaries, and relationships with other microservices. To successfully implement this pattern, practitioners need to understand the overall business (see Fig. 2). In contrast, if microservices need to be defined with respect to business capabilities, **Decomposed by business capabilities** pattern can be used.

Table 1. Application decomposition patterns and strategies

Name	Summary
Decomposed by subdomains [3, 14]	Define services corresponding to Domain-Driven Design (DDD) subdomains
Decomposed by business capabilities [3, 14]	Define services corresponding to business capabilities
Service per team [3, 14]	Break down the application into microservices that individual teams can manage
Decomposed by transactions [3]	An application typically needs to call multiple microservices to complete one business transaction. To avoid latency issues, services can be defined based on business transactions
Scenario analysis [16]	Identify the business capabilities by analyzing the nouns and verbs from given business scenarios
Graph-based approach [8]	Identify microservices from the source code of existing monolithic applications by graph clustering and visualization techniques
Data Flow-Driven (DFD) approach [11]	Follow a top-down approach in which data flow diagrams contain the business requirements that are later partitioned through a formal algebra algorithm for identifying microservices

Normally, business capabilities are organized into a multi-level hierarchy and generate business value. This pattern improves the *Granularity, Performance,* and *Security* of microservices if the business capabilities are identified by understanding the client organization's structure, purposes, and business processes. However, this pattern reduces *Flexibility* as the application design is tightly coupled with the business model. Another option that we can use for decomposing applications is **Service per team** pattern. This pattern enables practitioners to break applications into microservices that individual teams can manage. It also complements **Decomposed by subdomains** and **Decomposed by business capabilities** patterns. A constraint of **Service per team** pattern is that only one small team (e.g., 5–9 people) owns one microservice, meaning that each team independently develops, tests, deploys, and scales individual microservice. The teams also interact with other teams to negotiate APIs. **Service per team** pattern increases *Availability, Scalability, Cohesion, Deployment,* and *Performance,* and *Maintainability.* If the project is large and needs to hire more people, **Service per team** pattern negatively impacts the development cost of microservices.

Another exclusive pattern option in decomposition patterns is **Decompose by transactions**, in which applications are decomposed based on business transactions. Each business transaction carries one task, and each microservice has the functionalities for several business transactions (e.g., sales, marketing). This pattern allows grouping multiple microservices to avoid latency issues. **Decompose by transactions** pattern can help to improve *Response time, Data consistency,* and *Availability* of microservices. Meanwhile, decomposing applications based

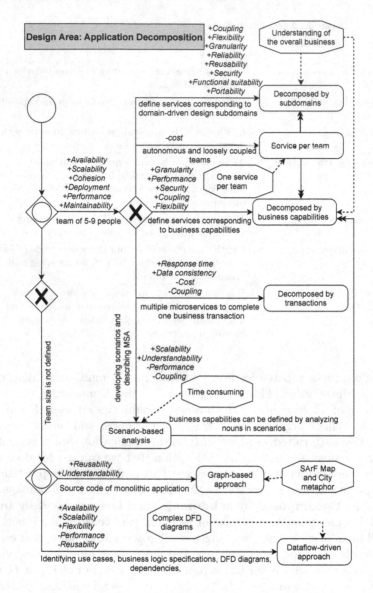

Fig. 2. Decision model for application decomposition

on transactions also increases *Execution cost* and *Coupling* of microservices due to multiple functionalities being implemented in one microservice. Another option to decompose an application is **Scenario-based analysis** which consists of several steps, such as developing scenarios, describing MSA, and evaluating scenarios. During the evaluation process of scenarios, practitioners identify the microservices and interactions between them. This pattern is appropriate if practitioners have enough time to develop and describe the scenarios and MSA, respectively. This strategy can also be used to identify the business capabilities of systems by analyzing the nouns and verbs from given business scenarios. The identified nouns represent the microservices, and the verbs describe the relationship among them. While this strategy increases *Scalability*, *Performance* and *Coupling* could be compromised because of the imprecise boundaries of microservices.

Suppose that the team size is not defined for designing and developing microservices, and we need to identify the microservices from the code of legacy applications. In that case, we can choose **Graph-based approach**. This approach uses the SArF clustering algorithm to decompose the system for comprehension [9] and the city metaphor techniques for visualizing the system structure [8]. **Graph-based approach** helps to identify microservices from the source code of existing monolithic applications. The use of this approach increases the *Reusability* of the existing code. **Graph-based approach** also visualizes the extracted microservices and their relationships along with the structure of the whole system. Hence, it also increases the *Understandability* about the MSA design. Finally, if the team size is not defined and applications need to be decomposed by using DFDs, in that case, **Data flow-driven** approach can be used, which consists of several steps, such as eliciting and analyzing the business requirements for identifying use cases and business logic specifications, creating fine-grained DFDs, identifying the dependencies between processes and datastores, and identifying microservices by clustering processes and related data stores. **Data flow-driven** approach increases *Availability*, *Scalability*, and *Flexibility*. In contrast, it decreases *Performance* and *Reusability* mainly because of complex DFDs.

4 Threats to Validity

The threats to *construct validity* are related to taking correct operational measures for collecting the data in this study. One potential threat is the inadequate use of the primary constructs of the decision model (i.e., MSA patterns and strategies, QAs, impact of the patterns on QAs). To mitigate this threat, we adopted the following operational measures: (i) we conducted a pilot search to ensure the correctness and appropriateness of the search terms, (ii) we used eight databases (i.e., ACM Digital Library, IEEE Explore, Springer Link, Science Direct, Wiley Online, Engineering Village, Web of Science, and Google Scholar) in software engineering research for retrieving the scientific studies, and (iii) we used Google for searching the grey literature. Additionally, we followed the guidelines [2] to review and extract data from the scientific and grey literature.

The threats to *internal validity* represent circumstances that could influence the results obtained from the research. We tried to mitigate this threat through collaborative work between the authors of this work. Regarding the collaborative work, one author proposed the decision model and the rest of the authors contributed to improving the models based on their knowledge and expertise.

5   Related Work

Decision Models for Architecting Microservices Systems: The study in [6] examines existing literature and provides guidance models for microservices discovery and fault tolerance. The study in [5] reports decision guidance models about generating, processing, and managing monitoring data, and disseminating monitoring data to stakeholders in the process automation domain. On the other hand, the study in [4] analyzes the strategies and provides guidelines to support architects in selecting suitable frontend architecture(s) for microservices systems.

Practitioners' Perspectives and Recommendations for Architecting Microservices Systems: The research in [13] derives a formal architecture decision model containing 325 elements and relations that can help to reduce the (i) efforts needed to understand the architectural decisions and (ii) uncertainty in the design process. An empirical study in [7] interviewed 10 microservices experts to find out the answers to (i) which design areas are relevant for microservices, (ii) how important they are, and (iii) why they are important.

Decision Models for Architectural Patterns Selection : The study [7] proposes a decision model that assists developers and architects in selecting appropriate patterns for blockchain-based applications. In a similar study [10], the authors present decision models for cyber-foraging systems that map functional and non-functional requirements to architectural tactics for designing and developing cyber-foraging systems.

Conclusive Summary: Our review of the related work suggests that there is a lack of research on decision models that can leverage patterns and strategies as reusable knowledge to address specific design area of microservices systems (i.e., application decomposition). To the best of our knowledge, our proposed decision model that supports decomposing applications into microservices is not covered in any existing studies. This decision model also provides an initial foundation to the research and practice in pattern-based architecting of microservices systems.

6   Conclusions

The paper proposes a decision model for selecting patterns and strategies to decompose applications into microservices. The proposed model is constructed by reviewing scientific and grey literature. The decision model provides MSA patterns, strategies, and their impact on QAs for selecting patterns and strategies in decomposing applications into microservices. In the next step, we aim to (1) propose decision models for other design areas, e.g., microservices security, communication, and service discovery, (2) validate the proposed decision models in an industrial setting, and (3) develop a recommendation system for selecting patterns and strategies for microservices systems.

Acknowledgments. This work has been supported by the National Key R&D Program of China under Grant No. 2018YFB1402800 and the NSFC under Grant No. 62172311.

References

1. Dragoni, N., Lanese, I., Larsen, S.T., Mazzara, M., Mustafin, R., Safina, L.: Microservices: how to make your application scale. In: Petrenko, A.K., Voronkov, A. (eds.) PSI 2017. LNCS, vol. 10742, pp. 95–104. Springer, Cham (2018). https://doi.org/10.1007/978-3-319-74313-4_8
2. Garousi, V., Felderer, M., Mäntylä, M.V.: Guidelines for including grey literature and conducting multivocal literature reviews in software engineering. Inf. Softw. Technol. **106**, 101–121 (2019)
3. Hari, O.P.R., Tabby, W., Dmitry, G.: Decomposing monoliths into microservices - AWS prescriptive (2021). http://alturl.com/5spq4
4. Harms, H., Rogowski, C., Lo Iacono, L.: Guidelines for adopting frontend architectures and patterns in microservices-based systems. In: Proceedings of the 11th ESEC/FSE, pp. 902–907. ACM (2017)
5. Haselböck, S., Weinreich, R.: Decision guidance models for microservice monitoring. In: Proceedings of the 14th ICSAW, pp. 54–61. IEEE (2017)
6. Haselböck, S., Weinreich, R., Buchgeher, G.: Decision guidance models for microservices: service discovery and fault tolerance. In: Proceedings of the 5th ECBS, pp. 1–10. ACM (2017)
7. Haselböck, S., Weinreich, R., Buchgeher, G.: An expert interview study on areas of microservice design. In: Proceedings of the 11th SOCA, pp. 137–144. IEEE (2018)
8. Kamimura, M., Yano, K., Hatano, T., Matsuo, A.: Extracting candidates of microservices from monolithic application code. In: Proceedings of the 25th APSEC, pp. 571–580. IEEE (2018)
9. Kobayashi, K., Kamimura, M., Yano, K., Kato, K., Matsuo, A.: SArF map: visualizing software architecture from feature and layer viewpoints. In: Proceedings of the 21st ICPC, pp. 43–52. IEEE (2013)
10. Lewis, G.A., Lago, P., Avgeriou, P.: A decision model for cyber-foraging systems. In: Proceedings of the 13th WICSA, pp. 51–60. IEEE (2016)
11. Li, S., et al.: A dataflow-driven approach to identifying microservices from monolithic applications. J. Syst. Softw. **157**, 110380 (2019)
12. Newman, S.: Building Microservices: Designing Fine-Grained Systems, 2nd edn. O'Reilly Media Inc., Newton (2020)
13. Ntentos, E., Zdun, U., Plakidas, K., Schall, D., Li, F., Meixner, S.: Supporting architectural decision making on data management in microservice architectures. In: Bures, T., Duchien, L., Inverardi, P. (eds.) ECSA 2019. LNCS, vol. 11681, pp. 20–36. Springer, Cham (2019). https://doi.org/10.1007/978-3-030-29983-5_2
14. Richardson, C.: Microservices Patterns: With Examples in Java. Manning, Shelter Island (2018)
15. Taibi, D., Auer, F., Lenarduzzi, V., Felderer, M.: From monolithic systems to microservices: an assessment framework. Inf. Softw. Technol. **137**, 106600 (2021)
16. Tusjunt, M., Vatanawood, W.: Refactoring orchestrated web services into microservices using decomposition pattern. In: Proceedings of the 4th ICCC, pp. 609–613. IEEE (2018)
17. Waseem, M., Liang, P., Shahin, M.: A systematic mapping study on microservices architecture in DevOps. J. Syst. Softw. **170**, 110798 (2020)

18. Waseem, M., Liang, P., Shahin, M., Ahmad, A., Nassab, A.R.: On the nature of issues in five open source microservices systems: an empirical study. In: Proceedings of the 25th EASE, pp. 201–210. ACM (2021)
19. Waseem, M., Liang, P., Shahin, M., Di Salle, A., Gastón, M.: Design, monitoring, and testing of microservices systems: the practitioners' perspective. J. Syst. Softw. **182**, 111061 (2021)

API-PROGRAM: An API Package Recommendation Model Based on the Graph Representation Learning Method

Qing Qi, Jian Cao$^{(\boxtimes)}$, and Yancen Liu

Shanghai Jiao Tong University, Shanghai, China
{qi_ng616,cao-jian,LiuYancen}@sjtu.edu.com

Abstract. To combine multiple services together using technologies such as mashup to produce a composite service has become a popular practice. However, with the increasing number of services and the diversification of service types, how to select suitable services and ensure these service combinations meet the needs of users has become an increasingly challenging topic. At present, although there are many recommendation algorithms for service selection, the semantics of the composed Web services have not been sufficiently modeled. This paper proposes an API package recommendation model based on the graph representation learning method (API-PROGRAM) which uses the historical data to learn more comprehensive semantics of Web APIs, construct the composite features of Web API collaborations and then recommend Web API packages for new mashups. The experimental results show that, compared with the existing algorithms, API-PROGRAM achieves better performance.

Keywords: Web API · Mashup · Service composition · Graph representation learning · Attention mechanism

1 Introduction

Web service is an important part of modern information systems. As a form of Web services, the number of Web APIs (Web Application Programming Interfaces) has grown exponentially on the network. The value of Web APIs not only comes from itself, but also from the potential to enable new and unique applications to be created from a mashup of several Web APIs.

When developing a mashup, we have to search for and select appropriate APIs. However, due to the huge number of APIs available on the Internet, it is a challenging task to select the Web APIs we need, especially when many Web APIs have similar functions. It is necessary to deliver personalized and customized services to users so developing applications which rely on composing Web APIs is becoming increasingly popular. Therefore, in recent years, a large number of mashups have been created. As a result, recommending Web APIs for mashup developers is necessary and has become a hot research topic [1].

© Springer Nature Switzerland AG 2021
H. Hacid et al. (Eds.): ICSOC 2021, LNCS 13121, pp. 859–866, 2021.
https://doi.org/10.1007/978-3-030-91431-8_63

Currently, most Web API recommendation approaches rely on the matching degree between the descriptions of the mashup to be developed and the descriptions of the Web APIs. Unfortunately, these methods only return related APIs with similar functions and developers must choose the most suitable API from them, which is still a difficult job. Moreover, when building mashups, we need to consider the compatibility between Web APIs and ideally, the selected Web APIs can satisfy the needs of the mashup in a complimentary way. Therefore, it is better to recommend multiple sets of APIs that can cooperate with each other, and each API set can cover the requirements of the target mashup. These sets of collaborative APIs are often referred to as API packages and each of them can be adopted entirely as a candidate solution to mashup development.

In this paper, we propose an API *P*ackage *R*ecommendation m*O*del based on the *G*raph *R*epresentation le*A*rning *M*ethod (API-PROGRAM). API-PROGRAM uses a graph neural network to learn the latent representations of Web APIs and mashups, which tries to capture more comprehensive semantics of Web APIs. Then, we apply another neural network with the attention mechanism to predict the adoption probability of a Web API in a new mashup based on the composite features of Web API pairs. Finally, Web API packages are generated and recommended. The experiment results show API-PROGRAM achieves better performance compared with other approaches.

2 Related Work

When publishing a Web API, the developer usually provides information including its name, description or tags. Therefore, traditional information retrieval methods, including distance calculation, the vector space model and TF-IDF methods for similarity evaluation between texts, can be applied to information retrieval-based Web API recommendation. Furthermore, services can be grouped into categories to enhance the recommendation process. Since Web APIs have a history of collaboration in many mashups, they are likely to collaborate again in the future so that this information can be used in recommendation. However, this approach cannot recommend Web APIs that have never cooperated before.

With the development of natural language processing technology, researchers began to use more advanced methods to extract the semantic relationship between mashups and Web APIs. Some researchers [2] explored the semantic relationship between mashups and Web APIs based on the topic model. However, these methods fail to learn the integral semantics of the composed services.

Moreover, most approaches only recommend an API list to users rather than a complementary API package that can meet their needs. Some researchers proposed a Multi-level Relational Network (MRN) method for mashup development by capturing the deep relationship between services on latent topics, tags and service networks [3]. However, this method ignored the semantic information of interactions from the perspective of service. API-Prefer [4] tries to model the interaction semantics of Web API pairs, which is similar to our research. But in API-Prefer, the semantics of Web APIs are derived from their own descriptions.

Differently, we apply a graph neural network to learn more informative embeddings of Web APIs in this paper. Furthermore, our model learns the semantic interactions of API pairs and applies a neural network with the attention mechanism to predict the adoption probability of Web API pairs, and finally to propose an API package recommendation method.

3   API-PROGRAM: An API Package Recommendation Model Based on the Graph Representation Learning Method

3.1   Model Structure

API-PROGRAM comprises three parts. The first part is a graph neural network where the embeddings of mashups and Web APIs can be learned. The second part is an adoption possibility prediction model for a pair of Web APIs based on a multi-layer neural network. The third part is the API package recommendation component which is responsible for generating potential API packages.

3.2   Graph Neural Network for Mashup and Web API Embeddings

The descriptions of Web APIs are not sufficient to describe their semantics for many reasons. Firstly, the descriptions provided by the Web API developers are often not detailed. Secondly, new functions can be discovered when a Web API is put into real applications. Thirdly, new functions can also emerge when it is used with other Web APIs. Therefore, in addition to learning semantics from descriptions, it is necessary to learn their semantics from their applications.

Mashups are applications of APIs and their descriptions are sources that can be applied to the process of learning the semantics of APIs. Compared with the semantic information contained only in the topic vector, graph embedded representation can contain both the semantic and the graph structure information.

Graph Network Construction   In our model, four types of nodes are considered, namely Web API, mashup, category and word. Then, we define six kinds of edges according to the different relationships between nodes:

- <Mashup, Word>: The TF-IDF value between mashup and word used in its description text.
- <API, Word>: The TF-IDF value between API and word used in its description text.
- <Word1, Word2>: The weighted frequency value of word1 and word2 co-occur in a certain size of sliding window.
- <Mashup, API>: The weighted value of API usage frequency by mashup.
- <Mashup, Category>: The category of mashup.
- <API, Category>: The category of API.

Node Embeddings. After constructing the entire graph, our goal is to use a convolutional neural network to get the node representation of Web APIs and mashups, which can be used for the training and application of the API pair adoption probability prediction model. As shown in Fig. 1, we use a node representation learning model including a two-layer graph convolution neural network, and finally get the node embeddings of mashups and Web APIs. The prediction task of links between APIs and mashups is used to learn the node representations and determine whether a mashup uses an API which is represented by a link between them in the graph. The input is the node representation of mashups and Web APIs, and the output is the prediction result. We select binary accuracy to evaluate our results.

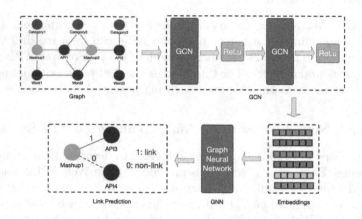

Fig. 1. Node representation learning based on link prediction.

3.3 Adoption Possibility Prediction for Web API Pairs

Figure 2 shows the process of adoption possibility prediction for Web API pairs. The vector of API_1, API_2 and target mashup can be represented as T_{a_1}, T_{a_2} and T_M. We need to extract more features from these representations to not only consider the interactions between Web APIs, but also the interactions between Web APIs and the target mashup. The attention mechanism [5] is a mainstream method which is inspired by the way that people receive information and is applied to deep learning. We make use of the attention mechanism to optimize the prediction model. The attention mechanism can be applied to the matrix after feature interactions. An attention network can be used to learn its related parameters, mainly using multi-layer perceptron (MLP) for learning. The input of the attention network is a combination of two feature vectors encoded in the embedding space. The attention network is defined as: $a'_{ij} = h^T ReLU(W(v_i \odot v_j)x_i x_j + b)$. The normalized attention scores can be calculated using the softmax function: $a_{ij} = \frac{exp(a'_{ij})}{\sum_{(i,j) \in R_x} exp(a'_{ij})}$, where, $W \in R^{t \times k}$, $b \in R^t$, and $h \in R^t$ are the parameters of the model, and t represents the size of the hidden layer of the

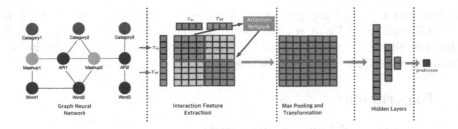

Fig. 2. Prediction model.

attention network, and v_i denotes the embedding vector of feature i. The input is the two interaction vectors of the pair-wise interaction layer, and the output is the attention score corresponding to the combined features. The attention-based pooling layer finally outputs a k dimensional vector, which is the result of considering the importance of different combinations of features.

We concatenate the semantic feature vector of Web APIs and the target mashup, then obtain an interactive matrix containing more information, which aims to provide a perspective of target mashup for the extraction of combined features. We use the attention mechanism on the basis of this matrix and then transform it to a fixed-length vector for later prediction. A max polling filter is used to get the API interaction feature matrix M_{TF} and then transform it to a vector. Then we take the feature vector of target mashup T_M and API interaction feature T_{IF} as the input of the multiple hidden layers. For each layer i, $f_{L_i}(T_x) = \sigma_{L_i}(W_{L_i}T_x + bias_{L_i})$, where T_x is the processed composition vector of API interaction and target mashup features, W is the corresponding weight vector. After three hidden layers, we use a sigmoid function to predict the adoption probability of the API pairs in the output layer, $P(T_x) = Sigmoid(t^T f_{L_3}(T_x))$. The prediction score P is from 0 to 1.

3.4 API Package Recommendation

We trained a network to predict the probability that a Web API pair can be adopted by this mashup. Therefore, to develop mashup T_M, we can test all API pairs for it. However, there are two problems. The first problem is there are too many Web APIs, so it is not possible for us to test all Web API pairs. The second problem is a mashup may need more than two APIs.

For the first problem, we try to select a Web API candidate set for mashup T_M. We can sort other mashups using their cosine similarities of embedding vectors with mashup T_M. Then, an appropriate number of Web APIs can be obtained from the most similar mashups.

For the second problem, we make an assumption that for a Web API package to be recommended to a mashup, any API pair in it must have a high adoption probability. Therefore, we can construct a graph whose nodes are APIs and edges are the adoption possibility predicted by the neural network. This can be represented as a complete graph identification problem. For a restriction, if the possibility of an API pair is larger than the edge between any API and itself, then this edge will remain, otherwise it will be removed. Then the nodes in each complete sub-graph form a Web API package.

4   Experiments

4.1   Datasets and Experimental Settings

Our data is from Programmable Web, the largest online repository of information on Web APIs and mashups. After screening, we finally crawled the information of 6,424 mashups and 20,541 Web APIs. Morever, we find that each mashup contains two Web APIs and each Web API has been used by eight mashups on average, indicating the cooperation of APIs are common.

In the node embedding process, we use the 200 dimensional vector representation. The interaction feature extraction layer units are 400×400. The configuration of the three hidden layers is (200, 100, 20). L2 regularization is used to avoid overfitting and the regularization strength is 0.001.

4.2   Evaluation Metrics

In this experiment, we use recall to measure how many previously adopted APIs are recommended to the mashup from the total number of adopted Web APIs. $Recall = \frac{TP}{TP+FN}$. Higher values indicate better performance.

4.3   Comparative Methods

We selected some existing methods and compared them with our methods.

- Word Vector Similarity Model (WVSM) is a recommendation method based on word level similarity.
- WJaccard is a word vector similarity model using Jaccard similarity. The collaborative filtering method (CF) recommends the APIs used by the mashup that are the most similar to the target mashup in the historical data.
- The enhanced relational topic model (ERTM) [6] method mixes and matches the relationship between mashup and API to extract the functional attributes of the API and then make recommendations.
- The TopicCF method [7] is a combination of the topic model and collaborative filtering.
- Social-aware service recommendation (SASR) [8] conducts in-depth exploration in the social relationship dimension to build a comprehensive service recommendation model.
- The multi-level relational network (MRN) method [3] is a mashup service recommendation method that builds a deep relationship network between services based on potential topics, tags, and service networks.
- API-Prefer model [4] is an API Package recommender system based on composition feature learning.

4.4   Results

Node Representation Learning Results. In the experiment, we divide the training set, verification set and test set in the ratio of 6:2:2. The results are shown in Fig. 3. After training 1000 epochs, the mean binary accuracy of link prediction is 0.8, which shows that node representation learning is effective in extracting the relationship between mashup and API.

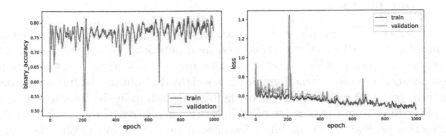

Fig. 3. Evaluation of node representation learning.

API Recommendation Results. The comparison of the recall results of the different models (the number of recommended APIs ranges from 10 to 50) is shown in Fig. 4.

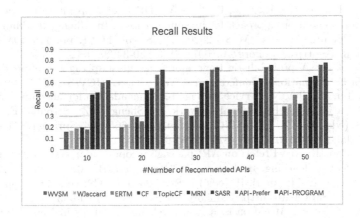

Fig. 4. Recommendation recall result.

It can be seen that the results of the three traditional algorithms, namely WVSM, WJaccard and CF, and the results of the ERTM and TopicCF methods which only consider simple features are not satisfactory. In contrast, the recommendation results of the in-depth mining method of relational networks have been greatly improved. Of these, API-PROGRAM replaces the LDA topic vector in API-Prefer with a graph to represent the effect of learning and also improves the interaction by adding an attention network. It can be seen that with the improvement of the method, the recall rate has also been improved. We observe that the results achieved by our method using graph representation learning and the attention mechanism are better than all the other methods. This verifies the effectiveness of our method and shows that our improvement direction is correct. It also indicates that our thinking and optimization of the deficiencies of the previous models in this section are effective.

5   Conclusion

In this paper, we use graph representation learning to mine the semantic features of mashup and API description texts and their network relationships. Then, the attention network is added. The attention score is obtained by using the attention network and the interaction matrix is weighted to obtain the final combined feature vector. The feature vector of the target mashup in the interaction layer is added to achieve the purpose of adding the perspective of the mashup in the extraction process of the combined features. After the aforementioned improvements, we compare the recommendation recall results of the different models and find that our results are the best of all the other methods.

Acknowledgment. This work is partially supported by National Key Research and Development Plan(No. 2018YFB1003800).

References

1. Xiao, Y., Liu, J., Hu, R., Cao, B., Cao, Y.: DINRec: deep interest network based API recommendation approach for mashup creation. In: Cheng, R., Mamoulis, N., Sun, Y., Huang, X. (eds.) WISE 2020. LNCS, vol. 11881, pp. 179–193. Springer, Cham (2019). https://doi.org/10.1007/978-3-030-34223-4_12
2. Shi, M., et al.: A probabilistic topic model for mashup tag recommendation. In: 2016 IEEE International Conference on Web Services (ICWS). IEEE (2016)
3. Cao, J., Lu, Y., Zhu, N.: Service package recommendation for mashup development based on a multi-level relational network. In: Sheng, Q.Z., Stroulia, E., Tata, S., Bhiri, S. (eds.) ICSOC 2016. LNCS, vol. 9936, pp. 666–674. Springer, Cham (2016). https://doi.org/10.1007/978-3-319-46295-0_46
4. Liu, Y., Cao, J.: API-Prefer: an API package recommender system based on composition feature learning. In: Kafeza, E., Benatallah, B., Martinelli, F., Hacid, H., Bouguettaya, A., Motahari, H. (eds.) ICSOC 2020. LNCS, vol. 12571, pp. 500–507. Springer, Cham (2020). https://doi.org/10.1007/978-3-030-65310-1_36
5. Vaswani, A., et al.: Attention is all you need. In: Advances in Neural Information Processing Systems (2017)
6. Li, C., et al.: A novel approach for API recommendation in mashup development. In: 2014 IEEE International Conference on Web Services. IEEE (2014)
7. Jain, A., Liu, X., Yu, Q.: Aggregating functionality, use history, and popularity of APIs to recommend mashup creation. In: Barros, A., Grigori, D., Narendra, N.C., Dam, H.K. (eds.) ICSOC 2015. LNCS, vol. 9435, pp. 188–202. Springer, Heidelberg (2015). https://doi.org/10.1007/978-3-662-48616-0_12
8. Xu, W., et al.: A social-aware service recommendation approach for mashup creation. In: 2013 IEEE 20th International Conference on Web Services. IEEE (2013)

H-STREAM: Composing Microservices for Enacting Stream and Histories Analytics Pipelines

Genoveva Vargas-Solar[1] and Javier A. Espinosa-Oviedo[2]([✉])

[1] French Council of Scientific Research, LIRIS Lab, Villeurbanne, France
genoveva.vargas-solar@cnrs.fr
[2] University of Lyon, ERIC Lab, Bron, France
javier.espinosa-oviedo@univ-lyon2.fr

Abstract. This paper introduces H-STREAM, a framework that proposes microservices to support the analytics of streams produced by systems collecting data stemming from IoT (Internet of Things) environments. Microservices implement operators that can be composed for implementing specific analytics pipelines as queries using a declarative language. Queries (i.e., microservices compositions) can synchronise online streams and histories to provide a continuous and evolving understanding of the environments they come from.

Keywords: Stream processing · Cloud · Microservices

1 Introduction

The Internet of Things (IoT) enables the construction of smart environments (grids, homes, and cities) where streams are produced at different paces. Analytics tasks must combine streams and persistent historical data to understand thoroughly, model, and predict smart environments behaviour. For example, "at 9:00, start computing the average number of people entering a shopping mall every morning and identify points of interest (POI) according to peoples flow in the last month". Answering this query is challenging because it implies determining: (i) the streams that must be discarded or persist into histories (do we store the average/hour or every event representing a person entering the mall? or the person visiting an area in the mall?); (ii) how to properly combine histories with streams within analytics tasks (do we combine the whole history with the average observation/hour? do we compute POIs of the last month and correlate them with new computed POIs observed online?). Existing stream platforms provide efficient solutions for collecting and processing streams with parallel execution backends. Programmers rely on these platforms to define stream processing

This work has been partially funded by the International emerging Action on DAta centred intelligent GEOsciences (ADAGEO), https://adageo.github.io.

H. Hacid et al. (Eds.): ICSOC 2021, LNCS 13121, pp. 867–874, 2021.
https://doi.org/10.1007/978-3-030-91431-8_64

operations that consume "mini"-batches of streams observed through temporal windows thanks to query engines. These engines use a list of passive queries to analyze and to storage or use by other processors. Analytics-based applications must build ad-hoc programs that process postmortem data and streams to perform online analytics tasks. Since programs are ad-hoc and queries are passive, the use of specific processing operations (e.g., clustering, windowing, aggregation) are (hard)coded, and they should be modified and calibrated if new requirements come up.

This paper introduces H-STREAM,[1] an analytics pipelines' enactment engine. It wraps operators as self-contained services and composes them into pipelines of analytics tasks as queries. Queries can continuously deliver aggregated streams/historical data to target applications. Accordingly, the remainder of the paper is organised as follows. Section 2 introduces related work regarding stream processing. Section 3 describes the general architecture of H-STREAM and its operators as microservices that are deployed on high-performance underlying infrastructures. Section 4 introduces the core of our contribution, a stream processing microservice and discusses experimental results. Section 5 concludes the paper.

2   Related Work

Stream processing refers to data processing in motion or computing on data directly as it is produced or received. In the early 2000s, academic and commercial approaches proposed stream operators for defining continuous queries (windows, joins, aggregation) that dealt with streams [3]. These solutions evolved towards stream processors that receive and send the data streams and execute the application or analytics logic. A stream processor ensures that data flows efficiently and the computation scales and is fault-tolerant. We analyse stream processing systems that emerged to process (i.e., query) streams from continuous data providers (e.g. sensors, things).

Apache Storm,[2] Apache Flink,[3] Apache Kafka,[4] Spring Cloud Data Flow,[5] Amazon Kinesis Streams,[6] Cloud Dataflow,[7] Apache Beam SDK,[8] Apache Pulsar,[9] IBM Streams[10] are distributed stream processing computation frameworks. Most of them enable the design of topologies of consuming and processing nodes represented as acyclic graphs that implement pipelines. These frameworks are

---

[1] https://github.com/javieraespinosa/hstream.
[2] https://storm.apache.org.
[3] https://flink.apache.org.
[4] https://kafka.apache.org.
[5] https://spring.io/projects/spring-cloud-dataflow.
[6] http://aws.amazon.com/kinesis/data-streams/.
[7] https://cloud.google.com/dataflow.
[8] https://beam.apache.org.
[9] https://pulsar.apache.org/.
[10] https://www.ibm.com/cloud/streaming-analytics.

often stateful to enable database integration and the event-driven/reactive application or analytics logic. Streams from many sources can be ingested, processed, and distributed across various nodes. The exchange of streams across nodes often adopt a publish and subscribe strategy. Many of these frameworks implement microservices that enable batch and continuous stream processing. Event stream query engines like Elasticsearch, Amazon Athena, Amazon Redshift, Cassandra define queries to analyze and sequence data for storage or use by other processors. They rely on "classic" ETL (extraction, transformation and loading) processes and use query engines to execute online search and aggregation. The real-time stream processing engines rely on distributed processing models, where unbounded data streams are processed. Much data are of no interest, and they can be filtered and compressed by orders of magnitude [5,6]. Stream querying and analytics are often performed after the complete scanning of representative data sets. Processing techniques must process streams on the fly and combine them with historical data to provide past and current analytics of observed environments. Despite solid platforms, solutions do not let programmers design their analytics pipelines without caring about the conditions in which streams are collected and stored. H-STREAM is a cartridge for defining stream analytics pipelines and enacting them by composing microservices that hide the underlying platforms dealing with low-level tasks for collecting and storing streams.

3   H-STREAM for Building and Querying Pipelines for Analysing Streams

We propose H-STREAM, an analytics' pipelines enactment engine with microservices composed for processing streams (see Fig. 1). H-STREAM operators implement aggregation, descriptive statistics, filtering, clustering, and visualisation wrapped as microservices. Microservices can be composed to define pipelines as queries that apply a series of analytics operations to streams collected by stream processing systems and stream histories. H-STREAM relies on (i) message queues for collecting streams online from IoT farms; and (ii) a backend execution environment that provides high-performance computing infrastructure (e.g., a virtual data centre [1], a cloud) with resources allocation strategies necessary for executing costly processes.

Composing Microservices. Microservices can work alone or be composed to implement simple or complex analytics pipelines (e.g., fetch, sliding window, average, etc.). A query is implemented by composing microservices. For example, consider observing download and upload speed variations within users' connections when working on different networks. Assume that observations are monitored online but that previous observations are also stored before the query is issued. A network analyst willing to determine if she obtains the expected bandwidth according to her subscription to a provider can ask *every two minutes give me the fastest download speed of the last 8 min* (see a) in Figure 2). Figure 2 b) shows the composition implementing this query example that starts calling a Fetch, and a Filter operators that retrieve respectively the streams produced

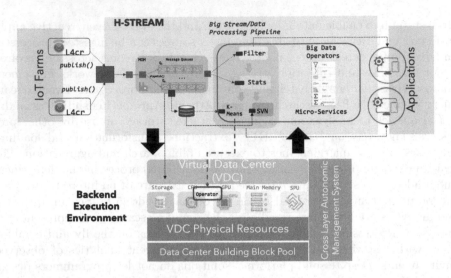

Fig. 1. H-STREAM general architecture.

online with a history filtering the *download_speed* collected the *last 8 min*. Results produced by these services are integrated by the operator MAX that synchronises the streams with the history to look for the maximum speed. The result is stored by a service Sink that contacts Grafana. This query is executed every two minutes by an operator window. The operator Fetch interacts with a RabbitMQ service that collects streams from devices and with a service that contacts InfluxDB[11] to store the streams for building a history. Finally, an operator window triggers the execution of the query every two minutes.

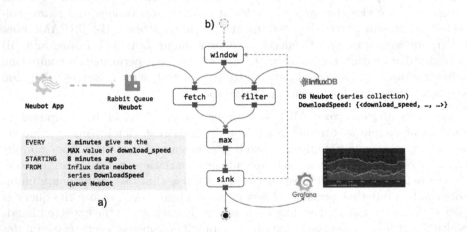

Fig. 2. Microservices composition example.

_____
[11] https://www.influxdata.com.

The approach for composing microservices is based on a composition operation that connects them by expressing a data flow (IN/OUT data). We currently compose aggregation services (min, max, mean) with temporal windowing services (landmark, sliding) that receive input data from storage support or a continuous data producer. We propose connectors, namely Fetch and Sink microservices that determine the way microservices exchange data from/to things, storage systems, or other microservices.

We proposed a simple query language used to express stream processing queries. A query expression is processed to generate a query-workflow that implements it (see Fig. 2). Activities represent calls to microservices; they are connected according to a control flow that defines the order they should be executed (i.e., in sequence or parallel). The control flow respects a data flow that defines data Input/Output dependencies. H-STREAM enacts the query-workflow coordinating the execution of microservices, retrieving partial output that serves as input or a result (see Fig. 2).

4   Stream Processing Microservice

Figure 3 shows the general architecture of a stream microservice operator with its components Buffer Manager, Fetch and Sink, and OperatorLogic. The microservice logic is based on a scheduler that ensures the recurrence rate in which the analytics operation implemented by the microservice is executed. Stream processing is based on "unlimited" consumption of data ensured by the component Fetch that works if a producer notifies streams. This specification is contained in the logic of the components OperatorLogic and Fetch.

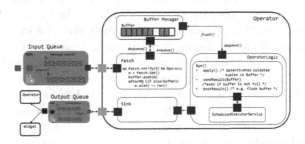

Fig. 3. Architecture of a stream processing microservice for processing data streams.

As shown in Fig. 3, a microservice communicates asynchronously with other microservices using a message-oriented middleware. As data is produced, the microservice fetches and copies the data to an internal buffer. Then, depending on its logic, it applies a processing algorithm and sends it to the microservices connected to it. The microservices adopt the tuple oriented data model as a stream exchange model among the IoT environment producing streams and other microservices. The general architecture of a microservice is specialised in concrete microservices processing streams using well-known window-based stream processing strategies: tumbling, sliding and landmark [4]. Microservices can also combine stream histories with continuous flows of streams of the same type (the average number of connections to the Internet by Bob of the last month until the next hour). Since RAM assigned to a microservice might be limited, every microservice implements a data management strategy by collaborating with the communication middleware to exploit buffer space, avoiding losing data and generating results on time. As data is produced, the microservice fetches and copies the data to an internal buffer. Then, depending on its logic, it applies a processing algorithm and sends it to the microservices connected to it. There are two possibilities: (i) on-line processing using tree window-based strategies [4] (tumbling, sliding and landmark) well known in the stream processing systems domain; (ii) combine stream histories with continuous flows of streams of the same type (the average number of connections to the Internet by Bob of the last month until the next hour).

4.1   Interval Oriented Storage Support for Consuming Streams

A microservice that aggregates historical data and streams includes a component named HistoricFetch. This component is responsible for performing a one-shot query for retrieving stored data according to an input query (for example, by a user or application). As described above, we have implemented a general/abstract microservice that contains a Fetch and Sink microservices. The historical fetch component has been specialized to interact with two stores: InfluxDB[12] and Cassandra[13].

Consider the query introduced previously *every two minutes give me the fastest download speed of the last* 8 min. It combines the history of observations of the *last 8* min with those produced continuously and this every two minutes. In technical terms, the query implies looking for the maximum down_load speed by defining windows of 8 min for observing the download_speed in the connections. To get the fastest speed every 2 min (as stated in the query), we divide the 8 min into buckets of 2 min and look within the window for the max value, that is, the fastest download_speed (i.e., the fastest speed within the 2 min buckets), and keep it as the "local" maximum speed. We combine every bucket with the historical data filtered according to the corresponding time interval. This strategy is valid only if the production timeliness of the stream producers and the operator microservice are synchronised. Finally, the global max will be the maximum of all this set of local maximum speeds that will be the fastest download speed in the last 8 min.

---

[12] InfluxDB is a time series system accepting temporal queries, useful for computing time-tagged tuples (https://www.influxdata.com).

[13] Cassandra is a key-value store that provides non-temporal read/write operations that might be interesting for storing vast quantities of data (http://cassandra.apache.org).

4.2 Microservices Execution

Microservices are executed on top of a Spark infrastructure deployed on a virtual machine provided by the cloud provider Microsoft Azure. A microservice exports two interfaces: the operator interface as a SpepsIoT Component with methods to manage it (e.g., start/stop, bind/unbind) and to produce results in a push/pull mode; the DB interface to connect and send temporal queries to a temporal database management system (e.g., Cassandra, InfluxDB). The microservice wraps the logic of a data processing operator that consumes time-stamped stream collections represented as series of tuples. We assume that it is possible to navigate through the tuple structure for accessing attribute values where one of the tuple attributes corresponds to its time-stamp. The time-stamp represents the arrival time of the stream to the communication infrastructure (i.e., rabbitMQ queue). The operator logic is implemented as a Spark program. Spark performs its parallel execution. Produced results can be collected by interacting with the operator through its interface; it can be connected to another microservice (e.g., the operator sink) as shown in the left part of Fig. 3.

4.3 Experimental Validation

We conducted experiments for validating the use of our microservices. For deploying our experiment, we built an IoT farm using our Azure Grant[14] and implemented a distributed version of the IoT environment to test a clustered version of RabbitMQ. Therefore, we address the scaling-up problem regarding the number of data producers (things) for our microservices. Using Azure Virtual Machines (VM), we implemented a realistic scenario for testing scalability in terms of: (i) Initial MOM (RabbitMQ) installed in the VM_2; (ii) Producers (Things) installed in the VM_1; (iii) microservices installed in the VM_3.

In this experiment, microservices and testbeds were running on separate VMs. This experiment leads to several cases scaling up to several machines hosting until 800 things with a clustered version of Rabbit using several nodes and queues that could consume millions of messages produced at rates in the order of milliseconds. Observations showed the behaviour of the IoT environment regarding the message-based communication middleware when the number of things increased, when the production rate varies and when it uses one or several queues for each consuming microservice. We also observed the behaviour of the IoT environment when several microservices were consuming and processing the data. The most agile behaviour is when nodes and virtual machines increase independently of the number of things. Indeed, the performance of 800 things against 3 things does not change a lot by increasing nodes, machines and queues. Note also that devoting one queue per thing does not lead to essential changes in performance. This scenario concerns an experiment conducted in the Neuroscience Laboratory at CINVESTAV Mexico (details can be found in [2]).

---

[14] The MS Azure Grant was associated with a project to perform data analytics on crowds flows in cities. It consisted of credits for using cloud resources for performing high-performance data processing.

Regarding connectivity in cities, with many people willing to connect devices in different networks available in different urban spaces, we configured more things and queues and nodes. The use case scenario gives insight into the way microservices can be composed to answer continuous queries[15]. The execution time of these queries is compared according to two settings: 800 things producing streams through 3 queues and 800 things and 1 queue deployed on one node. The query execution cost depends on its recurrence and the history size. The overhead implied by the streams' production pace is delegated to the message passing middleware. Through queries implemented by H-STREAM queries, we prove that it is possible to provide a hybrid post-mortem and online analytics.

5   Conclusions and Future Work

This paper proposed H-STREAM that composes microservices deployed on high-performance computing backends (e.g., cloud, HPC) to process data produced by farms of things producing streams at different paces. Microservices compositions can tailor data processing functions personalised to the requirements of the applications and IoT environments. Future work consists of developing a composition language used for expressing data processing workflows to be weaved within target application logics [1]. Current work includes two urban computing projects modelling and managing crowds and smart energy management.

References

1. Akoglu, A., Vargas-Solar, G.: Putting data science pipelines on the edge. arXiv preprint arXiv:2103.07978 (2021)
2. Arriaga-Varela, E., Espinosa-Oviedo, J.A., Vargas-Solar, G., Pérez, R.D.: Supporting real-time visual analytics in neuroscience. In: Advanced Vector Architectures for Future Applications - Book of Abstracts. Barcelona Supercomputing Center (2017)
3. Fragkoulis, M., Carbone, P., Kalavri, V., Katsifodimos, A.: A survey on the evolution of stream processing systems. arXiv preprint arXiv:2008.00842 (2020)
4. Golab, L., Özsu, M.T.: Data stream management. Synth. Lect. Data Manage. 2(1), 1–73 (2010)
5. Woo, M.Y.: What's the big deal about big data. Eng. Sci. 76(3), 16–23 (2013)
6. Zikopoulos, P., Eaton, C., et al.: Understanding Big Data: Analytics for Enterprise Class Hadoop and Streaming Data. McGraw-Hill Osborne Media, New York (2011)

---

[15] The HADAS group previously used the Neubot data collection in the context of the FP7 project S2EUNET in collaboration with Politecnico di Torino.

KG2Code: Correct Code Examples Mining Service Based on Knowledge Graph for Fixing API Misuses

Yangqi Zhang[✉], Zhirui Kuai, Wenjin Yao, Zhiyang Zhang, and Li Kuang[✉]

Department of Software Engineering, School of Computer Science and Engineering,
Central South University, Changsha, China
{zhangyangqi,8209180621,8209180518,zzy415573678,kuangli}@csu.edu.cn

Abstract. API misuse has become an important factor restricting the quality of software services. Existing API misuse detectors based on the API-constraint knowledge graph can not intuitively assist developers in fixing the API misuse. Correct code examples are more direct and straightforward for developers to modify and debug code. Therefore, we first enrich the API-constraint knowledge graph. Besides, we publish a service called KG2Code, which can map the API-constraint Knowledge Graph to the Correct Code examples. According to the different types of constraint relations in the API-constraint knowledge graph, we design a code snippet mining framework that extracts the corresponding correct API usage pattern from over 9528K Java repositories GitHub. KG2Code is implemented by the interactive visualization website. It helped users (1) learn how to use an unfamiliar API or fix an API misuse and (2) understand why API misuse occurs.

Keywords: Quality of software services · API-constraint knowledge graph · Mining software repositories

1 Introduction

If developers do not comply with API usage constraints in the actual software development, it will lead to API misuse or even software crash, which causes the software to be unreliable. For example, when using the *File* in Java, *File.createNewFile(String)* can only be called after *File.exist()* to avoid FileNotFoundException. Therefore, developers are often concerned with the solution to API misuse. In fact, whether in Github, in StackOverflow(SO), or the API reference documentation, there will be much implicit or explicit information to fix the API misuse.

The API reference documentation includes a wealth of knowledge in different aspects of the API, such as functionalities, constraints, directives, caveats, and resource specifications. The knowledge of constraint descriptions helps developers understand the correct usage of the API, making it easy to use the API. However, the constraint knowledge is scattered within the document of the API

© Springer Nature Switzerland AG 2021
H. Hacid et al. (Eds.): ICSOC 2021, LNCS 13121, pp. 875–882, 2021.
https://doi.org/10.1007/978-3-030-91431-8_65

elements (e.g., class), leading to many challenges for API constraint knowledge discovery and summarization. The Q&A knowledge forum (e.g., StackOverflow) also provides related API misuse questions and answers, but questions about API misuse are not necessarily correct, and many answers are not clear [1]. There are a large number of API usage examples in Github. Through these examples, developers can quickly understand the code and modify the incorrect usage of the API. However, it is difficult to locate the API we need from the massive Github repositories. Therefore, fixing the API misuse through the above three ways is not feasible in practice.

Inspired by the SO platform, we consider that correct code examples can better improve the efficiency and effectiveness of developers than API misuse description. Therefore, We publish a service called KG2Code, which can map an API-constraint knowledge graph to correct code examples. For a given API constraint triple, we extract correct code examples from the Java Github repositories. First, we crawl Java repositories and filter low-quality repositories by distributed software mining infrastructure [2]. And according to the class name and method name, each method in the repository can be found. Next, traverse the Abstract Syntax Trees (ASTs) of the two APIs with different constraint relations, and capture the correct code pattern of the API by converting different data such as control structure, calling sequence, guard conditions, etc. Finally, remove the part that we are not interested in by program slicing.

This paper makes the following contributions:

1. We expand the original API-constraint knowledge graph by adding constraint relations and merging more data;
2. We conduct an empirical study that reveals that correct code examples can effectively assist developers. We firstly propose an approach that can extract correct code examples from Github based on API-constraint knowledge graph, and we implement it as a visualization website;
3. Our manual inspection confirms the high quality of the correct examples mined by KG2Code.

2   Related Work

API pattern mining is our significant part of KG2Code. API pattern mining is divided into three parts: (1) By modeling the program as a code sequence or item set and inferring programming rules by mining frequent sequences, or frequent itemsets [3,4]. (2) Researchers apply formal concept analysis [5] to extract the call sequence in the program [6]. (3) Researchers mine the guard conditions of APIs by applying predicate mining technology [7].

Inspired by examplecheck [7], KG2code also mines the Github software code repositories, but the difference is that we mine through specific patterns in the knowledge graph. According to the knowledge graph, the calling sequence, guard conditions, and specific conditions of the control structure of the APIs correspond to different types of constraint relations. Besides, the SMT Solver [8] is used to determine the equivalence of the guard conditions.

3 Construction of API-Constraint Knowledge Graph

To mine correct code examples, we first need to construct the API constraint knowledge graph. Expect the four API constraint relations, which include call-order, state-checking, value-checking, and trigger, we add three types of fine-grained constraint relationships: redundant-checking, duplicate-checking, and synchronized-checking, which also corresponds to the frequent API misuse types in the MuBench [9]. We define the seven constraint relations which extend the prior work [10] for the first time. As the construction of the API constraint knowledge graph is similar to the prior work, A detailed description will not be given here. The overall construction framework of the API constraint knowledge graph is shown in Fig. 1.

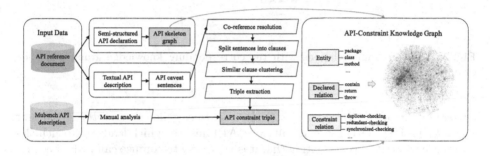

Fig. 1. The construction of API-constraint knowledge graph

The entity of knowledge graph consists of API elements: package, class, method, exception, parameter, return value, and value literals. Literal values such as null, −1, true, negative numbers, or a range such as [0, 9]. The knowledge graph contains two types of relations: declaration relations and constraint relations. Declare relations such as a package contains a class, a class contains a method, a method returns a numeric literal, or a method throws an exception. In terms of the constraint relations, by referring to the most frequent API misuse types of the MuBench, we added three fine-grained constraint relationships, and we expanded the constraint types to seven types. Now let's discuss the specific usage of these seven constraint types in the knowledge graph. (see Fig. 2.)

Call-Order: API misuse caused by missing an API call or incorrect call order. It means the method has to be called before a certain method or the method has to be called after a certain method to avoid API misuse. For example, the file should be closed after being written to prevent resource leakage, which means like *PrintWriter.close()* should be called after the PrintWriter method (close the PrintWriter after writing to avoid resource leak). The knowledge graph can also express chain calls through multi-hop relations.

State-Checking: API misuse caused by missing state-checking or incorrect state-checking. For example, we need to check the boolean value of *hasnext()*

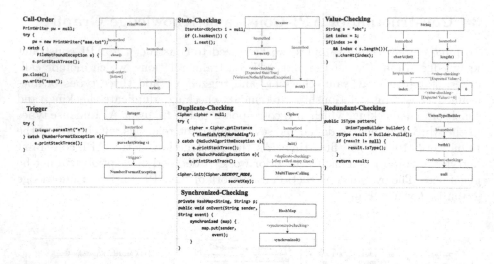

Fig. 2. The constraint relations with the corresponding knowledge graph and code example

or *isempty*() before *Iterator.next*(). It is correct when *hasnext*() is true, or *isempty*() is false. Otherwise, it will cause API misuse, which leads to NosuchElementexception. It is worth noting that it is very easy to confuse call-order because it seems to be an order relation between the two methods. We have to pay attention to that state-checking requiring state-checking on the method's return boolean value, while call-order does not need it.

Value-Checking: Determine whether the value of the parameter in the API follows API usage constraints of the method. For example: for the *ArrayList.Get*() method, and it is necessary to check if the index is out of bounds.

Trigger: Trigger is to check whether the exception handling is missing in the code, which leads to the API misuse. For example, *Interge.parseInt*(). If the string does not contain a parsable integer, *Interge.parseInt*() may throw a NumberFormatException.

Duplicate-Checking: If some APIs are called multiple times, they will be misused. For example, *cipher.init*() is called twice along one possible execution path, which causes an infinite loop.

Redundant-Checking: A method does a redundant checking, which prevents a necessary part of a usage and is executed along a certain execution path. One case is redundant null checks. For example: *UnionTypeBuilder.build*() returns a JSType that can never be null. Branching on a null check, therefore, results in dead code.

Synchronized-Checking: In multi-threaded environments, some container classes must be the thread-unsafe condition. For example, the *HashMap* in

JDK1.8 is thread-unsafe if a usage does not obtain a lock before updating a *HashMap* that is accessed from multiple threads.

4   KG2Code

KG2Code consists of two phases. One is the offline phase, which extracts the constraint triples in the knowledge graph and mines correct code examples from Github's high-quality repositories. While the other is the online phase, which generates the KG2Code results by the visualizing website. The KG2Code overview is shown in Fig. 3.

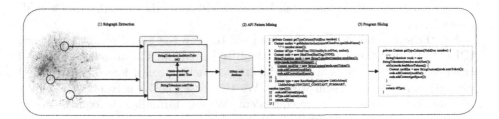

Fig. 3. Overview of KG2Code

4.1   Extract the Subgraph

It's simple to extract the subgraph from the API constraint knowledge graph. We extract the subgraph from neo4j by different relation types. However, we only extract the subgraph for four API constraint types of relations: call-order, state-checking, synchronized-checking, and trigger. This is because the relationship type needs to correspond to the code pattern that can be extracted-such as value-checking, the variables involved in a program change dynamically during the actual running of the program, and in some value-checking examples, getting the correct code structure requires checking if the variables are in an interval. However, it is represented by another variable in the range of the program, and it is difficult to ensure that the code snippet meets the requirements of value-checking.

4.2   Extract the Structure of the API

We only extract the subgraph for four API constraint types of relations: call-order, state-checking, synchronized-checking, and trigger.

For a given API, we search for code snippets on GitHub based on the constrained triples, which are from the knowledge graph. We used a distributed software mining infrastructure to filter out some of the low-quality Java repositories by some limits, such as the number of repository contributors and the number of version updates. We only consider repositories with at least 100 revisions and 2 contributors. Then we use the relevant syntax to traverse ASTs of Java files and match the methods and classes of interest by the name of the class and the name of the method. In order to extract API-specific patterns, KG2Code models each program as a structured call sequence, which extracts variable names, but still retains the call sequence, control structure, guard conditions. Furthermore, we extracted different API patterns for different constraint types.

For the call-order relation, we need to record the order of API calls properly. In some cases, the methods are not called sequentially, for example, $code().addContent(getSpace())$; this expression is a case of nested calls, we assume that the method inside the parentheses will complete the call first when it is run so that this sentence will be processed as 'code -> getSpace -> addContent'.

For the state-checking relation, we need to keep the guard condition of each API call. We use the conjunction of the lifted predicates in all relevant control structures. In other words, we record all the branching conditions on the method call path and connect them with &. We then use the Z3 solver to determine whether the two conditions are equivalent. We will formalize the equivalence of two guard conditions as a satisfiability problem.

For the synchronized-checking and trigger relation, we traverse the abstract syntax tree to retrain the method's control structure, including try-catch, switch-case, synchronized, return, various loops, and so on. For the synchronized-checking relation, we need to record whether the synchronized modifier is added. For the trigger relation, we need to check whether the API is contained within the associated try-catch block.

Finally, we matched the correct code pattern for each API by the constraint relation type and counted the number of correct code patterns conforming to each API. The GitHub link of this file is reserved.

4.3   Program Slicing

We need to do static code slicing to filter out any statements that are not related to the API method of interest. In this step, we retain the control structure of the method obtained in the previous step. On this basis, we record the variables involved in the API of interest, including the caller of the API, the receiver of the API, and the parameters used by the API. We use these variables for static code slicing.For example (see Fig. 3.), '$Contentmodifier = newStringContent(mods.nextToken())$;', this sentence contains the method of interest: $nextToken()$, so the variables we use to slice are '$mods$' and '$modifier$'. All statements that contain these two variables before and after this statement will be retained. The resulting statement and associated control structures make up the result of the slice.

5   Tool Implementation and Evaluation

We built an API knowledge graph for JDK 1.8[1]. The API constraint knowledge graph includes 52,754 entities and 85,196 relationships, which includes 2,397 classes, 26,902 API methods, 50,711 parameters, 648 exceptions. There are 58025 declared relationships and 27,171 constraint relationships, including 1586 call-order relations, 24,395 value-checking relations, 890 state-checking relations, 109 duplicate-checking relations, 85 redundant-checking relations, and 106 synchronized-checking relations. These API-constraint relations involve 19,385 methods, 6,823 parameters, and 5,347 return and 10,289 throw relations.

We scanned more than 9 million Java repositories on the 2019 October GitHub dataset. We have implemented KG2Code as an online website. The website front-end is implemented by using D3.js, and the back-end is implemented by built-in python and nodeJS. Developers can enter a search query of the required API. when querying *java.swing. StringTokenizer.nextToken*, it shows a description of the API, the display of the API constraint subgraph from the knowledge graph, the corresponding code example, and the number of code examples with the same pattern. Each API can also be accessed through the link to the original Github repository (see Fig. 4.).

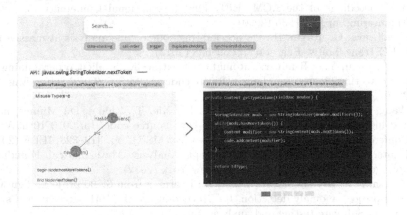

Fig. 4. A snapshot of the KG2Code website

We can map 108 API-constraint relations in the MuBench to correct examples that correspond to the API pattern. To check whether the correct examples mined by KG2Code indeed conform to the desirable API usage. We manually check 300 random code snippets mined by KG2code involving 30 API misuses from the MuBench. Each API misuse contains 10 correct examples. They all match the correct usage Java file provided. These results demonstrate that our proposed approach the correct examples mined by KG2Code are effective.

---

[1] https://docs.oracle.com/javase/8/docs/api.

6   Conclusions and Future Work

This paper first proposes a service named KG2Code, a mining framework based on API-constraint knowledge graph for correct code examples in Github. Furthermore, we expand the previous API-constraint knowledge graph with three more fine-grained types of constraint relations, derived from API reference documentation and the MuBench. The quality of correct examples has been demonstrated by manual inspection. In the future, we will tackle the challenges that the API reference documentation and Github code repositories will continue to evolve and update as time goes on.

Acknowledgement. This work has been supported by the National Key R&D Program of China (No. 2018YFB1402800), the National Natural Science Foundation of China (No. 61772560), and the Fundamental Research Funds for the Central Universities of Central South University (No. 2021zzts0746).

References

1. Ren, X., Sun, J., Xing, Z., Xia, X., Sun, J.: Demystify official API usage directives with crowdsourced API misuse scenarios, erroneous code examples and patches. In: Proceedings of the ACM/IEEE 42nd International Conference on Software Engineering, pp. 925–936 (2020)
2. Upadhyaya, G., Rajan, H.: On accelerating source code analysis at massive scale. IEEE Trans. Softw. Eng. **44**(7), 669–688 (2018)
3. Li, Z., Zhou, Y.: PR-miner: automatically extracting implicit programming rules and detecting violations in large software code. ACM SIGSOFT Softw. Eng. Notes **30**(5), 306–315 (2005)
4. Wang, J., Dang, Y., Zhang, H., Chen, K., Xie, T., Zhang, D.: Mining succinct and high-coverage API usage patterns from source code. In: 2013 10th Working Conference on Mining Software Repositories (MSR), pp. 319–328. IEEE (2013)
5. Ganter, B., Wille, R.: Formal Concept Analysis: Mathematical Foundations. Springer Science & Business Media, New York (2012)
6. Gruska, N., Wasylkowski, A., Zeller, A.: Learning from 6,000 projects: lightweight cross-project anomaly detection. In: Proceedings of the 19th international symposium on Software testing and analysis, pp. 119–130 (2010)
7. Zhang, T., Upadhyaya, G., Reinhardt, A., Rajan, H., Kim, M.: Are code examples on an online Q&A forum reliable? A study of API misuse on stack overflow. In: 2018 IEEE/ACM 40th International Conference on Software Engineering (ICSE), pp. 886–896. IEEE (2018)
8. Eén, N., Sörensson, N.: An extensible SAT-solver. In: Giunchiglia, E., Tacchella, A. (eds.) SAT 2003. LNCS, vol. 2919, pp. 502–518. Springer, Heidelberg (2004). https://doi.org/10.1007/978-3-540-24605-3_37
9. Amann, S., Nadi, S., Nguyen, H.A., Nguyen, T.N., Mezini, M.: MUBench: a benchmark for API-misuse detectors. In: Proceedings of the 13th International Conference on Mining Software Repositories, pp. 464–467 (2016)
10. Ren, X., et al.: API-misuse detection driven by fine-grained API-constraint knowledge graph. In: 2020 35th IEEE/ACM International Conference on Automated Software Engineering (ASE), pp. 461–472. IEEE (2020)

Industry Papers

An Embedded Representation Learning of Relational Clinical Codes

Suman Roy[1](✉), Amit Kumar[1], Ayan Sengupta[1], Riccardo Mattivi[2], Selim Ahmed[2], and Michael Bridges[2]

[1] Optum Global Advantage (OGA), UnitedHealth Group, Bangalore 560 103, India
{suman.roy,amit.kumar75,ayan_sengupta}@optum.com
[2] Optum Global Advantage (OGA), UnitedHealth Group, Dublin, Ireland
{riccardo.mattivi,ahmed.selim,michael.bridges}@optum.com

Abstract. Fraud, waste, abuse and error (FWAE) incidents lead to higher co-payments and premiums and other costs that can significantly impact the quality of care one receives. Curbing such incidents of overpayment in claims settlement is a major organizational goal for healthcare companies. As claims are settled by examining the combination of clinical codes assigned, the task at hand is to predict if a new claim would lead to overpayment. This prediction task can be solved by building a classification model that would accept a representation of the clinical codes (which form an ontology graph among themselves) and other feature vectors appearing in claims data. In this work, we learn the embedded representation of these clinical nodes and relations among them in the ontology graph (excerpts from Unified Medical Language System (UMLS)) by incorporating knowledge from the semantics of code descriptions and edge relations. We combine the Paragraph Vector (PV) model with translation-based models in a framework of multi-relational learning. We carry out intrinsic evaluations of these embedding models on different tasks. Finally, we apply this representation learning by detecting overpayment on claims in healthcare application and by computing the savings achieved in fraud prevention in healthcare.

Keywords: Healthcare systems · Fraud · Waste · Abuse and Error (FWAE) · Clinical codes · Embedding · Paragraph Vector Model · Ontology graph · Multi-relational learning

1 Introduction

FWAE incidents lead to pilferage of significant resources away from necessary health care services resulting in higher co-payments and premiums, and other costs. It can also impact the quality of care one receives and even deprive one of legitimate health benefits the person is entitled to. Billions of dollars are lost each year to healthcare fraud in the United States. In Payment Integrity Operations of a healthcare organization, one of the major aims is to reduce the amount of overpayment in claims settlement as a prevention measure to mitigate the effects of FWAE. Normally claims are settled by examining the combinations of clinical codes assigned to them. Let us consider the following collection of claim records as shown in Table 1. Here clm_id is a unique

© Springer Nature Switzerland AG 2021
H. Hacid et al. (Eds.): ICSOC 2021, LNCS 13121, pp. 885–899, 2021.
https://doi.org/10.1007/978-3-030-91431-8_66

identifier for a claim, drg_bil the drug code for which the provider has billed Optum, drg_pd the drug code that is used to pay the claim. Further dx1, ..., dx5 are the ICD-10-CM Diagnosis Codes, icd_proc1 and icd_proc2 the CPT codes, mbr_age_at_dos the age of the member, mbr_gender the gender of the member and amt_pd the amount paid for this particular claim. In addition, we can assume that we have a label (over_pmt) for each claim in the training data set, – it equals Y (1) if it is found to be an over-payment, N (0) if not. The task is to determine whether a new claim results in overpayment. In a supervised approach we can train a classification model, *e.g.*, a Deep Neural Network (DNN) to learn a label (1 or 0) with an appropriate input feature vector for each claim. This feature vector can be an embedded representation to be learned from the assigned clinical codes appended with other (categorical/continuous) features. However learning the vector representation for the clinical codes can be challenging, not only we need to consider the semantics of the short texts associated with each code, the relations between the codes in a code family and those between different code families also need to be taken into account. In this work we aim to learn the embedded representation of such ontology graph on these clinical nodes by incorporating knowledge originating from the semantics of the description of codes and their relations on the graph.

Table 1. A sample claim data in Payment Integrity application

clm_id	opt_proc_cd	drg_bil	drg_pd	dx1	dx2	dx3	dx4	dx5	icd_proc1	icd_proc2	mbr_age_at_dos	mbr_gender	amt_pd ($)	over_pmt
73237341601	None	00765	785	034211	01002	2302	23A38	2370	10D0021	OUT7022	20.0	F	7342.40	N
709375925701	None	00455	455	M4727	M5117	M532X7	G8929	K279	0SG30AJ	0SG3071	43.0	F	40215.44	Y
748308776301	None	00807	807	099824	Z370	09902	D649	0701	10EOx22	DKQMOZZ	28.0	F	8698.14	N
733395256901	None	00949	949	S065X9D	Z431	SQ020XXD	S2220XD	S32432D	OSPCX5Z	000000	21.0	M	36530.00	Y
756108875501	None	00807	807	O700	Z37D	Z3A38	None	None	10EQXZZ	DHQ9XZZ	37.0	F	4324.80	N
853629913502	None	00003	3	S36031A	S24103A	S24104A	R402312	R402112	02HV332	07TPOZZ	23.0	M	5977.50	N
840262672701	None	00755	755	O414	09912	Z6843	O102213	O34211	10DQQZ1	OUB70ZZ	37.0	F	15375.94	Y

The representation learning is based on the idea of integrating extra knowledge from ontology graph (built from the knowledge source in UMLS) into paragraph vector (PV) models for healthcare NLP tasks. In Paragraph Vector approach [10] paragraphs/texts are learned by training the vector representation of words in a paragraph. Because of the short nature of the texts and limited context information we feel bag of words models like PV models, would be adequate rather than using sequence to sequence models or transformer-based models which can lead to over-fitting. In the proposed approach we explore the idea of jointly learning texts (that describe the clinical codes) using paragraph vector models, and relations in a graph embedding framework. Thus we embed both the code descriptions and relations in low-dimensional vector spaces. We view the ontological graph structure on clinical codes as multi-relation data and integrate this extra knowledge into PV embedding to generate vector representations for both code entities and relations. For this we adopt TransH model (translation on hyperplanes) [22] for capturing multi-relational structure on clinical codes for illustration purposes although almost any translation model can be easily fitted into this framework. We carry out extensive experimentation to evaluate the quality of embedding produced for a certain combination of a few particular clinical codes. First, we undertake intrinsic evaluations of these embedding models on different tasks. We also demonstrate the utility of this representation learning by detecting overpayment on claims in a healthcare application and computing the savings achieved on labeled claims in healthcare fraud prevention.

Contribution of this Work: We contribute to the research work of embedding representation of short texts in many ways. It simultaneously learns the representation of codes as well as the representation of relations. It also exploits both semantical (description of codes) knowledge and syntactical information (ontological relations) to generate embedding representations.

Reproducibility: For reproducing our research we have uploaded all the codes into an anonymized repository https://github.com/DSRnD/UMLs.

1.1 Related Work

There are very few pieces of work available on multi-relational data model which, given an ontology graph/knowledge graph, learns the representation of textual description of each node (if any) and also the representation of relations. In [23] Weston *et al.* have introduced an approach to extract relation from free text which leverages text mention data and triples from a known KB. Although this method uses a function which embeds words and features into n-dimensional real vector space, it does not learn any representation of the textual content of a node in the KB. The authors [24] present a joint learning approach to embed entities of knowledge graph by leveraging resources of both text data and graph knowledge, however, the loss function for joint learning is not analyzed deeply. In [7] a novel framework is proposed to embed words, entities and relations in a knowledge graph into the same vector space, but it may not be applicable in translation models like TransR/TransC [11] which embeds texts and relations in different vector spaces. The idea of integrating knowledge from knowledge graph[1] to improve word embedding models in biomedical tasks is put forth by Ling *et al.* in [12]. They assume the existence of a knowledge graph and integrate this knowledge in the form of graph regularizer to the popular word embedding models. Mai *et al.* [15] combine paragraph vector and knowledge graph embedding to learn the representation of (academic) papers and entities for the purpose of searching papers in academics. They use these embeddings to learn the semantic similarity of papers and entities, however, they do not design any method to compute the combined loss function for paragraph vector and relational learning model. The other available prior art is discussed in two parts, text embedding and multi-relational learning for knowledge graph embedding.

Text Embedding. In recent past there have been lot of work of learning texts/documents. Recursive Deep Neural Network (RNN) has been the first approach using word vectors to generate paragraph vector representation from texts through the use of a parse tree called Sentiment Treebank [19]. Socher *et al.* [13, 18] have proposed distributed representations of phrases and sentences for sentence level representations through parsing. However, these methods are supervised and require more labeled data for efficient operation. Also it works for just one sentence. On the other hand, the approach of paragraph vector representation due to Le *et al.* [10] mostly uses unsupervised learning and can work well with less labeled data for learning fixed-length feature representation from variable-length pieces of texts such as sentences, paragraphs and documents.

---

[1] we use knowledge graph and ontology graph interchangeably.

Knowledge Graph Embedding. The models in knowledge graph embedding can be divided into three categories [14]: translation-based models, bi-linear models and external information learning models. In this work we mainly consider translation-based models. In one of these original models TransE [4], one regards a relation **r** as a translation from node **t** to node **s** for a triple (t, r, s) in the training set. This can model one-to-one relations very efficiently, but fails to adequately capture reflexive/one-to-many/many-to-one/many-to-many relationships. The TransH model [22] removes most of these drawbacks by treating relation **r** as a translation on hyperplane with u_r as the normal vector. However there are some issues with TransH model as it cannot capture the fact that some entities (nodes/relations) are similar in the entity space but comparably different in other specific aspects. These are addressed in TranR/TransC [11]. A transfer matrix M_r is defined for each relation **r** to map entity embedding to relation vector space. There is another translation-based model proposed in [9], *viz.* TransD, which considers different types of entities and relations at the same time. A mapping matrix M_{re} is assumed for each relation-entity pair (r, e) in order to map entity embedding into relation vector space. Many other translation-based models are proposed in the recent past, a survey of which can be found in [21].

2   Data Sets Used: Metathesaurus Ontology from UMLS

The Unified Medical Language System (UMLS [2]) consists of a collection of files and software that brings together many health and biomedical vocabularies and standards which can be used to enhance or develop applications, such as electronic health records, classification tools, dictionaries and language translators[2] etc. In healthcare industry UMLS is commonly employed in linking health information, medical terms, drug names, and billing codes across different computer systems through the knowledge source Metathesaurus. The Metathesaurus[3] is a very large, multi-purpose, and multi-lingual vocabulary database including clinical codes such as CPT, ICD-10-CM, LOINC, MeSH, RxNorm, and SNOMED-CT and so on, which contains information about biomedical and health related concepts, their various names, and the relationships among them. For our internal claim data occurring in Payment Integrity System the vocabulary consists of clinical codes, ICD-9/10-CM (International Classification of Diseases), ICD-10-PCS (Procedure Codes), and CPT (Current Procedural Terminology) codes, each of these codes are associated with a short description (a sample of them is shown in Table 2). Also each of them will be called a code family/code resource. For this purpose the scope of the Metathesaurus that will be used for representational learning of knowledge source entities will be restricted to the vocabulary of those clinical codes only and relations between them.

The Metathesaurus contains (not all possible) non-synonymous relationships between concepts from the same source vocabulary (intra-source/internal vocabulary relationships) and between concepts in different vocabularies (inter-source/external vocabulary relationships). In our case we consider all the original relationships enlisted in the code vocabularies that we describe, and additionally some intra/inter-source relations as listed by the Metathesaurus on them.

---

[2] Also see https://www.nlm.nih.gov/research/umls/quickstart.html.
[3] For more details see https://www.ncbi.nlm.nih.gov/books/NBK9684/.

We consider a total of about 300k codes consisting of 94833 ICD-10-CM, 190390 ICD-10-PCS, and 13869 CPT codes. The ICD-10-CM codes are organized in a hierarchical structure along a tree, thus the edges between codes can be labeled as *Par* (Parent), *Chd* (Child) and *Sib* (Sibling), and additionally

Table 2. A sample of clinical codes

Code family	Code name	Description
CPT	CPT-77013	Computed tomography guidance for, and monitoring of, parenchymal tissue ablation
CPT	CPT-1006116	Electrophysiologic Operative Procedures on the Heart and Pericardium
ICD10PCS	ICD10PCS-2W3PX1Z	Immobilization of Left Upper Leg using Splint
ICD10PCS	ICD10PCS-0PPQ	Medical and Surgical Upper Bones Removal Metacarpal, Left
ICD10CM	ICD10CM-Z82.61	Family history of arthritis
ICD10CM	ICD10CM-E13.61	Other specified diabetes mellitus with ketoacidosis

as *is_similar_to* for this code family. The ICD-10-PCS codes form a tree structure in which nodes are connected with edges with the same labels as that of ICD-10-CM. The Current Procedural Terminology (CPT) code, from the American Medical Association (maintained by CPT Editorial Panel [1]), contain edges with 11 labels such as *Par, Chd, Sib* (Sibling), *is_similar_to, RO/do_not_code_with, RO/has_add_on_code, RO/add_on_code_for* and so on. In Metathesaurus on this vocabulary there is only one external relation, *viz. is_similar_to* between the nodes of ICD-10-PCS and CPT codes (which has got 27 instances).

Notation. In rest of the discussion we adopt these notations. We use $[x]_+ \hat{=} \max(0, x)$, where x is any number/variable. We denote $t, t_1, t_2, \ldots, s, s_1, s_2, \ldots$ as texts (will be also called nodes later), these nodes together with relations to be introduced subsequently will also be referred to as entities. There are n number of such texts in our disposal, call this set $T = \{t_1, \ldots, t_n\}$. Each such text t_i is represented as a m-dimensional real-valued vector, written as $\mathbf{t}_i \in \mathbb{R}^m$. We assume that we have a fixed vocabulary represented in the form of the word-embedding matrix $\mathbf{D} \in \mathbb{R}^{v \times m}$, where each row j denotes the m dimensional vector representing the word w_j; the size of the vocabulary being v. Note that text representations and word representations are both captured using the same m dimensional space, although this is not necessary.

3   Paragraph Vector Models

There are two models for learning paragraph vectors [16], Distributed Memory model of Paragraph Vector (PV-DM) (it uses skip-gram approach) and Distributed Bag of Words model of Paragraph Vector (PV-DBoW) (uses distributed bag-of-words (DBoW) approach). We briefly describe them to facilitate the introduction of joint text and relation learning in Sect. 5.

PV-DM Model. In the PV-DM model one needs a 'predictor model' which utilizes the representation of a paragraph (also called text) and its constituent words for the task of predicting the center/next word in a window of length k. In our case we adopt a neural network with $\mathbf{W}_p \in \mathbb{R}^{v \times (2k+1)m}$ and $\mathbf{b}_p \in \mathbb{R}^v$ as weight and bias parameters respectively. The input to this network is a vector representation of text $\mathbf{t}_i$ concatenated with the word representation of k words which are placed to the left and to the right of the center word. This can be written as as $\left(\mathbf{t}_i, w^i_{h-k-1} \cdots w^i_{h-1} w_{h+1} \cdots w^i_{h+k+1}\right) \in \mathbb{R}^{(2k+1)m}$, where $w^i_{h-k-1} \cdots w^i_{h-1} w^i_{h+1} \cdots w^i_{h+k+1}$ is the context of length $2k$ around the center word w^i_h, which we abbreviate as $\mathbf{c}^i_h$, also here w^i_h is the index of hth word in the text t_i from the vocabulary $\mathbf{D}$.

We represent the text t_i as a sequence of words $w^i_1, w^i_2, \ldots, w^i_{l_i}$ which is of length l_i. Let $Pr(w^i_h | \mathbf{t}_i : \mathbf{c}^i_h)$ be the probability of the occurrence of the center word w^i_h under the text representation $\mathbf{t}_i$ along with context vector $\mathbf{c}^i_h$. We use the softmax function $Pr(w^i_h | \mathbf{t}_i : \mathbf{c}^i_h) = \sigma(\mathbf{W}_p[\mathbf{t}_i : \mathbf{c}^i_h] + \mathbf{b}_p) \mid_{w^i_h}$, where $\sigma(\mathbf{z})|_i = \frac{e^{z_i}}{\sum^v_{k=1} e^{z_k}}$ and $\mathbf{z} = (z_1, \cdots, z_v)$. Then the cross-entropy loss (log-loss) for text i at window location h will be $loss_{pr}(t_i, h) = -\ln(Pr(w^i_h | \mathbf{t}_i : \mathbf{c}^i_h))$.

Hence, the total loss for the model will be the sum of average loss per window. For a training set of size n this will be given as

$$Loss_{pvdm}(\mathbf{t}_1, \mathbf{t}_2, \ldots, \mathbf{t}_n, \mathbf{D}, \mathbf{W}_p, \mathbf{b}_p) = \sum_{i=1}^{n} \frac{1}{l_i - 2k} \sum_{h=k+1}^{l_i - k} loss_{pr}(t_i, h) \qquad (1)$$

For the purpose of training we minimize the loss function given by Eq. 1 over all variables, $\mathbf{W}_p, \mathbf{b}_p, \mathbf{D}$ and $\mathbf{t}_1, \mathbf{t}_2, \ldots, \mathbf{t}_n$. In the testing phase one random row vector is used for the representation of text for each test case and the optimization is carried out only over this representation for the same loss function.

PV-DBoW Model. In PV-DBoW model one sets up a 'classification model' which utilizes this representation of a paragraph and its constituent words for the task of predicting a word sampled from the text. For our purpose we take a neural network-based classifier with $\mathbf{W}_c \in \mathbb{R}^{v \times m}$ and $\mathbf{b}_c \in \mathbb{R}^v$ as weight and bias parameters respectively. This is used to predict a word w_h (in the vocabulary) sampled from the input text. The input to this network is a vector representation of the ith text $\mathbf{t}_i \in \mathbb{R}^m$. The text representation acts as a paragraph vector for this model. The cross-entropy loss (log-loss) for t_i at window location h will be $loss_c(t_i, h) = -\ln(Pr(w^i_h | \mathbf{t}_i))$.

Again we use softmax as the activation function on the cross-entropy loss (log-loss) for this model as before. The total loss for the model will be the sum of average loss per window. For a training set of size n this will be given as:

$$Loss_{pvdbow}(\mathbf{t}_1, \mathbf{t}_2, \ldots, \mathbf{t}_n, \mathbf{D}, \mathbf{W}_c, \mathbf{b}_c) = \sum_{i=1}^{n} \frac{1}{l_i} \sum_{h=1}^{l_i} loss_c(t_i, h) \qquad (2)$$

For the purpose of training we minimize this loss function given by Eq. 2 over all variables $\mathbf{W}_c, \mathbf{b}_c, \mathbf{D}$ and $\mathbf{t}_1, \mathbf{t}_2, \ldots, \mathbf{t}_n$.

4   Translating Embedding Modeling for Multi-relational Data

A typical embedding of multi-relational data represents an entity as a k-dimensional vector $\mathbf{t}$ (or $\mathbf{s}$) and formulates a scoring function $f_r(\mathbf{t}, \mathbf{s})$ to measure the plausibility of the triplet (t, r, s) in the embedding space, which denotes a transformation $\mathbf{r}$ characterising the relation $r \in R$ (R is the set of all relations) on the pair of entities

t and s. For instance, in the translation-based method TransE [4], the authors define $f_r(\mathbf{t}, \mathbf{s}) = \|\mathbf{t} + \mathbf{r} - \mathbf{s}\|_2$. Different translation transformations vary with different scoring functions [3–6,8,17,20]. There are other multi-relational learning models like structured embedding (SE) [5] or semantic matching energy (SME) [3], but we shall not employ them here as they involve multiple matrix multiplications and Hadamard products which can be quite time consuming. Among translation transformation-based models, TransE [4] provides a simple and efficient formalism which produces satisfactory predictive performance, However, TransE has shortcomings when it comes to dealing with relations capturing reflexive/one-to-many/may-to-one/many-to-many mappings. To address these issues Wang *et al.* have proposed TransH [22] which models a relation as a hyperplane with a translation operation on it and makes a good trade-off between model complexity and efficiency. For illustration of our embedding learning using multi-relational learning we shall use the TransH model only as discussed below. Other models can be fitted seamlessly in this framework.

In TransH model, for a triplet (t, r, s) the embedding vectors $\mathbf{t}$ and $\mathbf{s}$ are first projected onto the hyperplane $\mathbf{u_r}$ as $\mathbf{t}_\perp$ and $\mathbf{s}_\perp$ respectively. The embedded vectors $\mathbf{t}_\perp$ and $\mathbf{s}_\perp$ are expected to be connected by a translation vector $\mathbf{h_r}$ on the hyperplane with low error if (t, r, s) is a true triplet, also called a golden triplet. Subsequently one defines a scoring function as: $f_r(\mathbf{t}_\perp, \mathbf{s}_\perp) = \|\mathbf{t}_\perp + \mathbf{h_r} - \mathbf{s}_\perp\|_2$. Assuming $\|\mathbf{u_r}\|_2 = 1$ it is easy to deduce $\mathbf{t}_\perp = \mathbf{t} - \mathbf{u_r^T t u_r}$ and $\mathbf{s}_\perp = \mathbf{s} - \mathbf{u_r^T u h_r}$. Thus the scoring function now becomes, $f_r(\mathbf{t}_\perp, \mathbf{s}_\perp) = \|(\mathbf{t} - \mathbf{u_r^T t u_r}) + \mathbf{h_r} - (\mathbf{s} - \mathbf{u_r^T s u_r})\|_2$. The model parameters are all the entities $\{\mathbf{e_i}\}_{i=1}^{|E|}$ (e_i can be t_i, s_i or r_i etc.), and the hyperplanes and translation vectors of all the relations, $\{(\mathbf{u_r}, \mathbf{h_r})\}_{r=1}^{|R|}$. During training one works with the loss function that discriminates between positive (golden) and negative triplets by using margin-based ranking loss. Moreover some more constraints are added to the loss function as soft constraints while it is minimized in order to capture the following: all the entity vectors are scaled below 1, the translation vector is in the hyperplane, and normal vector should have length 1.

$$
\begin{aligned}
Loss_{transh}(\mathbf{t}, \mathbf{r}, \mathbf{s}, \mathbf{u_r}, \mathbf{h_r}) &= \sum_{(t,r,s)\in\Delta} \sum_{(t',r',s')\in\Delta'_{(t,r,s)}} [[f_r(\mathbf{t}_\perp, \mathbf{s}_\perp) + \gamma - f'_r(\mathbf{t}'_\perp, \mathbf{s}'_\perp)]_+ \\
&\quad + \eta \left\{ \sum_{e\in E}[\|e\|_2 - 1]_+ + \sum_{r\in R}\left[\frac{(\mathbf{u_r}^T\mathbf{h_r})^2}{\|\mathbf{h_r}\|_2^2} - \epsilon^2\right]_+ \right\}] \\
&= \sum_{(t,r,s)\in\Delta} \sum_{(t',r',s')\in\Delta'_{(t,r,s)}} \left(loss_{hplane} + \eta\, loss_{constr} \right)
\end{aligned}
$$
(3)

Above Δ is the set of positive (golden) triplets, $\Delta'_{(t,r,s)}$ is the set of negative triplets created by corrupting the triple (t, r, s), γ is the margin separating positive and negative triplets, and η is a hyper parameter weighing the importance of soft constraints (new notations are self-explanatory).

One constructs the set of corrupted triplets (as in Eq. 3) by replacing the head or tail of a true triplet with a random entity (but not both at the same time). The set of golden triplets (in the knowledge graph) is randomly traversed multiple times, in the process a corrupt triplet is randomly constructed. For details see [22].

5   Learning Texts and Relations Jointly

Finally we learn the representation of the description of entities (using the paragraph vector approach) together with the relations on these entities (using TransH approach) for multi-relational data. For that we formulate the loss function as a convex combination of loss due to paragraph vector model and that due to TransH model. We call them as PV-TransH learning models.

In the PV-DM model we use the predictor model to compute the loss function while predicting the center/next word in a window of length k for an entity text t. Along with this we embed text (in terms of node) t, and each text (captured as node only) s that are connected with t through the relation r in the TransH model, call this PV-DM-TransH model. The loss function for this combined model will be given as:

$$Loss_{pvdm-transh}(\mathbf{t}_1, \ldots, \mathbf{t}_n, \mathbf{D}, \mathbf{W}_p, \mathbf{b}_p, \mathbf{r}_1, \ldots, \mathbf{r}_{|R|}, \mathbf{h}_1, \ldots, \mathbf{h}_{|R|}, \mathbf{u}_1, \ldots, \mathbf{u}_{|R|})$$

$$= \sum_{t_i \in \{t_1, \ldots, t_n\}} \left[\frac{1}{l_i - 2k} \sum_{h=k+1}^{l_i-k} loss_{pr}(t_i, h) \right.$$

$$\left. + \frac{1}{|t_i|} \sum_{p=1}^{|ti|} \sum_{(r_j, s_k^p):(t_i, r_j, s_k^p) \in \Delta} \sum_{(r_j', s'_k^p):(t_i, r_j', s'_k^p) \in \Delta^{t_i}(r_j, s_k^p)} \left(loss_{hplane}^p + \eta\, loss_{constr} \right) \right]$$

$$(4)$$

Recall Δ is the set of positive (golden) triplets, $\Delta_{(r,s)}^t$ is the set of negative (corrupt) triplets created from the triplet (t, r, s) by changing the tail s of the original triplet while keeping its head t unchanged. For each window *wrt* a word in the text $|t_i|$ in the PV-DM model, we choose a negative triplet (where $|t_i|$ is the length of the text t_i) and

$$loss_{hplane}^p = \left[f_r(\mathbf{t}_\perp, \mathbf{s}_\perp^{\mathbf{P}}) + \gamma - \mathbf{f}_{\mathbf{r}'}(\mathbf{t}_\perp, \mathbf{s}'^{\mathbf{P}}_\perp) \right]_+$$

As usual we use stochastic gradient descent to minimize the loss function. In this we fix text t, update the parameters and repeat the process for all other texts. For a fixed text t we randomly choose a golden triplet and correspondingly choose a corrupt triplet by changing the tail of the triplet keeping the head t unchanged. For every mini-batch we compute the gradient and update the model parameters. See Algorithm 1 for details.

When we combine PV-DBoW with TransH (call this PV-DBoW-TransH) we use the classification model to predict a word sampled from an text entity t and also employ the TransH model which aids in learning the text t and the relations $\{r_i\}_{i \in R}$. Similarly one can formulate the loss function $Loss_{pvdbow-transh}(\cdot, \ldots, \cdot)$ along the lines of Eq. 4.

We describe how we reduce false negative labels in Algorithm 1. In our method for a fixed head t of a triplet (t, r, s) we corrupt the tail t and choose a node t' by random sampling of the collection of nodes. However, the knowledge graph on clinical nodes is not complete and this random sampling may introduce many false negative labels into training. We adopt a simple approach to solve this. For a fixed head $t \in T$ we construct a set of pair of relations and nodes, $\Gamma_t = \{(r, s) : (t, r, s) \in \Delta \text{ for some } r \in R, s \in T\}$. Now we randomly pick any $(r', s') \notin \Gamma_t$ and construct a negative/corrupt triplet (t, r', s').

Algorithm 1: Learning with PV-TransH models

Input	: `Training set`; Set of texts $T = \{t_1, \ldots t_n\}$, set of relations R, set of golden triplets $\Delta = \{(t, r, s) : t, s \in T, r \in R\}$ in the knowledge graph, hyperplane vector $\mathbf{u}_r$, translation vector $\mathbf{h}_r$, Word embedding matrix $\mathbf{D}$, margin γ, hyperparamater for modeling constraints η, embedding dimension v, Parameters for paragraph vector models $\mathbf{W}_p$, and $\mathbf{b}_p$
Initialization	: $r \leftarrow \text{uniform}(-\frac{5}{\sqrt{v}}, \frac{5}{\sqrt{v}})$, $\mathbf{r} \leftarrow \frac{\mathbf{r}}{\|\mathbf{r}\|}$, for each relation $r \in R$, $t \leftarrow \text{uniform}(-\frac{5}{\sqrt{v}}, \frac{5}{\sqrt{v}})$ for each text $t \in T$, $\mathbf{D} \leftarrow \text{rand}(1)$, $\mathbf{u}_r \leftarrow \text{randint}()$, $\mathbf{h}_r \leftarrow \text{randint}()$, $\mathbf{u}_r \leftarrow \frac{\mathbf{u}_r}{\|\mathbf{u}_r\|}$, $\mathbf{h}_r \leftarrow \frac{\mathbf{h}_r}{\|\mathbf{h}_r\|}$

1 **for** $t = t_1, \ldots, t_n$ **do**

2     $\mathbf{t}_i \leftarrow \frac{\mathbf{t}_i}{\|\mathbf{t}_i\|}$;

3     $\Delta_{\text{batch}} \leftarrow \text{sample}(\Delta, b)$; // sample of mini-batch size b

4     $\Gamma_{\text{batch}} \leftarrow \varnothing$; // initialize the set of pairs of gold and corrupt triplets

5   **for** $(t, r, s) \in \Delta_{\text{batch}}$ **do**

6        $(t, r, s') \leftarrow \text{sample}(\Delta^t(r, s))$; // sample a corrupt triplet

7        $\Gamma_{\text{batch}} \leftarrow \Gamma_{\text{batch}} \cup \{(t, r, s), (t, r, s')\}$;

8   **end**

9   update parameters wrt $\frac{1}{l_i - 2k} \sum_{h=k+1}^{l_i - k} loss_p(t_i, h) +$

$$\frac{1}{|t_i|} \sum_{p=1}^{|ti|} \sum_{(r_j, s_k^p):(t_i, r_j, s_k^p) \in \Delta} \sum_{(r_j', s'^p_k):(t_i, r_j', s'^p_k) \in \Delta^{t_i}(r_j, s_k^p)} \left(loss_{hplane}^p + \eta \, loss_{constr} \right)$$

    /* **PV-DM-TransH model**   */

10   or, update parameters wrt **PV-DBoW-TransH model**

11 **end**

---

6 Experiments

We evaluate our approach on two kinds of tasks, intrinsic and extrinsic. We produce the experimental results and the subsequent analysis on them. For experimental purposes we use the Metathesaurus Ontology clinical code vocabulary from UMLS as described in Sect. 2.

6.1 Baseline Methods Used

For experimental purposes, we use a few knowledge graph embedding models involving relations for learning embedding of codes and relations in ontology like TransH [22], TransR [11] and TransD [9]. Further we use Paragraph Vector Models (PV-DM and PV-DBoW) [16] and combine them with these embedding models. So in all, we use the following methods for benchmarking purposes, PV-DM, PM-DBoW, TransH, TransR and TransD, PV-DM-TransH, PV-DM-TransR, PV-DM-TransD, PV-DBoW-TransH, PV-DBoW-TransR, PV-DBoW-TransD etc.

We implement our joint text and relation learning models on all those baselines and evaluate on our Metathesaurus ontology on clinical codes in UMLS data set and compare the performance of these models. We are not able to use other data sets as most of them either do not contain much textual description for the nodes or do not incorporate a graph ontology.

Table 3. Experimental results on triplets classification

SI	Method	Accuracy	F-1 measure
1	PV-DBow	0.5	0.65
2	PV-DM	0.5	0.67
3	TransH	0.6	0.68
4	TransR	0.7	0.71
5	TransD	0.75	0.72
6	PV-DBoW-TransH	0.65	0.68
7	PV-DM-TransH	0.7	0.68
8	PV-DBoW-TransR	0.8	0.72
9	PV-DM-TransR	0.76	0.68
10	PV-DBoW-TransD	0.79	0.73
11	PV-DM-TransD	0.77	0.71

6.2   Intrinsic Evaluation

We perform intrinsic evaluation on the following tasks, - triplet classification and link prediction on Metathesaurus ontology only. We produce the embedding from the combined loss function involving texts and relations as given by Eq. 4. Most of the cases the models converge in less than 25 epochs. We exhibit one such convergence plot for PV-DM-TRansH model in Fig. 1. Both the training and validation losses converge after 17 epochs.

Triplets Classification

By the task of triplets classification [11, 17, 22] one tries to judge whether a given triplet (t, r, s) is correct or not, which is a binary classification task. A part of the Metathesaurus ontology on clinical code vocabulary is used for training. The test set contains only correct triplets, but for the evaluation of binary classification we need to construct negative triplets. In this case we create negative (incorrect) triplets by randomly choosing a tail s for a fixed head t in a correct triplet as described in Sect. 5.

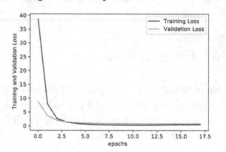

Fig. 1. Loss function for PV-DM-TransH model at optimal parameters

We adopt the commonly used decision rule for triplets classification [11, 22]. We first set a threshold δ_r for each relation r, which is obtained by maximizing the accuracy values for classification on the valid set. For the given triplet if the score (using the scoring function f_r) is lower than δ_r we mark it as positive, otherwise it is negative.

For training TransH model we use the learning rate λ for SGD to be among $\{0.1, 0.01, 0, 001\}$, the margin γ among $\{0.5, 1, 2\}$, the dimensions d of both entity and relations embedding among $\{50, 100, 150, 200, 250\}$, the importance of soft constraints $\eta \in \{0.0156, 0.0625, 0.25, 1.0\}$ and the batch size B among $\{64, 128, 256, 512\}$. The window size (on both sides of the context word) for PV-DM model is chosen in between $2k \in \{2, 4, 6\}$. The best configuration is chosen according to the accuracy in the test set. The optimal hyper parameters for TransH are as follows: the learning rate λ is 0.001, embedding dimension $d = 200$, margin $\gamma = 1$, the importance of soft constraints

$\eta = 0.25$, and the batch size $B = 512$. For TransR we select the parameters in the same range, however, we vary the margin separating positive and negative triplets γ_e, the margin for subclass triples γ_c and the margin for relational triples γ_l [14]: $\gamma_l, \gamma_e, \gamma_c \in \{0.1.03, 0.5, 1\}$, the dimension of entity embedding $d \in \{50, 100, 150, 200, 250\}$, and the dimension of relation embedding $d' \in \{25, 50, 100\}$. In TransR we get the best configuration as: the learning rate $\lambda = 0.001$, the margins $\gamma_l = 1, \gamma_e = 0.1, \gamma_c = 1$, the dimension of entity embedding $d = 200$ and the dimension of relation embedding $d' = 20$, and the batch size $B = 256$, also we take L_1 as the dissimilarity. In case of TransD we arrive at the following optimal parameters: For all other cases, the learning rate $\lambda = 0.001$, the margin $\gamma = 1$, the dimension of entity embedding $d = 200$ and the dimension of relation embedding $d' = 50$, and the batch size $B = 256$, and we chose L_2 as the dissimilarity.

The results of triplets classification are reported in Table 3 wherein we use metrics, accuracy and F1-measure. The combination of models PV-DBoW and TransD perform the best followed by PV-DM with TransD. In general, TransD models are performing well and DBoW models are better than DM models. And also when we are jointly learning entities and relations the accuracy and F-1 measure improve.

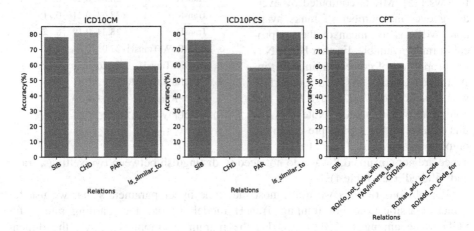

Fig. 2. Classification accuracies of different relations on three code families: ICD-10-CM, ICD-PCS and CPT

The prediction accuracy of different relations for the PV-DM-TransH model is shown in Fig. 2. We plot all the 5 relations available in ICD-10-CM and ICD-10-PCS codes. The CHD relation has the best accuracy followed by SIB for ICD-10-CM codes (almost 80%). Same phenomenon is observed for CHD and SIB relations in case of ICD-10-PCS codes, which have prediction accuracy close to 67% and 76% respectively. But the maximum accuracy of 81% is shown in case of is_similar_to relation which means synonyms for procedure codes are easier to predict. For CPT codes we focus on the relations which have higher accuracy values. The maximum accuracy is produced by RO/has_add_on_code which is close to 83%; it means that lot of CPT codes do have add on codes. Further CHD and PAR relations have nearby prediction accuracy values as PAR is the inverse of CHD relation.

Link Prediction. The task of link prediction is to predict a missing head h or tail t for a triplet (t, r, s), this task is originally proposed in [4,5]. In this task one attaches more importance to ranking a set of candidate entities from the ontology graph rather than requiring a unique answer saying which is the best. We follow the same evaluation protocol that is used for TransE modeling [4]. For each testing triplet (t, r, s) we replace tail s by each node e, different from s in the ontology graph and calculate the score on the corrupted triplet (t, r, e) using the scoring function f_r. By ranking these scores and aggregating over all the testing triplets in ascending order, we can obtain the rank of the correct triplet.

We report three measures as our eval-uation metrics: the average rank of all correct entities (*Mean Rank (MR)*), *Mean Reciprocal Rank (MRR)* and the propor-tion of correct entities ranked in top 10 (*Hits@10*). These metrics are defined as follows [25]. MR is computed by aver-aging over the number of ranks avail-able. MRR is the mean of the recipro-cal of ranks available. Further Hits@N is the proportion of correct entities in top-N ranked entities. A good embedding would yield a low *MR*, a high *MRR* and a high *Hits@10* values. Note that for this data set all the triplets present in the ontology graph are real word triplets and

Table 4. Experimental results on link prediction

SI	Method	MR	MRR	Hits@10
1	PV-DBoW	28.52	0.28	0.78
2	PV-DM	28.92	0.23	0.74
3	TransH	28.86	0.24	0.74
4	TransR	28.68	0.21	0.71
5	TransD	28.34	0.19	0.72
6	PV-DBoW-TransH	27.03	0.34	0.82
7	PV-DM-TransH	27.26	0.31	0.82
8	PV-DBoW-TransR	27.02	0.31	0.85
9	PV-DM-TransR	27.13	0.29	0.80
10	PV-DBoW-TransD	27.73	0.27	0.76
11	PV-DM-TransD	27.12	0.25	0.78

hence are not corrupted. So we do not need to distinguish between two settings, 'raw' and 'filtered' (see Table 4).

For obvious reasons we use almost the same hyper parameters that we use for triplets classification. For training TransH model we use the learning rate λ for SGD to be among $\{0.1, 0.01, 0, 001\}$, the margin γ among $\{1, 2, 4\}$, the dimen-sions of entity and relations embedding among $\{50, 100, 150, 200, 250\}$, the impor-tance of soft constraints $\eta \in \{0.0156, 0.0625, 0.25, 1.0\}$ and the batch size B among $\{64, 128, 256, 512\}$. The window size (on both sides of the context word) for PV-DM model is chosen in between $2k \in \{2, 4, 6, 8\}$. The best configuration is determined according to the MR in the validation set. For TransH the optimal hyper parameters are as follows: the learning rate λ is 0.01, margin $\gamma = 1$, embedding dimension $d = 100$, the importance of soft constraints $\eta = 0.25$, and the batch size $B = 512$, and the window size for PV-DM model to be 2 (for all the cases). For TransR we select the parameters in the same range, however, we vary the margin separating positive and negative triplets γ_e, the margin for subclass triples γ_c and the margin for relational triples γ_l [14] as: $\gamma_l, \gamma_e, \gamma_c \in \{0.1.03, 0.5, 1, 2\}$, the dimension of entity embedding $d \in \{50, 100, 150, 200, 250\}$; other parameters are: the dimension of relation embed-ding $d' \in \{25, 50, 100\}$. We arrive at best configuration for TransR as: the learning rate $\lambda = 0.01$, the margins $\gamma_l = 1, \gamma_e = 0.1, \gamma_c = 1$, the dimension of entity embedding $d = 100$ and the dimension of relation embedding $d' = 100$, and the batch size $B = 512$, we take L_2 as the dissimilarity. In case of TransD [9] by fixing the range of hyper parameters as in TransH, we arrive at the following optimal parameters: the learning rate $\lambda = 0.01$, the margin $\gamma = 1$, the dimension of entity embedding $d = 100$ and the dimension of relation embedding $d' = 50$, and the batch size $B = 256$, and we chose L_2 as the dissimilarity.

The results are depicted in Table 5. The simplest models like PV-DBow and PV-DM under-perform in comparison to other combined models. Also other plain translation models like TransH, TransR and TransD perform no better than the combined models for obvious reasons. Overall, combined TransH and TransR models seem to be performing well. Also DBoW models consistently perform better than DM models meaning that context would play little role in embedding models here.

Table 5. An extrinsic evaluation on internal claim data

SI	Method	Precision	Recall	AUC	Savings σ (in USD)
1	PV-DBoW	0.246	0.418	0.623	8,312,089
2	PV-DM	0.235	0.554	0.621	8,349,657
3	TransH	0.257	0.345	0.629	8,056,294
4	TransR	0.231	0.523	0.629	8,435,095
5	TransD	0.239	0.504	0.628	8,227,509
6	PV-DBoW-TransH	0.247	0.489	0.633	8,809,780
7	PV-DM-TransH	0.234	0.564	0.634	8,863,804
8	PV-DBoW-TransR	0.244	0.572	0.635	8,927,542
9	PV-DM-TransR	0.265	0.528	0.638	9,037,456
10	PV-DBoW-TransD	0.273	0.614	0.634	9,153,498
11	PV-DM-TransD	0.278	0.629	0.632	9,267,376

However, the improvements in performance for the combined models is not that appreciable which may be due to the fact that relations probably do not play much role in this particular data set.

6.3 Extrinsic Evaluation

We use internal claims data (courtesy Optum Global Advantage Payment Integrity Team) for extrinsic evaluation. These data sets contain a combination of 13k ICD-10-CM and 10k ICD-10-PCS codes. We use 188k claims (appearing from 2016-Q1 until 2017-Q4) with over-payment labels (0 or 1) as training data while test set contains 22k claims (from 2018-Q1 until 2018-Q2). We fit a feed forward deep neural network (FFDN) (with a threshold value of 0.5) for predicting if a new claim will lead to over-payment. We use the same hyper parameters that we employ for triplets classification and link prediction. We use the metrics, precision, recall and AUC for judging the efficacy of our approach. Further we formulate a savings metric σ which is computed as the sum of maximum savings on 1000 claims. The best configuration for different models are picked by examining the maximum amount of savings σ. The best configuration for FFDFN across the models has 4 layers with $300 \times 1500 \times 750 \times 1$ node sizes at different layers with dropout ratios of $0.5, 0.5$ and 0.3. The best configuration for TransH model turns to be as follows, the learning rate $\lambda = 0.001$, embedding dimension $= 100$, margin $\gamma = 2, \eta = 0.25$ and batch size $= 20$.

The results are shown in Table 5. Joint learning of entities and relations improves the savings in case all combined TransH, TransR and TransD models. Using these models one is able to predict claims which result in higher savings. Also the prediction ability remains almost the same for all the methods as witnessed by AUC metrics. The results could have been better if we had access to context historical data for claims and more number of clinical codes (only five ICD-10-CM codes and two ICD-10-PCS codes are used for each claim) would have been made available for classification purposes.

7 Conclusion

In this work we propose a new graph embedding model which jointly learns the representation of the texts describing the nodes in the graph and the representation of the relations connecting the nodes. Thus it exploits both semantic knowledge and syntactical information to generate embedding. Also the framework can adept to any translation model with Paragraph Vector models. This method is integrated within payment integrity solutions framework and is live now. This research can be used in other applications of representation learning beyond healthcare, specifically in classification of texts (containing short texts or domain specific abbreviation with hierarchical relationships between the texts), for example, using multi-relational data sets like WordNet (WN11 and WN18 [17]), although the texts embedded therein will consist of a single word without any context information in which case quality of embedding cannot be guaranteed.

References

1. (AMA), A.M.A.: CPT Process. Archived May 11, 2016 at the Wayback Machine (2016)
2. Bethesda (MD): UMLSReference Manual [Internet]. National Library of Medicine (US) (2009). https://www.ncbi.nlm.nih.gov/books/NBK9676/
3. Bordes, A., Glorot, X., Weston, J., Bengio, Y.: A semantic matching energy function for learning with multi-relational data - application to word-sense disambiguation. Mach. Learn. **94**(2), 233–259 (2014)
4. Bordes, A., Usunier, N., García-Durán, A., Weston, J., Yakhnenko, O.: Translating embeddings for modeling multi-relational data. In: Proceedings of 27th NIPS, pp. 2787–2795 (2013)
5. Bordes, A., Weston, J., Collobert, R., Bengio, Y.: Learning structured embeddings of knowledge bases. In: Burgard, W., Roth, D. (eds.) Proceedings of the Twenty-Fifth AAAI 2011. AAAI Press (2011)
6. Chang, K.W., Yih, W.t., Meek, C.: Multi-relational latent semantic analysis. In: Proceedings of EMNLP, pp. 1602–1612 (2013)
7. Han, X., Liu, Z., Sun, M.: Joint representation learning of text and knowledge for knowledge graph completion. CoRR arXiv:1611.04125 (2016)
8. Jenatton, R., Roux, N.L., Bordes, A., Obozinski, G.: A latent factor model for highly multi-relational data. In: Proceedings of the 26th NIPS, pp. 3176–3184 (2012)
9. Ji, G., He, S., Xu, L., Liu, K., Zhao, J.: Knowledge graph embedding via dynamic mapping matrix. In: Proceedings of the 53rd ACL, vol. 1, pp. 687–696 (2015)
10. Le, Q.V., Mikolov, T.: Distributed representations of sentences and documents. In: Proceedings of the 31th ICML, pp. 1188–1196 (2014)
11. Lin, Y., Liu, Z., Sun, M., Liu, Y., Zhu, X.: Learning entity and relation embeddings for knowledge graph completion. In: Proceedings of AAAI (2015)

12. Ling, Y., An, Y., Liu, M., Hasan, S.A., Fan, Y., Hu, X.: Integrating extra knowledge into word embedding models for biomedical NLP tasks. In: IJCNN, pp. 968–975. IEEE (2017)
13. Luong, T., Socher, R., Manning, C.D.: Better word representations with recursive neural networks for morphology. In: Proceedings the 17th CoNLL, pp. 104–113 (2013)
14. Lv, X., Hou, L., Li, J., Liu, Z.: Differentiating concepts and instances for knowledge graph embedding. In: Proceedings of EMNLP, pp. 1971–1979 (2018)
15. Mai, G., Janowicz, K., Yan, B.: Combining text embedding and knowledge graph embedding techniques for academic search engines. In: Joint proceedings of the 4th Workshop SemDeep-4 and NLIWoD4 and QALD-9 co-located with 17th ISWC, vol. 2241, pp. 77–88. CEUR-WS.org (2018)
16. Mikolov, T., Sutskever, I., Chen, K., Corrado, G.S., Dean, J.: Distributed representations of words and phrases and their compositionality. In: 27th NIPS, Proceedings, pp. 3111–3119 (2013)
17. Socher, R., Chen, D., Manning, C.D., Ng, A.Y.: Reasoning with neural tensor networks for knowledge base completion. In: 27th NIPS, Proceedings, pp. 926–934 (2013)
18. Socher, R., Huang, E.H., Pennington, J., Ng, A.Y., Manning, C.D.: Dynamic pooling and unfolding recursive autoencoders for paraphrase detection. In: 25th NIPS, Proceedings, pp. 801–809 (2011)
19. Socher, R., Lin, C.C., Ng, A.Y., Manning, C.D.: Parsing natural scenes and natural language with recursive neural networks. In: Proceedings of the 28th ICML, pp. 129–136 (2011)
20. Sutskever, I., Salakhutdinov, R., Tenenbaum, J.B.: Modelling relational data using bayesian clustered tensor factorization. In: 23rd NIPS, Proceedings, pp. 1821–1828 (2009)
21. Wang, Q., Mao, Z., Wang, B., Guo, L.: Knowledge graph embedding: a survey of approaches and applications. IEEE Trans. Knowl. Data Eng. 29(12), 2724–2743 (2017)
22. Wang, Z., Zhang, J., Feng, J., Chen, Z.: Knowledge graph embedding by translating on hyperplanes. In: Proceedings of the 28th AAAI, pp. 1112–1119 (2014)
23. Weston, J., Bordes, A., Yakhnenko, O., Usunier, N.: Connecting language and knowledge bases with embedding models for relation extraction. In: Proceedings of the EMNLP, pp. 1366–1371 (2013)
24. Zhang, D., Yuang, B., Wang, D., Liu, R.: Joint semantic relevance learning with text data and graph knowledge. Technical report, CSLT TECHNICAL REPORT-20150023 (2015)
25. Zhang, Y., Yao, Q., Shao, Y., Chen, L.: NSCaching: simple and efficient negative sampling for knowledge graph embedding. In: 35th IEEE ICDE, pp. 614–625 (2019)

An Attention-Based Forecasting Network for Intelligent Services in Manufacturing

Xinyi Zhou and Xiaofeng Gao[✉]

MoE Key Lab of Artificial Intelligence, Department of Computer Science
and Engineering, Shanghai Jiao Tong University, Shanghai 200240, China
zhouxy1003@sjtu.edu.cn, gao-xf@cs.sjtu.edu.cn

Abstract. Multivariate temporal data generally exists in the whole manufacturing process and forecasting lays the foundation for many intelligent services in industry. In this paper, we propose an end-to-end deep learning framework named dual-dimensional attention-based network (DANet) to solve the multivariate time series forecasting problem in industry. It leverages the strengths of recurrent neural network (RNN) structures to discover the underlying temporal patterns of the multi-dimensional input. A recurrent module is used for capturing sequential relationships between adjacent timesteps and embedding the original observations. Then, we apply a novel dual-dimensional attention mechanism to cope with the intrinsic characteristics of industrial big data. Feature-wise self-attention enables the network to adaptively learn the correlations between features, while time-wise attention captures complex long and short-term temporal dependencies. Our model shows its advantages over the baseline methods and a more stable and robust performance in the experiments on several real-world manufacturing datasets.

Keywords: Multivariate time series prediction · Recurrent neural network · Attention mechanism

1 Introduction

Nowadays, the deeper integration of new information technology and manufacturing is exerting a profound influence on industrial innovation [5], enabling the automatic collection and recording of massive sensor data in chronological order [8]. Multivariate temporal data generally exists in the whole manufacturing, warehousing, and marketing process. Making accurate predictions in advance lays the foundation for many intelligent services targeted at specific applications, such as enhancing productivity, monitoring equipment health, warning performance degradation and reducing costs. Therefore, it makes sense that multivariate time series forecasting can provide a real-time insight and foresight for process monitoring, which has become a fundamental and important subject of data mining in both academia and industry ever since [13].

© Springer Nature Switzerland AG 2021
H. Hacid et al. (Eds.): ICSOC 2021, LNCS 13121, pp. 900–914, 2021.
https://doi.org/10.1007/978-3-030-91431-8_67

Since the manufacturing industry has high requirements for model reliability, data mining techniques commonly used in the industry are still traditional mathematical and statistical methods (e.g., time series analysis and linear regression [4]) for their robustness and consistency. However, it is difficult for these models to discover the underlying correlations and causality when faced with huge data with noise and high dimensionality. On the other hand, data-driven deep learning models, despite weaker interpretability, have been explored as an effective approach to discovering complex nonlinear relationships between multivariate time series. Nevertheless, the following distinct characteristics of industrial time series make it challenging for existing forecasting models to be directly applied to.

- **Relevance:** Some models only focus on learning time-varying features in different steps and stages [13], caring little about variable-wise data associations.
- **Variety:** Some models consist of complex feature selection operations or need additional priori knowledge when tuning parameters [11], which makes them not scalable enough to handle multi-source heterogeneity in the complicated and noisy production environment.
- **Velocity:** Fast data generating and processing speed requires the model to generate accurate results under longer prediction horizon in order to reserve sufficient reaction time in applications. The capability of some models are not strong enough to maintain satisfactory performance when the forecast range is long [9].

In this paper, we propose an end-to-end deep learning framework named dual-dimensional attention-based network (DANet) to address the multivariate time series forecasting problem with the aforementioned characteristics. It mainly leverages the strengths of recurrent neural network (RNN) structures to discover the underlying temporal patterns of the multi-dimensional input. Firstly, the recurrent module is used for capturing sequential relationships between adjacent timesteps and embedding the original observations. Then, we apply a novel dual-dimensional attention mechanism to cope with the intrinsic characteristics of industrial big data. Feature-wise self-attention computed on the row vectors of hidden states enables the network to adaptively learn the correlations between features, while time-wise attention calculated on the hidden states of each timestep captures complex long and short-term temporal dependencies. Additionally, the DANet connects a conventional autoregressive linear model in parallel. The linear AR part captures scale and trend while the nonlinear neural network part captures fluctuations. They together make the overall model more robust when processing non-stationary time series with scale change.

Our contributions are summarized as follows:

- We proposed DANet, an end-to-end deep learning framework solving the multivariate time series forecasting problem in industry.
- We apply a novel dual-dimensional attention mechanism which helps the network to adaptively learns useful correlations between variables and better modeling long and short-term temporal dependencies.

– Our model shows its advantages over the baseline methods and a more stable and robust performance in the experiments on several real-world manufacturing datasets.

2   Related Work

2.1   Smart Manufacturing Applications

In the latest industrial revolution, namely Industry 4.0, the development of industrial internet of things (IIOT), machine learning (ML), and artificial intelligence (AI) technology is bringing new vitality to the manufacturing industry. As one of the most common types of sensor data in industrial environment, time series data contains rich information which can benefit research topics such as scheduling, monitoring, quality, and failure detection [3]. For example, supervised ML methods have been widely used to develop defect diagnosis and prognosis models in order to improve machine reliability [19]; Machine health monitoring involves predicting the occurrence time, duration and probability of equipment failure and performance degradation [12]; Management of product quality needs to identify key performance indicators (KPIs) and predict the final outputs according to intermediate results [20]. Therefore, time series forecasting plays an important role in laying the foundation for more sophisticated tasks in industry.

2.2   Time Series Prediction Models

Parametric Models. Conventional parametric model for time series forecast takes regression function as a premise and usually targets at univariate time series forecasting. The most popular models are autoregressive (AR) models and more advanced autoregressive integrated moving average models (ARIMA) [14], which determines the parameters by fitting the observations into a linear regression function. Vector autoregression (VAR) [7] models naturally extend AR models to the multivariate setting. Nevertheless, large parameter space of VAR is easy to cause overfitting due to insufficient sample size when dealing with long-term temporal patterns. These models have been successfully applied the economic and financial fields, but it is difficult for these models to overcome the interference of random events and model the nonlinear and uncertain characteristics of spatial-temporal data.

Deep Learning Models. In recent years, with the strengthening of computing power and the development of deep learning theory, the research of neural network models for time series prediction has become a hot spot. These data-driven methods do not analyze the physical properties and dynamic behaviors of the system. Instead, it infers future trend and tendency through the statistical regularity of data, thus having high flexibility. Recurrent neural network (RNN) is born to solve the time series forecasting problems. Its variants long short-term memory (LSTM) [6,15] and gated recurrent unit (GRU) [2] are so popular that they gradually take the place of RNN. Such self-circulation mechanism enables them to learn temporal dependencies well and get better prediction results.

Currently, a hot direction is to combine convolutional neural network (CNN) [16] and sequential models to acquire better predictions. LSTNet [11] performs a one-dimensional convolution to capture short-term local information and uses an RNN layer to capture long-term macro information. It improves RNNs by adding skip connections to distant cells to directly utilizes the periodic information. However, in order to take full advantage of this novel structure, the skip length need to be carefully selected, which may require additional manual effort or priori knowledge. TPA-LSTM [17] makes further improvements on the basis of LSTNet by changing the order of convolution and recurrence and proposes a novel attention mechanism to integrate information of one feature at all timesteps for multivariate forecasting. Nevertheless, more complex structure also introduces a great amount of hyperparameters which brings inconvenience under different real-world scenarios.

The attention mechanism was firstly applied to the field of natural language processing (NLP) and improved the word alignment of the encoder-decoder architecture in the translation task [1]. Many researchers have taken advantage of its sequence alignment ability and leveraged it in the time series forecasting problem. Informer [21] is a successful attempt to apply the popular self-attention structure Transformer to increase the prediction capacity and deal with the long sequence time series forecasting problem.

3 Preliminary

In this section, we give a formal definition of the multivariate time series (MTS) forecasting problem. Assume a fixed-size window is sliding over multiple observed time series, and the model input at time stamp t can be denoted as:

$$X_t = \{x_1, x_2, \cdots, x_T\} \in \mathbb{R}^{d \times T} \tag{1}$$

where T is the window size, $x_i = \{x_i^1, x_i^2, \cdots, x_i^m \mid x_i^{m+1}, \cdots, x_i^d\} \in \mathbb{R}^{d \times 1}$ represents d different variables observed at time stamp i, and x_i^j is the j-th variable of x_i. These variables are classified into two types and is divided by $|$. The last $(d - m)$ dimensions are the variables we are interested in and they are called target variables, such as key metrics and crucial stage outputs of the production line. The front m dimensions are called external variables, which may have potential relationship with target variables or among themselves. Our goal is to predict:

$$x_{T+\Delta} = \{x_{T+\Delta}^1, x_{T+\Delta}^2, \cdots, x_{T+\Delta}^m \mid x_{T+\Delta}^{m+1}, \cdots, x_{T+\Delta}^d\} \in \mathbb{R}^{d \times 1} \tag{2}$$

where Δ is a changeable horizon ahead of current time stamp. The determination of Δ depends on specific application scenarios. For example, measurements of machines on the production line are usually timed accurately to a second, while statistics about production rate or energy consumption are often recorded once an hour.

4   Methodology

In this section, we describe the structure of the proposed deep learning framework. Figure 1 shows an overview of DANet architecture.

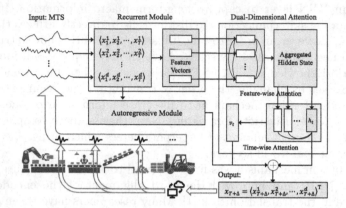

Fig. 1. An overview of the dual-dimensional attention network (DANet).

Statistics sampled from the industrial process are gathered and preprocessed to form a multivariate input. The MTS are firstly sent to a recurrent module and is embedded into a hidden state matrix. The row vectors are called feature vectors which incorporate dependencies of adjacent timesteps. The following is a dual-dimensional attention module, which consists of feature wise multi-head self-attention and time-wise dot product attention structures. The feature vectors enter a self-attention module to adaptively capture and aggregate the correlations between features and updates the hidden state matrix. After that, time-wise attention is calculated on the column vectors of hidden states to dynamically select timesteps mostly related to the last hidden state. We also connect an autoregressive module in parallel which is sensitive to the scale change in the input to add robustness to the whole structure. Finally, the forecasting results from both nonlinear part and linear part of the network are added up together to generate a final prediction, which can serve as a feedback for high-level optimization services for the industrial process.

4.1   Recurrent Module

The input time series containing d variables are split into snippets of the same length as the window size. The first layer of DANet utilizes LSTM cells to extract information and encode the original observations of variables into an embedding matrix $H_t = \{h_1, h_2, \cdots, h_T\} \in \mathbb{R}^{f \times T}$, where f is the number of hidden state features. An LSTM cell has four inputs and one output at each timestep. The vector x_t and a previous hidden state vector h_{t-1} is transformed by specific weight matrices to provide different input for each gate. For each element in X_t, the hidden state is calculated as:

$$i_t = \sigma(W_{xi}x_t + W_{hi}h_{t-1})$$
$$f_t = \sigma(W_{xf}x_t + W_{hf}h_{t-1})$$
$$o_t = \sigma(W_{xo}x_t + W_{ho}h_{t-1}) \tag{3}$$
$$c_t = i_t \odot tanh(W_{xg}x_t + W_{hg}h_{t-1}) + f_t \odot c_{t-1}$$
$$h_t = o_t \odot tanh(c_t)$$

where i_t, f_t, o_t, c_t, $h_t \in \mathbb{R}^{f \times 1}$ represent the value of input gate, forget gate, output gate, memory cell and hidden state at timestep t, respectively. W_{xi}, W_{xf}, W_{xo}, $W_{xg} \in \mathbb{R}^{f \times d}$ and W_{hi}, W_{hf}, W_{ho}, $W_{hg} \in \mathbb{R}^{f \times f}$ are the weight matrix to transform the input and hidden state. σ stands for the sigmoid function, and $\odot$ means element-wise multiplication.

4.2   Attention Module

The forecasting model should meet more requirements in terms of the inherent characteristics of industrial time series. The feature selection problem in time series can be seen from two perspectives. In the time dimension, there usually exists continuity or periodic temporal patterns in the feature sequence of a single variable. Generally, the shorter the time interval, the smaller the difference between the adjacent values. While in the variable dimension, most of the time the features are heterogeneous. Therefore, we design two kinds of attention structure to better model inter- and intra-variable temporal patterns in multivariate time series respectively.

The attention mechanism [18] is a general technique which maps a query and a set of key-value pairs to compute a weighted average of the values. The calculation process can be summarized as the following three steps:

1. Use a scoring function F to evaluate relevance between query q and keys K.

$$\text{relevance} = F(q, K_i), i = 1, 2, \cdots, m \tag{4}$$

2. Obtain the attention value by normalizing the scoring function by softmax so that each element of the vector represents a probability of considering K_i to be relevant to the query.

$$\alpha_i = \text{softmax}(F(q, K_i)), i = 1, 2, \cdots, m \tag{5}$$

3. Perform a weighted summation on all the values in V to obtain the context vector. Just as its name implies, the context vector incorporates historical information that is helpful in accomplishing subsequent tasks.

$$\text{context} = \sum_{i=1}^{m} \alpha_i V_i \tag{6}$$

Feature-Wise Attention. Although processing multivariate input brings more challenges compared with univariate time series, the prediction performance of one single variable can also benefit from its dependencies with other variables. For example, changes of environmental parameters of the former stages in an assembly line are likely to affect the measurements in the following process. Therefore, it is vital for a single variable to distinguish which features have causal effect on or synchronous relationship with itself. Otherwise, mixing and predicting features together may only introduce unnecessary noise to the result.

The row vectors of the hidden state matrix H_t has embedded input variables into feature vectors. Then, we perform self-attention among them to attend to hidden state features which are the most relevant to and helpful in forecasting each variable. We use the row vectors of H_t as query, key and value of each feature. They are divided into s parallel parts (or called heads) and each part performs self-attention individually to learn attention weights from different positions. We denote a feature vector in one part as $z_i \in \mathbb{R}^{1 \times T/s}, i = 1, 2, \cdots, f$ and Fig. 2 illustrates the calculation process.

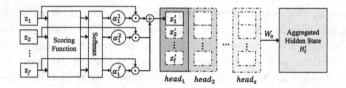

Fig. 2. Calculation process of feature-wise attention.

Feature-wise attention uses scaled dot product to evaluate the relevance between each feature and another. In most cases, the number of features is smaller than the length of representation vector. Scaling dot product by the square root of dimension of keys can prevent it from data overflow in magnitude. The left part of Fig. 2 takes z_1 as an example to show how to calculate z_1'. The computation results are normalized by a softmax function to obtain attention weights.

$$\alpha_i^j = \text{softmax}(\frac{z_i z_j^{\mathrm{T}}}{\sqrt{T/s}}) \tag{7}$$

Then, weights and values are multiplied and added together to form an updated feature vector z_i', which encodes underlying data associations.

$$z_i' = \sum_{j=1}^{f} \alpha_i^j z_j \tag{8}$$

After that, we concatenate all z_i' as the representation of one head. The multi-head output $H_t' \in \mathbb{R}^{f \times T}$ is the concatenation of all heads and multiplied by a transform matrix $W_o \in \mathbb{R}^{T \times T}$.

$$head_i = \text{concat}(z_1', z_2', \cdots, z_f') \tag{9}$$

$$H_t' = \text{concat}(head_1, head_2, \cdots, head_s)W_o \tag{10}$$

Feature-wise attention structure enables each feature to pay attention to those who are most correlated with itself instead of equally taking other features into consideration.

Time-Wise Attention. After weighting the importance of features, time-wise attention layer pays attention on the updated hidden states to select history information that are most related to the current timestep, so that it can extract more useful information from previous timesteps when the prediction horizon is longer.

Dot product is the most direct way to establish mapping between query and keys. Its advantage is that no parameter is required so the calculation complexity is greatly reduced and it demands that the number of dimensions of queries and keys should be the same. We use dot product as the scoring function measuring relevance between one hidden state and h_t. Then, the output of the scoring function goes through a softmax layer to acquire the time-wise attention. After that, values at corresponding locations of columns of H_t and time-wise attention are multiplied and added together. In other words, the column vectors of H_t are weighted by attention to obtain the time-wise context vector $v_t \in \mathbb{R}^{f \times 1}$.

$$v_t = \frac{\sum_i \exp(h_t^T h_i) h_i}{\sum_j \exp(h_t^T h_j)} \tag{11}$$

At last, we integrate the last hidden state vector h_t and time-wise context vector v_t through a set of weight matrices to yield the prediction from the non-linear network, which is denoted as $\hat{x}_{T+\Delta}^N \in \mathbb{R}^{d \times 1}$, where W_h and $W_t \in \mathbb{R}^{d \times f}$.

$$\hat{x}_{T+\Delta}^N = W_h h_t + W_t v_t \tag{12}$$

4.3 Autoregressive Module

The manufacturing environment constantly changes in a non-periodic manner when some controllable parameters are altered by engineers. The scale of target variables is closely connected with externalities. As is explored in the literature, nonlinear neural network components such as RNNs and CNNs are not sensitive enough to recognize the scale fluctuations of inputs [11], which significantly lowers the forecast accuracy. An effective approach to address this deficiency is to add a linear module which primarily focuses on capturing the local scale change. We bring the AR component in LSTNet to our model. The value at timestep t is a linear combination of the values in the immediately preceding window with size δ, which is usually smaller than the length of all timesteps. The prediction from linear AR module denoted as $\hat{x}^L_{T+\Delta}$ is formulated as follows, where $W_{ar} \in \mathbb{R}^{\delta \times 1}$, $b_{ar} \in \mathbb{R}^{\delta \times 1}$, and $\odot$ denotes the element-wise multiplication.

$$\hat{x}^L_{T+\Delta} = \sum_{i=1}^{\delta} W_{ar} \odot x_{T-i} + b_{ar} \tag{13}$$

The final prediction result is the combination of nonlinear and linear part.

$$\hat{x}_{T+\Delta} = \hat{x}^N_{T+\Delta} + \hat{x}^L_{T+\Delta} \tag{14}$$

5   Experiment

In this section, we conduct extensive experiments with five methods (including DANet) on three real-world industrial datasets for model evaluation.

5.1   Experimental Settings

Datasets

- **MP** [10] (Multi-stage continuous flow manufacturing process) was taken from an actual production line which contains high-speed, continuous manufacturing process with parallel and series stages. The input data includes pressure of different zones in the manufacturing environment, parameters of raw material feeders, amperage and revolutions per minute (RPM) of motors, etc. The forecast goal is to predict certain measurements of the line's output after going through a processing stage. We preprocessed the original dataset by filling in missing values and eliminating some unaltered series such as the material properties.
- **ETT** [21] (Electricity transformer temperature) is donated by the researchers of Informer for long sequence time series problem. We use the dataset **ETTh1** and **ETTm1**, which contains the data of one electricity transformer at one station. Measurement at each timestep consists of one target variable *oil temperature*, which is a crucial indicator in the electric power long-term deployment, and 6 power load features including quantity of useful load and useless load.

Table 1 lists the detailed statistics of all datasets, where N_e is the number of external variables and N_t is the number of target variables.

Table 1. Statistics of datasets

Dataset	Length	N_e	N_t	Sample rate
MP	4377	9	2	1 s
ETTh1	17420	6	1	1 h
ETTm1	69680	6	1	1 min

All datasets are split in chronological order and the ratio of training, validation and test set is 60%, 20% and 20%, respectively. The training set is zero-mean normalized. Then, the validation and test set are normalized by the mean and standard deviation of training set.

Baselines. We compare the performance of our model with VAR [7], LSTM [6], LSTNet [11] and TPA-LSTM [17], which are the state-of-the-art models solving multivariate time series forecasting problems. Details of baselines have been discussed in Sect. 2.

Evaluation Metrics. We use three conventional evaluation metrics. Denote x_t as the truth value at timestep t, $\hat{x}_t$ as the predicted value and d as the variable dimension, these metrics can be formulated as:

- Mean absolute error (MAE). It measures the mean of absolute value of difference between x_t and $\hat{x}_t$, which is the lower the better.

$$\text{MAE} = \frac{1}{d}\sum_{j=1}^{d}|x_t^j - \hat{x}_t^j| \tag{15}$$

- Mean square error (MSE). It measures the mean of square of difference between x_t and $\hat{x}_t$, which is the lower the better.

$$\text{MSE} = \frac{1}{d}\sum_{j=1}^{d}||x_t^j - \hat{x}_t^j||^2 \tag{16}$$

- Pearson correlation coefficient (CORR). It reflects the strength and direction of linear correlation between two variables. The closer the CORR is to 1, the stronger the positive correlation.

$$\text{CORR} = \frac{\sum_{j=1}^{d}(x_t^j - \overline{x}_t)(\hat{x}_t^j - \overline{\hat{x}}_t)}{\sqrt{\sum_{j=1}^{d}(x_t^j - \overline{x}_t)^2}\sqrt{\sum_{j=1}^{d}(\hat{x}_t^j - \overline{\hat{x}}_t)^2}} \tag{17}$$

Experimental Details

Objective Function: Mean absolute error (MAE) is one of the most commonly used objective function in time series forecast and we choose it as the default loss function of our model. **Hyper-parameter tuning:** We conduct grid search over all tunable hyperparameters on the validation set for each method and dataset. In light of different sample rates, the window size T of dataset MP and ETTm1 is chosen from $\{60, 120, 180, 240, 300\}$ and that of ETTh1 is chosen from $\{24, 48, 96, 168, 336\}$, respectively. All baseline models incorporate an RNN module. The number of hidden state features ranges in $\{2^3, 2^4, \cdots, 2^7\}$. Search of other hyperparameters of LSTNet and TPA-LSTM follows the way in the original papers. The default batch size is 128. We use stochastic gradient descent (SGD) algorithm to optimize the parameters of our model, and the learning rate is set to 1e-05. **Platform:** All models were trained and tested on a Nvidia K80 24 GB GPU.

5.2   Results and Analysis

Tables 2 and 3 summarize the multivariate evaluation results of five methods on three datasets. MAE, MSE and CORR are the metric values of all variables, while *MAE, *MSE and *CORR are the metric values of only target variables. We gradually prolong the prediction horizon to judge the change of performance with the growth of prediction capacity, which ranges in $\{12, 24, 48, 96\}$. The best results of each metric are highlighted in boldface.

The training process of deep neural networks is supervised learning. Assume that the horizon is Δ, the training set is transformed into batches where each batch contains multiple (input, output) pairs, namely input X_t of size T and $x_{T+\Delta}$ as label.

From the result tables, when the horizon is relatively small, the accuracy of LSTNet sometimes achieves the best. However, as the horizon gets longer and longer, DANet gradually surpasses the other methods. In addition, as horizon prolongs, the performance of all methods decreases as the condition of under-fitting and time delay gets worse, which accords with our common sense. The network can no longer generate accurate predictions of peaks and valleys and only produces smooth values shrinking in the upper and lower bounds of true values. Generally, our proposed model outperforms other approaches most of

Table 2. Prediction results of five methods on all variables in three datasets. The best performance of one experiment instance is highlighted in boldface.

Horizon	Method	MP			ETTh1			ETTm1		
		MAE	MSE	CORR	MAE	MSE	CORR	MAE	MSE	CORR
12	AR	0.6860	0.8756	0.3016	0.4014	0.3929	0.7732	0.5235	0.6688	0.6853
	LSTM	0.5864	0.6292	0.4370	0.6417	0.8247	0.5781	0.4617	0.4987	0.7331
	LSTNet	**0.5400**	**0.5640**	**0.4874**	0.4065	0.3809	0.7725	**0.4447**	**0.4518**	**0.7637**
	TPA	0.6832	0.8627	0.3103	0.3917	0.3925	0.7733	0.5221	0.6604	0.6864
	DANet	0.5747	0.6114	0.4421	**0.3911**	**0.3912**	**0.7790**	0.4574	0.5590	0.7309
24	AR	0.7154	0.9656	0.2638	**0.3872**	0.3852	**0.7760**	0.7565	1.2484	0.3591
	LSTM	0.5657	0.6093	0.4504	0.4883	0.5053	0.6836	0.5653	0.7815	0.5864
	LSTNet	0.5610	0.6175	0.4533	0.4011	**0.3841**	0.7753	**0.5461**	**0.5796**	**0.6757**
	TPA	0.7153	0.9705	0.2630	0.3875	0.3853	0.7759	0.7564	1.2495	0.3609
	DANet	**0.5558**	**0.5807**	**0.4910**	0.3926	0.3862	0.7735	0.5582	0.6855	0.6272
48	AR	0.7221	0.8671	0.1515	0.4497	0.5086	0.7034	0.7938	1.3038	0.2743
	LSTM	0.6991	0.8581	0.3262	0.5214	0.5720	0.6812	0.5774	0.7191	0.5807
	LSTNet	0.6808	0.7558	0.3232	0.4637	0.5088	0.7000	**0.5566**	**0.6701**	0.6190
	TPA	0.7209	0.8644	0.1517	0.4528	0.5124	0.7022	0.7914	1.2855	0.2768
	DANet	**0.6708**	**0.6903**	**0.3454**	**0.4496**	**0.5084**	**0.7032**	0.5630	0.6900	**0.6247**
96	AR	0.7599	0.9447	0.1180	0.5085	0.5815	0.6287	0.3987	0.4050	0.7700
	LSTM	0.6546	0.8154	0.2963	0.5772	0.6732	0.6004	0.4176	0.4141	0.7646
	LSTNet	0.6488	0.7718	0.3623	0.5246	0.5804	0.6268	0.4189	0.4155	0.7617
	TPA	0.7596	0.9434	0.1331	0.4960	0.5694	0.6366	**0.3883**	0.4026	0.7705
	DANet	**0.6444**	**0.7236**	**0.3681**	**0.4958**	**0.5659**	0.6368	0.3886	**0.4018**	**0.7709**

Table 3. Prediction results of five methods on target variables in three datasets. The best performance of one experiment instance is highlighted in boldface.

Horizon	Method	MP			ETTh1			ETTm1		
		*MAE	*MSE	*CORR	*MAE	*MSE	*CORR	*MAE	*MSE	*CORR
12	AR	0.2674	0.1598	0.2109	0.1857	0.0627	0.8100	0.1200	0.0244	0.9431
	LSTM	0.2630	0.1498	0.1959	0.3532	0.1813	0.7728	**0.1065**	0.0224	0.9423
	LSTNet	0.2527	0.1386	0.2460	0.1878	0.0666	0.8190	0.1070	**0.0185**	**0.9457**
	TPA	0.2653	0.1557	0.2239	0.1852	0.0624	0.8100	0.1323	0.0282	0.9427
	DANet	**0.2489**	**0.1326**	**0.2543**	**0.1801**	**0.0591**	**0.8253**	0.1145	0.0316	0.9363
24	AR	0.2847	0.1659	0.1661	**0.1992**	0.0696	0.7788	0.2591	0.0935	0.8865
	LSTM	0.2611	0.1465	0.1540	0.3177	0.1635	0.7215	0.1710	0.0498	0.8772
	LSTNet	0.2639	0.1627	0.1979	0.2178	0.0861	0.7768	0.1673	0.0503	0.8881
	TPA	0.2830	0.1655	0.1665	0.1993	0.0698	0.7789	0.2616	0.0951	0.8861
	DANet	**0.2541**	**0.1358**	**0.2005**	0.1997	**0.0649**	**0.7790**	**0.1579**	**0.0463**	**0.8954**
48	AR	0.3541	0.2237	0.0623	0.2674	0.1182	0.6237	0.3319	0.1548	0.8156
	LSTM	0.2807	0.1662	0.0705	0.4209	0.2629	0.5713	0.1909	0.0618	0.8036
	LSTNet	0.2861	0.1564	0.1129	0.2726	0.1258	0.6255	0.2391	0.0964	0.7875
	TPA	0.3505	0.2191	0.0695	0.2672	0.1179	**0.6241**	0.3302	0.1572	0.8148
	DANet	**0.2704**	**0.1387**	**0.1139**	**0.2629**	**0.1142**	0.6222	**0.1898**	**0.0617**	**0.8337**
96	AR	0.3617	0.2298	0.0463	0.3163	0.1656	0.4690	0.2420	0.1014	0.7848
	LSTM	0.3363	0.1909	0.1375	0.4171	0.2677	0.4233	0.2051	0.0732	0.7644
	LSTNet	0.3646	0.2015	0.1369	0.3736	0.2190	0.4176	0.2272	0.0915	0.7814
	TPA	0.3591	0.2276	0.0508	0.3150	0.1648	0.4689	0.1999	0.0736	0.7889
	DANet	**0.3288**	**0.1406**	**0.1484**	**0.3091**	**0.1585**	0.4818	**0.1976**	**0.0715**	0.7892

the times, especially when it comes to target variables. It shows that DANet is good at discovering relationships among multiple heterogeneous input series and previous timesteps, especially at capturing useful patterns in forecasting target variables.

5.3   Ablation Study

In this section, we carry out an ablation study to analyze the effectiveness of modules in our network. Table 4 compares the prediction results of DANet with its sub-models which have omitted some modules. **Feature-wise** and **Time-wise** are the models which only adopts a single kind of attention. **woAR** denotes that the network does not include the autoregression module. The horizon is 12 and hyperparameters are the same as when the model achieves the best performance.

Influence of Dual-Dimensional Attention. Results show that merely attends to one dimension cannot fully leverage the underlying correlations between different features and timesteps. Combining these two methods together boosts the forecast accuracy of the network and make the framework more robust when encountering different circumstances.

Table 4. Ablation study

Method	MP			ETTh1			ETTm1		
	MAE	MSE	CORR	MAE	MSE	CORR	MAE	MSE	CORR
Feature-wise	0.5816	0.6195	0.4304	0.3924	**0.3873**	0.7765	0.4696	0.5249	0.7358
Time-wise	0.5870	0.6206	0.4397	0.3958	0.3898	0.7762	0.4692	**0.4976**	**0.7436**
woAR	0.5877	0.6224	0.4372	0.5782	0.6947	0.5778	0.4698	0.4989	0.7402
DANet	**0.5747**	**0.6114**	**0.4421**	0.3911	0.3912	**0.7790**	**0.4574**	0.5590	0.7309
Method	MP			ETTh1			ETTm1		
	*MAE	*MSE	*CORR	*MAE	*MSE	*CORR	*MAE	*MSE	*CORR
Feature-wise	0.2664	0.1460	0.1563	0.1832	0.0692	0.8205	0.1224	0.0374	0.9323
Time-wise	0.2719	0.1401	0.1862	0.2356	0.1092	0.7884	0.1205	0.0335	0.9281
woAR	0.2617	0.1461	0.1833	0.3285	0.1855	0.7076	0.2155	0.1006	0.8386
DANet	**0.2489**	**0.1326**	**0.2543**	**0.1801**	**0.0591**	**0.8253**	**0.1145**	**0.0316**	**0.9363**

Influence of Autoregressive Module. Removing the AR module from the DANet causes the most significant drops in performance on all of the datasets, showing that AR module plays a crucial role in ensuring high accuracy. This is because the time series in the dataset are non-stationary. The simple linear AR layer is sensitive and flexible enough to quickly react to the scale change in data. The linear part mainly captures the general scale and trend of data, while the deep learning neural network aims to discover nonlinear fluctuations. They take on different roles and work together to produce an accurate result.

Figure 3 compares the prediction accuracy of the target variable on the test set of ETTh1. The blue line is the true value and red line is the predicted sequence. Among all methods, DANet shows the smallest gap and time delay between real observations and predictions.

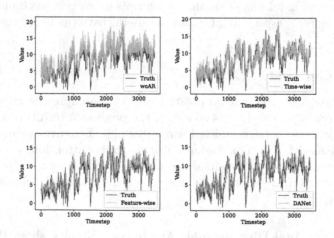

Fig. 3. The prediction value of target variable in ETTh1 from four models.

In summary, the ablation study adds interpretability to our work. It shows that all modules in our framework have a place and they altogether contribute to a robust and accurate time series forecasting model.

6 Conclusion

In this paper, we propose an end-to-end deep learning framework named dual-dimensional attention-based network (DANet) to solve the multivariate time series forecasting problem in industry. It mainly leverages the strengths of RNN structures to discover the underlying temporal patterns of the multi-dimensional input. We apply a novel dual-dimensional attention mechanism to cope with the intrinsic characteristics of industrial big data, where feature-wise self-attention enables the network to adaptively learn the correlations between features, and time-wise attention captures complex long and short-term temporal dependencies. We conduct extensive experiments on several real-world manufacturing datasets. Our model achieves smaller error, especially on target variables compared with other baseline methods, and shows a more robust performance when dealing with different datasets.

Acknowledgements. This work was supported by the National Key R&D Program of China [2020YFB1707903]; the National Natural Science Foundation of China [61872238, 61972254], Shanghai Municipal Science and Technology Major Project [2021SHZDZX0102], the Tencent Marketing Solution Rhino-Bird Focused Research Program [FR202001], and the CCF-Tencent Open Fund [RAGR20200105].

References

1. Bahdanau, D., Cho, K., Bengio, Y.: Neural machine translation by jointly learning to align and translate. In: International Conference on Learning Representations (ICLR) (2015)
2. Cho, K., et al.: Learning phrase representations using rnn encoder-decoder for statistical machine translation. In: Conference on Empirical Methods in Natural Language Processing (EMNLP), pp. 1724–1734 (2014)
3. Dogan, A., Birant, D.: Machine learning and data mining in manufacturing. Expert Syst. Appl. **166**, 114060 (2021)
4. Dudek, G.: Pattern-based local linear regression models for short-term load forecasting. Electric Power Syst. Res. **130**, 139–147 (2016)
5. Ghahramani, M., Qiao, Y., Zhou, M., O'Hagan, A., Sweeney, J.: AI-based modeling and data-driven evaluation for smart manufacturing processes. IEEE/CAA J. Automatica Sinica **7**(4), 1026–1037 (2020)
6. Hochreiter, S., Schmidhuber, J.: Long short-term memory. Neural Comput. **9**(8), 1735–1780 (1997)
7. Hsieh, T.Y., Sun, Y., Tang, X., Wang, S., Honavar, V.G.: SrVARM: state regularized vector autoregressive model for joint learning of hidden state transitions and state-dependent inter-variable dependencies from multi-variate time series. In: Proceedings of the Web Conference (WWW), pp. 2270–2280 (2021)

8. Hsu, C., Liu, W.: Multiple time-series convolutional neural network for fault detection and diagnosis and empirical study in semiconductor manufacturing. J. Intell. Manuf. **32**(3), 823–836 (2021)

9. Huang, S., Wang, D., Wu, X., Tang, A.: DSANet: dual self-attention network for multivariate time series forecasting. In: ACM International Conference on Information and Knowledge Management (CIKM), pp. 2129–2132 (2019)

10. Kaggle: multi-stage continuous flow manufacturing process. Website (2020). https://www.kaggle.com/supergus/multistage-continuousflow-manufacturing-process

11. Lai, G., Chang, W., Yang, Y., Liu, H.: Modeling long- and short-term temporal patterns with deep neural networks. In: ACM International Conference on Research and Development in Information Retrieval (SIGIR), pp. 95–104 (2018)

12. Lepenioti, K., et al.: Machine learning for predictive and prescriptive analytics of operational data in smart manufacturing. In: International Conference on Advanced Information Systems Engineering Workshops (CAiSE), vol. 382, pp. 5–16 (2020)

13. Li, J., Yang, B., Li, H., Wang, Y., Qi, C., Liu, Y.: DTDR-ALSTM: extracting dynamic time-delays to reconstruct multivariate data for improving attention-based LSTM industrial time series prediction models. Knowl.-Based Syst. **211**, 106508 (2021)

14. Li, M., Hua, Z., Zhao, J., Zou, Y., Xie, B.: ARIMA model-based web services trustworthiness evaluation and prediction. In: International Conference on Service-Oriented Computing (ICSOC), pp. 648–655 (2012)

15. Liu, C., Mao, W., Gao, Y., Gao, X., Li, S., Chen, G.: Adaptive recollected RNN for workload forecasting in database-as-a-service. In: International Conference on Service-Oriented Computing (ICSOC), pp. 431–438 (2020)

16. Sen, R., Yu, H., Dhillon, I.S.: Think globally, act locally: a deep neural network approach to high-dimensional time series forecasting. In: International Conference on Neural Information Processing Systems (NeurIPS), pp. 4838–4847 (2019)

17. Shih, S., Sun, F., Lee, H.: Temporal pattern attention for multivariate time series forecasting. Mach. Learn. **108**(8–9), 1421–1441 (2019)

18. Vaswani, A., et al.: Attention is all you need. In: International Conference on Neural Information Processing Systems (NeurIPS), pp. 6000–6010 (2017)

19. Wang, J., Wang, K., Wang, Y., Huang, Z., Xue, R.: Deep Boltzmann machine based condition prediction for smart manufacturing. J. Ambient. Intell. Humaniz. Comput. **10**(3), 851–861 (2019)

20. Wang, J., Yang, J., Zhang, J., Wang, X., Zhang, W.C.: Big Data Driven Cycle Time Parallel Prediction for Production Planning in Wafer Manufacturing. Enterprise Inf. Syst. **12**(6), 714–732 (2018)

21. Zhou, H., et al.: Informer: beyond efficient transformer for long sequence time-series forecasting. Computing Research Repository (CoRR) abs/2012.07436 (2020)

Author Index

Printed in the United States
by Baker & Taylor Publisher Services